Twelfth Workshop on Innovative Use of NLP for Building Educational Applications 2017

Copenhagen, Denmark
8 September 2017

ISBN: 978-1-5108-4756-9

Printed by Curran Associates, Inc. (2017)

For permission requests, please contact the Association for Computational Linguistics
at the address below.

Association for Computational Linguistics
209 N. Eighth Street
Stroudsburg, Pennsylvania 18360

Phone: 1-570-476-8006
Fax: 1-570-476-0860

acl@aclweb.org

Additional copies of this publication are available from:

Curran Associates, Inc.
57 Morehouse Lane
Red Hook, NY 12571 USA
Phone: 845-758-0400
Fax: 845-758-2633
Email: curran@proceedings.com
Web: www.proceedings.com

EMNLP 2017

The Twelfth Workshop
on Innovative Use of NLP for
Building Educational Applications

Proceedings of the Workshop

September 8, 2017
Copenhagen, Denmark

Gold Sponsors

turnitin | LightSide  grammarly 

Silver Sponsors

Bronze Sponsors

Introduction

This has been a momentous year for the BEA Workshop. In its 12th year, the BEA workshop is, for the first time, being held in conjunction with EMNLP. In addition, the workshop is being sponsored by the newly formed Special Interest Group: SIG EDU.[1]

Since the first workshop in 1997, BEA has become the leading venue for sharing and publishing innovative work that uses NLP to develop educational applications. The consistent interest and growth of the workshop has clear ties to challenges in education. The research presented at the workshop highlights advances in the technology and the maturity of the field of NLP in education. The capabilities serve as a response to educational challenges and are poised to support the needs of a variety of stakeholders, including educators, learners, parents, and administrators.

NLP capabilities now support an array of learning domains, including writing, speaking, reading, and mathematics. In the writing and speech domains, automated writing evaluation (AWE) and speech assessment applications, respectively, are commercially deployed in high-stakes assessment and instructional settings, including Massive Open Online Courses (MOOCs). We also see widely-used commercial applications for plagiarism detection and peer review and explosive growth of mobile applications for game-based applications for instruction and assessment. The current educational and assessment landscape continues to foster a strong interest and high demand that pushes the state of the art in AWE capabilities to expand the analysis of written responses to writing genres other than those traditionally found in standardized assessments, especially writing tasks requiring use of sources and argumentative discourse.

Steady growth in the development of NLP-based applications for education has prompted an increased number of workshops that typically focus on a single subfield. In BEA, we make an effort to have papers from many subfields, for example, tools for automated scoring, automated test-item generation, curriculum development, evaluation of text, dialogue, evaluation of genres beyond essays, feedback studies, and grammatical error correction.

This year we received a record 62 submissions, and accepted 9 papers as oral presentations and 25 as poster presentation and/or demos, for an overall acceptance rate of 55 percent. Each paper was reviewed by three members of the Program Committee who were believed to be most appropriate for each paper. We continue to have a very strong policy to deal with conflicts of interest. First, we made a concerted effort to not assign papers to reviewers to evaluate if the paper had an author from their institution. Second, with respect to the organizing committee, authors of papers for which there was a conflict of interest recused themselves from the discussions.

While the field is growing, we do recognize that there is a core group of institutions and researchers who work in this area. With a higher acceptance rate, we were able to include papers from a wider variety of topics and institutions. The papers accepted were selected on the basis of several factors, including the relevance to a core educational problem space, the novelty of the approach or domain, and the strength of the research. The accepted papers were highly diverse – an indicator of the growing variety of foci in this field. We continue to believe that the workshop framework designed to introduce work in progress and new ideas needs to be revived, and we hope that we have achieved this with the breadth and variety of research accepted for this workshop, a brief description of which is presented below.

The BEA12 workshop has presentations on Automated Writing Evaluation (AWE), item generation,

---

[1] https://www.aclweb.org/adminwiki/index.php?title=2017Q3_Reports:_SIGEDU

readability, dialogue and annotation/database schemas, among others:

AWE Written Assessments: Whereas much work in scoring at BEA focuses on learner language, Horbach et al. score essays written by proficient native German speakers in a complex writing task. Madnani et al. look at scoring for content in science, math, language arts and social studies. Rei looks at detecting off-topic essay responses to visual prompts. Riordan et al. examine neural architectures for scoring responses to short answer questions. Finally, looking at the bigger picture, Burstein et al. explore the relations between AWE and broader educational outcomes.

Domain-Specific AWE: Three papers look at assessments in specific subject domains. For language learning, Tolmachev and Kurohashi extract exemplar sentences to accompany flash cards. Tack et al. investigate the feasibility of automated learner English assessment in the CEFR (European) framework. In the science domain, Nadeem and Ostendorf look at language-based mapping of science assessment items to skills.

Error Detection and Correction: Rei and Yannakoudakis use a neural sequence labeling approach to grammatical error detection. Napoles and Callison-Burch adapt Machine Translation (MT) to grammatical error correction. In another use for machine translation, Rei et al. use MT to generate artificial errors for training machine learning systems. Chollampatt and Ng augment an MT approach with neural network models. Farag et al. develop an error-oriented word embedding approach that exploits errors in learner productions. Caines et al. collect crowd-sourced fluency corrections for transcripts of spoken learner English. Finally, Sakaguchi et al. present a position paper on error correction that discusses issues that need to be addressed and provide recommendations.

Item generation: Jiang and Lee develop distractors for fill-in-the-gap items in Chinese. Satria and Tokunaga evaluate automatically generated pronoun reference questions. Chinkina and Meurers generate questions for evaluating language learning. Finally, Stasaski and Hearst generate multiple choice questions using an ontology.

Estimating Item Difficulty: A last topic in the test domain is Pado's paper on estimating question difficulty in the domain of automatic grading.

Readability: Gonzalez-Garduño and Søgaard measure gaze to predict readability while Štajner et al. measure viewing time per word in autistic and neurotypical readers. Yaneva et al. also explore readability assessment for people with cognitive disabilities. Beigman Klebanov et al. study the challenges of varying text complexity in a read-aloud intervention program. Östling and Grigonyte use deep convolutional neural networks to measure text quality. Sheng et al. introduce the pedagogical roles of documents to study pedagogical values. Gordon et al. generate reading lists of technical text. Finally, Wolska and Clausen simplify metaphorical language for young readers.

Dialogue: There are two papers on dialogue, but with very different topics. In the first, Lugini and Litman predict specificity in classroom discussions. In the second, Jin et al. develop a system for interpreting questions in a virtual patient dialogue system.

Annotation/Databases: Loughnane et al. create a database that links learning content, linguistic annotation and open-source resources. Laarmann-Quante et al. develop a novel German learner corpus.

Finally there are two papers with content so original that they don't fit into any of the categories above: Kochmar and Shutova investigate how semantic knowledge is acquired in English as a second language and evaluate the pace of development across a number of dimensions. Chen and Lee predict an audience's laughter during an oral presentation.

This year, the workshop is hosting a Shared Task on Native Language Identification[2] (NLI). NLI is the process of automatically identifying the native language (L1) of a non-native speaker based solely on language that he or she produces in another language. Two previous shared tasks on NLI have been organized in which the task was to identify the native language of non-native speakers of English based on essays and spoken responses to a standardized assessment of academic English proficiency. The first shared task[3] was based on the essays only and was also held with the BEA workshop in 2013. Three years later, Computational Paralinguistics Challenge[4] at Interspeech 2016 hosted a sub-challenge on identifying the native language based solely on the *spoken* responses. This year's shared task combines the inputs from the two previous tasks. There are three tracks: NLI on the essay only, NLI on the speech response only, and NLI using both responses from a test taker. 19 teams competed in the NLI shared task, with 17 presenting their systems during the poster session. A summary report of the shared task (Malmasi et al.) will be presented orally.

We wish to thank everyone who showed interest and submitted a paper, all of the authors for their contributions, the members of the Program Committee for their thoughtful reviews, and everyone who is attending this workshop. We would especially like to thank our sponsors: at the Gold Level, Turnitin | LightSide, Grammarly and Duolingo; at the Silver level, Educational Testing Service (ETS), Pacific Metrics, National Board of Medical Examiners (NBME), and iLexIR; at the Bronze level, Cognii. Their contributions help fund workshop extras, such as the dinner which is a great social and networking event, especially for students.

Joel Tetreault, Grammarly
Jill Burstein, Educational Testing Services
Ekaterina Kochmar, University of Cambridge
Claudia Leacock, Grammarly
Helen Yannakoudakis, University of Cambridge

---

[2]https://sites.google.com/site/nlisharedtask/home
[3]https://sites.google.com/site/nlisharedtask2013/home
[4]http://emotion-research.net/sigs/speech-sig/is16-compare

Mariano Felice, University of Cambridge
Michael Flor, Educational Testing Service
Peter Foltz, Pearson
Hector-Hugo Franco-Penya, DIT
Thomas François, Université Catholique de Louvain
Michael Gamon, Microsoft Research
Dipesh Gautam, University of Memphis
Binyam Gebrekidan Gebre, Philips
Kallirroi Georgila, University of Southern California
Cyril Goutte, National Research Council Canada
Roman Grundkiewicz, Adam Mickiewicz University in Poznan
Iryna Gurevych, TU Darmstadt
Na-Rae Han, University of Pittsburgh
Jiangang Hao, Educational Testing Service
Rachel Harsley, University of Illinois at Chicago
Homa B. Hashemi, University of Pittsburgh
Marti A. Hearst, UC Berkeley
Trude Heift, Simon Fraser University
Derrick Higgins, American Family Insurance
Andrea Horbach, University of Duisburg-Essen
Chung-Chi Huang, Frostburg State University
Radu Tudor Ionescu, University of Bucharest
Ross Israel, Factual
Pamela Jordan, University of Pittsburgh
Marcin Junczys-Dowmunt, Adam Mickiewicz University in Poznan
Fazel Keshtkar, St. John's University
Levi King, Indiana University
Sigrid Klerke, University of Copenhagen
Ekaterina Kochmar, University of Cambridge
Mamoru Komachi, Tokyo Metropolitan University
Robert Krovetz, Lexical Research
Girish Kumar, Stanford University
Lun-Wei Ku, IIS, Academica Sinica
Kristopher Kyle, University of Hawaii
John Lee, City University of Hong Kong
Lung-Hao Lee, National Taiwan Normal University
James Lester, North Carolina State University
Chen Wee Leong, Educational Testing Service
Baoli Li, Henan University of Technology
Diane Litman, University of Pittsburgh
Annie Louis, University of Essex
Anastassia Loukina, Educational Testing Service
Xiaofei Lu, Pennsylvania State University
Fabiana MacMillan, Rosetta Stone
Nitin Madnani, Educational Testing Service
Shervin Malmasi, Harvard Medical School
Liliana Mamani Sanchez, University College Dublin
Montse Maritxalar, University of the Basque Country
Ditty Matthew, Indian Institute of Technology Madras
Julie Medero, Harvey Mudd College
Beata Megyesi, Uppsala University

Mohsen Mesgar, Heidelberg Institute for Theoretical Studies
Angeliki Metallinou, Amazon
Detmar Meurers, University of Tübingen
Christian M. Meyer, Technische Universität Darmstadt
Lisa Michaud, Aspect Software
Michael Mohler, Language Computer Corporation
Maria Moritz, Faculty of Mathematics and Computer Science
Smaranda Muresan, Columbia University
William Murray, Pearson
Courtney Napoles, Johns Hopkins University
Hwee Tou Ng, National University of Singapore
Huy Nguyen, University of Pittsburgh
Nobal Niraula, Boeing Research & Technology
Simon Ostermann, Saarland University
Alexis Palmer, University of North Texas
Siddharth Patwardhan, Apple
Ted Pedersen, University of Minnesota, Duluth
Isaac Persing, University of Texas at Dallas
Patti Price, PPRICE Speech and Language Technology Consulting
Martí Quixal, Universitat Oberta de Catalunya
Preethi Raghavan, IBM
Zahra Rahimi, University of Pittsburgh
Lakshmi Ramachandran, A9.com
David Randolph, University of Illinois at Chicago
Sudha Rao, University of Maryland
Livy Real, IBM Research
Marek Rei, University of Cambridge
Robert Reynolds, UiT The Arctic University of Norway
Brian Riordan, Educational Testing Service
Andrew Rosenberg, IBM
Alla Rozovskaya, Queens College (CUNY)
Alexander Rush, Harvard
Anton Rytting, University of Maryland
Keisuke Sakaguchi, Johns Hopkins University
Elizabeth Salesky, MIT LL
Allen Schmaltz, Harvard University
Swapna Somasundaran, Educational Testing Service
Helmer Strik, Radboud University Nijmegen
David Suendermann-Oeft, Educational Testing Service
Kaveh Taghipour, National University of Singapore
Fatemeh Torabi Asr, Indiana University
Yuen-Hsien Tseng, National Taiwan Normal University
Sowmya Vajjala, Iowa State University
Giulia Venturi, Istituto di Linguistica Computazionale (ILC-CNR)
Aline Villavicencio, Federal University of Rio Grande do Sul
Carl Vogel, Computational Linguistics Lab, O'Reilly Institute
Elena Volodina, University of Gothenburg
Michael White, The Ohio State University
Denise Whitelock, The Open University
David Wible, National Central University
Alistair Willis, The Open University

Magdelena Wolska, Eberhard Karls Universität Tübingen
Michael Wojatzki, University of Duisburg-Essen
Huichao Xue, Google
Zheng Yuan, University of Cambridge
Marcos Zampieri, Saarland University
Torsten Zesch, University of Duisburg-Essen
Fan Zhang, University of Pittsburgh
Xiaodan Zhu, National Research Council Canada

Table of Contents

Workshop Program

Friday, September 8, 2017

8:45–9:00   ***Load Oral Presentations***

9:00–10:30   **Session 1**

9:00–9:15   ***Opening Remarks***

9:15–9:40   *Question Difficulty – How to Estimate Without Norming, How to Use for Automated Grading*
Ulrike Pado

9:40–10:05   *Combining CNNs and Pattern Matching for Question Interpretation in a Virtual Patient Dialogue System*
Lifeng Jin, Michael White, Evan Jaffe, Laura Zimmerman and Douglas Danforth

10:05–10:30   *Continuous fluency tracking and the challenges of varying text complexity*
Beata Beigman Klebanov, Anastassia Loukina, John Sabatini and Tenaha O'Reilly

10:30–11:00   **Break**

11:00–12:35   **Session 2**

11:00–11:25   *Auxiliary Objectives for Neural Error Detection Models*
Marek Rei and Helen Yannakoudakis

11:25–11:50   *Linked Data for Language-Learning Applications*
Robyn Loughnane, Kate McCurdy, Peter Kolb and Stefan Selent

11:50–12:10   *Predicting Specificity in Classroom Discussion*
Luca Lugini and Diane Litman

12:10–12:35   *A Report on the 2017 Native Language Identification Shared Task*
Shervin Malmasi, Keelan Evanini, Aoife Cahill, Joel Tetreault, Robert Pugh, Christopher Hamill, Diane Napolitano and Yao Qian

12:35–14:00   **Lunch**

Friday, September 8, 2017 (continued)

15:30–16:00   **Break**

16:00–17:30   **Session 3**

16:00–16:25   *Using Gaze to Predict Text Readability*
Ana Valeria Gonzalez-Garduño and Anders Søgaard

16:25–16:50   *Annotating Orthographic Target Hypotheses in a German L1 Learner Corpus*
Ronja Laarmann-Quante, Katrin Ortmann, Anna Ehlert, Maurice Vogel and Stefanie
Dipper

16:50–17:15   *A Large Scale Quantitative Exploration of Modeling Strategies for Content Scoring*
Nitin Madnani, Anastassia Loukina and Aoife Cahill

17:15–17:30   ***Closing Remarks***

Question Difficulty – How to Estimate Without Norming, How to Use for Automated Grading

Ulrike Padó

ulrike.pado@hft-stuttgart.de
Hochschule für Technik Stuttgart
Schellingstr. 24
70174 Stuttgart, Germany

Abstract

Question difficulty estimates guide test creation, but are too costly for small-scale testing. We empirically verify that Bloom's Taxonomy, a standard tool for difficulty estimation during question creation, reliably predicts question difficulty observed after testing in a short-answer corpus. We also find that difficulty can be approximated by the amount of variation in student answers, which can be computed before grading.

We show that question difficulty and its approximations are useful for *automated grading*, allowing us to identify the optimal feature set for grading each question even in an unseen-question setting.

1 Introduction

Testing is a core component of teaching, and many tasks in NLP for education are concerned with creating good questions and correctly grading the answers. We look at how to estimate question difficulty from question wording as a link between the two tasks.

From a test creation point of view, knowing question difficulty levels is imperative: Too many easy questions, and the test will be unable to distinguish between the more able test-takers, who all achieve equally good results. Too many hard questions, and only the most able test-takers will be clearly distinguishable from the (low-performing) rest.

In large-scale testing, question difficulty and other measures of question quality are established through prior *norming* (Downey, 2010), where the questions are answered by a pool of test-takers in a dry run before definitive use with a similar demographic. Difficulty is then determined on the basis of the observed results using probabilistic test theory (PTT). Norming is usually not available in automated question creation or in ad-hoc testing in small classrooms, while the need for correctly determining question difficulty of course remains.

In this situation, teachers often use Bloom's Taxonomy (Bloom, 1956), a classification of the knowledge dimensions and cognitive processes involved in the completion of a test task, to formulate questions of appropriate difficulty. In the literature, the difficulty of multiple-choice questions has been successfully aligned with the cognitive process dimension of the Bloom hierarchy (Tiemeier et al. (2011); Kim et al. (2012), but see also Kibble and Johnson (2011)). In this paper, we empirically evaluate the predictive power of both Bloom dimensions for estimating the empirically observed difficulty of *short-answer questions*, which require the test-taker to freely formulate one to three sentence answers. We find that the Taxonomy allows a useful approximation of question difficulty at the time of question creation. We find clear empirical evidence that the *instructional context*, that is the teaching materials presented in instruction, has to be taken into account when determining difficulty using the Taxonomy.

Once test-taker answers are available, but before grading makes PTT analysis possible, another predictor for question difficulty becomes available: *Answer variation*, the average amount of variation within the student answers for each question, is computed based only on the answer strings.

We also look at question difficulty from the point of view of improving automated short-answer grading (SAG). To date, the focus of research has been on finding informative features, ranging from deep processing (Zesch et al., 2013; Hahn and Meurers, 2012) through text-based similarity (Sultan et al., 2016) to shallow, string-based approaches (Okoye et al., 2013; Jimenez et al., 2013). Padó (2016) has proposed to perform pre-grading model selection by tailoring feature sets to the characteristics of

1

Proceedings of the 12th Workshop on Innovative Use of NLP for Building Educational Applications, pages 1–10
Copenhagen, Denmark, September 8, 2017. ©2017 Association for Computational Linguistics

different short-answer corpora. We refine this idea and show that within the same corpus, questions with different difficulty levels also profit from different feature sets, and that the Bloom Taxonomy levels and student answer variation can be used as stand-ins for feature set prediction if difficulty estimates are not available. These results point to a new avenue of research in SAG.

The paper is structured as follows: We begin by providing some theoretical background on PTT and Bloom's Taxonomy in Section 2. Our first set of analyses tests the reliability of the Bloom's Taxonomy question difficulty predictions for our data set (Section 3). The second analysis in Section 4 focuses on the relationship between answer variation and question difficulty. Our final set of experiments investigates the use of question difficulty for question-level model selection in short-answer grading (Section 5). We end with a discussion and conclusions in Section 6.

2 Theoretical Background

Our analyses require defining ground truth question difficulty. We use the Rasch model from probabilistic test theory for this estimate. This Section also introduces Bloom's Taxonomy, a tool from the field of education intended for analysing the cognitive requirements for answering a question, and thereby its difficulty.

2.1 PTT Difficulty Estimation with the Rasch Model

Test theory is concerned with determining test-taker ability and analysing question quality and difficulty. Probabilistic test theory formulates latent trait models for these tasks. Latent trait models assume that a student's ability and a question's difficulty are not directly observable, but depend probabilistically on the observed scores. The two best-known proponents are the Rasch model (Rasch, 1960) and the related Item Response Theory models[1] (van der Linden, 2010).

The Rasch model fits a joint model of question difficulty and student ability on the basis of the manual grades awarded to student answers (i.e., after testing). The goal is to establish question difficulty independently of concrete test-takers and vice versa. Concretely, the Rasch model estimates question difficulty and student ability given the fol-

lowing relation (where B_n is the ability of student n and D_i is the difficulty of question i):

$$P_{ni}(x = 1|B_n, D_i) = \frac{e^{(B_n - D_i)}}{1 + e^{(B_n - D_i)}} \quad (1)$$

Success ($x = 1$) of a student n on a question i is linked to the difference between the student's ability and the question's difficulty. If the ability is greater than the difficulty, the student is likely to succeed, or if the inverse is true, the student is more likely to fail. Estimates of B and D are made iteratively from the test results.

The resulting measures are returned in logits and question difficulty is centered at 0, so that easy items have low or negative difficulty estimates and hard items have high difficulty estimates.

2.2 Bloom's Taxonomy

Bloom's Taxonomy (Bloom, 1956), revised by Anderson and Krathwohl (2014), is a well-known tool for creating and interpreting teaching objectives as well as writing test questions and estimating their difficulty. The Taxonomy has two independent dimensions: the *Cognitive Process* (CP) dimension and the *Knowledge* dimension (KD). The Cognitive Process dimension describes which type of cognitive activity is necessary to complete a task, in our case to answer a question. The least demanding process is Remember, followed by Understand (e.g., explain, compare, classify), Apply, Analyze and, the most demanding, Create.

The second dimension of the revised Taxonomy looks at the type of knowledge needed to complete the task. The simplest knowledge type is Factual (facts and terminology), followed by Conceptual (categories, principles and models), Procedural (algorithms, techniques and criteria) and Metacognitive (including strategic knowledge and self-knowledge).

Anderson et al. explicitly recommend that Taxonomy users infer the dimension levels from the question wording: Verbs like "compare" or "generalize" indicate the Understand level, while "identify" or most simply "name" belong to the Remember level. To assess the Knowledge dimension level needed to solve a task, Anderson et al. advise teachers to look at the direct object of the verb describing the required Cognitive Process. This explicit operationalization of level identification as analysis of the question formulation indicates the possibility of automating the process. Making these inferences however is complex for questions which set

---

[1]The most fundamental one-parameter IRT model is mathematically equivalent to the Rasch model.

Question	Warum hat jede Klasse die Methode `public String toString()`?
	Why does every class contain the method `public String toString()`?
Reference Answer	Die Methode wird von der Klasse `Object` an alle Klassen in Java vererbt.
	The method is inherited by all Java classes from class `Object`.

Bloom's CP	Understand	Bloom's KD	Conceptual
Bloom's CP text&question	Remember	Rasch Difficulty	0.89

Table 1: Example question with Bloom categories (original and re-assigned, see Section 3.3) and Rasch difficulty (centered at 0, larger means harder)

concrete tasks. For example, for the question "Calculate the voltage given I and R.", we need to infer that Ohm's law, a generalization, will be applied to a concrete problem to arrive at the Apply cognitive process on the Conceptual level.

3 Bloom's Taxonomy and Difficulty

We now empirically evaluate how accurately Bloom's Taxonomy (Bloom, 1956), revised by Anderson and Krathwohl (2014), predicts question difficulty as estimated from student performance in a manually graded short-answer corpus. We check whether questions on the different levels of the Taxonomy show different ground-truth difficulty, as provided by a Rasch model.

3.1 Data

We use the Computer Science Short Answers in German corpus (CSSAG, Padó and Kiefer (2015)). This corpus contains 31 content-assessment questions with reference answers as well as student answers by highly-proficient speakers of German (native or near-native). Anonymized student IDs are available to track answers by the same person, and there is sufficient person overlap between the questions to allow consistent PTT analysis.

We exclude question 6 from our data set. Rasch modelling uncovered an extreme mismatch of expected and actual difficulty, and further inspection of the answers shows that the question was often misunderstood and therefore skipped or answered incorrectly. Uncovering questions like this is one of the standard uses of PTT, so we feel justified in excluding the question after careful analysis.

3.2 Method

For the empirical evaluation of Bloom's Taxonomy levels, we annotated the CSSAG questions with the corresponding Cognitive Process and Knowledge dimension. The author's annotations were verified by comparison to the level annotations of

two colleagues familiar with the Taxonomy and the CSSAG subject matter, A and B.

The Cognitive Process annotations show substantial annotator agreement (UP-A: $\kappa = 73.7$; UP-B: $\kappa = 82.6$; A-B: $\kappa = 67.5$). Literature results, which mostly consider multiple choice questions, are often not this robust (Kibble and Johnson (2011): $\kappa = 33.3$, Cunnington et al. (1996): at most $\kappa = 48$ for a binary decision).[2]

The Knowledge dimension is much less consistent (UP-A: $\kappa = 11.8$; UP-B: $\kappa = 24.9$; A-B: $\kappa = 32.8$). Analysis showed that the annotators entertained substantially different interpretations of the levels, making adjudication impossible. Classifying the Knowledge levels involves the annotators' private conceptualisations of the question topic domain (What comprises procedural knowledge in Computer Science?), which leads to much greater inconsistency than classifying the process verb for the CP levels.

We use the author's level annotations, with the caveat that the Knowledge level annotations are noisy. We found questions on the Remember ($n = 10$) , Understand ($n = 17$) and Apply ($n = 3$) levels of the CP dimension and in the Factual ($n = 10$), Conceptual ($n = 18$) and Procedural ($n = 2$) levels of the Knowledge dimension.

We also estimated question difficulties on the basis of the student performance in the corpus. Table 1 shows a question from CSSAG with its reference answer and Bloom levels as well as its estimated difficulty.

Since we are doing data analysis and not building predictive models, we used the whole corpus without holding out test data.

For our analyses, we use the `lm` function in R[3] to induce linear models for question difficulty, us-

---

[2]Kim et al. (2012) argue that level assignment is harder for multiple choice questions because the answer choices may provide clues to the students, effectively reducing higher-level questions to Remember.

[3]`www.r-project.org`

	Estimate	Std. Error	Sig.
CP Remember	-0.388	0.205	ns
CP Understand	0.632	0.247	*
CP Apply	-0.780	0.473	ns

Table 2: Difficulty and the Cognitive Process levels, re-assigned using instructional context: Linear model coefficients. *: $p < 0.05$, ns: not significant.

ing the Bloom dimensions as factors. Since the difficulty estimates are centered on 0, we force the intercept to 0 in the models.

3.3 Analysis I: Bloom's Cognitive Processes and Difficulty

We begin by analysing the relationship between Bloom's CP dimension and ground-truth difficulty.

We train a linear model of difficulty, using the three CP levels present in the data as factors. However, the linear model is not significant, and neither are the coefficients. From this first analysis, it seems that Bloom's Cognitive Process dimension cannot predict observed question difficulties.

A closer look at the Taxonomy description reveals a problem. The Cognitive Process dimension was first annotated taking only the question into account. However, Anderson and Krathwohl (2014) (p.71) state that "If the assessment task is identical to a task or example used during instruction, we are probably assessing *remembering*, despite our efforts to the contrary." It is quite intuitive that, beyond the specific wording of the question, instructional context influences question difficulty. Therefore, we analysed the teaching materials (lecture slides) used for instruction before the CSSAG questions were answered in a test. The categories were then re-assigned with the teaching materials in mind: If for an Understand question, there was text presented on a single slide (or on several slides for a multi-component question) that would have been graded as a correct answer given the reference answer, the question was classified as Remember instead, since no active knowledge transfer was required by the student in this case. We re-classified six of originally 17 Understand questions as Remember (among them the example question in Table 1). The new classification based on this closer reading of Anderson et al. is called Bloom's CP text&question below.

Table 2 shows the results of another linear model of ground-truth difficulty using the three

CP text&question levels as factors. The model is significant on the $p < 0.05$ level, so the use of instructional context yields a quantifiable relationship between the Bloom levels and ground-truth difficulty. This relationship is carried by the Understand level - this model coefficient is significant and positive, meaning that Understand questions are predicted to have higher than average difficulty. The non-significant negative coefficient for Remember indicates a tendency for these questions to be less difficult than average. The estimate for the Apply level is based on only three data points, so the strong tendency for easier-than-average difficulty must be taken with a grain of salt. Unlike the findings for Remember and Understand, this last observation is not in line with the predictions of the Bloom Taxonomy. We return to this in Section 3.5.

In sum, the categories do show a significant difference in difficulty, but only if the explicit presentation of material during instruction is considered.

The Bloom CP text&question categories are by design strongly correlated with the existence of the answer in the teaching materials: Questions in category Remember always refer to explicitly presented material, while questions in category Understand never do.[4] Therefore, the predictive performance of the CP question&text levels could in principle be due just to the existence of the answer in the teaching materials. We therefore trained a linear model of difficulty using *answer presented* (1 if the answer was shown on the lecture slides, as defined for the category re-assignment above, 0 otherwise) as a factor. This model did not reach significance. We conclude that the predictive power of the Bloom dimensions (when assigned with the teaching materials in mind) is in fact at the core of our findings.

3.4 Analysis II: Bloom's Knowledge Dimension and Difficulty

We now turn to the Knowledge dimension of Bloom's Taxonomy. In the data, we find 10 questions on the Factual level, 18 on the Conceptual level and two on the Procedural level. The KD levels are not related to the *answer presented* measure: While answering a question may require knowledge that has been explicitly presented, the correct

---

[4]In category Apply, explicitly presented or inferrable facts have to be applied to a new situation, so there is no a priori relationship between the category and the answer having been presented. In our data, all Apply questions referred to presented material.

	Estimate	Std. Error	Sig.
KD Factual	-0.785	0.263	**
KD Conceptual	0.316	0.196	ns
KD Procedural	0.280	0.588	ns

Table 3: Difficulty and the Knowledge levels: Linear model coefficients. **: $p < 0.01$, ns: not significant.

answer need not have been.

Table 3 shows the coefficients of another linear model of difficulty, now using the Knowledge dimension levels and again fixing the intercept at 0. The model predictions are significantly correlated with difficulty ($p < 0.05$). The significant coefficient is Factual knowledge, which results in the prediction of easier-than-average difficulty. This, of course, agrees with the Bloom Taxonomy.

Despite the large disagreement between the three annotators on this dimension, the annotated Knowledge levels still hold relevant information with regard to question difficulty, and that information is in line with the predictions of the Bloom Taxonomy.

3.5 Analysis III: Both Bloom Dimensions and Difficulty

Next, we analyse the relationship between the two dimensions of Bloom's Taxonomy, which are conceptually independent. A linear model of difficulty using the levels of both dimensions as factors is significant. Factors CP Understand and KD Factual remain significant as in the individual models, but there are no significant interactions, probably due to sparse data. The raw data still show interesting patterns, though, which we will analyse next.

Table 4 shows the category difficulty means across both Bloom dimensions. Where the table cells are appropriately filled, the mean difficulties reflect the assumptions of the Taxonomy:

CP Remember questions are a lot easier than CP Understand questions (recall the coefficient estimates in Table 2). Within the Remember dimension (the only one to use all three Knowledge levels), mean difficulty rises monotonically in accord with the Knowledge dimension definition.

We now see that the reason for Apply questions overall appearing twice as easy as Remember questions may be the lack of Apply questions using Conceptual and Procedural knowledge. This seems more likely than an effect of noise, since all three

Apply questions are at most of difficulty -0.5, with an average of -0.78, which is clearly on the easy side of the spectrum.

It is also striking that there is an effect of CP level beyond Knowledge dimension for Conceptual, but not Factual questions: The Apply-Factual questions are as difficult on average as the Remember-Factual questions, while the Understand-Conceptual questions are much harder than the Remember-Conceptual questions. Further investigation with a larger data base and more closely standardized Knowledge level annotation would certainly be interesting given this pattern.

In the Knowledge Dimension grand averages, the Taxonomy is clearly mirrored: Questions using Factual knowledge are easier than questions using Conceptual knowledge (this corresponds to the model coefficients shown in Table 3 above). Questions for Procedural knowledge (with an n of just 2) appear overall a little too easy. Keep in mind, though, that the level annotations for the Knowledge dimension must be assumed to be noisy given the low inter-annotator κ values.

In sum, both dimensions of Bloom's Taxonomy taken together categorize the CSSAG questions into four categories of monotonously increasing difficulty in the raw data (ignoring for the moment the Apply-Factual category): Remember-Factual, Remember-Conceptual, Remember-Procedural and Understand-Conceptual. The data confirm that Bloom categories are predictive of question difficulty before testing, allowing teachers and test creators to balance their tests before or even without norming. Vitally, however, the instructional context of the question has to be taken into account for categorization.

4 Answer Variation

Our analyses so far have looked at predicting question difficulty solely from properties of the question (and instructional context), prior to testing. Once the question has been answered, but before grading, another potentially informative predictor of question difficulty becomes available: Answer variation, measured either as the average similarity of student answers among themselves or their average similarity with the reference answer.

We hypothesize a link between answer variation and question difficulty based on the assumption that easy questions (e.g. on the Bloom Remember-Factual levels) have clear-cut answers that many

	Factual	Conceptual	Procedural	Grand Avg
Remember	-0.79 ($n = 7$)	-0.18 ($n = 7$)	0.28 ($n = 2$)	-0.39
Understand	–	0.63 ($n = 11$)	–	0.63
Apply	-0.78 ($n = 3$)	–	–	-0.78
Grand Avg	-0.79	0.37	0.28	

Table 4: Cognitive Process text&question and Knowledge dimensions, Rasch difficulty averages (number of questions).

Model	Adjusted R^2	Model Sig.
KD + CP text & question	0.290	*
Avg. SAV	0.246	*
SAV + KD + CP text & question	0.312	*

Table 5: Difficulty predicted by the Bloom Knowledge dimension (KD) and Cognitive Process (CP) levels and SAV (student answer variation): Linear model R^2 values and significances. *: $p < 0.05$.

students know. This should lead to many highly similar student answers (mirroring the reference answer). Difficult questions that require understanding of conceptual knowledge should show higher variation in the phrasing of the correct answer as well as more incorrect answers, leading to higher answer variation both among student answers and with regard to the reference answer.

If such a link indeed exists, then discrepancies between a question's intended difficulty and its observed answer variation would help identify problematic questions even before grading.

We model average student answer variance through the Greedy String Tiling (GST) similarity measure (Wise, 1996), which ranges between 0 and 1 (where 0 indicates no overlap between the strings – high variation, and 1 indicates perfect overlap – low variation). Comparing the (non-empty) student answers and the reference answer is straightforward. For the average similarity within all non-empty student answers, we use each student answer in turn as the point of comparison since GST is non-symmetric. We use the same corpus as before (see Section 3.1).

Rasch question difficulty (the assumed ground truth) is indeed correlated with the average variation between student and reference answers at Spearman's $\rho = -0.372, p < 0.05$ and with the average variation of student answers among themselves at Spearman's $\rho = -0.668, p < 0.001$. For both measures, difficulty is low when answer similarity is high (and therefore, answer variation is low). Perhaps surprisingly, the variation of answers among themselves is a much stronger predictor

than variation with regard to the reference answer. This may be because the similarity measure does not account for valid paraphrases (e.g., by technical terms in the reference answer). Relying just on the student answers is more elegant in any case, as no assumptions are made about the quality (or even existence) of the reference answer.

Next, we train a linear model predicting difficulty, just as before, but using student answer variation (SAV) as a factor. Table 5 compares the results for SAV to a model using the Bloom KD and CP text&question levels. We also combine SAV and both Bloom dimensions. We find that all three models significantly predict difficulty. At $n = 30$, there were no significant differences between the models in an ANOVA. We do see some indication of differences between the models in the R^2 values, however, which reflect how much of the variance in the variable *difficulty* the model accounts for. For the combination of the Bloom dimensions, R^2 is somewhat higher than for SAV alone, but combining all factors yields another small increase.

We conclude that the Bloom levels, if known, are the best predictors of question difficulty. However, it can be difficult to assign the levels for existing questions if instructional materials are not available. In this case, the amount of within-answer variation for each question can be used to estimate question difficulty before grades and PTT estimates are available, or if the PTT assumptions are not met.

Results from Dueñas et al. (2015) suggest that flat features such as word and length information from the question and reference answer are also useful in predicting difficulty; for them, simplified taxonomy categories worked better than Bloom categories. Note that they had no information on the instructional materials used and so could not adjust the CP categories (see Section 3.3).

5 Automated Grading: Features and Difficulty

Having looked at difficulty and its predictability from the point of view of test creation in the previous section, we now turn to an analysis of the usefulness of question difficulty information for automated grading.

In Padó (2016), we found that on the corpus level, there are optimal feature combinations for different data sets. Learner corpora of text comprehension questions (lower on the Bloom hierarchy) can be graded well with shallow features close to the string level, while corpora for content assessment of native speakers (containing questions higher on the Bloom hierarchy) require features derived from syntactic and semantic analysis. Following this lead, we investigate the link between question difficulty and optimal feature sets for grading on the question level. We show that question difficulty can indeed be used for question-level model selection (of the optimal feature set). Since question difficulty is often not known at grading time, we also look at Bloom's Taxonomy levels and SAV as predictors for model selection.

5.1 Automated Grading Model and Features

For reasons of comparability, we use the automated binary grading model from Padó (2016). It consists of a decision tree algorithm that considers features from five feature groups. Table 6 lists them in order of increasing complexity of the linguistic analysis necessary to compute them. We will refer to the NGram as well as the Similarity features (consisting of the Greedy String Tiling, Cosine, and Levenshtein Edit Distance similarity algorithms) as *shallow* features, because only the character strings of the answers and possibly lemmatization are needed. The *deep* features are the overlap between student and reference answer in terms of Dependency relations or Lexical Resource Semantics (LRS) components (Richter and Sailer, 2004), as well as the output of the Excitement Open Platform Textual Entailment system (Magnini et al., 2014).

5.2 Method

We train the grading model in the leave-one-question-out setting on the CSSAG corpus (Section 3.1). This means the test questions and answers are completely unseen during training. We do five training and test runs for each question: First with only the NGram features, then adding the Similarity features and so on, until the full feature set is used. We then determine for each question which feature sets yield the best performance. We report per-question prediction accuracy, which ranges between 50 and 88.9%.

5.3 Feature Sets and Model Selection

We find that for 12 out of the 30 available questions, the best performance is only reached using deep features in addition to the shallow features. For the remaining 18 questions, the best performance is already reached using just the NGram or NGram and Similarity features. In seven of these 18 cases, model performance even declines when the deep features are added, for the remaining 11 cases, either feature set yields optimal performance. These results show that there is room for question-level feature optimization.

The short-answer grading model with the full feature set (the best choice for the corpus according to Padó (2016)) reaches an overall accuracy of 73.11%. If we choose the best-performing feature set for each question instead of the full model, overall accuracy increases to 74.35%.

These results indicate that automatic grading can be improved by choosing the best-performing grading model for each question instead of relying on a per-corpus choice. We expect greater improvements with fine-tuned features, because the feature implementations from Padó (2016) were left intentionally vanilla so the results would generalize more easily over the range of corpora used there.

5.4 Model Selection by Difficulty

We continue our analyses with the 19 questions with optimal behaviour for just one feature set. For the other 11 questions, either feature set works well, so they carry limited information for us. To verify that difficulty is indeed related to the optimal feature set for grading, we train a linear model of difficulty using the feature set (deep or shallow) that shows optimal performance for each question. The resulting model significantly ($p < 0.01$) predicts difficulty.

Feature Group	Features
NGram	Unigram, Bigram, Trigram overlap of student and reference answer
Similarity	Greedy String Tiling, Cosine, Levenshtein measures
Dependency	Dependency triple overlap of student and reference answer
Semantics	LRS component overlap of student and reference answer
TE	Textual Entailment of reference answer by student answer

Table 6: Overview of the feature set for automated grading

	Accuracy
Frequency Baseline	63.2
Difficulty	78.9

Table 7: Model Selection: Accuracy of predicting the best-performing feature set

We now change tasks and evaluate the usefulness of difficulty for model selection. We evaluate how well the best-performing feature set (shallow or deep) for each question can be predicted by a logistic regression model (R cv.glm) using difficulty as its only feature.[5] We use leave-one-out cross-validation.

Table 7 shows the classification accuracy of predicting when the shallow feature set will outperform the deep feature set. Using only ground-truth difficulty, the prediction is correct for roughly 80% of the 19 questions. This clearly outperforms the frequency baseline (always predict the deep feature set). Difficulty therefore is very informative with regard to the most useful features for SAG.

5.5 Model Selection: Bloom Levels and SAV

If difficulty estimates are not available, Bloom levels or SAV may still be obtainable. We have shown above that both can be used to predict difficulty. In the case of Bloom levels, we also see a promising pattern in the raw data: There is a clear tendency for questions low on the Bloom hierarchy to be optimally gradable with shallow features, while questions higher on the Bloom hierarchy require deep features. For three out of four Remember-Factual questions (out of the 19 questions with one optimal feature set), optimal grading performance is reached with shallow features. For the five Remember-Conceptual questions, two show optimal performance with shallow and three with deep features. Six out of seven Understand-

Conceptual questions require deep features, and there is one Remember-Procedural question, also optimally graded with deep features. (The two Apply-Factual questions are split between deep and shallow features, in keeping with their estimated difficulty, see Section 3.5).

We therefore use the Bloom levels to train a logistic regression models to predict the optimal feature set, just as above. A second model uses SAV. The left-hand side of Table 8 shows that for our small data set, these factors perform practically at chance level, much below the frequency baseline.[6]

This pessimistic result is not the whole picture. We also evaluate three simple, conservative heuristics based on the Taxonomy, SAV and difficulty, respectively, that do not require training. The results are on the right-hand side of Table 8.

The Bloom heuristic predicts the shallow feature set for all Remember-Factual questions, and the deep feature set otherwise. Its accuracy of 74% clearly outperforms the frequency baseline.

The SAV heuristic predicts the shallow feature set for the 20% of questions with the lowest student answer variation (i.e., highest within-answer similarity). We chose 20% for the boundary based on the observation that there are five Bloom dimension combinations present in the data and the Bloom heuristic assigns the shallow feature set for only one of them. The SAV heuristic performs at the level of the frequency baseline.

The difficulty heuristic predicts the shallow feature set for the easiest 20% of questions. At 84% accuracy, this prediction model even outperforms the linear difficulty model from Section 5.4.

The results underscore the usefulness of difficulty for model selection. In parallel to Sections 3 and 4 above, we find that difficulty can be approximated well by the levels of the Bloom Taxonomy,

---

[5] Note that our result is strictly speaking an upper bound, since difficulty was originally inferred using all questions.

[6] For the Bloom Taxonomy evaluation, one dimension level was represented only once, so the corresponding data point was unpredictable and was excluded, yielding $n = 18$ and a frequency baseline of 61.1.

	Accuracy			Accuracy
Frequency Baseline	63.2		Frequency Baseline	63.2
Difficulty	78.9		Difficulty heuristic	84.2
Bloom KD & CP	55.6		Bloom KD + CP heuristic	73.7
SAV	52.6		SAV heuristic	63.2

Table 8: Model Selection: Accuracy of predicting the best-performing feature set. Left: Logistic model, right: Heuristic

and to a degree by the variation within student answers, if the levels are not available. While for small data sets such as ours, learning a selection model may not be possible, difficulty and its stand-in measures contain sufficient information to formulate an informative, yet simple heuristic model.

6 Discussion and Conclusions

Question difficulty is important in test creation and question analysis (as our discovery and exclusion of an unsuitable question in Section 3.1 demonstrates). We have shown that is also an informative factor in optimizing automated grading: Question difficulty quite accurately predicts which feature set allows best grading performance. This insight allows us to use question difficulty to tailor models to specific questions and optimize SAG performance.

Difficulty, however, can only be estimated after grading, making it impractical to use in many SAG settings. We have shown that difficulty can be approximated by the question's levels on Bloom's Taxonomy, a standard tool in education, or, to a somewhat lesser extent, by SAV, the amount of variation present in student answers, measured in string similarity. These approximations are available before testing (Bloom) and grading (SAV).

In this context, we can refine the hypothesis put forward in Padó (2016) that the grading performance variation of different feature sets over different corpora is primarily due to differences in answer variation. Padó (2016) attributes these differences to different student populations (language learners have less ability to paraphrase than native or near-native speakers), which co-varied with elicitation tasks (learner reading understanding versus native content assessment). Our results here zoom in on native-level speakers in content assessment. We found a strong relationship between preferred grading features and question difficulty, while difficulty is partially expressed in answer variation.

The link between Bloom hierarchy levels and difficulty that we found provides more insight: Questions low on the Bloom hierarchy tend to be easier and are optimally graded with shallow features (close to the text level). Questions higher on the Bloom hierarchy require deep features (more extensive syntactic and semantic analysis). This matches the corpus-level results from Padó (2016) (on top of the effect of language ability): The corpora best graded with shallow features were learner corpora of text comprehension questions. Most of these questions are low on the Bloom hierarchy, since they ask the reader to repeat knowledge explicitly presented in the text.[7] On the other hand, content assessment corpora (such as CSSAG) contain more and higher Bloom levels and therefore more questions that require deep processing for grading.

An avenue for future work is the *automatic* inference of Bloom Taxonomy levels. In addition to facilitating SAG, knowing question difficulty levels without norming would increase the quality of manually created ad-hoc tests as well as automatically generated question sets. The guidelines from Anderson and Krathwohl (2014) suggest that the levels can be inferred from the question wording by Textual Entailment methods. Given the necessary inference steps and the patterns of human annotation consistency for the two dimensions, the Cognitive Process dimension lends itself more to automated assignment than the Knowledge dimension. Finally, we have shown that it is vital to identify cases of recall of instructional materials in level prediction.

Acknowledgements

The author would like to thank Sebastian Padó for helpful discussions and three anonymous reviewers for their insightful comments. Jan Seedorf and Sebastian Padó kindly provided Bloom annotations.

---

[7] A subset of text comprehension questions from CREG (Meurers et al., 2011) shows 59 Remember and 24 Understand questions out of 83 rated questions.

References

Lorin W. Anderson and David A. Krathwohl, editors. 2014. *A taxonomy for learning, teaching and assessing: A revision of Bloom's*. Pearson Education.

Benjamin. S. Bloom, editor. 1956. *The taxonomy of educational objectives, the classification of educational goals*, volume Handbook I: Cognitive Domain. David McKay, New York.

John Cunnington, Geoffrey Norman, Jennnifer Blake, Dale Dauphinee, and D. Blackmore. 1996. Applying learning taxonomies to test items: Is a fact an artifact? *Academic Medicine* 71(10).

Steven Downey. 2010. Test development. In Penelope Peterson, Eva Baker, and Barry McGaw, editors, *International Encyclopedia of Education*, Elsevier Ltd., pages 159–165.

George Dueñas, Sergio Jimenez, and Julia Baquero. 2015. Automatic prediction of item difficulty for short-answer questions. In *Proceedings of the 10th Colombian Computing Conference*.

Michael Hahn and Detmar Meurers. 2012. Evaluating the meaning of answers to reading comprehension questions: A semantics-based approach. In *Proceedings of the 7th Workshop on the Innovative Use of NLP for Building Educational Applications*. pages 326–336.

Sergio Jimenez, Claudia Becerra, and Alexander Gelbukh. 2013. Softcardinality: Hierarchical text overlap for student response analysis. In *Proceedings of SemEval-2013*.

Jonathan Kibble and Teresa Johnson. 2011. Are faculty predictions or item taxonomies useful for estimating the outcome of multiple-choice examinations? *Advances in Physiological Education* 35:396–401.

Myo Kyoung Kim, Rajul Patel, Jamoo Uohisono, and Lynn Beck. 2012. Incorporation of Bloom's taxonomy into multiple-choice examination questions for a pharmacotherapeutics course. *American Journal of Pharmaceutical Education* 76(6).

Bernardo Magnini, Roberto Zanoli, Ido Dagan, Katrin Eichler, Günter Neumann, Tae-Gil Noh, Sebastian Padó, Asher Stern, and Omer Levy. 2014. The Excitement Open Platform for textual inferences. In *Proceedings of the ACL demo session*.

Detmar Meurers, Ramon Ziai, Niels Ott, and Janina Kopp. 2011. Evaluating answers to reading comprehension questions in context: Results for German and the role of information structure. In *Proceedings of the TextInfer 2011 Workshop on Textual Entailment*. Edinburgh, Scottland, UK.

Ifeyinwa Okoye, Steven Bethard, and Tamara Sumner. 2013. Cu: Computational assessment of short free text answers - a tool for evaluating students' understanding. In *Proceedings of SemEval-2013*.

Ulrike Padó. 2016. Get semantic with me! The usefulness of different feature types for short-answer grading. In *Proceedings of COLING-2016*. Osaka, Japan.

Ulrike Padó and Cornelia Kiefer. 2015. Short answer grading: When sorting helps and when it doesn't. In *4th NLP4CALL workshop at Nodalida*. Vilnius, Lithuania.

Georg Rasch. 1960. *Probabilistic Models for Some Intelligence and Attainment Tests*. Danish Institute for Educational Research, Copenhagen.

Frank Richter and Manfred Sailer. 2004. Basic concepts of lexical resource semantics. In Arnold Beckmann and Norbert Preining, editors, *European Summer School in Logic, Language and Information 2003. Course Material I, volume 5 of Collegium Logicum*, Publication Series of the Kurt Gödel Society, Vienna, pages 87–143.

Md Arafat Sultan, Cristobal Salazar, and Tamara Sumner. 2016. Fast and easy short answer grading with high accuracy. In *Proceedings of NAACL-HLT 2016*. pages 1070–1075.

Amy Tiemeier, Zachary Stacy, and John Burke. 2011. Using multiple choice questions written at various Bloom's taxonomy levels to evaluate student performance across a therapeutics sequence. *Innovations in Pharmacy* 2(2).

Wim van der Linden. 2010. Item response theory. In Penelope Peterson, Eva Baker, and Barry McGaw, editors, *International Encyclopedia of Education*, Elsevier Ltd., pages 81–88.

Michael J. Wise. 1996. YAP3: Improved detection of similarities in computer program and other texts. In *SIGCSEB: SIGCSE Bulletin (ACM Special Interest Group on Computer Science Education)*. ACM Press, pages 130–134.

Torsten Zesch, Omer Levy, Iryna Gurevych, and Ido Dagan. 2013. UKP-BIU: Similarity and entailment metrics for student response analysis. In *Proceedings of SemEval-2013*.

Combining CNNs and Pattern Matching for Question Interpretation in a Virtual Patient Dialogue System

Lifeng Jin[1], Michael White[1], Evan Jaffe[1], Laura Zimmerman[2] and Douglas Danforth[2]
[1]Department of Linguistics, [2]Department of Family Medicine
The Ohio State University, Columbus, OH, USA
{jin, white, jaffe}@ling.osu.edu
zimmerman.411@osu.edu, doug.danforth@osumc.edu

Abstract

For medical students, virtual patient dialogue systems can provide useful training opportunities without the cost of employing actors to portray standardized patients. This work utilizes word- and character-based convolutional neural networks (CNNs) for question identification in a virtual patient dialogue system, outperforming a strong word- and character-based logistic regression baseline. While the CNNs perform well given sufficient training data, the best system performance is ultimately achieved by combining CNNs with a hand-crafted pattern matching system that is robust to label sparsity, providing a 10% boost in system accuracy and an error reduction of 47% as compared to the pattern-matching system alone.

1 Introduction

Standardized Patients (SPs) are actors who play the part of a patient with a specific medical history and pathology. Medical students interact with SPs to train skills like taking a patient history and developing a differential diagnosis. However, SPs are expensive and can behave inconsistently from student to student. A virtual patient dialogue system aims to overcome these issues as well as provide a means of automated evaluation of the medical student's interaction with the patient (see Figure 1).

Previous work with a hand-crafted pattern-matching system called ChatScript (Danforth et al., 2009, 2013) used a 3D avatar and allowed for students to input questions using text or speech. ChatScript matches input text using hand-written patterns and outputs a scripted re-

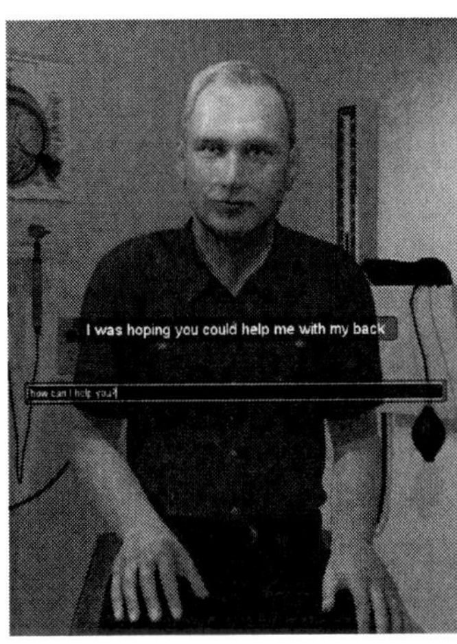

Figure 1: Virtual Patient avatar used to train medical students

sponse for each input question identified by the system. While pattern matching with ChatScript can achieve relatively high accuracy with sufficient pattern-writing skill and effort, it is unable to take advantage of large amounts of training data, somewhat brittle regarding misspellings, and difficult to maintain as new questions and patterns are added.

With an apparent plateau in system performance, this work explores new data-driven methods. In particular, we use convolutional neural networks with both words and characters as input, demonstrating a significant improvement in overall question identification accuracy relative to a strong multiclass logistic regression baseline. Furthermore, inspired by the different error patterns between the ChatScript and CNNs, we develop a simple system combination using a binary classifier that results in the highest overall performance, achieving a remarkable 47% reduction in error in comparison to the ChatScript sys-

11

Proceedings of the 12th Workshop on Innovative Use of NLP for Building Educational Applications, pages 11–21
Copenhagen, Denmark, September 8, 2017. ©2017 Association for Computational Linguistics

tem alone. Frequency quantile analysis shows that the hybrid system is able to leverage the relatively higher performance of ChatScript on the infrequent label items, while also taking advantage of the CNN system's superior accuracy where more data is available for training.

2 Related Work

Question identification has been formulated as at least two distinct tasks. Multi-class logistic regression is a standard approach that can take advantage of class-specific features but requires a good amount of training data for each class. A pairwise setup involves a more general binary classification decision which is then made for each label, choosing the highest confidence match.

Early work (Ravichandran et al., 2003) found that treating a question answering task as a maximum entropy re-ranking problem outperformed using the same system as a classifier. DeVault et al. (2011) observed maximum entropy systems performed well with simple n-gram features. Jaffe et al. (2015) explored a log-linear pairwise ranking model for question identification and found it to outperform a multiclass baseline along the lines of DeVault et al. However, Jaffe et al. (2015) used a much smaller dataset with only about 915 user turns, less than one-fourth as many as in the current dataset. For this larger dataset, multiclass logistic regression outperforms a pairwise ranking model. With no pairwise comparisons, a multiclass classifier is also much faster, lending itself to real-time use.

It is probable that multiclass vs. pairwise approaches' overall effectiveness depends on the amount of training data; pairwise ranking methods have potential advantages for cross-domain and one-shot learning tasks (Vinyals et al., 2016) where data is sparse or non-existent. In the closely related task of short-answer scoring, Sakaguchi et al. (2015a) found that pairwise methods could be effectively combined with regression-based approaches to improve performance in sparse-data cases.

Other work involving dialogue utterance classification has traditionally required a large amount of data. For example, Suendermann et al. (2009) acquired 500,000 dialogues with over 2 million utterances, observin that statistical systems outperform rule-based ones as the amount of data increases. Crowdsourcing for collecting additional dialogues (Ramanarayanan et al., 2017) could alleviate data sparsity problems for rare categories by providing additional training examples, but this technique is limited to more general domains that do not require special training/skills. In the current medical domain, workers on common crowdsourcing platforms are unlikely to have the expertise required to take a patient's medical history in a natural way, so any data collected with this method would likely suffer quality issues and fail to generalize to real medical student dialogues. Rossen and Lok (2012) have developed an approach for collecting dialogue data for virtual patient systems, but their approach does not directly address the issue that even as the number of dialogues collected increases, there can remain a long tail of relevant but infrequently asked questions.

CNNs have been used to great effect for image identification (Krizhevsky et al., 2012) and are becoming common for natural language processing. In general, CNNs are used for convolution over input language sequences, where the input is often a matrix representing a sequence word embeddings (Kim, 2014). Intuitively, word embedding kernels are convolving n-grams, ultimately generating features that represent n-grams over word vectors of length equal to the kernel width. CNNs are very popular in systems for tasks like paraphrase detection (Yin and Schütze, 2015; Yin et al., 2016; He et al., 2015), community question answering (Das et al., 2016; Barbosa et al., 2016) and even machine translation (Gehring et al., 2017). Character-based models that embed individual characters as input units are also possible, and have been used for language modeling (Kim et al., 2016) to good effect. It is worth noting that character sequences are more robust to spelling errors and potentially have the same expressive capability as word sequences given long enough character sequences.

3 Dataset

The dataset consists of 94 dialogues of medical students interacting with the ChatScript system. The ChatScript system has been deployed in a medical school to assess student's ability to interact with patients through a text-based interface and the questions typed by the students and the responses given by ChatScript, which then are hand-corrected by annotators, form this dataset. There are 4330 total user turns, with a mean of 46.1 turns per dialogue. Each turn consists of the question

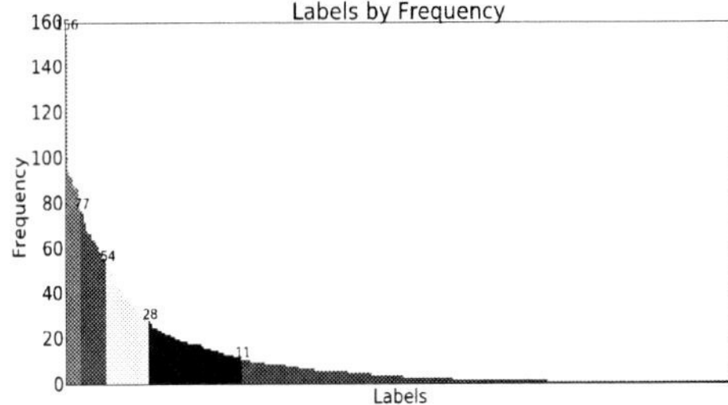

Figure 2: Label frequency distribution is extremely long-tailed, with few frequent labels and many infrequent labels. Values are shown above quintile boundaries.

the student asked, ChatScript's automatic label (with hand-correction) and the scripted response associated with the label. An example turn could be represented with the tuple, (*'hello mr. wilkins, how are you doing today?', 'how are you', 'well i would be doing pretty well if my back weren't hurting so badly.'*). The task is to predict the label of the asked question.

There are 359 unique labels, with a mean of 12 instances per label, median of 4, and large standard deviation of 20. Of note, the distribution of labels is extremely long-tailed (Figure 2), with 8 of the most common labels accounting for nearly 20% of the data, while the bottom 20% includes 265 infrequent labels. The most frequent label occurs 156 times.

4 The CNN model

We now turn to the structure of our model. The main model used in this work follows Kim (2014). There are four layers in the model: an embedding layer, a convolution layer, a max-pooling layer and a linear layer. Let $\mathbf{x}_i \in \mathbb{R}^k$ a k-dimensional embedding for the i-th element of the sequence, i.e. the i-th word or character. The representation of a sentence, $\mathbf{S}_j \in \mathbb{R}^{|s_j| \times k}$ is the concatenation of all the embeddings of the elements in the sentence s_j. The multichannel setup, shown in Kim (2014) as marginally effective, is not used in this work. The following equations will all work on sentence $\mathbf{S}_j$, thus j is dropped for clarity.

A convolutional kernel is defined as a filter $\mathbf{w} \in \mathbb{R}^{hk}$ which slides across the sentence matrix $\mathbf{S}$ to produce a feature map. Because the kernel is as wide as the embeddings, it will only produce one value for each window.

$$c_i = \sigma(\mathbf{w} \cdot \mathbf{x}_{i:i+h-1} + b) \tag{1}$$

In Eq. 1, b is a scalar and σ is a non-linearity. The feature map $\mathbf{c} \in \mathbb{R}^{|s|-h+1}$ for this kernel is the concatenation of all the feature values from the convolution. In order to maintain fixed dimension for the output, max-over-time pooling (Collobert et al., 2011) is applied to the feature map and the maximum value $\hat{c}$ is extracted from $\mathbf{c}$.

Because there are many kernels for each kernel height h, the output from a group of kernels with the same height is $\mathbf{o}_h = [\hat{c}_1, \hat{c}_2, \ldots, \hat{c}_{n_h}]$, where n_h is the number of kernels for the kernel width h.

We concatenate all the outputs from all the kernels into a single vector $\mathbf{o} \in \mathbb{R}^N$ where $N = \sum_h n_h$, and apply a linear transformation with the softmax non-linearity to it as the final fully-connected neural network layer for the CNN.

$$\hat{\mathbf{y}} = \text{softmax}(\mathbf{W}_l \mathbf{o} + \mathbf{b}_l) \tag{2}$$

where $W_l \in \mathbb{R}^{N \times m}$ is the weight matrix of the final layer, $\mathbf{b}_l \in \mathbb{R}^m$ is the bias term for the final layer, and m is the number of classes that we are trying to predict.

4.1 Regularization

We follow Kim (2014) for regularization strategies. Dropout (Srivastava et al., 2014) prevents the final layer from overfitting to training data by randomly setting some input values to zero according to a Bernoulli distribution with parameter p. We adopt this strategy and put a dropout layer between the max-pooling layer and the final linear layer.

Kim (2014) also applies a max norm constraint to the weight matrix of the final linear layer instead of using $l2$-regularization over all the parameters. In Kim (2014), a row in the weight matrix $\mathbf{W}_l$ is renormalized to the max-norm s if the 2-norm of the row exceeds s after a parameter update. However, in a recent reimplementation of Kim (2014)[1], the renormalization is always applied to the rows of W_l regardless of whether the 2-norm exceeds s or not. This change shows up as a 1% difference in accuracy on the development datasets. Therefore, we use this renormalization strategy instead of max-norm in the original paper

---

[1] https://github.com/harvardnlp/sent-conv-torch

and refer to it as max-renorm in this work.

5 Ensemble methods

In order to reduce variance of performance when training on different splits of data, models trained with different training datasets and models with different architecture are combined together. Previous research has shown that ensembling models improves performance (Sakaguchi et al., 2015b; Ju et al., 2017; He et al., 2017). We train different models with different splits of training and develop data, and ensemble them together. We use two methods to combine the submodels together: majority voting and stacking. The individual CNNs, or the submodels, first are ensembled together according to their input features into two ensembled models, and then the two ensembles are stacked together to form the final stacked model.

Majority voting

The majority voting strategy is adopted by the submodels to reduce variance and also to provide better generalizability. Each submodel gives one vote to the best class given some input according to their parameters, and whichever class has the most votes wins. Let $\hat{\mathbf{y}}_d$ be the output of d-th submodel in the ensemble, and the final output of the ensemble $\hat{\mathbf{y}}_e$ is

$$\hat{\mathbf{y}}_e = \sum_d \text{hardmax}(\hat{\mathbf{y}}_d) \tag{3}$$

where hardmax is the function that converts the argument of the function into a one-hot vector where the original maximum value of the argument is replaced by 1 and the rest by 0. In the case of ties, we pick the class that appears first in the vector. For the ensemble, the predicted class is $argmax(\hat{\mathbf{y}}_e)$. However, $\hat{\mathbf{y}}_e$ is also an unnormalized distribution used by the stacked model.

Stacking

We use stacking (Wolpert, 1992) to combine results from the ensembles. Stacking is essentially weighted linear interpolation of the ensemble results. Let $\hat{\mathbf{y}}_{e,r}$ be the output of the r-th ensemble, thus the final output of stacking $\hat{\mathbf{y}}_t$:

$$\hat{\mathbf{y}}_t = \text{softmax}(\sum_r \alpha_r \hat{\mathbf{y}}_{e,r}) \tag{4}$$

where α_r is the coefficient of the r-th ensemble. The coefficients need to be trained.

6 Model setup and training

We now explain preprocessing steps, the hyperparameters we used for training, model initialization as well as the training process.

6.1 Preprocessing

We represent a sentence with both a sequence of words and a sequence of characters. Using word sequences as input allows us to take advantage of pre-trained word embeddings so that even if a word never appears in the training set due to data sparsity, its embedding may still provide enough information for the models to classify correctly. Using character sequences allows the models to be robust to spelling variations. This helps the word-based models, which are susceptible to misspelled words. Therefore we train separate word- and character-based CNN models. We then ensemble the word CNN submodels into a word CNN ensemble, and also ensemble the character CNN submodels into a character CNN ensemble, using majority voting in both cases. The two ensembles are then combined together with stacking to form the stacked CNN model. All submodels are trained separately and remain fixed when the stacked model is being trained.

6.2 Hyperparameters

The hyperparameters for both the word CNN and the character CNN submodels are mostly the same. In the following paragraph, if not otherwise mentioned, all hyperparameters are shared. All hyperparameters are tuned on the development dataset of each fold. We set the number of submodels d to 5. We set the number of kernels of the character CNN to be 400, and the word CNN 300. We use kernels of widths 2 to 5 for the character CNN, and 3 to 5 for the word CNN. All non-linearities in the models are rectified linear units (Nair and Hinton, 2010). We use Adadelta (Zeiler, 2012) as the optimizer for the submodels, and use the recommended values for its hyperparameters ($\rho = 0.9, \epsilon = 1 \times 10^{-6}, learning\_rate = 1.0$). We set the max-renorm to be 3.0 and the dropout rate for the linear layer to be 0.5. We use negative log-likelihood as our training objective to minimize.

6.3 Initialization

For the word CNNs, we follow Kim (2014) to initialize the parameters. We use pre-trained word2vec word embeddings (Mikolov et al., 2013) for words that are in the whole dataset, and initialize embeddings of the other out-of-vocabulary words with $Unif(-0.25, 0.25)$. This keeps the variance of each randomly initialized embedding close to the word2vec embeddings. We also tried the GloVe embeddings Pennington et al. (2014) and found it to be slight worse in performance than word2vec embeddings. We initialize the convolutional kernels with $Unif(-0.01, 0.01)$ and the linear layer $N(0, 1e-4)$. We initialize all bias terms to 0.

For the character CNNs, we initialize all weights to follow $Unif(-1/\sqrt{n_{in}}, 1/\sqrt{n_{in}})$ (Glorot and Bengio, 2010) where n_{in} is the length of the input vector. For the convolutional kernels, the length of the input vector is hk. Additionally, we randomly initialize the embedding matrix with $N(0, 1)$.

6.4 Training

We use 10-fold cross validation for training and evaluation. Shuffling the original dataset reduces performance variance on the development sets, improving generalizability. For each fold, we split the whole dataset into training and testing sets with 90/10 ratio, and further split the training set into training and development sets with 90/10 ratio. For training the submodels, we split the training set into training and development sets at different places to create different training data for each submodel, and add all the labels as training instances to the training set. We use minibatch updates with batch size 50 and train each submodel for 40 epochs, shuffling the training set for each epoch. We evaluate the performance of the submodels after each epoch of training, using early stopping on development data to select the best-performing set of parameters.

Majority voting does not need training, but stacking does. We train the stacked model also for 40 epochs with the training/development split that is done for the first submodel. The optimizer is also Adadelta with recommended hyperparameter values.

	Simple	Ensembled
ChatScript	**79.8**	n/a
Baseline	77.2	n/a
CharCNN	76.16	78.20
WordCNN	76.92	77.67
Stacked	n/a	**79.02**

Table 1: Mean 10-fold Accuracy by System Type. Numbers reported are on the test set.

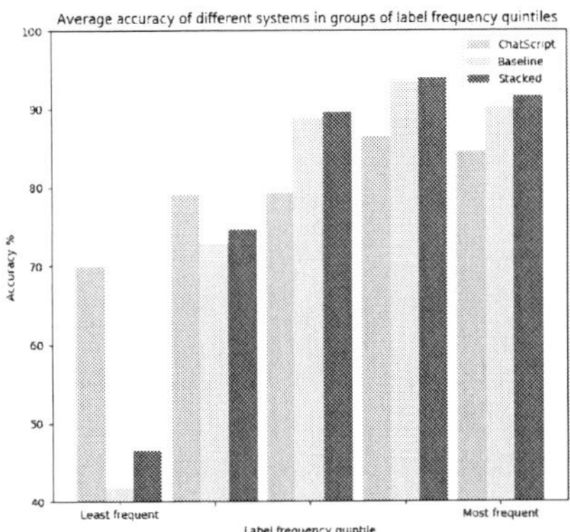

Figure 3: System Accuracy by Label Frequency, in Quintiles. Note the high performance in the least frequent labels for ChatScript, the hand-crafted pattern matching system. With more data, the CNNs perform better.

6.5 Baseline

We also create a simple baseline system for comparison. The baseline system is a logistic regression classifier that takes in one-hot representations of $1, 2, 3$-grams of words, word stems, and $1, 2, 3, 4, 5, 6$-grams of characters from a sentence as features and predict what class this sentence belongs to. The baseline system also follows the 10-fold cross validation training setup.

7 CNN Results

System performance is measured by correct question identification for each of the 4330 user turns. Accuracies reported are the average 10-fold cross-validation accuracies. Apart from performance results from the baseline logistic classifier and the stacked model, we also include results from the rule-based ChatScript system.

Table 1 shows the test accuracies of different systems averaged over the 10 folds. For machine learning systems, the stacked CNN model performs the best overall. For single models, the baseline system works the best. It is widely believed that deep learning models are generally data-hungry, and the training sets are small compared to popular training sets for deep learning models. In terms of single model performance, the simple logistic regression is better than the deep learning models and it is reasonable to believe that data sparsity is at issue. However, through ensembling and stacking, the final stacked model performs the best, and the performance gap between a machine learning system and a carefully created and actively maintained rule-based system on this task becomes very small. The 2-point difference between the baseline system and the stacked CNN model is highly significant ($p = 8.19 \times 10^{-6}$, McNemar's test).

System accuracies by label frequency show a striking difference between ChatScript and all other systems for the most infrequent labels. Fig. 3 shows a clear advantage for ChatScript in the quintile with the least frequent labels. ChatScript is not trained, so data sparsity does not affect performance of this system as much as the machine learning systems. Also, most of the time, the training instances for a rare label are very close to the label itself. Therefore by pattern matching, ChatScript performs best among all models for items with rare labels. The stacked CNN model performs slightly better than the baseline model in this quintile, but still is very low compared to ChatScript.

However, ChatScript does relatively worse to the other systems as label frequency increases. This is expected because when training instances increase in a dataset, it means that probabilistically variants of the label that differ substantially will also increase. Therefore more non-conflicting patterns need to be added and existing patterns need to be updated, which may be difficult or even impossible to do. Machine learning based systems are good at frequent labels. There are more training instances, and constraint of non-conflicting rules does not apply to such models. We can see in Figure 3 that the stacked CNN model outperforms the baseline in all quintiles, and outperforms ChatScript in the last three quintiles where training data is ample. The clear difference of model behavior of ChatScript and the stacked CNN shows that they may be combined together and perform even better in all quintiles.

The effectiveness of ensembling

Figure 4 shows accuracy numbers on the test set of each fold for the best individual submodels and ensembles. The best individual submodels are chosen based on performance on the development set. For the character CNN submodels and the ensemble, it is clear that the ensembled model always performs better than the best individual model. For all 10 folds, the ensembled character CNN model always outperforms the best model in the ensemble and the average performance gain is about 1.04%. For the word CNN submodels and the ensemble, the relation is less obvious. Although in 9 out of 10 folds, the ensemble outperforms the best individual model, the difference between performances of the two systems is smaller compared to the difference between best character CNN submodel and the character CNN ensemble, and the average performance gain is about 0.75%. A Student's t test on the accuracy numbers confirms this observation. The improvement gained from ensembling the character CNN submodels is significant ($p = 0.0045$), but the improvement gained from ensembling the word submodels is not ($p = 0.43$).

The result for the ensembles and the stacked model can also be seen in Figure 4. Except for fold 1, where the stacked model is outperformed by the character CNN ensemble, the stacked model outperforms all the ensembles in all the other folds. The performance gained from stacking the character CNN ensemble on top of the word CNN ensemble is significant ($p = 0.049$), but insignificant the other way around ($p = 0.11$). This could mean that the character CNN ensemble has all the information it can extract from text for prediction that the word CNN ensemble is not providing new information for it to do better.

Comparing the stacked model with the individual best model, stacking always provides significant performance gain ($p = 0.033$ for the best word CNN submodel and $p = 9 \times 10^{-4}$ for the best character CNN submodel).

Error analysis

One of the hypotheses of why the stacked CNN model works better is because it has access to word embeddings, and word embeddings are good at modeling words that are superficially different but synonymous. Table 2 shows a few examples where the baseline classifier makes the wrong pre-

No.	Question	Baseline predicted label	Stacked CNN predicted label
1	constipation	do you use any contraception	do you have any bowel problems
2	does anything aggravate your back pain	what makes the pain better	what makes the pain worse
3	are you employed	are you happy	what do you do for a living
4	have you taken any tylenol or done anything to help your back pain this time	what makes the pain better	are you taking any medication for the pain
5	have you ever had any psychotherapy treatment	have you tried any treatment	do you have a history of depression
6	have you injured your back previously	have you had back injury	when was your last period
7	can you stand up	are you able to stand	what do you do for a living

Table 2: Prediction examples. The stacked CNN model predicts the correct label for the first 4 cases and the wrong label for the last 3 cases. The baseline predicts the last 3 cases correctly.

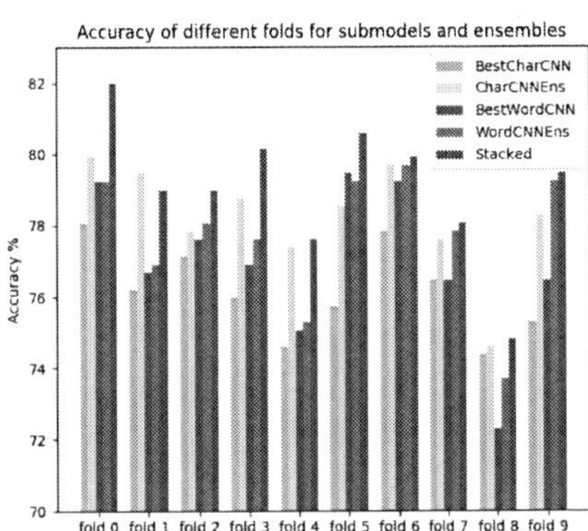

Figure 4: System Accuracy of the Submodels and Ensembles by Fold

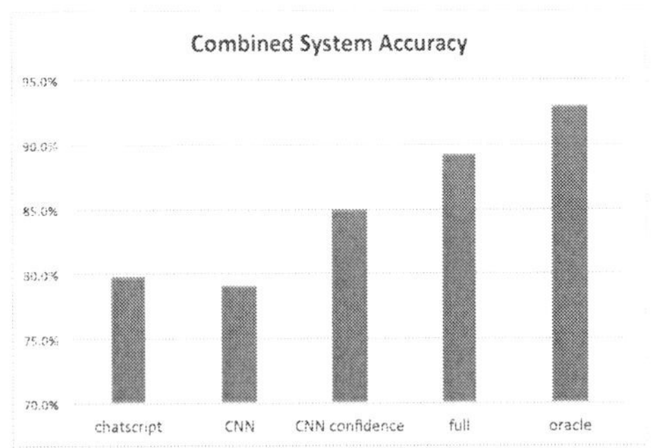

Figure 5: Accuracy of model trained to combine ChatScript and CNN predictions

diction but the stacked CNN model makes the correct prediction. These examples show how the stacked CNN model is able to use semantic information provided by the word embeddings to make the correct prediction whereas the baseline classifier can not. Example 1 requires the models to know 'constipation' is related to 'bowel'. The baseline classifier is confused by the spelling similarities between 'constipation' and 'contraception', but the stacked model is able to make the right prediction. Example 2 requires the models to know that 'aggravate' means 'get worse', not 'get better', and the stacked model makes the correct decision. Similarly, 'employed' and 'tylenol' in examples 3 and 4 all show that the stacked CNN can tap into the semantic information provided by the word embeddings and use them in prediction.

However, it appears that the semantic information in word vectors can sometimes backfire as well. In examples 5 and 6, the words that are similar in meaning are making unhelpful connections. The stacked CNN links 'psychotherapy treatment' to 'depression' in example 5, but the question as a whole is about treatment, so the prediction from the stacked model is wrong. Similarly, the stacked model predicts example 6 to be in the class 'when was your last period' maybe because 'last' and 'previously' are similar, apparently missing the 'injury' part of the question. The stacked CNN missed example 7 because of data sparsity. There are only two instances of the class 'are you able to stand' in the whole dataset, therefore the stacked CNN has low confidence in the gold class and instead chooses a class which has much more training examples.

8 Combining ChatScript with the CNN

While the fully ensembled and stacked CNN performs at 79% accuracy, which is slightly below that of ChatScript, its error pattern is distinct from ChatScript, as seen in Fig. 3. ChatScript, because it only uses pattern matching to do classification, is less affected by the imbalance of training instances belonging to target classes in the training data. The CNN, however, is affected by such imbalance and generally performs worse when training instances for one class is scarce. Meanwhile, despite the use of automatic spelling correction in ChatScript, a substantial portion (11.1%) of the

Chatscript errors were on questions with typos or other spelling errors in them; on these items, the CNN managed to make the correct prediction 74.1% of the time. This indicates that the character CNNs are more robust to spelling errors, as there is no need to make a possibly erroneous guess as to the correctly spelled word. Additionally, whereas the CNN always makes its best guess on test items, the ChatScript patterns failed to match (yielding no answer) on 7.4% of the questions, representing 36.5% of the ChatScript errors. On these questions, the CNN achieved 59.6% accuracy, indicating that they are considerably more difficult to recognize than the average question.

Given that our two methods make rather different errors, we investigated whether it would make sense to combine them, and found that an oracle that always chose the correct system if either was right could achieve 92.9% accuracy, much higher than the ChatScript systems 79.8% accuracy by itself. As such, we experimented with training a logistic regression binary classifier for automatically choosing between the two systems, again using 10-fold cross-validation. The binary classifier was trained to choose the CNN prediction when it was correct and ChatScript was wrong, otherwise to choose the ChatScript output—including in cases where the ChatScript patterns yielded no match, on the assumption that a no-match response would be preferable to an incorrect response. To make its choices, the binary classifier used the following features:[2]

Log Prob The log probability of the predicted class in the final output of the stacked model.

Entropy The entropy of the distribution over classes output by the stacked model.

Confidence For each submodel, the confidence score is the unnormalized score for the predicted class. For the stacked model, the confidence score is the average of all confidence scores from the submodels.

CNN Label The label predicted by the CNN.

CS Label The label matched by ChatScript.

CS Log Prob The log probability according to the CNN of the ChatScript prediction.

<hr>

[2]Note that ChatScript does not output scores for its matched patterns, so we did not pursue a stacking-based approach.

Note that an automatic method for choosing between the two systems could in principle do worse than simply always choosing the ChatScript system. Nevertheless, as shown in Fig. 5, a classifier trained to make the choice based on the log prob, entropy and confidence of the CNN's prediction achieves 85.0%, a large gain. This binary classifier can be improved further by taking into account how likely the logistic regression model considers the ChatScript choice, including the special case of no match from the ChatScript system, along with the specific label of both system predictions. The full model, making use of these additional features, achieves 89.3% accuracy, a huge gain that represents more than two-thirds of the potential gains revealed by the oracle analysis, and a **47% reduction in error** over the ChatScript system by itself. This shows that the stacked CNN effectively compliments the rule-based ChatScript system on the mid-to-high frequency labels, making the final system much stronger than either of the component systems.

We also investigated whether it would make sense to always choose the CNN prediction when the ChatScript system yielded no match. By allowing the binary combination classifier to choose the ChatScript system even when it yielded no match, the combined system reduced the number of no match outputs from 7.4% to 2.4%, close to the 3.0% oracle rate for cases where neither system is correct. Always choosing the CNN prediction in these cases increases the combined system accuracy by 0.6%, but at the cost of a 1.8% increase in erroneous responses rather than no-match responses. As such, it appears preferable to allow the binary combination classifier to make the choice even in the no-match cases.

9 Discussion and Future Work

CNNs are very sensitive to their hyperparameters and initializations. Differences in normal vs. uniform weight matrix initializations were observed to impact word- and character-based CNN models differently. He et al. (2017) use orthonormal initializations following Saxe et al. (2013), while Kim (2014) suggests initializing unknown word embeddings using parameters (e.g., variance) sampled from pre-trained word embeddings, etc.; further exploration of hyperparameter tuning and initialization strategies are left as future work.

Models with more complicated architecture,

such as Memory Networks (Weston et al., 2015), Highway Networks (Srivastava et al., 2015) and Convolutional sequence models (Gehring et al., 2017) can also be explored and integrated as well, although more data is needed to successfully train these models. Other ensemble methods like Super Learner (Ju et al., 2017) should be tried as well.

Since label sparsity is at the heart of the performance difference between ChatScript and the CNN models, a more direct way to deal with lack of training examples (possibly obviating the need for a hand-crafted system like ChatScript) could be to automatically generate paraphrases to augment available data, potentially with a content author in the loop; we are currently exploring strategies for doing so.

10 Conclusion

This work shows the value of combining a hand-authored pattern matching system with CNN models to overcome label sparsity in training. The stacked CNN model with ensembled word and character CNN submodels significantly outperforms the logistic regression baseline. Within the CNN models, ensembling is found to significantly improve performance for the character model, while stacking always provides significant improvement over the best word- or character-based submodels. The final system uses a binary classifier over ChatScript and a stacked CNN, improving overall accuracy by 10% and achieving an impressive 47% error reduction on a question identification task in a virtual patient dialogue system.

Acknowledgments

Thanks to Kellen Maicher for creating the virtual environment, Bruce Wilcox for authoring ChatScript, and Eric Fosler-Lussier and William Schuler for feedback and discussion. This project was supported by funding from the Department of Health and Human Services Health Resources and Services Administration (HRSA D56HP020687), the National Board of Medical Examiners Edward J. Stemmler Education Research Fund (NBME 1112-064), and the National Science Foundation (NSF IIS 1618336). This material is based upon work supported by the National Science Foundation Graduate Research Fellowship Program under grant no. DGE-1343012. Any opinion, findings, and conclusions or recommendations expressed in this material are those of the author(s) and do not necessarily reflect the views of the National Science Foundation. The project does not necessarily reflect NBME policy, and NBME support provides no official endorsement.

References

Luciano Barbosa, Dasha Bogdanova, Bianca Zadrozny, and Rio De Janeiro. 2016. Learning Hybrid Representations to Retrieve Semantically Equivalent Questions. In *Proceedings of the 54th Annual Meeting of the Association for Computational Linguistics (ACL 2016)*. 1, pages 694–699.

Ronan Collobert, Jason Weston, Léon Bottou, Michael Karlen, Koray Kavukcuoglu, and Pavel Kuksa. 2011. Natural Language Processing (Almost) from Scratch. *Journal of Machine Learning Research* 12:2493–2537.

Douglas Danforth, A. Price, K. Maicher, D. Post, B. Liston, D. Clinchot, C. Ledford, D. Way, and H. Cronau. 2013. Can virtual standardized patients be used to assess communication skills in medical students. In *Proceedings of the 17th Annual IAMSE Meeting, St. Andrews, Scotland*.

Douglas Danforth, Mike Procter, Richard Chen, Mary Johnson, and Robert Heller. 2009. Development of virtual patient simulations for medical education. *Journal For Virtual Worlds Research* 2(2).

Arpita Das, Harish Yenala, Manoj Chinnakotla, and Manish Shrivastava. 2016. Together We Stand : Siamese Networks for Similar Question Retrieval. In *Proceedings of the 54th Annual Meeting of the Association for Computational Linguistics (ACL 2016)*. pages 378–387.

David DeVault, Anton Leuski, and Kenji Sagae. 2011. An evaluation of alternative strategies for implementing dialogue policies using statistical classification and rules. In *Proceedings of the 5th International Joint Conference on Natural Language Processing (IJCNLP)*. pages 1341–1345.

Jonas Gehring, Michael Auli, David Grangier, Denis Yarats, and Yann N Dauphin. 2017. Convolutional Sequence to Sequence Learning. In *Proceedings of 34th International Conference on Machine Learning (ICML 2017)*.

Xavier Glorot and Yoshua Bengio. 2010. Understanding the difficulty of training deep feedforward neural networks. In *Proceedings of the 13th International Conference on Artificial Intelligence and Statistics (AISTATS)*. volume 9, pages 249–256.

Hua He, Kevin Gimpel, and Jimmy Lin. 2015. Multi-Perspective Sentence Similarity Modeling with Convolutional Neural Networks. *Proceedings of the*

2015 Conference on Empirical Methods in Natural Language Processing (EMNLP 2015) (1):1576–1586.

Luheng He, Kenton Lee, Mike Lewis, and Luke Zettlemoyer. 2017. Deep Semantic Role Labeling : What Works and What's Next. In *Proceedings of the 55th Annual Meeting of the Association for Computational Linguistics (ACL 2017)*.

Evan Jaffe, Michael White, William Schuler, Eric Fosler-Lussier, Alex Rosenfeld, and Douglas Danforth. 2015. Interpreting questions with a log-linear ranking model in a virtual patient dialogue system. In *Proceedings of the Tenth Workshop on Innovative Use of NLP for Building Educational Applications*. pages 86–96.

Cheng Ju, Aurélien Bibaut, and Mark J. van der Laan. 2017. The Relative Performance of Ensemble Methods with Deep Convolutional Neural Networks for Image Classification. *arXiv* page 1704.01664vi [stat.ML].

Yoon Kim. 2014. Convolutional Neural Networks for Sentence Classification. *Proceedings of the 2014 Conference on Empirical Methods in Natural Language Processing (EMNLP 2014)* pages 1746–1751.

Yoon Kim, Yacine Jernite, David Sontag, and Alexander M. Rush. 2016. Character-Aware Neural Language Models. In *Proceedings of the 30th AAAI Conference on Artificial Intelligence (AAAI 16)*. pages 2741–2749.

Alex Krizhevsky, Ilya Sutskever, and Geoffrey E Hinton. 2012. Imagenet classification with deep convolutional neural networks. In F. Pereira, C. J. C. Burges, L. Bottou, and K. Q. Weinberger, editors, *Advances in Neural Information Processing Systems 25*, Curran Associates, Inc., pages 1097–1105.

Tomas Mikolov, Ilya Sutskever, Kai Chen, Gregory S Corrado, and Jeffrey Dean. 2013. Distributed Representations of Words and Phrases and their Compositionality. In *Advances in Neural Information Processing Systems 26 (NIPS 2013)*. pages 3111–3119.

Vinod Nair and Geoffrey E Hinton. 2010. Rectified Linear Units Improve Restricted Boltzmann Machines. In *Proceedings of the 27th International Conference on Machine Learning (ICML 2010)*. 3, pages 807–814.

Jeffrey Pennington, Richard Socher, and Christopher D Manning. 2014. GloVe: Global Vectors for Word Representation. In *Proceedings of the Conference on Empirical Methods in Natural Language Processing (EMNLP 2014)*. pages 1532–1543.

Vikram Ramanarayanan, David Suendermann-Oeft, Hillary Molloy, Eugene Tsuprun, Patrick Lange, and Keelan Evanini. 2017. Crowdsourcing multimodal dialog interactions: Lessons learned from the HALEF case. In *Proceedings of the AAAI-17 Workshop on Crowdsourcing, Deep Learning, and Artificial Intelligence Agents*. pages 423–431.

Deepak Ravichandran, Eduard Hovy, and Franz Josef Och. 2003. Statistical qa-classifier vs. re-ranker: What's the difference? In *Proceedings of the ACL 2003 workshop on Multilingual summarization and question answering-Volume 12*. Association for Computational Linguistics, pages 69–75.

Brent Rossen and Benjamin Lok. 2012. A crowdsourcing method to develop virtual human conversational agents. *International Journal of HCS* 70(4):301–319.

Keisuke Sakaguchi, Michael Heilman, and Nitin Madnani. 2015a. Effective feature integration for automated short answer scoring. In *Proceedings of the 2015 Conference of the North American Chapter of the Association for Computational Linguistics: Human Language Technologies*. Association for Computational Linguistics, pages 1049–1054.

Keisuke Sakaguchi, Michael Heilman, and Nitin Madnani. 2015b. Effective Feature Integration for Automated Short Answer Scoring. In *Proceedings of the Conference of the North American Chapter of the Association of Computational Linguistics (NAACL 2015)*. pages 1049–1054.

Andrew M. Saxe, James L. McClelland, and Surya Ganguli. 2013. Exact solutions to the nonlinear dynamics of learning in deep linear neural networks. *Advances in Neural Information Processing Systems* pages 1–9.

Nitish Srivastava, Geoffrey Hinton, Alex Krizhevsky, Ilya Sutskever, and Ruslan Salakhutdinov. 2014. Dropout: A Simple Way to Prevent Neural Networks from Overfitting. *Journal of Machine Learning Research* 15:1929–1958.

Rupesh Kumar Srivastava, Klaus Greff, and Jürgen Schmidhuber. 2015. Highway Networks. In *Proceedings of the Deep Learning workshop (ICML 2015)*.

D. Suendermann, K. Evanini, J. Liscombe, P. Hunter, K. Dayanidhi, and R. Pieraccini. 2009. From rule-based to statistical grammars: Continuous improvement of large-scale spoken dialog systems. In *Proceedings of International Conference on Acoustics, Speech, and Signal Processing (ICASSP) 2009*. pages 4713–4716.

Oriol Vinyals, Charles Blundell, Timothy Lillcrap, Koray Kavukcuoglu, and Daan Wierstra. 2016. Matching Networks for One Shot Learning Oriol. In *Proceedings of Neural Information Processing Systems (NIPS 2016)*. pages 817–825.

Jason Weston, Sumit Chopra, and Antoine Bordes. 2015. Memory Networks. In *ICLR*. pages 1–15.

D.H. Wolpert. 1992. Stacked generalization. *Neural Networks* 5(2):241–259.

Wenpeng Yin and Hinrich Schütze. 2015. Convolutional Neural Network for Paraphrase Identification. *Proceedings of 2015 Conference of the North American Chapter of the Association for Computational Linguistics Human Language Technologies (NAACL HLT 2015)* pages 901–911.

Wenpeng Yin, Hinrich Schütze, Bing Xiang, and Bowen Zhou. 2016. ABCNN: Attention-Based Convolutional Neural Network for Modeling Sentence Pairs. *Transactions of the Association for Computational Linguistics* 4:259–272.

Matthew D. Zeiler. 2012. ADADELTA: An Adaptive Learning Rate Method. *CoRR* .

Continuous fluency tracking and the challenges of varying text complexity

Beata Beigman Klebanov, Anastassia Loukina, John Sabatini, Tenaha O'Reilly
Educational Testing Service
660, Rosedale Rd, Princeton NJ, USA
08541, NJ, USA
{bbeigmanklebanov, aloukina, jsabatini, toreilly}@ets.org

Abstract

This paper is a preliminary report on using text complexity measurement in the service of a new educational application. We describe a reading intervention where a child takes turns reading a book aloud with a virtual reading partner. Our ultimate goal is to provide meaningful feedback to the parent or the teacher by continuously tracking the child's improvement in reading fluency. We show that this would not be a simple endeavor, due to an intricate relationship between text complexity from the point of view of comprehension and reading rate.

1 Introduction

According to the 2015 report from the National Assessment of Educational Progress on reading achievement, 31% of U.S. 4th graders read below the Basic level.[1] Our goal is to help low-proficiency readers such as these improve their reading skill.

The critical transition from word-by-word reading to fluency, or from learning how to read to reading for learning or enjoyment, requires extended and sustained reading practice. To encourage such practice we propose an educational application which combines (1) an excellent story to achieve engagement (such as "Harry Potter and the Sorcerer's Stone" by J. K. Rowling), and (2) a virtual reading companion, implemented through an audiobook, who would take turns reading aloud with the child – "you read a page, I read the next one". The turn-taking allows the child to alternate between the more effortful reading and the less effortful listening, as well as supplies a model

reading of many of the words and phrases the child will encounter during his turn.

In addition to supporting sustained reading by children, the system will also provide the teacher or parent with a detailed picture of the child's developmental trajectory, by continuously tracking the child's reading fluency throughout his reading turns. Oral reading fluency is not only an important indicator of reading skill in itself (Hudson et al., 2008; Fuchs et al., 2001), for students in early elementary grades it is also strongly correlated (r around 0.7) with reading comprehension (Roberts et al., 2005; Good et al., 2001).

The standard measure of oral reading fluency is words correct per minute (henceforth, WCPM) (Wayman et al., 2007), combining aspects of speed and accuracy of oral reading.[2] Several studies (Balogh et al., 2007; Zechner et al., 2009) showed that WCPM can be accurately computed automatically using an automated speech recognizer (ASR) and a string matching algorithm; this approach has already been incorporated into many commercial and research systems for automated oral fluency assessment such as VersaReader (Balogh et al., 2012) or Project LISTEN (Mostow, 2012) (see also Eskenazi (2009) for a review).

Previous studies on reading fluency indicate that WCPM may vary across different texts (Ardoin et al., 2005; Compton et al., 2004). It seems reasonable to assume that variation in text complexity/readability might be one of the sources of variation in oral reading fluency across different passages: Texts that cause comprehension difficulties may also elicit less fluent reading. In fact, this assumption underlies text selection for tests of oral reading fluency such as DIBELS (Good and Kaminski, 2002) that rely on readability to select

---

[1] https://www.nationsreportcard.gov/reading_math_2015/#reading/acl?grade=4

[2] In some studies, reading rate (words per minute) is used as a separate measure while fluency is defined in terms of expressiveness and adherence to syntax (Danne et al., 2005).

Proceedings of the 12th Workshop on Innovative Use of NLP for Building Educational Applications, pages 22–32
Copenhagen, Denmark, September 8, 2017. ©2017 Association for Computational Linguistics

comparable passages (Francis et al., 2008). Since in our application the child will be reading different passages in the book on different days, it is possible that the differences between passages would confound the measurement of the child's progress. In this case, WCPM would need to be adjusted to account for such differences in order to produce interpretable feedback.

Previous work generally focused on text properties and WCPM in short texts that have already been controlled for grade-level appropriate readability. Little is known about the variability of text complexity across a whole book and how this may affect WCPM of a child reading the book. Therefore, the focus of this paper is to see whether an adjustment of WCPM to text is in fact necessary in our context, and, if so, whether it can be done using a state-of-the-art text complexity measure.

We address the following research questions: (1) What is the extent of variation in passage complexity in J. K. Rowling's "Harry Potter and the Sorcerer's Stone" (henceforth, **HP1**)? (2) Does the complexity of the text actually impact reading fluency as measured by WCPM? (3) Do automatically generated estimates of text complexity correspond to the observed fluency patterns?

The rest of the paper is organized as follows. We first introduce previous work related to text complexity measurement and the relationship between text complexity and oral reading fluency. We then present the results of two studies: In the first study we looked at variation in text complexity across passages selected from HP1. In the second study we investigate how text complexity estimates relate to WCPM of children reading selected passages from the book. Our findings are then discussed and implications for research on continuous tracking of fluency are drawn.

2 Related Work

Text Complexity Estimation: While for Dale and Chall (1949) the notion of text readability involved "the extent to which they [readers] understand it [the text], read it at an optimal speed, and find it interesting",[3] most classical (Flesch, 1948; Gunning, 1952; Kincaid et al., 1975; McLaughlin, 1969) and modern (Sheehan et al., 2014; Flor and Beigman Klebanov, 2014; Vajjala and Meurers, 2012; Schwarm and Ostendorf, 2005) measures of text readability/complexity focus on reading

comprehension, including special formulas and models designed for special populations, such as young children (Spache, 1953), learners of English as a second language (Beinborn et al., 2014; Heilman et al., 2007), adults with mental disabilities (Feng et al., 2009), among others.

While comprehension-based complexity estimation of relatively short reading passages has been the subject of extensive research for many decades, there is little research on estimating the complexity of long, book-level texts. In early work on readability, Fowler (1978) estimated readability of a novel using the mean of readability estimates of fifteen randomly selected 100-word passages from the novel. Milone (2012) generates book-level complexity estimates by combining complexity estimates for the text in the book with a measure based on the length of the book, following the observation that longer books tend to be more difficult, all else being equal. He decided to base the estimate of text complexity in the book on the analysis of the whole book, as opposed to samples from the book, based on the observation of extensive within-text variability in estimates of text complexity and the concomitant hazard of a large sampling error if only parts of the book are taken into account during complexity estimation (see Appendix E in Milone (2012)). For example, the book *Black Beauty* yields a grade-level estimate of 5.4 based on the text of the whole book; looking at 500-word slices yields estimates anywhere from 2.2 to 9.5 per slice – a range of 7 grade levels. This finding raises the question of a young reader's experience in the face of such variability. To our knowledge, our project is the first study to address variation in within-book reading experiences in general, and variation in oral reading performance specifically.

Relationship between oral reading fluency and text complexity: In Compton et al. (2004), 248 low and average-achieving second graders each read 15 passages of comparable readability levels; their reading performance was recorded in terms of accuracy (proportion of words read correctly) and fluency (WCPM). Analyzing the relationship between textual characteristics and performance, researchers found that Flesch-Kincaid measure, Spache measure, and average sentence length did not significantly correlate with performance. On the other hand, they found that percentage of high frequency words was significantly

---

[3]Quoted from DuBay (2004).

correlated with both performance measures. Ardoin et al. (2005) examined a number of readability formulas for their ability to predict WCPM and found generally fairly low correlations (r<0.5).

In Petscher and Kim (2011), about 35,000 students in grades 1-3 read three grade-level-appropriate passages (as measured by Spache formula) during each of 4 administrations of an oral reading fluency test throughout the year. The authors estimated the amount of variability in WCPM that was attributable to variation among students vs variability across the text passages. Their results showed that 2%-4% was attributable to variability in passages and/or order of passages for grade 1, with higher proportions for grades 2 (5%-6%) and 3 (3%-9%). Petscher and Kim (2011) also observed an increase in the reading rate from the first to the third administered passage within an assessment, consistently with other studies (Francis et al., 2008; Jenkins et al., 2009), pointing to the existence of practice effects in oral reading performance of consecutively read texts.

To summarize, the related work suggests that (1) some amount of variation in reading fluency is attributable to variation in text passages being read, for early elementary grade children; (2) classical readability formulas are not very effective predictors of oral reading fluency.

We note however that passage readability/complexity variation across texts used in previous studies tends to be limited, since texts selected for assessments are typically controlled for grade-level-appropriate readability. In contrast, we consider a case where children are reading a long novel that is not specifically designed to be grade-level controlled; we therefore expect more variation in complexity across different passages in a book. Larger variation may show better alignment between reading rates and text complexity estimates.

3 Study I: Text complexity in Harry Potter and the Sorcerer's Stone

3.1 Data and methodology

For this first study we considered the variation in text complexity in J. K. Rowling's "Harry Potter and the Sorcerer's Stone". We first split the book into a series of consecutive, non-overlapping 250 word chunks. These should take 2-3 minutes to read for our target population and constitute the approximate amount of text to be read by the child at each turn. For each chunk, after 250 words, we either extended or reduced the chunk to the end of a paragraph, thus ensuring that each passage had a natural break point.

The whole book consists of 79,508 words spread across 17 chapters. We created 318 consecutive passages, with a mean length of 250.0 words (SD=16.9). The shortest passage contained 177 words and the longest passage contained 309 words. Half of the passages (II and III quartiles) fell within 242-259 words range.

We used TextEvaluator,[4] a state-of-the-art measure of comprehension complexity of a text (Napolitano et al., 2015; Sheehan et al., 2014, 2013; Nelson et al., 2012),[5] to conduct text complexity analyses. TextEvaluator extracts a range of linguistic features and uses them to compute a complexity index on the scale of 100-2000, as well as an overall grade equivalent score. TextEvaluator computes three complexity scores based on the models optimized for literary, informational and mixed texts. We used the literary metric as the final complexity score for our passages since all texts were excerpts from a novel.[6]

In addition to the overall score, several dimension scores are provided, including: Syntactic Complexity (using features related to sentence complexity); Academic Vocabulary (the extent to which words in the text are characteristic of academic texts); Word Unfamiliarity (a composite measure of word frequency); Lexical Cohesion (measures the degree of overlap between concepts across adjacent sentences within paragraphs); Level of Argumentation (indexes the ease or difficulty of inferring connections across sentences when the underlying format of a text is argumentative); additional dimensions include Interactive/Conversational Style, Concreteness, Degree of Narrativity.

We note that passage lengths between 177 and

---

[4] https://textevaluator.ets.org/

[5] TextEvaluator appears in the Nelson et al. (2012) benchmark as SourceRater.

[6] A reviewer of this paper pointed out that Text Evaluator includes an automatic genre classifier which is used to determine the final complexity score (Sheehan et al., 2013), and that it is possible that some passages in a novel could be more on the informational side. In our study, 302 passages (95%) were classified as literary texts by TextEvaluator's genre classifier. Among the remaining 16 passages, 7 passages were classified as informational texts and 9 passages as mixed texts. None of the selected passages (in section 4.1) belong to these 16. Using final instead of literary scores had a negligible effect on statistics reported in section 3.2.

309 words are within scope for TextEvaluator, albeit on the shorter side of the range: Sheehan et al. (2013) report an evaluation with texts ranging in length from 112 to more than 2,000 words.

For this analysis, we treated each chunk from the book as an independent passage. Thus, TextEvaluator had no access to information about other passages. One might contend that there are limitations to such an approach, as some aspects of difficulty of the text may change as the reader accumulates knowledge about the world of the book. For example, words that are initially unfamiliar, such as names of characters, magic creatures and artifacts, spells and curses, would become increasingly familiar as the story progresses. In contrast, other aspects of complexity, such as the syntactic complexity of sentences, are less likely to become more or less challenging as one reads further into the book. In the current study, we have not attempted to capture any such text continuity effects.

3.2 Results

The overall TextEvaluator complexity of passages across the book varied from 160 to 1150 with average complexity 613.4 (SD=163.1). In terms of grade levels this corresponds to variation from second to eleventh grade, with the average around grade six.

The dimension scores also varied across the book although the patterns were different for different dimensions. Figure 1 shows the distributions for different dimension scores. The scale for all scores is 0-100. The score for Academic vocabulary was consistently low across all passages (Mean=27, SD=7.3), while the score for narrativity was consistently high (Mean=83, SD=5.8). The score for the Level of Argumentation showed the largest spread (Mean=53 and SD=19.8). We also note the substantial spread in Syntactic complexity (Mean=46.1 and SD=11.3).

We also considered how the complexity varies as one proceeds through the book (Figure 2). The red line shows values for each passage, the blue line shows a smoothed estimate calculated using lowess (Cleveland, 1979).[7] The plot shows there is a substantial fluctuation from passage to passage as well as potentially longer-range trends that may correspond to the book's narrative structure. Specifically, the peak around 130-140 corresponds to the description-heavy introduction to

---

[7] as implemented in (Seabold and Perktold, 2010)

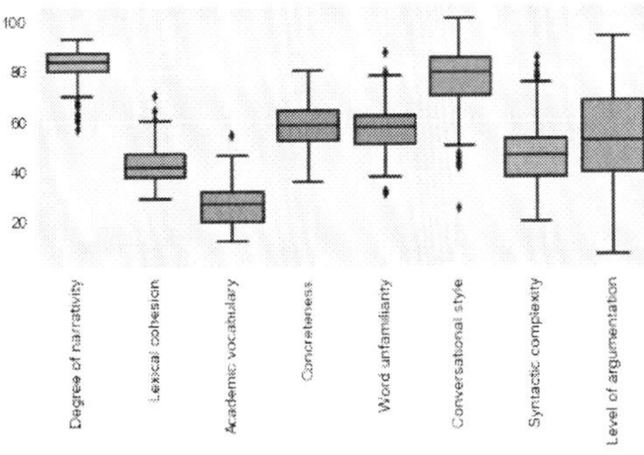

Figure 1: Distributions of scores for various dimensions of text complexity in HP1. The dimensions are ordered on the x-axis by spread (SD).

Hogwarts and Harry's first classes; the valley around 300 corresponds to the fast-moving final stand-off between Harry and Voldemort/Quirrell.

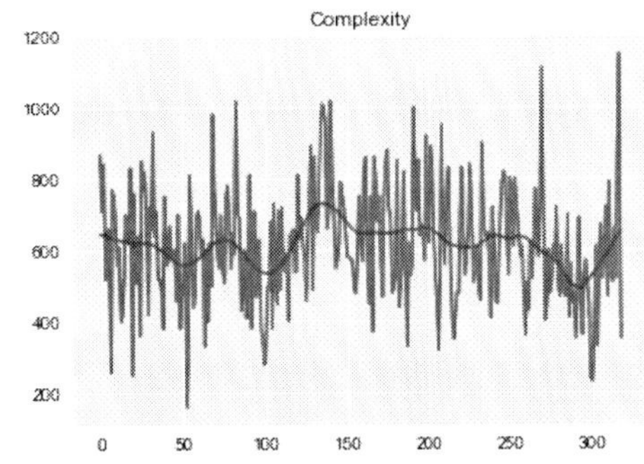

Figure 2: Distribution of holistic text complexity scores as one proceeds through HP1.

The answer to research question 1 is thus: The extent of variation in text complexity across passages in the book is very substantial. If text complexity has any systematic effect on the oral reading performance, the extent of variation in complexity suggests that it is likely to become a major confounding factor in tracking the child's progress in fluency while reading the book.

4 Study II: Text complexity and oral reading fluency

Our second question is: Does the complexity of the passage that is being read significantly impact children's reading fluency for the passage? In order to answer this question, we selected 3 passages with very large differences in text complexity as estimated by TextEvaluator, and collected oral reading fluency estimates for these passages from a sample of 2-4 graders. The details of the procedure and the results are described in this section.

4.1 Passage selection

We ordered all 318 passages by estimated text complexity, and selected passages from the middle of the distribution and from the lowest and highest deciles. In addition to TextEvaluator score, when selecting passages we also took into account whether a passage could be reasonably read as stand-alone text. Table 1 shows the characteristics of these three passages. All passages are from the first chapter of the book.

Passage	# words	TE score	Complexity Percentile
Easy	226	260	1.9%
Medium	282	580	51.5%
Hard	246	800	90.3%

Table 1: The characteristics of the passages used for the data collection: length in words, complexity, complexity relative to the whole book.

4.2 Data collection procedure

The recordings took place in an office with several children recorded simultaneously. The texts were presented on screen and the audio was captured using the head-set with a microphone.

Before reading the experimental passages, the child first listened to the passage that begins the first chapter of HP1 (starting with "Mr. and Mrs. Dursley of number four, ...") as narrated by the professional actor Jim Dale (Rowling and Dale, 2016). Then the child read aloud the passage immediately following the passage read by the narrator. Since all children read this passage first, this passage is used as a reference text to measure baseline WCPM for each child.

The experimental passages were then presented to children in a randomized order, to allow separation between text and order effects in subsequent analyses (Petscher and Kim, 2011; Francis et al., 2008; Jenkins et al., 2009). The children were asked to read at their natural pace.

A total of 30 children took part in this data collection selected via a convenience sample. Table 2 shows the distribution by grade and gender and

Grade	Girls	Boys	Mean age
2	7	3	8;3
3	3	7	9;0
4	6	4	10;2

Table 2: The demographic characteristics of participants.

the average age in each group. All recordings were done in April of 2017.

4.3 Computation of oral reading measures

To compute WCPM we used a professional transcription agency to obtain word-by-word transcriptions of each child's reading and aligned them to the passage text using an algorithm based on dynamic programming. We next computed how many words in the original passage matched those in the transcription. This algorithm is similar to that used to compute ASR word error rate, but following the standard practice in reading research we only penalized substitutions and deletions and did not take into account any insertions. Most children's reading closely followed the texts, with the average of 93.8% of all words in each text read correctly (SD=3.7, min=82.7%, max=99.6%).

We manually identified in each recording the time stamps where the child started and finished reading the text. WCPM was computed by dividing the total time it took the child to read the text by the total number of matched words in each text. The average WCPM in the experimental texts in our corpus was 117.1 (SD=27.3, min=57.2, max=196.0). To get an idea where these readers stand with respect to general population of U.S. children of comparable age, we consulted the WCPM norms in Table 1 of Hasbrouck and Tindal (2006), and found that a grade-stratified sample of children from grades 2-4 during spring term is expected to read, on average, at 106 WCPM. The observed rate of 117 WCPM corresponds to 60% percentile – somewhat above average. We note that this is only a rather rough estimate of these children's fluency relative to peers, since the experimental texts differ in complexity substantially from the grade-leveled materials used for oral reading fluency assessments. Still, this estimate accords with our observation during the data collection that these children generally read quite fluently and accurately for their age.

4.4 Results

To evaluate the effect of text on WCPM, we used a mixed effects linear model. These models offer a more powerful way to conduct repeated-measures analyses than a simple repeated-measures ANOVA, because they make it possible to combine both continuous and categorical predictors. We used WCPM as the dependent variable and speaker identity as a random factor. We included the following fixed factors: text identity (categorical), the baseline WCPM on the reference text (continuous), and order in which each text was read (continuous). In addition to the main effects, we also included the interaction between text identity and the baseline WCPM. Table 3 shows the standardized coefficients and significance values for the model. We took WCPM for the Medium text as the reference category.

	Variable	**Coeff.**	$\mathbf{P} > |z|$
1	Intercept	0.522	<0.001
2	text-easy	-0.814	<0.001
3	text-hard	-1.165	<0.001
4	base_wcpm	0.893	<0.001
5	text-easy:base_wcpm	-0.258	0.001
6	text-hard:base_wcpm	-0.132	0.089
7	order	0.046	0.236

Table 3: The standardized coefficients and their significance values for fixed effects used to predict WCPM on each text (N=90). In addition to the fixed effects, the model also included the random effect for speakers (not shown in the table).

First, we observe that the child's baseline reading fluency estimated from the reference text is a significant factor, as expected. Second, we note that the order in which the experimental texts were presented does not yield a significant effect.

The identity of the passage (Easy, Medium, Hard) has a significant effect on reading fluency. Thus, the Hard text is read 1.2 standard deviations less fluently than the Medium text (row 3); this result accords with expectations. The result in row 2 is surprising: There is a highly significant and large difference in WCPM between the Easy text and the Medium text, but it is in the *opposite* direction – the Medium text is read 0.8 standard deviations *more fluently* than the Easy text. Thus, while the results clearly attest to a substantial effect of the text on WCPM, the estimates of text complexity are in a rather dramatic mis-alignment with the

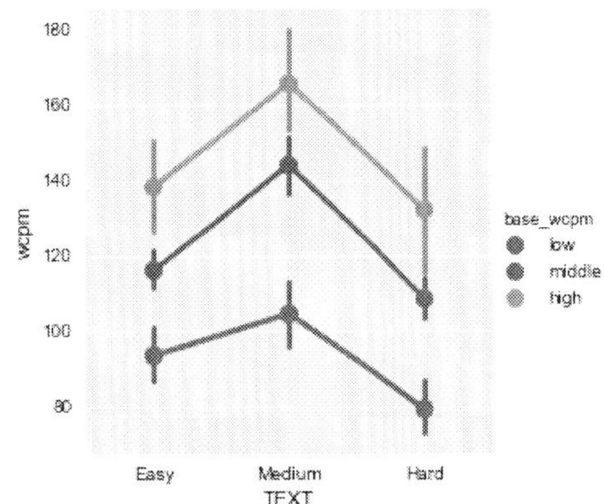

Figure 3: Average WCPM for the three texts in our study. To illustrate the interaction between fluency and text we divided all speakers into three equal bins based on 'base_wcpm'.

pattern of the oral reading.

Row 5 in Table 3 shows a significant interaction effect between text and base WCPM, for Medium vs Easy texts: The higher the base reading fluency of the child (base_wcpm), the bigger the difference in WCPM between Easy and Medium text. This effect is consistent with the tendency shown in row 6, though it does not reach significance: the more fluent readers also tended to differentiate more between the Medium and Hard texts. This finding suggests that more fluent readers seem to have a tendency to differentiate their oral reading pattern depending on the text they read to a larger extent than the less fluent readers. Indeed, there is a significant, medium-strength correlation between a child's *average* WCPM for the three texts and his or her *variance* in WCPM across these texts: $r = 0.47, p < 0.01$.

Figure 3 shows the average of WCPM across the three texts in our study. To illustrate the interaction between text and fluency we divided all children into three equal groups based on their base WCPM on the reference text.

In order to check whether the impact of the text is mostly about the accuracy aspect of the fluency measure (words read *correctly* per minute) or about the reading rate itself (words or syllables per minute), we repeated the analyses above using either words per minute or syllables per minute as the dependent variable instead of WCPM. The results are very similar to those reported in Table 3: Base reading rate has a significant effect; text identity has a significant effect, with one of the comparisons going in the opposite direction from that predicted; the interaction effect for base reading rate and text for Easy vs Medium is significant; order and the second interaction effects are not significant. This finding suggests that, at least for these readers, the basic speed of reading is systematically affected by the identity of the text.

5 Discussion

The main finding in our study is that while different passages consistently elicit different reading rates, text complexity as estimated by a state-of-the-art measure does not predict the differences correctly – a passage that is rated as 3.2 grade levels more difficult than another is in fact read significantly *faster*, consistently across readers. We consider several possible reasons for this effect:

- TextEvaluator's complexity estimates may not be accurate when applied to passages from a novel.

- *Oral* reading is not only a kind of reading, but also a kind of *speaking*. Reading rate might thus be affected by properties of speech, in a direction that differs, or even contradicts, the impact of text complexity.

- Reading *a story* aloud, or *narration*, is not only a kind of oral reading, but also a kind of *performance* for an audience. While children are not explicitly asked to narrate, the nature of the text might drive them to do so, as well as the model reading provided by the narrator of the audiobook (recall that the children listened to a passage narrated by the actor Jim Dale before reading aloud their own passages). Variation in WCPM across texts could be effected by demands of expressive narration that are unrelated, or at least not directly related, to comprehension complexity of the text.

5.1 Estimation of text complexity in book excerpts

One possible hypothesis for explaining the finding is that TextEvaluator scores may not provide an adequate estimate of complexity for book excerpts, since the engine, like many other complexity/readability measures, has been developed and validated for estimating reading comprehension difficulty of standalone passages meant for use in assessments. In particular, the guidelines for using TextEvaluator specifically exclude drama, yet the Easy text includes an informal conversation with punctuation used to indicate emotions of the interlocutors. The Easy text contains the following excerpts:

> (1) "Well, I just thought ... maybe ... it was something to do with ... you know ... her crowd."
> (2) "Funny stuff on the news," Mr. Dursley mumbled. "Owls ... shooting stars ... and there were a lot of funny-looking people in town today ... "

TextEvaluator treats "..." as if they were sentence-final periods, as in:

> (3) "Well, I just thought. Maybe. It was something to do with. You know. Her crowd."
> (4) "Funny stuff on the news," Mr. Dursley mumbled. "Owls. Shooting stars. And there were a lot of funny-looking people in town today."

This creates multiple very short sentences which in turns lowers the complexity score since average sentence length is one of the indicators of text complexity. However, an alternative interpretation where utterance-internal "..." are more akin to commas is also possible, as in:

> (5) "Well, I just thought, maybe, it was something to do with, you know, her crowd."
> (6) "Funny stuff on the news," Mr. Dursley mumbled. "Owls, shooting stars, and there were a lot of funny-looking people in town today."

After substituting (5) and (6) instead of (1) and (2), respectively, the estimation of the complexity of the text increased from 260 to 300, due to the increase in average sentence length. It is possible that there are other ambiguities that could be resolved in ways with differing levels of complexity, as well as other indicators of complexity that are not picked up or interpreted as such by TextEvaluator. We note that the particular issue pointed out above would not be specific to TextEvaluator, as many complexity indices include average sentence length as a component. Generally, it is possible that measures developed predominantly for analyzing passages for assessments would not account correctly for stylistic devices used in novels. Indeed, Nelson et al. (2012) observed that various measures of text complexity, including TextEvaluator, generally had better correlations with grade level for informational texts than for narrative texts.

5.2 Text complexity vs general properties of speech prosody

Average sentence length is a text complexity indicator used in both classical (such as Flesh-Kincaid) and modern text complexity measures – longer sentences tend to be more difficult from the point of view of comprehension. From the point of view of speech prosody, however, it is not clear that a long sentence would be uttered slower than a few shorter sentences covering, in total, the same number of words (or syllables). Studies of speech prosody have consistently demonstrated that the duration of segments increases at certain important locations within utterances, sentence boundaries being one such location (see White (2014) for a detailed review of this topic). As a result, the overall time it would take to read a text with many short sentences might in fact be longer than a text with the same number of words split into longer sentences.

We observe that the actor who is narrating the audiobook is unlikely to be influenced by text complexity to the same extent as young readers who are still learning to read. It is hard to imagine that any of the passages in HP1 are genuinely difficult for the narrator, as a reader who is not only proficient but highly skilled,[8] and also very familiar with the text he is narrating. Thus, if we observe substantial variation in reading rates across the three texts for the narrator, it is likely that the reason for the changes is something other than text complexity, as quantified by comprehension-related measures.

To test this hypothesis we compute the reading rate for the narrator following the same approach as described above. We found that the patterns of the reading rate of the narrator closely followed those we observed for children in our study: The Easy text was read slower than the Medium text which in turn was read faster than the Hard text. Figure 4 shows the WCPM for the narrator relative to the children in our study.

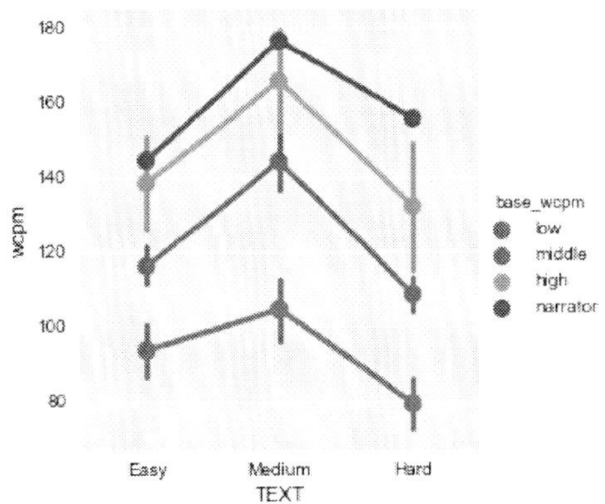

Figure 4: Average WCPM for children in our corpus and the audiobook narrator (purple).

It appears that readers with different levels of reading fluency (young learners and a performing professional), are affected by some aspect of the text *in a similar way*, which makes it less likely that this aspect is directly related to comprehension complexity, since complexity should pose much less of a challenge for a performing professional than for a second grader. General patterns of speech are one potential reason (as also mentioned in section 5.2); another possibility is that in the context of narrating a story, reading rate is affected by "directives" in the text that govern expressive oral reading performance of each passage (cf. Theune et al. (2006)). Such directives could include markers of hesitation, emphasis, surprise, stuttering, etc.; some of these might have a systematic effect on reading rate.

5.3 Interaction between base fluency and impact of text identity

Finally, we also observed an interaction effect between the reader's baseline fluency and the extent to which text identity impacts that reader's fluency. Specifically, for one of the pairs of texts, more fluent readers tend to have significantly larger differences in reading rates between the two texts. This finding is in agreement with the literature – Petscher and Kim (2011) found that the proportion of reading rate variance attributable to variation in passages tends to increase with grade, for grades 1 to 3. This could be due to more proficient readers reading more expressively by attending more closely to the rhetorical and prosodic clues that impact the reading rate. Lower profi-

---

[8]The narrator, Jim Dale, has won Grammy awards for his recordings of two of the seven Harry Potter books.

ciency readers are likely to be focused more on reading words, while better readers also attend to other structures in the text. Indeed, Schwanenflugel et al. (2015) found that more fluent readers communicate linguistic focus while reading aloud by prosodically marking direct quotes, exclamations, and contrastive words. This direction requires further exploration; if the finding is replicated with a larger sample of readers with more variation in reading proficiencies, it would suggest that the extent of adjustment for text effects needs to be moderated by the reader's baseline reading rate.

6 Conclusion

In this paper we discussed the challenges of continuous fluency tracking within an assisted-reading intervention where a child reads a long novel rather than a set of grade-controlled passages. We showed that there is substantial variation in passage difficulty across a single book as estimated by a state-of-the-art measure of text complexity for comprehension and a consistent variation in reading rates between passages. Continuous fluency tracking needs to account for this variability. The results of our small preliminary study suggest not only that a state-of-the-art measure of comprehension complexity does not predict reading rates well, but in fact substantial variation in reading rates may be unrelated to comprehension complexity of the text. Additional research needs to be done to further explore these relationships.

7 Acknowledgements

We would like to thank René Lawless, Kelsey Dreier, and Thomas Florek for their help with data collection; Diane Napolitano for her help with running TextEvaluator; Patrick Lange and Binod Gyawali for their help with preparing the narrator's data. We would also like to thank our many colleagues at ETS who discussed this work with us and provided useful comments.

References

Scott P. Ardoin, Shannon M. Suldo, Joseph Witt, Seth Aldrich, and Erin McDonald. 2005. Accuracy of readability estimates' predictions of CBM performance. *School Psychology Quarterly* 20(1):1–22.

Jennifer Balogh, Jared Bernstein, Jian Cheng, and Bren Townshend. 2007. Automatic evaluation of reading accuracy: Assessing machine scores. *Proceedings of SLaTE ITWR Workshop* .

Jennifer Balogh, Jared Bernstein, Jian Cheng, Alistair Van Moere, Brent Townshend, and Masanori Suzuki. 2012. Validation of automated scoring of oral reading. *Educational and Psychological Measurement* 72(3):435–452.

Lisa Beinborn, Torsten Zesch, and Iryna Gurevych. 2014. Readability for foreign language learning: The importance of cognates. *International Journal of Applied Linguistics* 165(2):136–162. https://doi.org/doi:10.1075/itl.165.2.02bei.

William S. Cleveland. 1979. Robust locally weighted regression and smoothing scatterplots. *Journal of the American Statistical Association* 74(368):829–836.

Donald Compton, Amanda Appleton, and Michelle Hosp. 2004. Exploring the relationship between text-leveling systems and reading accuracy and fluency in second-grade students who are average and poor decoders. *Learning Disabilities Research* 19(3):176–184.

Edgar Dale and Jeanne Chall. 1949. The concept of readability. *Elementary English* 26(23).

Mary C. Danne, Jay R. Campbell, Wendy S. Grigg, Madeline J. Goodman, and Andreas Oranje. 2005. Fourth-Grade Students Reading Aloud: NAEP 2002 Special Study of Oral Reading. The Nation's Report Card. NCES 2006-469. *National Center for Education Statistics* .

William DuBay. 2004. The principles of readability. http://files.eric.ed.gov/fulltext/ED490073.pdf.

Maxine Eskenazi. 2009. An overview of spoken language technology for education. *Speech Communication* 51(10):832–844.

Lijun Feng, Noémie Elhadad, and Matt Huenerfauth. 2009. Cognitively motivated features for readability assessment. In *Proceedings of the 12th Conference of the European Chapter of the ACL (EACL 2009)*. Association for Computational Linguistics, Athens, Greece, pages 229–237.

Rudolph Flesch. 1948. A new readability yardstick. *Journal of Applied Psychology* 32(3):221–233.

Michael Flor and Beata Beigman Klebanov. 2014. Associative lexical cohesion as a factor in text complexity. *International Journal of Applied Linguistics* 165(2):223–258.

Gilbert Fowler. 1978. The comparative readability of newspapers and novels. *Journalism Quarterly* 55(3):589–591.

David J. Francis, Kristi L. Santi, Christopher Barr, Jack M. Fletcher, Al Varisco, and Barbara F. Foorman. 2008. Form effects on the estimation of students' oral reading fluency using DIBELS. *Journal of School Psychology* 46:315–342.

Lynn S. Fuchs, Douglas Fuchs, Michelle K. Hosp, and Joseph R. Jenkins. 2001. Oral reading fluency as an indicator of reading competence: A theoretical, empirical, and historical analysis. *Scientific Studies of Reading* 5(3):239–256.

Roland H. Good, Deborah C. Simmons, and Edward J. Kame'enui. 2001. The importance and decision-making utility of a continuum of fluency-based indicators of foundational reading skills for third-grade high-stakes outcomes. *Scientific Studies of Reading* 5(3):257–288.

Ronald. H. Good and Ruth. A. Kaminski. 2002. DI-BELS oral reading fluency passages for first through third grades. *Technical Report* 10. Eugene, OR: University of Oregon.

Robert Gunning. 1952. *The Technique of Clear Writing*. McGraw-Hill.

Jan Hasbrouck and Gerald Tindal. 2006. Oral reading fluency norms: A valuable assessment tool for reading teachers. *The Reading Teacher* 59(7):636–644.

Michael Heilman, Kevyn Collins-Thompson, Jamie Callan, and Maxine Eskenazi. 2007. Combining lexical and grammatical features to improve readability measures for first and second language texts. In *Human Language Technologies 2007: The Conference of the North American Chapter of the Association for Computational Linguistics; Proceedings of the Main Conference*. Association for Computational Linguistics, Rochester, New York, pages 460–467.

Roxanne F. Hudson, Paige C. Pullen, Holly B. Lane, and Joseph K. Torgesen. 2008. The complex nature of reading fluency: A multidimensional view. *Reading & Writing Quarterly* 25(1):4–32.

Joseph R. Jenkins, J. Jason Graff, and Diana L. Miglioretti. 2009. Estimating reading growth using intermittent CBM progress monitoring. *Exceptional Children* 46:315–342.

J. Peter Kincaid, Robert P. Fishburne, Richard Rogers, and Brad Chissom. 1975. Derivation of new readability formulas (Automated Readability Index, Fog Count and Flesch Reading Ease Formula) for navy enlisted personnel. *Institute for Simulation and Training* 56.

G. Harry McLaughlin. 1969. SMOG grading - a new readability formula. *Journal of Reading* 12(8):639–646.

Michael Milone. 2012. The Development of ATOS: The Renaissance Readability Formula. http://mpemc.weebly.com/uploads/5/4/0/7/5407355/development_of_atos.pdf.

Jack Mostow. 2012. Why and how our automated reading tutor listens. *Proceedings of the International Symposium on Automatic Detection of Errors in Pronunciation Training* pages 43–52. https://www.cs.cmu.edu/listen/pdfs/2012-05-05 ISADEPT2012 keynote final.pdf.

Diane Napolitano, Kathleen M. Sheehan, and Robert Mundkowsky. 2015. Online readability and text complexity analysis with TextEvaluator. In *Proceedings of HLT-NAACL*. pages 96–100.

Jessica Nelson, Charles Perfetti, David Liben, and Meredith Liben. 2012. Measures of text difficulty: Testing their predictive value for grade levels and student performance. In *Technical Report to the Gates Foundation*. http://achievethecore.org/content/upload/nelson_perfetti_liben_measures_of_text_difficulty_research_ela.pdf.

Yaacov Petscher and Young-Suk Kim. 2011. The utility and accuracy of oral reading fluency score types in predicting reading comprehension. *Journal of School Psychology* 49(1):107–129.

Greg Roberts, Roland Good, and Stephanie Corcoran. 2005. Story retell: A fluency-based indicator of reading comprehension. *School Psychology Quarterly* 20(3):304–317.

Joanne K. Rowling and Jim Dale. 2016. *Harry Potter and the sorcerer's stone*. Listening Library/Penguin Random House, New York. https://usd.shop.pottermore.com/collections/audiobooks/products/harry_potter_and_the_sorcerers_stone_audio_book1_english.

Paula J. Schwanenflugel, Matthew R. Westmoreland, and Rebekah George Benjamin. 2015. Reading fluency skill and the prosodic marking of linguistic focus. *Reading and Writing* 28(1):9–30.

Sarah E. Schwarm and Mari Ostendorf. 2005. Reading level assessment using support vector machines and statistical language models. In *Proceedings of the 43rd Annual Meeting on Association for Computational Linguistics*. Association for Computational Linguistics, Stroudsburg, PA, USA, ACL '05, pages 523–530.

Skipper Seabold and Josef Perktold. 2010. Statsmodels: Econometric and Statistical Modeling with Python. In *Proceedings of the Python in Science Conference*. pages 57–61.

Kathleen M. Sheehan, Michael Flor, and Diane Napolitano. 2013. A two-stage approach for generating unbiased estimates of text complexity. In *Proceedings of the Workshop on Natural Language Processing for Improving Textual Accessibility*. Association for Computational Linguistics, Atlanta, Georgia, pages 49–58.

Kathleen M. Sheehan, Irene Kostin, Diane Napolitano, and Michael Flor. 2014. The TextEvaluator Tool: Helping teachers and test developers select texts for use in instruction and assessment. *Elementary School Journal* 115(2):184–209.

George Spache. 1953. A new readability formula for primary-grade reading materials. *The Elementary School Journal* 53(7):410–413.

Mariët Theune, Koen Meijs, Dirk Heylen, and Roeland Ordelman. 2006. Generating expressive speech for storytelling applications. *IEEE Transactions on Audio, Speech and Language Processing* 14(4):1137–1144.

Sowmya Vajjala and Detmar Meurers. 2012. On improving the accuracy of readability classification using insights from second language acquisition. In *Proceedings of the Seventh Workshop on Building Educational Applications Using NLP*. Association for Computational Linguistics, Stroudsburg, PA, USA, pages 163–173.

Miya Miura Wayman, Teri Wallace, Hilda Ives Wiley, Renta Tich, and Christine A. Espin. 2007. Literature synthesis on curriculum-based measurement in reading. *The Journal of Special Education* 41(2):85–120.

Laurence White. 2014. Communicative function and prosodic form in speech timing. *Speech Communication* 63-64:38–54.

Klaus Zechner, John Sabatini, and Lei Chen. 2009. Automatic scoring of children's read-aloud text passages and word lists. In *Proceedings of the NAACL-HLT Workshop on Innovative Use of NLP for Building Educational Applications*. Association for Computational Linguistics, pages 10–18.

Auxiliary Objectives for Neural Error Detection Models

Marek Rei
The ALTA Institute
Computer Laboratory
University of Cambridge
United Kingdom
marek.rei@cl.cam.ac.uk

Helen Yannakoudakis
The ALTA Institute
Computer Laboratory
University of Cambridge
United Kingdom
helen.yannakoudakis@cl.cam.ac.uk

Abstract

We investigate the utility of different auxiliary objectives and training strategies within a neural sequence labeling approach to error detection in learner writing. Auxiliary costs provide the model with additional linguistic information, allowing it to learn general-purpose compositional features that can then be exploited for other objectives. Our experiments show that a joint learning approach trained with parallel labels on in-domain data improves performance over the previous best error detection system. While the resulting model has the same number of parameters, the additional objectives allow it to be optimised more efficiently and achieve better performance.

1   Introduction

Automatic error detection systems for learner writing need to identify various types of error in text, ranging from incorrect uses of function words, such articles and prepositions, to semantic anomalies in content words, such as adjective–noun combinations. To tackle the scarcity of error-annotated training data, previous work has investigated the utility of automatically generated ungrammatical data (Foster and Andersen, 2009; Felice and Yuan, 2014), as well as explored learning from native well-formed data (Rozovskaya and Roth, 2016; Gamon, 2010).

In this work, we investigate the utility of supplementing error detection frameworks with additional linguistic information that can be extracted from the available error-annotated learner data. We construct a neural sequence labeling system for error detection that allows us to learn better representations of language composition and de-

tect errors in context more accurately. In addition to predicting the binary error labels, we experiment with also predicting additional information for each token, including token frequency and the specific error type, which can be extracted from the existing data, as well as part-of-speech (POS) tags and dependency relations, which can be generated automatically using readily available toolkits.

These auxiliary objectives provide the sequence labeling model with additional linguistic information, allowing it to learn useful compositional features that can then be exploited for error detection. This can be seen as a type of multi-task learning, where the model learns better compositional features via shared representations with related tasks. While common approaches to multi-task learning require randomly switching between different tasks and datasets, we demonstrate that a joint learning approach trained on in-domain data with parallel labels substantially improves error detection performance on two different datasets. In addition, the auxiliary labels are only required during the training process, resulting in a better model with the same number of parameters.

In the following sections, we describe our approach to the task, systematically compare the informativeness of various auxiliary loss functions, investigate alternative training strategies, and examine the effect of additional training data.

2   Error Detection Model

In addition to the scarcity of errors in the training data (i.e., the majority of tokens are correct), recent research has highlighted the variability in manual correction of writing errors: re-annotation of the CoNLL 2014 shared task test set by 10 annotators demonstrated that even humans have great difficulty in agreeing how to correct writ-

Proceedings of the 12th Workshop on Innovative Use of NLP for Building Educational Applications, pages 33–43
Copenhagen, Denmark, September 8, 2017. ©2017 Association for Computational Linguistics

ing errors (Bryant and Ng, 2015). Given the challenges of the all-errors correction task, previous research has demonstrated that detection models can *detect* more errors than systems focusing on correction (Rei and Yannakoudakis, 2016), and therefore provide more extensive feedback to the learner.

Following Rei and Yannakoudakis (2016), we treat error detection as a sequence labeling task – each token in the input sentence is assigned a label, indicating whether it is correct or incorrect given the current context – and construct a bidirectional recurrent neural network for detecting writing errors. The model is given a sequence of tokens as input, which are then mapped to a sequence of distributed word embeddings $[x_1, ..., x_T]$. These embeddings are then given as input to a bidirectional LSTM (Hochreiter and Schmidhuber, 1997) moving through the sentence in both directions. At each step, the LSTM calculates a new hidden representation based on the current token embedding and the hidden state from the previous step.

$$h_t^{(f)} = \text{LSTM}(x_t, h_{t-1}^{(f)}) \qquad (1)$$

$$h_t^{(b)} = \text{LSTM}(x_t, h_{t+1}^{(b)}) \qquad (2)$$

Next, the network includes a tanh-activated feedforward layer, using the hidden states from both LSTMs as input, allowing the model to learn more complex higher-level features. By combining the hidden states from both directions, we are able to have a vector that represents a specific token but also takes into account context on both sides:

$$d_t = \tanh(W_f h_t^{(f)} + W_b h_t^{(b)}) \qquad (3)$$

where W_f and W_b are fully-connected weight matrices.

The final layer calculates label predictions based on the layer d_t. The softmax activation function is used to output a normalised probability distribution over all the possible labels for each token:

$$y_t = \text{softmax}(W_y d_t) \qquad (4)$$

where W_y is a weight matrix and y_t is a vector with a position for each possible label. In order to find the predicted label, we return the element with the highest predicted value.

The model is optimised using cross entropy, which is equivalent to optimising the negative log-likelihood of the correct labels:

$$E = - \sum_t \sum_k \widetilde{y}_{t,k} \log(y_{t,k}) \qquad (5)$$

where $y_{t,k}$ is the predicted probability of token t having label k, and $\widetilde{y}_{t,k}$ has the value 1 if the correct label for token t is k, and the value 0 otherwise.

We also make use of the character-level extension described by Rei et al. (2016). Each token is separated into individual characters and mapped to character embeddings. Using a bidirectional LSTM and a hidden feedforward component, the character vectors are composed into a character-based token representation. Finally, a dynamic gating function is used to combine this representation with a regular token embedding, taking advantage of both approaches. This component allows the model to capture useful morphological and character-based patterns, in addition to learning individual token-level vectors of common tokens.

3 Auxiliary Loss Functions

The model in Section 2 learns to assign error labels to tokens based on the manual annotation available in the training data. However, there are nearly limitless ways of making writing errors and learning them all explicitly from hand-annotated examples is not feasible. In addition, writing errors can be very sparse, leaving the system with very little useful training data for learning error patterns. In order to train models that generalise well with limited training examples, we would want to encourage them to learn more generic patterns of language, grammar, syntax and composition, which can then be exploited for error detection.

Multi-task learning allows models to learn from multiple objectives via shared representations, using information from related tasks to boost performance on tasks for which there is limited target data. For example, Plank et al. (2016) explored the option of using word frequency as an auxiliary loss function for part-of-speech (POS) tagging. Rei (2017) describe a semi-supervised framework for multi-task learning, integrating language modeling as an additional objective. Following this work, we adapt auxiliary objectives for the task of error detection, and further experi-

words	My	husband	was	following	a	course	all	the	week	in	Berne	.
target	c	c	c	i	c	c	c	i	c	c	c	c
freq	5	3	8	4	8	5	7	9	5	8	0	10
lang	fr	fr	fr	fr	fr	fr	fr	fr	fr	fr	fr	fr
error	c	c	c	RV	c	c	c	UD	c	c	c	c
POS	APP$	NN1	VBDZ	VVG	AT1	NN1	DB	AT	NNT1	II	NP1	.
GR	det	ncsubj	aux	null	det	dobj	ncmod	det	ncmod	ncmod	dobj	null

Table 1: Alternative labels for an example sentence from the FCE training data.

ment with a larger set of possible objectives. Instead of only predicting the correctness of each token in context, we extend the system to predict additional information and labels for every token. The information from these auxiliary objectives is propagated into the weights of the model during training, without requiring the extra labels at testing time. While common neural approaches to multi-task learning switch randomly between different tasks and datasets, we use a joint learning approach trained on in-domain data only.

The lower parts of the model function similarly to the system described in Section 2. Token representations are first passed through a bidirectional LSTM in order to build context-specific representations. After that, each separate objective is assigned an individual hidden layer:

$$d_t^{(n)} = W_f^{(n)} h_t^{(f)} + W_b^{(n)} h_t^{(b)} \qquad (6)$$

where $W_f^{(n)}$ and $W_b^{(n)}$ are weight matrices specific to the n-th task. While the recurrent components are shared between all objectives, the hidden layers allow parts of the model to be customised for a specific task, learning higher-level features and controlling how the information from forward- and backward-moving LSTMs is combined.

Next, a task-specific output distribution is calculated based on $d_t^{(n)}$:

$$y_t^{(n)} = \text{softmax}(W_y^{(n)} d_t^{(n)}) \qquad (7)$$

where $W_y^{(n)}$ is a weight matrix and $y_t^{(n)}$ has the dimensionality of the total number of labels for the n-th task. Figure 1 presents a diagram of the network with $n = 2$, although the number of possible auxiliary tasks can also be larger.

The whole model is optimised by minimising the cross-entropy for every task and every token:

$$E = -\sum_t \sum_n \sum_k \alpha_n \cdot \widetilde{y}_{t,k}^{(n)} \cdot \log(y_{t,k}^{(n)}) \qquad (8)$$

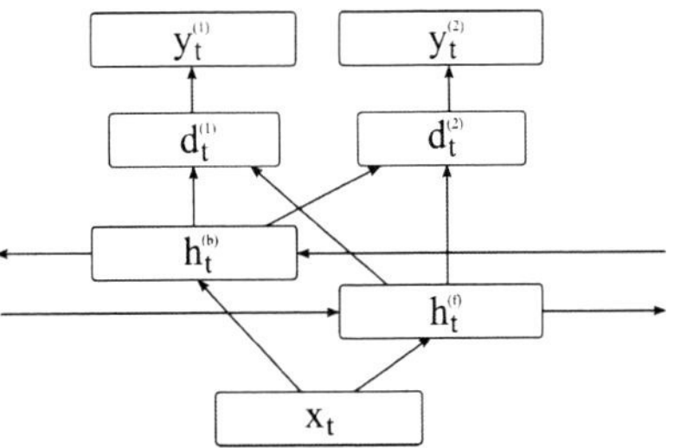

Figure 1: The bidirectional recurrent architecture for one time-step, using one main objective and one auxiliary objective.

where $y_{t,k}^{(n)}$ is the predicted probability of the t-th token having label k for the n-th task; $\widetilde{y}_{t,k}^{(n)}$ has value 1 only if that label is correct, and 0 otherwise; α_n is the weight for task n. Since our main goal is to develop more accurate error detection models, α_n allows us to control how much the model depends on the n-th auxiliary task. For example, setting the value of α_n to 0.1 means any updates for the n-th task will have 10 times less importance. We tune a specific weight for each task by trying values $[0.05, 0.1, 0.2, 0.5, 1.0]$ and choosing the ones that achieved the highest result on the development data.

The main goal of our system is to classify tokens as being correct or incorrect, and this objective is included in all configurations. In addition, we experiment with a number of auxiliary loss objectives that are only required during training:

- **frequency**: Plank et al. (2016) propose using word frequency as an additional objective for POS tagging, since words with certain POS tags can be more likely to belong to specific frequency groups. The frequency of a token w in the training corpus is discretized as $\text{int}(\log(\text{freq}_{\text{train}}(w))$ and used as an auxiliary label.

- **error type**: While the task is defined as binary classification, available learner data also

35

	FCE DEV					FCE TEST				
	predicted	correct	P	R	$F_{0.5}$	predicted	correct	P	R	$F_{0.5}$
R&Y (2016)	-	-	54.5	28.2	46.0	3898	1798	46.1	28.5	41.1
Main system	1837	1140	62.3	24.6	47.6	2653	1468	55.7	23.3	43.4
+ frequency	1870	1111	59.7	23.9	45.8	2702	1461	54.4	23.2	42.7
+ language	1929	1150	60.4	24.8	46.6	2690	1458	54.9	23.1	42.8
+ errors	1905	1206	**63.3**	26.0	49.2	2778	1584	57.0	25.1	45.5
+ POS	2199	1334	60.7	**28.8**	49.7	3322	1803	54.3	**28.6**	46.0
+ GR	1952	1207	62.1	26.0	48.4	2887	1654	**57.9**	26.2	46.4
+ err POS GR	2087	1320	63.2	28.4	**50.8**	3090	1781.0	57.7	28.3	**47.7**

Table 2: Error detection results on the FCE dataset using different auxiliary loss functions.

contains more fine-grained labels per error. For example, the FCE (Yannakoudakis et al., 2011) training set has 75 different labels for individual error types, such as missing determiners or incorrect verb forms. By giving the model access to these labels, the system can learn more fine-grained error patterns that are based on the individual error types.

- **first language**: Previous work has experimentally demonstrated that the distribution of writing errors depends on the first language (L1) of the learner (Rozovskaya and Roth, 2011; Chollampatt et al., 2016). We investigate the usefulness of L1 as an auxiliary objective during training.

- **part-of-speech**: POS tagging is a well-established sequence labeling task, requiring the model to disambiguate the word types based on their contexts. We use the RASP (Briscoe et al., 2006) parser to automatically generate POS labels for the training data, and include them as additional objectives.

- **grammatical relations**: We include as an auxiliary objective the type of the Grammatical Relation (GR) in which the current token is a dependent, in order to incentivise the model to learn more about semantic composition. Again we use the RASP parser, which is unlexicalised and therefore more suitable for learner data where spelling and grammatical errors are common.

Table 1 presents the labels for each of the auxiliary tasks for an example sentence from the FCE training data.

The auxiliary objectives introduce additional parameters into the model, in order to construct the hidden and output layers. However, these components are required only during the training process; at testing time, these can be removed and the resulting model has the same architecture and number of parameters as the baseline, with the only difference being in how the parameters were optimised.

4 Evaluation setup and datasets

Rei and Yannakoudakis (2016) investigate a number of compositional architectures for error detection, and present state-of-the-art results using a bidirectional LSTM. We follow their experimental setup and investigate the impact of auxiliary loss functions on the same datasets: the First Certificate in English (FCE) dataset (Yannakoudakis et al., 2011) and the CoNLL-14 shared task test set (Ng et al., 2014b).

FCE contains texts written by non-native learners of English in response to exam prompts eliciting free-text answers. The texts have been manually annotated with error types and error spans by professional examiners, which Rei and Yannakoudakis (2016) convert to a binary correct/incorrect token-level labeling for error detection. For missing-word errors, the error label is assigned to the next word in the sequence. The released version contains 28,731 sentences for training, 2,222 sentences for development and 2,720 sentences for testing. The development set was randomly sampled from the training data, and the test set contains texts from a different examination year.

The CoNLL-14 test set contains 50 texts annotated by two experts. Compared to FCE, the texts are more technical and are written by higher-proficiency learners. In order to make our results comparable to Rei and Yannakoudakis (2016), we

	predicted	CoNLL-14 TEST1				CoNLL-14 TEST2			
		correct	P	R	$F_{0.5}$	correct	P	R	$F_{0.5}$
R&Y (2016)	4449	683	15.4	**22.8**	16.4	1052	23.6	**25.1**	23.9
Main system	3222	452	14.1	15.1	14.3	750	23.3	17.9	21.9
+ frequency	3428	484	14.1	16.2	14.5	790	23.1	18.8	22.0
+ language	3633	502	13.8	16.8	14.2	828	22.8	19.7	22.0
+ errors	3582	557	15.6	18.6	16.1	890	25.0	21.2	24.0
+ POS	3938	657	**16.7**	22.0	**17.5**	1045	**26.5**	24.9	**26.2**
+ GR	3945	593	15.0	19.8	15.7	912	23.2	21.7	22.8
+ err POS GR	3722	621	**16.7**	20.8	17.4	979	26.3	23.3	25.6

Table 3: Error detection results on the CoNLL-14 test set using different auxiliary loss functions.

also evaluate our models on the two CoNLL-14 test annotations and train our models only on the public FCE dataset. This corresponds to their *FCE-public* model that treats the CoNLL-14 dataset as an out-of-domain test set corpus.

Following the CoNLL-14 shared task, we also report $F_{0.5}$ as the main evaluation metric. However, while the shared task focused on correction and calculated $F_{0.5}$ over error spans using multiple annotations, we evaluate token-level error detection performance. Following recommendations by Chodorow et al. (2012), we also report the raw counts for predicted and correct tokens.

For pre-processing, all the texts are lowercased and digits are replaced with zeros for the token-level representations, although the character-based component has access to the original version of each token. Tokens that occur only once are mapped to a single *OOV* token, which is then used to represent previously unseen tokens during testing. The word embeddings have size 300 and are initialised with publicly available word2vec (Mikolov et al., 2013) embeddings trained on Google News. The LSTM hidden layers have size 200 and the task-specific hidden layers have size 50 with *tanh* activation. The model is optimised using Adadelta (Zeiler, 2012) and training is stopped based on the error detection $F_{0.5}$ score on the development set. We implement the proposed framework using Theano and make the code publicly available online.[1]

5 Results

Table 2 presents the results for different system configurations trained and tested on the FCE dataset. The first row contains results from the current state-of-the-art system by Rei and Yan-

nakoudakis (2016), trained on the same FCE data. The main system in our experiments is the bi-directional LSTM error detection model with character-based representations, as described in Section 2. We then use this model and test the effect on performance when adding each of the auxiliary loss functions described in Section 3 to the training objective.

The auxiliary frequency loss improves performance for POS tagging (Plank et al., 2016); however in error detection the same objective does not help. While certain POS tags are more likely to belong to specific frequency classes, there is less reason to believe that word frequency provides a useful cue for error detection. A similar drop in performance is observed for the auxiliary loss involving the first language of the learner. It is likely that the system learns specific types of features for the L1 identification auxiliary task (such as the presence of certain words or phrases), and these are not directly useful for error detection. Investigating different architectures for incorporating the L1 as an auxiliary task is an avenue for future work.

The integration of fine-grained error types through an auxiliary loss function gives an absolute improvement of 2.1% on the FCE test set. While the baseline only differentiates between correct and incorrect tokens, the auxiliary loss allows the system to learn feature detectors that are specialised for individual error types, thereby also making these features available to the binary error detection component.

The inclusion of POS tags and GRs gives consistent improvements over the basic configuration. Both of these tasks require the system to understand how each token behaves in the sentence, thereby encouraging it to learn higher-quality compositional representations. If the ar-

[1] http://www.marekrei.com/projects/seqlabaux

| | FCE | CoNLL-14 | CoNLL-14 |
Aux dataset	TEST	TEST1	TEST2
None	43.4	14.3	21.9
CoNLL-00	42.5	**15.4**	**22.3**
CoNLL-03	39.4	12.5	20.0
PTB-POS	**44.4**	14.1	20.7

Table 4: Results on error detection when the model is pre-trained on different tasks.

| | FCE | CoNLL-14 | CoNLL-14 |
Aux dataset	TEST	TEST1	TEST2
None	**43.4**	**14.3**	**21.9**
CoNLL-00	30.3	13.0	17.6
CoNLL-03	31.0	13.1	18.2
PTB-POS	31.9	11.5	14.9

Table 5: Results on error detection when training is alternated between the two tasks (e.g., error detection and POS tagging) and datasets.

chitecture is able to predict the POS tags or GR type based on context, then it can use the same features to identify irregular sequences for error detection. The added advantage of these loss functions over the L1 and the fine-grained error types is that they can be automatically generated and require no additional manual annotation. As far as we know, this is the first time automatically generated GR labels have been explored as objectives in a multi-task sequence labeling setting.

Finally, we evaluate a combination system, integrating the auxiliary loss functions that performed the best on the development set. The combination architecture includes four different loss functions: the main binary incorrect/correct label, the fine-grained error type, the POS tag and the GR type. We left out frequency and L1, as these lowered performance on the development set. The resulting system achieves 47.7% $F_{0.5}$, which is a 4.3% absolute improvement over the baseline without auxiliary loss functions, and a 6.6% absolute improvement over the current state-of-the-art error detection system by Rei and Yannakoudakis (2016), trained on the same FCE dataset.

Table 3 contains the same set of evaluations on the two CoNLL-14 shared task annotations. Word frequency and L1 have nearly no effect, whereas the fine-grained error labels lead to roughly 2% absolute improvement over the basic system. The inclusion of POS tags in the auxiliary objective consistently leads to the highest $F_{0.5}$. While GRs also improve performance over the main system, their overall contribution is less compared to the FCE test set, which can be explained by the different writing style in the CoNLL data.

6 Alternative Training Strategies

In contrast to our approach, most previous work on multi-task learning has focused on optimising the same system on multiple datasets, each annotated with one specific type of labels. To evaluate the effectiveness of our approach, we implement two alternative multi-task learning strategies for error detection. For these experiments, we make use of three established sequence labeling datasets that have been manually annotated for different tasks:

- The CoNLL 2000 dataset (Tjong Kim Sang and Buchholz, 2000) for chunking, containing sections of the Wall Street Journal and annotated with 22 different labels.

- The CoNLL 2003 corpus (Tjong Kim Sang and De Meulder, 2003) contains texts from the Reuters Corpus and has been annotated with 8 labels for named entity recognition (NER).

- The Penn Treebank (PTB) POS corpus (Marcus et al., 1993) contains texts from the Wall Street Journal and has been annotated with 48 POS tags.

The CoNLL-00 dataset was identified by Bingel and Søgaard (2017) as being the most useful additional training resource in a multi-task setting; The CoNLL-03 NER dataset has a similar label density as the error detection task; and the PTB corpus was chosen as POS tags gave consistently good performance for error detection on both the development and test sets, as demonstrated in the previous section.

In the first setting, each of these datasets is used to train a sequence labeling model for their respective tasks, and the resulting model is used to initialise a network for training an error detection system. While it is common to preload word embeddings from a different model, this strategy extends the idea to the compositional components of the network. Results in Table 4 show the performance of the error detection model with and without pre-training. There is a slight improvement when pre-training the model on the CoNLL-00 dataset, but the increase is considerably smaller compared to the results in Section 5. One of the main advantages of multi-task learning is regularisation, actively encouraging the model to learn more general-purpose features, something which is not exploited in this setting since the training happens in separate stages.

In the second set of experiments, we explore the possibility of training on the second domain and task at the same time as error detection. Similar to Collobert and Weston (2008), we randomly sample a sentence from one of the datasets and update the model parameters for that specific task. By alternating between the two tasks, the model is able to retain the regularisation benefits. However, as shown in Table 5, this type of training does not improve error detection performance. One possible explanation is that the domain and writing style of these auxiliary datasets is very different from the learner writing corpus, and the model ends up optimising in an unnecessary direction. By including alternative labels on the same dataset, as in Section 5, the model is able to extract more information from the domain-relevant training data and thereby achieve better results.

7 Additional Training Data

The main benefits of multi-task learning are expected in scenarios where the available task-specific training data is limited. However, we also investigate the effect of auxiliary objectives when training on a substantially larger training set. More specifically, we follow Rei and Yannakoudakis (2016), who also experimented with augmenting the publicly available datasets with training data from a large proprietary corpus. In total, we train this large model on 17.8M tokens from the Cambridge Learner Corpus (CLC, Nicholls 2003), the NUS Corpus of Learner English (NUCLE, Dahlmeier et al. 2013), and the Lang-8 corpus (Mizumoto et al., 2011).

We use the same model architecture as Rei and Yannakoudakis (2016), adding only the auxiliary objective of predicting the automatically generated POS tag, which was the most successful additional objective based on the development experiments. Table 6 contains results for evaluating this model, when trained on the large training set. On the FCE test data, the auxiliary objective does not provide an improvement and the model performance is comparable to the results by Rei and Yannakoudakis (2016) (R&Y). Since most of the

	R&Y $F_{0.5}$	P	R	$F_{0.5}$
FCE DEV	60.7	75.1	35.1	**61.2**
FCE TEST	**64.3**	78.4	37.0	64.1
CoNLL TEST1	34.3	44.7	20.5	**36.1**
CoNLL TEST2	44.0	63.8	20.8	**45.1**

Table 6: Error detection results using auxiliary objectives, trained on additional data.

large training set comes from the CLC, which is quite similar to the FCE dataset, it is likely that the available training data is sufficient and the auxiliary objective does not offer an additional benefit. However, there are considerable improvements on the CoNLL test sets, with 1.8% and 1.1% absolute improvements on the corresponding benchmarks. Only small amounts of the training data are similar to the CoNLL dataset, and including the auxiliary objective has provided a more robust model that delivers better performance on different writing styles.

8 Previous Work

Error detection: Early error detection systems were based on manually constructed error grammars and mal-rules (e.g., Foster and Vogel 2004). More recent approaches have exploited error-annotated learner corpora and primarily treated the task as a classification problem over vectors of contextual, lexical and syntactic features extracted from a fixed window around the target token. Most work has focused on error-type specific detection models, and in particular on models detecting preposition and article errors, which are among the most frequent ones in non-native English learner writing (Chodorow et al., 2007; De Felice and Pulman, 2008; Han et al., 2010; Tetreault et al., 2010; Han et al., 2006; Tetreault and Chodorow, 2008; Gamon et al., 2008; Gamon, 2010; Kochmar and Briscoe, 2014; Leacock et al., 2014). Maximum entropy models along with rule-based filters account for a substantial proportion of utilized techniques. Error detection models have also been an integral component of essay scoring systems and writing instruction tools (Burstein et al., 2004; Andersen et al., 2013; Attali and Burstein, 2006).

The Helping Our Own (HOO) 2011 shared task on error detection and correction focused on a set of different errors (Dale and Kilgarriff, 2011), though most systems were type specific and targeted closed-class errors. In the following year, the HOO 2012 shared task only focused on correcting preposition and determiner errors (Dale et al., 2012). The recent CoNLL shared tasks (Ng et al., 2013, 2014a) focused on error correction rather than detection: CoNLL-13 targeted correcting noun number, verb form and subject-verb agreement errors, in addition to preposition and determiner errors made by non-native learners of English, whereas CoNLL-14 expanded to correction of all errors regardless of type. Core components of the top two systems across the CoNLL correction shared tasks include Average Perceptrons, L1 error correction priors in Naive Bayes models, and joint inference capturing interactions between errors (e.g., noun number and verb agreement errors) (Rozovskaya et al., 2014), as well as phrase-based statistical machine translation, under the hypothesis that incorrect source sentences can be "translated" to correct target sentences (Felice et al., 2014; Grundkiewicz, 2014).

The work that is most closely related to our own is the one by Rei and Yannakoudakis (2016), who investigate a number of compositional architectures for error detection, and propose a framework based on bidirectional LSTMs. In this work, we used their system architecture as a baseline, compared our model to their results in Sections 5 and 7, and showed that multi-task learning can further improve performance and allow the model to generalise better.

Multi-task learning: Multi-task learning was first proposed by Caruana (1998) and has since been applied to many language processing tasks and neural network architectures. For example, Collobert and Weston (2008) constructed a convolutional architecture that shared some weights between tasks such as POS tagging, NER and chunking. Whereas their model only shared word embeddings, our approach focuses on learning better compositional features through a shared bidirectional LSTM.

Luong et al. (2016) explored a multi-task architecture for sequence-to-sequence learning where encoders and decoders in different languages are trained jointly using the same semantic representation space. Klerke et al. (2016) used eye tracking measurements as a secondary task in order to improve a model for sentence compression. Bingel and Søgaard (2017) explored beneficial task relationships for training multitask models on different datasets. All of these architectures are trained

by randomly switching between different tasks and updating parameters based on the corresponding dataset. In contrast, we treat alternative tasks as auxiliary objectives on the same dataset, which is beneficial for error detection (Section 6).

There has been some research on using auxiliary training objectives in the context of other tasks. Cheng et al. (2015) described a system for detecting out-of-vocabulary names by also predicting the next word in the sequence. Plank et al. (2016) predicted the frequency of each word together with the POS, and showed that this can improve tagging accuracy on low-frequency words. However, we are the first to explore the auxiliary objectives described in Section 3 in the context of error detection.

9 Conclusion

We have described a method for integrating auxiliary loss functions with a neural sequence labeling framework, in order to improve error detection in learner writing. While predicting binary error labels, the model also learns to predict additional linguistic information for each token, allowing it to discover compositional features that can be exploited for error detection. We performed a systematic comparison of possible auxiliary labels, which are either available in existing annotations or can be generated automatically. Our experiments showed that POS tags, grammatical relations and error types gave the largest benefit for error detection, and combining them together improved the results further.

We compared this training method to two other multi-task approaches: learning sequence labeling models on related tasks and using them to initialise the error detection model; and training on multiple tasks and datasets by randomly switching between them. Both of these methods were outperformed by our proposed approach using auxiliary labels on the same dataset – the latter has the benefit of regularising the model with a different task, while also keeping the training data in-domain.

While the main benefits of multi-task learning are expected in scenarios where the available task-specific training data is limited, we found that error detection benefits from additional labels even with large training sets. Successful error detection systems have to learn about language composition, and introducing an additional objective encourages the model to train more general composition functions and better word representations. The error detection model, which also learns to predict automatically generated POS tags, achieved improved performance on both CoNLL-14 benchmarks. A useful direction for future work would be to investigate dynamic weighting strategies for auxiliary objectives that allow the network to initially benefit from various available labels, and then specialise to performing the main task.

References

Øistein E Andersen, Helen Yannakoudakis, Fiona Barker, and Tim Parish. 2013. Developing and testing a self-assessment and tutoring system. In *Proceedings of the Eighth Workshop on Innovative Use of NLP for Building Educational Applications, BEA*. Association for Computational Linguistics, pages 32–41.

Yigal Attali and Jill Burstein. 2006. Automated essay scoring with e-rater v. 2. *The Journal of Technology, Learning and Assessment* 4(3).

Joachim Bingel and Anders Søgaard. 2017. Identifying beneficial task relations for multi-task learning in deep neural networks. In *arXiv preprint*. http://arxiv.org/abs/1702.08303.

Ted Briscoe, John Carroll, and Rebecca Watson. 2006. The Second Release of the RASP System. In *Proceedings of the COLING/ACL on Interactive presentation sessions.*. Association for Computational Linguistics, Sydney, Australia, July, pages 77–80. https://doi.org/10.3115/1225403.1225423.

Christopher Bryant and Hwee Tou Ng. 2015. How far are we from fully automatic high quality grammatical error correction? In *Proceedings of the 53rd Annual Meeting of the Association for Computational Linguistics and the 7th International Joint Conference on Natural Language Processing*. Association for Computational Linguistics, pages 697–707.

Jill Burstein, Martin Chodorow, and Claudia Leacock. 2004. Automated essay evaluation: The Criterion online writing service. *AI Magazine* 25(3):27.

Rich Caruana. 1998. Multitask Learning. *Learning to learn* .

Hao Cheng, Hao Fang, and Mari Ostendorf. 2015. Open-Domain Name Error Detection using a Multi-Task RNN. In *Proceedings of the 2015 Conference on Empirical Methods in Natural Language Processing*.

Martin Chodorow, Markus Dickinson, Ross Israel, and Joel Tetreault. 2012. Problems in evaluating grammatical error detection systems. In *COLING 2012*.

Martin Chodorow, Joel R. Tetreault, and Na-Rae Han. 2007. Detection of grammatical errors involving prepositions. In *Proceedings of the 4th ACL-SIGSEM Workshop on Prepositions*. https://doi.org/10.3115/1654629.1654635.

Shamil Chollampatt, Duc Tam Hoang, and Hwee Tou Ng. 2016. Adapting Grammatical Error Correction Based on the Native Language of Writers with Neural Network Joint Models. *Proceedings of the 2016 Conference on Empirical Methods in Natural Language Processing (EMNLP-16)* pages 1901–1911.

Ronan Collobert and Jason Weston. 2008. A Unified Architecture for Natural Language Processing: Deep Neural Networks with Multitask Learning. *Proceedings of the 25th international conference on Machine learning (ICML '08)* https://doi.org/10.1145/1390156.1390177.

Daniel Dahlmeier, Hwee Tou Ng, and Siew Mei Wu. 2013. Building a large annotated corpus of learner English: The NUS corpus of learner English. *Proceedings of the Eighth Workshop on Innovative Use of NLP for Building Educational Applications* .

Robert Dale, Ilya Anisimoff, and George Narroway. 2012. HOO 2012: A report on the preposition and determiner error correction shared task. In *Proceedings of the Seventh Workshop on Building Educational Applications Using NLP*. Association for Computational Linguistics, pages 54–62.

Robert Dale and Adam Kilgarriff. 2011. Helping our own: The HOO 2011 pilot shared task. In *Proceedings of the 13th European Workshop on Natural Language Generation*. Association for Computational Linguistics, pages 242–249.

Rachele De Felice and Stephen G Pulman. 2008. A classifier-based approach to preposition and determiner error correction in L2 English. In *Proceedings of the 22nd International Conference on Computational Linguistics*. Association for Computational Linguistics, pages 169–176.

Mariano Felice and Zheng Yuan. 2014. Generating artificial errors for grammatical error correction. In *Proceedings of the Student Research Workshop at the 14th Conference of the European Chapter of the Association for Computational Linguistics*. pages 116–126.

Mariano Felice, Zheng Yuan, Øistein E. Andersen, Helen Yannakoudakis, and Ekaterina Kochmar. 2014. Grammatical error correction using hybrid systems and type filtering. *Conference on Computational Natural Language Learning: Shared Task (CoNLL-2014)* http://www.comp.nus.edu.sg/ nlp/conll14st/conll14st-book.pdf#page=25.

Jennifer Foster and Øistein E Andersen. 2009. GenERRate: generating errors for use in grammatical error detection. In *Proceedings of the fourth Workshop on Innovative use of NLP for Building Educational Applications*. Association for Computational Linguistics, pages 82–90.

Jennifer Foster and Carl Vogel. 2004. Parsing ill-formed text using an error grammar. *Artificial Intelligence Review* 21(3-4):269–291.

Michael Gamon. 2010. Using mostly native data to correct errors in learners' writing: a meta-classifier approach. In *Human Language Technologies: The 2010 Annual Conference of the North American Chapter of the Association for Computational Linguistics*. Association for Computational Linguistics, pages 163–171.

Michael Gamon, Jianfeng Gao, Chris Brockett, Alexandre Klementiev, William B Dolan, Dmitriy Belenko, and Lucy Vanderwende. 2008. Using contextual speller techniques and language modeling for ESL error correction. In *IJCNLP*. volume 8, pages 449–456.

Marcin Junczys-Dowmunt Roman Grundkiewicz. 2014. The AMU system in the CoNLL-2014 shared task: Grammatical error correction by data-intensive and feature-rich statistical machine translation. In *Proceedings of the Eighteenth Conference on Computational Natural Language Learning: Shared Task*. Association for Computational Linguistics, pages 25–33.

Na-Rae Han, Martin Chodorow, and Claudia Leacock. 2006. Detecting errors in English article usage by non-native speakers. *Natural Language Engineering* 12. https://doi.org/doi:10.1017/S1351324906004190.

Na-Rae Han, Joel Tetreault, Soo-Hwa Lee, and Jin-Young Ha. 2010. Using error-annotated ESL data to develop an ESL error correction system. In *In Proceedings of LREC. Emi Izumi, Kiyotaka Uchimoto und Hiroshi Isahara.*

Sepp Hochreiter and Jürgen Schmidhuber. 1997. Long Short-term Memory. *Neural Computation* 9. https://doi.org/10.1.1.56.7752.

Sigrid Klerke, Yoav Goldberg, and Anders Søgaard. 2016. Improving sentence compression by learning to predict gaze. In *The Annual Conference of the North American Chapter of the Association for Computational Linguistics (NAACL)*. http://arxiv.org/abs/1604.03357.

Ekaterina Kochmar and Ted Briscoe. 2014. Detecting learner errors in the choice of content words using compositional distributional semantics. In *Proceedings of the 25th International Conference on Computational Linguistics (COLING 2014): Technical Papers*. pages 1740–1751.

Claudia Leacock, Martin Chodorow, Michael Gamon, and Joel Tetreault. 2014. Automated grammatical error detection for language learners, second edition.

Synthesis lectures on human language technologies 7(1):1–170.

Minh-Thang Luong, Quoc V. Le, Ilya Sutskever, Oriol Vinyals, and Lukasz Kaiser. 2016. Multi-task Sequence to Sequence Learning. *ICLR 2017* http://arxiv.org/abs/1511.06114.

Mitchell P. Marcus, Beatrice Santorini, and Mary Ann Marcinkiewicz. 1993. Building a large annotated corpus of English: The Penn Treebank. *Computational Linguistics* 19. https://doi.org/10.1162/coli.2010.36.1.36100.

Tomáš Mikolov, Kai Chen, Greg Corrado, and Jeffrey Dean. 2013. Efficient Estimation of Word Representations in Vector Space. In *Proceedings of the International Conference on Learning Representations (ICLR 2013)*. https://doi.org/10.1162/153244303322533223.

Tomoya Mizumoto, Mamoru Komachi, Masaaki Nagata, and Yuji Matsumoto. 2011. Mining Revision Log of Language Learning SNS for Automated Japanese Error Correction of Second Language Learners. *Proceedings of the 5th International Joint Conference on Natural Language Processing 2011* https://doi.org/10.1527/tjsai.28.420.

Hwee Tou Ng, Siew Mei Wu, Ted Briscoe, Christian Hadiwinoto, Raymond Hendy Susanto, and Christopher Bryant. 2014a. The CoNLL-2014 shared task on grammatical error correction. In *Proceedings of the Eighteenth Conference on Computational Natural Language Learning: Shared Task*. Association for Computational Linguistics, Baltimore, Maryland, pages 1–14.

Hwee Tou Ng, Siew Mei Wu, Ted Briscoe, Christian Hadiwinoto, Raymond Hendy Susanto, and Christopher Bryant. 2014b. The CoNLL-2014 Shared Task on Grammatical Error Correction. In *Proceedings of the Eighteenth Conference on Computational Natural Language Learning: Shared Task*. http://www.aclweb.org/anthology/W/W14/W14-1701.

Hwee Tou Ng, Siew Mei Wu, Yuanbin Wu, Christian Hadiwinoto, and Joel Tetreault. 2013. The CoNLL-2013 shared task on grammatical error correction. In *Proceedings of the Seventeenth Conference on Computational Natural Language Learning: Shared Task*. Association for Computational Linguistics, pages 1–12.

Diane Nicholls. 2003. The Cambridge Learner Corpus - error coding and analysis for lexicography and ELT. *Proceedings of the Corpus Linguistics 2003 Conference* .

Barbara Plank, Anders Søgaard, and Yoav Goldberg. 2016. Multilingual Part-of-Speech Tagging with Bidirectional Long Short-Term Memory Models and Auxiliary Loss. In *Proceedings of the*

54th Annual Meeting of the Association for Computational Linguistics (ACL-16). pages 412–418. http://arxiv.org/abs/1604.05529.

Marek Rei. 2017. Semi-supervised Multitask Learning for Sequence Labeling. In *Proceedings of the 55th Annual Meeting of the Association for Computational Linguistics (ACL-2017)*.

Marek Rei, Gamal K. O. Crichton, and Sampo Pyysalo. 2016. Attending to Characters in Neural Sequence Labeling Models. In *Proceedings of the 26th International Conference on Computational Linguistics (COLING-2016)*. http://arxiv.org/abs/1611.04361.

Marek Rei and Helen Yannakoudakis. 2016. Compositional Sequence Labeling Models for Error Detection in Learner Writing. In *Proceedings of the 54th Annual Meeting of the Association for Computational Linguistics*. https://aclweb.org/anthology/P/P16/P16-1112.pdf.

Alla Rozovskaya, Kai-Wei Chang, Mark Sammons, Dan Roth, and Nizar Habash. 2014. The Illinois-Columbia system in the CoNLL-2014 shared task. In *Proceedings of the Eighteenth Conference on Computational Natural Language Learning: Shared Task*. Association for Computational Linguistics, pages 34–42.

Alla Rozovskaya and Dan Roth. 2011. Algorithm Selection and Model Adaptation for ESL Correction Tasks. *Proceedings of the 49th Annual Meeting of the Association for Computational Linguistics (ACL-2011)* http://www.aclweb.org/anthology-new/P/P11/P11-1093.pdf.

Alla Rozovskaya and Dan Roth. 2016. Grammatical error correction: Machine translation and classifiers. In *Proceedings of the 54th Annual Meeting of the Association for Computational Linguistics*. pages 2205–2215.

Joel Tetreault, Jennifer Foster, and Martin Chodorow. 2010. Using parse features for preposition selection and error detection. In *Proceedings of the acl 2010 conference short papers*. Association for Computational Linguistics, pages 353–358.

Joel R Tetreault and Martin Chodorow. 2008. The ups and downs of preposition error detection in ESL writing. In *Proceedings of the 22nd International Conference on Computational Linguistics*. Association for Computational Linguistics, pages 865–872.

Erik F. Tjong Kim Sang and Sabine Buchholz. 2000. Introduction to the CoNLL-2000 shared task: Chunking. *Proceedings of the 2nd Workshop on Learning Language in Logic and the 4th Conference on Computational Natural Language Learning* 7. https://doi.org/10.3115/1117601.1117631.

Erik F. Tjong Kim Sang and Fien De Meulder. 2003. Introduction to the CoNLL-2003 Shared Task: Language-Independent Named Entity Recognition. In *Proceedings of the seventh conference on Natural language learning at HLT-NAACL 2003*. http://arxiv.org/abs/cs/0306050.

Helen Yannakoudakis, Ted Briscoe, and Ben Medlock. 2011. A New Dataset and Method for Automatically Grading ESOL Texts. In *Proceedings of the 49th Annual Meeting of the Association for Computational Linguistics: Human Language Technologies*. http://www.aclweb.org/anthology/P11-1019.

Matthew D. Zeiler. 2012. ADADELTA: An Adaptive Learning Rate Method. *arXiv preprint arXiv:1212.5701* http://arxiv.org/abs/1212.5701.

Linked Data for Language-Learning Applications

Robyn Loughnane, Kate McCurdy, Peter Kolb, Stefan Selent
Babbel (Lesson Nine GmbH)
{rloughnane, kmccurdy, pkolb, sselent}@babbel.com

Abstract

The use of linked data within language-learning applications is an open research question. A research prototype is presented that applies linked-data principles to store linguistic annotation generated from language-learning content using a variety of NLP tools. The result is a database that links learning content, linguistic annotation and open-source resources, on top of which a diverse range of tools for language-learning applications can be built.

1 Introduction

Since Berners-Lee (2001) presented his vision of a Semantic Web at the turn of the century, there has been an explosion of technologies and tools made available to implement it[1]. The core idea of the Semantic Web is *linked data*, where data forms a giant graph spread across the internet, known as the Giant Global Graph or Web 3.0. In Berners Lee's original vision, this linked data should be open source and the resulting graph is freely available over the internet. Of course, the same principles and technologies can be applied to create a private graph database used for commercial purposes, for applications like a social network or knowledge base.

Use of linked data in linguistics in general is a burgeoning research topic (Section 2). In this paper, linked-data technology is applied in the context of a language-learning application, in order to create a prototype database of linguistic annotation for learning content (Section 3). The database further links learning content and linguistic annotation with resources from the Linguistic Linked Open Data (LLOD) cloud and other open-source linguistic resources. The resulting database is flexible enough to allow a variety of useful applications for the language learner to be built on top of it.

Although NLP tools for creating linguistic annotation on the fly are becoming more and more accurate[2] and are adequate for many purposes, this prototype tests storage of linguistic annotation with the future aim of storing high-quality, curated linguistic annotation. This linguistic annotation, to be derived from a combination of various NLP tools and human expertise, could then be updated or expanded as new technology becomes available. The result would be a database of linguistic annotation that is more accurate than the output of any single tool and can be used for a variety of purposes related to language-learning applications.

There are already a number of approaches available for automatically generating exercises for language learning, such as using Google *n*-grams (Hill and Simha, 2016) or a mix of techniques including crowdsourcing, measuring WordNet distance, and machine learning (Kumar et al., 2015). Although it is the focus of the evaluation of the prototype (Section 4), automatic generation of exercises is only one possible use of the database discussed here. Linking between learning content, linguistic annotation and the LLOD cloud creates a resource that can be used for a variety of purposes, for example assessing the number of lemmas seen in exercises completed by a user up to a certain point in time, or showing the user grammatical information for a particular exercise.

---

[1] https://www.w3.org/standards/semanticweb/

[2] The state of the art in automatic syntax parsing reports models with an upper limit of around to 95% accuracy for certain types of input (Andor et al., 2016). For part-of-speech tagging, the state of the art is around 97%, depending on the type of input. Accuracy rates can be much lower for low-frequency tokens, out-of-context text, and data that differs significantly from the training set.

Proceedings of the 12th Workshop on Innovative Use of NLP for Building Educational Applications, pages 44–51
Copenhagen, Denmark, September 8, 2017. ©2017 Association for Computational Linguistics

2 Linked Data in Linguistics

Recently, applications of linked-data technology in the field of linguistics in general have been gaining in popularity, as witnessed by the large amount of resources in the LLOD cloud (Section 2.1) and the growing number of linguistic ontologies (Section 2.2). In addition to being able to link to the LLOD cloud, Semantic Web has the advantage of a native graph-based data model (Section 2.3), namely the Resource Description Framework[3] (RDF).

The use of linked-data technology in applications for language learning has, however, been limited, meaning that the potential of the LLOD cloud has yet be fully exploited in this area. A notable exception is El Maarouf et al. (2015), who created a multilingual network of linguistic resources by using sense linking to bridge the language gap with the goal of facilitating the creation of language-learning content.

2.1 LLOD

The LLOD cloud diagram[4] (McCrae et al., 2016; Chiarcos et al., 2012) shows that there is already a wealth of free and open-source linguistic linked data available to use. Major resources are each represented by a single node in the LLOD cloud diagram. These include DBpedia (Mendes et al., 2012), consisting of structured information extracted from Wikipedia; WordNet RDF (McCrae et al., 2014), an RDF translation of Princeton's WordNet lexical database project; and DBnary (Sérasset, 2015), derived from Wiktionary.

2.2 Ontologies

An ontology is a document that specifies the structure of a system through entities and relations (Guarino et al., 2009). Complex abstract models can be specified precisely via ontologies in the Web Ontology Language[5] (OWL). A variety of ontologies have been proposed to describe the components of language analysis, each developed with a different purpose in mind.

ISOcat (Windhouwer and Wright, 2012) and GOLD (Farrar and Langendoen, 2003) were created with the aim of covering a large range of linguistic terminological categories. Ontologies of Linguistic Annotation (OLiA), an inter-

mediate level of representation between ISOcat and GOLD, addresses conceptual interoperability (Chiarcos, 2012; Chiarcos and Sukhareva, 2015).

POWLA (Chiarcos, 2012) represents any kind of linguistic annotation in a theory independent way. It is an adaptation of the PAULA XML exchange format (Zeldes et al., 2013).

Lemon (McCrae et al., 2012) is an ontology for exchanging lexical information on the Semantic Web. It is used, for example, in the DBnary project (Sérasset, 2015) and WordNet RDF (McCrae et al., 2014).

2.3 Linguistic Annotation as a Graph

Representing linguistic annotation as a graph has the advantage of avoiding undue influence from the data serialization format (e.g. XML) or the database type (e.g. relational). For example, Zipser (2009) describes how, when a format for exchanging linguistic annotation is specified without an abstract model being explicitly specified, it can lead to the format's implicit abstract model being influenced or limited by the data serialization format used. An example would be XML-based formats being influenced by the tree-based structure of XML to the extent that the implicit abstract model of the linguistic annotation format becomes tree based.

Semantic Web technology largely allows this problem to be avoided. RDF-based linguistic exchange formats are inherently graph based, so are only limited in structure to the extent that a labelled, directed multigraph is limited. Further, OWL is designed specifically for ontology specification, and allows complex models to be specified in a precise way. Although, of course, the XML syntax for RDF (Gandon and Schreiber, 2014) shows that a graph may be specified in the XML format, so the pitfall of influence from the data serialization format can also be avoided with clear specification of the abstract model independent of the data serialization format, e.g. in the Unified Modeling Language (UML).

The graph-based SALT model (Zipser and Romary, 2010) further shows that a graph structure preserves the abstract model for a wide range of linguistic annotation formats, including PAULA, ELAN, ANNIS and more.

Chiarcos (2012) likewise argues that a representation of linguistic annotation as a labelled, directed graph represented in OWL and RDF can

---

[3]https://www.w3.org/RDF/
[4]http://linguistic-lod.org/llod-cloud
[5]https://www.w3.org/OWL/

Resource	Type
Stanford CoreNLP	Language analysis
FreeLing	Language analysis
WebLicht	Annotation framework
WordNet RDF	Lexical database
DBnary	Lexical database
Specialist lexicon	Lexical database
Lemon	Ontology

Table 1: External Resources

solve interoperability issues and enables connection to the LLOD cloud.

Bird and Liberman (2001) also argued that it is of greatest importance to have a well-defined common conceptual framework and that the standardization of file formats is of secondary importance. They present an annotation graph as a common conceptual framework for a number of annotation formats.

3 Design of the Database

The starting point for the database was Babbel's learning content (Section 3.1). Linguistic annotation for the content was then created via NLP pipelines (Section 3.2). The learning content and its annotation was then converted to RDF and linked with LLOD resources and other open-source linguistic resources (Section 3.3). Table 1 summarizes the external dependencies.

3.1 Learning Content

Babbel is a language-learning application with over 1 million active subscribers and has been shown to be an effective way to learn a foreign language (Vesselinov and Grego, 2016). The language application is based on a large corpus of language exercises created by a team of didactic experts. There are a range of types of exercises, testing users' reading, writing, listening and speaking skills.

YAML files containing the exercises were used as the starting point for the database. Additionally, a variety of metadata for the learning content was available in an XML format.

3.2 Linguistic Annotation

Linguistic annotation was derived from NLP pipelines set up for each of the two learning languages, English and Spanish. These NLP pipe-

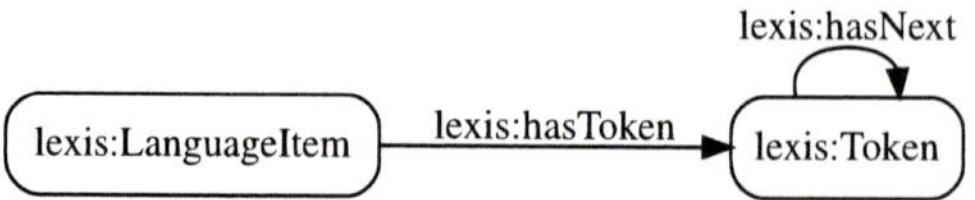

Figure 1: Lexis Language Item and Token

lines used a combination of custom implementations and open-source tools, including Stanford CoreNLP (Manning et al., 2014) and FreeLing (Padró and Stanilovsky, 2012). As the pipelines are used for a variety of research purposes, the resulting linguistic annotation was stored in WebLicht's Text Corpus Format (TCF) (Heid et al., 2010) in XML files, rather than directly in RDF. The NLP pipeline produces the following layers: text, tokens, sentences, lemmas, part-of-speech tags, morphological features, and dependency parsing.

3.3 Linking the Data

The learning content and linguistic annotation were converted to RDF (Section 3.3.1) and then linked to existing LLOD resources (Section 3.3.2), and other open-source linguistic resources converted to RDF (Section 3.3.2).

3.3.1 Linking Learning Content

Three ontologies were created with OWL to model the learning content from the three different sources: the Graph ontology for the XML metadata files; the Lesson ontology for the learning content YAML files; and the Lexis[6] ontology for the TCF XML files. A Java program was then created to convert the XML and YAML structures to RDF triples.

The Graph ontology models a variety of metadata, including the order of lessons within a learning module. The Lesson ontology models information within a lesson, like the parts of the language item that the user interacts with e.g. a gap in a sentence that the user fills in. Given that the learning content and metadata already had a well-defined underlying structure, a parallel structure was created in the Graph and Lesson ontologies.

The following OWL classes were defined within the Lexis ontology: `LanguageItem`, `Token`, `Dependency`, `Feature` and `Sense`. Figures 1 to 5 show the main OWL object property relations between the classes.

---

[6]From the Ancient Greek λέξης meaning 'word'

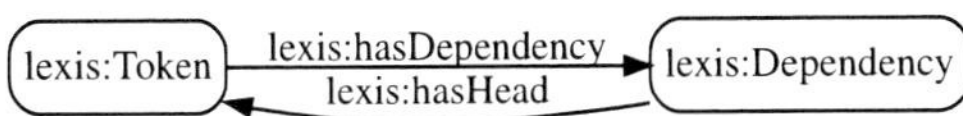

Figure 2: Lexis Token and Dependency Relation

Figure 3: Lexis Token and Feature

Figure 1 shows that a second language text fragment, namely a `LanguageItem`, may have one or more entities of type `Token` related to it by the `hasToken` property. The `hasNext` property points to the next ordered `Token` for the `LanguageItem`. A number of OWL datatype property relations are further defined for `Token`, e.g. the text value of the token.

The property `hasDependency` (Figure 2) connects a `Token` and a `Dependency` according to the dependency relations specified by the Universal Dependencies project (Nivre, 2016). The head of a dependency relation is another token, indicated by the `hasHead` object property. Morphological features of tokens, including part of speech and grammatical gender, are assigned to the `Feature` class, related to a token via the object property `hasFeature` (Figure 3).

The Lexis ontology imports the Lemon ontology (Section 2.2), which is used to connect word senses of tokens to the corresponding WordNet entries (Figures 4 and 5). The lemma of a token is saved as a datatype property of the token's sense.

For the Lexis ontology, in addition to Lemon, it would have been possible to reuse other existing ontologies designed for representing linguistic annotation, like POWLA, GOLD or OLiA (Section 2.2). For this initial research prototype, however, the design decision was made to create a new, minimal ontology and the mapping of Lexis to other ontologies is left for future research.

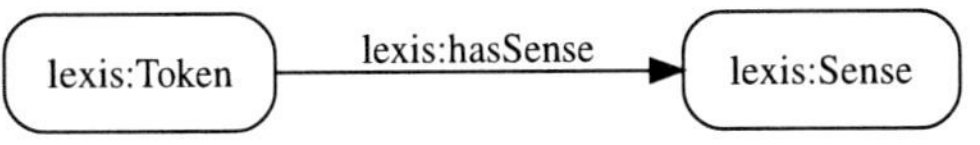

Figure 4: Lexis Token and Sense

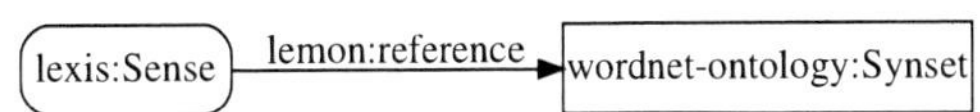

Figure 5: Lexis Sense and Lemon Reference

3.3.2 Linking LLOD Resources

As mentioned above, the RDF version (McCrae et al., 2014) of WordNet (Miller, 1995) was used, connecting synsets to tokens via lexical sense (Figure 5). As an expedient initial assignment, the part of speech and lemma of a token were used to search for the corresponding WordNet synset with the highest frequency (tag count). Links to DBnary (Sérasset, 2015) were created in a similar way.

3.3.3 Linking Other Linguistic Resources

The majority of open-source linguistic resources are currently not available as five-star linked open data according to Berners-Lee's (2006) definition. However, as long as the data is three star, then it can generally be meaningfully converted into linked data, usually with some manual work involved to create a mapping. Three-star data is available to use with an open licence; available as structured, machine-readable data; and available in a non-proprietary format (Berners-Lee, 2006). Indeed this is the source of many of the LLOD resources, like DBpedia, whose data were originally available in some other format. For the current research prototype, two main resources were converted to RDF, the Specialist lexicon[7] and the FreeLing Spanish dictionary[8]. These were then linked to the learning content in a similar way to the LLOD resources (Section 3.3.2).

The Specialist lexicon (Browne et al., 2000) is a large English lexicon developed within the Unified Medical Language System by the US National Library of Medicine (Bodenreider, 2004). The XML version of the lexicon was imported using the provided (but slightly adapted) XML format specification. A custom ontology was created in OWL that paralleled the underlying structure of the dictionary entries. A Java program was then written to convert the XML to RDF according to the ontology. The ontology and Java program have been made available as an open-source project[9].

The FreeLing Spanish dictionary entry files were converted into RDF triples according to the

---

[7] http://specialist.nlm.nih.gov/lexicon
[8] https://github.com/TALP-UPC/FreeLing
[9] https://github.com/babbel/specialist_rdf

Lemon ontology (McCrae et al., 2010).

3.4 Storing Linguistic Linked Data

With the recent rise in popularity of NoSQL data-bases, there are now a number of databases specifically designed for storing linked data as RDF triples, such as Ontotext's GraphDB (based on RDF4J, formerly Sesame) and Apache Jena Fuseki. The created and collected linguistic linked data described in Section 3.3 was stored in GraphDB.

4 Evaluation

A suite of example use cases were built on top of the database, serving as experimental evaluation. These use cases included a Spanish conjugation exercise (Section 4.1) and an English syntax display (Section 4.2). Apart from unit testing to assure the graph is produced as expected, the quality of the data produced was not evaluated. The quality of the linguistic annotation depends on the tools used to generate it, e.g. Stanford CoreNLP. The evaluation of the quality of the sense linking with WordNet and DBnary is left for further research.

4.1 Spanish Conjugation

A learning exercise for verb conjugation in Spanish was built on top of the existing learning content in the database[10]. Learning content for Spanish was searched for sentences in the present tense of the form subject–verb–direct object. Spanish verbs in the present tense have a different form depending on politeness (Helmbrecht, 2013) and the person and number of the subject. The verb was then replaced with its infinitive form and a drop-down menu showing all present tense verb forms for the same verb. The user is then asked to choose the correct form of the verb. For example, "Este piso tiene un jardín privado" becomes "Este piso tener un jardín privado", with a drop-down menu for "tener" displaying all the present tense forms of the verb. If the user selects the incorrect verb form from the drop-down menu, a message is displayed and they may try again. If the user selects the correct verb form from the drop-down menu, the exercise is complete.

---

[10]The authors thank Raphaela Wrede, Pierpaolo Frasa, Katharina Schoppa and Simon Kreiser for their help in testing a prototype of this idea.

4.2 English Syntax

A further use case was built on top of the database for selecting English language items containing auxiliary verbs. The SPARQL request shown in Listing 1 selects English language items that have a dependency relation where one verb acts as an auxiliary to another verb. This query returns URIs for languages items such as "Which pants should I buy?", where 'should' is the auxiliary verb and 'buy' is the main verb. A further SPARQL query retrieves the tokenization for this language item, enabling the auxiliary verb and main verb to be identified and highlighted for the user in the GUI. Such a use case could be extended to any other syntactic construction, so that the user could revise the construction in question, e.g. by highlighting the correct verb types.

Listing 1: SPARQL Query

```
 1  PREFIX lexis: <http://www.babbel.com/
        lexis#>
 2  PREFIX lesson: <http://www.babbel.com/
        lesson#>
 3  SELECT DISTINCT ?subject
 4  WHERE {
 5      ?subject a lexis:LanguageItem .
 6      ?subject lesson:alpha3 'eng' .
 7      ?subject lexis:hasToken ?token .
 8      ?token lexis:hasDependency ?dependency
            .
 9      ?dependency lexis:dependencyFunction '
            aux' .
10      ?dependency lexis:hasHead ?head .
11      ?head lexis:hasFeature ?feature .
12      ?feature lexis:featureValue ?pos .
13      ?feature lexis:featureName 'pos' .
14      FILTER regex(?pos, '^V')
15  } LIMIT 50
```

4.3 Performance

The technology for RDF triple stores is not as mature as for relational databases and this is reflected in their performance as witnessed by the so-called "RDF tax", although recent work has been done to improve this (Boncz et al., 2014). Performance for this prototype was also affected by the quality of the data contained in the database and the type of query performed. When the linguistic annotation saved in the database is clean and precise, the SPARQL query can be simpler and get the desired result faster.

The SPARQL query in Listing 1 sent via cURL took 0.035 seconds on average when run 100 times in a row on a MacBook Pro with 8GB RAM. The database stops searching and replies as soon as it has found 50 items that fulfill the request.

The SPARQL query in Section 4.1, however, took around seven seconds when executed in the GraphDB SPARQL GUI. This is not unexpected as the query searches through every single item in the database. A large number of complicated conditions were further required in the query, as the NLP tool did not distinguish between certain types of objects. For example, temporal phrases and direct objects were coded the same, so these had to be manually added as conditions to the SPARQL query, so as not to be included in the end result.

5 Conclusion and Further Work

The prototype database presented here combines RDF resources created from Babbel's learning content with linguistic annotation and existing resources from the LLOD cloud and elsewhere. The concept of the database was validated by experimental evaluation in the form of use cases built on top of it (Section 4).

In the first prototype, the minimal Lexis ontology was designed to test the concept. In future iterations, more work on this ontology could take place, including identification of areas where ontology design patterns (Blomqvist et al., 2016) could be used; and mapping to existing ontologies for linguistic annotation (Section 2.2). Likewise, work on conceptual (semantic) interoperability could take place, using ISOcat categories or similar, to enable use cases that incorporate linguistic annotation across more than one language, and to enable more use of external LLOD resources.

Future iterations could also incorporate improved word sense disambiguation techniques based on supervised machine learning (Navigli, 2009). Alternatively, the availability of translations of the learning content into multiple languages could be exploited to infer the correct mapping (Tufiş et al., 2004).

As seen in Section 4.1, query performance time suffers, when the query becomes too complex due to errors in the linguistic annotation or underspecification in annotation categories. Improving the quality of the linguistic annotation, either by swapping out a given NLP tool, or using a combination of multiple NLP tools and manual review, would further improve the efficiency and usefulness of the database. As the second-language text fragments generally do not have any context, manual review will likely always be necessary.

Future work could also be done on database performance in general, for example by exploring the use of the compact Header, Dictionary and Triples structure for storing RDF (Fernández et al., 2010).

References

Daniel Andor, Chris Alberti, David Weiss, Aliaksei Severyn, Alessandro Presta, Kuzman Ganchev, Slav Petrov, and Michael Collins. 2016. Globally normalized transition-based neural networks. arXiv:1603.06042 .

Tim Berners-Lee. 2006. Linked data. http://www.w3.org/DesignIssues/LinkedData.html.

Tim Berners-Lee, James Hendler, and Ora Lassila. 2001. The Semantic Web. Scientific American .

Steven Bird and Mark Liberman. 2001. A formal framework for linguistic annotation. Speech Communication 33(1):23–60.

Eva Blomqvist, Pascal Hitzler, Krzysztof Janowicz, Adila Krisnadhi, Tom Narock, and Monika Solanki. 2016. Considerations regarding ontology design patterns. Semantic Web 7(1):1–7.

Olivier Bodenreider. 2004. The Unified Medical Language System (UMLS): Integrating biomedical terminology. Nucleic Acids Research 32(1):D267–D270.

Peter Boncz, Orri Erling, and Minh-Duc Pham. 2014. Advances in large-scale RDF data management. In Sören Auer, Volha Bryl, and Sebastian Tramp, editors, Linked Open Data – Creating Knowledge Out of Interlinked Data, Springer, pages 21–44.

Allen C Browne, Alexa T McCray, and Suresh Srinivasan. 2000. The Specialist lexicon. Technical report, National Library of Medicine.

Christian Chiarcos. 2012. Interoperability of corpora and annotations. In Christian Chiarcos, Sebastian Nordhoff, and Sebastian Hellmann, editors, Linked Data in Linguistics, Springer-Verlag, Berlin, pages 161–179.

Christian Chiarcos, Sebastian Hellmann, and Sebastian Nordhoff. 2012. Linking linguistic resources: Examples from the Open Linguistics Working Group. In Christian Chiarcos, Sebastian Nordhoff, and Sebastian Hellmann, editors, Linked Data in Linguistics, Springer-Verlag, Berlin, pages 201–216.

Christian Chiarcos and Maria Sukhareva. 2015. OLiA – Ontologies of Linguistic Annotation. Semantic Web 6(4):379–386.

Ismail El Maarouf, Hatem Mousselly Sergieh, Eugene Alferov, Haofen Wang, Zhijia Fang, and Doug

Cooper. 2015. The GuanXi network: A new multilingual LLOD for language learning applications. In Second Workshop on Natural Language Processing and Linked Open Data. Hissar, Bulgaria, pages 42–51.

Scott Farrar and D Terence Langendoen. 2003. A linguistic ontology for the Semantic Web. GLOT International 7(3):97–100.

Javier D. Fernández, Miguel A. Martínez-Prieto, and Claudio Gutierrez. 2010. Compact representation of large RDF data sets for publishing and exchange. In Peter F. Patel-Schneider, Yue Pan, Pascal Hitzler, Peter Mika, Lei Zhang, Jeff Z. Pan, Ian Horrocks, and Birte Glimm, editors, The Semantic Web – ISWC 2010, Springer-Verlag, Berlin, pages 193–208.

Fabien Gandon and Guus Schreiber. 2014. RDF 1.1 XML syntax. W3C recommendation, W3C.

Nicola Guarino, Daniel Oberle, and Steffen Staab. 2009. What is an ontology? In Handbook on Ontologies, Springer-Verlag, Berlin, pages 1–17.

Ulrich Heid, Helmut Schmid, Kerstin Eckart, and Erhard Hinrichs. 2010. A corpus representation format for linguistic web services: The D-SPIN Text Corpus Format and its relationship with ISO standards. In Nicoletta Calzolari, Khalid Choukri, Bente Maegaard, Joseph Mariani, Jan Odijk, Stelios Piperidis, Mike Rosner, and Daniel Tapias, editors, LREC 2010, Seventh International Conference on Language Resources and Evaluation. Valletta, Malta.

Johannes Helmbrecht. 2013. Politeness distinctions in pronouns. In Matthew S. Dryer and Martin Haspelmath, editors, The World Atlas of Language Structures Online, Max Planck Institute for Evolutionary Anthropology, Leipzig. http://wals.info/chapter/45.

Jennifer Hill and Rahul Simha. 2016. Automatic generation of context-based fill-in-the-blank exercises using co-occurrence likelihoods and Google n-grams. In Proceedings of the 11th Workshop on Innovative Use of NLP for Building Educational Applications. San Diego, California, USA, pages 23–30.

Girish Kumar, Rafael E. Banchs, and Luis F. D'Haro. 2015. RevUP: Automatic gap-fill question generation from educational texts. In The Tenth Workshop on Innovative Use of NLP for Building Educational Applications. Denver, Colorado, USA, pages 154–161.

Christopher D. Manning, Mihai Surdeanu, John Bauer, Jenny Finkel, Steven J. Bethard, and David McClosky. 2014. The Stanford CoreNLP natural language processing toolkit. In Proceedings of 52nd Annual Meeting of the Association for Computational Linguistics: System Demonstrations. pages 55–60.

John McCrae, Guadalupe Aguado-de-Cea, Paul Buitelaar, Philipp Cimiano, Thierry Declerck, Asunción Gómez-Pérez, Jorge Gracia, Laura Hollink, Elena Montiel-Ponsoda, Dennis Spohr, and Tobias Wunner. 2012. Interchanging lexical resources on the Semantic Web. Language Resources and Evaluation 46(4):701–719.

John McCrae, Guadalupe Aguado-de-Cea, Paul Buitelaar, Philipp Cimiano, Thierry Declerck, Asunción Gómez Pérez, Jorge Gracia, Laura Hollink, Elena Montiel-Ponsoda, Dennis Spohr, and Tobias Wunner. 2010. The lemon cookbook. http://lemon-model.net/lemon-cookbook.pdf.

John Philip McCrae, Christian Chiarcos, Francis Bond, Philipp Cimiano, Thierry Declerck, Gerard de Melo, Jorge Gracia, Sebastian Hellmann, Bettina Klimek, Steven Moran, Petya Osenova, Antonio Pareja-Lora, and Jonathan Pool. 2016. The Open Linguistics Working Group: Developing the Linguistic Linked Open Data cloud. In LREC 2016, Tenth International Conference on Language Resources and Evaluation. Portorož, Slovenia, pages 2435–2441.

John Philip McCrae, Christiane Fellbaum, and Philipp Cimiano. 2014. Publishing and linking WordNet using lemon and RDF. In 3rd Workshop on Linked Data in Linguistics: Multilingual Knowledge Resources and Natural Language Processing. Reykjavík, Iceland.

Pablo Mendes, Max Jakob, and Christian Bizer. 2012. DBpedia: A multilingual cross-domain knowledge base. In Nicoletta Calzolari, Khalid Choukri, Thierry Declerck, Mehmet Uur Doan, Bente Maegaard, Joseph Mariani, Asuncion Moreno, Jan Odijk, and Stelios Piperidis, editors, LREC 2012, Eighth International Conference on Language Resources and Evaluation. Istanbul, Turkey.

George A Miller. 1995. WordNet: A lexical database for English. Communications of the ACM 38(11):39–41.

Roberto Navigli. 2009. Word sense disambiguation: A survey. ACM Computing Surveys 41(2):10.

Joakim Nivre. 2016. Universal Dependencies: A cross-linguistic perspective on grammar and lexicon. In Eva Hajičová and Igor Boguslavsky, editors, Grammar and Lexicon: Interactions and Interfaces. Osaka, Japan, pages 38–40.

Llus Padró and Evgeny Stanilovsky. 2012. FreeLing 3.0: Towards wider multilinguality. In LREC 2012, Eighth International Conference on Language Resources and Evaluation. Istanbul, Turkey, pages 2473–2479.

Gilles Sérasset. 2015. DBnary: Wiktionary as a lemon-based multilingual lexical resource in RDF. Semantic Web 6(4):355–361.

Dan Tufiş, Radu Ion, and Nancy Ide. 2004. Fine-grained word sense disambiguation based on parallel corpora, word alignment, word clustering and aligned wordnets. In COLING 2004: Proceedings of the 20th International Conference on Computational Linguistics. Geneva, Switzerland, 1192, pages 1312–1318.

Roumen Vesselinov and John Grego. 2016. The Babbel efficacy study. http://press.babbel.com/en/releases/downloads/ Babbel-Efficacy-Study.pdf.

Menzo Windhouwer and Sue Ellen Wright. 2012. Linking to linguistic data categories in ISOcat. In Christian Chiarcos, Sebastian Nordhoff, and Sebastian Hellmann, editors, Linked Data in Linguistics, Springer-Verlag, Berlin, pages 99–107.

Amir Zeldes, Florian Zipser, and Arne Neumann. 2013. PAULA XML documentation: Format version 1.1. Technical report, University of Potsdam.

Florian Zipser. 2009. Entwicklung eines Konverterframeworks für linguistisch annotierte Daten auf Basis eines gemeinsamen (Meta-)modells. Diplomarbeit, Humboldt-Universität zu Berlin.

Florian Zipser and Laurent Romary. 2010. A model oriented approach to the mapping of annotation formats using standards. In Language Resource and Language Technology Standards State of the Art, Emerging Needs, and Future Developments, LREC 2010. Valletta, Malta.

Predicting Specificity in Classroom Discussion

Luca Lugini and **Diane Litman**
Computer Science Department & Learning Research and Development Center
University of Pittsburgh
Pittsburgh, PA 15260
`{lucalugini,litman}@cs.pitt.edu`

Abstract

High quality classroom discussion is important to student development, enhancing abilities to express claims, reason about other students' claims, and retain information for longer periods of time. Previous small-scale studies have shown that one indicator of classroom discussion quality is specificity. In this paper we tackle the problem of predicting specificity for classroom discussions. We propose several methods and feature sets capable of outperforming the state of the art in specificity prediction. Additionally, we provide a set of meaningful, interpretable features that can be used to analyze classroom discussions at a pedagogical level.

1 Introduction

Classroom discussion plays an important role in the learning process. It has been shown that reasoning, reading, and writing skills can be positively affected by high-quality student-centered classroom discussion in the context of English Language Arts (ELA) classrooms (Reznitskaya and Gregory, 2013; Graham and Perin, 2007; Applebee et al., 2003). High quality discussions encourage student-to-student talk, negotiation of claims, supporting claims with evidence, and reasoning about those claims. Although the effectiveness of particular kinds of claims, evidence and reasoning can vary across disciplines, Chisholm and Godley (2011) and Lee (2006) showed that the specificity of these argument moves is related to discussion quality. These findings are based on a largely qualitative analysis of a single classroom discussion that relied on the manual annotation of specificity and discussion quality. The proposed method in this paper will help address this limitation by making the annotation of specificity automatic.

Specificity is defined by the Oxford Dictionary as "The quality of belonging or relating uniquely to a particular subject" [1]. Natural language processing (NLP) techniques can be used to facilitate the analysis of classroom discussion and of specificity. Chen et al. (2014) developed a tool for teacher self-assessment of classroom discussion through the analysis of the frequency of participation of students in the discussion, and teacher-student turn patterns. Blanchard et al. (2016) developed a system for detecting teacher questions from classroom discussion recordings. These works, however, do not take into account the actual student discussion content. Speciteller (Li and Nenkova, 2015) is a current state of the art method for predicting sentence specificity. It was developed by analyzing newspaper articles to distinguish between general and specific sentences. Spoken and written language differ in grammatical structure, contextual influence, and cognitive process and skills (Chafe and Tannen, 1987; Biber, 1988). As such we believe that using Speciteller as-is on classroom discussions will lead to suboptimal performance, which we can improve.

In this paper we propose a method to automatically determine specificity of student turns at talk in high school ELA classroom discussions of texts. The contributions of this paper are twofold. For the educational community this work will enable the exploration of hypotheses concerning specificity and discussion quality over large datasets, spanning multiple classes and including a large number of students, which would otherwise require a prohibitive amount of work for manually annotating data. Additionally, we develop a set of pedagogically meaningful features which can be

---

[1] https://en.oxforddictionaries.com/definition/specificity

Proceedings of the 12th Workshop on Innovative Use of NLP for Building Educational Applications, pages 52–61
Copenhagen, Denmark, September 8, 2017. ©2017 Association for Computational Linguistics

used to understand important elements of highly specific discussions. For the NLP community, we make the following contributions: we experimentally evaluate the performance of prior approaches for predicting specificity in a new domain; we compare between different feature sets and algorithms; finally, we provide a model for predicting specificity tailored to spoken dialogue and in an educational context, which outperforms the current state of the art.

2 Related Work

To the best of our knowledge, this is the first work to analyze specificity of spoken dialogue, and more precisely in classroom discussions. Louis and Nenkova (2011) analyzed specificity in news articles and their summarizations. Their proposed method leverages a combination of lexical and syntactic features and annotated data from the Penn Discourse Treebank to train a logistic regression classifier. They used the trained model to analyze differences in specificity between human-written and automatically-generated summaries of news articles. Li and Nenkova (2015) developed Speciteller, a tool for predicting the specificity score of sentences. Specificity was defined in relation to the amount of details in a sentence. This tool uses a set of shallow features (described in Section 4.2) and two dense word vector representations to train two logistic regression models on Wall Street Journal articles. Additionally, they improved classification accuracy by using a semi-supervised co-training method on over thirty thousand sentences from the Associated Press, New York Times, and Wall Street Journal. Finally, Li et al. (2016) improved the annotation scheme used in (Louis and Nenkova, 2011; Li and Nenkova, 2015) by considering contextual information, and by using a scale from 0 to 6 rather than binary specificity annotations. Our annotation scheme is based on prior educational work in coding specificity (Chisholm and Godley, 2011), and our prediction models will incorporate features used by Speciteller.

Like other machine learning-based methods, Speciteller is highly dependent on its training data. Since our objective is to analyze classroom discussion, we also draw on work that has used Speciteller to analyze data that is more similar to our corpus. Swanson et al. (2015) analyzed online forum dialogues in the context of argument mining.

By performing feature selection they observed that argument quality is highly correlated with specificity as measured by Speciteller across multiple topics. We believe there might be a correlation between specificity and other features used in their work (described in Section 4.3) to predict argument quality, therefore we used some of these features in our approach.

3 Dataset Description

The dataset for this work consists of manually transcribed text-based classroom discussions from English Language Arts high school classes. Text-based discussions are about a "text" (e.g., literature such as *Macbeth* and *Memoir of a Geisha*, a news article, a speech, etc.) and can either be mediated by a teacher or conducted exclusively among students. The number of students per discussion ranges from 5 to 13 in our dataset.

Motivated by Chisholm and Godley's (2011) and Lee's (2006) coding of classroom discussions, a codebook for manually annotating student argument moves and specificity has been developed. Each student turn at talk is labeled for: (i) specificity (low, medium, high); (ii) argument move (claim, evidence, warrant). Specificity was labeled at the level of argument move: each transcript was preprocessed by one of the annotators and a decision was made on whether to segment each turn at talk into multiple ones if the turn at talk could potentially contain multiple argument move types. The following aspects were considered when labeling specificity for a turn at talk:

1. it involves one character or scene;

2. it gives substantial qualifications or elaboration;

3. it uses content-specific vocabulary;

4. it provides a chain of reasons.

If none of the four elements was present, or if the turn at talk refers to all humans or the text in general, the turn at talk is labeled as low specificity. Medium specificity turns at talk contain one of the four elements, while high specificity ones contain at least two of the four elements.

Table 1 shows examples of specificity annotation from one of the discussions in our dataset about the book *Death of a Salesman*. The first turn at talk in the table was labeled as low specificity because the claim made by the student was

Turn at talk	Specificity
It's just kind of a maintaining personality	low
Yeah because she just couldn't- I mean, it's not a fake personality, but it's kind of like superficial	med
At one point, I don't even think she's concerned that like with her sons as much as she is with Willy, or you know, she's just focusing most of her attention and comfort on Willy and um, when Biff and Happy are there it makes him, like, [inaudible]. I think she's trying to like, you know, be the bridge between them and Willy.	high

Table 1: Examples of turns at talk for different specificity classes.

unsubstantiated. The student did not give a definition of what maintaining personality means in this context, nor did they mention the reasons for making such a claim. The second turn at talk in the table, although not providing considerable elaboration, is clearly about one individual character in the book. As such, it is classified as medium specificity. The third turn at talk is classified as high specificity because the statement is particular to one or a few selected characters, and the student shows a clear chain of reasoning.

The dataset spans 23 classroom discussions and over 2000 turns at talk. Two pairs of annotators coded specificity for 5 and 9 transcripts respectively, while the remaining 9 transcripts were single-coded. Inter-rater reliability on specificity labels for the two annotator pairs as measured by quadratic-weighted Cohen's Kappa is 0.714 and 0.9, indicating substantial agreement and almost perfect agreement, respectively.[2] A gold standard set of labels for each double-coded discussion was obtained by resolving the disagreements between the two annotators. Table 2 shows the distribution of specificity classes in our dataset.

Turns at talk	Specificity		
	Low	Medium	High
2057	730	974	353

Table 2: Dataset statistics.

4 Proposed Method

This section provides a description of Speciteller (Li and Nenkova, 2015) and additional features and models that we propose to predict specificity.

4.1 Speciteller tool

The baseline for testing our hypotheses consists of using Speciteller out of the box to predict the specificity of each turn at talk. Speciteller accepts a string as input and outputs a specificity score in the range $[0, 1]$, where 0 indicates general sentences and 1 indicates specific sentences. Since the unit of analysis for the current work is a turn at talk, which may consist of multiple sentences, we evaluated the performance of Speciteller in several scenarios (e.g. sentence, turn at talk). We found that the best results are obtained when using the complete turn at talk as input to Speciteller. In order to convert the numeric specificity score into a specificity class (i.e. low, medium, or high) we set two thresholds t_1 and t_2, then labeled turns at talk with specificity score $s \leq t_1$ as low, those with score $t_1 < s \leq t_2$ as medium, and those with score $s > t_2$ as high. The optimal thresholds were found by starting at 0 and iteratively increasing them by 0.001 at each step, while saving the best results. The values for the optimal thresholds are: $t_1 = 0.02$ and $t_2 = 0.70$. It is important to note that this represents the upper bound for Speciteller's performance. Finding the optimal thresholds is not trivial and in practice it could be done through cross-validation.

4.2 Speciteller feature set

The initial set of features we evaluated was that used in Speciteller. We extracted features from each turn at talk using the source code provided by Speciteller[3]. In their proposed method, Li and Nenkova extracted two categories of features, a shallow feature set and a word embeddings set, and used them for two separate classifiers. In this work, we concatenate both shallow features and word embeddings to form a single feature vector. We will refer to these features as the Speciteller

---

[3] https://www.cis.upenn.edu/ nlp/software/speciteller.html

set. Shallow features for each sentence consist of: number of connectives, sentence length (number of words), number of numbers, number of capital letters, number of symbols (including punctuation), average number of characters for the words in the sentence, number of stopwords (normalized by sentence length), number of strongly subjective and polar words (using the MPQA (Wilson et al., 2009) and the General Inquirer (Stone and Hunt, 1963) dictionaries), average word familiarity and imageability (using the MRC Psycholinguistic Database (Wilson, 1988)), average, maximum, minimum inverse document frequency values. Word embeddings features consist of the average of 100-dimensional vectors for each word in the sentence. The embeddings were provided by Turian et al. (2010) and trained on a corpus consisting of news articles.

4.3   Online dialogue features

While extracting arguments from online forum dialogues, Swanson at al. (2015) found that Speciteller scores (as a measure of specificity) are highly correlated with argument quality. In addition to Speciteller scores, their model used several feature sets. While not explicitly stated by the authors, we believe there might exist a correlation between specificity and the other feature sets. We will add the following sets of features to the features already present in Speciteller.

Semantic features[4]   The number of pronouns present in a given turn at talk. Descriptive statistics for word lengths: minimum, maximum, average, and median length of the words in a turn at talk. It is worth noting that the average word length differs from the one implemented in Speciteller as this feature keeps punctuation into account. Number of occurrences of words of length 1 to 20: one feature for each word length - words longer than 20 characters will be counted in the feature for length 20.

Lexical features   N-gram language models are often powerful features, but one drawback is their dependence on specific domains. Since we plan to build a model for predicting specificity which is able to generalize to multiple topics, we did not use the raw N-gram features. To alleviate this problem, we used the term frequency - inverse document frequency (tf-idf) feature for each uni-

gram and bigram in the corpus with frequency of at least 5. Descriptive statistics of lexical features for each turn at talk, namely minimum, maximum, and average, were also used.

Syntactic features   To mitigate the data sparsity that impacts word n-grams, and to get more generalizable features, we extracted unigrams, bigrams, and trigrams of Parts Of Speech (POS) tags, using the Natural Language Toolkit (Bird et al., 2009).

4.4   Additional feature sets

In addition to the previous feature sets, we also extracted the following feature sets which we believe are able to capture specificity with respect to the educational domain of ELA text-based classroom discussions.

Pronoun features   Pronouns are grammatical units that might help us gain useful information about the focus of a turn at talk. For example, if the pronoun "she" is present in a turn at talk, the student might likely be referring to one specific character, which is one of the aspects considered when annotating specificity. Therefore we extracted a set of the following pronoun features: binary feature indicating presence/absence of pronouns; total number of pronouns in the turn at talk[5]; the numbers of first, second, and third person pronouns; the number of singular and plural pronouns; the number of pronouns for each of the following categories: personal, possessive, reflexive, reciprocal, relative, demonstrative, interrogative, indefinite.

Named entities   Named entities might give us a sense of characters or places that students discuss, with respect to specificity. For example, saying "I did not like Biff" is more specific than saying "I did not like one of the characters" as it points out which of the characters a student might not like. For this task we used the Stanford Named Entity Recognizer (Finkel et al., 2005) (NER) with the pre-trained 3 class model detecting location, person and organization entities. We extracted the following features: a binary feature indicating the presence/absence of any named entity; a binary feature indicating presence/absence of each of the three named entity classes; the total number of named entities; the total number of named entities per class. We complemented the previous counts by adding a normalized feature, with respect to the

---

[4]The name of the feature set in the original paper is semantic-density features; we use semantic features for brevity.

[5]This feature differs from that described in section 4.3: the feature from the online dialogue set only considers deictic pronouns.

length of the turn at talk, for each of them.

Book features   Since our dataset consists of text-based discussions, we might be able to leverage information about the texts (i.e. books) for each discussion to understand how much each turn at talk is related to the book or its characters. First, a manually-created summary and a list of characters for each book were obtained from the web, using Wikipedia when possible or Sparknotes as an alternative. Then, the following character-related features were extracted from each turn at talk: a binary feature indicating the presence/absence of a character's name; the number of characters mentioned; the number of characters mentioned normalized by the length of the turn at talk. A character was counted by matching each word in the turn at talk to their first name, last name, or their nickname. Additionally the following summary related features were extracted: the number of overlapping words with the turn at talk; Jaccard similarity between the turn at talk and the summary; tf-idf based cosine similarity between the summary and the turn at talk. We extracted the summary related features in two different settings: considering the book summary as a single entity; computing the similarity between the turn at talk and each sentence in the summary, then picking the maximum. All features were extracted after removing stopwords from the turn and summary.

Embeddings   Li and Nenkova (2015) used sentence embeddings based on word embeddings in order to increase the accuracy of Speciteller. The sentence embeddings were obtained by computing the average of pre-trained word embeddings for each word in the sentence. We believe our method can further benefit from sentence embeddings specifically trained on our corpus and optimized for our target: predicting specificity. We generated embeddings by training a character-level Long-Short Term Memory (LSTM) network (Hochreiter and Schmidhuber, 1997), using it as an encoder on the turns at talk from our corpus. Each turn at talk, which might consist of multiple sentences, represents one sequence (training sample) for the LSTM training. Since punctuation is not very meaningful given that we are analyzing spoken discussions, all characters that are not letters or numbers are ignored. Inputs for the LSTM consist of one-hot (1 X N) encoding of individual characters.

The neural network is trained by using the hid-

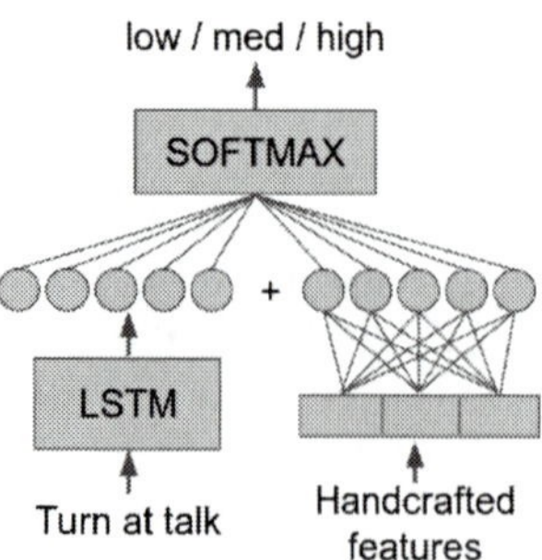

Figure 1: Network setup for training neural network-based embeddings.

den state of the LSTM unit at the end of the turn at talk as embedding, feeding it to a softmax classifier for predicting specificity, and back-propagating errors. Cross-entropy was used as the objective function to optimize during training. A disadvantage of neural network models is the fact that their large number of parameters requires extensive amount of data to show their expressive power. Given the size of our training data we try to mitigate this problem by merging the embeddings for a turn at talk with handcrafted features. Ideally we would combine embeddings with all the features described previously but the resulting model would be far too large for our dataset, therefore we chose to use the $Speciteller + Semantic$ feature set for this task. The training procedure changes slightly: a turn at talk is propagated through the LSTM resulting in a fixed size embedding; handcrafted features are extracted from the turn at talk, concatenated to form a vector, and a fully-connected layer is applied to those; the output of the fully-connected layer is concatenated with the embedding, and given as input to a softmax classifier to predict specificity. A graphical overview of the model is given in Figure 1.

It is important to note that the neural network for embeddings and the classifier are jointly trained, therefore the embeddings are specifically tailored to encode information regarding specificity. The Keras library (Chollet et al., 2015) was used for extracting sentence embeddings as well as for evaluating performance of the softmax classifier.

Pedagogical feature set   In addition to maximizing kappa for specificity prediction, an additional objective for this study is to find meaningful features that can help explain different aspects of highly specific discussions. Many of the features described above, like N-grams or tf-idf, might have good predictive power but they are not easily interpretable and bear little relation to our codebook.

When considering NLP techniques applied to the educational domain, there is an increasing interest in developing models that capture important components of the construct to measure. Rahimi et al. (2017), for example, developed a model for automated essay scoring using rubric-based features; Loukina et al. (2015) evaluated different feature selection methods to obtain interpretable features in an educational setting.

In order to create an interpretable feature set we started by manually selected meaningful features from Speciteller (imageability, subjectivity, polarity, and familiarity ratings, number of connectives, fraction of stopwords). At training/test time, this set is combined with features from the *Pronoun*, *Named entities*, and *Book* feature sets. Since all the features from the last 3 sets are interpretable, we only chose a few features from each set, selecting the ones with highest information gain with respect to specificity. For each fold, we first rank features in the *Pronoun*, *Named entities*, and *Book* sets by information gain, then select the top k (based on the number of features in each respective set), concatenate them to the interpretable Speciteller features and train a logistic regression model. Section 5.4 will give examples of selected features.

5 Experiments and Results

In this section we provide results for our experiments. All classifiers and feature sets were evaluated using 10-fold cross validation, and using quadratic-weighted Cohen's kappa as the performance metric since it is important to make a distinction between different classification errors (e.g. classifying a low specificity turn at talk as high should result in bigger error than classifying it as medium). We used the scikit-learn Python package[6] for training and evaluating classifiers, as well as performing feature selection. Specifically, sections 5.1 and 5.2 will be used to test our first hypothesis: that by retraining an existing model on our corpus we will obtain an improvement in performance. Sections 5.2 and 5.3 will be used to test our second hypothesis: that by using fea-

---

[6]http://scikit-learn.org/stable/

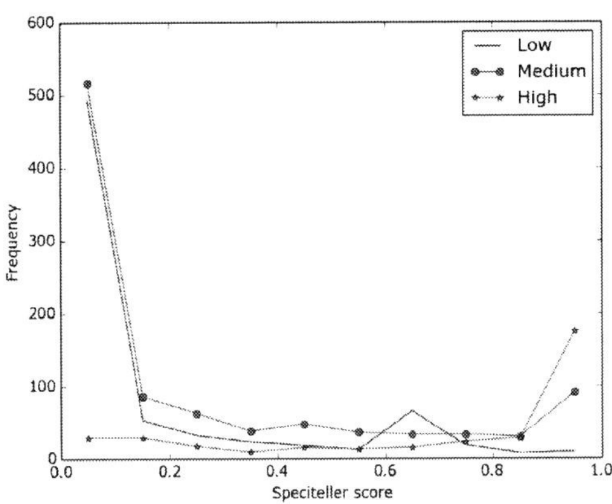

Figure 2: Speciteller scores by specificity class.

tures from additional NLP literature we can further improve the performance of a state-of-the-art model. Section 5.4 will test our third hypothesis: that the additional features we handcrafted to capture specificity with respect to verbal discussion in an educational setting will lead to better performance.

5.1 Baseline using Speciteller off-the-shelf

Since we plan to use Speciteller as a baseline for comparing the performance of our proposed method, we iteratively tested thresholds to find the set which results in the highest quadratic-weighted kappa in all scenarios described in Section 4.1. The best result was obtained when the input to Speciteller is the complete turn at talk, and the resulting quadratic-weighted kappa is 0.495, which represents Speciteller's upper bound performance. Figure 2 shows the frequency distribution of speciteller scores for each specificity class.

From the figure we can see that Speciteller is able to correctly capture specificity for a portion of the turns at talk in the dataset, as there is a peak in the low end of the spectrum for the distribution of low specificity scores and a peak in the high end of the spectrum for the distribution of high specificity scores. The medium specificity class seems to be the most problematic one, which has a similar trend as the low specificity class distribution in the low end of the spectrum, and a similar trend to the high specificity class distribution in the high end of the spectrum. Ideally we would expect the medium specificity distribution to have a peak towards the middle of the spectrum but that is not the case. Additionally, the low specificity class distribution shows a peak between 0.6 and 0.7 which

57

will further penalize accuracy.

Table 3 shows the confusion matrix when applying the optimal thresholds in order to get specificity labels from Speciteller scores. As we can see from the confusion matrix the overlap between the low and medium specificity classes and the medium and high specificity classes causes a large number of misclassifications: almost half of the low specificity turns at talk are classified as medium, over 40% of the medium specificity turns at talk are classified as either low or high, and almost 40% of high specificity turns at talk are classified as medium. We believe these errors stem from two main reasons: as with many data-driven approaches, Speciteller is highly dependent on its training corpus. Speciteller was trained on articles from the Wall Street Journal and the New York Times. Articles written by professional writers are inherently different from transcriptions of spoken discussions between high school students. Additionally, for training the model, Speciteller used a binary general/specific label, while we consider three labels in our work. Since Speciteller has no prior knowledge on medium specificity sentences, it is understandable that most of the misclassifications come from this class.

5.2 Training using Speciteller features

Our hypotheses as to why Speciteller does not work effectively out of the box are related to its corpora and the way it was trained. With respect to the features used by Speciteller, we believe they might be useful in the context of classroom discussion as well. We extracted the shallow feature set and the neural network word embeddings feature sets and combined them to train a logistic regression classifier on our dataset. This classifier was chosen because one of our objectives is to compare the importance of other feature sets in addition to the *Speciteller* one, and in order for this comparison to be fair we decided to use the same classifier Speciteller uses. Additionally, the classifier

		predictions		
		low	**med**	**high**
	low	352	360	18
ground truth	**med**	280	565	129
	high	4	139	210

Table 3: Confusion matrix using Speciteller scores to classify according to the optimal split points.

weights can be used to understand the importance of each feature. It is important to note that, unlike Speciteller, we will be using a single classifier on the combination of all features, and will not be able to leverage semi-supervised co-training.

Table 4 shows the performance of a logistic regression classifier trained on this feature set and others described in the previous section. As we

Feature sets	QWKappa
Speciteller	0.5758
Speciteller + Online dialogue	0.6347*
All: Speciteller + Online dialogue + Pronoun + NE + Book	0.6360*
Speciteller + Semantic + Embeddings	**0.6550***
Pedagogical	0.5886

Table 4: Classification performance of different feature sets. * indicates statistically significant improvement over Speciteller features with p-value < 0.001. Statistical significance was tested using a two-tailed paired t-test. Bold font highlights best results.

can see from the table, training a classifier using the Speciteller feature set on our corpus results in a considerable increase in performance, with QWKappa of 0.5758 which represents a 16% relative improvement over the 0.495 QWKappa obtained using Speciteller out of the box. This confirms our first hypothesis that Speciteller's performance, like many other methods, is highly dependent on its training corpus and using this model out of the box would give sub-optimal results.

5.3 Speciteller and online dialogue features

To test whether features from Section 4.3 are useful, we combined the Speciteller features with the Semantic, Lexical, and Syntactic features and trained a logistic regression classifier based on the concatenated feature vectors. Table 4 confirms our hypothesis that the 4 feature sets combined result in statistically significant (using a two-tailed paired t-test) higher kappa than using only Speciteller features. When combining Speciteller with each of the 3 other feature sets individually, kappa increases but not with statistical significance. We evaluated additional classifiers (Support Vector Machine, decision tree, random forest, Naive Bayes) but none of them outperformed logistic regression. Since the number of features is over 7000, we also tried using Recursive Feature Elimination (RFE) and Principal Component Analysis (PCA) for feature selection/reduction, but neither improved performance.

5.4 Additional features

To the feature set described in the previous section, we added the features described in Section 4.4. We then tested our third hypothesis by evaluating the performance of a logistic regression model trained with these features.

We can see from Table 4 that all additional feature sets yield better performance than the *Speciteller* feature set by itself. This result confirms our third hypothesis: the additional feature sets are able to capture aspects of specificity with respect to verbal discussion and the educational domain. In particular the feature set containing neural network-based sentence embedding achieved the best kappa measure of 0.6550, which suggests that sentence embeddings are also domain-dependent. Compared to using Speciteller off-the-shelf this method improves kappa by 32%. While the size of the neural network was constant during training/test (not optimized for each fold), we experimented with several numbers of hidden nodes (ranging from 50 to 200) for the LSTM and fully-connected layers, which resulted in kappa values in the range $0.6283 - 0.6550$.

The Pedagogical feature set is also able to marginally outperform the Speciteller feature set. Compared to the best result, the loss in kappa when using the Pedagogical set is 11%. At the expense of a slightly lower accuracy we gain the ability to use only informative features, which can be used to better understand highly specific versus general classroom discussions. The use of logistic regression also makes this possible: the model's coefficients give us an indication of how important features are. Table 5 shows the top 12 features in the Pedagogical feature set ranked by the magnitude of the model's coefficients.

The table shows the results of a model trained on the complete dataset. The number of connectives seems to be the most important feature for predicting high specificity. This seems straightforward, as more connectives translates into more clauses, which provide more information. While the annotators did not look for connectives during coding, one of the aspects they analyzed was the presence/absence of a chain of reasoning, and

Feature	Coefficient
Number of connectives	1.9168
Cosine similarity whole summary	0.9293
MRC imageability	0.8172
Number of characters	0.6931
MPQ subjectivity	-0.5440
Fraction of stopwords	-0.4087
MRC familiarity	0.3986
Number of possessive pronouns	0.2035
Number of named entities normalized	0.1865
Number of 3rd person pronouns	0.1755
Word overlap whole summary	0.1585
Number of personal pronouns	0.1476

Table 5: Pedagogical feature set and respective logistic regression coefficients. Italic font shows features developed in this study (Section 4.4).

the number of connectives might capture that aspect. The cosine similarity between the turn at talk and the book summary (considered as one entity) is another important feature in the model: higher similarity between the summary and what a student says means that they are using terms from the book. This feature seems to capture another aspect in our codebook, the use of book-specific vocabulary. We can use the information provided by these features to understand specificity, and to give feedback to teachers and students: if for example a student tends to produce low specificity turns at talk and the number of connectives used is generally low, that might be an indication that they should elaborate more on their statements. Conversely, if the number of connectives used is high but the number of characters mentioned is low, that might be an indication that the student should reference specific characters more often.

6 Conclusions and Future Work

We proposed several models for predicting specificity and evaluated them on text-based, high school classroom discussion data. We showed that an existing general-purpose system achieves significantly better performance when its features are used for retraining on educational data. We also showed that performance can be further improved by using additional features from the NLP literature (Swanson et al., 2015), especially when combined with neural network embeddings and other new features tailored to text-based classroom discussion. Finally we proposed a subset of pedagogical features which, even though slightly less performing, provide the ability to interpret the features, which is especially important for the educational community.

As more data becomes available, we will explore more advanced neural network models and examine method generalization (e.g., social science vs. ELA, middle vs. high school). We also plan to analyze features at a finer granularity than a turn at talk and to extract the book summary features automatically from the original texts. Since our dataset is already annotated for argument type, and will be annotated for discussion quality, we plan to investigate relationships between specificity, argumentation, and quality.

Acknowledgements

We want to thank Dr. Amanda Godley, Christopher Olshefski, Zane Denmon, Zinan Zhuang, Clare Miller, Keya Bartolomeo, and Annika Swallen for their contribution, and all the anonymous reviewers for their helpful suggestions.

This work was supported by the Learning Research and Development Center at the University of Pittsburgh.

References

Arthur N Applebee, Judith A Langer, Martin Nystrand, and Adam Gamoran. 2003. Discussion-based approaches to developing understanding: Classroom instruction and student performance in middle and high school english. *American Educational Research Journal*, 40(3):685–730.

Douglas Biber. 1988. *Variation across speech and writing*. Cambridge University Press.

Steven Bird, Ewan Klein, and Edward Loper. 2009. *Natural language processing with Python: analyzing text with the natural language toolkit.* " O'Reilly Media, Inc.".

Nathaniel Blanchard, Patrick J Donnelly, Andrew M Olney, Borhan Samei, Brooke Ward, Xiaoyi Sun, Sean Kelly, Martin Nystrand, and Sidney K DMello. 2016. Identifying teacher questions using automatic speech recognition in classrooms. In *17th Annual Meeting of the Special Interest Group on Discourse and Dialogue*, page 191.

W. Chafe and D. Tannen. 1987. The relation between written and spoken language. *Annual Review of Anthropology*, 16(1):383–407.

G Chen, SN Clarke, and LB Resnick. 2014. An analytic tool for supporting teachers reflection on classroom talk. In *Learning and becoming in practice: The International Conference of the Learning Sciences (ICLS) 2014*. International Society of the Learning Sciences.

James S Chisholm and Amanda J Godley. 2011. Learning about language through inquiry-based discussion: Three bidialectal high school students talk about dialect variation, identity, and power. *Journal of Literacy Research*, 43(4):430–468.

François Chollet et al. 2015. Keras. https://github.com/fchollet/keras.

Jenny Rose Finkel, Trond Grenager, and Christopher Manning. 2005. Incorporating non-local information into information extraction systems by gibbs sampling. In *Proceedings of the 43rd annual meeting on association for computational linguistics*, pages 363–370. Association for Computational Linguistics.

Steve Graham and Dolores Perin. 2007. A meta-analysis of writing instruction for adolescent students. *Journal of Educational Psychology*, 99(3):445–476.

Sepp Hochreiter and Jürgen Schmidhuber. 1997. Long short-term memory. *Neural computation*, 9(8):1735–1780.

Carol D Lee. 2006. every good-bye aint gone: analyzing the cultural underpinnings of classroom talk. *International Journal of Qualitative Studies in Education*, 19(3):305–327.

Junyi Jessy Li and Ani Nenkova. 2015. Fast and accurate prediction of sentence specificity. In *Proceedings of the Twenty-Ninth Conference on Artificial Intelligence (AAAI)*, pages 2281–2287.

Junyi Jessy Li, Bridget ODaniel, Yi Wu, Wenli Zhao, and Ani Nenkova. 2016. Improving the annotation of sentence specificity. In *Proceedings of the Tenth International Conference on Language Resources and Evaluation (LREC)*.

Annie Louis and Ani Nenkova. 2011. General versus specific sentences: automatic identification and application to analysis of news summaries. Technical Report MS-CIS-11-07, University of Pennsylvania.

Anastassia Loukina, Klaus Zechner, Lei Chen, and Michael Heilman. 2015. Feature selection for automated speech scoring. In *Proceedings of the Tenth Workshop on Innovative Use of NLP for Building Educational Applications*, pages 12–19.

Zahra Rahimi, Diane Litman, Richard Correnti, Elaine Wang, and Lindsay Clare Matsumura. 2017. Assessing students use of evidence and organization in response-to-text writing: Using natural language processing for rubric-based automated scoring. *International Journal of Artificial Intelligence in Education*, pages 1–35.

Alina Reznitskaya and Maughn Gregory. 2013. Student thought and classroom language: Examining the mechanisms of change in dialogic teaching. *Educational Psychologist*, 48(2):114–133.

Philip J Stone and Earl B Hunt. 1963. A computer approach to content analysis: studies using the general inquirer system. In *Proceedings of the May 21-23, 1963, spring joint computer conference*, pages 241–256. ACM.

Reid Swanson, Brian Ecker, and Marilyn Walker. 2015. Argument mining: Extracting arguments from online dialogue. In *Proceedings of the 16th Annual Meeting of the Special Interest Group on Discourse and Dialogue*, pages 217–226.

Joseph Turian, Lev Ratinov, and Yoshua Bengio. 2010. Word representations: a simple and general method for semi-supervised learning. In *Proceedings of the 48th annual meeting of the association for computational linguistics*, pages 384–394. Association for Computational Linguistics.

Michael Wilson. 1988. Mrc psycholinguistic database: Machine-usable dictionary, version 2.00. *Behavior Research Methods*, 20(1):6–10.

Theresa Wilson, Janyce Wiebe, and Paul Hoffmann. 2009. Recognizing contextual polarity: An exploration of features for phrase-level sentiment analysis. *Computational linguistics*, 35(3):399–433.

A Report on the 2017 Native Language Identification Shared Task

**Shervin Malmasi[1,2], Keelan Evanini[3], Aoife Cahill[3], Joel Tetreault[4]
Robert Pugh[5], Christopher Hamill[3], Diane Napolitano[3] and Yao Qian[5]**

[1]Harvard Medical School, Boston, MA, USA
[2]Macquarie University, Sydney, Australia
[3]Educational Testing Service, Princeton, NJ, USA
[4]Grammarly, New York, NY, USA
[5]Educational Testing Service, San Francisco, CA, USA

`shervin.malmasi@mq.edu.au`, `{kevanini,acahill}@ets.org`, `joel.tetreault@grammarly.com`

Abstract

Native Language Identification (NLI) is the task of automatically identifying the native language (L1) of an individual based on their language production in a learned language. It is typically framed as a classification task where the set of L1s is known *a priori*. Two previous shared tasks on NLI have been organized where the aim was to identify the L1 of learners of English based on essays (2013) and spoken responses (2016) they provided during a standardized assessment of academic English proficiency. The 2017 shared task combines the inputs from the two prior tasks for the first time. There are three tracks: NLI on the essay only, NLI on the spoken response only (based on a transcription of the response and i-vector acoustic features), and NLI using both responses. We believe this makes for a more interesting shared task while building on the methods and results from the previous two shared tasks. In this paper, we report the results of the shared task. A total of 19 teams competed across the three different sub-tasks. The fusion track showed that combining the written and spoken responses provides a large boost in prediction accuracy. Multiple classifier systems (*e.g.* ensembles and meta-classifiers) were the most effective in all tasks, with most based on traditional classifiers (*e.g.* SVMs) with lexical/syntactic features.

Visit the website for more info about the task:
https://sites.google.com/site/nlisharedtask/

1 Introduction

Native Language Identification (NLI) is the task of automatically identifying the native language (L1) of an individual based on their writing or speech in another language (L2). NLI works by identifying language use patterns that are common to certain groups of speakers that share the same native language. This process is underpinned by the presupposition that an author's linguistic background will dispose them towards particular language production patterns in their learned languages, as influenced by their mother tongue.

Predicting the native language of a writer has applications in different fields. It can be used for authorship identification (Estival et al., 2007), forensic analysis (Gibbons, 2003), tracing linguistic influence in potentially multi-author texts (Malmasi et al., 2017), and naturally to support Second Language Acquisition research (Malmasi and Dras, 2014). It can also be used in educational applications such as developing grammatical error correction systems which can personalize their feedback and model performance to the native language of the user (Rozovskaya and Roth, 2011).

Most work in NLI focused on predicting the native language of an ESL (English as a Second Language) writer based on a sample essay, although NLI has also been shown to work on other languages (Malmasi and Dras, 2015). Work by Koppel et al. (2005), Tsur and Rappoport (2007) Wong and Dras (2009), and Tetreault et al. (2012) set the stage for much of the recent research efforts. However, it was the 2013 Native Language Identification Shared Task (Tetreault et al., 2013) that led to an explosion of interest in this area by making public a large dataset developed specifically

Proceedings of the 12th Workshop on Innovative Use of NLP for Building Educational Applications, pages 62–75
Copenhagen, Denmark, September 8, 2017. ©2017 Association for Computational Linguistics

for this task called the TOEFL11 (Blanchard et al., 2013). In that shared task, 29 teams participated, making it one of the largest NLP competitions that year alone.

In addition to analyzing the written responses, a recent trend in NLP research has been the use of speech transcripts (generated manually or via Automatic Speech Recognition) and audio features for dialect identification (Malmasi et al., 2016), a task that involves identifying specific dialects of pluricentric languages, such as Spanish or Arabic.[1] The combination of transcripts and acoustic features has also provided good results for dialect identification (Zampieri et al., 2017b), demonstrating that it is possible to improve performance by combining this information.

While there has been growing interest in using such features, the use of speech transcripts for NLI is not entirely new. In fact, the very first NLI study by Tomokiyo and Jones (2001) was based on applying a Naive Bayes classifier to transcriptions of speech from native and non-native speakers, albeit using limited data. However, this strand of NLI research has not received much attention, most likely due to the costly and laborious nature of collecting and transcribing non-native speech. Following this trend, the 2016 Computational Paralinguistics Challenge (Schuller et al., 2016) also included an NLI task based on the spoken response using the raw audio.

The NLI Shared Task 2017 attempts to combine these approaches by including a written response (essay) and a spoken response (speech transcript and i-vector acoustic features) for each candidate. The competition also allows for the fusion of all features, a novel task that has not been previously tried. Another motivation for this task was the rapid growth of deep learning methods for natural language processing tasks (Manning, 2015). In prior shared tasks, there were several barriers to using deep learning for NLP. However, deep learning has now had a positive impact on many tasks across NLP and it is an area of investigation on whether the same successes can be found in NLI.

In the following section, we provide a summary of the prior work in Native Language Identification, for both text and speech based tracks. Next, in §3, we describe the data used for training, de-

velopment, and testing in this shared task. In §4 we describe the results of each sub-task, with a short description of each team's submission. Then in §5, we discuss the commonalities and trends in and across the three sub-tasks, and present an ensemble analysis of all submissions. Finally, in §6, we offer conclusions and ideas for avenues of research in this growing field.

2 Related Work

NLI is most commonly framed as a supervised classification task, where features are extracted from a linguistic response produced by non-native speakers, and used to train a classification model. NLI is a recent, but rapidly growing, area of research. While some early research was conducted in the early 2000s, most work has only appeared in the last few years.

2.1 Text-based NLI

Most NLI research has focused on English texts where both lexical and syntactic features (often based on n-gram frequency profiles) have been used. Popular lexical features include character, word and lemma n-grams, while syntactic features are based on constituent parse trees, dependency parse features and part-of-speech tags. Support Vector Machine (SVM) models have been the most prevalent classification approach. Researchers have mainly focused on experimenting with different features and methods of combining them. While a detailed analysis of previous work is beyond the scope of this report, a comprehensive exposition of NLI research from 2001-2015, including all of the systems from the first shared task, can be found in Malmasi (2016, Section 2.3).

The winning entry for the 2013 shared task was that of Jarvis et al. (2013), achieving 83.6% in terms of accuracy (the official metric). The features used in the system include n-grams of words, parts-of-speech, and lemmas. A logentropy weighting schema was used to normalize the frequencies. An L2-regularized SVM classifier was used to create a single-model system.

A notable trend in NLI has been the success of multiple classifier systems, such as ensemble classifiers (Tetreault et al., 2012). In fact, such approaches have consistently achieved state-of-the-art performance on the NLI Shared Task 2013 dataset. Bykh and Meurers (2014) applied a tuned and optimized ensemble, reporting an accuracy of

---

[1]NLI could also be framed as a dialect identification task if we assume that each L1 group has their own interlanguage/dialect which is influenced by their L1.

84.82% on this data. Ionescu et al. (2014) used string kernels to perform NLI. They create several string kernels which are then combined through multiple kernel learning. They report an accuracy of 85.3% on the 2013 Test set, 1.7% higher than the winning shared task system. More recently, Malmasi and Dras (2017) presented a thorough examination of meta-classification models for NLI, achieving state-of-the-art results on three datasets from different languages, including an accuracy of 87.1% on the 2013 data.

2.2 Speech-based NLI

The task of speech-based NLI is closely related to the tasks of language identification and dialect identification, for which substantially more research has been conducted. For those tasks, the two main types of approach are based on acoustic features (Dehak et al., 2011) and phonotactic features (Zissman, 1996). For further details we refer the reader to Rao and Nandi (2015) and Etman and Beex (2015) which provide comprehensive overviews of the different approaches that have been taken for speech-based language and dialect identification.

The 2016 Computational Paralinguistic Challenge on NLI was designed to explore the related task of speech-based NLI in more detail. The data set for that task contained 64 hours of speech from 5,132 non-native speakers of English (approximately 45 seconds per speaker) representing the same 11 L1 backgrounds as the 2013 NLI Shared Task corpus. Each language was represented by recordings ranging from 458 to 485 different speakers representing a range of English speaking proficiencies. The best performing system in the challenge was that of Abad et al. (2011): their system used i-vector features that were based on Phone Log-Likelihood Ratios and achieved a performance of 81.3% (in terms of Unweighted Average Recall, which was the evaluation metric for the challenge) on the test set.

3 Task Description and Data

There were three tracks in the NLI Shared Task 2017: essay-only, speech-only, and fusion. The corpus consists of both written essays and orthographic transcriptions of spoken responses. These were provided by test takers in the context of a standardized assessment of a non-native speaker's ability to use and understand English for academic purposes at the university level, TOEFL® iBT. There were 11,000 test takers included in the training data (1,000 per L1) and 1,100 each for development and test (100 per L1). The 11 L1 backgrounds included in the NLI Shared Task 2017 were identical to the 2013 and 2016 shared tasks: Arabic, Chinese, French, German, Hindi, Italian, Japanese, Korean, Spanish, Telugu, and Turkish. These L1s and their language families are shown in Figure 1.

The test takers' essays and spoken responses were elicited by test questions (hereafter referred to as *prompts*) asking about an opinion (e.g., which of two choices the test taker would prefer) or a personal experience. A total of 8 essay prompts were included in the training and development partitions and 7 of these were represented in the test partition; a total of 9 different speaking prompts were included in the training and development partitions and 7 of these were represented in the test partition. Prompt IDs for both the essays and the spoken responses were provided with the corpus. We tried to ensure the the data was as balanced as possible by prompt (in addition to by L1), though we did not always have enough data for all L1s for some prompts.

In the **essay-only** track, the task was to predict the L1 of a candidate based only on an essay written in English. The essay training data consisted of the training plus development data used in the NLI Shared Task 2013, while the development essay data consisted of the test data from the 2013 task. The test data for this track was new, previously unreleased data. The average length of the essays across all three partitions was 316.2 words (SD: 77.6, Min.: 2, Max.: 796).

In the **speech-only** track, the task was to predict the L1 of a candidate based only on a 45-second-long spoken response in English. The main source of data was a manually-created orthographic transcription of the spoken response. The average length of the speech transcriptions across all three partitions was 89.5 words (SD: 25.7, Min.: 0, Max.: 202). Unfortunately, it was not possible to distribute the raw audio for the responses. To provide a more realistic sense of the performance of a speech-based NLI system, a feature file of *i-vectors* was provided to participants who requested it. An i-vector is a fixed-length, low-dimensional representation of the sequence of frame-level acoustic measurements extracted from

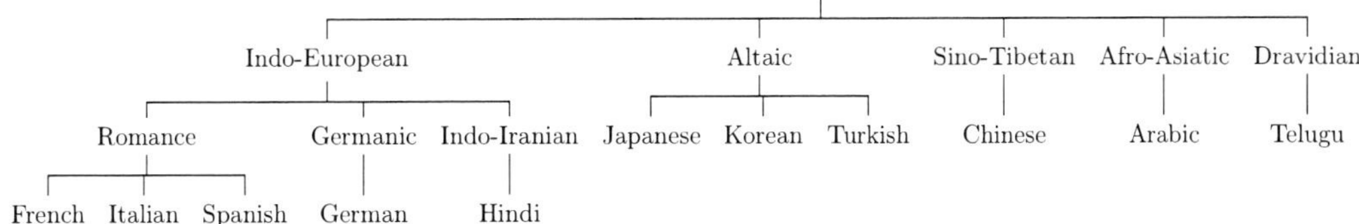

Figure 1: Language families in the task. The languages were selected to represent different families, but to also have several from within the same families. Diagram reproduced from Blanchard et al. (2013).

the speech signal (Dehak et al., 2011; Martinez et al., 2011). The dimensions of the i-vectors (800) and number of Gaussian components (1024) were tuned on the development set by using the Kaldi toolkit.[2] In order to be able to distinguish the effects of new features or approaches, participants were encouraged to clearly describe the relative contribution of their features on the task both with and without the i-vector features.

In the **fusion** track, the task was to predict the L1 of a candidate using the combination of their written essay and spoken response.

The training and development data were released in two phases. The first phase consisted of only the essays, while the second phase consisted of the spoken transcriptions and optionally i-vectors. Simple baseline scripts that used unigram features and an SVM learner were also provided for each track.

There were both open and closed competitions for each track. In the closed competition, only the data provided could be used for training (though *features* based on external data sources such as language models or parsers could be included). In the open competition, additional NLI training data could be used to help improve predictions. There were no submissions to the open competition.

The test period for each track lasted 3 days, and teams could submit up to 12 systems per track. The essay-only and speech-only test phases ran concurrently. The IDs for the essay data and transcription data were generated by separate random processes for this test period. For the fusion test period, an updated package providing linked IDs between the essay and spoken transcription data was released.

3.1 Evaluation and Ranking

The majority of NLI research to date has reported results using accuracy as the main metric. For this task, however, we decided to use the macro-averaged F1-score as the official evaluation metric. The macro-averaged F1-score is calculated by first computing the F1-score for each class, and then taking the average across all classes (Yang and Liu, 1999). This metric favors more consistent performance across classes rather than simply measuring global performance across all samples. Accuracy was still reported for completeness.

We also used statistical significance testing for ranking purposes. McNemar's test[3] (with an alpha value of 0.05) was applied to the ordered results to identify groups of teams where the highest and lowest results were not significantly different, and they were therefore assigned the same rank.

For comparison, we compare to two types of baselines: a random baseline and one that use a linear SVM classifier. There were three random baselines, one for each task, and five simple SVM baselines in total across the three tasks. For the essay-only task there was one baseline based on raw unigram frequencies from the essay texts. For the speech-only task there were two baselines: one an SVM based on raw unigram frequencies from the orthographic transcriptions alone, and a second SVM that combined the unigram features with the i-vectors using horizontal concatenation. For the fusion task there were two baselines: one, an SVM combining the unigrams from the essays and the transcriptions, and a second SVM combining the unigrams from the essays and the transcriptions with the i-vectors.

---

[2] http://kaldi-asr.org

[3] For more details see §7.3 of Malmasi and Dras (2017)

4 Results

A total of 19 teams participated in the task, 17 of which submitted system description papers. Participation across the three tracks varied, with 17 participants in the essay-only track, 9 in the speech-only track, and 10 in the fusion track. The results for each track are described in the following sections. For every track we briefly outline each team's best system. Interested readers can refer to the team's paper for more details.

4.1 Essay-only Track

The best essay-only submission for each team, along with rankings and other details, are listed in Table 4.1. Each team's best system is briefly described below, ordered by rankings.

ItaliaNLP Lab (Cimino and Dell'Orletta, 2017) utilize a novel classifier stacking approach based on a sentence-level classifier whose predictions are used by a second document-level classifier. The sentence classifier is based on a Logistic Regression model trained on standard lexical, stylistic, and syntactic NLI features. The document-classifier is an SVM, trained using the same features, as well as the sentence prediction labels. Their experiments indicate that inclusion of the sentence prediction features provides a small increase in performance.

CIC-FBK (Markov et al., 2017) build an SVM with multiple lexical and syntactic features. They introduce two new feature types – typed character n-grams and syntactic n-grams – and combine them with word, lemma, and POS n-grams, function words, and spelling error character n-grams. Features are weighted using log-entropy.

Groningen (Kulmizev et al., 2017) achieve their best results using a very simple system based on character 1-9 grams. Features are counted in a binary fashion and normalized via tf-idf. They also conducted experiments omitting data from some prompts during training and observe that performance can drop considerably, depending on which prompt is left out.

NRC (Goutte and Léger, 2017) explored various ways of building ensemble models to make the final prediction. Relatively simple features were used (character, word, and POS n-grams). Their best run for this track was a voting ensemble with 10 SVM models.

tubasfs (Rama and Çöltekin, 2017) used a single SVM classifier trained on word bigrams and character 7-grams. They tried a variety of n-gram combinations and found this to work best on the development data.

UnibucKernel (Ionescu and Popescu, 2017) use different types of character-level string kernels which are combined with multiple kernel learning.

WLZ (Li and Zou, 2017) build an ensemble of single-feature SVMs fed into a multi-layer perceptron (MLP), which is a meta-classifier trained on the outputs of the base SVM classifiers. The single features are based on lexical and syntactic information and the best submission includes character, word, stem, and function word n-grams as well as syntactic dependencies.

Uvic-NLP (Chan et al., 2017) trained a single SVM model on word n-grams (1–3) and character n-grams (4-5). They also conducted several post-evaluation experiments, improving their results to 0.8730 using an LDA meta-classifier trained on individual SVM classifiers.

ETRI-SLP (Oh et al., 2017) designed a system that was based on word n-gram features (with n ranging from 1 to 3) and character n-gram features (with n ranging from 4 to 6). The normalized count vectors based on these features were used to extract LSA features, which were then reduced using LDA. The count and LSA-LDA features were used to train SVM and DNN classifiers whose outputs were subsequently combined via late fusion in a DNN-based ensemble classifier.

CEMI (Ircing et al., 2017) use a Logistic Regression meta-classifier to achieve their best essay-only results. The meta-classifier is trained on the outputs of several base classifiers, which are trained on TF-IDF weighted word unigrams, word bigrams, character n-grams and POS n-grams.

RUG-SU (Bjerva et al., 2017) primarily focus on applying neural network models to NLI. Several systems are trained: A deep residual network based on word unigrams and character n-grams; a sentence-level LSTM based on POS-tagged sentences; a Logistic Regression model based on spelling error features; and a CBOW model based on document embeddings. Their best result is achieved by an ensemble combining these systems together with an SVM meta-classifier. Spelling error features did not improve overall performance.

Rank	Team	F1	Acc.	Approach
1	ItaliaNLP Lab	0.8818	0.8818	Stacked classifier w/ lexical and syntactic features
1	CIC-FBK	0.8808	0.8809	SVM with log-entropy weighted n-gram and syntactic features
1	Groningen	0.8756	0.8755	Linear SVM with character n-grams (1-9)
1	NRC	0.8740	0.8736	Voting ensemble w/ SVM models using lexical/syntactic features
1	tubasfs	0.8716	0.8718	SVM trained on word bigrams and char 7-grams
1	UnibucKernel	0.8695	0.8691	Character-level string kernels combined w/ multiple kernel learning
1	WLZ	0.8654	0.8655	MLP meta-classifier trained on SVMs w/ lexical/syntactic features
2	Uvic-NLP	0.8633	0.8636	SVM trained on word and character n-grams
2	ETRI-SLP	0.8601	0.8600	Ensemble of SVMs & DNNs using LSA-LDA features
2	CEMI	0.8536	0.8536	LogReg meta-classifier trained on word/char/POS base models
3	RUG-SU	0.8323	0.8318	Ensemble of resnets, LSTM and document embeddings
3	NLI-ISU	0.8264	0.8264	Logistic Regression model with word n-grams (1-3)
3	IUCL	0.8262	0.8264	Phonetic features combined in an SVM
3	GadjahMada	0.8107	0.8110	Char embeddings w/ a feed-forward NN classifier
4	superliuxz	0.7896	0.7900	No paper submitted.
4	ltl	0.7676	0.7673	No paper submitted.
5	ut.dsp	0.7609	0.7636	n-gram language models over characters (3-4) and words (1-2)
Word Unigram Baseline		0.7104	0.7109	Linear SVM trained on word unigrams
Random Baseline		0.0910	0.0910	Randomly select an L1

Table 1: Official results in the essay-only track. The official metric is the macro-averaged F1-score. Accuracy (Acc.) is also reported. Rankings are determined by statistical significance testing (see §3.1).

NLI-ISU (Vajjala and Banerjee, 2017) explored the use of n-grams and embeddings in their submissions. Their best run was a Logistic Regression model trained on word 1-3 grams. They also report that spell checking features, as well as word and document embeddings did not work well on the development data.

IUCL (Smiley and Kübler, 2017) investigated the use of phonetic features for the essay classification task based on the hypothesis that speakers from different L1 backgrounds may tend to use English words that match sounds in their own L1 more frequently than speakers from other L1 backgrounds. They explored three sets of phonetic features based on algorithms for fuzzy text matching (Soundex, Double Metaphone, and NYSIIS) as well as a set of features based on representations of the words using the CMU Pronouncing Dictionary. While none of these feature sets individually outperformed a system based on character n-grams, the addition of the Double Metaphone features to the character n-gram features led to a small performance improvement.

GadjahMada (Sari et al., 2017) apply a character embedding model with a feed-forward neural network classifier in the essay track. This is based on the relatively high performance of character n-grams in previous research. An embedding size of 25 was used with n-grams of length 2–5.

ut.dsp (Mohammadi et al., 2017) utilize n-gram language models over words and characters. For each L1, a language model over character 3- and 4-grams as well as word unigrams and bigrams is calculated and smoothing is applied. For each text in the test set, the probably of the whole text for all language models in each class is calculated and the class with the maximum probability is chosen as the predicted label. This approach does not involve any supervised learning.

4.2 Speech-only Track

The best speech-only submission for each team, along with rankings and other details, are listed in Table 4.2. Each team's best system is briefly described below, ordered by rankings.

Rank	Team	F1	Acc.	Approach
1	UnibucKernel	0.8755	0.8755	Character-level string kernels and i-vector features
1	ETRI-SLP	0.8664	0.8664	DNN ensemble with early fusion using LSA-LDA features
1	CEMI	0.8607	0.8609	Ensemble of transcript & i-vector features w/ softmax fusion
2	NRC	0.8448	0.8445	Single models trained on transcript char 6-grams and i-vectors
2	tubasfs	0.8333	0.8336	LDA classifier using only i-vector features
Baseline: transcript + i-vector		0.7980	0.7982	Linear SVM trained on word unigrams (transcripts) + i-vectors
Baseline: transcript only		0.5435	0.5464	Linear SVM trained on word unigrams (transcripts)
3	GadjahMada	0.5084	0.5073	FFNN classifier trained on character embeddings (transcripts)
4	ut.dsp	0.4530	0.4536	n-gram language models over transcript characters & words
4	NLI-ISU	0.4259	0.4282	Logistic Regression model w/ word n-grams (1-3) on transcripts
5	ltl	0.3714	0.3718	No paper submitted.
Random Baseline		0.0910	0.0910	Randomly select an L1

Table 2: Official results in the speech-only track. The official metric is the macro-averaged F1-score. Accuracy (Acc.) is also reported. Rankings are determined by statistical significance testing (see §3.1).

UnibucKernel (Ionescu and Popescu, 2017) extend their essay-only system based on character-level string kernels to include the transcription data, as well as an additional kernel for the i-vector features. The various models are combined using multiple kernel learning.

ETRI-SLP (Oh et al., 2017) submitted a system for the Speech task that was similar to their submission for the Essay task, although the SVM classifiers and one of the DNN classifiers were not used in the ensemble classifier. They experimented with both late fusion and early fusion for combining the text-based features with the i-vectors and obtained the best results with an early fusion ensemble classifier.

CEMI (Ircing et al., 2017) attained their best result with an ensemble consisting of a SGD classifier trained on transcript word features and a feedforward neural network trained on the i-vector features. The final prediction is selected via softmax combination.

NRC (Goutte and Léger, 2017) use a single classifier trained on transcript character 6-grams and the i-vector features to achieve their best speech-only results.

tubasfs (Rama and Çöltekin, 2017) used an LDA classifier using only the i-vector features, a simple approach that yielded good results.

GadjahMada (Sari et al., 2017) did not use the i-vector features for the speech track, applying their character embedding model from the essay track to the transcripts.

ut.dsp (Mohammadi et al., 2017) apply their n-gram language model from the essay-only track to the transcripts.

NLI-ISU (Vajjala and Banerjee, 2017) did not use the i-vector features for the speech track, instead applying their n-gram based model from the essay track. They report that the essay features do not work very well for transcripts, hypothesizing that this may be due to the shorter texts.

4.3 Fusion Track

The best fusion submission for each team, along with rankings and other details, are listed in Table 4.3. Each team's best system is briefly described below, ordered by rankings.

UnibucKernel (Ionescu and Popescu, 2017) extend their speech system to also include essays, in addition to the transcripts and i-vectors. The models are combined via multiple kernel learning.

CEMI (Ircing et al., 2017) obtain their best results using a neural network based meta-classifier. They use several isolated feed-forward neural network models, each trained on one feature type. Features include word, character, and POS n-grams (from transcripts/essays) plus i-vectors. The outputs from the networks are fused using softmax combination to predict the final label.

Rank	Team	F1	Acc.	Approach
1	UnibucKernel	0.9319	0.9318	Character-level string kernels and i-vector features
1	CEMI	0.9257	0.9255	NN meta-classifier over lexical/syntactic/i-vector features
1	ETRI-SLP	0.9220	0.9218	DNN ensemble with early fusion using LSA-LDA features
1	NRC	0.9193	0.9191	Voting ensemble w/ half sampling to choose the SVM models
2	tubasfs	0.9175	0.9173	Ensemble w/ word/char n-grams (essay/transcript) & i-vectors
3	GadjahMada	0.8414	0.8409	FFNN trained on essay character embeddings and i-vectors
3	L2F	0.8377	0.8391	BPE n-grams, NN fusion, i-vector post-processing
3	ZCD	0.8358	0.8355	Ensemble of word/char. n-gram and i-vector SVM classifiers
Baseline: essay/transcript/i-vector		0.7901	0.7909	SVM trained on word unigrams (essay/transcript) + i-vectors
Baseline: Essay + Transcript		0.7786	0.7791	Linear SVM trained on word unigrams (essays + transcripts)
4	ut.dsp	0.7748	0.7764	n-gram language models over chars/words (essay+transcript)
5	ltl	0.7346	0.7345	No paper submitted.
Random Baseline		0.0910	0.0910	Randomly select an L1

Table 3: Official results in the fusion track. The official metric is the macro-averaged F1-score. Accuracy (Acc.) is also reported. Team rankings are determined by statistical significance testing (see §3.1).

ETRI-SLP (Oh et al., 2017) submitted a system for the Fusion task that was similar to their submissions for the Essay and Speech tasks, although the SVM and DNN classifiers were not used in the ensemble classifier; their ensemble classifier for the fusion task only combined the LSA-LDA features and the i-vectors. As with the Speech task, they experimented with both late fusion and early fusion for combining the text-based features with the i-vectors and obtained the best results with an early-fusion ensemble classifier.

NRC (Goutte and Léger, 2017) explored various ways of building ensemble models to make the final prediction. Relatively simple features were used (character, word, and POS n-grams). For the fusion track, their best submission used *half sampling* which uses one half of the data to estimate the best number of models to include in the final voting ensemble, and the other half to estimate which models to include.

tubasfs (Rama and Çöltekin, 2017) obtain their best result with an ensemble model based on mean probability combination. The ensemble includes individual SVM models trained on word and character n-grams from essays and transcripts, and an LDA classifier trained on the i-vector features.

GadjahMada (Sari et al., 2017) extended their essay-based character embedding model to include i-vectors for the fusion track. They did not use the speech transcript data.

L2F (Kepler et al., 2017) designed a system that combined three types of text-based classifiers (an RNN with a bidirectional GRU layer, a Naive Bayes classifier with byte n-grams, and a Naive Bayes classifier with n-grams based on representations of the words using Byte Pair Encoding) with versions of the i-vector features that were post-processed using centering and whitening in an attempt to reduce channel variability. These classifiers were combined together in a Neural Network fusion approach and the authors demonstrated that the i-vector features were the main driver of performance.

ZCD (Zampieri et al., 2017a) used an approach based on ensembles of multiple SVM classifiers. Separate SVM classifiers were trained using character n-grams (with n ranging from 1 to 10) and word n-grams (with n ranging from 1 to 2). Individual classifiers with cross-validation performance lower than 0.8 were retained in the ensemble; the classifiers that were retained were based on character n-grams with n in $6, 7, 8$. These n-gram-based classifiers were then combined into an ensemble with a classifier based on the i-vector features and the majority vote from the ensemble was taken as the final prediction.

ut.dsp (Mohammadi et al., 2017) apply their n-gram language model from the essay-only track to the combination of essays and transcripts.

5 Discussion and Analysis

In this section we synthesize the overarching findings from this edition of the NLI shared task.

5.1 Primary Trends

Multiple Classifier Systems are very effective. Almost all of the top ranked teams employed some type of multiple classifier system, including meta-classifiers (classifier stacking), ensemble combination methods (voting and probability based fusion), and multiple kernel learning. Their use has become much more prevalent compared to the previous shared task.

Lexical n-grams are the best single feature type. Surface form features such as word and character n-grams continue to be the powerhouse feature for the text classification tasks. Evidence from various participants suggests that high-order character n-grams (as high as $n = 10$) are extremely useful for this task. This is likely because when extracted across word boundaries, these features capture not only sub-word (*e.g.* morphological) information, but also dependencies between words. However, it should also be noted that the top systems in all tracks made use of syntactic features which can give them a slight performance boost. This is not surprising as it has been shown that lexical and syntactic features each capture diverse types of information that are complementary (Malmasi and Cahill, 2015).

Feature weighting schemes are important. Similar to past results, many of the top teams apply a form of feature weighting (such as TF-IDF or log-entropy) to their data.

Acoustic features are highly informative for speech-based NLI. Using only text-based features over the transcripts did not work well, and teams that did not utilize the i-vector features performed much worse in the speech-only track. The top-ranked teams combined the transcripts and i-vectors.

Speech transcript features did not perform well. Teams that used only the transcript features did not fare well in the speech track. This could be due to the different types of linguistic phenomena that are present in spontaneous speech, which may be less informative than those found in the essays.

Various teams also hypothesize that this may potentially be due to their relatively shorter lengths compared to the essays (see §3 for stats).

Fusion of writing and speech features provides the best results. The substantial performance increase between the essay/speech tracks and the fusion track indicates that the acoustic features are complementary and lead to much more reliable results.

Traditional classifier models continue to dominate text classification tasks. It has been noted that traditional supervised learning models outperform newer deep learning approaches on high-dimensional text classification tasks (Malmasi et al., 2016, §6.2). The results from this NLI task do not provide any evidence to suggest otherwise; almost all of the top teams in the essay-only track used an SVM or similar linear model. Uvic-NLP (Chan et al., 2017) compared SVMs and neural network models, finding that SVM models achieve better results with shorter training times.

Average performance is much higher than 2013. Although much of the training data remains the same, the submissions were much more competitive than the first NLI shared tasks. This is likely due to NLI being a much more established task, as well as the aforementioned prevalence of more sophisticated models such as meta-classifiers.

A number of open questions remain. For example, it is not clear if any one approach is dominant across all tracks as most of the top-ranked teams in the essay track did not participate in the other tracks. It is hard to say how well their systems would have done in the other tracks, but the trends from the teams who did participate in all tracks suggest that their approaches could have done well.

It is also clear that ensemble-based systems attain some of the best results, but while we note that meta-classifiers were particularly popular, it is difficult to draw conclusions about the best approach as most teams used different configurations (*e.g.* different base classifiers and meta-classifier models). A comprehensive and detailed study is needed to provide an empirical comparison of the different methods.

	2013	2017		
		Essay	**Speech**	**Fusion**
# Systems	29	17	9	10
Shared Task Best	0.8359	0.8818	0.8755	0.9319
Oracle	0.9791	0.9628	0.9572	0.9809
Accuracy@3	0.9555	0.9592	0.9508	0.9764
Accuracy@2	0.9218	0.9501	0.9290	0.9700
Plurality Vote	0.8425	0.8793	0.8508	0.9319

Table 4: Oracle results on the NLI 2013 and 2017 shared task systems. The ensemble includes each team's best system in each track. Results are reported as the macro-averaged F1-score.

5.2 Ensemble Analysis

One interesting research question is to measure the upper-bound on accuracy for this year's task. This can be measured by treating each team's best submission as an independent system, and combining the results using ensemble methods such as a plurality vote or an oracle. This type of analysis has previously been applied to the NLI 2013 task and shown to be helpful in other work (Malmasi et al., 2015). Following the approach of Malmasi et al. (2015), we apply the following combination methods to the 2017 data.

Plurality Voting: This is the standard combination strategy that selects the label with the highest number of votes, regardless of the overall percentage of votes it received (Polikar, 2006). This differs from a *majority* vote combiner where a label must obtain over 50% of the votes.

Oracle: An oracle is a type of fusion method that assigns the correct class label for an instance if *any* of the classifiers in the ensemble produces the correct label for that data point. This method has previously been used to analyze the limits of majority vote classifier combination (Kuncheva et al., 2001). It can help quantify the *potential* upper limit of an ensemble's performance on the given data and how this performance varies with different ensemble configurations and combinations.

Accuracy@N: To account for the possibility that a classifier may randomly predict the correct label (with a probability determined by the random baseline) and thus exaggerate the oracle score, an Accuracy@N combiner has been proposed (Malmasi et al., 2015). This method is inspired by the "Precision at k" metric from Information Retrieval (Manning et al., 2008) which measures precision at fixed low levels of results (*e.g.* the top 10 re-

sults). Here, it is an extension of the Plurality vote combiner where instead of selecting the label with the highest votes, the labels are ranked by their vote counts and a sample is correctly classified if the true label is in the top N ranked candidates.[4] Another way to view it is as a more restricted version of the Oracle combiner that is limited to the top N ranked candidates in order to minimize the influence of a single classifier having chosen the correct label by chance. In this study we experiment with $N = 2$ and 3. We also note that setting $N = 1$ is the same as the Plurality voting method.

We applied the above combiners to all three tracks in the NLI 2017 task. The results are presented in Table 4. The results for each track are compared against the best system in the shared task. The equivalent results from the NLI 2013 shared task are also included for comparison.

We note that the 2017 oracle performance is similar to that of 2013, despite having fewer systems. The Accuracy@2 results are also substantially higher. Another difference in 2017 is that the voting ensemble did not outperform the single best system in any track, which was the case in 2013. Taken together, these trends seem to suggest that the 2017 entries were more accurate, rather than the test set being easier to classify (in which case we would have expected higher oracle results).

Results from the Accuracy@2 combiner show that a great majority of the texts are close to being correctly classified: this value is significantly higher than the plurality combiner and not much lower than the oracle itself. This shows that the correct label receives a significant portion of the votes, and when not the winning label, it is often the runner-up.

---

[4]In case of ties we choose randomly from the labels with the highest number of votes.

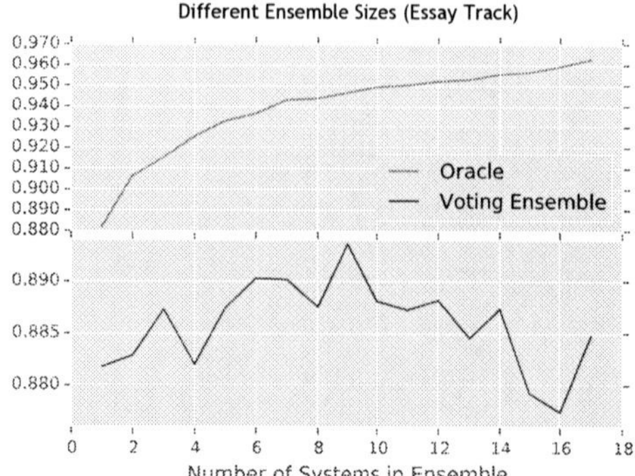

Figure 2: Results (macro-F1) for ensembles of different sizes using each team's best system in the Essay track. Systems are added according to their absolute rank. Oracle combination (top) and plurality voting (bottom) are shown.

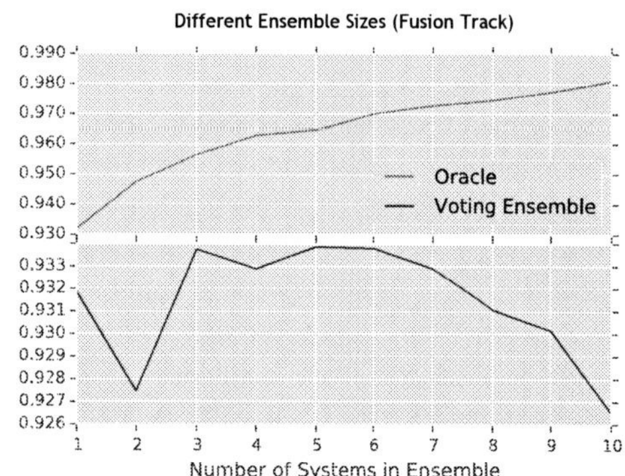

Figure 3: Results (macro-F1) for creating ensembles of different sizes using each team's best submission in the Fusion track. Systems are added according to their absolute rank. Oracle combination (top) and plurality voting (bottom) are shown.

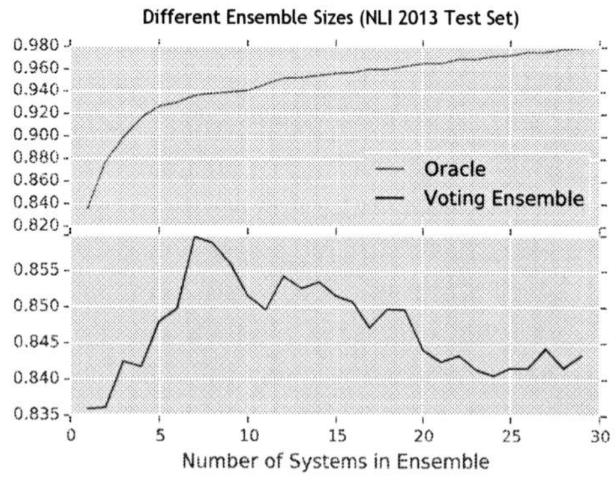

Figure 4: Results (macro-F1) for ensembles of different sizes using each team's best system in the NLI Shared Task 2013 (test set). Systems are added in order of their rank. Oracle combination (top) and plurality voting (bottom) are shown.

It is also evident that the results for the fusion track are much higher, again highlighting the utility of combining multiple modalities for NLI.

In addition to using each team's best system, We also experimented with creating ensembles of different sizes. For each track we created N ensembles $E_1 \ldots E_N$, with N being the number of systems in that track. Each ensemble E_n contains the top n systems in the given track, so that the first ensemble contains only the top system, the second contains the top two systems, and so on, with the final ensemble containing every team's system.

This analysis enables us to assess the ensemble performance as more predictions are added. The results for the Oracle and Plurality Vote ensembles in the essay and fusion tracks are shown in Figure 2 and Figure 3. For comparison we also include the ensemble combinations generated from the 2013 test set, as shown in Figure 4.

For both tracks we observe that oracle accuracy increases as more systems are added, which is to be expected. For voting combination, performance increases as the top systems are added, but then begins to drop off as errors are introduced from the less accurate systems. This suggests that it might be possible to develop a system that performs slightly better than the top-ranked system.

On balance, the analysis presented in this section suggests that it will be challenging to develop NLI systems that attain statistically significant gains on this data.

6 Conclusion and Future Work

We presented the results of the NLI Shared Task 2017. This edition of the task introduced the use of transcriptions and i-vector features for speech-based NLI, as well the as the fusion task which jointly uses the spoken and written responses.

The task attracted strong participation with 19 entrants, many of whom developed systems that built on recent research in the field. The fusion track demonstrated that the combination of the written and spoken response can provide a substantial boost in classification accuracy. Multiple classifier systems (such as ensembles and meta-classifiers) were the most effective across all tracks. Mainly using lexical and syntactic features, models were mostly based on traditional classification methods (*e.g.* SVMs) which were not outperformed by deep learning approaches. Taken together, their results have generated a number of new insights for this task, and serve as a building block for future work. The results obtained here will also provide an important benchmark for assessing future results.

There are a number of avenues for future NLI research. Although we were not able to include the raw audio data in this task, its inclusion in the speech and fusion tasks could be an interesting addition. The expansion of the L1 classes to include a larger number of linguistically diverse languages can also be insightful. Most NLI research to date has been limited to approximately a dozen languages, so it is not clear how these systems will fare as the number of classes increases.

The relatively low performance of transcription-based features also merits further investigation. A first step would be to assess whether the primary issue is related to the shorter lengths of the texts. This hypothesis can be tested by obtaining transcripts of longer spoken responses, or even artificially creating longer texts by concatenating the existing data.

Finally, the essay-based NLI results obtained on English L2 data have been replicated on a range of other languages (Malmasi and Dras, 2015). It would be interesting to see to what degree the speech-based NLI methodologies would work on other languages. The paucity of spoken responses from learners of languages other than English makes this a challenging research question.

References

Alberto Abad, Eugénio Ribeiro, Fábio Kepler, Ramon Astudillo, and Isabel Trancoso. 2011. Exploiting phone log-likelihood ratio features for the detection of the native language of non-native english speakers. In *Proceedings of Interspeech*. San Francisco, USA, pages 2413–2417.

Johannes Bjerva, Gintarė Grigonytė, Robert Östling, and Barbara Plank. 2017. Neural Networks and Spelling Features for Native Language Identification. In *Proceedings of the 12th Workshop on Building Educational Applications Using NLP*. Association for Computational Linguistics, Copenhagen, Denmark.

Daniel Blanchard, Joel Tetreault, Derrick Higgins, Aoife Cahill, and Martin Chodorow. 2013. TOEFL11: A Corpus of Non-Native English. Technical report, Educational Testing Service.

Serhiy Bykh and Detmar Meurers. 2014. Exploring Syntactic Features for Native Language Identification: A Variationist Perspective on Feature Encoding and Ensemble Optimization. In *Proceedings of COLING 2014, the 25th International Conference on Computational Linguistics: Technical Papers*. Dublin, Ireland, pages 1962–1973.

Sophia Chan, Maryam Honari Jahromi, Benjamin Benetti, Aazim Lakhani, and Alona Fyshe. 2017. Ensemble Methods for Native Language Identification. In *Proceedings of the 12th Workshop on Building Educational Applications Using NLP*. Association for Computational Linguistics, Copenhagen, Denmark.

Andrea Cimino and Felice Dell'Orletta. 2017. Stacked Sentence-Document Classifier Approach for Improving Native Language Identification. In *Proceedings of the 12th Workshop on Building Educational Applications Using NLP*. Association for Computational Linguistics, Copenhagen, Denmark.

Najim Dehak, Pedro A Torres-Carrasquillo, Douglas Reynolds, and Reda Dehak. 2011. Language recognition via i-vectors and dimensionality reduction. In *Twelfth Annual Conference of the International Speech Communication Association*.

Dominique Estival, Tanja Gaustad, Son Bao Pham, Will Radford, and Ben Hutchinson. 2007. Author profiling for English emails. In *Proceedings of the 10th Conference of the Pacific Association for Computational Linguistics*. Melbourne, Australia, pages 263–272.

Asmaa Etman and A. A. Louis Beex. 2015. Language and Dialect Identification: A survey. In *SAI Intelligent Systems Conference*. London, UK, pages 220–231.

J. Gibbons. 2003. *Forensic Linguistics: An Introduction to Language in the Justice System.*.

Cyril Goutte and Serge Léger. 2017. Exploring Optimal Voting in Native Language Identification. In *Proceedings of the 12th Workshop on Building Educational Applications Using NLP*. Association for Computational Linguistics, Copenhagen, Denmark.

Radu Tudor Ionescu and Marius Popescu. 2017. Can string kernels pass the test of time in Native Language Identification? In *Proceedings of the 12th Workshop on Building Educational Applications Using NLP*. Association for Computational Linguistics, Copenhagen, Denmark.

Radu Tudor Ionescu, Marius Popescu, and Aoife Cahill. 2014. Can characters reveal your native language? A language-independent approach to native language identification. In *Proceedings of the 2014 Conference on Empirical Methods in Natural Language Processing (EMNLP)*. Association for Computational Linguistics.

Pavel Ircing, Jan Švec, Zbyněk Zajíc, Barbora Hladká, and Martin Holub. 2017. Combining Textual and Speech Features in the NLI Task Using State-of-the-Art Machine Learning Techniques. In *Proceedings of the 12th Workshop on Building Educational Applications Using NLP*. Association for Computational Linguistics, Copenhagen, Denmark.

Scott Jarvis, Yves Bestgen, and Steve Pepper. 2013. Maximizing Classification Accuracy in Native Language Identification. In *Proceedings of the Eighth Workshop on Innovative Use of NLP for Building Educational Applications*. Association for Computational Linguistics, Atlanta, Georgia, pages 111–118.

Fabio N. Kepler, Ramon F. Astudillo, and Alberto Abad. 2017. Fusion of Simple Models for Native Language Identification. In *Proceedings of the 12th Workshop on Building Educational Applications Using NLP*. Association for Computational Linguistics, Copenhagen, Denmark.

Moshe Koppel, Jonathan Schler, and Kfir Zigdon. 2005. Automatically determining an anonymous author's native language. *Intelligence and Security Informatics* pages 41–76.

Artur Kulmizev, Bo Blankers, Johannes Bjerva, Malvina Nissim, Gertjan van Noord, Barbara Plank, and Martijn Wieling. 2017. The Power of Character N-grams in Native Language Identification. In *Proceedings of the 12th Workshop on Building Educational Applications Using NLP*. Association for Computational Linguistics, Copenhagen, Denmark.

Ludmila I Kuncheva, James C Bezdek, and Robert PW Duin. 2001. Decision templates for multiple classifier fusion: an experimental comparison. *Pattern Recognition* 34(2):299–314.

Wen Li and Liang Zou. 2017. Classifier Stacking for Native Language Identification. In *Proceedings of the 12th Workshop on Building Educational Applications Using NLP*. Association for Computational Linguistics, Copenhagen, Denmark.

Shervin Malmasi. 2016. *Native Language Identification: Explorations and Applications*. Ph.D. thesis. http://hdl.handle.net/1959.14/1110919.

Shervin Malmasi and Aoife Cahill. 2015. Measuring Feature Diversity in Native Language Identification. In *Proceedings of the Tenth Workshop on Innovative Use of NLP for Building Educational Applications*. Association for Computational Linguistics, Denver, Colorado, pages 49–55. http://aclweb.org/anthology/W15-0606.

Shervin Malmasi and Mark Dras. 2014. Language Transfer Hypotheses with Linear SVM Weights. In *Proceedings of the 2014 Conference on Empirical Methods in Natural Language Processing (EMNLP)*. Association for Computational Linguistics, Doha, Qatar, pages 1385–1390. http://aclweb.org/anthology/D14-1144.

Shervin Malmasi and Mark Dras. 2015. Multilingual Native Language Identification. In *Natural Language Engineering*.

Shervin Malmasi and Mark Dras. 2017. Native Language Identification using Stacked Generalization. *arXiv preprint arXiv:1703.06541* .

Shervin Malmasi, Mark Dras, Mark Johnson, Lan Du, and Magdalena Wolska. 2017. Unsupervised Text Segmentation Based on Native Language Characteristics. In *Proceedings of the 55th Annual Meeting of the Association for Computational Linguistics (ACL 2017)*. Vancouver, Canada.

Shervin Malmasi, Joel Tetreault, and Mark Dras. 2015. Oracle and Human Baselines for Native Language Identification. In *Proceedings of the 10th BEA workshop*. pages 172–178.

Shervin Malmasi, Marcos Zampieri, Nikola Ljubešić, Preslav Nakov, Ahmed Ali, and Jörg Tiedemann. 2016. Discriminating between Similar Languages and Arabic Dialect Identification: A Report on the Third DSL Shared Task. In *Proceedings of the VarDial Workshop*. Osaka, Japan.

Christopher D Manning. 2015. Computational linguistics and deep learning. *Computational Linguistics* 41(4):701–707.

Christopher D Manning, Prabhakar Raghavan, and Hinrich Schütze. 2008. Evaluation in information retrieval. In *Introduction to Information Retrieval*, Cambridge university press Cambridge, pages 151–175.

Ilia Markov, Lingzhen Chen, Carlo Strapparava, and Grigori Sidorov. 2017. CIC-FBK Approach to Native Language Identification. In *Proceedings of the 12th Workshop on Building Educational Applications Using NLP*. Association for Computational Linguistics, Copenhagen, Denmark.

David Martınez, Oldrich Plchot, Lukás Burget, Ondrej Glembek, and Pavel Matejka. 2011. Language recognition in ivectors space. In *Proceedings of Interspeech*. Firenze, Italy, pages 861–864.

Elham Mohammadi, Hadi Veisi, and Hessam Amini. 2017. Native Language Identification Using a Mixture of Character and Word N-grams. In *Proceedings of the 12th Workshop on Building Educational Applications Using NLP*. Association for Computational Linguistics, Copenhagen, Denmark.

Yoo Rhee Oh, Hyung-Bae Jeon, Hwa Jeon Song, Yun-Kyung Lee, Jeon-Gue Park, and Yun-Keun Lee. 2017. A deep-learning based native-language classification by using a latent semantic analysis for the NLI Shared Task 2017. In *Proceedings of the 12th Workshop on Building Educational Applications Using NLP*. Association for Computational Linguistics, Copenhagen, Denmark.

Robi Polikar. 2006. Ensemble based systems in decision making. *Circuits and systems magazine, IEEE* 6(3):21–45.

Taraka Rama and Çağrı Çöltekin. 2017. Fewer features perform well at Native Language Identification task. In *Proceedings of the 12th Workshop on Building Educational Applications Using NLP*. Association for Computational Linguistics, Copenhagen, Denmark.

K. Sreenivasa Rao and Dipanjan Nandi. 2015. Language identificationa brief review. In Wim Kouwenhoven, editor, *Language Identification Using Excitation Source Features*, Springe, chapter 2, pages 11–30.

Alla Rozovskaya and Dan Roth. 2011. Algorithm selection and model adaptation for esl correction tasks. In *Proceedings of the 49th Annual Meeting of the Association for Computational Linguistics: Human Language Technologies*. Association for Computational Linguistics, Portland, Oregon, USA, pages 924–933. http://www.aclweb.org/anthology/P11-1093.

Yunita Sari, Muhammad Rifqi Fatchurrahman, and Meisyarah Dwiastuti. 2017. A Shallow Neural Network for Native Language Identification with Character N-grams. In *Proceedings of the 12th Workshop on Building Educational Applications Using NLP*. Association for Computational Linguistics, Copenhagen, Denmark.

Björn Schuller, Stefan Steidl, Anton Batliner, Julia Hirschberg, Judee K. Burgoon, Alice Baird, Aaron Elkins, Yue Zhang, Eduardo Coutinho, and Keelan Evanini. 2016. The INTERSPEECH 2016 Computational Paralinguistics Challenge: Deception, Sincerity & Native Language. In *Interspeech 2016*. pages 2001–2005. https://doi.org/10.21437/Interspeech.2016-129.

Charese Smiley and Sandra Kübler. 2017. Native Language Identification using Phonetic Algorithms. In *Proceedings of the 12th Workshop on Building Educational Applications Using NLP*. Association for Computational Linguistics, Copenhagen, Denmark.

Joel Tetreault, Daniel Blanchard, and Aoife Cahill. 2013. A report on the first native language identification shared task. In *Proceedings of the Eighth Workshop on Innovative Use of NLP for Building Educational Applications*. Association for Computational Linguistics, Atlanta, GA, USA.

Joel Tetreault, Daniel Blanchard, Aoife Cahill, and Martin Chodorow. 2012. Native tongues, lost and found: Resources and empirical evaluations in native language identification. In *Proceedings of COLING 2012*. The COLING 2012 Organizing Committee, Mumbai, India, pages 2585–2602. http://www.aclweb.org/anthology/C12-1158.

Laura Mayfield Tomokiyo and Rosie Jones. 2001. You're not from 'Round here, are you?: Naive Bayes detection of Non-native utterance text. In *Proceedings of the second meeting of the North American Chapter of the ACL (NAACL)*. Association for Computational Linguistics, Pittsburgh, PA.

Oren Tsur and Ari Rappoport. 2007. Using Classifier Features for Studying the Effect of Native Language on the Choice of Written Second Language Words. In *Proceedings of the Workshop on Cognitive Aspects of Computational Language Acquisition*. Association for Computational Linguistics, Prague, Czech Republic, pages 9–16. http://www.aclweb.org/anthology/W/W07/W07-0602.

Sowmya Vajjala and Sagnik Banerjee. 2017. A study of N-gram and Embedding Representations for Native Language Identification. In *Proceedings of the 12th Workshop on Building Educational Applications Using NLP*. Association for Computational Linguistics, Copenhagen, Denmark.

Sze-Meng Jojo Wong and Mark Dras. 2009. Contrastive Analysis and Native Language Identification. In *Proceedings of the Australasian Language Technology Association Workshop 2009*. Sydney, Australia, pages 53–61. http://www.aclweb.org/anthology/U09-1008.

Yiming Yang and Xin Liu. 1999. A re-examination of text categorization methods. In *Proceedings of the 22nd annual international ACM SIGIR conference on Research and development in information retrieval*. ACM, pages 42–49.

Marcos Zampieri, Alina Maria Ciobanu, and Liviu P. Dinu. 2017a. Native Language Identification on Text and Speech. In *Proceedings of the 12th Workshop on Building Educational Applications Using NLP*. Association for Computational Linguistics, Copenhagen, Denmark.

Marcos Zampieri, Shervin Malmasi, Nikola Ljubešić, Preslav Nakov, Ahmed Ali, Jörg Tiedemann, Yves Scherrer, and Noëmi Aepli. 2017b. Findings of the VarDial Evaluation Campaign 2017. In *Proceedings of the Fourth Workshop on NLP for Similar Languages, Varieties and Dialects (VarDial)*. Valencia, Spain, pages 1–15.

Marc Zissman. 1996. Comparison of four approaches to automatic language identification of telephone speech. *IEEE Transactions on Speech and Audio Processing* 4(1):31–44.

Evaluation of Automatically Generated Pronoun Reference Questions

Arief Yudha Satria and **Takenobu Tokunaga**
School of Computing
Tokyo Institute of Technology
152-8550 Tokyo, Meguro, Ôokayama, 2-12-1, Japan
satria.a.aa@m.titech.ac.jp   take@c.titech.ac.jp

Abstract

This study provides a detailed analysis of evaluation of English pronoun reference questions which are created automatically by machine. Pronoun reference questions are multiple choice questions that ask test takers to choose an antecedent of a target pronoun in a reading passage from four options. The evaluation was performed from two perspectives: the perspective of English teachers and that of English learners. Item analysis suggests that machine-generated questions achieve comparable quality with human-made questions. Correlation analysis revealed a strong correlation between the scores of machine-generated questions and that of human-made questions.

1 Introduction

Asking questions has been widely used as a method to assess the effectiveness of teaching and learning activities. By asking questions, teachers can get feedback whether students understand about the teaching materials. In this context, creating questions becomes an important task in teaching and learning activities. Questions are usually made by human experts, which demands manual efforts; thus it is time-consuming and expensive. Automatic question generation is a solution to solve this problem.

Several past studies worked on various kinds of automatic question generation. Heilman and Smith (2009) worked on the automatic question generation for the purpose of reading comprehension assessment and practice. Liu and Calvo (2012) worked on the automatic generation of trigger questions (directive and facilitative) for supporting writing activities. Chali and Hasan (2015)

worked on the automatic generation of all possible questions given a topic of interest. Serban et al. (2016) worked on the automatic generation of questions about an image.

Research on automatic question generation has been active, yet there are few studies which elaborate the detailed evaluation process and in-depth analysis of the machine-generated questions. QG-STEC 2010 is the first shared task about question generation that comprises two subtasks: question generation from paragraphs and question generation from sentences (Rus et al., 2010). Human judges were utilised to evaluate question quality by considering five criteria: syntactic correctness and fluency, question type, relevance, ambiguity, and variety.

Liu and Calvo (2012) evaluated their trigger question generation system for academic writing support by comparing machine-generated trigger questions to human-made trigger questions based on five aspects: clarity, correctness, relevance, usefulness for learning concepts, and usefulness to improve the literature review documents. Twenty-three students were instructed to write essays and then to assess the trigger questions if these questions could improve their essays. Because the machine-generated trigger questions were created based on the collected student essays, their analysis showed that they were effective only for the collected student essays while the human-made trigger questions were effective for general essays as well as the collected essays.

Zhang and VanLehn (2016) employed students to rate machine-generated questions and human-made questions based on relevance, fluency, ambiguity, pedagogy and depth. Araki et al. (2016) evaluated their question generation system by judging the questions on three metrics: grammatical correctness, answer existence and inference steps.

Proceedings of the 12th Workshop on Innovative Use of NLP for Building Educational Applications, pages 76–85
Copenhagen, Denmark, September 8, 2017. ©2017 Association for Computational Linguistics

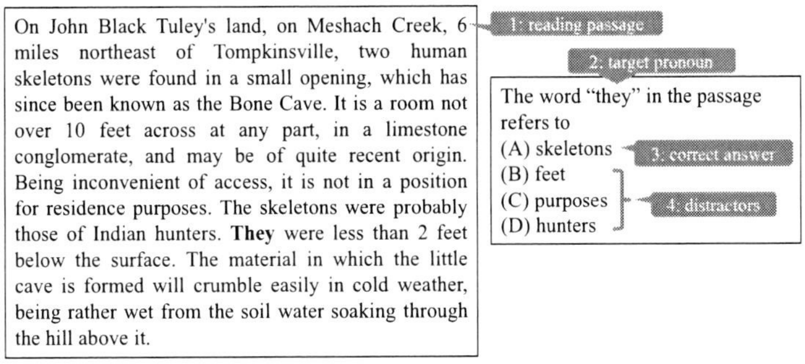
On John Black Tuley's land, on Meshach Creek, 6 miles northeast of Tompkinsville, two human skeletons were found in a small opening, which has since been known as the Bone Cave. It is a room not over 10 feet across at any part, in a limestone conglomerate, and may be of quite recent origin. Being inconvenient of access, it is not in a position for residence purposes. The skeletons were probably those of Indian hunters. **They** were less than 2 feet below the surface. The material in which the little cave is formed will crumble easily in cold weather, being rather wet from the soil water soaking through the hill above it.
1: reading passage
2: target pronoun
The word "they" in the passage refers to
(A) skeletons
(B) feet
(C) purposes
(D) hunters
3: correct answer
4: distractors

Figure 1: Example of pronoun reference question

Susanti et al. (2017) utilised English teachers and students to evaluate their question generation system. English teachers were asked to distinguish machine-generated questions from human-made questions apart. The English teachers also judged the questions on their usability in a real test and their difficulties using five scale rating. They also received suggestions to improve the questions from the English teachers. Furthermore, students were asked to answer the machine-generated questions and human-made questions; their answers were analysed using item analysis and the analysis based on Neural Test Theory (Shojima, 2007).

To sum up, the evaluation of automatic question generation systems in the past research was performed by utilising human judges and students. In this study, we provide detailed evaluation experiments and analysis of automatically generated pronoun reference questions. Pronoun reference questions consist of four components, i.e. a reading passage, a target pronoun, a correct answer, and three distractors as illustrated in Figure 1. We focus on pronoun reference questions because they measure the test taker's ability to resolve pronoun in reading passages. We argue that resolving pronoun is an important skill for reading comprehension.

The evaluation target of this study is the English pronoun reference questions generated by our system (Satria and Tokunaga, 2017). To the best of our knowledge, there is no other system for generating pronoun reference questions. The system generates questions from human-written texts by performing a sentence splitting technique on nonrestrictive relative clauses. The details of the question generation system are explained in Section 2. We evaluate the questions from two different perspectives following Susanti et al. (2017). The first perspective is from English teachers. We argue that English teachers have the ability to differentiate the good questions from the bad ones because creating questions is one of the teacher's responsibilities in the classroom; thus asking English teachers to judge the quality of machine-generated questions is reasonable. The second perspective is from English learners. Good questions can discriminate high proficiency learners from low proficiency learners. English learners were instructed to answer the questions and their responses were used for analysing the characteristics of the questions.

In what follows, we explain the automatic question generation system to be evaluated (Section 2), followed by the elaboration of the evaluation from the English teacher perspective (Section 3) and the English learner perspective (Section 4). We conclude the evaluation results and point out the possible future research direction (Section 5).

2 Generating pronoun reference questions

Pronoun reference questions such as in Figure 1 ask test takers to identify the antecedent of the target pronoun in the reading passage; thus the correct answer can be obtained by employing an anaphora resolution system to identify the antecedent of the target pronoun. Using this approach, the performance of the anaphora resolution system directly affects the quality of the generated questions. Since the performance of the state-of-the-arts anaphora resolution system is still insufficient to be employed for generating pronoun reference questions, we proposed to utilise nonrestrictive relative clauses to obtain pairs of the correct answer (antecedent) and the target pronoun (Satria and Tokunaga, 2017). The core idea of our method is transforming a sentence with a nonrestrictive relative clause into two sentences by applying a sentence splitting technique with replacing the relative pronoun with a personal pronoun. An assumption behind our method is that the antecedent identification of relative pronouns is relatively easier than that of personal pronouns because the antecedents of the relative pronouns appear in a restricted region in the sentence.

The system receives human-written texts from Project Gutenberg[1] that span several genres (i.e. science, technology and history) and produces question components based on the texts. The question generation process comprises four steps: correct answer generation, reading passage generation, target pronoun generation, and distractor generation.

The nonrestrictive relative clause is vital in our system because we transform human-written texts by applying the sentence splitting technique regarding nonrestrictive relative clauses to create the correct answer, the reading passage and the target pronoun. Nonrestrictive relative clauses are clauses that do not specify its modifying noun; they only give additional information to it instead. Thus, they can be detached from their main clauses. This property allows the sentence splitting technique to work most of the cases without changing the meaning of the texts.

There are cases, however, where the sentence splitting induces a change of text meaning, mostly due to the introduced pronoun refers to a different antecedent from that referred to by the relative pronoun in the original sentence. For instance, the text (2) is derived from the text (1) by extracting the nonrestrictive relative clause (underlined part) and replacing the relative pronoun "which" with a pronoun "it". The antecedent of "it" in the third sentence looks to be "legend", a subject in the previous sentence. But it should be "knowledge" in the previous sentence when we look at the original sentence where "which", the counterpart of "it" in (2), obviously refers to "knowledge". To exclude such spurious anaphora, we apply the Centering theory (Brennan et al., 1987; Grosz et al., 1995) to see the introduced pronoun refers to the same antecedent as in the original sentence. In this particular example, the Centering theory tells us that "legend" in the second sentence of (2) has a higher status than "knowledge" because the former is a

subject and the latter is an element in the prepositional phrase. Thus "legend" is a more probable antecedent of "it", which contradicts the original sentence of (1).

(1)   The church of S. Croce has seen another strange death of a Pope, that of Sylvester II. (999-1003), a Frenchman, Gerbert by name. A legend, related first by cardinal Benno in 1099, describes him as deep in necromantic **knowledge**, <u>which he had gathered during a journey through the Hispano-Arabic provinces.</u>

(2)   The church of S. Croce has seen another strange death of a Pope, that of Sylvester II. (999-1003), a Frenchman, Gerbert by name. A **legend**, related first by cardinal Benno in 1099, describes him as deep in necromantic **knowledge**. <u>He had gathered **it** during a journey through the Hispano-Arabic provinces.</u>

2.1   Correct answer generation

The identified antecedent of the relative pronoun is used as a correct answer. To identify the antecedent of the relative pronoun, we employed both lexical parser and dependency parser. The lexical parser produces a parse tree of the target sentence, i.e. a sentence that contains a nonrestrictive relative clause. The parse tree is traversed based on hand-made rules (Satria and Tokunaga, 2017) which consider the syntactic attachment and the linguistic feature, i.e. number. The dependency parser produces a set of dependencies which include the acl:relc[2] dependency relation. If only both results from the lexical parser together with hand-made rules and the dependency parser agree on the antecedent of the relative pronoun, the target sentence is further processed in the next steps. The system discards the target sentence which causes discordance on the antecedent of the relative pronoun.

2.2   Reading passage and target pronoun generation

We create a reading passage by splitting a sentence at a nonrestrictive relative clause. Sentence splitting divides the target sentence into two sentences: the main clause and the relative clause.

---

[1] https://www.gutenberg.org/

[2] http://universaldependencies.org/docs/en/dep/acl-relcl.html

Table 1: Example of the evaluation table filled by the evaluators

question	quality	reading passage	target pronoun	correct answer	distractors	comments
Q1	2	✓			✓	⋮
Q2	1			✓		⋮
⋮	⋮	⋮	⋮	⋮	⋮	⋮
Q60	3					⋮

When splitting the target sentence, the connection between two sentences must be maintained in order to retain the sentence meaning. The connection of those sentences is maintained through the target pronoun. The system creates the target pronoun by replacing the relative pronoun with a personal pronoun with considering linguistic features. Because the target pronoun resides in the reading passage, splitting target sentence and replacing the relative pronoun with the target pronoun complete the reading passage generation. For instance, the text (4) is derived from (3). The underlined non-restrictive relative clause in (3) is taken out into a separate sentence and placed after the main clause in (4). At the same time, the relative pronoun in the relative clause is replaced with the personal pronoun "they". We further confirm that the introduced pronoun "they" surely refers to the subject in the previous sentence regarding the Centering theory.

(3) The **flowers**, which are individually larger than those of the False Acacia, are of a beautiful rosy-pink, and produced in June and July.

(4) The **flowers** are of a beautiful rosy-pink, and produced in June and July. **They** are individually larger than those of the False Acacia.

2.3 Distractor generation

Distractor generation comprises the following three steps.

Candidate generation Since we restrict the antecedent of the pronoun, i.e. the correct answer, to a noun or a noun phrase, distractors must also be nouns or noun phrases. The part-of-speech tagger was employed to extract all nouns and noun phrases in the passage. The incompatible candidates on linguistic features are eliminated from the distractor candidates.

Coreference chain extraction A coreference chain consists of a list of expressions that refer to the same entity in a text. Thus, expressions in the same coreference chain with the correct answer are also a possible correct answer. Therefore, they are eliminated from the distractor candidates.

Candidate ranking Since we need only three distractors, the distractor candidates are ranked on the recency principle. Recently mentioned entities are likely to be maintained in human memory because they are still fresh; thus those entities are likely to be referred to by pronouns. More recently mentioned entities are ranked higher than the less recently mentioned entities. Finally, the three highest ranked candidates are selected as the distractors.

3 Evaluation from English teacher perspective

3.1 Experimental setting

We asked five English teachers[3] to evaluate the quality of 60 machine-generated questions by assigning a score of one, two or three to each question. The meaning of the scores is described below.

1. **problematic**, the question is not usable in a real test. Significant modifications are necessary for real use.

2. **acceptable but can be improved**, the question is usable in a real test as it is, but it can be further improved.

3. **acceptable**, the question has no problem to be used in a real test without any change.

If the question quality is judged to be one or two, the evaluators must further identify the problematic question components by checking

---

[3] They are non-native English speakers but the TESOL (http://www.tesol.org) certificate holders.

the corresponding columns as shown in Table 1. The evaluators leave the problematic components columns empty for acceptable quality questions. The evaluators may optionally give comments on problematic components or suggestions to improve the question quality.

Table 2: Distribution of pairwise disagreement

evaluator\score	{1,2}	{1,3}	{2,3}
(A, B)	7	4	28
(A, C)	2	7	14
(A, D)	4	6	24
(A, E)	2	8	20
(B, C)	1	1	28
(B, D)	1	0	28
(B, E)	3	4	30
(C, D)	1	0	27
(C, E)	4	3	22
(D, E)	1	5	19
total	26	38	240

Table 3: Distribution of rating

evaluator\score	1	2	3	total
A	10	18	32	60
B	1	35	24	60
C	1	20	39	60
D	0	18	42	60
E	6	16	38	60
total	18	107	175	300

3.2 Result and discussion

First, we investigated the agreement between the evaluators by computing the ordinal Krippendorff's alpha (Krippendorff, 1970); it was 0.05 indicating very low agreement between the evaluators. We further investigated the reason of the low agreement. We calculated the pairwise disagreement frequency between every pair of the evaluators as shown in Table 2. The table indicates that the disagreement between the judgement "acceptable but can be improved" and "acceptable" ($\{2, 3\}$) is dominant (80%). This fact suggests the decision on these two categories is highly subjective. Since they are both acceptable categories, we recalculated the Krippendorff's alpha after merging them into a single category to obtain the value 0.06. The average of the pairwise observation agreement was 0.89 after merging. Table 3 shows the distribution of scores judged by each evaluator. As the table shows, the highly skewed distribution of judgment can be considered as the main reason

of a very low alpha despite the fairly high observation agreement.

Table 4: Majority quality scores of 60 questions

majority score	frequency
1	0
2	12
3	39
tie	9
total	60

Table 4 shows the distribution of the quality score calculated by the majority principle. The majority principle means that when at least three evaluators rate a same value, that particular value is defined as the question quality score. Table 5 indicates that there are 39 questions (65%) which the majority of the evaluators rated "acceptable (3)". All nine tie cases get at most two "problematic" rating, i.e. the "problematic" can not be the majority. This means all generated questions were judged "usable in a real test" based on the majority principle.

Table 5: Average quality scores of 60 questions

average score	frequency
1.6	1
1.8	1
2.0	4
2.2	8
2.4	7
2.6	22
2.8	13
3.0	4
total	60

Table 5 summarises the average quality scores of five evaluators with their frequency. Even though the majority quality is the same, the actual rating may be different; thus it yields a different average quality. The question with the score 1.6 gets two ones and three twos. All evaluators agree that this particular question has an error in the correct answer. The question with the score 1.8 gets two ones, two twos and one three. Four evaluators agree that this particular question has an error in the correct answer.

Table 6 summarises the comments from the five evaluators with their frequency. The most common comments are related to the correct answer. This tendency is consistent with the component-wise evaluation of our past research (Satria and

Table 6: Evaluator's comments with frequency

comments	frequency
other option could be the correct answer	71
the reading passage is too long	28
the distractors do not distract	18
the distractors are too distracting	11
the reading passage offers little context	6
there are multiple correct answers	5
the reading passage has many technical word (i.e. too difficult)	4
the correct answer is too obvious	1
the target pronoun is inadequate	1

Tokunaga, 2017). We counted the number of questions with a checked cell in the "correct answer" column of the evaluation table (Table 1) to find 80 such cells in total. This number is roughly the same as that of the comments on correct answers. Among these 80 questions, 12 questions were rated 1 (problematic) and 68 were rated 2 (acceptable but can be improved). These cases suggest that the filtering with the Centering theory should be further improved.

4 Evaluation based on English learner perspective

The evaluation from the English learner perspective was conducted to evaluate the behaviour of machine-generated questions in measuring test taker's proficiency.

4.1 Experimental setting

We prepared three sets of questions each of which contains ten machine-generated questions (MGQs) and ten human-made questions (HMQs), in total 20 questions. These 30 HMQs were randomly selected from TOEFL preparation books while these 30 MGQs were randomly selected from the set of MGQs which were judged acceptable on the majority principle in the evaluation by the English teachers as described in Section 3. The question sets were created so that the difference of the average of question difficulty across the question sets was minimised. The balance of question difficulty among three groups, and between MGQs and HMQs is important because we calculate the student-wise score correlation between scores from MGQs and HMQs as explained later in 4.2.

To balance question difficulty among the question sets, we utilised the reading passage difficulty. A question is considered difficult if its read-

Dr.$_1$ M. Aurel$_9$ Stein$_9$, principal$_2$ of$_1$ the$_1$ Oriental$_7$ College$_1$ at$_1$ Lahore$_9$, has$_1$ now$_1$ ready$_1$ for$_1$ publication$_4$ the$_1$ first$_1$ volume$_2$ of$_1$ his$_1$ critical$_3$ edition$_4$ of$_1$ the$_1$ Rajatarangini$_9$, or$_1$ Chronicles$_8$ of$_1$ the$_1$ Kings$_1$ of$_1$ Kashmir$_9$, upon$_1$ which$_1$ he$_1$ has$_1$ been$_1$ engaged$_3$ for$_1$ some$_1$ years$_1$. This$_1$ work$_1$ is$_1$ of$_1$ special$_1$ interest$_1$ as$_1$ being$_1$ almost$_1$ the$_1$ sole$_4$ example$_1$ of$_1$ historical$_2$ literature$_2$ in$_1$ Sanskrit$_9$. It$_1$ was$_1$ written$_2$ by$_1$ the$_1$ poet$_2$ Kalhana$_9$ in$_1$ the$_1$ middle$_1$ of$_1$ the$_1$ twelfth$_1$ century$_1$.

Figure 2: Example of reading passage with word difficulty level (subscripts correspond to the level)

Table 7: Mean of reading passage difficulty

metric	question set	MGQ	HMQ
average JACET8000	Qs1	2.15	2.14
	Qs2	2.13	2.13
	Qs3	2.12	2.12
Flesch-Kincaid grade level	Qs1	9.9	11.2
	Qs2	10.0	9.8
	Qs3	9.6	10.7
Flesch-Kincaid reading ease	Qs1	60.3	46.1
	Qs2	59.9	58.9
	Qs3	65.2	50.5
Dale-Chall readability formula	Qs1	9.0	9.9
	Qs2	9.0	9.1
	Qs3	8.9	9.7

ing passage is difficult and vice versa. The reading passage difficulty is calculated based on the word difficulty in the passages. We employed JACET8000 (Uemura and Ishikawa, 2004), a list of 8,000 English words divided into eight levels of word difficulty based on their word frequency. Level 1 is the most frequent (i.e. the easiest) while level 8 is least frequent (i.e. the most difficult). Words that do not appear in the list are considered even less frequent than level 8; thus they are considered to be level 9. To obtain the reading passage difficulty, we assigned a JACET8000 word difficulty level to every word in the reading passage as illustrated in Figure 2 and calculated the average of the difficulty levels. The average of reading passage difficulty for each question set is presented in Table 7.

Many metrics to measure text readability have been proposed in the past, such as Flesch-Kincaid grade level (Kincaid et al., 1975), Flesch-Kincaid reading ease (Kincaid et al., 1975) and Dale-Chall readability formula (Dale and Chall, 1948). The first two calculate text difficulty with respect to the number of sentences, words and syllables in the text. The third one takes into account the difficulty of each word as well. Table 7 also shows

Table 8: TOEIC score of each group

student group	question set	TOEIC score mean	SD	number of students
1	Qs1	561	146	31
2	Qs2	559	123	25
3	Qs3	554	122	25

the mean values of these metrics for each question set and generation mode, i.e. machine-generated vs. human-made. Overall, the difficulty of reading passages in every question set is well balanced against every metric.

Eighty-one Japanese university students (57 first year and 24 second year students) were recruited and divided into three groups, 27 students for each group, considering their TOEIC scores; we did our best to minimise the difference of the score distribution and the mean of the scores across these three groups. Each student group was assigned a different question set and instructed to finish the assigned question set within 30 minutes.

4.2 Result and discussion

Although we made three groups of the same number of students (27) and assigned a different question set to each group, four students mistakenly worked on a wrong question set. Therefore the distribution of the number of students in a group was skewed as shown in Table 8. Table 8 also shows the average TOEIC score of each group with a standard deviation (SD).

Table 9: Item difficulty of MGQs and HMQs

	MGQ	HMQ
mean	0.59	0.60
standard deviation	0.24	0.17
minimum	0.20	0.26
maximum	0.96	0.90

The item analysis investigates the test taker's responses to individual question items to evaluate the quality of those items. It often uses two measures: the item difficulty and the item discrimination index. The item difficulty is a proportion of the number of test takers who answered correctly to the number of all test takers (Brown, 2013). The value ranges from 0 to 1 with a larger value representing an easier item. Table 9 shows the descriptive statistics of the item difficulty of the sets of 30 MGQs and 30 HMQs.

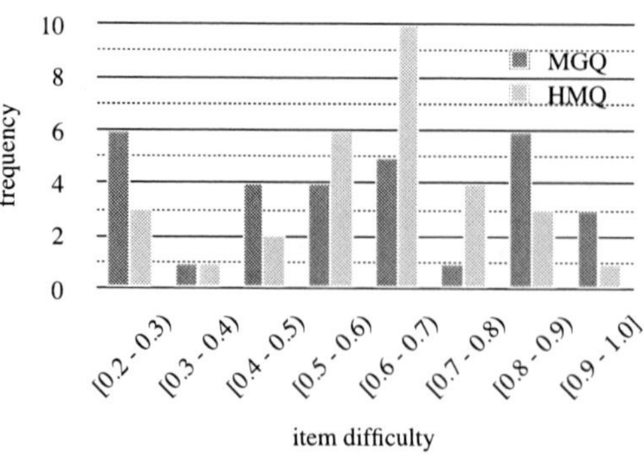

Figure 3: Distribution of item difficulty

Table 9 shows no big difference in mean of the item difficulty between MGQs and HMQs. This result suggests that MGQs have similar difficulty with HMQs. This is consistent with the fact we maintained the balance of question difficulty between MGQs and HMQs as explained in Subsection 4.1. We also provide the distribution of the item difficulty of the MGQs and HMQs in Figure 3. Although the mean is similar between the MGQs and HMQs as shown in Table 9, Figure 3 reveals that the distribution of the item difficulty for HMQs is closer to the normal distribution than that for MGQs. We conducted the Levene's test (Levene et al., 1960) to assess the item difficulty variance homogeneity between MGQs and HMQs to find that their variances are not homogeneous. As we do not care about controlling item difficulty when generating question items, this is a natural consequence.

Mexico, 1818. This species, though not hardy enough for every situation, is yet sufficiently so to stand unharmed as a wall plant. It grows from 10 feet to 12 feet high, with deep-green <u>leaves</u> that are hoary on the under <u>sides</u>. The <u>flowers</u> are bright blue, and produced in June and the following <u>months</u>. **They** are borne in large, axillary panicles. In a light, dry soil and sunny position this shrub does well as a wall plant, for which purpose it is one of the most ornamental. There are several good nursery forms, of which the following are amongst the best: C. azureus Albert Pettitt, C. azureus albidus, C. azureus Arnddii, one of the best, C. azureus Gloire de Versailles, and C. azureus Marie Simon.
(A) leaves
(B) sides
(C) flowers ← correct answer
(D) months

Figure 4: The easiest question

Figure 4 shows the easiest question item while

There are two recesses in the cliff on the opposite side of the little creek formed by the spring. They are 40 to 50 feet above the water, each with an irregular floor of 20 by 30 feet under shelter of the rock. No solid rock is visible in front of them, but a projecting <u>ledge</u> appears on either side about 6 feet below the present average level of the floor; and this is probably the <u>depth</u> of <u>accumulation</u> at the <u>front</u>. **It** seems continuous. It may be less toward the rear. The cavities are in a stratum which is somewhat shelly and crumbles easily.
(A) ledge ← correct answer
(B) depth
(C) accumulation
(D) front

Figure 5: The most difficult question

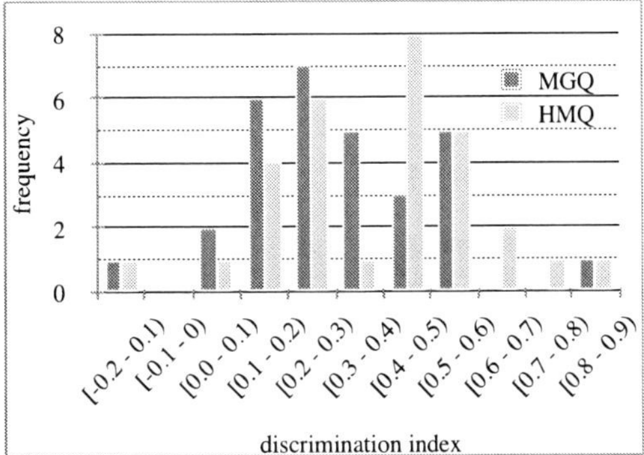

Figure 6: Distribution of item discrimination index

Figure 5 shows the most difficult one in the MGQs in which the target pronoun is in bold and the options are underlined in the reading passage for the readability purpose. Twenty-four out of 25 students answered correctly for the easiest one. This question item is easy because the subject pronoun refers to the subject of the previous sentence. Only five out of 25 students answered correctly for the most difficult question item. Both extremes are not preferable in measuring test taker's proficiency because too easy items lead to very high scores while too difficult items lead to very low scores for the most of test takers.

We calculated the Pearson correlation coefficient between the JACET8000 based reading passage difficulty as we defined in Table 7 and the item difficulty of the MGQs and obtained the value of 0.56. This result suggests that the reading passage difficulty can be one of the important factors for predicting and controlling the item difficulty of question items.

The item discrimination index is a metric to measure the discrimination power of question items (Brown, 2013). The discrimination power is the ability of question items in discriminating high-proficiency test takers from low-proficiency test takers. This metric is vital for language testing because a good test must be able to discriminate test taker's proficiency precisely. The item discrimination index of a question item i is computed as follows

$$ID_i = \frac{U_i - L_i}{n},$$

where U_i and L_i represent the number of test takers who correctly answered the question item i in the high proficiency group and the low proficiency group respectively, and n denotes the number of test takers in a group. The groups of high and low proficiency are defined as the top 27% of the test takers and bottom 27% of the test takers respectively. The threshold value of 27% is utilised to maximise two characteristics; those two groups must be as different as possible to discriminate clearly, and the number of test takers in each group must be as large as possible to achieve reliability (Popham, 1981; Kelley, 1939).

We computed the item discrimination index for each question item and the average of them. The average is 0.33 for the MGQs and 0.37 for the HMQs. A question item is considered to be acceptable if its discrimination index is greater than or equal to 0.2 (Brown, 1983). According to this criteria, we counted the number of question items of which the discrimination index is greater than or equal to 0.2. Out of 30 question items, the 22 MGQs and 24 HMQs items cleared this condition. Figure 6 shows the distribution of the discrimination index. There seems to be no big difference between the MGQs and HMQs in terms of

The region may be roughly characterized as a vast sandy plain, arid in the extreme; or rather as two such <u>plains</u>, separated by a chain of <u>mountains</u> running northwest and southeast. In the southern part of the reservation this mountain range is known as the Choiskai <u>mountains</u>, and here the top is flat and mesa-like in character, dotted with little <u>lakes</u> and covered with giant <u>pines</u>. **They** in the summer give it a park-like aspect. The general elevation of this plateau is a little less than 9,000 feet above the sea and about 3,000 feet above the valleys or plains east and west of it.
(A) plains
(B) mountains
(C) lakes
(D) pines ← correct answer

Figure 7: MGQ example with a poor discrimination index ($ID = 0.125$)

the average discrimination index (0.33 vs. 0.37) and the number of items clearing the 0.2 criterion (22 vs. 24). Their distribution reveals that the HMQs shows a slightly better distribution than the MGQs. However, the MGQs have comparable discrimination power as the HMQs.

Figure 7 shows an example of MGQ which has a poor discrimination index, i.e. $ID = 0.125$. Three test takers in the high proficiency group and two test takers in the low proficiency group answered correctly. The distractor "mountains" distracted test takers in the high proficiency group very much; thus the number of correctly answered test takers was almost the same between the two groups. The potential reason is that "mountains" appears twice in the text, so it lured the test takers to choose "mountains".

To assess the ability of the MGQs in measuring test taker's proficiency, we calculated the correlation between the test taker's score of the MGQs and other scores including that of the HMQs and TOEIC scores. We argue that the test taker's TOEIC scores provide their true English proficiency. The Pearson correlation coefficient (Pearson, 1896) was calculated, presented in Table 10. The p-value of all the correlation coefficients is less than 0.05.

Table 10 shows that there is no big difference between the MGQs and HMQs in terms of the correlation between the test taker's scores and their TOEIC scores. Furthermore, the correlation with the TOEIC Reading scores is stronger than that with the TOEIC Listening scores. This is a reasonable tendency because the pronoun reference questions are designed for assessing reading comprehension ability.

5 Conclusion

This paper presented the evaluation of automatically generated pronoun reference questions which ask test takers the antecedent of the specified pronoun in the reading passage. A pronoun reference question was automatically generated by splitting a sentence in a human-written text at a nonrestrictive relative clause and replacing the relative pronoun with a personal pronoun.

The evaluation was performed from two different perspectives: the English teacher perspective and the English learner perspective. Automatically generated 60 question items were evaluated by five English teachers, resulting in that 39 out

Table 10: Peason correlation coefficients between test taker's scores

	MGQ	HMQ
TOEIC Listening	0.56	0.57
TOEIC Reading	0.65	0.68
TOEIC Listening & Reading	0.74	0.77
HMQ	0.61	—

of 60 (65%) question items were considered acceptable to be used in a real test. We administered 30 MGQs from these acceptable question items together with 30 HMQs from TOEFL preparation books to the 81 university students. The analysis results of the test taker's responses showed that the MGQs achieved comparable quality with the HMQs on their item difficulty and item discrimination index. Furthermore, there was a strong correlation between the MGQ scores and the TOEIC scores of the same test takers.

Possible future work includes controlling item difficulty of the generated questions and generating other types of questions. For instance, our experimental result suggested that the item difficulty of the generated questions had a moderate correlation with the reading passage difficulty. Thus, controlling the passage difficulty might enable us to control the difficulty of the question items. We also need to further explore other factors affecting the item difficulty.

References

Jun Araki, Dheeraj Rajagopal, Sreecharan Sankaranarayanan, Susan Holm, Yukari Yamakawa, and Teruko Mitamura. 2016. Generating questions and multiple-choice answers using semantic analysis of texts. In *Proceedings of COLING 2016, the 26th International Conference on Computational Linguistics: Technical Papers*. The COLING 2016 Organizing Committee, Osaka, Japan, pages 1125–1136. http://aclweb.org/anthology/C16-1107.

Susan E. Brennan, Marilyn W. Friedman, and Carl J. Pollard. 1987. A centering approach to pronouns. In *Proceedings of the 25th Annual Meeting of the Association for Computational Linguistics*. Association for Computational Linguistics, Stanford, California, USA, pages 155–162. https://doi.org/10.3115/981175.981197.

Frederick Gramm Brown. 1983. *Principles of educational and psychological testing*. Holt, Rinehart, and Winston, 3 edition.

James Dean Brown. 2013. Classical test theory. In Glenn Fulcher and Fred Davidson, editors, *The*

Routledge handbook of language testing, Routledge, pages 323–335.

Yllias Chali and Sadid A. Hasan. 2015. Towards topic-to-question generation. *Computational Linguistics* 41(1):1–20. https://doi.org/10.1162/COLI_a_00206.

Edgar Dale and Jeanne S Chall. 1948. A formula for predicting readability: Instructions. *Educational research bulletin* pages 37–54. http://www.jstor.org/stable/1473669.

Barbara J. Grosz, Aravind K. Joshi, and Scott Weinstein. 1995. Centering: A framework for modeling the local coherence of discourse. *Computational Linguistics* 21(2):203–225. http://aclweb.org/anthology/J95-2003.

Michael Heilman and Noah A Smith. 2009. Question generation via overgenerating transformations and ranking. Technical report, DTIC Document.

Truman L Kelley. 1939. The selection of upper and lower groups for the validation of test items. *Journal of educational psychology* 30(1):17–24. http://dx.doi.org/10.1037/h0057123.

J Peter Kincaid, Robert P Fishburne Jr, Richard L Rogers, and Brad S Chissom. 1975. Derivation of new readability formulas (automated readability index, fog count and flesch reading ease formula) for navy enlisted personnel. Technical report, DTIC Document.

Klaus Krippendorff. 1970. Estimating the reliability, systematic error and random error of interval data. *Educational and Psychological Measurement* 30(1):61–70. https://doi.org/10.1177/001316447003000105.

Howard Levene et al. 1960. Robust tests for equality of variances. *Contributions to probability and statistics* 1:278–292.

Ming Liu and Rafael A. Calvo. 2012. Using information extraction to generate trigger questions for academic writing support. In Stefano A. Cerri, William J. Clancey, Giorgos Papadourakis, and Kitty Panourgia, editors, *Intelligent Tutoring Systems: 11th International Conference, ITS 2012, Chania, Crete, Greece, June 14-18, 2012. Proceedings*, Springer Berlin Heidelberg, Berlin, Heidelberg, pages 358–367.

Karl Pearson. 1896. Mathematical contributions to the theory of evolution. iii. regression, heredity, and panmixia. *Philosophical Transactions of the Royal Society of London. Series A, Containing Papers of a Mathematical or Physical Character* 187:253–318. http://www.jstor.org/stable/90707.

W.J. Popham. 1981. *Modern educational measurement*. Englewood Cliff, NJ: Prentice-Hall.

Vasile Rus, Brendan Wyse, Paul Piwek, Mihai Lintean, Svetlana Stoyanchev, and Cristian Moldovan. 2010. The first question generation shared task evaluation challenge. In *Proceedings of the 6th International Natural Language Generation Conference*. Association for Computational Linguistics, pages 251–257. http://www.aclweb.org/anthology/W10-4234.

Arief Yudha Satria and Takenobu Tokunaga. 2017. Automatic generation of english reference question by utilising nonrestrictive relative clause. In *Proceedings of the 9th International Conference on Computer Supported Education - Volume 1: CSEDU*. INSTICC, ScitePress, pages 379–386. https://doi.org/10.5220/0006320203790386.

Iulian Vlad Serban, Alberto García-Durán, Caglar Gulcehre, Sungjin Ahn, Sarath Chandar, Aaron Courville, and Yoshua Bengio. 2016. Generating factoid questions with recurrent neural networks: The 30m factoid question-answer corpus. In *Proceedings of the 54th Annual Meeting of the Association for Computational Linguistics (Volume 1: Long Papers)*. Association for Computational Linguistics, Berlin, Germany, pages 588–598. http://www.aclweb.org/anthology/P16-1056.

K Shojima. 2007. Neural test theory. *DNC Research Note* 7(02):1–12.

Yuni Susanti, Takenobu Tokunaga, Hitoshi Nishikawa, and Hiroyuki Obari. 2017. Evaluation of automatically generated english vocabulary questions. *Research and Practice in Technology Enhanced Learning* 12(1):11. https://doi.org/10.1186/s41039-017-0051-y.

Toshihiko Uemura and Shinichiro Ishikawa. 2004. Jacet 8000 and asia tefl vocabulary initiative. *Journal of Asia TEFL* 1(1):333–347.

Lishan Zhang and Kurt VanLehn. 2016. How do machine-generated questions compare to human-generated questions? *Research and Practice in Technology Enhanced Learning* 11(1):7. https://doi.org/10.1186/s41039-016-0031-7.

Predicting Audience's Laughter During Presentations Using Convolutional Neural Network

Lei Chen
Educational Testing Service (ETS)
Princeton, NJ USA
LChen@ets.org

Chong Min Lee
Educational Testing Service (ETS)
Princeton, NJ USA
CLee001@ets.org

Abstract

Public speakings play important roles in schools and work places and properly using humor contributes to effective presentations. For the purpose of automatically evaluating speakers' humor usage, we build a presentation corpus containing humorous utterances based on TED talks. Compared to previous data resources supporting humor recognition research, ours has several advantages, including (a) both positive and negative instances coming from a homogeneous data set, (b) containing a large number of speakers, and (c) being open. Focusing on using lexical cues for humor recognition, we systematically compare a newly emerging text classification method based on Convolutional Neural Networks (CNNs) with a well-established conventional method using linguistic knowledge. The advantages of the CNN method are both getting higher detection accuracies and being able to learn essential features automatically.

1 Introduction

The ability to make effective presentations has been found to be linked with success at school and in the workplace (Hill and Storey, 2003; Stevens, 2005). Humor plays an important role in successful public speaking, e.g., helping to reduce public speaking anxiety often regarded as the most prevalent type of social phobia, generating shared amusement to boost persuasive power, and serving as a means to attract attention and reduce tension (Xu, 2016).

Automatically simulating an audience's reactions to humor will not only be useful for presentation training, but also improve conversational sys-

tems by giving machines more empathetic power. The present study reports our efforts in recognizing utterances that cause laughter in presentations. These include building a corpus from TED talks and using Convolutional Neural Networks (CNNs) in the recognition.

The remainder of the paper is organized as follows: Section 2 briefly reviews the previous related research; Section 3 describes the corpus we collected from TED talks; Section 4 describes the text classification methods; Section 5 reports on our experiments; finally, Section 6 discusses the findings of our study and plans for future work.

2 Previous Research

Humor recognition refers to the task of deciding whether a sentence/spoken-utterance expresses a certain degree of humor. In most of the previous studies (Mihalcea and Strapparava, 2005; Purandare and Litman, 2006; Yang et al., 2015), humor recognition was modeled as a binary classification task.

In the seminal work (Mihalcea and Strapparava, 2005), a corpus of 16,000 "one-liners" was created using daily joke websites to collect humorous instances while using formal writing resources (e.g., news titles) to obtain non-humorous instances. Three humor-specific stylistic features, including *alliteration*, *antonymy*, and *adult slang* were utilized together with content-based features to build classifiers. In a recent work (Yang et al., 2015), a new corpus was constructed from the *Pun of the Day* website. Yang et al. (2015) explained and computed stylistic features based on the following four aspects: (a) Incongruity, (b) Ambiguity, (c) Interpersonal Effect, and (d) Phonetic Style. In addition, Word2Vec (Mikolov et al., 2013) distributed representations were utilized in the model building.

Proceedings of the 12th Workshop on Innovative Use of NLP for Building Educational Applications, pages 86–90
Copenhagen, Denmark, September 8, 2017. ©2017 Association for Computational Linguistics

Beyond lexical cues from text inputs, other research has also utilized speakers' acoustic cues (Purandare and Litman, 2006; Bertero and Fung, 2016b). These studies have typically used audio tracks from TV shows and their corresponding captions in order to categorize characters' speaking turns as humorous or non-humorous based on canned laughter.

Convolutional Neural Networks (CNNs) have recently been successfully used in several text categorization tasks (e.g., review rating, sentiment recognition, and question type recognition). Kim (2014); Johnson and Zhang (2015); Zhang and Wallace (2015) suggested that using a simple CNN setup, which entails one layer of convolution on top of word embedding vectors, achieves excellent results on multiple tasks. Deep learning recently has been applied to computational humor research (Bertero and Fung, 2016b,a). In Bertero and Fung (2016b), CNN was found to be the best model that uses both acoustic and lexical cues for humor recognition. However, it did not outperform the Logistical Regression (LR) model when using text inputs exclusively. Beyond treating humor detection as a binary classification task, Bertero and Fung (2016a) formulated the recognition to be a sequential labeling task and utilized Recurrent Neural Networks (RNNs) (Hochreiter and Schmidhuber, 1997) on top of CNN models (serving as feature extractors) to utilize context information among utterances.

From the brief review, it is clear that there is a great need for an open corpus that can support investigating humor in presentations.[1] CNN-based text categorization methods have been applied to humor recognition (e.g., in (Bertero and Fung, 2016b)) but with limitations: (a) a rigorous comparison with the state-of-the-art conventional method examined in Yang et al. (2015) is missing; (b) CNN's performance in the previous research is not quite clear; and (c) some important techniques that can improve CNN performance (e.g., using varied-sized filters and dropout regularization (Hinton et al., 2012)) were not applied. Therefore, the present study is meant to address these limitations.

3 TED Talk Data

TED Talks[2] are recordings from TED conferences and other special TED programs. Many effects in a presentation can cause audience laugh, such as speaking content, presenters' nonverbal behaviors, and so on. In the present study, we focused on the transcripts of the talks. Most transcripts of the talks contain the markup '(Laughter)', which represents where audiences laughed aloud during the talks. This special markup was used to determine utterance labels.

We collected 1,192 TED Talk transcripts[3]. An example transcription is given in Figure 1. The collected transcripts were split into sentences using the Stanford CoreNLP tool (Manning et al., 2014). In this study, sentences containing or immediately followed by '(Laughter)' were used as 'Laughter' sentences, as shown in Figure 1; all other sentences were defined as 'No-Laughter' sentences. Following Mihalcea and Strapparava (2005) and Yang et al. (2015), we selected the same numbers ($n = 4726$) of 'Laughter' and 'No-Laughter' sentences. To minimize possible topic shifts between positive and negative instances, for each positive instance, we randomly picked one negative instance nearby (the context window was 7 sentences in this study). For example, in Figure 1, a negative instance (corresponding to 'sent-2') was selected from the nearby sentences ranging from 'sent-7' to 'sent+7'. More details about this data set can refer to Lee et al. (2016). The TED data set can be obtained by contacting the authors.

4 Methods

4.1 Conventional Model

Following Yang et al. (2015), we applied Random Forest (Breiman, 2001) to perform humor recognition by using the following two groups of features. The first group are humor-specific stylistic features covering the following 4 categories[4]: *Incongruity* (2), *Ambiguity* (6), *Interpersonal Effect* (4), and *Phonetic Pattern* (4). The second group are semantic distance features, including the humor label classes from 5 sentences in the training set that are closest to the sentence being evaluated (found by using a *k*-Nearest Neighbors (kNN)

---

[1] While we were working on this paper, we found a recent Master's thesis (Acosta, 2016) that also conducted research on detecting laughter on the TED transcriptions. However, that study only explored conventional text classification approaches.

---

[2] http://www.ted.com
[3] The transcripts were collected on 7/9/2015.
[4] The number in parenthesis indicates how many features are in that category.

sent-7 ...

... ...

No-Laughter He has no memory of the past, no knowledge of the future, and he only cares about two
things: easy and fun.

sent-1 Now, in the animal world, that works fine.

Laughter *If you're a dog and you spend your whole life doing nothing other than easy and fun things,
you're a huge success!* (Laughter)

sent+1 And to the Monkey, humans are just another animal species.

... ...

sent+7 ...

Figure 1: An excerpt from TED talk *"Tim Urban: Inside the mind of a master procrastinator"* (`http:
//bit.ly/2l1P3RJ`)

method), and each sentence's averaged Word2Vec representations ($n = 300$). More details can be found in Yang et al. (2015).

4.2 CNN model

Our CNN-based text classification's setup follows Kim (2014). Figure 2 depicts the model's details. From the left side's input texts to the right side's prediction labels, different shapes of tensors flow through the entire network for solving the classification task in an end-to-end mode.

Firstly, tokenized text strings were converted to a $2D$ tensor with shape $(L \times d)$, where L represents sentences' maximum length while d represents the word-embedding dimension. In this study, we utilized the Word2Vec (Mikolov et al., 2013) embedding vectors ($d = 300$) that were trained on 100 billion words of Google News. Next, the embedding matrix was fed into a $1D$ convolution network with multiple filters. To cover varied reception fields, we used filters of sizes of $f_w - 1$, f_w, and $f_w + 1$. For each filter size, n_f filters were utilized. Then, max pooling, which stands for finding the largest value from a vector, was applied to each feature map (total $3 \times n_f$ feature maps) output by the $1D$ convolution. Finally, maximum values from all of $3 \times n_f$ filters were formed as a flattened vector to go through a fully connected (FC) layer to predict two possible labels (Laughter vs. No-Laughter). Note that for $1D$ convolution and FC layer's input, we applied 'dropout' (Hinton et al., 2012) regularization, which entails randomly setting a proportion of network weights to be zero during model training, to overcome over-fitting. By using cross-entropy as the learning metric, the whole sequential network (all weights and bias) could be optimized by using any SGD optimization, e.g., Adam (Kingma and Ba, 2014), Adadelta (Zeiler, 2012), and so on.

5 Experiments

We used two corpora: the TED Talk corpus (denoted as TED) and the Pun of the Day corpus[5] (denoted as Pun). Note that we normalized words in the Pun data to lowercase to avoid a possibly elevated result caused by a special pattern: in the original format, all negative instances started with capital letters. The Pun data allows us to verify that our implementation of the conventional model is consistent with the work reported in Yang et al. (2015).

In our experiment, we firstly divided each corpus into two parts. The smaller part (the Dev set) was used for setting various hyper-parameters used in text classifiers. The larger portion (the CV set) was then formulated as a 10 fold cross validation setup for obtaining a stable and comprehensive model evaluation result. For the PUN data, the Dev contains 482 sentences, while the CV set contains 4344 sentences. For the TED data, the Dev set contains 1046 utterances, while the CV set contains 8406 utterances. Note that, with a goal of building a speaker-independent humor detector, when partitioning our TED data set, we always kept all utterances of a single talk within the same partition.

When building conventional models, we developed our own feature extraction scripts and used the SKLL[6] python package for building Random Forest models. When implementing CNN,

---

[5] The authors of Yang et al. (2015) kindly shared their data with us. We would like to thank them for their generosity.

[6] `https://github.com/`
`EducationalTestingService/skll`

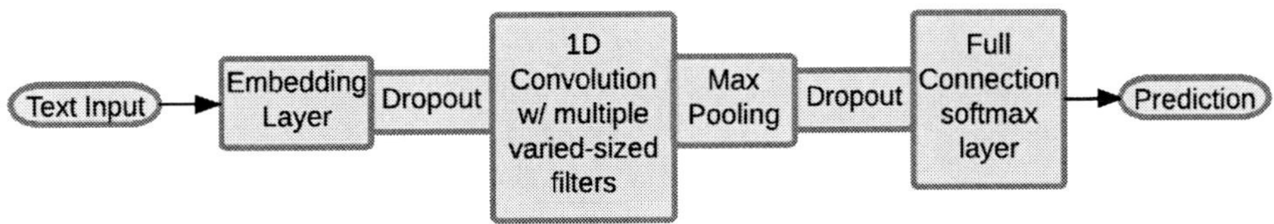

Figure 2: CNN network architecture

	Acc. (%)	F1	Precision	Recall
Pun set				
Chance	50.2	.498	.506	.497
Base	78.3	.795	.757	.839
CNN	**86.1**	**.857**	**.864**	**.864**
TED set				
Chance	51.0	.506	.510	.503
Base	52.0	.595	.515	.705
CNN	**58.9**	**.606**	**.582**	.632

Table 1: Humor recognition on both Pun and TED data sets by using (a) random prediction (Chance), conventional method (Base) and CNN method

we used the Keras Python package[7]. Regarding hyper-parameter tweaking, we utilized the Tree Parzen Estimation (TPE) method as detailed in Bergstra et al. (2013). After running 200 iterations of tweaking, we ended up with the following selection: f_w is 6 (entailing that the various filter sizes are $(5, 6, 7)$), n_f is 100, $dropout_1$ is 0.7 and $dropout_2$ is 0.35, optimization uses Adam (Kingma and Ba, 2014). When training the CNN model, we randomly selected 10% of the training data as the validation set for using early stopping to avoid over-fitting.

On the Pun data, the CNN model shows consistent improved performance over the conventional model, as suggested in Yang et al. (2015). In particular, precision has been greatly increased from 0.762 to 0.864. On the TED data, we also observed that the CNN model helps to increase precision (from 0.515 to 0.582) and accuracy (from 52.0% to 58.9%). The empirical evaluation results suggest that the CNN-based model has an advantage on the humor recognition task. In addition, focusing on the system development time, gener-

ating and implementing those features in the conventional model would take days or even weeks. However, the CNN model automatically learns its optimal feature representation and can adjust the features automatically across data sets. This makes the CNN model quite versatile for supporting different tasks and data domains. Compared with the humor recognition results on the Pun data, the results on the TED data are still quite low, and more research is needed to fully handle humor in authentic presentations.

6 Discussion

For the purpose of monitoring how well speakers can use humor during their presentations, we have created a corpus from TED talks. Compared to the existing corpora, ours has the following advantages: (a) it was collected from authentic talks, rather than from TV shows performed by professional actors based on scripts; (b) it contains about 100 times more speakers compared to the limited number of actors in existing corpora. We compared two types of leading text-based humor recognition methods: a conventional classifier (e.g., Random Forest) based on human-engineered features vs. an end-to-end CNN method, which relies on its inherent representation learning. We found that the CNN method has better performance. More importantly, the representation learning of the CNN method makes it very efficient when facing new data sets.

Stemming from the present study, we envision that more research is worth pursuing: (a) for presentations, cues from other modalities such as audio or video will be included, similar to Bertero and Fung (2016b); (b) context information from multiple utterances will be modeled by using sequential modeling methods.

---

[7]Our code implementation was based on
`https://github.com/shagunsodhani/`
`CNN-Sentence-Classifier`

References

Andrew D. Acosta. 2016. *Laff-O-Tron: Laugh Prediction in TED Talks*. Master's thesis, California Polytechnic State University, San Luis Obispo, CA.

James Bergstra, Daniel Yamins, and David D Cox. 2013. Making a science of model search: Hyperparameter optimization in hundreds of dimensions for vision architectures. *ICML (1)* 28:115–123.

D Bertero and P Fung. 2016a. A long short-term memory framework for predicting humor in dialogues. In *Proceedings of NAACL-HLT*. San Diego, CA.

D Bertero and P Fung. 2016b. Deep learning of audio and language features for humor prediction. In *International Conference on Language Resources and Evaluation (LREC)*. Portoroz, Slovenia.

L Breiman. 2001. Random forests. *Machine learning* 45(1):5–32.

Monica Hill and Anne Storey. 2003. Speakeasy: online support for oral presentation skills. *ELT Journal* 57(4):370–376.

GE Hinton, N Srivastava, and A Krizhevsky. 2012. Improving neural networks by preventing coadaptation of feature detectors. *arXiv preprint arXiv:1207.0580* .

Sepp Hochreiter and Jürgen Schmidhuber. 1997. Long Short-Term Memory. *Neural Computation* 9(8):1735–1780.

R Johnson and T Zhang. 2015. Semi-supervised convolutional neural networks for text categorization via region embedding. *Advances in neural information processing* .

Y Kim. 2014. Convolutional neural networks for sentence classification. In *Proc. EMNLP*. Doha, Qatar, pages 1746–1751.

D Kingma and J Ba. 2014. Adam: A method for stochastic optimization. *arXiv preprint arXiv:1412.6980* .

Chong Min Lee, Su-Youn Yoon, and Lei Chen. 2016. Can we make computers laugh at talks? In *Proceedings of the Workshop on Computational Modeling of People's Opinions, Personality, and Emotions in Social Media (PEOPLES)*. The COLING 2016 Organizing Committee, Osaka, Japan, pages 173–181.

Christopher D. Manning, Mihai Surdeanu, John Bauer, Jenny Finkel, Steven J. Bethard, and David McClosky. 2014. The Stanford CoreNLP natural language processing toolkit. In *Association for Computational Linguistics (ACL) System Demonstrations*. pages 55–60.

Rada Mihalcea and Carlo Strapparava. 2005. Making computers laugh: Investigations in automatic humor recognition. In *Proceedings of Human Language Technology Conference and Conference on Empirical Methods in Natural Language Processing*. Association for Computational Linguistics, Vancouver, British Columbia, Canada, pages 531–538.

T Mikolov, I Sutskever, and K Chen. 2013. Distributed representations of words and phrases and their compositionality. *Advances in neural information processing systems* .

Amruta Purandare and Diane J. Litman. 2006. Humor: Prosody analysis and automatic recognition for F*R*I*E*N*D*S*. In *EMNLP*. Sydney, Australia.

Betsy Stevens. 2005. What communication skills do employers want? silicon valley recruiters respond. *Journal of Employment Counseling* 42(1):2.

Z Xu. 2016. Laughing Matters: Humor Strategies in Public Speaking. *Asian Social Science* 12(1):117.

Diyi Yang, Alon Lavie, Chris Dyer, and Eduard Hovy. 2015. Humor recognition and humor anchor extraction. In *Proceedings of the 2015 Conference on Empirical Methods in Natural Language Processing*. Association for Computational Linguistics, Lisbon, Portugal, pages 2367–2376.

MD Zeiler. 2012. ADADELTA: an adaptive learning rate method. *arXiv preprint arXiv:1212.5701* .

Y Zhang and B Wallace. 2015. A sensitivity analysis of (and practitioners' guide to) convolutional neural networks for sentence classification. In *arXiv:1510.03820*.

Collecting fluency corrections for spoken learner English

Andrew Caines[1]   **Emma Flint**[1]   **Paula Buttery**[2]
[1] Department of Theoretical and Applied Linguistics
[2] Computer Laboratory
University of Cambridge, Cambridge, U.K.
`{apc38|emf40|pjb48}@cam.ac.uk`

Abstract

We present crowdsourced collection of error annotations for transcriptions of spoken learner English. Our emphasis in data collection is on *fluency* corrections, a more complete correction than has traditionally been aimed for in grammatical error correction research (GEC). Fluency corrections require improvements to the text, taking discourse and utterance level semantics into account: the result is a more naturalistic, holistic version of the original. We propose that this shifted emphasis be reflected in a new name for the task: 'holistic error correction' (HEC). We analyse crowdworker behaviour in HEC and conclude that the method is useful with certain amendments for future work.

1 Introduction

By convention, grammatical error detection and correction (GEC) systems depend on the availability of labelled training data in which tokens have been annotated with an error code and a correction. In (1) for example, taken from the open FCE subset of the Cambridge Learner Corpus (CLC) (Nicholls, 2003; Yannakoudakis et al., 2011), the original token 'waken' is coded as a 'TV' (verb tense) error and annotated with the correct token 'woken' on the right-hand side of the pipe.

(1) In the morning, you are <NS type="TV"> waken|woken </NS> up by a singing puppy.

Such efforts to annotate learner corpora are time-consuming and costly, but with sufficient quantities it is possible to train GEC systems to identify and correct errors in unseen texts. For example, 29 million tokens of the CLC have been

error-annotated, of which the FCE is a publicly-available 500k token subset (Yannakoudakis et al., 2011). The Write & Improve[1] GEC system (W&I) has been built on these resources (Andersen et al., 2013), providing automated assessment and per-token error feedback. In common with other GEC systems, W&I prizes precision ahead of recall – so as to avoid false positive corrections being presented to the user.

Indeed the field of GEC as a whole adopts a conservative stance on error correction (hence preferring precision to recall in the well-established $F_{0.5}$ metric), is focused at the token level, and has tended to train separate classifiers for each error type (De Felice and Pulman, 2008; Tetreault et al., 2010; Dahlmeier and Ng, 2012), has adopted a machine translation approach (Brockett et al., 2006; Park and Levy, 2011; Yuan et al., 2016), or a hybrid of the two (Rozovskaya and Roth, 2016). Ease of correction varies by class of error, with Table 1 showing best-to-worst recall of the top-performing system for each error type in the CoNLL-2014 shared task on GEC of NUCLE data (Ng et al., 2014).

It is apparent that detection rates are relatively high for certain error types, namely issues of register, subject-verb agreement, determiner errors and noun number. We note that there are several error types in the lower half of Table 1 – such as sentence fragments, linking words, redundancy, unclear meaning and wrong collocations – which relate to fluency broadly defined. This indicates that these error types are harder to solve, or at least have not been worked on so much. Either way they require further attention.

Some notable blind-spots of the current GEC approach are found above the token level, in sentence and discourse level semantics and coher-

---

[1] `https://writeandimprove.com`

Proceedings of the 12th Workshop on Innovative Use of NLP for Building Educational Applications, pages 91–100
Copenhagen, Denmark, September 8, 2017. ©2017 Association for Computational Linguistics

Code	Error	Training %	Recall %	System
Wtone	inappropriate register	1.3	81.8	AMU
SVA	subject-verb agreement	3.4	70.3	CUUI
ArtOrDet	article/determiner error	14.8	58.9	CUUI
Nn	noun number	8.4	58.7	AMU
Spar	parallelism	1.2	50.0	RAC
WOadv	adjective/adverb order	0.8	47.6	CAMB
Wform	word form	4.8	45.6	AMU
Mec	spelling & punctuation	7.0	43.5	RAC
Prep	preposition	5.4	38.3	CAMB
V0	missing verb	0.9	36.7	NARA
Vm	modal verb	1.0	35.9	RAC
Vform	verb form	3.2	27.6	NARA
Vt	verb tense	7.1	26.2	RAC
Sfrag	sentence fragment	0.6	25.0	UMC
Pform	pronoun form	0.4	22.6	CAMB
Trans	linking words	3.1	21.4	CAMB
Npos	possessive	0.5	20.0	NARA
Rloc–	redundancy	10.5	20.2	CAMB
Pref	pronoun reference	2.1	19.4	CAMB
Um	unclear meaning	2.6	15.8	PKU
Ssub	subordinate clause	0.8	15.4	NARA
Wci	wrong collocation	11.8	12.0	AMU
WOinc	word order	1.6	6.7	UMC
Others	miscellaneous	3.3	3.1	RAC
Cit	citation	1.5	0	–
Smod	dangling modifier	0.1	0	–
Srun	run on sentence	1.9	0	–
Wa	acronym	0.1	0	–

Table 1: Best recall by error type in the CoNLL-2014 shared task on GEC (Ng et al., 2014), including frequency of error type in the training data, and recall against gold-standard edits[3].

ence. Hence there has been a call for greater emphasis on *fluency* in error correction (Sakaguchi et al., 2016). We may think of fluency as encompassing the grammaticality-per-token focus of GEC thus far, with added layers of sentence and discourse level semantics and coherence. It is also more than just spoken fluency, which is a common usage of the term. Instead, it is a holistic notion of all-linguistic performance competence.

For example, in (2) we see the kind of sentence which in the GEC approach might only be corrected for the ungrammaticality of 'shorten', as in (3). But in fact the new version still lacks native-like fluency. The meaning is clear, a fact we can use to offer the fluent correction seen in (4).

(2) From this scope, social media has shorten our distance[4].

(3) From this scope, social media has shortened our distance.

(4) From this perspective, social media has shortened the distance between us.

Furthermore, in speech the problem is heightened by the fact that, relative to grammaticality,

fluency is arguably of greater importance than it is in writing. In the immediate communication scenario of spontaneous conversation – the default setting for speech, though there are others – the signal is ephemeral and interlocutors are both forgiving of errors and adept at rapid repair (Clark and Schaefer, 1987; Cahn and Brennan, 1999; Branigan et al., 2007).

Except in classroom settings or when explicitly asked to do so, the listener rarely corrects or points out the speaker's grammatical errors. Instead she tends to signal understanding, offer signs of agreement or other emotional reaction, and seek clarification – all of which have been listed among the typical acts of 'alignment' in dialogue (Pickering and Garrod, 2004). She focuses more on the meaning of what is said, and the fluency of linguistic construction plays an important role in how successfully meaning is conveyed. We work with spoken data from learners, and the implication is that fluency takes on added importance in our view.

We therefore support the call for greater emphasis on fluency rather than grammaticality (Sakaguchi et al., 2016), propose that we represent that changed emphasis with a changed label for the field – 'holistic error correction' (HEC) is our

---

[4]Examples (2)–(4) from Sakaguchi et al (2016).

suggestion – and finally we present and evaluate a crowdsourcing method for fluency correction of transcriptions of spoken learner English. We analyse crowdworker behaviour in this task, discuss how the data can be used, and assess how the method can be improved in future work with a view to creating an open dataset of fluency annotations.

2 Crowdsourcing

Annotation of language corpora is an expensive process in both cost and time. And yet the labelling of corpora is highly desired as it opens the data up to further linguistic analysis and machine learning experiments. We describe our efforts to use *the crowd* for fast, low-cost annotation tasks and conclude as others have done before that, 'they can help' (Madnani et al., 2011) – the resultant annotations are good enough to be useful.

We engaged 120 crowdworkers through Prolific Academic[5] to provide fluency corrections for transcriptions of spoken learner English. A recent evaluation of Prolific Academic and two other widely-used crowdsourcing services, CrowdFlower and Amazon Mechanical Turk, reported favourable comparisons for Prolific in terms of both data quality and participant diversity (Peer et al., 2017). We recruited workers from Prolific on condition that they had an approval rating of 95% or more, that they reported English to be their first language, and that they were educated to at least U.K. GCSE level or equivalent (normally taken at 16 years).

This meant that the worker pool was reduced to 17,363 from an original pool of 23,973 at the time of recruitment (January 2017). Nevertheless recruitment proceeded at a rapid pace and all tasks had been completed within 24 hours of launch. Workers were paid £1 for what was estimated to be 10 minutes of work correcting 16 items (plus the two test items we put in to catch pathological contributions[6]). In fact our 120 workers spent an average of 16 minutes on the task (max=43 mins, min=7.2 mins, st.dev=7.6 mins). Workers declared themselves to be 45% female and 55% male

and were in the age range 17–70 years (mean=33).

The data were language learner monologues from Cambridge English Language Assessment Business Language Testing Service (BULATS) oral exams[7]. The learners were prompted to discuss business topic scenarios and allowed to talk for up to a minute at a time. Recordings were transcribed by two different workers from the Amazon Mechanical Turk crowdsourcing service and subsequently combined into a single transcript by finding the best path through a word network constructed out of the two transcript versions, using automated speech recognition (van Dalen et al., 2015). This method is of course not error-free: van Dalen *et al* report a word error rate of 28% on a 55k token test set.

The learners' first languages (L1s) were Arabic, Dutch, French, Polish, Thai and Vietnamese (Table 2), and their proficiency was judged by two examiners such that they could be placed on the CEFR scale (Common European Framework of Reference for Languages) as shown in Table 3.

Whilst the learners are fairly well-balanced by L1 in terms of both speaker numbers and token counts, it is clear that there's a skew towards the middle ranks of the CEFR scale – namely, A2 to C1 – with fewer A1 learners and only two C2 level learners. As would be expected, the token-to-speaker ratio rises with increasing proficiency: thus there are more tokens for each proficiency level (excepting C2), even where speaker numbers do not go up.

We prepared a web application using R Shiny and shinyapps hosting (R Core Team, 2017; Chang et al., 2016; Allaire, 2016). We named it 'Correcting English' and directed crowdworkers to it from Prolific Academic. If necessary, transcriptions were divided into 'speech-units' (Moore et al., 2016) – analogous to the sentence in writing – and presented speech-unit by speech-unit (SU). Workers were greeted with a welcome page explaining that they would be shown transcriptions of spoken learner English, that the learners were talking about business topics, and that they could expect to see mistakes.

Workers were asked to make corrections so that, "it sounds like something you would expect to hear or produce yourself in English". Whether the target should be the proficiency of a native speaker or a high proficiency learner is a fraught ques-

---

[5] http://www.prolific.ac

[6] These were the straightforward grammatical errors in, 'The currency of the USA be dhollars', and, 'The capital of the UK are Londoin', where we could pattern match for the corrections we expected. The absence of such corrections warned us to check the worker's whole contribution and judge whether to reject it and refuse payment.

[7] http://www.bulats.org

L1	Speakers	Tokens	SUs
Arabic	40	12,181	425
Dutch	33	11,549	396
French	37	11,716	383
Polish	40	9729	393
Thai	37	10,207	414
Vietnamese	39	9858	361
Total		226	65,240	2372

Table 2: L1 of speakers in the BULATS corpus: number of tokens and speech-units per group.

CEFR	Speakers	Tokens	SUs
A1	38	4553	325
A2	48	9584	451
B1	48	14,766	520
B2	48	16,854	509
C1	42	17,749	541
C2	2	624	26
Total	226	65,240	2372

Table 3: CEFR proficiency level of speakers in the BULATS corpus: number of tokens and speech-units per group.

tion in second language acquisition research, so we avoid reference to any such target and instead ask the worker to envisage how they might express the information contained in the SU. We intended that this gave the worker a concrete standard of English to aim for, and we assume that they are native speakers in any case, since we filtered for that in the recruitment stage. Moreover it encourages them to think about how they would *speak* the same thought, the intention being that this would lead them to think more about fluency than about grammaticality. We added that they should make as many changes as necessary, echoing Sakaguchi and colleagues' instruction for 'fluency edits' as opposed to 'minimal edits' (2016).

On the annotation page, workers were also able to view the context of a learner's response: that is, a summary of the 'prompt' to which they had responded. They could opt to skip the given transcription if they could not make any sense of it (and it would be replaced with another: such a move did not 'run down' the 18 required annotations). They could indicate with a tick-box that the transcription needed no correction. And they could grade their own confidence in their judgements, from 'not sure' to 'very sure' with 'quite sure' in between. A screenshot of a Correcting English page is given in Figure 1.

Once the worker completed 18 annotations (the 16 BULATS items and 2 test items) they were redirected to Prolific Academic and we were re-

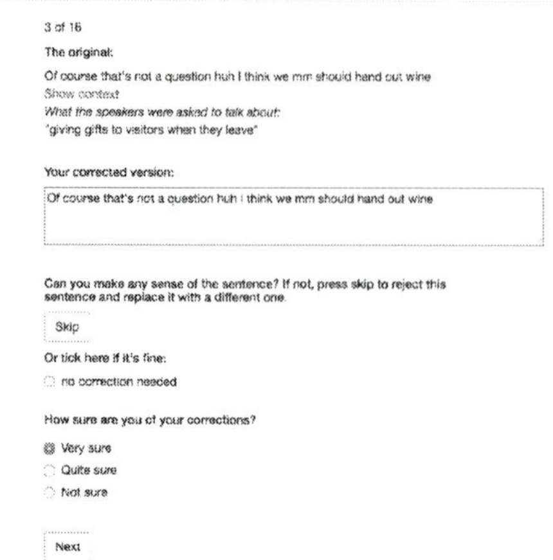

Figure 1: Screenshot from the Correcting English web application for crowdsourcing fluency corrections of spoken learner English: note that the original speech-unit is reproduced verbatim in the correction text-box, ready for the crowdworker to edit (or not).

quired to approve or reject their submission. In total we approved 120 submissions.

3 Results

The BULATS dataset is different to those previously submitted for crowdsourced error annotation, to the best of our knowledge, in that it is *spoken* data and it is *learner* English. In all, 1507 unique SUs were selected at random and presented to crowdworkers for annotation, representing 63.5% of the 2372 SUs in the corpus. Workers made a total of 5706 judgements, excluding the test items.

3.1 Skipped speech-units

The majority of judgements were 'skip' moves to reject the presented SU. Overall workers skipped almost two-and-a-half SUs for every one they annotated (Table 4).

We found that variation in proficiency level explains the SU skip rate to some extent. The ratio of skipped to annotated SUs decreases from 5.8:1 to 1.5:1 from level A1 to C1, indicating that workers were more willing to annotate SUs uttered by higher proficiency speakers. There is a non-significant correlation between the percen and the grade assigned to the recording ($r = -0.182, p <$

CEFR	Skips	Annotations	Skip:Annotation	Unique SUs	Corpus %
A1	507	87	5.8	46	14.2
A2	832	238	3.5	117	25.9
B1	948	387	2.4	162	31.2
B2	837	359	2.3	164	32.2
C1	870	582	1.5	232	42.9
C2	23	18	1.3	6	23.1
Total	4017	1671	2.4	727	30.6

Table 4: CEFR proficiency level of speakers in the BULATS corpus: number of tokens and speech-units per group.

$0.001, df = 1155$). As a consequence our corpus of annotations is skewed towards higher proficiency levels (ignoring the small C2 subset for now), with almost half of the C1 SUs in our corpus being annotated at least once, in contrast to just one-sixth of A1 SUs (Table 4).

Of the SUs presented to crowdworkers, 348 were never skipped (Table 5). Recall that the skip action was intended for workers to indicate that they could make no sense of the speech-unit, and therefore could not reasonably be expected to correct it. Of the skipped SUs, 282 were skipped once only. Since linguistic intuitions are highly subjective, we put these aside as singular opinions on the SUs while we wait for a second opinion. Therefore we have 877 SUs which have been skipped two or more times, and we pay attention to this subset in some way.

Skips	SUs	Skips	SUs
0	348	9	27
1	282	10	9
2	259	11	7
3	194	12	8
4	128	13	5
5	97	14	3
6	59	15	5
7	48	16	2
8	24	18	2

Table 5: Number of skips per speech-unit in the BULATS corpus.

Examples of highly-skipped SUs include the following:

(5) A lot of coaching ment mentor.

(6) Ah we work very very well together ah we uh very close we can share lots of things er we also have time to uh sit down and talk about how school is developing and ah whether we are doing the right things together or not.

(7) Uh so I think I think location of facility is where the is good to store it to store.

In (5) the SU is too short, disfluent and lacking in a main verb to make any sense of. In contrast (6) is very long, peppered with filled pauses ('ah', 'uh', 'er'), and made up of several main clauses run on to one another in a chain. Both are difficult to make sense of for different reasons. Both were spoken by learners of CEFR level C1, whereas in (7) the level is B1 and the difficulty in interpretation perhaps stems more from the low proficiency level of the speaker.

How can we make use of the information in crowdworkers' skipping actions? We could interpret them as judgements as to the futility of attempting automatic correction on these units. For example, we could choose to exclude those SUs which have been skipped on at least two of the occasions they have been presented to crowdworkers. These SUs would constitute a 'nonsensical' portion of the corpus which (for now) we might deem too hard to automatically correct, as it is not possible to infer what the speaker intended to say. With the proposed threshold, 282 SUs would have to be set aside – or, 38.8% of the 727 SUs in the current dataset.

The implication for HEC evaluation is that we are only judging system performance against those SUs which we can reasonably expect to be corrected. The implication for computer-assisted language learning (CALL) applications is that if such an utterance were automatically detected, the system could ask the learner to clarify what they said or ask them to try again, rather than attempting a correction and damaging the system's reputation through nonsensical corrections to nonsensical SUs. However, it is apparent that many SUs would be trimmed through this method and with the proposed threshold. Is this a sensible approach? We leave this as a matter for debate, and welcome feedback in this regard.

3.2 Corrected speech-units

In terms of annotations then, 727 (30.6%) of the 2372 SUs in the corpus were annotated at least once (Table 4). If all 120 crowdworkers had submitted 16 SU annotations of suitable quality, it would give us a corpus of 1920 annotated SUs. However, in a quality control stage we removed 249 units due to poor contributions by workers, thereby losing just over one-eighth of the total submissions and leaving us with 1671 remaining annotations. Data loss of 13% seems a reasonable amount to allow for in designing a crowdsourcing study, and certainly we never expected a 100% success rate in terms of data quality.

These 1671 remaining annotations represent 727 unique SUs. Thus we have approximately two annotations for each SU on average. How can we assess what changes crowdworkers made to the original texts? Firstly we note that on the whole SUs were shortened in correction: the mean character difference between the original and corrected SU is -9.2 characters, while the median was -4 characters.

Self-reported confidence levels are generally high: workers rated their confidence level as 'very sure' or 'quite sure' for 85% of their annotations. We could choose to exclude the remaining 15% of annotations of which the workers declared themselves unsure. This would reduce the 1671 annotations to 1425 and the number of included SUs from 727 to 632. That would be the conservative approach, and probably the decision one would take before training a HEC system. Nevertheless we can use this information in evaluating HEC outputs, weighting scoring so that hypotheses measured against gold-standard fluency edits (of which the worker is at least quite sure) are valued more highly than those measured against silver-standard edits (the 'not sure' annotations).

Moreover, confidence level tends to be lower the greater the character difference between original and corrected SUs: in Figure 2 we see that the character difference values are more widely spread around the zero mark for the lower confidence levels, 'not sure' and 'quite sure'. For 'very sure' on the other hand, there is a peak of character differences around the zero mark, suggesting that no change has been made in the majority of cases. This indicates that crowdworkers tended to feel unsure when they *took action*: whether this is a property of the dataset or human nature is a matter for further investigation. It could also be that where no change was needed, the worker felt no need to change the confidence level from its default setting ('very sure'). Thus in future work we will consider alternative methods of collecting confidence ratings: either with larger scales or an interface other than radio buttons.

Another indicator of the changes made by the crowdworkers comes from lexical diversity scores: the mean type-token ratio (TTR) of the original SUs is 0.872 (st.dev=0.114), whereas mean TTR of the corrected SUs is 0.915 (st.dev=0.089). This overall increase in diversity suggests that one way in which workers 'improved' the SUs was to make them more expressive in terms of vocabulary use.

Of the 727 SUs annotated by crowdworkers, 433 were annotated at least twice. For all pairwise comparisons within a set of SU annotations we measured identical corrections, like Sakaguchi and colleagues (2016) on the basis that interannotator agreement is difficult to operationalise and arguably an inappropriate measure for error annotation (Bryant and Ng, 2015). Having made 7676 comparisons in this way, we find that 14.8% of error corrections are identical, a figure close to the 15.3% reported for the 'expert' annotators in Sakaguchi et al's study (and well above the 5.9% for the 'non-expert' crowdworkers).

We also report translation edit rate (TER) – a measure of the number of edits needed to transform one text into another, where an edit is an insertion, deletion, substitution, or phrasal shift, and where TER is expressed as edits per token (Snover et al., 2006).

In Table 6 we selected a speech-unit from the BULATS corpus along with two crowdsourced corrections. In the first correction, minimal edits have been made to make the SU more acceptable in grammatical terms (*that's → is, a the → a, are → is*). In the second version the correction is more holistic, even with punctuation (which was not called for), and the resulting SU is fluent. This latter type of correction is the one we seek, though it's clear from this example that not all corrections were done in a holistic way. One method to determine the success of crowdsourcing fluency edits would be to sample and rate corrections for fluency. We will incorporate this approach into further inspection of speech-units and the way they were corrected in future work.

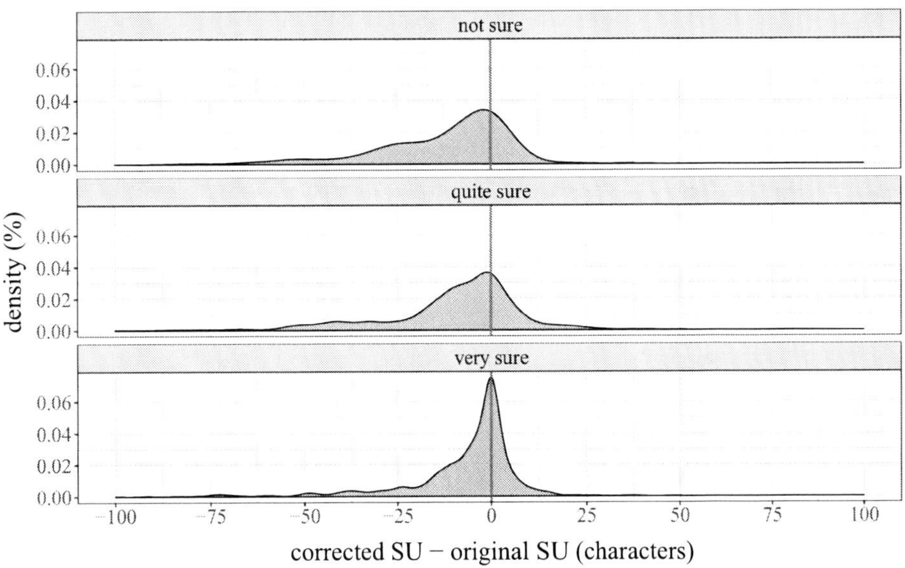

Figure 2: Density plot of the difference between corrected SU and original SU in characters, by crowd-workers' self-reported confidence level.

Version	Speech-unit	TER
original	I think in a newspaper that's an option and a the reference from a past employer are very important	0
corrected.1	I think in a newspaper is an option and a reference from a past employer is very important	3/19
corrected.2	I think that when advertising in a newspaper that's an option and also asking for a reference from a past employer is very important	10/19

Table 6: Example crowdsourced corrections for a speech-unit from the BULATS corpus.

In Figure 3 we show that for each CEFR level, firstly the proportion of SUs marked 'fine', or in need of no correction, tends to increase with increasing proficiency, and secondly mean TER scores for each SU rise from levels A1 to B1, and then fall again to C1 and C2. We hypothesise that the reason for this is that learners become more 'adventurous' in the linguistic constructions they attempt to use as they move from the A1 and A2 proficiency levels to B1 and B2. Thus their speech-units become in need of *more* correction, despite their improving capability with English. Part of their development into C1 and C2 level speakers is to become more accurate with the more complex construction types; hence SUs are in *less* need of correction. This is a 'U-shaped' developmental trajectory previously observed in language acquisition (Gershkoff-Stowe and Thelen, 2004).

4 Related work

Our work relates to previous attempts to collect error annotations through crowdsourcing (Tetreault et al., 2010; Madnani et al., 2011), which have concluded in its favour on the whole. Moreover we focus on *fluent* error corrections, as Sakaguchi and colleagues do (2016). Note also that crowdworkers were engaged in speech transcription, which is itself an established practice (Snow et al., 2008; Novotney and Callison-Burch, 2010).

Within second language acquisition research, we are focused on the *fluency* part of the well-established 'complexity accuracy fluency' framework (Housen and Kuiken, 2009). In future work we intend to turn to the complexity and accuracy dimensions as well. The framework gives us a useful way to consider automated assessment and feedback for language learners.

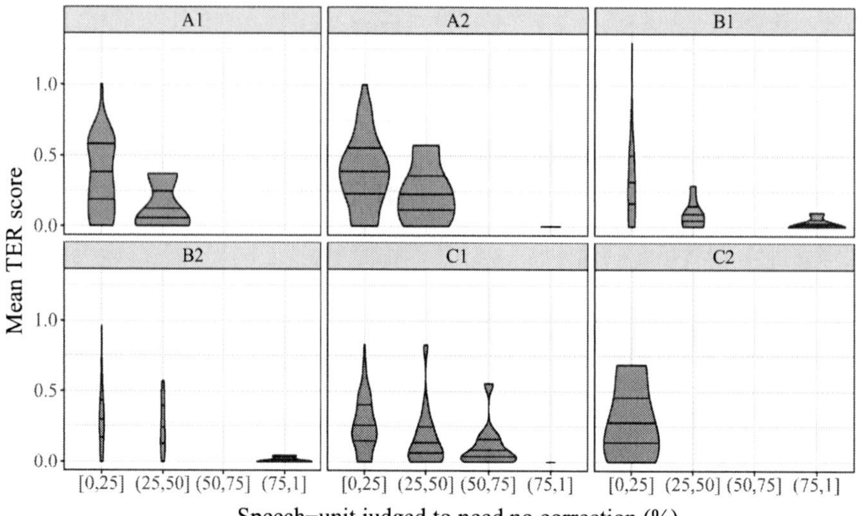

Figure 3: Proportion of SUs marked 'fine' by crowdworkers x Mean TER score for each CEFR level (width of 'violins' indicates density; horizontal lines mark first, second and third quartiles).

5 Conclusion and future work

In this paper we have presented our efforts to crowdsource fluency corrections of spoken learner English. We found that crowdworkers were tentative in applying corrections to SUs, more so for low CEFRs. When they did attempt to correct SUs though, we did find an overall decrease in SU length, an increase in lexical diversity, and TER scores which suggest U-shaped edit quantities by proficiency level.

Further evaluation of annotation quality remains to be carried out, including fluency ratings of the corrected versions. Also in future work we intend to repeat this work on an open dataset, such as the CrowdED Corpus (Caines et al., 2016), so that the resulting annotations can be released to others. Currently the BULATS corpus is not openly available.

One option for future annotations is to offer the original and corrected speech-units in parallel corpus format for machine translation approaches to error correction (Brockett et al., 2006; Park and Levy, 2011; Susanto et al., 2014; Junczys-Dowmunt and Grundkiewicz, 2016; Yuan et al., 2016), and with automatically aligned error annotations at the token level for classifier and rule-based approaches – the format used for GEC so far, as in the FCE and NUCLE datasets (Yannakoudakis et al., 2011; Dahlmeier et al., 2013).

This would be in line with the call by Sakaguchi and colleagues for new annotated corpora for HEC research (Sakaguchi et al., 2016). We believe that whole sentence or speech-unit corrections lend themselves well to the recent emergence of neural network MT systems for error correction, since these are essentially sequence-to-sequence translations (Yuan and Briscoe, 2016). The challenge would be to build a sufficiently large training corpus for NMT: crowdsourcing would seem to be a fast and good-enough data collection method. Moreover, a hybrid MT-classifier system (Rozovskaya and Roth, 2016) may suit the goal of automated feedback, whereby the learner can be informed of detected errors and how to avoid them.

In any future data collection we need to install controls against crowdworkers' tendency to annotate higher proficiency items in preference to lower proficiency items. For example, we could remove the facility for skipping items, or there could be only a limited facility to do so (since we do find this information useful too). We could also present more context than the prompt alone – for example, the preceding and following speech-units. Finally, we will further investigate correction behaviours: to what extent crowdworkers followed our request to consider *spoken* English as the model, rather than written norms, and to what extent they aimed for holistic fluency corrections rather than minimal grammatical edits.

98

Acknowledgments

This paper reports on research supported by Cambridge English, University of Cambridge. We are grateful to our colleagues Kate Knill, Calbert Graham and Russell Moore. The second author received funding to pay crowdworkers from Sidney Sussex College, Cambridge, and the Department of Theoretical & Applied Linguistics at the University of Cambridge. We thank the three reviewers for their very helpful comments and have attempted to improve the paper in line with their suggestions.

References

JJ Allaire. 2016. *rsconnect: Deployment Interface for R Markdown Documents and Shiny Applications*. R package version 0.5.

Øistein Andersen, Helen Yannakoudakis, Fiona Barker, and Tim Parish. 2013. Developing and testing a self-assessment and tutoring system. In *Proceedings of the Eighth Workshop on Innovative Use of NLP for Building Educational Applications*. Association for Computational Linguistics.

Holly P. Branigan, Martin J. Pickering, Janet F. McLean, and Alexandra A. Cleland. 2007. Syntactic alignment and participant role in dialogue. *Cognition* 104:163–197.

Chris Brockett, William B. Dolan, and Michael Gamon. 2006. Correcting ESL errors using phrasal SMT techniques. In *Proceedings of the 21st International Conference on Computational Linguistics and 44th Annual Meeting of the Association for Computational Linguistics*.

Christopher Bryant and Hwee Tou Ng. 2015. How far are we from fully automatic high quality grammatical error correction? In *Proceedings of the 53rd Annual Meeting of the Association for Computational Linguistics and the 7th International Joint Conference on Natural Language Processing (Volume 1: Long Papers)*.

Janet Cahn and Susan Brennan. 1999. A psychological model of grounding and repair in dialog. In *Proceedings, AAAI Fall Symposium on Psychological Models of Communication in Collaborative Systems*.

Andrew Caines, Christian Bentz, Calbert Graham, Tim Polzehl, and Paula Buttery. 2016. Crowdsourcing a multilingual speech corpus: recording, transcription and annotation of the CROWDED CORPUS. In *Proceedings of the Tenth International Conference on Language Resources and Evaluation (LREC 2016)*.

Winston Chang, Joe Cheng, JJ Allaire, Yihui Xie, and Jonathan McPherson. 2016. *shiny: Web Application Framework for R*. R package version 0.14.2.

Herbert Clark and Edward Schaefer. 1987. Collaborating on contributions to conversations. *Language and Cognitive Processes* 2:19–41.

Daniel Dahlmeier and Hwee Tou Ng. 2012. A beam-search decoder for grammatical error correction. In *Proceedings of the 2012 Joint Conference on Empirical Methods in Natural Language Processing and Computational Natural Language Learning*.

Daniel Dahlmeier, Hwee Tou Ng, and Siew Mei Wu. 2013. Building a large annotated corpus of learner English: the NUS Corpus of Learner English. In *Proceedings of the Eighth Workshop on Innovative Use of NLP for Building Educational Applications*.

Rachele De Felice and Stephen G. Pulman. 2008. A classifier-based approach to preposition and determiner error correction in L2 English. In *Proceedings of the 22nd International Conference on Computational Linguistics (Coling 2008)*.

Lisa Gershkoff-Stowe and Esther Thelen. 2004. U-shaped changes in behavior: A dynamic systems perspective. *Journal of Cognition and Development* 5(1):11–36.

Alex Housen and Folkert Kuiken. 2009. Complexity, fluency, and accuracy in second language acquisition. *Applied Linguistics* 30:461–473.

Marcin Junczys-Dowmunt and Roman Grundkiewicz. 2016. Phrase-based machine translation is state-of-the-art for automatic grammatical error correction. In *Proceedings of the 2016 Conference on Empirical Methods in Natural Language Processing*.

Nitin Madnani, Joel Tetreault, Martin Chodorow, and Alla Rozovskaya. 2011. They can help: using crowdsourcing to improve the evaluation of grammatical error detection systems. In *Proceedings of the 49th Annual Meeting of the Association for Computational Linguistics*. Association for Computational Linguistics.

Russell Moore, Andrew Caines, Calbert Graham, and Paula Buttery. 2016. Automated speech-unit delimitation in spoken learner English. In *Proceedings of COLING*.

Hwee Tou Ng, Siew Mei Wu, Ted Briscoe, Christian Hadiwinoto, Raymond Hendy Susanto, and Christopher Bryant. 2014. The conll-2014 shared task on grammatical error correction. In *Proceedings of the Eighteenth Conference on Computational Natural Language Learning: Shared Task*.

Diane Nicholls. 2003. The cambridge learner corpus: error coding and analysis for lexicography and elt. In Dawn Archer, Paul Rayson, Andrew Wilson, and Tony McEnery, editors, *Proceedings of the Corpus Linguistics 2003 conference; UCREL technical paper number 16*. Lancaster University.

Scott Novotney and Chris Callison-Burch. 2010. Cheap, fast and good enough: Automatic speech recognition with non-expert transcription. In *Human Language Technologies: The 2010 Annual Conference of the North American Chapter of the Association for Computational Linguistics*.

Y. Albert Park and Roger Levy. 2011. Automated whole sentence grammar correction using a noisy channel model. In *Proceedings of the 49th Annual Meeting of the Association for Computational Linguistics: Human Language Technologies*.

Eyal Peer, Laura Brandimarte, Sonam Samat, and Alessandro Acquisti. 2017. Beyond the turk: Alternative platforms for crowdsourcing behavioral research. *Journal of Experimental Social Psychology* 70:153–163.

Martin Pickering and Simon Garrod. 2004. Toward a mechanistic psychology of dialogue. *Behavioral and Brain Sciences* 27:169–190.

R Core Team. 2017. *R: a language and environment for statistical computing*. R Foundation for Statistical Computing, Vienna.

Alla Rozovskaya and Dan Roth. 2016. Grammatical error correction: Machine translation and classifiers. In *Proceedings of the 54th Annual Meeting of the Association for Computational Linguistics (Volume 1: Long Papers)*.

Keisuke Sakaguchi, Courtney Napoles, Matt Post, and Joel Tetreault. 2016. Reassessing the goals of grammatical error correction: fluency instead of grammaticality. *Transactions of the Association for Computational Linguistics* 4:169–182.

Matthew Snover, Bonnie Dorr, Richard Schwartz, Linnea Micciulla, and John Makhoul. 2006. A study of Translation Edit Rate with targeted human annotation. In *Proceedings of Association for Machine Translation in the Americas*.

Rion Snow, Brendan O'Connor, Daniel Jurafsky, and Andrew Ng. 2008. Cheap and fast – but is it good? evaluating non-expert annotations for natural language tasks. In *Proceedings of the 2008 Conference on Empirical Methods in Natural Language Processing*.

Raymond Hendy Susanto, Peter Phandi, and Hwee Tou Ng. 2014. System combination for grammatical error correction. In *Proceedings of the 2014 Conference on Empirical Methods in Natural Language Processing (EMNLP)*.

Joel Tetreault, Elena Filatova, and Martin Chodorow. 2010. Rethinking grammatical error annotation and evaluation with the Amazon Mechanical Turk. In *Proceedings of the NAACL HLT 2010 Fifth Workshop on Innovative Use of NLP for Building Educational Applications*.

Rogier van Dalen, Kate Knill, Pirros Tsiakoulis, and Mark Gales. 2015. Improving multiple-crowdsourced transcriptions using a speech recogniser. In *Proceedings of the International Conference on Acoustics, Speech and Signal Processing (ICASSP)*.

Helen Yannakoudakis, Ted Briscoe, and Ben Medlock. 2011. A new dataset and method for automatically grading ESOL texts. In *Proceedings of the 49th Annual Meeting of the Association for Computational Linguistics: Human Language Technologies-Volume 1*.

Zheng Yuan and Ted Briscoe. 2016. Grammatical error correction using neural machine translation. In *Proceedings of the 2016 Conference of the North American Chapter of the Association for Computational Linguistics: Human Language Technologies*.

Zheng Yuan, Ted Briscoe, and Mariano Felice. 2016. Candidate re-ranking for SMT-based grammatical error correction. In *Proceedings of the 11th Workshop on Innovative Use of NLP for Building Educational Applications*.

Exploring Relationships Between Writing & Broader Outcomes With Automated Writing Evaluation

Jill Burstein   Dan McCaffrey   Beata Beigman Klebanov   Guangming Ling
{jburstein, dmccaffrey, bbeigmanklebanov, gling}@ets.org

Educational Testing Service
Princeton, NJ 08541

Abstract

No significant body of research examines writing achievement and the specific skills and knowledge in the writing domain for postsecondary (college) students in the U.S., even though many at-risk students lack the prerequisite writing skills required to persist in their education. This paper addresses this gap through a novel *exploratory* study examining how automated writing evaluation (AWE) can inform our understanding of the relationship between postsecondary writing skill and broader indicators of college success. The exploratory study presented in this paper was conducted using test-taker essays from a standardized writing assessment of postsecondary student learning outcomes. Findings showed that for the essays, AWE features were found to be predictors of *broader outcomes* measures: college success indicators and learning outcomes measures. Study findings expose AWE's potential to support educational analytics -- i.e., relationships between writing skill and broader outcomes –moving AWE beyond writing assessment and instructional use cases.

1   Introduction

Writing is a challenge, especially for at-risk students who may lack the prerequisite writing skills required to persist in U.S. 4-year postsecondary (college) institutions (NCES, 2012). Educators teaching postsecondary courses that require writing could benefit from a better understanding of writing achievement and its role in postsecondary success (college completion). U.S K-12 research examines writing achievement and the specific skills and knowledge in the writing domain (Berninger, Nagy & Beers, 2011; Olinghouse, Graham, & Gillespie, 2015). No parallel significant body of research exists for postsecondary students. There has been research related to essay writing on standardized tests and college success

indicators for exams, such as the College Board Advanced Placement[1] (Bridgeman & Lewis, 1994). However, only the final overall essay score is evaluated. In this work, we try to *drill deeper* into essays to explore if specific features in the writing of college students is related to measures of broader outcomes.

Automated writing evaluation (AWE) systems typically support the measurement of pertinent writing skills for automated scoring of large-volume, high-stakes assessments (Attali & Burstein, 2006; Shermis et al, 2015) and online instruction (Burstein et al, 2004; Foltz et al, 2013; Roscoe et al, 2014). AWE has been used primarily for on-demand essay writing on standardized assessments. However, the real-time, dynamic nature of NLP-based AWE affords the ability to explore linguistic features and skill relationships across a range of writing genres in postsecondary education, such as, on-demand essay writing tasks, argumentative essays from the social sciences, and lab reports in STEM courses (Burstein et al, 2016). Such relationships can provide educational analytics that could be informative for various stakeholders, including students, instructors, parents, administrators and policy-makers.

This paper discusses an *exploratory* secondary data analysis, using AWE to examine interactions between writing and broader outcomes measures of student success. An evaluation was conducted using test-taker essays from a standardized writing assessment of postsecondary student learning outcomes. Findings suggested that AWE features from the essays were found to be predictors of broader outcomes measures: *college success indicators* and *learning outcomes measures*. Recent

---

[1] https://apstudent.collegeboard.org/home

Proceedings of the 12th Workshop on Innovative Use of NLP for Building Educational Applications, pages 101–108
Copenhagen, Denmark, September 8, 2017. ©2017 Association for Computational Linguistics

work has shown similar results, examining relationships between AWE and read ing skills (Allen et al, 2016) versus broader outcomes measures

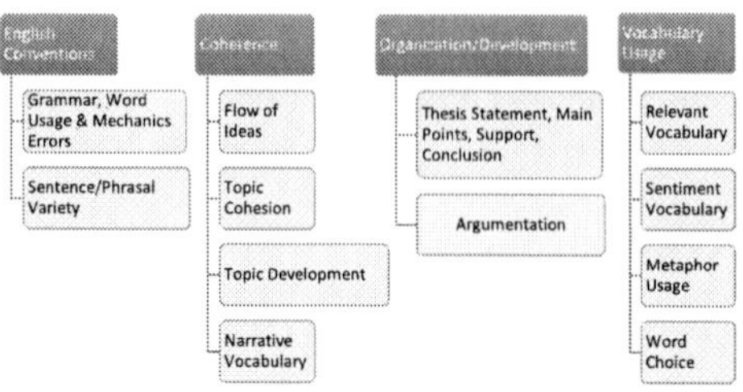

Figure 1. Construct representation of the AWE features extracted from pilot study essays.

(discussed here).

The work presented here broadens the lens -- exposing AWE's potential to inform our understanding of the relationship between writing and critical educational outcomes above and beyond prevalent use cases for assessment and instruction of writing itself.

2 The Study

An *exploratory* secondary data analysis was conducted to examine relationships between responses to a 45-minute, timed standardized *writing assessment* of postsecondary student learning. The writing assessment contains two components: an *on demand essay task* requiring students to compose an essay in response to a prompt wherein they must adopt or defend a position or a claim presented in the prompt; and 15 *selected-response* (SR) (multiple choice) items related to one reading passage. The SR portion measures writing domain knowledge skills, such as English conventions, vocabulary choice, evaluating evidence, analyzing arguments, understanding the language of argumentation, evaluating organization, distinguishing between valid and invalid arguments, and evaluating tone. The *writing assessment* is <u>one of three</u> component skills assessments from an outcomes assessment suite. A second *critical thinking* component test is also used for this study. It is also a 45-minute, timed assessment, composed of 27 or 29 selected-response items depending on the test form (i.e., version of a test). The pilot study includes 5 forms (versions) for the *critical thinking* test. The five forms were developed under the same test specification and their scores were linked to each other and can be used interchangeably (Liu, et al., 2016).

In this study, we examine relationships between AWE features found in essay responses of 4-year postsecondary students who took the writing assessment, and indicators of college success.

2.1 Data

To evaluate the psychometric properties of the assessment and to gather evidence on the reliability and validity of the test prior to its release, the authors' organization had previously conducted an extensive pilot test of the assessment at more than 33 colleges and universities. Analyses used all data collected from 929 students (37% first-year, 29% sophomores, 16% junior, and 18% seniors) enrolled at the institutions; students had completed one of two pilot forms of the *writing assessment*. Of the 929 students, 514 also had scores from the pilot *critical thinking assessment*.

In addition to the *writing assessment* essay text, the pilot test data includes human ratings for the essay responses, and selected-response items scores. We also had access to students' college GPA and some external measures such as, the *critical thinking assessment scores*, SAT[2] or ACT[3] scores, high school grade point average (GPA). Although these variables were missing for subsamples of students.

2.2 Methods

Several hundred AWE features were generated for the essay writing data. These features were drawn from a large portfolio of features used for analysis of student writing (including features from a commercial essay scoring engine). As this was an initial exploratory analysis, one of the authors selected an initial, manageable set of 61 construct-relevant features related to subconstructs, including English writing conventions (e.g., errors in grammar and mechanics), coherence (e.g., flow of ideas), organization and development, vocabulary, and topicality. See Figure 1 (above). The author hypothesized that this 61-feature subset would have strong predictive potential based on the subconstruct that each feature was intended

---

[2] https://collegereadiness.collegeboard.org/sat

[3] http://www.act.org/

Feature Name	Subconstruct Class	NLP-Based Feature / Resource Description
argumentation	argumentation	Detection of sentences containing argumentation (Beigman Klebanov et al, 2017)
dis_coh1	coherence	Aggregate discourse coherence quality measure (Somasundaran et al, 2014)
gen_max_lsa	coherence	Latent semantic analysis values computed for long-distance sentence pairs (Somasundaran et al, 2014)
dis_coh2, dis_coh3, dis_coh4	coherence	Three measures related to topic distribution in a text (Beigman Klebanov et al, 2013; Burstein et al, 2016)
fphajnp	collocation	Noun phrase collocations identified using a rank-ratio based collocation detection algorithm trained on the Google Web1T n-gram corpus (Futagi et al, 2008)
logdta	discourse	Aggregate value based on length of essay-based discourse element (Attali & Burstein, 2006) derived from a discourse structure detection method that identifies essay-based discourse elements (e.g., thesis statement) (Burstein et al, 2003)
grammaticality	English conventions	Aggregate value generated for relative grammaticality (Heilman et al, 2014)
logg	English conventions	Aggregate value from a set of 9 automatically-detected *grammar* error feature types (Attali & Burstein, 2006)
nsqm	English conventions	Aggregate value from a set of 12 automatically-detected *mechanics* error feature types (Attali & Burstein, 2006)
nsqu	English conventions	Aggregate value from a set of 10 automatically-detected *word usage* error feature types (Attali & Burstein, 2006)
statives	narrativity	Count measures using a manually-compiled list of *stative* verbs (i.e., express states vs. action, e.g., *feel*).
PR1, PR2	personal reflection	Aggregate scores generated related to use of personal reflection language (Beigman Klebanov et al, 2017)
complexnp	phrasal complexity	Noun phrases identified with a hyphenated adjective or a prepositional phrase modifier using regular expressions defined on constituency parses.
svf	sentence variety	Aggregate value generated based on sentence-type factors (Burstein et al, 2013)
topicdev	topic development	Detection of main topics and related words (Beigman Klebanov et al , 2013; Burstein et al, 2016)
nwf_median	vocabulary sophistication	Aggregate measure generated related to word frequency (Attali & Burstein (2006)
wordln_2	vocabulary sophistication	Aggregate measure generated related to average word length for all words in a text (Attali & Burstein, 2006)
variants1, variants2	vocabulary usage	Detection of morphologically complex inflectional (variants1) and derivational (variants2) word forms using an algorithm that first over-generates variants using rules and then filters using co-occurrence statistics computed over Gigaword. (Madnani et al, 2016)
metaphor	vocabulary usage	Detection of metaphor (Beigman Klebanov et al (2015); Beigman Klebanov et al (2016)
sentiment	vocabulary usage	Count measures based on VADER[4] sentiment lexicon entries.
vocab_richness	vocabulary usage	Aggregate feature composed of a number of text-based vocabulary-related measures (e.g., morphological complexity, relatedness of words in a text). This work is not yet published.
colprep	vocabulary usage	Aggregate measure related to collocation and preposition use (described in Burstein et al, 2013).

Table 1: The 26 Features, Subconstructs & Methods

---

[4] https://github.com/cjhutto/vaderSentiment

to address, and its alignment with the writing assessment construct Before modeling the interactions between the 61 AWE features and other measures, an analysis was conducted to identify features that were functionally related or strongly correlated to remove redundant features. This analysis identified 35 features that were monotonic functions of other features (e.g., one feature equaled the log of a second features), very highly linearly correlated, or have very small variance. Among features that were functionally related or highly correlated, the feature most highly correlated with human ratings of the essay were retained. The outcome of this analysis was the set of 26 features listed in Table 1 (below). Only the 26 features in this subset were used for the analysis reported here.

The analysis consisted of linear regression analyses with the AWE features as the independent (or predictor) variables and scores on the critical thinking assessment, SAT or ACT, *writing assessment* selected-response (SR) items, and college GPA as the dependent variables. Separate regression analyses were conducted for each dependent variable. For example, there was a model predicting GPA as a function of *argumentation*, another model predicting GPA as function of *dis_coh1*, another model predicting GPA as a function of *gen_max_lsa*, and so on for each of the features. This modeling process was repeated for each of the dependent variables. The goal of the analysis was to determine how strongly each feature was related to each outcome. However, since better writers will probably get better scores on other tests too, we wanted to know if the features contained unique information for predicting the dependent variables, above and beyond how well the essay was written. That is, we wanted to know if two students who appear to be comparable writers based on human scores can be further differentiated by the additional properties of their writing as captured by AWE. Therefore, for each dependent variable, a series of regression models were fit that predicted the dependent variable not only as a function of each of the feature values, but also included the length of the essay and the average of the human ratings on a 6-point scale (where 1 indicates the lowest proficiency and 6, the highest). The regression models included these two additional predictors because both are related to the quality of the essay. Essay length is generally a good predictor of human ratings of essays and related to many AWE features (Chodorow & Burstein, 2004). By including these two additional predictors in the model, we were better able to isolate the relationship between the features and the dependent variable distinct from quality of the essay.

3   Results

Tables 2 to 8 (below) present the results of the regression analyses for each of the 6 outcomes. For presentation purposes, the table for each dependent variable includes only those features where the coefficient for that feature was significantly greater than zero with a p-value less than 0.05. Across all the dependent variables, 25 of the 26 variables appear in the table for one or more dependent variables. Only one feature, *metaphor*, did not emerge from the analyses. Given that 26 features were tested for each dependent variable, there is a considerable chance that p-values below 0.05 were sometimes due to chance and did not indicate a statistically significant relationship. Controlling for multiple comparisons would be required to reduce the probability of spurious p-values of less than 0.05. P-values were used to reduce the size of the tables and focus on features with the strongest evidence of a relationship with each dependent variable.

Each row contains a standardized coefficient from a model that included 3 features: (1) the AWE feature, (2) the square root of the number of words (length), and (3) the raw average of 2-3 human ratings per essay. In addition to the coefficient for the AWE feature and its standard error, the table includes the overall R-squared (R^2) for the three independent variables (AWE feature, length, and average human rating) and the *part* of the R-squared attributable to the AWE features (Inc. R^2). The R^2 measures the variance explained by the predictor.

All features in the tables explain some amount of variance showing promise of relationships between AWE features and college success and learning outcomes. Results show that for all outcomes, a breadth of features emerge, covering the *English conventions, coherence* or *argumentation*, and *vocabulary* subconstructs. Features shown in *italics* in Tables 2-8 indicate relatively stronger predictors (i.e., greater explained variance), using Inc. R^2 of 0.05 as a "cutoff". *Vocabulary sophistication* ("wordln_2") and *vocabulary usage* ("vocab_richness") were the stronger predictors of the *critical thinking assessment* scores, the SAT/ACT Composite Score and SAT Verbal Score. *Vocabulary usage* ("sentiment") was a stronger predictor in ACT Science.

4   Discussion and Future Work

This *exploratory*, secondary data analysis illustrates that 1) writing can provide meaningful information about student knowledge related to broader outcomes (college success indicators and learning outcomes measures) and 2) AWE has greater potential for educational analytics above and beyond current prevalent uses for writing assessment and instruction. Vocabulary features were the most consistent and strongest predictors. This is not surprising since most of the college success predictors used in this study involved intensive reading, and vocabulary knowledge is shown to be related to reading comprehension (Qian & Schedl, 2004; Quinn et al, 2015). The detailed analyses illustrated in Tables 2 – 8 do show statistically significant relationships between the full set of writing skill feature measures and broader outcomes. The big picture is that this line of research could inform instructional curriculum, assessment development, and educational policy vis-à-vis the improvement of college student success factors.

The *limitations* of this project are the small size of the data set since students were missing some of the dependent variables, and the examination of writing data from a single writing genre – i.e., on-demand essay writing. However, these will be addressed in next steps, in Fall 2017-Spring 2018. The authors will conduct a larger study with seven 4-year postsecondary partner institutions. A larger sample of student writing will be collected from approximately 2,000 students from the sites. Student writing data collected will include not only on-demand essay writing, but students will each also provide multiple authentic writing assignments from their courses. Both writing and disciplinary courses will be included in the study. Student success factor

data, such as, SAT and ACT scores, college GPA, course grades, and course completion, will also be collected. We will administer the same *writing assessment* and *critical thinking assessment* to our outcomes measures. Using the new data, we will apply knowledge from this study to continue to evaluate how AWE can provide analytics related to broader outcomes measures. Further, this larger data set will span different genres which will afford the opportunity to 1) replicate this exploratory study on the same writing assessment as a baseline, and 2) apply current and enhanced analyses to authentic writing data collected from college students.

AWE has traditionally been used for writing assessment (automated essay scoring), and writing instruction (automated feedback about writing). The work presented in this paper explores new territory, and brings awareness to the potential impact of NLP in a bigger educational space – i.e., to support understanding of relationships between writing and broader outcomes of student success.

Variable	Coeffcient	Std. Error	R^2	Inc. R^2
logg	0.10	0.04	0.22	0.01
nsqu	0.17	0.04	0.24	0.02
nsqm	0.11	0.04	0.22	0.01
svf	0.27	0.06	0.25	0.03
nwf_median	0.18	0.04	0.24	0.03
wordln_2	*0.25*	*0.04*	*0.27*	*0.06*
PR1	-0.08	0.04	0.22	0.01
fphajnp	0.08	0.04	0.22	0.01
complexnp	0.12	0.04	0.23	0.01
variants1	0.23	0.04	0.26	0.04
vocab_richness	*0.27*	*0.05*	*0.26*	*0.05*
dis_coh1	0.40	0.13	0.23	0.01
sentiment	0.15	0.04	0.23	0.02

Table 2: *Critical Thinking* Composite Score; Baseline R^2 with human rating and length = 0.21

Variable	Coefficient	Std. Error	R^2	Inc. R^2
nsqu	0.12	0.03	0.23	0.01
nsqm	0.21	0.03	0.25	0.04
svf	0.11	0.04	0.22	0.01
wordln_2	0.19	0.03	0.24	0.03
grammaticality	0.12	0.03	0.22	0.01
colprep	0.08	0.03	0.22	0.01
dis_coh3	-0.10	0.03	0.22	0.01
dis_coh4	-0.11	0.05	0.22	0.00
fphajnp	0.11	0.03	0.22	0.01
complexnp	0.08	0.03	0.22	0.01
variants2	0.13	0.03	0.22	0.01
vocab_richness	0.13	0.03	0.22	0.01
dis_coh1	0.23	0.09	0.22	0.01
sentiment	0.06	0.03	0.22	0.00
statives	-0.13	0.03	0.23	0.02

Table 3: *Writing Assessment* Selected Response Score; Baseline R^2 with human rating and length = 0.21

Variable	Coefficient	Std. Error	R^2	Inc. R^2
logg	0.09	0.04	0.17	0.01
nsqu	0.10	0.04	0.17	0.01
nsqm	0.17	0.04	0.18	0.03
svf	0.25	0.05	0.19	0.03
nwf_median	0.14	0.04	0.18	0.02
wordln_2	*0.25*	*0.04*	*0.21*	*0.06*
grammaticality	0.08	0.04	0.16	0.01
colprep	0.10	0.04	0.17	0.01
PR1	-0.12	0.04	0.17	0.01
PR2	-0.12	0.04	0.17	0.01
fphajnp	0.13	0.04	0.18	0.02
complexnp	0.12	0.04	0.17	0.01
variants2	0.20	0.04	0.19	0.03
gen_max_lsa5	-0.12	0.06	0.16	0.01
vocab_richness	*0.31*	*0.04*	*0.22*	*0.06*
dis_coh1	0.26	0.12	0.16	0.01
sentiment	0.17	0.04	0.19	0.03

Table 4: SAT/ACT Composite Score (ACT rescaled to the SAT Scale); Baseline R^2 with human rating and length = 0.16

Variable	Coefficient	Std. Error	R^2	Inc. R^2
logg	0.11	0.04	0.18	0.01
nsqu	0.14	0.04	0.18	0.02
nsqm	0.15	0.04	0.18	0.02
svf	0.29	0.06	0.21	0.04
nwf_median	0.15	0.04	0.19	0.02
wordln_2	*0.29*	*0.04*	*0.24*	*0.07*
grammaticality	0.11	0.05	0.17	0.01
colprep	0.12	0.05	0.18	0.01
argumentation	0.13	0.05	0.18	0.01
PR1	-0.15	0.04	0.19	0.02
PR2	-0.12	0.05	0.18	0.01
fphajnp	0.11	0.05	0.17	0.01
complexnp	0.12	0.05	0.18	0.01
variants1	0.13	0.05	0.18	0.01
variants2	0.22	0.05	0.20	0.04
gen_max_lsa5	-0.13	0.06	0.17	0.01
vocab_richness	*0.33*	*0.05*	*0.23*	*0.07*
dis_coh1	0.28	0.13	0.17	0.01
sentiment	0.12	0.04	0.18	0.01

Table 5. SAT Verbal Score; Baseline R^2 with human rating and length = 0.16

Variable	Coefficient	Std. Error	R^2	Inc. R^2
nsqm	0.22	0.05	0.14	0.04
svf	0.19	0.06	0.12	0.02
nwf_median	0.14	0.05	0.12	0.02
wordln_2	0.20	0.05	0.14	0.03
colprep	0.10	0.05	0.11	0.01
PR1	-0.12	0.05	0.12	0.01
PR2	-0.13	0.05	0.11	0.01
fphajnp	0.10	0.05	0.11	0.01
complexnp	0.11	0.05	0.11	0.01
variants2	0.15	0.05	0.12	0.02
gen_max_lsa	-0.16	0.07	0.11	0.01
vocab_richness	0.24	0.05	0.14	0.04
sentiment	0.18	0.04	0.13	0.03

Table 6. SAT Math Score; Baseline R^2 with human rating and length = 0.10

ACT English				
Variable	**Coefficient**	**Std. Error**	**R^2**	**Inc. R^2**
nsqu	0.11	0.05	0.16	0.01
nsqm	0.15	0.05	0.17	0.02
logdta	-0.19	0.06	0.18	0.03
svf	0.17	0.07	0.17	0.02
wordln_2	0.16	0.06	0.18	0.02
dis_coh2	0.21	0.11	0.16	0.01
argumentation	0.16	0.07	0.17	0.01
variants1	0.13	0.05	0.17	0.02
vocab_richness	0.16	0.06	0.17	0.02
sentiment	0.24	0.07	0.19	0.03

ACT Math				
Variable	**Coefficient**	**Std. Error**	**R^2**	**Inc. R^2**
svf	0.18	0.07	0.12	0.02
wordln_2	0.15	0.06	0.13	0.02
complexnp	0.16	0.06	0.13	0.02
variants2	0.15	0.06	0.12	0.02
variants1	0.15	0.06	0.12	0.02
vocab_richness	0.21	0.07	0.13	0.03
dis_coh1	0.38	0.17	0.12	0.02
sentiment	0.19	0.06	0.14	0.03

ACT Reading				
Variable	**Coefficient**	**Std. Error**	**R^2**	**Inc. R^2**
logg	0.11	0.05	0.14	0.01
svf	0.17	0.07	0.15	0.02
wordln_2	0.17	0.06	0.16	0.03
PR1	-0.11	0.05	0.15	0.01
variants1	0.16	0.06	0.15	0.02
vocab_richness	0.23	0.07	0.16	0.03
sentiment	0.20	0.06	0.17	0.04
statives	-0.14	0.05	0.15	0.02

ACT Science				
Variable	**Coefficient**	**Std. Error**	**R^2**	**Inc. R^2**
logdta	-0.14	0.07	0.09	0.01
svf	0.22	0.08	0.10	0.03
wordln_2	0.14	0.06	0.09	0.02
fphajnp	0.15	0.06	0.10	0.02
complexnp	0.16	0.06	0.10	0.02
variants1	0.17	0.06	0.10	0.02
vocab_richness	0.26	0.07	0.12	0.04
sentiment	*0.23*	*0.06*	*0.12*	*0.05*

Table 7. ACT Subject Test Scores; Baseline R^2 with human rating and length: ACT English = 0.15; ACT Math = 0.11; ACT Reading = 0.13; ACT Science = 0.08

Variable	**Coefficient**	**Std. Error**	**R^2**	**Inc. R^2**
nsqu	0.09	0.05	0.05	0.01
nsqm	0.16	0.05	0.07	0.02
wordln_2	0.13	0.05	0.06	0.02
grammaticality	0.13	0.05	0.06	0.01
argumentation	0.13	0.06	0.05	0.01
topicdev	-0.10	0.05	0.05	0.01
vocab_richness	0.12	0.05	0.05	0.01

Table 8. Cumulative GPA; Baseline R^2 with human rating and length = 0.04

Acknowledgements

Research presented in this paper was supported by the Institute of Education Science, U.S. Department of Education, Award Number R305A160115. Many thanks to Binod Gyawali, Michael Flor, and Diane Napolitano for support with this work.

References

Allen, L.K., Dascalu,M., McNamara, D.S., , Crossley, S.A, Trausan-Matu, S. (2016). In Proceedings of EDULEARN16 Conference 4th-6th July 2016, Barcelona, Spain, 5269-5279. Attali, Y., & Burstein, J. (2006). Automated essay scoring with e-rater V.2. *Journal of Technology, Learning, and Assessment, 4*(3), 1-31.

Beigman Klebanov, B., Burstein, J., Harackiewicz, J., Prinski, S., Mullholland, M. (2017) Reflective writing as a tool for increasing STEM motivation and retention -- can AI help scale it up? *Special Issue for the International Journal of Artificial Intelligence in Education: MARWIDE: Multidisciplinary Approaches to*

Reading and Writing Integrated with Disciplinary Education (Eds. D. McNamara, S. Muresan, R. J. Passonneau, & D. Perin).

Beigman Klebanov, B., Leong, C., Gutierrez, D., Shutova, E., Flor, M. (2016). *Semantic classifications for detection of verb metaphors.* Proceedings of the 54th Annual Meeting of the Association for Computational Linguistics, Berlin, Germany, 101-106.

Berninger, V. W., Nagy, W., & Beers, S. (2011). Child writers' construction and reconstruction of single sentences and construction of multi-sentence texts: contributions of syntax and transcription to translation. *Reading and Writing, 24,* 151-182. doi 10.1007/s11145-010-9262-y.

Bridgeman, B. and Lewis, C. (1994). The Relationship of Essay and Multiple-Choice Scores with Grades in College Courses, *Journal of Educational Measurement, 31*(1): 37-50.

Burstein, J., Beigman Klebanov, B., Elliot, N., & Molloy, H. (2016). A Left Turn: Automated Feedback & Activity Generation for Student Writers. To appear in the *Proceedings of the 3rd Language Teaching, Language & Technology Workshop*, co-located with Interspeech, San Francisco, CA.

Burstein, J., Tetreault, J., & Madnani, N. (2013). The E-rater® Automated Essay Scoring System. In Shermis, M.D., & Burstein, J. (Eds.), Handbook of Automated Essay Scoring: Current Applications and Future Directions. New York: Routledge.

Burstein, J., Chodorow, M., & Leacock, C. (2004). Automated essay evaluation: The Criterion Service. *AI Magazine, 25*(3), 27–36.

Burstein, J., Marcu, D., & Knight, K. (2003). Finding the WRITE stuff: Automatic identification of discourse structure in student essays. *IEEE Intelligent Systems: Special Issue on Advances in Natural Language Processing, 18*(1), 32–39.

Chodorow, M. and Burstein, J. (2004). Beyond Essay Length: Evaluating e-rater's Performance on TOEFL Essays. TOEFL Research Report 73, RR-04-04, Educational Testing Service, Princeton, NJ.

Foltz, P. W., Streeter, L. A., Lochbaum, K. E., & Landauer, T. K (2013). Implementation and applications of the Intelligent Essay Assessor. Handbook of Automated Essay Evaluation, M. Shermis & J. Burstein, (Eds.). Pp. 68-88. Routledge, NY. NY.

Futagi, Y., Deane, P., Chodorow, M., and Tetreault, J. (2008). A computational approach to detecting collocation errors in the writing of non-native speakers of English. Computer Assisted Language Learning, 21(4).

Heilman, M., Cahill, A., Madnani,N., Lopez, M., Mulholland, M. and Tetreault, J. (2014) *Predicting Grammaticality on an Ordinal Scale* Proceedings of the 52nd Annual Meeting of the Association for Computational Linguistics (Volume 2: Short Papers), pages 174-180, Baltimore, MD.

Liu, O. L., Mao, L., Frankel, L., & Xu, J. (2016). Assessing critical thinking in higher education: the *HEIghten*[TM] approach and preliminary evidence. *Assessment & Evaluation in Higher Education, 41,* 677-694.

Madnani, N., Burstein, J., Sabatini, J., Biggers, K., & Andreyev, S. (2016). *Language Muse*[TM]*: Automated Linguistic Activity Generation for English Language Learners.* Proceedings of the Annual Meeting of the Association for Computational Linguistics, Berlin, Germany.

National Center for Education Statistics (2012). *The nation's report card: Writing 2011* (NCES 2012–470). Washington, DC: Institute of Education Sciences, U.S. Department of Education.

Olinghouse, N. G., Graham, S., & Gillespie, A. (2015). The relationship of discourse and topic knowledge to fifth graders' writing performance. *Journal of Educational Psychology,* 107(2), 391-406.

Qian, D. and Schedl, M. (2004). Evaluation of an in-depth vocabulary knowledge measure for assessing reading performance. *Language Testing*, 21(1), 28-52.

Quinn J.M., Wagner R.K., Petscher Y, Lopez D. (2015). Developmental Relations Between Vocabulary Knowledge and Reading Comprehension: A Latent Change Score Modeling Study. Child Development, 6(1):159-75.

Roscoe, R. D., Allen, L. K., Weston, J. L., Crossley, S. A., & McNamara, D. S. (2014). The Writing Pal intelligent tutoring system: Usability testing and development. *Computers and Composition, 34,* 39-59.

Somasundaran, S., Burstein, J. and Chodorow, M. (2014) Lexical Chaining for Measuring Discourse Coherence Quality in Test-taker Essays, COLING 2014, Dublin, Ireland.

An Investigation into the Pedagogical Features of Documents

Emily Sheng, **Prem Natarajan**, **Jonathan Gordon**, and **Gully Burns**
USC Information Sciences Institute
Marina del Rey, CA, USA
{ewsheng, pnataraj, jgordon, burns}@isi.edu

Abstract

Characterizing the content of a technical document in terms of its learning utility can be useful for applications related to education, such as generating reading lists from large collections of documents. We refer to this learning utility as the "pedagogical value" of the document to the learner. While pedagogical value is an important concept that has been studied extensively within the education domain, there has been little work exploring it from a computational, i.e., natural language processing (NLP), perspective. To allow a computational exploration of this concept, we introduce the notion of "pedagogical roles" of documents (e.g., *Tutorial* and *Survey*) as an intermediary component for the study of pedagogical value. Given the lack of available corpora for our exploration, we create the first annotated corpus of pedagogical roles and use it to test baseline techniques for automatic prediction of such roles.

1 Introduction

We define "pedagogical value" as the estimate of how useful a document is to an individual who seeks to learn about specific concepts described in the document. A computational task that operationalizes the concept of pedagogical value is generating an ordered reading list of documents that a learner can traverse in order to maximize understanding of a subject. When a professor manually constructs a reading list about a specific subject for a student, the professor incorporates substantial knowledge of the subject history and interdependencies with other related subjects. The student's background and the relative qualities of documents on similar subjects are also considered. Techniques for automatically

generating reading lists should also consider the extent to which a learner will be able to learn from a particular document.

Previously, Tang and McCalla (2009) have studied the "pedagogical value of papers" in the context of paper recommendation. In their work, they define the multiple "pedagogical values" of a paper as the paper's overall ratings, popularity, degree of peer recommendation, learner gain in new knowledge, learner interest, and learner background knowledge. Other efforts on generating reading lists and document recommendation have focused on modeling concepts represented in documents (Jardine, 2014), modeling concept dependencies (Gordon et al., 2016), and user modeling (Bollacker et al., 1999), but there appears to be very limited work on characterizing the learning utility between a learner and a document. The abstract nature of pedagogical value motivates us to identify explicit document features that are salient to pedagogical value. With graduate students as our target learners, we start with a simplified model of novice, intermediate, and advanced learners, and we focus on identifying pedagogical features of documents that could benefit different learners.

In our document annotation process, we collected annotations for the qualitative and largely objective judgments of categories that documents belong to: *Tutorial, Survey, Software Manual, Resource, Reference Work, Empirical Results,* and *Other*. We identify the seven categories based on document objectives in presenting content, e.g., *Tutorials* teach the reader step by step how to do something, *Resource* papers point the reader to datasets and implementations. Motivated by the need to conceptually organize information to be pedagogically useful, we refer to documents with different objectives as fulfilling different "pedagogical roles." In the rest of this paper, we will use the document category names to refer to the pedagogical roles.

Proceedings of the 12th Workshop on Innovative Use of NLP for Building Educational Applications, pages 109–120
Copenhagen, Denmark, September 8, 2017. ©2017 Association for Computational Linguistics

Identifying important qualitative features of pedagogical value, such as the pedagogical role, gives a greater degree of interoperability and insight into how we can help students learn more effectively. Education research explains the distinction between declarative and functioning knowledge: the former is knowledge of content and the latter is knowledge of how to interpret and put the content to work (Biggs, 2011). To apply content, learners must first understand the content; this explains why a novice and an advanced learner trying to learn the same subject would seek out documents with different pedagogical roles. *Tutorials, Reference Works*, and *Survey* papers are better introductions for a novice with no knowledge of a subject. In contrast, an expert would have enough background knowledge to dive right into advanced papers presenting state-of-the-art empirical results. Although pedagogical roles are not the same as pedagogical value, these pedagogical features offer some insight as a starting point for estimating learning utility. For our study, we collected annotations for over 1000 documents, which we document and make available for others to use.[1]

We also collected annotations for three ordinal-scale questions of document complexity and quality as an exercise to gauge the feasibility of the task despite its subjective nature. However, the resulting inter-annotator agreement results were too low to be meaningful. These results stress the importance of identifying more objective user and document features relevant to pedagogical value; in this initial work, we focus on document features.

Our contribution is twofold: We provide the first annotated corpus of pedagogical roles for the study of pedagogical value, and we present baseline classification results using state-of-the-art techniques for others to work with. Our goal is to establish a framework that can be extended to other domains, provide empirical results to validate our dataset and algorithms, and demonstrate the feasibility of the proposed role classification task. In the rest of this paper, we will describe our methods for collecting, evaluating, and automatically generating annotations in Section 2, the results of our evaluations in Section 3, related work in Section 4, and concluding remarks in Section 5.

---

[1]https://doi.org/10.6084/m9.figshare.5202424

2 Methods

2.1 Creating guidelines for annotation

We performed a few rounds of annotation to develop a set of roles that would be adequate and insightful for an initial investigation. We identified the following pedagogical roles:

- *Survey*: Is this document a broad survey? A broad survey examines or compares across a broad concept.

- *Tutorial*: Is this document a tutorial? *Tutorials* describe a coherent process about how to use tools or understand a concept, and teach by example.

- *Resource:* Does this document describe the authors' implementation of a system, corpus, or other resource that has been distributed (e.g., public data sets or tools that have been released under an open-source license or are commercially available)?

- *Reference Work*: Is this document a collection of authoritative facts intended for others to refer to? Reports of novel, experimental results are not authoritative facts; the statement "grass is green" is. *Reference Works* describe different subtopics within a concept.

- *Empirical Results*: Does this document describe results of the authors' experiments?

- *Software Manual*: Is this document a manual describing how to use different components of a software?

- *Other*: Other role. This includes theoretical papers, papers that present a rebuttal for a claim, thought experiments, etc.

Additionally, we developed annotation guidelines instructing annotators to select all applicable pedagogical roles for each document. A document could present results of a novel method and also direct readers to an implementation of the method, thus making the paper both an *Empirical Results* paper and a *Resource* paper. Another document could simultaneously give a step-by-step tutorial about how to use a system, present specific commands on how to use components of the system, and provide a link to where readers can download the system, making the document a *Tutorial, Software Manual*, and *Resource*. Although a document could validly belong to multiple pedagogical roles, we have carefully gone through several iterations of pedagogical roles to maximize the differences between roles. In other words, the distribution of the number of pedagogical roles per document is skewed such that most of the documents have one role. The *Other* role is an alternative category for all other possible pedagogical role types; we do not focus on documents with this role in this work. We believe most of the *Other* documents have high pedagogical value to a small group of experts and are beyond the scope of this initial investigation. In addition to these guidelines, we also provided a few examples of documents of each pedagogical role to annotators.

2.2 Annotation

The corpus of documents we annotated is drawn from a collection of pedagogically diverse documents related to natural language processing. The collection is based on the ACL Anthology, using the plain-text documents included in the ACL Anthology Network corpus (Radev et al., 2009). The ACL Anthology primarily consists of expert-level empirical research papers, so the collection was expanded to include other document types, as described in Gordon et al. (2017). Although we generally targeted specific document sources for specific pedagogical roles, we still found a variety of pedagogical roles from each source, i.e., not all documents from Wikipedia are *Reference Works*, and not all papers found while searching the web for "tutorials" are *Tutorials*. For annotation, we tried to identify a balanced sample of documents with different roles in this corpus by using simple regular expression pattern matching in document titles and abstracts. For example, to roughly target *Software Manuals*, we looked for documents with the phrase "software manual," "manual," or "technical manual" in the title or abstract.

To choose a reliable group of annotators, we internally annotated pedagogical roles for a set of documents and compared it with annotations done by a group of students pursuing master's degrees in computer science. We selected 11 students whose annotations had the highest correlation with our annotations. These annotators were instructed to read the abstract if there was one and to skim the rest of the document in enough detail such that they were able to annotate features for the document accurately and in a timely manner. We met regularly to discuss and come to a consensus on general document characteristics that were confusing to interpret.

We divided the documents for annotation into subsets of 100 to distribute among annotators so that each document was annotated by three annotators, and each subset was annotated by the same three annotators. We also manually filtered through and internally annotated 155 more supplementary documents to make up for a lack of documents that were annotated as *Surveys*, *Resources*, and *Software Manuals*. This supplementary set consists of 76 documents from the expanded ACL corpus and 79 additional documents collected from searching the web for more *Surveys*, *Resources*, and *Software Manuals*.[2]

2.3 Automatic prediction of pedagogical roles

We represent each document as a bag of sentence-embedding clusters. This technique embeds all sentences into vectors, clusters sentence vectors, and then represents documents as distributions over clusters. To evaluate the effectiveness of representing each document as a bag of sentence-embedding clusters and performing k-nearest neighbors classification, we also run two baseline techniques. One baseline technique is a multi-label centroid-based algorithm with sentence embeddings that is related to the single label centroid-based algorithm presented by Han and Karypis (2000) and the naïve Rocchio (1971) classification algorithm, a popular method for text classification (Rogati and Yang, 2002). The other baseline technique is a random forest classification of TF–IDF scores, which allows us to evaluate if sentence embeddings are more useful than word frequencies for this task.

We use sentence embeddings because specific sentences in documents are key indicators of the pedagogical roles of the document. As an explicit example, one might find the following in a *Survey* paper: "This paper presents a survey of the field of machine translation. . . " A more implicit example might be a *Resource* paper that mentions that one can find the corpus created by the authors at a specific link. We want to give much weight to the sentences that are the best indicators of the pedagogical roles of the document and leverage this information to automatically predict the pedagogical roles of documents. Skip-thought vectors[3] are able to effectively capture the semantics and syntax of sentences in several different tasks (Kiros et al.,

---

[2]Supplementary annotations are included in our publicly available annotation dataset.

[3]https://github.com/ryankiros/skip-thoughts

2015). To generate sentence embeddings needed for the centroid-based algorithm and the bag of sentence embedding clusters, we apply skip-thought vectors to embed each sentence from our annotated documents into a 4800-dimensional vector. We use the pre-trained skip-thought vector model to create sentence embeddings for each sentence.[4]

In our techniques, we do not pre-select sentences to include as features for classifying a document. We also do not treat sentences differently given their location in different sections of a document, e.g., introduction versus conclusion. Our corpus is composed of research papers, book chapters, Wikipedia articles, and web documents, so there is not a standard format that all documents follow. Our goal is to discover different types of sentences that could support our defined set of pedagogical roles as well as point to the existence of other roles.

Random Forest baseline classifier (RF): TF–IDF scores of words in our annotated documents are used as features for a random forest classifier. To calculate the TF–IDF scores, we included words that were in at least 10% and at most 90% of the documents. We used five-fold cross-validation to evaluate the results.[5]

Multi-label centroid-based algorithm with sentence embeddings (CEN): Each pedagogical role is represented by an average centroid vector, which is calculated by adding all sentence vectors in every document that belongs to the role, and then dividing the sum by the total number of sentence vectors added. When classifying a new document, we assign each sentence vector in the new document to a role label based on the nearest average vector. The role labels that are predicted for more than a third of the document's sentences are then predicted to be the document's role(s). Although this baseline method limits each document to two or fewer role predictions, it works as a rough baseline. 99.1% of the annotated documents have one or two pedagogical roles, and we assume our sample of annotated documents is representative of a larger collection of documents.

Bag of Sentence Embedding Clusters (BoSEC): Starting with the hypothesis that semantic and syntactic features of sentences are useful indicators of pedagogical roles, we employ k-means clustering[6]

over sentence vectors to generate a representation basis (of N clusters) for computing a single $N \times 1$ feature vector per document. Each entry in the feature vector is the relative frequency of the specific sentence vector cluster being observed in the document.

K-Nearest Neighbors with Bag of Sentence Embedding Clusters (KNN+BoSEC): We use k-nearest neighbors classification to search for documents which exhibit the most similar distributions of clusters and predict the pedagogical roles of documents. To predict the roles of document A, we look for the three nearest documents in the N-dimensional vector space as calculated by the Manhattan distance metric. The majority roles of the three nearest documents are then predicted to be the roles of document A. The details of KNN+BoSEC are shown in Figure 1.

KNN+BoSEC with custom sentence encoder (KNN+BoSEC+): The content and style of writing in the scientific papers in our corpus differs from that of books used to train the pre-trained skip-thoughts vector model. We also run experiments using the KNN+BoSEC technique with a custom sentence embedding model trained on our entire collection of (annotated and unannotated) NLP documents. The custom sentence embedding model is trained using the default parameters described in the skip-thoughts training code.[7]

3 Results

3.1 Annotation agreement evaluation

The kappa value, which measures the likelihood of annotator agreement occurring above chance, is 0.68 for the pedagogical role annotations. This kappa value was calculated as an average over the kappa values for each subset of 100 documents. Given the difficulty of annotating pedagogical roles, which was confirmed by annotators, we believe a kappa of 0.68 indicates substantial agreement between annotators (Landis and Koch, 1977).

Table 1 shows the details of inter-annotator agreement for annotated pedagogical roles from documents with only one majority role. The rows are the majority roles, which we take to be the ground truth pedagogical roles of documents. The columns show the third annotator's annotations; if the third

---

[4]Model parameter details in Supplemental Material A.1.

[5]Model parameter details in Supplemental Material A.2.

[6]http://scikit-learn.org, model parameter details in Supplemental Material A.3.

[7]https://github.com/ryankiros/skip-thoughts; model parameter details in Supplemental Material A.4.

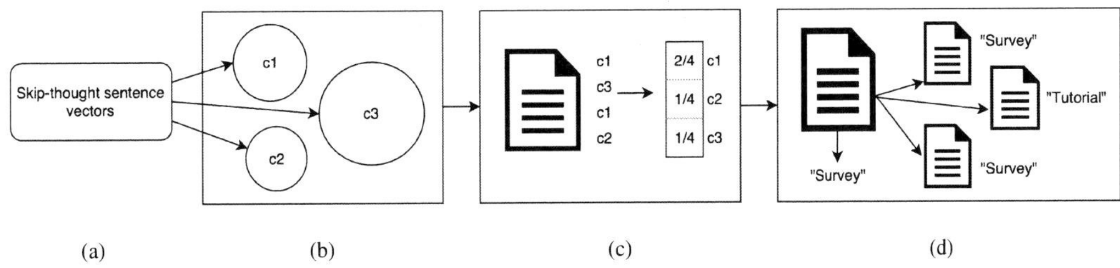

Figure 1: An end-to-end overview of the BoSEC+KNN technique. In (a), we generate skip-thought sentence vectors for every sentence in all documents. We partition all sentence vectors into clusters in (b). In (c), we represent each document as a distribution over the clusters formed in (b). (d) shows the KNN pedagogical role classification of documents based on the majority votes of annotated documents.

annotation matches the majority, then the particular annotation falls on the diagonal of Table 1. Although there are 1264 majority pedagogical role annotations, we calculated the confusion matrix for 1206 roles from documents with only one majority role each, for ease of interpretation. From the 1206 pedagogical roles, there are 1245 role pairs between the majority role and the third annotator's annotated role(s).

	Survey	Tutorial	Resource	Reference Work	Empirical Results	Software Manual	Other	Total
Sur.	**10**	1	0	7	4	0	5	27
Tut.	2	**44**	6	22	6	4	14	98
Res.	0	0	**5**	1	1	3	5	15
Ref.	36	20	3	**151**	4	1	28	243
Emp.	13	8	8	15	**526**	3	56	629
Sof.	0	1	0	0	2	**1**	2	6
Other	12	24	6	47	29	2	**107**	227
Total	73	98	28	243	572	14	217	**1245**

Table 1: Confusion matrix for annotated pedagogical roles from documents with only one majority role. Rows are the majority roles (chosen by two or three annotators) that we treat as ground truth. Columns are the third annotator's corresponding annotations.

From Table 1, we can see that *Survey* documents are sometimes confused with *Reference Works*, *Resource* papers are sometimes confused with *Other* documents, and *Software Manuals* are rare. We also see that *Other* documents have relatively higher rates of misclassification. These results are consistent with feedback from annotators. The reason why *Survey* documents are sometimes mistaken for *Reference Works* is because both examine a broad number of subjects in a domain; the distinction we make in our annotation guidelines is that *Reference Works* are a collection of established authoritative facts such as those one might find in an encyclopedia, whereas *Surveys* focus on the discoveries of other publications. When looking for *Resource* papers, annotators rely on looking for few indicator sentences that may be missed with a more superficial skim of the document. Also, the *Other* documents belong to a range of additional pedagogical roles, though we do not make finer distinctions here.

For each annotated document, we kept the pedagogical roles that had majority annotation agreement across the three annotators who annotated the document. If a document had no majority labels, the document was filtered out of the annotated document set. This filtered document set of 1235 documents with 1264 annotated pedagogical roles is the one we use along with a supplementary set for all pedagogical role prediction techniques.

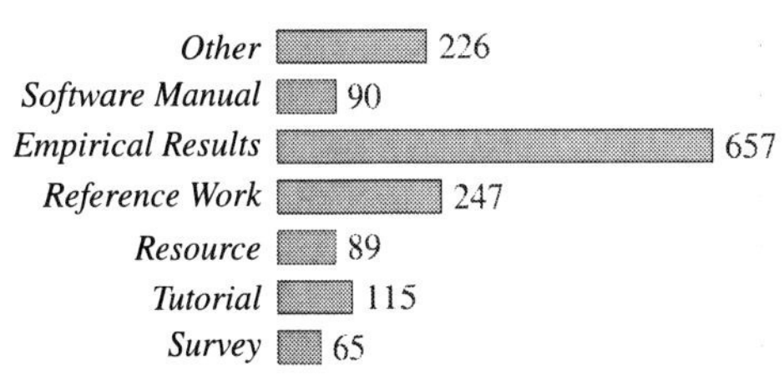

Figure 2: Distribution of all pedagogical role annotations in the full annotated corpus used for training classifiers

113

We noticed a lack of *Surveys*, *Resources*, and *Software Manuals*, so we internally annotated another supplementary set of 155 documents consisting mostly of documents of the underrepresented roles. The full annotated corpus we use for classification has the distribution of roles shown in Figure 2; this full corpus includes the filtered set of 1235 documents annotated by three annotators each and 155 internally annotated documents, for a total of 1489 pedagogical role annotations over 1390 documents. Given the corpora we selected our set of documents to annotate from, it is not surprising that most of the documents are *Empirical Results*, *Reference Works*, *Tutorials*, or *Other*. 94% of the annotated documents have just one pedagogical role, and 99.1% have one or two pedagogical roles.[8] The top three most common combinations of roles for a document are *Resource* and *Empirical Results*; *Resource* and *Software Manual*; *Tutorial*, *Resource*, and *Software Manual*.[9] Many documents with multiple pedagogical roles are *Resource* documents because the authors make their work publicly available.

3.2 Pedagogical role classification evaluation

In Table 2, we see that for both random forest classification of TF–IDF scores (RF) and sentence embedding methods (CEN, KNN+BoSEC, KNN+BoSEC+), the more samples there are for a pedagogical role, the higher the scores are for the role. The scores for *Other* documents are an anticipated exception to the trend, because we do not make more fine-grained distinctions between other pedagogical roles in this work. *Software Manuals* are also an exception to this trend, as their scores are relatively high for the number of samples; this is because *Software Manuals* are typically written in a very distinct style. CEN generally performs poorly across roles, doing worse than the baseline random forest classification with TF–IDF. This suggests that word frequency is more informative about the pedagogical roles of a document than a single representative vector per role.

With the exception of *Software Manuals*, RF is able to predict roles with more samples (*Reference Work*, *Empirical Results*, *Other*) with higher precision compared to roles with fewer samples (*Survey*, *Tutorial*, *Resource*). KNN+BoSEC and KNN+BoSEC+ have comparable precision for roles with more samples, but have significantly higher precision for roles with fewer samples. Compared

to RF, KNN+BoSEC and KNN+BoSEC+ also have higher recall across all roles. KNN+BoSEC+ has the highest F_1 scores for all pedagogical roles. We attribute the fact that KNN+BoSEC+ is generally able to do better than KNN+BoSEC to using a custom sentence encoder trained on scientific documents.

Given that we use keyphrases to find documents that likely belong to specific pedagogical roles, we also want to see if we could achieve performance similar to that of our sentence embedding-based methods by simply classifying documents based on keyphrases. We manually curate a list of keyphrases for two pedagogical roles: "software manual," "manual," and "technical manual" for *Software Manuals*, and "tutorial" for *Tutorials*. We then classify a document as a certain role if any of the role's keyphrases are present in the first five sentences of the document, where the title counts as the first sentence. Classifying *Software Manuals* with this method has a precision of 0.15, a recall of 0.09, and an F_1 score of 0.11. KNN+BoSEC+ dramatically outperforms this method with the specified keyphrases for *Software manuals*. Classifying *Tutorials* with this method has a precision of 0.60, a recall of 0.50, and an F_1 score of 0.55. While the keyphrase classification results for *Tutorials* are closer to the corresponding KNN+BoSEC+ results, we think that the KNN+BoSEC+ results would also improve if it had access to the list of keyphrases as features, though we leave that for future experimentation. These initial keyphrase classification experiments suggest that sentence-embedding-based methods are generally more effective and robust than hand-crafting keyphrases for each pedagogical role.

The confusion matrix in Table 3 allows us to make judgments about documents of different pedagogical roles, as predicted by KNN+BoSEC+. The rows are the ground truth roles, and the columns are the predicted roles. We can see that *Surveys*, *Resources*, and *Other* documents are often mistaken to be documents with *Empirical Results*. Additionally, there are relatively more instances of *Surveys*, *Resources*, and *Other* documents where the classifier is unable to make a prediction. Overall, these results suggest that the misclassifications are an effect of an unbalanced dataset with many more samples of *Empirical Results*, rather than an inherent lack of distinctness between documents of different roles.

Through a qualitative analysis of sentences from the clusters most frequently associated with each

---

[8]See Figure 3 in Supplemental Material for more details.
[9]See Figure 4 in Supplemental Material for more details.

Ped. role	Precision				Recall				F_1				Support
	RF	CEN	KNN+BoSEC	KNN+BoSEC+	RF	CEN	KNN+BoSEC	KNN+BoSEC+	RF	CEN	KNN+BoSEC	KNN+BoSEC+	All
Survey	0	0.02	0.23	**0.31**	0	**0.21**	0.20	0.18	0	0.03	0.21	**0.23**	13
Tutorial	0.50	0.10	0.64	**0.66**	0.05	0.21	**0.55**	0.52	0.08	0.11	0.57	**0.58**	23
Resource	0.20	0	**0.70**	0.53	0.01	0	0.19	**0.24**	0.03	0	0.29	**0.32**	17.8
Ref. Work	0.77	0.07	0.71	**0.78**	0.33	0.32	0.70	**0.71**	0.46	0.11	0.70	**0.74**	49.4
Emp. Res.	**0.86**	0	0.83	0.85	0.77	0	0.86	**0.89**	0.81	0	0.85	**0.87**	131.4
Sof. Man.	**0.98**	0.05	0.93	0.95	0.34	0.16	0.72	**0.86**	0.49	0.07	0.81	**0.90**	18
Other	0.63	0.06	0.57	**0.65**	0.10	0.40	0.27	**0.48**	0.17	0.10	0.36	**0.55**	45.2
avg / total	0.71	0.03	0.73	**0.76**	0.44	0.15	0.64	**0.70**	0.50	0.05	0.66	**0.72**	297.8

Table 2: Precision, recall, and F_1 scores by pedagogical roles for all methods. Support is the actual number of documents with each role. avg / total computes weighted averages of scores across all roles. All values are averaged over a five-fold cross validation.

	Survey	*Tutorial*	*Resource*	*Reference Work*	*Empirical Results*	*Software Manual*	*Other*	No prediction	Total
Sur.	**2**	0.2	0	0.8	4.2	0	1.2	1.6	10
Tut.	0.2	**9.4**	0	2.6	0.8	0.8	2	2.2	18
Res.	0.2	0	**1.2**	0	3	0	0.6	1.8	6.8
Ref.	1.2	1.6	0.2	**34**	3.6	0.2	3.2	4.2	48.2
Emp.	0.8	1.4	1.8	3	**109.2**	0	4	4.2	124.4
Sof.	0	1.6	0.6	0.2	0	**9.8**	0	0.4	12.6
Oth.	3.4	0.6	0.6	3.2	8	0	**21.8**	7.6	45.2
Tot.	7.8	14.8	4.4	43.8	128.8	10.8	32.8	22	265.2

Table 3: Ground truth pedagogical roles (rows) versus predicted roles (columns) using KNN+BoSEC+. We calculate the confusion matrix for documents with only one ground truth role. All values are averaged over a five-fold cross validation.

pedagogical role, we observe that example sentences from different roles align with our intuitions of what exemplary sentences from different roles should be. The *Survey* sentences describe progress in different areas of research; the *Tutorial* sentences explain details of specific concepts and methods; the *Software Manual* sentences give information about how to use a tool.[10] Sentences from the most

---

[10]For more details, see Table 4 in Supplemental Material.

frequent clusters of a role do not explicitly mention the roles of the paper, e.g., "This paper presents a tutorial..." This phenomenon makes sense for two reasons. One reason is that the majority of documents do not explicitly say what kind of document they are. The second reason is that even when documents do explicitly state their role, the actual content of the document may disagree with the declared role. For example, some papers are written to accompany tutorials presented at workshops. The papers will explicitly declare themselves to be tutorials, but the paper will only include an abstract and not the tutorial itself. Following our annotation guidelines, we do not label these documents as *Tutorials*. This implicit characterization of a document's pedagogical roles through sentences means that a method that merely searches for explicit mentions of keywords or declaration of the document's roles would not be an effective approach to this problem. Thus, these example sentences qualitatively validate our embedding and clustering approach to pedagogical role classification.

4 Related Work

To the best of our knowledge, there is not much prior work that is directly related to investigating relevant pedagogical features of documents through pedagogical roles. There are some document recommendation systems that try to find documents that are both conceptually relevant to a user's query and pertinent to the user's interest, level of background knowledge, etc. For example, Semantic Scholar[11] allows users to filter an automatically generated reading list by "overviews," which are analogous to our definition of Surveys. PageRank accounts for popularity when identifying documents of interest (Page et al., 1999). Tang and McCalla (2004) consider the user's background knowledge, interest towards specific topics, and motivation when making recommendations. Gori and Pucci (2006) present a research paper recommender system based on the random walk algorithm and a small set of papers that users mark as relevant. Santos and Boticario (2010) emphasize that recommendation systems in the e-learning domain should be "guided by educational objectives" and define a semantic model for recommendation objects.

Previous efforts at investigating the value of documents include evaluating the reading difficulty of documents, citation graphs, and surveys, though none really address the problem of estimating the pedagogical value of a document to a learner while focusing on the interpretability of the results. The interpretability of results is especially important in education because educators need to be able to provide clear feedback to students. In automatic essay scoring, researchers look at features such as word count, semantic and syntactic coherence, sentence length, vocabulary complexity, and the use of certain phrases that facilitate the flow of ideas, e.g., "first of all" (Burstein et al., 2004; Shermis and Burstein, 2013). These features are a starting point to estimate the value of a document, but to estimate pedagogical value, we must consider if and how these features would affect different learners. Other directions of research use the influence of a paper within a citation graph as a proxy for the value of the paper, following the reasoning that good quality papers would be more important "nodes" in a citation graph (Ekstrand et al., 2010); however, documents that are important "nodes" in the graph do not necessarily have high pedagogical value for all learners. Tang and McCalla (2009) present surveys to students as an annotation method to estimate the value of the paper to the learner. They annotate individual features of job-relatedness, interestingness, usefulness, etc., using ordinal-scale values, and study the partial correlations between features to analyze the composition of features that

contribute to the pedagogical value of a document. Our approach is different in that (a) we develop an intermediate representation of pedagogical value that can be largely objectively annotated, (b) we evaluate correlation between annotators and not between features, and (c) we additionally present baseline results of pedagogical role prediction.

The classification task described in this work is also related to text classification, a task with a long history in NLP. Sebastiani (2002) presents a detailed survey of tasks and techniques used in text classification up until the early 2000s. Joachims (1998) presents experimental results that justify the use of Support Vector Machines (SVMs) for text classification. Soucy and Mineau (2001) use TF–IDF scores and a KNN model to perform different text categorization tasks.

5 Conclusion

In this paper, we have described (a) our creation of the first annotated corpus of pedagogical roles for the study of pedagogical value and (b) our use of sentence embeddings and clustering techniques to develop a baseline for pedagogical role classification. The inter-annotator agreement for the annotation of pedagogical roles is substantial and thus a good basis to develop pedagogical role classification techniques and intuitions about pedagogical value upon. Analyses of our bag of sentence-embedding clusters technique support our intuition that certain sentences in a document are strong indicators of the pedagogical roles of the document. The next steps are to expand the set of roles as needed and apply our techniques to other domains in order to work towards a general approach to estimating pedagogical value. We believe it is important to make our corpus and annotations public, as feedback from other researchers will help improve the quality and scope of our corpus as we expand it.

Acknowledgments

The authors thank Yigal Arens, Aram Galstyan, and Linhong Zhu for their valuable feedback on this work.

This research is based upon work supported in part by the Office of the Director of National Intelligence (ODNI), Intelligence Advanced Research Projects Activity (IARPA), via Air Force Research Laboratory (AFRL). The views and conclusions contained herein are those of the authors and should not be interpreted as necessarily representing the

---

[11] https://www.semanticscholar.org

official policies or endorsements, either expressed or implied, of ODNI, IARPA, AFRL, or the U.S. Government. The U.S. Government is authorized to reproduce and distribute reprints for Governmental purposes notwithstanding any copyright annotation thereon.

References

John B. Biggs. 2011. *Teaching for quality learning at university: What the student does*. McGraw-Hill Education (UK).

Kurt D. Bollacker, Steve Lawrence, and C. Lee Giles. 1999. A system for automatic personalized tracking of scientific literature on the web. In *Proceedings of the Fourth ACM Conference on Digital Libraries*, DL '99, pages 105–113, New York, NY, USA. ACM.

Jill Burstein, Martin Chodorow, and Claudia Leacock. 2004. Automated essay evaluation: The criterion online writing service. *AI Magazine*, 25(3):27.

Michael D. Ekstrand, Praveen Kannan, James A. Stemper, John T. Butler, Joseph A. Konstan, and John T. Riedl. 2010. Automatically building research reading lists. In *Proceedings of the Fourth ACM Conference on Recommender systems*, pages 159–166. ACM.

Jonathan Gordon, Stephen Aguilar, Emily Sheng, and Gully Burns. 2017. Structured generation of technical reading lists. In *Proceedings of the 12th Workshop on Innovative Use of NLP for Building Educational Applications*.

Jonathan Gordon, Linhong Zhu, Aram Galstyan, Prem Natarajan, and Gully Burns. 2016. Modeling concept dependencies in a scientific corpus. In *Proceedings of ACL*.

Marco Gori and Augusto Pucci. 2006. Research paper recommender systems: A random-walk based approach. In *Web Intelligence, 2006. WI 2006. IEEE/WIC/ACM International Conference on*, pages 778–781. IEEE.

Eui-Hong Sam Han and George Karypis. 2000. Centroid-based document classification: Analysis and experimental results. In *European conference on principles of data mining and knowledge discovery*, pages 424–431. Springer.

James G. Jardine. 2014. Automatically generating reading lists. Technical Report UCAM-CL-TR-848, University of Cambridge Computer Laboratory.

Thorsten Joachims. 1998. Text categorization with support vector machines: Learning with many relevant features. *Machine learning: ECML-98*, pages 137–142.

Ryan Kiros, Yukun Zhu, Ruslan R. Salakhutdinov, Richard Zemel, Raquel Urtasun, Antonio Torralba, and Sanja Fidler. 2015. Skip-thought vectors. In *Advances in neural information processing systems*, pages 3294–3302.

J. Richard Landis and Gary G. Koch. 1977. The measurement of observer agreement for categorical data. *Biometrics*, pages 159–174.

Lawrence Page, Sergey Brin, Rajeev Motwani, and Terry Winograd. 1999. The PageRank citation ranking: Bringing order to the Web. Technical Report 1999-66, Stanford InfoLab.

Dragomir R. Radev, Pradeep Muthukrishnan, and Vahed Qazvinian. 2009. The ACL Anthology Network Corpus. In *Proceedings, ACL Workshop on Natural Language Processing and Information Retrieval for Digital Libraries*, Singapore.

Joseph J. Rocchio. 1971. Relevance feedback in information retrieval. In G. Salton, editor, *The SMART retrieval system: Experiments in automatic document processing*. Prentice-Hall, Englewood Cliffs, NJ.

Monica Rogati and Yiming Yang. 2002. High-performing feature selection for text classification. In *Proceedings of the eleventh international conference on Information and knowledge management*, pages 659–661. ACM.

Olga C. Santos and Jesus G. Boticario. 2010. Modeling recommendations for the educational domain. *Procedia Computer Science*, 1(2):2793–2800.

Fabrizio Sebastiani. 2002. Machine learning in automated text categorization. *ACM Computing Surveys (CSUR)*, 34(1):1–47.

Mark D. Shermis and Jill Burstein. 2013. *Handbook of automated essay evaluation: Current applications and new directions*. Routledge.

Pascal Soucy and Guy W. Mineau. 2001. A simple KNN algorithm for text categorization. In *Proceedings of the 2001 IEEE International Conference on Data Mining*, ICDM '01, pages 647–8, Washington, DC, USA. IEEE Computer Society.

Tiffany Y. Tang and Gordon McCalla. 2009. The pedagogical value of papers: a collaborative-filtering based paper recommender. *Journal of Digital Information*, 10(2).

Tiffany Ya Tang and Gordon I. McCalla. 2004. On the pedagogically guided paper recommendation for an evolving web-based learning system. In *FLAIRS Conference*, pages 86–92.

A Supplemental Material

A.1 Skip-thought vector parameters

Each sentence vector has 4800 dimensions, with the first 2400 dimensions as the uni-skip model, and the latter 2400 dimensions as the bi-skip model. The model has the following parameters: recurrent matrices initialized with orthogonal initialization, non-recurrent matrices initialized from a uniform distribution in $[-0.1, 0.1]$, mini-batches of size 128, gradients clipped when the norm of the parameter vector is greater than 10, and the Adam algorithm for optimization.

A.2 Random forest classification parameters

For the random forest classifier, we used the Gini impurity function to estimate the quality of splits. When looking for the best split, the classifier considers the square root of the total number of features. The maximum depth of the tree is 75, and the classifier splits on a minimum of 5 samples at the internal nodes. We use 10 trees and a minimum of 1 sample at each leaf node.

A.3 Mini-batch K-means parameters

In this clustering technique, random subsets of the feature vectors are used in each iteration. We train the model with 300 clusters, early stopping if there is no improvement in the last 50 mini batches, a mini batch size of 4800, and the fraction of the maximum number of counts for a cluster center to be reassigned is 0.0001. We had experimented with different cluster sizes, and found 300 clusters to be the right size to maintain coherency within and distinction across clusters.

A.4 Custom skip-thought vector model parameters

Specifically, the RNN word embeddings have 620 dimensions, and we use a uni-skip model with a hidden state size of 2400. Both the encoder and the decoder are GRUs. The size of the decoder vocabulary is 20000, and the maximum length of a sentence is 30 words; additional words in sentences are ignored. Our custom model is trained for 5 epochs, has a gradient clipping value of 5, has a batch size of 64, and uses the Adam optimization algorithm.

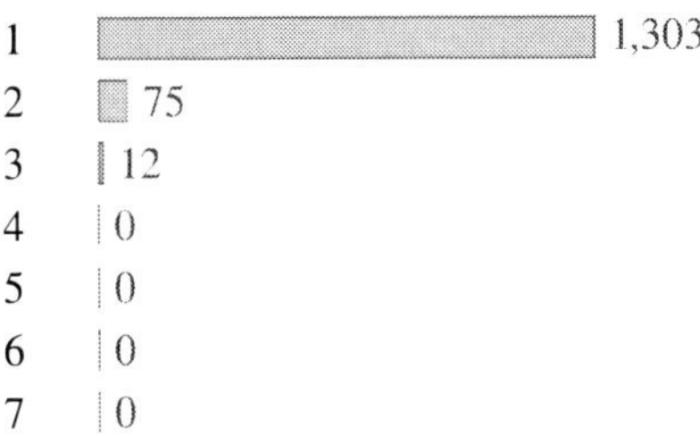

Figure 3: Distribution of number of pedagogical roles per document in full annotated corpus

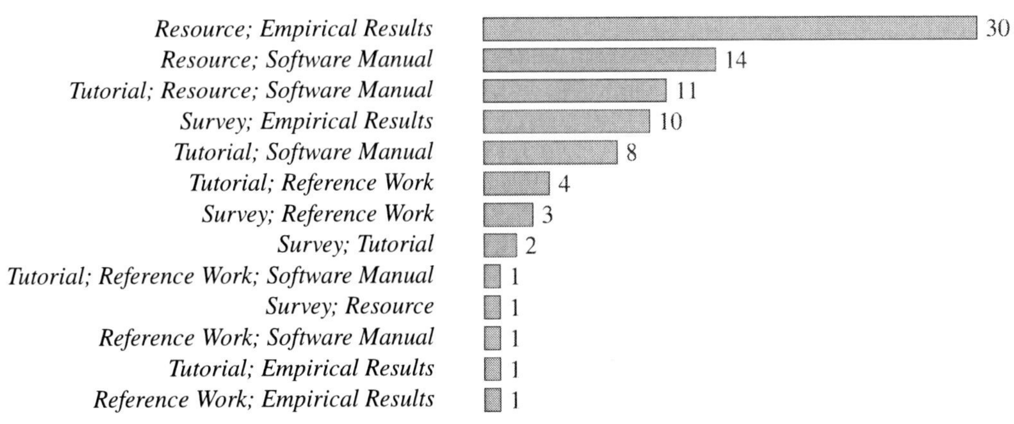

Figure 4: Distribution of pedagogical roles for documents in full annotated corpus with more than one role

Pedagogical role	Cluster ID	Example sentence
Survey	250	This view has been worked out in the text generation and dialog community more than in the text understanding community (Mann and Thompson, 1987; Hovy, 1993; Moore, 1994).
	123	Confronted with the claim that Game Theory should be the theoretical backbone to NLG, some people might respond that no new backbone is needed, because the theory of formal languages, conjoined with a properly expressive variant of Symbolic Logic, provides sufficient backbone already.
Tutorial	209	As you guessed from my explanations of different notations, different regex engine designers unfortunately have different ideas about the syntax to use.
	95	This information is incorporated in the tri-factorization model via a squared loss term, where the notation Tr (4) means trace of the matrix A.
Resource	147	`>>> windowdiff(s1, s1, 3)`
	255	`... print('', repr(corpus.fileids())[:60])`
Reference Work	155	The greater the resumption of the activity (i.e., mismatch negativity), the more different the neurological processing of the new item.
	86	A trajectory of an object is determined by its different centers of gravity relative to an underlying coordinate system.
Empirical Results	183	5.3 Using Multiple Knowledge Sources
	62	The NCC open track is shown in the following table 2.
Software Manual	147	`>>> clf.fit(X, Y)`
	152	An example of this approach can be found in the /verbi folder in the Italian MOR grammar.
Other	279	The problem in the cases (3) and (4) is how and why the hearer fails to derive implicatures.
	157	Proofs of the form suppose-absurd F D are called proofs by contradiction.

Table 4: Example sentences from the clusters most frequently associated with each pedagogical role. The clusters representing mostly punctuation, numbers, or incoherent strings were not included in calculating most frequently associated clusters.

Combining Multiple Corpora for Readability Assessment for People with Cognitive Disabilities

Victoria Yaneva, Constantin Orăsan, Richard Evans, and Omid Rohanian
Research Institute in Information and Language Processing,
University of Wolverhampton, UK
{v.yaneva, c.orasan, r.j.evans, omid.rohanian}@wlv.ac.uk

Abstract

Given the lack of large user-evaluated corpora in disability-related NLP research (e.g. text simplification or readability assessment for people with cognitive disabilities), the question of choosing suitable training data for NLP models is not straightforward. The use of large generic corpora may be problematic because such data may not reflect the needs of the target population. At the same time, the available user-evaluated corpora are not large enough to be used as training data. In this paper we explore a third approach, in which a large generic corpus is combined with a smaller population-specific corpus to train a classifier which is evaluated using two sets of unseen user-evaluated data. One of these sets, the ASD Comprehension corpus, is developed for the purposes of this study and made freely available. We explore the effects of the size and type of the training data used on the performance of the classifiers, and the effects of the type of the unseen test datasets on the classification performance.

1 Introduction

When developing educational tools and applications for students with cognitive disabilities, it is necessary to match the readability of the educational materials to the abilities of the students and to adapt the text content to their needs. Both text adaptation and readability research for people with cognitive disabilities are thus dependent on evaluation involving target users. However, there are two main difficulties in collecting data from users with cognitive disabilities: i) experiments involving those users are expensive to perform and ii)

the task of text evaluation is challenging for target users because of their cognitive disability.

Following from the first difficulty, user-evaluated data is scarce and the majority of NLP research for disabled groups is done by exploiting ratings or simplification provided by teachers and experts (Inui et al., 2001; Dell'Orletta et al., 2011; Jordanova et al., 2013). Examples of such a corpora are the FIRST corpus (Jordanova et al., 2013), which contains 31 original articles and versions of the articles that had been manually simplified for people with autism, and a corpus of manually simplified sentences for congenitally deaf Japanese readers (Inui et al., 2001). Henceforth in this paper, we refer to such manually simplified corpora as *population-specific corpora*. These corpora have not been evaluated by end users with disabilities.

As a result of the second difficulty, the fact that people with cognitive disabilities find text evaluation challenging, the size of user-evaluated datasets is rather limited. For example, to the best of our knowledge, there is currently only one readability corpus evaluated by people with intellectual disability, called LocalNews (Feng, 2009). This corpus contains 11 original and 11 simplified news stories. In this paper we present another corpus evaluated by people with autism containing a total of 27 documents. Henceforth in the paper, we refer to these type of corpora as *user-evaluated corpora*.

Given the lack of large population-specific or user-evaluated corpora in disability-related research, the question of choosing suitable training data for NLP models is not straightforward. While the use of large generic corpora as training data may be inadequate as such data may not reflect the needs of the target population, the use of population-specific and user-evaluated corpora as training data is problematic due to the scarcity

Proceedings of the 12th Workshop on Innovative Use of NLP for Building Educational Applications, pages 121–132
Copenhagen, Denmark, September 8, 2017. ©2017 Association for Computational Linguistics

of such data. In this paper we explore a third approach, in which a large generic corpus is combined with a smaller population-specific corpus to train

a system to predict the difficulty of text for people with autism. We compare the performance of this approach to: i) an approach exploiting only the large generic corpus and ii) an approach exploiting only the small population-specific corpus. We also compare the performance of the classification models derived from two different machine learning algorithms. All classifiers trained on the different corpora are then evaluated on two small sets of user-evaluated corpora (unseen data), one of which was developed for the purpose of this study (Section 3).

Contributions We developed the ASD Comprehension Corpus containing 27 educational articles evaluated by readers with autism and classified as *easy* and *difficult* based on participants' answers to comprehension questions. The texts and the answers of each participant for each question are currently available at: `https://github.com/victoria-ianeva/ASD-Comprehension-Corpus`[1]. Further, we explore i) the effects of the size and type of the training data on the external validity of the classifiers and ii) the effects of the type of unseen test datasets (only original versus original + simplified articles) on the classification performance. The system used in these experiments is available at: `http://rgcl.wlv.ac.uk/demos/autor_readability`

The rest of this paper is organised as follows. The next section presents related work relevant to this research, while Section 3 describes the process for the development of the ASD Comprehension corpus. Section 4 describes the corpora used in the study. Section 5 presents the derivation of the classification models, and Section 6 presents a discussion of the main findings, which are summarised in Section 7.

---

[1]The repository also contains the answers of participants from a control group (without autism), which were not explored in this article but may be useful to the community for investigating between-group differences. For more information about the control group see Yaneva (2016).

2 Related Work

Previous work from the fields of psycholinguistics, pertaining to language and autism, readability assessment, and domain adaptation are relevant to the research presented in our current paper.

2.1 Autism Spectrum Disorder

Autism Spectrum Disorder (ASD) is a neurodevelopmental condition affecting communication and social interaction. The reading difficulties of some people with ASD include, but are not limited to, difficulties resolving ambiguity in meaning (Happé and Frith, 2006; Happe, 1997; Frith and Snowling, 1983; O'Connor and Klein, 2004), difficulties comprehending abstract words (Happé, 1995), difficulties in the syntactic processing of long sentences (Whyte et al., 2014), difficulties identifying the referents of pronouns (O'Connor and Klein, 2004), difficulties in figurative language comprehension (MacKay and Shaw, 2004), and difficulties in making pragmatic inferences (Norbury, 2014). Adults with autism have also been shown to process images inserted in easy-to-read documents differently from non-autistic control participants (Yaneva et al., 2015).

2.2 Readability Assessment

Readability is a construct which has been defined as the ease of comprehension because of the style of writing (Harris and Hodges, 1995). Historically, the readability of texts has been estimated via formulae exploiting shallow features such as word and sentence length (Dubay, 2004); cognitive models exploiting features such as age of acquisition of words and text cohesion (McNamara et al., 2014) and, more recently, thanks to advances in Natural Language Processing (NLP), readability has also been estimated via computational models (Collins-Thompson, 2014; François, 2015). Advances in the fields of NLP and Artificial Intelligence have enabled both the faster computation of existing statistical features and the development of new NLP-enhanced features (e.g., average parse-tree height, average distance between pronouns and their anaphors, etc.) which can be used in more complex methods of assessment based on machine learning. An example of a readability model targeted to a specific application of readability assessment are the unigram models by Si and Callan (2001), which have been found particularly suitable for assessment of Web content, where the presence of links, email addresses and other elements biases the traditional formulae.

In terms of readability assessment for readers with cognitive disabilities, previous research has shown that readability features such as *entity density per sentence* and *lexical chains* (synonymy or hyponymy relations between nouns) are useful for estimating the readability of texts for readers with mild intellectual disability (Feng et al., 2010). This is due to the fact that these readers struggle to remember relations that hold within- and between-sentences (Feng et al., 2010). Similarly, features such as *word length* or *word frequency* are more relevant for readability assessment for people with dyslexia because they struggle with decoding particular letter and syllable combinations (Rello et al., 2012). In the case of autism, an important issue has been the lack of corpora whose reading difficulty levels have been evaluated by people with autism. For this reason most readability research for this population has so far focused on texts simplified by experts (Štajner et al., 2014). User-evaluated texts were used for the first time in a study, where the discriminatory power of a number of features was evaluated on a preliminary dataset of 16 texts considered easy or difficult to comprehend by people with autism (Yaneva and Evans, 2015).

2.3 Domain adaptation

Supervised machine learning and statistical methods like the ones used in this paper benefit from the availability of large amounts of training data. However, in many cases it is not easy to obtain enough training data for specific domains or applications. As a result it is not uncommon that researchers train on data from one domain and test on data from a different one. As would be expected, this usually leads to lower levels of performance. The field of domain adaptation is addressing this problem by proposing methods that can perform well even when the training and testing domains are different. In many cases this is achieved by exploiting a small training corpus of the same domain as the test documents. Domain adaptation has been used for a variety of tasks in NLP, including statistical machine translation (Axelrod et al., 2011), sentiment analysis (Blitzer et al., 2007; Glorot et al., 2011) and text classification (Xue et al., 2008).

Recent studies in the field of readability and language proficiency have used a similar approach to the one proposed in this paper. For example, Pilán et al. (2016) tackle the problem of data sparsity when classifying language proficiency levels of learner-written output by incorporating knowledge in the trained model from another domain consisting of input texts written by teaching professionals for learners. Their results indicated that the weighted combination of the two types of data performed best, even when compared to systems based on considerably larger amounts of in-domain data. In this paper we go a step further by applying this approach to readability classification for people with cognitive disabilities.

3 Evaluation of Text Passages by Readers with Autism

We present a collection of 27 individual documents for which the readability was evaluated by 27 different people with a formal diagnosis of autism. The collection is henceforth referred to as the *ASD Comprehension corpus* and is available at: `https://github.com/victoria-ianeva/ASD-Comprehension-Corpus`. Participants were asked to read text passages and answer three multiple choice questions (MCQs) per passage. Evaluation of the difficulty of the texts was then based on their answers to the questions[2].

Participants The evaluation of the texts was performed in three cycles of data collection and involved 27 different participants with autism. Texts 1-9 and 21-27 were evaluated by Group 1, consisting of 20 adult participants (13 male, 7 female) with mean age in years $\mu = 30.75$ and standard deviation $\sigma = 8.23$, while years spent in education, as a factor influencing reading skills, were $\mu = 15.31$, with $\sigma = 2.9$. Texts 10-17 were evaluated by Group 2, consisting of 18 adult participants (11 male and 7 female) with mean age $\mu = 36.83$, $\sigma = 10.8$ and years spent in education $\mu = 16$, $\sigma = 3.33$. Group 3 evaluated texts 18-20 and consisted of 18 adults (12 male and 6 female) with mean age $\mu = 37.22$, $\sigma = 10.3$ and years spent in education $\mu = 16$, $\sigma = 3.33$. All participants had a confirmed diagnosis of autism

---

[2]While reading the texts and answering the questions, the eye movements of the participants were recorded using an eye tracker; however, the recorded gaze data was not used in this study, hence we do not report details about the gaze data except when describing the data collection procedure. More details can be found in Yaneva (2016).

and were recruited through 4 local charity organisations. None of the 27 participants had other conditions affecting reading (e.g. dyslexia, intellectual disability, aphasia etc.). All participants were native speakers of English.

Materials A total of 27 text passages of varying complexity were collected from the Web. The registers were miscellaneous, covering educational (7 documents), news (10 documents) and general articles (3 documents), as well as easy-to-read texts (7 documents). The average number of words per text was $\mu = 156$ with standard deviation $\sigma = 49.94$. The texts covered a range of readability levels, where the average was $\mu = 65.07$ with $\sigma = 13.71$ according to the Flesch Reading Ease (FRE) score (Flesch, 1949), which is expressed on a scale from 0 to 100 (the higher the score, the easier the text).

A limitation of the study is the small size of the corpus, which was necessary in order to avoid fatigue in the participants and to comply with ethical considerations. By comparison, LocalNews (Feng, 2009), which is the only other corpus for English whose readability has been evaluated by people with cognitive disabilities contains 11 original and 11 simplified texts.

Design of the Multiple-Choice Questions Since people with ASD are generally known to understand many parts of what they read literally (Happé and Frith, 2006; Happe, 1997; Frith and Snowling, 1983; O'Connor and Klein, 2004), it is of interest to examine different types of comprehension of the texts in the ASD corpus. Impairment in specific types of reading comprehension merits the exploration of readability features related to those specific types. Table 1 shows the main types of comprehension we examine in our study following a taxonomy formulated by Day and Park (2005). The table also shows the relationship between the types of comprehension examined and the reading profile of people with autism.

These types of reading comprehension were examined through the inclusion of three multiple-choice questions per text passage, each of which contained three possible answers. The example below is a question examining the ability to make inferences:

Black peppered moths became more numerous in urban areas because:

a) They were mutants

c) They were camouflaged due to the airborne pollution

d) The airborne pollution blackened the white moths with soot

Apparatus and Procedure All participants were verbally instructed about the purpose and procedure of the experiment and given a participant information sheet. Once they were familiar with the implications of the research, they signed a consent form, verbal instruction was reinforced and demographic data about age, education and diagnosis was collected. Eye tracking data was recorded[3], hence the eye tracker was calibrated by each participant before the start of the experiment. Texts were presented on a 19" LCD monitor. In order to maximise the internal validity of the experiment, the texts were presented in random order to each participant. This controlled for factors such as fatigue or participants becoming accustomed to the types of questions asked. The order of questions after each text was also randomised, so that it would not influence the answers given by the participants. The effects of memory were controlled by having the relevant passage constantly displayed on the screen. Participants could therefore refer to it whenever they were not sure about the information it contained. While the effects of background knowledge could not be eliminated entirely, the selection of texts was made in such a way as to ensure that this effect would be minimised as far as possible. The participants read all texts and answered all questions, taking as many breaks as they requested. At the end of the experiment, participants were debriefed.

Development of the Gold Standard for ASD The 27 texts from the ASD corpus were used for evaluation of the document-level classifiers. They were divided into classes of *easy* and *difficult* texts based on the answers to the multiple choice questions (MCQs). Each text was evaluated by three MCQs and each correct answer was given 1 point, while each incorrect answer was awarded 0 points. Thus, if a participant had answered two out of three questions correctly for a given text, then that text had an answering score of two for this participant. After that, all answering scores for the participants were summed for each text. The texts

---

[3]The recorded eye tracking data is not examined in this study.

Comprehension	Characteristics (Day and Park, 2005)	Relation to ASD
Literal	Understanding of the straightforward meaning of the text: facts, dates, vocabulary, etc	Readers with ASD have predominantly literal understanding of language (MacKay and Shaw, 2004).
Reorganisation	The ability to combine *explicitly* given information from different parts of the text: *"Maria Kim was born in 1945"*; *"Maria Kim died in 1990"*. How old was Maria Kim when she died?".	Since this type of question is based on literal understanding it could provide insights exclusively into the role of context, the use of which is challenging for people with ASD (O'Connor and Klein, 2004).
Inference	The ability to use two or more pieces of information to arrive at a third piece of information that is *implicit*: *"He rushed off, leaving his bike unchained"* => He left his bicycle vulnerable to theft.	Types of inferences challenging for ASD: Inferring given or presupposed knowledge as well as new or implied knowledge derived from mental state words, bridging inferences, figurative language.

Table 1: Types of comprehension examined and their relation to ASD

were then ranked and partitioned at a threshold into two groups. Application of a Shapiro-Wilk test showed that the data was non-normally distributed and the two groups were thus compared using the non-parametric Wilcoxon Signed Rank test. The results indicated that the two groups of texts were significantly different from one another ($z = -6.091$, $p < 0.0001$). Thus 18 texts were classified as *easy* and 9 texts were classified as *difficult*.

4 Corpora

This section describes the corpora used for training and evaluation of the readability classifiers. We train classifiers on three corpora, presented below: i) **the WeeBit corpus** (Vajjala and Meurers, 2012), a comparatively large generic corpus used in readability research; ii) **the FIRST corpus**, a small corpus containing original and manually simplified texts, a subset of which have been evaluated in terms of readability in experiments involving 100 people with autism (Jordanova et al., 2013) and finally, iii) **a combination of the two**. After that we tested our classifiers by applying them to previously unseen user-evaluated data. These data consist of two corpora, the readability of which has been evaluated by people with autism (**The ASD Comprehension corpus**, presented above), and by people with intellectual disability (**LocalNews corpus** (Feng et al., 2009)).

4.1 The WeeBit Corpus

The WeeBit corpus (Vajjala and Meurers, 2012) contains educational documents obtained from the Weekly Reader[4] and BBC-BiteSize[5] web-

sites and comprises two sub-corpora of the same names. The Weekly Reader is an educational web-newspaper containing fiction, news and science articles. The WeeklyReader is intended for children aged 7-8 (Level 2), 8-9 (Level 3), 9-10 (Level 4) and 9-12 (Senior level). BBC-BiteSize is also an educational site containing articles at 4 levels corresponding to educational key stages (KS) for children between ages 5-7 (KS1), 7-11 (KS2), 11-14 (KS3) and 14-16 (GCSE). The combined WeeBit corpus comprises 5 readability levels corresponding to the Weekly Reader's Level 2, Level 3 and Level 4 and BBC-BiteSize KS4 and GCSE levels. The corpus contains 615 documents per level. The average document length measured in number of sentences is 23.4 sentences at the lowest level and 27.8 sentences at the highest level.

The WeeBit corpus was the most appropriate to use for the purpose of our work due to the fact that it contains educational and generally informative articles and due to its large size relative to other readability corpora for English. Examples of other corpora include Encyclopedia Britannica (Barzilay and Elhadad, 2003) (40 documents), Literacyworks (Petersen and Ostendorf, 2007) (around 200 documents) or the WeeklyReader (Allen, 2009) on its own. An alternative was to use Wikipedia and Simple English Wikipedia[6] as they contain a very large number of articles; however, claims that Simple English Wikipedia articles are more accessible than English Wikipedia articles have been disputed (Xu et al., 2015; Štajner et al., 2012; Yaneva, 2015).

As the primary purpose of our work is to build two-level readability classifiers, we normalized the WeeBit corpus to include texts of only two

---

[4]http://www.weeklyreader.com/

[5]http://www.bbc.co.uk/education

[6]http://simple.wikipedia.org/wiki/Main Page

readability levels: *easy* and *difficult*. Thus, the *difficult* texts in our corpus were the ones with class labels BitGCSE and BitKS3 (age 11-16) and the *easy* documents were the ones with class labels WRLevel2 and WRLevel3 (age 9 -11). Texts from Weekly Reader Level4 were excluded from the dataset, as they were intended for students aged 9-12, which overlaps with Weekly Reader Level3 (9-10), BitKS2 (7-11), and BitKS3 (11-14). Thus, the remaining data consisted of 1,610 documents divided into two equally sized classes of *easy* and *difficult* documents.

4.2 The FIRST corpus

The FIRST corpus consists of 25 documents of the registers of popular science and literature (13 texts) and newspaper articles (12 texts) (Jordanova et al., 2013). These texts were presented in both their original and simplified forms, so that the corpus contains 25 paired original and simplified documents (50 documents in total). The simplification was performed by 5 experts working with autistic people, who were given ASD-specific text simplification guidelines, specified in (Jordanova et al., 2013), which contains full details of the simplification procedure and the characteristics of the corpus. In addition to the 50 texts contained in that corpus, original and simplified versions of 6 additional texts were produced in accordance with the specified guidelines. These 12 texts were then evaluated on a sample of 100 adults with autism as part of the evaluation method in the EC-funded FIRST project.[7] Statistically significant differences in the levels of comprehension for texts from the two classes are reported (Jordanova et al., 2013). These texts were added to the FIRST corpus, which thus contains 31 original and 31 simplified versions of documents, of which 6 documents per class were evaluated by people with autism.

4.3 LocalNews Corpus

Similar to the ASD Comprehension corpus, the LocalNews corpus (Feng et al., 2009) is used as test data for evaluating the classifiers. The LocalNews corpus consists of 11 original and 11 simplified news stories and is, to the best of our knowledge, the only other resource in English, for which text complexity has been evaluated by people with intellectual disability. The articles were first manually simplified by humans, a process in which

long and complex sentences were split and important information contained in complex prepositional phrases was integrated in separate sentences. Lexical simplification included the substitution of rare words with more frequent ones and the deletion of sentences and phrases not closely related to the meaning of the text. The texts were then evaluated by 19 adults with mild intellectual disability, who showed significant differences in their comprehension scores for the two classes of documents (Feng et al., 2009).

5 Model Training and Evaluation

This section presents the experiments comparing the performance of the different classifiers.

5.1 Algorithms

The document-level classifier was built using supervised learning algorithms implemented in the Weka toolkit (Frank and Witten, 1998). We evaluated a number of algorithms in the WEKA toolkit and selected the two which performed best when evaluated using 10-fold cross validation over the WeeBit corpus (Random Forests) and the FIRST corpus (Bayes Net). The Random Forest algorithm (Breiman, 2001) is a decision tree algorithm which uses multiple random trees to vote for an overall classification of the given input. The Bayes Net classifier is the implementation of a Bayesian Network classifier (Heckerman et al., 1995) available in Weka. Bayesian networks are probabilistic graphical models which were shown to be very successful in domain adaptation problems (for example Finkel and Manning (2009)). For both learning algorithms we used the default values for their parameters as provided by Weka. Although there is scope for tuning of these parameters, we did not have access to enough data to explore this direction.

5.2 Baseline

We use the Flesch-Kincaid Grade Level readability formula (Kincaid et al., 1981) as a baseline for document classification due to the fact that it is one of the best-performing predictors of text difficulty, and has been used as a baseline in other readability estimation models (Vajjala Balakrishna, 2015). The baseline values are computed by using the score of the formula as a single feature in the classification model.

---

[7]FIRST project. [online] available at: http://www.first-asd.eu/[Last accessed: 19/05/2017]

Feature	Description	Random Forests			Bayes Net		
		W	F	WF	W	F	WF
1. Long words	Proportion of words with 3 or more syllables	−	+	−	−	−	−
2. Average word length	Average number of syllables, all words	−	+	−	−	−	−
3. Possible senses	Sum of all senses for all words in the text	−	+	−	−	−	−
4. Polysemous words	Words with more than one sense in WordNet	−	+	−	−	−	−
5. Polysemous type ratio	Ratio polysemous word types / all word types	−	+	+	+	−	+
6. Type-token ratio	Total number of types/number of tokens	−	−	−	−	−	−
7. Vocabulary variation	Word types/ common words not in the text	−	−	−	−	−	−
8. Numerical expressions	Number of numerical expressions	−	+	−	−	−	−
9. Infrequent words	Not in 5,000 most freq. words in English	−	+	−	−	−	−
10. Total number of words	Total number of words in the text	−	−	−	−	−	−
11. Dolch-Fry Index	*Fry 1000 Instant Word List/Dolch Word List*	−	−	−	−	−	−
12. Number of passive verbs	Number of passive verbs	−	+	−	−	−	−
13. Agentless passive density	Incidence score of passive voice	−	−	−	−	−	−
14. Negations	Number of negations	+	+	+	+	+	+
15. Negation density	Incidence score of negations	+	−	+	+	−	−
16. Long sentences	Proportion of sentences longer than 15 words	+	+	+	+	−	+
17. Words per sentence	Total words / total sentences	−	+	+	+	+	−
18. Average sentence length	Sentence length in words	−	+	+	+	+	+
19. Number of sentences	Total number of sentences	−	+	−	−	+	−
20. Paragraph index	10 x total paragraphs / total words	−	+	−	−	−	−
21. Semicolons	Number of semicolons	−	+	−	−	+	−
22. Unusual punctuation	Number of occurences of &, %,	+	+	+	+	−	−
23. Comma index	10 x total commas / total words	−	+	−	−	+	−
24. Pronoun Score	Occurence of pron. per 1,000 words	−	+	−	−	−	−
25. Definite description score	Occurence of def. descr. per 1,000 words	−	+	−	−	−	−
26. Illative conjunctions	Number of illative conjunctions	−	+	+	+	−	+
27. Comparative conjunctions	Number of comparative conjunctions	−	+	−	−	−	−
28. Adversative conjunctions	Number of adversative conjunctions	−	+	+	+	−	−
29. Word frequency	Average frequency of words	−	+	−	−	−	−
30. Age of Acquisition (aver.)	AOA norms from the MRC database	+	−	+	+	−	+
31. Familiarity (average)	Familiarity norms from the MRC database	−	+	−	−	−	−
32. Concreteness (average)	Concreteness norms from the MRC database	−	+	−	−	−	−
33. Imagability (average)	Imagability norms from the MRC database	−	+	+	+	−	−
34. 1st pronominal reference	Number of 1st pronominal ref.	−	−	−	−	−	−
35. 2nd pronominal ref.	Number of 2nd pronominal reference	+	−	+	+	−	+
36. ARI	ARI readability formula (Smith et al., 1989)	−	+	−	−	+	−
37. Coleman-Liau	Coleman-Liau formula (Coleman, 1971)	−	+	−	−	−	−
38. Fog Index	Fog Index formula (Gunning, 1952)	+	+	+	+	+	+
39. Lix	Lix readability formula (Anderson, 1983)	−	−	+	+	−	−
40. SMOG	SMOG formula (McLaughlin, 1969)	−	+	−	−	−	−
41. FRE	Flesch Reading Ease (Flesch, 1948)	−	+	−	−	−	−
42. FKGL	Flesch-Kincaid GL (Kincaid et al., 1981)	−	−	−	−	+	−
43. FIRST readability index	FIRST readability ind. (Jordanova et al., 2013)	−	+	−	−	−	−

Table 2: A list of features, their description and their selection for the Random Forests and BayesNet classifiers, where 'W' stands for WeeBit, 'F' stands for FIRST and 'WF' stands for WeeBit + FIRST

5.3 Features and feature selection

A total of 43 features were used in the experiments. Table 2 presents the features, their descriptions, and an indication of whether or not each individual feature was selected for use in the final model of the different readability classifiers. The features used in this study included lexico-semantic (numbers 1 - 14), syntactic (numbers 15-22), cohesion (numbers 23 - 27), and cognitively-motivated features (numbers 28 - 34), as well as 8 readability formulae (numbers 35 - 43) (Table 2). The cohesion and cognitively motivated features were inspired by those used in the Coh-Metrix tool (McNamara et al., 2014). The source for cognitively-motivated features were the word lists in the MRC Psycholinguistic database (Coltheart, 1981), in which each word has an assigned score based on human rankings. The number of personal words in a text is hypothesised to improve ease of comprehension (Freyhoff et al., 1998), which is why evaluation of the *number of first and second person pronominal references* were included as features in the classification model.

Initially, the full-feature sets were used to obtain the baseline models, which were subsequently optimised using the attribute selection filter for su-

Table 3: *F* Score Results for 10-fold cross validation

	Random Forests			Bayes Net		
	Baseline	All features	Selected features	Baseline	All features	Selected features
WeeBit	0.78	**0.988**	0.984	0.838	0.968	**0.978**
FIRST	0.651	0.794	0.825	0.778	0.810	0.841
WeeBit+FIRST	0.77	0.957	0.973	0.831	0.953	0.966

Table 4: *F* Score Results for the ASD Comprehension corpus and the LocalNews corpus

ASD Comprehension	Random Forests			Bayes Net		
	Baseline	All features	Selected features	Baseline	All features	Selected features
WeeBit	0.673	**0.927**	0.820	0.667	0.746	0.820
FIRST	0.747	0.782	0.782	0.817	0.782	0.784
WeeBit+FIRST	0.746	0.817	0.855	0.667	0.746	**0.892**
LocalNews	Random Forests			Bayes Net		
	Baseline	All features	Selected features	Baseline	All features	Selected features
WeeBit	0.818	0.861	**0.954**	0.817	0.908	0.954
FIRST	0.676	0.76	0.705	0.705	0.705	0.760
WeeBit+FIRST	0.818	0.861	0.908	0.817	0.908	**1**

pervised learning which is distributed with Weka (Frank and Witten, 1998) and through iterative elimination of redundant features. This was done at the stage of model evaluation through ten-fold cross validation. The last six columns of Table 2 indicate the lists of selected features for each model. It can be argued that the Random Forest model is already performing a certain degree of feature selection and therefore it may be not necessary to carry out this task on the experiments involving Random Forest. However, analysis of the Random Trees generated by the algorithm revealed that they contain a larger number of features than those selected by our feature selection step. In addition, by performing feature selection we wanted to learn which linguistic features are good indicators of text complexity.

5.4 Evaluation

First, all classifiers were evaluated using 10-fold cross-validation, using the WeeBit, FIRST and WeeBit + FIRST corpora as training sets (Table 3). After that each classifier was tested on previously unseen user-evaluated data. The two sets of unseen data are the ASD Comprehension corpus described in Section 3 and the LocalNews corpus described in Section 4.3. Results for the evaluation on unseen data are presented in Table 4.

For Random Forests we notice that the model trained on the WeeBit corpus performs best when classifying texts from the ASD Comprehension corpus ($F = 0.927$) and from the LocalNews corpus ($F = 0.954$). However, when using the model trained on the Bayes Net algorithm, we see that best external validity for both the ASD Compre-

hension corpus ($F = 0.892$) and the LocalNews corpus ($F = 1$) is achieved by using the combined WeeBit + FIRST training set.

6 Discussion

In terms of the effects of the size and type of training data used, the results indicate that, in isolation, smaller, population-specific corpora (e.g. FIRST) are not sufficient to achieve optimal classification accuracy; however, in certain cases such as the classification of the LocalNews texts, they do have the potential to boost the performance of a classification model when combined with larger generic corpora ($F = 1$) . Nevertheless, this improvement is subject to choosing a classification algorithm that has optimal performance when trained on the smaller corpus. It is important to note that the most accurate classification of the ASD Comprehension corpus was achieved by training the Random Forests classifier on the WeeBit corpus alone ($F = 0.927$). Hence, the infusion of population-specific and generic corpora is only useful in certain cases, as discussed below. This is in line with results in other fields. For example, Blitzer et al. (2007) investigate domain adaptation for sentiment analysis. Given a pair of source and target domains, they show how it is possible to improve the performance of a sentiment classifier on the target domain when it is trained on data from the source domain with the help of a small annotated corpus from the target domain. However, they show that it is necessary to consider the distance between the two domains as not any pair will lead to good results. For future research, we will consider how it is possible to define a distance metric that can prove useful in our context.

Regarding the effect of the type of the unseen data, we notice that, surprisingly, the pairs of original and simplified articles contained in the LocalNews corpus were predicted 100% correctly by the classifier trained on the combination of texts from WeeBit + FIRST. A possible reason for this is that the introduction of the FIRST corpus together with the larger WeeBit one enables the classifier to capture certain simplification operations (e.g. sentence splitting and lexical simplification) that are common in both LocalNews and FIRST. Achieving such a high score could also have been complemented by the fact that the genre of the documents contained in the LocalNews corpus is closer to the textual genre of the ones of both the WeeBit and of the FIRST corpora. However, this result was only achieved when combining FIRST with the larger WeeBit corpus and was not otherwise replicated by a classifier trained only on the FIRST data. This implies that relatively large data sets are still a prerequisite for the accurate classification of pairs of original and simplified texts. In both cases, when using Random Forests and Bayes Net, a better classification accuracy was achieved for LocalNews ($F = 0.954$ and $F = 1$, respectively) than for the ASD Comprehension corpus ($F = 0.927$ and $F = 0.892$, respectively). This suggests that corpora containing pairs of texts in their original and simplified forms are generally easier to classify than corpora containing only of texts in their original form. This finding has implications for general readability and text simplification research where pairs of texts in their original and manually simplified forms are commonly used for evaluation purposes. In other words, evaluating on such corpora may result in overly optimistic classification results which are less likely to be replicated in a "real-world scenario" with naturally written texts.

The experiments presented above have several limitations. First, the small size of the corpora (a key problem in disability-related research which we target in this article) means that the texts used in this study do not account for the great heterogeneity of natural language. In an attempt to compensate for the small number of texts, we have tried to include documents from miscellaneous registers and with varying levels of readability. Second, both the ASD Comprehension corpus and the LocalNews corpus were evaluated by a relatively small number of participants, which is why individual differences in comprehension may have larger effects on the definition of the gold standard compared to generic readability studies. Nevertheless, as mentioned at the beginning of this article, collecting data from readers with cognitive disabilities is a much needed but challenging task, and the corpora used in this study are currently the only ones of their kind. We contribute to future research in this area by making available the ASD Comprehension corpus.

7 Conclusion

This paper discussed the effects of algorithm selection, training corpora and evaluation corpora for readability research for people with cognitive disabilities, with a view to addressing the problem of the scarcity of user-evaluated data in this setting. First, we presented a collection of 27 individual documents, the readability of which was evaluated by readers with Autism Spectrum Disorder. We then showed that the corpora used for algorithm selection have an effect on the classification performance of the models and that combining large generic readability corpora with small population-specific ones has the potential to boost the classification performance. Finally, we discuss the effects of the type of evaluation data (original articles versus pairs of original and simplified articles) on the classification accuracy and we show that original and simplified documents are easier to classify, and that the combination of generic and population-specific corpora is particularly useful for the classification of such text pairs.

Acknowledgements

This research is part of the AUTOR project partially supported by University Innovation Funds awarded to the University of Wolverhampton.

References

Melissa L Allen. 2009. Brief report: decoding representations: how children with autism understand drawings. *Journal of autism and developmental disorders* 39(3):539–43. https://doi.org/10.1007/s10803-008-0650-y.

Jonathan Anderson. 1983. Lix and rix: Variations on a little-known readability index. *Journal of Reading* 26(6):490–496.

Amittai Axelrod, Xiaodong He, and Jianfeng Gao. 2011. Domain adaptation via pseudo in-domain data selection. In *Proceedings of the Conference on Empirical Methods in Natural Language Processing*. pages 355–362.

Regina Barzilay and Noemie Elhadad. 2003. Sentence alignment for monolingual comparable corpora. In *Proceedings of the 2003 Conference on Empirical Methods in Natural Language Processing*. Association for Computational Linguistics, Stroudsburg, PA, USA, EMNLP '03, pages 25–32. https://doi.org/10.3115/1119355.1119359.

John Blitzer, Mark Dredze, and Fernando Pereira. 2007. Biographies, bollywood, boom-boxes and blenders: Domain adaptation for sentiment classification. In *Proceedings of the 45th Annual Meeting of the Association of Computational Linguistics*. Prague, Czech Republic, pages 440–447.

Leo Breiman. 2001. Random forests. *Machine Learning* 45(1):5–32.

E. B. Coleman. 1971. *Developing a technology of written instruction: some determiners of the complexity of prose*, Teachers College Press, Columbia University, New York.

Kevyn Collins-Thompson. 2014. Computational assessment of text readability: A survey of current and future research. *ITL-International Journal of Applied Linguistics* 165(2):97–135.

Max Coltheart. 1981. The mrc psycholinguistic database. *The Quarterly Journal of Experimental Psychology Section A* 33(4):497–505. https://doi.org/10.1080/14640748108400805.

Richard R. Day and Jeong-Suk Park. 2005. Developing Reading Comprehension Questions. *Reading in a Foreign Language* 17(1).

Felice Dell'Orletta, Simonetta Montemagni, and Giulia Venturi. 2011. Read-it: Assessing readability of italian texts with a view to text simplification. In *Proceedings of the second workshop on speech and language processing for assistive technologies*. Association for Computational Linguistics, pages 73–83.

William H. Dubay. 2004. *The Principles of Readability*. Impact Information. http://www.impact-information.com/.

Lijun Feng. 2009. Automatic readability assessment for people with intellectual disabilities. *SIGACCESS Access. Comput.* (93):84–91. https://doi.org/10.1145/1531930.1531940.

Lijun Feng, Noémie Elhadad, and Matt Huenerfauth. 2009. Cognitively motivated features for readability assessment. In *Proceedings of the 12th Conference of the European Chapter of the Association for Computational Linguistics*. Association for Computational Linguistics, pages 229–237.

Lijun Feng, Martin Jansche, Matt Huenerfauth, and Noémie Elhadad. 2010. A comparison of features for automatic readability assessment. In *Proceedings of the 23rd International Conference on Computational Linguistics: Posters*. Association for Computational Linguistics, pages 276–284.

Jenny Rose Finkel and Christopher D. Manning. 2009. Hierarchical bayesian domain adaptation. In *Proceedings of Human Language Technologies: The 2009 Annual Conference of the North American Chapter of the Association for Computational Linguistics*. pages 602–610.

R. Flesch. 1949. *The art of readable writing*. Harper, New York.

Rudolf Flesch. 1948. A new readability yardstick. *Journal of applied psychology* 32(3):221–233.

Thomas François. 2015. When readability meets computational linguistics: a new paradigm in readability. *Revue française de linguistique appliquée* 20(2):79–97.

Eibe Frank and Ian H. Witten. 1998. Generating accurate rule sets without global optimization. In J. Shavlik, editor, *Fifteenth International Conference on Machine Learning*. Morgan Kaufmann, pages 144–151.

G. Freyhoff, G. Hess, L. Kerr, B. Tronbacke, and K. Van Der Veken. 1998. Make it simple. european guidelines for the production of easy-to-read information for people with learning disability. Technical report, ILSMH European Association.

Uta Frith and Maggie Snowling. 1983. Reading for meaning and reading for sound in autistic and dyslexic children. *Journal of Developmental Psychology* 1:329–342.

Xavier Glorot, Antoine Bordes, and Yoshua Bengio. 2011. Domain adaptation for large-scale sentiment classification: A deep learning approach. In *ICML*.

Robert Gunning. 1952. *The technique of clear writing*. McGraw-Hill, New York.

F Happe. 1997. Central coherence and theory of mind in autism: Reading homographs in context. *British Journal of Developmental Psychology* 15:1–12.

Francesca Happé and Uta Frith. 2006. The weak coherence account: Detail focused cognitive style in autism spectrum disorder. *Journal of Autism and Developmental Disorders* 36:5–25.

Francesca GE Happé. 1995. The role of age and verbal ability in the theory of mind task performance of subjects with autism. *Child development* 66(3):843–855.

T. L. Harris and R. E. Hodges. 1995. *The Literacy Dictionary: The Vocabulary of Reading and Writing*. International Reading Association.

David Heckerman, Dan Geiger, and David M. Chickering. 1995. Learning bayesian networks: The combination of knowledge and statistical data. *Machine Learning* 20(3):197–243.

Kentaro Inui, Satomi Yamamoto, and Hiroko Inui. 2001. Corpus-based acquisition of sentence readability ranking models for deaf people. In *NLPRS*. pages 159–166.

Vesna Jordanova, Richard Evans, and Arlinda Cerga Pashoja. 2013. First project - benchmark report (result of piloting task). Central and Northwest London NHS Foundation Trust. London, UK.

J. Peter Kincaid, James A. Aagard, John W. O'Hara, and Larry K. Cottrell. 1981. Computer readability editing system. *IEEE transactions on professional communications* .

Gilbert MacKay and Adrienne Shaw. 2004. A comparative study of figurative language in children with autistic spectrum disorders. *Child Language Teaching and Therapy* 20(13).

Harry G. McLaughlin. 1969. SMOG grading - a new readability formula. *Journal of Reading* pages 639–646.

Danielle S McNamara, Arthur C Graesser, Philip M McCarthy, and Zhiqiang Cai. 2014. *Automated evaluation of text and discourse with Coh-Metrix*. Cambridge University Press.

Courtenay Frazier Norbury. 2014. Atypical pragmatic development. *Pragmatic Development in First Language Acquisition* 10:343.

Irene M O'Connor and Perry D Klein. 2004. Exploration of strategies for facilitating the reading comprehension of high-functioning students with autism spectrum disorders. *Journal of autism and developmental disorders* 34(2):115–127.

Sarah E Petersen and Mari Ostendorf. 2007. Text simplification for language learners: a corpus analysis. In *SLaTE*. Citeseer, pages 69–72.

Ildikó Pilán, Elena Volodina, and Torsten Zesch. 2016. Predicting proficiency levels in learner writings by transferring a linguistic complexity model from expert-written coursebooks. In *COLING*. pages 2101–2111.

Luz Rello, Ricardo Baeza-yates, Laura Dempere-marco, and Horacio Saggion. 2012. Frequent Words Improve Readability and Shorter Words Improve Understandability for People with Dyslexia (1):22–24.

Luo Si and Jamie Callan. 2001. A statistical model for scientific readability. In *Proceedings of the Tenth International Conference on Information and Knowledge Management*. ACM, New York, NY, USA, CIKM '01, pages 574–576. https://doi.org/10.1145/502585.502695.

Dean R. Smith, A. Jackson Stenner, Ivan Horabin, and III Malbert Smith. 1989. The lexile scale in theory and practice: Final report. Technical report, MetaMetrics (ERIC Document Reproduction Service No. ED307577)., Washington, DC:.

S. Vajjala and D Meurers. 2012. On improving the accuracy of readability classification using insights from second language acquisition. In *In Proceedings of the Seventh Workshop on Building Educational Applications Using NLP*. Association for Computational Linguistics, Stroudsburg, PA, USA, pages 163–173.

Sowmya Vajjala Balakrishna. 2015. *Analyzing Text Complexity and Text Simplification: Connecting Linguistics, Processing and Educational Applications*. Ph.D. thesis, Universität Tübingen.

Sanja Štajner, Richard Evans, Constantin Orasan, and Ruslan Mitkov. 2012. What can readability measures really tell us about text complexity? In Luz Rello and Horacio Saggion, editors, *Proceedings of the LREC'12 Workshop: Natural Language Processing for Improving Textual Accessibility (NLP4ITA)*. European Language Resources Association (ELRA), Istanbul, Turkey.

Sanja Štajner, Ruslan Mitkov, and Gloria Corpas Pastor. 2014. *Simple or not simple? A readability question*, Springer-Verlag, Berlin.

Elisabeth M Whyte, Keith E Nelson, and K Suzanne Scherf. 2014. Idiom, syntax, and advanced theory of mind abilities in children with autism spectrum disorders. *Journal of Speech, Language, and Hearing Research* 57(1):120–130.

Wei Xu, Chris Callison-Burch, and Courtney Napoles. 2015. Problems in current text simplification research: New data can help. *Transactions of the Association for Computational Linguistics* 3:283–297.

Gui-Rong Xue, Wenyuan Dai, Qiang Yang, and Yong Yu. 2008. Topic-bridged plsa for cross-domain text classification. In *Proceedings of the 31st Annual International ACM SIGIR Conference on Research and Development in Information Retrieval*. SIGIR '08, pages 627–634.

Victoria Yaneva. 2015. Easy-read documents as a gold standard for evaluation of text simplification output. In *Proceedings of the Student Research Workshop*. INCOMA Ltd. Shoumen, BULGARIA, Hissar, Bulgaria, pages 30–36. http://www.aclweb.org/anthology/R15-2005.

Victoria Yaneva. 2016. *Assessing text and web accessibility for people with autism spectrum disorder*. Ph.D. thesis.

Victoria Yaneva and Richard Evans. 2015. Six good predictors of autistic text comprehension. In *Proceedings of the International Conference Recent Advances in Natural Language Processing*. INCOMA

Ltd. Shoumen, BULGARIA, Hissar, Bulgaria, pages 697–706. http://www.aclweb.org/anthology/R15-1089.

Victoria Yaneva, Irina Temnikova, and Ruslan Mitkov. 2015. Accessible texts for autism: An eye-tracking study. In *Proceedings of the 17th International ACM SIGACCESS Conference on Computers & Accessibility*. ACM, New York, NY, USA, ASSETS '15, pages 49–57. https://doi.org/10.1145/2700648.2809852.

Automatic Extraction of High-Quality Example Sentences for Word Learning Using a Determinantal Point Process

Arseny Tolmachev
Graduate School of Informatics
Kyoto University
Yoshida-honmachi, Sakyo-ku
Kyoto, 606-8501, Japan
`arseny@nlp.ist.i.kyoto-u.ac.jp`

Sadao Kurohashi
Graduate School of Informatics
Kyoto University
Yoshida-honmachi, Sakyo-ku
Kyoto, 606-8501, Japan
`kuro@i.kyoto-u.ac.jp`

Abstract

Flashcard systems are effective tools for learning words but have their limitations in teaching word usage. To overcome this problem, we propose a novel flashcard system that shows a new example sentence on each repetition. This extension requires high-quality example sentences, automatically extracted from a huge corpus. To do this, we use a Determinantal Point Process which scales well to large data and allows to naturally represent sentence similarity and quality as features. Our human evaluation experiment on Japanese language indicates that the proposed method successfully extracted high-quality example sentences.

1 Introduction

Learning vocabulary is a crucial step in learning foreign languages and it requires substantial time and effort. Word learning is often done using flashcards: a way of organizing information into question-answer pairs. An example of a flashcard for the Japanese word "柿" is shown on Figure 1 (a, b). Flashcard systems frequently use Spaced Repetition technique to optimize the learning process. The technique is based on the observation that people tend to remember things more effectively if they study in short periods spread over time (*spaced repetition practice*) opposed to *massed practice* (i.e. cramming) (Pavlik and Anderson, 2008; Cepeda et al., 2006). Anki[1] is one of the most well known open source Spaced Repetition System (SRS).

One major drawback of building a vocabulary with flashcards is that most of the time cards look like the one displayed on Figure 1 (top): flashcards

[1] `http://ankisrs.net`

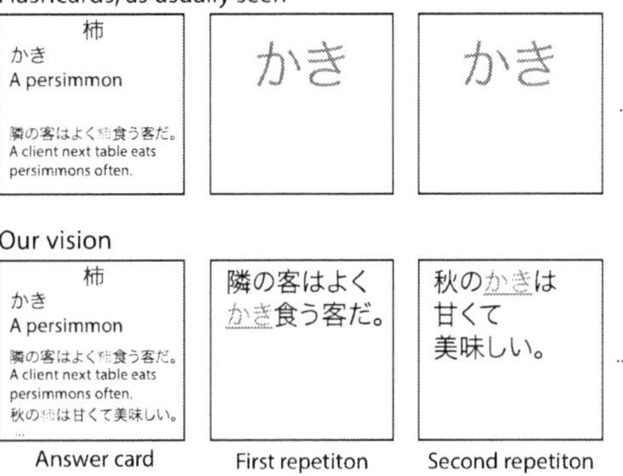

Figure 1: Flashcards for the word "柿"

often lack usage context information. A question card is usually *a word alone*, an answer card could contain a *fixed single* example sentence present. The example does not change from repetition to repetition, and as a result does not show the full spectrum of word usage. However, humans do not use isolated words for communicating. Words are always surrounded by other words, forming word usages. Learning these word usages is as important as learning words themselves.

To enhance the learning experience, we propose a novel framework of learning words using flashcards. Instead of showing only a single field like reading or writing of a flashcard in the question card similarly to the Figure 1 (top), we propose to use *example sentences* in both types of cards, see Figure 1 (bottom). Moreover, we want to show a *new* example sentence on each repetition as the question. This approach gives users an opportunity to learn correct word usages together with the words themselves. Obviously, implementing it requires a huge number of example sentences.

Because of this, we focus on automatic extraction of high-quality example sentences to be

133

Proceedings of the 12th Workshop on Innovative Use of NLP for Building Educational Applications, pages 133–142
Copenhagen, Denmark, September 8, 2017. ©2017 Association for Computational Linguistics

used in a flashcard system as questions. Collecting an enormous number of high-quality example sentences manually does not scale well. Words can have multiple senses and different usage patterns. A database containing dozens of sentences for each sense of each word would need to contain millions of different sentences. For a set of example sentences, we say that they are of high-quality if the sentences have the following properties.

- (Intrinsic) Value: Each individual example sentence should not be bad, for example ungrammatical, a fragment or unrelated to target word. Additionally, the sentences should not be too difficult for learners to understand them.

- Diversity: Inside a set, the sentences should cover different usage patterns, and word senses.

In addition we would like our method to support rare words and rare word senses.

For the task of example extraction, we are given a huge monolingual text corpora and a **target** word or a phrase to output a set of high-quality example sentences.

We propose a system architecture consisting of two components: a **search engine** which indexes a huge raw corpus and can produce a relatively high number of example sentence candidates, and the **selection part**, which takes the list of candidates and selects only a few of them. The search system is designed in a way so the selected sentences are syntactically rich near the target word (the target word has parents/children).

The DPP allows us to naturally represent data in terms of scalar quality and vector similarity. Additionally, the DPP has several interesting properties. For example, it is possible to compute a *marginal* probability of drawing a subset of items from a DPP efficiently. Marginal here means a probability of inclusion of a given set in *any subset drawn from the DPP*. Furthermore, it is proven that this marginal probability measure is submodular. Because of this, it is possible to build a greedy algorithm with reasonable guarantees, which selects items one by one, using the marginal probability measure as a weight. Also, the DPP is computationally and memory efficient. The computation of marginal probabilities can be performed linearly in respect to number of sentence candidates. This makes it possible to use

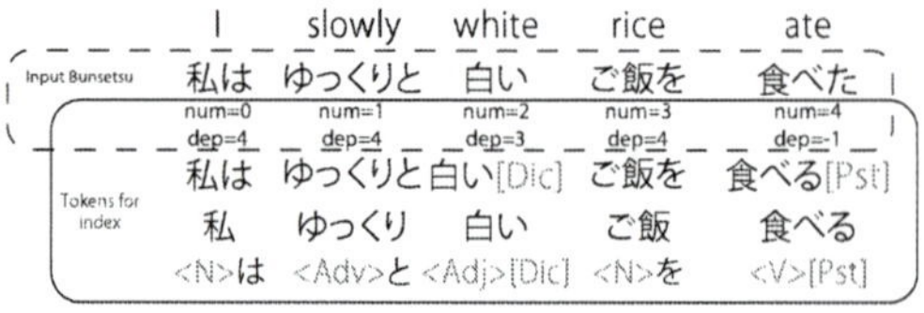

Figure 2: Word to token conversion for indexing a sentence. Tokens contain lexical information (black), POS tags (green) and conjugation forms (magenta). Dependency information is common for a set of tokens spawned from a single word. This information consists of word position and dependency position.

the DPP with tens thousands of candidates in near-realtime scenarios.

We have performed a human evaluation experiment which has shown that our method was preferred by Japanese learners and a teacher compared to two baselines.

2 Dependency Aware Search Engine

We want example sentences to have different possible usages of a target word. For example, verbs should have multiple arguments with different roles and in general it is better to have the vicinity of a target word syntactically rich. We use dependency information for approximating this information. For accessing syntactic information, we automatically tokenize raw text, extract lemmas, perform POS tagging and parse sentences into dependency trees.

To select syntactically rich sentences on a scale of a huge corpus, we have developed a distributed Apache Lucene-based search engine (Tolmachev et al., 2016) which allows to query not only on keywords as most systems do, but on dependency relations and grammatical information as well. We use this search engine to retrieve a relatively large set of example sentence candidates.

Search engines usually build a reverse index based on tokens, which are computed from the original document. We encode seed tokens for our engine as concatenation of lemma form and conjugation form tags, which are derived from the original text. For example, the verb 帰った (kaetta – "to leave" in past form) would be represented as "帰る+PAST". Each token also stores the position of its parent.

The next step generates rewritten tokens from the seed tokens until no more new tokens can be

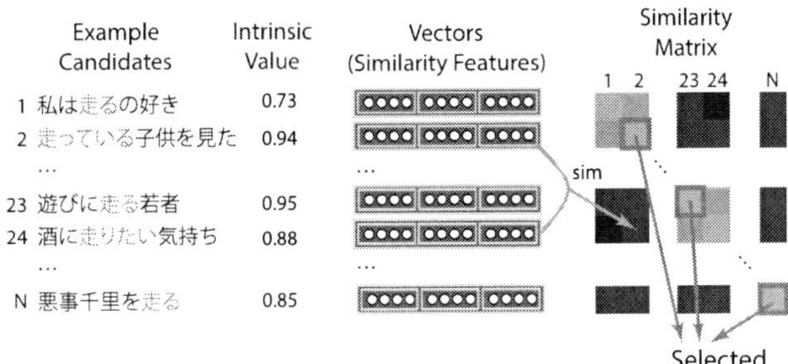

Figure 3: Example sentence selection. The objective is to select "best" and non-similar example sentences from the input list. Target word is marked red.

created using rewriting rules. Rewriting is done by replacing content word lexical information with part of speech information or removing some parts of tokens. For example, case markers of nouns are removed for some rules.

This representation allows to easily match same forms of different words while getting the benefits of reverse index in terms of performance. A list of created tokens for a raw sentence is shown in Figure 2. This example spawns three tokens for each of its word.

For selecting candidates we use queries which match a target word with up to 3 children or parents. The exact types of parents of children depend on POS of the target word. The number 3 was chosen to have balance with different arguments and to keep the syntactic vicinity of the target word diverse between the example sentence candidates.

3 Example sentence selection

After we have a relatively large list of example sentence candidates, we select a few of them as example sentences. The outline of the selection part is shown in Figure 3. In this section we describe the ideas behind the DPP and the way how we compute individual features.

3.1 Determinantal Point Process

In this section we provide a very basic explanation of the DPP inner workings. We invite interested readers to refer the original paper (Kulesza and Taskar, 2012) which gives a comprehensive overview of the DPP. In the supplementary material we show a toy task of greedily selecting a diverse subset of points from a plane to give an insight into how the DPP works.

Suppose we have a ground set $\mathcal{Y} = \{1...N\}$ of N items (in our case items are example sentence candidates from the search engine). In this stage we want to select a subset $Y \subseteq \mathcal{Y}$ s.t. $|Y| = k$. In its basic form, the DPP defines the probability of drawing a subset Y from a ground set as

$$\mathcal{P}_L(Y) \propto \det(L_Y) \tag{1}$$

Here L_Y denotes restriction of matrix L to the elements of Y, $L_Y = [L_{i,j}] : i, j \in Y$. L generally can be any semi-positive definite matrix, but for our task we compose it from two types of features: a **quality** scalar q_i and a **similarity** unit vector ϕ_i. Elements of L becomes a cosine similarity between the similarity features scaled by the quality features

$$L_{i,j} = q_i \phi_i^T \phi_j q_j. \tag{2}$$

The intuition behind the DPP as follows: because the right part of (1) contains determinant, when off-diagonal elements of L_Y get larger (meaning the cosine similarity of similarity features is large), then the determinant value, or in the other words, the probability of drawing Y, gets lower. At the same time, the DPP prefers elements with large values of quality features.

The DPP has a very interesting property. It is easy to compute **marginal** probabilities of inclusion of a set A in all subsets of the ground set $\mathcal{Y}$:

$$\mathcal{P}_L(A \subseteq \mathcal{Y}) = \frac{\sum_{Y:A\subseteq Y\subseteq \mathcal{Y}} \det(L_Y)}{\sum_{Y:Y\subseteq \mathcal{Y}} \det(L_Y)} = \det(K_A).$$

K_A is restriction of K with the elements of the set A (similar to (1)). K itself is called *marginal kernel* of the DPP and it can be computed as $K = L(L + I)^{-1}$, where I is an identity matrix.

Selecting diverse items

Because the elements of K can be used to compute the marginal probability of selecting a subset of items from the ground set, it is possible to use the marginal probabilities as a weight for a greedy selection algorithm.

In the beginning we have an empty set $A = \emptyset$. Then we repeatedly add an item i into the set A s.t. $i = \arg\max_i \det(K_{A \cup i})$ until the set A reaches the required size. Please note that this algorithm does not find a MAP answer, that problem is shown to be NP-complete.

Computational complexity

Dealing with L and K directly requires $O(N^3)$ floating point operations and $O(N^2)$ memory, which can be unwieldy for sufficiently large N.

Fortunately, if L is formulated as (2), it is possible to work around these requirements. Let B be a feature matrix with rows $B_i = q_i \phi_i$, so $L = B^T B$. Instead of computing $N \times N$ matrix L, we compute a $D \times D$ matrix $C = BB^T$. Note that if we have an eigendecomposition $L = \sum_{n=1}^{N} \lambda_n v_n v_n^T$, we can get the marginal kernel K by rescaling eigenvalues of L:

$$K = \sum_{n=1}^{N} \frac{\lambda_n}{\lambda_n + 1} v_n v_n^T.$$

Remember that non-zero eigenvalues of L and C are the same and their eigenvectors are related as well. Namely, the eigendecomposition of L is also

$$\left\{ \lambda_n, \frac{1}{\sqrt{\lambda_n}} B^T \hat{v}_n \right\}_{n=1}^{D},$$

where $\hat{v}_n$ are eigenvectors of C. Using this fact, we can compute the elements of marginal kernel K directly from the eigendecomposition of C and the feature matrix B:

$$K_{ij} = \sum_{n=1}^{D} \frac{(B_i^T \hat{v}_n)(B_j^T \hat{v}_n)}{\lambda_n + 1}.$$

Computation of a single element of K takes $O(D^2)$ floating point operations. For each step of the selection algorithm, we need to compute N new elements of K and compute N determinants of $|A| \times |A|$ size. In addition we need to compute an eigendecomposition of D. This leads to a total complexity of $O(D^3 + ND^2 k + Nk^3)$ for selecting k items using the DPP, which is linear of N.

3.2 Similarity Features

We construct similarity feature vector as a weighted stacking of three individual feature parts

$$\phi_i = f([w_1 s_i^{\text{lex}} \,;\, w_2 s_i^{\text{synt}} \,;\, w_3 s_i^{\text{sema}} \,;\, r])$$

and a parameter r which makes all sentences similar to each other, following the text summarization task in (Kulesza and Taskar, 2012). We set $r = 0.7$ in our experiments.

Three similarity feature parts are lexical, syntactic and semantic similarity. Feature weights w_i allow us to prioritize similarity feature components. Lexical and syntactic similarity features are created as count-based vectors and have large dimensionality. Transformation f here is a compression into a 600-dimensional vector using Gaussian random projections as recommended by Kulesza and Taskar (2012) to make the dimensionality of ϕ_i, D, small.

Lexical similarity features measure word overlap between two sentences, syntactic features measure structural (POS, grammar and dependency) similarity between two sentences and semantic features measure sense similarity of two sentences. Lexical similarity uses tf weighting inside example sentence candidate batch when inclusion of a content word is given a weight of 1.0; non-content words are given a weight of 0.1.

A **syntactic similarity** for two sentences should be higher if they have similar syntactic structure near the target word, meaning that it was used in a similar syntactic way. In other words, dependency structure, POS tags and grammatical words should be similar near the target word. For instance, let's consider sentences: "He is a fast runner", "She is a slow runner" and "John isn't a good runner". These three sentences have small content word overlap, but have exactly the same syntactic structure.

The idea for the syntactic similarity method is based on efficient calculation of graph similarity using graphlets. Graphlets are parts of graph, and it is shown by (Shervashidze et al., 2009) that they can be used for the fast approximate computation of graph similarity.

The main idea is to generate subtrees up to a certain size, by growing them from the target word and use those subtrees as features in the vector space. Overall, the syntactic similarity model can be thought of as a bag-of-subtrees model. Dependency trees in Japanese is build of *bunsetsu* – a unit which consist of a lemma with attached functional morphemes. Subtrees are treated as unordered because bunsetsu in Japanese can be moved on the same dependency level.

In the first step, the parse tree is *stripped* from

lexical information for open parts of speech by replacing them with part of speech tags. Function words are left as they were.

Secondly, a set of bunsetsu subtrees up to size of 3 is generated from the stripped tree. The generation starts from the bunsetsu containing the target word and continues until no new subtrees can be created.

Finally, the feature space is expanded by deriving new subtrees. Bunsetsu can contain compound nouns like "参政権" (a right to vote) or "積み上げる" (to place on top of something) which are analyzed to consist of two lexical units. Grammatically, they are not much different from single unit words. This step ensures that sentences containing both several-unit and single-unit words are still going to be structurally similar.

A **semantic similarity** score should be higher if the target word is used in the same or a close sense. For computing semantic similarity from a context we use prototype projections (Tsubaki et al., 2013) on word2vec word representations (Mikolov et al., 2013).

Prototype projections assume that for triples of (A, relation, B) there exist prototypes in the form of frequently occurring and semantically related groups words at the end of each relation. For example, it is possible to run company, business or marathon. The computed representation makes it possible to distinguish between the distant senses. For a given triple (e.g run, object, marathon), you compute frequently occurring words of **run** and **marathon** over the same relation and compute SVD in each group. The top n right singular vectors in each end of the relation form a prototype subspace, and the original vector is projected into it.

For the actual feature we use a sum of prototype projections over all possible arguments of a target word. For instance, we use all present Japanese case relations if the target word is a verb, case relation and genitive case for nouns, and dependencies for adverbs and adjectives. For the each end of a relation use top 200 words to compute SVDs.

3.3 Quality Features

Quality features represent an *intrinsic value* of individual sentences as examples of word usage. Our quality feature is defined as a product of four components: $q_i = q_i^{\text{cse}} q_i^{\text{csy}} q_i^{\text{d}} q_i^{\text{g}}$.

Centrality

q_i^{cse} and q_i^{csy} are semantic and syntactic centrality, respectively. We want example sentences to be representative of usage patterns and meaning. Centrality captures that idea. It is computed using a respective similarity feature component (s_i^{synt} and s_i^{sema}) as a cosine similarity to a nearest centroid of a K-means++ clustering. We take $k = 30$ for semantic and $k = 10$ for syntactic centralities.

Relative difficulty

The next quality feature is relative difficulty. It is estimated from the difficulty of content words. Sentence difficulty d_s is computed from the word difficulty d_{w_i} using the formula

$$d_s = \left(\sum_{w_i \in s} d_{w_i}^4 \right)^{\frac{1}{4}}.$$

We used the fourth power to give the sum a light softmax effect: smaller values should have less effect on the final result, but the sentence length should still be a certain factor in the difficulty score. Word difficulties are estimated using web corpus word frequencies and Japanese Language Proficiency Test (JLPT) word lists.

Frequency component of word difficulty is computed as $d_w^{\text{freq}} = \lfloor \log_2(1 + w_f/500) \rfloor$. Words which should be known for JLPT N5 were given the difficulty $d_w^{\text{JLPT}} = 1$, words for N1 were assigned $d_w^{\text{JLPT}} = 5$ respectively with other values in between. The final word difficulty score is computed as $d_w = \min(d_w^{\text{freq}}, d_w^{\text{JLPT}})$.

Sentence difficulty is then converted into the quality feature component using a piecewise linear function $q_i^{\text{d}} = T(d_s + \text{bias}_d)$, which is defined as $T = [0, 0.6, 1, 0.9, 0.7, 0.6, 0.2, 0]$ at $[-\infty, -1, 0, 3, 5, 6, 8, \infty]$. The function is rather adhoc. It has a maximum of 1 at 0 and decreases to the left and right. We wanted to have positive and negative parts to decrease with the different rate. A bias value bias_d can shift the area of acceptable difficulties for a learner. For example, a bias value of $\text{bias}_d = -3$ would make the quality to be near 1 for the sentences which have the words with the difficulty at most for JLPT N3.

Goodness

The last part is goodness feature q_i^{g} which is 1 by default and assigns a low score to garbage sentences which are present in the web corpus. It also assigns low score to sentence fragments (some

sentences from raw corpus start with case particles which in Japanese always comes after a noun)
or clearly sentences which are useless for example
sentences, for instance ones that contain random
digits or alphabet.

4 Related Work

There exist human-curated databases of example
sentences. Dictionaries contain example sentences
which explain word usage, but usually those are
fragments and not full sentences. Also, dictionary
content usually has copyright restrictions. The
Tatoeba Project[2] is a wiki-style database of example sentences maintained by human volunteers under open license. However, most of the sentences
focus on relatively easy words and many of the
sentences are very similar to each other.

Automated extraction of example sentences
from a corpora has also been proposed. GDEX
(Kilgarriff et al., 2008) describes semi-automated
example extraction. The objective is to select example sentences for English learners and define a
suitable example sentence as: (a) typical, showing frequent and dispersed patterns of usage, (b)
informative, helping to educate the definition, (c)
readable, meaning intelligible to learners, avoiding difficult words, anaphora and other structures
that makes it difficult to understand a sentence
without access to wider context. Sentence length,
word frequency, information about the presence
of pronouns and some other heuristics were used
to judge the quality of sentences. Subsequently,
the final example sentences for the dictionary were
manually selected by editors

There are numerous works which approach the
problem of selecting example sentences mostly
as a word sense disambiguation (WSD) problem
(de Melo and Weikum, 2009; Shinnou and Sasaki,
2008; Kathuria and Shirai, 2012). Specifically,
de Melo and Weikum (2009) proposed the use
of parallel corpora to extract disambiguated sentences from an aligned subtitle database. One
more important feature of that work is a concern
about *diversity* of example sentences. They generate a set of 1,2,3-grams for each example sentence and use them for scoring example sentences,
setting to zero scores for n-gram for the selected
sentences. This approach used aligned corpora for
WSD, which usually are small or belong to a specific domain, whereas example sentences should

be from different domains and cover rare words.
Also, the work does not consider sentence difficulty. In the evaluation by language learners we
found out that sentence difficulty is a major factor
for example sentence quality.

Kathuria and Shirai (2012) explore the use of
disambiguated example sentences in a reading as-
sistant system for Japanese learners. They create a system that assists reading by showing disambiguated example sentences that have the same
sense as the word in the text.

Huang et al. (2016) have used neural network
models to show example sentences which would
help disambiguate close synonyms. However, this
work does not try to extract globally diverse example sentences which cover the usage of a target
word.

The DPP itself (Kulesza and Taskar, 2012) was
used for document summarization by selecting
sentences from a text and showing a diverse image search result tasks. We use several tricks from
the former application.

5 Evaluation

Evaluating the suitability of example sentences for
learning a foreign language is difficult. Firstly,
it is not possible to assess the diversity of a sentence set when showing them to evaluators one
by one. Also, the automatic evaluation of example sentences is possible if the problem is formulated such that the only criterion is that example
sentences should be present for every sense of a
word. However, such evaluation does not determine whether the example sentences are actually
useful for learners.

5.1 Experiment Setup

We perform an evaluation experiment with
Japanese language learners and a native teacher
with two distinct main goals: to assess the performance of the example extraction system and to
validate the assumptions on the meaning of the
"quality" of example sentences. We use a web
corpus with 0.8B sentences lexically analyzed by
JUMAN and parsed by KNP.

The first goal is achieved by having participants
vote on lists of example sentences and select their
preferred lists. We deliberately use lists for the
evaluation instead of showing single examples to
make the spectrum of possible example sentences
visible for each method. Showing sentences one

---

[2]http://tatoeba.org/eng/

by one would make it difficult to compare the diversity of different lists.

For the second goal, the evaluation was performed in the form of an interview. Participants were asked why they have or have not chosen specific lists of example sentences after the initial preference selection.

Three methods were used in the evaluation: the proposed one and two baselines. The proposed method is labeled **DPP** in the evaluation results. We have used a difficulty bias value $bias_d = -3$ to make the sentence difficulty appropriate for the learners around JLPT N3 level.

The first baseline was a method by de Melo and Weikum (2009). However, because our setting uses only monolingual corpora, only lexical centrality and diversity parts were used from this method. The method received the same set of example sentences as the DPP, namely search results biased towards syntactically rich sentences near a target word. The method is referred as **DeMelo**.

The second baseline was a simple uniform random sampling without replacement. The data, again, was a list of example sentence candidates from the search system, not raw examples. This method is referred as **Rand**.

For the experiment we have used 14 Japanese words. Each chosen word has more than one sense and different usages. Words were also chosen to be relatively easy, to be likely familiar to language learners of lower intermediate level.

For each of the words, top 10k search results from the search engine were extracted as example sentence candidates. Each of the words had more than 10k containing sentences. After that, 12 sentences were extracted by each method from each list. That yields a total of $14 \times 12 \times 3$ sentences which were presented to participants of the experiment.

The first part of the evaluation experiment used Japanese language learners as participants. For each word, participants were presented three lists of example sentences produced by three methods. The lists were placed side by side in a random order to force participants to read sentence lists in a different order every time. Participants were asked to select a list which was more useful from their point for putting sentences on flashcards. After a participant would select a personally preferable list, anonymized names for methods were displayed and the participant was asked to explain the

#	FC	Level	Rand	DeMelo	DPP
1		N1	**7**	4	3
2		N1	**8**	0	6
3		N1	4	**7**	3
4	*	N1	2	3	**9**
5	*	N1	3	2	**9**
6	*	N2	5	3	**6**
7		N2	4	**6**	4
8		N2	5	2	**7**
9	*	N2	3	4	**7**
10	*	N3	0	1	**13**
11	*	N4	3	1	**10**
Total			44	33	77
Percentage			29%	21%	50%

Table 1: Learners' votes on the best example lists. Bold numbers are the majority for a person. FC means the experience of using flashcards. Level is approximate JLPT-style Japanese language proficiency from N5 (lowest) to N1 (highest).

reasons behind the selection.

The second part experiment was performed by showing the same example sentence lists to a native Japanese language teacher. In addition to selecting the best list, a teacher was asked to rank from 1 to 5 how appropriate the list was for students of approximately N3 and N2 JLPT levels. N3 is similar to intermediate and N2 to upper-intermediate levels in English. Similarly to the learners' case, no explicit criteria were given. Unfortunately, because of time limitations only one teacher have participated in the second part of the evaluation.

5.2 Results

The first part of the evaluation was performed with 11 learners. The evaluation took about 1.5 hours per learner in average. Vote counts for users and aggregated counts are shown in the Table 1. DPP got about a half of all votes, which is a positive aspect of the proposed method. It also got a majority for every participant who had the experience of using flashcards or spaced repetition systems. This shows that these example sentences are going to be useful inside the flashcards.

For the initial selection, the teacher commented that the best list was selected as if examples were for learners of N3 level. The votes on the initial selection were 0, 4, 10 for Rand, DeMelo and DPP respectively. Average lists ranks were 3.36, 3.79, 4.64 for N3 and 3.86, 4.21 and 4.36 for N2 learner levels.

Evaluation by the teacher assigns the DPP system as the best for N3 learners both by votes and by average rank. For N2 learners a score for DPP was lower, at the same time the score for DeMelo has raised. Score for Rand was the lowest.

The teacher explained the reason for selection as the following. Non-target words in a sentence should not be too difficult. A sentence should not depend on outer context like as if it was inside the conversation or about current affairs. The sentences should be short and the usages of the target words should be common. This criteria are strongly aligned with the objectives DPP uses for sentence extraction, which seems to be the reason for its high appraisal by the teacher.

If examples would be selected for N2-like learners, a sentence should include more diverse structures and usage. However, some high-level students had a different point of view.

There were cases when learners discarded a list because of a sentence they did not like or selected a list because of a sentence they liked very much. We tried to analyze the patterns of such sentences with a possibility for the further improvement of example sentence extraction.

6 Discussion

During the evaluation experiment, participants were asked to explain their choices about lists and criteria they were using.

Generally, list diversity was regarded as one of the main criteria for the selection. Semantic and lexical diversity was the mainly referred part. However, grammatical diversity was named as well. By grammatical diversity participants meant, usually, usage of words in different grammatical forms. Other themes that frequently came into criteria for the selection were sentence difficulty and *how interesting* were the sentences. Each of the points is discussed in greater detail below.

Diversity Diversity was the main idea behind the work for the present study and it was validated by answers of the participants. Most of them have stated that non-similarity of a sentence list was one of the main criteria for the selection.

All three used methods were specialized to produce non-similar sentences. DeMelo explicitly tries to select sentences with frequent words and penalize such words in next selections. Diversity of sentences using random sampling depends on the distribution in the candidate set.

For DPP, features were explicitly crafted to deal with semantic and syntactic similarity in addition to lexical similarity. Based on the results, there were cases where DPP was better in terms of diversity and the cases when it was worse.

One example of good performance in this regard was the word "卵" (an egg). In addition to the usual meaning of an egg in a sentence like "それには多くの卵を割る必要があります" (You would need to break a lot of eggs to make that), DPP also displayed several sentences for the usage like "医師の卵に期待が集まっている" (There are a lot of expectations in the future doctors) with the meaning of "future profession". Other methods did not produce example sentences with this sense.

A similar, but mixed result is sentences for the word "頭" (a head). DPP selected 6 sentences that have the regular meaning of the word as "head" like "彼女は僕の頭に手をかける" (She puts a hand on my head). However, the other 6 had the meaning of beginning of a time period like in the sentence "今年の頭に撮った写真です" ([This is] a photo I've taken in the beginning of this year).

Difficulty Sentence difficulty was also one criterion experiment participants used for selecting lists. The initial assumption for the creation of the system is that example sentences should be easy to understand and as short as possible. We designed an algorithm which selects example sentences for flashcard questions and thought that it was good to minimize question reading time.

The feedback of participants on this topic was divided. Learners of lower proficiency levels have agreed with our vision, while learners of higher proficiency levels have shown preference for more difficult example sentences. For the last user group, there were several opinions that example sentences selected by DPP were plain as if they come from a textbook. In comparison to that such learners preferred, more difficult, natural (in contrast to artificially created examples), and interesting example sentences.

We believe that this effect can be explained with learners' familiarity with the target word of example sentence. If a learner is not familiar with the target word, then the other words are expected to serve mostly as explanation for the target's meaning and the sentence itself should be easier. If a learner is generally familiar with the word, that context given by an example sentence helps learner to learn and remember usage situations of the target. Sentences in this period of the familiarity could be harder.

It seems that we should talk not about good example sentences *in general*, but about good example sentences *for a learner at some point in a learning process*. Static example lists are not going to solve this problem efficiently, but an educational tool like an SRS can. It has access not only to learner's general knowledge level, but for the learning process data for individual words as well. Using this information about learners, an example extraction system can provide the best examples learner needs at that point of time.

Interestingness Another criteria that was used by learners for selecting sentences was if the sentences were *interesting*. During the evaluation, there were the cases when the choice between lists was made on a single interesting sentence, disregarding the fact that the list have contained mostly inferior and low-quality sentences like complete fragments. There were 3 main types of such sentences.

The first type had sentences, interesting or unusual for a certain participant. We could not generalize this category further.

The second type was sentences having a story. For example, "画像が汚いのは、携帯カメラで撮ったからです、今度綺麗な写真でも撮っておきましょう" (Image quality is bad because it was taken by a mobile phone. Let's take a good picture next time.) vs "画像が汚かったりしたら買う気しませんからね" (I don't want to buy it since the image quality is bad). These two sentences have the same word usage of "dirty" (image is dirty = image quality is bad). However the first one has a cause-effect relation and was more liked because of that.

The third type as sentences displaying a vivid image. For instance, "旧ソ連の宇宙飛行士ガガーリンの有人宇宙飛行「地球は青かった」" (A famous Soviet astronaut Gagarin have said: "The Earth is blue").

Interesting content usually occurs only in relatively lengthy sentences containing many different words. Because of the conservative difficulty settings we used for the experiment, the DPP method was heavily biased against such sentences. Interestingness is difficult to define and measure, but we believe that it is worth investigating in the future.

7 Conclusion and Future Work

We have implemented an example extraction system for usage in a flashcard system for Japanese language learners. It uses Determinantal Point Process — a method for modeling diverse datasets as a framework which allows to select non-similar and high quality sentences at the same time.

While the example extraction system is developed for Japanese, but the underlying methods have little Japanese specific parts. The system itself is unsupervised and has only a tokenizer, morphologic analyzer and dependency parser as software dependencies. All other data can be created from a raw corpus analyzed by these three tools.

Experiments have shown that the proposed DPP-based method is useful for extracting example sentences. However the content and difficulty of example sentences are a non-trivial problem and it would be promising to consider ways to further improve the content and quality of example sentences. We also want to perform evaluation experiments using an actual SRS (Tolmachev and Kurohashi, 2017).

Acknowledgments

The first author thanks Japanese government and the Ministry of Education, Culture, Sports, Science and Technology for the MEXT scholarship which made this work possible. We thank Yugo Murawaki and Raj Dabre for proofreading and very helpful comments. We would also like to thank anonymous reviewers for their feedback.

References

Nicholas J. Cepeda, Harold Pashler, Edward Vul, John T. Wixted, and Doug Rohrer. 2006. Distributed practice in verbal recall tasks: A review and quantitative synthesis. *Psychological Bulletin*, 132(3):354–380.

Chieh-Yang Huang, Nicole Peinelt, and Lun-Wei Ku. 2016. Automatically suggesting example sentences of near-synonyms for language learners. In *Proceedings of COLING 2016, the 26th International Conference on Computational Linguistics: System Demonstrations*, pages 302–306. The COLING 2016 Organizing Committee.

Pulkit Kathuria and Kiyoaki Shirai. 2012. Word Sense Disambiguation Based on Example Sentences in Dictionary and Automatically Acquired from Parallel Corpus. In *Advances in Natural Language Processing*, number 7614 in Lecture Notes in Computer Science, pages 210–221.

Adam Kilgarriff, Milo Husk, Katy McAdam, Michael Rundell, and Pavel Rychl. 2008. GDEX: Automatically finding good dictionary examples in a corpus. In *Proceedings of the 13th EURALEX International Congress*, pages 425–432, Barcelona, Spain. Institut Universitari de Linguistica Aplicada, Universitat Pompeu Fabra.

Alex Kulesza and Ben Taskar. 2012. Determinantal Point Processes for Machine Learning. *Foundations and Trends in Machine Learning*, 5(2–3):123–286.

Gerard de Melo and Gerhard Weikum. 2009. Extracting sense-disambiguated example sentences from parallel corpora. In *Proceedings of the 1st Workshop on Definition Extraction*, WDE '09, pages 40–46, Stroudsburg, PA, USA. Association for Computational Linguistics.

Tomas Mikolov, Wen-tau Yih, and Geoffrey Zweig. 2013. Linguistic regularities in continuous space word representations. In *Proceedings of NAACL-HLT*, pages 746–751.

Philip I. Pavlik and John R. Anderson. 2008. Using a model to compute the optimal schedule of practice. *Journal of Experimental Psychology. Applied*, 14(2):101–117.

Nino Shervashidze, SVN Vishwanathan, Tobias Petri, Kurt Mehlhorn, and Karsten Borgwardt. 2009. Efficient graphlet kernels for large graph comparison. In *Proceedings of the Twelth International Conference on Artificial Intelligence and Statistics*, volume 5, pages 488–495. PMLR.

Hiroyuki Shinnou and Minoru Sasaki. 2008. Division of Example Sentences Based on the Meaning of a Target Word Using Semi-Supervised Clustering. In *LREC 2008*.

Arseny Tolmachev and Sadao Kurohashi. 2017. Kotonoha: An example sentence based spaced repetition system. In *Proceedings of the Twenty-third Annual Meeting of the Association for Natural Language Processing*, pages 847–850, Tsukuba, Japan.

Arseny Tolmachev, Hajime Morita, and Sadao Kurohashi. 2016. A grammar and dependency aware search system for japanese sentences. In *Proceedings of the Twenty-second Annual Meeting of the Association for Natural Language Processing*, pages 593–596, Sendai, Japan.

Masashi Tsubaki, Kevin Duh, Masashi Shimbo, and Yuji Matsumoto. 2013. Modeling and learning semantic co-compositionality through prototype projections and neural networks. In *Proceedings of the 2013 Conference on Empirical Methods in Natural Language Processing (EMNLP)*, pages 130–140, Seattle, Washington, USA. Association for Computational Linguistics.

Distractor Generation for Chinese Fill-in-the-blank Items

Shu Jiang
Department of
Computer Science and Engineering
Shanghai Jiao Tong University
Shanghai, China
jshmjs45@gmail.com

John Lee
Department of
Linguistics and Translation
City University of Hong Kong
Hong Kong SAR, China
jsylee@cityu.edu.hk

Abstract

This paper reports the first study on automatic generation of distractors for fill-in-the-blank items for learning Chinese vocabulary. We investigate the quality of distractors generated by a number of criteria, including part-of-speech, difficulty level, spelling, word co-occurrence and semantic similarity. Evaluations show that a semantic similarity measure, based on the word2vec model, yields distractors that are significantly more plausible than those generated by baseline methods.

1 Introduction

The fill-in-the-blank item is a common form of exercise in computer-assisted language learning (CALL) systems. Also known as a cloze or gap-fill item, a fill-in-the-blank item is constructed on the basis of a carrier sentence. One word in the sentence — called the *target word*, or *key* — is blanked out, and the learner attempts to fill it. The top of Table 1 shows an example carrier sentence whose target word is *tiaojian* 'condition'.[1]

To enable automatic feedback, a fill-in-the-blank item often specifies choices, including the target word itself and several distractors, as shown at the bottom of Table 1. Distractors need to be carefully chosen: they must be sufficiently plausible, but must not be acceptable answers. Literature in language pedagogy generally recommends the following criteria to authors of fill-in-the-blank items: a distractor should belong to the same word class and same difficult level, and have approximately the same length, as the target word (Heaton, 1989); it should collocate strongly with a word in the sentence (Hoshino, 2013); and it should be semantically related with the target word, ideally a

---

<table>
<tr><td colspan="2">他因爲那裏的 ___ 不好，所以不去
那裏上大學。
He chose not to attend that university
because its ___ are not good.</td></tr>
<tr><td>1. 條件 tiaojian 'condition'</td><td>← Target word
↓ Distractors</td></tr>
<tr><td>2. 原因 yuanyin 'reason'</td><td>Human</td></tr>
<tr><td>3. 頻道 pindao 'channel'</td><td>Baseline</td></tr>
<tr><td>4. 條約 tiaoyue 'agreement'</td><td>+Spell</td></tr>
<tr><td>5. 函數 hanshu 'function'</td><td>+Co-occur</td></tr>
<tr><td>6. 因素 yinsu 'factor'</td><td>+Similar</td></tr>
</table>

Table 1: An example fill-in-the-blank item, with a carrier sentence with a blank (top); and six choices for the blank (bottom), including the target word (correct answer), and distractors generated by five different methods (see Section 4).

"false synonym" (Goodrich, 1977). An empirical study confirmed that distractors indeed tend to be syntactically and semantically homogenous (Pho et al., 2014).

To automate the time-consuming process of selecting distractors, there has been much interest in developing algorithms that, given a carrier sentence and a target word, can find appropriate distractors. To-date, most research effort on distractor generation for language learning has focused on English.

This paper presents the first attempt to automatically generate distractors in fill-in-the-blank items for learners of Chinese as a foreign language. In Section 2, we review related research areas. In Section 3, we present our datasets. In Section 4, we outline our criteria for distractor generation. In Section 5, we describe the evaluation procedure. In Section 6, we report evaluation results, show-

---

[1]This example is taken from (Liu, 2004).

Proceedings of the 12th Workshop on Innovative Use of NLP for Building Educational Applications, pages 143–148
Copenhagen, Denmark, September 8, 2017. ©2017 Association for Computational Linguistics

ing that a semantic similarity measure based on the `word2vec` model yields distractors that are significantly more plausible than those generated by baseline methods.

2 Previous work

An algorithm for generating distractors must attempt a trade-off between two objectives. One objective is plausibility. Most approaches require the distractor and the target word to have the same part-of-speech (POS) and similar level of difficulty, often approximated by word frequency (Coniam, 1997; Shei, 2001; Brown et al., 2005). They must also be semantically close, which can be quantified with semantic distance in WordNet (Lin et al., 2007; Pino et al., 2008; Chen et al., 2015; Susanti et al., 2015), thesauri (Sumita et al., 2005; Smith et al., 2010), ontologies (Karamanis et al., 2006; Ding and Gu, 2010), or hand-crafted rules (Chen et al., 2006). Another approach generates distractors that are semantically similar to the target word in some sense, but not in the particular sense in the carrier sentence (Zesch and Melamud, 2014). Others directly extract frequent mistakes in learner corpora to serve as distractors (Sakaguchi et al., 2013; Lee et al., 2016). Error-annotated Chinese learner corpora are still not large enough, however, to support broad-coverage distractor generation.

A second, often competing objective is to ensure that the distractor, however plausible, is not an acceptable answer. Most approaches require that the distractor never, or only rarely, collocate with other words in the carrier sentence. Some define collocation as n-grams in a context window centered on the distractor (Liu et al., 2005). Others also consider words elsewhere in the carrier sentence, for example those present in the Word Sketch of the distractor (Smith et al., 2010) or those that are grammatically related to the distractor in dependencies (Sakaguchi et al., 2013). Still others restrict potential distractors to antonyms of the target word, words with the same hypernym, and synonym of synonyms in WordNet (Knoop and Wilske, 2013).

To the best of our knowledge, there is not yet any reported attempt to generate distractors for learning Chinese vocabulary. The only previous work on Chinese distractor generation was designed for testing knowledge in the aviation domain, and leveraged a domain-specific ontology (Ding and Gu, 2010).

3 Data

To facilitate our study, we compiled two datasets:

Textbook Corpus We collected 299 fill-in-the-blank items, each with a target word and two to three distractors, from three Chinese textbooks (Liu, 2004, 2010; Wang, 2007). An analysis on this corpus confirms many of the criteria proposed in the literature: in 63% of the items, all distractors have the same POS as the target word; and in 45% of the items, at least one distractor shares a common character with the target word.

Wiki Corpus We extracted 14 million sentences from Chinese Wikipedia for calculating word frequency, similarity and co-occurrence statistics in the Candidate Generation step. We then performed word segmentation, POS tagging and dependency analysis on a subset of 5.5 million sentences with the Stanford Chinese parser (Levy and Manning, 2003) for use in the Candidate Filtering step.

4 Approach

We follow a two-step process where the first step, Candidate Generation, optimizes distractor plausibility; and the second step, Candidate Filtering, aims to filter out distractor candidates that are acceptable answers.

4.1 Candidate Generation

We implemented the following criteria for generating a ranked list of distractor candidates:

Baseline (`Baseline`) The baseline re-implements the criteria proposed by Coniam (1997): the distractor must have the same POS and the similar difficulty level as the target word. We extract all words in the Wiki corpus with the same POS, and then rank them by the proximity of their word frequency and that of the target word. In Table 1, for example, *pindao* 'channel' was chosen because, among all nouns, its word frequency is closest to that of the target word *tiaojian*.

Spelling similarity (`+Spell`) Many Chinese words contain multiple characters; two words that have one or more characters in common may be easily confusable for learners. This method requires the candidate to share at least one common character with the target word. In our running example in Table 1, *tiaoyue* 'agreement' was chosen because, among all words that contain the character *tiao* or *jian* (which combine to form the target word *tiaojian*), it has the most similar word frequency.

Word co-occurrence (+Co-occur) A distractor that often co-occurs with the target word may be easily confusable for learners. We ranked the candidate distractors according to their pointwise mutual information (PMI) score with the target word, as estimated on the Wiki corpus. In our running example in Table 1, *hanshu* 'function' was chosen because of its frequent co-occurrence with *tiaojian* 'condition'.

Word similarity (+Similar) Words that are semantically close to the target word tend to be plausible candidates. We ranked candidate distractors according to their similarity score with the target word. We obtained these scores by training a word2vec model (Mikolov et al., 2013) on the Wiki corpus.[2] We opted for word2vec over thesauri or Chinese lexical databases such as HowNet because of its broader coverage. In the example in Table 1, the distractor *yinsu* 因素 'factor' was chosen because it has the highest similarity score with *tiaojian* in the word2vec model.

4.2 Candidate Filtering

A distractor is called "reliable" if it yields an incorrect sentence. This step aims to remove those candidates that are also acceptable answers, leaving only the reliable distractors. We do so by examining whether the distractor can collocate with words in the rest of the carrier sentence. The system examines the candidates in the ranked list produced by the Candidate Generation step (Section 4.1), and removes candidates that are rejected by both filters below:

Trigram The word trigram, formed by the distractor, the previous word and the following word in the carrier sentence, must not appear in the

---

[2]We trained a bag-of-words (CBOW) model of 400 dimensions and window size 5 with word2vec.

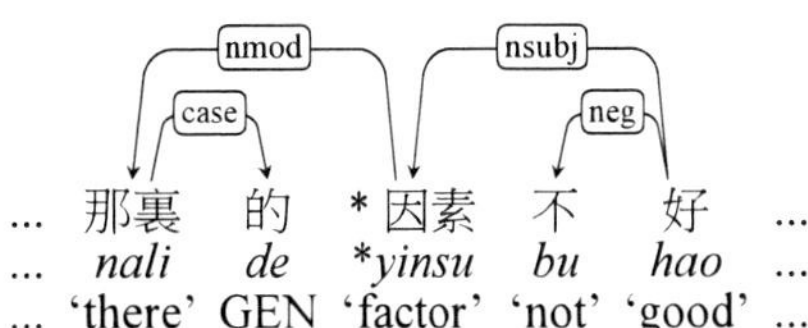

Figure 1: In the Candidate Filtering step (Section 4.2), candidate distractors whose dependency relations are attested in the corpus are rejected. To determine whether *yinsu* can serve as a distractor in the carrier sentence in Table 1, the system determines whether the dependency relations nmod(*yinsu*, *nali*) or nsubj(*hao*, *yinsu*) is attested in a large corpus of Chinese texts.

Wiki corpus. In the example in Figure 1, the trigram "*de yinsu bu*" must not be attested.

Dependency The Trigram filter alone might be too strict, since words that are grammatically related to the distractor may be further away. Among dependency relations in the parse tree of the carrier sentence, we extract all those with the distractor as head or child, and require that these relation must not be attested in the Wiki corpus. This filter is similar to the approach by Smith et al. (2010), but instead of the grammatical relations in Word Sketches, we consider all dependency relations. In our running example in Table 1, the candidate 情况 *qingkuang* 'situation' was rejected because it is attested to serve as the subject of *hao* 'good'. The next distractor in the ranked list, *yinsu* 'factor', was chosen instead since it never served as the subject of *hao* 'good', and was never modified by the noun *nali* 'there'.

5 Evaluation

5.1 Test data

According to Da (2007), basic ability in Chinese news reading require a vocabulary of around 20,000 words. Among the target words in the Textbook Corpus, we selected 37 nouns and verbs such that they were roughly equally spaced among the 20,000 most frequent words in the Wiki Corpus.

For each of these 37 words, we generated distractors using each of the four criteria in Section 4 (Baseline, +Spell, +Co-occur, and +Similar). In addition, we randomly picked one

Method	Reliability
Baseline	100%
+Co-occur	98.6%
+Spell	93.2%
+Similar	93.2%
Human	100%

Table 2: Reliability of the various distractor generation methods.

distractor from the corresponding fill-in-the-blank item in the Textbook corpus (Human). We thus have 37 items, each with six choices[3]: one correct answer, and five distractors. Table 1 shows an example.

5.2 Human annotation

We asked two human judges, both native Chinese speakers, to annotate these choices, without revealing the target word. For each choice in the item, the judges decided whether it was correct or incorrect; they may identify zero, one or multiple correct answers. For an incorrect answer, they further assessed its plausibility as a distractor on a three-point scale: "Plausible" (3), "Somewhat plausible' (2)', or "Obviously wrong" (1).

The kappa for the human annotation is 0.529, which is considered a "moderate" level of agreement (Landis and Koch, 1977). As a annotation quality check, we found that overall, in 6.8% of the times, a judge labels the target word as a distractor.

6 Results

6.1 Reliability

As shown in Table 2, the Baseline and +Co-occur methods performed best in terms of reliability: 100% and 98.6% of their respective distractors can be used. The +Spell and +Similar methods, at 93.2%, were more prone to generating distractors that yield correct sentences. This is not unexpected since the +Similar method explicitly tries to find distractors that are semantically similar to the target word.

The reliability rate would have been lower if not for the Candidate Filtering step. The Trigram and Dependency filters rejected 16 of the 37 top candidates returned by the +Similar method. A post-

Method	Average score	Plausible or somewhat plausible
Baseline	1.06	5.2%
+Co-occur	1.27	8.6%
+Spell	1.66	39.7%
+Similar	**1.76**	**46.6%**
Human	**1.68**	**53.4%**

Table 3: Average scores, out of a 3-point scale (see Section 5.2), of distractors generated by the various methods in the human evaluation.

hoc analysis found that 11 of the 16 rejected candidates would indeed have been acceptable answers. The filters thus boosted the reliability rate by 30%, at the cost of falsely rejecting 5 top-ranked candidates.

6.2 Plausibility

Table 3 shows the results on plausibility. Both the +Similar method[4] and the +Spell method[5] outperformed the baseline, both in terms of the average score and the proportion of distractors considered at least somewhat plausible.

Distractors of the +Similar method have very competitive quality, scoring on average 1.76, slightly higher than the average score of the Human method (1.68). A qualitative review found that while the +Similar method can sometimes yield distractors that are even more plausible than those given by humans[6], they are also more likely overall to be rated "Obviously Wrong", especially when the model fails to take into account word sense ambiguity. 53.4% of the Human distractors are rated Plausible or Somewhat Plausible, versus only 46.6% for the +Similar method.

7 Conclusions

We presented the first study on automatic generation of distractors for fill-in-the-blank items for learning Chinese. Evaluations showed that a semantic similarity measure, based on the word2vec model, offers a significant improvement over a baseline that considers only part-of-speech and word frequency, and achieves competitive plausibility in comparison to human-crafted items.

---

[3]Except that in 5 items, the +Co-occur and +Similar methods generated the same distractor; in another item, Baseline and +Co-occur generated the same distractor.

[4]$p < 0.001$, by McNemar's test.

[5]$p < 0.021$ by McNemar's test.

[6]Since we randomly selected one distractor out of three in the Textbook Corpus, the Human score reflects the average plausibility of the human-authored distractors, rather than the best one.

Acknowledgments

This work is funded by the Language Fund under Research and Development Projects 2015-2016 of the Standing Committee on Language Education and Research (SCOLAR), Hong Kong SAR.

References

Jonathan C. Brown, Gwen A. Frishkoff, and Maxine Eskenazi. 2005. Automatic Question Generation for Vocabulary Assessment. In *Proc. HLT-EMNLP*.

Chia-Yin Chen, Hsien-Chin Liou, and Jason S. Chang. 2006. FAST: An Automatic Generation System for Grammar Tests. In *Proc. COLING/ACL Interactive Presentation Sessions*.

Tao Chen, Naijia Zheng, Yue Zhao, Muthu Kumar Chandrasekaran, and Min-Yen Kan. 2015. Interactive Second Language Learning from News Websites. In *Proc. 2nd Workshop on Natural Language Processing Techniques for Educational Applications*.

David Coniam. 1997. A Preliminary Inquiry into Using Corpus Word Frequency Data in the Automatic Generation of English Language Cloze Tests. *CALICO Journal* 14(2-4):15–33.

Jun Da. 2007. Reading News for Information: How Much Vocabulary a CFL Learner Should Know. In Andreas Guder, Jiang Xin, and Yexin Wan, editors, *The Cognition, Learning and Teaching of Chinese Characters*. Beijing Language and Culture University Press, pages 251–277.

Xiangmin Ding and Hongbin Gu. 2010. Automatic Generation Technology of Chinese Multiple-choice Items based on Ontology [in Chinese]. *Computer Engineering and Design* 31(6):1397–1400.

Hubbard C. Goodrich. 1977. Distractor Efficiency in Foreign Language Testing. *TESOL Quarterly* 11(1):69–78.

J. B. Heaton. 1989. *Writing English Language Tests*. Longman.

Yuko Hoshino. 2013. Relationship between Types of Distractor and Difficulty of Multiple-Choice Vocabulary Tests in Sentential Context. *Language Testing in Asia* 3(16).

Nikiforos Karamanis, Le An Ha, and Ruslan Mitkov. 2006. Generating Multiple-Choice Test Items from Medical Text: A Pilot Study. In *Proc. 4th International Natural Language Generation Conference*.

S. Knoop and S. Wilske. 2013. WordGap: Automatic Generation of Gap-Filling Vocabulary Exercises for Mobile Learning. In *Proc. Second Workshop on NLP for Computer-assisted Language Learning, NODALIDA*.

J. Richard Landis and Gary G. Koch. 1977. The Measurement of Observer Agreement for Categorical Data. *Biometrics* 33:159–174.

John Lee, Donald Sturgeon, and Mengqi Luo. 2016. A CALL System for Learning Preposition Usage. In *Proc. ACL*.

Roger Levy and Christopher D. Manning. 2003. Is it harder to parse Chinese, or the Chinese Treebank? In *Proc. ACL*.

Y.-C. Lin, L.-C. Sung, and M.-C. Chen. 2007. An Automatic Multiple-Choice Question Generation Scheme for English Adjective Understanding. In *Proc. Workshop on Modeling, Management and Generation of Problems/Questions in eLearning, 15th International Conference on Computers in Education*.

Chao-Lin Liu, Chun-Hung Wang, Zhao-Ming Gao, and Shang-Ming Huang. 2005. Applications of Lexical Information for Algorithmically Composing Multiple-Choice Cloze Items. In *Proc. 2nd Workshop on Building Educational Applications Using NLP*. pages 1–8.

Jennifer Lichia Liu. 2004. *Connections I: a Cognitive Approach to Intermediate Chinese*. Indiana University Press, Bloomington, IN.

Jennifer Lichia Liu. 2010. *Encounters I/II: a Cognitive Approach to Advanced Chinese*. Indiana University Press, Bloomington, IN.

Tomas Mikolov, Kai Chen, Greg Corrado, and Jeffrey Dean. 2013. Efficient estimation of word representations in vector space. In *Proc. ICLR*.

Van-Minh Pho, Thibault André, Anne-Laure Ligozat, B. Grau, G. Illouz, and Thomas François. 2014. Multiple Choice Question Corpus Analysis for Distractor Characterization. In *Proc. LREC*.

Juan Pino, M. Heilman, and Maxine Eskenazi. 2008. A Selection Strategy to Improve Cloze Question Quality. In *Proc. Workshop on Intelligent Tutoring Systems for Ill-Defined Domains., 9th International Conference on Intelligent Tutoring Systems*.

Keisuke Sakaguchi, Yuki Arase, and Mamoru Komachi. 2013. Discriminative Approach to Fill-in-the-Blank Quiz Generation for Language Learners. In *Proc. ACL*.

Chi-Chiang Shei. 2001. FollowYou!: An Automatic Language Lesson Generation System. *Computer Assisted Language Learning* 14(2):129–144.

Simon Smith, P. V. S. Avinesh, and Adam Kilgarriff. 2010. Gap-fill Tests for Language Learners: Corpus-Driven Item Generation. In *Proc. 8th International Conference on Natural Language Processing (ICON)*.

Eiichiro Sumita, Fumiaki Sugaya, and Seiichi Yamamoto. 2005. Measuring Non-native Speakers' Proficiency of English by Using a Test with
Automatically-Generated Fill-in-the-Blank Questions. In *Proc. 2nd Workshop on Building Educational Applications using NLP*.

Yuni Susanti, Ryu Iida, and Takenobu Tokunaga. 2015.
Automatic Generation of English Vocabulary Tests.
In *Proc. 7th International Conference on Computer
Supported Education (CSEDU)*.

Youmin Wang. 2007. 實用商務漢語課本（漢韓版）
準高級篇／高級篇. Commercial Press, Beijing.

Torsten Zesch and Oren Melamud. 2014. Automatic Generation of Challenging Distractors Using
Context-Sensitive Inference Rules. In *Proc. Workshop on Innovative Use of NLP for Building Educational Applications (BEA)*.

An Error-Oriented Approach to Word Embedding Pre-Training

Youmna Farag[1]   Marek Rei[1,2]   Ted Briscoe[1,2]

[1]Computer Laboratory, University of Cambridge, United Kingdom
[2]The ALTA Institute, Cambridge, United Kingdom
{youmna.farag,marek.rei,ted.briscoe}@cl.cam.ac.uk

Abstract

We propose a novel word embedding pre-training approach that exploits writing errors in learners' scripts. We compare our method to previous models that tune the embeddings based on script scores and the discrimination between correct and corrupt word contexts in addition to the generic commonly-used embeddings pre-trained on large corpora. The comparison is achieved by using the aforementioned models to bootstrap a neural network that learns to predict a holistic score for scripts. Furthermore, we investigate augmenting our model with error corrections and monitor the impact on performance. Our results show that our error-oriented approach outperforms other comparable ones which is further demonstrated when training on more data. Additionally, extending the model with corrections provides further performance gains when data sparsity is an issue.

1 Introduction

Assessing students' writing plays an inherent pedagogical role in the overall evaluation of learning outcomes. Traditionally, human graders are required to mark essays, which is cost- and time-inefficient, especially with the growing numbers of students. Moreover, the evaluation process is subjective, which leads to possible variations in the awarded scores when more than one human assessor is employed. To remedy this, the automated assessment (AA) of writing has been motivated in order to automatically evaluate writing competence and hence not only reduce grader workload, but also bypass grader inconsistencies as only one system would be responsible for the

assessment. Numerous AA systems have been developed for research purposes or deployed for commercial use, including Project Essay Grade (PEG) (Page, 2003), e-Rater (Attali and Burstein, 2006), Intelligent Essay Assessor (IEA) (Landauer et al., 2003) and Bayesian Essay Test Scoring sYstem (BETSY) (Rudner and Liang, 2002) among others. They employ statistical approaches that exploit a wide range of textual features.

A recent direction of research has focused on applying deep learning to the AA task in order to circumvent the heavy feature engineering involved in traditional systems. Several neural architectures have been employed including variants of Long Short-Term Memory (LSTM) (Alikaniotis et al., 2016; Taghipour and Ng, 2016) and Convolutional Neural Networks (CNN) (Dong and Zhang, 2016). They were all applied to the Automated Student Assessment Prize (ASAP) dataset, released in a Kaggle contest[1], which contains essays written by middle-school English speaking students. On this dataset, neural models that only operate on word embeddings outperformed state-of-the-art statistical methods that rely on rich linguistic features (Yannakoudakis et al., 2011; Phandi et al., 2015).

The results obtained by neural networks on the ASAP dataset demonstrate their ability to capture properties of writing quality without recourse to handcrafted features. However, other AA datasets pose a challenge to neural models and they still fail to beat state-of-the-art methods when evaluated on these sets. An example of such datasets is the First Certificate in English (FCE) set where applying a rank preference Support Vector Machine (SVM) trained on various lexical and grammatical features achieved the best results (Yannakoudakis et al., 2011). This motivates further investigation

---

[1]https://www.kaggle.com/c/asap-aes/

Proceedings of the 12th Workshop on Innovative Use of NLP for Building Educational Applications, pages 149–158
Copenhagen, Denmark, September 8, 2017. ©2017 Association for Computational Linguistics

into neural networks to determine what minimum useful information they can utilize to enhance their predictive power.

Initializing neural models with contextually rich word embeddings pre-trained on large corpora (Mikolov et al., 2013; Pennington et al., 2014; Turian et al., 2010) has been used to feed the networks with meaningful embeddings rather than random initialization. Those embeddings are generic and widely employed in Natural Language Processing (NLP) tasks, yet few attempts have been made to learn more task-specific embeddings. For instance, Alikaniotis et al. (2016) developed *score-specific word embeddings* (SSWE) to address the AA task on the ASAP dataset. Their embeddings are constructed by ranking correct ngrams against their "noisy" counterparts, in addition to capturing words' informativeness measured by their contribution to the overall score of the essay.

We propose a task-specific approach to pre-train word embeddings, utilized by neural AA models, in an error-oriented fashion. Writing errors are strong indicators of the quality of writing competence and good predictors for the overall script score, especially in scripts written by language learners, which is the case for the FCE dataset. For example, the Spearman's rank correlation coefficient between the FCE script scores and the ratio of errors is -0.63 which is indicative of the importance of errors in writing evaluation:

$$\text{ratio of errors} = \frac{\text{number of erroneous script words}}{\text{script length}}$$

This correlation could even be higher if error severity is accounted for as some errors could be more serious than others. Therefore, it seems plausible to exploit writing errors and integrate them into AA systems, as was successfully done by Yannakoudakis et al. (2011) and Rei and Yannakoudakis (2016), but not by capturing this information directly in word embeddings in a neural AA model.

Our pre-training model learns to predict a score for each ngram based on the errors it contains and modifies the word vectors accordingly. The idea is to arrange the embedding space in a way that discriminates between "good" and "bad" ngrams based on their contribution to writing errors. Bootstrapping the assessment neural model with those learned embeddings could help detect wrong patterns in writing which should improve its accuracy of predicting the script's holistic score.

We implement a CNN as the AA model and compare its performance when initialized with our embeddings, tuned based on natural writing errors, to the one obtained when bootstrapped with the SSWE, proposed by Alikaniotis et al. (2016), that relies on random noisy contexts and script scores. Furthermore, we implement another version of our model that augments ngram errors with their corrections and investigate the effect on performance. Additionally, we compare the aforementioned pre-training approaches to the commonly used embeddings trained on large corpora (Google or Wikipedea). The results show that our approach outperforms other initialization methods and augmenting the model with error corrections helps alleviate the effects of data sparsity. Finally, we further analyse the pre-trained representations and demonstrate that our embeddings are better at detecting errors which is inherent for AA.

2   Related Work

There have been various attempts to employ neural networks to assess the essays in the ASAP dataset. Taghipour and Ng (2016) compared the performance of a few neural network variants and obtained the best results with an LSTM followed by a *mean over time* layer that averages the output of the LSTM layer. Alikaniotis et al. (2016) assessed the same dataset by building a bidirectional double-layer LSTM which outperformed Distributed Memory Model of Paragraph Vectors (PV-DM) (Le and Mikolov, 2014) and Support Vector Machines (SVM) baselines. Dong and Zhang (2016) implemented a CNN where the first layer convolves a filter of weights over the words in each sentence followed by an aggregative pooling function to construct sentence representations. Subsequently, a second filter is applied over sentence representations followed by a pooling operation then a fully-connected layer to predict the final score. Their CNN was applied to the ASAP dataset and its efficacy in in-domain and domain-adaptation essay evaluation was demonstrated in comparison to traditional state-of-the-art baselines.

Several AA approaches in the literature have exploited the "quality" or "correctness" of ngrams as a feature to discriminate between good and poor essays. Phandi et al. (2015) defined good essays

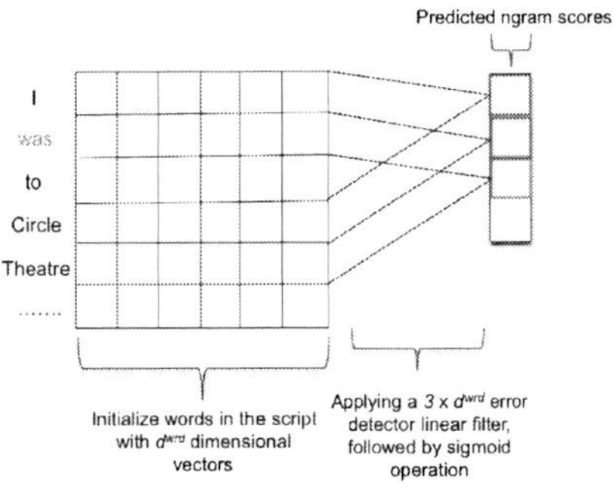

Figure 1: Error-specific Word Embeddings (ESWE).

as the ones with grades above or equal to the average score and the rest as poor ones. They calculated the Fisher scores (Fisher, 1922) of ngrams and selected 201 with the highest scores as *"useful ngrams"*. Similarly, they generated correct POS ngrams from grammatically correct texts, classified the rest as "bad POS ngrams" and used them along with the useful ngrams and other shallow lexical features as bag-of-words features. They applied Bayesian linear ridge regression (BLRR) and SVM regression for domain-adaptation essay scoring using the ASAP dataset. Alikaniotis et al. (2016) applied a similar idea; in their SSWE model, they trained word embeddings to distinguish between correct and noisy contexts in addition to focusing more on each word's contribution to the overall text score. Bootsrapping their LSTM model with those embeddings offered further performance gains.

Other models have directly leveraged error information exhibited in text. For example, Yannakoudakis et al. (2011) demonstrated that adding an *"error-rate"* feature to their SVM ranking model that uses a wide range of lexical and grammatical writing competence features further improves the AA performance. They calculated the error-rate using the error annotations in the Cambridge Learner Corpus (CLC) in addition to classifying a trigram as erroneous if it does not occur in the large ukWaC corpus (Ferraresi et al., 2008) or highly scoring CLC scripts. Rei and Yannakoudakis (2016) proposed a bidirectional LSTM for error detection in learner data, where the model predicts the probability of a word being correct for each word in text. As an extension to their experiment, they incorporated the average predicted probability of word correctness as an additional feature to the self-assessment and tutoring system

(SAT) (Andersen et al., 2013) that applied a supervised ranking perceptron to rich linguistic features. Adding their correctness probability feature successfully enhanced the predictive power of the SAT.

3 Approach

3.1 Word Embedding Pre-training

In this section, we describe three different neural networks to pre-train word representations: the model implemented by Alikaniotis et al. (2016) and the two error-oriented models we propose in this work. The models' output embeddings – referred to as *AA-specific* embeddings – are used later to bootstrap the AA system.

Score-specific Word Embeddings (SSWE). We compare our pre-training models to the SSWE developed by Alikaniotis et al. (2016). Their method is inspired by the work of Collobert and Weston (2008) which learns word representations by distinguishing between a target word's context (window of surrounding words) and its noisy counterparts. These counterparts are generated by replacing the target word with a randomly selected word from the vocabulary. The network is trained to rank the positive correct contexts higher than the negative corrupt ones. Additionally, the model is augmented with score specific information to focus on the informative words that contribute to the overall score of essays rather than the frequent words that occur equally in good and bad essays. They optimize the overall loss function as a weighted sum of the ranking loss between correct and noisy ngrams and the score specific loss:

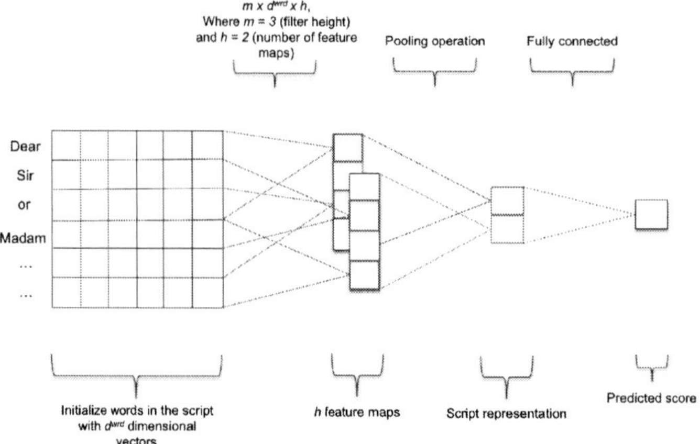

Figure 2: A CNN for AA where the final score is predicted by applying a convolutional operation followed by a pooling function.

$$Loss_{(SSWE)} = \alpha \cdot loss_{(ranking)} + (1 - \alpha) \cdot loss_{(score)} \tag{1}$$

where α is a hyperparameter. In their experiment, they set α to 0.1 giving most of the weight to score-related information.

Error-specific Word Embeddings (ESWE). We propose a model that fine-tunes the embedding space using a supervised method that leverages the errors appearing in the training data. It modifies the embedding space to discriminate between erroneous ngrams and correct ones. The core difference between this approach and SSWE is that it relies on the writing errors occurring naturally in the training data instead of randomly generating incorrect ngrams or capturing words' informativeness. The motivation for adopting this approach is twofold. First, we believe that the model could learn more useful AA features from actual errors rather than introducing random contexts that are unlikely to happen. Second, SSWE ignores the frequent words as they have less predictive power (they are used equally in highly and lowly scored texts). However, despite the fact that frequent words (e.g. function words) carry less topical information than content ones, the errors associated with them constitute a substantial portion of the errors committed by non-native English speakers. For instance, *determiner errors* account for more than 9% of the total errors in public FCE training data. Therefore, learning representations from both function and content word errors in their contexts could be advantageous.

The ESWE model predicts error scores for word ngrams. First, we demonstrate how the true error scores for ngrams are calculated and second, we describe the approach applied to estimate these scores. Each word w_i in a training document is given an error indicating score $e_i \in \{1, 0\}$ based on whether it is part of an error or not, respectively. Subsequently, an ngram gold score (n_score) is calculated based on the sum of the errors it contains as follows:

$$n\_score = \frac{1}{1 + \sum_i^n e_i} \tag{2}$$

where n is the ngram length. For the model to estimate the ngram scores, a convolutional operation is applied as depicted in Figure 1. First, each word is mapped to a unique vector $v_i^{wrd} \in \mathbb{R}^{d^{wrd}}$ retrieved from an embedding space $E \in \mathbb{R}^{|V| \times d^{wrd}}$, where $|V|$ is the vocabulary size. Consequently, an ngram is represented as a concatenation of its word vectors $v^{ng} = [v_i^{wrd}; ...; v_{i+n-1}^{wrd}]$. Scoring the ngrams is accomplished by sliding a convolutional linear filter $W^e \in \mathbb{R}^{n \times d^{wrd}}$ – hereafter *error filter*[2] – over all the ngrams in the script, followed by a sigmoid non-linearity to map the predicted score to a $[0, 1]$ probability space:

$$n\_\hat{score} = \sigma(W^e \cdot v^{ng}) \tag{3}$$

---

[2] We also refer to the window size used in SSWE as error filter for simplicity.

where σ is the sigmoid function.[3] The error filter should work as an error detector that evaluates the correctness of words given their contexts and arranges them in the embedding space accordingly. For optimization, the sum of squared errors loss is minimized between the gold ngram scores and the estimated ones and the error gradients are back-propagated to the embedding matrix E building the ESWE space:

$$Loss = \sum_k \left(n\_score_k - n\_\hat{score}_k\right)^2 \quad (4)$$

where k is the ngram index.

Error-correction-specific Word Embeddings (ECSWE). As an extension to ESWE, we propose augmenting it with the errors' corrections as follows. We build a corrected version of each script by replacing all its errors with their suggested corrections and train the ESWE model using the corrected scripts together with the original ones. In the corrected version, all the ngrams are given $e_i = 0$ and consequently, $n\_score = 1$ according to Equation 2. All the above ESWE equations are applied and the loss for each script is calculated as the sum of both the loss of the original script and its corrected version (Equation 4 applied to obtain both). The motivation for this model is twofold. First, it could enrich the embedding space by allowing the model to learn from faulty ngrams and their correct counterparts (both occur naturally in text) and construct ECSWE which is a modified version of ESWE that is more capable of distinguishing between good and bad contexts. Second, it could alleviate the effects of data sparsity, when training on small datasets, by learning from more representations.[4]

3.2 AA Model

The previous section discusses pre-training approaches for word embeddings that are later used to initialize the AA model. For this model, we use a second CNN to predict a holistic score for the script (Figure 2) as follows. Each word in an input script is initialized with its vector $v_i^{wrd'} \in \mathbb{R}^{d^{wrd}}$ from a pre-trained embedding matrix, resulting in a script embedding $[v_1^{wrd'}; ....; v_l^{wrd'}]$, where l is the length of the script. A convolutional filter $W^s \in \mathbb{R}^{m \times d^{wrd} \times h}$ is slid over all the

Model	Dataset	Error	Script
Google Word2Vec	FCE		3
& GloVe	FCE$_{ext}$	-	
SSWE, ESWE &	FCE	3	3
ECSWE	FCE$_{ext}$	9	9

Table 1: Error and script refer to their filter sizes. For each of the 5 pre-training models on the two datasets, the error filter size is displayed (if applicable) along with the script filter size used in the AA network initialized with the embeddings on the left. FCE refers to the public FCE.

script's subsequences to generate the feature maps $M \in \mathbb{R}^{h \times (l-m+1)}$, where m is the filter height (window size) and h is the number of the output feature maps. We refer to this filter as the *script filter*. Previously, for the error filter used in the ESWE and ECSWE approaches, h was set to 1 which represents the predicted ngram score ($n\_\hat{score}$), whereas here, the system extracts various contextual features from each ngram as a pre-step towards predicting the script's score, hence setting h to a large value. The convolutional operation is followed by a *ReLU* non-linearity to capture more complex linguistic phenomena:[5]

$$M_i = ReLU(W^s \cdot v_{i:i+m-1}^{wrd'}) \quad (5)$$

$$M = [M_1, M_2, ...M_{l-m+1}] \quad (6)$$

Subsequently, an average pooling function is applied to the output feature maps in order to select the useful features and unify the scripts' representations to a vector $S \in \mathbb{R}^h$ of fixed length. Finally, the last layer of the network is a fully connected one by applying linear regression to the script representation in order to predict the final score:

$$s\_\hat{score} = W^{reg} \cdot S \quad (7)$$

where $W^{reg} \in \mathbb{R}^h$ is a learned parameter matrix. The network optimizes the sum of squared errors loss between the scripts' predicted scores and the gold ones.

4 Experimental Setup

Baselines. We compare our error-oriented approaches to the SSWE model as well as generic pre-trained models commonly used to initialize

---

[3] Biases are removed from equations for simplicity.

[4] We refer to ESWE and ECSWE as *error-oriented* models.

[5] Initial experimentation showed that *ReLU* performs better than *tanh* in the AA model.

Bootstrapping Model	Pearson (r)	Spearman (ρ)	RMSE
Google Word2Vec 300d	0.488	0.446	5.339
GloVe 50d	0.475	0.427	5.308
SSWE	0.494	0.445	5.182
ESWE	0.521	0.481	5.194
ECSWE	**0.538**	**0.499**	**5.033**

Table 2: AA results when bootstrapped from different word embeddings and trained on public FCE. The bold values indicate the best results.

neural networks for different NLP tasks. The generic models are trained on large corpora to capture general semantic and syntactic regularities, hence creating richer, more meaningful word vectors, as opposed to random vectors. In particular, Google News Word2Vec ($d^{wrd} = 300$) (Mikolov et al., 2013) and GloVe ($d^{wrd} = 50$) (Pennington et al., 2014) pre-trained models are used. Google Word2Vec[6] is a Skip-gram model that learns to predict the context of a given word. It is trained on Google News articles which contain around 100 billion words with 3 million unique words. On the other hand, GloVe[7] vectors are learned by leveraging word-word cooccurrence statistics in a corpus. We use the GloVe embeddings trained on a 2014 Wikipedia dump in addition to Gigaword 5 with a total of 6 billion words.

Evaluation. We replicate the SSWE model, implement our ESWE and ECSWE models, use Google and GloVe embeddings and conduct a comparison between the 5 initilization approaches by feeding their output embeddings to the AA system from Section 3.2. All the models are implemented using the open-source Python library Theano (Al-Rfou et al., 2016). For evaluation, we calculate Spearman's rank correlation coefficient (ρ), Pearson's product-moment correlation coefficient (r) and root mean square error ($RMSE$) between the final predicted script scores and the ground-truth values (Yannakoudakis and Cummins, 2015).

Dataset. For our experiments, we use the FCE dataset (Yannakoudakis et al., 2011) which consists of exam scripts written by English learners of upper-intermediate proficiency and graded with scores ranging from 1 to 40.[8] Each script contains two answers corresponding to two different prompts asking the learner to write either an article, a letter, a report, a composition or a short story. We apply script-level evaluation by concatenating the two answers and using a special $answer\_end$ token to separate the answers in the same script.

The writing errors committed in the scripts are manually annotated using a taxonomy of 80 error types (Nicholls, 2003) together with suggested corrections. An example of error annotations is:

The problems started <e type="RT"> <i>in</i><c>at</c></e> *the box office.*

where <i></i> is the error, <c></c> is the suggested correction and the error type *"RT"* refers to *"replace preposition"*. For error-oriented models, a word is considered an error if it occurs inside an error tag and the correction is retrieved according to the correction tag.

We train the models on the released public FCE dataset which contains $1,141$ scripts for training and 97 scripts for testing. In order to examine the effects of training with extra data, we conduct experiments where we augment the public set with additional FCE scripts and refer to this extended version as FCE$_{ext}$, which contains $9,822$ scripts. We report the results of both datasets on the released test set. The public FCE dataset is divided into $1,061$ scripts for training and 80 for development while for FCE$_{ext}$, $8,842$ scripts are used for training and 980 are held out for development. The only data preprocessing employed is word tokenization which is achieved using the Robust Accurate Statistical Parsing (RASP) system (Briscoe et al., 2006).

Training. Hyperparameter tuning is done for each model separately. The SSWE, ESWE and ECSWE models are initialized with GloVe ($d^{wrd} = 50$) vectors, trained for 20 epochs and the learning rate is set to 0.01. For SSWE, α is set to 0.1, batch size to 128, the number of randomly gen-

---

[6] https://code.google.com/archive/p/word2vec/

[7] https://nlp.stanford.edu/projects/glove/

[8] We only evaluate on FCE and not the ASAP dataset because the latter does not contain error annotations.

Bootstrapping Model	Pearson (r)	Spearman (ρ)	RMSE
Google Word2Vec 300d	0.626	0.567	4.930
GloVe 50d	0.568	0.518	5.200
SSWE	0.624	0.583	4.872
ESWE	0.667	0.637	**4.536**
ECSWE	**0.674**	**0.642**	4.692

Table 3: AA results when bootstrapped from different word embeddings and trained on the extended FCE version (FCE$_{ext}$). The bold values indicate the best results.

erated counterparts per ngram to 20 and the size of hidden layer to 100.[9] For the AA network, initialized with any of the 5 models, h is set to 100, and learning rate to 0.001 when training on public FCE and 0.0001 on FCE$_{ext}$. The sizes used for error and script filters are shown in Table 1.[10] All the networks are optimized using Stochastic Gradient Descent (SGD). The AA system is regularized with $L2$ regularization with rate = 0.0001 and trained for 50 epochs during which performance is monitored on the dev sets. Finally, the AA model with the best mean square error over the dev sets is selected.

5 Results and Discussion

The public FCE results shown in Table 2 reveal that AA-specific embedding pre-training offers further gains in performance over the traditional embeddings trained on large corpora (Google and GloVe embeddings), which suggests that they are more suited for the AA task. The table also demonstrates that the ESWE model outperforms the SSWE one on correlation metrics, with a slight difference in the RMSE value. While the variance in the correlations between the two models is noticeable and suggests that the ESWE model is a more powerful one, the RMSE values weaken this assumption. This result could be attributed to the fact that public FCE is a small dataset with sparse error representations and SSWE is trained on 20 times more data as each ngram is paired with 20 randomly generated counterparts. Therefore, a more relevant comparison is needed and could be achieved by either training on more data, as will be discussed later, or further enriching the embedding space with corrections (ECSWE). Table 2 demonstrates that learning from the er-

rors and their corrections enhances the error pre-training performance on public FCE which indicates the usefulness of the approach and its ability to mitigate the effects of data sparsity. According to the results, training the model based on naturally occurring errors and their correct counterparts is better suited to the AA task rather than introducing artificial noisy contexts and tuning the embeddings according to scripts' scores or relying on word distributions learned from large corpora.

For a more robust analysis, we examine the performance when training on additional data (FCE$_{ext}$) as shown in Table 3. Comparing the results in Tables 2 and 3 proves that training with more data boosts the predictive power of all the models. It is also clear from Table 3 that with more data, the discrepancy in the performance between SSWE and ESWE models becomes more prominent and ESWE provides a superior performance on all evaluation metrics which suggests that, qualitatively, learning from learners' errors is a more efficient bootstrapping method. However, with FCE$_{ext}$, the ECSWE approach outperforms ESWE on correlation metrics while giving a worse RMSE value. This change in the results when training on a bigger dataset indicates that the effect of incorporating the corrections in training becomes less obvious with enough data as the distribution of correct and incorrect ngrams is enough to learn from.

6 Analysis

We conduct further analysis to the scores predicted by AA-specific embeddings by investigating the ability of the ESWE and SSWE models to detect errors in text. We run each model for 20 epochs on the public FCE (ngram size = 3) and FCE$_{ext}$ (ngram size = 9) training sets, then test the models on the respective dev sets and examine the output predictions. For simplicity, we assign a binary true score for each ngram with a

---

[9]Using the same parameters as Alikaniotis et al. (2016).

[10]Tuning the filter sizes was done for each model separately; for the Glove and Word2Vec models, a filter of size 3 performed better than 9, on both datasets.

Model	Public FCE	FCE$_{ext}$
Random Baseline	0.258	0.494
SSWE	0.251	0.480
ESWE	**0.472**	**0.539**

Table 4: AP results of the random baseline and SSWE and EWE models when trained on public and extended FCE sets and tested on the respective dev sets. The AP is calculated with respect to the error class.

zero value if it contains any errors and one otherwise. ESWE predicts a score $\in [0, 1]$ for each ngram indicating its correctness and hence could be used directly in the evaluation. On the other hand, SSWE predicts two scores for each ngram: *correct score* that it maximizes in comparison to the noisy ngrams and *script score* that should be high for good ngrams that occur in highly-graded scripts. The two scores are hence expected to be high for high-quality ngrams and low otherwise, which suggests that they can be used as proxies for error detection. We calculate the ngram predicted score of the SSWE model as a weighted sum of the correct and script scores, similar to its loss function (Equation 1 with $\alpha = 0.1$), and map the output to a $[0, 1]$ probability based on the minimum and maximum generated scores.[11] We calculate the average precision (AP) between the true scores and predicted ones with respect to the error representing class (true score $= 0$) and compare it to a random baseline, where random probability scores are generated. The results are displayed in Table 4 which shows that ESWE achieves a higher AP score on all evaluation sets, particularly with public FCE, and SSWE's performance is similar to the random baseline. This result is expected since the ESWE model is trained to predict actual errors, yet an empirical verification was required. We conclude from this analysis that tuning the embeddings based on training writing errors increases their sensitivity to unseen errors which is key for learners' data assessment and yields better performance than comparable pre-training approaches.

7   Conclusion and Future Work

In this work, we have presented two error-oriented approaches to train the word embeddings used by writing assessment neural networks. The first approach learns to discriminate between good and bad ngrams by leveraging writing errors occurring in learner data. The second extends the first by combining the error representations with their suggested corrections and tuning the embedding space accordingly. Our motivation for applying these models is to provide neural assessment systems with the minimum features useful for the task in an attempt to boost their performance on challenging datasets while still avoiding heavy feature engineering. The presented results demonstrate that our error-oriented embeddings are better suited for learners' script assessment than generic embeddings trained on large corpora when both are used to bootstrap a neural assessment model. Additionally, our embeddings have yielded superior performance to those that rely on ranking correct and noisy contexts as well as words' contributions to the script's overall score. Furthermore, extending our error embeddings with error corrections has enhanced the performance when trained on small data, while having a less obvious effect when trained on greater amounts of data which shows their efficacy to enrich the embedding space and mitigate data sparsity issues. We further analysed our embeddings and the score-specific ones and showed empirically that error-oriented representations are better at error detection which explicates their superior performance in learners' data evaluation.

Our best performing model still underperforms the state-of-the-art system by Yannakoudakis et al. (2011) that utilises a wide variety of features, even when they exclude error related features. However, the improvement obtained by error-oriented models over employing generic embeddings or score-specifc ones suggests that our pre-training approach is a promising avenue of research as it provides neural network assessment with useful information and motivates learning relevant properties associated with language proficiency.

For future work, it will be interesting to jointly train the score-specific model with the error-oriented one and test if this could further improve the performance. We also suggest fully automating the assessment process by using the outputs of automated error detection and correction systems to build the embeddings rather than relying on handcrafted error annotations. Finally, we encourage further examination for other types of fea-

---

[11]Different score combinations were implemented including using only one score, but they all led to similar results.

tures that could be useful for assessment models and incorporating them in the pre-training stage. This way the performance could be further enhanced with less information than what heavily engineered systems require.

References

Rami Al-Rfou, Guillaume Alain, Amjad Almahairi, et al. 2016. Theano: A Python framework for fast computation of mathematical expressions .

Dimitrios Alikaniotis, Helen Yannakoudakis, and Marek Rei. 2016. Automatic text scoring using neural networks. In *Proceedings of the 54th Annual Meeting of the Association for Computational Linguistics (Volume 1: Long Papers)*. Association for Computational Linguistics, pages 715–725.

Øistein E Andersen, Helen Yannakoudakis, Fiona Barker, and Tim Parish. 2013. Developing and testing a self-assessment and tutoring system. In *Proceedings of the Eighth Workshop on Innovative Use of NLP for Building Educational Applications, BEA*. pages 32–41.

Yigal Attali and Jill Burstein. 2006. Automated essay scoring with e-rater® v. 2. *The Journal of Technology, Learning and Assessment* 4(3).

Ted Briscoe, John Carroll, and Rebecca Watson. 2006. The second release of the rasp system. In *Proceedings of the COLING/ACL on Interactive presentation sessions*. Association for Computational Linguistics, pages 77–80.

Ronan Collobert and Jason Weston. 2008. A unified architecture for natural language processing: Deep neural networks with multitask learning. In *Proceedings of the 25th international conference on Machine learning*. ACM, pages 160–167.

Fei Dong and Yue Zhang. 2016. Automatic features for essay scoring – an empirical study. In *Proceedings of the 2016 Conference on Empirical Methods in Natural Language Processing*. pages 1072–1077.

Adriano Ferraresi, Eros Zanchetta, Marco Baroni, and Silvia Bernardini. 2008. Introducing and evaluating ukwac, a very large web-derived corpus of english. In *Proceedings of the 4th Web as Corpus Workshop (WAC-4) Can we beat Google*. sn, pages 47–54.

Ronald A Fisher. 1922. On the interpretation of $\chi 2$ from contingency tables, and the calculation of p. *Journal of the Royal Statistical Society* 85(1):87–94.

Thomas K Landauer, Darrell Laham, and Peter W Foltz. 2003. Automated scoring and annotation of essays with the intelligent essay assessor. *Automated essay scoring: A cross-disciplinary perspective* pages 87–112.

Quoc Le and Tomas Mikolov. 2014. Distributed representations of sentences and documents. In *Proceedings of the 31st International Conference on Machine Learning (ICML-14)*. pages 1188–1196.

Tomas Mikolov, Ilya Sutskever, Kai Chen, Greg S Corrado, and Jeff Dean. 2013. Distributed representations of words and phrases and their compositionality. In *Advances in neural information processing systems*. pages 3111–3119.

Diane Nicholls. 2003. The cambridge learner corpus: Error coding and analysis for lexicography and elt. In *Proceedings of the Corpus Linguistics 2003 conference*. volume 16, pages 572–581.

Ellis Batten Page. 2003. Project essay grade: Peg. *Automated essay scoring: A cross-disciplinary perspective* pages 43–54.

Jeffrey Pennington, Richard Socher, and Christopher D. Manning. 2014. Glove: Global vectors for word representation. In *Empirical Methods in Natural Language Processing (EMNLP)*. pages 1532–1543.

Peter Phandi, Kian Ming Adam Chai, and Hwee Tou Ng. 2015. Flexible domain adaptation for automated essay scoring using correlated linear regression. In *EMNLP*. pages 431–439.

Marek Rei and Helen Yannakoudakis. 2016. Compositional sequence labeling models for error detection in learner writing. In *Proceedings of the 54th Annual Meeting of the Association for Computational Linguistics (Volume 1: Long Papers)*. Association for Computational Linguistics, pages 1181–1191.

Lawrence M Rudner and Tahung Liang. 2002. Automated essay scoring using bayes' theorem. *The Journal of Technology, Learning and Assessment* 1(2).

Kaveh Taghipour and Hwee Tou Ng. 2016. A neural approach to automated essay scoring. In *Proceedings of the 2016 Conference on Empirical Methods in Natural Language Processing*. Association for Computational Linguistics, pages 1882–1891.

Joseph Turian, Lev Ratinov, and Yoshua Bengio. 2010. Word representations: a simple and general method for semi-supervised learning. In *Proceedings of the 48th annual meeting of the association for computational linguistics*. pages 384–394.

Helen Yannakoudakis, Ted Briscoe, and Ben Medlock. 2011. A new dataset and method for automatically grading esol texts. In *Proceedings of the 49th Annual Meeting of the Association for Computational Linguistics: Human Language Technologies-Volume 1*. Association for Computational Linguistics, pages 180–189.

Helen Yannakoudakis and Ronan Cummins. 2015. Evaluating the performance of automated text scoring systems. In *Proceedings of the Tenth Workshop* on Innovative Use of NLP for Building Educational Applications. pages 213–223.

Investigating neural architectures for short answer scoring

Brian Riordan[1], Andrea Horbach[2], Aoife Cahill[1], Torsten Zesch[2], Chong Min Lee[1]
[1]Educational Testing Service, Princeton, NJ 08541, USA
[2]Language Technology Lab, University of Duisburg-Essen, Duisburg, Germany

Abstract

Neural approaches to automated essay scoring have recently shown state-of-the-art performance. The automated essay scoring task typically involves a broad notion of writing quality that encompasses content, grammar, organization, and conventions. This differs from the *short answer content scoring* task, which focuses on content accuracy. The inputs to neural essay scoring models – ngrams and embeddings – are arguably well-suited to evaluate content in short answer scoring tasks. We investigate how several basic neural approaches similar to those used for automated essay scoring perform on short answer scoring. We show that neural architectures can outperform a strong non-neural baseline, but performance and optimal parameter settings vary across the more diverse types of prompts typical of short answer scoring.

1 Introduction

Deep neural network approaches have recently been successfully developed for several educational applications, including automated essay assessment. In several cases, neural network approaches exceeded the previous state of the art on essay scoring (Taghipour and Ng, 2016).

The task of *automated essay scoring* (AES) is generally different from the task of automated *short answer scoring* (SAS). Essay scoring generally focuses on *writing quality*, a multidimensional construct that includes ideas and elaboration, organization, style, and writing conventions such as grammar and spelling (Burstein et al., 2013). Short answer scoring, by contrast, typically focuses only on the accuracy

of the content of responses (Burrows et al., 2015). Analyzing the rubrics of prompts from the Automated Student Assessment Prize shared tasks on AES and SAS, while there is some overlap across essay scoring and short answer scoring, there are three main dimensions of differences:

1. *Response length.* Responses in SAS tasks are typically shorter. For example, while the ASAP-AES data contains essays that average between about 100 and 600 tokens (Shermis, 2014), short answer scoring datasets may have average answer lengths of just several words (Basu et al., 2013) to almost 60 words (Shermis, 2015).

2. *Rubrics* focus on content only in SAS vs. broader writing quality in AES.

3. *Purpose and genre.* AES tasks cover persuasive, narrative, and source-dependent reading comprehension and English Language Arts (ELA), while SAS tasks tend to be from science, math, and ELA reading comprehension.

Given these differences, the feature sets for AES and SAS systems are often different, with AES incorporating a larger set of features to capture writing quality (Shermis and Hamner, 2013). Nevertheless, deep learning approaches to AES have thus far demonstrated strong performance with minimal inputs consisting of unigrams and word embeddings. For example, Taghipour and Ng (2016) explore simple LSTM and CNN-based architectures with regression and evaluate on the ASAP-AES data. Alikaniotis et al. (2016) train score-specific word embeddings with several LSTM architectures. Dong and Zhang (2016) demonstrate that a hierarchical CNN architecture produces

159

strong results on the ASAP-AES data. Recently, Zhao et al. (2017) show state-of-the-art performance on the ASAP-AES dataset with a memory network architecture.

In this work, we investigate whether deep neural network approaches with similarly minimal feature sets can produce good performance on the SAS task, including whether they can exceed a strong non-neural baseline. Unigram embedding-based neural network approaches to essay scoring capture content signals from their input features, but the extent to which they capture other aspects of writing quality rubrics has not been established. These approaches as implemented would seem to lend themselves even better to the purely content-focused rubrics in SAS, where content signals should dominate in achieving good human-machine agreement. On the other hand, recurrent neural networks may derive some of their predictive power in AES from more redundant signals in longer input sequences (as sketched by Taghipour and Ng (2016)). As a result, the shorter responses in SAS may hinder the ability of recurrent networks to achieve state-of-the-art results.

To explore the effectiveness of neural network architectures on SAS, we use the basic architecture and parameters of Taghipour and Ng (2016) on three publicly available short answer datasets: ASAP-SAS (Shermis, 2015), Powergrading (Basu et al., 2013), and SRA (Dzikovska et al., 2016, 2013). While these datasets differ with respect to the length and complexity of student responses, all prompts in the datasets focus on content accuracy. We explore how well the optimal parameters for AES from Taghipour and Ng (2016) fare on these datasets, and whether different architectures and parameters perform better on the SAS task.

2 Datasets

The three datasets we use cover different kinds of prompts and vary considerably in the length of the answers as well as their well-formedness. Table 1 shows basic statistics for each dataset. Figures 1, 2 and 3 show examples for each of the datasets.

2.1 ASAP-SAS

The Automated Student Assessment Prize Short Answer Scoring (ASAP-SAS) dataset[1] contains 10 individual prompts, covering science, biology,

and ELA. The prompts were administered to U.S. high school students in several state-level assessments. Each prompt has an average of 2,200 individual responses, typically consisting of one or a few sentences. Responses are scored by two human annotators on a scale from 0 to 2 or 0 to 3 depending on the prompt (Shermis, 2015). Following the guidelines from the Kaggle competition, we always use the score assigned by the first annotator.

2.2 Powergrading

The Powergrading dataset (Basu et al., 2013) contains 10 individual prompts from U.S. immigration exams with about 700 responses each. Each prompt is accompanied by one or more reference responses. As responses are very short (typically a few words – see Figure 2) and because the percentage of correct responses is very high, responses in the Powergrading dataset are to some extent repetitive. The Powergrading dataset tests models' ability to perform well on extremely short responses.

The Powergrading dataset was originally used for the task of (unsupervised) clustering (Basu et al., 2013), so that there are no state-of-the-art scoring results available for this dataset. For simplicity, we use the first out of three binary human-annotated correctness scores.

2.3 SRA

The SRA dataset (Dzikovska et al., 2012) became widely known as the dataset used in SemEval-2013 Shared Task 7 "The Joint Student Response Analysis and 8th Recognizing Textual Entailment Challenge" (Dzikovska et al., 2013). It consists of two subsets: *Beetle*, with student responses from interacting with a tutorial dialogue system, and *SciEntsBank (SEB)* with science assessment questions. We use two label sets from the shared task: the 2-way labels classify responses as correct or incorrect, while the 5-way labels provide a more fine-grained classification of responses into the categories *non_domain*, *correct*, *partially_correct_incomplete*, *contradictory* and *irrelevant*. In contrast with most SAS datasets, the SRA dataset contains a large number of prompts and with relatively few responses per prompt (see Table 1). Following the procedure from the shared task, we train models for each SRA dataset (Beetle, SEB) across all responses to all prompts.

---

[1] https://www.kaggle.com/c/asap-sas

ASAP - Prompt 1

QUESTION: After reading the groups procedure, describe what additional information you would need in order to replicate the experiment. Make sure to include at least three pieces of information.

SCORING RUBRIC FOR A 3 POINT RESPONSE: The response is an excellent answer to the question. It is correct, complete, and appropriate and contains elaboration, extension, and/or evidence of higher-order thinking and relevant prior knowledge. There is no evidence of misconceptions. Minor errors will not necessarily lower the score.

STUDENT RESPONSES:

- **3 points:** Some additional information you will need are the material. You also need to know the size of the contaneir to measure how the acid rain effected it. You need to know how much vineager is used for each sample. Another thing that would help is to know how big the sample stones are by measureing the best possible way.

- **1 point:** After reading the expirement, I realized that the additional information you need to replicate the expireiment is one, the amant of vinegar you poured in each container, two, label the containers before you start yar expirement and three, write a conclusion to make sure yar results are accurate.

- **0 points:** The student should list what rock is better and what rock is the worse in the procedure.

Figure 1: **ASAP-SAS example:** Question, partial scoring rubric, and example student responses for Prompt 1. (Spelling errors in the student responses are in the original. Source text used in the prompt is omitted here for space reasons.)

PG - PROMPT 1

QUESTION: What is one right or freedom from the First Amendment of the U.S. Constitution?

REFERENCE RESPONSES:
- speech
- religion
- assembly
- press
- petition the government

STUDENT RESPONSES:

- **correct:** freedom of speech
- **correct:** free speech
- **correct:** freedom to talk freely
- **correct:** freedome of religeon
- **incorrect:** the right to bear arms
- **incorrect:** life

Figure 2: **Powergrading example:** Question, reference responses, and example student responses for Prompt 1.

SRA - BEETLE dataset

QUESTION: What are the conditions that are required to make a bulb light up

REFERENCE RESPONSES: the bulb and the battery are in a closed path

STUDENT RESPONSES:

- **correct:** a complete circuit of electricty
- **incorrect:** connection to a battery

Figure 3: **SRA example:** Question, reference response, and example student responses from Beetle subset.

Dataset	# prompts	Scores / Labels	# train responses (mean)	# dev responses (mean)	# test responses (mean)	Mean length (train)
ASAP-SAS	10	0/1/2(/3)	1363	341	522	48.4
PG	10	0/1	418	140	140	3.9
SRA Beetle	47	2 or 5-way	3153 (67.1)	788 (16.8)	449 (9.4)	9.8
SRA SEB	135	2 or 5-way	2968 (29.4)	1001 (7.4)	540 (4.0)	12.5

Table 1: Overview of the datasets used in this work. Since we train prompt-specific models for ASAP-SAS and PG, we report the mean number of responses per set per prompt. For SRA, we train one model per label set across prompts and report the overall number of prompts per set as well as the mean number of responses per prompt per set (in parentheses).

3 Experiments

3.1 Method

We carried out a series of experiments across datasets to discern the effect of specific parameters in the SAS setting. We took the best parameter set from Taghipour and Ng (2016) as our reference since it performed best on the AES data. We looked at the effect of varying several important parameters to discern the effectiveness of each for SAS:

- the role of the mean-over-time layer, which was crucial for good performance in Taghipour and Ng (2016)

- the utility of pretrained embeddings

- the contribution of features derived from a convolutional layer

- the needs for network representational capacity via recurrent hidden layer size

- the role of bidirectional architectures for short response lengths

- regression versus classification

- the effect of attention

To explore the effect of specific parameters, we trained models on the training set and evaluated on the development set only. Following these experiments, we trained a model on the training and development sets and evaluated on the test set. We report prompt-level results for this model in Section 3.6.

For evaluation, we use quadratic weighted kappa (QWK) for the ASAP-SAS and Powergrading datasets. Because the class labels in the SRA dataset are unordered, we report the weighted F1 score, which was the preferred metric in the Semeval shared task (Dzikovska et al., 2016).

3.2 Baseline

As a baseline system, we use a supervised learner based on a hand-crafted feature set. This baseline is based on DkPro TC (Daxenberger et al., 2014) and relies on support vector classification using Weka (Hall et al., 2009). We preprocess the data using the ClearNlp Segmenter [2] via DKPro Core (Eckart de Castilho and Gurevych, 2014). The features used in the baseline system comprise a commonly used and effective feature set for the SAS task. We use both binary word and character uni- to trigram occurrence features, using the top 10,000 most frequent ngrams in the training data, as well as answer length, measured by the number of tokens in a response.

3.3 Neural networks

We work with the basic neural network architecture explored by Taghipour and Ng (2016) (Figure 4).[3] First, the word tokens of each response are converted to embeddings. Optionally, features are extracted from the embeddings by a convolutional network layer. This output forms the input to an LSTM layer. The hidden states of the LSTM are aggregated in either a "mean-over-time" (MoT) layer or attention layer. The MoT layer simply averages the hidden states of the LSTM across the input. We use the same attention mechanism employed in Taghipour and Ng (2016), which involves taking the dot product of each LSTM hidden state and a vector that is trained with the network. The aggregation layer output is a single vector, which is input to a fully connected layer. This layer computes a scalar (regression) or class label (classification).

---

[2]https://github.com/clir/clearnlp

[3]The networks are implemented in Keras and use the Theano backend.

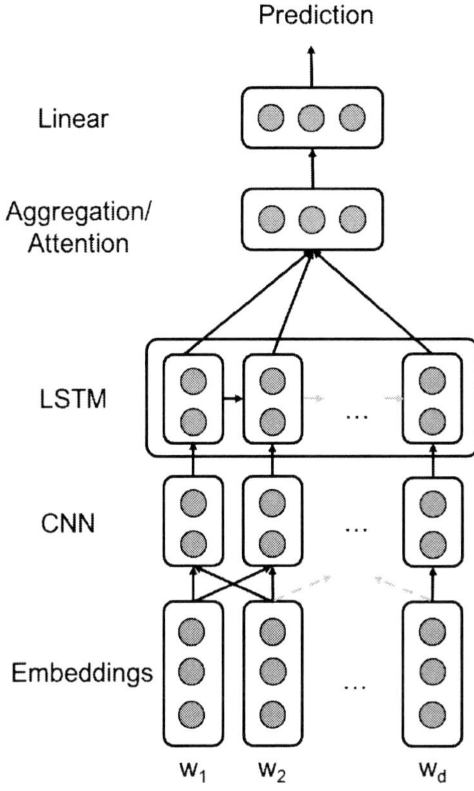

Figure 4: The basic neural architecture explored in this work for short answer scoring.

3.4 Setup, training, and evaluation

The text is lightly preprocessed as input to the neural networks following Taghipour and Ng (2016). The text is tokenized with the standard NLTK tokenizer and lowercased. All numbers are mapped to a single <num> symbol.[4] Each response is padded with a dummy token to uniform length, but these dummy tokens are masked out during model training.

For the ASAP-SAS and Powergrading datasets, prior to training, we scale all scores of responses to [0, 1] and use these scaled scores as input to the networks. For evaluation, the scaled scores are converted back to their original range. The SRA class labels are used as is.

We fix a number of neural network parame-

---

[4]It may be the case that relevant content information is thus ignored. However, since many numbers occur with units of measurement, e.g. 1g, we do not have word embeddings for them either and so the embeddings would simply be random initializations. We leave a full exploration of this issue to future work.

ters for our experiments. For pretrained embeddings, in preliminary experiments the GloVe 100 dimension vectors (Pennington et al., 2014) performed slightly better than a selection of other off-the-shelf embeddings, and hence we use these for all conditions that involve pretrained embeddings. Embeddings for word tokens that are not found in the embeddings are randomly initialized from a uniform distribution. The convolutional layer uses a window length of 3 or 5 and 50 filters. We use a mean squared error loss for regression models and a cross-entropy loss for classification models. To train the network, we use RMSProp with ρ set to 0.9 and learning rate of 0.001. We clip the norm of the gradient to 10. The fully connected layer's bias is initialized to the mean score for the training data, and the layer is regularized with dropout of 0.5. We use a batch size of 32, which provided a good compromise between performance and runtime in preliminary experiments.

To obtain more consistent results and improve predictive performance, we evaluate the models by keeping an exponential moving average of the model's weights during training. The moving average weights w_{EMA} are updated after each batch by

$$w_{EMA} \mathrel{-}= (1.0 - d) * (w_{EMA} - w_{current}).$$

d is a decay rate that is updated dynamically at each batch by taking into account the number of batches so far:

$$min(decay, (1 + \#batches)/(10 + \#batches))$$

where *decay* is a maximum decay rate, which we set to 0.999. This decay rate updating procedure allows the weights to be updated quickly at first while stabilizing across time.

All models are trained for 50 epochs for parameter exploration on the development set (Section 3.5) and 50 epochs for the final models on the test set (Section 3.6). Following Taghipour and Ng (2016), for our parameter exploration experiments on the development set, we report the best performance across epochs. When we train final models on the combined training and development set and evaluate on the test set, we report the results from the last epoch.

During development, we observed that even after employing best practices for ensuring reproducibility of results[5], there was still some small variation between runs of the same parameter settings. The reasons for this variability were not clear.

3.5 Parameter exploration results

Our focus in this section is comparing different architecture and parameter choices for the neural networks with the best parameters from Taghipour and Ng (2016). Table 2 shows the results of our experiments on the *development* set for ASAP-SAS and Powergrading, and Table 3 shows the corresponding results for SRA.

Does the mean-over-time layer improve performance? Taghipour and Ng (2016) demonstrate a large performance gain with the mean-over-time layer that averages the LSTM hidden states across the response tokens. Comparing "T&N best" with "no MoT" across the datasets, we see mixed results. The mean-over-time layer performs relatively well across datasets, but achieves the best results only on the SRA-SEB dataset. We hypothesized that the mean-over-time layer is helpful when the input consists of longer responses (as was the case for the essay data in Taghipour and Ng (2016)). We computed the Pearson's correlation on the ASAP-SAS data between the difference on each prompt of the two conditions and the mean response length in the development set. However, the correlation was modest at 0.437.

Do pretrained embeddings with tuning outperform fixed or randomly initialized embeddings? On all datasets, the pretrained embeddings with tuning (among the "T&N best" parameters) performed better than fixed pretrained or learned embeddings.[6] Tuned embeddings were especially important for the ASAP-SAS and Powergrading datasets.

Does a convolutional layer produce useful features for the SAS task? The results for convolutional features are mixed: convolutional features contribute small performance improvements on Powergrading and one of the SRA label sets (SRA SEB 2-way).

Can smaller hidden layers be used for the SAS task? Although LSTMs with smaller hidden states

often outperformed the 300-dimensional LSTM in the T&N best parameter set (compare 'T&N best' performance with performance for 'LSTM dims' conditions), the improvements were all quite small.

Do bidirectional LSTMs improve performance? Bidirectional LSTM architectures produced solid gains over the T&N best parameters on ASAP-SAS, Powergrading, and two of the four SRA label sets.

Can classification improve performance? The T&N model used regression. While the labels in SRA allow only for classification, ASAP-SAS and PG work with both regression and classification. However, we found consistently better results using regression.

Can attention improve performance? The attention mechanism we considered in this paper yielded strong performance improvements over the mean-over-time layer on all datasets except SRA-SEB 5-way. The largest improvements were on Powergrading and SRA-Beetle 5-way, where increases were almost 3 points weighted F1.

We also report the results of the combinations of individual parameters that performed well on the development data at the bottom of Table 2 and Table 3. While these combinations performed better than any individual parameter variation on ASAP-SAS and Powergrading, the combination performed *worse* on three of the four label sets in the SRA data. These results underscore that these parameters do not always produce additive effects in practice.

We examined the predictions from the baseline system and the T&N system for the ASAP-SAS development set and conducted a brief error analysis. In general, across the 10 prompts, it can be observed that when the baseline system is incorrect it tends to under-predict the scores, whereas the T&N system tends to slightly over-predict scores when it is incorrect. These effects are typically small, but consistent.

3.6 Test performance

We selected the top parameter settings on the development set and trained models on the full training set (i.e. training and development sets) for each dataset:

- *ASAP-SAS:* 250-dimensional bidirectional LSTM, attention mechanism

---

[5]The Numpy random seed was set. Since we used Theano, in run scripts, we used `PYTHONHASHSEED=0`.

[6]We also did experiments with a much larger number of epochs for the "learned" condition, but performance did not approach that of the tuned embeddings.

Experiment	Condition	Emb	CNN	Dim	Dir	MoT	Att	ASAP-SAS Mean QWK	Powergrading Mean QWK
Benchmark	Baseline							0.6529	**0.9049**
	T&N best	tun	no	300	uni	yes	no	0.7381	0.8724
MoT	no MoT	tun	no	300	uni	no	no	0.7197	**0.8753**
Embeddings	fixed	fix	no	300	uni	yes	no	0.7126	0.8376
	learned	lea	no	300	uni	yes	no	0.6687	0.8482
CNN	win len 5	tun	len 5	300	uni	yes	no	0.7224	**0.8748**
Directionality	bi	tun	no	300	bi	yes	no	**0.7396**	**0.8798**
LSTM dims	50	tun	no	50	uni	yes	no	0.7169	0.8514
	100	tun	no	100	uni	yes	no	0.7341	0.8567
	150	tun	no	150	uni	yes	no	0.7377	**0.8797**
	200	tun	no	200	uni	yes	no	0.7343	0.8669
	250	tun	no	250	uni	yes	no	**0.7429**	0.8547
Classification		tun	no	300	uni	yes	no	0.7164	0.8299
Attention	T&N-sum	tun	no	300	uni	no	yes	**0.7436**	**0.9005**
Best combination	ASAP-SAS	tun	no	250	bi	no	yes	**0.7439**	
Best combination	PG	tun	len 5	150	bi	no	yes		**0.9036**

Table 2: Parameter experiment results on ASAP-SAS and Powergrading on the *development* set. "Baseline" is the baseline non-neural system. "T&N best" is the best-performing parameter set in Taghipour and Ng (2016): tuned embeddings (here, GLOVE 100 dimensions), 300-dimensional LSTM, unidirectional, mean-over-time layer. Scores are bolded if they outperform the score for the "T&N best" parameter setting.

- *Powergrading:* CNN features with window length 5, 150-dimensional bidirectional LSTM, attention mechanism

- *SRA:* Because of the decreased performance of the combined best individual parameters on the development data, we use a 300-dimensional *uni*directional LSTM with attention mechanism.

These models are "T&N tuned" in Table 4, which appear along with the non-neural baseline system. On ASAP-SAS, the "T&N tuned" parameter configuration outperformed the baseline system and the "T&N best" parameters. The tuned system does not reach the state-of-the-art Fisher-transformed mean score on the ASAP-SAS dataset (Ramachandran et al., 2015)[7], which, like the winner of the ASAP-SAS competition (Tandalla, 2012), employed prompt-specific regular expressions. Other top performing systems used prompt-specific preprocessing and ensemble-based approaches over rich feature spaces (Higgins et al., 2014).

On the Powergrading dataset, the "T&N tuned" system did not match the performance of the baseline system, consistent with the results on the development set (Table 2). It appears that on the very short and redundant data in this dataset, the character- and n-gram based system can learn somewhat more efficiently than the neural systems.

On the SRA datasets, the "T&N tuned" model outperformed the baseline and the "T&N best" settings on average across prompts, by a larger margin than the other datasets. On the SRA data, as on the ASAP-SAS data, a gap remains between the tuned model's performance and the state of the art. On SRA, this may be partly due to the use of "question indicator" features by the top performing systems (Heilman and Madnani, 2013; Ott et al., 2013).

The performance improvement over the baseline system was larger on the development sets than on the test sets. Part of the reason for this is that the test set evaluation procedure likely did not choose the best-performing epoch for the neural models.

---

[7]Ramachandran et al. (2015) state that their mean QWK is 0.0053 higher than the Tandalla result, so in Table 4 we report that score truncated to 3 decimal places rather than the rounded result reported in Ramachandran et al. (2015).

								SRA Beetle 2-way	5-way	SRA SEB 2-way	5-way
Experiment	**Condition**	**Emb**	**CNN**	**Dim**	**Dir**	**MoT**	**Att**	**Mean wF1**	**Mean wF1**	**Mean wF1**	**Mean wF1**
Benchmark	Baseline							0.7438	0.5815	0.7011	0.5415
	T&N best	tun	no	300	uni	yes	no	0.7805	0.6184	0.7386	0.6175
MoT	no MoT	tun	no	300	uni	no	no	0.7803	0.6163	0.7384	0.6159
Embeddings	fixed	fix	no	300	uni	yes	no	0.7803	0.6119	0.7112	0.5730
	learned	lea	no	300	uni	yes	no	0.7396	0.5929	0.7285	0.5855
CNN	win len 3	tun	no	300	uni	yes	no	0.7786	0.6048	**0.7431**	0.5874
Directionality	bi	tun	no	300	bi	yes	no	0.7699	**0.6461**	**0.7511**	0.6171
LSTM dims	50	tun	no	50	uni	yes	no	0.7603	0.5954	**0.7395**	0.5992
	100	tun	no	100	uni	yes	no	0.7679	**0.6192**	0.7341	0.5925
	150	tun	no	150	uni	yes	no	**0.7816**	0.6168	**0.7389**	0.6039
	200	tun	no	200	uni	yes	no	0.7768	**0.6186**	0.7336	0.6080
	250	tun	no	250	uni	yes	no	0.7663	0.6106	0.7334	0.6160
Attention	T&N-sum	tun	no	300	uni	no	yes	**0.7915**	**0.6469**	**0.7454**	0.5941
Combination		tun				no	yes	0.7691	**0.6246**	0.7308	0.6109

Table 3: Parameter experiment results on SRA datasets on the *development* set. "wF1" is the weighted F1 score. "Baseline" is the baseline non-neural system. "T&N best" is the best-performing parameter set in Taghipour & Ng (2016): tuned embeddings (here, GLOVE 100 dimensions), 300-dimensional LSTM, unidirectional, mean-over-time layer. Scores are bolded if they outperform the score for the "T&N best" parameter setting.

4 Discussion

Our results establish that the basic neural architecture of pretrained embeddings with tuning across model training and LSTMs is a reasonably effective architecture for the short answer content scoring task. The architecture performs well enough to exceed a non-neural content scoring baseline system in most cases.

Given the diversity of prompts in SAS, there was a good deal of variation in the effectiveness of parameter choices in this neural architecture. Still, some basic trends emerged. First, pretrained embeddings tuned across model training were crucial for competitive performance on most datasets. Second, neural models for SAS generally benefit from similar size hidden dimensions as models for AES. Only the Powergrading dataset, with very short answers and a small vocabulary for each prompt, benefitted from a significantly smaller LSTM dimensionality. The relationship between task, rubrics, vocabulary size, and the representational capacity of neural models for SAS need further exploration.

Third, a mean-over-time aggregation mechanism on top of the LSTM generally performed well, but notably this mechanism was not nearly as important as in the AES task. Mean-over-time produced competitive results on many prompts, but contrary to Taghipour and Ng (2016), *bidirectional* LSTMS and *attention* produced some of the best results, which is consistent with results for neural models on other text classification tasks (e.g., Longpre et al. (2016)).

Research is needed to explain these emerging differences in effective neural architectures for AES vs. SAS, including model-specific factors such as the interaction of an LSTM's integration of features over time and the redundancy of predictive signals in essays vs. short answers, along with data-specific factors such as the consistency of human scoring, the demands of different rubrics, and the homogeneity or diversity of prompts in each setting. At the same time, different from the AES task, the family of neural architectures explored here needs further augmenting to achieve state-of-the-art results on the SAS task. Moreover, more experiments are needed to document how well neural systems perform relative to highly optimized non-neural systems. While further parameter optimizations and different architectures may yield better results, it may be the case that the

Dataset	Prompt	Baseline	T&N best	T&N tuned	State of the art
ASAP-SAS	1	0.719	0.784	**0.795**	
	2	0.719	**0.742**	0.718	
	3	0.592	**0.702**	0.684	
	4	0.688	0.697	**0.700**	
	5	0.752	0.821	**0.830**	
	6	0.775	0.774	**0.790**	
	7	0.606	0.638	**0.648**	
	8	**0.571**	0.566	0.554	
	9	0.760	**0.791**	0.777	
	10	0.691	0.681	**0.735**	
	Mean	0.687	0.720	**0.723**	
	Mean$_{Fisher}$	0.693	0.728	0.732	**0.776**
PG	1	**1.000**	**1.000**	**1.000**	-
	2	0.866	**0.897**	0.844	-
	3	**0.743**	0.597	0.614	-
	4	**0.926**	0.903	0.887	-
	5	**0.930**	0.759	0.759	-
	6	**0.930**	0.880	0.906	-
	7	0.831	0.831	**0.881**	-
	8	0.985	0.970	**1.000**	-
	13	**0.576**	0.553	0.554	-
	20	**0.949**	**0.949**	**0.949**	-
	Mean	**0.873**	0.834	0.839	-
SRA	Beetle 2-way	0.742	0.776	0.790	**0.845**
	Beetle 5-way	0.583	0.630	0.633	**0.715**
	SEB 2-way	0.661	0.670	0.712	**0.773**
	SEB 5-way	0.503	0.521	0.533	**0.643**
	Mean	0.622	0.649	0.667	**0.744**

Table 4: *Test* set results for all datasets across prompts. Scores for ASAP-SAS and PG are QWK. Mean$_{Fisher}$ is the Fisher-transformed mean QWK used in the ASAP-SAS competition. Scores for SRA are weighted F1 scores.

SAS task of content scoring with relatively short response sequences requires neural approaches to employ a larger set of features (Pado, 2016) or a greater level of prompt-specific tuning, or pairing with methods from active learning (Horbach and Palmer, 2016).

Acknowledgements

We thank Nitin Madnani, Swapna Somasundaran, Beata Beigman Klebanov and the anonymous reviewers for their detailed comments. Part of this work was funded by the German Federal Ministry of Education and Research under grant no. FKZ 01PL16075.

References

Dimitrios Alikaniotis, Helen Yannakoudakis, and Marek Rei. 2016. Automatic text scoring using neural networks. In *Proceedings of the 54th Annual Meeting of the Association of Computational Linguistics*.

Sumit Basu, Chuck Jacobs, and Lucy Vanderwende. 2013. Powergrading: a Clustering Approach to Amplify Human Effort for Short Answer Grading. *Transactions of the Association for Computational Linguistics (TACL)* 1:391–402.

Steven Burrows, Iryna Gurevych, and Benno Stein. 2015. The eras and trends of automatic short answer grading. *International Journal of Artificial Intelligence in Education* 25(1):60–117.

Jill Burstein, Joel Tetreault, and Nitin Madnani. 2013. The e-rater automated essay scoring system. *Handbook of automated essay evaluation: Current applications and new directions* pages 55–67.

Johannes Daxenberger, Oliver Ferschke, Iryna Gurevych, and Torsten Zesch. 2014. Dkpro TC: A java-based framework for supervised learning experiments on textual data. In *Proceedings of the 52nd Annual Meeting of the Association for Computational Linguistics*.

Fei Dong and Yue Zhang. 2016. Automatic features for essay scoring - an empirical study. In *Proceedings of the 2016 Conference on Empirical Methods in Natural Language Processing*.

Myroslava O. Dzikovska, Rodney Nielsen, Chris Brew, Claudia Leacock, Danilo Giampiccolo, Luisa Bentivogli, Peter Clark, Ido Dagan, and Hoa Trang Dang. 2013. SemEval-2013 Task 7: The Joint Student Response Analysis and 8th Recognizing Textual Entailment Challenge. **SEM 2013: The First Joint Conference on Lexical and Computational Semantics* .

Myroslava O Dzikovska, Rodney D Nielsen, and Chris Brew. 2012. Towards effective tutorial feedback for explanation questions: A dataset and baselines. In *Proceedings of the 2012 Conference of the North American Chapter of the Association for Computational Linguistics: Human Language Technologies*.

Myroslava O Dzikovska, Rodney D Nielsen, and Claudia Leacock. 2016. The joint student response analysis and recognizing textual entailment challenge: making sense of student responses in educational applications. *Language Resources and Evaluation* 50(1):67–93.

Richard Eckart de Castilho and Iryna Gurevych. 2014. A broad-coverage collection of portable nlp components for building shareable analysis pipelines. In *Proceedings of the Workshop on Open Infrastructures and Analysis Frameworks for HLT*. Association for Computational Linguistics and Dublin City University, Dublin, Ireland, pages 1–11.

Mark Hall, Eibe Frank, Geoffrey Holmes, Bernhard Pfahringer, Peter Reutemann, and Ian H. Witten. 2009. The weka data mining software: An update. *SIGKDD Explorer Newsletter* 11(1):10–18.

Michael Heilman and Nitin Madnani. 2013. ETS: Domain adaptation and stacking for short answer scoring. In *Second Joint Conference on Lexical and Computational Semantics (*SEM), Volume 2: Proceedings of the Seventh International Workshop on Semantic Evaluation (SemEval)*. pages 275–279.

Derrick Higgins, Chris Brew, Michael Heilman, Ramon Ziai, Lei Chen, Aoife Cahill, Michael Flor, Nitin Madnani, Joel R Tetreault, Daniel Blanchard, Diane Napolitano, Chong Min Lee, and John Blackmore. 2014. Is getting the right answer just about choosing the right words? The role of syntactically-informed features in short answer scoring http://arxiv.org/abs/1403.0801.

Andrea Horbach and Alexis Palmer. 2016. Investigating active learning for short-answer scoring. In *Proceedings of the 11th Workshop on Innovative Use of NLP for Building Educational Applications*.

Shayne Longpre, Sabeek Pradhan, Caiming Xiong, and Richard Socher. 2016. A way out of the odyssey: Analyzing and combining recent insights for lstms. *arXiv preprint arXiv:1611.05104* .

Niels Ott, Ramon Ziai, Michael Hahn, and Walt Detmar Meurers. 2013. CoMeT: Integrating different levels of linguistic modeling for meaning assessment. In *Second Joint Conference on Lexical and Computational Semantics (*SEM), Volume 2: Proceedings of the Seventh InternationalWorkshop on Semantic Evaluation (SemEval 2013)*. pages 608–616.

Ulrike Pado. 2016. Get semantic with me! the usefulness of different feature types for short-answer grading. In *Proceedings of the 25th International Conference on Computational Linguistics (COLING)*.

Jeffrey Pennington, Richard Socher, and Christopher D. Manning. 2014. Glove: Global vectors for word representation. In *Proceedings of the 2014 Conference on Empirical Methods in Natural Language Processing*.

Lakshmi Ramachandran, Jian Cheng, and Peter W Foltz. 2015. Identifying patterns for short answer scoring using graph-based lexico-semantic text matching. In *Proceedings of the 10th Workshop on Innovative Use of NLP for Building Educational Applications*.

Mark D Shermis. 2014. State-of-the-art automated essay scoring: Competition, results, and future directions from a united states demonstration. *Assessing Writing* 20:53–76.

Mark D Shermis. 2015. Contrasting state-of-the-art in the machine scoring of short-form constructed responses. *Educational Assessment* 20(1):46–65.

Mark D. Shermis and Ben Hamner. 2013. Contrasting state-of-the-art automated scoring of essays. In *Handbook of Automated Essay Evaluation*, Taylor and Francis, New York.

Kaveh Taghipour and Hwee Tou Ng. 2016. A neural approach to automated essay scoring. In *Proceedings of the 2016 Conference on Empirical Methods in Natural Language Processing*.

Luis Tandalla. 2012. Scoring short answer essays.

Siyuan Zhao, Yaqiong Zhang, Xiaolu Xiong, Anthony Botelho, and Neil Heffernan. 2017. A memory-augmented neural model for automated grading. In *Proceedings of the Fourth ACM Conference on Learning @ Scale*.

Human and Automated CEFR-based Grading of Short Answers

Anaïs Tack[1,2,4a]   **Thomas François**[1,4b]   **Sophie Roekhaut**[3]   **Cédrick Fairon**[1]

[1] CENTAL, UCL, Place Blaise Pascal 1, B-1348 Louvain-la-Neuve, Belgium
[2] ITEC, imec, KU Leuven Kulak, Etienne Sabbelaan 51, B-8500 Kortrijk, Belgium
[3] ALTISSIA International, Place de l'Université 16, B-1348 Louvain-la-Neuve, Belgium
[4] F.R.S.-FNRS [a] Research Fellow, [b] Postdoctoral Researcher

anais.tack@uclouvain.be   thomas.francois@uclouvain.be
sroekhaut@altissia.com   cedrick.fairon@uclouvain.be

Abstract

This paper is concerned with the task of automatically assessing the written proficiency level of non-native (L2) learners of English. Drawing on previous research on automated L2 writing assessment following the Common European Framework of Reference for Languages (CEFR), we investigate the possibilities and difficulties of deriving the CEFR level from short answers to open-ended questions, which has not yet been subjected to numerous studies up to date.

The object of our study is twofold: to examine the intricacy involved with both human and automated CEFR-based grading of short answers. On the one hand, we describe the compilation of a learner corpus of short answers graded with CEFR levels by three certified Cambridge examiners. We mainly observe that, although the shortness of the answers is reported as undermining a clear-cut evaluation, the length of the answer does not necessarily correlate with inter-examiner disagreement. On the other hand, we explore the development of a soft-voting system for the automated CEFR-based grading of short answers and draw tentative conclusions about its use in a computer-assisted testing (CAT) setting.

1 Introduction

The recent years have seen a growth of interest in Automated Writing Evaluation (AWE) for levelling non-native (L2) writing proficiency. Among the variety of assessment scales used, a number of studies have focused on levelling the writing proficiency following the Common European Framework of Reference (CEFR) (Council of Europe, 2001) through a combination of machine learning techniques and linguistic complexity features (Vajjala and Lõo, 2014; Volodina et al., 2016a; Pilán et al., 2016). One of the often cited benefits for using such assistive systems is that they could increase the effectiveness of large-scale testing procedures where a large panel of examiners are grading a mass of responses in a short period of time.

One application that comes to mind is the validation of the required writing skills of a large group of university students. In this scenario, implementing an expert-only testing procedure is costly for two reasons. On the one hand, a sufficiently large panel of experts evaluating the same text is needed to guarantee the validity of the evaluation. On the other hand, the large number of students who are participating in the programme makes the procedure even more time-consuming. Integrating an automated evaluator in the panel of examiners could therefore contribute to an increase in effectiveness of the evaluation procedure.

The present study takes part in a broader project which very aim is to research the possibility of using a computer-assisted setting for evaluating the level of written proficiency in English of non-native university students. The main idea of the project is to validate whether the students have the writing skills matching the CEFR descriptors of the proficiency level in which they have been placed. As a follow-up to a more general placement test, the students are queried to write an original short answer (ranging from 30 to 200 words) to an open-ended question, on the basis of

169

which a panel of examiners validate or adapt the CEFR level resulting from the global evaluation. In this context, we investigated the possibilities of partially automatising the short answer evaluation procedure, which is the general subject of the current paper.

The paper is structured as follows. After a brief review of the previous work on automated grading and the CEFR (Section 2), we will introduce our work on (i) the collection of a CEFR-graded learner corpus of short answers (Section 3) and (ii) the development of an automated grading system through ensemble learning (Section 4). In Section 5, we will compare the human and automated grading of short answers.

2 Background

2.1 Learner Writing Proficiency

The Common European Framework of Reference for Languages (CEFR) (Council of Europe, 2001) is one of the most commonly used scale for measuring the proficiency of L2 users, dividing them into three groups: the basic (levels A1 and A2), independent (levels B1 and B2) and proficient users (levels C1 and C2). For various dimensions of proficiency (i.e. speaking, writing, etc.), it lists 'can-do' descriptors that can be used to assign a level to a learner. Although these criteria have been widely used in L2 teaching and research, studies have also stressed the need for more empirical research on how the different levels are linked with particular aspects of L2 proficiency (Hulstijn, 2007) (f.i. writing proficiency). Indeed, it is important to evaluate the learners' writing proficiency regardless of their overall L2 proficiency, since there is no proof that the overall CEFR level is necessarily transferred to the various dimensions composing L2 proficiency.

Over more than the past two decades, the most indispensable resource for gaining empirical insight into learner writing proficiency has been the learner corpus (Granger, 2009), as shown by the continuous emergence of written and spoken corpora available for numerous target languages and discourse types. For English in particular, the *International Corpus of Learner English* (ICLE) (Granger et al., 2009) and the *Cambridge Learner Corpus* (CLC) have been the go-to standard. Moreover, the recent years have also seen an increasing availability of learner corpora aligned with the CEFR (Boyd et al., 2014; Vajjala and

Lõo, 2014; Volodina et al., 2016b), including the subsets of the CLC used by the English Profile (Salamoura and Saville, 2010).

Drawing on these developments, many studies have aimed at identifying the linguistic variables that are indicative (or *criterial*) of a particular L2 proficiency level (Díaz-Negrillo et al., 2013) and in particular those that are predictive of qualitative L2 writing (Crossley and McNamara, 2011; Vajjala, 2017). As a result, we know lexical complexity features, such as lexical diversity, word familiarity, meaningfulness and imageability, to be good predictors of L2 writing. As for the criterial features that apply specifically to the CEFR, important advances have been made in the context of the English Profile with the creation of a valuable inventory of structural patterns and learner errors (Hawkins and Buttery, 2010).

2.2 Automated Learner Writing Assessment

The advances made towards developing error-annotated and human-graded learner corpora (such as the CLC), as well as understanding the features underlying L2 proficiency, have subsequently furthered the development of systems for automated learner writing assessment, which include intelligent writing assistants (e.g. Andersen et al., 2013) and automated scoring systems (e.g. Yannakoudakis et al., 2011). In the case of automated scoring, two kinds of systems are generally distinguished, viz. automated essay grading (AEG) and automated short answer grading (ASAG)[1], depending on the length and type of texts as well as the kind of scoring method used. However, Burrows et al. (2015, p. 66) observe that '[t]he difference between these types can be fuzzy'.

Essay grading, on the one hand, is concerned with the evaluation of the quality or proficiency – often by means of a standard scale – of writings spanning several paragraphs or pages. In the context of L2 essay grading, a number of recently developed systems have achieved promising results with a wide range of complexity features and machine learning techniques for English, using the Cambridge English Scale (Yannakoudakis et al., 2011)[2] or the TOEFL scale (Vajjala,

---

[1] For a more extensive overview of the fields, see Shermis and Burstein (2013) and Burrows et al. (2015).

[2] The scores of the scale are aligned with the CEFR. The Cambridge English First (FCE) corpus used by Yannakoudakis et al. (2011) is known to correlate with a B1/B2 level.

2017). Other CEFR-based grading systems have been developed for German (Hancke and Meurers, 2013), Estonian (Vajjala and Lõo, 2014) and Swedish (Pilán et al., 2016).

The specificity of short answer grading, on the other hand, is the fact that it deals with 'objective questions' and length-restricted answers ranging 'between one phrase and one paragraph' (Burrows et al., 2015, p. 61). Its goal is to evaluate the learner responses as regards their correctness with respect to the initial question. The adequacy of the answer is thus compared to a model answer and graded either on a pass/fail basis or along a scale of correctness, using a range of concept and pattern matching techniques, alignment-based evaluation metrics (e.g. BLEU) or machine learning algorithms. In the context of L2 short answer grading, we mainly find systems developed for evaluating responses to reading comprehension questions, such as the CoMiC systems developed for English and German (Meurers et al., 2011).

The writing task underlying the current study can be situated between the extreme ends of essay and short answer grading presented above, aiming at assessing the CEFR level associated with short texts. On the one hand, the task is based on a series of questions (e.g."What is the best book you ever read?") which are more open-ended than the objective questions generally used in ASAG. On the other hand, contrary to essay writing, the task aims to assess writing proficiency based on a shorter display of writing, by adding more restrictions on the length of the answers (approximately one paragraph, or between 30 and 200 words).

3 A Corpus of Short Answers Graded per CEFR Level

In the context of the writing proficiency test we introduced in Section 1, we conducted a pilot study for collecting a CEFR-graded learner corpus that was representative of the task at hand.

3.1 Design

CEFR levels We defined a pool of questions (Table 1) that were used for querying the students' based on the result of the placement test. We will refer to the CEFR level defined by the placement test as the *initial proficiency level*. Note that although we defined the same set of questions for both the advanced C1 and C2 levels, hence grouping them in a common C level, we decided to

level	min. words	topics
A1	30	(A) family (B) daily habits (C) hobbies
A2	60	(A) holiday memories (B) birthday invitation (C) lifetime goals
B1	80	(A) book reading (B) spending 1 million euros (C) blog writing
B2	100	(A) improve the environment (B) enjoy work or earn money (C) study abroad
C	150	(A) social networks (B) leading a healthy life (C) living in the public eye

Table 1: Question types per initial CEFR level

keep the original six-level distinction in the graded learner corpus in order to ensure the reusability of the collected data.

Question types The questions were all open-ended questions intended to trigger as wide a range of answers as possible. In order to vary the range of topics targeted by each question, we defined a pool of three different topics per initial level, which were construed bearing the CEFR guidelines in mind.

Length During the corpus collection procedure, each question trigger was followed by an indication of the minimal word limit required for submitting an answer. We mainly targeted answers ranging from 30 words at the A1 levels to 150 words at the C levels.

3.2 Collection

To collect a corpus of short answers, we conducted an on-line survey where each participant answered a question based on the CEFR level of the course in which they were enrolled. Each question was chosen in a circular fashion from the pool of questions previously defined. The minimal word limit of each answer was controlled so as to only allow a submission when the minimal word limit had been reached. After having submitted a valid answer, the students also responded to a short sociological questionnaire and were given the opportunity to enter in a raffle as a reward for participating.

We targeted learners coming from two different learning environments. On the one hand, we contacted participants who were enrolled in an e-learning platform. Their initial level was defined based on the CEFR level of the course they were

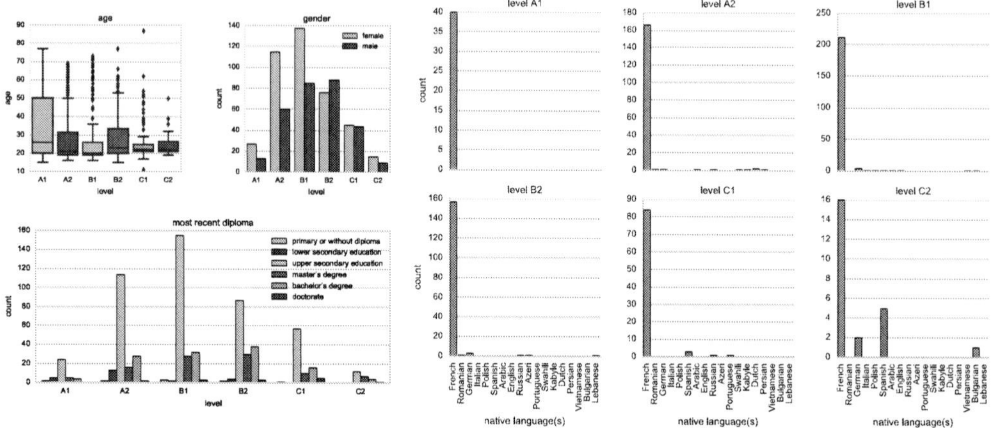

Figure 1: Sociological variables of the participants.

(a) original

	question			
initial level	A	B	C	all
A1	14	8	17	39
A2	65	50	60	175
B1	75	88	60	223
B2	42	66	54	162
C1	40	27	22	89
C2	11	8	5	24
all	247	247	218	712

(b) resampled

	question			
initial level	A	B	C	all
A1	14	7	17	38
A2	35	19	18	72
B1	19	19	18	56
B2	18	19	19	56
C1	20	17	16	53
C2	11	8	5	24
all	117	89	93	299

Table 2: The number of answers collected per initial level and per question type

following after having completed a general proficiency placement test with vocabulary, grammar, reading and listening exercises. On the other hand, we also contacted a group of participants enrolled in university-level English language classrooms targeting a particular CEFR level.

In all, we collected a total of 712 responses (Table 2). Based on the responses given in the questionnaire (Figure 1), we can observe that the majority of the participants were French-speaking learners of English studying at the bachelor's and master's level (all disciplines included).

3.3 Grading

The data used in this study contains a sample of the learner responses graded (i) according to their initial level and (ii) according to their *assessed proficiency level* as evaluated by majority voting[3] of a panel of three certified CEFR-expert Cambridge examiners. We will referred to them as examiners $\mathcal{X}$, $\mathcal{Y}$ and $\mathcal{Z}$ respectively.

Before assessing the written proficiency level of the learner responses, we decided to keep the dataset as balanced as possible. Indeed, as we observe from the number of responses per initial CEFR level (Table 2b), there is an important difference between the number of texts collected for the beginner (A1) and advanced levels (C1 and C2) and the number of texts collected for the intermediate levels (A2, B1 and B2). We therefore performed a stratified random sampling of the data to balance the number of texts per initial level and question type, (i) by randomly selecting an equivalent number of texts per individual level ($\pm$ 25 texts) and (ii) by randomly supplying additional texts per grouped levels A, B, and C (60, 62, and 28 texts respectively) with the aim of having as similar a distribution per group as possible. As a result, a sample of 299 texts was used for the remainder of the study.

The panel of examiners used an on-line evaluation interface for grading. The examiners were prompted with the initial question and submitted

---

[3]In cases without agreement, the assessed level was derived by taking the nearest integer of the mean of the votes. These cases were then manually verified taking the hesitations observed in the examiners' comments into account.

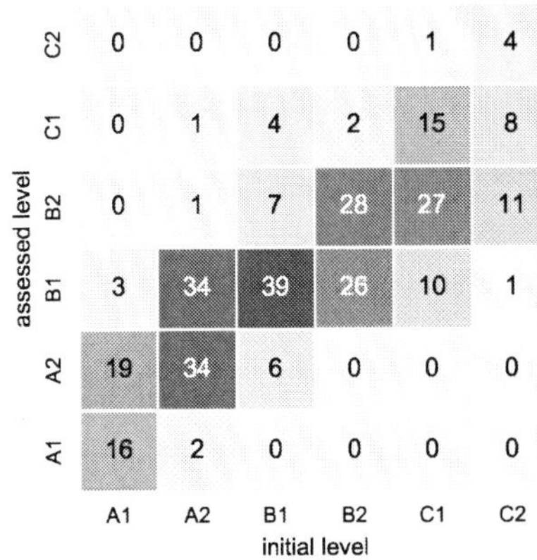

Figure 2: A comparison of the distribution between the initial and assessed CEFR levels.

answer, but did not receive any indication of the initial question level. They were then asked to evaluate the proficiency level of the answer based on the CEFR scale (ranging from A1 to C2), which they could turn back to and review as much as possible. The examiners could also flag the text as "Impossible to evaluate" in case they were, for whatever reason, unable to derive its proficiency level. Finally, they were also given the option of adding a comment to provide further details and justifications of their choice.

Figure 2 shows the number of texts distributed per initial and assessed levels. We observe that particularly the initial B1 answers were assessed as being indicative of a B1 written proficiency level (70%), whereas the initial C1 and C2 levels seem to have been relatively overestimated with only 28% and 17% of them assessed as having the C1 and C2 levels respectively.

4 A Soft-Voting CEFR-based Grader

In this section, we describe the general architecture of the system developed for the automated grading of the collected learner texts on a 5-point scale (A1, A2, B1, B2 and C). We decided to collapse the C1 and C2 levels into one C label for two reasons. First, although the small number of observatons that received an assessed C2 level (N=5) was considered insufficient, we did not want them to be discarded. Second, the original test setup on which this study was based did not aim to make a distinction between these assessed levels.

Features As preprocessing step to feature extraction, we used the Stanford CoreNLP suite (Manning et al., 2014) for performing tokenisation, lemmatisation, part-of-speech tagging, constituency and dependency parsing as well as coreferential resolution.

We defined a feature set of 18 different families, counting 695 individual feature configurations. We included a number of traditional readability features (François and Fairon, 2012; Vajjala and Lõo, 2014), including lexical features (word length, number of syllables, lexical frequency from SUBTLEX (Brysbaert and New, 2009), lexical likelihood based on Simple-Good Turing Smoothing (Gale and Sampson, 1995), lexical variation, lexical sophistication and part-of-speech tag ratios), syntactic features (sentence length and constituency tree structural patterns), WordNet-based (Fellbaum, 1998) and discursive features (synonyms, number of referential expressions and degree of content overlap), as well as a number of psycholinguistic norms (age of acquisition, imageability, familiarity, etc.) extracted from the MRC database (Wilson, 1988). We also included additional features for L2 complexity such as the types of (shallow) spelling and grammar errors as well as corpus-driven criterial features based on the English Profile (Hawkins and Buttery, 2010).

We should note that, contrary to previous work on Swedish L2 essay grading where the learner texts were normalised for error correction (Pilán et al., 2016), we only included error-based features without performing any error normalisation – apart from sentence segmentation errors and run-on sentences in particular – as preprocessing step to feature extraction. The error-based features were computed based on a noisy channel spelling correction (Kernighan et al., 1990) and handcrafted orthographic and syntactic (constituency- and dependency-based) patterns.

By means of a Spearman rank correlation test and a randomised logistic regression stability selection procedure on the entire sample, we found a set of 29 features to be of significant importance for the task at hand (Table 3 on the next page). This procedure was then reapplied on each of the model training folds before model fitting during nested cross-validation (cf. *infra*). Not surprisingly, we find that the most informative predictors of writing proficiency are the lexical ones

family	feature	μ_{A1}	μ_{A2}	μ_{B1}	μ_{B2}	μ_{C}	ρ
AoA	*Bristol lem*	−0.8	−0.8	−0.1	0.7	0.6	0.57***
	Kup lem	−1.1	−0.7	−0.2	0.7	0.8	0.62***
CEFR	*B1*	−0.7	−0.6	−0.2	0.7	0.7	0.53***
Disc	*global content overlap*	−1.0	−0.8	−0.2	0.7	0.9	0.73***
	global noun overlap	−0.9	−0.5	−0.2	0.6	0.7	0.56***
GrCorr	*missing subject*	−0.8	−0.7	−0.2	0.7	0.8	0.63***
LexFreq	*all mean*	−0.6	−0.4	0.3	0.0	−0.1	0.13*
	all mean $\mathcal{L}$	−0.8	−0.4	0.3	0.0	−0.1	0.18**
	grammatical 75P $\mathcal{L}$	−0.6	−0.6	0.3	0.2	0.0	0.22***
LexLike	*all $\mathcal{L}$*	0.0	0.2	0.3	−0.3	−0.6	−0.29***
LexVar	*adjective UberIndex $\mathcal{L}$*	−1.5	−0.9	−0.1	0.8	1.0	0.75***
	all UberIndex	−1.9	−0.9	0.0	0.8	1.0	0.78***
	modifier LogTTR	−2.2	−0.7	0.0	0.7	0.8	0.74***
	modifier SquaredTTR	−1.1	−0.8	−0.2	0.7	1.1	0.72***
	modifier UberIndex	−1.7	−0.9	−0.1	0.8	1.0	0.78***
	verb1 LogTTR	−2.1	−0.7	0.1	0.6	0.8	0.71***
	verb1 SquaredTTR	−1.4	−0.8	−0.1	0.6	1.2	0.71***
	verb1 UberIndex	−1.9	−0.9	0.0	0.7	1.0	0.77***
	verb2 UberIndex	−1.9	−0.9	0.0	0.7	1.0	0.78***
POSTag	*noun : grammatical*	1.3	0.2	−0.3	0.1	−0.1	−0.12*
	noun : preposition	1.8	0.3	−0.2	−0.2	−0.3	−0.26***
	determiner : noun	−0.8	−0.3	0.3	0.0	−0.1	0.14*
	grammatical : noun	−1.0	−0.1	0.3	−0.2	−0.1	0.12*
	lexical : grammatical	0.4	−0.1	−0.4	0.3	0.3	0.19***
	nominal : preposition	1.8	0.3	−0.2	−0.2	−0.3	−0.33***
	past part. : wh pron.	−0.4	−0.4	−0.2	0.2	0.9	0.43***
SentLen	*median*	−0.8	−0.5	−0.1	0.4	0.9	0.52***
WordLen	*mean*	−0.8	−0.6	−0.3	0.7	0.7	0.54***
	proportion 5 letters	−0.3	−0.4	−0.3	0.5	0.6	0.40***

$$***p < 0.001, **p < 0.01, *p < 0.05$$

Table 3: Features selected through a Spearman rank correlation test and a stability selection procedure. All features are standardised to a Gaussian scale and their average is reported per assessed level. Lemma-based indices are marked with $\mathcal{L}$.

and in particular lexical diversity features, which is in line with previous studies (Crossley and Mc-Namara, 2011; Hancke and Meurers, 2013; Vajjala and Lõo, 2014; Pilán et al., 2016). Furthermore, we find that the sentence length and word length, as well as the average age of acquisition of the words used by the learners display a strong positive correlation with the assessed CEFR level. We also observe that the frequent use of B1 criterial feature patterns are indicative of the learner writings from the B2 levels onwards. One surprising observation, however, can be drawn from the apparent positive correlation of lexical frequencies. This could be explained by the fact that beginners (A1 and A2) quite commonly display a use of L1 interference in their texts – as can be seen in the use of the French *caractères* ("characters") in Figure 3 – which are subsequently tagged as foreign (infrequent) words.

Model Figure 3 illustrates the model architecture used for the automated CEFR-based grading of a short answer (initial A1 level and assessed A2 level). Our system used the *Scikit-learn* library (Pedregosa et al., 2011) for training an ensemble learning approach via a soft-voting classifier integrating a panel of five traditional models: a

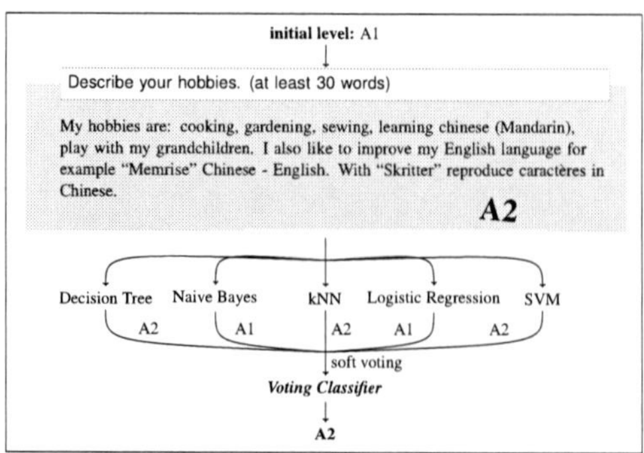

Figure 3: Example of the ensemble learning approach to the automated scoring of short answers.

Gaussian Naive Bayes classifier, a CART Decision Tree, a kNN classifier, a one-vs.-rest (OvR) Logistic Regressor and a OvR polynomial LibSVM Support Vector Machine. The system was developed via a nested cross-validation procedure and its hyperparameters were optimised via a two-stage model selection procedure on the training fold, performing a 10-fold grid search on the individual models first and then on the ensemble method.

5 Results

5.1 Expert Grading

Reliability To measure the inter-rater reliability of the assessed proficiency levels, we use Krippendorff's α with interval metric.[4] Krippendorff's statistic suggests a strong agreement ($\alpha = .81$; $.80 < \alpha < .90$) between our examiners, which ensures the reliability of the CEFR-labelled corpus. The strong agreement is also reflected by the fact that all three examiners gave the same proficiency level (i.e. perfect agreement) to 44% of the texts and that for 50% of the texts at least one pair of examiners gave the same proficiency level (Table 4 on the following page). Only for 6% of the texts do they seem to not agree at all. Furthermore, the high agreement score for the interval metric indicates that, in the cases where our examiners did not perfectly agree on the target proficiency level, the distance between the given levels was not large.

---

[4] Although we could have used Fleiss' κ for comparing the CEFR categories, we decided to use the former because it enables us not only to compare the assessed levels on a *scale*, but also to properly deal with missing values (cf. *supra*, "Impossible to evaluate") instead of discarding them as would Fleiss' κ. We should also note that only two missing values were observed for one examiner.

		initial level						
agreement	*%*	A1	A2	B1	B2	C1	C2	all
perfect	**43.8**	19	29	28	25	22	8	131
partial	**50.2**	17	41	27	27	26	12	150
no	**6.0**	2	2	1	4	5	4	18
		38	72	56	56	53	24	299

Table 4: Inter-examiner agreement scores.

Put differently, the examiners tended to disagree more on adjacent proficiency levels (such as B1 and B2) than between levels at the extreme ends of the scale (such as A1 and C2).

Grading difficulty and disagreement Although we observe a strong human-human agreement (HHA) between the three examiners, we also noted their comments with respect to the difficulty of the task of assigning a CEFR level to a very short text. Indeed, for the A1 and A2 levels (counting minimally 30 and 60 words respectively) they frequently reported needing more context to correctly assess the proficiency level, in particular for those texts that displayed "no errors" and were written in "mainly accurate English". This is illustrated in the few texts where the initial A2 level seemed to have been underestimated in favour of a B2 or C1 level. We were therefore interested in examining what characteristics define the texts that were difficult to grade.

We measured the difficulty of grading a text on the basis of the per item observed disagreement $D^{\alpha}_{o_i}$ on the label x given by coder c on item i (5.1.1). We derived this measure by decomposing Krippendorff's formula for the observed disagreement D^{α}_o (Artstein and Poesio, 2008, pp. 564-7) , which amounts to two times the per-item empirical variance s^2_i.

$$D^{\alpha}_{o_i} = \frac{1}{\mathbf{c}(\mathbf{c}-1)} \sum_{m=1}^{\mathbf{c}} \sum_{n=1}^{\mathbf{c}} \delta_{interval}(x_{ic_m}, x_{ic_n})$$

$$= 2s^2_i \tag{5.1.1}$$

Interestingly, we find that, although the examiners reported having difficulties evaluating the CEFR level of the shortest answers, the length of the answer was not significantly correlated with the amount of per-item disagreement (Pearson's $r = .04$; $p = .455$) In fact, Pearson's r as well as the number of agreeing or disagreeing cases per initial level (Table 4) show that the annotators tended to

	acc.	adj. acc.	$F_{1\,macro}$	RMSE	α
Soft Voting	$.530 \pm .115$	$.978 \pm .040$	$.495 \pm .142$	$.721 \pm .124$	.757
Decision Tree	$.504 \pm .103$	$.946 \pm .053$	$.438 \pm .126$	$.802 \pm .125$	.713
kNN	$.500 \pm .084$	$.972 \pm .047$	$.403 \pm .107$	$.758 \pm .104$	.690
Logistic Regression	$.462 \pm .138$	$.958 \pm .044$	$.422 \pm .142$	$.807 \pm .120$	.717
Naive Bayes	$.486 \pm .117$	$.952 \pm .047$	$.487 \pm .132$	$.802 \pm .173$	.742
SVM	$.496 \pm .129$	$.977 \pm .041$	$.451 \pm .135$	$.750 \pm .164$	.737
baseline (prior)	$.378 \pm .013$	$.824 \pm .017$	$.110 \pm .003$	1.072 ± 0.031	$-.010$
baseline (stratified)	$.282 \pm .041$	$.606 \pm .024$	$.201 \pm .046$	1.524 ± 0.057	$-.161$
baseline (random)	$.191 \pm .015$	$.484 \pm .027$	$.163 \pm .020$	1.930 ± 0.058	$-.131$

Table 5: Performance of the system compared to a set of baselines on 10-fold cross-validation.

disagree more on the longer ones, as most of the texts where no agreement was observed were concerned with the initial level ranging from the C1 to C2 levels (min. 150 words).

Multiple semipartial Spearman correlation tests were then carried out as a way of investigating which complexity features might be characteristic of the per-item grading difficulty D (as previously defined by $D^{\alpha}_{o_i}$), while controlling for text length L (in number of words). We observed a number of significant effects with a small set of lexical features, such as the overall lexical diversity ($r_{D(X.L)} = .142$; $p < .05$), the variation in use of modifiers ($r_{D(X.L)} = .183$; $p < .01$) and adjectives ($r_{D(X.L)} = .182$; $p < .01$), as well as the average lexical likelihood ($r_{D(X.L)} = -.151$; $p < .01$).

5.2 Automated Scoring

Performance The voting classifier described in Section 4 achieves a good human-system agreement[5] (HSA) ($\alpha = .76$, $.67 < \alpha < .80$) with respect to the answers' assessed CEFR level obtained by majority voting (Table 5). Although our system did not surpass the strong HHA ceiling we observed earlier (which amounts to $\alpha = .82$ when using a 5-point scale), the HSA of our ensemble method still outperformed the HSA of its individual classifiers. What is more, in cases where there is a human-system *dis*agreement, we find that the output mainly differs by an adjacent level, leading to an adjacent accuracy of 98% and an RMSE of .7 on a scale of five (A1, A2, B1, B2 and C).

A Friedman test with a post-hoc Holm correction was then carried out as a means of comparing the performance of our voting classifier with respect to the models it is composed of as well as to the most performant baseline. Our system achieved a significant gain in perform-

---

[5]The α values were computed by aggregating the predictions on all 10 test folds and by comparing them to the true labels obtained after majority voting.

ance (RMSE) with respect to a prior baseline[6] ($F_F = 4.865$, $p < .01$, $k = 6$, $\alpha = .05$). Although the test did not reveal any other significant gain beyond the one observed over the baseline, we find that the system's performance is comparable to previous work for Swedish CEFR-based essay grading where an F_1 of .438 is attained on original (not error-normalised) learner texts (Pilán et al., 2016).

Nevertheless, we do observe a difficulty of attaining a perfect HSA with the system's accuracy peaking at 53%. Even though this result may seem inferior to previous CEFR-based essay grading systems (Vajjala and Lõo, 2014; Volodina et al., 2016a), we should note that the data sets used in these studies were slightly different from our data set and mainly included longer texts graded on either a 4-point scale (A2, B1, B2 and C1) (Vajjala and Lõo, 2014; Pilán et al., 2016) or a 5-point scale (A1, A2, B1, B2 and C1) (Volodina et al., 2016a). Furthermore, we should also note the parallel between the difficulty of deriving the exact CEFR level from the answers and the difficulty experienced by our human raters of achieving a perfect agreement (43.8%) (see Table 4 on the previous page).

However, linking the length of the answers with the per-item human-system disagreement (cf. formula 5.1.1 on the preceding page), we observe yet again a non-significant correlation between both (Pearson's $r = .07$; $p = .22$). Thus, it seems that, similarly to the expert graders, our system did not particularly have a difficulty grading the shortest answers. In addition, the system did not have any particular difficulties in correctly predicting the lowest CEFR levels either (Figure 4).

For enhancing our automated CEFR-based scoring of short answers, the two following options could be explored. First, we could explore the possibility of pinpointing and resolving the difficulties involved with attaining a high HHA and HSA using more high-level learner features indicative of the advanced CEFR levels. Second, similarly to Pilán et al. (2016), we could examine the effect of applying (automatic) learner error normalisation on the system's performance, provided that the applied normalisation technique is accur-

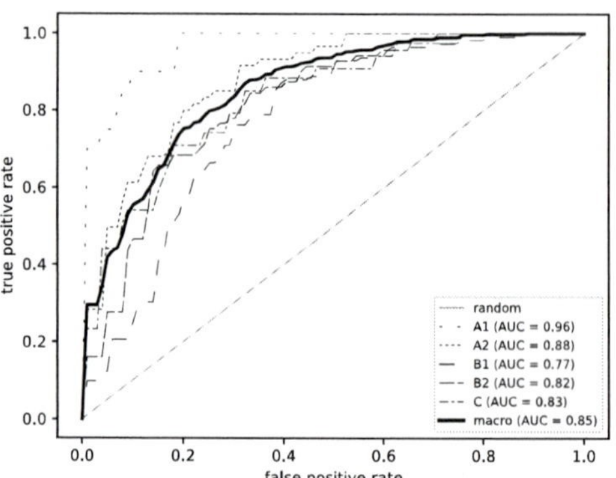

Figure 4: Receiver operating characteristic for the voting classifier.

ate enough for correctly dealing with learner language. However, we should note that the absence of error normalisation did not seem to have impacted the grading accuracy of the A1 and A2 levels (see Figure 4) where the presence of errors is known to be particularly prevalent (Hulstijn, 2007).

Computer-assisted testing simulation To explore the possibility of using the system in a computer-assisted setting, we simulated the reliability of replacing one of the three examiners by our system. Table 6 on the next page shows the performance scores and reliability coefficients of all possible configurations using a panel of three examiners where we replaced one examiner with a soft-voting short answer grader which was retrained on the examiner's evaluations.

The good agreement scores for Krippendorff's α[7] enable us to draw tentative conclusions as to the possibility of using the system in a panel of examiners. Replacing one examiner by our system could therefore be possible, but the simulation did not reveal any configurations ($\alpha = .75$ on average) that topped the strong agreement of having three human examiners ($\alpha = .82$ when using a 5-point scale).

Interestingly, we also observed that the best results were achieved when training the system on examiner $\mathcal{Z}$, who could be typed as being neither too "demanding" nor too "lenient" compared to the other examiners (Table 7 on the following page). To perform this comparison, we ranked the exam-

---

[6]The prior baseline predicts the class with the maximum prior probability, which is the B1 level (113 out of 299 observations; Figure 2 on page 5). The stratified baseline gives random predictions based on the class distribution as observed on the training set.

[7]As before, the α values were computed by aggregating the predictions on all 10 test folds, but now comparing them to the individual labels given by the two other examiners.

trained on	$\mathcal{X}$	$\mathcal{Y}$	$\mathcal{Z}$	avg.
acc.	.51	.37	.56	.48
adj. acc.	.97	.84	.99	.93
F_1	.48	.33	.52	.44
RMSE	.77	1.05	.67	.83
agreeing with (%)	$\left(\begin{array}{c}\mathcal{Y}\\\mathcal{Z}\end{array}\right)$	$\left(\begin{array}{c}\mathcal{X}\\\mathcal{Z}\end{array}\right)$	$\left(\begin{array}{c}\mathcal{X}\\\mathcal{Y}\end{array}\right)$	
perfect	33.78	31.42	34.11	33.10
partial	60.54	61.49	60.87	60.97
HHA	47.51	53.85	42.86	48.07
HSA	52.49	46.15	57.14	51.93
no	5.69	7.09	5.02	5.93
Krippendorff's α	.76	.74	.75	.75

Table 6: Reliability of replacing one examiner with the system. The partial agreement scores are further broken down into percentages per human-human agreement (HHA) and human-system agreement (HSA).

examiner	average rank
$\mathcal{X}$	1.81
$\mathcal{Z}$	1.96
$\mathcal{Y}$	2.23

rank 1: gave the lowest level ("demanding")
rank 2: gave neither one, or all scores tied
rank 3: gave the highest level ("lenient")

Table 7: Comparative ranking of the examiners according to their evaluations.

iners according to their evaluation for each text and used 'average' ranking for tied labels (i.e. for perfect or pairwise agreement).

Moreover, it appears that training the system on examiner $\mathcal{Z}$ even bettered the performance of the voting classifier trained on the data labelled by the entire panel of examiners (see Table 5 on page 7). However, for future endeavours, we argue that we should not solely rely on such idiosyncratic evaluations merely because they enhance a system's performance – however appealing that may be – and that we should therefore continue to use the labelled data obtained via majority voting.

6   Conclusion

In this paper, we compared human and automated scoring of short answers using the Common European Framework of Reference (CEFR). For this purpose, we compiled a learner corpus of short answers, written by non-native learners of English and evaluated by a panel of three certified Cambridge examiners, and which will be made available for non-commercial use. Furthermore, we de-

veloped a soft-voting CEFR-based classifier based on a set of traditional linguistic complexity features as well as some more specific L2 complexity features.

We obtained positive results, although more work is needed to further examine the difficulties involved with predicting the CEFR written proficiency level from short texts. Indeed, our findings showed that the shortness of the answer is not necessarily correlated with the amount of human-human or human-system disagreement. Yet, our results were inconclusive as to what indicators could explain the difficulty of grading a short answer according to the CEFR scale.

We therefore propose to continue investigating the influence of more advanced L2 complexity features on explaining the intricacy involved with the current task. As regards our system, we propose to examine the impact of error normalisation on its performance. Finally, other aspects associated with the task still remain to be considered as well, such as the replication of the results to other target L2 languages as well as to groups with more diverse L1 backgrounds.

Acknowledgements

This work received the financial support of the ALTISSIA e-learning company. We would also like to thank the *Centres de Langues* (CLL) and the *Institut des langues vivantes* (ILV) of Louvain-la-Neuve, Belgium for their indispensable contributions to the corpus collection and annotation.

References

Øistein E. Andersen, Helen Yannakoudakis, Fiona Barker, and Tim Parish. 2013. Developing and testing a self-assessment and tutoring system. In *Proceedings of the Eighth Workshop on Innovative Use of NLP for Building Educational Applications*, pages 32–41, Atlanta, Georgia. Association for Computational Linguistics.

Ron Artstein and Massimo Poesio. 2008. Inter-Coder Agreement for Computational Linguistics. *Computational Linguistics*, 34(4):555–596.

Adriane Boyd, Jirka Hana, Lionel Nicolas, Detmar Meurers, Katrin Wisniewski, Andrea Abel, Karin Schöne, Barbora Štindlová, and Chiara Vettori. 2014. The MERLIN corpus: Learner Language and the CEFR. In *Proceedings of the Ninth International Conference on Language Resources and Evaluation (LREC'14)*, pages 1281–88, Reykjavik, Iceland. European Language Resources Association (ELRA).

Marc Brysbaert and Boris New. 2009. Moving beyond Kučera and Francis: A critical evaluation of current word frequency norms and the introduction of a new and improved word frequency measure for American English. *Behavior Research Methods*, 41(4):977–990.

Steven Burrows, Iryna Gurevych, and Benno Stein. 2015. The Eras and Trends of Automatic Short Answer Grading. *International Journal of Artificial Intelligence in Education*, 25(1):60–117.

Council of Europe. 2001. *Common European Framework of Reference for Languages*. Cambridge University Press, Cambridge, UK.

Scott A. Crossley and Danielle S. McNamara. 2011. Understanding expert ratings of essay quality: Coh-Metrix analyses of first and second language writing. *International Journal of Continuing Engineering Education and Life-Long Learning*, 21(2-3):170–191.

Ana Díaz-Negrillo, Nicolas Ballier, and Paul Thompson, editors. 2013. *Automatic Treatment and Analysis of Learner Corpus Data*, volume 59 of *Studies in Corpus Linguistics*. John Benjamins Publishing Company, Amsterdam.

Christiane Fellbaum. 1998. *WordNet: An Electronic Lexical Database*. MIT Press, Cambridge, MA.

Thomas François and Cédrick Fairon. 2012. An "AI Readability" Formula for French As a Foreign Language. In *Proceedings of the 2012 Joint Conference on Empirical Methods in Natural Language Processing and Computational Natural Language Learning*, pages 466–477, Stroudsburg, PA, USA. Association for Computational Linguistics.

William A. Gale and Geoffrey Sampson. 1995. Good-Turing frequency estimation without tears. *Journal of Quantitative Linguistics*, 2(3):217–237.

Sylviane Granger. 2009. The contribution of learner corpora to second language acquisition and foreign language teaching: A critical evaluation. In Karin Aijmer, editor, *Studies in Corpus Linguistics*, volume 33, pages 13–332. John Benjamins Publishing Company, Amsterdam.

Sylviane Granger, Estelle Dagneaux, Fanny Meunier, and Magali Paquot. 2009. *International Corpus of Learner English. Version 2. Handbook and CD-ROM*. Presses Universitaires de Louvain, Louvain-la-Neuve, Belgium.

Julia Hancke and Detmar Meurers. 2013. Exploring CEFR classification for German based on rich linguistic modeling. In *Learner Corpus Research 2013, Book of Abstracts*, pages 54–56, Bergen, Norway.

John A. Hawkins and Paula Buttery. 2010. Criterial Features in Learner Corpora: Theory and Illustrations. *English Profile Journal*, 1(01):1–23.

Jan H. Hulstijn. 2007. The Shaky Ground Beneath the CEFR: Quantitative and Qualitative Dimensions of Language Proficiency. *The Modern Language Journal*, 91(4):663–667.

Mark D. Kernighan, Kenneth W. Church, and William A. Gale. 1990. A Spelling Correction Program Based on a Noisy Channel Model. In *Proceedings of the 13th Conference on Computational Linguistics - Volume 2*, pages 205–210, Stroudsburg, PA, USA. Association for Computational Linguistics.

Christopher D. Manning, Mihai Surdeanu, John Bauer, Jenny Finkel, Steven J. Bethard, and David Mcclosky. 2014. The Stanford CoreNLP Natural Language Processing Toolkit. In *Proceedings of the 52nd Annual Meeting of the Association for Computational Linguistics: System Demonstrations*, pages 55–60, Baltimore, Maryland USA. Association for Computational Linguistics.

Detmar Meurers, Ramon Ziai, Niels Ott, and Janina Kopp. 2011. Evaluating Answers to Reading Comprehension Questions in Context: Results for German and the Role of Information Structure. In *Proceedings of the TextInfer 2011 Workshop on Textual Entailment*, pages 1–9, Stroudsburg, PA, USA. Association for Computational Linguistics.

Fabian Pedregosa, Gaël Varoquaux, Alexandre Gramfort, Vincent Michel, Bertrand Thirion, Olivier Grisel, Mathieu Blondel, Peter Prettenhofer, Ron Weiss, Vincent Dubourg, Jake Vanderplas, Alexandre Passos, David Cournapeau, Matthieu Brucher, Matthieu Perrot, and Édouard Duchesnay. 2011. Scikit-learn: Machine Learning in Python. *Journal of Machine Learning Research*, 12:2825–2830.

Ildikó Pilán, Elena Volodina, and Torsten Zesch. 2016. Predicting proficiency levels in learner writings by transferring a linguistic complexity model from expert-written coursebooks. In *Proceedings of the 26th International Conference on Computational Linguistics (COLING'16)*, pages 2101–2111, Osaka, Japan. Association for Computational Linguistics.

Angeliki Salamoura and Nick Saville. 2010. Exemplifying the CEFR: Criterial features of written learner English from the English Profile Programme. In Inge Bartning, Maisa Martin, and Ineke Vedder, editors, *Communicative proficiency and linguistic development: Intersections between SLA and language testing research*, number 1 in Eurosla Monographs Series, pages 101–132. European Second Language Association.

Mark D. Shermis and Jill Burstein, editors. 2013. *Handbook of Automated Essay Evaluation: Current Applications and New Directions*. Routledge, New York, NY.

Sowmya Vajjala. 2017. Automated Assessment of Non-Native Learner Essays: Investigating the Role of Linguistic Features. *International Journal of Artificial Intelligence in Education*, pages 1–27.

Sowmya Vajjala and Kaidi Lõo. 2014. Automatic CEFR Level Prediction for Estonian Learner Text. In *Proceedings of the third workshop on NLP for computer-assisted language learning*, NEALT Proceedings Series 22, pages 113–127.

Elena Volodina, Ildikó Pilán, and David Alfter. 2016a. Classification of Swedish learner essays by CEFR levels. In *CALL communities and culture – short papers from EUROCALL 2016*, pages 456–461, Limassol, Cyprus. European Association for Computer Assisted Language Learning.

Elena Volodina, Ildikó Pilán, Ingegerd Enström, Lorena Llozhi, Peter Lundkvist, Gunlög Sundberg, and Monica Sandell. 2016b. SweLL on the rise: Swedish Learner Language corpus for European Reference Level studies. In *Proceedings of the Tenth International Conference on Language Resources and Evaluation (LREC'16)*, pages 206–212, Portorož, Slovenia. European Language Resources Association (ELRA).

Michael Wilson. 1988. MRC Psycholinguistic Database: Machine Usable Dictionary, version 2.00. *Behavior Research Methods, Instruments, & Computers*, 20(1):6–10.

Helen Yannakoudakis, Ted Briscoe, and Ben Medlock. 2011. A New Dataset and Method for Automatically Grading ESOL Texts. In *Proceedings of the 49th Annual Meeting of the Association for Computational Linguistics: Human Language Technologies - Volume 1*, pages 180–189, Stroudsburg, PA, USA. Association for Computational Linguistics.

GEC into the future:
Where are we going and how do we get there?

Keisuke Sakaguchi,[1] **Courtney Napoles,**[1] and **Joel Tetreault**[2]
[1]Center for Language and Speech Processing, Johns Hopkins University
[2]Grammarly
{keisuke,napoles}@cs.jhu.edu, joel.tetreault@grammarly.com

Abstract

The field of grammatical error correction (GEC) has made tremendous bounds in the last ten years, but new questions and obstacles are revealing themselves. In this position paper, we discuss the issues that need to be addressed and provide recommendations for the field to continue to make progress, and propose a new shared task. We invite suggestions and critiques from the audience to make the new shared task a community-driven venture.

1 Introduction

In the field of grammatical error correction (GEC), the Helping Our Own shared tasks in 2011 (Dale and Kilgarriff, 2011) and 2012 (Dale et al., 2012), and then the CoNLL shared tasks of 2013 (Ng et al., 2013) and 2014 (Ng et al., 2014) marked a sea change. For the first time there were public datasets, most notably the NUS Corpus of Learner English (NUCLE; Dahlmeier et al., 2013), and evaluation metrics, of which the most commonly used to date is M^2 (Dahlmeier and Ng, 2012). This has allowed researchers from other fields, such as machine translation, to enter GEC more easily. It has also enabled new developments, with many papers published on metrics, new algorithms (most recently neural methods), and occasionally new datasets.

Even with the accelerated progress in GEC, problems yet remain in the field. The use of specific datasets may be GEC's worst enemy, as system and even evaluation metric development rely too heavily on the NUCLE test set. While probably one of the most important contributions to the field's development to date, the lack of publicly available alternatives has caused some over-optimization. Other issues have also gone undis-

cussed. For example, nearly all work that has been published in the NLP community has focused on standalone systems, and very few investigate their impact on downstream users, except, e.g., Nagata and Nakatani (2010); Chodorow et al. (2010).

In this short paper, we take stock of the current state of GEC (§2) and its limitations (§3), and outline where we believe the field should be five years from now (§4). We finish with a recommendation for a new *community-driven* shared task that will help the field progress even further (§5). We look forward to discussing this proposal with the community and to refine a shared task for 2018.

2 GEC: A Quick Retrospective

A complete retrospective is outside the scope of this paper and thus we focus on two key aspects of the field: For a more detailed review of the field, we refer the reader to Leacock et al. (2014).

2.1 Datasets

There are several error-annotated corpora, and for the purposes of this paper, we only focus on the most recent public datasets. The size and characteristics of each corpus is summarized in Table 1. The most frequently used corpus for GEC is NUCLE, which was the official dataset of the 2013 and 2014 shared tasks. It is a collection of essays written by students at the National University of Singapore (Dahlmeier et al., 2013). The test set and system results from the most recent shared task were released to the community (Ng et al., 2014), and have been the focus of recent work on automatic metrics (see §2.2). Additionally, this test set has been augmented with eight additional annotations from Bryant and Ng (2015) and eight from Sakaguchi et al. (2016).

The Cambridge Learner Corpus (CLC) contains a broader representation of native languages than the NUCLE, however only the First Certificate in

Proceedings of the 12th Workshop on Innovative Use of NLP for Building Educational Applications, pages 180–187
Copenhagen, Denmark, September 8, 2017. ©2017 Association for Computational Linguistics

Corpus	Num. refs.	Num. sent.	Sents. changed	Err. type labeled	Fluency edits	Err. span >1 sent.	Diverse proficiency	Diverse topic	Diverse L1	Native speakers
NUCLE	59k	2	38%	✓	(✗)	✓	✗	✗	✗	✗
FCE	34k	1	62%	✓	✗	✓	✓	✓	✓	✗
Lang-8	2.5M	≥1	42%	✗	✓	✓	✓	✓	✓	✗
AESW	1.2M	1	39%	✗	✗	✓	✗	✗	✓	✓ + ✗
JFLEG	1.5k	4	86%	✗	✓	✗	✓	✓	✓	✗

Table 1: GEC corpora available for free (for research purposes) and desired properties, identified in §3.1. ✓ and ✗ indicate whether the corpus exhibits each property. Fluency edits for the NUCLE test set were added by Sakaguchi et al. (2016).

English (FCE) portion is publicly available (Yannakoudakis et al., 2011). The FCE is approximately the same size as NUCLE and was used for the 2012 shared task. However it has not been used to the same extent as NUCLE, presumably because it lacks multiple annotations and the 2012 shared task system outputs were not released.

All of the corpora described above have been annotated with spans of text containing an error and assigned an error code. Unlike these, the Lang-8 Learner Corpora Corpus of Learner English (Tajiri et al., 2012) is a parallel set of original and corrected sentences from `lang-8.com`, an online community of language learners who post text that is corrected by other users. It is also the largest public GEC corpora, with more than 2 million English sentences.[1] Another large corpus currently available was released for the first Automatic Evaluation of Scientific Writing shared task (AESW; Daudaravicius et al., 2016). Unlike the other corpora, it contains scientific writing by native and non-native English speakers, corrected by professional editors. Because the writers are highly proficient, there is a lower diversity of errors than the other corpora. More than half of the errors are related to punctuation (Flickinger et al., 2016), which compose less than 7% of NUCLE errors.

Finally, the JHU FLuency-Extended GUG corpus (JFLEG) is a small dataset for tuning and evaluating GEC systems. 1.5k sentences are taken from the GUG corpus (Heilman et al., 2014), which labels sentences with an ordinal grammaticality score. In JFLEG, each sentence is corrected four times for grammaticality and *fluency* (Sakaguchi et al., 2016).

2.2 Evaluation

Precision, recall, and F-score have been used to evaluate GEC systems that correct targeted error types. Three additional evaluation metrics have been proposed for GEC: MaxMatch (M^2; Dahlmeier and Ng, 2012), I-measure (Felice and Briscoe, 2015), and GLEU (Napoles et al., 2015). The first two metrics compare the changes made in the output to error-coded spans of the reference corrections. M^2 was the metric used for the 2013 and 2014 CoNLL GEC shared tasks (Ng et al., 2013, 2014). It captures word- and phrase-level edits by building an edit lattice and calculating an F-score over the lattice. I-measure (IM) is based on token-level alignment-based accuracy among the source, hypothesis, and gold-standard. IM considers the distinction between "do-nothing (already grammatical) baseline" and systems that only propose wrong corrections (i.e., make the source sentence worse). Unlike these two approaches, GLEU does not need error-coded references (Napoles et al., 2015). Based on BLEU (Papineni et al., 2002), it computes n-gram precision of the system output against reference sentences, and additionally penalizes n-grams in the hypothesis that should have been corrected but failed.

3 Limitations

3.1 Problems with Datasets

As we saw in the previous section, the majority of the commonly used datasets are limited to students, specifically college-level ESL writers. To date, the overwhelmingly majority of publications benchmark on NUCLE, save for a few exceptions such as Cahill et al. (2013) and Rei and Yannakoudakis (2016) which means that research efforts are becoming over-optimized for one set. This lack of diversity means that it is not clear how systems perform on other genres under different training conditions. We should look to the parsing community as a warning sign. For well over a decade, the field was heavily focused on improving parsing accuracy on the Penn Treebank (Marcus et al., 1993), but robustness was greatly improved with the advent of Ontonotes (Hovy et al., 2006) and the Google Web Treebank (Petrov and

---

[1] Because of noise and implementation differences in sentence extraction, the size varies from 2–2.5 million sentences.

System	GLEU [0,100]	IM [-100, 100]	M^2 [0, 100]		
			P	R	$F_{0.5}$
"a"	0.2	0.0	28.4	31.3	28.9
"a a"	0.6	0.0	28.7	31.8	29.3
"a a a"	1.6	0.0	28.7	32.0	29.4
Source	57.4	0.0	100.0	0.0	0.0
CAMB14	64.3	-5.3	39.7	30.1	37.3
CUUI14	64.6	-2.2	41.8	24.9	36.8
AMU14	64.6	-2.5	41.6	21.4	35.0
Src>Game	✓	✗	✓	✗	✗
Src<Sys	✓	✗	✗	✓	✓

Table 2: Metric scores of three artificially contrived systems (Game), input source sentences (Src), and top 3 system outputs (Sys) on CoNLL14 data. The bottom two rows show whether each metric scores the systems better than Game or worse than Source. Humans judge all systems be better than over Source.

McDonald, 2012).

Another issue is training data size. The sister field of machine translation (MT) usually has datasets in the orders of millions or even tens of millions of sentence pairs. The largest GEC datasets barely approach that figure, with 2.5 million sentences at a maximum, a number which includes sentences that were not corrected.

Table 1 summarizes the strengths and weaknesses of the most commonly used GEC corpora across different properties ranging from size to diversity in native language (L1). The most notable weakness across corpora is the lack of multiple reference corrections. NUCLE contains two corrections per sentence and JFLEG 4. M^2 and GLEU scores increase with more references but at a diminishing rate (Bryant and Ng, 2015; Sakaguchi et al., 2016). Further investigation is warranted to determine what an ideal number of references is, given the trade off between cost and reliability. Some corpora contain little diversity in proficiency, topic, and/or native language of the writers (namely NUCLE and AESW), however AESW is the only corpus to contain sentences by native English speakers.

3.2 Problems with Evaluation

The 2014 CoNLL shared task has enabled, for the first time, the development of evaluation metrics. These metrics are evaluated by comparing their ranking of the shared task systems with the ranking done by human annotators. Sakaguchi et al. (2016) showed that GLEU could rank systems closer to a human ranking than M^2 and IM, and a higher correlation could be found when combining GLEU with a reference-less fluency met-

ric (Napoles et al., 2017). However, it is important to take these results with a grain of salt—all benchmarking of the metrics was done with the CoNLL 2014 systems and data, and it remains to be seen if this ranking would hold on other, larger datasets.

Another issue with the metrics is the number of references available for comparison. As in machine translation, the more references (human-generated gold-standard corrections) one has, the better one can evaluate a system. The CoNLL 2014 test set has 18 references annotated, but one can find examples where a system produces a correction which is not reflected in the references. This gets more complicated when human raters feel it is necessary to rewrite a sentence.

A third issue is that no metric directly measures meaning preservation. This means that a system could produce a more fluent version of the original but accidentally change one word, and that could change the meaning of the whole sentence. For example, if a system accidentally corrected *documentary* to *document* in "The documentary gave a nice summary of global warming." By current metrics, that error would have the same penalty as a minor spelling mistake.

Finally, the most commonly used GEC metric, M^2, has a serious weakness, which has been noted in earlier papers (Felice and Briscoe, 2015; Sakaguchi et al., 2016; Bryant et al., 2017). The phrasal alignments under-penalize a sequence of incorrect tokens, and to illustrate how troubling this is, we tested a series of dummy systems, where each system produces the same sentence regardless of input (the sentences produced by each system are *a*, *a a*, and *a a a*). Table 2 shows their scores on the CoNLL 2014 test set evaluated on the official NUCLE references (without alternatives), compared to the top 3 systems in the shared task, CAMB14 (Felice et al., 2014), CUUI14 (Rozovskaya et al., 2014), and AMU14 (Junczys-Dowmunt and Grundkiewicz, 2014). The reader will notice that GLEU and IM score these sentences at or near zero, however according to M^2, the dummy system that only returns the string "a a" scores higher than 7/13 systems participating in the 2014 Shared Task. The IM score is also problematic in that the gamed sentences have the same score as the source.

System	Sentence	Metric score (rank)		
		GLEU	**IM**	**M^2**
System	**Sentence**	[0,100]	[-100,100]	[0,100]
Source	In both advertisements is said that these tooth pastes will make your teeth briliant and brighter .	15.7 (4)	0.0 (4)	0.0 (5)
Reference	☐ Both advertisements ☐ say that the toothpaste will make your teeth brilliant and brighter .	50.7 (1)	17.4 (3)	65.2 (3)
AMU16 & NUS16	In both advertisements is said that these tooth pastes will make your teeth briliant and brighter .	15.7 (4)	0.0 (4)	0.0 (5)
CAMB14	In both advertisements is said that these tooth pastes will make your teeth brilliant and brighter .	35.5 (3)	100.0 (1)	83.3 (1)
CAMB16	In both advertisements it is said that these tooth problems will make your teeth brilliant and brighter .	39.5 (2)	56.1 (2)	71.4 (2)
Dummy	a a a .	2.9 (5)	-47.7 (5)	52.6 (4)

Table 3: An original source sentence and candidate corrections, along with the score of each sentence from different metrics. Changed or inserted spans are underlined and ☐ indicates deletions.

4 Looking into the Future

In this section we outline our recommendations for how the field should develop.

4.1 Data

As the world's communication is not limited to college-level essays, it is important that we have datasets which better represent as much breadth as possible. Ideally, datasets should span different genres (such as emails, blog posts, and official documents) and include content from both native and non-native speakers, as well as from different proficiency levels. All of these changes will enable the field to better assess how we are helping *more* of the world's writers under different conditions, and also enable one to test adaptation between domains.

4.2 Evaluation

We envision evaluation metrics which check that corrections are not only grammatically valid, but also check that the corrections are native-sounding and preserve the original meaning or intent of the writer. Future metrics should be easy to compute and be interpretable. For instance, a range between -1 and 1 may be preferred (like IM uses), since it is possible a suggested set of corrections could produce a sentence which is *worse* than the original. If multiple references are used, metrics should assign credit to corrections which match different references in different places, assuming the outcome is overall coherent. In addition, most (if not all) evaluation schemes to date have focused on the sentence as the minimal unit. It would be good to take the entire document into account and allow for more global rewrites, such as consistent tense.

Ultimately, a metric should say whether or not a system has attained the same level of performance as a human judge. One way of doing this is through a GEC Turing Test, where system outputs are blindly judged alongside human corrections of the same sentences. If human adjudicators think the system outputs are indistinguishable in quality from the human corrections (for example, given a set of criteria such as being good corrections, meaning preserving and native-sounding) then that is a very strong signal that GEC has attained human-level performance.

To illustrate the shortcomings of current metrics, Table 3 contains a JFLEG sentence corrected by current leading systems (AMU16 (Junczys-Dowmunt and Grundkiewicz, 2016); NUS16 (Chollampatt et al., 2016); CAMB16 (Yuan and Briscoe, 2016)) and the automatic metric scores.[2] Notice that the CAMB16 sentence, which changes *tooth pastes → tooth problems*, is ranked the highest system output by GLEU and the second highest by IM and M^2. All metrics score it higher than the unchanged Source sentence. Another issues evidenced in the table is that IM and M^2 score the imperfect correction (CAMB14) as better than Reference; and according to M^2, the Dummy output is better than Source.

We believe that the GEC field should take

---

[2] All metrics run with default settings. Reference is evaluated against the other 3 references; other sentences are evaluated against all 4 references.

notes from the Workshop on Machine Translation (WMT) (Bojar et al., 2016). There the participants in the evaluation shared tasks are also responsible for contributing system ranking judgments. This makes the whole effort more community-driven and takes the pressure off one group from having to supply all annotations.

4.3   Consensus on Goals and Applications

As a corollary to data and metrics, the end-goal of GEC also needs to be refined within the community. Initial approaches to GEC seemed to focus on providing feedback to English language learners where specific error types would be targeted and feedback would be given in terms of detection or possible corrections. The work was also motivated by concurrent work in using NLP for automatic essay scoring (for example, Attali and Burstein (2006)). Chodorow et al. (2012) noted several other applications for GEC: improving overall writing quality for both native and non-native writers, assistive language learning, and applications within NLP (such as post-editing in MT). More recently the field has drifted to "whole sentence GEC" using statistical or neural MT approaches. In this situation, the writer simply gets a complete rewrite of their sentence, which may be useful as an instructional tool in some circumstances, but not all.

There is no consensus on what the focus application(s) should be. Which application determines which methods and which evaluation metrics one uses. For example, if one wants to provide feedback to language learners, then a high-precision, interpretable method is preferred. Conversely, if the application is simply to automatically clean up one's writing without any feedback, then a whole sentence approach may be preferred. Very few papers delve into error detection and correction for goals other than whole-sentence error correction or targeted feedback for ESL writers. Datasets and metrics should be created with a specific goal in mind. Thus, the field should reassess what are the goals and how we evaluate with respect to these goals.

5   Proposal for a New Shared Task

We believe it is time for another shared task in the field, this one designed with consideration the field should be several years from now. The CoNLL shared tasks were instrumental in unifying the field with a common benchmark corpus and metric, and the AESW shared task provided data from a new domain to evaluate on. We recommend the following:

- **Data**: A new corpus for training and evaluation that spans different genres. We have already begun collecting conversational data from native and non-native writers and from genres other than essays, such as emails. Our aim is to construct a corpus larger than the NUCLE to support the development of data-hungry methods such as neural MT.
- **Annotation**: The data is corrected for fluency with crowdsourcing as in Sakaguchi et al. (2016) which is a cheap and efficient way of collecting annotations of reasonable quality. Error types can be automatically tagged using a method such as that described in Bryant et al. (2017)
- **Metric Evaluation**: Borrowing from the WMT community, the shared task should also be a venue to improve automatic GEC evaluation. Participants will provide judgments on system rankings.

We invite discussion from the community and seek others to help contribute data, annotations and other resources to make this a community-driven event. Our goal is to host a shared task in 2018. We believe that this type of collaboration has made the WMT evaluations a success, and will similarly benefit GEC. We have set up a public mailing list where others can post their comments and suggestions: `https://groups.google.com/forum/#!forum/gec-sharedtask`.

6   Conclusions

The goal of this paper is to laud the progress that the GEC field has made, but also highlight the limitations that must be addressed for the field to grow further. The reliance on a few narrow datasets is problematic as it has a major impact on system development and metric development, as well as robustness when applying these approaches in the real world. Our concern is that unless data and metrics are improved, it will be hard to assess the value of new algorithms optimized for a small set of datasets and metrics. We list a recommendation for a new shared task to fuel discussion offline as well as at the BEA12 Workshop in Copenhagen.[3]

---

[3] `https://www.cs.rochester.edu/~tetreaul/emnlp-bea12.html`

References

Yigal Attali and Jill Burstein. 2006. Automated essay scoring with e-rater® v. 2. *The Journal of Technology, Learning and Assessment* 4(3).

Ondřej Bojar, Rajen Chatterjee, Christian Federmann, Yvette Graham, Barry Haddow, Matthias Huck, Antonio Jimeno Yepes, Philipp Koehn, Varvara Logacheva, Christof Monz, Matteo Negri, Aurelie Neveol, Mariana Neves, Martin Popel, Matt Post, Raphael Rubino, Carolina Scarton, Lucia Specia, Marco Turchi, Karin Verspoor, and Marcos Zampieri. 2016. Findings of the 2016 conference on machine translation. In *Proceedings of the First Conference on Machine Translation*. Association for Computational Linguistics, Berlin, Germany, pages 131–198. http://www.aclweb.org/anthology/W16-2301.

Christopher Bryant, Mariano Felice, and Ted Briscoe. 2017. Automatic annotation and evaluation of error types for grammatical error correction. In *Proceedings of the 55th Annual Meeting of the Association for Computational Linguistics*. Association for Computational Linguistics, Vancouver, Canada.

Christopher Bryant and Hwee Tou Ng. 2015. How far are we from fully automatic high quality grammatical error correction? In *Proceedings of the 53rd Annual Meeting of the Association for Computational Linguistics and the 7th International Joint Conference on Natural Language Processing*. Association for Computational Linguistics, Beijing, China, pages 697–707. http://www.aclweb.org/anthology/P15-1068.

Aoife Cahill, Nitin Madnani, Joel Tetreault, and Diane Napolitano. 2013. Robust systems for preposition error correction using wikipedia revisions. In *Proceedings of the 2013 Conference of the North American Chapter of the Association for Computational Linguistics: Human Language Technologies*. Association for Computational Linguistics, Atlanta, Georgia, pages 507–517. http://www.aclweb.org/anthology/N13-1055.

Martin Chodorow, Markus Dickinson, Ross Israel, and Joel Tetreault. 2012. Problems in evaluating grammatical error detection systems. In *Proceedings of COLING 2012*. The COLING 2012 Organizing Committee, Mumbai, India, pages 611–628. http://www.aclweb.org/anthology/C12-1038.

Martin Chodorow, Michael Gamon, and Joel Tetreault. 2010. The utility of grammatical error detection systems for English language learners: Feedback and assessment. *Language Testing* 27(3).

Shamil Chollampatt, Duc Tam Hoang, and Hwee Tou Ng. 2016. Adapting grammatical error correction based on the native language of writers with neural network joint models. In *Proceedings of the 2016 Conference on Empirical Methods in Natural Language Processing*. Association for Computational Linguistics, Austin, Texas, pages 1901–1911. https://aclweb.org/anthology/D16-1195.

Daniel Dahlmeier and Hwee Tou Ng. 2012. Better evaluation for grammatical error correction. In *Proceedings of the 2012 Conference of the North American Chapter of the Association for Computational Linguistics: Human Language Technologies*. Association for Computational Linguistics, Montréal, Canada, pages 568–572.

Daniel Dahlmeier, Hwee Tou Ng, and Siew Mei Wu. 2013. Building a large annotated corpus of learner english: The NUS Corpus of Learner English. In *Proceedings of the Eighth Workshop on Innovative Use of NLP for Building Educational Applications*. Association for Computational Linguistics, Atlanta, Georgia, pages 22–31. http://www.aclweb.org/anthology/W13-1703.

Robert Dale, Ilya Anisimoff, and George Narroway. 2012. Hoo 2012: A report on the preposition and determiner error correction shared task. In *Proceedings of the Seventh Workshop on Building Educational Applications Using NLP*. Association for Computational Linguistics, Montréal, Canada, pages 54–62. http://www.aclweb.org/anthology/W12-2006.

Robert Dale and Adam Kilgarriff. 2011. Helping our own: The hoo 2011 pilot shared task. In *Proceedings of the Generation Challenges Session at the 13th European Workshop on Natural Language Generation*. Association for Computational Linguistics, Nancy, France, pages 242–249. http://www.aclweb.org/anthology/W11-2838.

Vidas Daudaravicius, Rafael E. Banchs, Elena Volodina, and Courtney Napoles. 2016. A report on the automatic evaluation of scientific writing shared task. In *Proceedings of the 11th Workshop on Innovative Use of NLP for Building Educational Applications*. Association for Computational Linguistics, San Diego, CA, pages 53–62. http://www.aclweb.org/anthology/W16-0506.

Mariano Felice and Ted Briscoe. 2015. Towards a standard evaluation method for grammatical error detection and correction. In *Proceedings of the 2015 Conference of the North American Chapter of the Association for Computational Linguistics*. Association for Computational Linguistics, Denver, CO.

Mariano Felice, Zheng Yuan, Øistein E. Andersen, Helen Yannakoudakis, and Ekaterina Kochmar. 2014. Grammatical error correction using hybrid systems and type filtering. In *Proceedings of the Eighteenth Conference on Computational Natural Language Learning: Shared Task*. Association for Computational Linguistics, Baltimore, Maryland, pages 15–24. http://www.aclweb.org/anthology/W14-1702.

Dan Flickinger, Michael Goodman, and Woodley Packard. 2016. Uw-stanford system description for aesw 2016 shared task on grammatical error detection. In *Proceedings of the 11th Workshop on Innovative Use of NLP for Building Educational Applications*. Association for Computational Linguistics, San Diego, CA, pages 105–111. http://www.aclweb.org/anthology/W16-0511.

Michael Heilman, Aoife Cahill, Nitin Madnani, Melissa Lopez, Matthew Mulholland, and Joel Tetreault. 2014. Predicting grammaticality on an ordinal scale. In *Proceedings of the 52nd Annual Meeting of the Association for Computational Linguistics*. Association for Computational Linguistics, Baltimore, Maryland, pages 174–180. http://www.aclweb.org/anthology/P14-2029.

Eduard Hovy, Mitchell Marcus, Martha Palmer, Lance Ramshaw, and Ralph Weischedel. 2006. Ontonotes: the 90% solution. In *Proceedings of the human language technology conference of the NAACL, Companion Volume: Short Papers*. Association for Computational Linguistics, pages 57–60.

Marcin Junczys-Dowmunt and Roman Grundkiewicz. 2014. The AMU System in the CoNLL-2014 shared task: Grammatical error correction by data-intensive and feature-rich statistical machine translation. In *Proceedings of the Eighteenth Conference on Computational Natural Language Learning: Shared Task*. Association for Computational Linguistics, Baltimore, Maryland, pages 25–33. http://www.aclweb.org/anthology/W14-1703.

Marcin Junczys-Dowmunt and Roman Grundkiewicz. 2016. Phrase-based machine translation is state-of-the-art for automatic grammatical error correction. In *Proceedings of the 2016 Conference on Empirical Methods in Natural Language Processing*. Association for Computational Linguistics, Austin, Texas, pages 1546–1556. https://aclweb.org/anthology/D16-1161.

C. Leacock, M. Chodorow, M. Gamon, and J. Tetreault. 2014. *Automated Grammatical Error Detection for Language Learners, Second Edition*. Synthesis Lectures on Human Language Technologies. Morgan & Claypool Publishers. https://books.google.com/books?id=bi0QAwAAQBAJ.

Mitchell P Marcus, Mary Ann Marcinkiewicz, and Beatrice Santorini. 1993. Building a large annotated corpus of english: The penn treebank. *Computational linguistics* 19(2):313–330.

Ryo Nagata and Kazuhide Nakatani. 2010. Evaluating performance of grammatical error detection to maximize learning effect. In *Coling 2010: Posters*. Coling 2010 Organizing Committee, Beijing, China, pages 894–900. http://www.aclweb.org/anthology/C10-2103.

Courtney Napoles, Keisuke Sakaguchi, Matt Post, and Joel Tetreault. 2015. Ground truth for grammatical error correction metrics. In *Proceedings of the 53rd Annual Meeting of the Association for Computational Linguistics and the 7th International Joint Conference on Natural Language Processing*. Association for Computational Linguistics, Beijing, China, pages 588–593. http://www.aclweb.org/anthology/P15-2097.

Courtney Napoles, Keisuke Sakaguchi, and Joel Tetreault. 2017. Jfleg: A fluency corpus and benchmark for grammatical error correction. In *Proceedings of the 15th Conference of the European Chapter of the Association for Computational Linguistics: Volume 2, Short Papers*. Association for Computational Linguistics, Valencia, Spain, pages 229–234. http://www.aclweb.org/anthology/E17-2037.

Hwee Tou Ng, Siew Mei Wu, Ted Briscoe, Christian Hadiwinoto, Raymond Hendy Susanto, and Christopher Bryant. 2014. The CoNLL-2014 Shared Task on grammatical error correction. In *Proceedings of the Eighteenth Conference on Computational Natural Language Learning: Shared Task*. Association for Computational Linguistics, Baltimore, Maryland, pages 1–14.

Hwee Tou Ng, Siew Mei Wu, Yuanbin Wu, Christian Hadiwinoto, and Joel Tetreault. 2013. The CoNLL-2013 Shared Task on grammatical error correction. In *Proceedings of the Seventeenth Conference on Computational Natural Language Learning: Shared Task*. Association for Computational Linguistics, Sofia, Bulgaria, pages 1–12.

Kishore Papineni, Salim Roukos, Todd Ward, and Wei-Jing Zhu. 2002. Bleu: a method for automatic evaluation of machine translation. In *Proceedings of 40th Annual Meeting of the Association for Computational Linguistics*. Association for Computational Linguistics, Philadelphia, Pennsylvania, USA, pages 311–318.

Slav Petrov and Ryan McDonald. 2012. Overview of the 2012 shared task on parsing the web. In *SANCL*.

Marek Rei and Helen Yannakoudakis. 2016. Compositional sequence labeling models for error detection in learner writing. In *Proceedings of the 54th Annual Meeting of the Association for Computational Linguistics (Volume 1: Long Papers)*. Association for Computational Linguistics, Berlin, Germany, pages 1181–1191. http://www.aclweb.org/anthology/P16-1112.

Alla Rozovskaya, Kai-Wei Chang, Mark Sammons, Dan Roth, and Nizar Habash. 2014. The Illinois-Columbia System in the CoNLL-2014 shared task. In *Proceedings of the Eighteenth Conference on Computational Natural Language Learning: Shared Task*. Association for Computational Linguistics, Baltimore, Maryland, pages 34–42. http://www.aclweb.org/anthology/W14-1704.

Keisuke Sakaguchi, Courtney Napoles, Matt Post, and Joel Tetreault. 2016. Reassessing the goals of grammatical error correction: Fluency instead of grammaticality. *Transactions of the Association for Computational Linguistics* 4:169–182.

Toshikazu Tajiri, Mamoru Komachi, and Yuji Matsumoto. 2012. Tense and aspect error correction for ESL learners using global context. In *Proceedings of the 50th Annual Meeting of the Association for Computational Linguistics*. Association for Computational Linguistics, Jeju Island, Korea, pages 198–202. http://www.aclweb.org/anthology/P12-2039.

Helen Yannakoudakis, Ted Briscoe, and Ben Medlock. 2011. A new dataset and method for automatically grading ESOL texts. In *Proceedings of the 49th Annual Meeting of the Association for Computational Linguistics: Human Language Technologies*. Association for Computational Linguistics, Portland, Oregon, USA, pages 180–189. http://www.aclweb.org/anthology/P11-1019.

Zheng Yuan and Ted Briscoe. 2016. Grammatical error correction using neural machine translation. In *Proceedings of the 2016 Conference of the North American Chapter of the Association for Computational Linguistics: Human Language Technologies*. Association for Computational Linguistics, San Diego, California, pages 380–386. http://www.aclweb.org/anthology/N16-1042.

Detecting Off-topic Responses to Visual Prompts

Marek Rei
The ALTA Institute
Computer Laboratory
University of Cambridge
United Kingdom
marek.rei@cl.cam.ac.uk

Abstract

Automated methods for essay scoring have made great progress in recent years, achieving accuracies very close to human annotators. However, a known weakness of such automated scorers is not taking into account the semantic relevance of the submitted text. While there is existing work on detecting answer relevance given a textual prompt, very little previous research has been done to incorporate visual writing prompts. We propose a neural architecture and several extensions for detecting off-topic responses to visual prompts and evaluate it on a dataset of texts written by language learners.

1 Introduction

Evaluating the relevance of learner essays with respect to the assigned prompt is an important part of automated writing assessment (Higgins et al., 2006; Briscoe et al., 2010). Existing systems are able to assign high-quality assessments based on grammaticality (Yannakoudakis et al., 2011; Ng et al., 2014), but are known to be vulnerable to memorised off-topic answers which can be a critical weakness in high-stakes testing. In addition, students who have limited relevant vocabulary may try to shift the topic of their answer in a more familiar direction, which most automated assessment systems are not able to capture. Solutions for detecting topical relevance can help prevent these weaknesses and provide informative feedback to the students.

While there is previous work on assessing the relevance of answers given a textual prompt (Persing and Ng, 2014; Cummins et al., 2015; Rei and Cummins, 2016), very little research has been done to incorporate visual writing prompts. In

this setting, students are asked to write a short description about an image in order to assess their language skills, and we would like to automatically evaluate the semantic relevance of their answers. An intuitive method for comparing multiple modalities is to map them into a shared distributed space – semantically similar entities will get mapped to similar vector representations, regardless of the information source. Frome et al. (2013) used this principle to improve image recognition, by first training separate visual and textual components, and then mapping the images into the same space as word embeddings. Ma et al. (2015) performed information retrieval tasks with a related model based on convolutional networks. Klein et al. (2015) learned to associate word embeddings to images using Fisher vectors.

In this paper, we start with a similar architecture, based on the approach used by Kiros et al. (2014) for image caption generation, and propose modifications that make the model more suitable for discriminating between relevant and irrelevant answers. The framework uses an LSTM for text composition and a pre-trained image recognition model for extracting visual features. Both representations are mapped to the same space and a prediction is made about the relevance of the text given the image. We propose a novel gating component that decides which parts of the image should be considered for the current similarity calculation, based on first reading the input sentence. Application of dropout to word embeddings and visual features helps increase robustness on an otherwise noisy dataset and assisted in regularising the model. Finally, the standard loss function is replaced with a version of cross-entropy, encouraging the model to jointly optimise over batches. We evaluate on a dataset of short answers by language learners, written in response to visual prompts and our experiments show perfor-

Proceedings of the 12th Workshop on Innovative Use of NLP for Building Educational Applications, pages 188–197
Copenhagen, Denmark, September 8, 2017. ©2017 Association for Computational Linguistics

mance improvements for each of the model modifications.

2   Relevance Detection Model

Automated methods for scoring essays and short answers have made great progress in recent years (Yannakoudakis et al., 2011; Sakaguchi et al., 2015; Alikaniotis et al., 2016; Hussein et al., 2017), achieving accuracies very close to human annotators. However, a known weakness of such automated scorers is not taking into account the topical relevance of the submitted text. Students with limited language skills may attempt to shift the topic of the response in a more familiar direction, which automated systems would not be able to detect. In a high-stakes examination framework, this weakness could be further exploited by memorising a grammatically correct answer and presenting it in response to any prompt. Being able to detect topical relevance can help prevent such weaknesses, provide useful feedback to the students, and is also a step towards evaluating more creative aspects of learner writing. While there is existing work on detecting answer relevance given a textual prompt (Persing and Ng, 2014; Cummins et al., 2015; Rei and Cummins, 2016), only limited previous research has been done to extend this to visual prompts. Some recent work has investigated answer relevance to visual prompts as part of automated scoring systems (Somasundaran et al., 2015; King and Dickinson, 2016), but they reduced the problem to a textual similarity task by relying on hand-written reference descriptions for each image without directly incorporating visual information.

Our proposed relevance detection model takes an image and a sentence as input, and assigns a score indicating how relevant the image is to the text. Formulating this as a scoring problem instead of binary classification allows us to treat the model output as a confidence score, and the classification threshold can be selected at a later stage based on the specific application.

Kiros et al. (2014) describe a supervised method for mapping an image and a sentence into the same space, which allows them to generate similar vector representations for images that have semantically similar descriptions. We base our approach for multimodal relevance scoring on this architecture, and introduce several modifications in order to adapt it to the task of discriminating between relevant and irrelevant textual answers.

The outline of our framework can be seen in Figure 1. The input sentence is first passed through a Long Short-Term Memory (LSTM, Hochreiter and Schmidhuber (1997)) component, mapping it to a vector representation u. The visual features for the input image are extracted using a model trained for image recognition. The visual representation is then conditioned on the input sentence and mapped to a vector representation v. Both u and v are given as input to a function that predicts a confidence score for the answer being relevant to the image. In the next sections we will describe each of these components in more detail.

2.1   Text Composition

The input to the text composition component is a tokenised sentence. We first map these tokens to an embedding space, resulting in a sequence of vector representations:

$$[w_1, w_2, ..., w_N] \quad (1)$$

Next, we apply dropout (Srivastava et al., 2014) to each of the word embeddings in the sentence. Dropout is a method of regularising neural networks, shown to provide performance imrovements. Neuron activations in a layer are set to zero with probability p, preventing the model from excessively relying on the presence of specific features. The process can also be thought of as training a randomly constructed smaller network at each training iteration, resulting in a full combination model. At test time, all the values are retained, but scaled with $(1 - p)$ to compensate for the difference. While dropout is commonly applied to weights inside the network (Tai et al., 2015; Zhang et al., 2015; Kalchbrenner et al., 2015; Kim et al., 2016), there is also some recent work that deploy dropout directly on the word embeddings (Rocktäschel et al., 2016; Chen et al., 2016). The relevance scoring model needs to handle texts from different domains, including error-prone sentences from language learners, and dropout on the embeddings allows us to introduce robustness into the training process.

We use an LSTM component for processing the word embeddings, building up a sentence representation. It is similar to a traditional recurrent neural network, with specialised gating functions that allow it to dynamically decide which information to carry forward or forget. The LSTM calcu-

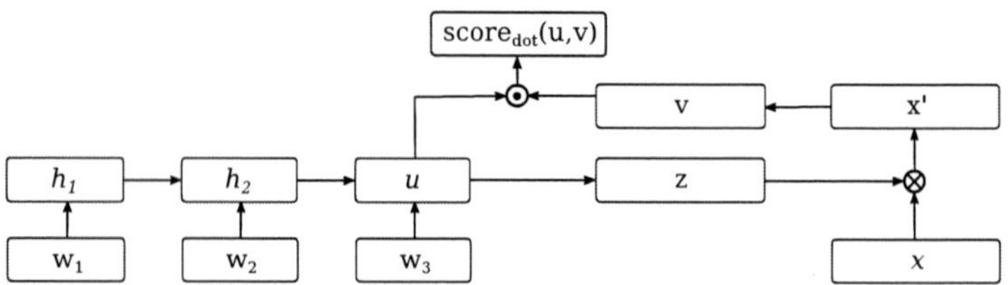

Figure 1: The outline of the relevance detection model. The input sentence and image are mapped to vector representations u and v using modality-specific functions. These vectors are then given to a relevance function which assigns a real-valued score based on their similarity.

lates a hidden representation at word n based on the current word embedding and the previous hidden representation at time step $n - 1$:

$$h_n = LSTM(w_n, h_{n-1}) \qquad (2)$$

The last hidden representation h_N is calculated based on all the words in the sequence, thereby allowing the model to iteratively construct a semantic representation of the whole sentence. We use this vector $u = h_N$ to represent a given input sentence in the relevance scoring model. Since word-level processing is not ideal for handling spelling errors in learner texts, future work could also investigate character-based extensions for text composition, such as those described by Rei et al. (2016) and Wieting et al. (2016).

2.2 Image Processing

In order to map images to feature vectors, a pre-trained image recognition model is combined with a supervised transformation component. We make use of the BVLC GoogLeNet image recognition model, which is based on an architecture described by Szegedy et al. (2015) and provided by the Caffe toolkit (Jia et al., 2014). The GoogLeNet is a 22-layer deep convolutional network, trained on ImageNet (Deng et al., 2009) data to detect 1,000 different image classes.

An input image is passed through the network and a probability distribution over the possible classes is produced. Instead of using the output layer, we extract the neuron activations at the second-to-last layer in the network – this takes advantage of all the visual feature processing on various levels of the network, but retains a more general distributed representation of the image compared to using the output layer. Similarly to the word embeddings in textual composition, we apply dropout with probability p directly to the image vectors – this introduces variance to the other-

wise limited training data, and prevents the model from overfitting on specific features.

The previous process maps the image to a 1024-dimensional vector x, which contains useful visual information but is not optimised for the relevance scoring task. We introduce a gating component which modulates the image vector, based on the textual vector representation from the input sentence. A vector of gating weights is calculated as a nonlinear weighted transformation of the sentence vector u:

$$z = \sigma(uW_z + b_z) \qquad (3)$$

where W_z is a weight matrix, b_z is a bias vector, and $\sigma()$ is the logistic activation function with values between 0 and 1. A new image representation x' is then calculated by applying these element-wise weights to the visual vector x:

$$x' = z * x \qquad (4)$$

where $*$ indicates an element-wise multiplication. This architecture allows the model to first read the input sentence, determine what to look for in the corresponding image, and block out irrelevant information in the image vector. We also disconnect the backpropagation between vector u and the gating weights z – this forces the model to optimise u only for score prediction, leaving W_z and b_z to specialise on handling the gating.

Finally, we pass the image representation through a fully connected non-linear layer – this allows the model to transform the pre-trained GoogLeNet space to a representation that is specialised for relevance scoring:

$$v = tanh(x'W_x) \qquad (5)$$

where W_x is a weight matrix that is optimised during training, and v is the final image vector that is used as input to the relevance scoring component.

2.3 Scoring and optimisation

Based on vector representations for the input sentence (u) and image (v) we now want to assign a score which indicates how related they are. Kiros et al. (2014) used the cosine measure as the similarity function – it measures the angle between two vectors, returning a value in the range $[-1, 1]$, and is commonly used for similarity calculations in language processing:

$$score_{cos}(u, v) = cos(u, v) = \frac{uv}{|u||v|} \quad (6)$$

The model can then be optimised to predict a high score for image-sentence pairs where the image and sentence and related, and a low score for randomly constructed pairs. The loss function is a hinge loss with a margin m; if the score difference between the positive and negative example is greater than m, then no training is required, otherwise the error is backpropagated and weights are updated accordingly:

$$Loss_{hinge} = \sum_{i \in I} \sum_{j \in J(i)} max(-score_{cos}(u_i, v_i)$$
$$+ score_{cos}(u_j, v_i) + m, 0) \quad (7)$$

where I is the set of related image-text pairs for training, and $J(i)$ is a set of randomly constructed pairs for entry i. When generating the negative examples, we make sure the resulting set $J(i)$ does not contain any examples with the same image as i – otherwise the model would accidentally optimise related examples towards a low score.

In this work we propose using an alternative scoring function, in order to help discriminate between the answers. We first replace the cosine similarity with a dot-product:

$$score_{dot}(u, v) = uv \quad (8)$$

Next, we create a scoring function by calculating a probability distribution over the current minibatch of examples:

$$score_{exp}(u_i, v_i) = \frac{\exp(score_{dot}(u_i, v_i))}{Z} \quad (9)$$

$$Z = \exp(score_{dot}(u_i, v_i))$$
$$+ \sum_{j \in J(i)} \exp(score_{dot}(u_j, v_i)) \quad (10)$$

	images	sentences
TRAIN	29,000	145,000
DEV	1,014	5,070
TEST	1,000	5,000

Table 1: Number of images and descriptions in the Flickr30k dataset.

The model is then optimised for cross-entropy, which is equivalent to optimising the negative log-likelihood:

$$Loss_{ce} = -\sum_{i \in I} log(score_{exp}(u_i, v_i)) \quad (11)$$

The transition from cosine to dot-product is required in order to facilitate the new scoring function. In this setting, $score_{exp}(u_i, v_i)$ acts as a softmax layer, requiring the input values to be unbounded for functioning correctly, whereas cosine would restrict values to a range between -1 and 1.

The new scoring function based on softmax encourages the model to further distinguish between relevant and irrelevant images. While the hinge loss function is also optimised in minibatches, it independently optimises the relevance score of each training pair, whereas softmax connects the scores for all the pairs into a probability distribution. When this distribution is optimised using cross-entropy, it specifically focuses more on instances that incorrectly have relatively high scores compared to other pairs in the dataset. In addition, optimising towards a larger score for the known correct example also reduces the scores for all other pairs in the batch.

3 Evaluation Setup

Given an image and a text written in response to this image, the goal of the system is to assign a score and return a decision about the relevance of this text. We evaluate the framework on an experimental dataset collected by the English Profile[1], containing 543 answers written by language learners in response to visual prompts in the form of photographs. As part of the instructions, the students were able to select the image that they wanted to write about, and were then free to choose what to write. The length of the collected answers ranges from 1 to 44 sentences.

---

[1] http://www.englishprofile.org/

This dataset contains real-world examples for the task of visual relevance detection, and therefore also proposes a range of challenges. The answers are provided by students in various stages of learning English, which means the texts contain numerous writing errors. Spelling mistakes prevent the model from making full use of word embeddings, and previously unseen grammatical mistakes will cause trouble for the LSTM composition function. The students have also interpreted the open writing task in various different ways – while some have answered by describing the content of the image, others have instead talked about personal memories triggered by the image, or even created a short fictional story inspired by the photo. This has led to answers that vary quite a bit in writing style, vocabulary size and sentence length.

Ideally, we would like to train the model on examples where pairs of images and sentences are specifically annotated for their semantic relevance. However, since the collected dataset is not large enough for training neural networks, we make use of the Flickr30k (Young et al., 2014) dataset which contains implicitly relevant pairs of images and their corresponding descriptions. Flickr30k is an image captioning dataset, containing 31,014 images and 5 hand-written sentences describing each image. We use the same splits as Karpathy and Li (2015) for training and development; the dataset sizes are shown in Table 1. During training, the model is presented with 32 sentences and their corresponding images in each batch, making sure all the images within a batch are unique. The loss function from Section 2.3 is then minimised to maximise the predicted scores for the 32 relevant pairs, and minimise the scores for the $32 * 32 - 32 = 992$ random combinations.

Theano (Bergstra et al., 2010) was used to implement the neural network model. The texts were tokenised and lowercased, and sentences were padded with special markers for start and end positions. The vocabulary includes all words that appeared in the training set at least twice, plus an extra token for any unseen words. Words were represented with 300-dimensional embeddings and initialised with the publicly available vectors trained with CBOW (Mikolov et al., 2013). All other parameters were initialised with random values from a normal distribution with mean 0 and standard deviation 0.1.

	ACC	AP	P@50
Random	50.0	50.0	50.0
LSTM-COS	68.2	71.6	81.0
+ gating	69.6	74.6	84.4
+ cross-ent	71.1	79.0	**92.2**
+ dropout	**75.4**	**81.9**	89.8

Table 3: Results on the dataset of short answers written by language learners in response to visual prompts. Reporting accuracy, average precision, and precision at rank 50.

We trained for 300 epochs, measuring performance on the development set after every full pass over the data, and used the best model for evaluating on the test set. The parameters were optimised using gradient descent with the initial learning rate at 0.001 and the ADAM algorithm (Kingma and Ba, 2015) for dynamically adapting the learning rate during training. Dropout was applied to both word embeddings and image vectors with $p = 0.5$. In order to avoid any outlier results due to randomness in the model, which affects both the random initialisation and the sampling of negative image examples, we trained each configuration with 10 different random seeds and present here the averaged results.

4   Experiments

We evaluate the visual relevance detection model by training on Flickr30k and testing on the dataset of learner responses to visual prompts. In order to handle multiple sentences in the written responses, every sentence is first scored individually and the scores are then averaged over all the sentences. For every textual answer in the dataset, we create a negative datapoint by pairing it with a random image. The task is then to accurately detect whether the pair is truly relevant or randomly created, by assigning it high or low relevance scores. In order to convert the model output to a binary classification, we employ leave-one-out optimisation – one example at a time is used for testing, while the others are used to calculate the optimal threshold for accuracy. We also report average precision and precision at detecting irrelevant answers in the top 50 returned instances, which measure the quality of the ranking and do not require a fixed threshold.

Results for the different system architectures

0.65	In this picture there are lot of people and each one has a different attitude.
0.81	In the foreground, people are waiting for the green light in order to cross the street.
-2.75	While a child is talking with an adult about something that is on the other side of the road, instead a women, with lots of bag in her left hand, is chatting with her mobile telephone.
0.63	Generally speaking, the picture is full of bright colours and it conveys the idea of crowded city.
-2.38	Looking at this pictures reminds me of the time I went scuba diving in the sea.
-2.16	It's fascinating, because you are surrounded by water and fishes and everything seems so coulorful and adventurous.
-1.40	Another good part of diving is coming up.
-1.70	You swim to the surface and you see the sunlight coming nearer and nearer until you get out and can breathe "real" air again.

Table 2: Predicted scores from the best relevance scoring model, given example sentences from the learner dataset and the included photo as a prompt. The first 4 sentences were written in response to this image, whereas the last 4 were written about a different photo.

can be seen in Table 3. The baseline LSTM-COS system is based on the framework by Kiros et al. (2014) – it uses an LSTM for composing a sentence into a vector, calculates the relevance score by finding the cosine similarity between the sentence vector and the image vector, and optimises the model using the hinge loss function. This model already performs relatively well and is able to distinguish between relevant and random image-text pairs with 68.2% accuracy.

On top of this model we incrementally add 3 modifications and measure their impact on the performance. First, we augment the model with the gating architecture described in Section 2.2. The vector representation of the text is used to calculate a dynamic mask, which is then applied to the image vector. This allows the model to first read the sentence, and then decide which parts of the image are more important for the similarity calculation. The inclusion of the gating component improves accuracy by 1.4% and average precision by 3%.

Next, we change the scoring and optimisation functions as described in Section 2.3. Cosine similarity measure is substituted with a dot product between the vectors, removing useful bounds on the score, but allowing more flexibility in the model. In addition, the hinge loss function is exchanged for calculating the negative cross-entropy over a softmax. While the hinge loss performs only pairwise comparisons and applies a sharp cut-off, softmax ties all the examples into a probability distribution and provides a more gradual prioritisa-

| | DEV | | TEST | |
	ACC	POS	NEG	ACC
Random	16.7	0.5	0.5	16.7
LSTM-COS	70.8	0.7	0.0	72.6
+ gating	75.6	0.5	-0.6	76.5
+ cross-ent	82.8	5.8	-5.2	83.8
+ dropout	**87.0**	5.6	-3.7	**87.4**

Table 4: Results for different system configurations on the Flickr30k development and test sets. We report accuracy and the average predicted scores for positive and negative examples.

tion for the parameter optimisation. By introducing these changes, the accuracy is again increased by 1.5% and average precision by 4.4%.

Finally, we apply dropout with probability 0.5 to both the 300-dimensional word embeddings in the input sentence and the 1024-dimensional image representation produced by the BVLC GoogLeNet. By randomly setting half of the values to 0 during training, additional variance is introduced to the available data and the model is becomes more robust for handling noisy learner-generated text. Integrating dropout improves the performance further by 4.3% and average precision by 2.9%.

Table 2 contains examples of the predicted scores from the final model, given example sentences written by language learners. For most sentences, the model successfully distinguishes between relevant and irrelevant topics, assigning

Figure 2: Relevance scores for two example sentences, using the best model from Section 4. Higher values indicate higher confidence in the text being relevant to the image.

lower scores to the last 4 sentences that describe a different image. However, the model also makes a mistake and incorrectly assigns a low score to the third sentence – this likely happens due to the sentence being much longer and more convoluted than most examples in the training data, leading the LSTM to lose some important information in the sentence representation.

For comparison, we also evaluate the system architectures on the Flickr30k dataset in Table 4. In this setting, we present the model with a sentence and 6 images from the Flickr30k test set, one of which is known to be relevant while the others are selected randomly. Accuracy is then measured as the proportion of test cases where the model chooses the correct image as the most relevant one. A random baseline has a 1 in 6 chance of finding the correct image for an input sentence, as there are 5 negative examples for every positive example. We also report the average scores assigned by the models to positive (relevant) and negative (not relevant) pairs of images and sentences. As can be seen by the averaged predicted scores in Table 4, the final system is free to push positive and negative examples apart by a larger margin, increasing the average score difference by an order of magnitude.

5 Analysis

Figure 2 contains predicted scores for different images, given example sentences as input. As can be seen, the system returns high scores when the sentences are paired with very relevant images, and also offers an intuitive grading of relevance. For the first sentence describing an orange shirt and a bicycle, the model has assigned reasonably high scores to other images containing bikes and orange objects. Similarly, for the second sentence the system has found alternative images containing dogs and wooden floors.

In order to analyse the possible weaknesses of the model, we manually examined cases that are difficult for the system. Figure 3 contains 4 examples from the Flickr30k development set where a valid image-description pair received a negative score from the relevance model. While a negative score does not necessarily mean an error, as that depends on the chosen threshold, it indicates that the model has low confidence in this being a correct pairing. The use of rare terms is a source of confusion for the model – if a word was not used in the training data sufficiently, it will make the relevance calculation more difficult. For example, "unicycle" and "fire lit batons" are relatively rare terms that can cause confusion in example A. In addition, the description mentions only the man, while most of the photo depicts a crowd and a building.

An alternative source of confusion comes from the visual component, with GoogLeNet having more trouble with certain images. Out of 5,070 image-sentence pairs in the development data, the best model assigned negative scores to 222. Out of those, only 140 had a unique image, indicating that the visual component has more trouble detecting the content of certain unusual images, such as examples C and D, regardless of the textual composition. Both of these issues represent cases where the model is faced with input that is substantially different from the training examples, and therefore

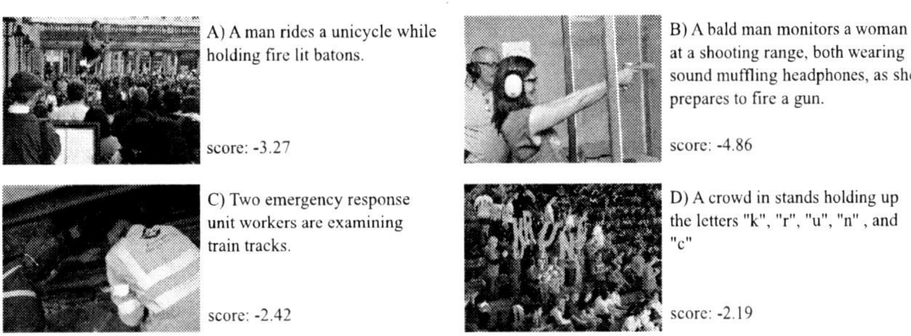

Figure 3: Example valid pairs of images and sentences from the Flickr30k development set where the system incorrectly predicts a low relevance score.

Figure 4: Visualisation of the 1,024 visual gating weights for two example sentences. Lighter areas indicate features where the model chooses to discard the visual information.

fails to perform as well as possible. This can be remedied by either creating models that are able to generalise better to unseen examples, or by expanding the sources of available training data.

We also analysed the gating component, which is conditioned on the text vector and applied to the image vector. The calculation of the gating weights includes a bias term and a logistic function, which means it could easily adapt to always predicting a vector of 1-s, effectively leaving the image vector unmodified. Instead, we found that the model actively makes use of this additional architecture, choosing to switch off many features in the image vector. Figure 4 shows a visualisation of the 1024 gating weights for the two example sentences used in Figure 2. Values close to 0 are represented by white, and values close to 1 are shown in blue. As can be seen, quite a few features receive weights close to zero, therefore effectively being turned off. In addition, the two sentences have fairly different gating signatures, demonstrating that weights are being calculated dynamically based on the input sentence.

6 Conclusion

We presented a system for mapping images and sentences into a shared distributed vector space and evaluating their semantic similarity. The task is motivated by applications in automated language assessment, where scoring systems focusing on grammaticality are otherwise vulnerable to memorised off-topic answers.

The model starts by learning embeddings for words in the input sentence, then composing them to a vector representation using an LSTM. In parallel, the image is first passed through a pre-trained image detection model to extract visual features, and then a further supervised layer to transform the representation to a suitable space. We found that applying dropout on both word embeddings and visual features allowed the model to generalise better, providing consistent improvements in accuracy.

Next, we introduced a novel gating component which first reads the input sentence and then decides which visual features from the image pipeline are important for that specific sentence. We found that the model actively makes use of this component, predicting different gating patterns depending on the input sentence, and substantially improves the overall performance in the evaluations. Finally, we moved from a pairwise hinge loss to optimising a probability distribution over the possible candidates, and found that this further improved relevance accuracy.

The experiments were performed on two different datasets – a collection of short answers written by language learners in response to visual prompts, and an image captioning dataset which pairs single sentences to photos. The relevance assessment model was able to distinguish unsuitable image-sentence pairs on both datasets, and the model modifications showed consistent improvements on both tasks. We conclude that automated relevance detection of short textual answers to visual prompts can be performed by mapping images and sentences into the same distributed vector space, and it is a potentially useful addition for preventing off-topic responses in automated assessment systems.

References

Dimitrios Alikaniotis, Helen Yannakoudakis, and Marek Rei. 2016. Automatic Text Scoring Using Neural Networks. *Proceedings of the 54th Annual Meeting of the Association for Computational Linguistics* .

James Bergstra, Olivier Breuleux, Frederic Frédéric Bastien, Pascal Lamblin, Razvan Pascanu, Guillaume Desjardins, Joseph Turian, David Warde-Farley, and Yoshua Bengio. 2010. Theano: a CPU and GPU math compiler in Python. *Proceedings of the Python for Scientific Computing Conference (SciPy)* http://www-etud.iro.umontreal.ca/ wardefar/publications/theano_scipy2010.pdf.

Ted Briscoe, Ben Medlock, and Øistein Andersen. 2010. Automated Assessment of ESOL Free Text Examinations. Technical report.

Danqi Chen, Jason Bolton, and Christopher D. Manning. 2016. A Thorough Examination of the CNN / Daily Mail Reading Comprehension Task. In *Proceedings of the 54th Annual Meeting of the Association for Computational Linguistics*.

Ronan Cummins, Helen Yannakoudakis, and Ted Briscoe. 2015. Unsupervised Modeling of Topical Relevance in L2 Learner Text. In *In Proceedings of the 11th Workshop on Innovative Use of NLP for Building Educational Applications*.

Jia Deng, Wei Dong, Richard Socher, Li-Jia Li, Kai Li, and Li Fei-Fei. 2009. ImageNet: A large-scale hierarchical image database. *2009 IEEE Conference on Computer Vision and Pattern Recognition* https://doi.org/10.1109/CVPR.2009.5206848.

Andrea Frome, Greg S. Corrado, Jonathon Shlens, Samy Bengio, Jeffrey Dean, Marc' Aurelio Ranzato, and Tomas Mikolov. 2013. Devise: A deep visual-semantic embedding model. *Advances in neural information processing systems* http://papers.nips.cc/paper/5204-devise-a-deep-visual-semantic-embedding-model.

Derrick Higgins, Jill Burstein, and Yigal Attali. 2006. Identifying Off-topic Student Essays Without Topic-specific Training Data. *Natural Language Engineering* 12. https://doi.org/10.1017/S1351324906004189.

Sepp Hochreiter and Jürgen Schmidhuber. 1997. Long Short-term Memory. *Neural Computation* 9. https://doi.org/10.1.1.56.7752.

Youmna Hussein, Marek Rei, and Ted Briscoe. 2017. An Error-Oriented Approach to Word Embedding Pre-Training. In *Proceedings of the 12th Workshop on Innovative Use of NLP for Building Educational Applications*.

Yangqing Jia, Evan Shelhamer, Jeff Donahue, Sergey Karayev, Jonathan Long, Ross Girshick, Sergio Guadarrama, and Trevor Darrell. 2014. Caffe: Convolutional Architecture for Fast Feature Embedding. In *ACM International Conference on Multimedia*. https://doi.org/10.1145/2647868.2654889.

Nal Kalchbrenner, Ivo Danihelka, and Alex Graves. 2015. Grid Long Short-Term Memory. *arXiv preprint arXiv:1507.01526* http://arxiv.org/abs/1507.01526.

Andrej Karpathy and Fei Fei Li. 2015. Deep visual-semantic alignments for generating image descriptions. *Proceedings of the IEEE Computer Society Conference on Computer Vision and Pattern Recognition* https://doi.org/10.1109/CVPR.2015.7298932.

Yoon Kim, Yacine Jernite, David Sontag, and Alexander M. Rush. 2016. Character-Aware Neural Language Models. *In Proceedings of the 30th AAAI Conference on Artificial Intelligence (AAAI'16)* http://arxiv.org/abs/1508.06615.

Levi King and Markus Dickinson. 2016. Shallow Semantic Reasoning from an Incomplete Gold Standard for Learner Language. In *Proceedings of the 11th Workshop on Innovative Use of NLP for Building Educational Applications*.

Diederik P. Kingma and Jimmy Lei Ba. 2015. Adam: a Method for Stochastic Optimization. In *International Conference on Learning Representations*.

Ryan Kiros, Ruslan Salakhutdinov, and Richard S Zemel. 2014. Unifying Visual-Semantic Embeddings with Multimodal Neural Language Models. *arXiv preprint arXiv:1411.2539* http://arxiv.org/abs/1411.2539v1.

Benjamin Klein, Guy Lev, Gil Sadeh, and Lior Wolf. 2015. Associating neural word embeddings with deep image representations using Fisher Vectors. *Proceedings of the IEEE Computer Society Conference on Computer Vision and Pattern Recognition* pages 4437–4446. https://doi.org/10.1109/CVPR.2015.7299073.

Lin Ma, Zhengdong Lu, Lifeng Shang, and Hang Li. 2015. Multimodal convolutional neural networks for matching image and sentence. In *Proceedings of the IEEE International Conference on Computer Vision*. pages 2623–2631. https://doi.org/10.1109/ICCV.2015.301.

Tomáš Mikolov, Kai Chen, Greg Corrado, and Jeffrey Dean. 2013. Efficient Estimation of Word Representations in Vector Space. In *Proceedings of the International Conference on Learning Representations (ICLR 2013)*. https://doi.org/10.1162/153244303322533223.

Hwee Tou Ng, Siew Mei Wu, Ted Briscoe, Christian Hadiwinoto, Raymond Hendy Susanto, and Christopher Bryant. 2014. The CoNLL-2014 Shared Task on Grammatical Error Correction. In *Proceedings of the Eighteenth Conference on Computational Natural Language Learning: Shared Task*. http://www.aclweb.org/anthology/W/W14/W14-1701.

Isaac Persing and Vincent Ng. 2014. Modeling prompt adherence in student essays. In *52nd Annual Meeting of the Association for Computational Linguistics (ACL 2014)*.

Marek Rei, Gamal K. O. Crichton, and Sampo Pyysalo. 2016. Attending to Characters in Neural Sequence Labeling Models. In *Proceedings of the 26th International Conference on Computational Linguistics (COLING-2016)*. http://arxiv.org/abs/1611.04361.

Marek Rei and Ronan Cummins. 2016. Sentence Similarity Measures for Fine-Grained Estimation of Topical Relevance in Learner Essays. In *Proceedings of the 11th Workshop on Innovative Use of NLP for Building Educational Applications (BEA)*. http://ir.dcs.gla.ac.uk/ ronanc/papers/reiBEA2016.pdf.

Tim Rocktäschel, Edward Grefenstette, Karl Moritz Hermann, and Phil Blunsom. 2016. Reasoning about Entailment with Neural Attention. *International Conference on Learning Representations* .

Keisuke Sakaguchi, Michael Heilman, and Nitin Madnani. 2015. Effective Feature Integration for Automated Short Answer Scoring. *HLT-NAACL 2015 - Human Language Technology Conference of the North American Chapter of the Association of Computational Linguistics, Proceedings of the Main Conference* http://www.scopus.com/inward/record.url?eid=2-s2.0-84960119751&partnerID=tZOtx3y1.

Swapna Somasundaran, Chong Min Lee, Martin Chodorow, and Xinhao Wang. 2015. Automated Scoring of Picture-based Story Narration. *Proceedings of the Tenth Workshop on Innovative Use of NLP for Building Educational Applications* .

Nitish Srivastava, Geoffrey E. Hinton, Alex Krizhevsky, Ilya Sutskever, and Ruslan Salakhutdinov. 2014. Dropout : A Simple Way to Prevent Neural Networks from Overfitting. *Journal of Machine Learning Research (JMLR)* 15. https://doi.org/10.1214/12-AOS1000.

Christian Szegedy, Wei Liu, Yangqing Jia, Pierre Sermanet, Scott Reed, Dragomir Anguelov, Dumitru Erhan, Vincent Vanhoucke, and Andrew Rabinovich. 2015. Going deeper with convolutions.

Computer Vision and Pattern Recognition (CVPR) https://doi.org/10.1109/CVPR.2015.7298594.

Kai Sheng Tai, Richard Socher, and Christopher D. Manning. 2015. Improved Semantic Representations From Tree-Structured Long Short-Term Memory Networks. *Proceedings of the 53rd Annual Meeting of the Association for Computational Linguistics and the 7th International Joint Conference on Natural Language Processing* .

John Wieting, Mohit Bansal, Kevin Gimpel, and Karen Livescu. 2016. Charagram: Embedding Words and Sentences via Character n-grams. In *Proceedings of the 2016 Conference on Empirical Methods in Natural Language Processing*. http://arxiv.org/abs/1607.02789.

Helen Yannakoudakis, Ted Briscoe, and Ben Medlock. 2011. A New Dataset and Method for Automatically Grading ESOL Texts. In *Proceedings of the 49th Annual Meeting of the Association for Computational Linguistics: Human Language Technologies*. http://www.aclweb.org/anthology/P11-1019.

Peter Young, Alice Lai, Micah Hodosh, and Julia Hockenmaier. 2014. From image descriptions to visual denotations: New similarity metrics for semantic inference over event descriptions. In *Transactions of the Association for Computational Linguistics*. http://web.engr.illinois.edu/ aylai2/publications/TACL2014DenotationGraph.pdf.

Xiang Zhang, Junbo Zhao, and Yann LeCun. 2015. Character-level Convolutional Networks for Text Classification. In *Advances in Neural Information Processing Systems*. http://arxiv.org/abs/1509.01626#.

Combining Textual and Speech Features in the NLI Task Using State-of-the-Art Machine Learning Techniques

Pavel Ircing, Jan Švec, Zbyněk Zajíc
University of West Bohemia
Univerzitní 8
306 14 Plzeň
Czech Republic
{ircing, honzas, zzajic}@kky.zcu.cz

Barbora Hladká, Martin Holub
Charles University
Malostranské nám. 25
118 00 Prague 1
Czech Republic
{hladka, holub}@ufal.mff.cuni.cz

Abstract

We summarize the involvement of our CEMI team in the "NLI Shared Task 2017", which deals with both textual and speech input data. We submitted the results achieved by using three different system architectures; each of them combines multiple supervised learning models trained on various feature sets. As expected, better results are achieved with the systems that use both the textual data and the spoken responses. Combining the input data of two different modalities led to a rather dramatic improvement in classification performance. Our best performing method is based on a set of feed-forward neural networks whose hidden-layer outputs are combined together using a softmax layer. We achieved a macro-averaged F1 score of 0.9257 on the evaluation (unseen) test set and our team placed first in the main task together with other three teams.

1 Native Language Identification

We think of learning a second language L2 by people with their native language L1. The Native Language Identification (NLI) task is to recognize the L1 of an L2 author's text or speech. Most work in the NLI field has focused on identifying the native language of students learning English as a second language, which is also reflected in the very first experiments with written responses and spoken responses, see (Koppel et al., 2005) and (Schuller et al., 2016), respectively.

With respect to the form of analyzed responses, written ones and spoken ones, we distinguish between text-based NLI and speech-based NLI, respectively. In text-based NLI, all experiments performed so far are based on searching patterns in texts that are common to groups of speakers of the same L1. This idea naturally arises from general awareness that L1 speakers use typical grammatical constructions or make typical mistakes when using L2.

Speech-based NLI is naturally being approached differently, mainly by analyzing the acoustic properties of a speech utterance by the acoustic signal processing methods. Very recently (Schuller et al., 2016) organized the *Native Language Sub-Challenge* with spoken responses.

While most NLI research has focused on English as L2, there is also a growing trend to apply the techniques to other L2 languages, e.g. Norwegian (Malmasi et al., 2015a), Chinese (Malmasi and Dras, 2014a), Finnish (Malmasi and Dras, 2014b).

NLI has a wide variety of potential applications and both its techniques and findings can be used in areas such as Second-Language Acquisition (Ortega, 2009), author profiling (Rangel et al., 2013), and authorship contribution (Halvani et al., 2016). Typically, NLI is employed as a starting point for investigations into crosslinguistic influence, see e.g. (Jarvis and Paquot, 2012).

In this paper, we summarize the involvement of the CEMI team in the NLI Shared Task 2017 co-located with the *12th Workshop on Innovative Use of NLP for Building Educational Applications* held in September 2017 in Copenhagen, Denmark. The NLI task is typically framed as a classification problem where the set of L1s is known a priori. The NLI Shared Task 2017 deals with 11 output classes $C = \{$ARA, CHI, FRE, GER, HIN, ITA, JPN, KOR, SPA, TEL, TUR$\}$,[1] and defines three sub-tasks that differ in data sources available:

---

[1]The classes correspond to 11 different L1 languages, namely Arabic, Chinese, French, German, Hindi, Italian, Japanese, Korean, Spanish, Telugu, and Turkish, respectively.

Proceedings of the 12th Workshop on Innovative Use of NLP for Building Educational Applications, pages 198–209
Copenhagen, Denmark, September 8, 2017. ©2017 Association for Computational Linguistics

	ICLEv2	**Lang-8**	**TOEFL11**
	Granger et al. (2009)	Mizumoto et al. (2011)	Blanchard et al. (2013)
number of documents	6,085	154,702	12,100
average document length	617	150	348
number of L1s	16	65	11
number of topics	variation	variation	8
proficiency level	inter, high	variation	low, inter, high

Table 1: Some of the NLI English textual datasets.

- ESSAY *Task* – the L1 identification is based solely on the written essays
- SPEECH *Task* – the L1 identification is based on the speech utterances (their transcripts and/or extracted i-vectors capturing the acoustic properties of the recorded speech)
- *(Main)* FUSION *Task* – the NLI system is allowed to use both sources listed above

We participated in each track and used only the available labelled data. The data collection consists of 13,200 English essays (written texts) and spoken responses (written transcriptions and pre-processed i-vectors) and its pairwise disjoint subsets of 11,000 training examples, 1,100 development test examples, and 1,100 evaluation test examples. Both training and development test sets were provided to the shared task participants, while the evaluation test set was the unseen data portion kept only for the final evaluation performed by the organizers. The i-vectors are computed from 45-second audio files corresponding to orthographic transcriptions. The results of the NLI Shared Task 2017 are reported in Malmasi et al. (2017).

In the rest of this paper, we first review related works in Section 2. Other works on feature engineering inspired us to choose features for our experiments. More details about the features we used are provided in Section 3. Our approach focuses mainly on different machine learning algorithms explained in Section 4. We design a two-step procedure consisting of training stand-alone classifiers (see Section 4.1), and training additional parameters of fused models (see Section 4.2). In total, we submitted three different system architectures described in Section 4.3. In Section 5 we present and discuss our results, and in the last Section 6 we make some final comments.

2 Related work

Text-based NLI has been addressed since 2005 and speech-based NLI since 2016. We give a picture of which results have been produced since the very beginning to date. Given the scope of the NLI Shared Task 2017, we focus on studies having English as a second language.

2.1 Text-based NLI

An exhaustive overview of NLI until 2014 has been provided by Massung and Zhai (2016). In Table 1 we show the basic characteristics of the datasets widely used so far. Now we mention only some works with respect to three milestones.

The very beginning Koppel et al. (2005) implemented a fully automated method to address text-based NLI for the first time ever. They experimented with the sub-part of the ICLEv2 corpus containing only five L1s.[2] Their feature set included relative frequencies of function words, character n-grams, error types and rare POS bi-grams so that each document was represented as a vector of 1,035 features. Their SVM-based method achieved just above 80% accuracy.

Seven years later There were three papers alone on text-based NLI at the COLING 2012 conference: Brooke and Hirst (2012) developed a robust model that works with 79.3% accuracy when used across the ICLEv2 and Lang-8 corpora. They extracted a set of 800,000 features,[3] which was extremely large in comparison to the set used by Koppel et al. (2005). They also discuss the inadequacy of ICLEv2 as a training corpus and recommended to pay more attention to the overall validity of NLI experiments, rather than to

---

[2]Bulgarian, Czech, French, Russian, Spanish

[3]Function words, character {1-3}-grams, word {1-2}-grams, POS {1-3}-grams, context-free grammar production rules, dependencies, proper nouns.

specific technical approaches. Bykh and Meurers (2012) experimented with ICLEv2 as well but their seven target classes were different from those used in (Brooke and Hirst, 2012). They explored recurring word and POS n-grams and they achieved 89.71% accuracy that was later surpassed by Tetreault et al. (2012) who used (Koppel et al., 2005)'s feature set enriched with the Tree Substitution Grammar features (Swanson and Charniak, 2012), the Stanford dependency features (de Marneffe et al., 2006) and language model perplexity scores to achieve an accuracy of 90.1%.

The TOEFL11 corpus available The First Native Language Identification Shared Task in 2013 (Tetreault et al., 2013) marks an important stage in the text-based NLI research mainly because of making available the TOEFL11 corpus. This corpus consists of essays on eight different topics written by non-native speakers of three proficiency levels (low/medium/high); the essays' authors have 11 different native languages listed in Section 1. The corpus contains 1,100 essays per language with an average of 348 word tokens per essay. A corpus description and the motivation to build such corpus can be found in (Blanchard et al., 2013). The report by Tetreault et al. (2013) summarizes the techniques used and the results achieved by the competing teams in the shared task.

TOEFL11 has become a common evaluation resource for the text-based NLI task. Nicolai et al. (2013) used a subset of the corpus with only five L1s to train probabilistic graphical models.[4] Bykh and Meurers (2014) systematically explored non-lexicalized and lexicalized context-free grammar production rules. They combined them with word-based and POS-based n-grams and they achieved accuracy of 84.8%, the best result reported by that time. Later on, Ionescu et al. (2014) obtained a new state-of-the-art result, 85.3% accuracy, so that they combined several string kernels using multiple kernel learning to do feature selection. Their method is completely language independent, and texts are treated as a sequence of characters.

Kříž et al. (2015) measure similarity between general English and English used by L1 speakers using cross-entropy scores, which then serve as features for an SVM classifier. It requires 12 language models of English – one model of general

---

System	# features	Acc.
1 (Malmasi and Dras, 2017)	?	85.3
2 (Bykh and Meurers, 2016)	?	85.4*
3 (Gebre et al., 2013)	73,626	84.6
4 (Jarvis et al., 2013)	400K	84.5
5 (Ionescu et al., 2014)	?	84.1
...	...	...
(Kříž et al., 2015)	55	82.4

Table 2: Top 5 written NLI systems on TOEFL11, and for comparison the system with the lowest number of (entropy-based) features. A 10-fold cross-validation accuracy is provided (Acc. in %). *The authors report the 85.4% accuracy on the evaluation test set.

English based on Wikipedia data and eleven special models, each based on a particular L1 group. The best classification accuracy of 82.4% has been achieved by a combination of language models built upon four different n-gram types — tokens, characters, suffixes, and POS tags. These 44 (= 4x11) cross-entropy scores completed with other nine numerical and two categorical features result in the final set of 55 features. In fact, this compact feature set comprises a big amount of statistical information about a huge number of n-grams hidden in the language models consisting of smoothed linear n-grams combinations.

In contrast, (Malmasi and Cahill, 2015) extracted a much bigger feature set and they focused on measuring association between two feature sets through classification errors.

The very last work on text-based NLI focuses on systematic examination of ensemble methods for addressing NLI with three L2s, namely English, Norwegian, and Jinan Chinese (Malmasi and Dras, 2017).

Table 2 presents the top 5 text-based NLI systems on TOEFL11. We also provide the same figures for the system (Kříž et al., 2015) with an extremely low number of features. Here is a brief description of the algorithms and the features used:

- (Malmasi and Dras, 2017) – ensemble classifier, bagging, linear discriminant analysis; n-grams of lemmas, words, function words, POS tags, dependencies, CFG rules, Adaptor Grammar, TSG fragments

- (Bykh and Meurers, 2016) – ensemble classifier; n-grams of lemmas, words, POS tags

---

[4]Chinese, French, German, Japanese, and Turkish.

where $1 \leq n \leq 10$, dependencies, suffixes, verb subcategorization patterns

- (Gebre et al., 2013) – SVM; tf-idf of word unigrams and bigrams, df $\geq$ 5, normalized feature vectors

- (Jarvis et al., 2013) – SVM; $\{1,2,3\}$-grams of words, lemmas, POS tags, df $\geq$ 2, normalized feature vectors

- (Ionescu et al., 2014) – Kernel-based learning; character $\{5\text{-}8\}$-grams

- (Kríž et al., 2015) – SVM; entropy-based features using language modeling (tokens, characters, POS, suffixes)

Malmasi et al. (2016) analyze the results of the *Discriminating between Similar Languages* shared task and they state that numerous teams attempted to use new deep learning-based approaches, and that most of them ended with a poor performance compared to traditional classifiers. To the best of our knowledge, there has been no published paper on using deep learning in text-based NLI yet. We can only speculate that researchers have already applied deep learning techniques to text-based NLI but they did not beat traditional classifiers.

2.2 Speech-based NLI

The speech-based NLI shared task was organized under the name *Native Language Sub challenge* as one of the subtasks of the IN-TERSPEECH 2016 Computational Paralinguistics Challenge (Schuller et al., 2016).

The ETS Corpus of Non-native Spoken English was provided for the task consisting of 5,132 examples in total – 3,300 examples were selected for training, 965 examples for the development test set, and 867 examples for the evaluation test set. The corpus includes spoken responses from non-native speakers of English drawn from 11 different L1 backgrounds that are identical to the TOEFL11 L1s. The recorded utterances are 45-second long for each speaker. The participants were provided with the audio files (amplitude normalized) and were also pointed to the toolkit that was used to extract the audio features for the baseline system provided by the sub-challenge organizers. It is obvious that the extracted features did not reflect only the actual content of the utterances but also – and possibly more prominently – the

System	UAR (%)
1 (Abad et al., 2016)	84.6
2 (Shivakumar et al., 2016)	78.6
3 (Gosztolya et al., 2016)	70.7
4 (Huckvale, 2016)	69.8
5 (Senoussaoui et al., 2016)	68.4
6 (Keren et al., 2016)	61.5
7 (Jiao et al., 2016)	52.2
8 (Rajpal et al., 2016)	39.8
baseline	45.1

Table 3: Spoken NLI systems submitted to the 2016 NLI shared task. UAR stands for Unweighted Average Recall.

acoustic properties of the speech that are supposedly and significantly influenced by the speaker's native language. Given the usual background of the INTERSPEECH attendees, it is only natural that most participants of the sub-challenge had a strong background in speech signal processing and (at least the top teams) concentrated on their own sophisticated methods for feature extraction.

According to our knowledge, no transcriptions of the recorded utterances were provided and none of the participants attempted to use an automatic speech recognition system in order to create transcripts that could be used as the source of textual features. Given the poor performance of the system based solely on the (manual) speech transcriptions in the NLI Shared Task 2017, it seems that ignoring the textual content of the utterances was a wise decision.

Table 3 presents the systems submitted to the sub-challenge. Since the top two teams, whose systems outperformed the rest by a large margin, employed the i-vector feature representation, the organizers have decided to provide the i-vectors directly to the NLI Shared Task 2017 participants, supposedly in order to lower the entry threshold for participants without the speech processing background. A short high-level description of the i-vector principles is given in Section 3.

3 Feature extraction

Textual features Since our work concentrates mainly on the different machine learning algorithms (described in detail in the later sections), we did not perform any sophisticated feature engineering. Instead, we picked the textual features that have been proven to be effective in the experiments performed by other researchers previously, being mostly inspired by Gebre et al. (2013). We have employed n-grams of various lengths from the following "data streams":

- Word unigrams, bigrams and trigrams extracted from both essays and speech transcriptions.

- Character n-grams with n ranging from 3 to 5, extracted from the essays only.

- POS n-grams with n ranging from 1 to 5, also extracted only from the essays.

All features were weighted using the well-known *tf-idf* weighting scheme, with the sublinear *tf* scaling and the standard *idf*, that is, the weight w of each feature i in the document j is given by:

$$w_{i,j} = (1 + \log(tf_{i,j})) \cdot \log \frac{N}{n_i} \qquad (1)$$

where N denotes the total number of documents and n_i the number of documents containing the feature i. Then the resulting feature vectors are normalized to unit length. Quick experiments on the development data have shown that:

- Sublinear *tf* scaling substantially outperforms the unscaled *tf*.

- The number of n-gram based-features used in the classification can be reduced to top 30,000 features (ordered by decreasing *tf*) without hurting the performance.[5] The feature vector dimension was thus limited to 30k for all textual features described above.

Speech features   Here we did not have any other choice than using the i-vectors provided by the Shared Task organizers. The i-vectors were originally developed as a representation of speech utterances in a low-dimensional subspace, which efficiently conveys speaker's "vocal" characteristics and is therefore suitable for speaker recognition (Dehak et al., 2011). The i-vectors of course contain also the information about the acoustic environment, transmission channel or phonetic content of the utterance. Intuitively, the phonetic content appears to be an important factor distinguishing

the L1 of the speaker as the native language naturally influences the way the speaker pronounces English phonemes. The i-vectors were extracted from the 45-second audio files by the task organizers, employing a state-of-the-art approach and using the Kaldi[6] toolkit. The dimension of the i-vectors is 800, reduced by factor analysis from supervector of statistics accumulated on the universal background model with 1,024 components.

Several experiments (and the description of the the state-of-the-art NLI in (Malmasi and Dras, 2017)) confirmed our intuition that simply concatenating the individual feature vectors and training a single classifier does not yield the best results. We therefore concentrated mainly on the development of the fused (ensemble) classifiers, described in details in the following section.

Finally, let us point out that we have decided not to use the character and POS n-grams from the speech transcription data in our final systems. The reason is the fact that 1) word n-grams are by far the best performing textual features, yet their performance was rather poor on the speech transcriptions, and 2) any performance gain from character and POS n-grams was clearly overshadowed by the i-vectors contribution in both speech and fusion tasks.

4   Prediction model

We used multiple supervised models to process each type of input features. Then, we fused the predictions of such models, i.e. we combined the *outputs* of the classifiers instead of combining the input features and training one joint model. This approach consists of two steps: (1) training the stand-alone classifiers, and (2) training the additional parameters of the fused model. Optionally, the step (2) could employ additional retraining of the stand-alone classifiers.

4.1   Stand-alone classifiers

The term "stand-alone classifiers" is herein used for the systems whose internal parameters are trained with a standard supervised machine learning algorithm (e.g., gradient descent) and which take the input feature vector and output a vector of $|C|$ probabilities. The decision about the class membership is then determined solely by the index of the maximum value of such output vector.

---

[5]Note that the total number of features would exceed 2.5 million in the case of word trigrams.

[6]http://kaldi-asr.org

Linear models To perform the classification using textual features, we widely used linear models. The training procedure of such model varied – we experimented with a linear SVM and stochastic gradient descent training implemented using the `LinearSVC` and `SGDClassifier` classes from the *scikit-learn* toolkit (Pedregosa et al., 2011). Both implementations support sparse feature representation and therefore in our experiments the full feature vector could be used.

Non-linear models We also used non-linear models implemented as feed-forward neural networks (FFNN) containing hidden layers with non-linear functions. In our experiments we also tried the very deep architectures such as ResNets and DenseNets, but they were outperformed by a relatively simple FFNN with one hidden layer. This is probably caused by a relatively low number of training examples and a high number of parameters of deeper networks. The FFNNs were used to classify both textual and speech-related features. The size of the textual feature vectors was reduced to 30k as explained in Section 3. The FFNNs were implemented in the *Keras* system (Chollet et al., 2015). To optimize the FFNNs, we used the ADAM algorithm (Kingma, 2015) with a categorical cross-entropy loss.

Probabilistic Linear Discriminant Analysis (PLDA) is a state-of-the-art system for i-vector based speaker verification (Kenny, 2005) and can by easily used for representation of another information, the L1 in our case. I-vectors also contain some noisy information not relevant to the L1 identity (e.g. influence of the channel, speaker etc.). If structured training data (more than one session for each L1) are available, PLDA can be trained to model L1 and session variability separately. Then, only the L1 domain is used for identification. Moreover, the PLDA model itself can be used as a powerful tool for compute the similarity between two i-vectors (only in L1 domain). In our case, the test i-vector is compared to $|C|$ L1 i-vectors representing the models of particular L1 languages. The similarities are normalized to sum up to one. The L1 i-vector is computed as the mean of all i-vectors belonging to a given class. The PLDA classifier was used to classify i-vector features in the *ensemble* systems used in the SPEECH and FUSION tasks.

4.2 Model combinations

To combine the outputs of the stand-alone classifiers, we experimented with three different schemas: (1) discriminative logistic regression, (2) softmax combination of hidden layer's outputs, and (3) softmax combination of classifier's outputs. Since the development data set provides an additional valuable source of labelled data, special attention has to be paid to the correct estimation of the fusion parameters, as described below.

Discriminative logistic regression for fusing system's outputs was implemented using an open-source *FoCal Multi-class toolkit* (Brümmer, 2007). This MATLAB toolkit allows evaluation, calibration and fusion of, and decision-making with, multi-class statistical pattern recognition scores. This toolkit is different from, but similar in design principles to the original FoCal Toolkit that was used by several NIST Speaker Recognition Evaluation 2006 participants to fuse and calibrate their scores (Brümmer et al., 2007). For the fusion we used the tool based on calibration and discriminative logistic regression of K classifiers

$$\hat{y}(x) = \sum_{k=1}^{K} \alpha_k y_k(x) + \beta, \qquad (2)$$

where $y_k(x) \in \Re^{|C|}$ is a vector of posterior probabilities obtained from k-classifier, $\hat{y}(x)$ is a vector of fused probabilities and vectors $\alpha \in \Re^K$ and $\beta \in \Re^{|C|}$ are parameters of the fusion. These parameters were first estimated on the held-out data (data not used to train the stand-alone classifiers), then the classifiers were retrained to employ all available labelled data (train and development) and the previously estimated vectors α and β were used.

Softmax combination The softmax combination is implemented as a neural network without hidden layers. The vector of fused probabilities $\hat{y}(x)$ is given by:

$$a(x) = W \cdot \begin{pmatrix} y_1(x) \\ \vdots \\ y_K(x) \end{pmatrix} + b \qquad (3)$$

$$\hat{y}(x) = \mathrm{softmax}(a(x)) \qquad (4)$$

where W is a weight matrix and b is a bias vector. The values of W and b are optimized using

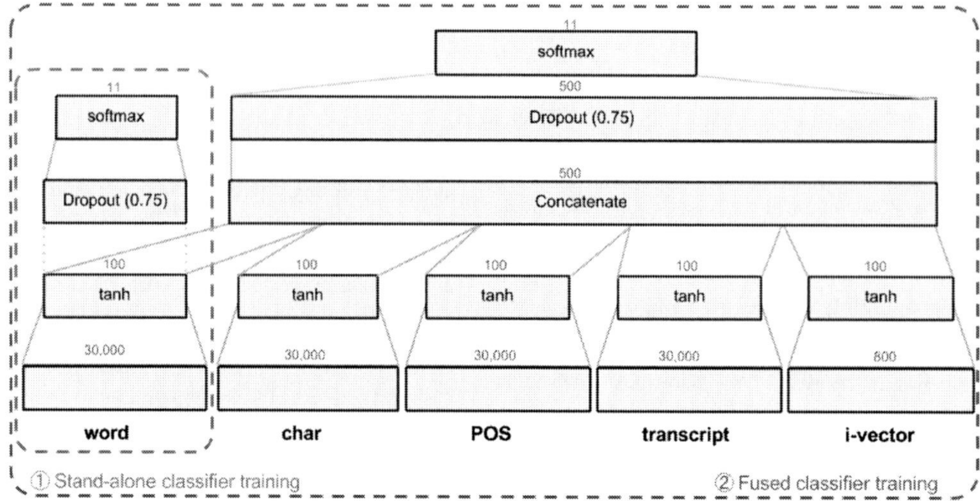

Figure 1: Architecture of the *homogeneous* neural network for the FUSION task.

the ADAM algorithm and the categorical cross-entropy loss. We experimented with two different choices of y_k:

- The output of the hidden layer from the FFNN corresponding to a specific feature set. In this case, we merged the trained stand-alone FFNNs to form a fused FFNN according to Figure 1 and the parameters of the stand-alone FFNNs were trained using the back-propagation errors. The stand-alone FFNNs and the fused FFNN were trained on the union of train and development datasets.

- The $|C|$-dimensional output of the stand-alone classifier. For the linear models the output consists of the values of decision functions, for the FFNN such output is the potential of the output layer before applying the softmax activation. In this case, we first trained the stand-alone classifiers on the train dataset, and then we trained just the fusion parameters W and b on the development dataset.

4.3 Submitted systems

Based on the experiments with the development data set, we finally decided to submit three different system architectures. Each architecture is a combination of multiple systems trained on different features, even in the ESSAY and SPEECH tasks.

- *Classical model ensemble* (*"ensemble"*) consists of different stand-alone models trained

separately and combined using the discriminative logistic regression.

- *Homogeneous FFNN* (*"homogeneous"*) uses a set of stand-alone FFNNs trained separately. The number of hidden layers, number of neurons in hidden layers, and activation functions are identical for each stand-alone FFNN. The outputs of hidden layers in the trained FFNNs are combined using softmax combination. The resulting network is retrained. To avoid overfitting, we used the dropout layer before the softmax layer.

- *Heterogeneous FFNN* (*"heterogeneous"*) employs a set of FFNNs with different architectures. The stand-alone classifiers are trained separately using different objectives. The $|C|$-dimensional outputs are then combined using softmax combination. The resulting network is not retrained during estimating the softmax weights and biases.

For different tasks we used the following different sets of features and classifiers:

ESSAY task – the *ensemble* system used word, char and POS features and FFNN and `SGDClassifier` models for each feature set (= 3×2 stand-alone models). The *homogeneous* system used word, char and POS features and FFNN with 1 hidden layer containing 100 neurons. The *heterogeneous* system used the same features and `SGDClassifier` only.

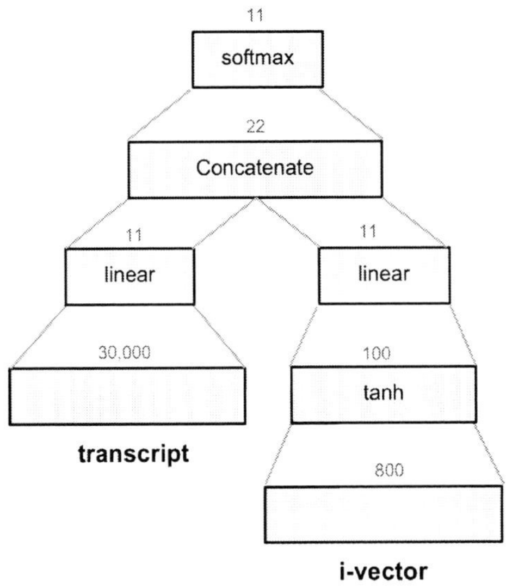

Figure 2: Architecture of the *heterogeneous* neural network for the SPEECH task.

SPEECH task – the *ensemble* system used FFNN classifiers trained on word and char features extracted from transcripts and PLDA and FFNN trained from i-vectors. The *homogeneous* system used word features from transcripts and i-vectors and FFNN (1 hidden layer, 100 neurons). The *heterogeneous* system contained `SGDClassifier` trained from transcript word features and FFNN (1 hidden layer, 100 neurons) trained on i-vectors (see Figure 2).

FUSION task – for each system we used a combination of the stand-alone classifiers used in the ESSAY and SPEECH tasks. An example of such a combination for the *homogeneous* system is given in Figure 1.

5 Results and discussion

The final results of the submitted systems measured on the unseen evaluation test set are shown in Table 4. In this paper, all F1 values are macro-averaged over all 11 output classes. It should be noted that the relatively low number of test examples combined with a higher number of classes resulted in quite wide confidence intervals. For example, we evaluated the F1 measure for the homogeneous system on the FUSION task. Using the development data set and a bootstrapping approach with 550 samples and 1,000 repetitions we found that the resulting average F1 0.9112 has associated a 95 % confidence interval of $<0.8850;$

Task	System	F1
ESSAY	ensemble	**0.8536**
	homogeneous	0.8491
	heterogeneous	0.8464
SPEECH	ensemble	0.8570
	homogeneous	0.7987
	heterogeneous	**0.8607**
FUSION	ensemble	0.9238
	homogeneous	**0.9257**
	heterogeneous	0.9244

Table 4: Summary of the results for each task and our three architectures. The macro-averaged F1 value was measured on the unseen evaluation test set by the shared task organizers.

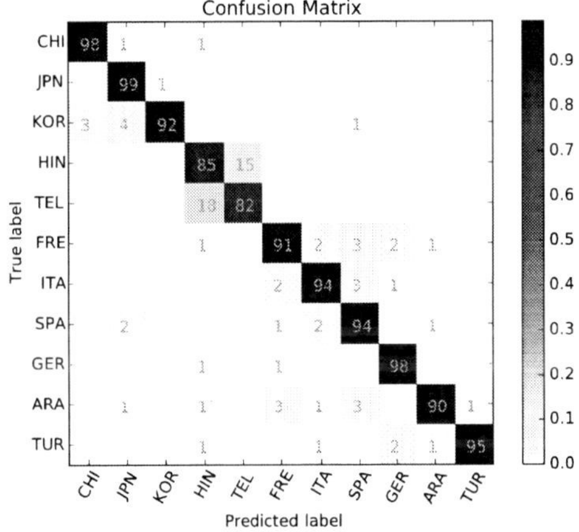

Figure 3: Confusion matrix for the FUSION task, *homogeneous* system. Measured on the unseen evaluation test set.

$0.9345>$ (!). Even the variations caused by the random seed selection are noticeable: for ten different seeds the F1 value varies between 0.9075 and 0.9166. For proper perspective, it is important to keep in mind that the difference of 0.001 in F1 evaluated on test data means that the systems mismatch in approximately 1 correctly classified test example.

Table 4 also shows another interesting fact that the F1 value in the SPEECH task is higher than in the ESSAY task. We assume this is caused by the availability of two modalities – the speech alone (i-vectors) and the lexical information (transcripts). On the development test set, the stand-alone classifier trained solely on i-vectors achieved an F1 value of only 0.8080, while the classifier trained solely on transcribed text features achieved only 0.5787. In this case, the combination of a relatively weak predictor with a strong model further improved the performance to 0.8610. We also observed that training classifiers on the union of the training and development data sets consistently improves performance – the increase in the F1 value (evaluated on the unseen test data) is approximately 0.004. To illustrate the performance on different feature types, we evaluated the stand-alone classifiers of the homogeneous system trained for the FUSION task on the development data. The results are summarized in Table 5.

We also used the Local Interpretable Model-agnostic Explanations (LIME) method (Ribeiro et al., 2016) to extract the most informative features for a given L1 class. The results showed that just the presence of certain words very often leaks significant information about the L1 language (this effect was already observed by (Gebre et al., 2013)) – for example essays labelled as JPN contain words *Japan*, *Japanese*, KOR mention *Korea* and *Korean*. Also, there are some typos that have origin in the L1 language (e.g., ITA: *pubblic* from Italian *pubblico* – 52 examples in the training data, FRE: *exemple* from French *exemple* – 174 examples). The confusion matrix in Figure 3 shows that 40 % of all errors are confusions between the HIN and TEL classes. This is probably caused by the fact that the L1 speakers of these languages have gone through the same educational system of India. In addition, the geographic references mentioned above do not allow to discriminate between them. During the system development, we also experimented with the advanced architectures of neural networks, such as convolutional networks, recurrent networks, ResNets, DenseNets and pretrained word embeddings but none of them performed better than the linear SVM baseline.

6 Conclusion

Malmasi et al. (2015b) previously showed that even NLI systems working with just written essays can outperform human decisions. Our experiments revealed that adding information extracted from the spoken responses of non-native English speakers results into a substantial improvement in

	Features	**F1**
ESSAY	word	0.8151
	char	0.8025
	POS	0.5012
SPEECH	transcript words	0.5591
	i-vectors	0.7962

Table 5: Performance of five stand-alone classifiers used in the homogeneous FUSION system measured on the development test set. The stand-alone classifiers are FFNNs, 1 hidden layer with 100 neurons. In the FUSION model they were further trained by the softmax combination training.

classification performance (about 5 % relative[7]). It corroborates our initial intuition that the textual and spoken data really complement well as the source of information about the L1 language.

To sum up our results measured on the unseen evaluation test set, we attained the following macro-averaged F1 scores:

- ESSAY task: 0.8536
  – shared second place in the task,

- SPEECH task: 0.8607
  – shared first place in the task,

- main FUSION task: 0.9257
  – shared first place in the task.

Let us stress out that those results were achieved by rather straightforward (yet at the same time informed and careful) application of state-of-the-art machine learning algorithms, using feature extraction methods that have already been proven efficient both in previous NLI shared tasks and in our NLP and speech processing research.

7 Acknowledgements

We really appreciate the hard work done by the organizers. They prepared the high-quality data that motivated the participants to work on an interesting project. This research was supported by the Grant Agency of the Czech Republic, projects No. GAČR GBP103/12/G084 and ID 16-10185S, and by the Charles University project No. SVV 260 333.

---

[7]Measured as the relative difference between our best system using both text and speech data and the best system based solely on essays submitted to the NLI Shared Task 2017.

References

Alberto Abad, Eugénio Ribeiro, Fábio Kepler, Ramon Astudillo, and Isabel Trancoso. 2016. Exploiting Phone Log-Likelihood Ratio Features for the Detection of the Native Language of Non-Native English Speakers. In *Interspeech 2016*. pages 2413–2417.

Daniel Blanchard, Joel Tetreault, Derrick Higgins, Aoife Cahill, and Martin Chodorow. 2013. TOEFL11: A Corpus of Non-Native English. *ETS Research Report Series* 2013(2):i–15.

Julian Brooke and Graeme Hirst. 2012. Robust, Lexicalized Native Language Identification. In *Proceedings of COLING 2012*. Mumbai, India, pages 391–408.

Niko Brümmer. 2007. Focal Multi-Class: Toolkit for Evaluation, Fusion and Calibration of Multi-Class Recognition Scores. In *Spescom DataVoice*.

Niko Brümmer, Lukáš Burget, Jan Černocký, Ondřej Glembek, František Grézl, Martin Karafiát, David Leeuwen van, Pavel Matějka, Petr Schwarz, and Albert Strasheim. 2007. Fusion of heterogeneous speaker recognition systems in the stbu submission for the nist speaker recognition evaluation 2006. *IEEE Transactions on Audio, Speech, and Language Processing* 15(7):2072–2084.

Serhiy Bykh and Detmar Meurers. 2012. Native Language Identification using Recurring n-grams – Investigating Abstraction and Domain Dependence. In *Proceedings of COLING 2012*. Mumbai, India, pages 425–440.

Serhiy Bykh and Detmar Meurers. 2014. Exploring Syntactic Features for Native Language Identification: A Variationist Perspective on Feature Encoding and Ensemble Optimization. In *Proceedings of COLING 2014: Technical Papers*. Dublin City University and ACL, Dublin, Ireland, pages 1962–1973.

Serhiy Bykh and Detmar Meurers. 2016. Advancing Linguistic Features and Insights by Label-informed Feature Grouping: An Exploration in the Context of Native Language Identification. In *Proceedings of COLING 2016, the 26th International Conference on Computational Linguistics: Technical Papers*. The COLING 2016 Organizing Committee, Osaka, Japan, pages 739–749.

François Chollet et al. 2015. Keras. `https://github.com/fchollet/keras`.

Marie-Catherine de Marneffe, Bill MacCartney, and Christopher D. Manning. 2006. Generating Typed Dependency Parses from Phrase Structure Parses. In *Proceedings of the Fifth International Conference on Language Resources and Evaluation*. pages 449–454.

Najim Dehak, Patrick J Kenny, Réda Dehak, Pierre Dumouchel, and Pierre Ouellet. 2011. Front-End Factor Analysis for Speaker Verification. *IEEE Transactions on Audio, Speech, and Language Processing* 19(4):788–798.

Binyam Gebrekidan Gebre, Marcos Zampieri, Peter Wittenburg, and Tom Heskes. 2013. Improving Native Language Identification with TF-IDF Weighting. In *Proceedings of the Eighth Workshop on Innovative Use of NLP for Building Educational Applications*. ACL, Atlanta, Georgia, pages 216–223.

Gábor Gosztolya, Tamás Grósz, Róbert Busa-Fekete, and László Tóth. 2016. Determining Native Language and Deception Using Phonetic Features and Classifier Combination. In *Interspeech 2016*. pages 2418–2422.

Sylviane Granger, Estelle Dagneaux, Fanny Meunier, and Magali Paquot. 2009. *International Corpus of Learner English v2 (Handbook + CD-ROM)*. Presses universitaires de Louvain, Louvain-la-Neuve.

Oren Halvani, Christian Winter, and Anika Pflug. 2016. Authorship Verification for Different Languages, Genres and Topics. *Digital Investigation* 16, Supplement:S33 – S43. {DFRWS} 2016 EuropeProceedings of the Third Annual {DFRWS} Europe.

Mark Huckvale. 2016. Within-Speaker Features for Native Language Recognition in the Interspeech 2016 Computational Paralinguistics Challenge. In *Interspeech 2016*. pages 2403–2407.

Radu Tudor Ionescu, Marius Popescu, and Aoife Cahill. 2014. Can Characters Reveal Your Native Language? A Language-Independent Approach to Native Language Identification. In *Proceedings of the 2014 Conference on EMNLP*. ACL, Doha, Qatar, pages 1363–1373.

Scott Jarvis, Yves Bestgen, and Steve Pepper. 2013. Maximizing Classification Accuracy in Native Language Identification. In *Proceedings of the Eighth Workshop on Innovative Use of NLP for Building Educational Applications*. ACL, Atlanta, Georgia, pages 111–118.

Scott Jarvis and Magali Paquot. 2012. Exploring the Role of n-grams in L1 Identification. In Scott Jarvis and Scott A. Crossley, editors, *Approaching Transfer through Text Classification: Explorations in the Detection-based Approach*, Bristol, UK: Multilingual Matters, pages 71—-105.

Yishan Jiao, Ming Tu, Visar Berisha, and Julie Liss. 2016. Accent Identification by Combining Deep Neural Networks and Recurrent Neural Networks Trained on Long and Short Term Features. In *Interspeech 2016*. pages 2388–2392.

Patrick Kenny. 2005. Joint Factor Analysis of Speaker and Session Variability: Theory and Algorithms. Technical report, Centre de Recherche Informatique de Montreal.

Gil Keren, Jun Deng, Jouni Pohjalainen, and Björn Schuller. 2016. Convolutional Neural Networks with Data Augmentation for Classifying Speakers' Native Language. In *Interspeech 2016*. pages 2393–2397.

Diederik P Kingma. 2015. ADAM: A Method for Stochastic Optimization pages 1–15.

Moshe Koppel, Jonathan Schler, and Kfir Zigdon. 2005. Determining an Author's Native Language by Mining a Text for Errors. In *Proceedings of the Eleventh ACM SIGKDD International Conference on Knowledge Discovery in Data Mining*. ACM, New York, NY, USA, KDD '05, pages 624–628.

Vincent Kríž, Martin Holub, and Pavel Pecina. 2015. Feature Extraction for Native Language Identification Using Language Modeling. In Galia Angelova, Kalina Boncheva, and Ruslan Mitkov, editors, *Proceedings of Recent Advances in Natural Language Processing*. Hisarja, Bulgaria, pages 298–306.

Shervin Malmasi and Aoife Cahill. 2015. Measuring Feature Diversity in Native Language Identification. In *Proceedings of the Tenth Workshop on Innovative Use of NLP for Building Educational Applications*. ACL, Denver, Colorado, pages 49–55.

Shervin Malmasi and Mark Dras. 2014a. Chinese Native Language Identification. In *Proceedings of the EACL-14*. ACL, Gothenburg, Sweden, pages 95–99.

Shervin Malmasi and Mark Dras. 2014b. Finnish Native Language Identification. In *Proceedings of the Australasian Language Technology Workshop (ALTA)*. Melbourne, Australia, pages 139–144.

Shervin Malmasi and Mark Dras. 2017. Native Language Identification using Stacked Generalization. *CoRR* abs/1703.06541.

Shervin Malmasi, Mark Dras, and Irina Temnikova. 2015a. Norwegian Native Language Identification. In *Proceedings of RANLP 2015*. ACL, Hissar, Bulgaria, pages 404–412.

Shervin Malmasi, Keelan Evanini, Aoife Cahill, Joel Tetreault, Robert Pugh, Christopher Hamill, Diane Napolitano, and Yao Qian. 2017. A Report on the 2017 Native Language Identification Shared Task. In *Proceedings of the 12th Workshop on Building Educational Applications Using NLP*. Association for Computational Linguistics, Copenhagen, Denmark.

Shervin Malmasi, Joel Tetreault, and Mark Dras. 2015b. Oracle and Human Baselines for Native Language Identification. In *Proceedings of the Tenth Workshop on Innovative Use of NLP for Building Educational Applications*. Association for Computational Linguistics, Denver, Colorado, pages 172–178.

Shervin Malmasi, Marcos Zampieri, Nikola Ljubešić, Preslav Nakov, Ahmed Ali, and Jörg Tiedemann. 2016. Discriminating between Similar Languages and Arabic Dialect Identification: A Report on the Third DSL Shared Task. In *Proceedings of the Third Workshop on NLP for Similar Languages, Varieties and Dialects (VarDial3)*. The COLING 2016 Organizing Committee, Osaka, Japan, pages 1–14.

Sean Massung and ChengXiang Zhai. 2016. Non-Native Text Analysis: A Survey. *Natural Language Engineering* 22(2):163–186.

Tomoya Mizumoto, Mamoru Komachi, and Masaaki Nagata. 2011. Mining Revision Log of Language Learning SNS for Automated Japanese Error Correction of Second Language Learners. In *In Proceedings of the Fifth International Joint Conference on Natural Language Processing*. pages 147–155.

Garrett Nicolai, Md Asadul Islam, and Russ Greiner. 2013. Native Language Identification Using Probabilistic Graphical Models. In *International Conference on Electrical Information and Communication Technology (EICT)*. Khulna, Bangladesh, pages 0–1.

Lourdes Ortega. 2009. *Understanding Second Language Acquisition / Rod Ellis*. Hodder Education, Oxford, UK.

F. Pedregosa, G. Varoquaux, A. Gramfort, V. Michel, B. Thirion, O. Grisel, M. Blondel, P. Prettenhofer, R. Weiss, V. Dubourg, J. Vanderplas, A. Passos, D. Cournapeau, M. Brucher, M. Perrot, and E. Duchesnay. 2011. Scikit-learn: Machine learning in Python. *Journal of Machine Learning Research* 12:2825–2830.

Avni Rajpal, Tanvina B. Patel, Hardik B. Sailor, Maulik C. Madhavi, Hemant A. Patil, and Hiroya Fujisaki. 2016. Native Language Identification Using Spectral and Source-Based Features. In *Interspeech 2016*. pages 2383–2387.

Francisco Rangel, Paolo Rosso, Moshe Moshe Koppel, Efstathios Stamatatos, and Giacomo Inches. 2013. Overview of the Author Profiling Task at PAN 2013. In *CLEF Conference on Multilingual and Multimodal Information Access Evaluation*. CELCT, pages 352–365.

Marco Tulio Ribeiro, Sameer Singh, and Carlos Guestrin. 2016. "Why Should I Trust You?": Explaining the Predictions of Any Classifier. In *Proceedings of the 22Nd ACM SIGKDD International Conference on Knowledge Discovery and Data Mining*. ACM, New York, NY, USA, KDD '16, pages 1135–1144.

Björn Schuller, Stefan Steidl, Anton Batliner, Julia Hirschberg, Judee K. Burgoon, Alice Baird, Aaron Elkins, Yue Zhang, Eduardo Coutinho, and Keelan Evanini. 2016. The INTERSPEECH 2016 Computational Paralinguistics Challenge: Deception, Sincerity and Native Language. In *Interspeech 2016*. pages 2001–2005.

Mohammed Senoussaoui, Patrick Cardinal, Najim Dehak, and Alessandro L. Koerich. 2016. Native Language Detection Using the I-Vector Framework. In *Interspeech 2016*. pages 2398–2402.

Prashanth Gurunath Shivakumar, Sandeep Nallan Chakravarthula, and Panayiotis Georgiou. 2016. Multimodal Fusion of Multirate Acoustic, Prosodic, and Lexical Speaker Characteristics for Native Language Identification. In *Interspeech 2016*. pages 2408–2412.

Ben Swanson and Eugene Charniak. 2012. Native Language Detection with Tree Substitution Grammars. In *Proceedings of the 50th Annual Meeting of the Association for Computational Linguistics: Short Papers - Volume 2*. Association for Computational Linguistics, Stroudsburg, PA, USA, ACL '12, pages 193–197.

Joel Tetreault, Daniel Blanchard, and Aoife Cahill. 2013. A Report on the First Native Language Identification Shared Task. In *Proceedings of the Eighth Workshop on Innovative Use of NLP for Building Educational Applications*. ACL, Atlanta, Georgia, pages 48–57.

Joel Tetreault, Daniel Blanchard, Aoife Cahill, and Martin Chodorow. 2012. Native Tongues, Lost and Found: Resources and Empirical Evaluations in Native Language Identification. In *Proceedings of COLING 2012*. The COLING 2012 Organizing Committee, Mumbai, India, pages 2585–2602.

Native Language Identification
Using a Mixture of Character and Word N-grams

Elham Mohammadi, Hadi Veisi and Hessam Amini
Data and Signal Processing Lab (DSP Lab)
Faculty of New Sciences and Technologies (FNST)
University of Tehran (UT), Tehran, Iran
{elham.mohammadi;h.veisi;hessam.amini}@ut.ac.ir

Abstract

Native language identification (NLI) is the task of determining an author's native language, based on a piece of his/her writing in a second language. In recent years, NLI has received much attention due to its challenging nature and its applications in language pedagogy and forensic linguistics. We participated in the NLI Shared Task 2017 under the name UT-DSP. In our effort to implement a method for native language identification, we made use of a mixture of character and word N-grams, and achieved an optimal F1-score of 0.7748, using both essay and speech transcription datasets.

1 Introduction

Native Language Identification (NLI) is the task of using a piece of writing in a second language in order to determine the writers native language. The main applications of NLI are in language teaching and also in forensic linguistics (Kochmar, 2011).

In language teaching, NLI can help in determining the role of native language transfer in second language acquisition, so that course designers can change the material based on the native language of the learners (Laufer and Girsai, 2008).

In forensic linguistics, NLI can be the starting point in making assumptions about the authors identity of a text which is of some interest to intelligence agencies, yielding the linguistic background of the author (Tsvetkov et al., 2013).

The 2017 shared task contains 3 sub-challenges (Malmasi et al., 2017). The first challenge is predicting the native language of an English language leaner using a standardized assessment of English proficiency for academic purposes. The second challenge is native language identification using the transcriptions of spoken responses produced by test takers. The last sub-part of the NLI Shared Task 2017 is a fusion of the two, i.e. we have both written and spoken responses from test takers at our disposal in order to make a prediction about their native language.

Our team, UT-DSP participated in the NLI Shared Task 2017. An account of our participation is given in this paper.

2 Related Work

The first NLI Shared Task was organized in 2013 (Tetreault et al., 2013). The task was designed to predict the native language of an English learner based only on his/her English writing. The corpus used for the training phase of the task was the TOEFL11 corpus (Blanchard et al., 2013) which contained 11000 English texts written by native speakers of 11 different languages.

29 teams participated in total, achieving an overall accuracy rate between 0.836 and 0.319. According to the NLI Shared Task 2013 report, the prevailing trend among different teams was using character, word, and POS N-grams (Jarvis et al., 2013; Henderson et al., 2013; Bykh et al., 2013). The leading team (Jarvis) used the support vector machine (SVM) method with as many as more than 400,000 unique features including lexical and POS N-grams.

A number of teams employed simple N-gram-based methods as the implementation of these approaches can be simpler and, as a result, less time-consuming. (Gyawali et al., 2013) developed four different models using character n-grams, word n-grams, POS n-grams, and the perplexity rates of character n-grams. They used an ensemble of these 4 different models to achieve an accuracy rate of 0.75. (Kyle et al., 2013) used an approach employing key N-grams. They could outperform

210

the random baseline with an accuracy of 0.59.

Three years after the first NLI Shared Task, in 2016, the Computational Paralinguistics Challenge included a sub-task aiming at the prediction of native language based on recordings of spoken responses. The accuracy rates reported by participating teams ranged from 30.9 to 47.5 per cent (Schuller et al., 2016).

3 Data Description

The datasets for the NLI Shared Task 2017 were released by the Educational Testing Service (ETS). These datasets were released in 4 phases, two of which belonged to the training, and the remaining two belonging to the testing phases. Each dataset released contained an equal number of files belonging to each of the following 11 languages: Araic, Chinese, French, German, Hindi, Italian, Japanese, Korean, Spanish, Telugu, and Turkish.

3.1 Train - Phase 1

In this phase, a dataset containing 12,100 essay files was released, 1,100 of which were included in a collection named *dev* chosen for evaluation purposes, and the rest were used for training the method.

3.2 Train - Phase 2

The dataset released in this phase contained a collection of 12,100 speech files, which were added to the essay files released in the previous phase. Similar to the previous phase, 1,100 of the speech files were chosen as the *dev* collection, in order to be used for evaluation. The remaining files were used to train the method.

As, in this stage, both essay and speech files were at our disposal, we could train a method to predict the test taker's native language, using both essay and speech datasets simultaneously, as well as using them separately.

3.3 Test - Phase 1

The first test phase's purpose was to test the implemented methods for native language prediction, using speech and train collections separately. The essay and speech collections contained 1,100 files each, with no overlap among the files in the two.

3.4 Test - Phase 2

The aim of this phase was to test the fusion method on a collection of files, belonging to 1,100 test takers. For each test taker, an essay and a speech file were included in the collection.

4 Methodology

An N-gram-based language model is used to estimate the probability of the occurance of the next language particle (i.e. character, word, etc.) given its N previous particles of the same type, by using a maximum likelihood estimation (MLE) approach (Amini et al., 2016; Brown et al., 1992). For example, considering $N(w_{i-n+1}^i)$ as the number of occurances of the word sequence $w_{i-n+1}w_{i-n+2}...w_{i-1}w_i$ in a corpus, the n-gram probability of word w_i based on the sequence of words $w_{i-n+1}w_{i-n+2}...w_{i-1}$ which come before it, is computed using formula 1:

$$P_w(w_i|w_{i-n+1}^{i-1}) = \frac{N(w_{i-n+1}^i)}{N(w_{i-n+1}^{i-1})} \quad (1)$$

Our work employed a simple approach using a mixture of character and word N-grams. In order to do so, we had to train N-grams for each of the essay and speech transcription datasets in each language. The method was implemented without the use of i-vectors.

To compute the character N-grams, we first extracted two separate lists of characters from the essay and speech files. Then, for each language within each of the essay and speech groups, we computed the character trigrams and 4-grams, smoothed using the additive smoothing method with $\alpha = 0.1$.

In order to compute the word N-grams, two separate lists of words from the essay and speech files were extracted. These two lists were then limited to the words which were encountered more than once. Afterwards, we computed the word monograms and bigrams (considering out-of-vocabulary words), which were smoothed using the additive smoothing method with $\alpha = 0.01$.

In order to predict the native language for a text file, considering it as an essay/speech transcription, we have to compute its probabilities using character and word N-grams of essay/speech for each language. The character-level probabilities are computed using the formulas 2 and 3:

$$Prob_{l,c-3}(C) = \sum_{i=3}^{m} \log P_{l,c-3}(c_i|c_{i-2}c_{i-1}) \quad (2)$$

$$Prob_{l,c-4}(C) = \sum_{i=4}^{m} \log P_{l,c-4}(c_i|c_{i-3}c_{i-2}c_{i-1}) \tag{3}$$

In which $Prob_{l,c-N}(C)$ stands for the character-level probability of the text by the character N-gram for language l, m is the number of characters in the text, $P_{l,c-3}(c_i|c_{i-2}c_{i-1})$ represents the character trigram probability of language l for character c_i given its two previous characters, and $P_{l,c-4}(c_i|c_{i-3}c_{i-2}c_{i-1})$ represents the character 4-gram probability of language l for character c_i given its three previous characters.

The word-level probabilities are computed using the formulas 4 and 5:

$$Prob_{l,w-1}(W) = \sum_{i=1}^{n} \log P_{l,w-1}(w_i) \tag{4}$$

$$Prob_{l,w-2}(W) = \sum_{i=2}^{n} \log P_{l,w-2}(w_i|w_{i-1}) \tag{5}$$

In which $Prob_{l,w-N}(W)$ stands for the word-level probability of the text by the word N-gram for language l, n is the number of words in the text, $P_{l,w-1}(w_i)$ represents the word monogram probability of language l for word w_i, and $P_{l,w-2}(w_i|c_{i-1})$ represents the word bigram probability of language l for word w_i given its previous word.

In order to compute the character-level N-grams, we used the 4-gram probability to predict the language of an essay file, while for speech files, we used the summation of trigram and 4-gram character probabilities. In both essay and speech files, we used the sum of word-level monogram and bigram probabilities. These N-grams were chosen in a way that they could achieve the best results on the *dev* dataset, when trained using the *train* one.

In order to compute the final probability of a text file for each language, we added the character-level and word-level probabilities together. The language with the highest probability was chosen as the predicted language for the text. To test our system on the *test* dataset, we trained our system using both *train* and *dev* datasets.

5 Results

In the first test phase, we achieved the macro F1-score of 0.7609 and the overall accuracy of 0.7636 on the Essay track, and the macro F1-score of 0.4530 and the overall accuracy of 0.4536 on the Speech track. Tables 1 and 2 show our method's performance on each class, and Figure 1 and 2 show the confusion matrices yielded in the first test phase.

In the second test phase, we tested our system using both essay, speech, and the fusion of both essay and speech datasets. Table 3 shows the results achieved in each test. As you can see, the best result was achieved in the fusion test. Table 4 shows our method's performance on each class, and Figure 3 shows the confusion matrix from the fusion result in the second test phase.

All results reported in this section were officially submitted as part of the NLI Shared Task 2017.

6 Discussion

First of all, it is worth mentioning that all the results reported in this paper were achieved without the use of i-vectors, and therefore the comparisons between the results of our method with the baseline results are done only for essay, speech (transcriptions-only) and the fusion of essay and speech transcriptions.

Our implemented method is useful in the native language identification of essays (outperforming the baseline F1-score of 0.710), it does not perform well on speech transcriptions (whose baseline F1-score is 0.544), and as a result the fusion of essays and transcriptions (with a baseline F1-score of 0.779). The reason for this can be the fact that in speech transcriptions, the file lengths vary much more than those of the essay files. The fact that, in our method, the length of the file can affect the probabilities can lead to this result.

As evident in Figure 1 to 3, most of the performance reduction was due to complications in telling Telugu and Hindi apart. Figure 2 shows that, in the speech track, both of these languages have very often been mistaken for each other; however, Figure 1 and 3 point to the fact that in the essay and fusion tracks, Hindi has been detected more accurately, while Telugu has often been labeled as Hindi.

An interesting point worth mentioning is that, although our method did not yield a decent perfor-

Language	Precision	Recall	F1-Score
ARA	0.8333	0.6500	0.7303
CHI	0.7944	0.8500	0.8213
FRE	0.8400	0.8400	0.8400
GER	0.8125	0.9100	0.8585
HIN	0.5590	0.9000	0.6897
ITA	0.8966	0.7800	0.8342
JPN	0.8506	0.7400	0.7914
KOR	0.8182	0.7200	0.7660
SPA	0.7345	0.8300	0.7793
TEL	0.7778	0.4200	0.5455
TUR	0.6726	0.7600	0.7136
Avg	0.7809	0.7636	0.7609

Table 1: Per Class Performance for the Essay Track

Language	Precision	Recall	F1-Score
ARA	0.3204	0.3300	0.3251
CHI	0.5440	0.6800	0.6044
FRE	0.4343	0.4300	0.4322
GER	0.4907	0.5300	0.5096
HIN	0.3507	0.4700	0.4017
ITA	0.4444	0.4000	0.4211
JPN	0.5417	0.5200	0.5306
KOR	0.5176	0.4400	0.4757
SPA	0.4045	0.3600	0.3810
TEL	0.4040	0.4000	0.4020
TUR	0.5972	0.4300	0.5000
Avg	0.4591	0.4536	0.4530

Table 2: Per Class Performance for the Speech Track

mance on the speech dataset, it achieved optimal performance when implemented on the combination of both essay and speech files in the fusion phase.

As explained in Section 3, our method is a rather simple one, compared to SVM and artificial neural networks. The combination of character N-grams and word N-grams used in our method is purely experimental, and does not take advantage of a strong mathematical basis.

All that being said, our method could still be used in combination with a form of supervised learning, in order to be more effective and achieve a decent accuracy rate.

7 Acknowledgement

We would like to express our sincere gratitude to Professor Leila Kosseim from Concordia University, for her support and encouragement through this task.

References

Hessam Amini, Hadi Veisi, and Elham Mohammadi. 2016. Target words selection for a persian brain-computer-interface-based speller using language model. In *Information and Knowledge Technology (IKT), 2016 Eighth International Conference on*. IEEE, pages 216–220.

Daniel Blanchard, Joel Tetreault, Derrick Higgins, Aoife Cahill, and Martin Chodorow. 2013. Toefl11: A corpus of non-native english. Technical report, Educational Testing Service.

Peter F Brown, Peter V Desouza, Robert L Mercer, Vincent J Della Pietra, and Jenifer C Lai. 1992. Class-based n-gram models of natural language. *Computational Linguistics* 18(4):467–479.

Serhiy Bykh, Sowmya Vajjala, Julia Krivanek, and Detmar Meurers. 2013. Combining shallow and linguistically motivated features in native language identification. *NAACL/HLT 2013* page 197.

Binod Gyawali, Gabriela Ramírez-de-la Rosa, and Thamar Solorio. 2013. Native language identifica-

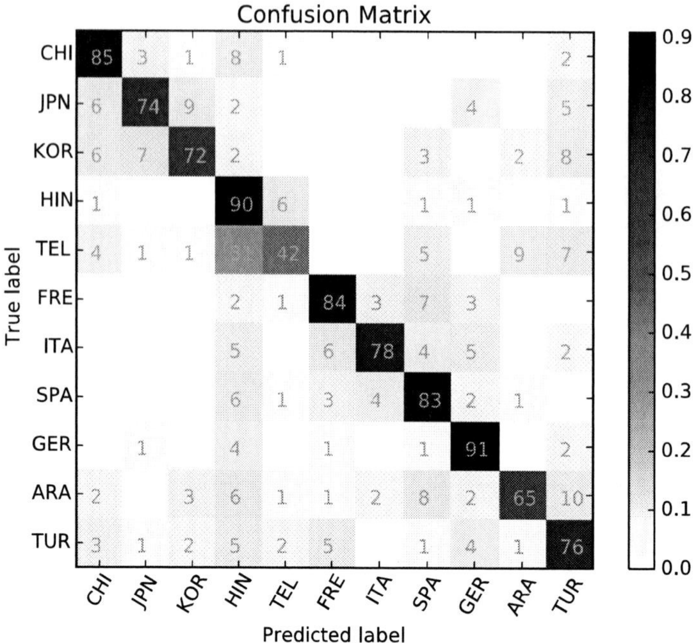

Figure 1: The Confusion Matrix in the Essay Track

System	F1-Score	Accuracy
Essay	0.7609	0.7636
Speech	0.4530	0.4536
Fusion	0.7748	0.7764

Table 3: Results in the Second Test Phase

tion: a simple n-gram based approach. In *BEA@ NAACL-HLT*. pages 224–231.

John C Henderson, Guido Zarrella, Craig Pfeifer, and John D Burger. 2013. Discriminating non-native english with 350 words. In *BEA@ NAACL-HLT*. pages 101–110.

Scott Jarvis, Yves Bestgen, and Steve Pepper. 2013. Maximizing Classification Accuracy in Native Language Identification. In *Proceedings of the Eighth Workshop on Innovative Use of NLP for Building Educational Applications*. Association for Computational Linguistics, Atlanta, Georgia, pages 111–118.

Ekaterina Kochmar. 2011. *Identification of a writer's native language by error analysis*. Master's thesis, University of Cambridge.

Kristopher Kyle, Scott A Crossley, Jianmin Dai, and Danielle S McNamara. 2013. Native language identification: A key n-gram category approach. In *BEA@ NAACL-HLT*. pages 242–250.

Batia Laufer and Nany Girsai. 2008. Form-focused instruction in second language vocabulary learning: A case for contrastive analysis and translation. *Applied Linguistics* 29(4):694–716.

Shervin Malmasi, Keelan Evanini, Aoife Cahill, Joel Tetreault, Robert Pugh, Christopher Hamill, Diane Napolitano, and Yao Qian. 2017. A Report on the 2017 Native Language Identification Shared Task. In *Proceedings of the 12th Workshop on Building Educational Applications Using NLP*. Association for Computational Linguistics, Copenhagen, Denmark.

Bjrn Schuller, Stefan Steidl, Anton Batliner, Julia Hirschberg, Judee K. Burgoon, Alice Baird, Aaron Elkins, Yue Zhang, Eduardo Coutinho, and Keelan Evanini. 2016. The INTER-SPEECH 2016 Computational Paralinguistics Challenge: Deception, Sincerity & Native Language. In *Interspeech 2016*. pages 2001–2005. https://doi.org/10.21437/Interspeech.2016-129.

Joel Tetreault, Daniel Blanchard, and Aoife Cahill. 2013. A Report on the First Native Language Identification Shared Task. In *Proceedings of the Eighth Workshop on Building Educational Applications Us-*

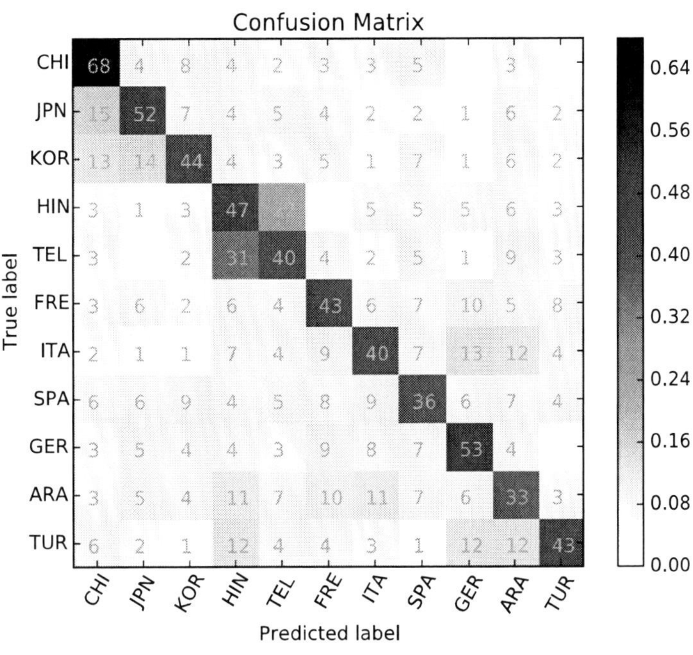

Figure 2: The Confusion Matrix in the Speech Track

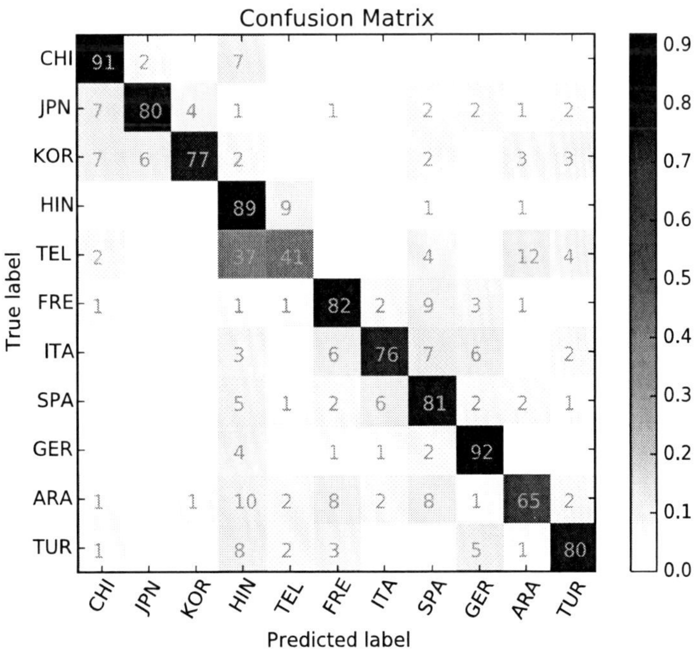

Figure 3: The Confusion Matrix in the Fusion Track (Best Result)

Language	Precision	Recall	F1-Score
ARA	0.7558	0.6500	0.6989
CHI	0.8273	0.9100	0.8667
FRE	0.7961	0.8200	0.8079
GER	0.8288	0.9200	0.8720
HIN	0.5329	0.8900	0.6667
ITA	0.8736	0.7600	0.8128
JPN	0.9091	0.8000	0.8511
KOR	0.9390	0.7700	0.8462
SPA	0.6983	0.8100	0.7500
TEL	0.7321	0.4100	0.5256
TUR	0.8511	0.8000	0.8247
Avg	0.7949	0.7764	0.7748

Table 4: Per Class Performance for the Fusion Track (Best Result)

ing NLP. Association for Computational Linguistics, Atlanta, GA, USA.

Yulia Tsvetkov, Naama Twitto, Nathan Schneider, Noam Ordan, Manaal Faruqui, Victor Chahuneau, Shuly Wintner, and Chris Dyer. 2013. Identifying the 11 of non-native writers: the cmu-haifa system. In *BEA@ NAACL-HLT*. pages 279–287.

Ensemble Methods for Native Language Identification

Sophia Chan,* Maryam Honari Jahromi,* Benjamin Benetti,* Aazim Lakhani, Alona Fyshe
Department of Computer Science
University of Victoria
Victoria, BC, Canada
`{schan1,mhonari,bbenetti,aazimlakhani,afyshe}@uvic.ca`

Abstract

Our team—Uvic-NLP—explored and evaluated a variety of lexical features for Native Language Identification (NLI) within the framework of ensemble methods. Using a subset of the highest-performing features, we train Support Vector Machines (SVM) and Fully Connected Neural Networks (FCNN) as base classifiers, and test different methods for combining their outputs. Restricting our scope to the closed essay track in the NLI Shared Task 2017, we find that our best SVM ensemble achieves an F1 score of 0.8730 on the test set.

1 Introduction

Native Language Identification (NLI) is the task of identifying a person's native language (L1) based on a sample of their writing or speech in a second language (L2). The underlying intuition is that those with the same L1 tend to use similar language patterns during L2 production. This is known as cross-linguistic influence (Ortega, 2014).

NLI can accelerate second language acquisition by giving students L1-specific feedback on their written or spoken samples (Malmasi et al., 2014). In forensic linguistics, NLI can be applied to identify the L1 of anonymous texts (Perkins, 2015).

The NLI Shared Task 2013—the first of its kind—was based on written essays (Tetreault et al., 2013), while the 2016 Computational Paralinguistics Challenge was based on spoken responses (Schuller et al., 2016). The NLI Shared Task 2017 organizers provided a dataset of both essays and transcriptions of verbal responses

(Malmasi et al., 2017). As our team—Uvic-NLP—participated in the closed essay track, we performed classification on essays only.

We begin our analysis by comparing various lexical features and focus on two high-performing classifiers: Support Vector Machines (SVM) and Fully Connected Neural Networks (FCNN). Then, we explore different ensemble methods for combining outputs of individual classifiers. We present and discuss three of our best systems for this task: a single SVM classifier, an SVM ensemble, and an FCNN ensemble.

2 Related Work

NLI is generally conceptualized as a multiclass supervised classification problem, where the classes represent the set of possible L1s. One of the first NLI systems trained SVMs on a variety of stylistic features (Koppel et al., 2005).

The NLI Shared Task 2013 introduced a corpus designed specifically for NLI (Blanchard et al., 2013). Use of a standardized dataset and evaluation metric allowed for the effective comparison of different models, and the results confirmed the usefulness of SVMs for NLI (Tetreault et al., 2013). Popular features included word, part of speech (POS), and character n-grams; higher-order n-grams were shown to be especially useful. Four of the top five teams used at least 4-grams, with the top team using up to 9-grams. String kernels using 5- to 8-grams at the character-level also worked well, and were one of the best performing models for this task (Ionescu et al., 2014).

A trend in recent work is the use of ensemble methods, which combine the predictions of a set of classifiers, giving more accurate results than a single classifier trained on a combination of different features (Tetreault et al., 2012; Malmasi et al., 2013). Malmasi and Dras (2017) used meta-

---

*These authors contributed equally to this work.

217

Proceedings of the 12th Workshop on Innovative Use of NLP for Building Educational Applications, pages 217–223
Copenhagen, Denmark, September 8, 2017. ©2017 Association for Computational Linguistics

classifier ensembles, where results from base classifiers are fed to an ensemble of meta-classifiers. Such models are the current state of the art for NLI.

3 Data

The dataset for the essay track of the NLI Shared Task 2017 was collected by Educational Testing Services, and consists of written responses to a standardized assessment of English proficiency for academic purposes.

13,200 response essays from test takers were separated into three sets: 11,000 for training (TRAIN), 1,100 for development (DEV), and 1,100 for testing (TEST). Each set of documents is equally distributed among eleven L1s: Arabic (ARA), Chinese (CHI), French (FRE), German (GER), Hindi (HIN), Italian (ITA), Japanese (JPN), Korean (KOR), Spanish (SPA), Telugu (TEL), and Turkish (TUR).

4 Features

Previous work demonstrates that a variety of lexical and syntactic features are useful for NLI (Tetreault et al., 2012). In addition to incorporating lexical features known to be effective for this task, we also extract phonemes. Here, we describe each of the features in turn.

Word n-grams Where topic bias is pervasive, word n-grams are not useful features for classification (Brooke and Hirst, 2011), but have been used successfully in topic-balanced corpora (Tetreault et al., 2012). Our dataset is balanced across topics, making word n-grams useful.

Lemma n-grams Lemmas are the dictionary representation of words, i.e. words that are stripped of morphological marking. The lemmatized versions of all words in our corpus were attained using Natural Language Toolkit's WordNet interface (Bird et al., 2009; Feinerer and Hornik, 2016; Wallace, 2007; Fellbaum, 1998).

Character n-grams Tsur and Rappoport (2007) achieved good results on the NLI task using only character bigrams as features. Methods working at the character level were also the previous state of the art (Ionescu et al., 2014). Character n-grams can be generated from text within or across word boundaries.

Part of speech n-grams Koppel et al. (2005) found rare part of speech (POS) bigrams to be a useful feature; many teams in the 2013 Shared Task also made use of this feature (Tetreault et al., 2013). We use the Stanford Tagger to extract POS features (Toutanova et al., 2003).

Function words Function words are a closed class of words that serve a grammatical function in sentences, whose use for NLI was explored early on (Koppel et al., 2005). These include articles, determiners, conjunctions, and auxiliaries. These were extracted based on a list provided in the ModErn Text Analysis Toolkit (Massung et al., 2016).

Spelling errors Spelling errors were extracted by finding the difference between misspelled words before and after they were corrected using the autocorrect package (Jonas, 2013). We coded a subset of the spelling errors defined by Koppel et al. (2005): repeated letter, double letter appears only once, letter replacement, letter inversion, inserted letter, and missing letter.

Phoneme n-grams Phonemes are representations of sounds in a language. In English, one sound can be represented using many different letters (e.g. *c*at and *k*ick). For mapping orthography onto phonemes, we used the Carnegie Mellon Pronouncing Dictionary (Weide, 2005). To our knowledge, phonemes have not yet been explored as a feature.

5 Classifiers

We evaluated classifier performance across features types and found that the SVM and FCNN classifiers consistently outperformed other classifiers, such as Perceptron and Multinomial Naive Bayes. As such, we focus on these two classifiers in subsequent experiments.

Ensemble methods involve combining the outputs of multiple classifiers to yield a final prediction (Polikar, 2006). Three types of ensemble methods which have been shown to be useful for NLI are explored here (Malmasi and Dras, 2017). At a high level, SVM and FCNN outputs are combined using (1) a voting scheme, (2) a Linear Discriminant Analysis (LDA) classifier trained on the outputs, and (3) multiple LDA classifiers—trained on random subsets of the outputs—whose predictions are in turn combined using a voting scheme.

Table 1: Comparison of individual feature types using SVM and FCNN classifiers, using F1 scores on DEV. The highest F1 score for each feature set is indicated in bold.

Feature type	SVM	FCNN
Word unigram	0.6936	0.7645
Word bigram	0.7228	**0.8027**
Word trigram	0.6705	0.6790
Lemma	0.6703	**0.7481**
Character bigram	0.4787	0.5818
Character trigram	0.6360	0.7381
Character 4-gram	0.7213	0.7836
Character 5-gram	0.7363	**0.8081**
POS bigram	0.4286	0.4081
POS trigram	**0.4723**	0.4472
Function words	0.3036	**0.5646**
Spelling errors	0.2201	**0.2509**
Phoneme bigram	0.5356	0.5509
Phoneme trigram	0.6697	0.6654
Phoneme 4-gram	0.7089	0.6727
Phoneme 5-gram	**0.7241**	0.6654
Combined	**0.8183**	0.7784

5.1 Support Vector Machine (SVM)

SVMs (Joachims, 1998) are frequently used for text classification and have been applied successfully to NLI (Tetreault et al., 2013). We use a scikit-learn SVM implementation: LinearSVC (Pedregosa et al., 2011).

5.2 Neural Networks

Since we found little previous work applying neural networks to NLI, this paper strives to fill this gap by constructing a FCNN using TensorFlow (Allaire et al., 2016) and the Keras (Chollet et al., 2015) framework.

The network is comprised of one hidden layer of 128 nodes that uses a tanh activation function and an input dropout of 0.2. The optimal dropout value was established empirically. Following the hidden layer, there is an 11 node output layer that uses the softmax activation function. The entire network uses a cross entropy loss function and the Adam optimization algorithm.

Due to memory constraints, we limit analysis to only the 100,000 most important features, selected by performing an ANOVA F-test on the entire fea-

ture set (Harwell et al., 1992).

In addition to the FCNN, we test another type of neural network for this task. Following the architecture described by Wang et al. (2016), we train a pipeline consisting of a convolutional neural network (CNN) which transforms the input data at the character-level and a Long Term Short Memory (LSTM) neural network which performs classification on the output of the CNN. We also trained an LSTM on word vectors (Mikolov et al., 2013). In both cases, however, we found results to be lacking in accuracy.

5.3 Ensemble construction

For any given SVM or FCNN, the output for 11-way classification can be represented as a vector of 11 numbers. For the SVM, output is in the form of confidence scores for each class, which is equivalent to the signed distance of that sample to each class's hyperplane (Weston and Watkins, 1998). Similarly, each FCNN prediction is in the form of confidence values for each class, derived from the softmax output layer.

Using the best feature combination and representation from the previous experiments, we trained two sets of base classifiers—FCNNs and SVMs—on different features and combined each set of outputs using three different voting schemes (Polikar, 2006):

- **Mean**: Final label is the class corresponding to the greatest average confidence score.

- **Median**: Final label is the class corresponding to the greatest median confidence score.

- **Plurality vote**: Final label is the class with the greatest number of votes. In a tie, we choose the class that comes first alphabetically.

In line with previous work, we achieve the highest accuracy using the mean rule (Malmasi et al., 2013), as shown in Table 3.

5.4 Meta-classifier

Another way to combine the outputs of several base classifiers is to feed their outputs into another classifier, also known as a meta-classifier. To obtain outputs from SVMs and FCNNs, we split the training set into ten folds and perform cross-validation. This gave us a set of meta-features that were then used as input to an LDA meta-classifier, which was found to outperform other algorithms for meta-classification in Malmasi and Dras (2017).

5.5 Meta-classifier ensembles

Building on the idea of ensembles and meta-classification, we experiment with ensembles of meta-classifiers (Malmasi and Dras, 2017). SVM and FCNN outputs—meta-features—are generated in the same way as in section 5.4. However, instead of training a single meta-classifier on these features, we use bagging (bootstrap aggregating) to train multiple LDAs on random subsets of the base classifier outputs. A grid search was performed to find the optimal number of meta-classifiers and optimal percentage of samples to train each LDA on. The predictions from multiple LDAs were then combined using voting schemes described in section 5.3.

6 Results and Discussion

In this section we present our results on single features, feature combinations, single classifiers, and classifier ensembles.

6.1 Individual features

The results of SVM and FCNN classifiers trained on different features are shown in Table 1. For these experiments, features were represented by their frequency count. We observe a general trend within different feature types: F1 scores increase as n-gram order increases (see Table 1). This is not unexpected, given the success of NLI models that make use of higher-order n-grams (Jarvis et al., 2013; Tetreault et al., 2013). One exception to this trend is that there seems to be a upper-bound for word n-grams at the bigram level, where accuracy drops for word trigrams. This may be attributed in part to the increased sparsity of features when we move from bigrams to trigrams at the word-level.

Interestingly, spelling errors were less informative than what we had expected. Although we did not evaluate the accuracy of the autocorrect package we used for spelling correction, we suspect that it did not perform well since it operates naively, without looking at context (Jonas, 2013). Additionally, the types of errors we defined might have not been fine-grained enough to capture differences unique to groups of L1 writers.

6.2 Single classifier results

As in Malmasi et al. (2013), we measure the effectiveness of different feature representations. Of the feature types described above, we include in our final system only a subset of the highest performing features. Thus, analysis is limited to this subset of features.

With frequency counts as a baseline, we compare the performance of classifiers trained on three different combinations of high-performing features. These groups are:

- **Word**: Lemmas, words (1-, 2-, and 3-grams).

- **Char**: Characters (4- and 5-grams).

- **Phoneme**: Phonemes (4- and 5-grams).

Each group of features is tested with and without term frequency-inverse document frequency (TF-IDF) weighting. Further, we examine the effects of binarization, L1 normalization, and L2 normalization on the same feature set. Note that L1 and L2 normalization refer to the vector norms across each input row. These results are summarized in Table 2.

Comparing classifiers trained on individual features (Table 1) to those trained on combinations of features (Table 2), it is evident that better results are achieved by training a single classifier on multiple features than on any single feature type. Further, Table 2 shows that the best performing classifiers use L2-normalized features with TF-IDF.

Our official submission to the NLI Shared Task 2017 used a single SVM classifier, which requires less time and fewer computational resources to train compared to a FCNN. An SVM on words (1-, 2-, and 3-grams) and characters (4- and 5-grams) achieves an F1 score of 0.8633 on TEST (see Table 4). The features were binarized, L2-normalized and TF-IDF weighted. The confusion matrix is shown in Figure 1.

6.3 Ensembles

The results detailed in this section were not submitted as part of the NLI Shared Task 2017, and were obtained after the test phase ended.

At the most basic level, individual classifiers are combined in a straightforward manner using a voting scheme. As we increase the complexity of the model, first by training an LDA meta-classifier on

Table 2: Comparison of feature representations for SVM and FCNN classifiers, using F1 scores on DEV. The best feature representation for each classifier is indicated in bold.

		Word		Char		Phoneme	
		SVM	FCNN	SVM	FCNN	SVM	FCNN
TF	*Binarized*	0.7983	**0.8190**	0.6932	**0.8172**	0.7550	0.6950
	Frequency counts	0.8090	0.8090	0.6931	0.8003	0.7056	0.6971
	L1 Normalized	0.6167	0.6372	0.4921	0.4427	0.4270	0.4604
	L2 Normalized	0.7736	0.7854	0.7629	0.7610	0.7677	0.6971
TF-IDF	*Binarized*	**0.8092**	0.7872	0.6837	0.7693	0.7489	0.6623
	Frequency counts	0.7772	0.7579	0.6834	0.7560	0.7085	0.6578
	L1 Normalized	0.6954	0.7845	0.5911	0.3794	0.5325	0.2919
	L2 Normalized	0.8049	0.8155	**0.7709**	0.8048	**0.7812**	**0.7059**

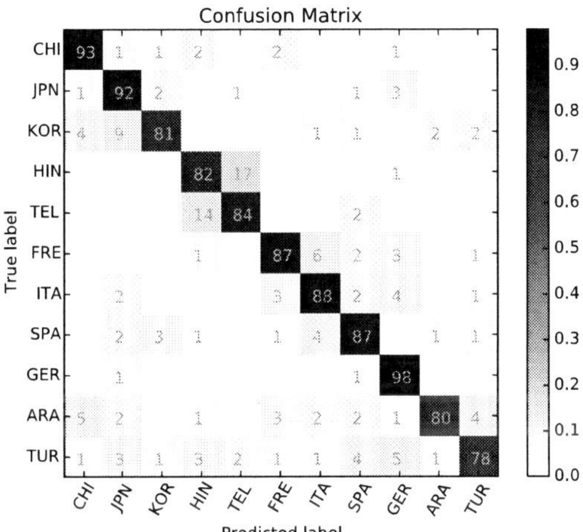

Figure 1: SVM confusion matrix on TEST. The SVM was trained on words (1-, 2-, and 3-grams) and characters within word boundaries (4- and 5-grams).

the outputs, and then by constructing an ensemble of meta-classifiers, we observe a slight performance gain for both SVMs and FCNNs at each step, consistent with the results in Malmasi and Dras (2017). Table 3 summarizes our results from using different ensemble methods to combine individual classifiers trained on words (2- and 3-grams), characters (4- and 5-grams) and phonemes (4- and 5-grams).

Further experiments with SVMs and FCNNs were conducted by selecting different features to combine on a trial and error basis. The decision to use character *n*-grams within as opposed to across word boundaries was made arbitrarily. All features are binarized, L2-normalized, and TF-IDF

Table 3: Comparison of different ensemble methods to combine outputs of SVM and FCNN classifiers: voting schemes, LDA meta-classifier, and an ensemble of LDA meta-classifiers. F1 scores on DEV are shown. The best result for each classifier is indicated in bold.

		SVM	FCNN
Voting scheme	Plurality vote	0.8285	0.8109
	Mean	0.8417	0.8345
	Median	0.8313	0.8363
Meta-classifier	LDA	0.8448	0.8534
Meta-classifier ensembles	Plurality-LDA	0.8449	0.8507
	Mean-LDA	**0.8475**	**0.8544**
	Median-LDA	**0.8475**	**0.8544**

weighted. The results of our best ensemble classifiers on DEV and TEST are displayed in Table 4.

While an ensemble of meta-classifiers outperforms both a simple voting scheme and a single meta-classifier, we do not observe the same performance gain with respect to FCNNs (see Table 3).

Our best SVM ensemble consists of an ensemble of meta-classifiers. SVMs are trained on words (2- and 3-grams), characters within word boundaries (4- and 5-grams), and phonemes (4- and 5-grams), giving a total of six classifiers. The outputs of these individual classifiers are fed to an ensemble of LDAs, as described in 5.5. Finally, the LDA predictions are combined using the mean rule. The F1 score on TEST for this model is 0.8730.

Our best FCNN ensemble applies a voting scheme to classifier outputs. Four FCNN networks

Table 4: F1 scores on TEST and on DEV for final systems. Ensemble results were obtained after the test phase. The best result for each dataset is indicated in bold. * = Official submission to the NLI Shared Task 2017.

System	DEV	TEST
Random baseline	0.9090	—
Official baseline	0.7104	—
*SVM**	0.8168	0.8633
SVM ensemble	0.8475	**0.8730**
FCNN ensemble	0.8576	0.8560

are trained on the following combination of features: (1) word bigrams and lemma trigrams, (2) word bigrams, (3) character 5-grams, (4) character 5-grams within word boundaries. The outputs from these individual networks are combined using the mean rule, yielding an F1 score of 0.8560 on TEST.

Additionally, we created an ensemble of different SVM and FCNN classifiers but found no improvement over pure ensembles of either type.

7 Future work

We excluded from our system individual features that did not perform well in our experiments. It would be helpful to evaluate the influence of these less accurate features and determine whether they would be useful to include in ensemble classifiers. Further, we tested a limited number of combinations of features. One facet of the problem involves developing a systematic approach to search for a good feature set.

Although we trained several FCNNs on different feature types, its utility as a meta-classifier has not been examined.

A CNN-LSTM model shown to perform well for sentiment analysis (Wang et al., 2016) did not achieve good results for NLI. While sentiment classification typically involves five or fewer classes, there were 11 classes for the NLI Shared Task 2017. It may may be that additional classes increase the possibility of error. Further investigation is required to explain why a CNN-LSTM architecture performs worse relative to a FCNN model.

Our results show the utility of various features for this task and confirm that ensemble methods perform better than single classifiers trained on multiple features. They also offer several new directions to further improve NLI systems.

References

Joseph Allaire, Dirk Eddelbuettel, Nick Golding, and Yuan Tang. 2016. tensorflow: R interface to tensorflow. https://github.com/rstudio/tensorflow.

Steven Bird, Ewan Klein, and Edward Loper. 2009. *Natural Language Processing with Python.* O'Reilly Media.

Daniel Blanchard, Joel Tetreault, Derrick Higgins, Aoife Cahill, and Martin Chodorow. 2013. Toefl11: A corpus of non-native english. Technical report, Educational Testing Service.

Julian Brooke and Graeme Hirst. 2011. Native language detection with 'cheap' learner corpora. In *Conference of Learner Corpus Research.* Presses universitaires de Louvain.

François Chollet et al. 2015. Keras. https://github.com/fchollet/keras.

Ingo Feinerer and Kurt Hornik. 2016. *wordnet: WordNet Interface.* R package version 0.1-11. https://CRAN.R-project.org/package=wordnet.

Christiane Fellbaum. 1998. *WordNet: An Electronic Lexical Database.* Bradford Books.

Michael Harwell, Elaine Rubinstein, William Hayes, and Corley Olds. 1992. Summarizing monte carlo results in methodological research: The one-and two-factor fixed effects ANOVA cases. *Journal of Educational Statistics* 17(4):315–339.

Radu Ionescu, Marius Popescu, and Aoife Cahill. 2014. Can characters reveal your native language? a language-independent approach to native language identification. In *Proceedings of the 2014 Conference on Empirical Methods in Natural Language Processing.* Association for Computational Linguistics.

Scott Jarvis, Yves Bestgen, and Steve Pepper. 2013. Maximizing classification accuracy in native language identification. In *Proceedings of the Eighth Workshop on Innovative Use of NLP for Building Educational Applications.* pages 111–118.

Thorsten Joachims. 1998. Text categorization with support vector machines: Learning with many relevant features. In *Proceedings of the 10th European Conference on Machine Learning.* Springer, pages 137–142.

McCallum Jonas. 2013. autocorrect spelling. https://github.com/phatpiglet/autocorrect.

Moshe Koppel, Jonathan Schler, and Kfir Zigdon. 2005. Automatically determining an anonymous author's native language. *Intelligence and Security Informatics* pages 41–76.

Shervin Malmasi and Mark Dras. 2017. Native language identification using stacked generalization abs/1703.06541. http://arxiv.org/abs/1703.06541.

Shervin Malmasi, Mark Dras, et al. 2014. Language transfer hypotheses with linear SVM weights. In *Proceedings of the 2014 Conference on Empirical Methods in Natural Language Processing*. Association for Computational Linguistics, pages 1385–1390.

Shervin Malmasi, Keelan Evanini, Aoife Cahill, Joel Tetreault, Robert Pugh, Christopher Hamill, Diane Napolitano, and Yao Qian. 2017. A Report on the 2017 Native Language Identification Shared Task. In *Proceedings of the 12th Workshop on Building Educational Applications Using NLP*. Association for Computational Linguistics.

Shervin Malmasi, Sze-Meng Jojo Wong, and Mark Dras. 2013. NLI shared task 2013: MQ submission. In *Proceedings of the Eighth Workshop on Innovative Use of NLP for Building Educational Applications*. Association for Computational Linguistics, pages 124–133.

Sean Massung, Chase Geigle, and ChengXiang Zhai. 2016. MeTA: A Unified Toolkit for Text Retrieval and Analysis. In *Proceedings of ACL-2016 System Demonstrations*. Association for Computational Linguistics, pages 91–96.

Tomas Mikolov, Kai Chen, Greg Corrado, and Jeffrey Dean. 2013. Efficient estimation of word representations in vector space http://arxiv.org/abs/1301.3781.

Lourdes Ortega. 2014. *Understanding second language acquisition*. Routledge.

Fabian Pedregosa, Gaël Varoquaux, Alexandre Gramfort, Vincent Michel, Bertrand Thirion, Olivier Grisel, Mathieu Blondel, Peter Prettenhofer, Ron Weiss, Vincent Dubourg, et al. 2011. Scikit-learn: Machine learning in Python. *Journal of Machine Learning Research* 12:2825–2830.

Ria Perkins. 2015. Native language identification (NLID) for forensic authorship analysis of weblogs. *New Threats and Countermeasures in Digital Crime and Cyber Terrorism* pages 213–234.

Robi Polikar. 2006. Ensemble based systems in decision making. *IEEE Circuits and systems magazine* 6(3):21–45.

Björn Schuller, Stefan Steidl, Anton Batliner, Julia Hirschberg, Judee Burgoon, Alice Baird, Aaron Elkins, Yue Zhang, Eduardo Coutinho, and Keelan Evanini. 2016. The INTERSPEECH 2016 computational paralinguistics challenge: Deception, sincerity & native language. pages 2001–2005.

Joel Tetreault, Daniel Blanchard, and Aoife Cahill. 2013. A Report on the First Native Language Identification Shared Task. In *Proceedings of the Eighth Workshop on Building Educational Applications Using NLP*. Association for Computational Linguistics.

Joel Tetreault, Daniel Blanchard, Aoife Cahill, and Martin Chodorow. 2012. Native tongues, lost and found: Resources and empirical evaluations in native language identification. In *Proceedings of the 24th International Conference on Computational Linguistics*. Association for Computational Linguistics, pages 2585–2602.

Kristina Toutanova, Dan Klein, Christopher Manning, and Yoram Singer. 2003. Feature-rich part-of-speech tagging with a cyclic dependency network. In *Proceedings of the 2003 Conference of the North American Chapter of the Association for Computational Linguistics on Human Language Technology*. Association for Computational Linguistics, pages 173–180.

Oren Tsur and Ari Rappoport. 2007. Using classifier features for studying the effect of native language on the choice of written second language words. In *Proceedings of the Workshop on Cognitive Aspects of Computational Language Acquisition*. Association for Computational Linguistics, pages 9–16.

Mike Wallace. 2007. *Jawbone Java WordNet API*. http://mfwallace.googlepages.com/jawbone.

Xingyou Wang, Weijie Jiang, and Zhiyong Luo. 2016. Combination of convolutional and recurrent neural network for sentiment analysis of short texts. In *Proceedings of the 26th International Conference on Computational Linguistics*. pages 2428–2437.

Robert Weide. 2005. The Carnegie Mellon pronouncing dictionary. http://www.speech.cs.cmu.edu/cgi-bin/cmudict.

Jason Weston and Chris Watkins. 1998. Multi-class support vector machines. Technical report, Department of Computer Science, University of London.

Can string kernels pass the test of time in Native Language Identification?

Radu Tudor Ionescu[*] and **Marius Popescu**[*]

University of Bucharest
Department of Computer Science
14 Academiei, Bucharest, Romania
raducu.ionescu@gmail.com
popescunmarius@gmail.com

Abstract

We describe a machine learning approach
for the 2017 shared task on Native Language Identification (NLI). The proposed
approach combines several kernels using
multiple kernel learning. While most
of our kernels are based on character
p-grams (also known as n-grams) extracted from essays or speech transcripts,
we also use a kernel based on i-vectors,
a low-dimensional representation of audio recordings, provided by the shared
task organizers. For the learning stage,
we choose Kernel Discriminant Analysis (KDA) over Kernel Ridge Regression
(KRR), because the former classifier obtains better results than the latter one
on the development set. In our previous work, we have used a similar machine learning approach to achieve state-of-the-art NLI results. The goal of this
paper is to demonstrate that our shallow
and simple approach based on string kernels (with minor improvements) can pass
the test of time and reach state-of-the-art performance in the 2017 NLI shared
task, despite the recent advances in natural language processing. We participated
in all three tracks, in which the competitors were allowed to use only the essays
(essay track), only the speech transcripts
(speech track), or both (fusion track). Using only the data provided by the organizers for training our models, we have
reached a macro F_1 score of 86.95% in
the closed essay track, a macro F_1 score
of 87.55% in the closed speech track, and
a macro F_1 score of 93.19% in the closed

fusion track. With these scores, our team
(UnibucKernel) ranked in the first group
of teams in all three tracks, while attaining the best scores in the speech and the
fusion tracks.

1 Introduction

Native Language Identification (NLI) is the task of
identifying the native language (L1) of a person,
based on a sample of text or speech they have produced in a language (L2) other than their mother
tongue. This is an interesting sub-task in forensic
linguistic applications such as plagiarism detection and authorship identification, where the native
language of an author is just one piece of the puzzle (Estival et al., 2007). NLI can also play a key
role in second language acquisition (SLA) applications where NLI techniques are used to identify
language transfer patterns that help teachers and
students focus feedback and learning on particular areas of interest (Rozovskaya and Roth, 2010;
Jarvis and Crossley, 2012).

In 2013, Tetreault et al. (2013) organized the
first NLI shared task, providing the participants
written essays of non-native English learners. In
2016, the Computational Paralinguistics Challenge (Schuller et al., 2016) included a shared task
on NLI based on the spoken response of non-native English speakers. The 2017 NLI shared
task (Malmasi et al., 2017) attempts to combine
these approaches by including a written response
(essay) and a spoken response (speech transcript
and i-vector acoustic features) for each subject.
Our team (UnibucKernel) participated in all three
tracks proposed by the organizers of the 2017 NLI
shared task, in which the competitors were allowed to use only the essays (closed essay track),
only the speech transcripts (closed speech track),
or both modalities (closed fusion track).

Our approach in each track combines two or

---

[*] The authors have equally contributed to this work.

Proceedings of the 12th Workshop on Innovative Use of NLP for Building Educational Applications, pages 224–234
Copenhagen, Denmark, September 8, 2017. ©2017 Association for Computational Linguistics

more kernels using multiple kernel learning. The first kernel that we considered is the p-grams presence bits kernel[1], which takes into account only the presence of p-grams instead of their frequency. The second kernel is the (histogram) intersection string kernel[2], which was first used in a text mining task by Ionescu et al. (2014). While these kernels are based on character p-grams extracted from essays or speech transcrips, we also use an RBF kernel (Shawe-Taylor and Cristianini, 2004) based on i-vectors (Dehak et al., 2011), a low-dimensional representation of audio recordings, made available by the 2017 NLI shared task organizers (Malmasi et al., 2017). We have also considered squared RBF kernel versions of the string kernels and the kernel based on i-vectors. We have taken into consideration two kernel classifiers (Shawe-Taylor and Cristianini, 2004) for the learning task, namely Kernel Ridge Regression (KRR) and Kernel Discriminant Analysis (KDA). In a set of preliminary experiments performed on the development set, we found that KDA gives better results than KRR, which is consistent with our previous work (Ionescu et al., 2014, 2016). Therefore, we decided to submit results using just the KDA classifier. We have also tuned the range of p-grams for the string kernels. Using only the data provided by the organizers for training our models, we have reached a weighted F_1 score of 86.95% in the essay track, a weighted F_1 score of 87.55% in the speech track, and a weighted F_1 score of 93.19% in the fusion track.

The first time we used string kernels for NLI, we placed third in the 2013 NLI shared task (Popescu and Ionescu, 2013). In 2014, we improved our method and reached state-of-the-art performance (Ionescu et al., 2014). More recently, we have shown that our method is language independent and robust to topic bias (Ionescu et al., 2016). However, with all the improvements since 2013, our method remained a simple and shallow approach. In spite of its simplicity, the aim of this paper is to demonstrate that our approach can still achieve state-of-the-art NLI results, 4 years after its conception.

The paper is organized as follows. Related work on native language identification and string kernels is presented in Section 2. Section 3 presents

the kernels that we used in our approach. The learning methods used in the experiments are described in Section 4. Details about the NLI experiments are provided in Section 5. Finally, we draw conclusions and discuss future work in Section 6.

2 Related Work

2.1 Native Language Identification

As defined in the introduction, the goal of automatic native language identification (NLI) is to determine the native language of a language learner, based on a piece of writing or speech in a foreign language. Most research has focused on identifying the native language of English language learners, though there have been some efforts recently to identify the native language of writing in other languages, such as Chinese (Malmasi and Dras, 2014b) or Arabic (Malmasi and Dras, 2014a).

The first work to study automated NLI was that of Tomokiyo and Jones (2001). In their study, a Naïve Bayes model is trained to distinguish speech transcripts produced by native versus non-native English speakers. A few years later, a second study on NLI appeared (Jarvis et al., 2004). In their work, Jarvis et al. (2004) tried to determine how well a Discriminant Analysis classifier could predict the L1 language of nearly five hundred English learners from different backgrounds. To make the task more challenging, they included pairs of closely related L1 languages, such as Portuguese and Spanish. The seminal paper by Koppel et al. (2005) introduced some of the best-performing features for the NLI task: character, word and part-of-speech n-grams along with features inspired by the work in the area of second language acquisition such as spelling and grammatical errors. In general, most approaches to NLI have used multi-way classification with SVM or similar models along with a range of linguistic features. The book of Jarvis and Crossley (2012) presents some of the state-of-the-art approaches used up until 2012. Being the first book of its kind, it focuses on the automated detection of L2 language-use patterns that are specific to different L1 backgrounds, with the help of text classification methods. Additionally, the book presents methodological tools to empirically test language transfer hypotheses, with the aim of explaining how the languages that a person knows interact in the mind.

In 2013, Tetreault et al. (2013) organized the

---

[1]We computed the p-grams presence bits kernel using the code available at http://string-kernels.herokuapp.com.

[2]We computed the intersection string kernel using the code available at http://string-kernels.herokuapp.com.

first shared task in the field. This allowed researchers to compare approaches for the first time on a specifically designed NLI corpus that was much larger than previously available data sets. In the shared task, 29 teams submitted results for the test set, and one of the most successful aspects of the competition was that it drew submissions from teams working in a variety of research fields. The submitted systems utilized a wide range of machine learning approaches, combined with several innovative feature contributions. The best performing system in the closed task achieved an overall accuracy of 83.6% on the 11-way classification of the test set, although there was no significant difference between the top teams. Since the 2013 NLI shared task, several systems (Bykh and Meurers, 2014, 2016; Ionescu et al., 2014, 2016) have reported results above the top scoring system of the 2013 NLI shared task.

Another interesting linguistic interpretation of native language identification data was only recently addressed, specifically the analysis of second language usage patterns caused by native language interference. Usually, language transfer is studied by Second Language Acquisition researchers using manual tools. Language transfer analysis based on automated native language identification methods has been the approach of Jarvis and Crossley (2012). Swanson and Charniak (2014) also define a computational methodology that produces a ranked list of syntactic patterns that are correlated with language transfer. Their methodology allows the detection of fairly obvious language transfer effects, without being able to detect underused patterns. The first work to address the automatic extraction of underused and overused features on a per native language basis is that of Malmasi and Dras (2014c). The work of Ionescu et al. (2016) also addressed the automatic extraction of underused and overused features captured by character p-grams.

2.2 String Kernels

In recent years, methods of handling text at the character level have demonstrated impressive performance levels in various text analysis tasks (Lodhi et al., 2002; Sanderson and Guenter, 2006; Kate and Mooney, 2006; Grozea et al., 2009; Popescu, 2011; Escalante et al., 2011; Popescu and Grozea, 2012; Popescu and Ionescu, 2013; Ionescu et al., 2014, 2016; Giménez-Pérez et al., 2017; Ionescu and Butnaru, 2017). String kernels are a common form of using information at the character level. They are a particular case of the more general convolution kernels (Haussler, 1999). Lodhi et al. (2002) used string kernels for document categorization with very good results. String kernels were also successfully used in authorship identification (Sanderson and Guenter, 2006; Popescu and Grozea, 2012). For example, the system described by Popescu and Grozea (2012) ranked first in most problems and overall in the PAN 2012 Traditional Authorship Attribution tasks. More recently, various blended string kernels reached state-of-the-art accuracy rates for native language identification (Ionescu et al., 2014, 2016) and Arabic dialect identification (Ionescu and Popescu, 2016; Ionescu and Butnaru, 2017). String kernels have also been used for sentiment analysis in various languages (Popescu et al., 2017) and in cross-domain settings (Giménez-Pérez et al., 2017).

3 Kernels for Native Language Identification

3.1 String Kernels

The kernel function captures the intuitive notion of similarity between objects in a specific domain and can be any function defined on the respective domain that is symmetric and positive definite. For strings, many such kernel functions exist with various applications in computational biology and computational linguistics (Shawe-Taylor and Cristianini, 2004). String kernels embed the texts in a very large feature space, given by all the substrings of length p, and leave it to the learning algorithm to select important features for the specific task, by highly weighting these features.

The first kernel that we use in the NLI experiments is the character p-grams presence bits kernel. The feature map defined by this kernel associates to each string a vector of dimension $|\Sigma|^p$ containing the presence bits of all its substrings of length p (p-grams). Formally, for two strings over an alphabet Σ, $s, t \in \Sigma^*$, the character p-grams presence bits kernel is defined as:

$$k_p^{0/1}(s, t) = \sum_{v \in \Sigma^p} \text{in}_v(s) \cdot \text{in}_v(t),$$

where $\text{in}_v(s)$ is 1 if string v occurs as a substring in s, and 0 otherwise.

The second kernel that we employ is the intersection string kernel introduced in (Ionescu et al., 2014). The intersection string kernel is defined as follows:

$$k_p^{\cap}(s, t) = \sum_{v \in \Sigma^p} \min\{\mathrm{num}_v(s), \mathrm{num}_v(t)\},$$

where $\mathrm{num}_v(s)$ is the number of occurrences of string v as a substring in s. Further details about the string kernels for NLI are given in (Ionescu et al., 2016). The efficient algorithm for computing the string kernels is presented in (Popescu et al., 2017).

Data normalization helps to improve machine learning performance for various applications. Since the value range of raw data can have large variation, classifier objective functions will not work properly without normalization. After normalization, each feature has an approximately equal contribution to the similarity between two samples. To ensure a fair comparison of strings of different lengths, normalized versions of the p-grams presence bits kernel and the intersection kernel are being used:

$$\hat{k}_p^{0/1}(s, t) = \frac{k_p^{0/1}(s, t)}{\sqrt{k_p^{0/1}(s, s) \cdot k_p^{0/1}(t, t)}},$$

$$\hat{k}_p^{\cap}(s, t) = \frac{k_p^{\cap}(s, t)}{\sqrt{k_p^{\cap}(s, s) \cdot k_p^{\cap}(t, t)}}.$$

Taking into account p-grams of different lengths and summing up the corresponding kernels, new kernels, termed *blended spectrum kernels*, can be obtained. We have used various blended spectrum kernels in the experiments in order to find the best combination. Inspired by the success of Ionescu and Butnaru (2017) in using a squared RBF kernel based on i-vectors for Arabic dialect identification, we have also tried out squared RBF versions of the above kernels. We first compute the standard RBF kernels as follows:

$$\bar{k}_p^{0/1}(s, t) = exp\left(-\frac{1 - \hat{k}_p^{0/1}(s, t)}{2\sigma^2}\right),$$

$$\bar{k}_p^{\cap}(s, t) = exp\left(-\frac{1 - \hat{k}_p^{\cap}(s, t)}{2\sigma^2}\right).$$

We then interpret the RBF kernel matrix as a feature matrix, and apply the dot product to obtain a linear kernel for this new representation:

$$\bar{K} = K \cdot K'.$$

The resulted squared RBF kernels are denoted by $(\bar{k}_p^{0/1})^2$ and $(\bar{k}_p^{\cap})^2$, respectively.

3.2 Kernel based on Acoustic Features

For the speech and the fusion tracks, we also build a kernel from the i-vectors provided by the organizers (Malmasi et al., 2017). The i-vector approach (Dehak et al., 2011) is a powerful speech modeling technique that comprises all the updates happening during the adaptation of a Gaussian mixture model (GMM) mean components to a given utterance. The provided i-vectors have 800 dimensions. In order to build a kernel from the i-vectors, we first normalize the i-vectors using the L_2-norm, then we compute the euclidean distance between each pair of i-vectors. We next employ the RBF kernel (Shawe-Taylor and Cristianini, 2004) to transform the distance into a similarity measure:

$$\hat{k}^{i\text{-}vec}(x, y) = exp\left(-\frac{\sqrt{\sum_{j=1}^{m}(x_j - y_j)^2}}{2\sigma^2}\right),$$

where x and y are two i-vectors and m represents the size of the two i-vectors, 800 in our case. For optimal results, we have tuned the parameter σ in a set of preliminary experiments. We also interpret the resulted similarity matrix as a feature matrix, and we compute the product between the matrix and its transpose to obtain the squared RBF kernel based on i-vectors, denoted by $(\bar{k}^{i\text{-}vec})^2$.

4 Learning Methods

Kernel-based learning algorithms work by embedding the data into a Hilbert feature space and by searching for linear relations in that space. The embedding is performed implicitly, by specifying the inner product between each pair of points rather than by giving their coordinates explicitly. More precisely, a kernel matrix that contains the pairwise similarities between every pair of training samples is used in the learning stage to assign a vector of weights to the training samples.

Various kernel methods differ in the way they learn to separate the samples. In the case of binary classification problems, kernel-based learning algorithms look for a discriminant function, a function that assigns $+1$ to examples belonging to one class and -1 to examples belonging to the other class. In the NLI experiments, we employed the Kernel Ridge Regression (KRR) binary classifier. Kernel Ridge Regression selects the vector of weights that simultaneously has small empirical error and small norm in the Reproducing Kernel Hilbert Space generated by the kernel function. KRR is a binary classifier, but native language identification is usually a multi-class classification problem. There are many approaches for combining binary classifiers to solve multi-class problems. Typically, the multi-class problem is broken down into multiple binary classification problems using common decomposition schemes such as: one-versus-all and one-versus-one. We considered the one-versus-all scheme for our NLI task. There are also kernel methods that take the multi-class nature of the problem directly into account, for instance Kernel Discriminant Analysis. The KDA classifier is sometimes able to improve accuracy by avoiding the masking problem (Hastie and Tibshirani, 2003). More details about the kernel classifiers employed for NLI are discussed in (Ionescu et al., 2016).

5 Experiments

5.1 Data Set

The corpus provided for the 2017 NLI shared task contains 13,200 multi-modal samples produces by speakers of the following 11 languages: Arabic, Chinese, French, German, Hindi, Italian, Japanese, Korean, Spanish, Telugu and Turkish. The samples are split into 11,000 for training, 1100 for development and 1100 for testing. The distribution of samples per prompt (topic) per native language is balanced. Each sample is composed of an essay and an audio recording of a non-native English learner. For privacy reasons, the shared task organizers were not able to provide the original audio recordings. Instead, they provided a speech transcript and an i-vector representation derived from the audio file.

5.2 Parameter and System Choices

In our approach, we treat essays or speech transcripts as strings. Because the approach works at the character level, there is no need to split the texts into words, or to do any NLP-specific processing before computing the string kernels. Hence, we apply string kernels on the raw text

Kernel	Accuracy	
	KRR	**KDA**
$\hat{k}_{5-9}^{0/1}$	82.18%	84.55%
$\hat{k}_{5-9}^{\cap}$	81.91%	84.18%

Table 1: Accuracy rates of KRR versus KDA on the essay development set.

samples, disregarding the tokenized version of the samples. The only editing done to the texts was the replacing of sequences of consecutive space characters (space, tab, and so on) with a single space character. This normalization was needed in order to prevent the artificial increase or decrease of the similarity between texts, as a result of different spacing.

We used the development set for tuning the parameters of our approach. Although we have some intuition from our previous work (Ionescu et al., 2016) about the optimal range of p-grams that can be used for NLI from essays, we decided to carry out preliminary experiments in order to confirm our intuition. We also carried out preliminary experiments to determine the optimal range of p-grams to be used for speech transcripts, a different kind of representation that captures other features of the non-native English speakers. We fixed the learning method to KDA based on the presence bits kernel and we evaluated all the p-grams in the range 3-9. For essays, we found that p-grams in the range 5-9 work best, which confirms our previous results on raw text documents reported in (Ionescu et al., 2016). For speech transcripts, we found that longer p-grams are not helpful. Thus, the optimal range of p-grams is 5-7. In order to decide which classifier gives higher accuracy rates, we carried out some preliminary experiments using only the essays. The KRR and the KDA classifiers are compared in Table 1. We observe that KDA yields better results for both the blended p-grams presence bits kernel ($\hat{k}_{5-9}^{0/1}$) and the blended p-grams intersection kernel ($\hat{k}_{5-9}^{\cap}$). Therefore, we employ KDA for the subsequent experiments. An interesting remark is that we also obtained better performance with KDA instead of KRR for the English L2, in our previous work (Ionescu et al., 2016).

After fixing the classifier and the range of p-grams for each modality, we conducted further experiments to establish what type of kernel works better, namely the blended p-grams presence bits

Kernel	Accuracy	Track
$\hat{k}^{0/1}_{5-9}$	84.55%	Essay
$\hat{k}^{\cap}_{5-9}$	84.18%	Essay
$\hat{k}^{0/1}_{5-9} + \hat{k}^{\cap}_{5-9}$	**85.18%**	Essay
$(\bar{k}^{0/1}_{5-9})^2$	85.45%	Essay
$(\bar{k}^{\cap}_{5-9})^2$	85.09%	Essay
$(\bar{k}^{0/1}_{5-9})^2 + (\bar{k}^{\cap}_{5-9})^2$	**85.55%**	Essay
$\hat{k}^{0/1}_{5-7}$	58.73%	Speech
$\hat{k}^{\cap}_{5-7}$	58.55%	Speech
$\hat{k}^{i\text{-}vec}$	81.64%	Speech
$\hat{k}^{0/1}_{5-7} + \hat{k}^{\cap}_{5-7}$	58.73%	Speech
$\hat{k}^{0/1}_{5-7} + \hat{k}^{i\text{-}vec}$	**85.27%**	Speech
$\hat{k}^{\cap}_{5-7} + \hat{k}^{i\text{-}vec}$	85.18%	Speech
$\hat{k}^{0/1}_{5-7} + \hat{k}^{\cap}_{5-7} + \hat{k}^{i\text{-}vec}$	84.91%	Speech
$(\bar{k}^{0/1}_{5-7})^2$	59.00%	Speech
$(\bar{k}^{\cap}_{5-7})^2$	59.82%	Speech
$(\bar{k}^{i\text{-}vec})^2$	81.55%	Speech
$(\bar{k}^{0/1}_{5-7})^2 + (\bar{k}^{\cap}_{5-7})^2$	59.91%	Speech
$(\bar{k}^{0/1}_{5-7})^2 + (\bar{k}^{i\text{-}vec})^2$	85.36%	Speech
$(\bar{k}^{\cap}_{5-7})^2 + (\bar{k}^{i\text{-}vec})^2$	85.27%	Speech
$(\bar{k}^{0/1}_{5-7})^2 + (\bar{k}^{\cap}_{5-7})^2 + (\bar{k}^{i\text{-}vec})^2$	**85.45%**	Speech
$\hat{k}^{0/1}_{5-9} + \hat{k}^{\cap}_{5-9} + \hat{k}^{0/1}_{5-7} + \hat{k}^{i\text{-}vec}$	91.64%	Fusion
$\hat{k}^{0/1}_{5-9} + \hat{k}^{0/1}_{5-7} + \hat{k}^{i\text{-}vec}$	**92.09%**	Fusion
$(\bar{k}^{0/1}_{5-9})^2 + (\bar{k}^{\cap}_{5-9})^2 + (\bar{k}^{0/1}_{5-7})^2 + (\bar{k}^{\cap}_{5-7})^2 + (\bar{k}^{i\text{-}vec})^2$	**91.72%**	Fusion

Table 2: Accuracy rates on the NLI development set obtained by KDA based on various kernels for the essay, the speech and the fusion tracks. The submitted systems are highlighted in bold.

kernel, the blended p-grams intersection kernel, or the kernel based on i-vectors. We also included squared RBF versions of these kernels. Since these different kernel representations are obtained either from essays, speech transcripts or from low-level audio features, a good approach for improving the performance is combining the kernels. When multiple kernels are combined, the features are actually embedded in a higher-dimensional space. As a consequence, the search space of linear patterns grows, which helps the classifier in selecting a better discriminant function. The most natural way of combining two or more kernels is to sum them up. Summing up kernels or kernel matrices is equivalent to feature vector concatenation. The kernels were evaluated alone and in various combinations, by employing KDA for the learning task. All the results obtained on the development set are given in Table 2.

The empirical results presented in Table 2 reveal several interesting patterns of the proposed methods. On the essay development set, the presence bits kernel gives slightly better results than the intersection kernel. The combined kernels yield better performance than each of the individual components, which is remarkably consistent with our previous works (Ionescu et al., 2014, 2016). For each kernel, we obtain an improvement of up to 1% by using the squared RBF version. The best performance on the essay development set (85.55%) is obtained by sum of the squared RBF presence bits kernel and the squared RBF intersection kernel. On the speech track, the results are fairly similar among the string kernels, but the kernel based on i-vectors definitely stands out. Indeed, the best individual kernel is the kernel based on i-vectors with an accuracy of 81.64%. By contrast, the best individual string kernel is the squared RBF intersection kernel, which yields an accuracy of 59.82%. Thus, it seems that the character p-grams extracted from speech transcripts do not provide enough information to accurately

Kernel	Accuracy	F_1 (macro)	Track	Rank
$\hat{k}^{0/1}_{5-9} + \hat{k}^{\cap}_{5-9}$	86.91%	**86.95%**	Essay	1st
$(\bar{k}^{0/1}_{5-9})^2 + (\bar{k}^{\cap}_{5-9})^2$	86.91%	**86.95%**	Essay	1st
$\hat{k}^{0/1}_{5-7} + \hat{k}^{i\text{-}vec}$	87.55%	**87.55%**	Speech	1st
$(\bar{k}^{0/1}_{5-7})^2 + (\bar{k}^{\cap}_{5-7})^2 + (\bar{k}^{i\text{-}vec})^2$	87.45%	87.45%	Speech	1st
$\hat{k}^{0/1}_{5-9} + \hat{k}^{0/1}_{5-7} + \hat{k}^{i\text{-}vec}$	93.18%	**93.19%**	Fusion	1st
$(\bar{k}^{0/1}_{5-9})^2 + (\bar{k}^{\cap}_{5-9})^2 + (\bar{k}^{0/1}_{5-7})^2 + (\bar{k}^{\cap}_{5-7})^2 + (\bar{k}^{i\text{-}vec})^2$	93.00%	93.01%	Fusion	1st

Table 3: Accuracy rates on the NLI test set obtained by KDA based on various kernels for the essay, the speech and the fusion tracks. The best marco F_1 score in each track is highlighted in bold. The final rank of each kernel combination in the 2017 NLI shared task is presented on the last column.

distinguish the native languages. On the other hand, the i-vector representation extracted from audio recordings is much more suitable for the NLI task. Interestingly, we obtain consistently better results when we combine the kernels based on i-vectors with one or both of the string kernels. The best performance on the speech development set (85.45%) is obtained by sum of the squared RBF presence bits kernel, the squared RBF intersection kernel and the squared RBF kernel based on i-vectors. The top accuracy levels on the essay and speech development sets are remarkably close. Nevertheless, when we fuse the features captured by the kernels constructed for the two modalities, we obtain considerably better results. This suggests that essays and speech provide complementary information, boosting the accuracy of the KDA classifier by more than 6% on the fusion development set. It is important to note that we tried to fuse the kernel combinations that provided the best performance on the essay and the speech development sets, while keeping the original and the squared RBF versions separated. We also tried out a combination that does not include the intersection string kernel, an idea that seems to improve the performance. Actually, the best performance on the fusion development set (92.09%) is obtained by sum of the presence bits kernel ($\hat{k}^{0/1}_{5-9}$) computed from essays, the presence bits kernel ($\hat{k}^{0/1}_{5-7}$) computed from speech transcripts, and the kernel based on i-vectors ($\hat{k}^{i\text{-}vec}$). In each track, we submitted the top two kernel combinations for the final test evaluation.

5.3 Results

The results on the test set are presented in Table 3. Although we tuned our approach to optimize the accuracy rate, the official evaluation metric for the NLI task is the macro F_1 score. Therefore, we have reported both the accuracy rate and the macro F_1 score in Table 3. Both kernel combinations submitted to the essay track obtain equally good results (86.95%). For the speech and the fusion tracks, the squared RBF kernels reach slightly lower performance than the original kernels. The best submission to the speech track is the KDA classifier based on the sum of the presence bits kernel ($\hat{k}^{0/1}_{5-7}$) and the kernel based on i-vectors ($\hat{k}^{i\text{-}vec}$), a combination that reaches a macro F_1 score of 87.55%. These two kernels are also included in the sum of kernels that gives our top performance in the fusion track (93.19%). Along with the two kernels, the best submission to the fusion track also includes the presence bits kernel ($\hat{k}^{0/1}_{5-9}$) computed from essays. An interesting remark is that the results on the test set (Table 3) are generally more than 1% better than the results on the development set (Table 2), perhaps because we have included the development samples in the training set for the final test evaluation.

The organizers have grouped the teams based on statistically significant differences between each team's best submission, calculated using McNemar's test with an alpha value of 0.05. The macro F_1 score of 86.95% places us in the first group of methods in the essay track, although we reach only the sixth best performance within the group. Remarkably, we also rank in the first group of methods in the speech and the fusion tracks, while also reaching the best performance in each of these two tracks. It is important to note that UnibucKernel is the only team ranked in first group of teams in each and every track of the 2017 NLI shared task, indicating that our shallow and simple approach is still state-of-the-art in the field.

To better visualize our results, we have included

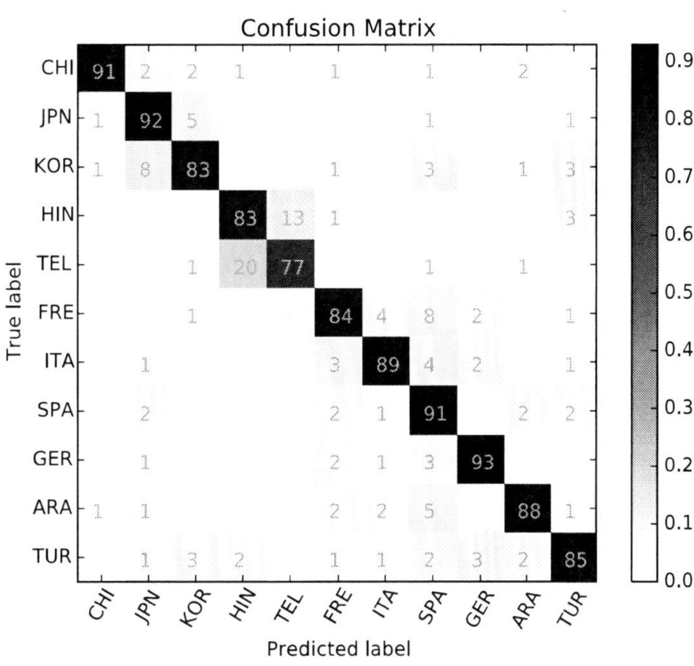

Figure 1: Confusion matrix of the system based on squared RBF kernels on the essay track.

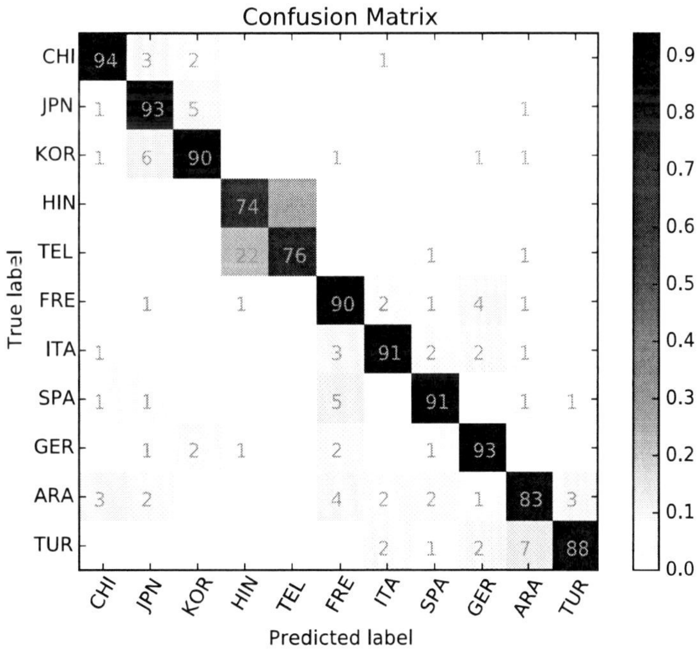

Figure 2: Confusion matrix of the best system on the speech track.

the confusion matrices for our best runs in each track. The confusion matrix presented in Figure 1 shows that our approach for the essay track has a higher misclassification rate for Telugu, Hindi and Korean, while the confusion matrix shown in Figure 2 indicates that our approach for the speech track has a higher misclassification rate for Hindi, Telugu and Arabic. Finally, the confusion matrix illustrated in Figure 3, shows that we are able to obtain the highest correct classification rate for

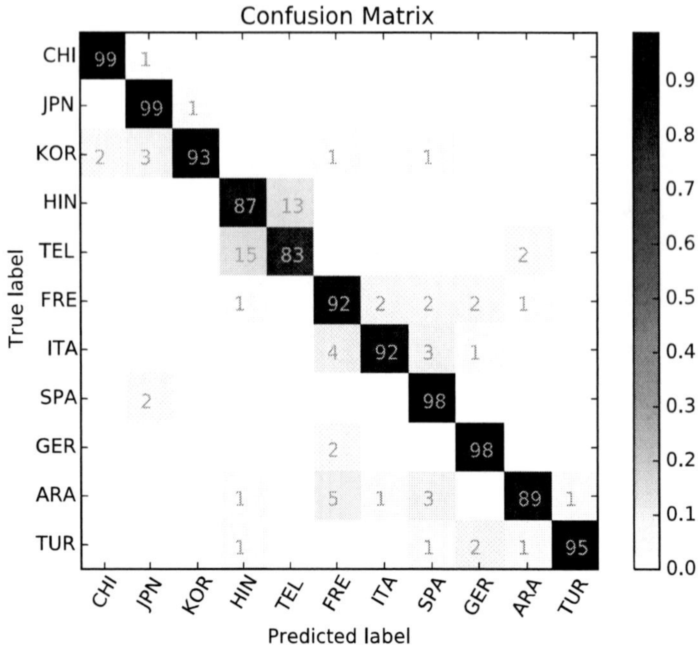

Figure 3: Confusion matrix of the best system on the fusion track.

each and every L1 language (with respect to the other two confusion matrices) by fusing the essay and speech information. While there are no more than two misclassified samples for Chinese, Japanese, Spanish and German, our fusion-based approach still has some trouble in distinguishing Hindi and Telugu. Another interesting remark is that 5 native Arabic speakers are wrongly classified as French, perhaps because these Arabic speakers are from Maghreb, a region in which French arrived as a colonial language. As many people in this region speak French as a second language, it seems that our system gets confused by the mixed Arabic (L1) and French (L2) language transfer patterns that are observable in English (L3).

6 Conclusion and Future Work

In this paper, we have described our approach based on learning with multiple kernels for the 2017 NLI shared task (Malmasi et al., 2017). Our approach attained generally good results, consistent with those reported in our previous works (Ionescu et al., 2014, 2016). Indeed, our team (UnibucKernel) ranked in the first group of teams in all three tracks, while reaching the best marco F_1 scores in the speech (87.55%) and the fusion (93.19%) tracks. As we are the only team

that ranked in first group of teams in each and every track of the 2017 NLI shared task, we consider that our approach has passed the test of time in native language identification.

Although we refrained from including other types of features in order to keep our approach shallow and simple, and to prove that we can achieve state-of-the-art results using character p-grams alone, we will consider combining string kernels with other features in future work.

Acknowledgments

This research is supported by University of Bucharest, Faculty of Mathematics and Computer Science, through the 2017 Mobility Fund.

References

Serhiy Bykh and Detmar Meurers. 2014. Exploring Syntactic Features for Native Language Identification: A Variationist Perspective on Feature Encoding and Ensemble Optimization. *Proceedings of COLING* pages 1962–1973.

Serhiy Bykh and Detmar Meurers. 2016. Advancing Linguistic Features and Insights by Label-informed Feature Grouping: An Exploration in the Context of Native Language Identification. *Proceedings of COLING 2016* pages 739–749.

Najim Dehak, Pedro A. Torres-Carrasquillo, Douglas A. Reynolds, and Rda Dehak. 2011. Language recognition via i-vectors and dimensionality reduction. *Proceedings of INTERSPEECH* pages 857–860.

Hugo Jair Escalante, Thamar Solorio, and Manuel Montes-y-Gómez. 2011. Local histograms of character n-grams for authorship attribution. *Proceedings of ACL: HLT* 1:288–298.

Dominique Estival, Tanja Gaustad, Son-Bao Pham, Will Radford, and Ben Hutchinson. 2007. Author profiling for English emails. *Proceedings of PACLING* pages 263–272.

Rosa M. Giménez-Pérez, Marc Franco-Salvador, and Paolo Rosso. 2017. Single and Cross-domain Polarity Classification using String Kernels. *Proceedings of EACL* pages 558–563.

Cristian Grozea, Christian Gehl, and Marius Popescu. 2009. ENCOPLOT: Pairwise Sequence Matching in Linear Time Applied to Plagiarism Detection. In *3rd PAN Workshop. Uncovering Plagiarism, Authorship, and Social Software Misuse*. page 10.

Trevor Hastie and Robert Tibshirani. 2003. *The Elements of Statistical Learning*. Springer, corrected edition.

David Haussler. 1999. Convolution Kernels on Discrete Structures. Technical Report UCS-CRL-99-10, University of California at Santa Cruz, Santa Cruz, CA, USA.

Radu Tudor Ionescu and Andrei Butnaru. 2017. Learning to Identify Arabic and German Dialects using Multiple Kernels. *Proceedings of VarDial Workshop of EACL* pages 200–209.

Radu Tudor Ionescu and Marius Popescu. 2016. UnibucKernel: An Approach for Arabic Dialect Identification based on Multiple String Kernels. *Proceedings of VarDial Workshop of COLING* pages 135–144.

Radu Tudor Ionescu, Marius Popescu, and Aoife Cahill. 2014. Can characters reveal your native language? a language-independent approach to native language identification. *Proceedings of EMNLP* pages 1363–1373.

Radu Tudor Ionescu, Marius Popescu, and Aoife Cahill. 2016. String kernels for native language identification: Insights from behind the curtains. *Computational Linguistics* 42(3):491–525.

Scott Jarvis, Gabriela Castañeda Jiménez, and Rasmus Nielsen. 2004. Investigating L1 lexical transfer through learners' wordprints. *Second Language Research Forum (SLRF)* .

Scott Jarvis and Scott Crossley, editors. 2012. *Approaching Language Transfer Through Text Classification: Explorations in the Detection-based Approach*, volume 64. Multilingual Matters Limited, Bristol, UK.

Rohit J. Kate and Raymond J. Mooney. 2006. Using String-kernels for Learning Semantic Parsers. *Proceedings of ACL* pages 913–920.

Moshe Koppel, Jonathan Schler, and Kfir Zigdon. 2005. Automatically Determining an Anonymous Author's Native Language. *Proceedings of ISI* pages 209–217.

Huma Lodhi, Craig Saunders, John Shawe-Taylor, Nello Cristianini, and Christopher J. C. H. Watkins. 2002. Text classification using string kernels. *Journal of Machine Learning Research* 2:419–444.

Shervin Malmasi and Mark Dras. 2014a. Arabic Native Language Identification. *Proceedings of the EMNLP 2014 Workshop on Arabic Natural Language Processing (ANLP)* pages 180–186.

Shervin Malmasi and Mark Dras. 2014b. Chinese Native Language Identification. *Proceedings of EACL* 2:95–99.

Shervin Malmasi and Mark Dras. 2014c. Language Transfer Hypotheses with Linear SVM Weights. *Proceedings of EMNLP* pages 1385–1390.

Shervin Malmasi, Keelan Evanini, Aoife Cahill, Joel Tetreault, Robert Pugh, Christopher Hamill, Diane Napolitano, and Yao Qian. 2017. A Report on the 2017 Native Language Identification Shared Task. *Proceedings of the 12th Workshop on Building Educational Applications Using NLP* .

Marius Popescu. 2011. Studying translationese at the character level. *Proceedings of RANLP* pages 634–639.

Marius Popescu and Cristian Grozea. 2012. Kernel methods and string kernels for authorship analysis. *CLEF (Online Working Notes/Labs/Workshop)* .

Marius Popescu, Cristian Grozea, and Radu Tudor Ionescu. 2017. HASKER: An efficient algorithm for string kernels. Application to polarity classification in various languages. *Proceedings of KES* .

Marius Popescu and Radu Tudor Ionescu. 2013. The Story of the Characters, the DNA and the Native Language. *Proceedings of the Eighth Workshop on Innovative Use of NLP for Building Educational Applications* pages 270–278.

Alla Rozovskaya and Dan Roth. 2010. Generating Confusion Sets for Context-Sensitive Error Correction. *Proceedings of EMNLP* pages 961–970.

Conrad Sanderson and Simon Guenter. 2006. Short text authorship attribution via sequence kernels, markov chains and author unmasking: An investigation. *Proceedings of EMNLP* pages 482–491.

Bjrn Schuller, Stefan Steidl, Anton Batliner, Julia Hirschberg, Judee K. Burgoon, Alice Baird, Aaron Elkins, Yue Zhang, Eduardo Coutinho, and Keelan

Evanini. 2016. The INTERSPEECH 2016 Computational Paralinguistics Challenge: Deception, Sincerity & Native Language. *Proceedings of INTERSPEECH* pages 2001–2005.

John Shawe-Taylor and Nello Cristianini. 2004. *Kernel Methods for Pattern Analysis.* Cambridge University Press.

Ben Swanson and Eugene Charniak. 2014. Data driven language transfer hypotheses. *Proceedings of EACL* pages 169–173.

Joel Tetreault, Daniel Blanchard, and Aoife Cahill. 2013. A report on the first native language identification shared task. *Proceedings of the Eighth Workshop on Innovative Use of NLP for Building Educational Applications* pages 48–57.

Laura Mayfield Tomokiyo and Rosie Jones. 2001. You're Not From 'Round Here, Are You? Naive Bayes Detection of Non-Native Utterances. *Proceedings of NAACL* .

Neural Networks and Spelling Features for Native Language Identification

Johannes Bjerva
CLCG
University of Groningen
j.bjerva@rug.nl

Gintarė Grigonytė
Department of Linguistics
Stockholm University
gintare@ling.su.se

Robert Östling
Department of Linguistics
Stockholm University
robert@ling.su.se

Barbara Plank
CLCG
University of Groningen
b.plank@rug.nl

Abstract

We present the RUG-SU team's submission at the Native Language Identification Shared Task 2017. We combine several approaches into an ensemble, based on spelling error features, a simple neural network using word representations, a deep residual network using word and character features, and a system based on a recurrent neural network. Our best system is an ensemble of neural networks, reaching an F1 score of 0.8323. Although our system is not the highest ranking one, we do outperform the baseline by far.

1 Introduction

Native Language Identification (NLI) is the task of identifying the native language of, e.g., the writer of an English text. In this paper, we describe the University of Groningen / Stockholm University (team RUG-SU) submission to NLI Shared Task 2017 (Malmasi et al., 2017). Neural networks constitute one of the most popular methods in natural language processing these days (Manning, 2015), but appear not to have been previously used for NLI. Our goal in this paper is therefore twofold. On the one hand, we wish to investigate how well a neural system can perform the task. On the other hand, we wish to investigate the effect of using features based on spelling errors.

2 Related Work

NLI is an increasingly popular task, which has been the subject of several shared tasks in recent years (Tetreault et al., 2013; Schuller et al., 2016; Malmasi et al., 2017). Although earlier shared task editions have focussed on English, NLI has recently also turned to including non-English languages (Malmasi and Dras, 2015). Additionally, although the focus in the past has been on using written text, speech transcripts and audio features have also been included in recent editions, for instance in the 2016 Computational Paralinguistics Challenge (Schuller et al., 2016). Although these aspects are combined in the NLI Shared Task 2017, with both written and spoken responses available, we only utilise written responses in this work. For a further overview of NLI, we refer the reader to Malmasi (2016).

Previous approaches to NLI have used syntactic features (Bykh and Meurers, 2014), string kernels (Ionescu et al., 2014), and variations of ensemble models (Malmasi and Dras, 2017; Tetreault et al., 2013). No systems used neural networks in the 2013 shared task (Tetreault et al., 2013), hence ours is one of the first works using a neural approach for this task, along with concurrent submissions in this shared task (Malmasi et al., 2017).

3 External data

3.1 PoS-tagged sentences

We indirectly use the training data for the Stanford PoS tagger (Manning et al., 2014), and for initialising word embeddings we use GloVe embeddings from 840 billion tokens of web data.[1]

3.2 Spelling features

We investigate learner misspellings, which is mainly motivated by two assumptions. For one, spelling errors are quite prevalent in learners' written production (Kochmar, 2011). Additionally, spelling errors have been shown to be influenced by phonological L1 transfer (Grigonytė and Hammarberg, 2014). We use the Aspell spell checker to detect misspelled words.[2]

---

[1]https://nlp.stanford.edu/projects/glove/

[2]http://aspell.net

Proceedings of the 12th Workshop on Innovative Use of NLP for Building Educational Applications, pages 235–239
Copenhagen, Denmark, September 8, 2017. ©2017 Association for Computational Linguistics

4 Systems

4.1 Deep Residual Networks

Deep residual networks, or *resnets*, are a class of convolutional neural networks, which consist of several convolutional blocks with skip connections in between (He et al., 2015, 2016). Such skip connections facilitate error propagation to earlier layers in the network, which allows for building deeper networks. Although their primary application is image recognition and related tasks, recent work has found deep residual networks to be useful for a range of NLP tasks. Examples of this include morphological re-inflection (Östling, 2016), semantic tagging (Bjerva et al., 2016), and other text classification tasks (Conneau et al., 2016).

We apply resnets with four residual blocks. Each residual block contains two successive one-dimensional convolutions, with a kernel size and stride of 2. Each such block is followed by an average pooling layer and dropout ($p = 0.5$, Srivastava et al. (2014)). The resnets are applied to several input representations: word unigrams, and character 4- to 6-grams. These input representations are first embedded into a 64-dimensional space, and trained together with the task. We do not use any pre-trained embeddings for this subsystem. The outputs of each resnet are concatenated before passing through two fully connected layers, with 1024 and 256 hidden units respectively. We use the rectified linear unit (ReLU, Glorot et al. (2011)) activation function. We train the resnet over 50 epochs with the Adam optimisation algorithm (Kingma and Ba, 2014), using the model with the lowest validation loss. In addition to dropout, we use weight decay for regularisation ($\epsilon = 10^{-4}$, Krogh and Hertz (1992)).

4.2 PoS-tagged sentences

In order to easier capture general syntactic patterns, we use a sentence-level bidirectional LSTM over tokens and their corresponding part of speech tags from the Stanford CoreNLP toolkit (Manning et al., 2014). PoS tags are represented by 64-dimensional embeddings, initialised randomly; word tokens by 300-dimensional embeddings, initialised with GloVe (Pennington et al., 2014) embeddings trained on 840 billion words of English web data from the Common Crawl project.[3]

[3]`https://nlp.stanford.edu/projects/glove/`

To reduce overfitting, we perform training by choosing a random subset of 50% of the sentences in an essay, concatenating their PoS tag and token embeddings, and running the resulting vector sequence through a bidirectional LSTM layer with 256 units per direction. We then average the final output vector of the LSTM over all the selected sentences from the essay, pass it through a hidden layer with 1024 units and rectified linear activations, then make the final predictions through a linear layer with softmax activations. We apply dropout ($p = 0.5$) on the final hidden layer.

4.3 Spelling features

Essays are checked with the Aspell spell checker for any misspelled words. If misspellings occur, we simply consider the first suggestion of the spell checker to be the most likely correction. The features for NLI classification are derived entirely from misspelled words. We consider deletion, insertion, and replacement type of corrections. Features are represented as pairs of original and corrected character sequences (uni, bi, tri), for instance:

```
visiters visitors
{(e,o),(te,to),(ter,tor)}
travellers travelers
{(l,0),(ll,l0),(ole,l0e)}
```

These features are fed to a logistic regression classifier with builtin cross-validation, as implemented in the scikit-learn library.[4]

4.4 CBOW features

We complement the neural approaches with a simple neural network that uses word representations, namely a *continuous bag-of-words* (CBOW) model (Mikolov et al., 2013). It represents each essay simply as the average embedding of all words in the essay. The intuition is that this simple model provides complementary evidence to the models that use sequential information. Our CBOW model was tuned on the DEV data and consists of an input layer of 512 input nodes, followed by a dropout layer ($p = 0.1$) and a single softmax output layer. The model was trained for 20 epochs with Adam using a batch size of 50. No pre-trained embeddings were used in this model. We additionally experiment with a simple multiplayer perceptron (MLP). In contrast to CBOW it uses n-hot features (of the size of the vocabulary),

[4]`http://scikit-learn.org/`

Table 1: Official results for the essay task, with and without external resources (ext. res.).

Setting	System	F1 (macro)	Accuracy
Baselines	Random Baseline	0.0909	0.0909
	Official Baseline	0.7100	0.7100
No ext. res.	01 – Resnet (w_1+c_5)	0.8016	0.8027
	02 – Resnet (w_1+c_5)	0.7776	0.7782
	03 – Ensemble (Resnet (w_1+c_5), Resnet (c_4))	0.7969	0.7964
	04 – Ensemble (Resnet (w_1+c_5), Resnet (c_6), Resnet (c_4), Resnet (c_3))	0.8023	0.8018
	05 – Ensemble (Resnet (w_1+c_5), Resnet (c_6), Resnet (c_4), CBOW)	0.8149	0.8145
	06 – Ensemble (Resnet (w_1+c_5), Resnet (c_6), MLP, CBOW)	**0.8323**	**0.8318**
With ext. res.	01 – Ensemble (LSTM, Resnet (w_1+c_5))	**0.8191**	**0.8186**
	02 – Ensemble (LSTM, Resnet (w_1+c_5), Resnet (c_4))	0.8191	0.8195
	03 – Ensemble (Spell, LSTM, Resnet (w_1+c_5), Resnet (c_6), CBOW)	0.8173	0.8175
	04 – Ensemble (Spell, Resnet (w_1+c_5), Resnet (c_6), CBOW)	0.8055	0.8051
	05 – Ensemble (Spell, Spell, Resnet (w_1+c_5), Resnet (c_6), Resnet (c_4), CBOW)	0.8045	0.8048
	06 – Ensemble (LSTM, Resnet (w_1+c_5), Resnet (c_6), Resnet (c_4), CBOW)	0.8009	0.8007

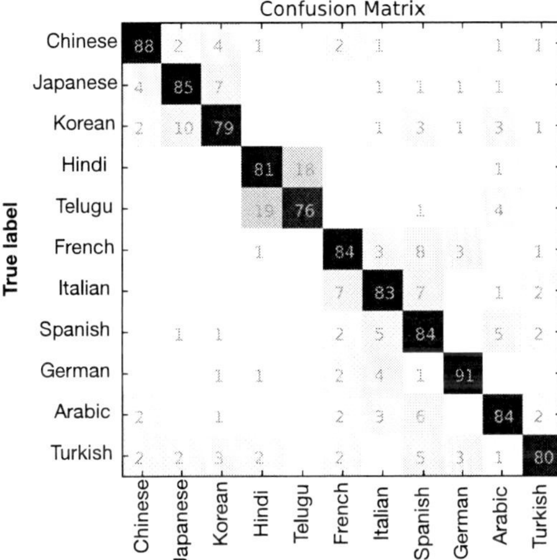

Figure 1: Confusion matrix for our best run (closed track, run 06)

a single layer with 512 nodes, sigmoid activation and dropout ($p = 0.1$). The remaining training parameters are the same as for CBOW. We see that this model adds complementary knowledge in the closed-track ensemble (run 06).

4.5 Ensemble

The systems are combined into an ensemble, consisting of a linear SVM. We use the probability distributions over the labels, as output by each system, as features for the SVM, as in meta-classification (Malmasi and Dras, 2017). The ensemble is trained and tuned on a random subset of the development set (70/30 split). For the selection of systems to include in the ensemble, we use the combination of systems resulting in the highest mean accuracy over five such random splits.

5 Results

The results when using external resources are lower than when not using them (Table 1). Our best result without external resources is an F1 score of 83.23, whereas we obtain F1 score of 81.91 with such resources. Figure 1 shows the confusion matrix of our best system's predictions (run 06). Most confusions occur in three groups: *Hindi* and *Telugu* (South Asian), *Japanese* and *Korean* (East Asian), and *French*, *Italian* and *Spanish* (South European).

6 Discussion

In isolation, the ResNet system yields a relatively high F1 score of 80.16. This indicates that, although simpler methods yield better results for this task, deep neural networks are also applicable. However, further experimentation is needed before such a system can outperform the more traditional feature-based systems. This is in line with previous findings for the related task of language identification (Medvedeva et al., 2017; Zampieri et al., 2017). Combining all of our systems without external data yields an F1 score of 83.23, which places our system in the third best performing group of the NLI Shared Task 2017 (Malmasi et al., 2017).

When adding external data, the best performing systems are those including the spelling system predictions and/or the LSTM predictions. However, the highest F1 score obtained (81.91) is lower than our best score without external resources. This can attributed to overfitting of the ensemble on the development data. It is nonetheless interesting that adding spelling features does boost performance within the external resources setting.

The main confusions of our system were within three groups. We suggest two reasons for this bias. On the one hand, the South European group also encompasses only Romance languages, hence the confusion could be attributed to the learners making similar mistakes in the grammar. However, both the South Asian group and the East Asian group comprise languages which are not related to one another. Therefore, it is reasonable to assume that the confusion is also due to a cultural bias, such as South European learners using more vacation-related words, or South Asian learners using words related to India (in which both of the languages in question are spoken).

7 Conclusions

We describe our system for the NLI Shared Task 2017, which is one the first system to involve a neural approach to this task. Although deep neural networks are able to perform this task, traditional methods still appear to be better.

Acknowledgments

This work was partially funded by the NWO–VICI grant 'Lost in Translation – Found in Meaning' (288-89-003).

References

Johannes Bjerva, Barbara Plank, and Johan Bos. 2016. Semantic tagging with deep residual networks. In *Proceedings of COLING 2016, the 26th International Conference on Computational Linguistics: Technical Papers*. The COLING 2016 Organizing Committee, pages 3531–3541. http://aclweb.org/anthology/C16-1333.

Serhiy Bykh and Detmar Meurers. 2014. Exploring Syntactic Features for Native Language Identification: A Variationist Perspective on Feature Encoding and Ensemble Optimization. In *Proceedings of COLING 2014, the 25th International Conference on Computational Linguistics: Technical Papers*. Dublin, Ireland, pages 1962–1973.

Alexis Conneau, Holger Schwenk, Loïc Barrault, and Yann Lecun. 2016. Very deep convolutional networks for natural language processing. *arXiv preprint arXiv:1606.01781* .

Xavier Glorot, Antoine Bordes, and Yoshua Bengio. 2011. Deep sparse rectifier neural networks. In *International Conference on Artificial Intelligence and Statistics*. pages 315–323.

Gintarė Grigonytė and Björn Hammarberg. 2014. Pronunciation and spelling: the case of misspellings in swedish l2 written essays. In *6th International Conference on Human Language Technologies-The Baltic Perspective (Baltic HLT), Kaunas, Lithuania, September 26-27, 2014*. IOS Press, pages 95–98.

Kaiming He, Xiangyu Zhang, Shaoqing Ren, and Jian Sun. 2015. Deep residual learning for image recognition. *arXiv preprint arXiv:1512.03385* .

Kaiming He, Xiangyu Zhang, Shaoqing Ren, and Jian Sun. 2016. Identity mappings in deep residual networks. *CoRR abs/1603.05027*.

Radu Tudor Ionescu, Marius Popescu, and Aoife Cahill. 2014. Can characters reveal your native language? A language-independent approach to native language identification. In *Proceedings of the 2014 Conference on Empirical Methods in Natural Language Processing (EMNLP)*. Association for Computational Linguistics.

Diederik Kingma and Jimmy Ba. 2014. Adam: A method for stochastic optimization. *arXiv preprint arXiv:1412.6980* .

Ekaterina Kochmar. 2011. *Identification of a Writers Native Language by Error Analysis*. Master's thesis, University of Cambridge.

Anders Krogh and John A Hertz. 1992. A simple weight decay can improve generalization. In *Advances in neural information processing systems*. pages 950–957.

Shervin Malmasi. 2016. *Native Language Identification: Explorations and Applications*. Ph.D. thesis. http://hdl.handle.net/1959.14/1110919.

Shervin Malmasi and Mark Dras. 2015. Multilingual Native Language Identification. In *Natural Language Engineering*.

Shervin Malmasi and Mark Dras. 2017. Native Language Identification using Stacked Generalization. *arXiv preprint arXiv:1703.06541* .

Shervin Malmasi, Keelan Evanini, Aoife Cahill, Joel Tetreault, Robert Pugh, Christopher Hamill, Diane Napolitano, and Yao Qian. 2017. A Report on the 2017 Native Language Identification Shared Task. In *Proceedings of the 12th Workshop on Building Educational Applications Using NLP*. Association for Computational Linguistics, Copenhagen, Denmark.

Christopher D. Manning. 2015. Computational linguistics and deep learning. *Computational Linguistics* 41(4):701–707.

Christopher D. Manning, Mihai Surdeanu, John Bauer, Jenny Finkel, Steven J. Bethard, and David McClosky. 2014. The Stanford CoreNLP natural language processing toolkit. In *Association for Computational Linguistics (ACL) System Demonstrations*. pages 55–60. http://www.aclweb.org/anthology/P/P14/P14-5010.

Maria Medvedeva, Martin Kroon, and Barbara Plank. 2017. When sparse traditional models outperform dense neural networks: the curious case of discriminating between similar languages. In *Proceedings of VarDial 2017*. page 156.

Tomas Mikolov, Kai Chen, Greg Corrado, and Jeffrey Dean. 2013. Efficient estimation of word representations in vector space. *arXiv preprint arXiv:1301.3781* .

Robert Östling. 2016. Morphological reinflection with convolutional neural networks. In *Proceedings of the 2016 Meeting of SIGMORPHON*. Association for Computational Linguistics, Berlin, Germany.

Jeffrey Pennington, Richard Socher, and Christopher D. Manning. 2014. Glove: Global vectors for word representation. In *Empirical Methods in Natural Language Processing (EMNLP)*. pages 1532–1543. http://www.aclweb.org/anthology/D14-1162.

Björn Schuller, Stefan Steidl, Anton Batliner, Julia Hirschberg, Judee K. Burgoon, Alice Baird, Aaron Elkins, Yue Zhang, Eduardo Coutinho, and Keelan Evanini. 2016. The INTER-SPEECH 2016 Computational Paralinguistics Challenge: Deception, Sincerity & Native Language. In *Interspeech 2016*. pages 2001–2005. https://doi.org/10.21437/Interspeech.2016-129.

Nitish Srivastava, Geoffrey E Hinton, Alex Krizhevsky, Ilya Sutskever, and Ruslan Salakhutdinov. 2014. Dropout: a simple way to prevent neural networks from overfitting. *Journal of Machine Learning Research* 15(1):1929–1958.

Joel Tetreault, Daniel Blanchard, and Aoife Cahill. 2013. A Report on the First Native Language Identification Shared Task. In *Proceedings of the Eighth Workshop on Building Educational Applications Using NLP*. Association for Computational Linguistics, Atlanta, GA, USA.

Marcos Zampieri, Shervin Malmasi, Nikola Ljubešić, Preslav Nakov, Ahmed Ali, Jörg Tiedemann, Yves Scherrer, and Noëmi Aepli. 2017. Findings of the VarDial Evaluation Campaign 2017. In *Proceedings of the Fourth Workshop on NLP for Similar Languages, Varieties and Dialects (VarDial)*. Valencia, Spain, pages 1–15.

A study of N-gram and Embedding Representations
for Native Language Identification

Sowmya Vajjala   **Sagnik Banerjee**

Iowa State University, USA

sowmya,sagnik@iastate.edu

Abstract

We report on our experiments with N-
gram and embedding based feature representations for Native Language Identification (NLI) as a part of the NLI Shared
Task 2017 (team name: NLI-ISU). Our
best performing system on the test set for
written essays had a macro F1 of 0.8264
and was based on word uni, bi and trigram features. We explored n-grams covering word, character, POS and word-POS
mixed representations for this task. For
embedding based feature representations,
we employed both word and document
embeddings. We had a relatively poor performance with all embedding representations compared to n-grams, which could
be because of the fact that embeddings
capture semantic similarities whereas L1
differences are more stylistic in nature.

1   Introduction

Native Language Identification (NLI) refers to the
task of identifying the native language (L1) of a
writer based on their writings in another language
(L2). Identifying the L1 of a writer is useful in
applications such as authorship attribution, forensic linguistics, language instruction and Second
Language Acquisition (SLA) (Koppel et al., 2005;
Estival et al., 2007; Jarvis and Crossley, 2012).
While early work on this problem began at the
beginning of this century (Tomokiyo and Jones,
2001; Jarvis et al., 2004), there has been an increased interest in this task since 2012, with the
availability of some publicly accessible corpora
(Brooke and Hirst, 2012; Tetreault et al., 2012;
Bykh and Meurers, 2012).

The First NLI Shared Task (Tetreault et al.,
2013) and the release of large corpora such as

TOEFL11 corpus of non-native English (Blanchard et al., 2013) and EFCAMDAT corpus
(Geertzen et al., 2013) resulted in a surge of research in this area in the past few years. While
most of the NLI research has been on English,
there is a significant amount of work on other language texts such as Chinese, Finnish and Arabic
(Malmasi and Dras, 2015; Malmasi, 2016). Starting form surface linguistic forms such as words
and characters to deeper syntactic structures, a
range of features have been explored for this task
in the past five years.

The last few years saw the field of NLI advance
in both the directions of feature engineering and
modeling. However, irrespective of what modeling choices were made, results seem to show that
word level features still are the most predictive
ones as a single group (e.g., Jarvis et al., 2013;
Gebre et al., 2013) for this data. So, in this paper, we take a step back from complex feature and
model engineering, and explore how far can we get
by doing classification using simpler feature rep
resentations based on words, characters and POS
tags. While our current experiments (team name:
NLI-ISU), done as a part of the NLI Shared Task
2017 (Malmasi et al., 2017), do not result in any
improvements over existing approaches, we believe they provide insights into the nature of the
task and why n-grams may still be needed for this
task despite the presence of more compact embedding representations for texts.

The rest of this paper is organized as follows:
The next section describes some of the related
work and puts our experiments in context. Section 3 briefly describes the corpus used. We describe our methodology including feature description in Section 4. Our experiments and results are
discussed in Section 5. Section 6 concludes the
paper with pointers to future work.

Proceedings of the 12th Workshop on Innovative Use of NLP for Building Educational Applications, pages 240–248
Copenhagen, Denmark, September 8, 2017. ©2017 Association for Computational Linguistics

2   Related Work

Native Language Identification is generally treated as a supervised text classification problem in computational linguistics literature. (Koppel et al., 2005) can be described as one of the early works that considers NLI as a supervised machine learning problem. Using a corpus of texts from International Corpus of Learner English (ICLE) along with word and letter n-grams and errors made by the learners as features, they achieved a classification accuracy of over 80%.

Along with n-grams, syntactic features based on parse structures were also shown to be useful for the task in the past (Wong and Dras, 2011) resulting in accuracies in the range of 80-85% with ICLE data. Extending the n-gram based feature sets to larger n-gram sizes and using a combination of word and POS tag n-grams, Bykh and Meurers (2012) achieved an accuracy of 89.7% on the same dataset. With combinations of n-grams, lexical and syntactic features, Brooke and Hirst (2012) explored NLI with multiple corpora, and achieved accuracies of over 90% on ICLE data. Summarizing the research on NLI until then, Tetreault et al. (2012) explored a range of features on ICLE and introduced the TOEFL11 corpus for NLI (Blanchard et al., 2013).

This corpus was used in the first Native Language Identification shared task (Tetreault et al., 2013). 29 teams participating in the task, and wide range of lexical and syntactic feature representations were explored. The best performing system (Jarvis et al., 2013) resulted in an accuracy of 83.6% and used word, char, POS n-gram features.

After this shared task, interest in NLI continued with different groups exploring both finer feature representations and diverse ensemble methods for combining multiple classification models. These explorations resulted in an accuracy gain of up to 2% on the 2013 shared task test set (Ionescu et al., 2014; Bykh and Meurers, 2014, 2016). More recently, (Malmasi and Dras, 2017) reported an accuracy of 87.1% on the 2013 test set, using an ensemble of meta classifiers and a range of word level and syntactic features. Apart from TOEFL11, other corpora such as EFCAM-DAT (Geertzen et al., 2013) were also used for NLI in the recent past (e.g., Nisioi, 2015).

While most of the work in NLI happened in English, a substantial body of NLI research happened in the past two years covering at least six other languages (cf. Malmasi and Dras, 2015; Malmasi, 2016). In addition to using the written responses, a recent development has been the use of speech transcripts and audio features for dialect identification (Malmasi et al., 2016) and native language identification (Schuller et al., 2016). In this background, the NLI Shared Task 2017 was proposed, with an additional spoken language component.

While a range of feature representations and modeling representations have been explored from this task, it has been shown that word/character level n-grams have been unreasonably effective as a single feature group (e.g., Jarvis et al., 2013; Gebre et al., 2013; Bykh et al., 2013). As Jarvis et al. (2013) concluded, "complex features" such as suffixes, length, lexical variety etc did not result in any major improvement over n-gram features. Further, other complex and memory intensive representations such as constituency and dependency parses did not result in large performance improvements without the support of stronger models and ensemble learners.

In this background, in this paper, we take a step back from exploring new feature extraction methods and new modeling techniques, and re-investigate the role of surface feature representations in NLI. Word and document embeddings became popular and useful alternatives to n-gram features in several classification tasks in the recent past as they result in dense representation compared to sparse n-gram features. Hence, in addition to word, character and POS n-grams, we also explored the use of embedding based feature representations for this task.

3   Data

We used a corpus of standardized assessment of English proficiency for academic purposes provided by the shared task organizers. It is a corpus of non-native speaker English essays and speech transcripts. The written corpus has a training data of 11000 essays written by learners with 11 native language backgrounds (Arabic, Chinese, French, German, Hindi, Italian, Japanese, Korean, Spanish, Telugu, Turkish). The essays are written in response to 8 prompts, and essays are evenly distributed across L1s (1000 essays per L1). The development set had 1100 essays (100 per L1) and the prompt information was provided. Exact text for the prompts was not provided in the corpus. No information was given about the proficiency scores for the essays. We discarded two texts from the training data which had only two-three token responses (e.g., "I agree") before starting with feature extraction.

The shared task task also had a speech track, where the goal is to predict the speaker's L1 based on a transcription of a 45 second recording. There were 11000 spoken transcriptions (1000 per L1) in the training data and 1100 (100 per L1) in the development set, similar to the essay section of the corpus. The transcriptions were produced in response to 9 prompts. While the original recordings were not provided, i-vectors, which are low-dimensional representations of the speech signals were provided using the Kaldi toolkit (`http://kaldi-asr.org`). We did not use the i-vectors and only did preliminary n-gram based experiments on that data as well.

Test Data: Test data for both written and spoken texts had 1100 texts each (100 per L1 in each case). i-vectors were provided for the spoken files in the test data as well.

4   Features

As mentioned earlier, we explored two kinds of feature representations in this task: n-grams and embeddings.[1]

4.1   N-gram Representations

We explored N-gram representations at the level of words, characters, POS tags and mixed word-POS representations. Binary feature representation with a minimum n-gram frequency of 10 was used as a common setting for across all features. The maximum number of features was capped at 100K for most of the experiments, to limit feature explosion and over-fitting to rare n-grams. We did not find any significant differences between using binary, count and TF-IDF representations.

Word n-grams :   Word n-grams are used in almost all the previous NLI approaches, and we start with them as well.   We explored 1–8 lower cased n-grams with/without punctuation, with/without stemming and with/without spell check. We used the Enchant spell checker through the PyEnchant library (`http://pyenchant.readthedocs.io`). We considered two n-gram representations using spell-checker:

- replace the spelling error with the most likely word suggested by the checker

- replace the error with a pseudo-word

Spelling errors were used as features in earlier NLI approaches (Koppel et al., 2005; Gebre et al., 2013).   But we are not aware of any previous work that pre-processed for spelling errors before n-gram extraction.

Char n-grams :   We explored 2–10 character grams (lower cased), with/without crossing over word boundaries for n-gram extraction. Punctuation was not included while extracting character n-grams.

POS n-grams :   We explored 1–5 POS grams. We extracted features using both NLTK tagger and Stanford POS tagger.

Word-POS mixed n-grams :   (Bykh and Meurers, 2012) in the past used Open Class POS n-grams where n-grams for open class words (nouns, verbs, adjectives, and cardinal numbers) were replaced by their POS tags and the other words are left as is while calculating n-grams. Similarly, skip word n-grams have also been explored in NLI research before (Malmasi and Cahill, 2015).   We extended such feature representations further by other Word-POS mixed representations such as: replacing only nouns, or only verbs with their tags, or replacing all except prepositions etc. We consider such mixed representations as a form of skip gram representations, where the gap has a name (POS tag, for example). We used NLTK tagger for feature extraction.

4.2   Embedding Representations

Embedding based representations are seen as an alternative to the sparse n-gram based representations in the recent past as they resulted in dense feature representations for text. Hence, we explored word and document level embeddings for this task, using several models. We used gensim[2] to train and classify using embedding features.

Word Embeddings :   We trained the embeddings using the entire training corpus, and tuning the number of dimensions using cross validation. We tried with both CBOW (continuous bag-of-words) and skip-gram. In our experience, CBOW generated the vector representations better

---

[1] code for the feature extraction and classification is hosted at: `https://github.com/nishkalavallabhi/NLIST2017/` for replication purposes.

[2] `https://radimrehurek.com/gensim/`

than skip-grams. For all the settings a minimum word count of 5 was set. The negative sampling rate, for all the settings, was left at default. We did change the negative sampling rate in the hope of obtaining better results but the results we obtained was not significantly better than the default case. For each of the settings, we explored 100 to 1000 features in an increment of 100 and a window setting of 5 to 15 in increments of 2.

Three different methods were used to get the vector representations for documents using these word embeddings:

- summed vector of all the word embeddings

- averaged vector for all the word embeddings

- a combination of average and standard deviation

For building these word embeddings, we used Word2Vec (Mikolov et al., 2013) and FastText (Joulin et al., 2016).

Document Embeddings : In addition to word embeddings, vector representations were also generated for an entire document with distributed memory (dm) and distributed bag-of-words (dbow) architectures (Le and Mikolov, 2014) using Doc2Vec tool. Number of dimensions ranged from 100 to 500 in 100 increments and the window size ranged from 5 to 50. We did not use negative sampling as it was shown in previous research that negative sampling will result in a document embedding that is biased to content words (Lau and Baldwin, 2016) whereas function words are important in the task of NLI.

For document embeddings, we used two representations:

- Doc2Vec-Full: Using the entire training data to construct an unsupervised Doc2Vec model

- Doc2Vec-PerL1: Using training data per L1 to build 11 Doc2Vec models, and use the concatenation of vectors from all 11 models per text during classification training and testing.

Additionally, we also explored the use of Efficient, Compositional, Order-sensitive n-gram Embeddings (ECO) proposed recently by Poliak et al. (2017) for constructing the document embeddings. In ECO embeddings, vector representation of neighbouring words (both occurring before and after) are averaged to obtain the numeric representation of the current word. We used the pre-trained word vectors from Wikipedia dump with dimensionality ranging from 100 to 700 as provided by Poliak et al. (2017).[3] to generate document embeddings

5 Results

We used Logistic Regression and SVMs with default parameters to train our classification models. While there are no significant differences between both the algorithms, logistic regression was much faster. So, unless otherwise stated, we report the results with logistic regression in the rest of this paper. We submitted runs for both the ESSAY track and the SPEECH track. For the SPEECH track we worked with the transcripts directly and not with the i-vectors. macro-F1 and classification accuracy were used as the evaluation measures for this task.

- Run 1: Word 1-3 grams + incl. punctuation + no stemming

- Run 2: Word 1-3 grams + POS Bi, Tri grams

- Run 3: Character n-grams (2–10), crossing word boundaries.

Table 1 shows the results on test set for our submitted systems using Logistic Regression.

System	F1 (macro)	Accuracy
Random Baseline	0.0909	0.0909
Official Baseline (Essay)	0.7104	0.7109
Official Baseline (Speech-transcriptions only)	0.5435	0.5464
Official Baseline (Speech-with ivectors)	0.7980	0.7982
Run 1-Essay	**0.8264**	**0.8264**
Run 2-Essay	0.8201	0.8200
Run 3-Essay	0.7829	0.7836
Run 1-Speech	**0.4282**	**0.4259**
Run 2-Speech	0.4036	0.4000

Table 1: Official Submissions for the ESSAY and SPEECH tracks

Word n-grams (range: 1–3) turned out to be most predictive feature representation among the ones we tried. N-grams beyond 3 did not result

[3]https://zenodo.org/record/439387

in a significant improvement in accuracy. While adding bi-, tri-grams resulted in about 9% improvement in accuracy over unigrams, adding 4-8 grams did not result in any significant performance difference on development set.

Stemming consistently resulted in a decrease in performance compared to non-stemmed features, and including punctuation always resulted in a 2-3% increase in accuracy on the development set for all settings we explored.[4] Adding POS based features to word n-grams did not result in any significant difference in the accuracy. For character n-grams, there was a 3.2% decrease in accuracy on the development set when we did not consider n-grams across word boundaries.

Spell checking: We did not find spell checking particularly useful for this task. Both our spell check feature representations did not result in any improvement in the results on the development set. It could be because we set our minimum frequency threshold to 10 and the error patterns are not frequent and consistent enough in the dataset. On the other hand, this may also imply that the people from the same native language may not always have a consistent spelling error pattern significant enough to be distinguishable from another native language group.

Using only POS n-grams did not result in an accuracy beyond 60% using both the taggers, for n = 1 to 8. Combining them with word n-grams did not result in any improvement either, as it was seen in Run 2 results in Table 1.

Mixed Word-POS representations: In terms of mixed word-POS representations, we explored the following representations using the NLTK tagger:

- Rep 1: Replace all nouns, pronouns and punctuation markers with a single string for each category.

- Rep 2: Same as the above representation, but having retaining punctuation tags for all punctuation markers

- Rep 3: Same as Rep 2, but replacing all verb tags with a single string.

- Rep 4: All words except prepositions were replaced with a common tag, and all punctuations were replaced with a common tag.

- Rep 5: OCPOS representation as described in Bykh and Meurers (2012).

For all these cases, we trained classification models with 1–8 n-grams, minimum frequency of 10, and up to 300K features. While some of these mixed word-POS representations were not explored for this task before, none of the models give an accuracy beyond 75% on the development set. It has to be noted that we used only Logistic Regression and SVM for classification. But, it is unlikely that another classification algorithm would result in a dramatic increase with these feature representations. We did not explore ensemble models where different feature representations are combined as multiple models instead of a large single model.

In addition to training classifiers, we also briefly explored using distance measures from stylistics and authorship attribution research such as Burrow's Delta (Burrows, 2002) and other related measures (Evert et al., 2015) using 100-1000 most frequent word, character and POS n-grams in the corpus. We did not find them particularly useful for this task, with highest accuracies of less than 60% on the development set. This could be due to the fact that Delta based measures are usually used on much longer texts, typically full length texts or novels.[5]

Speech Data: As mentioned earlier, for speech transcripts, we did not use the i-vectors and only used the above mentioned n-gram features. They were not as useful predictors for speech as they were for essays. One possible reason could be the fact that we have much smaller texts compared to written texts. However, i-vectors, which capture the acoustic features, clearly play an important role in NLI for speech data, as it was seen from the improvement over baseline they achieved on development set, as it was indicated in the documentation for corpus release.

5.1 With Embeddings on Development Set

In addition to the submitted runs, we explored word and document embedding based feature rep-

---

[4]Since the classification accuracy was very sensitive to decisions such as stemming and punctuation, and to how the features are extracted, we are sharing our final list of word trigram features for both essay and speech tracks extracted using LightSide (Mayfield and Rosé, 2013) on github for replication purposes.

[5]We used Stylo (Eder et al., 2016) and JGAAP (`https://github.com/evllabs/JGAAP`) libraries for calculating Delta scores

resentations that were described in Section 4 for this task. Our experiments with these representations did not result in better results than word and character n-grams. Table 2 shows a summary of the most predictive results with embedding features in our experiments.

System	F1 (macro)	Accuracy
Random Baseline	0.0909	0.0909
Word2vec (dim:200,window:11)	0.6311	0.6312
Word2vec (Nouns and Numbers sub.) (dim:200,window:11)	0.6311	0.6312
ECO	0.5744	0.5742
Doc2Vec-full (dim:100,window:10)	0.5440	0.5463
Doc2Vec-full (dim:500,window:25)	0.6276	0.6291
Doc2Vec-byL1 (dim:100,window:10)	0.6169	0.6190
Doc2Vec-byL1 (dim:500,window:25)	**0.7119**	**0.7127**

Table 2: Results for the ESSAY track with Embedding Features on Development data

For word embeddings, we achieved a macro F1 of 0.63 with Word2Vec (number of features 200 and window size 11), using SVM. We experimented with various levels of negative sampling but we could not attain any improvement. What is more interesting to note is that the system performance remains the same even when nouns and numbers are substituted. We repeated our experiments by averaging the word vectors with their corresponding TF-IDF values but we did not any improvement of performance. Training the embeddings on spell corrected data did not produce better results.

For larger number of features we noticed that the system performed better on the training set than it did on the development set clearly hinting at over-fitting. We performed 5 fold cross-validation, with multiple parameter settings and using linear, rbf and polynomial kernels, in a bid to find optimum parameter settings which would lead to the best classifier. Linear kernel emerged out as the winner for the optimum parameter settings for Word2Vec.

We got a macro F1 of 0.57 with ECO embed-

dings (number of features 700 and window size 4) using SVM. The reason for a poorer performance of ECO embeddings compared to Word2Vec could be the training corpus. ECO embeddings were trained on Wikipedia dump and not the training corpus as was the case for Word2Vec embeddings. Training embeddings on the shared task's training corpus could have possibly captured the specific features of the corpus instead of more general language features from Wikipedia corpus.

FastText performed much worse than Word2Vec and ECO, and was even below baseline with some of the parameter settings. We found that the performance of the system did not change appreciably when the number of features was increased, indicating that a large number of features may not be essential or desirable to capture all the stylistic differences in the corpus.

With Doc2Vec, concatenating the vectors from L1 specific doc2vec models performed much better than training a single Doc2Vec model on the entire dataset, giving a macro F1 of 0.7119 (500 features per L1, window size 25, dbow representation) using Logistic Regression. Doc2Vec-byL1 was consistently better than Doc2Vec-full in all the parameter settings we explored, always resulting in over 7% increase in accuracy.

Number of features and window size seemed to have a good influence on the classification performance and window sizes below 10 resulted in low performance for L1 classification. It was also shown in a previous empirical evaluation that dbow favors larger window sizes (Lau and Baldwin, 2016), although the longest they had was 15. Overall, from what we observed so far, training L1 specific Doc2Vec models may result in better performance for this task. Finding a better way to combine L1 specific features instead of just concatenating everything may boost the performance further.

5.2 Prompt based classification

Our results so far seem to show that embedding based representations are not particularly useful for this task. We hypothesized that this could be due to the fact that most of what embeddings capture is semantic similarity, while NLI involves capturing stylistic choices such as use of function words, punctuation markers etc, along with content word choices. To test this hypothesis, we did prompt based classification instead of L1 classification.

Doc2Vec-Full models for prompt based classification achieved accuracy of over 95% on the development for smaller feature/dimension sizes (10–20) and window sizes (5–10) using logistic regression. A dimensionality of 5 already gave an accuracy of 73% on the development set for prompt classification (8 prompts in essays corpus). This clearly indicates that the embeddings were able to capture topical differences between prompts easily even in a low dimensional space.

From a comparison of Doc2vec experiments for L1 and prompt classification, we can conclude that embeddings are more suitable when the categories have more semantic and less stylistic differences. However, an interesting observation from L1 classification using Doc2Vec was the influence of window size on classification performance. Performance steadily improved with both larger dimensions and larger window sizes. Whether this captures something unique about stylistic variation is something that should be more systematically explored in future.

6 Discussion

We described some of our experiments that study the usefulness of n-gram and embedding based feature representations for Native Language Identification as a part of the NLI Shared Task 2017. Our main conclusions so far are:

- Word uni–trigram features performed the best as a single group for classifying written texts, and there is no significant improvement in terms of adding infrequent trigrams or adding n-grams beyond 3.

- Character n-grams (n=2–10) were the second best performing feature group for written texts.

- Results with word and character n-grams could not be replicated with speech transcripts.

- Word and document embedding features did not give better results than n-grams, possibly because they capture semantic similarities instead of stylistic aspects.

6.1 Outlook

While modeling innovations may result in performance improvement, they make predictions more and more opaque. For NLI to be useful in applications such as language instruction or in language generation (e.g. generating texts with individual writing style in applications such as machine translation) we may need interpretable models. More qualitative analysis and eventually more concrete stylistic features for specific L1 backgrounds need to be developed. With this goal, and inspired by previous work on learning stylistic variation for language generation (Lin, 2012) and learning to segment phrasal features (instead of words) for sentiment analysis (Tang et al., 2014), we plan to focus on working towards better feature representations that may result in generalizable insights into the nature of L1 influence on L2 writing.

References

Daniel Blanchard, Joel Tetreault, Derrick Higgins, Aoife Cahill, and Martin Chodorow. 2013. Toefl11: A corpus of non-native english. Technical report, Educational Testing Service.

Julian Brooke and Graeme Hirst. 2012. Robust, Lexicalized Native Language Identification. In *Proceedings of COLING 2012*. The COLING 2012 Organizing Committee, Mumbai, India, pages 391–408. http://www.aclweb.org/anthology/C12-1025.

John Burrows. 2002. delta: a measure of stylistic difference and a guide to likely authorship. *Literary and linguistic computing* 17(3):267–287.

Serhiy Bykh and Detmar Meurers. 2012. Native Language Identification using Recurring n-grams – Investigating Abstraction and Domain Dependence. In *Proceedings of COLING 2012*. The COLING 2012 Organizing Committee, Mumbai, India, pages 425–440. http://www.aclweb.org/anthology/C12-1027.

Serhiy Bykh and Detmar Meurers. 2014. Exploring Syntactic Features for Native Language Identification: A Variationist Perspective on Feature Encoding and Ensemble Optimization. In *Proceedings of COLING 2014, the 25th International Conference on Computational Linguistics: Technical Papers*. Dublin, Ireland, pages 1962–1973.

Serhiy Bykh and Detmar Meurers. 2016. Advancing linguistic features and insights by label-informed feature grouping: An exploration in the context of native language identification. In *Proceedings of COLING 2016, the 26th International Conference on Computational Linguistics: Technical Papers*. The COLING 2016 Organizing Committee, Osaka, Japan, pages 739–749.

Serhiy Bykh, Sowmya Vajjala, Julia Krivanek, and Detmar Meurers. 2013. Combining shallow and linguistically motivated features in native language identification. *the 8th NAACL Workshop on Innovative Use of NLP for Building Educational Applications (BEA8)* pages 197–206.

Maciej Eder, Jan Rybicki, and Mike Kestemont. 2016. Stylometry with r: a package for computational text analysis. *R Journal* 8(1):107–121. http://journal.r-project.org/archive/2016-1/eder-rybicki-kestemont.pdf.

Dominique Estival, Tanja Gaustad, Son Bao Pham, Will Radford, and Ben Hutchinson. 2007. Author profiling for English emails. In *Proceedings of the 10th Conference of the Pacific Association for Computational Linguistics*. Melbourne, Australia, pages 263–272.

Stefan Evert, Thomas Proisl, Thorsten Vitt, Christof Schöch, Fotis Jannidis, and Steffen Pielström. 2015. Towards a better understanding of burrows's delta in literary authorship attribution. In *Proceedings of the Fourth Workshop on Computational Linguistics for Literature*. Association for Computational Linguistics, Denver, Colorado, USA, pages 79–88. http://www.aclweb.org/anthology/W15-0709.

Binyam Gebrekidan Gebre, Marcos Zampieri, Peter Wittenburg, and Tom Heskes. 2013. Improving native language identification with tf-idf weighting. In *the 8th NAACL Workshop on Innovative Use of NLP for Building Educational Applications (BEA8)*. pages 216–223.

Jeroen Geertzen, Theodora Alexopoulou, and Anna Korhonen. 2013. Automatic linguistic annotation of large scale l2 databases: The ef-cambridge open language database (efcamdat). In *Proceedings of the 31st Second Language Research Forum. Somerville, MA: Cascadilla Proceedings Project*.

Radu Tudor Ionescu, Marius Popescu, and Aoife Cahill. 2014. Can characters reveal your native language? A language-independent approach to native language identification. In *Proceedings of the 2014 Conference on Empirical Methods in Natural Language Processing (EMNLP)*. Association for Computational Linguistics.

Scott Jarvis, Yves Bestgen, and Steve Pepper. 2013. Maximizing Classification Accuracy in Native Language Identification. In *Proceedings of the Eighth Workshop on Innovative Use of NLP for Building Educational Applications*. Association for Computational Linguistics, Atlanta, Georgia, pages 111–118.

Scott Jarvis, Gabriela Castaneda-Jiménez, and Rasmus Nielsen. 2004. Investigating l1 lexical transfer through learners wordprints. In *Second Language Research Forum (SLRF). State College, PA*.

Scott Jarvis and Scott Crossley, editors. 2012. *Approaching Language Transfer Through Text Classification: Explorations in the Detection-based Approach*, volume 64. Multilingual Matters Limited, Bristol, UK.

Armand Joulin, Edouard Grave, Piotr Bojanowski, and Tomas Mikolov. 2016. Bag of tricks for efficient text classification. *arXiv preprint arXiv:1607.01759* .

Moshe Koppel, Jonathan Schler, and Kfir Zigdon. 2005. Determining an author's native language by mining a text for errors. In *Proceedings of the eleventh ACM SIGKDD international conference on Knowledge discovery in data mining*. ACM, Chicago, IL, pages 624–628.

Jey Han Lau and Timothy Baldwin. 2016. An empirical evaluation of doc2vec with practical insights into document embedding generation. In *Proceedings of the 1st Workshop on Representation Learning for NLP*. Association for Computational Linguistics, Berlin, Germany, pages 78–86. http://anthology.aclweb.org/W16-1609.

Quoc Le and Tomas Mikolov. 2014. Distributed representations of sentences and documents. In *Proceedings of the 31st International Conference on Machine Learning (ICML-14)*. pages 1188–1196.

Jing Lin. 2012. *Using a rewriting system to model individual writing styles*. Ph.D. thesis, University of Aberdeen.

Shervin Malmasi. 2016. *Native Language Identification: Explorations and Applications*. Ph.D. thesis, Macquarie University. http://hdl.handle.net/1959.14/1110919.

Shervin Malmasi and Aoife Cahill. 2015. Measuring feature diversity in native language identification. In *Proceedings of the Tenth Workshop on Innovative Use of NLP for Building Educational Applications*. Association for Computational Linguistics, Denver, Colorado, pages 49–55. http://www.aclweb.org/anthology/W15-0606.

Shervin Malmasi and Mark Dras. 2015. Multilingual native language identification. *Natural Language Engineering* pages 1–53.

Shervin Malmasi and Mark Dras. 2017. Native language identification using stacked generalization. *CoRR* abs/1703.06541. http://arxiv.org/abs/1703.06541.

Shervin Malmasi, Keelan Evanini, Aoife Cahill, Joel Tetreault, Robert Pugh, Christopher Hamill, Diane Napolitano, and Yao Qian. 2017. A Report on the 2017 Native Language Identification Shared Task. In *Proceedings of the 12th Workshop on Building Educational Applications Using NLP*. Association for Computational Linguistics, Copenhagen, Denmark.

Shervin Malmasi, Marcos Zampieri, Nikola Ljubešić, Preslav Nakov, Ahmed Ali, and Jörg Tiedemann. 2016. Discriminating between Similar Languages and Arabic Dialect Identification: A Report on the Third DSL Shared Task. In *Proceedings of the VarDial Workshop*. Osaka, Japan.

Elijah Mayfield and Carolyn Penstein Rosé. 2013. 8 lightside. *Handbook of Automated Essay Evaluation: Current Applications and New Directions* page 124.

Tomas Mikolov, Ilya Sutskever, Kai Chen, Greg S Corrado, and Jeff Dean. 2013. Distributed representations of words and phrases and their compositionality. In *Advances in neural information processing systems*. pages 3111–3119.

Sergiu Nisioi. 2015. *Feature Analysis for Native Language Identification*, Springer International Publishing, Cham, pages 644–657. https://doi.org/10.1007/978-3-319-18111-0$_4$9.

Adam Poliak, Pushpendre Rastogi, M. Patrick Martin, and Benjamin Van Durme. 2017. Efficient, compositional, order-sensitive n-gram embeddings. In *Proceedings of the 15th Conference of the European Chapter of the Association for Computational Linguistics: Volume 2, Short Papers*. Association for Computational Linguistics, Valencia, Spain, pages 503–508. http://www.aclweb.org/anthology/E17-2081.

Bjrn Schuller, Stefan Steidl, Anton Batliner, Julia Hirschberg, Judee K. Burgoon, Alice Baird, Aaron Elkins, Yue Zhang, Eduardo Coutinho, and Keelan Evanini. 2016. The INTER-SPEECH 2016 Computational Paralinguistics Challenge: Deception, Sincerity & Native Language. In *Interspeech 2016*. pages 2001–2005. https://doi.org/10.21437/Interspeech.2016-129.

Duyu Tang, Furu Wei, Bing Qin, Li Dong, Ting Liu, and Ming Zhou. 2014. A joint segmentation and classification framework for sentiment analysis. In *Proceedings of the 2014 Conference on Empirical Methods in Natural Language Processing (EMNLP)*. Association for Computational Linguistics, Doha, Qatar, pages 477–487. http://www.aclweb.org/anthology/D14-1054.

Joel Tetreault, Daniel Blanchard, and Aoife Cahill. 2013. A Report on the First Native Language Identification Shared Task. In *Proceedings of the Eighth Workshop on Building Educational Applications Using NLP*. Association for Computational Linguistics, Atlanta, GA, USA.

Joel Tetreault, Daniel Blanchard, Aoife Cahill, and Martin Chodorow. 2012. Native tongues, lost and found: Resources and empirical evaluations in native language identification. In *Proceedings of COLING 2012*. The COLING 2012 Organizing Committee, Mumbai, India, pages 2585–2602. http://www.aclweb.org/anthology/C12-1158.

Laura Mayfield Tomokiyo and Rosie Jones. 2001. You're not from'round here, are you?: naive bayes detection of non-native utterance text. In *Proceedings of the second meeting of the North American Chapter of the Association for Computational Linguistics on Language technologies*. Association for Computational Linguistics, pages 1–8.

Sze-Meng Jojo Wong and Mark Dras. 2011. Exploiting Parse Structures for Native Language Identification. In *Proceedings of the 2011 Conference on Empirical Methods in Natural Language Processing*. Association for Computational Linguistics, Edinburgh, Scotland, UK., pages 1600–1610. http://www.aclweb.org/anthology/D11-1148.

A Shallow Neural Network for Native Language Identification with Character N-grams

Yunita Sari
Department of Computer Science
University of Sheffield, UK
y.sari@sheffield.ac.uk

Muhammad Rifqi Fatchurrahman and **Meisyarah Dwiastuti**
Department of Computer Sciences and Electronics
Universitas Gadjah Mada, Indonesia
{muh.rifqi.fatchurrahman, meisyarah.dwiastuti}@gmail.com

Abstract

This paper describes the systems submitted by GadjahMada team to the Native Language Identification (NLI) Shared Task 2017. Our models used a continuous representation of character n-grams which are learned jointly with feed-forward neural network classifier. Character n-grams have been proved to be effective for style-based identification tasks including NLI. Results on the test set demonstrate that the proposed model performs very well on essay and fusion tracks by obtaining more than 0.8 on both F-macro score and accuracy.

1 Introduction

Native Language Identification (NLI) is the task of identifying the native language (L1) of the speakers in which English is usually their second language (L2). Given $F = \{f_1, f_2, ..., f_3\}$ be a set of written or speech responses and $K = \{k_1, k_2, k_m\}$ a pre-defined set of native languages (L1), the NLI task is to assign L1 to each of the responses in F. This task is often considered as a subset of author profiling task which currently focuses more on age and gender identification (Lopez-Monroy et al., 2014; Johannsen et al., 2015; Rangel Pardo et al., 2016).

The growing interest in this field is due to the applicability of this task to support language learners by providing a tailored feed-back about their errors. Swan and Smith (2001) argued that speakers of different native languages tend to make different mistakes. Thus, targeted feed-back is ex-

pected to improve the process of language learning (Tetreault et al., 2013).

The NLI Shared Task 2017 (Malmasi et al., 2017) is the continuation of the first task that has been held in 2013 (Tetreault et al., 2013). This year's task aims to combine written responses (essay) and spoken responses (speech transcript and i-vector acoustic features) for identifying 11 native language classes.

To address the NLI Shared Task 2017 problem, we adopted an approach that has been applied for authorship attribution task (Sari et al., 2017). In this approach, continuous representations of character n-grams are used jointly with feed-forward neural network classifier. The methods performed very well on essay and fusion tracks by obtaining more than 0.8 on both F-macro score and accuracy. However, due to the poor hyper-parameter setting and the limitation of training data, we only managed to get around 0.5 on speech track for both evaluation scores, using only the speech transcripts.

The paper is organised as follows: Section 2 provides a review of relevant work in NLI. We then explain our methodology in Section 3. The next section describes our experiments including the description of the dataset and the details of training and hyper-parameter tuning. Result and discussion are presented in Section 5. Finally, conclusion and future work are drawn in Section 6.

2 Related Work

The first NLI shared task (Tetreault et al., 2013) was introduced in 2013 with a total of 29 teams participated across three different subtasks. The dataset for the task was TOEFL11 corpus (Blan-

Proceedings of the 12th Workshop on Innovative Use of NLP for Building Educational Applications, pages 249–254
Copenhagen, Denmark, September 8, 2017. ©2017 Association for Computational Linguistics

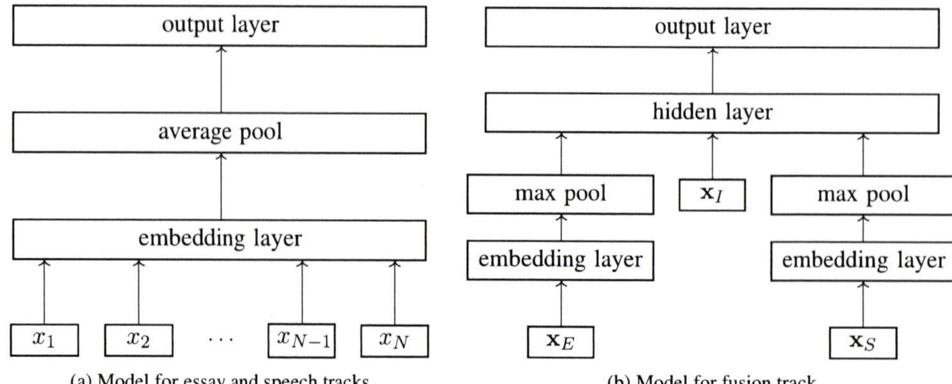

(a) Model for essay and speech tracks (b) Model for fusion track

chard et al., 2013) consists of 11,000 essays written by a high-stakes college-entrance test taker. Same as this year's task, there are 11 native languages covered. Tetreault, et. al reported that majority of the participant addressed the problem by utilising powerful machine learning algorithms such as Support Vector Machine (SVM) and Logistic Regression. In term of features, word, character and POS n-grams were the most common used features.

One of the interesting findings from the first NLI task is simple features such as words, word forms, sequential word combinations, and sequential POS combinations turn out to be effective indicators for identifying L1. Jarvis et al. (2013) who implemented those features successfully secured the best systems in the first NLI task by obtaining 10-fold cross-validated accuracy of 84.5% and overall accuracy of 83.6% on the test set. In addition, they reported that a model with character n-grams achieved similar accuracy to the best model involving lexical and POS n-grams.

Following the first NLI task, Ionescu et al. (2014) extended their submission system by implementing character n-grams with two kernel classifiers namely Kernel Ridge Regression (KRR) and Kernel Discriminant Analysis (KDA). Their result outperformed Jarvis, et. al by 1.7% on the overall accuracy. Character n-grams have been known for its impressive performance in style-based text analysis task such as authorship attribution (Peng et al., 2003; Stamatatos, 2013; Schwartz et al., 2013). It has advantages of capturing stylistic and morphological information (Koppel et al., 2011; Sapkota et al., 2015) regardless of the language. This has motivated us to utilised character n-grams in our system.

In addition to written responses, recent trend starts to consider spoken responses (speech transcripts and audio features) for NLI task. Incorporating spoken responses has produced good result for dialect identification (Malmasi et al., 2016; Zampieri et al., 2017). However compared to audio features, speech transcripts are less useful since ambiguity is more pronounced in written transcripts.

3 Methodology

In this section, we describe our models and features used in our NLI system. First, we present the details of the features. Then we explain our model architectures which use shallow feed-forward neural network.

3.1 Features

There are two types of features used in our system: character n-grams and i-vectors. We used only character n-grams features in essay and speech tracks and combined them with i-vectors for fusion track. The details of the features are explained as follows:

- **Character n-grams:** This substring takes n characters constructing the text along the whole text as features. We set the vocabulary to 70 most common characters including letters, digits, and some punctuation marks as conducted by Zhang et al. (2015). We followed Sari et al. (2017) who represented the features as continuous vectors. The idea of representing n-grams in continuous space was introduced by Joulin et al. (2017) who proposed an efficient model for text classification called fastText. Instead of using a single value of n, we applied a range of n values from three to six grams.

- **i-vectors:** i-vector or identity vector is one of feature representation that commonly used in speech processing. It is a low-dimensional vector derived from mapping sequence of speech frames (Dehak et al., 2011). The i-vectors correspond to the speech transcriptions and have a length of 800. We used the provided i-vectors without any additional pre-processing.

3.2 Model Architecture

Our model adopted fastText architecture which was proposed by Joulin et al. (2017). FastText represents a document with an average of feature embeddings for the features present. The probability distribution over the labels then is simply predicted using *softmax* function. However, instead of working on word level, we chose to work on character level, since it is found to be more suitable for the task. Figure 1a shows the model that we used for both essay and speech tracks. In that figure, x_n represents a single character n-gram, while N is the maximum sequence which the value is fixed. In our experiment, feature embeddings are learned during training.

For fusion track, we extended the first model with an auxiliary input to accommodate i-vectors as presented in Figure 1b. We also added one hidden layer with the size of 128 right before the output layer. Slightly different with the first model, in the fusion track we used *max pooling* as it produced higher performances. Both of the models were implemented using Keras (Chollet et al., 2015) with Tensorflow backend.

3.3 Baseline Systems

As a benchmark, the organiser developed baseline systems which use SVM as the classifier. Essay and speech transcript are represented as bag-of-words (BoW). The baseline results on the test set are presented in the Table 1.

4 Experiments

4.1 Dataset

The dataset provided by Educational Testing Service (ETS) contains test responses from a standardised assessment of English proficiency for academic purposes. It consists of 13,200 English essays (written responses) and 13,200 of 45 seconds English speech transcriptions (spoken responses). In addition to that, i-vectors of the speech audios are generated in lieu of the audio files. The essays typically range in length from 300 to 400 words and the transcriptions typically contain approximately 100 words.

The test responses are from 13,200 different test takers. Each test taker contributed one essay and one speech transcription. There are 11 native languages (L1) covered, including Arabic (ARA), Chinese (CHI), French (FR), German (GER), Hindi (HIN), Italian (ITA), Japanese (JPN), Korean (KOR), Spanish (SPA), Telugu (TEL), and Turkish (TUR). The organiser set the 11,000 samples from the dataset for training purpose, 1,100 for development and the rest as the test set.

4.2 Hyper-parameter Tuning and Training Details

During training, we tried different combinations of hyper-parameter configurations. However, only the configurations of the best run are reported in this paper.

Feature hyper-parameters. For essay and speech tracks, we only used character n-grams features. We set the range of n-gram values from 2 to 5. The sequence lengths were set to 6,000 for essay and 4,000 for speech. Meanwhile, for fusion track in addition to the character n-grams, i-vectors were used. The n-grams range was set to 3 to 5. In order to reduce the input dimensions, we decreased the length of the sequence to 1,500 for essays and 300 for speech transcriptions.

Model hyper-parameters. The best run for essay and speech tracks used embedding size of 25 with dropout rate of 0.75. For fusion model, embedding size for both essay and speech representation was set to 128. Between the layers, we put dropout with the probability of 0.5.

Training. For all sub-tracks, the models were trained using Adam Optimizer (Kingma and Ba, 2015) with cross-entropy loss. We also implemented early stopping procedure in order to avoid over-fitting. We set batch size of 64 for essay and fusion tracks; and 32 for speech track. Number of epochs for essay, speech, and fusion tracks were set to 80, 50, and 100 respectively. For both essay and speech tracks, learning rate of 0.005 was used.

Track	Baseline System		GadjahMada System	
	F1-score	Accuracy	F1-score (macro)	Accuracy
Essay	0.7104	0.7109	**0.8107**	**0.8109**
Speech (transcription only)	**0.5435**	**0.5464**	0.5084	0.5073
Fusion (essay, speech transcripts, i-vectors)	0.7901	0.7909	**0.8414**	**0.8409**

Table 1: Submission Results

While fusion track used learning rate of 0.0002, higher rates did not make any improvement.

5 Results and Discussion

Table 1 shows our submission results for all the sub-tracks. We participated in closed- training subtask in which we only used provided training data to train our models. Results on the table present that our systems performed very well on the essay and fusion tracks. Our systems outperformed the baseline systems with accuracy of 0.8109 and 0.8409 on the essay and fusion tracks respectively. However, the system failed to produce similar performances on speech track. Our system produced accuracy of 0.5073 which is lower than the baseline. This might happen due to the poor hyper-parameter tuning. Note that on speech track, we only utilised speech transcripts.

Similar to the previous NLI shared task results, character n-grams demonstrate their effectiveness for capturing style in written responses. We believe that speakers of each native language have their own learning experiences which are reflected in their responses. The speaker's characteristics are better captured in written responses than speech transcripts. Written responses are significantly longer compared to speech transcripts which make it better on providing information about the speaker. In addition to that, speech transcripts are less useful since ambiguity is more pronounced (Malmasi et al., 2016). Audio features in the form of i-vectors help to improve the performance. Our results on the fusion track are higher than the results on other tracks.

In order to get more insight into the classification results, confusion matrices for the best run in each sub-track are presented in Figure 2. In the essay and fusion tracks, it can be seen that German (GER) speaker are the easiest class to identify with more than 90% on the accuracy. It is also interesting to highlight that the system is mistakenly identified several native language classes that have morphological and lexical similarities, for exam-

ple: Chinese (CHI), Japanese (JPN) and Korean (KOR); Hindi (HIN) and Telugu (TEL); French (FRE), Italian (ITA) and Spanish (SPA). However in the speech track as shown in Figure 2b, in most classes the system made correct predictions no more than 50% of the total samples. It demonstrates that spoken response in the form of speech transcripts is not good enough to be used as feature.

6 Conclusion and Future Work

This paper presents our submission approaches for NLI Shared Task 2017. Results on the test set show our model that utilises shallow feed-forward neural network with character n-grams features could effectively identify the native language (L1) of the speaker. Our proposed model performed very well on the essay and fusion tracks but failed to achieve similar scores on the speech track. It is interesting to note that character n-grams mostly works for any style-based classification tasks including NLI. More details analysis on the languages with similar lexical and morphological forms can be an interesting work to explore. Indicative features for those languages are essential since most incorrect predictions were made on those groups.

References

Daniel Blanchard, Joel Tetreault, Derrick Higgins, Aoife Cahill, and Martin Chodorow. 2013. Toefl11: A corpus of non-native english. Technical report, Educational Testing Service.

François Chollet et al. 2015. Keras. https://github.com/fchollet/keras.

Najim Dehak, Pedro A Torres-Carrasquillo, Douglas Reynolds, and Reda Dehak. 2011. Language recognition via i-vectors and dimensionality reduction. In *Twelfth Annual Conference of the International Speech Communication Association*.

Radu Tudor Ionescu, Marius Popescu, and Aoife Cahill. 2014. Can characters reveal your native language? A language-independent approach to native

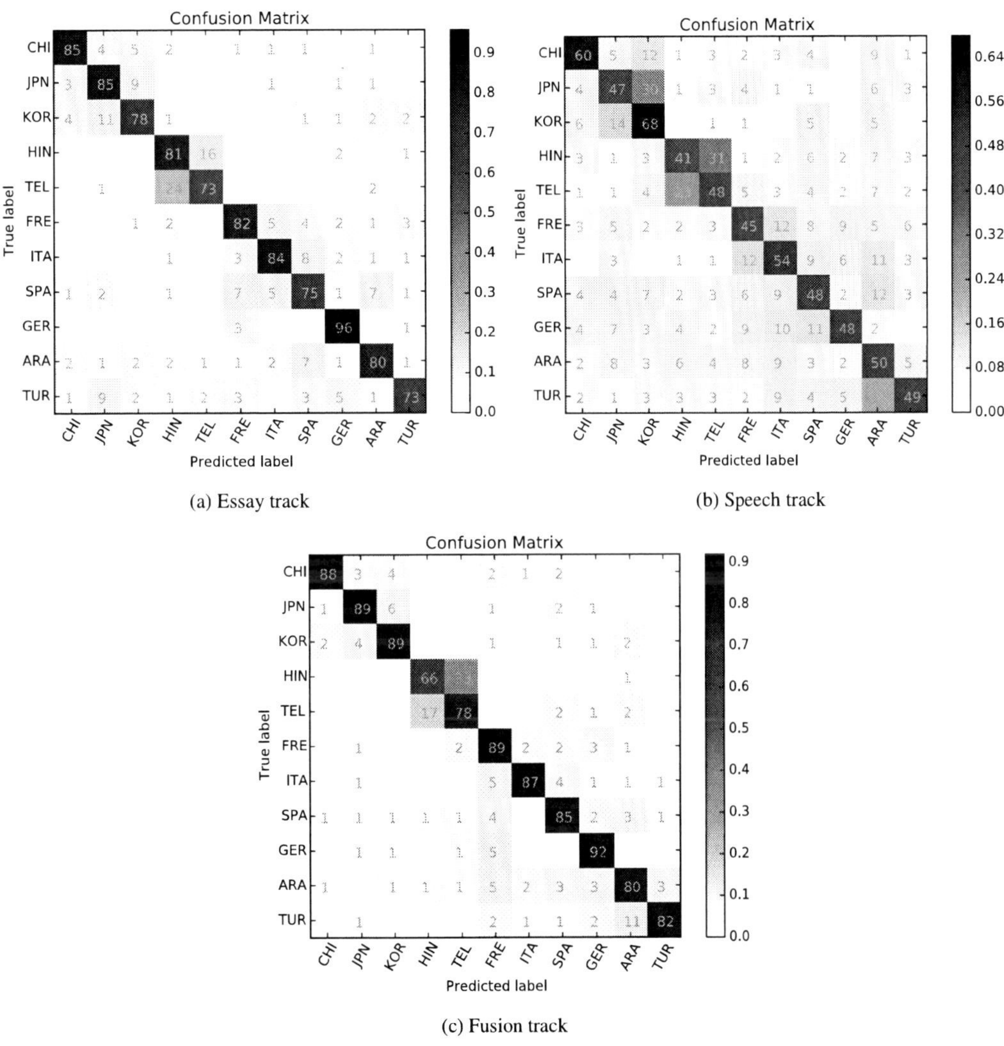

(a) Essay track

(b) Speech track

(c) Fusion track

Figure 2: Confusion matrices for the best run in each sub-track

language identification. In *Proceedings of the 2014 Conference on Empirical Methods in Natural Language Processing (EMNLP)*. Association for Computational Linguistics.

Scott Jarvis, Yves Bestgen, and Steve Pepper. 2013. Maximizing Classification Accuracy in Native Language Identification. In *Proceedings of the Eighth Workshop on Innovative Use of NLP for Building Educational Applications*. Association for Computational Linguistics, Atlanta, Georgia, pages 111–118.

Anders Johannsen, Dirk Hovy, and Anders Søgaard. 2015. Cross-lingual syntactic variation over age and gender. In *Proceedings of the Nineteenth Conference on Computational Natural Language Learning*. Association for Computational Linguistics, Beijing, China, pages 103–112.

Armand Joulin, Edouard Grave, Piotr Bojanowski, and Tomas Mikolov. 2017. Bag of tricks for efficient text classification. In *Proceedings of the 15th Conference of the European Chapter of the Association for Computational Linguistics: Volume 2, Short Papers*. Association for Computational Linguistics, Valencia, Spain, pages 427–431.

Diederik P. Kingma and Jimmy Ba. 2015. Adam: A method for stochastic optimization. In *Proceeding of the 3rd International Conference for Learning Representations, ICLR 2015*. San Diego, CA.

Moshe Koppel, Jonathan Schler, and Shlomo Argamon. 2011. Authorship attribution in the wild. *Language Resources and Evaluation* 45(1):83–94.

A. Pastor Lopez-Monroy, Manuel Montes Gomez, and Hugo Jair-Escalante. 2014. Using Intra-Profile Information for Author Profiling. In *Notebook for PAN at CLEF 2014*.

Shervin Malmasi, Keelan Evanini, Aoife Cahill, Joel Tetreault, Robert Pugh, Christopher Hamill, Diane Napolitano, and Yao Qian. 2017. A Report on the 2017 Native Language Identification Shared Task. In *Proceedings of the 12th Workshop on Building Educational Applications Using NLP*. Association for Computational Linguistics, Copenhagen, Denmark.

Shervin Malmasi, Marcos Zampieri, Nikola Ljubešić, Preslav Nakov, Ahmed Ali, and Jörg Tiedemann. 2016. Discriminating between Similar Languages and Arabic Dialect Identification: A Report on the Third DSL Shared Task. In *Proceedings of the VarDial Workshop*. Osaka, Japan.

Fuchun Peng, Dale Schuurmanst, Vlado Kesel, and Shaojun Wan. 2003. Language Independent Authorship Attribution using Character Level Language Models. In *Proceedings of the 10th Conference on European Chapter of the Association for Computational Linguistics, EACL 2003*. Budapest, Hungary.

Francisco Manuel Rangel Pardo, Paolo Rosso, Ben Verhoeven, Walter Daelemans, Martin Potthast, and Benno Stein. 2016. Overview of the 4th Author Profiling Task at PAN 2016: Cross-Genre Evaluations. In *Working Notes Papers of the CLEF 2016 Evaluation Labs*. CLEF and CEUR-WS.org, CEUR Workshop Proceedings.

Upendra Sapkota, Steven Bethard, Manuel Montes, and Thamar Solorio. 2015. Not all character n-grams are created equal: A study in authorship attribution. In *Proceedings of the 2015 Conference of the North American Chapter of the Association for Computational Linguistics: Human Language Technologies, ACL HLT 2015*. Association for Computational Linguistics, Denver, Colorado, pages 93–102.

Yunita Sari, Andreas Vlachos, and Mark Stevenson. 2017. Continuous n-gram representations for authorship attribution. In *Proceedings of the 15th Conference of the European Chapter of the Association for Computational Linguistics: Volume 2, Short Papers*. Association for Computational Linguistics, pages 267–273.

Roy Schwartz, Oren Tsur, Ari Rappoport, and Moshe Koppel. 2013. Authorship attribution of micromessages. In *Proceedings of the 2013 Conference on Empirical Methods in Natural Language Processing, EMNLP 2013*. Association for Computational Linguistics, Seattle, Washington, USA, pages 1880–1891.

Efstathios Stamatatos. 2013. On the Robustness of Authorship Attribution Based on Character n-gram Features. *Journal of Law and Policy* 21(2):421–439.

Michael Swan and Bernard 1937 Smith. 2001. *Learner English : a teacher's guide to interference and other problems*. Cambridge (U.K.) Cambridge University Press, 2nd ed edition. :A Teacher's Guide to Interfernce and Other Problems.

Joel Tetreault, Daniel Blanchard, and Aoife Cahill. 2013. A report on the first native language identification shared task. In *Proceedings of the Eighth Workshop on Innovative Use of NLP for Building Educational Applications*. Association for Computational Linguistics, Atlanta, GA, USA.

Marcos Zampieri, Shervin Malmasi, Nikola Ljubešić, Preslav Nakov, Ahmed Ali, Jörg Tiedemann, Yves Scherrer, and Noëmi Aepli. 2017. Findings of the VarDial Evaluation Campaign 2017. In *Proceedings of the Fourth Workshop on NLP for Similar Languages, Varieties and Dialects (VarDial)*. Valencia, Spain, pages 1–15.

Xiang Zhang, Junbo Zhao, and Yann LeCun. 2015. Character-level convolutional networks for text classification. In *Proceedings of the 28th International Conference on Neural Information Processing Systems, NIPS 2015*. MIT Press, Cambridge, MA, USA, pages 649–657.

Fewer features perform well at Native Language Identification task

Taraka Rama and **Çağrı Çöltekin**
Department of Linguistics
University of Tübingen, Germany
`taraka-rama.kasicheyanula@uni-tuebingen.de`
`ccoltekin@sfs.uni-tuebingen.de`

Abstract

This paper describes our results at the NLI shared task 2017. We participated in essays, speech, and fusion task that uses text, speech, and i-vectors for the task of identifying the native language of the given input. In the essay track, a linear SVM system using word bigrams and character 7-grams performed the best. In the speech track, an LDA classifier based only on i-vectors performed better than a combination system using text features from speech transcriptions and i-vectors. In the fusion task, we experimented with systems that used combination of i-vectors with higher order n-grams features, combination of i-vectors with word unigrams, a mean probability ensemble, and a stacked ensemble system. Our finding is that word unigrams in combination with i-vectors achieve higher score than systems trained with larger number of n-gram features. Our best-performing systems achieved F1-scores of 87.16 %, 83.33 % and 91.75 % on the essay track, the speech track and the fusion track respectively.

1 Introduction

In this paper, we describe our (team tubafs) efforts in three different tasks during our participation in NLI shared task 2017 (Malmasi et al., 2017). All the three tasks aim at identifying native language using essays (*essay track*), speech transcriptions along with i-vectors (*speech track*) and *fusion track* that allows the participants to use all the three data sources to design and test a system for the purpose of NLI.

The first NLI task employed only essays written in English for the identification of native language.

To date, all NLI shared tasks have been based on L2 English data, but NLI research has been extended to at least six other non-English languages (Malmasi and Dras, 2015). In addition to using the written responses, a recent trend has been the use of speech transcriptions and audio features for dialect identification (Malmasi et al., 2016). The combination of transcriptions and acoustic features has also provided good results for dialect identification (Zampieri et al., 2017). Following this trend, the 2016 Computational Paralinguistics Challenge (Schuller et al., 2016) also included an NLI task based on the spoken response. The NLI 2017 shared task attempts to combine these approaches by including a written response (essay) and a spoken response (speech transcriptions and i-vector acoustic features) for each subject. The task also allows for the fusion of all features.

Recent years have seen a large amount of work on employing text based features for the purpose of native language identification. The winning system (Jarvis et al., 2013) of NLI shared task 2013 featured a single model SVM system that used n-grams of lemmas, words, and part-of-speech tags. The authors normalized each text to unit length and obtained an accuracy of 83.60 %. In another work, Ionescu et al. (2014) applied a union of character n-gram based string kernels and obtained an accuracy of 85.30 % on the dataset from NLI shared task 2013.

Using the data from NLI shared task 2013, Bykh and Meurers (2014) explored the use of phrase structure rules for the purpose of NLI. The authors obtained an accuracy of 84.82 % which is similar to the results reported by previous authors. In another paper, Goutte et al. (2013) employed an ensemble of SVM classifiers trained on character, word, part-of-speech n-grams, and syntactic dependencies and showed that the system achieves an accuracy of 81.82 % at NLI task. Recently,

255

Proceedings of the 12th Workshop on Innovative Use of NLP for Building Educational Applications, pages 255–260
Copenhagen, Denmark, September 8, 2017. ©2017 Association for Computational Linguistics

Malmasi and Dras (2017) explored ensemble related classifiers using word, character, lemma, and grammar based features and found that stacking the classifiers' ensemble achieves an accuracy of 87.10 %.

In this paper, we used the single SVM model of Çöltekin and Rama (2016) that combines character n-grams with word n-grams for the essay task. We explored different ensemble models such as hard majority ensemble, mean majority ensemble, and stacked ensemble for the fusion task. In the case of speech task, we found that a linear classifier trained on i-vectors (alone) achieves an accuracy greater than 80 % on the test data. We also found that i-vectors combined with word unigrams from essays and speech transcriptions achieve an accuracy of 90.64 % on the test data. The main result from our experiments is that i-vectors contribute towards improving the performance of NLI systems.

We also experimented with adding POS tags as features, and a number of neural network classifiers. However, within our efforts, neither options improve the results. As a result we only submitted results with the linear models noted above, and we only discuss these models in detail in this paper.

The remainder of the paper is organized as follows. In section 2, we describe the different tasks and systems. In section 3, we describe the results of our experiments. We conclude our paper in section 4.

2 Methodology and Data

2.1 Task description

In this subsection, we provide a description of the three subtasks in NLI shared task 2017 (Malmasi and Dras, 2017). The goal of the shared task is to produce a system that can identify the native language of the test giver based on written response (essays), speech transcriptions, and audio files (i-vectors). The native languages are known beforehand and are as follows: Arabic, Chinese, French, German, Hindi, Italian, Japanese, Korean, Spanish, Telugu, Turkish.

The *essays* task is limited to using (only) written response for identifying the native language of the individual. The *speech* task consists of using speech transcriptions and i-vectors (fixed-length vectors representing some acoustic properties of whole utterances) for NLI. In the *fusion* task, we use essays, speech transcriptions, and i-vectors for

the purpose of NLI.

The organizers provided separate training and development datasets for each task. The training dataset consisted of 11 000 examples and the development dataset consisted of 1 100 examples.

2.2 NLI with a single classifier

In this paper, we extracted character n-grams, word n-grams, and word skip-grams from essays and speech transcriptions for training our classifiers. Specifically, we used the following features in our experiments. We used a simple regular expression based tokenizer for extracting words and did not apply any filtering (e.g., case normalization).

- Word n-grams: Unigrams and bigrams.
- Character n-grams: We extracted character substrings of length from 1–9.
- Word skip-grams: We extracted word bigrams by skipping a intermediary word for extracting 1-skip word bigram (Ionescu et al., 2014).

For each task, we extracted the following features:

- *Essays task*: Each document is represented as a combination of word and character n-grams which are weighted using sub-linear tf-idf scaling (Jurafsky and Martin, 2009, p.805).
- *Speech task*: We used a combination of i-vectors, word and character n-grams (extracted from speech transcriptions). The word/character n-grams are weighted separately using sublinear tf-idf scaling and then combined with the i-vectors.
- *Fusion task*: We extracted word and character n-grams from both essays and speech transcriptions and, then, applied sublinear tf-idf scaling to the combined word and character n-gram vectors. Finally, we combined the i-vectors with the sublinear tf-idf scaled speech & transcriptions n-grams.

In all the tracks, we normalize the combined document vectors to unit length. We also tuned the number of character and word n-grams, as well as the SVM margin parameter 'C' for each task separately. The SVMs were not very sensitive to the changes in 'C' parameter. All linear SVM models were implemented with scikit-learn (Pedregosa et al., 2011) and trained and tested using Liblinear backend (Fan et al., 2008). All our multi-class classifiers are trained in a one-vs-many fashion.

2.3 Ensemble classifiers

In a recent paper, Malmasi and Dras (2017) showed that ensemble classifiers perform the best at NLI task. Specifically, Malmasi and Dras (2017) showed that ensemble of linear classifiers trained on multiple feature types performed better than a single classifier trained on a combination of feature types. We trained an SVM classifier on each of the above listed feature types extracted from essays and speech transcriptions. In the case of i-vectors, we trained an LDA classifier (Hastie et al., 2009, p.106) since it performed better than the SVM classifier on the development data. A classifier trained on a feature type predicts both the label and the probability score for each class. Based on this, we created two ensembles as follows:

- Majority Ensemble: In this system, each classifier labels an example and the class with the highest frequency is chosen as the label for the instance.

- Mean probability Ensemble: In this system, the probability estimates for each class are added and the class with the highest sum is chosen as the label for the instance.

- Meta Classifier: Following Malmasi (2016), we train a linear SVM classifier for each feature type through ten-fold cross-validation on the training data. This step results in 10 classifiers for each feature type. For each feature type, we average the class probability estimates of the ten classifiers and then train a linear SVM classifier with the probability estimates as features and the corresponding class label as target class.

2.4 Submitted systems

- *Essay task:* We trained SVM classifiers on combinations of word n-grams (ranging from 1 to 3) and character n-grams (ranging from 1-9) and found that the SVM system trained with word bigrams and character 7-grams performed the best at F1-score on the development data. We submitted the results of the trained model as **w2c7**.

- *Speech track:* We submitted the following two systems:

  - *only i-vectors:* In our experiments, we found that a Linear Discriminant Classifier (LDA) trained on i-vectors performed better than an SVM model on the development data. We submitted the system as **LDA (only i-vectors)**.

  - *Transcripts + i-vectors:* We submitted the results of the SVM model trained on a combination of i-vectors, word bigrams, and character 7-grams (extracted from speech transcriptions) as **SVM (i+t)**.

- *Fusion track:* We submitted four systems in this task. The first two systems are based on two SVM models trained on different combinations of word- and character-ngrams. The third system is a mean majority ensemble based on different feature types. The fourth system is a meta classifier model based on different feature types.

3 Results

In this section, we describe the results of the submitted systems in each track.

3.1 Essay task

In this track, the best performing model is a linear SVM model trained with word bigrams and character 7-grams (*w2c7* model). We explored the effect of using higher order word and character n-grams for this task by training a linear SVM model on the training data and testing the model on the development data. In the case of development data, with w2c7 model, we report an accuracy of 84.09% and an F1 score of 84.04%. The results on the test data for the same model is given in table 1. The results suggest that the model performed better on the testing data than development data. We also explored the effect of tuning the SVM hyperparameter 'C' and found that the F1-score on the development data are not sensitive to the 'C' parameter.

The confusion matrix for the essay task is given in figure 1. The confusion matrix shows that model makes most of the mistakes occur at the classification of Telugu vs. Hindi and Japanese vs. Korean language pairs. More generally, the system makes mistakes between languages that have a history of long geographical contact (Chinese-Japanese–Korean; Hindi–Telugu) or belong to the same language subgroup (French–

System	F1 (macro)	Accuracy
w2c7	0.871 6	0.871 8
Official baseline	0.710 4	0.710 9
Random baseline	0.090 9	0.090 9

Table 1: The results for word bigrams and character 7-grams using Linear SVMs for essay task.

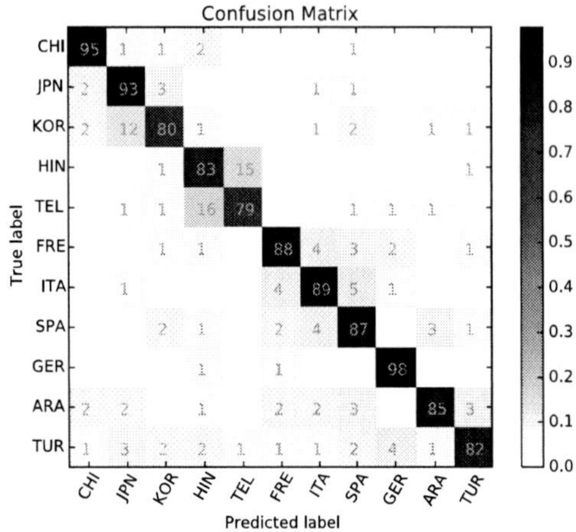

Figure 1: Confusion matrix for the *essay* track.

Italian–Spanish). In the case of Turkish, the model errs uniformly at classifying Turkish instances as instances of other classes.

3.2 Speech task

We submitted two systems in the case of speech task: an LDA classifier based on i-vectors and an SVM classifier based on the combined features of speech transcriptions and i-vectors. We expected that a combination of transcriptions and i-vectors might capture the acoustic features that would discriminate the highly confused language pairs such as Hindi–Telugu. However, the F1-scores in table 2 show that i-vectors alone perform better than a combination of transcriptions and i-vectors at NLI task. Although the combination model of transcriptions and i-vector features yield an F1-score of 81.57 % on the development data, the combined model performs poorly with test data. In contrast, the LDA model trained on i-vectors yielded an F1-score of 83.33 % on the test data.

The confusion matrix for the LDA model is presented in figure 2. The results suggest that the model makes most of its mistake at classifying Telugu–Hindi language pair. We hypothe-

System	F1 (macro)	Accuracy
LDA (only i-vectors)	0.833 3	0.833 6
SVM (combined)	0.280 1	0.293 6
Official Baseline		
transcriptions	0.543 5	0.546 4
combined	0.798 0	0.798 2
Random Baseline	0.909 0	0.909 0

Table 2: Results of LDA classifier on i-vectors and the results on combined transcriptions and i-vectors.

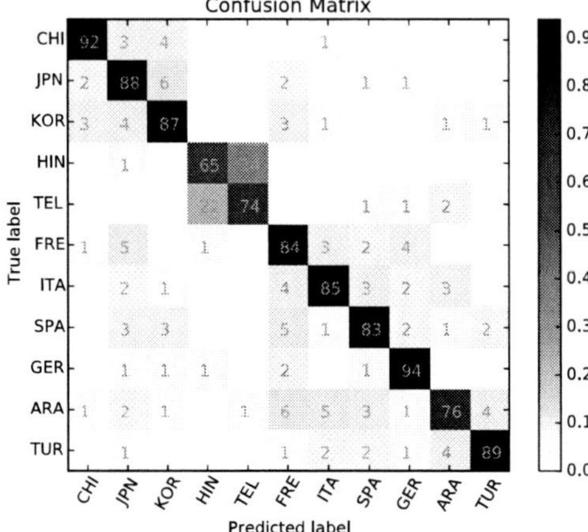

Figure 2: Confusion matrix for the *speech* task (i-vectors only).

sized that i-vectors might be useful to discriminate Telugu–Hindi language pair since they might capture differences between languages that are in contact. However, the *LDA (only i-vector)* model errs more than the essay-based SVM model for the test dataset originating from the same set of individuals.

3.3 Fusion task

We submitted four systems in this task.

The first system is a *Combined* feature system is a combination of the following features:

- Word bigrams and character 7-grams from essays (*w2c7* model)
- Word bigrams from transcriptions
- i-vectors

The combined feature system achieved an F1-score of 85.24 % on the development data and an F1-score of 88.71 % on the test data. The difference between the performance on the development

258

and test data is similar to that of the SVM model trained on essays data. We attribute the improvement from essay model SVM mainly to i-vector based features.

Due to the poor performance of the combination of transcriptions and i-vectors, we also explored if reducing the features would improve the performance of the model. After exploring different combinations of n-grams in essays and transcriptions, we found that the following feature combination (a 66 881 dimension vector) yielded an F1-score of 88.20 % on the development data and 90.65 % on the test data.

- Both Essays and transcriptions: Word unigrams and *no* character n-grams
- i-vectors

The third system is a mean probability ensemble trained on the following features:

- Essays: char ngrams (n ranging from 2–5), word ngrams (n ranging from 1–2), 1-skip word bigram
- Transcripts: word 1gram, 1-skip word bigram
- i-vectors

The mean probability ensemble yielded an F1-score of 89.93 % on the development data and a score of 91.75 % on the test data. The mean probability ensemble made the most number of mistakes in classifying Telugu–Hindi language pair but erred less than the essay based SVM model at other language pairs.

The meta classifier described in section 2.3 was trained on the following feature types and yielded an F1-score of 90.54 % on the development data.

- essays: character ngrams 2–7, word ngrams 1–2
- transcriptions: word 1-gram
- i-vectors: LDA

The meta classifier performed better than the mean probability ensemble on the development data. This result is in line with the previously reported results of Malmasi and Dras (2017). Surprisingly, the meta classifier performs worse on the test data.

4 Discussion

In this paper, we described our systems participating in the NLI shared task 2017. We participated in all the three tasks offered during this shared task campaign. We find that word unigram features in conjunction with i-vectors perform better than a combination of word or character based higher order n-gram features. We also find that transcription-based features do not improve the performance on the test data as is in the case of the combination system. All the systems make errors when discriminating between Hindi vs. Telugu. Another surprising result from experiments is that the Meta Classifier approach does not perform better than the mean probability ensemble which is not in line with the result of Malmasi and Dras (2017).

Besides the models we describe above, we also experimented with additional linguistic features (POS tags) and neural network classifiers. The POS tag n-gram features used together with our best-performing models did not improve the results. Furthermore, the best performing neural network architectures performed a few percentage scores worse than the linear models described in this paper in all of our experiments. Although this

System	F1 (macro)	Accuracy
Combined system	0.887 1	0.887 3
Simple system	0.906 5	0.906 4
Mean probability ensemble	0.917 5	0.917 3
Meta Classifier	0.848 1	0.848 2
Official Baseline		
essays and trans.	0.778 6	0.779 1
all	0.790 1	0.790 9
Random Baseline	0.909 0	0.909 0

Table 3: Results of different submissions for Fusion track.

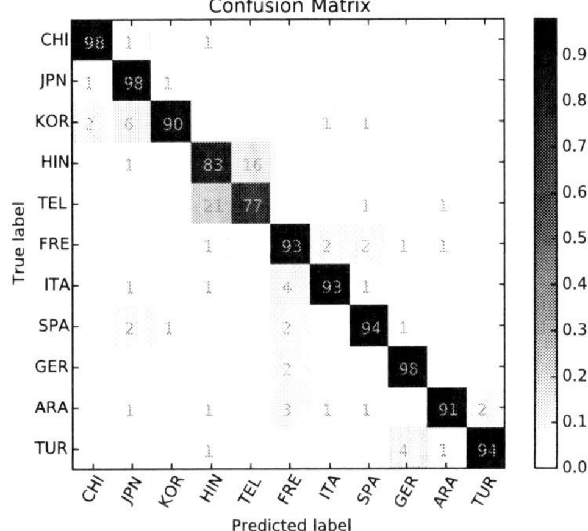

Figure 3: Confusion matrix of Mean probability ensemble for the *fusion* track.

is in line with our earlier experiments (Çöltekin and Rama, 2016, 2017) in a similar task, discriminating between similar languages and dialects (Malmasi et al., 2016; Zampieri et al., 2017), our experiments were not exhaustive and it is likely that one can get better results with neural networks with different architectures, and/or more data.

Acknowledgements

The first author is supported by the ERC Advanced Grant 324246 EVOLAEMP, which is gratefully acknowledged.

References

Serhiy Bykh and Detmar Meurers. 2014. Exploring Syntactic Features for Native Language Identification: A Variationist Perspective on Feature Encoding and Ensemble Optimization. In *Proceedings of COLING 2014, the 25th International Conference on Computational Linguistics: Technical Papers*. Dublin, Ireland, pages 1962–1973.

Çağrı Çöltekin and Taraka Rama. 2016. Discriminating Similar Languages with Linear SVMs and Neural Networks. In *Proceedings of the Third Workshop on NLP for Similar Languages, Varieties and Dialects (VarDial3)*. Osaka, Japan, pages 15–24.

Çağrı Çöltekin and Taraka Rama. 2017. Tübingen system in VarDial 2017 shared task: experiments with language identification and cross-lingual parsing. In *Proceedings of the Fourth Workshop on NLP for Similar Languages, Varieties and Dialects (VarDial)*. Valencia, Spain, pages 146–155. http://www.aclweb.org/anthology/W17-1218.

Rong-En Fan, Kai-Wei Chang, Cho-Jui Hsieh, Xiang-Rui Wang, and Chih-Jen Lin. 2008. LIBLINEAR: A library for large linear classification. *Journal of Machine Learning Research* 9:1871–1874.

Cyril Goutte, Serge Léger, and Marine Carpuat. 2013. Feature space selection and combination for native language identification. In *BEA@ NAACL-HLT*. pages 96–100.

Trevor Hastie, Robert Tibshirani, and Jerome Friedman. 2009. *The Elements of Statistical Learning: Data Mining, Inference, and Prediction*. Springer series in statistics. Springer-Verlag New York, second edition.

Radu Tudor Ionescu, Marius Popescu, and Aoife Cahill. 2014. Can characters reveal your native language? A language-independent approach to native language identification. In *Proceedings of the 2014 Conference on Empirical Methods in Natural Language Processing (EMNLP)*.

Scott Jarvis, Yves Bestgen, and Steve Pepper. 2013. Maximizing Classification Accuracy in Native Language Identification. In *Proceedings of the Eighth Workshop on Innovative Use of NLP for Building Educational Applications*. Atlanta, Georgia, pages 111–118.

Daniel Jurafsky and James H. Martin. 2009. *Speech and Language Processing: An Introduction to Natural Language Processing, Computational Linguistics, and Speech Recognition*. Pearson Prentice Hall, second edition.

Shervin Malmasi. 2016. *Native Language Identification: Explorations and Applications*. Ph.D. thesis. http://hdl.handle.net/1959.14/1110919.

Shervin Malmasi and Mark Dras. 2015. Multilingual Native Language Identification. In *Natural Language Engineering*.

Shervin Malmasi and Mark Dras. 2017. Native Language Identification using Stacked Generalization. *arXiv preprint arXiv:1703.06541* .

Shervin Malmasi, Keelan Evanini, Aoife Cahill, Joel Tetreault, Robert Pugh, Christopher Hamill, Diane Napolitano, and Yao Qian. 2017. A Report on the 2017 Native Language Identification Shared Task. In *Proceedings of the 12th Workshop on Building Educational Applications Using NLP*. Copenhagen, Denmark.

Shervin Malmasi, Marcos Zampieri, Nikola Ljubešić, Preslav Nakov, Ahmed Ali, and Jörg Tiedemann. 2016. Discriminating between Similar Languages and Arabic Dialect Identification: A Report on the Third DSL Shared Task. In *Proceedings of the VarDial Workshop*. Osaka, Japan.

F. Pedregosa, G. Varoquaux, A. Gramfort, V. Michel, B. Thirion, O. Grisel, M. Blondel, P. Prettenhofer, R. Weiss, V. Dubourg, J. Vanderplas, A. Passos, D. Cournapeau, M. Brucher, M. Perrot, and E. Duchesnay. 2011. Scikit-learn: Machine learning in Python. *Journal of Machine Learning Research* 12:2825–2830.

Björn Schuller, Stefan Steidl, Anton Batliner, Julia Hirschberg, Judee K. Burgoon, Alice Baird, Aaron Elkins, Yue Zhang, Eduardo Coutinho, and Keelan Evanini. 2016. The INTERSPEECH 2016 Computational Paralinguistics Challenge: Deception, Sincerity & Native Language. In *Interspeech 2016*. pages 2001–2005. https://doi.org/10.21437/Interspeech.2016-129.

Marcos Zampieri, Shervin Malmasi, Nikola Ljubešić, Preslav Nakov, Ahmed Ali, Jörg Tiedemann, Yves Scherrer, and Noëmi Aepli. 2017. Findings of the VarDial Evaluation Campaign 2017. In *Proceedings of the Fourth Workshop on NLP for Similar Languages, Varieties and Dialects (VarDial)*. Valencia, Spain, pages 1–15.

Structured Generation of Technical Reading Lists

Jonathan Gordon
USC Information Sciences Institute
Marina del Rey, CA, USA
jgordon@isi.edu

Stephen Aguilar
USC Rossier School of Education
Los Angeles, CA, USA
aguilars@usc.edu

Emily Sheng
USC Information Sciences Institute
Marina del Rey, CA, USA
ewsheng@isi.edu

Gully Burns
USC Information Sciences Institute
Marina del Rey, CA, USA
burns@isi.edu

Abstract

Learners need to find suitable documents to read and prioritize them in an appropriate order. We present a method of automatically generating reading lists, selecting documents based on their pedagogical value to the learner and ordering them using the structure of concepts in the domain. Resulting reading lists related to computational linguistics were evaluated by advanced learners and judged to be near the quality of those generated by domain experts. We provide an open-source implementation of our method to enable future work on reading list generation.

1 Introduction

More scientific and technical literature is instantly accessible than ever before, but this means that it can also be harder than ever to determine what sequence of documents would be most helpful for a learner to read. Standard information retrieval tools, e.g., a search engine, will find documents that are highly relevant, but they will not return documents about concepts that must be learned first, and they will not identify which documents are appropriate for a particular user. Learners would greatly benefit from an automated approximation of the sort of personalized reading list an expert tutor would create for them. We have developed TechKnAcq – short for Technical Knowledge Acquisition – to automatically construct this kind of pedagogically useful reading list for technical subjects.

Presented with only a "core corpus" of technical material that represents the subject under study, without any additional semantic annotation, TechKnAcq generates a reading list in response to a simple query. For instance, given a corpus of documents related to natural language processing, a reading list can be generated for the query "machine translation." The reading list should be similar to what a PhD student might be given by her advisor: it should include prerequisite subjects that need to be understood before attempting to learn material about the query, and it should be tailored to the individual needs of the student.

To generate such a reading list, we first infer the conceptual structure of the domain from the core corpus. We then expand this corpus to include a greater amount of relevant, pedagogically useful documents, and we relate concepts to one another and to the individual documents in a *concept graph* structure. Using this graph and a model of the learner's expertise, we generate personalized reading lists for the user's queries. In the following sections, we describe these steps and then evaluate the resulting reading lists for several concepts in computational linguistics, compared to reading lists generated by domain experts.

2 Generating a Concept Graph

A *concept graph* (Gordon et al., 2016) is a model of a knowledge domain and related documents. To generate a concept graph, we start with a *core corpus*, consisting of technical documents, e.g., the archives of an academic journal. We identify technical phrases in the core corpus and use these to find additional, potentially pedagogically valuable documents, such as reference works or tutorials. For each document in the resulting *expanded corpus*, we infer a distribution over a set of pedagogical roles. We model the concepts in the domain using topic modeling techniques and apply information-theoretic measures to predict *concept dependency* (roughly, prerequisite) relations among them. Associating the documents of the expanded corpus with these concepts results in a rich graph representation that enables structured reading list generation.

261

Proceedings of the 12th Workshop on Innovative Use of NLP for Building Educational Applications, pages 261–270
Copenhagen, Denmark, September 8, 2017. ©2017 Association for Computational Linguistics

2.1 Pedagogical Corpus Expansion

Most technical corpora are directed at experts, so they typically focus on presenting new methods and results. They often lack more introductory or instructional documents, and those covering fundamental concepts. Therefore, before generating a reading list, we want to automatically expand a core technical corpus to include relevant documents that are directed at learners at different levels.

Identifying terms Given a collection of documents, our first step is to identify a list of technical terms that can be used as queries. We adapt the lightweight, corpus-independent method presented by Jardine (2014):

1. Generate a list of n-grams that occur two or more times in the titles of papers in the corpus.
2. Filter unigrams that appear in a Scrabble dictionary (e.g., common nouns).
3. Filter n-grams that begin or end with stop words, such as conjunctions or prepositions. (Remove "part of" but not "part of speech".)
4. Filter any n-gram whose number of occurrences is within 25% of the occurrences of a subsuming $n+1$-gram. E.g., remove "statistical machine" because "statistical machine translation" is nearly as frequent.

Based on manual inspection of the results, we increased the threshold for subsumption to 30% and added two steps:

5. Filter regular plurals if the list includes the singular.
6. Order technical terms based on the density of the citation graph for documents containing them (Jo et al., 2007).

Jardine (2014) removes the bottom 75% of unigrams and bigrams by frequency (but keeps all longer n-grams). The Jo et al. (2007) method is better for comparing terms than simple frequency, but most technical terms we discover are also of high quality, making aggressive filtering of unigrams and bigrams unnecessary. Jardine also adds acronyms (uppercase words in mixed-case titles), regardless of frequency. We find acronyms from the initial collection of terms and do not consider it necessary to add singleton acronyms to our results – or those that are also a common noun, e.g., TRIPS, since we cannot assure case sensitivity in our searches.

Wikipedia and ScienceDirect We retrieve book chapters from Elsevier's ScienceDirect full-text document service and encyclopedia articles from Wikipedia. For Wikipedia, each term is queried individually, but only the top two results are included. For ScienceDirect, terms are used to retrieve batches of 50 results for each disjunction of 100 technical terms. This identifies documents that are central to the set of query terms rather than those with minimal shared content, and it reduces the number of API requests required. These documents are filtered based on heuristic relevance criteria: For Wikipedia, we keep documents if they contain at least 15 occurrences of at least five unique technical terms. For ScienceDirect, we require at least 20 occurrences of at least 10 unique technical terms since these documents tend to be longer.

Given this initial set of matching documents, we can then exploit their natural groupings: For Wikipedia, these are the categories that articles belong to, while for ScienceDirect, they are the books the chapters are from. For each grouping of the matched documents, ordered by size, we add the most relevant 75% of the documents that belong to the grouping and pass a weaker threshold of relevance to the query terms (four occurrences of two unique technical terms). This adds back in documents that would not pass the more stringent filters above but are likely to be relevant based on these groupings. These thresholds were manually tuned to balance the accuracy and coverage of expansion documents for these sources, but a full consideration of the parameter space is left for future work.

Tutorials Tutorials are often written by researchers for use within their own groups or for teaching a course and are then made available to the broader community online. For developing scientists in the field, these serve as valuable training resources, but they are not indexed or collected in any centralized way. Our approach for downloading tutorials from the Web is as follows:

1. Search Google or Bing for each of the top-200 technical terms and for randomized disjunctions of 10 technical terms for the full list.
2. Filter the results with the ".pdf" file extension and containing the phrase "this tutorial."
3. For each result found for more than one query, perform OCR and export the document.

2.2 Computing Pedagogical Roles

Given an expanded corpus of pedagogically diverse documents, we would like to infer a distribution for each document of how well it fulfills different pedagogical roles. Sheng et al. (2017) have created an annotated corpus and trained a classifier to predict these roles:

- **Survey**: A survey examines or compares across a broad concept.
- **Tutorial**: Tutorials describe a coherent process about how to use tools or understand a concept, and teach by example.
- **Resource**: Does this document describe the authors' implementation of a tool, corpus, or other resource that has been distributed?
- **Reference work**: Is this document a collection of authoritative facts intended for others to refer to? Reports of novel, experimental results are not considered authoritative facts.
- **Empirical results**: Does this document describe results of the authors' experiments?
- **Software manual**: Is this document a manual describing how to use different components of a piece of software?
- **Other**: This includes theoretical papers, papers that present a rebuttal for a claim, thought experiments, etc.

For the training corpus – a subset of the pedagogically expanded corpus – annotators were instructed to select all applicable pedagogical roles for each document. In the experiments we report, we use a combination of the predicted roles and manually set prior probabilities for the different document sources (e.g., an article from Wikipedia is most likely to be a *Reference work*).

2.3 Computing Concepts and Dependencies

To infer conceptual structure in a collection of documents, TechKnAcq must first identify the *concepts* that are important in the document domain. We model concepts as probability distributions over words or phrases, known as *topics* (Griffiths and Steyvers, 2004). Specifically, we use latent Dirichlet allocation (LDA) (Blei et al., 2003), implemented in MALLET (McCallum, 2002), to discover topics in the core corpus.[1]

Many relations can hold between concepts, but for reading list generation we are most interested in *concept dependency*, which holds whenever one concept would help you to understand another. This is strongest in the case of prerequisites (e.g., *First-order logic* is a prerequisite for understanding *Markov logic networks*). Gordon et al. (2016)

---

[1] Concepts are not tied to standard topic modeling, e.g., they can also come from running Explicit Semantic Analysis (Gabrilovich and Markovitch, 2007) using Wikipedia pages.

propose and evaluate approaches to predict concept dependency relations between LDA topics, and we adopt the average of their best-performing methods:

Word-similarity method   The strength of dependency between two topics is the Jaccard similarity coefficient $J(t_1, t_2) = \frac{t_1 \cap t_2}{t_1 \cup t_2}$, using the top 20 words in the associated topic distributions. A limitation of this method is that it is symmetric, while dependency relations can be asymmetric.

Cross-entropy method   Topic t_1 depends on topic t_2 if the distribution (e.g., of top-k associated words) for t_1 is better approximated by that of t_2 than vice versa – for cross entropy H function, $H(t_1, t_2) > H(t_2, t_1)$ – and their joint entropy is lower than a chosen threshold, namely, the average joint entropy of topics known not to be dependent.

2.4 Concept Graphs

In a concept graph, concepts are nodes, which may be connected by weighted, directed edges for relations including concept dependency. These concepts have associated features, most importantly their distribution over words or phrases, which will be used to match learners' queries. Documents are also represented as nodes, which have as their features basic bibliographic information and their pedagogical role distributions. Documents are connected to concepts by weighted edges indicating their relevance.

A natural basis for identifying the most relevant documents for a concept is the distribution over topics that LDA produces for each document. However, high relevance of a topic to a document does not entail that the document is highly relevant to the topic. In particular, the LDA document–topic composition gives anomalous results for documents that are not well aligned with the topic model. Therefore, we also compute scores for a document's relevance to a topic based on the importance of each word in the document to the topic. For each document, we sum the weight of each word or phrase for the topic (i.e., the number of times LDA assigned the word to that topic in the entire corpus). This score is then normalized by dividing by the length of the document and then by the maximum score of any document for that topic. The algorithm is given in Figure 1. In the concept graph, we use the average of the original document–topic composition weight and this alternative measure.

```
Input: topic model T, corpus C, document d
scores ← nested hash table
foreach topic t ∈ T do
    scores[t][d] ← 0
    max_score ← 0
    foreach document d ∈ C do
        foreach word w ∈ d do
            scores[t][d] ← scores[t][d] +
                topic_weight(w, t)
        scores[t][d] ← scores[t][d] / length(d)
        if scores[t][d] > max_score then
            max_score ← scores[t][d]
    foreach document d ∈ C do
        scores[t][d] ← scores[t][d] / max_score
return scores
```

Figure 1: Algorithm to score the relevance of documents to concepts.

3 Generating a Reading List

Given a concept graph linking each concept to the concepts it depends upon and to the documents that describe it, we generate a reading list by

1. computing the relevance of each concept to the user's query string,
2. performing a depth-first traversal of the dependencies, starting from the best match, and
3. selecting documents for each concept based on our model of the user's expertise and the documents' pedagogical roles.

Learner models   The *learner model* gives the user's level of familiarity with each concept in the concept graph for the domain. By modeling the user's familiarity with concepts when we generate personalized reading lists, we can prefer introductory material for new concepts and more advanced documents for the user's areas of expertise, omitting them when they would be included only as dependencies for another concept. Such a model can be built from an initial questionnaire or inferred from other inputs, such as documents the user has marked as read. In the absence of a model of the specific user, we fall back to generic "beginner," "intermediate," and "advanced" preferences, where all concepts are assigned the same level of familiarity.

Concept relevance   Given a query, we match concepts based on lexical overlap with their associated word distribution. For each concept with a match score over a threshold, if the learner model indicates that the user is a beginner at that concept, we traverse concept dependencies until the relevance score drops below a threshold. If concept d is a prerequisite of the matched topic m with weight $P(d, m)$, the

relevance $R(d) = M(d) + M(m) \cdot P(d, m)$, where M is the function giving the lexical overlap strength.

Document selection   When we include concept dependencies, we bookend their presentation on the reading list by presenting one or more introductory or overview documents, presenting documents about the dependencies, and then proceeding to more advanced documents about the original concept. So, for instance, a reading list might include an overview about *Markov logic networks*, then present documents about the prerequisite concepts *First-order logic* and *Markov network*, and end with more advanced documents about *Markov logic networks*. This avoids the confusion of presenting documents in strict concept dependency order, where the learner may not have the basic understanding of a subject to recognize why the prerequisites are in the reading list and how they relate to the query concept.

If the user already has advanced knowledge of a concept, we do not follow dependencies. Instead, we present three papers for that concept: a survey and two empirical results papers. We keep track of the concepts and documents that have been covered by the reading list generation so that, for instance, a matching topic that is also a dependency of a stronger match will be included as a dependency but not repeated later.

4 Evaluation

To enable comparison to an existing gold standard, we evaluated TechKnAcq on the domain of computational linguistics and natural language processing. Our evaluation covers 16 topics: For eight topics, we evaluate the expert-generated Jardine (2014) gold standard (JGS) reading lists and reading lists generated by TechKnAcq for the same topics. We additionally evaluated reading lists generated by TechKnAcq for eight topics of central importance in the domain, sampled from the list of "Major evaluations and tasks" on the Wikipedia article on natural language processing.[2] In this section, we describe the generation of a concept graph for the evaluation domain, the evaluation methodology and participants, and the results.

4.1 Evaluation Domain

As our core corpus, we used the ACL Anthology, which consists of PDFs – many of them scanned –

---

[2]   https://en.wikipedia.org/wiki/Natural_language_
processing#Major_evaluations_and_tasks

of conference and workshop papers and journal articles. There have been multiple attempts to produce machine-readable versions of the corpus, but all suffer from problems of text quality and extraction coverage. We used the December 2016 release of the ACL Anthology Network corpus (Radev et al., 2009), which includes papers published through 2014. We automatically and manually enhanced this corpus by adding missing text, removing documents not primarily written in English and ones with only abstracts, and joining words split across lines. After running the corpus expansion method described in Section 2.1, the corpus includes:

- 22,084 papers from the ACL Anthology
- 1,949 encyclopedia articles from Wikipedia
- 1,172 book chapters from ScienceDirect
- 114 tutorials retrieved from the Web

The concept graph was generated using a 300-topic LDA model, defined over bigrams. Names were manually assigned to 238 topics, and 62 topics that could not be assigned a name were excluded from the concept graph.

4.2 Evaluation Method

We recruited 33 NLP researchers to take part in the evaluation, primarily from an online mailing list for the computational linguistics community. Participants were required to have institutional affiliations and expertise in NLP. In the evaluation, participants were presented with the reading lists[3] and asked to change the order of documents to the order they would recommend a novice in NLP to read, i.e., ensuring that the first documents require limited knowledge and the documents that follow are predicated on the ones that came before. The participants could also remove documents from the reading list and suggest new documents be added in any position. By tracking changes in the reading lists, we can measure how many entries had to be changed for the list to be satisfactory.

Three sets of reading lists were evaluated. The first two were comparable lists, consisting of expert-generated lists, and their TechKnAcq counterparts. Together, these constitute the "comparison" set. The third set consisted of additional TechKnAcq-generated reading lists; this constitutes the "stand-alone" set. In addition to this edit-based evaluation, for the stand-alone set participants were asked to rate their agreement with statements about read-

ing lists generated by TechKnAcq for a qualitative measure of a reading list's pedagogical value.

4.3 Evaluation Results

The similarity of TechKnAcq reading lists to expert-generated ones in terms of pedagogical value was assessed based on the changes participants made to the lists – the fewer documents that were moved, deleted, or added, the better the participant considered the reading list. The total number of changes to a reading list was measured using edit distance, but we are also interested specifically in the stability of document positions, the number of documents deleted, and the number of documents added to the reading lists.

Edit distance   One of the most natural ways to compute how much a participant modified a given reading list overall is to use Levenshtein (1966) edit distance. This is a method of computing the fewest edit operations necessary to turn one sequence into another, classically applied to spell-checking. The operations are insertion, deletion, and substitution of an item. So, for instance, if the participant removes a paper and adds another in the same location in the reading list, she has performed a substitution, with an edit distance of one. If she then moves a paper from the end of the reading list to the beginning, that is a deletion from the old location followed by an insertion. A limitation of edit distance is that it does not take into account the length of the sequence being modified. E.g., a long reading list that is mostly considered to be good may have the same number of edits as a shorter reading list that is much worse. As such, we also normalized the edit distance scores by dividing by the length of the original reading list. For the comparable set, the average edit distance was 0.22 for an expert reading list and 0.33 for a TechKnAcq-generated one. The edit distance for TechKnAcq reading lists for the stand-alone set was 0.38. These results are shown in Figure 2.

List stability   One indicator of reading list quality is how stable a list is, i.e., whether a document changes position within a list. This is computed as the number of documents whose absolute position in the reading list has changed, not including documents that were added (written in) by the participants. The mean level of stability for reading lists is given in Table 1. Smaller means, paired with smaller standard deviations indicate more stability within the reading list for a query. Minimums and

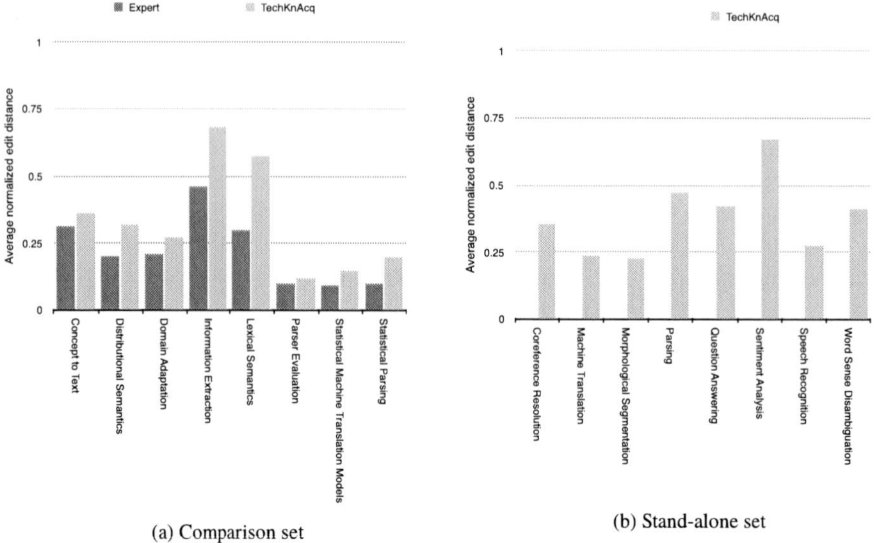

(a) Comparison set   (b) Stand-alone set

Figure 2: Average Levenshtein edit distances for reading lists produced by domain experts and by TechKnAcq, normalized by dividing by the original length of each reading list.

Domain	TechKnAcq-generated reading lists						Expert-generated reading lists					
	Norm	Mean	SD	Min	Max	Len.	Norm	Mean	SD	Min	Max	Len.
Concept to Text	0.63	3.75	2.01	0	6	6	0.80	12.83	4.26	0	16	16
Distributional Semantics	0.66	4.62	2.93	0	7	7	0.71	10.00	4.73	0	14	14
Domain Adaptation	0.69	4.13	1.55	2	6	6	0.80	8.78	1.64	6	10	11
Information Extraction	0.64	7.04	3.25	0	10	11	0.65	5.85	3.72	0	9	9
Lexical Semantics	0.60	5.93	3.93	0	10	10	0.30	7.90	3.04	0	14	14
Parser Evaluation	0.77	10.00	1.41	9	12	13	0.75	3.00	1.41	1	4	4
Stat. Machine Trans. Models	0.84	15.88	3.40	10	19	19	0.55	2.75	2.05	0	5	5
Statistical Parsing	0.79	10.29	4.64	0	13	13	0.66	14.57	10.03	0	22	22
Average	0.70						0.69					
Coreference Resolution	0.60	3.58	1.98	0	6	6						
Machine Translation	0.55	8.25	4.74	0	13	15						
Morphological Segmentation	0.67	6.00	2.78	0	9	9						
Parsing	0.54	5.40	4.81	0	10	10						
Question Answering	0.56	3.36	2.17	0	6	6						
Sentiment Analysis	0.68	4.05	1.86	0	6	6						
Speech Recognition	0.73	8.00	4.18	0	11	11						
Word Sense Disambiguation	0.64	3.81	2.04	0	6	6						
Average	0.62											

Table 1: Changes to document positions in expert and TechKnAcq reading lists, for the comparison and stand-alone sets. Lower numbers indicate greater list stability. *Norm* is the mean number of changes normalized by dividing by the reading list length to allow comparison across lists.

maximums are also reported, with TechKnAcq scoring a minimum of zero more often, indicating that participants left these lists unchanged more often than the expert (JGS) lists. Note that, unlike for edit distance, some changes to reading lists, such as moving the first document to the end, have an outsize effect on the stability score compared with others, like swapping the first and last documents. This indicator is also sensitive to list length – the longer the list, the more potential there is for changes within the list. For the comparison set, the average stability for TechKnAcq reading lists, normalized by length, is 0.70 vs 0.69 for expert-generated reading lists, indicating a similar level of document movement.

Deletions Fewer deletions signals a judgment that the reading list contents are appropriate. Table 2 presents the mean number of deletions. When deletions are normalized by reading list length, there are fewer (0.16) for expert-generated reading lists than for for TechKnAcq (0.23) on the comparison set. While the stability scores were similar for the comparison set, the deletions suggest that TechKnAcq does worse at selecting documents than experts do. This may be a limitation of computing relevance using a coarse-grained topic model or it may reflect that TechKnAcq includes more documents for concept dependencies than the participants felt necessary.

Additions Participants were encouraged to add any documents they felt belonged in the reading list that were not present. However, this was relatively labor-intensive, requiring the participant to either remember or look up relevant papers and then enter information about them. As such, relatively few documents were added. Statistics for additions are given in Table 3, but the rate with which documents were added is similar for TechKnAcq and expert-generated reading lists.

Qualitative For reading lists generated for the stand-alone set, participants qualitatively evaluated whether they were appropriate to use in a pedagogical setting. They were asked to rate their agreement with these statements on a scale from 1 (strongly disagree) to 7 (strongly agree):

1. This reading list is complete.
2. This is a good reading list for a PhD student.
3. I would use this reading list in one of my classes.
4. I would send this reading list to a colleague of mine.
5. This is a good reading list for a master's student.
6. I could come up with a more complete reading list than the one provided.
7. If a PhD read the articles in this reading list in order, they would master the concepts.

Cronbach's α was calculated for each set of questions; high values ($\alpha > .8$) indicate that each set of items were internally consistent, and closely related as a set (Santos, 1999). Thus, we averaged these ratings (with responses to Statement 6 inverted) for a composite measure of the pedagogical value of each reading list. Results indicate that, on average, the reading lists have moderate-to-high potential. These results are in Table 4.

5 Related Work

Research on information retrieval provides a historically sizable literature describing methods to catalog, index, and query document collections, but it focuses on the task of finding the most relevant documents for a given query (Witten et al., 1999). Wang et al. (2007) build a repository of learning objects characterized by metadata and then personalize recommendations based on a user's preferences. Tang (2008) introduces the problem of reading list generation and addresses it using collaborative filtering techniques. Ekstrand et al. (2010) provide a good run-through of possible competition based on collaborative filtering.

The doctoral work of Jardine (2014) addresses the question of building reading lists over corpora of technical papers. Given an input word, phrase, or entire document, Jardine identifies a weighted set of relevant topics using an LDA model trained on a corpus and then selects the most relevant papers for each topic using his ThemedPageRank metric. This is an unstructured method for reading list generation, while TechKnAcq uses concept dependency relations to order the presentation of topics. Jardine's method selects documents based on their importance to a topic but without consideration of the pedagogical roles the documents serve for different learner models.

Jardine's work provides a set of expert-generated gold-standard reading lists, which we have reused in our evaluation. Jardine asked experts to compose gold standard reading lists and compared these to the reading lists generated by his system, using a citation substitution coefficient to judge how similar a paper in his output is to that chosen by an expert.

Domain	TechKnAcq-generated reading lists						Expert-generated reading lists					
	Norm	*Mean*	*SD*	*Min*	*Max*	*Len.*	*Norm*	*Mean*	*SD*	*Min*	*Max*	*Len.*
Concept to Text	0.17	1.00	1.28	0	4	6	0.31	4.92	4.27	0	14	16
Distributional Semantics	0.73	5.08	1.04	3	7	7	0.09	1.23	1.59	0	4	14
Domain Adaptation	0.11	0.78	1.09	0	3	7	0.19	2.11	1.05	0	4	11
Information Extraction	0.12	1.37	1.71	0	5	11	0.50	4.48	1.19	2	7	9
Lexical Semantics	0.26	2.55	3.43	0	10	10	0.07	1.00	1.62	0	5	14
Parser Evaluation	0.08	1.00	1.41	0	3	13	0.00	0.00	0.00	0	0	4
Stat. Machine Trans. Models	0.18	3.50	2.33	1	7	19	0.05	0.25	0.71	0	2	5
Statistical Parsing	0.19	2.43	1.81	0	4	13	0.11	2.43	2.37	0	7	22
Average	0.23						0.16					
Coreference Resolution	0.05	0.27	0.47	0	1	6						
Machine Translation	0.08	1.13	2.80	0	8	15						
Morphological Segmentation	0.23	2.11	2.32	0	6	9						
Parsing	0.08	0.83	1.60	0	4	10						
Question Answering	0.06	0.36	0.63	0	2	6						
Sentiment Analysis	0.07	0.41	0.80	0	3	6						
Speech Recognition	0.18	2.00	1.80	0	5	11						
Word Sense Disambiguation	0.07	0.44	0.89	0	3	6						
Average	0.10											

Table 2: Number of documents participants deleted from expert and TechKnAcq reading lists, for the comparison and stand-alone sets. Lower numbers indicate better document selection. *Norm* is the mean number of deletions normalized by dividing by the reading list length to allow comparison across lists.

Domain	TechKnAcq-generated reading lists						Expert-generated reading lists					
	Norm	*Mean*	*SD*	*Min*	*Max*	*Len.*	*Norm*	*Mean*	*SD*	*Min*	*Max*	*Len.*
Concept to Text	0.00	0.00	0.00	0	0	6	0.00	0.00	0.00	0	0	16
Distributional Semantics	0.11	0.77	1.17	0	3	7	0.04	0.54	0.78	0	2	14
Domain Adaptation	0.06	0.44	1.01	0	3	7	0.04	0.44	1.01	0	3	11
Information Extraction	0.04	0.48	0.98	0	4	11	0.02	0.19	0.48	0	2	9
Lexical Semantics	0.09	0.85	1.69	0	5	10	0.00	0.00	0.00	0	0	14
Parser Evaluation	0.08	1.00	1.41	0	3	13	0.13	0.50	0.58	0	1	4
Stat. Machine Trans. Models	0.07	1.38	1.41	0	4	19	0.08	0.38	0.74	0	2	5
Statistical Parsing	0.07	0.86	1.46	0	3	13	0.02	0.43	1.13	0	3	22
Average	0.06						0.04					
Coreference Resolution	0.10	0.58	1.24	0	4	6						
Machine Translation	0.01	0.13	0.35	0	1	15						
Morphological Segmentation	0.06	0.56	1.01	0	3	9						
Parsing	0.04	0.40	0.97	0	3	10						
Question Answering	0.02	0.14	0.53	0	2	6						
Sentiment Analysis	0.08	0.48	0.93	0	3	6						
Speech Recognition	0.05	0.56	1.33	0	4	11						
Word Sense Disambiguation	0.05	0.31	0.70	0	2	6						
Average	0.05											

Table 3: Number of documents participants added to expert and TechKnAcq reading lists, for the comparison and stand-alone sets. Lower numbers indicate better original reading lists. *Norm* is the mean number of additions normalized by dividing by the reading list length to allow comparison across lists.

	N	Mean	SD	Min	Max	α
Coreference Resolution	12	4.22	1.18	1.33	5.50	0.89
Machine Translation	8	4.04	1.95	1.00	5.83	0.97
Morphological Segmentation	9	3.41	1.73	1.00	5.50	0.96
Parsing	10	4.32	1.63	1.17	6.83	0.97
Question Answering	14	3.80	1.51	1.33	5.50	0.93
Sentiment Analysis	22	4.18	1.25	1.00	6.67	0.93
Speech Recognition	9	4.41	1.35	2.00	6.83	0.91
Word Sense Disambiguation	16	4.40	1.23	1.17	6.50	0.92

Table 4: Descriptive statistics for the pedagogical value of each TechKnAcq reading list, with 1 = weak pedagogical potential and 7 = strong pedagogical potential. N is the number of participants who rated the reading list for each query.

He also performed user satisfaction evaluations, where thousands of users of the Qiqqa document management system evaluated the quality of the technical terms and documents generated from their libraries.

In Section 2.1, we use a variant of Jardine's method for identifying technical terms in a set of documents, in order to run queries for expanding a core technical corpus to include more pedagogically helpful documents. There is significant prior work on identifying key phrases or technical terminology, e.g., Justeson and Katz (1995). We could also select phrases based on TF–IDF weighting of n-grams or using the highest weighted phrases in the LDA topic model. However, since the technical terms are only used to find additional documents, whose relevance is then determined by the LDA topic model and the document–topic relevance algorithm (Figure 1), the accuracy of technical term identification is not critical to our results. As this was not a focus of our research, Jardine's method was chosen largely for its simplicity.

6   Conclusions

We have presented the first system for generating reading lists based on inferred domain structure and models of learners. Our method builds a topic-based index for a technical corpus, expands that corpus with relevant pedagogically oriented documents, provides a preliminary encoding of the pedagogical roles played by individual documents, and builds a personalized, structured reading list for use by learners.

We predict that the greatest performance gains to be generated in future work are likely to come from more detailed and complete studies of the pedagogical value of specific documents (and types of documents) for individual learners. Thus, an important direction for future investigation may be to characterize a learner's knowledge in order to be able to score the pedagogical value of reading material for that person rather than for the generic learner models used in our evaluation.

We have demonstrated that the quality of reading lists generated in this way may be quantitatively compared to existing expert-generated lists and that our system approaches the performance of human experts. We are releasing our implementation[4] to support future efforts and serve as a basis for comparison.

Acknowledgments

The authors thank Yigal Arens, Aram Galstyan, Vishnu Karthik, Prem Natarajan, and Linhong Zhu for their contributions and feedback on this work.

This research is based upon work supported in part by the Office of the Director of National Intelligence (ODNI), Intelligence Advanced Research Projects Activity (IARPA), via Air Force Research Laboratory (AFRL). The views and conclusions contained herein are those of the authors and should not be interpreted as necessarily representing the official policies or endorsements, either expressed or implied, of ODNI, IARPA, AFRL, or the U.S. Government. The U.S. Government is authorized to reproduce and distribute reprints for Governmental purposes notwithstanding any copyright annotation thereon.

References

David M. Blei, Andrew Y. Ng, and Michael I. Jordan. 2003. Latent Dirichlet allocation. *Journal of Machine Learning Research*, 3:993–1022.

Michael D. Ekstrand, Praveen Kannan, James A. Stemper, John T. Butler, Joseph A. Konstan, and John T.

---

[4] http://techknacq.isi.edu

Riedl. 2010. Automatically building research reading lists. In *Proceedings of the Fourth ACM Conference on Recommender Systems*, pages 159–66.

Evgeniy Gabrilovich and Shaul Markovitch. 2007. Computing semantic relatedness using Wikipedia-based explicit semantic analysis. In *Proceedings of the 20th International Joint Conference on Artifical Intelligence*, IJCAI'07, pages 1606–11, San Francisco, CA, USA. Morgan Kaufmann.

Jonathan Gordon, Linhong Zhu, Aram Galstyan, Prem Natarajan, and Gully Burns. 2016. Modeling concept dependencies in a scientific corpus. In *Proceedings of the Annual Meeting of the Association for Computational Linguistics (ACL 2016)*, pages 866–75.

Thomas L. Griffiths and Mark Steyvers. 2004. Finding scientific topics. In *Proceedings of the National Academy of Sciences of the USA*, volume 101, pages 5228–35. Supplement 1.

James G. Jardine. 2014. Automatically generating reading lists. Technical Report UCAM-CL-TR-848, University of Cambridge Computer Laboratory.

Yookyung Jo, Carl Lagoze, and C. Lee Giles. 2007. Detecting research topics via the correlation between graphs and texts. In *Proceedings of the 13th ACM SIGKDD International Conference on Knowledge Discovery and Data Mining*, pages 370–9, New York, NY, USA. ACM.

John S. Justeson and Slava M. Katz. 1995. Technical terminology: some linguistic properties and an algorithm for identification in text. 1:9–27.

V. I. Levenshtein. 1966. Binary codes capable of correcting deletions, insertions, and reversals. *Soviet Physics Doklady*, 10:707–10.

Andrew McCallum. 2002. MALLET: A machine learning for language toolkit.

Dragomir R. Radev, Pradeep Muthukrishnan, and Vahed Qazvinian. 2009. The ACL anthology network corpus. In *Proceedings of the 2009 Workshop on Text and Citation Analysis for Scholarly Digital Libraries*, pages 54–61.

J. Reynaldo A. Santos. 1999. Cronbach's alpha: A tool for assessing the reliability of scales. *Journal of Extension*, 37:1–5.

Emily Sheng, Prem Natarajan, Jonathan Gordon, and Gully Burns. 2017. An investigation into the pedagogical features of documents. In *Proceedings of the 12th Workshop on Innovative Use of NLP for Building Educational Applications*.

Tiffany Ya Tang. 2008. *The Design and Study of Pedagogical Paper Recommendation*. Ph.D. thesis, University of Saskatchewan.

Tzone I. Wang, Kun Hua Tsai, Ming Che Lee, and Ti Kai Chiu. 2007. Personalized learning objects recommendation based on the semantic-aware discovery and the learner preference pattern. *Educational Technology & Society*, 10:84–105.

Ian H. Witten, Alistair Moffat, and Timothy C. Bell. 1999. *Managing Gigabytes: Compressing and Indexing Documents and Images*. Morgan Kaufmann.

Effects of Lexical Properties on Viewing Time per Word in Autistic and Neurotypical Readers

Sanja Štajner[1]   Victoria Yaneva[2]   Ruslan Mitkov[2]   Simone Paolo Ponzetto[1]

[1]Data and Web Science Group, University of Mannheim, Germany
`{sanja, simone}@informatik.uni-mannheim.de`
[2]Research Group in Computational Linguistics, University of Wolverhampton, UK
`{v.yaneva, r.mitkov}@wlv.ac.uk`

Abstract

Eye tracking studies from the past few decades have shaped the way we think of word complexity and cognitive load: words that are long, rare and ambiguous are more difficult to read. However, online processing techniques have been scarcely applied to investigating the reading difficulties of people with autism and what vocabulary is challenging for them. We present parallel gaze data obtained from adult readers with autism and a control group of neurotypical readers and show that the former required higher cognitive effort to comprehend the texts as evidenced by three gaze-based measures. We divide all words into four classes based on their viewing times for both groups and investigate the relationship between longer viewing times and word length, word frequency, and four cognitively-based measures (word concreteness, familiarity, age of acquisition and imagability).

1 Introduction

Online methodologies such as eye tracking and event-related potentials have been extensively used to investigate word processing among neurotypical readers (Rayner et al., 2012; Dehaene and Cohen, 2011). The idea that the duration of gaze fixations and revisits (go-back fixations to a previously fixated object) could be used as a proxy for measuring cognitive load dates back to the *strong eye-mind hypothesis* by Just and Carpenter (1980), according to which, "there is no appreciable lag between what is fixated and what is processed" (Just and Carpenter, 1980). That is, when a subject looks at something, he/she also processes it cognitively and the amount of time the subject spends on processing the particular object is equal to the amount of time his/her gaze stays fixated on this object. According to this hypothesis, gaze duration metrics allow measuring the cognitive load imposed on the reader by certain words, clauses and sentences (Just and Carpenter, 1980).

A series of studies investigating the effects of word frequency, verb complexity and lexical ambiguity (Juhasz and Rayner, 2003; Rayner et al., 2012), as well as contextual effects on word perception (Ehrlich and Rayner, 1981) concluded that long, rare and ambiguous words are more likely to be fixated longer and their processing requires more cognitive effort from the reader. These are also words that are likely to be replaced with shorter and more frequent ones during lexical simplification aimed at making text more accessible to wider populations (Bott et al., 2012; Glavaš and Štajner, 2015).

Eye tracking has also been extensively used for the investigation of reading-related disorders owing to its capacity to provide information about the online processing of the text. For example, aphasic readers show "qualitatively different gaze fixation patterns" when answering comprehension questions (Dickey et al., 2007) and readers with dyslexia have been found to exhibit longer fixation durations and less efficient scanning techniques (Kim and Lombardino, 2016).

In spite of the decades-long tradition of using gaze data to investigate word processing among neurotypical readers and readers with reading-related disorders, this methodology has been scarcely used to investigate reading among people with Autism Spectrum Disorder (ASD). People with ASD have been shown to experience comprehension difficulties at lexical, syntactic and pragmatic level (Frith and Snowling, 1983; Happe, 1997; O'Connor and Klein, 2004; Happé and Frith, 2006; Whyte et al., 2014) and thus studies

Proceedings of the 12th Workshop on Innovative Use of NLP for Building Educational Applications, pages 271–281
Copenhagen, Denmark, September 8, 2017. ©2017 Association for Computational Linguistics

employing online processing techniques have the potential to cast light on the particular linguistic constructions which people with autism find challenging.

1.1 Autism Spectrum Disorder

Autism Spectrum Disorder (ASD) is a neurodevelopmental disorder characterised by impairment in communication and social interaction (American Psychiatric Association, 2013). A majority of children on the spectrum experience language delay, which results in reading comprehension difficulties later on in their lives, such as resolving ambiguity in meaning (Frith and Snowling, 1983; Happé and Frith, 2006), syntax processing of long sentences (Whyte et al., 2014) and identifying pronoun referents (O'Connor and Klein, 2004).

Unlike people with other developmental conditions such as dyslexia, autistic readers are not considered to have deficits in word decoding, successfully applying both lexical (look-and-say) and phonological (grapheme-to-phoneme conversion) strategies for reading words (Frith and Snowling, 1983; Smith Gabig, 2010). This implies that in the case of readers with autism, decoding difficulties are unlikely to be the reason for longer fixation times. However, while decoding skills are considered intact, there is an evidence of semantic deficit in ASD (Henderson et al., 2011; Löfkvist et al., 2014), and more specifically in word comprehension rather than word production (Charman et al., 2003; Luyster et al., 2008). This suggests that a difficulty with accessing and integrating the semantic representation of words could pose higher cognitive load on readers with autism.

This hypothesis is supported through an online measurement of word processing using gaze data. Sansosti et al. (2013) provide evidence for significant differences between the total fixation durations, number of fixations and number of regressions between autistic and non-autistic adolescents while reading individual sentences, suggesting that the reading task imposed an overall heavier cognitive load on the participants from the ASD group.

Brock et al. (2008) also used gaze data[1] and showed that both the ASD and the control participants were able to use context to successfully dis-

ambiguate the ambiguous target words. The studies by Sansosti et al. (2013) and Brock et al. (2008) are, to the best of our knowledge, the only two existing studies investigating reading among people with autism using gaze data; we advance this by i) using a larger dataset from a natural reading task as opposed to individual sentences, ii) identifying which words impose heavier cognitive load on the participants and what their lexical properties are.

1.2 Complex Word Identification

Complex Word Identification (CWI) task received high attention only recently, with findings suggesting that using a CWI module at the beginning of a lexical simplification (LS) pipeline significantly improves performances of LS systems (Paetzold and Specia, 2016c) and with the recently organised SemEval-2016 CWI shared task.[2] The goal of the shared task was building CWI systems which would identify challenging words for non-native English speakers. The dataset consisted of sentences (without context), each with one content word (noun, verb, adjective, or adverb) marked as a target word. The training dataset contained 200 sentences, where each target word was annotated by 20 non-native English speakers as 'easy' or 'complex', depending on whether they understood its meaning or not. The participants were asked to mark the word as 'complex' even if they understood the meaning of the sentence as a whole, as long as they did not understand the word itself. The test set consisted of 9,000 sentences, this time each sentence annotated only by one non-native speaker (300 different annotators in total). The main goal of the task was to predict potentially complex words for a non-native English speaker based on the annotations collected from 20 non-native speakers. The analysis of the crowdsourced annotations revealed that 'complex' words are on average shorter, less ambiguous, and less frequent in Simple English Wikipedia[3]. The results of the shared task (Paetzold and Specia, 2016b) showed that the use of features focused only on isolated words and not their context lead to best performing CWI systems. Among many investigated lexical and syntactic features, some of them taking into account the context of the target word and some not, the word frequency of the target word in Simple English Wikipedia was identified as the best

---

[1]The study by Brock et al. (2008) did not contain gaze data produced during a reading task. Instead, the participants were asked to look at an image on the screen which was either relevant or irrelevant to the target word they were hearing.

[2]http://alt.qcri.org/semeval2016/task11/
[3]https://simple.wikipedia.org

feature (Wróbel, 2016).

In an earlier organised shared task on English Lexical Substitution at SemEval-2012,[4] which had the aim of providing a framework for evaluation of lexical simplification systems, for each given sentence containing one target 'complex' word and four substitution candidates, participating systems were competing in ranking the four given substitution candidates according to their simplicity, i.e. how easy they are to be understood by fluent but non-native English speakers. The best performing system (Jauhar and Specia, 2012) used a combination of collocational features and four psycholinguistic measures extracted from the MRC (Machine Readable Dictionary) Psycholinguistic Database (Coltheart, 1981):

- Concreteness – the level of abstraction associated with the concept a word describes.

- Imageability – the ability of a given word to arouse mental images.

- Familiarity – the frequency of exposure to a word.

- Age of Acquisition – the age at which a given word is appropriated by a speaker.

1.3 Study Aims and Contributions

We advance previous approaches to CWI by focusing on a new, less-studied population of target readers with autism, and by using a more sophisticated approach based on eye tracking data.

In this study, we use parallel gaze data to study the differences in word processing between participants with autism and a control group of neurotypical (non-autistic) participants in a natural reading task. Our aim is to find out which words could potentially be considered challenging for both groups of readers for the purposes of automatic text simplification (ATS) and to explore which lexical properties underpin the differences in word processing. The contributions of this study are as follows.

We first show that in spite of the fact that both groups achieved similar level of reading comprehension, the reading task imposed significantly heavier cognitive load on the participants with autism as measured by three different gaze measures (Section 3). This finding is consistent with the results of Sansosti et al. (2013) (Section 1.1).

Next, we identify which particular words (in their specific contexts) impose heavier cognitive load on each group of participants by clustering them as challenging or not, based on viewing time of each participant individually (Section 4.1), and then classifying them into four classes depending on the number of participants who found them challenging (Section 4.2).

Finally, we investigate the lexical properties which underpin the different processing times for the different word classes in two groups of participants, using both statistical (word frequency and length) and cognitively-based (familiarity, age of acquisition, concreteness, and imagability) features. To account for the context in which the words appear, we treat the same word in different contexts as different entries in our clustering and classification tasks, i.e. we are actually clustering and classifying the Areas of Interest (AOIs) and not the words (Section 4.3).

Identifying such lexical properties has both theoretical and practical implications. On one hand, understanding into what makes a word challenging for a reader with autism could inform future writing guidelines for easy-to-read content and the design of exams and test items for students with autism (Elliott et al., 2010). On the other hand, as shown is Section 1.2, the identification of challenging words based on their lexical properties is on a high demand in the field of Natural Language Processing (NLP) for the purpose of automated text simplification for people with autism and other disorders (Martos et al., 2013; Siddharthan, 2014) as well as for non-native speakers.

2 Data Collection

An experimental group of participants with a diagnosis of autism and a control group of non-autistic participants were asked to read 20 texts while their eye movements were recorded by an eye tracker. In order to explore between-group differences in reading patterns, the groups were matched based on their reading comprehension, as follows. It was important to ensure that i) all participants had understood the presented texts at a similar level and ii) that they read for meaning as opposed to simply skimming through the text, which is why they were asked to answer three multiple-choice (MCQ) questions per passage with three possible answers each. The questions assessed both literal

---

[4]https://www.cs.york.ac.uk/semeval-2012/task1/index.html

273

Texts	Group	Participants	Age in years	Years of schooling
1 - 9	ASD	9 (5 male, 4 female)	m = 33, SD = 9.18	m = 15.66, SD = 2.12
1 - 9	Control	9 (5 male, 4 female)	m = 31.33, SD = 7.48	m = 16.88, SD = 1.83
10 - 17	ASD	14 (8 male, 6 female)	m = 37.9 , SD = 9.6	m = 16, SD = 3.77
10 - 17	Control	13 (9 male, 4 female)	m = 33.84, SD = 9.02	m = 18.54, SD = 3.13
18 - 20	ASD	8 (7 male, 1 female)	m = 36.5, SD = 9.78	m = 15.63, SD = 3.74
18 - 20	Control	10 (6 male, 4 female)	m = 31.3, SD = 6.4	m = 18.1, SD = 2.6

Table 1: Mean age and years spent in formal education for the participants whose gaze data was retained

and inferential reading comprehension and were developed following the taxonomy and guidelines of Day and Park 2005. Gaze data from both groups were collected for 3,636 words.

Materials: A total of 20 text passages with varying complexity were obtained from the Web[5]. The registers were miscellaneous, covering educational (7 documents), news (10 documents) and general informational articles (3 documents). Each text passage was self-contained and coherent (did not refer to information given in the rest of the article and could be comprehended independently of it), did not require specific cultural background to be comprehended and did not contain highly specialised terms, unless they were explained within the text. The average number of words per text was 156 with a standard deviation of 49.94 (min = 74 words and max = 242 words). The texts covered a range of readability levels, with an average Flesch Reading Ease score[6] (Flesch, 1948) of 65.07 and a standard deviation (SD) of 13.71 (min = 40.66, max = 95).

Participants: All participants were native speakers of English, had no diagnosed conditions affecting reading (other than autism in the ASD group) and no diagnosed developmental delay. The participants from the two groups had similar age and similar number of years spent in formal education (Table 1). All participants had normal or corrected vision.

The participants with autism had a confirmed clinical diagnosis obtained in the UK after a referral from a general practitioner and based on the the ADOS diagnostic criteria (Gotham et al., 2007). Out of a total of 27 participants in the ASD group, 11 had a diagnosis of ASD and 15 had a diagnosis of Asperger's syndrome (obtained before the introduction of DSM-5 in 2013). Some participants were diagnosed also with depression (four in ASD group; one in control group) and anxiety (six in ASD group).

The gaze recordings were obtained in three cycles of data collection and the 20 text passages were initially read by a total of 27 different people with a formal diagnosis of autism (texts 1-9 by 20 people, texts 10-17 by 18 people and texts 18-20 by 18 people) and by 31 different neurotypical participants (texts 1-9 by 20 people, texts 10-17 by 18 people and texts 18-20 by 14 people). Participants who performed poorly on comprehension testing, had missing or inaccurate gaze data or were unable to calibrate the eye tracker, were subsequently excluded from the study. The final number of participants whose data was retained and analysed were 21 participants with autism and 19 participants without autism.

Apparatus and Procedure: Texts were presented on a 19 LCD monitor. The device used for recording the gaze of the participants was a Gazepoint GP3 video-based eye tracker[7] (60Hz sampling rate and accuracy of 0.5 - 1 degree of visual angle). The eye tracker was calibrated individually for each participant using a 9-point calibration procedure. The distance between each participant and the eye tracker was controlled by a sensor integrated within the Gazepoint software, and was approximately 65 cm. The software randomised both the order of presentation of the texts and the questions pertaining to texts for each participant, to avoid bias. Participants were instructed about the purpose and the procedure of the experiment, signed a consent form and then read all texts and answered all questions, taking breaks if needed. At the end of the experiment, demographic data was collected and participants were debriefed.

Data Post-Processing: Each word in the texts

---

[5]The data are available at `https://github.com/victoria-ianeva/ASD-Comprehension-Corpus`. For more information about the data see Yaneva (2016).

[6]Expressed on a scale from 0 to 100 (the higher the score, the easier the text).

[7]Available at: https://www.gazept.com/

was defined as an Area of Interest (AOI) using the in-built Gazepoint analysis software. The output contains three gaze based measures for a total of 3,636 words for each participant separately: Time Viewed (TV) (the time an AOI was viewed, measured in seconds), Fixations (F) (the number of gaze fixations in a given AOI) and Revisits (R) (the number of go-back fixations in a given AOI, after the eyes have left the AOI and have moved to the right). Cognitive load is usually studied through the temporal aspects of the gaze data. In this paper, we identify challenging words by using the late measure of time viewed per word as opposed to early processing measures such as first fixation duration. This is done in order to account for the overall cognitive load rather than the individual stages of visual word recognition.

3 Between-group Differences in Comprehension and Cognitive Effort

In this section we compare the level of comprehension of the two groups, as well as the duration and number of their fixations and revisits for each word for each participant. A chi-square test for independence revealed that there was no statistically significant association between the group type (ASD vs. Control) and the level of comprehension ($\chi^2(1) = 3.442$; $p = 0.064$). Nevertheless, while both groups achieved similar levels of text comprehension, it took significantly more cognitive effort for the ASD participants to comprehend the text, as shown by all three gaze-based measures (Table 2).[8] This means that identification and simplification of words which pose higher cognitive load on readers with autism could potentially reduce the time and effort required for reading a text, completing an exam, etc.

In order to gain some preliminary insights into the between-group differences we examined the box-plots with outliers and extreme values for TV for each of the 20 texts. We observed that the participants with ASD were more heterogeneous than the control group participants in the words that they viewed extremely long. In contrast, within

the control group, the words with extreme TV values were similar for most participants, suggesting that the existing differences between the two groups were not merely based on individual differences between the participants.

To better understand the reasons behind certain words been viewed so long and differences between the two groups of participants, we took a systematic approach. We classified all words into four classes using the procedure explained in the next section and then explored the lexical properties of each word class and for each group of participants separately.

4 Between-group Differences in Words Found Challenging

Motivated by the need of automatically recognising potentially challenging words (i.e. CWI task) which should then be replaced by their simpler synonyms in the task of automated text simplification, and the need for ranking substitution candidates according to their simplicity for intended reader (Section 1.2), we wanted to classify all AOIs into different classes according to their potential challenge to the intended reader. Taking into account that different readers might find different words challenging, instead of just classifying words into challenging or not, we wanted to have more fine-grained classes depending on how many readers found them challenging. Therefore, we had a two-step procedure:

1. We divided the words into *challenging* and *not challenging*, according to the TV feature, for each reader separately.

2. We divided the words into four classes, depending on how many readers found them challenging.

4.1 Challenging vs. Not Challenging

The division of words into *challenging* and *not challenging* according to the time viewed could be done in different ways, e.g. by finding a cut-off

Statistic	TV (sec)		Fix.		Rev.	
	ASD	Con.	ASD	Con.	ASD	Con.
Mean	0.20	0.16	1.71	1.46	1.22	0.94
SD	0.29	0.21	1.78	1.41	1.88	1.44
Skewness	5.40	2.47	1.91	1.45	2.55	2.26

Table 2: Eye-tracking data statistics

---

[8]Differences in means between the fixations of the two groups of participants for each word were found statistically significant on all three gaze measures using the two-tailed t-test for equality of means in independent samples, where equal variances are not assumed (for TV: $t = 19.842$, df= 61652.575, $p = 0.000$ with 95% CI (0.035, 0.042); for F: $t = 20.781$, df= 64963.384, $p = 0.000$ with 95% CI (0.229, 0.277); and for R: $t = 22.666$, df= 63955.256, $p = 0.000$ with 95% CI (0.263, 0.313)).

Group	Mean	SD	Var.	Min.	Max.
ASD	17.68	4.62	21.37	8.94	27.69
Control	19.81	3.04	9.21	15.14	26.12

Table 3: Percentage of words clustered as challenging (per participant-session combination)

Class	# words		% words	
	ASD	Control	ASD	Control
NOT	1,845	1,608	54.51%	47.31%
P-CH	1,158	1,344	34.10%	39.54%
CH	381	444	11.26%	13.06%
E-CH	1	3	3e-4%	9e-4%

Table 4: Distribution of classes

point based on the feature distribution and standard deviation, or by using a parameter-free clustering approach. As there have been no previous studies trying to divide words into those two groups according to the time viewed, and thus no evidence on which approach is better, we opted for the second approach which is parameter-free.

We thus clustered the words from 20 texts into two clusters (*challenging* vs. *not challenging*) for each participant-session combination separately by applying the K-Means algorithm in SPSS, taking only into consideration the TV feature. We applied the iterative KMeans algorithm with two clusters (until convergence, i.e. no change in cluster centers). In a few cases, where there was an extreme outlier (extremely long gazed word) in the given participant-session combination, the clustering resulted in two clusters where one cluster contained only the outlier and the other all other words. In such cases, we applied the K-Means with three clusters, which resulted in having one cluster with *not challenging* words, another with *challenging* words, and the third one with the outlier. We then added the outlier to the cluster of *challenging* words and retained the two resulting clusters.

The average percentage of *challenging* AOIs (out of all words read) was lower, on average, within the ASD group than within the Control group (Table 3).[9] Although this might seem contradictory to the overall higher cognitive load (viewing time) in the ASD group, it is actually a result of the significantly stronger skewness of the TV in the ASD group (Table 2); the participants in the ASD group find fewer AOIs challenging, but they focus on them longer.

4.2 Word Classes

In the second step, for each AOI-id and for each group of participants separately, we assigned one

of the following four classes:

- **EXTREMELY CHALLENGING (E-CH)** if that AOI-id was clustered as *challenging* for all participants;

- **CHALLENGING (CH)** if that AOI-id was clustered as *challenging* for at least half of the participants (in the case of the texts read by an odd number of participants, the half was the mean value rounded to the lower integer) but not for all;

- **POTENTIALLY CHALLENGING (P-CH)** if that AOI-id was clustered as *challenging* for at least two participants, but less than a half of the participants;

- **NOT CHALLENGING (NOT)** if none of above (i.e. that AOI-id was clustered as *challenging* for one participant at the most).

The number of AOIs found in each class for each group of participants is presented in Table 4. The distribution of AOIs among classes was similar for both groups of participants, while the numbers supported our hypothesis that the participants in the ASD group are more heterogeneous in the AOIs they find challenging (i.e. the AOIs they viewed long), which results in a lower overlap of challenging AOIs among the participants (i.e. the lower number of POTENTIALLY CHALLENGING (P-CH) and CHALLENGING (CH) AOIs than in the Control group).

Extremely challenging words (E-CH) for the Control group were: *conservative*, *Academicians*, and *iconoclasm*, whereas for the ASD group it was only the word *acquaintance*.

4.3 Importance of Context

In order to account for the influence that the context can have on certain word requiring greater cognitive effort, we were classifying AOIs, allowing thus for the same word (but different AOI) to be classified in different classes.

---

[9]The between-group differences in percentage of words found challenging were statistically significant using the two-tailed t-test for equality of means in independent samples, where equal variances are not assumed ($t = -2.084$; $df = 45.252$; $p = 0.043$ with 95% CI $(-4.184, -0.072)$).

Word	Context	Class
computer	Experts in Namibia are using a **computer** system to identify and track...	CH
computer	Next, they store the photos on a **computer**.	NOT
computer	Whenever a new print is added, the **computer** compares it to all the other prints...	NOT
comes	Secondhand smoke (SHS) **comes** from burning cigarettes, pipes, or cigars.	NOT
comes	... where an excellent music policy **comes** complete with a decent pint of Guinness.	CH

Table 5: Examples of same words placed in different classes depending on their context.

Class	Age of aquisition (AoA)		Familiarity (Fam)	
	ASD	Control	ASD	Control
NOT CHALLENGING (NOT)	235.1 ± 108.7	230.4 ± 107.5	600.5 ± 71.7	602.8 ± 70.3
POTENTIALLY CHALLENGING (P-CH)	331.0 ± 122.0	317.6 ± 122.4	548.0 ± 83.9	555.5 ± 82.9
CHALLENGING (CH)	427.9 ± 114.3	420.0 ± 115.6	489.5 ± 94.4	495.1 ± 97.6
EXTREMELY CHALLENGING (E-CH)	NotFound	604.7 ± 113.5	NotFound	317.2 ± 162.6

Table 6: Age of aquisition and familiarity of the words in different classes (mean $\pm$ standard deviation)

Among the total of 3398 AOIs, 1495 were unique words. Out of those 1495, 1048 appeared only once in the whole corpus (20 texts), 224 appeared twice, 187 appeared between three and ten times, while 36 words appeared more than ten times (stop words only).

For each of the two groups of participants, we closely examined all words that appeared more than once searching for those which (appearing in different contexts) were classified in different levels of difficulty, and especially for those that appear in two not-neighbouring levels (e.g. NOT CHALLENGING and CHALLENGING).

In the case of non-autistic readers, out of 347 words which appeared more than once in the presented texts, 175 were placed always in the same level of difficulty (irrespective of their context), 18 of them (which repeated at least three times) were placed in three different classes (three neighbouring classes – NOT CHALLENGING, POTENTIALLY CHALLENGING, and CHALLENGING), whereas six words (*comes, won, Foxes, provides, artists, computer*) were placed in two non-neighbouring difficulty levels (NOT CHALLENGING and CHALLENGING).

Two examples of the same words (but different AOIs) classified into two non-neighbouring classes are presented in Table 5 together with contexts.

4.4 Analysis of Word Classes

The mean value with the standard deviation of the cognitively-based features (age of acquisition, familiarity, imagability, and concreteness) in each word class are presented in Tables 6 and 7.

Given that the manually created MRC psycholinguistic database (Coltheart, 1981) covered only 4.76% of words in our texts, we used the bootstrapped larger version of it (Paetzold and Specia, 2016a) which covered 95% of the words.[10]

While the cognitively-based features (age of aquisition, familiarity, imagability and concreteness) were obtained from non-ASD college students, we argue that these properties transfer between subject groups. The reason for this is that our participants were all high-functioning (none of them attended a specialised school) and thus they have all been exposed to a similar vocabulary by going through the national curricula. In addition, both groups understood the texts equally well and we did not observe large between-group differences in the correlation of these metrics with the gaze data.

No significant differences between the values obtained for the same word classes between the two groups of participants were observed. However, it is interesting to note that the extremely

---

[10]The words not covered by the bootstrapped MRC database (Paetzold and Specia, 2016a) were excluded from the analysis.

Class	Imagability (Img)		Concreteness (Con)	
	ASD	Control	ASD	Control
NOT CHALLENGING (NOT)	354.3 ± 90.3	353.3 ± 90.0	322.4 ± 92.9	322.0 ± 92.8
POTENTIALLY CHALLENGING (P-CH)	390.0 ± 97.4	385.3 ± 96.6	360.9 ± 100.6	355.3 ± 99.9
CHALLENGING (CH)	399.7 ± 89.6	396.6 ± 93.3	376.8 ± 90.9	372.1 ± 95.6
EXTREMELY CHALLENGING (E-CH)	NotFound	302.4 ± 87.1	NotFound	333.3 ± 36.4

Table 7: Imagability and Concreteness of the words in different classes (mean $\pm$ standard deviation)

Class	Length		SWiki	
	ASD	Control	ASD	Control
NOT CHALLENGING (NOT)	3.6 ± 1.7	3.5 ± 1.7	0.012 ± 0.018	0.012 ± 0.018
POTENTIALLY CHALLENGING (P-CH)	5.6 ± 2.3	5.3 ± 2.3	0.004 ± 0.012	0.005 ± 0.013
CHALLENGING (CH)	7.8 ± 2.3	7.6 ± 2.4	0.001 ± 0.004	0.001 ± 0.004
EXTREMELY CHALLENGING (E-CH)	$11.0 \pm NA$	11.3 ± 1.2	NotFound	$1e\text{-}5 \pm 2e\text{-}5$

Table 8: Length and frequency of words in different classes (mean $\pm$ standard deviation)

challenging words (E-CH) for the Control group had lower imagability and concreteness than the words classified as less challenging (Table 7). Moreover, the imagability and concreteness values seem to have the opposite correlations with the "challenging" classifications; i.e. the average imagability and concreteness values increase from the NOT to the CH groups. These results imply that the imagability and concreteness may not be well correlated with the cognitive load measured as TV.

The mean value with the standard deviation of the statistically-based measures (length in characters and frequency in Simple Wikipedia) in each word class are presented in Table 8. It is interesting to note that the relative word frequencies in Simple Wikipedia had extremely high standard deviations (Table 8), thus implicating that this feature is not the main characteristic of whether the word is challenging or not.

4.5 Correlation of TV and Word Classes with Lexical Complexity Features

Finally, for each group of participants separately, we tested how the time viewed (taking each participant-AOI combination as a separate data point) and word classes are correlated (using the Spearman's rho coefficient) with both statistical and cognitively-based lexical properties of the words (Table 9).

As can be observed, all investigated lexical properties are better correlated with the word classes than with the raw viewing times (TV). This

Feature	TV		Classes	
	ASD	Control	ASD	Control
Len (char.)	$+0.297$	$+0.308$	$+0.563$	$+0.556$
Con	$+0.113$	$+0.116$	$+0.241$	$+0.217$
Img	$+0.103$	$+0.107$	$+0.223$	$+0.206$
AoA	$+0.252$	$+0.261$	$+0.465$	$+0.479$
Fam	-0.231	-0.235	-0.448	-0.433
SWiki	-0.235	-0.242	-0.457	-0.446

Table 9: Correlation (Spearman's rho) of TV and word classes with lexical complexity features (all statistically significant at a 0.001 level of significance)

is probably due to the fact that word classes eliminate the influences of individual differences in reading speed among the participants, which dilute the correlations with the TV.

5 Discussion

We collected parallel gaze data to study the differences in word processing between participants with autism and a control group of neurotypical participants in a natural reading task.

The presented results indicated that even though both groups understood the texts at a similar level, participants with autism had significantly longer viewing times, more fixations and more revisits per word, indicative of heavier cognitive load. Even when individuals on the spectrum appear highly able and achieve comprehension similar to their peers, they put more cognitive effort into doing so. Another possible explanation of this result could be that the pattern of results observed in the ASD readers reflects a different, perhaps more cautious reading strategy rather than reflecting greater cognitive load associated with lexical processing. In other words, it is possible that given the same instructions, readers with ASD are more careful than control participants to ensure that they have read the text thoroughly and understood the sentences completely. Under this alternative, its not that ASD readers are spending more time and making more fixations because reading is challenging, but instead because they are simply reading more cautiously. Whichever one of these interpretations of the result is valid, this finding provides experimental evidence for the need to allow extra time for exams and for rewriting texts in a way that reduces cognitive load. Both of these accommodations are important steps towards the inclusion of students with ASD.

Although the readers with ASD had significantly longer viewing times, they did not fixate long on as many words as the control participants did. Their overall longer viewing times were heavily skewed towards the words they find challenging. This result reveals differences in the reading patterns between the two groups.

Finally, other than word length which is naturally highly correlated with viewing time, the age of acquisition (AoA) seems to be an important factor related to the viewing times of both groups, followed by frequency and familiarity. This result is consistent with Juhasz and Rayner (2003), who also reported that the effect age of acquisition had on fixation duration was above and beyond the effect of word frequency. Furthermore, the large standard deviation in the word frequency implies that this measure is not suitable for choosing alternative words for lexical substitution in text simplification. Based on our data, an improved strategy for lexical simplification would be basing the word substitutes on the age of acquisition or familiarity ratings. Concreteness and imagability were only weakly related to viewing time. There were no between-group differences observed with regards to the importance of lexical features.

Another important conclusion of this study is that the absolute measures such as concreteness and imagability, which were obtained based on rating of individual words, might not be suitable for complex word identification task, as the gaze data showed that the same word presented in different contexts could be identified as both challenging or not.

One limitation of this study is the fact that it explores only the lexical effects on viewing times and does not explore the effect of contextual features. While we acknowledge the high importance of context for the duration of gaze fixations, the focus on the lexical component in the present study allows for future comparisons between lexical and context-based effects on viewing times. Another limitation is the low speed of the eye tracker used for data collection, which reduces the precision of the recordings and does not allow for comparison of early and late gaze features. However, the data used in this study is the only existing resource of its kind to date and it would be interesting to compare the results obtained from this study with future results based on more sophisticated sets of text and gaze features.

6 Conclusion

This paper presented a study investigating which words are found challenging by readers with high-functioning autism and a control group of non-autistic readers based on gaze data from a natural reading task. We fist showed that even though there were no differences between the level of comprehension of the texts between the two groups, the analysis of the gaze data showed that the readers with autism produced significantly more fixations and revisits, as well as longer viewing times per word. We then clustered the viewing times for each participant-session combination and classified the words into four classes of difficulty based on the gaze data. Finally, we investigated the relationship between those classes and cognitively-based features commonly used in text simplification such as age of acquisition, familiarity, imagability, concreteness, and word frequency and length. Our results showed that relying on such absolute measures for the complex word identification task is not always justified because a given word could be perceived as challenging or not based on the surrounding context.

Acknowledgments

This work has been partially supported by the SFB 884 on the Political Economy of Reforms at the University of Mannheim (project C4), funded by the German Research Foundation (DFG) and the

AUTOR project funded by University Innovation Funds (University of Wolverhampton).

References

American Psychiatric Association. 2013. Diagnostic and Statistical Manual of Mental Disorders (5th ed.).

Stefan Bott, Luz Rello, Biljana Drndarevic, and Horacio Saggion. 2012. Can Spanish be simpler? LexSiS: Lexical simplification for Spanish. In *Proceedings of the 24th International Conference on Computational Linguistics (COLING)*. pages 357–374.

Jon Brock, Courtenay Norbury, Shiri Einav, and Kate Nation. 2008. Do individuals with autism process words in context? evidence from language-mediated eye-movements. *Cognition* 108(3):896–904.

Tony Charman, Auriol Drew, Claire Baird, and Gillian Baird. 2003. Measuring early language development in preschool children with autism spectrum disorder using the macarthur communicative development inventory (infant form). *Journal of child language* 30(1):213.

M. Coltheart. 1981. The mrc psycholinguistic database. *Quarterly Journal of Experimental Psychology* 33A:497–505.

Richard R. Day and Jeong-Suk Park. 2005. Developing Reading Comprehension Questions. *Reading in a Foreign Language* 17(1).

Stanislas Dehaene and Laurent Cohen. 2011. The unique role of the visual word form area in reading. *Trends in cognitive sciences* 15(6):254–262.

Michael Walsh Dickey, JungWon Janet Choy, and Cynthia K Thompson. 2007. Real-time comprehension of wh-movement in aphasia: Evidence from eyetracking while listening. *Brain and language* 100(1):1–22.

Susan F Ehrlich and Keith Rayner. 1981. Contextual effects on word perception and eye movements during reading. *Journal of verbal learning and verbal behavior* 20(6):641–655.

Stephen N Elliott, Ryan J Kettler, Peter A Beddow, Alexander Kurz, Elizabeth Compton, Dawn McGrath, Charles Bruen, Kent Hinton, Porter Palmer, Michael C Rodriguez, et al. 2010. Effects of using modified items to test students with persistent academic difficulties. *Exceptional Children* 76(4):475–495.

Rudolph Flesch. 1948. A new readability yardstick. *Journal of applied psychology* 32(3):221.

Uta Frith and Maggie Snowling. 1983. Reading for meaning and reading for sound in autistic and dyslexic children. *British Journal of Developmental Psychology* 1(4):329–342.

Goran Glavaš and Sanja Štajner. 2015. Simplifying Lexical Simplification: Do We Need Simplified Corpora? In *Proceedings of the 53rd Annual Meeting of the Association for Computational Linguistics and the 7th International Joint Conference on Natural Language Processing (ACL-IJCNLP), Volume 2: Short Papers*. pages 63–68.

Katherine Gotham, Susan Risi, Andrew Pickles, and Catherine Lord. 2007. The autism diagnostic observation schedule: revised algorithms for improved diagnostic validity. *Journal of autism and developmental disorders* 37(4):613–627.

F Happe. 1997. Central coherence and theory of mind in autism: Reading homographs in context. *British Journal of Developmental Psychology* 15:1–12.

Francesca Happé and Uta Frith. 2006. The weak coherence account: Detail focused cognitive style in autism spectrum disorder. *Journal of Autism and Developmental Disorders* 36:5–25.

LM Henderson, PJ Clarke, and MJ Snowling. 2011. Accessing and selecting word meaning in autism spectrum disorder. *Journal of Child Psychology and Psychiatry* 52(9):964–973.

Sujay Jauhar and Lucia Specia. 2012. Uow-shef: Simplex lexical simplicity ranking based on contextual and psycholinguistic features. In *Proceedings of the 6th International Workshop on Semantic Evaluation (SemEval-2012)*. pages 477–481.

Barbara J Juhasz and Keith Rayner. 2003. Investigating the effects of a set of intercorrelated variables on eye fixation durations in reading. *Journal of Experimental Psychology: Learning, Memory, and Cognition* 29(6):1312.

Marcel A Just and Patricia A Carpenter. 1980. A theory of reading: From eye fixations to comprehension. *Psychological review* 87(4):329.

Sunjung Kim and Linda J Lombardino. 2016. Simple sentence reading and specific cognitive functions in college students with dyslexia: An eye-tracking study. *Clinical Archives of Communication Disorders* 1(1):48–61.

Ulrika Löfkvist, Ove Almkvist, Björn Lyxell, and Mari Tallberg. 2014. Lexical and semantic ability in groups of children with cochlear implants, language impairment and autism spectrum disorder. *International journal of pediatric otorhinolaryngology* 78(2):253–263.

Rhiannon J Luyster, Mary Beth Kadlec, Alice Carter, and Helen Tager-Flusberg. 2008. Language assessment and development in toddlers with autism spectrum disorders. *Journal of autism and developmental disorders* 38(8):1426–1438.

Juan Martos, Sandra Freire, Ana González, David Gil, Richard Evans, Vesna Jordanova, Arlinda Cerga, Antoneta Shishkova, and Constantin Orasan. 2013.

FIRST Deliverable - User preferences: Updated. Technical Report D2.2, Deletrea, Madrid, Spain.

I.M. O'Connor and P.D. Klein. 2004. Exploration of Strategies for Facilitating the Reading Comprehension of High-Functioning Students with Autism Spectrum Disorders. *Journal of autism and developmental disorders* 34(2).

Gustavo Paetzold and Lucia Specia. 2016a. Inferring psycholinguistic properties of words. In *Proceedings of the 2016 Conference of the North American Chapter of the Association for Computational Linguistics: Human Language Technologies.* pages 435–440.

Gustavo Paetzold and Lucia Specia. 2016b. SemEval 2016 Task 11: Complex Word Identification. In *Proceedings of the 10th International Workshop on Semantic Evaluation (SemEval-2016).* San Diego, California, USA, pages 560–569.

Gustavo Henrique Paetzold and Lucia Specia. 2016c. Benchmarking lexical simplification systems. In *Proceedings of LREC.* pages 3074–3080.

Keith Rayner, Alexander Pollatsek, Jane Ashby, and Charles Clifton Jr. 2012. *Psychology of reading.* Psychology Press.

Frank J Sansosti, Christopher Was, Katherine A Rawson, and Brittany L Rcmaklus. 2013. Eye movements during processing of text requiring bridging inferences in adolescents with higher functioning autism spectrum disorders: A preliminary investigation. *Research in Autism Spectrum Disorders* 7(12):1535–1542.

Advaith Siddharthan. 2014. A survey of research on text simplification. *ITL-International Journal of Applied Linguistics* 165(2):259–298.

Cheryl Smith Gabig. 2010. Phonological awareness and word recognition in reading by children with autism. *Communication Disorders Quarterly* 31(2):67–85.

Elisabeth M Whyte, Keith E Nelson, and K Suzanne Scherf. 2014. Idiom, syntax, and advanced theory of mind abilities in children with autism spectrum disorders. *Journal of Speech, Language, and Hearing Research* 57(1):120–130.

Krzysztof Wróbel. 2016. PLUJAGH at SemEval-2016 Task 11: Simple System for Complex Word Identification. In *Proceedings of the 10th International Workshop on Semantic Evaluation (SemEval-2016).* San Diego, California, USA, pages 953–957.

Victoria Yaneva. 2016. *Assessing text and web accessibility for people with autism spectrum disorder.* Ph.D. thesis.

Transparent text quality assessment with convolutional neural networks[*]

Robert Östling and **Gintare Grigonyte**
Department of Linguistics, Stockholm University
`robert,gintare@ling.su.se`

Abstract

We present a very simple model for text quality assessment based on a deep convolutional neural network, where the only supervision required is one corpus of user-generated text of varying quality, and one contrasting text corpus of consistently high quality. Our model is able to provide local quality assessments in different parts of a text, which allows visual feedback about where potentially problematic parts of the text are located, as well as a way to evaluate which textual features are captured by our model. We evaluate our method on two corpora: a large corpus of manually graded student essays and a longitudinal corpus of language learner written production, and find that the text quality metric learned by our model is a fairly strong predictor of both essay grade and learner proficiency level.

1 Introduction and related work

What makes a text good? A confluence of diverse qualities: coherent narrative, correct grammar, absence of spelling mistakes, a rich vocabulary and set of idioms. Some of these are simple to detect automatically, while others seem to require a deep understanding of the text.

Early attempts to measure text quality were pioneered by approaching it as an aggregate of distinct text features that were easy to specify manually, such as type/token ratio, average length of sentences or words, and so on. More recently, machine learning techniques have been applied that can learn such features from data.

Our primary goals in this work are to investigate how well a model for textual quality can be trained without any labeled data, and to see whether the quality model agrees with human essay graders or is able to predict second language learner proficiency.

1.1 Automated text assessment

Recent work on automated assessment mainly covers English learners' written text and it aims at assigning grades based on textual features that try to balance performance errors and language competency. Most of the work in this area falls into a category of a supervised text classification (Attali and Burstein, 2006; Landauer, 2003; Rudner and Liang, 2002; Yannakoudakis et al., 2011). Of particular interest are methods that, like ours, are based on neural networks and require little or no manual feature engineering.

1.2 Neural network approaches

Alikaniotis et al. (2016) present a model for essay scoring based on recurrent neural networks at the word level. This is trained by supervision from a graded essay corpus, and allows basic visualization of the contribution of individual words on the overall grade through error gradients. Dong and Zhang (2016) similarly train a hierarchical neural network that encodes word sequences to sentence representations, and sentence representations to essay representations, in both cases through convolution and pooling layers. The same type of approach is taken by Taghipour and Ng (2016), who however explore a wider range of models.

Cummins et al. (2016) exploit external resources through multi-task learning for automated essay scoring. This is also one of our primary motivations, but our methods are quite different.

Our method is based on deep convolutional neural networks with residual connections, which

---

* The source code for our system is available at `https://github.com/robertostling/bea12-textquality`

Proceedings of the 12th Workshop on Innovative Use of NLP for Building Educational Applications, pages 282–286
Copenhagen, Denmark, September 8, 2017. ©2017 Association for Computational Linguistics

have recently gained popularity in natural language processing (Östling, 2016; Bjerva et al., 2016; Johnson and Zhang, 2016; Conneau et al., 2017).

2 Model

Since one of our primary concerns is transparency, we choose a fixed-width convolutional neural network so that it is easy to infer how each part of the text contributes to the model's estimate. In short, the whole text is passed through a one-dimensional convolutional network with residual connections, followed by a global mean pooling operation and a single fully connected layer which produces a scalar prediction of text quality. We now proceed to describe this in more detail.

Assume that the input text is a sequence of symbols (in our case characters) $s_1, s_2, \ldots, s_N$. Each symbol is represented by a row in an embedding matrix W_e of size $V \times d$, where V is the vocabulary size and d is the dimensionality of the embeddings. For convenience, we denote the embedding vector of s_i by w_i.

The sequence $w_1, w_2, \ldots, w_N$ is passed through a number of blocks with one-dimensional convolutions and residual connections (He et al., 2016). For simplicity, we let the sequence length and number of filters remain constant throughout the network (in our experiments, 512). For the first block, we use kernels of size 3, 5, 7 and 9 in order to capture character n-grams of varying size. The outputs of these are concatenated for each position in the text, similar to the encoder used by Lee et al. (2016) for character-level machine translation. This is followed by a number of blocks with only size-3 kernels. All our models use 10 blocks in total, each containing two convolutions with batch normalization layers (Ioffe and Szegedy, 2015) and rectifier non-linearities following each convolution. Let the vector x_i^l be the d-dimensional output after layer l at text position i. The final quality score of a text is computed as $q(s_{1...N}) = W_o \cdot \frac{1}{N} \sum_i^N x_i^L$, that is, the dot product of the output weight vector W_o and the mean value of the outputs at the final residual layer L. In our experiments, $L = 10$.

This structure implies that the model's score for a text is the mean score over each symbol, which means that the score $q(s_{i...j})$ can be computed for any subsequence $s_{i...j}$ of a text without depending on the length of the sequence. This allows visualizing the low- and high-scoring sections of a text by coloring it according to the local scores.

2.1 Training

We base our model training on pairwise comparison between text snippets from different corpora or authors. We use a pseudo-probabilistic framework, where the probability of text a being better than b is defined as $P(a > b) = \sigma(q(a) - q(b))$, where $\sigma(x) = \frac{1}{1+\exp(-x)}$ is the logistic function and $q(\cdot)$ is the quality score from our network, as detailed above. We should point out here that "better" is used from the perspective of formal written Swedish, and that "poor" text could either be informal, or due to lack of competence. During training we use cross-entropy loss, with the following axioms:

1. $P(a > b) = 0$ if a is user-generated text (**Blogs**) and b is professional prose (**News** or **SUC**).

2. $P(a > b) = 0.5$ if both a and b are professional prose.

3. $P(a > a') = 0.5$ if $\langle a, a' \rangle$ is a pair of blog texts from the same author.

4. $P(a > b) = \sigma(q(a') - q(b'))$ if $\langle a, a' \rangle$ and $\langle b, b' \rangle$ are pairs of blog texts, such that $\langle a, a' \rangle$ is from one author and $\langle b, b' \rangle$ is from another.

In plain English, these could be summarized as three general assumptions: *all authors (professional or not) are consistent, professional authors are better than blog authors*, and *all professional authors are equal*. Furthermore, the motivation behind point 4 is that blog authors are *not* equal, so that we can exploit the variation among them.

We initialize all model parameters, including the embeddings, randomly (orthogonal matrices for recurrent connections, Gaussian distributions for all other parameters). Due to time constraints, we did not perform hyperparameter tuning and used conservative values that worked well for similar tasks in the literature.

We train our model with stochastic gradient descent using Adam (Kingma and Ba, 2014) for learning rate adaptation. The system is implemented with Chainer (Tokui et al., 2015). In our experiments we use mini-batches of size 16, and choose an equal number of examples based for each axiom used. All text samples during training are 512 characters long. We train models for two configurations: one using all axioms, and one only using 1+2. For the examples using axiom 4, we use a two-step procedure where the model is first use to compute $\sigma(q(a') - q(b'))$, which is then used as ground truth for those examples. We also take care to sample examples for axiom 2 from different corpora, to ensure that the model sees as different examples as possible of the same quality, avoiding that domain-specific vocabulary is mistaken for quality predictors.

2.2 Data

For model training, we use three different raw text corpora (**Blogs**, **News** and **SUC**) described below. For evaluation, we use a corpus of student essays with human-assigned grades (**Essays**), and a corpus of learner Swedish (**ASU**).

Blogs   6 billion tokens of Swedish blog posts, crawled from the web. The available metadata indicates which blog each post is sourced from, so that we can group the posts by author (assuming one author per blog).

News   100 million tokens of crawled Swedish news articles and opinion pieces, crawled from the web.

SUC   7 million tokens of published text of various genres from the Stockholm-Umeå Corpus (Källgren, 2006). This includes news, novels and academic texts.

Essays   A corpus of Swedish high-school essays described in (Östling et al., 2013), containing 1,702 essays with a total of 1,1 million tokens. The data is from Swedish high school students (around age 17) with native or near-native command of Swedish. Each essay has two grades assigned by two independent human graders. While these generally have low agreement (Cohen's $\kappa = 0.399$), this is mainly due to a systematic bias by teachers assigning higher grades to their own students. We use the mean of the two grades in our analysis. Since the grading criteria mainly focus on the quality of the written language, we use this grade as a proxy for text quality.

ASU   The ASU corpus (Hammarberg, 2010) is a longitudinal corpus of university-level learners of Swedish, containing two texts per session, from 11 sessions with 10 students. The progress of students is tracked from the absolute beginner stage to a level acceptable for Swedish university studies, after one or two years. The total size is about 50,000 tokens.

3   Experimental Setup and Results

We train two models, as described in Section 2.1: one using only the professional-amateur distinction (axioms 1+2) and one also using the variation in the blog corpus (axioms 1+2+3+4). The former turns out to be very poor at estimating text quality, and is only briefly discussed in Section 3.2. For the rest of this section, the 1+2+3+4 model is used throughout.

3.1   Qualitative evaluation

To illustrate the transparency of the model, Table 1 contains example sentences sampled from two text corpora (**Blogs** and **News**). In general we can see that the news examples are ranked higher than the blog examples, which is to be expected since the model was trained in part to distinguish between these corpora. The only exception is the second news sentence, whose score the visualization indicates is pulled down by the first word, 'domen' (*the sentence*). This turns out to be a homograph of 'dom', a spoken-language form of the third person plural pronoun, which is generally avoided in written Swedish and a strong indicator of either an informal style or poor command of Swedish (since the written language makes a case distinction which does not exist in the modern spoken language). Other low-scoring features include smileys, frequent use of ellipsis, and informal spellings such as 'oxa' for 'ocksa' (*also*). Some of these are typical for informal Internet text, and would easily be avoided in e.g. a high-stakes essay setting. However, rather than low scores stemming from occasional features of poor or informal writing, it seems that the consistent lack of a richer vocabulary is a more important factor.

3.2   Native language essay grades

We compute the scores for each of the 1,702 essays in the **Essays** dataset. Since the essays were produced during a fixed-time test situation, length is a strong predictor of grade ($R^2 = 0.308$ for the 4th root of essay length in characters, $L^{0.25}$; we report adjusted R^2 from multiple linear regression). Controlling for length, the 1+2 model is not a significant predictor of grade. The 1+2+3+4

Table 1: Mean scores (left) and color-coded partial scores (right) for a sample of sentences from the blog corpus (top) and news corpus (bottom). Red encodes low scores, blue encodes high scores. Faded colors are used for scores near zero.

Blogs
1.475 Resten av veckan blir det jag som VAB:ar. Men det tycks inte bli så tråkigt som det låter...
0.530 Och på torsdag ska vi hem till Neos dagiskompis som oxå åkt på skiten, yeey!
-0.256 Någon mer som vill leka med oss och kanske bli smittad? Bara att hojta! :D
0.143 Spännande att få äta med sked och känna liiiite motstånd i munnen för en gång skull, haha! :D

News
2.310 Rättegången mot Geert Wilders direktsänds i holländsk tv. Det hör inte till vanligheterna.
0.613 Domen väntas i början av november.
2.428 I Storbritannien finns fem miljoner katoliker, vilket motsvarar en tolftedel av befolkningen.
2.611 Allt annat skulle betyda att det nyvunna förtroendet för Lettland går förlorat.

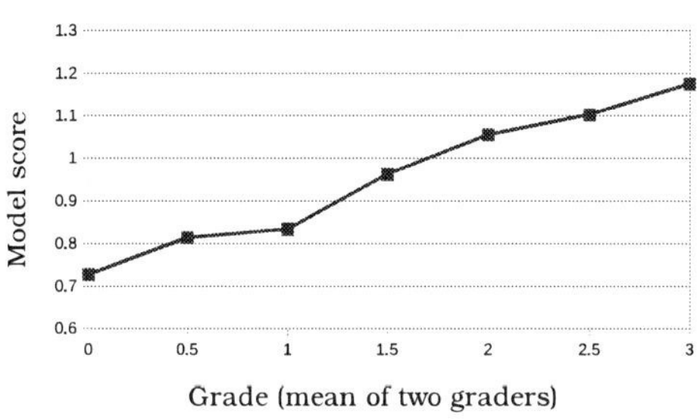

Figure 1: Relation between human-assigned grades and scores from our model.

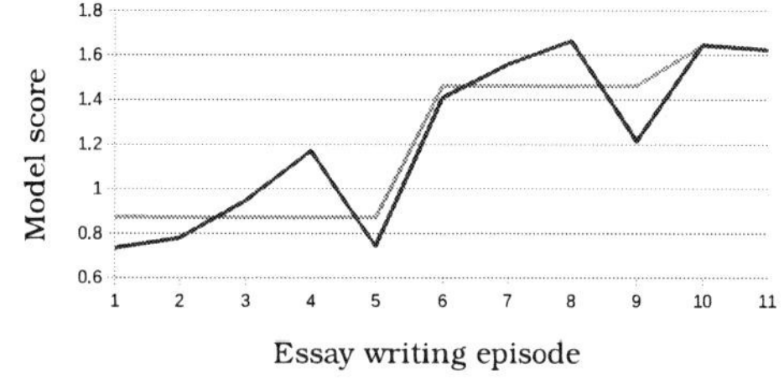

Figure 2: The progress of Swedish learner essay scores' during 11 writing episodes. Both curves display the same data, but averaged over writing episodes or semesters (i.e. down-sampled to smooth the curve), respectively.

model is a moderately strong predictor of grade ($R^2 = 0.127$ on its own, $R^2 = 0.355$ together with $L^{0.25}$).

The relation between essay grade and model score is illustrated in Figure 1, where for each of the seven possible grade means (0.0–3.0 in half-point intervals) the mean score of all essays with that grade is shown.

3.3 Second language learner progress

We use the **ASU** corpus (Hammarberg, 2010) to investigate whether our model can estimate the progress made by second-language learners during their early stages of acquiring Swedish as a second language.

Figure 2 shows how our model's score changes over the 11 sessions that the participants took part in. We compute the scores by pooling the essays from each session (20 essays, 2 each for 10 students). There is a clear increasing trend.

4 Conclusions

We have presented a model based on deep convolutional neural networks, which is able to estimate text quality at both the local and global scale, allowing easy visualization of weak or strong points of the text. Our method is using only unlabeled text corpora as training data, but its predictions align well with human-assigned grades for native-language essays and the time progression for second language learners. We expect this to be a useful component in systems for automated essay scoring and feedback.

Acknowledgments

We thank the reviewers for their constructive comments. Computing resources were provided by the Finnish IT Center for Science (CSC).

References

Dimitrios Alikaniotis, Helen Yannakoudakis, and Marek Rei. 2016. Automatic text scoring using neural networks. In *Proceedings of the 54th Annual Meeting of the Association for Computational Linguistics (Volume 1: Long Papers)*. Association for Computational Linguistics, Berlin, Germany, pages 715–725. http://www.aclweb.org/anthology/P16-1068.

Yigal Attali and Jill Burstein. 2006. Automated essay scoring with e-rater® v. 2. *The Journal of Technology, Learning and Assessment* 4(3).

Johannes Bjerva, Barbara Plank, and Johan Bos. 2016. Semantic tagging with deep residual networks. In *Proceedings of COLING 2016, the 26th International Conference on Computational Linguistics: Technical Papers*. The COLING 2016 Organizing Committee, Osaka, Japan, pages 3531–3541. http://aclweb.org/anthology/C16-1333.

Alexis Conneau, Holger Schwenk, Loïc Barrault, and Yann Lecun. 2017. Very deep convolutional networks for text classification. In *Proceedings of the 15th Conference of the European Chapter of the Association for Computational Linguistics: Volume 1, Long Papers*. Association for Computational Linguistics, Valencia, Spain, pages 1107–1116. http://www.aclweb.org/anthology/E17-1104.

Ronan Cummins, Meng Zhang, and Ted Briscoe. 2016. Constrained multi-task learning for automated essay scoring. In *Proceedings of the 54th Annual Meeting of the Association for Computational Linguistics (Volume 1: Long Papers)*. Association for Computational Linguistics, Berlin, Germany, pages 789–799. http://www.aclweb.org/anthology/P16-1075.

Fei Dong and Yue Zhang. 2016. Automatic features for essay scoring – an empirical study. In *Proceedings of the 2016 Conference on Empirical Methods in Natural Language Processing*. Association for Computational Linguistics, Austin, Texas, pages 1072–1077. https://aclweb.org/anthology/D16-1115.

Björn Hammarberg. 2010. Introduction to the asu corpus: A longitudinal oral and written text corpus of adult learner swedish with a corresponding part from native swedes. white paper. version 2010-11-16. .

Kaiming He, Xiangyu Zhang, Shaoqing Ren, and Jian Sun. 2016. Identity mappings in deep residual networks. *CoRR* abs/1603.05027. http://arxiv.org/abs/1603.05027.

Sergey Ioffe and Christian Szegedy. 2015. Batch normalization: Accelerating deep network training by reducing internal covariate shift. In David Blei and Francis Bach, editors, *Proceedings of the 32nd International Conference on Machine Learning (ICML-15)*. JMLR Workshop and Conference Proceedings, pages 448–456. http://jmlr.org/proceedings/papers/v37/ioffe15.pdf.

Rie Johnson and Tong Zhang. 2016. Convolutional neural networks for text categorization: Shallow word-level vs. deep character-level. *CoRR* abs/1609.00718. http://arxiv.org/abs/1609.00718.

Gunnel Källgren. 2006. *Manual of the Stockholm Umeå Corpus version 2.0*. Department of Linguistics, Stockholm University. Sofia Gustafson-Capková and Britt Hartmann (eds.).

Diederik P. Kingma and Jimmy Ba. 2014. Adam: A method for stochastic optimization. *CoRR* abs/1412.6980. http://arxiv.org/abs/1412.6980.

Thomas K Landauer. 2003. Automatic essay assessment. *Assessment in education: Principles, policy & practice* 10(3):295–308.

Jason Lee, Kyunghyun Cho, and Thomas Hofmann. 2016. Fully character-level neural machine translation without explicit segmentation. *CoRR* abs/1610.03017. http://arxiv.org/abs/1610.03017.

Robert Östling. 2016. Morphological reinflection with convolutional neural networks. In *Proceedings of the 14th SIGMORPHON Workshop on Computational Research in Phonetics, Phonology, and Morphology*. http://aclweb.org/anthology/W/W16/W16-2003.pdf.

Robert Östling, André Smolentzov, Björn Tyrefors Hinnerich, and Erik Höglin. 2013. Automated essay scoring for Swedish. In *Proceedings of the Eighth Workshop on Innovative Use of NLP for Building Educational Applications*. Association for Computational Linguistics, Atlanta, Georgia, pages 42–47. http://www.aclweb.org/anthology/W13-1705.

Lawrence M Rudner and Tahung Liang. 2002. Automated essay scoring using bayes' theorem. *The Journal of Technology, Learning and Assessment* 1(2).

Kaveh Taghipour and Hwee Tou Ng. 2016. A neural approach to automated essay scoring. In *Proceedings of the 2016 Conference on Empirical Methods in Natural Language Processing*. Association for Computational Linguistics, Austin, Texas, pages 1882–1891. https://aclweb.org/anthology/D16-1193.

Seiya Tokui, Kenta Oono, Shohei Hido, and Justin Clayton. 2015. Chainer: a next-generation open source framework for deep learning. In *Proceedings of Workshop on Machine Learning Systems (LearningSys) in The Twenty-ninth Annual Conference on Neural Information Processing Systems (NIPS)*.

Helen Yannakoudakis, Ted Briscoe, and Ben Medlock. 2011. A new dataset and method for automatically grading esol texts. In *Human Language Technologies-Volume 1*. ACL, pages 180–189.

Artificial Error Generation
with Machine Translation and Syntactic Patterns

Marek Rei   **Mariano Felice**   **Zheng Yuan**   **Ted Briscoe**

The ALTA Institute
Computer Laboratory
University of Cambridge
United Kingdom
`firstname.lastname@cl.cam.ac.uk`

Abstract

Shortage of available training data is holding back progress in the area of automated error detection. This paper investigates two alternative methods for artificially generating writing errors, in order to create additional resources. We propose treating error generation as a machine translation task, where grammatically correct text is translated to contain errors. In addition, we explore a system for extracting textual patterns from an annotated corpus, which can then be used to insert errors into grammatically correct sentences. Our experiments show that the inclusion of artificially generated errors significantly improves error detection accuracy on both FCE and CoNLL 2014 datasets.

1   Introduction

Writing errors can occur in many different forms – from relatively simple punctuation and determiner errors, to mistakes including word tense and form, incorrect collocations and erroneous idioms. Automatically identifying all of these errors is a challenging task, especially as the amount of available annotated data is very limited. Rei and Yannakoudakis (2016) showed that while some error detection algorithms perform better than others, it is additional training data that has the biggest impact on improving performance.

Being able to generate realistic artificial data would allow for any grammatically correct text to be transformed into annotated examples containing writing errors, producing large amounts of additional training examples. Supervised error generation systems would also provide an efficient method for anonymising the source corpus – error statistics from a private corpus can be aggre-

gated and applied to a different target text, obscuring sensitive information in the original examination scripts. However, the task of creating incorrect data is somewhat more difficult than might initially appear – naive methods for error generation can create data that does not resemble natural errors, thereby making downstream systems learn misleading or uninformative patterns.

Previous work on artificial error generation (AEG) has focused on specific error types, such as prepositions and determiners (Rozovskaya and Roth, 2010, 2011), or noun number errors (Brockett et al., 2006). Felice and Yuan (2014) investigated the use of linguistic information when generating artificial data for error correction, but also restricting the approach to only five error types. There has been very limited research on generating artificial data for all types, which is important for general-purpose error detection systems. For example, the error types investigated by Felice and Yuan (2014) cover only 35.74% of all errors present in the CoNLL 2014 training dataset, providing no additional information for the majority of errors.

In this paper, we investigate two supervised approaches for generating all types of artificial errors. We propose a framework for generating errors based on statistical machine translation (SMT), training a model to translate from correct into incorrect sentences. In addition, we describe a method for learning error patterns from an annotated corpus and transplanting them into error-free text. We evaluate the effect of introducing artificial data on two error detection benchmarks. Our results show that each method provides significant improvements over using only the available training set, and a combination of both gives an absolute improvement of 4.3% in $F_{0.5}$, without requiring any additional annotated data.

Proceedings of the 12th Workshop on Innovative Use of NLP for Building Educational Applications, pages 287–292
Copenhagen, Denmark, September 8, 2017. ©2017 Association for Computational Linguistics

Original	We are a well-mixed class with equal numbers of boys and girls, all about 20 years old.
FY14	We **am** a well-mixed class with equal numbers of boys and girls, all about 20 years old.
PAT	We are a well-mixed class with equal numbers of boys **an** girls, all about 20 **year** old.
MT	We are a well-mixed class with **equals** numbers of boys and girls, all about 20 years old.

Table 1: Example artificial errors generated by three systems: the error generation method by Felice and Yuan (2014) (FY14), our pattern-based method covering all error types (PAT), and the machine translation approach to artificial error generation (MT).

2 Error Generation Methods

We investigate two alternative methods for AEG. The models receive grammatically correct text as input and modify certain tokens to produce incorrect sequences. The alternative versions of each sentence are aligned using Levenshtein distance, allowing us to identify specific words that need to be marked as errors. While these alignments are not always perfect, we found them to be sufficient for practical purposes, since alternative alignments of similar sentences often result in the same binary labeling. Future work could explore more advanced alignment methods, such as proposed by Felice et al. (2016).

In Section 4, this automatically labeled data is then used for training error detection models.

2.1 Machine Translation

We treat AEG as a translation task – given a correct sentence as input, the system would learn to translate it to contain likely errors, based on a training corpus of parallel data. Existing SMT approaches are already optimised for identifying context patterns that correspond to specific output sequences, which is also required for generating human-like errors. The reverse of this idea, translating from incorrect to correct sentences, has been shown to work well for error correction tasks (Brockett et al., 2006; Ng et al., 2014), and round-trip translation has also been shown to be promising for correcting grammatical errors (Madnani et al., 2012).

Following previous work (Brockett et al., 2006; Yuan and Felice, 2013), we build a phrase-based SMT error generation system. During training, error-corrected sentences in the training data are treated as the source, and the original sentences written by language learners as the target. Pialign (Neubig et al., 2011) is used to create a phrase translation table directly from model probabilities. In addition to default features, we add character-level Levenshtein distance to each map-

ping in the phrase table, as proposed by Felice et al. (2014). Decoding is performed using Moses (Koehn et al., 2007) and the language model used during decoding is built from the original erroneous sentences in the learner corpus. The IRSTLM Toolkit (Federico et al., 2008) is used for building a 5-gram language model with modified Kneser-Ney smoothing (Kneser and Ney, 1995).

2.2 Pattern Extraction

We also describe a method for AEG using patterns over words and part-of-speech (POS) tags, extracting known incorrect sequences from a corpus of annotated corrections. This approach is based on the best method identified by Felice and Yuan (2014), using error type distributions; while they covered only 5 error types, we relax this restriction and learn patterns for generating all types of errors.

The original and corrected sentences in the corpus are aligned and used to identify short transformation patterns in the form of *(incorrect phrase, correct phrase)*. The length of each pattern is the affected phrase, plus up to one token of context on both sides. If a word form changes between the incorrect and correct text, it is fully saved in the pattern, otherwise the POS tags are used for matching.

For example, the original sentence '*We went shop on Saturday*' and the corrected version '*We went shopping on Saturday*' would produce the following pattern:

(VVD shop_VV0 II, VVD shopping_VVG II)

After collecting statistics from the background corpus, errors can be inserted into error-free text. The learned patterns are now reversed, looking for the correct side of the tuple in the input sentence. We only use patterns with frequency $>= 5$, which yields a total of 35,625 patterns from our training data. For each input sentence, we first decide how many errors will be generated (using probabilities from the background corpus) and attempt to create them by sampling from the collection of applicable patterns. This process is repeated until all the required errors have been generated or the sentence is exhausted. During generation, we try to balance the distribution of error types as well as keeping the same proportion of incorrect and correct sentences as in the background corpus (Felice, 2016). The required POS tags were generated with RASP (Briscoe et al., 2006), using the CLAWS2 tagset.

3 Error Detection Model

We construct a neural sequence labeling model for error detection, following the previous work (Rei and Yannakoudakis, 2016; Rei, 2017). The model receives a sequence of tokens as input and outputs a prediction for each position, indicating whether the token is correct or incorrect in the current context. The tokens are first mapped to a distributed vector space, resulting in a sequence of word embeddings. Next, the embeddings are given as input to a bidirectional LSTM (Hochreiter and Schmidhuber, 1997), in order to create context-dependent representations for every token. The hidden states from forward- and backward-LSTMs are concatenated for each word position, resulting in representations that are conditioned on the whole sequence. This concatenated vector is then passed through an additional feedforward layer, and a softmax over the two possible labels (*correct* and *incorrect*) is used to output a probability distribution for each token. The model is optimised by minimising categorical cross-entropy with respect to the correct labels. We use AdaDelta (Zeiler, 2012) for calculating an adaptive learning rate during training, which accounts for a higher baseline performance compared to previous results.

4 Evaluation

We trained our error generation models on the public FCE training set (Yannakoudakis et al., 2011) and used them to generate additional artificial training data. Grammatically correct text is needed as the starting point for inserting artificial errors, and we used two different sources: 1) the corrected version of the same FCE training set on which the system is trained (450K tokens), and 2) example sentences extracted from the English Vocabulary Profile (270K tokens).[1] While there are other text corpora that could be used (e.g.,

Wikipedia and news articles), our development experiments showed that keeping the writing style and vocabulary close to the target domain gives better results compared to simply including more data.

We evaluated our detection models on three benchmarks: the FCE test data (41K tokens) and the two alternative annotations of the CoNLL 2014 Shared Task dataset (30K tokens) (Ng et al., 2014). Each artificial error generation system was used to generate 3 different versions of the artificial data, which were then combined with the original annotated dataset and used for training an error detection system. Table 1 contains example sentences from the error generation systems, highlighting each of the edits that are marked as errors.

The error detection results can be seen in Table 2. We use $F_{0.5}$ as the main evaluation measure, which was established as the preferred measure for error correction and detection by the CoNLL-14 shared task (Ng et al., 2014). $F_{0.5}$ calculates a weighted harmonic mean of precision and recall, which assigns twice as much importance to precision – this is motivated by practical applications, where accurate predictions from an error detection system are more important compared to coverage. For comparison, we also report the performance of the error detection system by Rei and Yannakoudakis (2016), trained using the same FCE dataset.

The results show that error detection performance is substantially improved by making use of artificially generated data, created by any of the described methods. When comparing the error generation system by Felice and Yuan (2014) (FY14) with our pattern-based (PAT) and machine translation (MT) approaches, we see that the latter methods covering all error types consistently improve performance. While the added error types tend to be less frequent and more complicated to capture, the added coverage is indeed beneficial for error detection. Combining the pattern-based approach with the machine translation system (Ann+PAT+MT) gave the best overall performance on all datasets. The two frameworks learn to generate different types of errors, and taking advantage of both leads to substantial improvements in error detection.

We used the Approximate Randomisation Test (Noreen, 1989; Cohen, 1995) to calculate statistical significance and found that the improvement

---

[1] http://www.englishprofile.org/wordlists

	FCE			CoNLL-14 TEST1			CoNLL-14 TEST2		
	P	R	$F_{0.5}$	P	R	$F_{0.5}$	P	R	$F_{0.5}$
R&Y (2016)	46.10	28.50	41.10	15.40	**22.80**	16.40	23.60	**25.10**	23.90
Annotation	53.91	26.88	44.84	16.12	18.42	16.52	25.72	20.92	24.57
Ann+FY14	58.77	25.55	46.54	20.48	14.41	18.88	33.25	16.67	27.72
Ann+PAT	**62.47**	24.70	47.81	21.07	15.02	19.47	34.04	17.32	28.49
Ann+MT	58.38	**28.84**	48.37	19.52	20.79	19.73	30.24	22.96	28.39
Ann+PAT+MT	60.67	28.08	**49.11**	**23.28**	18.01	**21.87**	**35.28**	19.42	**30.13**

Table 2: Error detection performance when combining manually annotated and artificial training data.

for each of the systems using artificial data was significant over using only manual annotation. In addition, the final combination system is also significantly better compared to the Felice and Yuan (2014) system, on all three datasets. While Rei and Yannakoudakis (2016) also report separate experiments that achieve even higher performance, these models were trained on a considerably larger proprietary corpus. In this paper we compare error detection frameworks trained on the same publicly available FCE dataset, thereby removing the confounding factor of dataset size and only focusing on the model architectures.

The error generation methods can generate alternative versions of the same input text – the pattern-based method randomly samples the error locations, and the SMT system can provide an n-best list of alternative translations. Therefore, we also investigated the combination of multiple error-generated versions of the input files when training error detection models. Figure 1 shows the $F_{0.5}$ score on the development set, as the training data is increased by using more translations from the n-best list of the SMT system. These results reveal that allowing the model to see multiple alternative versions of the same file gives a distinct improvement – showing the model both correct and incorrect variations of the same sentences likely assists in learning a discriminative model.

5 Related Work

Our work builds on prior research into AEG. Brockett et al. (2006) constructed regular expressions for transforming correct sentences to contain noun number errors. Rozovskaya and Roth (2010) learned confusion sets from an annotated corpus in order to generate preposition errors. Foster and Andersen (2009) devised a tool for generating errors for different types using patterns provided by the user or collected automatically from

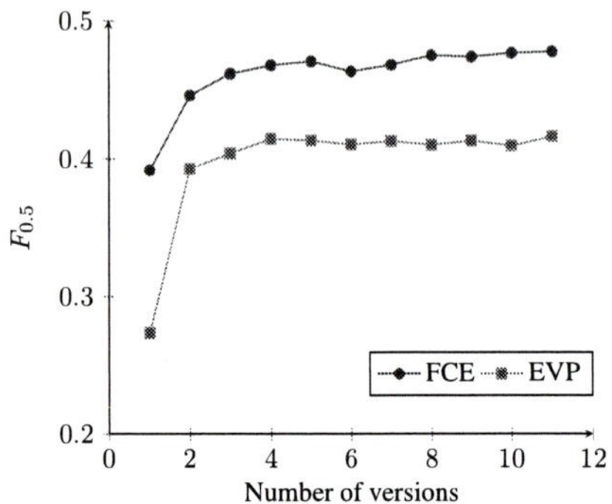

Figure 1: $F_{0.5}$ on FCE development set with increasing amounts of artificial data from SMT.

an annotated corpus. However, their method uses a limited number of edit operations and is thus unable to generate complex errors. Cahill et al. (2013) compared different training methodologies and showed that artificial errors helped correct prepositions. Felice and Yuan (2014) learned error type distributions for generating five types of errors, and the system in Section 2.2 is an extension of this model. While previous work focused on generating a specific subset of error types, we explored two holistic approaches to AEG and showed that they are able to significantly improve error detection performance.

6 Conclusion

This paper investigated two AEG methods, in order to create additional training data for error detection. First, we explored a method using textual patterns learned from an annotated corpus, which are used for inserting errors into correct input text. In addition, we proposed formulating error generation as an MT framework, learning to translate from grammatically correct to incorrect sentences.

The addition of artificial data to the training process was evaluated on three error detection annotations, using the FCE and CoNLL 2014 datasets. Making use of artificial data provided improvements for all data generation methods. By relaxing the type restrictions and generating all types of errors, our pattern-based method consistently outperformed the system by Felice and Yuan (2014). The combination of the pattern-based method with the machine translation approach gave further substantial improvements and the best performance on all datasets.

References

Ted Briscoe, John Carroll, and Rebecca Watson. 2006. The Second Release of the RASP System. In *Proceedings of the COLING/ACL on Interactive presentation sessions.*. Association for Computational Linguistics, Sydney, Australia, July, pages 77–80. https://doi.org/10.3115/1225403.1225423.

Chris Brockett, William B. Dolan, and Michael Gamon. 2006. Correcting ESL errors using phrasal SMT techniques. *Proceedings of the 21st International Conference on Computational Linguistics and 44th Annual Meeting of the Association for Computational Linguistics* https://doi.org/10.3115/1220175.1220207.

Aoife Cahill, Nitin Madnani, Joel Tetreault, and Diane Napolitano. 2013. Robust Systems for Preposition Error Correction Using Wikipedia Revisions. In *Proceedings of the 2013 Conference of the North American Chapter of the Association for Computational Linguistics: Human Language Technologies.* http://www.aclweb.org/anthology/N13-1055.

Paul Cohen. 1995. *Empirical Methods for Artificial Intelligence.* The MIT Press, Cambridge, MA.

Marcello Federico, Nicola Bertoldi, and Mauro Cettolo. 2008. IRSTLM: an open source toolkit for handling large scale language models. In *Proceedings of the 9th Annual Conference of the International Speech Communication Association.*

Mariano Felice. 2016. Artificial error generation for translation-based grammatical error correction. Technical Report UCAM-CL-TR-895, University of Cambridge, Computer Laboratory. http://www.cl.cam.ac.uk/techreports/UCAM-CL-TR-895.pdf.

Mariano Felice, Christopher Bryant, and Ted Briscoe. 2016. Automatic extraction of learner errors in esl sentences using linguistically enhanced alignments. In *Proceedings of COLING 2016, the 26th International Conference on Computational Linguistics: Technical Papers.* The COLING 2016 Organizing Committee, Osaka, Japan, pages 825–835. http://aclweb.org/anthology/C16-1079.

Mariano Felice and Zheng Yuan. 2014. Generating artificial errors for grammatical error correction. *Proceedings of the Student Research Workshop at the 14th Conference of the European Chapter of the Association for Computational Linguistics (EACL 2014)*.

Mariano Felice, Zheng Yuan, Øistein E. Andersen, Helen Yannakoudakis, and Ekaterina Kochmar. 2014. Grammatical error correction using hybrid systems and type filtering. In *Proceedings of the 18th Conference on Computational Natural Language Learning: Shared Task.*

Jennifer Foster and Øistein E. Andersen. 2009. GenERRate: generating errors for use in grammatical error detection. In *Proceedings of the Fourth Workshop on Innovative Use of NLP for Building Educational Applications.* http://dl.acm.org/citation.cfm?id=1609855.

Sepp Hochreiter and Jürgen Schmidhuber. 1997. Long Short-term Memory. *Neural Computation* 9. https://doi.org/10.1.1.56.7752.

Reinhard Kneser and Hermann Ney. 1995. Improved backing-off for M-gram language modeling. In *Proceedings of the IEEE International Conference on Acoustics, Speech, and Signal Processing.*

Philipp Koehn, Hieu Hoang, Alexandra Birch, Chris Callison-Burch, Marcello Federico, Nicola Bertoldi, Brooke Cowan, Wade Shen, Christine Moran, Richard Zens, Chris Dyer, Ondřej Bojar, Alexandra Constantin, and Evan Herbst. 2007. Moses: open source toolkit for statistical machine translation. In *Proceedings of the 45th Annual Meeting of the ACL on Interactive Poster and Demonstration Sessions.*

Nitin Madnani, Joel Tetreault, and Martin Chodorow. 2012. Exploring grammatical error correction with not-so-crummy machine translation. In *Proceedings of the Seventh Workshop on Building Educational Applications Using NLP.* Association for Computational Linguistics, Montréal, Canada, pages 44–53. http://www.aclweb.org/anthology/W12-2005.

Graham Neubig, Taro Watanabe, Eiichiro Sumita, Shinsuke Mori, and Tatsuya Kawahara. 2011. An unsupervised model for joint phrase alignment and extraction. In *Proceedings of the 49th Annual Meeting of the Association for Computational Linguistics: Human Language Technologies.*

Hwee Tou Ng, Siew Mei Wu, Ted Briscoe, Christian Hadiwinoto, Raymond Hendy Susanto, and Christopher Bryant. 2014. The CoNLL-2014 Shared Task on Grammatical Error Correction. In *Proceedings of the Eighteenth Conference on Computational Natural Language Learning: Shared Task.* http://www.aclweb.org/anthology/W/W14/W14-1701.

Eric W. Noreen. 1989. *Computer Intensive Methods for Testing Hypotheses.* Wiley, New York.

Marek Rei. 2017. Semi-supervised Multitask Learning for Sequence Labeling. In *Proceedings of the 55th Annual Meeting of the Association for Computational Linguistics (ACL-2017)*.

Marek Rei and Helen Yannakoudakis. 2016. Compositional Sequence Labeling Models for Error Detection in Learner Writing. In *Proceedings of the 54th Annual Meeting of the Association for Computational Linguistics*. https://aclweb.org/anthology/P/P16/P16-1112.pdf.

Alla Rozovskaya and Dan Roth. 2010. Generating confusion sets for context-sensitive error correction. *Proceedings of the 2010 Conference on Empirical Methods in Natural Language Processing* http://dl.acm.org/citation.cfm?id=1870752.

Alla Rozovskaya and Dan Roth. 2011. Algorithm Selection and Model Adaptation for ESL Correction Tasks. *Proceedings of the 49th Annual Meeting of the Association for Computational Linguistics (ACL-2011)* http://www.aclweb.org/anthology-new/P/P11/P11-1093.pdf.

Helen Yannakoudakis, Ted Briscoe, and Ben Medlock. 2011. A New Dataset and Method for Automatically Grading ESOL Texts. In *Proceedings of the 49th Annual Meeting of the Association for Computational Linguistics: Human Language Technologies*. http://www.aclweb.org/anthology/P11-1019.

Zheng Yuan and Mariano Felice. 2013. Constrained grammatical error correction using statistical machine translation. In *Proceedings of the 17th Conference on Computational Natural Language Learning: Shared Task*.

Matthew D. Zeiler. 2012. ADADELTA: An Adaptive Learning Rate Method. *arXiv preprint arXiv:1212.5701* http://arxiv.org/abs/1212.5701.

Modelling semantic acquisition in second language learning

Ekaterina Kochmar
The ALTA Institute
University of Cambridge
ek358@cam.ac.uk

Ekaterina Shutova
Computer Laboratory
University of Cambridge
es407@cam.ac.uk

Abstract

Using methods of statistical analysis, we investigate how semantic knowledge is acquired in English as a second language and evaluate the pace of development across a number of predicate types and content word combinations, as well as across the levels of language proficiency and native languages. Our exploratory study helps identify the most problematic areas for language learners with different backgrounds and at different stages of learning.

1 Introduction

Acquisition of semantic knowledge and vocabulary of a second language (L2), including appropriate word choice and awareness of selectional preference restrictions, are widely recognised as important aspects of L2 learning by native speakers, language teachers and learners themselves. Previous research demonstrated strong correlation between semantic knowledge and proficiency level (Shei and Pain, 2000; Alderson, 2005), and argued that the use of collocations makes one's speech more native-like (Kjellmer, 1991; Aston, 1995; Granger and Bestgen, 2014). James (1998) noted that learners often equate L2 mastery with mastery of L2 vocabulary, and Leacock et al. (2014) mention an experiment in which teachers of English ranked word choice errors among the most serious errors in L2 writing. At the same time, it has also been argued that acquisition of semantic knowledge proceeds on a word-by-word basis with each word being acquired as a separate construct (Gyllstad et al., 2015), and acquisition of content word combinations knowledge is slow and uneven, presenting challenges even at high proficiency levels (Bahns and Eldaw, 1993; Laufer and Waldman, 2011; Thewissen, 2013).

Native speakers are believed to be experts in their own language (James, 1998), and the language norm is usually set based on their preferences (Wulff and Gries, 2011). Apart from errors, learner English is often characterised by differences in the probabilistic distribution of lexical items which are expressed in under- or overuse of certain constructions (De Cock, 2004; Durrant and Schmitt, 2009; Laufer and Waldman, 2011; Wulff and Gries, 2011). In this paper, we adopt statistical approach and assume that native and learner language are characterised by different distributions. We investigate how non-native use of language develops and how closely it approximates native use at different levels of proficiency.

The native language distribution is modelled using a combination of the *British National Corpus* (*BNC*) and *ukWaC*, while learner language distributions are modelled using *Cambridge Learner Corpus* (*CLC*). CLC covers various L1 backgrounds as well as 6 language proficiency levels defined by the *Common European Framework of Reference for Languages* (*CEFR*) (Council of Europe, 2011a), ranging from "basic" (A1-A2) to "independent" (B1-B2) to "proficient" (C1-C2). In contrast to much of previous research, we run the experiments both on a wider scale, using a large corpus of learner English, and to finer level of granularity, exploring learner development across proficiency levels. Table 1 defines the amount and range of linguistic constructions that the learners are expected to be familiar with at different levels. Specifically, we explore:

(1) the pace of semantic knowledge and vocabulary acquisition across levels;

(2) the influence of one's L1 on the development of semantic knowledge;

(3) acquisition and development of selectional preference patterns across levels.

293

Proceedings of the 12th Workshop on Innovative Use of NLP for Building Educational Applications, pages 293–302
Copenhagen, Denmark, September 8, 2017. ©2017 Association for Computational Linguistics

Level	Descriptor
A1	Has a very *basic repertoire of words* and *simple phrases* related to *personal details* and *particular concrete situations.*
A2	Uses basic sentence patterns with *memorised phrases, groups of a few words* and formulae in order to communicate limited information in *simple everyday situations.*
B1	Has enough language to get by, with *sufficient vocabulary* to express him/herself with some hesitation and circumlocutions on topics such as *family, hobbies and interests, work, travel, and current events.*
B2	Has a *sufficient range of language* to be able to give clear descriptions, express viewpoints on *most general topics*, without much conspicuous searching for words, using some complex sentence forms to do so.
C1	Has *a good command of a broad range of language* allowing him/her to select a formulation to express him/ herself clearly in an appropriate style on *a wide range of general, academic, professional or leisure topics* without having to restrict what he/she wants to say.
C2	Shows great flexibility reformulating ideas in differing linguistic forms to convey *finer shades of meaning* precisely, to give emphasis, to differentiate and to eliminate ambiguity. Also has a *good command of idiomatic expressions and colloquialisms.*

Table 1: CEFR descriptors of general linguistic and vocabulary range (Council of Europe, 2011b)

2   Previous research

Within NLP, it is more typical to explore learner language from the perspective of automated assessment or error detection and correction (Leacock et al., 2014) which focus on the contrast between learner and native language in terms of errors in L2, rather than from a language development perspective. The latter was studied more extensively by Second Language Acquisition (SLA) researchers. Previous research looked into vocabulary acquisition and language development assessing passive, or *receptive*, vocabulary knowledge (Gyllstad et al., 2015) and trying to estimate the vocabulary that the learners might understand at different proficiency levels (Nation, 2006; Bergsma and Yarowsky, 2013). The vocabulary size tests of the type proposed by Nation (2012) were shown to not be appropriate to test *productive vocabulary knowledge* as they suffer from overestimation of the vocabulary size (Gyllstad et al., 2015). Using learner writing to estimate the productive vocabulary size provides more reliable results, but previous studies in this area were performed on a smaller scale, either focusing on a limited number of proficiency levels (Gilquin and Granger, 2011; Granger and Bestgen, 2014), L1s (Gilquin and Granger, 2011; Granger and Bestgen, 2014; Siyanova-Chanturia, 2015), or on overall smaller datasets (Grant and Ginther, 2000; Granger and Bestgen, 2014).

It is widely accepted that vocabulary develops over time, and richer vocabulary is characteristic of better language knowledge (Laufer and Waldman, 1995; Grant and Ginther, 2000). Moreover, as students become more proficient writers, they do not only start operating with an overall larger

vocabulary, but also become more precise in their word choice which is reflected in the increase of the type-token ratio (TTR) (Ferris, 1994; Engber, 1995; Frase et al., 1999; Grant and Ginther, 2000). However, the methodology of tagging the word choice and measuring TTR similar to that adopted in Grant and Ginther (2000) fails taking the *omissions* into account, while the method proposed in this paper helps alleviate this problem.

With respect to the development of selectional preference patterns and phraseological knowledge, Siyanova-Chanturia (2015) show that L2 learners even at lower levels do not just focus on single words acquisition but also attend to combinatorial linguistic mechanisms. The studies of Durrant and Schmitt (2009) and Granger and Bestgen (2014) suggest that intermediate learners tend to overuse high frequency collocations (such as *hard work*) and underuse lower-frequency collocations (such as *immortal souls*), while as proficiency in the language increases, this balance changes. Durrant and Schmitt (2009) argue that learners at the lower proficiency levels seem to over-rely on forms which are common in the language, and Paquot and Granger (2012) note that this might be related to the fact that learners feel confident using such common forms.

An interesting observation concerns the pace of semantic knowledge development: for instance, Laufer and Waldman (1995) observed that advanced learners' vocabulary is too varied to remain stable across different samples of writing. Laufer and Waldman (2011) and Nesselhauf (2005) investigated the development of collocational knowledge and came to a somewhat counterintuitive conclusion that more proficient learners produce more deviant collocations than their less proficient counterparts. Thewissen (2008) argue that higher-level learners attempt a much wider range of lexical phrases which are not always error-free, and produce a large number of near-hits as compared to their lower intermediate counterparts. Paquot and Granger (2012) conclude that at an advanced level, learners take more risks, try out more complex lexical phrases and as a result, produce errors, but those are of a different, more 'advanced' nature than the basic errors typical of earlier stages.

A number of studies looked into L1 influence on L2 development (Siyanova-Chanturia, 2015; Paquot and Granger, 2012). Typically, researchers report negative effects of L1 transfer (Lorenz, 1999; Gilquin, 2007; Nesselhauf, 2005; Laufer and Waldman, 2011; Paquot and Granger, 2012), but some research also suggests that the learners whose L1 belongs to the same language family as English are more likely to make fewer mistakes than the learners from other L1 backgrounds (Waibel, 2008; Alejo Gonzalez, 2010; Gilquin and Granger, 2011).

3 Experimental setup

We focus on three types of content word combinations that are some of the most frequent in learner writing and have previously been found challenging for language learners (Lorenz, 1999; Paquot and Granger, 2012): adjective–noun (AN), verb–direct object (VO) and subject–verb (SV). We (1) investigate how the use of the predicating words (*adjectives* and *verbs*) within these combinations develops over time,[1] and (2) look into how their selectional preference patterns change across levels of language proficiency. We do not focus on *collocations* specifically for two reasons: firstly, there is a lot of disagreement in defining collocations (cf. Foster (2010), Nesselhauf (2005), Hoey (1991)), and secondly, learners have been shown to have difficulties with all types of content word combinations, including those that are referred to as 'free' (Paquot and Granger, 2012).

3.1 Data

Learner data: We have extracted the data for our experiments from the Cambridge Learner Corpus (CLC), which is a 52.5 million-word corpus of

	Lvl	Types	Tokens	TTR	#Preds
AN	A1	7,053	41,502	0.1699	720
	A2	12,365	69,161	0.1788	1,010
	B1	37,198	179,791	0.2069	2,198
	B2	54,782	250,807	0.2184	2,699
	C1	59,965	250,263	0.2396	2,832
	C2	63,937	209,984	0.3045	3,664
VO	A1	9,690	58,399	0.1659	761
	A2	19,413	104,123	0.1864	1,238
	B1	45,826	217,100	0.2111	2,133
	B2	66,621	288,129	0.2312	2,499
	C1	67,235	247,842	0.2713	2,607
	C2	63,223	200,038	0.3161	2,764
SV	A1	7,553	40,657	0.1858	776
	A2	15,825	75,749	0.2089	1,323
	B1	49,282	187,378	0.2630	2,370
	B2	75,109	281,490	0.2668	2,867
	C1	83,832	293,654	0.2855	3,070
	C2	80,779	232,702	0.3471	3,283

Table 2: Overall statistics

learner English collected by Cambridge University Press and Cambridge English Language Assessment (Nicholls, 2003). It comprises essays written during examinations in English by language learners with over 80 L1s and representing all 6 CEFR levels (Council of Europe, 2011a). Since the learners are not restricted in the word choice,[2] we believe that the range of vocabulary used in the essays is representative of what is in learners' active lexicon and, therefore, reflects semantic knowledge internalised at this point.

We have extracted the word combinations from the full CLC parsed with the RASP (Briscoe et al., 2006). Table 2 summarises learner data: we include the number of *types* (unique combinations), *tokens* (overall number of combinations), *type-token ratio* (TTR) as well as the number of predicates for each level. Table 2 demonstrates that the overall number of the combinations and predicates as well as TTR constantly increase from A1 through to C2, with the largest increase between levels A2 and B1,[3] when the learners transfer from *beginners* to *intermediate* and start using the vocabulary beyond *basic* and *simple*, and between levels C1 and C2, when learners are expected to master *idiomatic expressions* and *colloquialisms*.

Native data: To estimate the general linguistic and vocabulary range of a native speaker, we have extracted the statistics on the use of ANs, VOs and SVs and the predicates from a combination of the BNC (Burnard, 2007) and ukWaC (Ferraresi et al.,

---

[1] We combine adjectives in AN and verbs in VO and SV combinations under the term of *predicating words* because we assume that they impose the selectional restrictions on the arguments (nouns) within the corresponding combinations.

[2] It can be argued that vocabulary selection is restricted by essay prompts; we address this issue in §5.

[3] The increase is statistically significant at 0.05 with t-test.

2008), which together amount to more than 2 billion words. For consistency, the native data has also been parsed with RASP (Briscoe et al., 2006).

3.2 Statistical methods

Distribution similarity: We measure the similarity between two distributions using Kullback-Leibler (KL) divergence (MacKay, 2003) which for distributions Q and P is defined as:

$$D_{\mathrm{KL}}(P||Q) = \sum_i P(i) log \frac{P(i)}{Q(i)} \qquad (1)$$

In our experiments, P is the distribution in the learner data and Q is the distribution in the native data. The closer the two distributions are, the lower the value of D_{KL}. To support the results, we additionally measure the Pearson correlation coefficient (PCC) between the predicates and content word combinations in the learner and native data. PCC is higher for the more similar distributions.

Argument clustering: To address the issue of data sparsity, we estimate selectional preferences (*SP*) over *argument classes* as well as *individual arguments*. We obtain SP classes using spectral clustering of nouns with lexico-syntactic features, which has been shown effective in previous lexical classification tasks (Brew and Schulte im Walde, 2002; Sun and Korhonen, 2009). Spectral clustering partitions the data relying on a matrix that records similarities between all pairs of data points. We use *Jensen-Shannon divergence* to measure the similarity between feature vectors for nouns w_i and w_j as follows:

$$d_{\mathrm{JS}}(w_i, w_j) = \frac{1}{2} d_{\mathrm{KL}}(w_i||m) + \frac{1}{2} d_{\mathrm{KL}}(w_j||m), \qquad (2)$$

where d_{KL} is the KL divergence, and m is the average of w_i and w_j. We construct the similarity matrix S computing similarities S_{ij} as $S_{ij} = \exp(-d_{\mathrm{JS}}(w_i, w_j))$. The matrix S encodes a similarity graph G over the nouns, where S_{ij} are the adjacency weights. The clustering problem can then be defined as identifying the optimal partition, or *cut*, of the graph into clusters, such that the intra-cluster weights are high and the inter-cluster weights are low. We cluster $2,000$ most frequent nouns in the BNC, using their grammatical relations as features. The features consist of verb lemmas occurring in the subject, direct object and indirect object relations with the given nouns in the RASP-parsed BNC. The feature vectors are constructed from the corpus counts and normalized by the sum of the feature values.

Selectional preference model: Once the SP classes are obtained, we quantify the strength of association between a given predicate and each of the classes. We adopt an information theoretic measure proposed by Resnik (1993) for this purpose. Resnik first measures *selectional preference strength* (*SPS*) of a predicate in terms of KL divergence between the distribution of noun classes occurring as arguments of the predicate, $p(c|v)$, and the prior distribution of the noun classes, $p(c)$:

$$\mathrm{SPS}_R(v) = \sum_c p(c|v) \log \frac{p(c|v)}{p(c)}, \qquad (3)$$

where R is the grammatical relation for which SPs are computed. SPS measures how strongly the predicate constrains its arguments. Selectional association with a particular argument class is then defined as a relative contribution of that argument class to the overall SPS of the predicate:

$$\mathrm{Ass}_R(v, c) = \frac{1}{\mathrm{SPS}_R(v)} p(c|v) \log \frac{p(c|v)}{p(c)} \qquad (4)$$

We extract VO and SV relations, map the argument heads to SP classes and quantify selectional association of a given predicate with each SP class.

4 Experimental results

We run a series of experiments to test the aspects of semantic knowledge acquisition outlined in §1.

4.1 Pace of semantic knowledge acquisition

Table 2 shows that at the lower levels learners operate with quite a small vocabulary. Many previous studies argued that learners at lower levels tend to overuse high frequency lexical items, whereas over time they expand their vocabulary with less frequent lexical items. It has also been argued that semantic knowledge acquisition is an unsteady process (see §2). First, we explore how exactly the semantic knowledge develops across proficiency levels, and investigate whether content word choice error rates – the proportion of word combinations where the predicate in chosen inappropriately as, for example, in *choose decision* instead of *make decision*, or *actual room* instead of *current room* – decrease over time.

For that, we identify 10 frequency bands for predicating words within each combination type using native English data. Each band covers from 363 (within band 1 of the most frequent predicates) up to $7,672$ (within band 10 of the least frequent ones) unique adjectives in ANs, and similarly from 281 to $3,676$ verbs in VOs, and 297 to $3,367$ verbs in SVs. For instance, band 1 contains such adjectives as *big* and *good*, and verbs *give*, *go* and *see*, while band 10 contains adjectives *behaviouristic* and *decipherable*, and verbs *factor*, *garnish* and *mesmerise*. It is reasonable to expect that learners are familiar with the "simpler" words from band 1 even at the lower proficiency levels, while they might find words from band 10 much more challenging. In order to quantitatively assess this, we measure the proportion of new predicating words used at each level and map it to the identified frequency bands. Next, we estimate the error rates for each level and for each frequency band.

Figure 1 shows the distribution of the new vocabulary acquired at each level mapped against the frequency bands, as well as the distribution of the error rates across the frequency bands at each level.[4] While we observe that, as expected, learners expand their vocabulary acquiring words from lower frequency bands, the following trends are worth noting: most of the verb predicates in VOs and SVs that the learners know at level A1 are covered by frequency band 1. At A2 and B1 they still expand their vocabulary with some verbs from band 1, but starting with level B2 none of the new vocabulary comes from this band. Most new verbs in VOs at level C2 are covered by band 10, and in SVs by band 4. For adjectives, most new vocabulary at A1 and A2 comes from band 1, at B1 – band 3, at B2 – band 5, at C1 – band 8 and at C2 – band 10. Predictably, the error rates decrease towards the higher proficiency levels and within the higher frequency bands. The highest error rates are observed on the bands covering less frequent words: for example, even though the error rates are overall lower for C2 level, the highest error rate for C2 is associated with band 10 for all three types of combinations which confirms that semantic acquisition is challenging even at advanced levels.

While these results corroborate previous findings and show quantitatively how semantic knowledge develops across levels, we look further into how it approximates native English. In particular, it is reasonable to assume that the variety of English used by language learners at the lower proficiency levels is more dissimilar to the native English both for predicates and content word com-

	Lvl	PCC_{pred}	KL_{pred}	PCC_{comb}	KL_{comb}
AN	A1	0.3497	2.8737	0.1052	4.2909
	A2	0.4338	2.5073	0.1382	3.6463
	B1	0.7036	1.3101	0.2785	2.6212
	B2	0.7968	0.9408	0.4627	2.2058
	C1	0.8482	0.7959	0.4896	2.1183
	C2	**0.8188**	**0.7990**	**0.4817**	2.0451
VO	A1	0.6226	1.8469	0.0975	4.5220
	A2	0.7811	1.3115	0.1973	3.5465
	B1	0.8749	0.9080	0.3339	2.5350
	B2	0.9270	0.5965	0.5454	1.9129
	C1	0.9395	0.5541	0.6082	1.7994
	C2	**0.9262**	**0.6106**	**0.5736**	**1.8145**
SV	A1	0.9669	1.2729	0.1660	4.2648
	A2	0.9716	1.0038	0.2336	3.3381
	B1	0.9824	0.6898	0.4758	2.3194
	B2	0.9859	0.5623	0.6306	1.9506
	C1	0.9873	0.5141	0.6637	1.8733
	C2	**0.9870**	**0.5230**	**0.5954**	**1.9079**

Table 3: Predicates (*pred*) and combinations (*comb*) distributions

binations, while it approximates native language distributions at upper levels. To test that, we calculate PCC and KL (see §3.2) and expect that towards C2 level PCC increases and approximates 1.0, while KL decreases and approximates 0.0.

Table 3 presents the PCC and KL values for the distribution of the adjectives and verbs in columns marked with *pred* for predicating words, and for combinations in columns marked with *comb*. These values show that PCC steadily increases while KL steadily decreases from level A1 through to level C1, with the biggest "jump" between levels A2 and B1 for the adjectives and verbs in SVs, and A1 and A2 for the verbs in VOs. However, we note that at level C2 predicating words distribution is less similar to native English distribution than at level C1 for all types of combinations – we mark these values in the table in bold. We hypothesise that at level C2 the learners are already familiar with the basic vocabulary and start experimenting with the use of novel constructions which might result in a quite distinct variety of English (see Thewissen (2008) and Paquot and Granger (2012) for similar hypotheses). To investigate this further, we identify 10 predicates per combination type such that after removing them from the list of predicates, KL between the learner and native distribution improves (see Table 4).

What makes the use of these predicates by learners different from native use? Column "#B" in Table 4 presents the mean of the frequency bands and shows that most of these predicates come from the first two frequency bands, so they

---

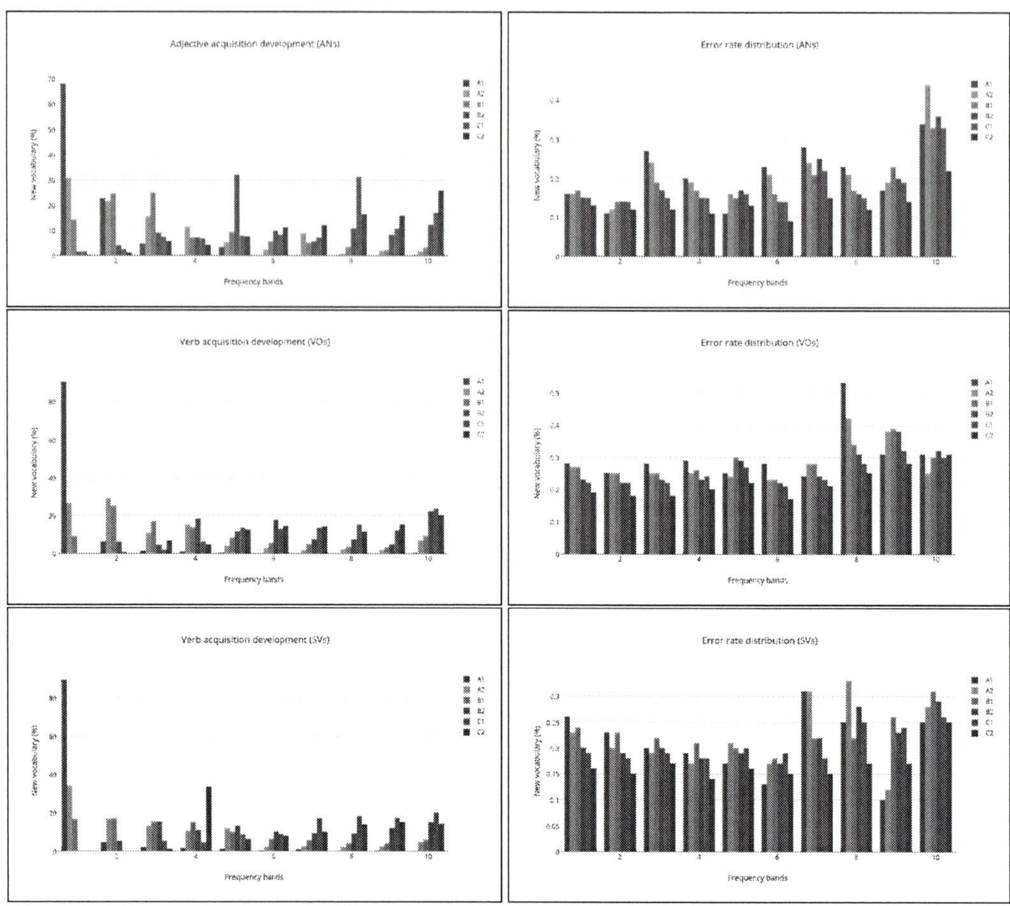

Figure 1: Predicates acquisition and error rate distribution across levels.

represent frequent words that are overused by the learners. We calculate the average error rates for the combinations with these predicates (column "*ErR*") and compare them to the average error rate over all predicates for each level (in parentheses). For adjectives and verbs in VOs the error rates are comparable or below the average error rate at the lower levels, and higher than the average at the upper levels. Verbs in SVs demonstrate an opposite trend: at the lower levels error rates associated with the use of these predicates are higher than average, while at the upper levels they are comparable or lower. We conclude that the differences in the distributions at the lower levels are caused by the overuse of the basic vocabulary, while towards the upper levels it is due to occasionally incorrect use of more diverse vocabulary.

The rightmost columns of Table 3 also compare the distribution of the ANs, VOs and SVs in the learner data to those in the native English data. We note that, similarly to the distribution of the predicates, the use of the content word combinations becomes more similar to native use towards higher levels of language proficiency, and to further confirm our hypothesis about the peculiar use of language at C2, we observe a disruption of this trend at C2 level for VOs and SVs. We also note that the development goes at quicker pace between A1 through to B2, and slows down at the upper levels.

4.2 L1 effects

L1 influence on the word choice has been extensively studied by SLA researchers (Siyanova-Chanturia, 2015; Paquot and Granger, 2012). It seems reasonable to expect that the similarity between one's L1 and L2 should facilitate semantic acquisition in L2: for example, if L1 and L2 belong to the same language group, they can be expected to bear considerable semantic similarities that might help learners acquire semantic knowl-

	Lvl	Predicates	#B	ErR
adj	A1	dear, mobile, favorite, other, national, blue, nice, pink, international, young	1.5	0.15 (0.16)
	A2	dear, mobile, favorite, local, national, nice, social, blue, pink, young	1.5	0.14 (0.16)
	B1	dear, best, nice, national, wealthy, beautiful, big, good, english, funny	1.4	0.15 (0.17)
	B2	dear, good, british, nice, wealthy, best, national, wonderful, important, big	1.3	0.15 (0.16)
	C1	dear, national, upward, wealthy, british, english, negative, bad, full, important	1.8	0.17 (0.15)
	C2	wealthy, national, dear, full, british, important, further, current, serial, european	1.4	0.15 (0.13)
v_{VO}	A1	buy, paint, like, watch, go, wear, bring, play, provide, make	1.1	0.28 (0.28)
	A2	buy, paint, provide, like, go, watch, attend, wear, book, confirm	1.2	0.26 (0.27)
	B1	buy, watch, include, provide, like, go, spend, offer, film, love	1.2	0.22 (0.27)
	B2	include, provide, spend, rent, support, contain, follow, raise, create, cover	1.1	0.26 (0.24)
	C1	include, excel, improve, concern, provide, solve, show, reach, spend, allow	1.4	0.21 (0.22)
	C2	spend, broaden, offer, earn, solve, allow, require, cover, use, enable	1.3	0.21 (0.19)
v_{SV}	A1	cost, make, use, park, have, show, find, say, wish, take	1.1	0.31 (0.25)
	A2	cost, use, include, make, provide, park, say, attend, find, show	1.1	0.27 (0.22)
	B1	include, like, wish, watch, provide, require, spend, set, decrease, amaze	1.4	0.22 (0.23)
	B2	increase, like, include, reward, decrease, interest, spend, provide, require, involve	1.4	0.20 (0.20)
	C1	increase, decrease, include, spend, like, change, say, show, improve, apply	1.2	0.20 (0.19)
	C2	include, increase, spend, frame, live, like, require, provide, set, base	1.3	0.16 (0.16)

Table 4: Top 10 predicates contributing to the difference between learner and native language distribution

	Lvl	GE	RM	AS
adj	A1	4.3318	3.5133	3.8219
	A2	3.3723	3.2955	3.2837
	B1	2.3309	2.3874	1.7002
	B2	1.4971	1.4109	1.3849
	C1	1.1840	1.1088	1.2562
	C2	**1.2880**	1.0543	**1.3716**
v_{VO}	A1	2.1994	2.0347	2.0446
	A2	1.6371	1.6478	1.6204
	B1	1.3751	1.2139	0.9772
	B2	0.9280	0.7363	0.8622
	C1	**0.9389**	0.7050	0.8164
	C2	**0.9806**	**0.7512**	**0.9465**
v_{SV}	A1	2.2841	1.3059	1.3300
	A2	1.6275	1.1930	1.2918
	B1	1.1583	0.9629	0.8604
	B2	0.8576	0.6862	**0.8636**
	C1	**0.8631**	0.6326	0.8158
	C2	**0.8818**	**0.7098**	**0.9283**

Table 5: Predicate distributions per language groups (*KL*)

speakers. We hypothesise that since Asian L1s are very different from English, the speakers of these languages may prefer to use prefabricated phrases more often than speakers of Germanic L1s, which makes their language more native-like. Similar hypotheses have been formulated earlier: for example, Gilquin and Granger (2011) noted that learners, especially at the lower levels, are likely to repeat expressions that are familiar to them and appear to be safe, and Hulstijn and Marchena (1989) noted that learners tend to rely on "play-it-safe" strategy rather than experiment unless they are confident in their vocabulary knowledge. We assume that speakers of Germanic L1s might feel more confident in their semantic knowledge and as a result be more "adventurous" in their use of English than speakers of Asian L1s. Our experiments on the individual L1s within each group show same trends as observed for L1 groups.

4.3 Selectional preference patterns

Finally, we investigate how selectional preference patterns develop across proficiency levels and whether they approximate native English patterns. For each predicate in learner and native data, we form argument clusters using the methodology described in §3.2, estimate SP strength for the predicates at each level using eq. 3, and then apply KL divergence and PCC to measure the difference.

Table 6 overviews the similarity between the SP models in learner and native data for the arguments and argument clusters (see columns with *cl*). As before, we observe that the SP models in

edge in L2, while one may expect to observe slower learning pace for speakers of more distant L1s (Gilquin and Granger, 2011).

To test to what extent L1 exerts influence on L2 semantic knowledge acquisition, we consider three language groups – Germanic L1s (GE) that belong to the same group as English (EN), Romance L1s (RM) that represent a different group within the same family of the Indo-European languages, and Asian L1s (AS) representing a group of languages most distant from English among the three.[5] We measure KL divergence for the three pairs, GE–EN, RM–EN and AS–EN, on the distribution of the predicates.

The results reported in Table 5 contradict our original assumption as we observe that the variety of English used by speakers of Romance L1s is closer to native English than the variety used by speakers of Germanic L1s. Furthermore, the variety of English used by speakers of Asian L1s, especially at the lower levels, is more similar to native English than the variety used by Germanic L1

---

[5] GE include Danish, Dutch, German, Norwegian and Swedish; RM include French, Italian, Portuguese, Romanian and Spanish; AS include Thai, Vietnamese and different varieties of Chinese.

	Lvl	PCC	KL	PCC_{cl}	KL_{cl}
AN	A1	0.1661	0.1481	0.2835	0.1980
	A2	0.4375	0.0843	0.5449	0.1149
	B1	0.5808	0.0494	0.5597	0.0897
	B2	0.6133	0.0395	0.5940	0.0765
	C1	0.6526	0.0372	0.6408	0.0729
	C2	**0.6428**	0.0364	**0.5866**	**0.0762**
VO	A1	0.4959	0.0966	0.5976	0.1533
	A2	**0.3893**	0.0917	**0.5414**	0.1430
	B1	0.6181	0.0579	0.7429	0.0810
	B2	0.6759	0.0412	**0.6987**	0.0749
	C1	0.7172	0.0354	0.7576	0.0634
	C2	**0.7168**	**0.0379**	0.7609	**0.0645**
SV	A1	0.6069	0.1254	0.4475	0.1722
	A2	**0.6061**	0.0956	0.4934	0.1604
	B1	**0.6053**	0.0837	0.5008	0.1538
	B2	0.6500	0.0612	**0.4248**	0.1515
	C1	0.6539	0.0553	0.4972	0.1306
	C2	0.6599	**0.0595**	0.5164	**0.1418**

Table 6: Selectional preference distribution

	Predicate	Learner language	Native language
AN	additional	worker, teacher, staff	information, item, detail
	kind	girl, woman, person	consent, permission, approval
VO	reserve	bathroom, hall, room	privilege, right, status
	stipulate	price, rent, salary	rule, need, norm
SV	bind	treaty, contract, deal	gene, tissue, cell
	reflect	gear, clothes, mask	rise, change, improvement

Table 7: Examples of the most strongly associated arguments

learner data become more similar to those in native language towards upper levels. Both ANs and VOs show the biggest improvements between A2 and B1, and we observe the disruption in this trend at the levels A2 and C2 (we mark those in bold).

Next, we look into the set of predicates that have the most different SP patterns in the learner and native language, and using eq. 4, identify the argument cluster that is most strongly associated with each of these predicates in the learner and native data. For the sake of space, in Table 7 we present only some illustrative examples from different levels and combination types.[6] The experiments suggest that the difference between the learner and native SP models might be due to the learners' use of concrete nouns with the adjectives and verbs where native speakers prefer abstract nouns.

To further investigate this hypothesis, we identify 10 predicates per combination type and proficiency level with the most distinct selectional preference patterns. Using the MRC Psycholinguistic Database (Wilson, 1988), we calculate the average concreteness score for the arguments clusters in learner and native data. Our results show that at the lower levels learners use more concrete arguments than native speakers, with the difference statistically significant at 0.05 with t-test, while the difference becomes less pronounced towards C1-C2 levels. Our results for productive vocabulary knowledge corroborate previous findings on the relation between receptive vocabulary knowledge and acquisition of abstract concepts (Tanaka et al., 2013; Vajjala and Meurers, 2014).

The results show that the difference in selectional preference patterns between the learner and native language is due to the concreteness of the selected arguments. This may reflect (1) the difficulty in acquiring semantics of abstract concepts in L2, or, alternatively, (2) L1-based instructional practices that may focus first on teaching concrete concepts before abstract concepts. The awareness of this discrepancy can serve as further guidance for language instructors and learners, and help make one's language use more native-like.

5   Discussion and conclusions

This paper reports the results of a large-scale corpus-based exploratory study of semantic knowledge acquisition by L2 learners. In contrast to previous work, we ran experiments on a wider scale, using a large learner corpus, and at finer granularity, investigating L2 development across 6 CEFR proficiency levels. We show that (1) the learners tend to overuse highly frequent English words across all proficiency levels, although towards the higher levels the lexical distributions in learner and in native language become more similar; (2) the two peaks of vocabulary acquisition are associated with the transition between beginner and intermediate levels (A2-B1), and between the two proficient levels (C1-C2); (3) lexical distribution at upper proficient level (C2) is less similar to native distribution than at lower proficient level (C1) which may be due to the more creative language use at C2; (4) the variety of English used by speakers of more distant L1s at lower levels of proficiency is closer to native English than the variety used by speakers of closer L1s, which might be an effect of "play-it-safe" strategy adopted by learners; (5) concrete nouns tend to be more strongly associated with the predicates in learner language than abstract nouns. The methodology presented in this paper can help identify the gaps in learner vocabulary knowledge and tailor vocabulary acquisition exercises to the needs of learners at dif-

---

[6]Full lists are available at `www.cl.cam.ac.uk/~ek358/vocab-acquisition.html`.

ferent proficiency levels.

We admit that potential topic and genre bias of learner exams data is a limitation of our corpus-based approach. We believe that corpus-based studies of the type presented in this paper will facilitate further research into semantic knowledge development, although it is possible that learner corpora provide only limited access to productive learner vocabulary. As Siyanova-Chanturia (2015) notes "in an ideal world, one would use the same topic across and within all tested levels, but in a language classroom, this is hardly possible". The future work will investigate possible solutions for this problem such as (1) augmentation of the data with other learner corpora, (2) use of fill-in-the-gaps exercises that test vocabulary knowledge directly, and (3) sampling of the native data to more closely reflect the selection of topics in the learner data.

Acknowledgments

We are grateful to the BEA reviewers for their helpful and instructive feedback. Ekaterina Kochmar's research is supported by Cambridge English Language Assessment via the ALTA Institute. Ekaterina Shutova's research is supported by the Leverhulme Trust Early Career Fellowship.

References

J. C. Alderson, editor. 2005. *Diagnosing Foreign Language Proficiency: The Interface between Learning and Assessment*. London; New York: Continuum.

R. A. Alejo Gonzalez. 2010. L2 Spanish acquisition of English phrasal verbs: a cognitive linguistic analysis of L1 influence. In *M. C. Campoy-Cubillo, B. Belles-Fortuno, & M. L. Gea-Valor (eds.), Corpus-based approaches to English language teaching*, London, UK: Continuum, pages 149–166.

G. Aston. 1995. *Corpora in language pedagogy: Matching theory and practice. In G. Cook & B. Seidlhofer (eds.), Principle and Practice in Applied Linguistics: Studies in Honour of H.G. Widdowson*, Oxford: Oxford University Press, pages 257–270.

J. Bahns and M. Eldaw. 1993. Should we teach EFL students collocations? *System* 21:101–114.

S. Bergsma and D. Yarowsky. 2013. Learning Domain-Specific, L1-Specific Measures of Word Readability. *TAL* 54(1):203–226.

C. Brew and S. Schulte im Walde. 2002. Spectral clustering for German verbs. In *Proceedings of EMNLP*. pages 117–124.

E. Briscoe, J. Carroll, and R. Watson. 2006. The Second Release of the RASP System. In *Proceedings of the 21st International Conference on Computational Linguistics and 44th Annual Meeting of the Association for Computational Linguistics (COLING-ACL 2006) Interactive Presentation Sessions*. pages 59–68.

L. Burnard, editor. 2007. *Reference Guide for the British National Corpus*. Research Technologies Service at Oxford University Computing Services.

The Council of Europe. 2011a. Common European Framework of Reference for Languages: Learning, Teaching, Assessment.

The Council of Europe. 2011b. Forms for detailed analysis of examinations or tests.

S. De Cock. 2004. Preferred sequences of words in NS and NNS speech. *Belgian Journal of English Language and Literature (BELL), New Series* 2:225–246.

P. Durrant and N. Schmitt. 2009. To what extent do native and non-native writers make use of collocations? *International Review of Applied Linguistics* 47:157–177.

C. Engber. 1995. The relationship of lexical proficiency to the quality of ESL compositions. *Journal of Second Language Writing* 4:139–155.

A. Ferraresi, E. Zanchetta, M. Baroni, and S. Bernardini. 2008. Introducing and evaluating ukWaC, a very large web-derived corpus of English. In *Proceedings of the 4th Web as Corpus Workshop (WAC-4)*. pages 47–54.

D. Ferris. 1994. Lexical and syntactic features of ESL writing by students at different levels of L2 proficiency. *TESOL Quarterly* 28:414–420.

P. Foster. 2010. Rules and routines: a consideration of their role in the task-based language production of native and non-native speakers. In *M. Bygate, P. Skehan, & M. Swain (eds.), Researching pedagogic tasks: Second language learning, teaching and testing*, Harlow, UK: Longman, pages 75–93.

L. Frase, J. Faletti, A. Ginther, and L. Grant. 1999. Computer Analysis of the TOEFL Test of Written English. Technical report, Princeton, NJ: Educational Testing Service.

G. Gilquin. 2007. To err is not all. What corpus and elicitation can reveal about the use of collocations by learners. *Zeitschrift fur Anglistik und Amerikanistik* 55:273–291.

G. Gilquin and S. Granger. 2011. From EFL to ESL: Evidence from the International Corpus of Learner English. In *Mukherjee J., Exploring Second-Language Varieties of English and Learner Englishes: Bridging a Paradigm Gap*, John Benjamins Publishing Company: Amsterdam and Philadelphia, pages 55–78.

S. Granger and Y. Bestgen. 2014. The use of collocations by intermediate vs. advanced non-native writers: A bigram-based study. *International Review of Applied Linguistics in Language Teaching (IRAL)* 52:229–252.

L. Grant and A. Ginther. 2000. Using Computer-Tagged Linguistic Features to Describe L2 Writing Differences. *Journal of Second Language Writing* 9(2):123–145.

H. Gyllstad, L. Vilkait/e, and N. Schmitt. 2015. Assessing vocabulary size through multiple-choice formats: issues with guessing and sampling rates. *International Journal of Applied Linguistics (ITL)* 166(2):278–306.

M. Hoey. 1991. *Patterns of lexis in text*. Oxford: Oxford University Press.

J. Hulstijn and E. Marchena. 1989. Avoidance: Grammatical or semantic causes? *Studies in Second Language Acquisition* 11(3):241–255.

C. James. 1998. *Errors in Language Learning and Use: Exploring Error Analysis*. London: Longman.

G. Kjellmer. 1991. *A mint of phrases. In K. Aijmer & B. Altenberg (eds.), English Corpus Linguistics: Studies in Honour of Jan Svartvik*, Harlow, Essex: Longman, pages 111–127.

B. Laufer and T. Waldman. 1995. Vocabulary Size and Use: Lexical Richness in L2 Written Production. *Applied Linguistics* 16(3):307–322.

B. Laufer and T. Waldman. 2011. Verb-noun collocations in second language writing: a corpus analysis of learners' English. *Language Learning* 61:647–672.

C. Leacock, M. Chodorow, M. Gamon, and J. Tetreault. 2014. *Automated Grammatical Error Detection for Language Learners*. Morgan & Claypool Publishers, second edition.

G. Lorenz. 1999. *Adjective intensification e Learners versus native speakers. A corpus study of argumentative writing*. Rodopi, Amsterdam.

D. J. C. MacKay. 2003. *Information Theory, Inference, and Learning Algorithms (First ed.)*. Cambridge University Press.

I. S. P. Nation. 2006. How Large a Vocabulary Is Needed For Reading and Listening? *The Canadian Modern Language Review/La Revue canadienne des langues vivantes* 63(1):59–82.

I. S. P. Nation. 2012. Vocabulary Size Test Instructions and Description. https://www.victoria.ac.nz/lals/about/staff/paul-nation.

N. Nesselhauf. 2005. *Collocations in a learner corpus*. John Benjamins, Amsterdam.

D. Nicholls. 2003. The Cambridge Learner Corpus: Error coding and analysis for lexicography and ELT. In *Proceedings of the Corpus Linguistics 2003 Conference*. pages 572–581.

M. Paquot and S. Granger. 2012. Formulaic language in learner corpora. *Annual Review of Applied Linguistics* 32:130–149.

P. Resnik. 1993. Selection and Information: A Class-based Approach to Lexical Relationships. Technical report, University of Pennsylvania.

C. C. Shei and H. Pain. 2000. An ESL Writer's Collocation Aid. *Computer Assisted Language Learning* 13(2):167–182.

A. Siyanova-Chanturia. 2015. Collocation in beginner learner writing: A longitudinal study. *System* 53:148–160.

L. Sun and A. Korhonen. 2009. Improving Verb Clustering with Automatically Acquired Selectional Preferences. In *Proceedings of EMNLP*. pages 638–647.

S. Tanaka, A. Jatowt, M. P. Kato, and K. Tanaka. 2013. Estimating Content Concreteness for Finding Comprehensible Documents. In *Proceedings of the sixth ACM international conference on Web search and data mining (WSDM'13)*. pages 475–484.

J. Thewissen. 2008. The phraseological errors of French-, German-, and Spanish speaking EFL learners: Evidence from an error-tagged learner corpus. In *Proceedings from the 8th Teaching and Language Corpora Conference (TaLC8)*. pages 300–306.

J. Thewissen. 2013. Capturing L2 Development Through Learner Corpus Analysis. *Modern Language Journal (special issue on capturing the dynamics of L2 development through learner corpus analysis)* 97:77–101.

S. Vajjala and D. Meurers. 2014. Readability Assessment for Text Simplification: From Analyzing Documents to Identifying Sentential Simplifications. *International Journal of Applied Linguistics, Special Issue on Current Research in Readability and Text Simplification* pages 1–23.

B. Waibel. 2008. *Phrasal verbs: German and Italian learners of English compared*. VDM, Saarbrucken, Germany.

M. D. Wilson. 1988. The MRC Psycholinguistic Database: Machine Readable Dictionary, Version 2. *Behavioral Research Methods, Instruments and Computers* 20:6–11.

S. Wulff and S. T. Gries. 2011. Corpus-driven methods for assessing accuracy in learner production. In *Second Language Task Complexity: Researching the Cognition Hypothesis of language learning and performance*, Peter Robinson (eds.): John Benjamins Publishing, pages 61–87.

Multiple Choice Question Generation Utilizing An Ontology

Katherine Stasaski and **Marti Hearst**
UC Berkeley
{katie_stasaski, hearst}@berkeley.edu

Abstract

Ontologies provide a structured representation of concepts and the relationships which connect them. This work investigates how a pre-existing educational Biology ontology can be used to generate useful practice questions for students by using the connectivity structure in a novel way. It also introduces a novel way to generate multiple-choice distractors from the ontology, and compares this to a baseline of using embedding representations of nodes.

An assessment by an experienced science teacher shows a significant advantage over a baseline when using the ontology for distractor generation. A subsequent study with three science teachers on the results of a modified question generation algorithm finds significant improvements. An in-depth analysis of the teachers' comments yields useful insights for any researcher working on automated question generation for educational applications.

1 Introduction

An important educational application of NLP is the generation of study questions to help students practice and study a topic, as a step toward mastery learning (Polozov et al., 2015). Although much research exists in automated question generation the techniques needed for educational applications require a level of precision that is not always present in these approaches.

Ontologies have the potential to be uniquely beneficial for educational question generation because they allow concepts to be connected in non-traditional ways. Questions can be generated about different concepts' properties which span different areas of a textbook or even different educational resources.

However, ontologies are not commonly used in NLP approaches to generate complex, multi-part questions. This may be due to concern about ontology's incompleteness and the fact that they are usually structured for other purposes.

In this work, we describe a novel method for generating complex multiple choice questions using an ontology, with the aim of testing a student's understanding of the bigger picture of how concepts interact, beyond just a definition question. This technique generates questions that help achieve understanding at the second level of Bloom's taxonomy (Bloom et al., 1956). We also generate multiple choice distractors using several ontology- and embedding-based approaches.

We report on two different studies. The first assesses both the questions and the question distractors with one domain expert, a middle school science teacher. This finds evidence that the ontology-based approach generates novel and useful practice questions. Based on the findings from that study, we adjust the question generation algorithm and report on a subsequent evaluation in which three experts quantitatively rank and qualitatively comment on a larger selection of questions. The results are strong, with more than 60 questions out of 90 receiving positive ratings from two of the judges. Additionally, we categorize and provide in-depth analysis of qualitative feedback and use this to inform multiple future directions to improve educational practice question generation.

2 Related Work

Prior work has explored both automatically generating educational ontologies from text and utilizing expert-created ontologies for other tasks. For instance, Olney et al. (2011) explored extracting

Proceedings of the 12th Workshop on Innovative Use of NLP for Building Educational Applications, pages 303–312
Copenhagen, Denmark, September 8, 2017. ©2017 Association for Computational Linguistics

nodes and relationships from text to build a concept map ontology automatically from textbooks. Other work has also attempted to build ontologies from non-educational texts (Benafia et al., 2015; Szulman et al., 2010) and has explored utilizing crowd-sourcing to build an ontology from text (Getman and Karasiuk, 2014).

Prior approaches to question generation from ontologies have involved hand-crafted rules to transform a relationship into a question (Olney et al., 2012b; Papasalouros et al., 2008; Ou et al., 2008). However, these approaches mainly generate questions for a single fact and do not combine multiple pieces of information together to create more complex questions. There is the potential to explore other, more complex, types of question generation procedures from the ontology. Approaches have also utilized online questions for ontology-driven generation, but this is less generalizable (Abacha et al., 2016).

Prior work aimed at generating educational practice questions has generated questions directly from text using a series of manual translations and a ranking procedure to determine quality (Heilman and Smith, 2010, 2009; Heilman, 2011).

Other work has focused on question generation, independent of an educational context. A large-scale question generation task posed to the community prompted a focus on factual question generation from texts and knowledge bases (Rus et al., 2008; Graesser et al., 2012). Approaches have included factual generation directly from text (Brown et al., 2005; Mannem et al., 2010; Mazidi and Tarau, 2016; Yao et al., 2012) as well as generation from knowledge bases (Olney et al., 2012a).

Recent advances in text generation have used neural generative models to create interestingly worded questions (Serban et al., 2016; Indurthi et al., 2017). However, because we are using a human created ontology and lack specialized training data, we utilize hand-crafted rules for generation.

3 Question Generation

We utilize an educational Biology ontology to generate multiple choice questions, which consist of the text of a question, the correct answer, and three distractor multiple choice candidates.

3.1 Dataset

We use an expert-curated ontology documenting K-12 Biology concepts (Fisher, 2010) designed

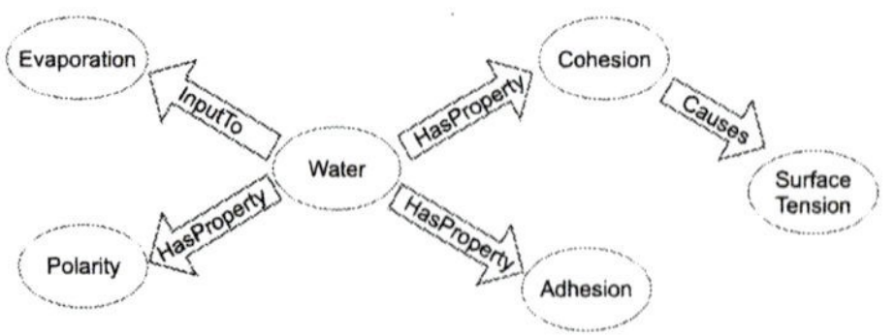

Figure 1: Selected part of the Biology ontology.

for educational applications. While more resources could be used to accomplish this task, we only utilize the ontology to explore the efficacy of this question generation approach. By utilizing an expert-curated ontology instead of an automatically generated one, we operate under the assumption that the ontology is correct and complete. Future work can explore utilizing this method in conjunction with other educational resources and techniques.

The ontology contains 1,260 unique concept nodes and 227 unique relationship types with a total of 3,873 node-relationship-node triples. The average outgoing degree is 7. Figure 1 shows a small sample.

3.2 Using The Structure of the Ontology

The novel aspect of our approach is the manner in which we use an ontology to go beyond simple factoid question generation. Rather than generating a question from a node-relation-node triple, this algorithm makes use of the graph structure of the ontology to create complex questions that link different concepts, with the aim of challenging the student to piece together different concepts.

The goal of this evaluation was to determine if this novel way of combining concepts would be judged as creating useful, coherent questions for testing students.

To create these novel structured questions, the algorithm chooses a node to act as the answer, and from three randomly-chosen outgoing links it generates a question. The relations of the outgoing links and the nodes on the other ends are used to form the question words. For instance, from the node "Water" emanates the links (DissolvesIn, "salt"), (HasProperty, "cohesion"), and (InputTo, "evaporation") from which is generated the question "What dissolves salt, has cohesion, and is an input to evaporation? (Water)"

A total of 992,926 questions can be generated via this method from the ontology. These questions are distributed over 426 nodes, with the average number of questions that can be generated per node being 2,330. While 834 nodes do not have three outgoing links to generate a question from, these nodes can be chosen as properties to commpose other questions.

3.3 Generating Distractors

Good multiple choice questions should have distractors (alternative answers to distract the student from the correct answer). These should not be synonymous with the correct answer, but should be a plausible answer which should not be so far-fetched as to be obviously incorrect.

We experimented with several different ways of generating multiple choice distractors using the structure of the ontology, and compared these with two embedding based methods. In each case, if the text of a distractor overlaps with the correct answer, we do not use it.

3.4 Ontology Distractor Generation

We experimented with 5 different ontology-based distractor methods. For each distractor generation method, the correct answer node, n is connected to three property nodes $n1, n2$, and $n3$ via relationships $r1, r2$, and $r3$ respectively. In order to ensure that distractor node m does not correctly answer the question, we make sure at least one of $n1, n2$, or $n3$ does not connect to m. The following methods are illustrated in Figure 2.

Two Matching Relationships: This method chooses m such that m is connected to $n1$ via $r1$ and m is connected to $n2$ via $r2$.

One Matching and One New Relationship: This method chooses m such that m is connected to $n1$ via $r1$ and m is connected to $n2$ via a different relationship, $r4 \neq r2$.

Two New Relationships: This method chooses m such that m is connected to $n1$ via a different relationship type $r4 \neq r2$ and m is connected to $n2$ via a different relationship, $r5 \neq r3$.

One Matching Relationship: This method chooses m such that m is connected to $n1$ via $r1$.

We also examined an additional question-independent ontology-grounded approach.

Node Structure: This approach rates pairs of nodes by similarity, where similarity is determined by their tendency to link to similar relation types and to link to the same intermediate nodes. More formally, let c_n denote the set of nodes which are connected to any node n and let $l_{n,r}$ denote the

number of connections that n has of type r. The similarity between n and m is computed as:

$$s_{n,m} = count(c_n \cap c_m) - \sum_r |l_{n,r} - l_{m,r}|$$

3.5 Embedding Distractors

We implemented two methods to generate distractors grounded in the embeddings of the nodes. Both utilize pre-trained word embeddings (Mikolov et al., 2013). A given node n consists of a series of words, $w_1, w_2, ..., w_n$. We create a multi-word embedding by distributing weight and placing more emphasis on the last word in a sequence, which we assume to be the head word. The similarity s between the two embedded nodes e_n and e_m is determined by cosine similarity.

Correct Answer Embeddings: are generated by comparing the correct answer, n with the most similar node in the graph G:

$$\text{distractor} = \arg\max_{m \in G} s_{e_n, e_m}$$

Question Component Embeddings: are generated by finding the most similar node to the question components n_1, n_2, and n_3. The above equation is computed for each component.

3.6 Ontology Coverage

Each of these methods is applicable to a subset of nodes in the ontology. From a randomly sampled selection of 10,000 questions, 15.6% met requirements for Two Matching Relationship Distractors, 16.2% met requirements for One Matching, One New Distractors, 29.1% met requirements for Two New Relationship Distractors, and 25.6% met requirements for One Matching Relationship Distractors. Node Structure, Correct Answer Embeddings, and Question Component Embeddings all had complete coverage due to the nature of the methods.

3.7 Pedagogical Motivation

This question generated method is similar to an inverse of the "Feature Specification" questions described by Graessner et al (1992) in which students are asked to describe properties of a concept. An example format of this type of question is "Which qualitative attributes does entity X have?" (Graesser et al., 1992). Instead of prompting students to list properties of a concept, we provide

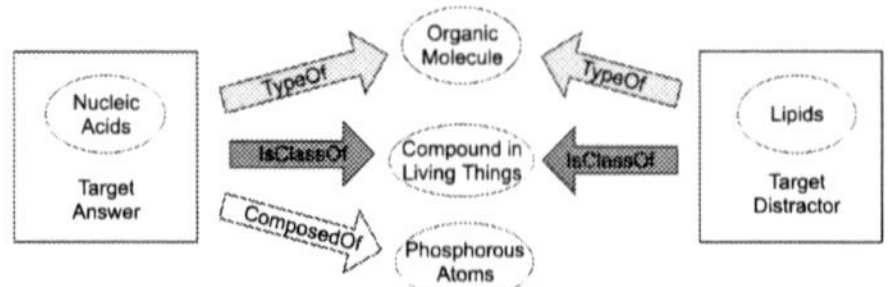

Two Matching Relationships: "What is a type of organic molecule, is a class of compound in living things, and is composed of phosphorous atoms?"

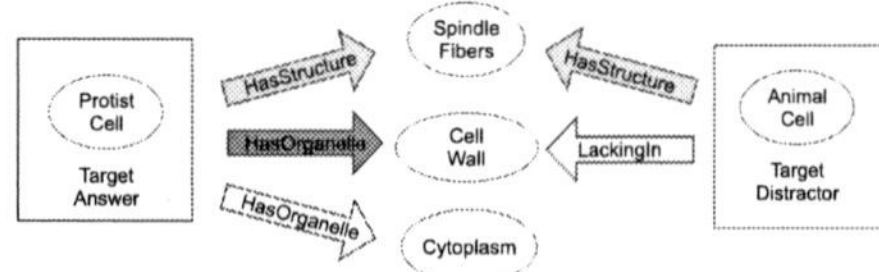

One Matching, One New Relationship: "What has structure spindle fibers, has organelle cell wall, and has organelle cytoplasm?"

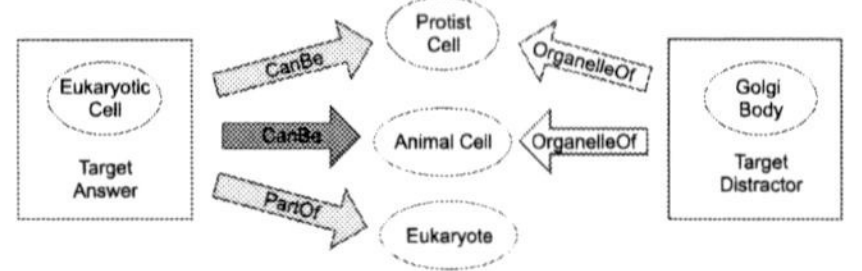

Two New Relationships: "What can be protist cell, can be animal cell, and is a part of a Eukaryote?"

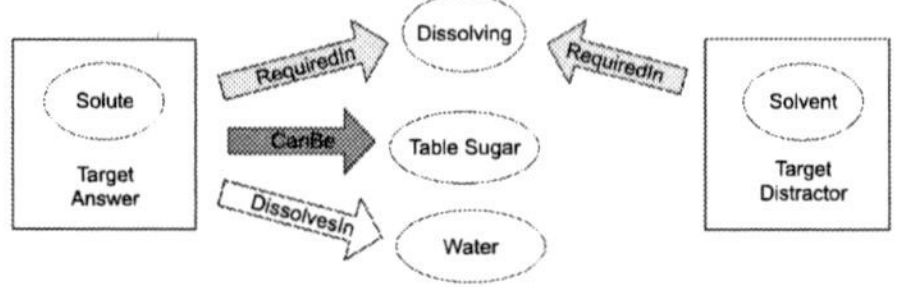

One Matching Relationship: "What is required in dissolving, can be table sugar, and dissolves in water?"

Figure 2: Question-specific distractor generation methods. Correct answer nodes are leftmost in each graph, and chosen distractor nodes are rightmost.

three features of concepts and ask the students to choose the correct concept given the features.

Through these questions, we aim to challenge students to connect different features of a concept while working within the constraints that the questions and corresponding answers be able to be generated via the ontology. The type of questions that arise are intended for mastery learning, in which students learn simpler facts about a concept before tackling more difficult conceptual problems (Polozov et al., 2015). While the questions are not critical thinking ones, they are designed to be more complex than a simple definition question and to be a gateway to more difficult questions.

Another potential application of these questions is preparation for extracurricular trivia competitions, such as Quiz Bowl[1]. One type of question asked at these competitions is one which lists many characteristics of a concept and challenges students to quickly identify the concept. Connecting multiple facets of a concept are essential to answer these questions.

3.8 Generating the Text

Because the purpose of this study was to examine the feasibility of the ontology structure for question generation, we use hand-crafted rules to produce the question text. The human-generated ontology has nodes and relationships that are worded

Relationship	Rule
Has Characteristic -	If n = verb → "n."
	If n = noun → "has n. "
	If n = adjective → "is n."
HasProcess	"has a process called n."
CanBe	"can be a/an n."

Table 1: Common relationship types and rule-methods used to generate the question segment.

somewhat naturally, which helped this process. We devised simple relationship-to-text translations rules; examples are shown in Table 1.

4 Study 1

4.1 Method

We conducted a study to assess the quality of the questions and distractors. We asked a middle school science teacher with 20 years of experience to rate the quality of 20 complex questions on a scale of 1-7. The scale was explained such that 1 was "Poor," 4 was "OK," and 7 was "Excellent." To create the test set, we randomly selected nodes and generated questions about them [2].

We also asked the teacher to rate distractors on a scale of 1-5 (a narrower scale was chosen as it was thought these would be more difficult to differen-

---

[1] https://www.naqt.com/about-quiz-bowl.html

[2] Full text of questions evaluated in both studies can be found in an appendix in the supplementary materials.

tiate than the questions). Each distractor method was tested with 10 different questions (each with 3 distractors). Questions were randomly chosen from all possible questions that could be generated from the ontology, and were disregarded if a given distractor method was not able to generate three valid distractors. For both processes described above, the teacher was prompted to enter optional comments about the question or distractors.

4.2 Results

Quantitative distractor generation results can be seen in Table 2. The difference in ontology-generated distractors compared to embedding-generated distractors was significant using a t-test with p value < 0.001. Comparing the highest-performing ontology and embedding methods (One Matching, One New Relationship and Correct Answer Embedding) is also significant under the t-test with $p < 0.05$. This indicates that while the overall feedback was critical, there is promise in using ontology over embedding distractors.

The questions' ratings averaged 2.25 out of 7. After analyzing the qualitative comments, this can be attributed primarily to the unnatural wording of the questions. Qualitative comments about the questions are categorized in Table 3.

4.3 Discussion

All ontology distractor methods except for One Matching Relationship received explicit comments pointing out that the distractors were "good," while no embedding approach received these comments. This indicates that the combination of different methods have strengths that contribute to a good set of distractors. The Node Structure method provides broad distractors, while the other methods provide question-specific ones. For example, the distractors "cell wall," "chloroplast," and "central vacuole" for the question "What is an organelle of eukaryotic cell, is an organelle of animal cell, and is an organelle of fungal cell? (Golgi body)" are plausible but incorrect.

However, the teacher also commented that some distractors of both embedding and ontology methods were "poor." Examining the "poor" distractors for embedding questions shows that the distractors can come from concept areas unrelated to the question. For instance, for the question "What contains chromosome, is an organelle of eukaryotic cell, and is a type of organelle? (nucleus),"

Distractor Type	Avg
Two Matching Relationships	2.37
One Matching, One New Relationship	2.78
Two New Relationships	2.03
One Matching Relationship	2.07
Node Structure	2.63
Correct Answer Embedding	2.10
Question Component Embedding	1.60

Table 2: Averaged distractor scores.

Type of Comment	Count
Unnatural Wording of Question	31
Good question	24
OK question	17
Unnatural Grouping of Characteristics	2
Text of Node was Confusing	2
Imprecise Relationship	1
Not Middle School Level	1

Table 3: Categorization of qualitative feedback for questions. Feedback was included for all questions, including those in the distractor section.

the Question Component Embeddings generated "new genetic recombinations" as a distractor.

By contrast, the ontology-generated distractors were marked "poor" when the question included one unique property. For example, for the question "What eats mice, eats deer, and is a type of predator? (mountain lion)," the improbable distractor "vole" was chosen because it eats mice and is a predator. This suggests the necessity of more formal reasoning and real world knowledge coupled with the ontology information.

There were also instances in which the proposed distractors were unintentionally correct answers. For the embedding-generated distractors, this happened because the method favors distractors that are more similar to the correct answer. For the ontology-generated distractors, this occurred where the ontology was incomplete.

While the distractor evaluation is quite preliminary as it only involves one expert evaluating 10 sets of distractors per generation method, these results suggest the potential to explore an ontology method of distractor generation in future work.

5 Study 2

Based on these initial results, we extended the work in several ways. First, based on the results of Study 1, we found that the teacher was sensitive to any flaws of the wording of the questions, so we modified the assessment with questions that were manually touched up to remove grammatical errors. Second, although we had evidence that the ontology-based method was producing high-quality questions, we noticed that the target answers of many of the questions were quite general (e.g. "solids", "water"). Therefore, we modified the algorithm to take out-degree and relation commonality into account. We also decided to investigate questions composed of only two relations as well as three relations. Finally, we wanted to improve the evaluation in two ways: (i) by assessing more questions, and (ii) by having more independent judges per question. We accomplished this by finding assessors with appropriate backgrounds on an expert-oriented crowdwork site. Each of these modifications is described in detail below, along with results of this second evaluation.

5.1 Modifications to Generation Algorithm

We wanted to assess if the ontology generation method worked well, but were wondering if perhaps including three relations made the questions too complex or unusual. For this reason, we decided to include questions with only two relations in Study 2.

After adapting the question generation method to generate questions with two properties as opposed to three, given that the node "Evaporation" is connected to the two relations (Outputs, "water vapor") and (OppositeOf, "condensation"), the question generated from these two properties is: "What yields water vapor and is the opposite of condensation? (evaporation)."

Improving diversity of questions and coverage of the ontology were priorities in this study. We modified our question generation algorithm to prioritize these goals. We placed restrictions on the number of outgoing connections of a node $conn_n$ such that $5 < conn_n < 30$.

In addition, for two-property questions, we imposed the constraint that the collection of chosen properties yields exactly one unique correct answer. This added an additional check that the question generated was not about general properties that multiple nodes in the ontology fulfill.

For a random selection of 45 questions, we do not allow the algorithm to generate more than 2 questions about the same concept, to evaluate a more diverse set of questions. We also do not allow a node to be asked as a property involved in a question more than 5 times. This procedure was used for the selection of questions for the study below.

5.2 Manual Adjustments of Question Expression

The first experiment showed that the grammatical errors were distracting and affected the evaluation of the content of the questions. Therefore, we adjusted the grammatical correction rules as well as made minor edits by hand to ensure grammatical correctness. Some minor grammatical errors still exist, but major ones which obscure the meaning of the question were manually corrected. So, for instance, we fixed errors in the specification of articles, as seen in the removal of *a* and addition of *s* when transforming the question "What yields a RNA and is contained in chromosome? (gene)" to "What yields RNA and is contained in chromosomes? (gene)." These changes were made to a total of 16 questions. When a question was modified, the average number of changed characters was 3.3.

5.3 Evaluation of Question Quality

Three middle school science teachers, each with at least 10 years of experience, were recruited to evaluate the generated questions via Upwork[3], an expert-oriented freelance work matching site. Each teacher evaluated 90 questions (45 two-property and 45 three-property) both quantitatively on a scale from 1 to 7 and qualitatively via open-ended comments.

The title shown to the assessors was "Middle School Science Practice Question Evaluation" and the instructions for the assessment were:

> Below are shown some automatically generated biology questions, intended for practice studying. Please rate the quality of these questions for these purposes. Use the rating 1 to 7 where 1 = Poor, 4 = OK, and 7 = Excellent.
>
> Please ignore grammatical errors. For each question, please briefly explain your rating in one sentence.

We recognize that by informing teachers that the questions were generated automatically, they

---

[3] http://www.upwork.com

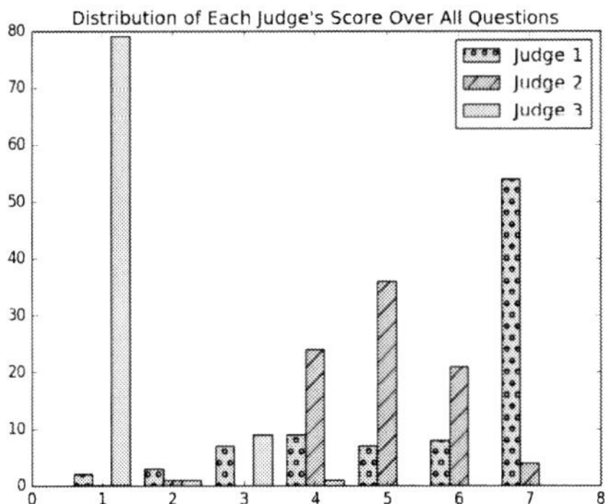

Figure 3: Distribution of judges' quantitative score over the 90 evaluated questions.

Evaluator	2R Questions	3R Questions
Evaluator 1	5.76	5.94
Evaluator 2	5.33	4.63
Evaluator 3	1.36	1.13
Average Score	**4.15**	**3.89**

Table 4: Quantitative feedback of question quality from the second study, scored on a scale from 1 to 7. 2R Questions are created from two relationships, 3R from three relationships.

could potentially be biased (either positively or negatively) when evaluating. However, because the generated questions are a new type of multiple-choice question, there is no naturally-arising human-generated baseline.

5.4 Results

Quantitative results from the second study can be viewed in Table 4. Both 2R and 3R questions achieved similar rankings, with no significant differences between the two (t-test, p=0.37). A histogram with judges' score distribution can be seen in Figure 3.

The qualitative results were analyzed and categorized in Table 5 and are discussed in the next subsection.

5.5 Discussion

Compared to the previous study, the fixing of grammatical errors allowed us to better determine the quality of the content of questions. While the evaluators did comment on the grammar of the questions and suggested corrections a total of 37 times, the quality of the content was able to be evaluated.

On the positive side, 77 questions were praised as being clear and easy to understand (see Table 5). We believe this is due to a combination of the two changes we made in response to the first study–improving the syntax and orienting the questions towards more specific answers.

Additionally, one teacher commented that 10 questions had particularly good properties. Two examples are: "What has a deoxyribose and occurs at the mitochondria? (DNA)" and "What includes carbon, is a part of organic molecule, and includes oxygen? (CHNOPS)." The updated algorithm ensured that the chosen properties were less vague and also not too specific.

In some cases, the evaluators had an explicit positive response to questions' logically grouping properties within questions. One teacher specifically pointed out that certain questions contained valuable properties which guide the students to the correct answer, as in: "What contrasts with plant cell and has an organelle called rough ER? (animal cell)". This provides positive support for the goal of this style of generating questions by include multiple pieces of information from the ontology.

The descriptive vocabulary of 8 questions was also pointed out by one evaluator, such as "What includes glucose, includes deoxyribose, and is a type of sugar? (monosaccharide)." Since we utilize a human-created ontology to generate questions, the nodes and relationships are often descriptive. Our generation method leverages this to create questions. Given an ontology with descriptive, precisely-worded relationships and nodes, questions generate via our method will reflect the diverse vocabulary.

On the negative side, one teacher was particularly skeptical of the ability of this method of questions to prepare students for standardized testing. She pointed out that this factual question style did not challenge students to think critically. While this is true, this is not the main focus of this work. We aim to over-generate simple practice questions to ensure students have adequate materials to practice and study with, before they have mastered a concept.

Two teachers specifically mentioned that the style of questions were repetitive. The lack of diversity of questions is something which can be addressed in future work. However, these stud-

Qualitative Feedback	Evaluator 1	Evaluator 2	Evaluator 3	Total
Clear and easy to understand	13	64	–	**77**
Simple to answer	20	–	–	**20**
Poor wording	–	3	16	**19**
Does not prepare for standardized test	–	–	19	**19**
Too many "What" questions	17	–	–	**17**
Vague/Broad	–	2	15	**17**
Confusing/Poor properties chosen	1	4	10	**15**
Too many options in question	9	1	1	**11**
Good chosen properties	10	–	–	**10**
Small rewording suggestion	–	8	2	**10**
Ontology flaw pointed out	–	5	4	**9**
More precise rewording suggestion	–	3	6	**9**
Descriptive vocab	8	–	–	**8**
Detailed question	7	–	–	**7**
"Trivia" question	–	–	6	**6**
Simple vocab	4	–	–	**4**
Too specific	–	–	4	**4**
Not a critical thinking question	–	–	4	**4**
Visual diagram needed	–	–	4	**4**
Good intermediate steps to guide to correct answer	4	–	–	**4**
Alternate phrasing for ontology node	–	2	1	**3**
Academic language	2	–	–	**2**
Redundant concepts chosen	2	–	–	**2**
Poor format of multiple choice	–	–	2	**2**
Too many similar questions	1	–	–	**1**
OK questions	1	–	–	**1**
Confusing property represented in the ontology	–	1	–	**1**
Should be a higher Bloom's Taxonomy question	–	–	1	**1**

Table 5: Qualitative feedback from evaluators, categorized by type of comment.

ies show promise for using an ontology to inform factual question generation, and future work can extend this method to other question types.

Two of the teachers also pointed out parts of the generated questions that were scientifically incorrect. Examining these questions shows that the ontology contains incorrect information. This points to the necessity of validating and updating created ontologies. Our method, while generalizable to other ontologies, assumes the correctness of the information represented. Future work can examine verifying ontologies, via methods such as dialogue, parsing educational materials, or direct validation from experts.

In nine of the comments, the wording of questions was stated as being imprecise. For instance, *solid* is linked to (CharacteristicOf, "Solvent"). It was pointed out that while most solvents are solid, some can be liquids or gases. This underscores the finding of the first study that errors in the ontology can lead to errors in the questions.

It also seems that the selection of nodes to form questions can be improved. Certain questions were pointed out to have poor groupings of properties. For instance, "What is produced by an ovary and via fertilization creates an embryo? (egg)"was thought not to be a good question, perhaps because to know either portions of the question one must know what an egg is.

6 Conclusion

We presented a novel way of generating complex multiple choice questions and distractors from an educational ontology. We showed significant improvement when the ontology was used to generate distractors compared to an embedding approach. Insights gained from evaluation indicate a necessity of ontology augmentation and a more advanced reasoning model.

We also showed in a subsequent study that question content, when adapted to account for potentially vague questions, has promising results. Future work may benefit from incorporating more knowledge rich approaches such as Berant et al.'s (2014) work on deep analysis of biology texts.

Our algorithm for choosing properties to include in questions and generating distractors is generalizable to other ontologies, although our method assumes a near-complete ontology, as distractors are generated via assumptions that the absence of a link implies the absence of a relationship. Changing the text-generating rules may be necessary to generalize our approach as these are tied to the specific relationships of our ontology. Our ontology contains many naturally-worded relationships, which aided this process. Other text generation methods can be explored in future work, as well, to rectify this.

Insights gained from the teachers' qualitative feedback are applicable to other question generation methods as well. Future work should focus on generating increasingly more complex questions which focus on higher levels of Bloom's taxonomy. External knowledge not represented in the ontology can be used to both increase the difficulty of the questions as well as improve simpler methods of question generation. Finally, verifying the completeness and accuracy of ontologies as well as wording questions diversely and precisely should be a focus going forward.

Acknowledgments

We thank Ann Peterson and the three Upwork science teachers for assessing the results of this analysis, Yiyi Chen for coding support, as well as Jonathan Gillick, David Bamman, Julian Park, and the anonymous reviewers for helpful comments. This work was supported by a UC Berkeley Chancellor's Fellowship.

References

Asma Ben Abacha, Julio Cesar Dos Reis, Yassine Mrabet, Cédric Pruski, and Marcos Da Silveira. 2016. Towards natural language question generation for the validation of ontologies and mappings. *Journal of biomedical semantics* 7(1):48.

Ali Benafia, Smaine Mazouzi, and Sara Benafia. 2015. Building ontologies from text corpora. In *ICEMIS '15 Proceedings of the The International Conference on Engineering MIS 2015*.

Jonathan Berant, Vivek Srikumar, Pei-Chun Chen, Abby Vander Linden, Brittany Harding, Brad Huang, Peter Clark, and Christopher D Manning. 2014. Modeling biological processes for reading comprehension. In *EMNLP*.

Benjamin S. Bloom, David Krathwohl, and Bertram B. Masia. 1956. *Taxonomy of educational objectives: The classification of educational goals. Handbook I: Cognitive domain..* Green.

Jonathan C. Brown, Gwen A. Frishkoff, and Maxine Eskenazi. 2005. Automatic question generation for vocabulary assessment. In *Proceedings of the Conference on Human Language Technology and Empirical Methods in Natural Language Processing*. HLT '05, pages 819–826.

Kathleen Fisher. 2010. Biology lessons at sdsu. http://naturalsciences.sdsu.edu/.

Anatoly P. Getman and Volodymyr V. Karasiuk. 2014. A crowdsourcing approach to building a legal ontology from text. *Artificial Intelligence and Law* 22:313–335.

Arthur C. Graesser, Natalie Person, and John Huber. 1992. Mechanisms that generate questions. In Thomas W. Lauer, Eileen Peacock, and Arthur C. Graesser, editors, *Questions and Information Systems*, Lawrence Erlbaum Associates, Inc., Hillsdale, New Jersey, chapter 9, pages 167–187.

Arthur C. Graesser, Vasile Rus, and Zhiqiang Cai. 2012. Question answering and generation question answering and generation. In *Applied Natural Language Processing: Identification, Investigation and Resolution*.

Michael Heilman. 2011. *Automatic Factual Question Generation from Text*. Ph.D. thesis, Carnegie Mellon University.

Michael Heilman and Noah A. Smith. 2009. Question generation via overgenerating transformations and ranking. Technical Report CMU-LTI-09-013, Carnegie Mellon University.

Michael Heilman and Noah A Smith. 2010. Good question! statistical ranking for question generation. In *Human Language Technologies: The 2010 Annual Conference of the North American Chapter of the Association for Computational Linguistics*. Association for Computational Linguistics, pages 609–617.

Sathish Indurthi, Dinesh Raghu, Mitesh M. Khapra, and Sachindra Joshi. 2017. Generating natural language question-answer pairs from a knowledge graph using a rnn based question generation model. In *ACL 2016*.

Prashanth Mannem, Rashmi Prasad, and Aravind Joshi. 2010. Question generation from paragraphs at upenn: Qgstec system description. In *Proceedings of QG2010: The Third Workshop on Question Generation*.

Karen Mazidi and Paul Tarau. 2016. Infusing nlu into automatic question generation. In *INLG*.

Tomas Mikolov, Ilya Sutskever, Kai Chen, Gregory S. Corrado, and Jeffrey Dean. 2013. Distributed representations of words and phrases and their compositionality. *CoRR* abs/1310.4546.

Andrew Olney, Arthur C. Graesser, and Natalie K. Person. 2012a. Question generation from concept maps. *DD* 3:75–99.

Andrew M Olney, Whitney L Cade, and Claire Williams. 2011. Generating concept map exercises from textbooks. In *Proceedings of the 6th workshop on innovative use of NLP for building educational applications*. Association for Computational Linguistics, pages 111–119.

Andrew McGregor Olney, Arthur C Graesser, and Natalie K Person. 2012b. Question generation from concept maps. *Dialogue & Discourse* 3(2):75–99.

Shiyan Ou, Constantin Orasan, Dalila Mekhaldi, and Laura Hasler. 2008. Automatic question pattern generation for ontology-based question answering. In *FLAIRS Conference*. pages 183–188.

Andreas Papasalouros, Konstantinos Kanaris, and Konstantinos Kotis. 2008. Automatic generation of multiple choice questions from domain ontologies. In *e-Learning*. pages 427–434.

Oleksandr Polozov, Eleanor O'Rourke, Adam M. Smith, Luke S. Zettlemoyer, Sumit Gulwani, and Zoran Popovic. 2015. Personalized mathematical word problem generation. In *IJCAI*.

Vasile Rus, Zhiqiang Cai, and Art Graesser. 2008. Question generation: Example of a multi-year evaluation campaign. *Proc WS on the QGSTEC* .

Iulian Vlad Serban, Alberto García-Durán, Caglar Gulcehre, Sungjin Ahn, Sarath Chandar, Aaron Courville, and Yoshua Bengio. 2016. Generating factoid questions with recurrent neural networks: The 30m factoid question-answer corpus. In *Proceedings of the 54th Annual Meeting of the Association for Computational Linguistics*. pages 588–598.

Sylvie Szulman, Nathalie Aussenac-Gilles, Adeline Nazarenko, Henry Valéry Teguiak, Eric Sardet, and Jean Charlet. 2010. Dafoe: A platform for building ontologies from texts. In *EKAW 2010 Knowledge Engineering and Knowledge Management by the Masses*.

Xuchen Yao, Gosse Bouma, and Yi Zhang. 2012. Semantics-based question generation and implementation. *DD* 3:11–42.

Simplifying metaphorical language for young readers:
A corpus study on news text

Magdalena Wolska
Eberhard Karls Universität Tübingen
LEAD Graduate School
magdalena.wolska@uni-tuebingen.de

Yulia Clausen
Ruprecht-Karls-Universität Heidelberg
Computational Linguistics
yulia.clausen@gmail.com

Abstract

The paper presents first results of an on-going project on text simplification focusing on linguistic metaphors. Based on an analysis of a parallel corpus of news text professionally simplified for different grade levels, we identify six types of simplification choices falling into two broad categories: preserving metaphors or dropping them. An annotation study on almost 300 source sentences with metaphors (grade level 12) and their simplified counterparts (grade 4) is conducted. The results show that most metaphors are preserved and when they are dropped, the semantic content tends to be preserved rather than dropped, however, it is reworded without metaphorical language. In general, some of the expected tendencies in complexity reduction, measured with psycholinguistic variables linked to metaphor comprehension, are observed, suggesting good prospect for machine learning-based metaphor simplification.

1 Motivation and problem statement

Text simplification is the process of meaning preserving reduction of discourse complexity whose purpose is to adapt text for specific populations of readers, for instance, children or language learners. The idea has been around since "My Weekly Reader" in the 1920s and Palmer's work (1932) and over the past 20 years has attracted attention of the computational linguistics community. While broadly interpreted "lexical simplification" – in general understood as substitution of "difficult" words with "simpler" ones – is a common component of automated simplification systems (see, for instance, (Siddharthan, 2014)), studies of text sim-

plification dedicated to specific lexis-related semantic phenomena are lacking. One class of such understudied phenomena are those related to figurative language; a surprising gap in the simplification research considering that metaphors have been shown to cause difficulties in text comprehension and that developing metaphor interpretation competence is a complex developmental process (for an overview, see, for instance, (Winner, 1997)). Since automated systems are trained on corpora of simplified text, understanding patterns of metaphor simplification based on corpus data could help improve simplification models.

In this paper we present a study that is our first step in this direction. We analyze linguistic metaphors in a corpus of news texts professionally simplified for different grade levels. While editors' guidelines instructed to avoid vivid metaphors, such as "paint into a corner", our goal was to find out whether, and if so, how, linguistic metaphors in general are simplified by professional editors. Since ultimately we want to build automated metaphor simplification models, the purpose of this study is to investigate whether metaphors in a corpus of professionally simplified text, that is, potential training data, are simplified in systematic ways. Specifically, we were interested in two questions: 1) What types of discourse modifications do editors perform when simplifying metaphorical language? (in other words, whether a well-defined set of classes for the metaphor simplification task can be specified). 2) Do professional editors simplify metaphor phenomena in systematic ways? (if not, training simplification models using machine learning based on corpus data may not be promising).

The paper's structure follows the data-driven methodology adopted for this study: We first define the criteria used to identify the phenomenon in question: linguistic metaphor. Next, we present

313

Proceedings of the 12th Workshop on Innovative Use of NLP for Building Educational Applications, pages 313–318
Copenhagen, Denmark, September 8, 2017. ©2017 Association for Computational Linguistics

the setup of an annotation study and a typology of simplification choices derived based on an analysis of a corpus of simplified news text. Finally, we present results of an exploratory analysis of the annotated data.

2 Data

2.1 The source corpus

Our data comes from Newsela,[1] a company producing professionally simplified news articles in English and Spanish intended for classroom use. Each Newsela article is available at 5 reading levels spanning grades 2 through 12 of the US school system (elementary school (grades K-4), middle school (grades 5-8), and high school (grades 9-12)). Two levels were used for this first study: the source articles (we will refer to this version as V0) and the most simplified version (V4), since between these versions we expect to see most differences.[2]

Documents were sampled from a subset of Newsela compiled by Xu et al. This is a parallel corpus of 1130 documents from the English portion of Newsela where each article has been automatically aligned sentence-wise with the four simplified versions using Jaccard similarity; for details on the aligned corpus see (Xu et al., 2015).

2.2 Sample selection

The sample of V0 (source) and V4 (simplified) sentences was drawn from the Xu et al.'s corpus as follows: As shown in Figure 1, different Newsela versions span multiple unevenly distributed grade levels. In order to avoid effects due to differences between grade levels within versions, from V0 only articles at grade level 12 were used and from V4 only articles at grade level 4 (the largest subsets). One sentence from each V0 document was selected with its corresponding V4 sentence(s); only sentences that were not identical between V0 and V4 were included in the sample. Sampling was randomized across all documents to avoid effects due to specific editors' decisions. This resulted in 582 V0 sentences. Automatic sentence alignments between the versions were manually checked and corrected where necessary; for instance, unaligned V4 sentences were linked appropriately, as in the following example ("i" marks

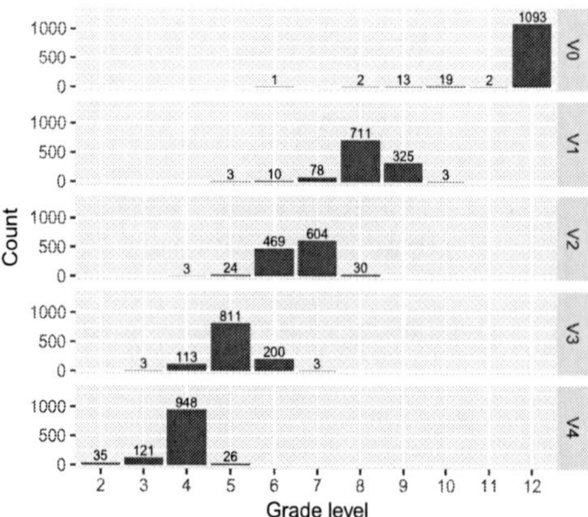

Figure 1: Distribution of grade levels by version in the (Xu et al., 2015) corpus[3]

the inserted segment):

V0   Parts of the nation experienced severe but not unprecedented drought during the study, the researchers noted, which might have reduced the amount of rain sustaining their wetlands and ponds

V4-i   Parts of the nation had very little snow or rain while the study was going on.

V4   That might have meant that there was less water in the wetlands and ponds where amphibians live.

The resulting corpus comprises 582 V0 sentences and their V4 counterparts correctly aligned; 267 alignments have been manually corrected.

2.3 Metaphor identification

We identify linguistic metaphors using Steen et al.'s (2010) refined Metaphor Identification Procedure known as MIPVU.[4] MIPVU provides guidelines for annotation of potentially metaphorical words, where "words" are linguistic units which receive a separate part-of-speech tag. Phrasal verbs, compounds, and proper names (multiword expressions) can be treated as lexical units as exceptions. For the simplification study we focus on the most common classes of content words: nouns and verbs.

In MIPVU, a lexical unit is considered to be metaphorically used when its meaning in a given context can be contrasted as well as understood in comparison with a more basic meaning that it can have in other contexts. MIPVU strives not to determine the most basic meaning of a word,

---

[1] https://newsela.com

[2] Analysis of metaphor simplification across other levels is planned as further work.

[3] Both plots were created using R's (R Core Team, 2017) ggplot2 package (Wickham, 2009)

[4] "VU" stands for Vrije Universiteit Amsterdam where the authors of the procedure are based.

	Simplification	Source sentence	Simplified sentence
Preserved	same metaphor	*... like the magnetized nails, unable to resist a powerful magnetic **force** in the galactic bulge ...*	*Like the magnetized nails, they would have been unable to resist a powerful magnetic **force** in the galactic bulge ...*
	other metaphor	*Obama also has **grappled** publicly with reconciling King's teachings on nonviolence ...*	*Obama has **wrestled** publicly with living up to King's teachings on nonviolence ...*
	phrase with metaphor(s)	*But now she's **struggling** to obtain documents required by the new law.*	*But now she's **having a hard time** getting the papers that the new law requires.*
Dropped	content dropped	*Our goal is to provide Internet service to people in areas that can't afford to **throw down** fiber lines ...*	*Our goal is to provide Internet service to people in areas that can't afford ◊ usual Internet lines ...*
	changed to non-metaphor	*In exchange for a 4 percent **piece** of their companies, entrepreneurs in the program will gain access ...*	*... people in the program will give up a 4 percent **share** of their companies. In exchange they will get ...*
	phrase without metaphor(s)	*Utah officials say that since 2008, highway crashes have **dropped** annually on stretches of rural Interstate ...*	*They say there have **been fewer** accidents where the speed limit was raised.*

Table 1: Metaphor simplification types.

but rather a meaning that is more basic that the one in the given context. A more basic sense is defined as a "more concrete, specific, and human-oriented sense in the contemporary language use" (Steen et al., 2010, p. 35). A corpus-based dictionary, here: the Macmillan English Dictionary for Advanced Learners,[5] is consulted for the basic and the contextual senses of lexical units. Two senses of one lexical unit are considered significantly distinct if they are listed under separate numbers in the dictionary. MIPVU defines three metaphor types: indirect (example (1)), direct (2) and implicit (3):

Indirect metaphors occur when contrast as well as comparison exists between the contextual and a more basic meaning:

(1) *Political cartoons engage and enrage more than articles do because they are visual and transcend language **barriers**.*

Direct metaphors display no contrast between the contextual and a more basic meaning. In this case contextual meaning is the basic meaning and comparison is expressed explicitly, for instance, by the so-called metaphor flags (words such as *like, as, so-called, -shaped*):

(2) *Like the **magnetized nails**, they would have been unable to resist a powerful magnetic force in the galactic bulge ...*

Implicit metaphors represent words pointing back to recoverable metaphorical material:

(3) *... unable to resist a powerful magnetic force in the galactic bulge around when **it** was forming stars around 8-13 billion years ago.*

Measure	Count
No. of sentences containing metaphors	272
No. of metaphor occurrences	416
Verbs	267
Nouns	149
Mean No. of metaphors per sentence	1.53
No. of unique lexemes	314

Table 2: Quantitative information on the annotated metaphor set

In the present study we focus on indirect metaphors (the prevalent type; see (Steen et al., 2010)) and identify metaphorical uses of all nouns and verbs in the sampled original sentences (V0).

Metaphor annotation proceeded as follows: Identification of candidate metaphor occurrences was carried out by one of the authors. All unclear cases were marked and discussed by both authors until agreement was reached. If agreement could not be reached, the case was excluded from further analysis. The final set of metaphorical word uses comprises only clear cases as per MIPVU.[6]

Quantitative information on the annotated metaphors is summarized in Table 2.

---

[5]http://www.macmillandictionary.com

[6]As one of the reviewers pointed out, MIPVU is not an easy protocol to apply. It it precisely for this reason that, since the focus of the present study was not on the metaphor identification task, but on simplification types, we opted to select only clear cases of metaphors in V0, as per agreement on metaphor status by both authors. Because this agreement was reached though a discussion in all cases, inter-annotator agreement on metaphor annotation was not calculated. We are planning to conduct a separate metaphor identification study as part of further work.

3 Simplification types

Identification and annotation of simplification types proceeded as follows: Both authors initially analyzed and discussed smaller subsets of the metaphor-annotated corpus (20-30 instances). Once the set of types stabilized to the final set (below) one author annotated all the remaining instances and the other author 99 instances in total (1 erroneous instance had to be excluded). Both annotators are non-native, but fluent, speakers of English. Inter-annotator agreement on the common subset of 99 instances was 0.93 proportion agreement (kappa=0.87) and was deemed reliable. The 7 disagreement cases in the common subset were discussed and resolved for the analysis.[7]

A typology of editors' simplification choices was derived in a data-driven fashion starting off of two basic options: a metaphor can be **preserved** in the simplified version or **dropped**. Corpus analysis revealed three subtypes of metaphor-related discourse modifications within each of these high-level categories: A metaphorically used word can be preserved unchanged (**same metaphor**), replaced with another single word used metaphorically (**other metaphor**), or reworded using multi-word phrasing containing metaphor(s) (**phrase with metaphor(s)**). It can be dropped by replacing it with a single different word in a more basic sense (**changed to non-metaphor**), with multi-word phrasing not containing metaphors (**phrase without metaphor(s)**), or the meaning portion expressed by the metaphor can be omitted altogether (**content dropped**). Table 1 provides a summary of the simplification types with examples.

4 Corpus analysis

Analysis of the annotated simplification types is split into two parts: We start with a high-level overview of the distribution of the simplification types. Then, we perform an exploratory analysis to investigate how four psycholinguistic variables – age of acquisition (AoA), familiarity, concreteness, and imageability –, previously linked to metaphor comprehension (see, for instance, (Paivio et al., 1968; Paivio and Walsh, 1993; Gibbs, 2006; Ureña and Faber, 2010)) and also used in simplification models (e.g. (Cross-

---

[7]Further annotation will be conducted and inter-annotator agreement recalculated for categories other than the prevalent Preserved.same in order to reduce class imbalance and to add instances of the smaller classes.

Simplification type	Count
Preserved	288
same metaphor	240
other metaphor	34
phrase with metaphor(s)	14
Dropped	128
changed to non-metaphor	81
content dropped	37
phrase without metaphor	10

Table 3: Distribution of simplification types

ley et al., 2007; Jauhar and Specia, 2012; Crossley et al., 2012; Vajjala and Meurers, 2014)), behave across simplification categories. The scores have been extracted from the MRC Psycholinguistic Database (Wilson, 1988) and the Bristol Norms (Kuperman et al., 2012).

Distribution of simplification types is shown in Table 3. Most metaphors, 69%, are preserved in V4, the majority with the same wording. Where metaphorical words are omitted, they tend to be replaced with their literal counterparts. Rewording consisting of longer phrases is dispreferred.

Distributions of psycholinguistic variables are shown in Figure 2. Since for the automated classification task the class imbalance (see Table 3) will need to be countered, we reduce the class imbalance already for distributions visualization by randomly downsampling the largest class (Preserved.same) to 80 instances such that the two basic classes, Preserved and Dropped, are of the same size; Preserved.same mean was estimated by randomly resampling the 80 instances 20 times. Dependent variables are ordered by complexity of intervention into the source semantics that the manipulation they denote involves; for the Preserved class: preserving same meaning at one end vs. paraphrasing by adding lexical material at the other and for the Dropped class: merely replacing the metaphorical lexeme with a non-metaphorical one vs. omitting content altogether.

Within the Preserved type, low-AoA metaphors tend to be preserved and high-AoA are rephrased. In the Dropped class, low-AoA metaphors are rephrased and high are dropped; also on average, as expected, lower AoA metaphors are preserved and higher dropped. Explicable pattern of Imageability can be observed: within both basic types, the higher the score, the more radical

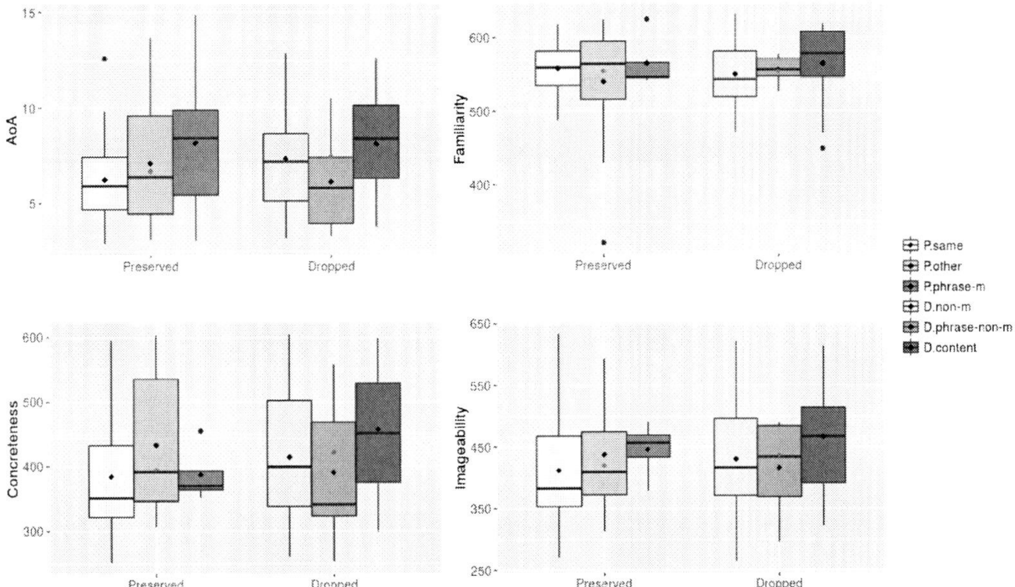

Figure 2: Distribution of psycholinguistic variables by simplification type (legend labels shortened for space reasons; the red dots indicate **P**reserved and **D**ropped group means (20 resamplings of P.same))

the modification (rephrasing and dropping content, respectively); aggregated means display the same pattern. This is consistent with the guideline on avoiding vivid metaphors. The pattern of Concreteness measure is unclear. Familiarity scores are the least discriminating.

5 Discussion and further work

Overall, some of the psycholinguistic variables do exhibit patterns confirming systematicity of professional simplification and good prospect for training machine learning models based on professionally simplified data; Xu et al. (2015) argue likewise. AoA and Imageability exhibit a consistent explicable pattern within and between the two basic types suggesting they can be used as predictors. This is not the case with the Familiarity measure. Interestingly, in the Preserved class, lexical elaboration (Preserved.other) is performed within narrow ranges of 3 of the variables, which could be exploited. The high prevalence of the Preserved class is surprising. On the one hand, it provides a safe default for a basic automated system, on the other hand, sets a high majority-based baseline.

Future work will involve investigating further linguistically and cognitively-motivated variables for metaphor simplification. Likewise, interactions between psycholinguistic variables and their relation to syntactic complexity variables require further study. We also plan to annotate further data, also at other grade levels, and train models (2-way classification, Preserve vs. Drop, in the first instance). Finally, the categorical approach to metaphor simplification might be entirely reconsidered in view of recent studies showing evidence that the literal-metaphorical distinction is a graded (scalar) phenomenon ((Cameron et al., 2009; Müller and Tag, 2010; Dunn, 2014), among others). Simplification might be thus seen as continuous "reduction of metaphoricity".[8]

Acknowledgments

We would like to thank Newsela for making their data available to the community and Wei Xu, Chris Callison-Burch, and Courtney Napoles for sharing their aligned corpus via Newsela; we are planning to make our final annotations available in the same way. We would also like to thank the reviewers for the interesting comments. Magdalena Wolska was supported by the Institutional Strategy of the University of Tübingen (Deutsche Forschungsgemeinschaft, ZUK 63). Part of this work was conducted while she was on a visiting appointment at the Ruprecht-Karls-Universität Heidelberg.

---

[8]This interesting suggestion for follow-up work and pointer to Dunn's papers is due to one of the reviewers.

References

L. Cameron, R. Maslen, Z. Todd, J. Maule, P. Stratton, and N. Stanley. 2009. The discourse dynamics approach to metaphor and metaphor-led discourse analysis. *Metaphor and Symbol* doi:10.1080/10926480902830821.

S.A. Crossley, D. Allen, and D.S. McNamara. 2012. Text simplification and comprehensible input: A case for an intuitive approach. *Language Teaching Research* doi:10.1177/1362168811423456.

S.A. Crossley, M.M. Louwerse, P.M. McCarthy, and D.S. McNamara. 2007. A linguistic analysis of simplified and authentic texts. *The Modern Language Journal* doi:10.1111/j.1540-4781.2007.00507.x.

J. Dunn. 2014. Measuring metaphoricity. In *Proceedings of the 52nd Annual Meeting of the ACL.* http://www.aclweb.org/anthology/P14-2121.

R.W. Gibbs. 2006. Metaphor interpretation as embodied simulation. *Mind & Language* doi:10.1111/j.1468-0017.2006.00285.x.

S.K. Jauhar and L. Specia. 2012. PUOW-SHEF: SimpLex-lexical simplicity ranking based on contextual and psycholinguistic features. In *Proceedings of the 1st Joint Conference on Lexical and Computational Semantics (*SEM-12).* http://www.aclweb.org/anthology/S12-1066.

V. Kuperman, H. Stadthagen-Gonzalez, and M. Brysbaert. 2012. Age-of-acquisition (AoA) norms for over 50 thousand English words. In *Behavior Research Methods.* http://crr.ugent.be/archives/806.

C. Müller and S. Tag. 2010. The dynamics of metaphor: Foregrounding and activating metaphoricity in conversational interaction. *Cognitive Semiotics* doi:10.1515/cogsem.2010.6.spring2010.85.

A. Paivio and M. Walsh. 1993. Psychological processes in metaphor comprehension and memory. In *Metaphor and thought* doi:10.1017/CBO9781139173865.016.

A. Paivio, J.C. Yuille, and S.A. Madigan. 1968. Concreteness, imagery, and meaningfulness values for 925 nouns. *Journal of experimental psychology* doi:10.1037/h0025327.

Harold E. Palmer. 1932. *The Grading and Simplifying of Literary Material.* Institute for Research in English Teaching.

R Core Team. 2017. *R: A Language and Environment for Statistical Computing.* R Foundation for Statistical Computing, Vienna, Austria. https://www.R-project.org.

A. Siddharthan. 2014. A survey of research on text simplification. *International Journal of Applied Linguistics* doi:10.1075/itl.165.2.06sid.

G.J. Steen, A.G. Dorst, J.B. Herrmann, A.A. Kaal, T. Krennmayr, and T. Pasma. 2010. *A Method for Linguistic Metaphor Identification: From MIP to MIPVU.* John Benjamins.

J.M. Ureña and P. Faber. 2010. Reviewing imagery in resemblance and non-resemblance metaphors. *Cognitive Linguistics* doi:10.1515/cogl.2010.004.

S. Vajjala and D. Meurers. 2014. Readability assessment for text simplification: From analysing documents to identifying sentential simplifications. *ITL–International Journal of Applied Linguistics* doi:10.1075/itl.165.2.04vaj.

H. Wickham. 2009. *ggplot2: Elegant Graphics for Data Analysis.* Springer. http://ggplot2.org.

M. Wilson. 1988. MRC Psycholinguistic Database: Machine-usable dictionary, version 2.00. In *Behavior Research Methods, Instruments, & Computers.* http://ota.ox.ac.uk/headers/1054.xml.

E. Winner. 1997. *The Point of Words.* Harvard University Press.

W. Xu, C. Callison-Burch, and C. Napoles. 2015. Problems in Current Text Simplification Research: New Data Can Help. In *Transactions of the Association for Computational Linguistics.* https://www.transacl.org/ojs/index.php/tacl/article/view/549.

Language Based Mapping of Science Assessment Items to Skills

Farah Nadeem and **Mari Ostendorf**
Dept. of Electrical Engineering
University of Washington
{farahn,ostendor}@uw.edu

Abstract

Knowledge of the association between assessment questions and the skills required to solve them is necessary for analysis of student learning. This association, often represented as a Q-matrix, is either hand-labeled by domain experts or learned as latent variables given a large student response data set. As a means of automating the match to formal standards, this paper uses neural text classification methods, leveraging the language in the standards documents to identify online text for a proxy training task. Experiments involve identifying the topic and crosscutting concepts of middle school science questions leveraging multi-task training. Results show that it is possible to automatically build a Q-matrix without student response data and using a modest number of hand-labeled questions.

1 Introduction

In both traditional and online contexts, fine grain diagnostic information can play a crucial role in employing formative assessment to improve student learning outcomes as observed by National Research Council (2012), and for creating scalable systems that provide individualized instruction (Barnes, 2005). A key requirement for this inference is association of each of the assessment tasks, which we will refer to as questions, with attributes, which are the skills (knowledge, concepts and/or strategies) needed to solve the tasks. The association of skills to questions is represented as a Q-matrix (Tatsuoka, 1983).

Hand crafted Q-matrices are created by domain experts who label each assessment task with the required skill(s). While this provides an inter-pretable matrix for educators, in the sense that the skills are associated with a documented standard or cognitive model, the question annotation process is time consuming and not scalable. When standards change, the old question annotation is no longer useful. The cost of question annotation is a key issue with the domain models in intelligent tutoring systems (ITS), which are created by experts for each subject area and grade level, limiting reusability (Burns et al., 2014).

As an alternative, there has been work on automated discovery of an association of (latent) skills to questions using student response data (Lan et al., 2014; Barnes, 2005; Desmarais, 2010). While these unsupervised automated methods can provide a good fit for the student response data, they are limited by the requirement of a large data set of student scores on a given test, which is not available for individual classroom assessments and hard to obtain for standardized testing. In addition, the latent skills offer limited interpretability for teachers. The results cannot easily be used to identify practice questions to help a student improve in areas of weakness.

It was observed in a report by National Research Council (2001) that fine grained diagnostic models are not widely used due to scalability, reusability and/or interpretability issues, which is still a problem today as stated by National Research Council (2012).

This work aims to develop interpretable and automatic methods for mapping science assessment tasks to underlying skills by using text classification methods that leverage the language in standards documents and teacher training materials. The experiments here use the Framework for K-12 Science education laid out in the framework by National Research Council (2012), but the method is designed to work for any well documented standard and the questions used in this study are not

319

Proceedings of the 12th Workshop on Innovative Use of NLP for Building Educational Applications, pages 319–326
Copenhagen, Denmark, September 8, 2017. ©2017 Association for Computational Linguistics

explicitly designed for that standard.

Specifically, we look at the core disciplinary ideas (topics) and crosscutting concepts described in the standard as the attributes needed to respond to assessment tasks. A multi-task convolutional neural network is designed to jointly label topics and concepts. The greater challenge is in recognizing concepts, for which there is no annotated data available. A key contribution is in the use of standards documentation to automate training annotation and obtain online text for use as a proxy task in an intermediate training stage.

The rest of the paper is organized as follows. Sec. 2 provides a detailed task description, which is followed in Sec. 3 by an overview of prior text classification work that we build on. Experiment details are provided in Sec. 4 with results in Sec. 5. Related work leveraging question text in latent skill learning is discussed in Sec. 6. Findings and open questions are summarized in Sec. 7.

2 Task

From the perspective of formal standards, student learning is measured along specified content areas and concepts. The goal of both classroom teaching and online instruction systems is to ultimately increase proficiency in these areas. This work considers the Framework for K-12 science education presented by National Research Council (2012), and the associated Next Generation Science Standard (NGSS Lead States, 2013). The framework measures student learning along three dimensions: i) disciplinary core areas, ii) crosscutting concepts, and iii) science and engineering practices. For this work, we aim to identify the core content areas (topics) and crosscutting concepts associated with a question. The dimension of science and engineering practices is reflected more in the text of student response, hence we do not consider it here.

NGSS provides content and learning progression descriptions for each dimension. The standard specifies a hierarchy of disciplinary core ideas from physical sciences (PS), life sciences (LS), earth and space sciences (ESS), and engineering, technology and application of sciences (ETS).[1] Our study operates at the middle level of the hierarchy, with 12 topics, focusing on the middle school level. Seven crosscutting concepts are

described.[2] Examples of descriptions in the standard are given below.

Topic: ESS3 Earth and human activity - Human activities have altered the biosphere, sometimes damaging it, although changes to ...

Concept: Energy and Matter Tracking energy and matter flows, into, out of, and within systems helps one understand their systems behavior.

The specific task addressed in this work is: given a question, identify the topic and concepts associated with that question. For example, the question:

What happens to the sun's energy in the greenhouse effect?

would be be associated with the topic ESS3 and the concept "Energy and Matter." Topic labeling corresponds to a multi-class decision (which one of 12 topics), and concept labeling involves 7 binary decisions. It is possible for a question to involve none of the concepts in the inventory.

More examples of topic and concept descriptions with sample questions are provided in supplementary materials.

3 Text Classification

Text classification is an established problem, with many different techniques available, including naive Bayes, support vector classifiers, decision trees and k nearest neighbors, which are summarized in (Ikonomakis et al., 2005). For longer documents, a bag-of-words approach is often used, but sequence models can be more useful for classifying sentences or short documents. A variety of neural techniques have been proposed, including (Wiener et al., 1995; Ruiz and Srinivasan, 1998; Nam et al., 2014; Lai et al., 2015). In our study, we build on the convolutional neural network (CNN) presented in (Kim, 2014), which achieves high accuracy for short texts. We briefly describe the model below.

The model takes a sequence of pre-trained word embeddings as input: each word x_i is represented by a k dimensional embedding vector, $x_i \in \mathbf{R}^k$. A sequence of n word embeddings are concatenated to form a $n \times k$ matrix that is input to the network.

The concatenated sequence is convolved with filters that span the entire embedding and h words.

---

[1] https://www.nextgenscience.org/get-to-know, **Appendices E and J**

[2] https://www.nextgenscience.org/get-to-know, **Appendix G**

A $h \times k$ filter w_l is convolved with a concatenated sequence of h words, generating an $n-h+1$ length output sequence, where the ith element of the sequence is given by

$$c_i(l) = f(w_l \circ x_{i:i+h-1} + b_l). \qquad (1)$$

where $\circ$ indicates a Hadamard product, and f is a non-linear or piece-wise linear function such as a rectified linear unit (ReLU). Using max-pooling over time results in one feature produced by one filter:

$$\hat{c}(l) = \max\{c_1(l), c_2(l), ..., c_{n-h+1}(l)\} \qquad (2)$$

The output from max-pooling for each filter is concatenated into a feature set, resulting in an m dimensional feature vector for m filters.

$$z = [\hat{c}(1), \hat{c}(2), ..., \hat{c}(m)] \qquad (3)$$

The output used to predict the label is given by

$$y = g(Yz + b) \qquad (4)$$

where g is a non-linear function, e.g. softmax for multi-class problems.

4 Methods

This section first describes the different data sets used in training and testing, and then the modifications to the above CNN for identifying question attributes.

4.1 Data

For our work we consider three sets of resources: science questions, Wikipedia science and mathematics articles, and standard related resources. Middle school science questions are the main training and testing data. Wikipedia articles provide a supplemental source of data for pre-training and for a proxy task for concepts. Standard related resources include descriptions of disciplinary core ideas and crosscutting concepts laid out in the standard, and question templates developed to aid teachers in assessing crosscutting concept proficiency.

The main data consists of 14,985 middle school science questions (Kembhavi et al., 2017), with questions divided into 629 generic science modules. This data represents a generic set of middle school science questions, and is not aligned with the dimensions of NGSS. For our study, the modules were hand-labeled as belonging to one of the

12 topics using NGSS descriptions, and topic labels for questions were determined based on the module label. All questions have module labels. The test data consists of 750 questions (5% of the total data); the rest is for training and validation. Only the test data is hand-labeled with crosscutting concepts.

In order to obtain concept labels for the training data, we used question templates that have been developed for each of the seven concepts,[3] which were designed to aid teachers in implementing these concepts into their own assessments. For example, one of the templates for the **Patterns** concept is:

What patterns do you observe in the
data presented above in the chart?

We pick keywords from each of the templates (e.g. "patterns", "presented", "observe", "data" and "chart" in the above question), and search for questions in the training data that contain at least two keywords associated with a concept. This results in labels for 890 questions, approximately 6% of the training set, of which 44 questions are assigned multiple concept labels. Keyword matching returned few matches since the questions have not been developed to test for crosscutting concepts specifically. Twenty percent of the results from the keyword search were randomly sampled and hand checked to ensure they matched the assigned concepts, and found to be correct.

The distribution of topics and counts of concepts in the question training and test sets are shown in tables 1 and 2, respectively. Both tables indicate that the class distributions are not balanced. This is expected, since the topics and concepts are designed for all grades (K-12), and some skills are more applicable to high school science curriculum.

Since only 6% of the training data has concept labels, we use external data to create an additional proxy training task for concepts. Using phrases from the concept descriptions from NGSS and the STEM Teaching Tools templates, we hand selected 122 Wikipedia science articles associated with the seven concepts, with 8 of these articles spanning multiple concepts. Sample article titles include:

---

[3] STEM teaching tools 2014-2017: `http://stemteachingtools.org/`

Topic	Train	Test
Matter and its interactions	12.0%	10.7%
From molecules to organisms	30.2%	31.2%
Engineering design	2.0%	2.4%
Heredity	1.1%	0.9%
Earth's place in the universe	13.7%	13.1%
Motion and stability	5.0%	4.3%
Earth and human activity	7.1%	6.7%
Waves and energy transfer	5.6%	5.6%
Earths systems	17.0%	18.6%
Energy	2.4%	2.0%
Ecosystems	3.1%	3.6%
Evolution	0.8%	0.9%

Table 1: Topic distribution in train and test sets

Concept	Train	Test
Stability & change (S&C)	46	5
Scale, proportion & quantity (SP&Q)	150	77
Patterns (P)	166	93
Structure & function (S&F)	24	9
Systems & system models (Sys)	88	27
Cause & effect (C&E)	97	41
Energy & matter (E&M)	365	116

Table 2: Concept counts in train and test sets

Patterns: Patterns in nature, Taxonomy, Correlation and dependence

System and system models: System, Systems modeling, System design

The articles are split into smaller "documents" based on linebreaks, yielding a set of 16,892 documents with concept labels. These documents correspond to paragraphs, section heads, related links and references, so they are not a good match to the style of a science question but they provide training examples of important keywords and phrases.

In addition to these sources, we use a pool of 40,000 general Wikipedia science and mathematics articles for pre-training word embeddings.

In summary, four data sources are used in training: questions labeled with both topic and concept D_{TC}, questions labeled with topic D_T (a superset of D_{TC}), concept-labeled Wikipedia paragraphs D_C, and unlabeled Wikipedia articles D_W, as shown in table 3.

Data	Number of Samples
D_{TC}	890 questions
D_T	14,235 questions
D_C	16,892 documents
D_W	40,000 articles
Test set	750 questions with topic and concept labels

Table 3: Data

4.2 Multi-task Topic-Concept Classification

Our use of the CNN for text classification involves multiple outputs:

$$y_t = g_t(Y_t z + b_t) \tag{5}$$
$$y_c = g_c(Y_c z + b_c) \tag{6}$$

where z is the output of the max-pooling layer, $Y_t \in \mathbf{R}^{m \times n_t}$, $b_t \in \mathbf{R}^{n_t}$, $Y_c \in \mathbf{R}^{m \times n_c}$, and $b_c \in \mathbf{R}^{n_c}$. For topics, g_t is a softmax layer, giving the per-class probabilities y_{ti}, from which the topic is chosen according to $argmax_i(y_{ti})$. For detecting multi-label concepts, g_c is a sigmoid, which outputs the concept probability without assuming that concepts are mutually exclusive. The labels are decided by thresholding the sigmoid output, $c_i = \{\mathbf{1}_{y_{ci}(k) > thr}\}^{n_c}$ for $k = 1, \ldots, n_c$. As noted earlier, there are 12 topics ($n_t = 12$) and 7 concepts ($n_c = 7$). The CNN for multi-task training is shown in figure 1.

The training loss function is multi-class cross-entropy for the topic output and binary cross-entropy for each of the concept outputs. Multi-task training uses a sum of topic and concept loss. 10% of the training data was used for validation at a time, using ten fold cross validation. This was used to tune drop out, set number of filters and filter sizes. The entire labeled data set was then used for training.

Training was done with both pre-trained and randomly initialized word embeddings. We used 128 dimensional word embeddings, and a vocabulary size of 75,000. The filter lengths used were [1, 3, 4, 5], with 64 filters for each size. Drop out of 50% was used for regularization. For concept classification, a threshold of 0.2 was set for positive label detection. This was empirically chosen on the training data.

Experiments are conducted to compare: i) random initialization vs. pre-training, ii) independent vs. multi-task training, and iii) different methods

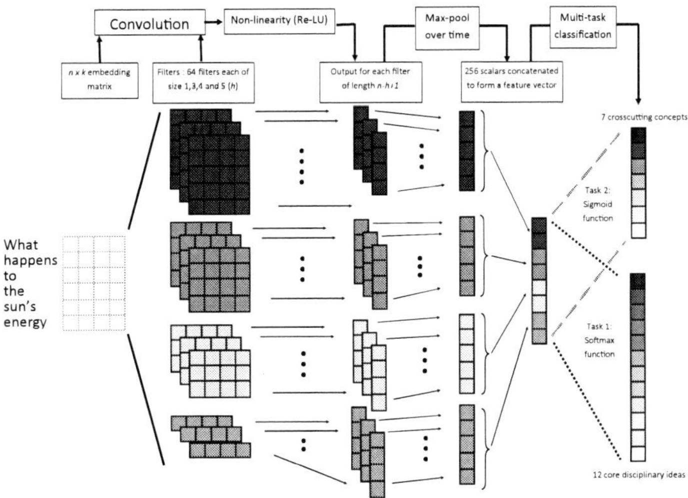

Figure 1: CNN for Multi-task Classification

of using the labeled training sets. Pre-training is based on D_W for both multi-task and independent classifiers.

For independent classifier training, D_T is used for topics, and D_{TC} is used for concepts. In addition, we explored a two-stage approach to training the concept model, using D_C in a first pass of training, followed by D_{TC} for fine tuning ($C \rightarrow TC$).

For multi-task training, three alternatives are explored:

- Stage 1: run single task training (with D_T). Stage 2: run multi-task training with D_{TC}. Do not use D_C. ($T \rightarrow TC$)

- Stage 1: alternate between batches of single task training (with D_T and D_C), starting with D_T. Stage 2: run multi-task training with D_{TC}. ($T/C \rightarrow TC$)

- Alternate between batches of the different labeled sets, starting with D_T and ending with D_{TC}. ($T/C/TC$)

All multi-task models are pre-trained using D_W.

5 Results and Discussion

Results for the different training schemes are shown in table 4. The first four rows correspond to systems with topic and concept classifiers trained separately, and the last three involve multi-task training. The first row indicates baseline performance using n-gram features in an SVM. Comparing the next two rows in the table shows that

pre-training word embeddings with the unlabeled Wikipedia articles benefits both topic and concept classifiers, so it was used in all subsequent experiments with multi-task training. The fourth row uses the two-stage concept training, which slightly hurts performance. All the different options for multi-task training (rows 5-7) improve over learning independent classifiers (row 3 for the case with pre-training). Unlike the independent training case, the proxy concepts represented by the Wikipedia article paragraphs benefit both topic and concept labeling when used in multi-task training.

The precision, recall and F1 scores for crosscutting concepts are shown in table 5. As expected, the best performance is observed for the class that dominates the training data. The topic confusion matrix also shows that topics which are well represented in the training data tend to be more reliably identified.

In order to ensure that the independent CNN classifiers provided a strong baseline, we also ran experiments with other approaches using the same training data. Specifically, we implemented an SVM with n-gram features ($n = 1, 2, 3$) and a k-nearest neighbor classifier using a vector space representation of questions based on latent semantic analysis (LSA). Two independent SVMs were trained, one using D_T for topic classification, and one using D_{TC} for concept classification. Performance on topic classification was slightly worse than the CNN result, but results for concept recog-

Training	Initialize	Topic	Concept
SVM	-	73.4	14.2
Separate T, TC	Random	81.3	34.7
Separate T, TC	Pre-train	84.1	38.2
$C \to TC$	Pre-train	-	35.8
$T \to TC$	Pre-train	84.5	41.2
$T/C/TC$	Pre-train	84.5	44.4
$T/C \to TC$	Pre-train	86.2	57.7

Table 4: Classifier Performance: Topic (accuracy) and concept (macro F1 score)

Concept	F1 Score	Precision	Recall
S&C	54.54	50.00	60.00
SP&Q	55.62	51.08	61.03
P	60.96	60.63	61.29
S&F	66.67	66.67	66.67
Sys	43.47	52.63	37.03
C&E	50.57	47.82	61.03
E&M	72.16	60.00	90.51

Table 5: Per-Concept Classification Performance

nition with the best macro F1 being 14.2 with an SVM. The LSA-based model gave much worse results when trained using D_{TC} and tested for concept accuracy; presumably topic factors dominate this unsupervised representation.

An additional factor that impacts performance for concept labeling is ignoring the data in figures accompanying the questions. Generally, for crosscutting concepts, some information is presented graphically, which we are not using in the current work. Hand annotating 200 questions from the test set, we find that roughly a quarter of the questions have associated images. Not all crosscutting concepts are impacted by the presence of an accompanying image. The categories that do worse are scale proportion and quantity, where questions are accompanied by graphs, energy and matter flows, with questions related to water, carbon and nitrogen cycles, and system and system models, which have associated block diagrams. It would be possible to achieve higher accuracy by combining information from the text and features from associated figures, since using text alone is not always enough to identify the correct concept. Consider the following question: *"Which gas is represented by letter F?"* Without the accompanying figure that depicts the carbon cycle, it is not possible to identify the underlying concept of matter and energy flow.

6 Related Work

As noted earlier, automated discovery of latent skills to question mapping provide a good fit to student response data, but the skills are abstract and cannot be easily used by teachers. In (Barnes, 2005; Lan et al., 2014), this problem is addressed by hand-labeling questions with topics and associating the latent concepts learned the different topics that are most frequently represented in the cor-

responding data. Interpretation of the latent factors is in terms of these topic combinations. This requires hand labeling of training data. The results may generalize to other data, but this was not evaluated. In related work, (Lan et al., 2013) uses multi-objective optimization to learn both skill-to-item and student-to-skill proficiency mappings, as well finding a list of keywords associated with each estimated skill. While both solutions add to the interpretability of the model, the skills are not aligned with formal standards or cognitive models.

Non-negative matrix factorization is used by (Desmarais, 2010) to associate questions with skills using student response data. The data sets consist of 4 subject (mathematics, biology, world history and French). The number of latent skills are 4, the hypothesis is that matrix factorization should separate student proficiency in the four subjects. This work does not provide fine grained proficiency within individual subjects. The model achieves 72% accuracy on all four subjects, and 96% on only mathematics and French, which are the most separable. Results on a set of trivia questions are also reported, where latent skill to topic matching achieves an accuracy of 35% for 4 topics.

7 Conclusion

In summary, this work provides a method for identifying skills required to solve specific science questions based on the text of the question, where skills associated with documented standards are characterized with a relatively small amount of manual annotation. We use state-of-the-art text classification methods that are made more effective by: i) leveraging standards documentation to harvest and automatically annotate training data, and ii) applying multi-task learning to jointly classify both topics and concepts. The best case models achieve 86% topic accuracy and 57.7 concept F1 score. Compared to current data driven models that are unsupervised and do not provide an explicit connection to standards, our approach is interpretable. In addition, it does not require student response data and can be used with any question set. Compared to frameworks that require human experts to align questions with attributes, our approach is scalable to large question sets. It enables teachers to leverage a variety of assessment materials and provide more individualized feedback to students. While the experiments described here are based on NGSS documentation, the methods are general and can be used with any well-documented standard or cognitive model.

The ability to automatically build a Q-matrix is promising for student learning evaluation and statistical models for online systems, particularly intelligent tutoring systems. Aligning the Q-matrix to elements of learning outcomes specified in standards gives the ability to automatically adapt existing material to new standards and curricula without extensive input from domain experts, improving reusability of tutoring system material. It can also provide new tools for educators analyzing learning across larger populations. In particular, the concept annotation work can help educators study learning progression along crosscutting concepts, which is largely undocumented at this point as stated in the report by National Research Council (2012). It can also provide a complementary tool that may be useful for interpreting unsupervised analyses based on large student response data sets. For example, it may be interesting to look for factors that are predictive of question difficulty based on classifier predictions or confidence of different skills.

Whether the level of accuracy is sufficient for downstream tasks is an open question, since goodness of fit is generally evaluated using student response data, which is not used in the current work. However, there are multiple opportunities for improvement, particularly for concept classification. For example, semantic similarity can be leveraged in using question templates to select articles associated with concepts, and the data could be filtered to exclude sections that are not well matched to questions. Semi-supervised training could increase the number of actual questions used in training. In addition, the use of information in tables and figures represents an important direction for future work. Neural classifiers are well suited to integrating features from different modalities, and we expect that significant gains may be possible with this approach.

References

Tiffany Barnes. 2005. The q-matrix method: Mining student response data for knowledge. In *American Association for Artificial Intelligence 2005 Educational Data Mining Workshop*. pages 1–8.

Hugh Burns, Carol A Luckhardt, James W Parlett, and Carol L Redfield. 2014. *Intelligent tutoring systems: Evolutions in design*. Psychology Press.

Michel Desmarais. 2010. Conditions for effectively deriving a q-matrix from data with non-negative matrix factorization. In *Educational Data Mining 2011*.

M Ikonomakis, S Kotsiantis, and V Tampakas. 2005. Text classification using machine learning techniques. *WSEAS transactions on computers* 4(8):966–974.

Aniruddha Kembhavi, Minjoon Seo, Dustin Schwenk, Jonghyun Choi, Ali Farhadi, and Hannaneh Hajishirzi. 2017. Are you smarter than a sixth grader? textbook question answering for multimodal machine comprehension. In *Conference on Computer Vision and Pattern Recognition (CVPR)*.

Yoon Kim. 2014. Convolutional neural networks for sentence classification. *arXiv preprint arXiv:1408.5882* .

Siwei Lai, Liheng Xu, Kang Liu, and Jun Zhao. 2015. Recurrent convolutional neural networks for text classification. In *AAAI*. volume 333, pages 2267–2273.

Andrew S Lan, Christoph Studer, Andrew E Waters, and Richard G Baraniuk. 2013. Joint topic modeling and factor analysis of textual information and graded response data. *arXiv preprint arXiv:1305.1956* .

Andrew S Lan, Andrew E Waters, Christoph Studer, and Richard G Baraniuk. 2014. Sparse factor analysis for learning and content analytics. *Journal of Machine Learning Research* 15(1):1959–2008.

Jinseok Nam, Jungi Kim, Eneldo Loza Mencía, Iryna Gurevych, and Johannes Fürnkranz. 2014. Large-scale multi-label text classification - revisiting neural networks. In *Joint European Conference on Machine Learning and Knowledge Discovery in Databases*. Springer, pages 437–452.

National Research Council. 2001. *Knowing what students know: The science and design of educational assessment*. National Academies Press.

National Research Council. 2012. *A framework for K-12 science education: Practices, crosscutting concepts, and core ideas.* National Academies Press.

NGSS Lead States. 2013. Next generation science standards: For states, by states http://www.nextgenscience.org/.

Miguel E Ruiz and Padmini Srinivasan. 1998. Automatic text categorization using neural networks. In *Proceedings of the 8th ASIS SIG/CR Workshop on Classification Research*. pages 59–72.

Kikumi K Tatsuoka. 1983. Rule space: An approach for dealing with misconceptions based on item response theory. *Journal of educational measurement* 20(4):345–354.

Erik Wiener, Jan O Pedersen, Andreas S Weigend, et al. 1995. A neural network approach to topic spotting. In *Proceedings of SDAIR-95, 4th annual symposium on document analysis and information retrieval*. Las Vegas, NV, volume 317, page 332.

Connecting the Dots: Towards Human-Level
Grammatical Error Correction

Shamil Chollampatt[1] and **Hwee Tou Ng**[1,2]
[1]NUS Graduate School for Integrative Sciences and Engineering
[2]Department of Computer Science
National University of Singapore
`shamil@u.nus.edu, nght@comp.nus.edu.sg`

Abstract

We build a grammatical error correction (GEC) system primarily based on the state-of-the-art statistical machine translation (SMT) approach, using task-specific features and tuning, and further enhance it with the modeling power of neural network joint models. The SMT-based system is weak in generalizing beyond patterns seen during training and lacks granularity below the word level. To address this issue, we incorporate a character-level SMT component targeting the misspelled words that the original SMT-based system fails to correct. Our final system achieves 53.14% $F_{0.5}$ score on the benchmark CoNLL-2014 test set, an improvement of 3.62% $F_{0.5}$ over the best previous published score.

1 Introduction

Grammatical error correction (GEC) is the task of correcting various textual errors including spelling, grammar, and collocation errors. The phrase-based statistical machine translation (SMT) approach is able to achieve state-of-the-art performance on GEC (Junczys-Dowmunt and Grundkiewicz, 2016). In this approach, error correction is treated as a machine translation task from the language of "bad English" to the language of "good English". SMT-based systems do not rely on language-specific tools and hence they can be trained for any language with adequate parallel data (i.e., erroneous and corrected sentence pairs). They are also capable of correcting complex errors which are difficult for classifier systems that target specific error types. The generalization of SMT-based GEC systems has been shown to improve further by adding neural network models (Chollampatt et al., 2016b).

Though SMT provides a strong framework for GEC, the traditional word-level SMT is weak in generalizing beyond patterns seen in the training data (Susanto et al., 2014; Rozovskaya and Roth, 2016). This effect is particularly evident for spelling errors, since a large number of misspelled words produced by learners are not observed in the training data. We propose improving the SMT approach by adding a character-level SMT component to a word-level SMT-based GEC system, with the aim of correcting misspelled words.

Our word-level SMT-based GEC system utilizes task-specific features described in (Junczys-Dowmunt and Grundkiewicz, 2016). We show in this paper that performance continues to improve further after adding neural network joint models (NNJMs), as introduced in (Chollampatt et al., 2016b). NNJMs can leverage the continuous space representation of words and phrases and can capture a larger context from the source sentence, which enables them to make better predictions than traditional language models (Devlin et al., 2014). The NNJM is further improved using the regularized adaptive training method described in (Chollampatt et al., 2016a) on a higher quality training dataset, which has a higher error-per-sentence ratio. In addition, we add a character-level SMT component to generate candidate corrections for misspelled words. These candidate corrections are rescored with n-gram language model features to prune away non-word candidates and select the candidate that best fits the context. Our final system outperforms the best prior published system when evaluated on the benchmark CoNLL-2014 test set. For better replicability, we release our source code and model files publicly at `https://github.com/nusnlp/smtgec2017`.

Proceedings of the 12th Workshop on Innovative Use of NLP for Building Educational Applications, pages 327–333
Copenhagen, Denmark, September 8, 2017. ©2017 Association for Computational Linguistics

2   Related Work

GEC has gained popularity since the CoNLL-2014 (Ng et al., 2014) shared task was organized. Unlike previous shared tasks (Dale and Kilgarriff, 2011; Dale et al., 2012; Ng et al., 2013) that focused only on a few error types, the CoNLL-2014 shared task dealt with correction of all kinds of textual errors. The SMT approach, which was first used for correcting countability errors of mass nouns (Brockett et al., 2006), became popular during the CoNLL-2014 shared task. Two of the top three teams used this approach in their systems. It later became the most widely used approach and was used in state-of-the-art GEC systems (Susanto et al., 2014; Chollampatt et al., 2016b; Junczys-Dowmunt and Grundkiewicz, 2016; Rozovskaya and Roth, 2016). Neural machine translation approaches have also showed some promise (Xie et al., 2016; Yuan and Briscoe, 2016).

A number of papers on GEC were published in 2016. Chollampatt et al. (2016b) showed that using neural network translation models in phrase-based SMT decoding improves performance. Other works focused on re-ranking and combination of the n-best hypotheses produced by an SMT system using classifiers to generate better corrections (Mizumoto and Matsumoto, 2016; Yuan et al., 2016; Hoang et al., 2016). Rozovskaya and Roth (2016) compared the SMT and classifier approaches by performing error analysis of outputs and described a pipeline system using classifier-based error type-specific components, a context sensitive spelling correction system (Flor and Futagi, 2012), punctuation and casing correction systems, and SMT. Junczys-Dowmunt and Grundkiewicz (2016) described a state-of-the-art SMT-based GEC system using task-specific features, better language models, and task-specific tuning of the SMT system. Their system achieved the best published score to date on the CoNLL-2014 test set. We use the features proposed in their work to enhance the SMT component in our system as well. Additionally, we use neural network joint models (Devlin et al., 2014) introduced in (Chollampatt et al., 2016b) and a character-level SMT component.

Character-level SMT systems are used in transliteration and machine translation (Tiedemann, 2009; Nakov and Tiedemann, 2012; Durrani et al., 2014). It has been previously used for spelling correction in Arabic (Bougares and Bouamor, 2015) and for pre-processing noisy input to an SMT system (Formiga and Fonollosa, 2012).

3   Statistical Machine Translation

We use the popular phrase-based SMT toolkit Moses (Koehn et al., 2007), which employs a log-linear model for combination of features. We use the task-specific tuning and features proposed in (Junczys-Dowmunt and Grundkiewicz, 2016) to further improve the system. The features include edit operation counts, a word class language model (WCLM), the Operation Sequence Model (OSM) (Durrani et al., 2013), and sparse edit operations. Moreover, Junczys-Dowmunt and Grundkiewicz (2016) trained a web-scale language model (LM) using large corpora from the Common Crawl data (Buck et al., 2014). We train an LM of similar size from the same corpora and use it to improve our GEC performance.

4   Neural Network Joint Models and Adaptation

Following Chollampatt et al. (2016b), we add a neural network joint model (NNJM) feature to further improve the SMT component. We train the neural networks on GPUs using log-likelihood objective function with self-normalization, following (Devlin et al., 2014). Training of the neural network joint model is done using a Theano-based (Theano Development Team, 2016) implementation, CoreLM[1]. Chollampatt et al. (2016a) proposed adapting SMT-based GEC based on the native language of writers, by adaptive training of a pre-trained NNJM on in-domain data (written by authors sharing the same native language) using a regularized loss function. We follow this adaptation method and perform subsequent adaptive training of the NNJM, but on a subset of training data with better annotation quality and a higher error-per-sentence ratio, favoring more corrections and thus increasing recall.

5   Spelling Error Correction using SMT

Due to the inherent weakness of SMT-based GEC systems in correcting unknown words (mainly consisting of misspelled words), we add a character-level SMT component for spelling error correction. A character in this character-level

---

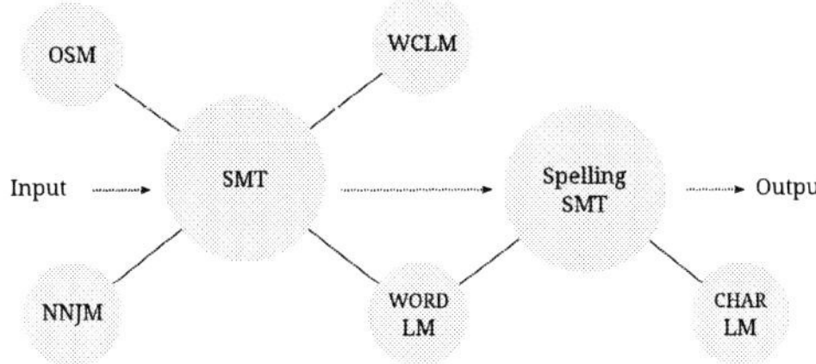

Figure 1: Architecture of our complete SMT-based system.

SMT component is equivalent to a word in word-level SMT, and a sequence of characters (i.e., a word) in the former is equivalent to a sequence of words (i.e., a sentence) in the latter. Input to our character-level SMT component is a sequence of characters that make up the unknown (misspelled) word and output is a list of correction candidates (words). Note that unknown words are words unseen in the source side of the parallel training data used to train the translation model. For training the character-level SMT component, alignments are computed based on a Levenshtein matrix, instead of using GIZA++ (Och and Ney, 2003). Our character-level SMT is tuned using the M^2 metric (Dahlmeier and Ng, 2012) on characters, with character-level edit operation features and a 5-gram character LM. For each unknown word, character-level SMT produces 100 candidates that are then rescored to select the best candidate based on the context. This rescoring is done following Durrani et al. (2014) and uses word-level n-gram LM features: LM probability and the LM OOV (out-of-vocabulary) count denoting the number of words in the sentence that are not in the LM's vocabulary. The architecture of our final system is shown in Figure 1.

6 Experiments

6.1 Data and Evaluation

The parallel data for training our word-level SMT system consist of two corpora: the NUS Corpus of Learner English (NUCLE) (Dahlmeier et al., 2013) and Lang-8 Learner Corpora v2 (Lang-8) (Mizumoto et al., 2011). From NUCLE, we extract sentences with at least one annotation (edit) in a sentence. We use one-fourth of these sentences as our development data (5,458 sentences with 141,978 source tokens). The remainder of NUCLE, including sentences without annotations

(i.e., error-free sentences), are used for training. We extract the English portion of Lang-8 by selecting sentences written by English learners via filtering using a language identification tool, langid.py (Lui and Baldwin, 2012). This filtered data set and the training portion of NUCLE are combined to form the training set, consisting of 2.21M sentences (26.77M source tokens and 30.87M target tokens). We use two corpora to train the LMs: Wikipedia texts (1.78B tokens) and a subset of the Common Crawl corpus (94B tokens). To train the character-level SMT component, we obtain a corpus of misspelled words and their corrections[2], of which the misspelling-correction pairs from Holbrook are used as the development set and the remaining pairs together with the unique words in the NUCLE training data (replicated on the source side to get parallel data) are used for training.

We evaluate our system on the official CoNLL-2014 test set, using the MaxMatch (Dahlmeier and Ng, 2012) scorer v3.2 which computes the $F_{0.5}$ score, as well as on the JFLEG corpus (Napoles et al., 2017), an error-corrected subset of the GUG corpus (Heilman et al., 2014), using the $F_{0.5}$ and GLEU (Napoles et al., 2015) metrics.

6.2 SMT-Based GEC System

Our SMT-based GEC system uses a phrase table trained on the complete parallel data. In our word-level SMT system, we use two 5-gram LMs, one of them trained on the target side of the parallel training data and the other trained on Wikipedia texts (Wiki LM). We add all the *dense* features proposed in (Junczys-Dowmunt and Grundkiewicz, 2016) and *sparse* edit features on words (with one word context). We further improve the system by replacing Wiki LM with a 5-gram LM trained on Common Crawl data (94BCC LM). NNJM is trained on the complete parallel data. We further adapt the NNJM following the adaptation method proposed by Chollampatt et al. (2016a) on sentences from the training portion of NUCLE that contain at least one error annotation (edit) in a sentence. We use the same hyper-parameters as (Chollampatt et al., 2016a). The SMT-based GEC system with all the features, 94BCC LM, and adapted NNJM, is referred to as "Word SMT-GEC".

---

[2]http://www.dcs.bbk.ac.uk/~ROGER/corpora.html

System	CoNLL-2014		
	Prec.	Recall	$F_{0.5}$
SMT-GEC	55.96	22.54	43.16
+ dense + sparse features	58.24	24.84	45.90
− Wiki LM + 94BCC LM	61.02	27.80	49.25
+ NNJM	61.65	29.11	50.39
+ adaptation **[Word SMT-GEC]**	62.14	30.92	51.70
+ Spelling SMT **[Word&Char SMT-GEC]**	**62.74**	**32.96**	**53.14**

Table 1: Results of incremental addition of features and components.

6.3 SMT for Spelling Error Correction

The character-level SMT component that generates candidates for misspelled words uses a 5-gram character-level LM trained on the target side of the spelling corpora. 5-gram Wiki LM is used during rescoring. The final system is referred to as "Word&Char SMT-GEC".

7 Results and Discussions

Table 1 shows the results of incrementally adding features and components to the SMT-GEC system, measuring performance on the official CoNLL-2014 test set. All SMT systems are tuned five times and the feature weights are averaged in order to account for optimizer instability. The improvement obtained for each incremental modification is statistically significant ($p < 0.01$) over its previous system.

The addition of NNJM improves by 1.14% $F_{0.5}$ on top of a high-performing SMT-based GEC system with task-specific features and a web-scale LM. Adaptation of NNJM on a subset of NUCLE improves the results by a notable margin (1.31% $F_{0.5}$). The NUCLE data set is manually annotated by experts and is of higher quality than Lang-8 data. Also, choosing sentences with a higher error rate encourages NNJM to favor more corrections.

Adding the SMT component for spelling error correction ("Spelling SMT") further improves $F_{0.5}$ to 53.14%. We use Wiki LM to rescore the candidates, since using 94BCC LM yielded slightly worse results (53.06% $F_{0.5}$). 94BCC LM, trained on noisy web texts, includes many misspellings in its vocabulary and hence misspelled translation candidates are not effectively pruned away by the OOV feature compared to using Wiki LM.

7.1 Comparison to the State of the Art

Table 2 shows the comparison of our systems to other top-performing systems: Junczys-Dowmunt

System	Official Test ($F_{0.5}$)	Bryant and Ng (2015)		
		10 ann. ($F_{0.5}$)	SvH ($F_{0.5}$)	Ratio (%)
Word SMT-GEC	51.70	68.38	67.51	93.02
Word&Char SMT-GEC	**53.14**	**69.12**	**68.29**	**94.09**
J&G (2016)	49.52	66.83	65.90	90.79
R&R (2016)	47.40	62.45	61.50	84.73
CoNLL-2014 Top System				
Felice et al. (2014)	37.33	54.30	53.47	73.67

Table 2: Comparison on the CoNLL-2014 test set.

System	Dev		Test	
	$F_{0.5}$	GLEU	$F_{0.5}$	GLEU
Word SMT-GEC	58.17	48.17	60.95	53.18
Word&Char SMT-GEC	**61.51**	**51.01**	**64.25**	**56.78**
Yuan and Briscoe (2016)	50.8	47.20	–	52.05
Chollampatt et al. (2016a)	52.7	46.27	–	50.13

Table 3: Results on the JFLEG corpus.

and Grundkiewicz (2016) (J&G) and Rozovskaya and Roth (2016) (R&R)[3]. "Word SMT-GEC" is better than the previous best system (J&G) by a margin of 2.18% $F_{0.5}$. This improvement is without using any additional datasets compared to J&G. "Word&Char SMT-GEC", which additionally uses "Spelling SMT" trained using spelling corpora, increases the margin of improvement to 3.62% $F_{0.5}$ and becomes the new state of the art.

We also evaluate using 10 sets of human annotations of the CoNLL-2014 test set released by Bryant and Ng (2015) ("10 ann."). We measure a system's performance compared to human using the ratio metric ("Ratio"), which is the average system-vs-human score ("SvH") divided by average human-vs-human score ($F_{0.5}$ of 72.58%). "SvH" is computed by removing one set of human annotations at a time and evaluating the system against the remaining 9 sets, and finally averaging over all 10 repetitions. The results show that "Word&Char SMT-GEC" achieves 94.09% of the human-level performance, substantially closing the gap between system and human performance for this task by 36%.

To ascertain the generalizability of our results, we also evaluate our system on the JFLEG development and test sets without re-tuning. Table 3 compares our systems with top-performing systems[4]. Our systems outperform the previous best systems by large margins.

---

[3] We re-run the official scorer (v3.2) on the released outputs of these systems against the official test set as well as the annotations released by Bryant and Ng (2015).

[4] Results are obtained from (Napoles et al., 2017) and https://github.com/keisks/jfleg

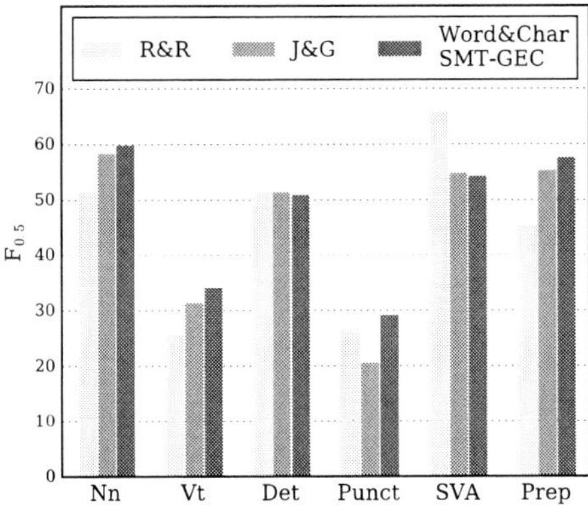

Figure 2: Per-error-type $F_{0.5}$ on CoNLL-2014 test set.

7.2 Error Type Analysis

We analyze the performance of our final system and the top systems on specific error types on the CoNLL-2014 test set. To do this, we compare the per-error-type $F_{0.5}$ using the ERRANT toolkit (Bryant et al., 2017). ERRANT uses a rule-based framework primarily relying on part-of-speech (POS) tags to classify the error types. The error type classification has been shown to achieve 95% acceptance by human raters.

We analyze the performance on six common error types, namely, noun number (*Nn*), verb tense (*Vt*), determiner (*Det*), punctuation (*Punct*), subject-verb agreement (*SVA*), and preposition (*Prep*) errors. The results are shown in Figure 2. Our system outperforms the other systems on four of these six error types, and achieves comparable performance on the determiner errors. It is interesting to note that R&R outperforms our system and J&G on subject-verb agreement errors by a notable margin. This is because R&R uses a classification-based system for subject-verb agreement errors that uses rich linguistic features including syntactic and dependency parse information. SMT-based systems are weaker in correcting such errors as they do not explicitly identify and model the relationship between a verb and its subject.

7.3 Performance on Spelling Errors

We perform comparative analysis on spelling error correction on the CoNLL-2014 test set using ERRANT. The results are summarized in Table 4. Our final system with the character-level SMT

System	Precision	Recall	$F_{0.5}$
J&G (2016)	82.35	46.15	71.19
R&R (2016)	74.19	85.98	76.29
Word SMT-GEC	76.36	46.67	67.74
Word SMT-GEC + Hunspell	58.94	86.41	62.94
Word&Char SMT-GEC	75.40	91.35	78.12

Table 4: Performance on spelling error correction.

component, "Word&Char SMT-GEC", achieves the highest recall (91.35) and $F_{0.5}$ (78.12) compared to the other systems. J&G and 'Word SMT-GEC" rely solely on misspelling-correction patterns seen during training for spelling correction. These two systems achieve the highest precision values (82.35 and 76.36, respectively) but have very low recall values (46.15 and 46.67, respectively) as they do not generalize to unseen misspellings. R&R, on the other hand, uses a specialized context-sensitive spelling error correction component, ConSpel (Flor and Futagi, 2012). ConSpel is a proprietary non-word spell checker that has been shown to outperform off-the-shelf spell checkers such as MS Word and Aspell. Despite using ConSpel, R&R achieves a lower precision (74.19 vs. 75.40) and recall (85.98 vs. 91.35) compared to our final system. We also compare against a baseline where our spelling correction component is replaced by an off-the-shelf spell checker Hunspell ("Word SMT-GEC + Hunspell"). Using Hunspell causes a drastic drop in precision due to a large number of spurious corrections that it proposes and results in a lower $F_{0.5}$ score.

8 Conclusion

We have improved a state-of-the-art SMT-based GEC system by incorporating and adapting neural network joint models. The weakness of SMT-based GEC in correcting misspellings is addressed by adding a character-level SMT component. Our final best system achieves 53.14% $F_{0.5}$ on the CoNLL-2014 test set, outperforming the previous best system by 3.62%, and achieves 94% of human performance on this task.

Acknowledgements

We thank the anonymous reviewers for their valuable feedback. This research was supported by Singapore Ministry of Education Academic Research Fund Tier 2 grant MOE2013-T2-1-150.

References

Fethi Bougares and Houda Bouamor. 2015. UMMU@QALB-2015 shared task: Character and word level SMT pipeline for automatic error correction of Arabic text. In *Proceedings of the Second Workshop on Arabic Natural Language Processing*.

Chris Brockett, William B. Dolan, and Michael Gamon. 2006. Correcting ESL errors using phrasal SMT techniques. In *Proceedings of the 21st International Conference on Computational Linguistics and 44th Annual Meeting of the Association for Computational Linguistics*.

Christopher Bryant, Mariano Felice, and Ted Briscoe. 2017. Automatic annotation and evaluation of error types for grammatical error correction. In *Proceedings of the 55th Annual Meeting of the Association for Computational Linguistics (Volume 1: Long Papers)*.

Christopher Bryant and Hwee Tou Ng. 2015. How far are we from fully automatic high quality grammatical error correction? In *Proceedings of the 53rd Annual Meeting of the Association for Computational Linguistics and the 7th International Joint Conference on Natural Language Processing (Volume 1: Long Papers)*.

Christian Buck, Kenneth Heafield, and Bas van Ooyen. 2014. N-gram counts and language models from the Common Crawl. In *Proceedings of the Ninth International Conference on Language Resources and Evaluation*.

Shamil Chollampatt, Duc Tam Hoang, and Hwee Tou Ng. 2016a. Adapting grammatical error correction based on the native language of writers with neural network joint models. In *Proceedings of the 2016 Conference on Empirical Methods in Natural Language Processing*.

Shamil Chollampatt, Kaveh Taghipour, and Hwee Tou Ng. 2016b. Neural network translation models for grammatical error correction. In *Proceedings of the 25th International Joint Conference on Artificial Intelligence*.

Daniel Dahlmeier and Hwee Tou Ng. 2012. Better evaluation for grammatical error correction. In *Proceedings of the 2012 Conference of the North American Chapter of the Association for Computational Linguistics: Human Language Technologies*.

Daniel Dahlmeier, Hwee Tou Ng, and Siew Mei Wu. 2013. Building a large annotated corpus of learner English: The NUS corpus of learner English. In *Proceedings of the Eighth Workshop on Innovative Use of NLP for Building Educational Applications*.

Robert Dale, Ilya Anisimoff, and George Narroway. 2012. HOO 2012: A report on the preposition and determiner error correction shared task. In *Proceedings of the Seventh Workshop on Building Educational Applications Using NLP*.

Robert Dale and Adam Kilgarriff. 2011. Helping our own: The HOO 2011 pilot shared task. In *Proceedings of the 13th European Workshop on Natural Language Generation*.

Jacob Devlin, Rabih Zbib, Zhongqiang Huang, Thomas Lamar, Richard Schwartz, and John Makhoul. 2014. Fast and robust neural network joint models for statistical machine translation. In *Proceedings of the 52nd Annual Meeting of the Association for Computational Linguistics*.

Nadir Durrani, Alexander Fraser, Helmut Schmid, Hieu Hoang, and Philipp Koehn. 2013. Can Markov models over minimal translation units help phrase-based SMT? In *Proceedings of the 51st Annual Meeting of the Association for Computational Linguistics (Volume 2: Short Papers)*.

Nadir Durrani, Hassan Sajjad, Hieu Hoang, and Philipp Koehn. 2014. Integrating an unsupervised transliteration model into statistical machine translation. In *Proceedings of the 14th Conference of the European Chapter of the Association for Computational Linguistics, Volume 2: Short Papers*.

Mariano Felice, Zheng Yuan, Øistein E. Andersen, Helen Yannakoudakis, and Ekaterina Kochmar. 2014. Grammatical error correction using hybrid systems and type filtering. In *Proceedings of the Eighteenth Conference on Computational Natural Language Learning: Shared Task*.

Michael Flor and Yoko Futagi. 2012. On using context for automatic correction of non-word misspellings in student essays. In *Proceedings of the Seventh Workshop on Building Educational Applications Using NLP*.

Lluís Formiga and José A. R. Fonollosa. 2012. Dealing with input noise in statistical machine translation. In *Proceedings of COLING 2012: Posters*.

Michael Heilman, Aoife Cahill, Nitin Madnani, Melissa Lopez, Matthew Mulholland, and Joel Tetreault. 2014. Predicting grammaticality on an ordinal scale. In *Proceedings of the 52nd Annual Meeting of the Association for Computational Linguistics (Volume 2: Short Papers)*.

Duc Tam Hoang, Shamil Chollampatt, and Hwee Tou Ng. 2016. Exploiting n-best hypotheses to improve an SMT approach to grammatical error correction. In *Proceedings of the 25th International Joint Conference on Artificial Intelligence*.

Marcin Junczys-Dowmunt and Roman Grundkiewicz. 2016. Phrase-based machine translation is state-of-the-art for automatic grammatical error correction. In *Proceedings of the 2016 Conference on Empirical Methods in Natural Language Processing*.

Philipp Koehn, Hieu Hoang, Alexandra Birch, Chris Callison-Burch, Marcello Federico, Nicola Bertoldi, Brooke Cowan, Wade Shen, Christine Moran, Richard Zens, Chris Dyer, Ondrej Bojar, Alexandra

Constantin, and Evan Herbst. 2007. Moses: Open source toolkit for statistical machine translation. In *Proceedings of the 45th Annual Meeting of the Association for Computational Linguistics (Interactive Poster and Demonstration Sessions)*.

Marco Lui and Timothy Baldwin. 2012. langid.py: An off-the-shelf language identification tool. In *Proceedings of the ACL 2012 System Demonstrations*.

Tomoya Mizumoto, Mamoru Komachi, Masaaki Nagata, and Yuji Matsumoto. 2011. Mining revision log of language learning SNS for automated Japanese error correction of second language learners. In *Proceedings of the Fifth International Joint Conference on Natural Language Processing*.

Tomoya Mizumoto and Yuji Matsumoto. 2016. Discriminative reranking for grammatical error correction with statistical machine translation. In *Proceedings of the 2016 Conference of the North American Chapter of the Association for Computational Linguistics: Human Language Technologies*.

Preslav Nakov and Jörg Tiedemann. 2012. Combining word-level and character-level models for machine translation between closely-related languages. In *Proceedings of the 50th Annual Meeting of the Association for Computational Linguistics (Volume 2: Short Papers)*.

Courtney Napoles, Keisuke Sakaguchi, Matt Post, and Joel Tetreault. 2015. Ground truth for grammatical error correction metrics. In *Proceedings of the 53rd Annual Meeting of the Association for Computational Linguistics and the 7th International Joint Conference on Natural Language Processing (Volume 2: Short Papers)*.

Courtney Napoles, Keisuke Sakaguchi, and Joel Tetreault. 2017. JFLEG: A fluency corpus and benchmark for grammatical error correction. In *Proceedings of the 15th Conference of the European Chapter of the Association for Computational Linguistics: Volume 2, Short Papers*.

Hwee Tou Ng, Siew Mei Wu, Ted Briscoe, Christian Hadiwinoto, Raymond Hendy Susanto, and Christopher Bryant. 2014. The CoNLL-2014 shared task on grammatical error correction. In *Proceedings of the Eighteenth Conference on Computational Natural Language Learning: Shared Task*.

Hwee Tou Ng, Siew Mei Wu, Yuanbin Wu, Christian Hadiwinoto, and Joel Tetreault. 2013. The CoNLL-2013 shared task on grammatical error correction. In *Proceedings of the Seventeenth Conference on Computational Natural Language Learning: Shared Task*.

Franz Josef Och and Hermann Ney. 2003. A systematic comparison of various statistical alignment models. *Computational Linguistics*, 29(1):19–51.

Alla Rozovskaya and Dan Roth. 2016. Grammatical error correction: Machine translation and classifiers. In *Proceedings of the 54th Annual Meeting of the Association for Computational Linguistics (Volume 1: Long Papers)*.

Raymond Hendy Susanto, Peter Phandi, and Hwee Tou Ng. 2014. System combination for grammatical error correction. In *Proceedings of the 2014 Conference on Empirical Methods in Natural Language Processing*.

Theano Development Team. 2016. Theano: A Python framework for fast computation of mathematical expressions. *arXiv preprint arXiv:1605.02688*.

Jörg Tiedemann. 2009. Character-based PSMT for closely related languages. In *Proceedings of the 13th Conference of the European Association for Machine Translation*.

Ziang Xie, Anand Avati, Naveen Arivazhagan, Dan Jurafsky, and Andrew Y. Ng. 2016. Neural language correction with character-based attention. *arXiv preprint arXiv:1603.09727*.

Zheng Yuan and Ted Briscoe. 2016. Grammatical error correction using neural machine translation. In *Proceedings of the 15th Annual Conference of the North American Chapter of the Association for Computational Linguistics*.

Zheng Yuan, Ted Briscoe, and Mariano Felice. 2016. Candidate re-ranking for SMT-based grammatical error correction. In *Proceedings of the 11th Workshop on Innovative Use of NLP for Building Educational Applications*.

Question Generation for Language Learning:
From ensuring texts are read to supporting learning

Maria Chinkina   **Detmar Meurers**
LEAD Graduate School & Research Network
Department of Linguistics
Eberhard Karls Universität Tübingen
{maria.chinkina,detmar.meurers}@uni-tuebingen.de

Abstract

In Foreign Language Teaching and Learning (FLTL), questions are systematically used to assess the learner's understanding of a text. Computational linguistic (CL) approaches have been developed to generate such questions automatically given a text (e.g., Heilman, 2011). In this paper, we want to broaden the perspective on the different functions questions can play in FLTL and discuss how automatic question generation can support the different uses.

Complementing the focus on meaning and comprehension, we want to highlight the fact that questions can also be used to make learners notice form aspects of the linguistic system and their interpretation. Automatically generating questions that target linguistic forms and grammatical categories in a text in essence supports incidental focus-on-form (Loewen, 2005) in a meaning-focused reading task. We discuss two types of questions serving this purpose, how they can be generated automatically; and we report on a crowdsourcing evaluation comparing automatically generated to manually written questions targeting particle verbs, a challenging linguistic form for learners of English.

1 Introduction

"Learning is goal-oriented ... Teaching therefore becomes an active thinking and decision-making process in which the teacher is constantly assessing what students already know, what they need to know, and how to provide for successful learning." (O'Malley and Chamot, 1990)

One of the most common ways to find out what students do and do not know is to ask questions.

In communicative and task-based language teaching, where the meaning and function of language drives the pedagogy, questions are asked to support the task at hand. Relatedly, when dealing with written language material, recall or comprehension questions can spell out typical goals for reading a text: searching for specific information or more comprehensively integrating the information provided in the text into the reader's background knowledge to draw inferences on that basis.

An increasing body of CL research supports the automatic generation of questions in order to assist teachers in constructing practice exercises and tests. For example, Heilman (2011) is a prominent approach for the generation of factual, low-level questions suitable for beginner or intermediate students. His goal is to assess the reader's knowledge of the information in the text, which is relevant for both content and language teaching.

At the same time, Second Language Acquisition (SLA) research since the 90s has emphasized that language input and meaning-based tasks alone are not sufficient to ensure successful language acquisition. Learners must also notice linguistic forms and grammatical categories (Schmidt, 1990) and teaching can facilitate such noticing through so-called focus on form (Doughty and Williams, 1998). Focus on form is designed to draw the learner's attention to relevant linguistic features of the language as they arise, while keeping the overriding focus on meaning (Long, 1991, pp. 45f). For written language, input enhancement (Sharwood Smith, 1993) has been proposed to make relevant forms more salient in the input, e.g., by coloring or font choices. Such visual input enhancement has also been automated using CL methods (Meurers et al., 2010), as part of a system also generating in-text exercises.

One problem with *form-based visual input enhancement* is that coloring a form or otherwise

Proceedings of the 12th Workshop on Innovative Use of NLP for Building Educational Applications, pages 334–344
Copenhagen, Denmark, September 8, 2017. ©2017 Association for Computational Linguistics

making it visually more salient neither ensures that it is noticed and cognitively processed more thoroughly nor do we know which aspect of that form the reader will notice and how it is interpreted. For example, coloring the form *has been raining* in a text may draw the reader's attention to any aspect of those forms (e.g., number or length of the words, or the *-ing* suffix of the last word), and noticing the form does not necessarily map it to its present perfect continuous interpretation.

In this paper, we propose another option for providing input enhancement, *functionally-driven input enhancement*. Concretely, we propose to generate two types of questions creating a functional need to process the targeted linguistic features. The first type of questions we generate are content questions about the clause containing the targeted form. So these questions are like Heilman's factual questions, but they are targeting sentences containing particular linguistic features to be acquired. To answer such questions, the learner must process form and meaning of the clause, ensuring increased activation of the targeted form. The goal of these questions is to ensure more exposure to the forms, so we will refer to them as *form exposure questions*.

The second type of functionally-driven input enhancement is designed to also ensure interpretation of the targeted form. For this, the nature of the question that is generated must be changed from asking about the content of the text to asking about the interpretation of the form being targeted. In the spirit of the concept questions of Workman (2008), we will refer to such questions as *grammar concept questions*.

The goal of this paper is to combine insights from SLA research with CL techniques to explore new options for question generation in support of language learning. In section 2, we first characterize the overall spectrum of questions we consider to be of relevance to FLTL, from supporting communication via ensuring texts are read to supporting learning of linguistic forms and their function. Section 3.1 then surveys the computational linguistic work on automatic question generation, which has focused on the content-side of the spectrum. Section 3.2 spells out the SLA background needed to motivate our research on question generation targeting linguistic forms and their interpretation. In section 4 we then present the question generation approach we developed, mostly

concentrating on the two new types of questions designed to provide functionally-driven input enhancement. For such questions to be effective, they must be reasonably well-formed and answerable, so in section 5 we present the results from a crowd sourcing experiment we conducted to evaluate whether the automatically generated form exposure questions are comparable to manually written questions in those two respects. Finally, section 6 provides a conclusion and outlook.

2 A spectrum of questions for FLTL

In an FLTL context, questions can be asked to serve a broad range of different goals:

1. We can ask about the learner's experience or general knowledge (e.g., "What do you know about Japan?"), which can serve a communicative goal.

2. Comprehension or recall questions can be asked to check whether the learner has understood a text or read it at all.

3. Questions can also be asked with the goal of eliciting a linguistic form from the learner (e.g., the question "What would you do if you won in a lottery?" requires the learner to produce conditionals.)

4. As introduced in the previous section, we can use questions to provide functionally-driven input enhancement drawing the learner's attention to the linguistic forms used in a given text. *Form exposure questions* ensure that the sentence containing the targeted forms are read and generally understood. Answering *grammar-concept questions* in addition requires an understanding of the interpretation of the targeted form.

5. Finally, there also are meta-linguistic questions checking the learner's explicit knowledge of the language system (e.g., "From which verb is the noun *decision* derived?" or "What is the synonym of *staff*?").

The aforementioned goals are presented in a particular order, from more communicative to more formal ones. In the work presented in this paper, we primarily focus on the idea of functionally-driven input enhancement captured by the fourth type: questions drawing the learner's attention to particular linguistic forms in the reading material and their interpretation. To contextualize our approach, we first provide some background on automatic question generation and the SLA concepts grounding our proposal.

3 Background

3.1 Automatic Question Generation

A typical text-based Question Generation (QG) system consists of three components: target selection (sentences and words), generation of questions (and answers), and the generation of distractors, which is applicable for a multiple choice answer setup. Most of work on *target selection* follows a top-down perspective on the text: First, a set of suitable sentences is selected based on different criteria (e.g., Pino et al., 2008; Pilán et al., 2013). Then the target words or linguistic forms are selected within the set of suitable sentences (e.g., Becker et al., 2012). Given our focus on input enhancement for language learning, we instead pursue a bottom-up approach: Given one or more target linguistic forms (e.g., the passive voice, or the present perfect tense), we automatically select all the candidate sentences in a text containing the target forms, apply basic constraints to filter out unsuitable sentences (such as those containing unresolvable pronouns), and then generate questions to the remaining ones.

Once the target sentence has been selected, it can be used to *generate questions* targeting particular linguistic forms contained in the sentence. Heilman (2011) discusses the generation of factual, low-level questions suitable for beginner or intermediate students and gives a comprehensive overview of QG methods. Among the most prominent ones are: replacing the target form with a gap (Agarwal et al., 2011; Becker et al., 2012), applying transformation rules (Mitkov et al., 2006), filling templates (Curto et al., 2012), and generating all possible questions to a sentence and ranking them afterwards using a supervised learning algorithm (Heilman and Smith, 2009). Finally, QG is not an exception to the wave of neural networks, and Du et al. (2017) have recently approached automatic generation of reading comprehension questions on that basis. All of the mentioned QG systems either assess vocabulary or target reading comprehension, which contrasts with the focus of our work on functionally supporting focus on form in language learning.

Distractor generation is a separate complex task that has received some attention in the QG community. It supports the provision of answers in a multiple-choice setup, and the choice of distractors is closely tied to what is intended to be assessed by the question. Traditionally, distractors are selected among words that are semantically related to the correct answer (Mitkov et al., 2006; Araki et al., 2016). Brown et al. (2005) select the distractors among the most frequent words that have the same part of speech as the correct answer. Pino and Eskenazi (2009) inform the distractor generation component by the wrong answers provided by the users of their system. Given that we do not focus on the multiple choice answer format here, distractor generation is not discussed further in this paper.

3.2 Relevant SLA concepts

Attention, *input*, and *form-meaning mapping* are key SLA concepts that are directly related to our work. We already saw in our introduction in section 1 that both meaning and form play important roles in SLA. Pushing this discussion one step further, work in the Input Processing paradigm (VanPatten and Cadierno, 1993), based on Krashen's (1977) input hypothesis, provides several relevant studies showing that "learners process input for meaning before they process it for form" (VanPatten, 1990; Wong, 2001). However, Norris and Ortega (2000) argued that simultaneously directing the learner's attention to form and meaning in the input does not hinder L2 development or reading comprehension. Leow et al. (2008) came to the same conclusion after revisiting the methodology used in the replication studies mentioned above and conducting a new study. Their results did not show any statistically significant differences in comprehension between different intervention groups. Finally, a study by Morgan-Short et al. (2012) demonstrated that learners who attended to and processed linguistic forms while reading for meaning scored higher on comprehension than those only reading for meaning.

In line with the Noticing Hypothesis (Schmidt, 1990), the most straightforward way to draw the learner's attention to particular linguistic forms in a text is to increase their salience. As the meta-analysis of Lee and Huang (2008) shows, results on the isolated effect of visual input enhancement on L2 development has been mixed. One option for pushing this research further is to investigate other types of input enhancement and the combination of visual input enhancement with other input activities.

The Input Processing approach to SLA has given rise to a pedagogical intervention called *processing instruction* (VanPatten, 2004). Its goal is to ensure that learners make form-meaning connections during reading. This goes beyond textual enhancement, which only ensures noticing (Benati, 2016). One of the components of processing instruction, structured input practice, has been identified as particularly effective in fostering L2 development (VanPatten and Oikkenon, 1996; Benati, 2004; Wong, 2004). Structured input is "input that is manipulated in particular ways to push learners to become dependent on form and structure to get meaning" (Lee and VanPatten, 1995).

Structured input activities can be seen as an umbrella term for a wide range of language teaching techniques. They provide the learners with enriched input and prompt them to process and eventually produce the target linguistic forms. While in the original approach, the input enrichment and development of structured input activities is done manually, CL methods can support this process. We have developed a system for automatic input enrichment, FLAIR (Chinkina and Meurers, 2016), which supports retrieval of documents containing targeted linguistic features. The linguistic features covered by the system include the full set of grammatical constructions spelled out in the official English language curriculum of schools in Baden-Württemberg (Germany). On this enriched input basis, automating the generation of questions as structured input activities is the logical next step. In the next section, we spell out the different types of questions that we are able to generate automatically and discuss the algorithms and challenges behind their generation.

4 Generating questions for FLTL

As mentioned in section 3.1, most of the work on QG has dealt with vocabulary (Brown et al., 2005) and comprehension questions (Mostow et al., 2004), not on linguistic form and grammar. For approaches automatically generating exercises that facilitate grammar acquisition and practice, cloze sentences are the most ubiquitous type. They are generated by substituting the target linguistic form with a gap, and the challenge usually lies in the selection of good sentences and gaps (Becker et al., 2012; Niraula and Rus, 2015).

(1)　The advisory group had ________ a list of all the different territorial arrangements in the EU. (draw up)

Metalinguistic questions, which are designed to test learners' explicit knowledge of the language system, have not received much attention in the QG community. The reason probably lies in the fact that they require the use of a limited number of templates and only a minimal amount of NLP. Their frequent use by teachers is also widely criticized by educators and researchers alike, mainly because they do not serve a communicative goal. For example, in order to generate question (2), one would only need a POS-tagger and the WordNet database (Miller, 1995).

(2)　From which verb is the noun *generation* derived?

To cover the whole spectrum of exercises facilitating the acquisition and practice of grammar, we also generate cloze and metalinguistic questions. However, the focus of the paper is on questions providing functionally-driven input enhancement, so we limit the discussion to those two types for space reasons.

4.1 Form Exposure Questions

Form exposure questions focus on a particular linguistic form, which can either be part of the question or be expected in the learner's production. They can take the form of a *wh-*, yes/no, or an alternative question. For example, when asking a question about the source text (3), one can think of different linguistic targets: relative clauses, past forms of irregular and regular verbs, etc. Question (3a) is asked about the subject and targets the particle verb *brought in*.

(3)　Indeed, Semel and the media executives he brought in by all accounts turned a scrappy young internet startup into a highly profitable company that brought old-line advertising to a new medium.

　　a.　Who turned a scrappy young internet startup into a highly profitable company? Semel and the media executives he ________.

Generation　We generate form exposure questions to subjects, objects, and predicates. The main linguistic form we focus on is the grammatical tense, so our form exposure questions target verbs and verb phrases.

We use the Java implementation of Stanford CoreNLP 3.7.0 for part-of-speech tagging, parsing, and resolving coreferences (Manning et al., 2014). After extracting a sentence or a clause containing the target form, we perform the following steps: adjust and normalize the auxiliaries, resolve pronouns and other referential expressions, and detect quotation sources, if any. Then the algorithm proceeds to detect specific syntactic components of the sentence, to modify them if necessary, and finally *transformation rules* are used to turn a sentence into a question. Let us inspect the algorithm for generating questions to predicates.

A. Active

(e.g., *What have Chinese retailers done?*)

1) Insert the question word "What" at the beginning of the sentence.
2) Identify or generate an auxiliary verb.
   - If there is an auxiliary verb modifying the main verb, identify it.
   - Otherwise, identify the grammatical tense of the main verb and generate an appropriate auxiliary verb.
3) Move the auxiliary verb to right after "What".
4) Identify the grammatical form of the main verb and replace the rest of the sentence with the same form of the verb *do*.

B. Passive

(e.g., *What happened to the staff?*)

1) Insert the question word "What" at the beginning of the sentence.
2) Identify the grammatical tense of the main verb and replace the whole predicate with the same form of the verb *happen* (including the auxiliary verb, if any).
3) Insert the preposition *to* left of the subject.
4) Remove the rest of the sentence.

In addition to generating questions, we also generate gap sentences (e.g., for particle verbs, *Chinese retailers have ______ staff.*). These question items can be used as fill-in-the-blanks or multiple choice exercises. In the latter case, one can ensure a deeper level of processing of the target linguistic form by having its synonym as the solution and semantically related words as distractors.

Challenges There is a two-stage process identifying the main syntactic components, POS- and dependency-based, and both of these are obligatory for the system to be able to generate a question. If there is an error, a syntactic component may not be detected. For instance, in example (4), *Skype* was identified as a verb by the statistical parser. Consequently, no subject was detected, and it was not possible to generate a question.

(4)   Skype was snapped up by eBay Inc.

The most challenging case that results in generating ungrammatical questions is when the parser incorrectly identifies secondary parts of speech, which does not prevent the system from generating a question. Given the source text (5) below, the question (5a) was generated. The parse tree of the source includes the noun phrase *(NP (VBG meaning) (NNS fans))*, which was then identified as the subject of the sentence.

(5)   Internet access in the Communist-ruled island is restricted, meaning fans can not easily look up series and mangas on the web.

   a. What can *meaning* fans not do? *Meaning fans can not ______ series and mangas on the web.*

Another type of error occurs when the coreference resolution component maps a referring expression to the wrong noun phrase. Given the source sentence (6), the program generated the question in (6a). *The manager* is resolved incorrectly as Dean Saunders instead of Chris Coleman.

(6)   Former Wales striker Dean Saunders says his country will struggle to hang on to Chris Coleman after their startling run to the Euro 2016 semi-finals and believes the manager could be tempted away soon.

   a. According to the article, what could happen to *former Wales striker Dean Saunders*? Former Wales striker Dean Saunders could be ______ soon.

In questions to subjects and objects, coreference resolution was originally used to determine the question word, *Who* or *What*. However, the error rate was high for rare names that occasionally occur in news articles at the beginning of sentences. Thus, we now combine the two question words in one question phrase *Who or what*. The English teachers we consulted preferred this solution over erroneously generated question words. To further minimize the effect of errors caused by coreference resolution, we do not substitute the subject of a gap sentence with a pronoun, which often leads to repetition of subject noun phrases.

4.2 Grammar-concept Questions

When it comes to grammar, questions can either focus the reader's attention on the form or the meaning of linguistic forms. In addition to testing the learner's understanding of text, meaning-driven questions also help raise the learner's (meta-)linguistic awareness and read and learn the language in a focused way. Rephrasing and form manipulation is one example of such meaning-driven grammar questions. The passive voice, for instance, is normally substituted with the active voice (or vice versa) to make the learner make inferences based on its semantics.

Similarly, grammar-concept questions make the learner infer information by isolating defining semantic characteristics of linguistic forms. Once the grammatical concept of a linguistic form is broken down into a series of semantic statements, yes/no or alternative questions can be asked about each of these statements. Consider the following example by Workman (2008):

Sentence: He *used to* play football.
Concept: *Used to* expresses a discontinued past habit. It highlights the fact that the person does not do this anymore in the present.
Concept questions:

1. Does he play football now? (No)
2. Did he play football in the past? (Yes)
3. Did he play once or often? (Often)

One important application of grammar-concept questions is scaffolding feedback. The questions can incrementally guide the learner towards task completion by scaffolding the use of correct forms. Grammar-concept questions then not only make the learners aware of the form but also guide them towards production.

Generation Depending on the linguistic form, we use different templates to generate the grammar-concept questions, and we transform the target verb into the appropriate tense form.[1]

Let us take a closer look at the case of the present perfect tense. Its two key characteristics are (i) the finished state of the action and (ii) the irrelevance of the exact time in the past when the action took place. The templates (7) and (8) are used for generating grammar-concept questions about these aspects.

(7)   `Be-form subject still verbing (particle)(dir-obj)(indir-obj)?`

     e.g., *Are Chinese retailers still cutting staff?*

(8)   Is it more important when exactly `subject verb-past (particle) (dir-obj) (indir-obj)` or that `verbing (dir-obj) (indir-obj)` took place at all?

     e.g., *Is it more important when exactly Chinese retailers cut staff or that cutting staff took place at all?*

Since the correct answers are known for each template, they can be hard-coded there. As the templates show, a target sentence should always contain a subject and a verb. The particle element is there for the case of particle verbs, and the object elements are optional.

Challenges One limitation of the current implementation of grammar-concept questions is that without identifying the specific interpretation of a grammatical tense, we can only specify rather general templates, one or two per grammatical tense. The task of tense sense disambiguation (Reichart and Rappoport, 2010) is very relevant to our work and can facilitate the creation of more fine-grained templates. For example, in case of the past simple tense, one could also ask about the repetitive versus single occurrence of an action in the past; in case of the present perfect continuous tense, a question about the (in)completeness of an action would be plausible.

5 Comparing computer-generated and human-written questions

For questions to be effective in real-life FLTL, they must be reasonably well-formed and answerable. We therefore conducted a crowdsourcing study[2] to determine how automatically generated questions and manually written questions are perceived in those two respects.

We started with a corpus of 40 news articles and 96 questions written by Simón Ruiz, an English

---

[1] For this step, we make use of the Java library `https://github.com/simplenlg/simplenlg`.

[2] For this study, we used the CrowdFlower platform: `https://crowdflower.com`

teacher and SLA researcher, to test the learner's knowledge of particle verbs. We used the question generation approach introduced in section 4 and generated 69 form exposure questions to particle verbs. To obtain an equal number of questions for the experiment, we randomly selected 69 questions from the manually created ones.

The crowd workers were selected among proficient speakers of English. This requirement was enforced by a website functionality restricting participating countries, three so-called test questions asking the participants about their level of English and self-perceived reliability of their judgements, and other test questions assessing their proficiency in English, which we now turn to.

In a crowdsourcing experiment, test questions are crucial because they limit the set of workers to those satisfying the requirements and make it possible to verify they are paying attention and follow the instructions. To create test questions assessing the workers' proficiency in English, we first created eight ungrammatical or unanswerable question items as follows: We edited four out of the 27 human-written questions not used in the study and four automatically generated questions to make them either ungrammatical or unanswerable. To obtain test questions on the clearly grammatical and answerable side of the spectrum, we ran a pilot study and selected sentences rated high with a high agreement among the contributors. Four human-written and four computer-generated ones were chosen as good examples of well-formed and answerable test questions. In order for the crowd workers to be eligible to start judging non-test questions, they had to pass through the so-called quiz mode and achieve 70% accuracy on five randomly selected test question items.

We investigated whether computer-generated questions are on a par with human-written ones based on two criteria, well-formedness and answerability. In other words, whether the question is written in acceptable English and whether it can be answered given the information in the source text. In addition, we asked the crowd workers whether they thought the question was written by an English teacher or generated automatically by a computer. Concretely, each task presented to the crowd workers consisted of an excerpt from the source news text and the human-written or automatically-generated question. The workers were asked to answer four questions:

1. How well-formed is this question item? Is it written in good English? (5-point Likert scale)

2. Can this question item be completed with the information from the source text? (5-point Likert scale)

3. Please, answer this question – in your words, in as few words as possible – based on the information from the source text. (free input)

4. Do you think this question was written by an English teacher or generated by a computer? (binary choice)

There also was an optional comment field.

Below you can find an example for a news excerpt (9) and the questions which were written manually (9a) and automatically-generated (9b).

(9) "Scotland is a part of the UK," a spokesman for the European Commission said. "All parts of the UK should sort out what they want to do," he added, calling the options "speculation".

    a. What did a spokesman for the European Commission say about the UK? He said that all parts of the UK should __________ what they want to do.

    b. According to a spokesman for the European Commission, what should all parts of the UK do? All parts of the UK should __________ what they want to do.

We received 1,384 judgements by 364 crowd workers classified as reliable, who identified as proficient English speakers and passed the quiz mode with the test questions. On the well-formedness scale, the means were 4.53 for human-written and 4.40 for computer-generated questions. On the answerability scale, the means were 4.44 and 4.47, respectively. We calculated the intra-class correlation (ICC) for the contributors and got 0.08 and 0.09 for well-formedness and answerability, respectively. The low contributor ICC ($< .1$) implies that the contributors provided different ratings for different question items, so we can ignore the dependencies among the observations and did not need a multi-level analysis.

To find out whether the difference in ratings between computer-generated and human-written questions is statistically significant, we ran Welch's t-test. On the well-formedness scale, the results turned out to be statistically significant, but the effect size was small: $t(913) = 2.06$, $p = .03$, Cohen's $d = 0.13$. On the answerability scale, the results were non-significant: $t(944) = -0.42$, $p \geq .1$, Cohen's $d = 0.02$.

However, the absence of evidence does not imply the evidence of absence. To test whether the computer-generated and human-written questions are equivalent in quality (well-formedness and answerability), we used Schuirmann's (1987) two one-sided test (TOST). The TOST is commonly used in medical research to determine if one treatment is as effective as another one. To prove our alternative hypothesis that computer-generated and human-written questions are comparable in quality, we needed to reject two parts of the null hypothesis:

$H0_1$: Computer-generated questions are inferior in quality to human-written ones.

$H0_2$: Computer-generated questions are superior in quality to human-written ones.

In statistical terms, the null hypothesis is that there is a true effect larger than a Smallest Effect Size of Interest (SESOS) between the two samples (Lakens, 2014). For this task, we opted for an SESOS of 0.5, a medium effect size according to Cohen (1977), and an alpha level of .05 (Lakens, 2017). We used the R package TOSTER[3] to conduct TOST testing for equivalence of the samples. All results were statistically significant on both scales ($p \leq .001$), so we could reject the null hypothesis (for more details, see Table 1).

Scale	t_1	t_2	p_1 and p_2	90% CI
well-formed	9.81	-5.68	$\leq.001$	[0.02;0.22]
answerable	7.32	-8.17	$\leq.001$	[-0.13;0.08]

Table 1: Results of Schuirmann's TOST for equivalence of computer-generated and human-written questions. Effect size d = 0.5; alpha = 0.05.

The results indicate that any difference in the ratings for well-formedness and answerability of the human-written and computer-generated questions is of an effect size smaller than the SESOS. In line with this finding, the contributors' answers guessing whether a question was written by an English teacher or generated by a computer were similar for both question classes: 74% of human-written and 67% of computer-generated questions were thought to be written by an English teacher. Our goal at this stage was to identify whether the questions as generated can effectively be used on a par with manually written questions – which indeed seems to be the case.

6 Conclusion and Outlook

We discussed question generation for FLTL and proposed that, in addition to the typical focus of such work on meaning and understanding, questions can also play an important role for functionally-driven input enhancement. In line with the focus-on-form perspective in Second Language Acquisition research and the notion of structured input activities, such questions help the learner in processing relevant forms and draw form-meaning connections while engaging in a meaning-based activity.

We proposed two types of questions designed to provide functionally-driven input enhancement of a text. *Form exposure questions* serve to engage a learner in more thoroughly processing a sentence containing a targeted form. *Grammar-concept questions* require the learner to interpret the targeted form in addition to processing it. We discussed the transformation- and template-based question generation approach we implemented for this purpose and exemplified the approach for particular tenses and verb classes. To evaluate whether the automatically generated form exposure questions are up to real-life use, we compared the well-formedness and answerability of automatically generated questions targeting particle verbs to human-written questions of the same type. The crowd sourcing results suggest that the automatic question generation can meaningfully be put to real-life use in a system, thereby paving the way for an external evaluation in terms of the learning outcomes that can be achieved by a functionally-driven input enhancement approach.

Using NLP technology integrated in web-based tools to support the intervention, a large-scale randomized controlled field study can be set up and run over an entire semester or school year, which is significantly longer than typical interventions, but it is the time span in which real-life foreign language learning takes place. Crucially, such a setup can also include collection of measures of individ-

---

[3]https://cran.r-project.org/web/packages/TOSTER/

ual differences and other relevant factors. For example, grammar-concept questions may be particularly valuable when the learner's first language does not have a particular linguistic form, as suggested by Workman (2008). The data from such an NLP-supported intervention study will stand to showcase the synergy that can result at the intersection of SLA and CL research (Meurers and Dickinson, 2017). In addition to empirically testing and advancing SLA hypotheses, the insights could further improve CL applications by integrating a learner model to parametrize the generation of questions for those target forms that are particularly relevant for a given user.

From the CL perspective, the task of generating such questions is feasible yet challenging and is interestingly intertwined with other NLP tasks. For instance, the tasks of named entity recognition and coreference resolution can be used to make questions more precise. However, there often is a trade-off between allowing for somewhat general phrases ("who or what" as a question phrase) and using a coreference resolution component with a suboptimal accuracy. We intend to explore this trade-off further in the future. In a similar vein, we also intend to develop filters to further reduce the number of generated questions that are suboptimal in terms of well-formedness, typically resulting from errors in parsing the sentence to be questioned.

In terms of conceptual outlook, there also are some issues we intend to pursue. When grammar-concept questions are asked, they may or may not draw the reader's attention to the target linguistic form, especially if semantic redundancy is present. The issue is exemplified by (10).

(10)   John *used to* play football, but since moving back to Tuvalu doesn't do so anymore.

    a. Does John still play football?

As the semantics of *used to* implies a discontinued past habit, the grammar-concept question shown in (10a) could be generated. However, the clause *doesn't do so anymore* has exactly the same implication, which can interfere with the learner noticing and processing the target linguistic form *used to*. This issue is reminiscent of VanPatten's Preference for Non-redundancy Principle (VanPatten, 2004). Short of changing the text as such, one option for ensure noticing of the relevant target is to combine the function-driven input enhancement with visual input enhancement. In practice,

automatic question generation here can be combined with automatic visual input enhancement (Meurers et al., 2010) by both asking a question about the semantics of a targeted linguistic form and highlighting it. Arguably, both types of input enhancement should be preceded by a text selection step that ensures a rich representation of the form to be targeted in the text. A linguistically-aware search engine, such as FLAIR (Chinkina and Meurers, 2016), can provide automatic input enrichment to support teachers and learners in text selection.

In terms of practical plans, we plan to integrate automatic visual and function-driven input enhancement into the FLAIR system. Going further towards activity generation, it could also be attractive to provide an interface from input enrichment and enhancement tools to applications supporting activity generation, such as the Language Muse Activity Palette (Burstein et al., 2017).

Acknowledgments

This research was supported by the LEAD Graduate School & Research Network [GSC1028], a project of the Excellence Initiative of the German federal and state governments. Maria Chinkina is a doctoral student at the LEAD Graduate School & Research Network.

We would like to thank our LEAD colleagues Michael Grosz and Johann Jacoby for sharing their expertise and insights in the field of statistical analysis.

The crowd sourcing experiment was made possible by the manual gold-standard questions targeting English particle verbs, which are a part of the PhD research of Simón Ruiz. We are grateful to him for providing us with the questions and allowing us to use them in the experiment.

Finally, we would like to thank the anonymous reviewers and the organizers whose feedback helped us improve the paper.

References

Manish Agarwal, Rakshit Shah, and Prashanth Mannem. 2011. Automatic question generation using discourse cues. In *Proceedings of the 6th Workshop on Innovative Use of NLP for Building Educational Applications*. Portland, OR, pages 1–9. http://aclweb.org/anthology/W11-1401.

Jun Araki, Dheeraj Rajagopal, Sreecharan Sankaranarayanan, Susan Holm, Yukari Yamakawa, and

Teruko Mitamura. 2016. Generating questions and multiple-choice answers using semantic analysis of texts. In *COLING*. pages 1125–1136. http://aclweb.org/anthology/C16-1107.

Lee Becker, Sumit Basu, and Lucy Vanderwende. 2012. Mind the gap: learning to choose gaps for question generation. In *Proceedings of the 2012 Conference of the North American Chapter of the Association for Computational Linguistics: Human Language Technologies*. Association for Computational Linguistics, pages 742–751. http://aclweb.org/anthology/N12-1092.

Alessandro Benati. 2004. The effects of structured input activities and explicit information on the acquisition of the italian future tense. *Processing instruction: Theory, research, and commentary* pages 207–225.

Alessandro Benati. 2016. Input manipulation, enhancement and processing: Theoretical views and empirical research. *Studies in Second Language Learning and Teaching* 6(1):65–88. https://doi.org/10.14746/ssllt.2016.6.1.4.

Jonathan Brown, Gwen Frishkoff, and Maxine Eskenazi. 2005. Automatic question generation for vocabulary assessment. In *Proceedings of Human Language Technology Conference and Conference on Empirical Methods in Natural Language Processing*. Vancouver, British Columbia, Canada, pages 819–826. http://aclweb.org/anthology/H05-1103.

Jill Burstein, Nitin Madnani, John Sabatini, Dan McCaffrey, Kietha Biggers, and Kelsey Dreier. 2017. Generating language activities in real-time for english learners using language muse. In *Proceedings of the Fourth (2017) ACM Conference on Learning @ Scale*. ACM, New York, NY, USA, L@S '17, pages 213–215. https://doi.org/10.1145/3051457.3053988.

Maria Chinkina and Detmar Meurers. 2016. Linguistically-aware information retrieval: Providing input enrichment for second language learners. In *Proceedings of the 11th Workshop on Innovative Use of NLP for Building Educational Applications*. San Diego, CA, pages 188–198. http://aclweb.org/anthology/W16-0521.pdf.

Jacob Cohen. 1977. *Statistical power analysis for the behavioral sciences*. Academic Press, New York.

Sérgio Curto, Ana Cristina Mendes, and Luísa Coheur. 2012. Question generation based on lexico-syntactic patterns learned from the web. *Dialogue & Discourse* 3(2):147–175. https://doi.org/10.5087/dad.2012.207.

Catherine Doughty and John Williams, editors. 1998. *Focus on form in classroom second language acquisition*. Cambridge University Press, Cambridge.

Xinya Du, Junru Shao, and Claire Cardie. 2017. Learning to ask: Neural question generation for reading comprehension. *arXiv preprint* https://arxiv.org/pdf/1705.00106.

Michael Heilman. 2011. *Automatic factual question generation from text*. Ph.D. thesis, Carnegie Mellon University.

Michael Heilman and Noah A. Smith. 2009. Question generation via overgenerating transformations and ranking. Technical report, DTIC Document.

Stephen Krashen. 1977. Some issues relating to the monitor model. *On Tesol* 77(144-158).

Daniël Lakens. 2014. Performing high-powered studies efficiently with sequential analyses. *European Journal of Social Psychology* 44(7):701–710.

Daniel Lakens. 2017. Equivalence tests: A practical primer for t tests, correlations, and meta-analyses. *Social Psychological and Personality Science* .

James F. Lee and Bill VanPatten. 1995. *Making communicative language teaching happen*, volume 1: Directions for Language Learning and Teaching. ERIC. https://doi.org/10.2307/328644.

Sang-Ki Lee and Hung-Tzu Huang. 2008. Visual Input Enhancement and Grammar Learning: A meta-analytic review. *Studies in Second Language Acquisition* 30:307–331. https://doi.org/10.1017/s0272263108080479.

Ronald P. Leow, Hui-Chen Hsieh, and Nina Moreno. 2008. Attention to form and meaning revisited. *Language Learning* 58(3):665–695. https://doi.org/10.1111/j.1467-9922.2008.00453.x.

Shawn Loewen. 2005. Incidental focus on form and second language learning. *Studies in Second Language Acquisition* 27(3):361–386. https://doi.org/10.1017/S0272263105050163.

Michael H. Long. 1991. Focus on form: A design feature in language teaching methodology. In K. De Bot, C. Kramsch, and R. Ginsberg, editors, *Foreign language research in cross-cultural perspective*, John Benjamins, Amsterdam, pages 39–52.

Christopher D. Manning, Mihai Surdeanu, John Bauer, Jenny Finkel, Steven J. Bethard, and David McClosky. 2014. The Stanford CoreNLP natural language processing toolkit. In *Proceedings of 52nd Annual Meeting of the Association for Computational Linguistics: System Demonstrations*. Baltimore, Maryland, pages 55–60. https://doi.org/10.3115/v1/p14-5010.

Detmar Meurers and Markus Dickinson. 2017. Evidence and interpretation in language learning research: Opportunities for collaboration with computational linguistics. *Language Learning* S1(2). http://dx.doi.org/10.1111/lang.12233.

Detmar Meurers, Ramon Ziai, Luiz Amaral, Adriane Boyd, Aleksandar Dimitrov, Vanessa Metcalf, and Niels Ott. 2010. Enhancing authentic web pages for language learners. In *Proceedings of the 5th Workshop on Innovative Use of NLP for Building Educational Applications (BEA-5) at NAACL-HLT 2010*. Los Angeles, pages 10–18. http://aclweb.org/anthology/W10-1002.pdf.

George Miller. 1995. Wordnet: a lexical database for English. *Communications of the ACM* 38(11):39–41. http://aclweb.org/anthology/H94-1111.

Ruslan Mitkov, Le An Ha, and Nikiforos Karamanis. 2006. A computer-aided environment for generating multiple-choice test items. *Natural Language Engineering* 12(2):177–194. https://doi.org/10.1017/S1351324906004177.

Kara Morgan-Short, Jeanne Heil, Andrea Botero-Moriarty, and Shane Ebert. 2012. Allocation of attention to second language form and meaning. *Studies in Second Language Acquisition* 34(04):659–685. https://doi.org/10.1017/s027226311200037x.

J. Mostow, J. E. Beck, J. Bey, A. Cuneo, J. Sison, B. Tobin, and J. Valeri. 2004. Using automated questions to assess readingcomprehension, vocabulary, and effects of tutorial interventions. *Technology, Instruction, Cognition and Learning* 2(1-2):97–134.

Bikram Nobal Niraula and Vasile Rus. 2015. *Proceedings of the Tenth Workshop on Innovative Use of NLP for Building Educational Applications*, Association for Computational Linguistics, chapter Judging the Quality of Automatically Generated Gapfill Question using Active Learning, pages 196–206. https://doi.org/10.3115/v1/W15-0623.

John M. Norris and Lourdes Ortega. 2000. Effectiveness of L2 instruction: A research synthesis and quantitative meta-analysis. *Language Learning* 50(3):417–528. https://doi.org/10.1111/0023-8333.00136.

Michael O'Malley and Anna Chamot. 1990. *Learning Strategies in Second Language Acquisition*. Cambridge University Press, New York.

Ildikó Pilán, Elena Volodina, and Richard Johansson. 2013. Automatic selection of suitable sentences for language learning exercises. In L. Bradley and S. Thouësny, editors, *20 Years of EUROCALL: Learning from the Past, Looking to the Future. Proceedings of the 2013 EUROCALL Conference*. pages 218–225. https://doi.org/10.14705/rpnet.2013.000164.

Juan Pino and Maxine Eskenazi. 2009. Semi-automatic generation of cloze question distractors effect of students' l1. In *SLaTE*. pages 65–68.

Juan Pino, Michael Heilman, and Maxine Eskenazi. 2008. A selection strategy to improve cloze question quality. In *Proceedings of the Workshop on Intelligent Tutoring Systems for Ill-Defined Domains.*

9th International Conference on Intelligent Tutoring Systems. Montreal, Canada, pages 22–34.

Roi Reichart and Ari Rappoport. 2010. Tense sense disambiguation: a new syntactic polysemy task. In *Proceedings of the 2010 Conference on Empirical Methods in Natural Language Processing*. Association for Computational Linguistics, pages 325–334. http://aclweb.org/anthology/D10-1032.

R. Schmidt. 1990. The role of consciousness in second language learning. *Applied Linguistics* 11:206–226.

Donald J Schuirmann. 1987. A comparison of the two one-sided tests procedure and the power approach for assessing the equivalence of average bioavailability. *Journal of Pharmacokinetics and Pharmacodynamics* 15(6):657–680.

Michael Sharwood Smith. 1993. Input enhancement in instructed SLA: Theoretical bases. *Studies in Second Language Acquisition* 15:165–179. https://doi.org/10.1017/s0272263100011943.

Bill VanPatten. 1990. Attending to form and content in the input. *Studies in second language acquisition* 12(03):287–301. https://doi.org/10.1017/s0272263100009177.

Bill VanPatten. 2004. *Processing instruction: Theory, research, and commentary*. Routledge. https://doi.org/10.4324/9781410610195.

Bill VanPatten and Teresa Cadierno. 1993. Explicit instruction and input processing. *Studies in Second Language Acquisition* 15(02):225–243. https://doi.org/10.1017/S0272263100011979.

Bill VanPatten and Soile Oikkenon. 1996. Explanation versus structured input in processing instruction. *Studies in Second Language Acquisition* 18(04):495–510. https://doi.org/10.1017/s0272263100015394.

Wynne Wong. 2001. Modality and attention to meaning and form in the input. *Studies in Second Language Acquisition* 23(03):345–368. https://doi.org/10.1017/s0272263101003023.

Wynne Wong. 2004. Processing instruction in French: The roles of explicit information and structured input. *Processing instruction: Theory, research, and commentary* pages 187–205. https://doi.org/10.4324/9781410610195.

Graham Workman. 2008. *Concept questions and time lines*. Gem Publishing.

Systematically Adapting Machine Translation for Grammatical Error Correction

Courtney Napoles[*] and **Chris Callison-Burch**[†]
[*]Center for Language and Speech Processing, Johns Hopkins University
[†]Computer and Information Science Department, University of Pennsylvania
napoles@cs.jhu.edu, ccb@cis.upenn.edu

Abstract

In this work we adapt machine translation (MT) to grammatical error correction, identifying how components of the statistical MT pipeline can be modified for this task and analyzing how each modification impacts system performance. We evaluate the contribution of each of these components with standard evaluation metrics and automatically characterize the morphological and lexical transformations made in system output. Our model rivals the current state of the art using a fraction of the training data.

1 Introduction

This work presents a systematic investigation for automatic grammatical error correction (GEC) inspired by machine translation (MT). The task of grammatical error correction can be viewed as a noisy channel model, and therefore a MT approach makes sense, and has been applied to the task since Brockett et al. (2006). Currently, the best GEC systems all use machine translation in some form, whether statistical MT (SMT) as a component of a larger pipeline (Rozovskaya and Roth, 2016) or neural MT (Yuan and Briscoe, 2016). These approaches make use of a great deal of resources, and in this work we propose a lighter-weight approach to GEC by methodically examining different aspects of the SMT pipeline, identifying and applying modifications tailored for GEC, introducing artificial data, and evaluating how each of these specializations contributes to the overall performance.

Specifically, we demonstrate that

- Artificially generated rules improve performance by nearly 10%.

- Custom features describing morphological and lexical changes provide a small performance gain.
- Tuning to a specialized GEC metric is slightly better than tuning to a traditional MT metric.
- Larger training data leads to better performance, but there is no conclusive difference between training on a clean corpus with minimal corrections and a noisy corpus with potential sentence rewrites.

We have developed and will release a tool to automatically characterize the types of transformations made in a corrected text, which are used as features in our model. The features identify general changes such as insertions, substitutions, and deletions, and the number of each of these operations by part of speech. Substitutions are further classified by whether the substitution contains a different inflected form of the original word, such as change in verb tense or noun number; if substitution has the same part of speech as the original; and if it is a spelling correction. We additionally use these features to analyze the outputs generated by different systems and characterize their performance with the types of transformations it makes and how they compare to manually written corrections in addition to automatic metric evaluation.

Our approach, Specialized Machine translation for Error Correction (SMEC), represents a single model that handles morphological changes, spelling corrections, and phrasal substitutions, and it rivals the performance of the state-of-the-art neural MT system (Yuan and Briscoe, 2016), which uses twice the amount of training data, most of which is not publicly available. The analysis provided in this work will help improve future efforts in GEC, and can be used to inform approaches rooted in both neural and statistical MT.

Proceedings of the 12th Workshop on Innovative Use of NLP for Building Educational Applications, pages 345–356
Copenhagen, Denmark, September 8, 2017. ©2017 Association for Computational Linguistics

2 Related work

Earlier approaches to grammatical error correction developed rule-based systems or classifiers targeting specific error types such as prepositions or determiners, (e.g., Eeg-Olofsson and Knutsson, 2003; Tetreault and Chodorow, 2008; Rozovskaya et al., 2014), and few approaches were rooted in machine translation, though some exceptions exist (Brockett et al., 2006; Park and Levy, 2011, e.g.,). The 2012 and 2013 shared tasks in GEC both targeted only certain error types (Dale et al., 2012; Ng et al., 2013), to which classification was appropriately suited. However, the goal of the 2014 CoNLL Shared Task was correcting all 28 types of grammatical errors, encouraging several MT-based approaches to GEC, (e.g., Felice et al., 2014; Junczys-Dowmunt and Grundkiewicz, 2014). Two of the best CoNLL 2014 systems used MT as a black box, reranking output (Felice et al., 2014), and customizing the tuning algorithm and using lexical features (Junczys-Dowmunt and Grundkiewicz, 2014). The other leading system was classification-based and only targeted certain error types (Rozovskaya et al., 2014). Performing less well, Wang et al. (2014) used factored SMT, representing words as factored units to more adeptly handle morphological changes. Shortly after the shared task, a system combining classifiers and SMT with no further customizations reported better performance than all competing systems (Susanto et al., 2014)

The current leading GEC systems all use MT in some form, including hybrid approaches that use the output of error-type classifiers as MT input (Rozovskaya and Roth, 2016) or include a neural model of learner text as a feature in SMT (Chollampatt et al., 2016); phrase-based MT with sparse features tuned to a GEC metric (Junczys-Dowmunt and Grundkiewicz, 2016); and neural MT (Yuan and Briscoe, 2016). Three of these model have been evaluated on a separate test corpus and, while the PBMT system reported the highest scores on the CoNLL-14 test set, it was outperformed by the systems with neural components on the new test set (Napoles et al., 2017).

2.1 GEC corpora

There are two broad categories of parallel data for GEC. The first is error-coded text, in which annotators have coded spans of learner text containing an error, and which includes the NUS Cor-

pus of Learner English (NUCLE; 57k sentence pairs) (Dahlmeier et al., 2013), the Cambridge Learner Corpus (CLC; 1.9M pairs per Yuan and Briscoe (2016)) (Nicholls, 2003), and a subset of the CLC, the First Certificate in English (FCE; 34k pairs) (Yannakoudakis et al., 2011). MT systems are trained on parallel text, which can be extracted from error-coded corpora by applying the annotated corrections, resulting a clean corpus with nearly-perfect word and sentence alignments.[1] These corpora are small by MT training standards and constrained by the coding approach, leading to minimal changes that may result in ungrammatical or awkward-sounding text (Sakaguchi et al., 2016).

The second class of GEC corpora are parallel datasets, which contain the original text and a corrected version of the text, without explicitly coded error corrections. These corpora need to be aligned by sentences and tokens, and automatic alignment introduces noise. However, these datasets are cheaper to collect, significantly larger than the error-coded corpora, and may contain more extensive rewrites. Additionally, corrections of sentences made without error coding are perceived to be more grammatical. Two corpora of this type are the Automatic Evaluation of Scientific Writing corpus, with more than 1 million sentences of scientific writing corrected by professional proofreaders (Daudaravicius et al., 2016), and the Lang-8 Corpus of Learner English, which contains 1 million sentence pairs scraped from an online forum for language learners, which were corrected by other members of the `lang-8.com` online community (Tajiri et al., 2012). Twice that many English sentence pairs can be extracted from version 2 of the Lang-8 Learner Corpora (Tomoya et al., 2011).

We will include both types of corpora in our experiments in Section 4.

2.2 Evaluation

GEC systems are automatically evaluated by comparing their output on sentences that have been manually annotated corpora. The Max-Match metric (M^2) is the most widely used, and calculates the $F_{0.5}$ over phrasal edits (Dahlmeier and Ng, 2012). Napoles et al. (2015) proposed a

---

[1]Alignment mistakes may occur when sentences are split or joined, or when errors and corrections span multiple tokens, in which the automatic alignment within that span may err.

new metric, GLEU, which has stronger correlation with human judgments. GLEU is based on BLEU and therefore is well-suited for MT. It calculates the n-gram overlap, rewarding n-grams that systems correctly changed and penalizing n-grams that were incorrectly left unchanged. Unlike M^2, it does not require token-aligned input and therefore is able to evaluate sentential rewrites instead of minimal error spans. Since both metrics are commonly used, we will report the scores of both metrics in our results. A new test set for GEC was recently released, JFLEG (Napoles et al., 2017), Unlike the CoNLL 2014 test set, which is a part of the NUCLE corpus, JFLEG contains fluency-based edits instead of error-coded corrections. Like the Lang-8 and AESW corpora, fluency edits allow full sentence rewrites and do not constrain corrections to be error coded, and humans perceive sentences corrected with fluency edits to be more grammatical than those corrected with error-coded edits alone (Sakaguchi et al., 2016). Four leading systems were evaluated on JFLEG, and the best system by both automatic metric and human evaluation is the neural MT system of Yuan and Briscoe (2016) (henceforth referred to as *YB16*).

3 Customizing statistical machine translation

Statistical MT contains various components, including the training data, feature functions, and an optimization metric. This section describes how we customized each of these components.

3.1 Training data

A translation grammar is extracted from the training data, which is a large parallel corpus of ungrammatical and corrected sentences. Each rule is of the form

left-hand side (LHS) → right-hand side (RHS)

and has a feature vector, the weights of which are set to optimize an objective function, which in MT is metric like BLEU. A limiting factor on MT-based GEC is the available training data, which is small when compared to the data available for bilingual MT, which commonly uses 100s of thousands or millions of aligned sentence pairs. We hypothesize that artificially generating transformation rules may overcome the limit imposed by lack of sufficiently large training data and improve performance. Particularly, the prevalence of spelling errors is amplified in sparse data due to the potentially infinite possible misspellings and large number of OOVs. Previous work has approached this issue by including spelling correction as a step in a pipeline (Rozovskaya and Roth, 2016).

Our solution is to artificially generate grammar rules for spelling corrections and morphological changes. For each word in the input, we query the Aspell dictionary with PyEnchant[2] for spelling suggestions and create new rules for each correction, e.g.

publically → public ally

publically → publicly

Additionally, sparsity in morphological variations may arise in datasets. Wang et al. (2014) approached this issue with factored MT, which translates at the sub-word level. Instead, we also generate artificial translation rules representing morphological transformations using RASP's morphological generator, `morphg` (Minnen et al., 2001). We perform POS tagging with the Stanford POS tagger (Toutanova et al., 2003) and create rules to switch the plurality of nouns (e.g., singular ↔ plural). For verbs, we generate rules that change that verb to every other inflected form, specifically the base form, third-person singular, past tense, past participle, and progressive tense (e.g., *wake, wakes, woke, woken, waking*). Generated words that did not appear in the PyEnchant dictionary were excluded.

3.2 Features

Each grammar rule has scores assigned by several feature functions $\vec{\varphi} = \{\varphi_1...\varphi_N\}$ that are combined in a log-linear model as that rule's weight, with parameters $\vec{\lambda}$ set during tuning.

$$w = -\sum_{i=1}^{N} \lambda_i \log \varphi_i$$

In SMT, these features typically include a phrase penalty, lexical and phrase translation probabilities, a language model probability, binary indicators for purely lexical and monotonic rules, and counters of unaligned words and rule length. Previous work in other monolingual "translation" tasks has achieved success in using features tailored to that task, such as a measure of the relative lengths for sentence compression (Ganitkevitch et al., 2011) or lexical complexity for sentence simplification (Xu et al., 2016). For GEC,

<hr>

[2] https://pythonhosted.org/pyenchant/

Junczys-Dowmunt and Grundkiewicz (2016) used a large number of sparse features for a phrase-based MT system that achieved state of the art performance on the CoNLL-2014 test set. Unlike that work, which uses a potentially infinite amount of sparse features, we choose to use a discrete set of feature functions that are informed by this task. Our feature extraction relies on a variety of pre-existing tools, including fast-align for word alignment (Dyer et al., 2013), trained over the parallel FCE, Lang-8, and NUCLE corpora; PyEnchant for detecting spelling changes; the Stanford POS tagger; the RASP morphological analyzer, `morpha` (Minnen et al., 2001); and the NLTK WordNet lemmatizer (Bird et al., 2009).

Given a grammatical rule and an alignment between tokens on the LHS and RHS, we tag the tokens with their part of speech and label the lemma and inflection of nouns and verbs with `morpha` and the lemma of each adjective and adverb with the WordNet lemmatizer. We then collect count-based features for individual operations and rule-level qualities. An operation is defined as a deletion, insertion, or substitution of a pair of aligned tokens (or a token aligned with ϵ). An aligned token pair is represented as (l_i, r_j), where l_i is a token on the LHS at index i, and similarly r_j for the RHS. The operation features, below, are calculated for each (un)aligned token and summed to attain the value for a given rule.

- **All operations**
    - CLASS-error(l_i) for deletions and substitutions
    - CLASS-error(r_j) for insertions

    CLASS refers to the broad word class of a token, such as *noun* or *verb*.
- **Deletions**
    - is-deleted(l_i)
    - TAG-deleted(l_i)

    TAG is the PTB part-of-speech tag of a token (e.g., *NN, NNS, NNP*, etc.),
- **Insertions**
    - is-inserted(r_j)
    - TAG-inserted(r_j)
- **Substitutions**
    - is-substituted(r_j)
    - TAG-substituted(r_j)
    - TAG-substituted-with-TAG(l_i, r_j)

    Morphological features:
    - inflection-change-same-lemma(l_i, r_j)
    - inflection-and-lemma-change(l_i, r_j)
    - lemma-change-same-inflection(l_i, r_j)

    Spelling features:
    - not-in-dictionary(l_i)
    - spelling-correction(l_i, r_j)

    Counts of spelling corrections are weighted by the probability of r_j in an English Giga-word language model.

We also calculate the following rule-level features:

- character Levenshtein distance(LHS, RHS)
- token Levenshtein distance(LHS, RHS)
- $\dfrac{\text{\# tokens(RHS)}}{\text{\# tokens(LHS)}}$
- $\dfrac{\text{\# characters(RHS)}}{\text{\# characters(LHS)}}$

In total, we use 24 classes and 45 tags. The total number of features 2,214 but only 266 were seen in training (due to unseen TAG-TAG substitutions). We additionally include 19 MT features calculated during grammar extraction.[3] Previous MT approaches to GEC, have included Levenshtein distance as a feature for tuning (Felice et al., 2014; Junczys-Dowmunt and Grundkiewicz, 2014, 2016), and Junczys-Dowmunt and Grundkiewicz (2016) also used counts of deletions, insertions, and substitutions by word class. They additionally had sparse features with counts of each lexicalized operation, e.g. substitute(*run, ran*), which we avoid by abstracting away from the lemmas and instead counting the operations by part of speech and indicating if the lemmas matched or differed for substitutions. An example rule with its feature values is found in Table 1. For artificially generated rules, the MT features are all assigned a 0-value rather than estimating what that value should be, since the artificial rules are unseen in the training data.

3.3 Metric

The decoder identifies the most probable derivation of an input sentence from the translation grammar. Derivations are scored by a combination of a language model score and weighted feature functions, and the weights are optimized to a specific metric during the tuning phase. Recent work has shown that MT metrics like BLEU are not sufficient for evaluating GEC (Grundkiewicz et al., 2015; Napoles et al., 2015) or tuning MT systems for GEC (Junczys-Dowmunt and Grundkiewicz,

---

[3]More details about the features can be found at `https://github.com/cnap/smt-for-gec`.

Rule	
argued that $\rightarrow$ may argue that	

Alignment	
(ϵ, may), (argued, argue), (that, that)	

Feature	Value
Verb error	2
Substituted	1
Inserted	1
MD inserted	1
VB is substituted	1
VBD substituted with VB	1
Inflection change, same lemma	1
Token LD	2
Character LD	5

Table 1: An example rule from our grammar and the non-zero feature values from Section 3.2.

2016). Fundamentally, MT metrics do not work for GEC because the output is usually very similar to the input, and therefore the input already has a high metric score. To address this issue, we tune to GLEU, which was specifically designed for evaluating GEC output. We chose GLEU instead of M^2 because the latter requires a token alignment between the input, output, and gold-standard references, and assumes only minimal, non-overlapping changes have been made. GLEU, on the other hand, measures n-gram overlap and therefore is better equipped to handle movement and changes to larger spans of text.

4 Experiments

For our experiments, we use the Joshua 6 toolkit (Post et al., 2015). Tokenization is done with Joshua and token-level alignment with fast-align (Dyer et al., 2013). All text is lowercased, and we use a simple algorithm to recase the output (Table 2). We extract a hierarchical phrase-based translation model with Thrax (Weese et al., 2011) and perform parameter tuning with pairwise ranked optimization in Joshua. Our training data is from the Lang-8 corpus (Tomoya et al., 2011), which contains 1 million parallel sentences, and grammar is extracted from the 563k sentence pairs that contain corrections. Systems are tuned to the JFLEG tuning set (751 sentences) and evaluated on the JFLEG test set (747 sentences). We use an English Gigaword 5-gram language model.

We evaluate performance with two metrics, GLEU and M^2, which have similar rankings and

1. Generate POS tags of the cased input sentence
2. Label proper nouns in the input
3. Align the cased input tokens with the output
4. Capitalize the first alphanumeric character of the output sentence (if a letter).
5. For each pair of aligned tokens (l_i, r_j), capitalize r_j if l_i is labeled a proper noun or r_j is the token "i".

Table 2: A simple recasing algorithm, which relies on token alignments between the input and output.

match human judgments on the JFLEG corpus (Napoles et al., 2017). We use two baselines: the first has misspellings corrected with Enchant (Sp. Baseline), and the second is an unmodified MT pipeline trained on the Lang-8 corpus, optimized to BLEU with no specialized features (MT Baseline), and we compare our performance to the current state of the art, YB16. While we train on about half a million sentence pairs, YB16 had nearly 2 million sentence pairs for training.[4] We additionally report metric scores for the human corrections, which we determine by evaluating each reference set against the other three and reporting the mean score.

All systems outperform both baselines, and the spelling baseline is stronger than the MT baseline. The spelling baseline also has the highest precision except for the best automatic system, YB16, demonstrating that spelling correction is an important component in this corpus. There is a disparity in the GLEU and M^2 scores for the baseline: the baseline GLEU is about 5% lower than the other systems but the M^2 is 30% lower. This can be attributed to the lesser extent of changes made by the baseline system which results in low recall for M^2 but which is not penalized by GLEU, which is a precision-based metric. The human corrections have the highest metric scores, and make changes to 77% of the sentences, which is in between the number of sentences changed by YB16 and SMEC, however the human corrections have a higher mean edit distance, because the annotators made more extensive changes when a sentence needed to be corrected than any of the models.

Our fully customized model with all modifications, Specialized Machine translation for Er-

---

[4]Drawn from the CLC, which is not public.

ror Correction (SMEC$^{+\text{morph}}$), scores lower than YB16 according to GLEU but has the same M^2 score. SMEC$^{+\text{morph}}$ has higher M^2 recall, and visual examination of the output supports this, showing many incorrect or unnecessary number of tense changes. Automatic analysis reveals that it makes significantly more inflection changes than the humans or YB16 (detected with the same method described in Section 3.2), from which we can conclude that the morphological rules errors are applied too liberally. If we remove the generated morphological rules but keep the spelling rules (SMEC), performance improves by 0.4 GLEU points and decreases by 0.1 M^2 points—but, more importantly, this system has higher precision and lower recall, and makes more conservative morphological changes. Therefore, we consider SMEC, the model without artificial morphological rules, to be our best system.

The metrics only give us a high-level overview of the changes made in the output. With error-coded text, the performance by feature type can be examined with M^2, but this is not possible with GLEU or the un-coded JFLEG corpus. To investigate the types of changes systems make on a more granular level, we apply the feature extraction method described in Section 3.2 to quantify the morphological and lexical transformations. While we developed this method for scoring translation rules, it can work on any aligned text, and is similar to the forthcoming ERRANT toolkit, which is uses a rule-based framework for automatically categorizes grammatical edits (Bryant et al., 2017). We calculate the number of each of these transformations made by to the input by each system and the human references, determining significant differences with a paired t-test ($p < 0.05$). Figure 1 contains the mean number of these transformations per sentence made by SMEC, YB16, and the human-corrected references, and Figure 2 shows the number of operations by part of speech. Even though the GLEU and M^2 scores of the two systems are nearly identical, they are significantly different in all of the transformations in Figure 1, with SMEC having a higher edit distance from the original, but YB16 making more insertions and substitutions. Overall, the human corrections have a significantly more inserted tokens than either system, while YB16 makes the most substitutions and fewer deletions than SMEC or the human corrections. The bottom plot displays the

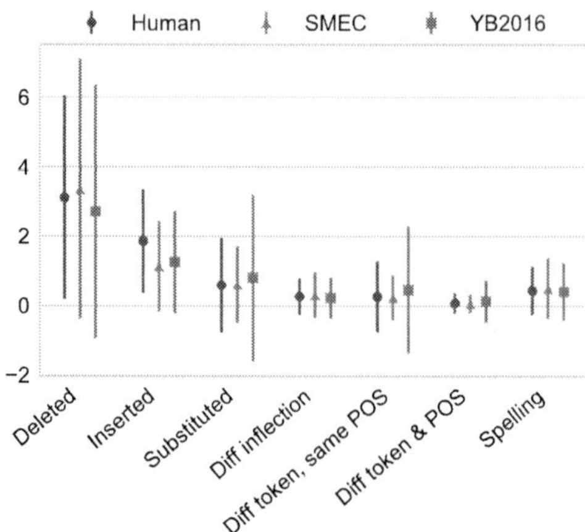

Figure 1: Mean tokens per sentence displaying certain changes from the input sentence.

mean number of operations by part of speech (operations include deletion, insertion, and substitution). Both systems and the human corrections display similar rates of substitutions across different parts of speech, however the human references have significantly more preposition and verb operations and there are significant differences between the determiner and noun operations made by YB16 compared to SMEC and the references. This information can be further analyzed by part of speech and edit operation, and the same information is available for other word classes.

5 Model analysis

We wish to understand how each component of our model contributes to its performance, and therefore train a series of variations of the model, each time removing a single customization, specifically: the optimization metric (tuning to BLEU instead of GLEU; SMEC$^{-\text{GLEU}}$), the features (only using the standard MT features; SMEC$^{-\text{feats}}$), and eliminating artificial rules (SMEC$^{-\text{sp}}$). The impact of training data size will be investigated separately in Section 5.1. We computed the automatic metric scores of each model variation and performed the automatic edit analysis described in Section 3.2. In Table 4, we report the net metric increase or decrease compared to the full model, and the percent increase or decrease for each of the features. Changing the metric from GLEU to BLEU significantly decreases the amount of change made by the model,

| System | GLEU | M² | | | Edit distance | |
		P	R	$F_{0.5}$	Sents. changed	(tokens)
Sp. Baseline	55.5	57.7	16.6	38.4	42%	0.8
MT Baseline	54.9	56.7	14.6	36.0	39%	0.7
SMEC^{+morph}	57.9	54.7	**44.2**	**52.3**	**88%**	**2.8**
SMEC	58.3	55.9	41.1	52.2	85%	2.5
YB16	**58.4**	**59.4**	35.3	**52.3**	73%	1.9
Human	62.1	67.0	52.9	63.6	77%	3.1

Table 3: Results on the JFLEG test set. In addition to the GLEU and M² scores, we also report the percent of sentences changed from the input and the mean Levensthein distance.

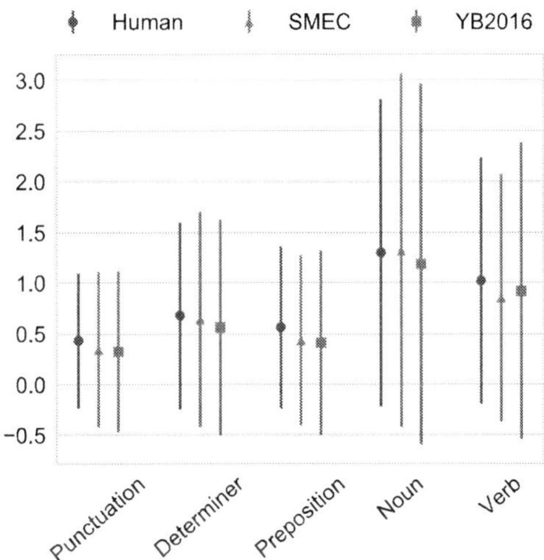

Figure 2: Mean number of operations (deletions, insertions, and substitutions) per sentence by part of speech.

SMEC^{-GLEU}, with a 60% lower edit distance than SMEC, and at least 50% fewer of almost all transformations. The GLEU score of this system is nearly 1 point lower, however there is almost no change in the M² score, indicating that the changes made were appropriate, even though they were fewer in number. Tuning to BLEU causes fewer changes because the input sentence already has a high BLEU score due to the high overlap between the input and reference sentences. GLEU encourages more changes by penalizing text that should have been changed in the output.

Removing the custom features (SMEC^{-feats}) makes less of a difference in the GLEU score, however there are significantly more determiners added and more tokens are substituted with words that have different lemmas and parts of speech. This suggests that the specialized features encouraged morphologically-aware substitutions, reduc-

ing changes that did not have semantic or functional overlap with the original content. Removing the artificially generated spelling rules (SMEC^{-sp}) had the greatest impact on performance, with a nearly 4-point decrease in GLEU score and 9.5-decrease in M². Without spelling rules, significantly fewer tokens were inserted in the corrections across all word classes. We also see a significantly greater number of substitutions made with words that had neither the same part of speech or lemma as the original word, which could be due to sparsity in the presence of spelling errors which is addressed with the artificial grammar.

Table 5 contains example sentences from the test set with system outputs that illustrate these observations. These ungrammatical sentences range from one that can easily be corrected using *minimal* edits; to a sentence that requires more significant changes and inference but has an obvious meaning; to a sentence that is garbled and does not have an immediately obvious correction, even to a native speaker. The reference correction contains more extensive changes than the automatic systems and makes spelling corrections not found by the decoder (*engy → energy*) or inferences in the instance of the garbled third sentence, changing *lrenikg → Ranking*. SMEC makes many spelling corrections and makes more insertions, substitutions, and deletions than the two SMEC variations. However, the artificial rules also cause some bad corrections, found in the third example changing *studens → stud-ens*, while the intended word, *students*, is obvious to a human reader. When optimizing to BLEU instead of the custom metric (SMEC^{-GLEU}), there are fewer changes and therefore output is less fluent. In the first example, SMEC^{-GLEU} applies only one spelling change even though the rest of the sentence has many small errors that were all corrected in SMEC, such as missing determiner and extra auxiliary. The

Score				
	SMEC	SMEC −GLEU	SMEC −feats	SMEC −sp
GLEU	58.3	57.6	58.1	54.4
M^2	52.2	44.9	47.7	42.7
Transformation				
Edit dist		−60%		−11%
Deleted		−51%	−7%	−4%
Inserted		−46%		−24%
Substituted		−37%		+9%
Diff inflection		−53%		
Diff token		−18%	+9%	
Diff token&POS		−29%	+24%	+31%
Spelling		−35%	+8%	
Determiner		−51%		−7%
del		−47%	−5%	
ins		−70%	+39%	−30%
sub		−56%		
Preposition		−52%		
del		−51%		
ins		−45%	−10%	−22%
sub		−42%		
Noun		−40%	−6%	−10%
del		−45%	−9%	−12%
ins		−38%	−7%	−13%
sub		−30%		
Verb		−57%	−5%	−11%
del		−61%	−6%	−7%
ins		−53%	−13%	−40%
sub		−50%		
Punctuation		−52%		
del		−47%	−5%	
ins		−84%		−30%
sub				

Table 4: Modifications of SMEC, reporting the mean occurrence of each transformation per sentence, when there is a significant difference ($p < 0.05$ by a paired t-test). We report the difference with percentages because each transformation occurs with different frequency.

same pattern is visible in the other two examples. Finally, without the artificial rules, SMEC^{-sp} fixes only a fraction of the spelling mistakes—however it is the only system that correctly changes *studens* → *students*. Independent from these modifications, the capitalization issues present in the input were all remedied by our recasing algorithm, which improves the metric score.

5.1 Impact of training data

Lang-8 is the largest publicly available parallel corpus for GEC, with 1 million tokens and approximately 563k corrected sentence pairs, however this corpus may contain noise due to automatic

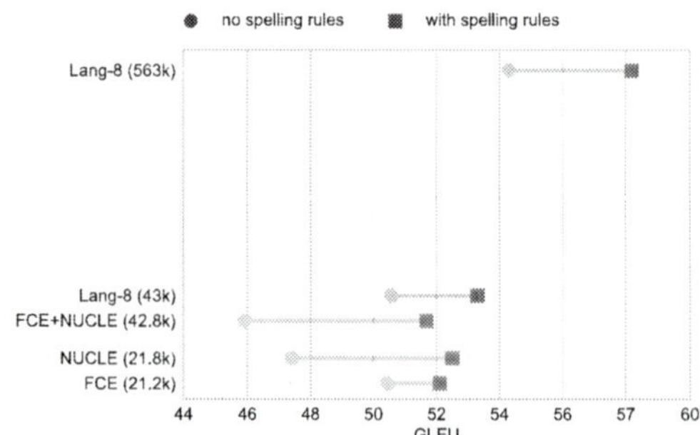

Figure 3: GLEU scores of SMEC with different training sizes, with and without artificial rules.

alignment and the annotators, who were users of the online Lang-8 service and may not necessarily have provided accurate or complete corrections. Two other corpora, FCE and NUCLE, contain annotations by trained English instructors and absolute alignments between sentences, however each is approximately 20-times smaller than Lang-8. We wish to isolate the effect of size and source of training data has on system performance, and therefore randomly sample the Lang-8 corpus to create a training set the same size as FCE and NU-CLE (43k corrected sentence pairs), train a model following the same procedure described above. We hypothesized that including artificial rules may help address problems of sparsity in the training data, and therefore we also train additional models with and without spelling rules to determine how artificial data affects performance as the amount of training data increases. Figure 3 shows the relative GLEU scores of systems with different training data sizes and sources, before and after adding artificial spelling rules.

More data increases performance for Lang-8, however there is no clear relationship between size and performance on the FCE+NUCLE data. Models trained on FCE, NUCLE, and FCE/NUCLE all have similar performance. And, training on 43k Lang-8 sentence pairs slightly improves performance over training on just FCE/NUCLE, suggesting that more data negates the presence of noise and the sentential rewrites present in Lang-8 are better for training a GEC system. The rewrites in Lang-8 could be more similar to those found in JFLEG since both datasets allow for broader fluency changes instead of corrections to coded spans of text. In future work, we will train on version 2 of the Lang-8 Learner Corpus, which has twice

Orig	Unforturntly , almost older people can not use internet , in spite of benefit of internet .
Human	**Unfortunately** , **most** older people can not use **the** internet , in spite of **benefits** of **the** internet .
SMEC	**Unfortunately** , **most** older people can not use **the** internet , in spite of **the benefits** of **the** internet .
SMEC$^{-\mathrm{GLEU}}$	**Unfortunately** , almost older people can not use internet , in spite of benefit of internet .
SMEC^{-sp}	Unforturntly , □ older people can not use **the** internet , in spite of **the benefits** of **the** internet .
Orig	becuse if i see some one did somthing to may safe me time and engy and it wok 's i will do it .
Human	**Because** if **I** see **that someone** did **something that** may **save** me time and **energy** and it **works I** will **also** do it .
SMEC	**Because** if **I** see □ one did **something** □ may **save** me time and **edgy** and □ **work** □ , **I** will do it .
SMEC$^{-\mathrm{GLEU}}$	**Because** if **I** see some one did **something** to may **save** me time and **edgy** and it wok 's **I** will do it .
SMEC^{-sp}	**Because** if **I** see □ one **somthings** □ may **save** me time and engy □ **work** □ **I** will do it .
Orig	lrenikg the studens the ideas have many advantegis :
Human	**Ranking** the **students '** □ ideas **has** many **advantages** .
SMEC	**Linking** the **stud-ens** □ ideas have many **advantages** :
SMEC$^{-\mathrm{GLEU}}$	**Linking** the **stud-ens** the ideas have many **advantages** :
SMEC^{-sp}	**Lrenikg** □ **students** □ ideas have □ advantegis :

Table 5: Example corrections made by a human annotator, SMEC, and two variations: trained on BLEU instead of GLEU SMEC$^{-\mathrm{GLEU}}$ and without artificial spelling rules (SMEC^{-sp}). Inserted or changed text is in **bold** and deleted text is indicated with □.

as much data as the version used in this work, to determine whether performance continues to improve. For all models, adding artificial spelling rules improves performance by about 4 GLEU points (adding spelling rules to FCE training data only causes a 2-point GLEU improvement). The amount of performance does not change related to the size of the training data, however the consistent improvement supports our hypothesis that artificial rules are useful to address problems of data sparsity.

6 Conclusion

This paper has presented a systematic investigation into the components of a standard statistical MT pipeline that can be customized for GEC. The analysis performed on the contribution of each component of the system can inform the design of future GEC models. We have found that extending the translation grammar with artificially generated rules for spelling correction can increase the M^2 score by as much as 20%. The amount of training data also has a substantial impact on performance, increasing GLEU and M^2 scores by approximately 10%. Tuning to a specialized GEC metric and using custom features both help performance but yield less considerable gains. The performance of our model, SMEC, is on par with the current state-of-the-art GEC system, which is neural MT trained on twice the training data, and our analysis suggests that the performance of SMEC would continue to improve if trained on that amount of data. In future work we will test this hypothesis with the larger parallel corpus extracted from version 2 of the Lang-8 Learner Corpora. Our code will be available for automatic feature extraction and edit analysis, as well as more details about the model implementation.[5]

Acknowledgments

We are grateful to the anonymous reviewers for their detailed and thoughtful feedback.

---

[5] https://github.com/cnap/smt-for-gec

References

Steven Bird, Ewan Klein, and Edward Loper. 2009. *Natural language processing with Python: Analyzing text with the natural language toolkit.* " O'Reilly Media, Inc.".

Chris Brockett, William B. Dolan, and Michael Gamon. 2006. Correcting esl errors using phrasal smt techniques. In *Proceedings of the 21st International Conference on Computational Linguistics and 44th Annual Meeting of the Association for Computational Linguistics.* Association for Computational Linguistics, Sydney, Australia, pages 249–256. https://doi.org/10.3115/1220175.1220207.

Christopher Bryant, Mariano Felice, and Ted Briscoe. 2017. Automatic annotation and evaluation of error types for grammatical error correction. In *Proceedings of the 55th Annual Meeting of the Association for Computational Linguistics.* Association for Computational Linguistics, Vancouver, Canada.

Shamil Chollampatt, Duc Tam Hoang, and Hwee Tou Ng. 2016. Adapting grammatical error correction based on the native language of writers with neural network joint models. In *Proceedings of the 2016 Conference on Empirical Methods in Natural Language Processing.* Association for Computational Linguistics, Austin, Texas, pages 1901–1911. https://aclweb.org/anthology/D16-1195.

Daniel Dahlmeier and Hwee Tou Ng. 2012. Better evaluation for grammatical error correction. In *Proceedings of the 2012 Conference of the North American Chapter of the Association for Computational Linguistics: Human Language Technologies.* Association for Computational Linguistics, Montréal, Canada, pages 568–572. http://www.aclweb.org/anthology/N12-1067.

Daniel Dahlmeier, Hwee Tou Ng, and Siew Mei Wu. 2013. Building a large annotated corpus of learner english: The NUS Corpus of Learner English. In *Proceedings of the Eighth Workshop on Innovative Use of NLP for Building Educational Applications.* Association for Computational Linguistics, Atlanta, Georgia, pages 22–31. http://www.aclweb.org/anthology/W13-1703.

Robert Dale, Ilya Anisimoff, and George Narroway. 2012. HOO 2012: A report on the preposition and determiner error correction shared task. In *Proceedings of the Seventh Workshop on Building Educational Applications Using NLP.* Association for Computational Linguistics, Montréal, Canada, pages 54–62. http://www.aclweb.org/anthology/W12-2006.

Vidas Daudaravicius, Rafael E. Banchs, Elena Volodina, and Courtney Napoles. 2016. A report on the automatic evaluation of scientific writing shared task. In *Proceedings of the 11th Workshop on Innovative Use of NLP for Building Educational Applications.* Association for Computational Linguistics, San Diego, CA, pages 53–62. http://www.aclweb.org/anthology/W16-0506.

Chris Dyer, Victor Chahuneau, and Noah A. Smith. 2013. A simple, fast, and effective reparameterization of IBM Model 2. In *Proceedings of the 2013 Conference of the North American Chapter of the Association for Computational Linguistics: Human Language Technologies.* Association for Computational Linguistics, Atlanta, Georgia, pages 644–648. http://www.aclweb.org/anthology/N13-1073.

Jens Eeg-Olofsson and Ola Knutsson. 2003. Automatic grammar checking for second language learners—the use of prepositions. In *Proceedings of NoDaLida 2003.*

Mariano Felice, Zheng Yuan, Øistein E. Andersen, Helen Yannakoudakis, and Ekaterina Kochmar. 2014. Grammatical error correction using hybrid systems and type filtering. In *Proceedings of the Eighteenth Conference on Computational Natural Language Learning: Shared Task.* Association for Computational Linguistics, Baltimore, Maryland, pages 15–24. http://www.aclweb.org/anthology/W14-1702.

Juri Ganitkevitch, Chris Callison-Burch, Courtney Napoles, and Benjamin Van Durme. 2011. Learning sentential paraphrases from bilingual parallel corpora for text-to-text generation. In *Proceedings of the 2011 Conference on Empirical Methods in Natural Language Processing.* Association for Computational Linguistics, Edinburgh, Scotland, UK., pages 1168–1179. http://www.aclweb.org/anthology/D11-1108.

Roman Grundkiewicz, Marcin Junczys-Dowmunt, and Edward Gillian. 2015. Human evaluation of grammatical error correction systems. In *Proceedings of the 2015 Conference on Empirical Methods in Natural Language Processing.* Association for Computational Linguistics, Lisbon, Portugal, pages 461–470. http://aclweb.org/anthology/D15-1052.

Marcin Junczys-Dowmunt and Roman Grundkiewicz. 2014. The AMU system in the CoNLL-2014 shared task: Grammatical error correction by data-intensive and feature-rich statistical machine translation. In *Proceedings of the Eighteenth Conference on Computational Natural Language Learning: Shared Task.* Association for Computational Linguistics, Baltimore, Maryland, pages 25–33. http://www.aclweb.org/anthology/W14-1703.

Marcin Junczys-Dowmunt and Roman Grundkiewicz. 2016. Phrase-based machine translation is state-of-the-art for automatic grammatical error correction. In *Proceedings of the 2016 Conference on Empirical Methods in Natural Language Processing.* Association for Computational Linguistics, Austin, Texas, pages 1546–1556. https://aclweb.org/anthology/D16-1161.

Guido Minnen, John Carroll, and Darren Pearce. 2001. Applied morphological processing of english. *Natural Language Engineering* 7(03):207–223.

Courtney Napoles, Keisuke Sakaguchi, Matt Post, and Joel Tetreault. 2015. Ground truth for grammatical error correction metrics. In *Proceedings of the 53rd Annual Meeting of the Association for Computational Linguistics and the 7th International Joint Conference on Natural Language Processing (Volume 2: Short Papers)*. Association for Computational Linguistics, Beijing, China, pages 588–593. http://www.aclweb.org/anthology/P15-2097.

Courtney Napoles, Keisuke Sakaguchi, and Joel Tetreault. 2017. JFLEG: A fluency corpus and benchmark for grammatical error correction. In *Proceedings of the 15th Meeting of the European Chapter of the Association for Computational Linguistics*. Association for Computational Linguistics.

Hwee Tou Ng, Siew Mei Wu, Yuanbin Wu, Christian Hadiwinoto, and Joel Tetreault. 2013. The CoNLL-2013 Shared Task on grammatical error correction. In *Proceedings of the Seventeenth Conference on Computational Natural Language Learning: Shared Task*. Association for Computational Linguistics, Sofia, Bulgaria, pages 1–12.

Diane Nicholls. 2003. The Cambridge Learner Corpus: Error coding and analysis for lexicography and ELT. In *Proceedings of the Corpus Linguistics 2003 conference*. volume 16, pages 572–581.

Y Albert Park and Roger Levy. 2011. Automated whole sentence grammar correction using a noisy channel model. In *Proceedings of the 49th Annual Meeting of the Association for Computational Linguistics: Human Language Technologies-Volume 1*. Association for Computational Linguistics, pages 934–944.

Matt Post, Yuan Cao, and Gaurav Kumar. 2015. Joshua 6: A phrase-based and hierarchical statistical machine translation system. *The Prague Bulletin of Mathematical Linguistics* 104(1):5–16.

Alla Rozovskaya, Kai-Wei Chang, Mark Sammons, Dan Roth, and Nizar Habash. 2014. The Illinois-Columbia system in the CoNLL-2014 shared task. In *Proceedings of the Eighteenth Conference on Computational Natural Language Learning: Shared Task*. Association for Computational Linguistics, Baltimore, Maryland, pages 34–42. http://www.aclweb.org/anthology/W14-1704.

Alla Rozovskaya and Dan Roth. 2016. Grammatical error correction: Machine translation and classifiers. In *Proceedings of the 54th Annual Meeting of the Association for Computational Linguistics (Volume 1: Long Papers)*. Association for Computational Linguistics, Berlin, Germany, pages 2205–2215. http://www.aclweb.org/anthology/P16-1208.

Keisuke Sakaguchi, Courtney Napoles, Matt Post, and Joel Tetreault. 2016. Reassessing the goals of grammatical error correction: Fluency instead of grammaticality. *Transactions of the Association for Computational Linguistics* 4:169–182.

Raymond Hendy Susanto, Peter Phandi, and Hwee Tou Ng. 2014. System combination for grammatical error correction. In *Proceedings of the 2014 Conference on Empirical Methods in Natural Language Processing (EMNLP)*. Association for Computational Linguistics, Doha, Qatar, pages 951–962. http://www.aclweb.org/anthology/D14-1102.

Toshikazu Tajiri, Mamoru Komachi, and Yuji Matsumoto. 2012. Tense and aspect error correction for ESL learners using global context. In *Proceedings of the 50th Annual Meeting of the Association for Computational Linguistics (Volume 2: Short Papers)*. Association for Computational Linguistics, Jeju Island, Korea, pages 198–202. http://www.aclweb.org/anthology/P12-2039.

Joel Tetreault and Martin Chodorow. 2008. Native judgments of non-native usage: Experiments in preposition error detection. In *Coling 2008: Proceedings of the workshop on Human Judgements in Computational Linguistics*. Coling 2008 Organizing Committee, Manchester, UK, pages 24–32. http://www.aclweb.org/anthology/W08-1205.

Mizumoto Tomoya, Mamoru Komachi, Masaaki Nagata, and Yuji Matsumoto. 2011. Mining revision log of language learning SNS for automated Japanese error correction of second language learners. In *Proceedings of 5th International Joint Conference on Natural Language Processing*. Asian Federation of Natural Language Processing, Chiang Mai, Thailand, pages 147–155. http://www.aclweb.org/anthology/I11-1017.

Kristina Toutanova, Dan Klein, Christopher D Manning, and Yoram Singer. 2003. Feature-rich part-of-speech tagging with a cyclic dependency network. In *Proceedings of the 2003 Conference of the North American Chapter of the Association for Computational Linguistics on Human Language Technology-Volume 1*. Association for Computational Linguistics, pages 173–180.

Yiming Wang, Longyue Wang, Xiaodong Zeng, Derek F. Wong, Lidia S. Chao, and Yi Lu. 2014. Factored statistical machine translation for grammatical error correction. In *Proceedings of the Eighteenth Conference on Computational Natural Language Learning: Shared Task*. Association for Computational Linguistics, Baltimore, Maryland, pages 83–90. http://www.aclweb.org/anthology/W14-1711.

Jonathan Weese, Juri Ganitkevitch, Chris Callison-Burch, Matt Post, and Adam Lopez. 2011. Joshua 3.0: Syntax-based machine translation with the Thrax grammar extractor. In *Proceedings of the Sixth Workshop on Statistical Machine Translation*. Association for Computational Linguistics, pages 478–484.

Wei Xu, Courtney Napoles, Ellie Pavlick, Quanze Chen, and Chris Callison-Burch. 2016. Optimizing statistical machine translation for text simplification.

Transactions of the Association for Computational Linguistics 4:401–415.

Helen Yannakoudakis, Ted Briscoe, and Ben Medlock. 2011. A new dataset and method for automatically grading ESOL texts. In *Proceedings of the 49th Annual Meeting of the Association for Computational Linguistics: Human Language Technologies*. Association for Computational Linguistics, Portland, Oregon, USA, pages 180–189. http://www.aclweb.org/anthology/P11-1019.

Zheng Yuan and Ted Briscoe. 2016. Grammatical error correction using neural machine translation. In *Proceedings of the 2016 Conference of the North American Chapter of the Association for Computational Linguistics: Human Language Technologies*. Association for Computational Linguistics, San Diego, California, pages 380–386. http://www.aclweb.org/anthology/N16-1042.

Fine-grained essay scoring of a complex writing task for native speakers

Andrea Horbach[1], Dirk Scholten-Akoun[2], Yuning Ding[1], Torsten Zesch[1]
[1] Language Technology Lab, Department of Computer Science and Applied Cognitive Science,
University of Duisburg-Essen, Germany
[2] Center of Teachers' Education, University of Duisburg-Essen,
{andrea.horbach|dirk.scholten|torsten.zesch}@uni-due.de
yuning.ding@stud.uni-due.de

Abstract

Automatic essay scoring is nowadays successfully used even in high-stakes tests, but this is mainly limited to holistic scoring of learner essays. We present a new dataset of essays written by highly proficient German native speakers that is scored using a fine-grained rubric with the goal to provide detailed feedback. Our experiments with two state-of-the-art scoring systems (a neural and a SVM-based one) show a large drop in performance compared to existing datasets. This demonstrates the need for such datasets that allow to guide research on more elaborate essay scoring methods.

1 Introduction

Automatic essay scoring is the task of automatically rating free-form writings. The scores assigned are often holistic and are based both on content and form. Automatic essay scoring is nowadays successfully used to reduce human scoring workload (Dikli, 2006), for example for the assessment of language proficiency (Weigle, 2013). Automatically assigned scores are considered reliable enough that they have replaced one out of two human annotators even in high-stakes language proficiency tests such as TOEFL for many years now (Attali and Burstein, 2006).

Essay scoring approaches in recent years have mainly focused on a small number of publicly available datasets, especially the ASAP dataset from the Kaggle competition. On this dataset, many approaches reach very competitive results, comparable to human scoring performance (Shermis and Hamner, 2012), so that the impression might arise that automatic essay scoring is a solved problem.

In this paper, we present experiments on a new dataset that we consider to be more challenging than currently available ones. We score essays written by prospective teachers, before starting their university education in Germany. These essays in German language are collected to assess whether these native-speaking students might need additional language training in order to become a teacher. While other datasets either measure the full range of language proficiency from novice learners to (near-)natives, or measure the writings of high-school students, our dataset shows much less variety in language proficiency. As almost all test-takers are native speakers and possess a general qualification for university entrance, differences between good and a not so good essays are much less pronounced.

When applying state-of-the-art essay scoring systems on this dataset, we find that a feature set working well on a standard dataset shows a considerably worse performance on our data. This makes it very questionable whether automatic scoring techniques could currently be applied in a real-life scenario, thus confirming the need for deeper methods able to handle such datasets.

We first present an overview of related work, especially publicly available datasets and present our corpus in detail. We then asses the scorability of the corpus by a series of experiments using a supervised machine learning system with a standard feature set. We first confirm that our system reaches state-of-the-art performance by evaluating it on the ASAP corpus and scores in our corpus assessing the writing globally. Subsequently, we assess how well such a feature set is suited to model the different scoring variables annotated in our data and find that the global scores are modeled best. Concentrating on these scores, we investigate the influence of various feature settings and different amounts of training data on the scor-

Proceedings of the 12th Workshop on Innovative Use of NLP for Building Educational Applications, pages 357–366
Copenhagen, Denmark, September 8, 2017. ©2017 Association for Computational Linguistics

ing performance.

2   Related Work

Automatic essay scoring is almost always tackled as a machine learning task (Dikli, 2006; Valenti et al., 2003). A wide range of features representing different aspects contributing to a good essay have been proposed such, as n-grams (Chen and He, 2013) or LSA (Foltz et al., 1999), length (Mahana et al., 2012; Östling, 2013), linguistic correctness in terms of spelling and grammar (Mahana et al., 2012; Östling, 2013), or cohesion and coherence of a text through identifying overlap between sentences and usage of connective devices (Lei et al., 2014). Recently, also neural methods have been proposed and successfully used for essay scoring (Taghipour and Ng, 2016).

Most essay scoring approaches in recent years have been evaluated either on proprietary datasets or on a few publicly available ones. Not publicly available data include datasets used by Klebanov et al. (2016) with large amounts of college level exam data, or data from music teacher proficiency test (Madnani et al., 2016). Responses in this last dataset are in length on the borderline between short answers and essays and are interesting because they, as well as our corpus, target writings by generally language-proficient population. The dominating publicly available dataset for essay scoring in recent year has been the data of the ASAP essay scoring challenge.[1] It contains both source-based and opinion tasks targeting US students from grade 7 to 10 for 8 different prompts with up to 3000 responses per prompt. Since its release in 2012, the dataset has been widely used in a number of approaches (Alikaniotis et al., 2016; Taghipour and Ng, 2016; Cummins et al., 2016). Another dataset, the CLC-FCE corpus (Yannakoudakis et al., 2011) contains essays written by ESOL test takers, but relatively little data per individual prompt (1,244 essays across 10 prompts), making it not the first choice for prompt-specific approaches. Because of its extensive error annotations, it has also been used for the task of grammatical error detection and correction (e.g. Cahill et al. (2013) and Seo et al. (2012)).

In Swedish, a corpus of high school essays has been released by Östling (2013) with an overall

number of 1,702 essay for 19 different prompts. This means, also this dataset contains few essays per prompt, such that their automatic scoring mainly focuses on form (which can be assessed across prompts) rather than content (which is to a higher degree prompt-specific).

Some other corpora were originally not designed for the task of essay scoring, but each sample comes with a language proficiency level of its writer, therefore allowing to use them for language proficiency assessment. That means their labels do not necessarily reflect the proficiency of the current essay, but rather the general language proficiency of the writer. For example, the ETS corpus of non-native written English (Blanchard et al., 2013) contains 12,100 TOEFL test essays and has originally been published for the task of native-language identification (Tetreault et al., 2013), but also comes with coarse proficiency levels and has been used for the task of proficiency classification (Klebanov et al., 2016; Vajjala, 2017). Similarly the ICNALE corpus (Ishikawa, 2011) contains English essays from Asian writers where each essay has an assigned proficiency level. Beyond the English language, proficiency classification has been performed on the Swedish SweLL corpus (Volodina et al., 2016; Pilán et al., 2016), and for Estonian (Vajjala and Lõo, 2014).

3   A more Challenging Essay Dataset

As described above, most datasets are either small or target a wide range of proficiency levels, so that relatively shallow features are sufficient to achieve quite good performance. To overcome this problem, we have created a new dataset from essays written in German by prospective university students, mostly native speakers. The essays are one part of a large-scale assessment project at the University of Duisburg-Essen, SkaLa (Bremerich-Vos and Scholten-Akoun, 2016). All students who intend to enroll in a degree program for future teachers have to participate in a compulsory language assessment. A major constituent of this assessment is an open writing task with two parts. First, students are asked to summarize a newspaper article dealing with an education-related topic (which we call the *source text*), in our datasets, an article about the pros and cons of study fees. This part of the response is the *summary* part of the essay. Second, the students shall briefly discuss a particular

---

[1] https://www.kaggle.com/c/asap-aes

358

statement from the prompt (the *discussion* part). The time limit for this task is 120 minutes and the produced text is supposed to consist of at least 350 words.

The aim of the fine-grained evaluation is to identify the participants' strengths and weaknesses as precisely as possible. After a manual evaluation of the essays, students receive detailed feedback about their performance in each of the manually scored variables and –if need be– are informed about relevant available training programs at the university designed to foster written language competencies.

In this way, 2,020 essays with an average of around 600 tokens per essay were collected and scored as described next.

Scoring Rubric While many essay-scoring corpora provide only a holistic score, this dataset has been scored using a fine-grained rubric, targeting different aspects of writing.

The raters were asked to evaluate the students' texts with regard to a total of 41 variables. The writing skills ratings are based upon analytical descriptors (cf. Weigle (2002, p. 114) and Weir (2005, p. 183)). Table 1 provides an overview of the annotated variables. 11 variables measured content-related aspects, i.e. whether a certain argument regarding the topic of the source text is mentioned in the essay, 3 formal, 5 structural and 10 measured linguistic aspects. In addition, there arc 6 dimension variables and one overall variable.

Before the annotators scored the texts according to the fine-grained rubric, they evaluated the texts in a subjective-holistic overall rating (*G1 – written language competence*). This evaluation was always carried out immediately after the first reading of the text, hence before the extensive analytical evaluation.

The rating scheme includes three types of variables: a) *descriptors* are variables for the evaluation of specific individual aspects of an essay (e.g. whether a certain argument from the source text is covered in the summary, whether the central thesis is correctly identified or whether grammar is proficiently used). The descriptors are directly annotated. b) *Dimension ratings (G2–G7)* are weighted aggregations of individual descriptors, i.e. they are not annotated but computed based on the descriptor annotations (e.g. G4–Discussion is an aggregation of the descriptors for the discussion part D1 to D4). c) Finally, a *superordinate rating (G8*

– informed overall judgment) emerges from the weighted aggregation of the dimension ratings and therefore relates to the entire text in all of its aspects covered by the rating scheme. (Annotators were allowed to change the aggregated G8 score, if they felt it did not adequately represent the essay.)

The essays were annotated by one out of 6 annotators each. The annotators received extensive training on a subset of randomly selected 120 essays. After training, annotators reached an inter-annotator agreement between 52 and 100% ModAgree (cf. Harsch and Martin (2012, p. 228-250) and Harsch and Martin (2013)) for the different descriptor variables. Percentage ModAgree is computed by measuring per essay and variable what percentage of all ratings assigned by the different annotators for this essay agrees with the mode, i.e. the value assigned most often. These values are then aggregated across all essays. For the subjective-holistic G1 score, annotators reached 59% ModAgree, for the aggregated G8 score 60% ModAgree was reached . Note that higher agreement values for the descriptor variables are partially due to fewer categories available for annotation.

In very few cases (up to four essays per variable), it was not possible for the annotator to encode a certain variable for a category (e.g. discussion variables could not be annotated if the discussion part was missing). We do not represent those essays in the label distributions and exclude them from the training and test data when performing machine learning experiments for that variable.

4 Experimental Setup

We split the data randomly into 90% training data and reserve 10%, i.e. 202 essays, as held-out test set. If not reported otherwise, our results are based on ten-fold cross-validation on the training section. In accordance with previous work, we evaluate using quadratically weighted kappa (QWK). For a more intuitive interpretation of the results, we also report accuracy. All data is preprocessed using a DKPro pipeline (Eckart de Castilho and Gurevych, 2014) consisting of segmentation, POS-tagging (both OpenNLP[2]), lemmatization using the MateLemmatizer (Anders et al., 2010) and parsing using the StanfordParser (Rafferty and Manning, 2008).

---

[2]https://opennlp.apache.org

	Score	Description	Range	% Mod-Agree	Relevant Essay Part	Distribution
	G1	Written language competence based on first impression	1/2/3/4/5/6	59	Both	
Form	F1	Appropriateness: Does the text address the task?	1/2/3/4	100	Both	
	F2	Plagiarism: Does the text copy the prompt?	1/2	100	Both	
	F3	Running text vs. bullet points	1/2	100	Both	
Content	C1	Central question	1/2/3	86	Summary	
	C2	Central thesis	1/2/3	79	Summary	
	C3	Political background	1/2/3	85	Summary	
	C4	Effect of study fees	1/2/3	90	Summary	
	C5	Securing academic educ. financially	1/2/3	92	Summary	
	C6	Beneficiaries	1/2/3	93	Summary	
	C7	Primary education (finances)	1/2/3	89	Summary	
	C8	Primary education (career)	1/2/3	85	Summary	
	C9	Academics vs. non aademics	1/2/3	91	Summary	
	C10	Overtaxing the poor	1/2/3	86	Summary	
	C11	Paying later	1/2/3	88	Summary	
	G2	Coherence – overall score	1/2/3/4/5/6	65	Summary	
	G3	Summary –aggregated score	1/2/3/4/5/6	74	Summary	
Discussion	D1	Are there own contributions (aspects not mentioned in source)?	1/2	92	Discussion	
	D2	Is an own point of view present and is it motivated?	1/2/3	75	Discussion	
	D3	Quality of argumentation	1/2/3	85	Discussion	
	D4	Rigor of discussion	1/2/3/4/5/6	59	Discussion	
	G4	Discussion – aggregated score	1/2/3/4/5/6	55	Discussion	
Structure	S1	Introduction present and marked?	1/2/3	94	Both	
	S2	Summary present and marked?	1/2/3	79	Both	
	S3	Discussion present and marked?	1/2/3	88	Both	
	S4	Conclusion present and marked?	1/2/3	78	Both	
	S5	Formatting	1/2/3/4	68	Both	
	G5	Structure – aggregated score	1/2/3/4/5/6	67	Both	
Language	L1	Spelling: no / up to 5 / 6 to 10 /more	1/2/3/4	76	Both	
	L2	Typos: no / up to 5 / more	1/2/3	86	Both	
	L3	Grammar: no / up to 5 / more	1/2/3	79	Both	
	L4	Punctuation errors: no / up to 5 / more	1/2/3	80	Both	
	L5	Word usage (correctness)	1/2/3	68	Both	
	L6	Word usage (variance)	1/2	91	Both	
	L7	Is there conceptually oral language?	1/2/3	76	Both	
	L8	Sentence structure (variability)	1/2	98	Both	
	L9	Citations (formal aspects): use of quotation marks, references…	1/2	75	Summary	
	L10	Citations (content): Are direct citations used for central points?	1/2	86	Summary	
	G6	Stilistic skills – aggregated score	1/2/3/4/5/6	52	Both	
	G7	Verbal skills – aggregated score	1/2/3/4/5/6	64	Both	
	G8	Overall Impression, aggregated from G2 to G8	1/2/3/4/5/6	60	Both	

Table 1: Scoring categories in our corpus. Note that a lower score corresponds to a better essay.

For our experiments, we rely on two state-of-the-art systems: A classical supervised system based on hand-crafted features, and an SVM classifier, and an LSTM neural model based on embeddings.

4.1 SVM Classifier

We use Weka's (Hall et al., 2009) Support Vector classifier (SMO) in standard configuration as provided through DKPro TC (Daxenberger et al., 2014). We utilize a number of state-of-the-art features: As the essays in our dataset were written within a certain time limit, the **length** of an essay is an indicator of its quality. We measure length by the number of sentences, tokens and characters per essay. Additionally, we measure average sentence length in tokens and average token length in characters. **N-gram** features model words and phrases or constructions – in the case of POS n-grams – in an essay. We use boolean occurrence features for token and POS uni- to trigrams and token skip bi- to 5-grams. We count the **occurrence** of linguistic features, such as certain punctuations (commas, exclamation marks, quotation marks) as well as formal references to the source text and occurrences of reported speech.

Another set of features is based on **syntax**. We count the number of subordinate clauses in general, as well as the number of temporal and causal subordinate clauses using lists of indicator words for the latter two. We model syntactic variability through the average and maximal depth of parse trees in an essay and the distribution of individual POS tags. We also cover the linguistic variance in an essay through type-token-ratio. Also **language errors** are usually considered informative. We use the rule-based LanguageTool[3] checker to identify the number of spelling mistakes, punctuation errors and other grammatical errors. The number of **cohesive devices**, i.e. connectives, normalized by the essay length in tokens. Additionally, the average similarity between adjacent sentences measured both through greedy string tiling and the number of shared nouns between two sentences represents **coherence**.

4.2 Neural System

As the neural system, we use the Neural Essays Assessor (NEA) (Taghipour and Ng, 2016)[4], a

LSTM architecture using a mean-over-time layer for aggregation in its reported best configuration exchanging the English word embeddings for German polyglot embeddings (Al-Rfou et al., 2013) and using 50 LSTM units for run-time efficiency. We also perform 10-fold cross-validation using 8 folds for training and 1 fold as development set to determine which of 50 epochs to use per run.

5 Experiments & Results

This section presents our experimental results. We first evaluate state-of-the-art systems on the two global variables G1 and G8 in our data and compare to the performance on ASAP. We then investigate the performance on all variables to measure to what factors our model is sensitive. In subsequent experiments we address the influence of using the essay's summary and discussion part separately, of individual feature groups and the size of training data on the scoring performance.

5.1 Experiment 1: Performance of State-of-the-Art Systems

In our first experiment, we assess the overall performance of the scoring system on the two global variables G1 (holistic) and G8 (aggregated) under different feature settings. We apply the neural system and for the SVM-based system we test several conditions: As n-grams are known to be strong features (Yannakoudakis et al., 2011), we evaluate a baseline taking only token n-grams into consideration. We use two versions of the feature, one where we consider the top 1,000 most frequent n-grams (*n-gram 1,000*) and one where we consider the top 10,000 n-grams (*n-gram 10,000*). We next evaluate the full system with and without stacking of the three groups of n-gram features individually in order to avoid that these feature groups might overpower the other features.

In Table 2, we report the performance of the different setups for the variables G1 and G8. We see that we always reach a higher performance when predicting the informed overall score G8 than the holistic G1. Remember that G1 is assigned before scoring the other essay variables while G8 is a score based on the other variables. It seems plausible that G8 is more consistent and easier to predict automatically, although we do not find that reflected in agreement scores between human annotators.

We further observe that the performances of

---

[3]https://languagetool.org/de/
[4]https://github.com/nusnlp/nea

Paradigm	Configuration	Our corpus				ASAP	
		G1 (holistic)		G8 (aggregated)			
		acc.	QWK	acc.	QWK	acc.	QWK
Neural	NEA (Taghipour and Ng, 2016)	.43	**.45**	**.59**	**.53**	n/a	**.76**
SVM	n-grams – top 1000	.36	.36	.47	.40	.44	.64
	n-grams – top 10000	.45	.44	.56	.48	.49	.67
	full + n-grams top 1000	.40	.39	.54	.45	.46	.66
	full + n-grams top 10000	.45	**.45**	.57	.48	.49	.68
	full + stacked n-grams 1000	.47	.39	.58	.47	.53	.72
	full + stacked n-grams 10000	**.48**	.42	**.59**	.46	**.54**	.72

Table 2: Scoring performance for G1 (intuitive holistic) and G8 (aggregated holistic). For comparison, we also provide the performance of a comparable English model for the ASAP dataset (averaged over all 8 prompts).

both variables benefit from a larger number of n-grams. However, additional features in the full model are only beneficial if we have lower numbers of n-grams. These findings suggest that there is some redundancy between the n-grams and the remaining features.

We observe that using the out-of-the-box neural system is at least on par with the best supervised configuration. While this shows the potential of neural approaches on the global variables, in the following experiments, we concentrate on the SVM system that can be more easily targeted towards the individual variables.

Verification Using ASAP Data For comparison, we also evaluate our feature set (with minor adaptations from German to English) on the ASAP corpus, a well-known dataset for essay scoring (see Section 2). As labeled test data is not available, we evaluate using 5-fold cross validation on the training data – Table 2, the two rightmost columns. For the neural system, we report results by Taghipour and Ng (2016). Both the neural system .76 QWK and the SVM .72 QWK are on par with the best open-source system participating in the ASAP shared task that reached .71 QWK.[5]

These results show that the applied systems are state of the art on established datasets and are thus probably also state of the art on our new dataset. However, the performance level is much lower, as the task is more challenging.

5.2 Experiment 2: Scoring Performance for Different Variables

Next, we want to assess how well our essay scoring system is able to predict the different variables.

---

[5]Results are not directly comparable, as the official test data from the challenge is not publicly available.

We repeat Experiment 1 in the best-performing feature setting using the full model with 10,000 n-grams for each scoring variable separately, i.e. we use always the same features to train different models.

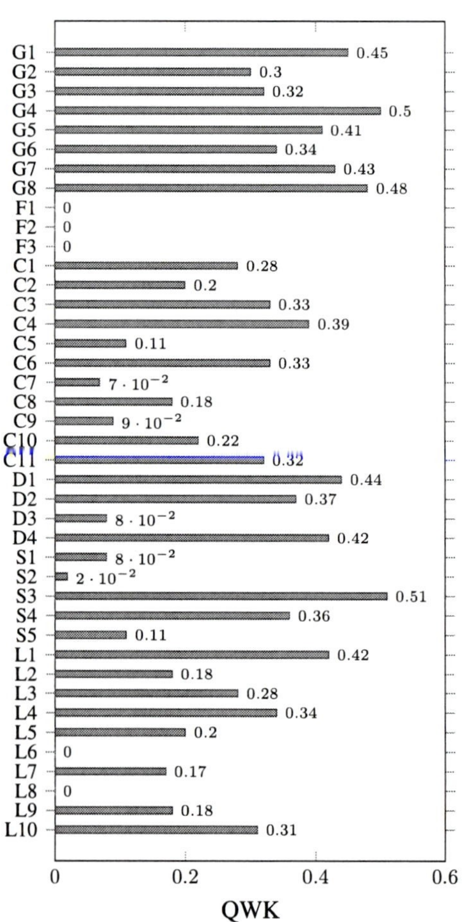

Figure 1: Scoring performance in quadratically weighted kappa for models trained separately using the same features on each scoring variable.

362

feature set	G1 (holistic)	G8 (aggregated)
merged	**.449**	.481
split	.441	**.522**

Table 3: Scoring performance measured in quadratically weighted kappa for G1 and G8 with features computed on the complete essay text (*merged*) and with features computed on the summary and discussion part separately (*split*).

It is clear that our one-fits-all approach can be improved by using feature sets tailored towards the individual variables. With this experiment we rather want to investigate which variables are sensitive to our model which uses features used for predicting global scores. This could help to answer the question which aspects of a global score an essay scoring system actually measures. Figure 1 shows the results.

We see that the feature set predicts at a very moderate level for many of the variables. For the very skewed variables F1 to F3, L6 and L8, performance is particularly bad. We also see that variables from each of the four categories (content, discussion, structure, and language) can be learnt to a very limited degree. Interestingly, the model performs a bit better on the aggregated scores G2 to G7 and the two global variables G1 and G8 although still on a level that prohibits a practical use of the system. In the following, we concentrate on G1 an G8. In doing so, we can also compare to scores in other essay datasets that use only holistic scores.

5.3 Experiment 3: Splitting Essays into Summary and Discussion Part

The prompt in our task asks for essays with a specific structure: a summarization and a discussion part. Some of the variables are measured on only one of those two parts (cf. Table 1). Therefore it seems reasonable to measure not only if a feature occurs, but also in which part of the essay. For example, the trigram *in my opinion* might be an indicator for a good essay if it occurs in the discussion, but not in the summary. Therefore, we also determine n-gram features (token, pos, and skip) separately for both essay parts.[6] In the *split* condition in Table 3, we duplicate each n-gram feature and compute it individually on the summary and

---

[6]There are essays where only one part was present. In such cases all features for the other part have been set to 0.

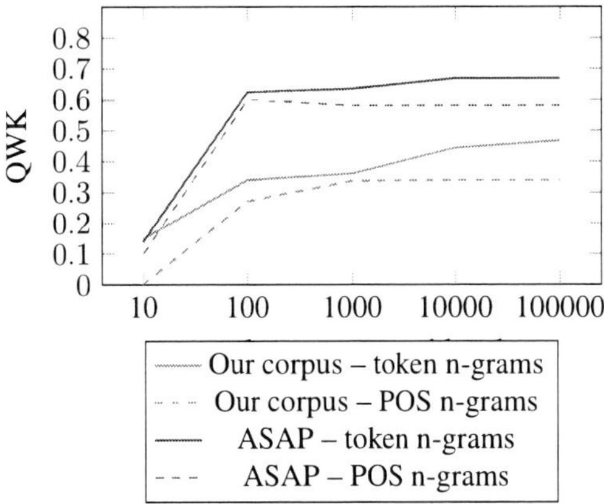

Figure 2: Assessing various numbers of token or POS n-grams as features for the scoring performance of G8.

the discussion part, the *merged* condition repeats values from Table 2 for the best-performing SVM, the full model with 10,000 n-grams.

We see that for G8 we profit from that split, while for G1 we do not. We do not have a good intuition why this is the case, but suspect that the more informed G8 score takes this additional information better into account. What we learn from this experiment is that it is helpful to take additional prompt-specific structure in the data into consideration. Identifying further automatically detectable sub-parts of the essay and treating them separately is a promising step for future work.

5.4 Experiment 4: Number and Type of N-grams

We have seen that a major contribution to the performance for both ASAP and our dataset comes from token n-gram features and that we benefit from a higher number of n-grams. To further assess this influence, we take the number of available n-grams to their extremes and perform experiments using token n-grams and POS n-grams individually while varying the number of k top-frequent n-grams to extract from 10 to 10,000. Note that it can happen for POS n-grams and for token n-grams on ASAP that k is bigger than the actual number of n-grams present in the data. In that case, we take all available n-grams.

In Figure 2, we see a huge difference between ASAP and our corpus: in ASAP, a steep performance increase can be observed already with low numbers of n-grams and the curve flattens out early. In our corpus, we see a steady increase of

Configuration	G8 (aggregated)
full model	.47
– token n-grams	.41
– skip n-grams	.47
– POS n-grams	.45
– length	.46
– coherence	.47
– cohesion	.46
– syntax	.46
– occurrence	.47
– error	.44

Table 4: Ablation test (QWK) for the global G8 variable.

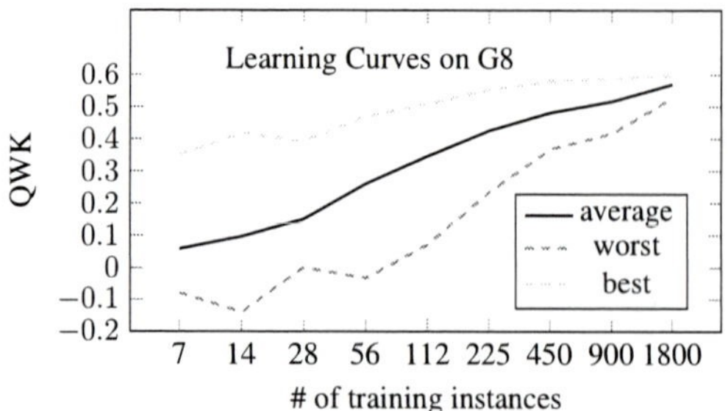

Figure 3: Learning curve experiments using different numbers of training instances, always testing on the same test set for G8.

performance that is less pronounced in the beginning and in general on a much lower level. One corpus variable explaining this effect is the average length of the essay. ASAP essays are shorter (the average number of tokens per prompt varies between 100 and 600) while our essays have a general average around 600 tokens. Even if we add more n-gram features the performance gap never closes and shows the difficulty in our data.

5.5 Experiment 5: Feature Ablation

We perform an ablation test to discern the contribution of individual feature groups. Table 4 shows the performance for the full model (using top 1,000 token, POS and skip n-grams, and stacking) and for the model with individual feature groups ablated. We chose this model because our models with more n-gram features show very similar results for the full model in comparison to n-grams only and the current settings seems most suitable to highlight potential contributions of individual features.

We can see that the feature group with the highest effect are unsurprisingly token n-grams. Most of the other features have only a minor effect. However, we saw in the comparison between the full model and n-grams only, that the additional features have a beneficial effect in our setting. We assume that our feature set is quite redundant, so that e.g. the occurrence of a connective can also be learnt from the respective unigram.

5.6 Experiment 6: Amount of Training Data

In a practical setting it is important to know how many training instances have to be available to reach a certain performance and at which amount of training data the performance levels off. This helps us to decide whether we can already fully as-

sess the performance of our method on the given data or whether more training data would be helpful. We therefore perform a learning curve experiment showing the correlation between the number of training data and the scoring performance. In this experiment, we keep the test data constant and use the 10% held-out data for this purpose. We use the split feature set with 10,000 n-gram features which showed the best performance on the cross-validation experiments. We always double the number of training data, starting from 7 until we reach 1,800. We sample each number of training instances randomly 100 times from the pool of unlabeled data and report average, worst and best performance across those 100 runs. The resulting learning curves are shown in Figure 3 We can see that the performance varies tremendously between the best and worst runs for smaller amounts of training data. This highlights that a careful selection of training data can help when only limited human annotation effort is available. We also see that the curve starts to flatten out in the end for the best case, so that we will not profit much more from more training data.

6 Conclusions and Future Work

We have presented a set of experiments on a new challenging dataset and have shown that standard features that perform well on a standard essay scoring dataset do not perform so well here. We attribute our results to the high proficiency of our writers. Of course, we cannot be sure that some of the differences might be due to the language of the essays being German, not English and we expect that some features of the German language, such as compounds, are indeed an additional challenge. Nevertheless, we have demonstrated that essay scoring still can be a challenging problem, calling for deeper linguistic analysis. Future work needs to concentrate on finding better representations for this kind of data, e.g. we hypothesize that recognizing argumentative structure might be helpful, as e.g. done in (Stab and Gurevych, 2016).

While the current set of essay data cannot be published for copyright reasons, we are preparing to collect and release a set of essays from the same setting from the next cohort. Essays of a similar type and in similar amounts are being collected at the beginning of each semester and we are preparing ways of getting the students' consent to publishing their anonymized essays in a corpus. In doing so, we aim at providing a challenging dataset to the community and broaden the range of available essay data.

Acknowledgements

This work is funded by the German Federal Ministry of Education and Research under grant no. FKZ 01PL16075.

References

Rami Al-Rfou, Bryan Perozzi, and Steven Skiena. 2013. Polyglot: Distributed word representations for multilingual nlp. In *Proceedings of the Seventeenth Conference on Computational Natural Language Learning*. Association for Computational Linguistics, Sofia, Bulgaria, pages 183–192. http://www.aclweb.org/anthology/W13-3520.

Dimitrios Alikaniotis, Helen Yannakoudakis, and Marek Rei. 2016. Automatic text scoring using neural networks. In *Proceedings of the 54th Annual Meeting of the Association for Computational Linguistics, ACL 2016, August 7-12, 2016, Berlin, Germany, Volume 1: Long Papers*. The Association for Computer Linguistics. http://aclweb.org/anthology/P/P16/P16-1068.pdf.

Björkelund Anders, Bohnet Bernd, Love Hafdell, and Pierre Nugues. 2010. A high-performance syntactic and semantic dependency parser. In *Coling 2010: Demonstrations*. Coling 2010 Organizing Committee, pages 33–36. http://aclweb.org/anthology/C10-3009.

Yigal Attali and Jill Burstein. 2006. Automated essay scoring with e-rater® v. 2. *The Journal of Technology, Learning and Assessment* 4(3).

Daniel Blanchard, Joel Tetreault, Derrick Higgins, Aoife Cahill, and Martin Chodorow. 2013. Toefl11: A corpus of non-native english. *ETS Research Report Series* 2013(2):i–15. https://doi.org/10.1002/j.2333-8504.2013.tb02331.x.

Albert Bremerich-Vos and Dirk Scholten-Akoun. 2016. *Schriftsprachliche Kompetenzen von Lehramtsstudierenden in der Studieneingangsphase, Eine empirische Untersuchung*. Schneider Verlag Hohengehren, Baltmannsweiler.

Aoife Cahill, Martin Chodorow, Susanne Wolff, and Nitin Madnani. 2013. Detecting missing hyphens in learner text. *NAACL/HLT 2013* page 300.

Hongbo Chen and Ben He. 2013. Automated essay scoring by maximizing human-machine agreement. In *EMNLP*. pages 1741–1752.

Ronan Cummins, Meng Zhang, and Ted Briscoe. 2016. Constrained multi-task learning for automated essay scoring. In *Proceedings of the 54th Annual Meeting of the Association for Computational Linguistics*. Association for Computational Linguistics.

Johannes Daxenberger, Oliver Ferschke, Iryna Gurevych, and Torsten Zesch. 2014. Dkpro tc: A java-based framework for supervised learning experiments on textual data. In *Proceedings of 52nd Annual Meeting of the Association for Computational Linguistics: System Demonstrations*. Association for Computational Linguistics, Baltimore, Maryland, pages 61–66. http://www.aclweb.org/anthology/P14-5011.

Semire Dikli. 2006. An overview of automated scoring of essays. *The Journal of Technology, Learning and Assessment* 5(1).

Richard Eckart de Castilho and Iryna Gurevych. 2014. A broad-coverage collection of portable nlp components for building shareable analysis pipelines. In *Proceedings of the Workshop on Open Infrastructures and Analysis Frameworks for HLT*. Association for Computational Linguistics and Dublin City University, Dublin, Ireland, pages 1–11. http://www.aclweb.org/anthology/W14-5201.

Peter W Foltz, Darrell Laham, and Thomas K Landauer. 1999. The intelligent essay assessor: Applications to educational technology. *Interactive Multimedia Electronic Journal of Computer-Enhanced Learning* 1(2):939–944.

Mark Hall, Eibe Frank, Geoffrey Holmes, Bernhard Pfahringer, Peter Reutemann, and Ian H. Witten. 2009. The weka data mining software: An update. *SIGKDD Explor. Newsl.* 11(1):10–18. https://doi.org/10.1145/1656274.1656278.

Claudia Harsch and Guido Martin. 2012. Adapting cef-descriptors for rating purposes: Validation by a combined rater training and scale revision approach. *Assessing Writing* 17(4):228–250.

Claudia Harsch and Guido Martin. 2013. Comparing holistic and analytic scoring methods: Issues of validity and reliability. *Assessment in Education: Principles, Policy & Practice* 20(3):281–307.

Shinichiro Ishikawa. 2011. A new horizon in learner corpus studies: The aim of the icnale project. *Corpora and language technologies in teaching, learning and research* pages 3–11.

Beata Beigman Klebanov, Michael Flor, and Binod Gyawali. 2016. Topicality-based indices for essay scoring. In (Tetreault et al., 2016), pages 63–72. http://aclweb.org/anthology/W/W16/W16-0507.pdf.

Chi-Un Lei, Ka Lok Man, and TO Ting. 2014. Using learning analytics to analyze writing skills of students: A case study in a technological common core curriculum course. *IAENG International Journal of Computer Science* 41(3).

Nitin Madnani, Aoife Cahill, and Brian Riordan. 2016. Automatically scoring tests of proficiency in music instruction. In (Tetreault et al., 2016), pages 217–222. http://aclweb.org/anthology/W/W16/W16-0524.pdf.

Manvi Mahana, Mishel Johns, and Ashwin Apte. 2012. Automated essay grading using machine learning. *Mach. Learn. Session, Stanford University* .

Robert Östling. 2013. Automated essay scoring for swedish. In *Proceedings of the Eighth Workshop on Innovative Use of NLP for Building Educational Applications*. pages 42–47.

Ildik Pilán, Elena Volodina, and Torsten Zesch. 2016. Predicting proficiency levels in learner writings by transferring a linguistic complexity model from expert-written coursebooks.

Anna N. Rafferty and Christopher D. Manning. 2008. Parsing three german treebanks: Lexicalized and unlexicalized baselines. In *Proceedings of the Workshop on Parsing German*. Association for Computational Linguistics, Stroudsburg, PA, USA, PaGe '08, pages 40–46. http://dl.acm.org/citation.cfm?id=1621401.1621407.

Hongsuck Seo, Jonghoon Lee, Seokhwan Kim, Kyusong Lee, Sechun Kang, and Gary Geunbae Lee. 2012. A meta learning approach to grammatical error correction. In *Proceedings of the 50th Annual Meeting of the Association for Computational Linguistics: Short Papers-Volume 2*. Association for Computational Linguistics, pages 328–332.

Mark D Shermis and Ben Hamner. 2012. Contrasting state-of-the-art automated scoring of essays: Analysis. In Mark D Shermis and Jill C Burstein, editors, *Handbook of automated essay evaluation: Current applications and new directions*, Routledge, pages 313–346.

Christian Stab and Iryna Gurevych. 2016. Parsing argumentation structures in persuasive essays. *CoRR* abs/1604.07370.

Kaveh Taghipour and Hwee Tou Ng. 2016. A neural approach to automated essay scoring. In Jian Su, Xavier Carreras, and Kevin Duh, editors, *Proceedings of the 2016 Conference on Empirical Methods in Natural Language Processing, EMNLP 2016, Austin, Texas, USA, November 1-4, 2016*. The Association for Computational Linguistics, pages 1882–1891. http://aclweb.org/anthology/D/D16/D16-1193.pdf.

Joel Tetreault, Daniel Blanchard, and Aoife Cahill. 2013. A report on the first native language identification shared task. In *In Proceedings of the Eighth Workshop on Innovative Use of NLP for Building Educational Applications*.

Joel R. Tetreault, Jill Burstein, Claudia Leacock, and Helen Yannakoudakis, editors. 2016. *Proceedings of the 11th Workshop on Innovative Use of NLP for Building Educational Applications, BEA@NAACL-HLT 2016, June 16, 2016, San Diego, California, USA*. The Association for Computer Linguistics. http://aclweb.org/anthology/W/W16/.

Sowmya Vajjala. 2017. Automated assessment of non-native learner essays: Investigating the role of linguistic features. *International Journal of Artificial Intelligence in Education* pages 1–27. https://doi.org/10.1007/s40593-017-0142-3.

Sowmya Vajjala and Kaidi Léo. 2014. Automatic cefr level prediction for estonian learner text. In *Proceedings of the third workshop on NLP for computer-assisted language learning at SLTC 2014, Uppsala University*. Linköping University Electronic Press, 107.

Salvatore Valenti, Francesca Neri, and Alessandro Cucchiarelli. 2003. An overview of current research on automated essay grading. *Journal of Information Technology Education: Research* 2(1):319–330.

Elena Volodina, Ildik Piln, Ingegerd Enstrm, Lorena Llozhi, Peter Lundkvist, Gunlg Sundberg, and Monica Sandell. 2016. Swell on the rise: Swedish learner language corpus for european reference level studies.

Sara C Weigle. 2013. English as a second language writing and automated essay evaluation. *Handbook of automated essay evaluation: Current application and new directions* pages 36–54.

Sara Cushing Weigle. 2002. *Assessing Writing*. Cambridge University Press, Cambridge.

Cyril J. Weir. 2005. *Language Testing and Validation*. Palgrave Macmillan, Basingstoke.

Helen Yannakoudakis, Ted Briscoe, and Ben Medlock. 2011. A new dataset and method for automatically grading esol texts. In *Proceedings of the 49th Annual Meeting of the Association for Computational Linguistics: Human Language Technologies - Volume 1*. Association for Computational Linguistics, Stroudsburg, PA, USA, HLT '11, pages 180–189. http://dl.acm.org/citation.cfm?id=2002472.2002496.

Exploring Optimal Voting in Native Language Identification

Cyril Goutte
Multilingual Text Processing
National Research Council Canada
1200 Montréal Rd, Ottawa, ON, Canada
Cyril.Goutte@gmail.com

Serge Léger
Human Computer Interaction
National Research Council Canada
100 Aboiteaux, Moncton, NB, Canada
Serge.Leger@nrc.ca

Abstract

We describe the submissions entered by
the National Research Council Canada in
the Native Language Identification Shared
Task 2017. We mainly explored the use
of voting, and various ways to optimize
the choice and number of voting systems.
We also explored the use of features that
rely on no linguistic preprocessing. Long
ngrams of characters obtained from raw
text turned out to yield the best performance on all textual input (written essays and speech transcripts). Voting ensembles turned out to produce small performance gains, with little difference between the various optimization strategies
we tried. Our top systems achieved accuracies of 87% on the ESSAY track, 84%
on the SPEECH track, and close to 92% by
combining essays, speech and i-vectors in
the FUSION track.

1 Introduction

This paper describes the system entered by the
National Research Council Canada in the Native
Language Identification (NLI) Shared Task 2017
(Malmasi et al., 2017).

The task of Native Language Identification consists of predicting the native (L1) language of a
foreign speaker, from textual and speech clues
in a second (L2) language. Applications of this
task are mostly in language learning and foren-
sic/security, see (Malmasi, 2016, Section 1.1) for
a good overview. This is an interesting example of a task that is difficult to perform for humans, especially when the number of target native languages is large. In fact, in a comparison
between automated and human evaluation, Malmasi et al. (2015) could only use 5 L1 languages,

whereas the automated classifier covered 11 languages. They also found that, even in these limited settings, humans generally under-performed
the automated systems.

An international evaluation in 2013 (Tetreault
et al., 2013) showed that statistical methods could
reach a high level of performance on this task
(close to 84% accuracy) using a mixture of surface form features, linguistic features, and model
combination. Ensemble methods, in particular,
have proved crucial to reach top performance on
this task and other related document categorization tasks like the discrimination of language variants (Goutte et al., 2014). Recent work has confirmed this; we refer the reader to Malmasi and
Dras (2017) for an overview and evaluation of
many combination approaches.

Our best attempts at the NLI-2013 evaluation
used model combination by voting, a simple strategy in which each base model contributes a vote
towards a category, and final prediction goes to
the category with the most votes. In this evaluation, we therefore explore this strategy further,
looking into important aspects of the process: selecting the models to add to the combination, as
well as their number. An attractive perk of the
voting/combination approach is that it provides a
natural way to handle multimodal data such as the
text and speech data available in the evaluation.
One can train models using either modality, and
combine their predictions using voting. This is
known as the *late fusion* approach. By contrast,
the *early fusion* approach combines different sets
of features and trains a single model on those. We
test and compare a simple early fusion model in
the FUSION track below.

Our second investigation is on the feature side.
In particular, we investigate the use of long character ngram, without any other linguistic processing. Previous work reached state-of-the-art perfor-

Proceedings of the 12th Workshop on Innovative Use of NLP for Building Educational Applications, pages 367–373
Copenhagen, Denmark, September 8, 2017. ©2017 Association for Computational Linguistics

mance on the 2013 NLI Shared Task using string kernels (Ionescu et al., 2016), considering subsequences of 5 to 9 characters. On the task of discriminating similar languages (Goutte et al., 2016), long character ngrams also reach top performance (Goutte and Léger, 2016) using subsequences of 5 and 6 characters. We looked in more detail into how useful this type of feature could be in the context of NLI. This contrasts with many systems used in the 2013 evaluation, including ours, which used a combination of lexical and syntactic features, including short character and word ngrams, part-of-speech and syntactic dependencies. We test character ngrams up to 6grams, extracted from raw text without any linguistic preprocessing (no tokenization or casing normalization).

In the following section, we quickly review the data and introduce the approaches we tested for the NLI Shared Task 2017. Section 3 presents our results, both during development and evaluated on the final test data.

2 Data and Methods

2.1 Data

The NLI-2017 collection covers 11 native languages: Arabic, Chinese, French German, Hindi, Italian, Japanese, Korean, Spanish, Telugu and Turkish, stratified across categories (Table 1). It was obtained from a standardized assessment of English proficiency for academic purposes. Each document contains three parts:

1. The text of an essay written in English by a native L1 speaker, in response to a prompt;

2. The orthographic transcript of a 45-second English spoken reply given by the native L1 speaker in response to a prompt;[1]

3. 800-dimensional i-vectors, computed from the 45s audio file recording the spoken reply.

The i-vectors (Verma and Das, 2015) are a compact representation of the audio signal, typically used in speaker recognition. The raw audio file is not available for this task. The prompts for the text and spoken replies are also provided for both training and test data, but we did not use that information in our work.

| L1 | (Estimation) | | |
	Train	Dev	Test
ARA	1000	100	100
CHI	1000	100	100
FRE	1000	100	100
GER	1000	100	100
HIN	1000	100	100
ITA	1000	100	100
JPN	1000	100	100
KOR	1000	100	100
SPA	1000	100	100
TEL	1000	100	100
TUR	1000	100	100
Total	11000	1100	1100

Table 1: NLI-2017 collection: #doc per L1.

In the NLI Shared Task 2017, the ESSAY track uses the text of the essay alone; The SPEECH track uses the transcript as well as the i-vectors; In the FUSION track, all information can be used. Finally, note that we only participated in the closed data condition, where only the provided collection may be used for modelling.

2.2 Features

For the text data (essays and transcripts), we generated a number of fairly standard textual features. Each type of feature results in a specific feature space that we denote by a tag indicating the type of feature, and a number indicating the size, e.g. `char3` for trigrams of characters.

Characters: We extracted subsequences of 3 to 6 characters from the text. This was done first on the tokenized text (as provided by the orgnizers), resulting in 4 feature spaces: `char3`, `char4`, `char5` and `char6`. We extracted the same features from the raw, untokenized text, resulting in another four sets of features: `rchar3`, `rchar4`, `rchar5` and `rchar6`.

Words: We extracted subsequences of 1 to 4 words from the tokenized text, ignoring punctuation, resulting in 4 feature sets: `bow1`, `bow2`, `bow3` and `bow4`.

POS: We extracted subsequences of 1 to 3 part-of-speech tags, as produced by the freely available Stanford POS tagger,[2] v3.7.0

---

[1] Speech and text prompts are different.

[2] http://www-nlp.stanford.edu/software/tagger.shtml

(Toutanova et al., 2003). This produced three feature sets: `pos1, pos2, pos3`.

For the character and word ngrams, we use a *tf-idf* weighting corresponding to the ltc weighting scheme (i.e. log term frequency, (log) inverse document frequency, and cosine normalization) in SMART (Manning et al., 2008, Fig. 6.7). Because most part-of-speech tags tend to occur in most documents, we did not use idf on the part-of-speech ngrams, and only perform scaling to unit length (nnc weighting in SMART).

Finally, in the SPEECH and FUSION tracks, the i-vectors were used as provided, either alone or in conjunction with another transcript feature. In that case, we scaled the i-vectors to unit length (cosine normalization).

2.3 Models

Equipped with multiple ways to generate features from documents, we will now review the models we estimated on those, as well as the approaches we investigated to improve the voting combination.

Model Estimation

We addressed the problem of identifying the native language as a document categorization problem with 11 classes (one per native language). We use 11 binary classifiers trained in a one-versus-all fashion, with a calibration layer on the classifier output in order to provide proper multilabel predictions.

Each of the base one-vs-all classifier is a Support Vector Machine trained using SVM^{light} (Joachims, 1998) with linear kernels, all default parameters and cost factor ($-j$) set to 10 in order to balance positive and negative examples. Once a classifier is trained, its output is calibrated in order to output proper probabilities, using a mixture of Gaussian distributions (Bennett, 2003). This allows the output of the 11 classifiers to be well-behaved probabilities that we can compare in order to predict the most probable class, or use in further post-processing in combination with other classifier's outputs.

Our first submission in each of Tables 2–4 is a single model trained that way, all other submissions are voting combinations, as described below.

Model Combination

Leveraging ensembles of models has proven effective in order to improve performance on Na-

tive Language Identification (Tetreault et al., 2013; Malmasi and Dras, 2017) and many other NLP tasks (Goutte et al., 2014). Among many alternatives, we focus on *voting*, a conceptually and practically simple approach where each model in the ensemble casts a vote towards a class, votes are tallied and prediction goes to the most voted class. In *plurality voting*, all models cast a single, identical vote towards one class. Other variants weigh votes according to, for example, how confident each model is in its prediction. Two important hyper-parameters influence the resulting prediction and its quality: 1) the number of voting systems, and 2) the way these systems are selected.

In a typical learning setup, it makes sense to let both of these choices be led by the resulting estimated prediction error. In previous work, we simply ranked models according to prediction error, estimated on either a separate validation/dev set or by cross-validation, and selected models in descending order of performance until the resulting combined performance started to drop.

For this evaluation, we experimented with a greedy selection approach: instead of considering all models in descending order of performance, we

1. Start with an ensemble containing only the highest performing model; place all remaining models in a candidate pool.

2. Add each candidate from the pool in turn to the current ensemble; compute resulting estimated performance.

3. Pick the candidate that produce the best performance, remove it from the pool and place it in the ensemble.

4. Iterate Steps 2–3 until pool is empty.

This greedy algorithm performs the optimal choice at each step but does not reconsider previous choices in order to further improve the model. It provides a one-step-optimal order in which models are added to the ensemble. In order to pick the number of models to include in the ensemble, we again look at the estimated prediction error. The simplest method is to look again at dev set or cross-validation performance. There are two issues with this, however:

1. When the order and number of models are set using the same prediction performance esti-

mate, these choices are clearly not independant, so our results will be biased. Typically, the number of models will be over-estimated.

2. We are essentially performing multiple comparisons between ensembles based on the same performance estimate. Unless we correct for multiple comparison, this will again lead to overestimate the ensemble size.

In order to partly address these concerns, we proceed with a selection method inspired by *half sampling* (Mccarthy, 1969). We split the evaluation data in two balanced halves (half the dev set, or half the full set in cross-validation). We use one half to estimate the best models to add to the ensemble, as above, and use the other half to get an unbiased estimate of the gain in performance from each addition, in order to select the best ensemble size. Of course we can swap the two halves, and there are many (correlated) ways to split the evaluation data. In our experiment we only considered one split in half, and swapped the two halves, resulting in two ensembles (last two submissions in Table 4).

Another combination approach is *stacking* (Wolpert, 1992), where a meta-classifer is trained to predict on the basis of base model scores. This approach was shown to be effective on Native Language Identification (Malmasi and Dras, 2017), and when several meta-classifiers are available, they can again be combined for further gains. The main drawback is that there are more parameters to estimate than in a simple ensemble combination approach.

3 Results

3.1 Explorations

In our preliminary experiments, we validated all design decisions by evaluating performance in two ways:

1. Building models on the official train set, and testing on the official dev set containing 1100 examples;

2. Joining the official train and dev data into one training set on which we run 10-fold cross-validation.

We later present both performance estimates for our submitted systems, together with the official test performance.

	Dev	CV	Test	
System	**Acc.**	**Acc.**	**m-F1**	**Acc.**
Org. baseline	.724	n/a	.710	.710
(rchar6) single	.835	.836	.862	.862
Best Dev Vote	.847	.842	***.874***	***.874***
Best CV Vote	.842	.845	.870	.869
Closed Task Best	n/a	n/a	**.882**	**.882**

Table 2: Results for the closed ESSAY track: organizer's baseline, our three submissions (our best result emphasized, best results in bold) and the best ranked system. 'Acc.' is accuracy and 'm-F1' is macro-averaged F1.

3.2 ESSAY track

Our three submissions to the ESSAY track are simple and typical illustrations of the ideas we explored for this evaluation:

1. Best single feature set (`rchar6`): the use of 6-grams on raw text (no tokenization or casing) provides the best performance estimates on both the dev set and in cross-validation.

2. The best vote, optimized on dev set performance, includes 10 models trained on the following feature sets: `rchar6`, `char6`, `pos3`, `bow2`, `bow4`, `char3`, `bow1`, `bow3`, `char4`, `pos2`.

3. The best vote, optimized on cross-validation performance, includes 7 models trained on the following feature sets: `rchar6`, `char6`, `bow3`, `rchar3`, `bow1`, `bow2`, `pos3`

The performance of our three submissions on the test set is shown in Table 2. The first outcome is that the single model based on raw text character 6-grams performs very significantly above the organizer-provided baseline. It is also our best performing single system, outperforming bag-of-words, bag of word $n$grams, part-of-speech $n$grams, or character $n$grams extracted from tokenized text. This suggests that large character $n$grams, without any linguistic pre-processing, are more than competitive with any of the typical textual features. The test performance of this simple model is around 86%, which is higher than any performance reported at the NLI-2013 evaluation (on a different dataset, of course).

As expected, ensemble prediction allows to improve the performance further. Gains are small,

System	Dev Acc.	CV Acc.	Test m-F1	Test Acc.
Org. baseline	.755	n/a	.798	.798
(rchar6+ivec)	.826	.737	*.845*	*.845*
Best Dev vote	.843	.810	.841	.841
Closed Task Best	n/a	n/a	**.876**	**.876**

Table 3: Results for the closed SPEECH track: organizer's baseline, our two submissions (our best result emphasized, best result in bold) and the best ranked system. 'Acc.' is accuracy and 'm-F1' is macro-averaged F1.

System	Dev Acc.	CV Acc.	Test m-F1	Test Acc.
Org. baseline	.783	n/a	.790	.790
Early fusion	.886	.886	.906	.906
Best Dev vote	.910	.893	.903	.903
Best CV vote	.902	.901	.917	.917
Top10 vote	.891	.894	.912	.912
Top15 vote	.896	.899	.917	.917
Best $\frac{1}{2}$Sample#1	.898	.901	*.919*	*.919*
Best $\frac{1}{2}$Sample#2	.901	.899	.916	.916
Closed Task Best	n/a	n/a	**.932**	**.932**

Table 4: Results for the closed FUSION track: organizer's baseline, our two submissions (our best result emphasized, best result in bold) and the best ranked system.

however: our best voting combination reached 87.4% accuracy, a gain of 1.2% over our best single system. This was obtained by optimizing the number of voting systems on the dev set, although the cross-validation-optimized vote performs less than 0.5% below our top submission on this track.

Our best result is 0.78% below the top ranked system in the closed ESSAY track, a difference that is not statistically significant and places our result in a set of 7 groups tied for first (out of 17 groups). We believe that this shows both how sophisticated and how mature statistical models for NLI have become. The confusion table for our best entry in shown in Figure 1 (left).

3.3 SPEECH track

For the SPEECH track, we only considered the use of transcripts and i-vectors, either together in a joint feature space, or within a voting ensemble. Also, we do not present the results of our first three submissions, due to an incorrect scaling of the i-vectors. The two systems we report here are:

1. A system with a single feature set (`rchar6`) together with the unit-scaled i-vectors: the use of 6-grams alone on the transcript clearly under-performs, topping at 58% in our experiments; the addition of i-vectors proved necessary to get competitive performance.

2. The best vote, optimized on dev set performance, includes 9 models: five with scaled i-vectors (with `rchar6`, `bow2`, `pos3`, `bow1`, `pos2`) and four using transcripts alone (`pos2`, `rchar5`, `rchar3`, `char3`). This shows that even though transcript features underperform, they may be useful in an ensemble.

Results from Table 3 show that both submissions outperform the baseline. The voting ensemble actually achieved slightly lower performance than the single system (by a handful of examples), the accuracy of which is 2.9% below our best ESSAY track submission.

Our best result is 3.07% below the top ranked system in the closed SPEECH track, a difference that is statistically significant and places our result alone below a set of 3 groups tied for first (out of 10 groups). The confusion table for our best entry in shown in Figure 1 (middle).

3.4 FUSION track

For the FUSION track, we submitted several systems, as this was the core of our investigation:

1. A simple early fusion system plays the role of the "single feature set" for the FUSION track: it uses `rchar6` on the essay text, `char6` on the transcripts and scaled i-vectors.

2. The best ensemble, selected to maximize dev set performance (both order and number of base models), contains 23 base models mixing essay, transcripts and i-vector features.

3. The best ensemble, selected to maximize cross-validation performance, contains 24 base models mixing essay, transcripts and i-vector features.

4. The top-10 and top-15 ensembles of base models, based on the order optimized on dev set performance. The idea is to evaluate whether optimizing the number of models in

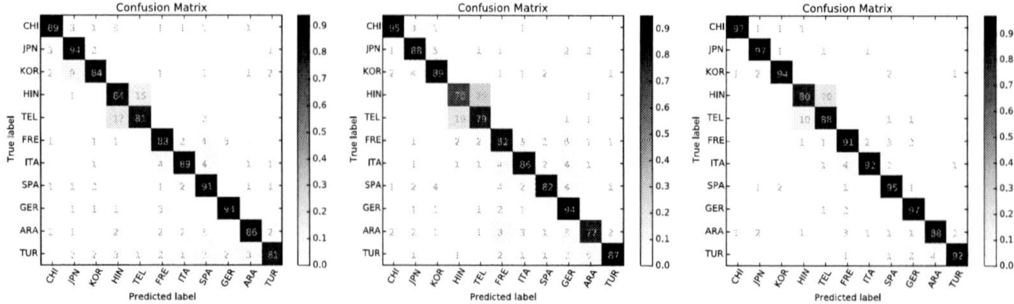

Figure 1: Confusion tables of our best system in each track: ESSAY (left), SPEECH and FUSION (right).

the ensemble on the same performance indeed overestimates the ensemble size.

5. Two half-sample ensembles, estimated by splitting the cross-validated predictions in halves, as described in Section 2.3 and swapping the halves for ordering and selecting the models.

Table 4 shows that most ensembles gain over the early fusion approach, but the improvement is limited to less than 1.5%. Only the "Best Dev vote" ensemble displays a drop in performance. This suggests that, as expected, the smaller dev set provides a less reliable estimate of performance, and performance improvements, than the cross-validation or half-sampling approaches. The Top-15 ensemble yields the same performance as the "Best CV" vote, which contains 24 base models. This shows that several of those base models bring no actual gain in predictive performance, confirming that selecting the order and number of base models in the ensemble tends to over-estimate the ensemble size. The best overall result is provided by the first half-sampling ensemble, which reaches 91.9% accuracy. This is less than .3% above, and likely not significant compared to the three closest following ensembles ("Best CV", "Top15" and "Best $\frac{1}{2}$Sample#2").

We also note that all FUSION systems, even the simple early fusion, are clearly above the ESSAY and SPEECH results, suggesting that using multiple sources of information is indeed beneficial.

Our best result is 1.26% below the top ranked system in the closed FUSION track, a difference that is not statistically significant and places our result in a set of 4 groups tied for first (out of 4 groups). Again, this shows that several approaches are able to yield high accuracy and state-of-the-

art results on this difficult NLI task. The confusion table for our best entry in shown in Figure 1 (right). This suggest a high level of predictive performance, except for the confusion between Hindi and Telugu, which was already noted in the 2013 evaluation.

4 Discussion

4.1 Voting and Optimal Ensembles

Our results confirm that ensemble methods, and voting in particular, provide small, but systematic gains in predictive performance. Our work suggests, however, that there is some variability in results depending on how the ensemble is estimated, and in particular on what estimator of predictive performance is used. For example, the assessment of performance improvement is hardly consistent across the dev, CV and test estimators, although each estimator usually will produce ensembles that gain over a single system. We feel that there may be room to improve the design on ensembles, and voting ensembles in particular.

4.2 Are Characters the New Words?

Our work on Native Language Identification confirms that long character ngrams can yield state-of-the-art performance, and often outperform word ngrams. This confirms earlier work on similar tasks such as Discriminating Similar Languages. Clearly, the fact that we are able to handle large ngram sizes allows the index to cover many word tokens, as frequent words are typically also short. Character ngrams may also be able to model word stems, in many situations, without any linguistic modelling or heuristics. The big advantage of this approach is that it requires no linguistic preprocessing, not even tokenization, and may be applicable to languages with rich morphology, on which word-based approaches typically suffer. The downside is the need to index many ngrams. This is partly offset by 1) the fact that the number of actually observed ngrams grows much slower than the number of possible ngrams, and 2) modern indexing techniques such as hashing are essentially insensitive to the theoretical feature set size. Working with long ngrams offers the prospect of developping versatile document categorizers that work on several languages and character sets with no prior linguistic tools (eg no segmentation for Chinese or no vowelization for Arabic).

Acknowledgements

This work was carried out as part of the Multimedia Analytics Tools for Security (MATS) program at the National Research Council Canada. We wish to thank the organizers for providing useful baselines and formatting results in a way that made our work so much easier.

References

Paul N. Bennett. 2003. Using asymmetric distributions to improve text classifier probability estimates. In *Proceedings of the 26th Annual International ACM SIGIR Conference on Research and Development in Informaion Retrieval*. ACM, New York, NY, USA, SIGIR '03, pages 111–118. https://doi.org/10.1145/860435.860457.

Cyril Goutte and Serge Léger. 2016. Advances in ngram-based discrimination of similar languages. In *Proceedings of the Third Workshop on NLP for Similar Languages, Varieties and Dialects*. pages 178–184.

Cyril Goutte, Serge Léger, and Marine Carpuat. 2014. The NRC system for discriminating similar languages. In *Proceedings of the First Workshop on Applying NLP Tools to Similar Languages, Varieties and Dialects (VarDial)*. Dublin, Ireland, pages 139–145.

Cyril Goutte, Serge Léger, Shervin Malmasi, and Marcos Zampieri. 2016. Discriminating similar languages: Evaluations and explorations. In *Proceedings of the 10th International Conference on Language Resources and Evaluation (LREC 2016)*.

Radu Tudor Ionescu, Marius Popescu, and Aoife Cahill. 2016. String kernels for native language identification: Insights from behind the curtains. *Computational Linguistics* 42(3):491–525.

Thorsten Joachims. 1998. Text categorization with Suport Vector Machines: Learning with many relevant features. In Claire Nédellec and Céline Rouveirol, editors, *Proceedings of ECML-98, 10th European Conference on Machine Learning*. Springer, volume 1398 of *Lecture Notes in Computer Science*, pages 137–142.

Shervin Malmasi. 2016. *Native Language Identification: Explorations and Applications*. Ph.D. thesis, Macquarie University Center for Language Technology. http://hdl.handle.net/1959.14/1110919.

Shervin Malmasi and Mark Dras. 2017. Native language identification using stacked generalization. *arXiv preprint arXiv:1703.06541*.

Shervin Malmasi, Keelan Evanini, Aoife Cahill, Joel Tetreault, Robert Pugh, Christopher Hamill, Diane Napolitano, and Yao Qian. 2017. A Report on the 2017 Native Language Identification Shared Task. In *Proceedings of the 12th Workshop on Building Educational Applications Using NLP*. Association for Computational Linguistics, Copenhagen, Denmark.

Shervin Malmasi, Joel Tetreault, and Mark Dras. 2015. Oracle and Human Baselines for Native Language Identification. In *Proceedings of the Tenth Workshop on Innovative Use of NLP for Building Educational Applications (BEA-10)*. pages 172–178.

Christopher D. Manning, Prabhakar Raghavan, and Hinrich Schütze. 2008. *Introduction to Information Retrieval*. Cambridge University Press.

P. J. Mccarthy. 1969. Pseudo-replication: Half sample. *Review of the International Statistical Institute* 37(3):239–264.

Joel Tetreault, Daniel Blanchard, and Aoife Cahill. 2013. A report on the first native language identification shared task. In *Proceedings of the Eighth Workshop on Innovative Use of NLP for Building Educational Applications*. Association for Computational Linguistics, Atlanta, GA, USA.

Kristina Toutanova, Dan Klein, Christopher Manning, and Yoram Singer. 2003. Feature-rich part-of-speech tagging with a cyclic dependency network. In *Proceedings of the HLT-NAACL 2003*. pages 252–259.

Pulkit Verma and Pradip K. Das. 2015. i-vectors in speech processing applications: a survey. *International Journal of Speech Technology* 18(4):529–546. https://doi.org/10.1007/s10772-015-9295-3.

David H. Wolpert. 1992. Stacked generalization. *Neural Networks,* 5(2):241–259.

CIC-FBK Approach to Native Language Identification

Ilia Markov[1], Lingzhen Chen[2], Carlo Strapparava[3], Grigori Sidorov[1]

[1]Instituto Politécnico Nacional, CIC, Mexico City, Mexico
[2]University of Trento, DISI, Trento, Italy
[3]FBK-irst, Trento, Italy
imarkov@nlp.cic.ipn.mx, lzchen.cs@gmail.com,
strappa@fbk.eu, sidorov@cic.ipn.mx

Abstract

We present the CIC-FBK system, which took part in the Native Language Identification (NLI) Shared Task 2017. Our approach combines features commonly used in previous NLI research, i.e., word n-grams, lemma n-grams, part-of-speech n-grams, and function words, with recently introduced character n-grams from misspelled words, and features that are novel in this task, such as typed character n-grams, and syntactic n-grams of words and of syntactic relation tags. We use log-entropy weighting scheme and perform classification using the Support Vector Machines (SVM) algorithm. Our system achieved 0.8808 macro-averaged F1-score and shared the 1st rank in the NLI Shared Task 2017 scoring.

1 Introduction

Native language identification (NLI) is a natural language processing (NLP) task that aims at automatically identifying the native language (L1) of a language learner based on his/her writing in the second language (L2). Identifying the native language is based on the hypothesis that the L1 of a learner impacts his/her L2 writing due to the language transfer effect. NLI can be used for a variety of purposes, including marketing, security, and educational applications. From the machine-learning perspective, the NLI task is viewed as a multi-class, single-label classification problem, in which automatic methods have to assign class labels (L1s) to objects (texts).

Recent trends in NLI include cross-genre and cross-corpus NLI scenarios (Malmasi and Dras, 2015a), as well as identifying the L1 based on writings in other non-English L2s and cross-lingual NLI research (Malmasi and Dras, 2015b). However, following the practice of the first NLI shared task (Tetreault et al., 2013), this year's task focuses on L2 English data (Malmasi et al., 2017). This can be related to the use of English as *lingua franca* on the Internet and academia, when NLI methods are particularly useful for languages with a large number of foreign speakers. Moreover, following the 2016 Computational Paralinguistics Challenge (Schuller et al., 2016) and the VarDial workshop (Malmasi et al., 2016), this year's competition covers an NLI task based on the spoken response. Overall, this year's task consists of three tracks: NLI on the essay only, NLI on the spoken response only, and NLI on both essay and spoken response. In this paper, we describe the CIC-FBK approach to the essay-only track.

Previous works on identifying the native language from texts explored a large variety of features, including lexical and part-of-speech (POS) features (Koppel et al., 2005a), character n-grams (Ionescu et al., 2014), spelling errors (Koppel et al., 2005b), and syntactic features (Wong and Dras, 2011). Following previous research on the NLI task, we incorporate commonly used word n-grams, lemma n-grams, POS n-grams, and function words. In order to capture the L1 influences at the character level, we use recently introduced character n-grams from misspelled words (Chen et al., 2017), as well as 10 categories of character n-gram features proposed by Sapkota et al. (2015). We also include syntactic features by extracting syntactic dependency-based n-grams of words and of syntactic relation tags (Sidorov et al., 2014) using the algorithm designed by Posadas-Durán et al. (2014, 2017). We describe the features used by the CIC-FBK system in more detail in subsection 3.1.

Our system achieved 0.8808 macro-averaged F1-score and 0.8809 accuracy in the essay-only

Proceedings of the 12th Workshop on Innovative Use of NLP for Building Educational Applications, pages 374–381
Copenhagen, Denmark, September 8, 2017. ©2017 Association for Computational Linguistics

track and shared the 1st rank in the NLI Shared Task 2017 scoring, obtaining the 2nd absolute score with the difference of 0.0010 F1-score and 0.0009 accuracy with the 1st place.

2 Data

The dataset used in the NLI Shared Task 2017 is composed of English essays written by non-native learners in a standardized assessment of English proficiency for academic purposes. The corpus consists of 13,200 essays (1,000 essays per L1 for training, 100 for development, and 100 for testing). The essays are sampled from 8 prompts, and score levels (low/medium/high) are provided for each essay. The training, development, and test sets are balanced in terms of the number of essays per L1 group. The 11 L1s covered by the corpus are: Arabic (ARA), Chinese (CHI), French (FRE), German (GER), Hindi (HIN), Italian (ITA), Japanese (JAP), Korean (KOR), Spanish (SPA), Telugu (TEL), and Turkish (TUR). The detailed description of the corpus and its statistics can be found in Malmasi et al. (2017).

3 Methodology

Our system incorporates a wide range of features, i.e., word, lemma, and POS n-grams, spelling error character n-grams, typed character n-grams, and syntactic n-grams. We used the tokenized version of essays provided by the organizers. For the evaluation of our approach, we merged the training and development sets, and conducted experiments under 10-fold cross-validation. System performance was measured in terms of both classification accuracy and F1 (macro) score. The former was used as evaluation metric in the majority of previous works on NLI, whilst the later is the official evaluation metric in the NLI Shared Task 2017.

3.1 Features

3.1.1 Word, lemma, and POS n-grams

Word and lemma features represent the lexical choice of a writer, while part-of-speech (POS) features capture the morpho-syntactic patterns in a text. Following previous works on the NLI task (Jarvis et al., 2013; Malmasi and Dras, 2017), we use word, lemma, and POS n-grams with n ranging from 1 to 3. We include punctuation marks and split n-grams by a full stop. We lowercase word and lemma n-grams and replace each

digit by the same symbol (e.g., 12,345 → 00,000), as proposed in Markov et al. (2017), to capture the format (e.g., 00.000 vs. 00,000), which reflects stylistic choice of a learner and not the value of a number that does not carry stylistic information. Lemmas and POS tags were obtained using the TreeTagger software package (Schmid, 1995).

3.1.2 Function words

Function words are the most common words in a language (e.g., articles, determiners, conjunctions). They are considered one of the most important stylometric features (Kestemont, 2014). Function words can be seen as indicators of the grammatical relations between other words. We use a set of 318 English function words from the scikit-learn package (Pedregosa et al., 2011). Other examined function word lists obtained from the Natural Language Toolkit[1] (127 function words) and the Onix Text Retrieval Toolkit[2] (429 function words), as well as function word skip-grams (Guthrie et al., 2006) did not lead to an improvement in accuracy.

3.1.3 Spelling error character n-grams

Spelling errors have been used as features for NLI since Koppel et al. (2005b). They are considered a strong indicator of an author's L1, since they reflect L1 influences, such as sound-to-character mappings in L1. Recently, Chen et al. (2017) introduced the use of character n-grams from misspelled words. The authors showed that adding spelling error character n-grams to other commonly used features (word and lemma n-grams) improves NLI classification accuracy. We extract 39,512 unique misspelled words from the training and development sets using the *spell* shell command. Then we build character n-grams ($n = 4$) from the extracted misspelled words. Other examined size of spelling error character n-grams ($n = 1$, 2, 3, and 5), as well as their combinations did not lead to an improvement in system performance.

3.1.4 Typed character n-grams

Character level features are sensitive to both the content and the form of a text and able to cap-

---

[1] http://www.nltk.org
[2] http://www.lextek.com/manuals/onix/functionwords1.html

ture lexical and syntactic information, punctuation and capitalization information related with the authors' style (Stamatatos, 2013). The effectiveness of character n-gram features for representing the stylistic properties of a text has been demonstrated in previous NLI studies (Ionescu et al., 2014; Chen et al., 2017). Their effectiveness in NLI is hypothesized to be a result of phoneme transfer from the learner's L1, and by their ability to capture orthographic conventions of a language (Tsur and Rappoport, 2007).

Sapkota et al. (2015) defined 10 different character n-gram categories based on affixes, words, and punctuation. In this approach, instances of the same n-gram may refer to different typed n-gram features. For example, in the phrase *less carelessness*, the two instances of the 4-gram *less* are assigned to different character n-gram categories. As an example, consider the following sample sentence:

(1) *Lisa said, "John should repair it tomorrow."*

The character n-grams (n = 4) for the sample sentence (1) for each of the categories proposed by Sapkota et al. (2015) are shown in Table 1. For clarity, spaces are represented by the underscore.

SC	Category	N-grams
affix	*prefix*	shou repa tomo
	suffix	ould pair rrow
	space-prefix	_sai _sho _rep _it_ _tom
	space-suffix	isa_ ohn_ uld_ air_
word	*whole-word*	Lisa said John
	mid-word	houl epai omor morr orro
	multi-word *	sa_s hn_s ld_r ir_1 it_t
punct	*beg-punct*	"Joh
	mid-punct **	_,_ _"_ _._ _"_
	end-punct	aid, row.

* If the previous word is more than one character long, two characters are considered; otherwise, only one character is considered.
** We use the tokenized version of essays and set the size of n-grams to 3 for this category. For other categories of typed character n-grams, the size is set to 4.

Table 1: Typed character 4-grams per category for the sample sentence (1) after applying the algorithm proposed by Sapkota et al. (2015).

Typed character n-grams have shown to be predictive features for other classification tasks, such as authorship attribution (Sapkota et al., 2015), author profiling (Markov et al., 2016), and discriminating between similar languages (Gómez-Adorno et al., 2017). In our experiments, typed character n-grams (n = 4) outperformed traditional character n-grams of the same size in most system configurations. In addition, we compared the performance of typed and traditional character n-grams on the 7-way ICLEv2 corpus (Granger et al., 2009), following the corpus splitting as described in Ionescu et al. (2014). In this experiment, typed character n-grams proved to be more indicative than traditional character n-grams when used in combination with features described in this paper.

3.1.5 Syntactic *n*-grams

Syntactic features, including production rules (Wong and Dras, 2011) and Tree Substitution Grammars (TSGs) (Swanson and Charniak, 2012), have been previously explored for NLI. Tetreault et al. (2012) experimented with the Stanford parser (de Marneffe et al., 2006) dependency features and concluded that they are strong indicators of structural differences in L2 writing. We exploit the Stanford dependencies to build syntactic n-gram features by using the algorithm designed and made available by Posadas-Durán et al. (2014, 2017).[3] Consider the following sample sentence:

(2) *I remember this great experience.*

The dependencies generated by the Standard parser for the the sample sentence (2) are the following:
```
root(ROOT, remember),
nsubj(remember, I),
dobj(remember, experience),
det(experience, this),
amod(experience, great).
```
These dependencies, including backoff transformation based on POS, were used as features for NLI in Tetreault et al. (2012). According to the metalanguage proposed in Sidorov (2013a), the syntactic 2-grams of words are the following:
```
remember[I],
remember[experience],
experience[this],
experience[great];
```
when the syntactic 3-grams of words are:
```
remember[I,experience],
remember[experience[this]],
remember[experience[great]],
```

---

[3]The Python implementation of the algorithm is available on http://www.cic.ipn.mx/ sidorov/MultiSNgrams_3.py

```
experience[this,great];
```
the syntactic 2-grams of syntactic relation tags are:
```
root[nsubj],
root[dobj],
dobj[det],
dobj[amod];
```
the syntactic 3-grams of syntactic relation tags are:
```
root[nsubj,dobj],
root[dobj[det]],
root[dobj[amod]],
dobj[det,amod].
```

Here, the head element is on the left of a square parenthesis and inside there are the dependent elements; the elements separated by a coma refer to non-continuous syntactic n-grams, that is, the elements are at the same level in a syntactic tree.

Syntactic n-grams can be used in any task where traditional n-grams are applied. They allow to introduce syntactic information into machine-learning methods (obviously, at cost of previous syntactic parsing). Syntactic n-grams outperformed traditional n-grams in the task of authorship attribution (Sidorov et al., 2014) and were applied in tasks related with L2, for example, automatic English as L2 grammar correction (Sidorov, 2013b). In our system, we use only continuous syntactic n-grams of words and of syntactic relation tags with n ranging from 2 to 3. The inclusion of non-continuous syntactic n-grams improved 10-fold cross-validation accuracy; however, did not perform well on the test set.

3.2 Frequency threshold

The fine-tuning of feature set size has proved to be a useful strategy for NLI (Jarvis et al., 2013) and other NLP tasks (Stamatatos, 2013; Markov et al., 2017). In our approach, we selected the frequency threshold value that provided the highest 10-fold cross-validation result. We consider only those features that occur in at least two documents in the training corpus and that occur at least 4 times in the entire training corpus. This frequency threshold improves 10-fold cross-validation accuracy by about 1%, compared to the configuration when all the features are considered, and reduces the size of the feature set by approximately 90% of the original. The final size of our feature set is 726,494.

3.3 Weighting scheme

We use log-entropy weighting scheme, which showed good results in previous studies on NLI (Jarvis et al., 2013; Chen et al., 2017).

Log-entropy weighting scheme consists of local weighting (denoted as $L_{log}(i, j)$) and global weighting (denoted as $G_{ent}(i)$). The local weighting is calculated by taking the logarithm value of adding-one smoothed term frequency:

$$L_{log}(i, j) = \log(frequency(i, j) + 1), \quad (1)$$

where $frequency(i, j)$ is the frequency of term i with regard to document j. The global entropy weighting is calculated by the following formula:

$$G_{ent}(i) = 1 + \frac{\sum_{j=1}^{J} p_{ij} \log p_{ij}}{\log(J + 1)}, \quad (2)$$

where J is the total number of documents in the corpus. $\sum_{j=1}^{J} p_{ij} \log p_{ij}$ is the additive inverse of entropy of the conditional distribution given i and

$$p_{ij} = \frac{frequency(i, j)}{\sum_{j} frequency(i, j)}. \quad (3)$$

The final weighting W is calculated as follows:

$$W = L_{log}(i, j) \times G_{ent}(i). \quad (4)$$

Other examined feature representations, i.e., binary feature representation, tf, $tf\text{-}idf$, and normalized feature representation did not enhance system performance. Using log-entropy weighting scheme outperforms $tf\text{-}idf$, the second best scheme in our experiments, by 2.6% in 10-fold cross-validation accuracy.

3.4 Classifier

Support Vector Machines (SVM) is considered among the best performing classification algorithms for text categorization tasks; moreover, it was the classifier of choice for the majority of the teams in the previous edition of the NLI shared task. We use the liblinear scikit-learn (Pedregosa et al., 2011) implementation of SVM with 'ovr' multi-class strategy. We set the penalty hyper-parameter C to 100 based on our model selection result.

4 Results

We present the results of our experiments in two phases. First, we show the performance of each type of features in isolation under 10-fold cross validation on the merged training and development sets. Then, we compare the performance obtained on the test set with other participating teams. We present the 10-fold cross-validation results in terms of classification accuracy. For each experiment, the difference between accuracy and F1 (macro) score was less than 0.0003.

The individual performance of the features used in our system with the configurations described in the previous section, as well as the number of features (N) of each type are shown in Table 2.

Features	Accuracy	N
words n-grams ($n = 1$–3)	0.8463	230,714
lemma n-grams ($n = 1$–3)	0.8454	228,229
POS n-grams ($n = 1$–3)	0.4930	14,510
function words	0.5004	302
spelling error character 4-grams	0.3779	12,322
typed character 4-grams	0.7779	35,480
syntactic n-grams of words ($n = 2$–3)	0.7064	148,728
syntactic n-grams of SR tags ($n = 2$–3)	0.2361	5,344
combination of the above	0.8640	726,494

Table 2: 10-fold cross-validation accuracy of each feature type individually on the merged training and development sets.

In line with the previous works on the NLI task (Tetreault et al., 2013; Jarvis et al., 2013; Chen et al., 2017), in our configurations word and lemma n-grams are the most predictive features. They showed 0.8463 and 0.8454 10-fold cross-validation accuracy, respectively, when evaluated in isolation. Typed character n-grams also performed well with a much smaller feature size, achieving 0.7779 accuracy. Syntactic n-grams of syntactic relation tags showed the lower accuracy when evaluated in isolation; however, when used in combination with other features, they improve 10-fold cross-validation accuracy by 0.2%. The combination of all the features showed 0.8640 10-fold cross-validation accuracy on the merged training and development sets.

The NLI Shared Task 2017 organizers reported several 1st ranked teams based on McNemar's statistical significance test with an alpha value of 0.05. The official results for the essay-only track in terms of F1 (macro) score and classification accuracy for the 1st ranked teams, as well as the baseline results are shown in Table 3.

The CIC-FBK best run differs 0.0009 in terms of classification accuracy from the highest result achieved by the ItaliaNLP Lab system, which corresponds to one correctly predicted label. All the 17 participating teams in the NLI Shared Task 2017 achieved higher level of F1 (macro) score than the official baseline of 0.7104.

Rank	Team	F1 (macro)	Accuracy
1	ItaliaNLP Lab	0.8818	0.8818
1	**CIC-FBK**	**0.8808**	**0.8809**
1	Groningen	0.8756	0.8755
1	NRC	0.8740	0.8736
1	taraka_rama	0.8716	0.8718
1	UnibucKernel	0.8695	0.8691
1	WLZ	0.8654	0.8655
-	Official baseline	0.7104	0.7109
-	Random baseline	0.0909	0.0909

Table 3: Results for the essay-only track for the 1st ranked teams. The results for our team are highlighted in bold typeface.

The CIC-FBK system showed 0.8639 F1 (macro) score and 0.8640 accuracy under 10-fold cross-validation on the merged training and development sets. Our other runs in the NLI Shared Task 2017 included small modifications in system configurations, such as variations in frequency threshold values and different strategy for dealing with digits (e.g., $12,345 \rightarrow 0,0$). However, since these modifications showed only marginal accuracy variations and did not improve system performance on the test set, the results for these runs are omitted in this paper.

The confusion matrix for our best run is shown in Figure 1. The highest level of confusion is between Hindi and Telugu classes. Korean and Japanese is another problematic language pair, in which Korean native speakers are often classified as Japanese. The highest accuracy of 0.9800 was achieved for German native speakers. These results are in line with the ones reported in the previous edition of the NLI share task (Tetreault et al., 2013), where the teams achieved low levels of accuracy for the Hindi/Telugu (none of the systems was able to reach 0.8000 accuracy for Hidni) and the Korean/Japanese pairs. In future work, we intend to tackle these two language pairs in isolation in order to improve the overall system performance.

5   Conclusions

We presented the description of the best submission of the CIC-FBK team to the NLI Shared Task 2017. Our approach combines features commonly used in the NLI task with recently introduced spelling error character n-grams, as well as with typed character n-grams, and syntactic n-grams of words and of syntactic relation tags.

Figure 1: Confusion matrix for the best CIC-FBK run.

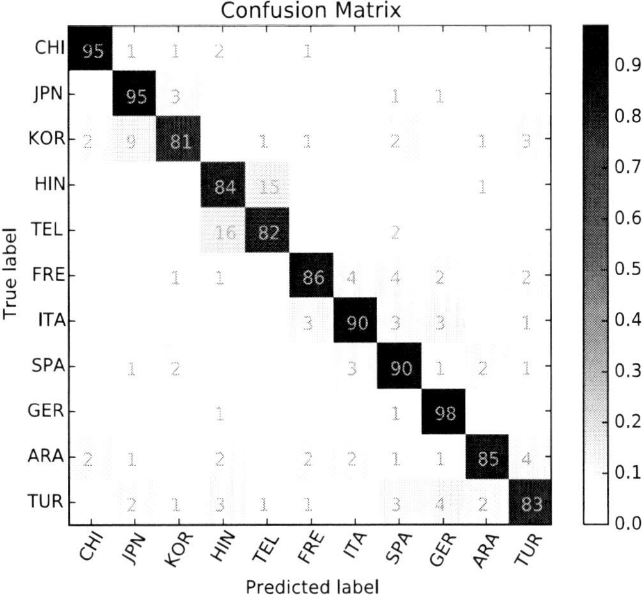

Typed character n-grams and syntactic n-grams are new types of features that are introduced in the NLI task for the first time. It was found during the preliminary experiments on the training and development sets that these features improve the classification accuracy when used in combination with other types of features, such as word n-grams, lemma n-grams, part-of-speech n-grams, spelling error character n-grams, and function words. The CIC-FBK system achieved 0.8808 F1 (macro) score and 0.8809 accuracy and shared the 1st rank in the competition.

Acknowledgements

This work was partially supported by the Mexican Government (CONACYT project 240844, SNI, COFAA-IPN, and SIP-IPN 20171813, 20171344, 20172008). We would like to thank Vivi Nastase for the discussion about spelling errors.

References

Lingzhen Chen, Carlo Strapparava, and Vivi Nastase. 2017. Improving native language identification by using spelling errors. In *Proceedings of the 55th annual meeting of the Association for Computational Linguistics (ACL 2017)*. ACL, Vancouver, Canada.

Marie-Catherine de Marneffe, Bill MacCartney, and Christopher D. Manning. 2006. Generating typed dependency parses from phrase structure parses. In *Proceedings of the Fifth International Conference on Language Resources and Evaluation (LREC 2006)*. ELRA, Genoa, Italy, pages 449–454.

Helena Gómez-Adorno, Ilia Markov, Jorge Baptista, Grigori Sidorov, and David Pinto. 2017. Discriminating between similar languages using a combination of typed and untyped character n-grams and words. In *Proceedings of the Fourth Workshop on NLP for Similar Languages, Varieties and Dialects (VarDial 2017)*. ACL, Valencia, Spain, pages 137–145.

Sylviane Granger, Estelle Dagneaux, and Fanny Meunier. 2009. *The International Corpus of Learner English. Version 2*. Presses Universitaires de Louvain.

David Guthrie, Ben Allison, Wei Liu, Louise Guthrie, and Yorick Wilks. 2006. A close look at skip-gram modelling. In *Proceedings of the Fifth International Conference on Language Resources and Evaluation (LREC 2006)*. ELRA, Genoa, Italy, pages 1222–1225.

Radu Tudor Ionescu, Marius Popescu, and Aoife Cahill. 2014. Can characters reveal your native language? A language-independent approach to native language identification. In *Proceedings of the 2014 Conference on Empirical Methods in Natural Language Processing (EMNLP 2014)*. ACL, Doha, Qatar, pages 1363–1373.

Scott Jarvis, Yves Bestgen, and Steve Pepper. 2013. Maximizing classification accuracy in native language identification. In *Proceedings of the Eighth*

Workshop on Innovative Use of NLP for Building Educational Applications. ACL, Atlanta, Georgia, USA, pages 111–118.

Mike Kestemont. 2014. Function words in authorship attribution. From black magic to theory? In *Proceedings of the 3rd Workshop on Computational Linguistics for Literature (EACL 2014)*. ACL, Gothenburg, Sweden, pages 59–66.

Moshe Koppel, Jonathan Schler, and Kfir Zigdon. 2005a. Automatically determining an anonymous author's native language. In *Proceedings of the IEEE International Conference on Intelligence and Security Informatics (ISI 2005)*. Springer, Atlanta, Georgia, USA, pages 209–217.

Moshe Koppel, Jonathan Schler, and Kfir Zigdon. 2005b. Determining an author's native language by mining a text for errors. In *Proceedings of the Eleventh ACM SIGKDD International Conference on Knowledge Discovery in Data Mining (KDD 2005)*. ACM, Chicago, Illinois, USA, pages 624–628.

Shervin Malmasi and Mark Dras. 2015a. Large-scale native language identification with cross-corpus evaluation. In *Proceedings of the 2015 Annual Conference of the North American Chapter of the ACL: Human Language Technologies (NAACL-HLT 2015)*. ACL, Denver, Colorado, USA, pages 1403–1409.

Shervin Malmasi and Mark Dras. 2015b. Multilingual native language identification. *Natural Language Engineering* 1:1–56.

Shervin Malmasi and Mark Dras. 2017. Native language identification using stacked generalization. *arXiv preprint arXiv:1703.06541* .

Shervin Malmasi, Keelan Evanini, Aoife Cahill, Joel Tetreault, Robert Pugh, Christopher Hamill, Diane Napolitano, and Yao Qian. 2017. A report on the 2017 native language identification shared task. In *Proceedings of the 12th Workshop on Building Educational Applications Using NLP*. ACL, Copenhagen, Denmark.

Shervin Malmasi, Marcos Zampieri, Nikola Ljubešić, Preslav Nakov, Ahmed Ali, and Jörg Tiedemann. 2016. Discriminating between similar languages and Arabic dialect identification: A report on the third DSL shared task. In *Proceedings of the VarDial Workshop*. Osaka, Japan.

Ilia Markov, Helena Gómez-Adorno, Grigori Sidorov, and Alexander Gelbukh. 2016. Adapting cross-genre author profiling to language and corpus. In *Working Notes Papers of the CLEF 2016 Evaluation Labs*. CLEF and CEUR-WS.org, Évora, Portugal, volume 1609, pages 947–955.

Ilia Markov, Efstathios Stamatatos, and Grigori Sidorov. 2017. Improving cross-topic authorship attribution: The role of pre-processing. In *Proceedings of the 18th International Conference on Computational Linguistics and Intelligent Text Processing (CICLing 2017)*. Springer, Budapest, Hungary, in press.

Fabian Pedregosa, Gaël Varoquaux, Alexandre Gramfort, Vincent Michel, Bertrand Thirion, Olivier Grisel, Mathieu Blondel, Peter Prettenhofer, Ron Weiss, Vincent Dubourg, Jake Vanderplas, Alexandre Passos, David Cournapeau, Matthieu Brucher, Matthieu Perrot, and Édouard Duchesnay. 2011. Scikit-learn: Machine learning in Python. *Journal of Machine Learning Research* 12:2825–2830.

Juan-Pablo Posadas-Durán, Grigori Sidorov, and Ildar Batyrshin. 2014. Complete syntactic n-grams as style markers for authorship attribution. In *Proceedings of the 13th Mexican International Conference on Artificial Intelligence (MICAI 2014)*. Springer, Tuxtla Gutiérrez, Mexico, pages 9–17.

Juan-Pablo Posadas-Durán, Grigori Sidorov, Helena Gómez-Adorno, Ildar Batyrshin, Elibeth Mirasol-Mélendez, Gabriela Posadas-Durán, and Liliana Chanona-Hernández. 2017. Algorithm for extraction of subtrees of a sentence dependency parse tree. *Acta Polytechnica Hungarica* in press.

Upendra Sapkota, Steven Bethard, Manuel Montes-y-Gómez, and Thamar Solorio. 2015. Not all character n-grams are created equal: A study in authorship attribution. In *Proceedings of the 2015 Annual Conference of the North American Chapter of the ACL: Human Language Technologies (NAACL-HLT 2015)*. ACL, Denver, Colorado, USA, pages 93–102.

Helmut Schmid. 1995. Improvements in part-of-speech tagging with an application to German. In *Proceedings of the ACL SIGDAT-Workshop*. ACL, Dublin, Ireland, pages 47–50.

Björn Schuller, Stefan Steidl, Anton Batliner, Julia Hirschberg, Judee K. Burgoon, Alice Baird, Aaron Elkins, Yue Zhang, Eduardo Coutinho, and Keelan Evanini. 2016. The INTERSPEECH 2016 computational paralinguistics challenge: Deception, sincerity & native language. In *Interspeech 2016*. pages 2001–2005.

Grigori Sidorov. 2013a. *Non-linear Construction of N-grams in Computational Linguistics*. SMIA.

Grigori Sidorov. 2013b. Syntactic dependency based n-grams in rule based automatic English as second language grammar correction. *International Journal of Computational Linguistics and Applications* 4(2):169–188.

Grigori Sidorov, Francisco Velasquez, Efstathios Stamatatos, Alexander Gelbukh, and Liliana Chanona-Hernández. 2014. Syntactic n-grams as machine learning features for natural language processing. *Expert Systems with Applications* 41(3):653–860.

Efstathios Stamatatos. 2013. On the robustness of authorship attribution based on character n-gram features. *Journal of Law & Policy* 21(2):427–439.

Ben Swanson and Eugene Charniak. 2012. Native language detection with tree substitution grammars. In
*Proceedings of the 50th Annual Meeting of the As-
sociation for Computational Linguistics: Short Papers – Volume 2 (ACL 2012)*. ACL, Jeju Island, Korea, pages 193–197.

Joel Tetreault, Daniel Blanchard, and Aoife Cahill.
2013. A report on the first native language identification shared task. In *Proceedings of the Eighth
Workshop on Building Educational Applications Using NLP*. ACL, Atlanta, GA, USA.

Joel Tetreault, Daniel Blanchard, Aoife Cahill, and
Martin Chodorow. 2012. Native tongues, lost and
found: Resources and empirical evaluations in native language identification. In *Proceedings of
the 24st International Conference on Computational
Linguistics (COLING 2012)*. The COLING 2012 Organizing Committee, Mumbai, India, pages 2585–
2602.

Oren Tsur and Ari Rappoport. 2007. Using classifier
features for studying the effect of native language
on the choice of written second language words.
In *Proceedings of the Workshop on Cognitive Aspects of Computational Language Acquisition (CA-
CLA 2007)*. ACL, Prague, Czech Republic, pages 9–
16.

Sze-Meng Jojo Wong and Mark Dras. 2011. Exploiting parse structures for native language identification. In *Proceedings of the Conference on Empirical
Methods in Natural Language Processing (EMNLP
2011)*. ACL, Edinburgh, Scotland, UK, pages 1600–
1610.

The Power of Character N-grams in Native Language Identification

Artur Kulmizev, Bo Blankers, Johannes Bjerva, Malvina Nissim,
Gertjan van Noord, Barbara Plank, Martijn Wieling
University of Groningen
Oude Kijk in 't Jatstraat 26
9712 EK Groningen
{a.kulmizev,b.blankers}@student.rug.nl
{j.bjerva,m.nissim,g.j.m.van.noord,b.plank,m.b.wieling}@rug.nl

Abstract

In this paper, we explore the performance of a linear SVM trained on language-independent character features for the NLI Shared Task 2017. Our basic system (GRONINGEN) achieves the best performance (87.56 F1-score) on the evaluation set using only 1-9 character n-grams as features. We compare this against several ensemble and meta-classifiers in order to examine how the linear system fares when combined with other, especially non-linear classifiers. Special emphasis is placed on the topic bias that exists by virtue of the assessment essay prompt distribution.

1 Introduction

Native Language Identification (NLI) is the task of identifying a writer's native language (L1) based on their writings in another language. Typically, low-to-medium proficiency writers exhibit a tendency to "borrow" linguistic constructions from their native language and apply them to the language in which they are communicating. A native Russian speaker, for example, may forego the use of articles such as "the" when writing in English. This phenomenon, widely referred to as Language Transfer, allows for a common set of linguistic features to emerge between speakers of the same native language (Odlin, 1989). NLI is thus concerned with applying machine learning approaches using these features in order to automatically identify the L1 of writers communicating in another language.

There are many practical applications for NLI. Second language (L2) education is a field in which NLI can offer much potential aid. For instance, in identifying the native language of a learner by their writing, it is possible to isolate the linguistic features they employ when communicating. This could subsequently be integrated in language-specific error-correction systems, in which a user receives L1-based suggestions to correct their L2 writing. At a large scale, this could be extended to enhance existing teaching pedagogies and tailor them towards students of a particular L1. NLI is another natural fit for forensic linguistics, where it can be used to detect the native language (and potentially the nationality) of an anonymous writer.

NLI is typically framed as a multi-class classification problem, wherein a classifier is trained on more than two native languages simultaneously. As with many text-classification tasks, Support Vector Machines (SVM) have consistently produced the best results for the task, e.g., (Brooke and Hirst, 2012). However, other classifiers, such as Random Forests and Logistic Regression, have also been explored (Tetreault et al., 2013). Ensemble systems, which combine the predictions of several classifiers and output the most likely class label via voting or probability-averaging, have further been shown to provide a boost in accuracy compared to the single-classifier approach. Such systems, however, are not light-weight. In training several classifiers simultaneously, quick training speeds are typically sacrificed in favor of a (usually marginal) performance gain. This paper is thus concerned with exploring each of these classification methods as they pertain to the NLI Shared Task 2017 (Malmasi et al., 2017).

2 Related Work

In 2005, Koppel et al. (2005) begun exploring methods for NLI by exploring the International Corpus of Learner English (Granger et al., 2009). In this work, they evaluated the effect of several features, including function words, letter n-grams, part-of-speech bigrams and error types.

Proceedings of the 12th Workshop on Innovative Use of NLP for Building Educational Applications, pages 382–389
Copenhagen, Denmark, September 8, 2017. ©2017 Association for Computational Linguistics

Training an SVM on the combination of these yielded an accuracy score of 80.0%. Several years later, a shared task in NLI was organized by Tetreault et al. (2013). A total of 29 teams participated in this competition, with the winning system implementing a combination of lexeme, lemma, and POS-tagged 1-3grams for their model (Jarvis et al., 2013). This system produced an accuracy of 83.6% discriminating between 11 different native languages. Ionescu et al. (2014) later improved on this result by applying Kernel Ridge Regression and Kernel Discriminant Analysis in order to extract character n-gram features from the NLI Shared Task 2013 data. This approached yielded an 85.3% accuracy score on the 2013 shared task's test set.

In the years between the initial NLI shared task and the current one, teams have continued to produce new state-of-the-art systems. Most recently, Malmasi and Dras (2017), presented an exhaustive survey of potentially relevant features for NLI. These included character, word, lemma, and POS n-grams, function words, context-free grammar production rules, and dependency tags, among others. Separate SVMs were trained on each of these features and their outputs were fed into a mean probability ensemble. A meta Linear Discriminant Analysis (LDA) classifier was then trained on the probability distributions generated by the ensemble, yielding an accuracy of 87.1%.

3 Methodology and Data

3.1 Data

The provided data set consists of 13,200 English-language essays submitted for a standardized assessment of English proficiency for academic purposes. The essays are equally divided into 11 native languages (L1s), totalling 1,200 essays per language. The languages represented therein are as follows: Arabic (ARA), Chinese (CHI), French (FRE), German (GER), Italian (ITA), Hindi (HIN), Japanese (JPN), Korean (KOR), Telugu (TEL), and Turkish (TUR). The full data set is divided into three parts, with 11,000, 1,100, and 1,100 essays constituting the training, development, and test set, respectively. The number of words per essay varies between 300 and 400.

In participating in the assessment, all participants were instructed to write their essay about a specific prompt topic. The data set is thus divided over 8 different prompts as well as L1s. While the L1s are evenly distributed over the data, the distribution of the prompts is skewed by both language and overall, as shown in Table 1. The table represents the distribution of the prompts for the training and the development set combined, since this constitutes all of the data that our final system is trained on. Noteworthy is the fact that Hindi and Telugu have similar distributions over all the prompts, which is a different distribution than the the other languages. It is also interesting that only a small portion (12 essays) are written about P1 for Italian, which could cause a discrepancy in the later classification of the language.

Due to these factors, we pay particular attention to the prompt distribution during our analysis.

3.2 Features

Our main classifier is a Linear Support Vector Machine, which has been shown to perform well in prior NLI tasks. We performed a grid search over the C, loss, and penalty parameters of the Linear SVM in order to obtain the best-performing variant. However, tuning these parameters failed to produce any noteworthy results and we thus opted for a non-parametric SVM. We also evaluated the performance of the classifier with an RBF kernel in order to examine whether a non-linear approach would generalize better over the data. Ultimately, this resulted in significantly longer training times as well as much lower performance accuracy and was discarded in favor of the linear alternative. The non-parametric classifier is based on several combinations or stand-alone models of the features described below.

3.2.1 Character n-grams

Large ranges of character n-grams contain characteristic information about the writing style of an author. Compared to word n-grams, which only capture the identity of a word and its possible neighbors, character n-grams are additionally capable of detecting the morphological makeup of a word. In a task such as NLI, where many words are likely to be misspelled, character n-grams are especially powerful at detecting patterns in such misspellings, and substantially less sparse than word n-grams. In this paper, we experimented with several ranges of character n-grams. Even though prior research in NLI has largely focused on character n-grams of up to 5 characters, this range did not perform well in this task. Instead, increasing the upper bound of the range to between

Table 1: Overview of prompt distribution per language for the data set

	ARA		CHI		FRE		GER		HIN		ITA		JPN		KOR		SPA		TEL		TUR	
	#	%	#	%	#	%	#	%	#	%	#	%	#	%	#	%	#	%	#	%	#	%
P0	139	12.6%	140	12.7%	156	14.2%	151	13.7%	86	7.8%	187	17.0%	138	12.5%	128	11.6%	159	14.5%	55	5.0%	170	15.5%
P1	133	12.1%	141	12.8%	68	6.2%	28	2.5%	53	4.8%	12	1.1%	142	12.9%	142	12.9%	157	14.3%	41	3.7%	43	3.9%
P2	141	12.8%	139	12.6%	160	14.5%	153	13.9%	161	14.6%	141	12.8%	143	13.0%	143	13.0%	162	14.7%	171	15.5%	169	15.4%
P3	138	12.5%	139	12.6%	151	13.7%	152	13.8%	158	14.4%	173	15.7%	141	12.8%	141	12.8%	160	14.5%	166	15.1%	167	15.2%
P4	138	12.5%	140	12.7%	158	14.4%	155	14.1%	161	14.6%	173	15.7%	116	10.5%	140	12.7%	141	12.8%	165	15.0%	169	15.4%
P5	136	12.4%	134	12.2%	160	14.5%	150	13.6%	156	14.2%	187	17.0%	138	12.5%	137	12.5%	134	12.2%	169	15.4%	147	13.4%
P6	138	12.5%	126	11.5%	87	7.9%	157	14.3%	163	14.8%	138	12.5%	140	12.7%	136	12.4%	54	4.9%	167	15.2%	90	8.2%
P7	137	12.5%	141	12.8%	160	14.5%	154	14.0%	162	14.7%	89	8.1%	142	12.9%	133	12.1%	133	12.1%	166	15.1%	145	13.2%
Total:	1100		1100		1100		1100		1100		1100		1100		1100		1100		1100		1100	

8 and 10 characters yielded very encouraging results. In training a classifier on character n-grams ranging from 1 to 10, this effectively models the effect of word unigrams, bigrams, and, in cases of very short words, trigrams. Indeed, the most informative features in these cases are 7-9 character n-grams in which the author discusses his or her own country (Japanese people talk about Japan, etc.). When combined with the morphological insight of the lower-range character n-grams, this approach proved to be simultaneously very powerful and simple. Though the performance difference between ranges of 1-8, 1-9, 1-10, 2-8, etc. is marginal, we choose the 1-9 range for our system as it provided the best results for Hindi and Telugu on the dev set - the languages which were most often confused in our case. It is important to note that we also employ a binary-counting approach, where a feature is either present (if it appears at least once in a document) or absent (if it did not appear). These counts are normalized via term-frequency, inverse-document frequency (tf-idf) as implemented by the scikit-learn[1] machine learning package for Python.

3.2.2 Part-of-speech tags

Part-of-speech tags provide information about how ESL learners approach English at a morpho-syntactic level. Intuitively, then, it is likely that the native distribution and usage of POS tags might affect a learner's production of English. For example, native speakers of Turkish are known for the difficulty they experience with appropriately inserting definite articles in English. This difficulty could thus surface in terms of observed POS sequences or distributions in Turkish-native production of English texts. Furthermore, this could be notably different from what is observed in the production of speakers whose native language features a usage of determiners that is more similar to English.

Although countless POS-taggers exist, one major problem in acquiring reliable tags is intrinsic to the non-native nature of the texts we deal with. As POS models for English are trained on native English data, it is not granted that they will perform as well on non-native writing as they do on canonical texts. For this reason, we trained a POS tagger (Plank et al., 2016) on POS-tagged English learner data obtained from the Universal Dependencies project (Nivre et al., 2016), i.e., `English-ESL` (78k training tokens), tuning its parameters on the corresponding UD dev data. We experimented with several combinations of POS n-grams on our data, and found that a range of 1–4 yielded the best results on the development set.

3.2.3 Prompt word extraction

In an attempt to remove topic bias, we extracted words that appear to be typical of each prompt topic. This was done with the intuition that such words would ultimately confuse the classifier towards modeling prompt instead of native language. As such, we concatenated every essay per topic (resulting in 8 large prompt documents) as well as every essay in total. Each of the prompt documents was then passed to a sparse additive generative model (SAGE) (Eisenstein et al., 2011), with the concatenated corpus acting as a comparison corpus. This allowed us to identify the top keywords per topic (P0: "advertiser"; P1: "tourist", etc.). We then combined these prompt lists into a single keyword list (ranked by SAGE-score), which we considered to be representative of the total number of prompt words written in the corpus. In training our classifier, we then replaced the top 100 of such words (if correctly spelled) in the individual essays with a dummy token (*). We retained misspelled prompt words, as our intuition is that these represent (incorrect) information about the writers' understanding of English morphology. Using this approach resulted in a slight drop in performance accuracy ($\sim$2%) for every

[1] http://scikit-learn.org/stable/

model it was tested with, thereby confirming our intuition that our systems were indeed modeling topics, too.

3.2.4 P7 Omission

In examining the prompt distribution for the test data, we noticed that Prompt 7 was excluded entirely from the provided essays. As such, we hypothesized that omitting P7 from the training data would remove a degree of confusion introduced by the P7 prompt lexicon. To check this assumption, we first removed all essays with P7 as a prompt from the dev data (143 documents). This resulted in a slight drop in F1-score (from 84% to 83%) on the dev set. We then repeated this experiment with the P7 essays also omitted from the training data (1,419 documents). Doing so reproduced the initial f1-score of 84%, albeit with different (less) training and dev data. We replicated this for the test submission, removing P7 from the concatenated train and dev data (1,562 documents) in order to balance our system in terms of prompt with respect to the actual test set.

3.3 Meta-classification and Ensembles

Meta-classification is the process of training a classifier on the probability distributions output by another classifier. Doing so has the effect of revealing the classification patterns of the latter classifier, including cases where it experienced the most confusion in assigning a label. In seeing enough of these patterns, a meta classifier can effectively learn from the label probability distributions and correct the decisions of the main classifier. We experimented with an SVM meta classifier trained on both the output of the character n-gram classifier, as well as the output of a combined character n-gram and a simple neural network (CBOW, see Section 3.3.1). We performed 5-fold cross-validation on the training set in order to obtain the label probabilities for the documents in the training data. Though this approach improves upon the performance of both classifiers we evaluated, it is important to note that it may lead to over-fitting (Thornton et al., 2013).

We separately trained an ensemble and meta-classifier on the probability distributions output by several systems as features. The goal in doing so was to examine how the aforementioned linear SVM fares when combined with other, non-linear classifiers. The classifier employed is an ensemble linear SVM, which is trained on the pre-

dicted probability distributions of a randomly chosen 60% of the dev set and tuned on the remaining 40%. We use the standard hyperparameters of the SVM implementation in scikit-learn, without any tuning. The maximum of the predicted probability distribution on the test set is then used as the system's label prediction.

We evaluated the performance of three ensembles. The first two ensembles included the character 1-9-gram system, the CBOW system, and a CNN system (see Section 3.3.2). The CNN systems in the two runs differed in the input representations used. In first case (CNN1), the CNN used word unigrams and character 4-5grams, whereas in the second case (CNN2), it used word unigrams and character 6-grams. The third ensemble (Submission #8) concatenated the probability distributions generated by both character 1-9-gram and CBOW models (i.e. `ARA_CBOW: 0.1234; ARA_CHAR: 0.1432; etc.`) and trained a meta-classifier on these probabilities.

Each of the systems included in the ensembles (excluding the character 1-9-gram SVM) as well as the meta-classifier are described below.

3.3.1 CBOW system

We incorporated a simple neural baseline that combines word embeddings with a feedforward neural architecture similar to the *continous bag-of-words* (CBOW) model introduced in (Mikolov et al., 2013). This system represents each document as the average embedding of all words in the document. We used a shallow model (no deep layers), with a single dropout layer followed by the softmax output layer. The parameters of this model were set based on the dev set: 512 input dimensions, 0.1 dropout, 20 epochs, trained with the `adam` optimization algorithm (Kingma and Ba, 2014) for 20 iterations with a batch size of 50.

3.3.2 Deep Residual Networks

Deep residual networks (resnets) are a class of convolutional neural networks (CNNs), which consist of several convolutional blocks with skip connections in between (He et al., 2016). Such skip connections facilitate error propagation to earlier layers in the network, which allows for building deeper networks. Resnets have been shown to be useful for NLP tasks, such as text classification (Conneau et al., 2016), and sequence labelling (Bjerva et al., 2016). We applied resnets with four residual blocks in our ensemble experiments, each containing two successive one-dimensional convolutions. Each such block is followed by an average pooling layer and dropout ($p = 0.5$, Srivastava et al. (2014)). The resnets were applied to several input representations: word unigrams, and character 4-6-grams. The outputs of each resnet are concatenated before passing through two fully connected layers. We trained the resnet over 50 epochs with `adam`, using the model with the lowest validation loss. In addition to dropout, we used weight decay for regularization ($\epsilon = 10^{-4}$).

3.4 Discarded features

All previous features and systems have been used for the final submissions and will be discussed in the results section of this paper. However, it is noteworthy to mention which features were evaluated but nonetheless failed to provide a performance improvement. These were tested on the development set of the data as standalone features as well as in combination with others. However, in none of the cases were these features able to improve the performance of any of the submitted systems.

3.4.1 Word, lemma, and POS n-grams

Given the relative success of prior work in NLI, such as (Jarvis et al., 2013), we decided to experiment with traditional n-gram features. In these experiments, we employed the spaCy[2] NLP toolkit in order to generate the lemma and POS representations of words tokens. Several combinations of these features were evaluated, such as WORD + LEMMA + POS bigrams/trigrams, WORD/LEMMA unigrams + POS bigrams/trigrams, etc. Combinations of binary features and frequency-based features were evaluated for all aforementioned feature types. The inclusion of any of the features, however, decreased the performance of our system by at least 2% and they were therefore excluded from any of our final submissions.

3.4.2 Skipgrams

Skipgrams are a relatively new approach in NLP, most notable for their effectiveness in approximating word meaning in vector space models (Mikolov et al., 2013). In addition to calculating the n consecutive units in a sequence, skipgrams introduce another parameter, k, which calculates

n-grams of units separated by a distance of k. For example, the character bigram $k = 1$ representation of `apple` would thus be: `(a, p)`, `(p, l)`, `(p, e)`. As such, we experimented with skipgrams for several of our systems. Most notably, we evaluated character 2-9-grams with skips of 2 and 3. These results, however, were largely identical to our simpler 1-9-gram system and were thus discarded due to significantly longer training times and exceedingly sparse feature matrices.

3.4.3 IPA representation

Due to the success of the character n-gram models in capturing morphological details, we tested a feature that transcribed every essay into its phonetic representation. Even though we knew this would largely reproduce the same information captured by the raw text of the essays, we nonetheless hypothesized that an IPA-transcription would reveal further insights about how learners impose the morpho-phonetic features of their native language onto their spelling in English. For example, while dipthongization is not represented by the orthography of a word, a phonetic transcription is able to capture it. Thus, we employed the eSpeak text-to-speech software[3], which reproduced words according to how an English speaker would pronounce them. When tested against our best-performing character-level system, this approach produced a slight drop in F1-score ($\sim 1\%$). This factor, combined with very long training time, led us to ultimately discard the feature.

3.4.4 Misspellings

In examining the essays in the training set, we observed a large number of misspelled words. As such, we experimented with incorporating word misspellings into our system. These words were identified via the PyEnchant Python library[4] and replaced with a dummy token ($\star$). We posited that this would have the effect of identifying misspellings and capturing their distributions per language. The character-level features of misspelled words were also retained by the combined character 1-9-n-gram model. We attempted various feature representations for this method, including 1-9 character n-grams as well as word unigrams combined with non-filtered 1-9 character n-grams. None of these results were noteworthy, however.

---

[2]https://spacy.io/

[3]http://espeak.sourceforge.net/
[4]http://pythonhosted.org/pyenchant/

4 Results

Table 2 provides an overview of all submissions with results obtained both on the development and on the final evaluation sets.

The results show that our best-performing system was the character 1-9-gram system trained on the concatenation of training and development data. This is a notable improvement on the development set, which was 84%. The system for the first submission is the same as for the second submission. However the first submission was only trained on the training data set and the second also included the dev set. This resulted in more documents for training, which improved the performance of the system. This resulted in our overall best system. The confusion matrix for this system is given in Figure 1.

Here, the most confused cases are Hindi and Telugu, replicating what we observed (at a higher rate) during the development of our system. This discrepancy has also been reported by various prior studies, including Jarvis et al. (2013), whose system was trained and evaluated on different data than ours. The other noteworthy cases are Turkish and Arabic, which are confused at least once for all but one and two languages, respectively. Even though Korean is mislabeled as Japanese eight times, the same does not apply for the reverse situation: Japanese is the second most accurately-labeled class, with only German faring better. Interestingly, the meta classifier over the character 1-9-gram probabilities fares slightly worse than the standalone system. This, however, could likely be due to overfitting the system on the training data, which is a risk posed by any meta-classification approach.

Both of the prompt-based systems produced largely similar results. In the case of prompt-word omission, the confusion between Hindi and Telugu is slightly reduced, but also moved to other classes. The omission of P7 documents from training also resulted in a larger drop in accuracy from the character 1-9-n-gram system, which was not observed during development. Of course a drop would be expected, but not as large as it would likely be if a prompt topic written about in the test data had been omitted from the training data instead. Also, it is possible that the omission of 1,562 total documents from training is responsible for this result, prompt-effect notwithstanding.

Each of the ensemble methods failed to match the performance of the character 1-9-n-gram system. Though the intuition in assembling the ensemble classifiers was that they would provide extra insight for the main classifier by virtue of being non-linear, this is not reflected in terms of accuracy. It is noteworthy, however, that the system including the CNN trained on character 4-5-n-grams and word unigrams (CNN1) improved much on Arabic (88% F1-score) and Turkish (83% F1-score), suggesting that further refinement of this system (perhaps extending the character n-gram ranges) may be fruitful. Unfortunately, due to time constraints, we did not have a chance to explore other configurations, as CNNs take a considerably long time to train.

Finally, we note that the native-trained POS-approach did not produce encouraging results. Unlike the ensemble, which improved the classifier's performance on some classes despite yielding a lower F1-score, the POS tags failed to provide any notable insight relative to the character classifier. However, this is not to say that this approach should be entirely discarded. Rather, it would be interesting to combine the POS features with other feature types, such as word or lemma n-grams, as opposed to character n-grams.

5 Discussion

Our first submission (i.e., standalone 1-9 character n-grams), which was trained on both the training and development data yielded the best test-set performance out of all our submitted systems. As we received the results of our primary submissions from the organizers during the testing period, it was confirmed that the 1-9 character n-gram features were very powerful when evaluated on the test set. We thus continued to include these features in subsequent system submissions. The insight regarding the performance of these initial systems against the test set has certainly impacted the decisions we made about which features to include later. It must be noted, however, that our best performing system was submitted before we had received any such feedback, since it was one of the first systems we submitted. Therefore we did not tweak any aspect of the system for the test set. The system we developed initially without any knowledge of the test set performed best and also proved to be the most compact system.

As mentioned in the features section, topic bias was one of our major concerns during the sys-

Submission	Char. 1-9-grams	Char. 1-10-grams	POS tags	PW omitted	Meta	CBOW	CNN1	CNN2	P7 Omitted	Dev F1	Test F1
Random baseline:										0.0700	0.0909
Essay baseline:										0.6907	0.7104
1	x									0.8374	0.8684
2	x									0.8374	**0.8756**
3	x			x						0.8165	0.8682
4	x				x					**0.8459**	0.8737
5	x					x		x		-	0.8515
6	x					x	x			-	0.8616
7	x								x	0.8410	0.8613
8	x				x	x				0.8321	(0.5302)
9	x		x							0.8212	0.8414
10	x	x								0.8385	0.8720

Table 2: Overview of submissions to the NLI Shared Task 2017. Test scores were received during the test phase. As CNN1 and CNN2 were evaluated against 30% of the development set, their results are excluded from the performance on the development set. (The low test performance for Submission 8 suggests that something went wrong with uploading the correct system.)

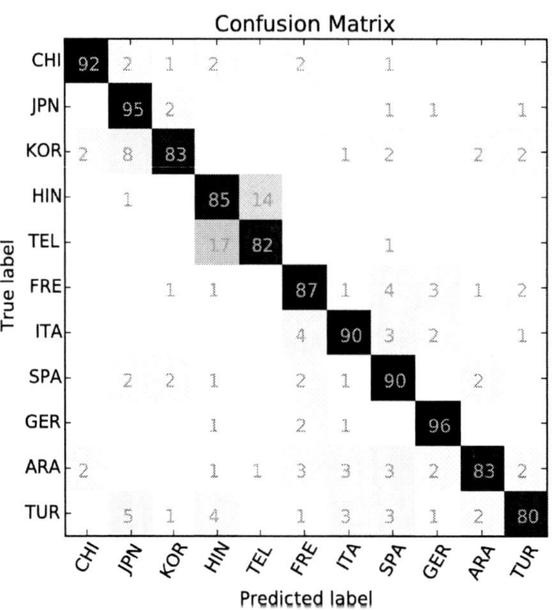

Figure 1: Confusion matrix for character 1-9-grams trained on train+dev

tem evaluation process. Our experiments with the prompt-word feature revealed that our system was indeed modeling prompt topic in addition to native language. In order to further validate this, we ran a series of experiments in which we omitted a prompt from the training set in a leave-one-prompt out scenario. We then fit a classifier on this truncated training data and evaluated it against the entire dev set (i.e., with all prompt information retained). The performance of the classifier varied greatly depending on which prompt was omitted, dropping in accuracy between 3% and 20%.

Interestingly, our experiments with omitting prompt information from the test set (both dev and test, in separate instances) did not reproduce such drastic drops in performance. Instead, the system's accuracy declined only slightly (as in the case of P7 omission), if at all. This suggests that, in evaluating the assessment submissions, the evaluation data can consist of a smaller prompt distribution than the training data, with only minimal prompt-overfitting observed for the latter. Conversely, this also means that a system must be trained on at least the same prompts that the data against which it is evaluated. Otherwise, the drop in performance may be unpredictable.

These prompt-omission experiments led us to conclude that, while it is possible to build a state-of-the-art model, the fact that it is trained and tested against the same prompt topics likely renders it unable to generalize towards other, potentially unseen future prompts. Furthermore, it is improbable that a system trained on one year's assessments will come close to replicating similar results when tested against essays from other years, due to the discrepancy in potential prompts. Certainly, this is to say that, in order to obtain a true metric of how well any of the submitted systems would fare in practical scenarios (i.e. NLI on future year's TOEFL essays), it is vital that they be tested against a data set that contains different and unseen prompts.

References

Johannes Bjerva, Barbara Plank, and Johan Bos. 2016. Semantic tagging with deep residual networks. In *Proceedings of COLING 2016, the 26th International Conference on Computational Linguistics: Technical Papers*. The COLING 2016 Organizing Committee, pages 3531–3541. http://aclweb.org/anthology/C16-1333.

Julian Brooke and Graeme Hirst. 2012. Robust, lexicalized native language identification. In *Proceedings of COLING 2012*.

Alexis Conneau, Holger Schwenk, Loïc Barrault, and Yann Lecun. 2016. Very deep convolutional networks for natural language processing. *arXiv preprint arXiv:1606.01781* .

Jacob Eisenstein, Amr Ahmed, and Eric P Xing. 2011. Sparse additive generative models of text .

Sylviane Granger, Estelle Dagneaux, Fanny Meunier, and Magali Paquot. 2009. International corpus of learner english.

Kaiming He, Xiangyu Zhang, Shaoqing Ren, and Jian Sun. 2016. Identity mappings in deep residual networks. *arXiv preprint arXiv:1603.05027* .

Radu Tudor Ionescu, Marius Popescu, and Aoife Cahill. 2014. Can characters reveal your native language? A language-independent approach to native language identification. In *Proceedings of the 2014 Conference on Empirical Methods in Natural Language Processing (EMNLP)*. Association for Computational Linguistics.

Scott Jarvis, Yves Bestgen, and Steve Pepper. 2013. Maximizing classification accuracy in native language identification. In *BEA@ NAACL-HLT*. pages 111–118.

Diederik Kingma and Jimmy Ba. 2014. Adam: A method for stochastic optimization. *arXiv preprint arXiv:1412.6980* .

Moshe Koppel, Jonathan Schler, and Kfir Zigdon. 2005. Determining an author's native language by mining a text for errors. In *Proceedings of the eleventh ACM SIGKDD international conference on Knowledge discovery in data mining*. ACM, pages 624–628.

Shervin Malmasi and Mark Dras. 2017. Native language identification using stacked generalization. *arXiv preprint arXiv:1703.06541* .

Shervin Malmasi, Keelan Evanini, Aoife Cahill, Joel Tetreault, Robert Pugh, Christopher Hamill, Diane Napolitano, and Yao Qian. 2017. A Report on the 2017 Native Language Identification Shared Task. In *Proceedings of the 12th Workshop on Building Educational Applications Using NLP*. Association for Computational Linguistics, Copenhagen, Denmark.

Tomas Mikolov, Kai Chen, Greg Corrado, and Jeffrey Dean. 2013. Efficient estimation of word representations in vector space. *arXiv preprint arXiv:1301.3781* .

Joakim Nivre, Marie-Catherine de Marneffe, Filip Ginter, Yoav Goldberg, Jan Hajic, Christopher D Manning, Ryan T McDonald, Slav Petrov, Sampo Pyysalo, Natalia Silveira, et al. 2016. Universal dependencies v1: A multilingual treebank collection. In *LREC*.

Terence Odlin. 1989. *Language transfer: Cross-linguistic influence in language learning*. Cambridge University Press.

Barbara Plank, Anders Søgaard, and Yoav Goldberg. 2016. Multilingual Part-of-Speech Tagging with Bidirectional Long Short-Term Memory Models and Auxiliary Loss. In *ACL 2016, arXiv preprint arXiv:1604.05529*. http://arxiv.org/abs/1604.05529.

Nitish Srivastava, Geoffrey E Hinton, Alex Krizhevsky, Ilya Sutskever, and Ruslan Salakhutdinov. 2014. Dropout: a simple way to prevent neural networks from overfitting. *Journal of Machine Learning Research* 15(1):1929–1958.

Joel R Tetreault, Daniel Blanchard, and Aoife Cahill. 2013. A report on the first native language identification shared task. In *BEA@ NAACL-HLT*. pages 48–57.

Chris Thornton, Frank Hutter, Holger H Hoos, and Kevin Leyton-Brown. 2013. Auto-weka: Combined selection and hyperparameter optimization of classification algorithms. In *Proceedings of the 19th ACM SIGKDD international conference on Knowledge discovery and data mining*. ACM, pages 847–855.

Classifier Stacking for Native Language Identification

Wen Li
Department of Linguistics
Indiana University
Bloomington, IN, USA
wl9@indiana.edu

Liang Zou
Department of Mathematics
Indiana University
Bloomington, IN, USA
liazou@indiana.edu

Abstract

This paper reports our contribution (team WLZ) to the NLI Shared Task 2017 (essay track). We first extract lexical and syntactic features from the essays, perform feature weighting and selection, and train linear support vector machine (SVM) classifiers each on an individual feature type. The output of base classifiers, as probabilities for each class, are then fed into a multilayer perceptron to predict the native language of the author. We also report the performance of each feature type, as well as the best features of a type. Our system achieves an accuracy of 86.55%, which is among the best performing systems of this shared task.

1 Introduction

Native language identification (NLI) is the task of determining an author's native language (L1) based on their writings in a second language (L2). NLI works under the assumption that an author's L1 will dispose them towards particular language production patterns in their L2, as influenced by their native language. This relates to cross-linguistic influence (CLI), a key topic in the field of second language acquisition (SLA) that analyzes transfer effects from the L1 on later learned languages (Malmasi, 2016). The identification of L1-specific features has been used to study language transfer effects in second-language acquisition (Malmasi and Dras, 2014), which is useful for developing pedagogical material, teaching methods, L1-specific instructions and generating learner feedback that is tailored to their native language.

The first NLI shared task was held in 2013 (Tetreault et al., 2013), and the winner team re-

ported an accuracy of 83.6% on the test data using an SVM classifier with over 400,000 unique features consisting of lexical and POS n-grams occurring in at least two texts in the training set (Jarvis et al., 2013). In addition to n-gram features, other researchers have also explored syntactic features (Bykh and Meurers, 2014) and the use of string kernels (Ionescu et al., 2014).

All NLI shared tasks to date have been based on L2 English data, but NLI research has been extended to at least six other non-English languages (Malmasi and Dras, 2015). In addition to using the written responses, a recent trend has been the use of speech transcripts and audio features for dialect identification (Malmasi et al., 2016). The combination of transcripts and acoustic features has also provided good results for dialect identification (Zampieri et al., 2017). Following this trend, the 2016 Computational Paralinguistics Challenge (Schuller et al., 2016) also included an NLI task based on the spoken response. The NLI Shared Task 2017 attempts to combine these approaches by including a written response (essay) and a spoken response (speech transcript and i-vector acoustic features) for each subject. The task also allows for the fusion of all features.

Ensemble methods using multiple classifiers have proven to be one of the most successful approaches for the task of NLI (Malmasi and Dras, 2017), and researchers have reported better results using stacking than a single classifier in other text classification tasks (e.g., Liu et al., 2016). In this work we present a stacking model using lexical and syntactic features for NLI Shared Task 2017 (Malmasi et al., 2017), report the performance of different feature types, and show the best features in each type. The features we use in the final model include character/word/stem n-grams, function word n-grams, and dependency parses.

Proceedings of the 12th Workshop on Innovative Use of NLP for Building Educational Applications, pages 390–397
Copenhagen, Denmark, September 8, 2017. ©2017 Association for Computational Linguistics

2 Data

The data set we use for NLI Shared Task 2017 (see details in Malmasi et al., 2017) includes English essays written by test takers who participated in a standardized assessment of English proficiency for academic purposes. The 11 native languages of the test takers are: Arabic (ARA), Chinese (CHI), French (FRE), German (GER), Hindi (HIN), Italian (ITA), Japanese (JPN), Korean (KOR), Spanish (SPA), Telugu (TEL), and Turkish (TUR). There are 11,000 essays (1,000 per L1) in the training partition (Train), 1,100 (100 per L1) in the development partition (Dev), and 1,100 (100 per L1) in the test partition (Test). All essays are available in both original and tokenized texts.

3 Methods

3.1 Features

We use **tf-idf weighting** for all the features in this work, since we observe better results than other feature representations, namely binary representation and frequency-based representation. For most of the feature types, we also **select k-best features** with chi-square metric instead of using all of them. Previous research has reported feature selection could improve the classification accuracy (Liu et al., 2014), and we notice the same trend for this task. In preliminary experiments feature selection increases the accuracy by around 1-3% for each feature type. The k value for each feature type varies with regard to the total number of features, and we choose the selected number of features based on their performance on the Dev set (trained on Train set). Both tf-idf weighting and feature selection are realized with Scikit-Learn (Pedregosa et al., 2011).

Character n-grams We extract character 3-7 grams from the tokenized text, and each is represented as a feature type (denoted by Char3-7). We also experiment with character 8-9 grams but do not include them in the final model, since adding them does not improve the accuracy.

Word n-grams We extract word uni-, bi-, and tri-grams from the tokenized text, and each is represented as a feature type (denoted by Word1-3).

Lemma n-grams We use the WordNet Lemmatizer in NLTK (Bird, 2006) to lemmatize the tokenized essays, and then extract lemma uni-, bi-, and tri-grams as feature types (denoted by Lemma1-3). However, we do not include these features in the final model, since adding them does not improve the accuracy.

Stem n-grams We first stem the tokenized text with Porter stemmer using NLTK, and then extract stem uni-, bi-, and tri-grams as feature types (denoted by Stem1-3).

POS n-grams We use the Stanford POS tagger (Toutanova et al., 2003) to tag the tokenized essays, and then extract POS uni-, bi-, and tri-grams as feature types (denoted by POS1-3). However, we do not include these features in the final model, since adding them does not improve the accuracy.

Function word n-grams We use the Stanford POS tagger to tag the tokenized essays first, and then extract the function words by their POS tags (which are tagged as auxiliary verbs, conjunctions, determiners, pronouns, etc.). Function word uni-, bi-, and tri-grams are used as features (denoted by FW1-3).

Dependency parses We use the Stanford dependency parser (Klein and Manning, 2003) to extract the dependencies from the tokenized essays. Three types of dependencies are included in the experiments (taking "I agree" as an example): original dependency (Dep0), e.g., (agree, nsubj, I); dependency where one of the word is replaced by its POS tag (Dep1), e.g., (VBP, nsubj, I) and (agree, nsubj, PRP); dependency where both of the words are replaced by their POS tags (Dep2), e.g., (VBP, nsubj, PRP). We include the POS-replaced dependencies, since we believe they would generalize better, as noted by Malmasi and Dras (2017).

Word embeddings We use the Common Crawl (42B tokens, 1.9M vocab, uncased, 300d vectors) in GloVe (global vectors for word representation) (Pennington et al., 2014) to produce feature vectors for each essay, with the help of Gensim (Řehůřek and Sojka, 2010). For all the words in an essay, we average their word vectors if they occur in the GloVe vocabulary as well. We observe that word vectors with larger dimension perform better than those with lower dimension when experimenting with different dimensions (e.g., 50d, 100d, 200d, 300d). However, we do not include the word embedding features (denoted by WV300) in the final model, since adding them does not improve the accuracy.

Feature type	Total #	Selected #	CV	Dev	Test
Char3	11,320	10,000	0.7327	0.7447	0.7555
Char4	51,072	30,000	0.7944	0.7827	0.8145
Char5	145,575	30,000	0.8158	0.8045	0.8264
Char6	334,117	30,000	0.8260	0.8000	0.8309
Char7	631,139	50,000	0.8386	0.8018	**0.8336**
Word1	25,950	20,000	0.7699	0.7627	0.8136
Word2	205,625	50,000	0.8417	0.7809	**0.8245**
Word3	384,184	50,000	0.8227	0.7082	0.7218
Stem1	145,575	10,000	0.7572	0.7618	0.7827
Stem2	334,117	30,000	0.8276	0.7791	**0.8118**
Stem3	631,139	30,000	0.7982	0.6964	0.7127
FW1	511	all	0.4199	0.4309	0.4227
FW2	12,385	all	0.4623	0.4764	**0.4900**
FW3	104,770	all	0.4174	0.4300	0.4464
Dep0	253,719	30,000	0.7868	0.6718	0.7473
Dep1	256,271	30,000	0.7996	0.7336	**0.7709**
Dep2	4,426	4,000	0.4598	0.4645	0.4745
Lemma1	22,541	20,000	0.7614	0.7627	–
Lemma2	181,533	50,000	0.8389	0.7891	–
Lemma3	355,414	50,000	0.8242	0.7082	–
POS1	44	all	0.3516	0.3800	–
POS2	12,385	all	0.5297	0.5173	–
POS3	18,961	15,000	0.5741	0.5710	–
WV300	300	300	0.5645	0.5673	–

Table 1: Total number of features, selected number of features, and accuracy of each feature type. CV: 10-fold cross validation on Train; Dev: trained on Train, tested on Dev; Test: trained on Train and Dev, tested on Test. Best performance of a feature group on Test is in bold.

3.2 Classifiers

We use **linear SVM** (implemented by Scikit-Learn) as the base classifier for the feature types mentioned above. We set C=0.8 for Char3, Word1, Stem1, FW1-3, and Dep2, and use default settings for other parameters. Experiments on other feature types use the default setting: C=1.0, L2 penalty, squared hinge loss, etc. For each feature type, we run 10-fold cross validation on Train and test on Dev to decide the number of selected features we would like to use for the final system.

To combine the output of probabilities from base classifiers and predict the final label, one method is to concatenate all the probabilities and feed into a classifier to generate the final prediction. We examine the performance of **multilayer perceptron** (MLP), linear SVM, Linear Discriminant Analysis (LDA), and MLP performs the best. We try different hidden layer sizes, and finally use one hidden layer of 100 perceptrons. Since MLP produces different results in every run, our final results using MLP contains the average results of 10 runs to reduce the variance.

We also try combining the probabilities mathematically. 1) summing up the probabilities from all feature types and taking the maximum as final prediction (denoted by SumProbs); 2) summing up the logarithmized probabilities from all feature types and taking the maximum as final prediction (denoted by LogSumProbs).

We run cross validation on Train and Dev to decide which feature types to include in the final model.

4 Results

4.1 Results by feature type

We report the performance of each feature type in Table 1. The upper part contains the 17 features we use in the final model, and the lower part contains some features we would like to explore but do not include in the final submissions.

We can see that the total number of features is very large for some feature types, which makes feature selection necessary. However, we choose the number of features by their performance on Dev and cross validation on Train, so there is no guarantee that we have the optimal number of selected features.

The features that perform comparatively well on Test set are: Char7, Word2, Stem2, FW2, and Dep1. We believe that bigrams perform better than unigrams or trigrams in general, because they consider context more than unigrams and generalize better than trigrams.

We also show the top features for each feature type ranked by Chi-square in Table 4, in the hope that it would be helpful for researchers interested in SLA or at least provide some insights to the readers. We notice that among the word n-grams are some country related words such as "italy" and "in japan", as well as some common expressions such as "in order to" and "more and more".

4.2 Final results

The Word Unigram baseline in Table 2 is achieved by using normalized frequency of all the word unigrams (which occurred at least three times in the essays) as features, and linear SVM as the classifier.

We try different methods of combining the output of probabilities by base classifiers and report their performance in Table 2. MLP and linear SVM are the best combiners among our experiments (other classifiers include random forest, LDA, logistic regression). When not using a classifier, summing up the logarithmized probabilities achieves better results than summing up the probabilities directly. The detailed evaluation of our best performing system is shown in Table 3, and the confusion matrix is shown in Figure 1.

From the confusion matrix we observe a few quite distinctive language groups: CHI, JPN, and KOR; HIN and TEL; FRE, ITA, and SPA. We suppose the confusion between languages results more from cultural than linguistic reasons. For instance, HIN and TEL are mutually misclassified in a lot of cases, while HIN belongs to Indo-European language family and TEL belongs to Dravidian. Similarly, CHI, JPN, and KOR come from three different language families, but they are in a cluster where one is often misclassified as another.

System	F1 (macro)	Accuracy
Random Baseline	0.0909	0.0909
Word Unigram	0.7104	0.7109
MLP	**0.8654**	**0.8655**
LinearSVM	0.8593	0.8591
LogSumProbs	0.8564	0.8565
SumProbs	0.8554	0.8555
LDA	0.8446	0.8445

Table 2: Final results using different combining methods. Trained on Train and Dev, tested on Test.

	Precision	Recall	F1
ARA	0.8673	0.8500	0.8586
CHI	0.9388	0.9200	0.9293
FRE	0.8600	0.8600	0.8600
GER	0.9406	0.9500	**0.9453**
HIN	0.7843	0.8000	*0.7921*
ITA	0.8878	0.8700	0.8788
JPN	0.8679	0.9200	0.8932
KOR	0.8632	0.8200	0.8410
SPA	0.8173	0.8500	0.8333
TEL	0.8265	0.8100	0.8182
TUR	0.8700	0.8700	0.8700
avg / total	0.8658	0.8655	0.8654

Table 3: Detailed evaluation of our best performing system. Trained on Train and Dev, tested on Test. Best and worst F1 in bold and italics.

5 Discussion and future work

We explore the performance of different feature types for NLI in this work. Among the features types we examine, character/word/lemma/stem n-grams have the best individual performance. Dependency parses are also informative with respect to the native language of the author. POS n-grams might be too general for this task, achieving around 50% accuracy alone. Word embeddings are good indicators for text classification tasks such as sentiment analysis, which relies heavily on the semantics of the content. NLI is not only about the semantics of the text but also involves writing style (e.g., the use of expressions and sentence structure). We suppose this justifies the performance of using word embeddings as features.

When we combine the output of base classifiers using different feature types to predict the final label, we have to decide which feature types to include. It is not practical to try all the combinations of features, so we start with the feature types

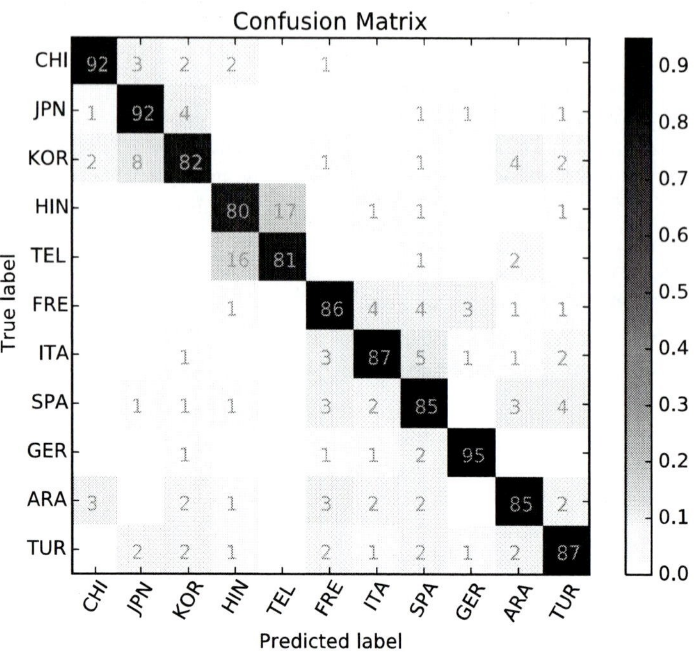

Figure 1: Confusion matrix of our best performing model.

with best individual performance, adding one and another. We do not include a feature type if it does not improve the accuracy on cross validation, and thus we cannot guarantee the optimization of performance on the test data. This process is very time consuming, and we believe there should be a better way of doing so. At the same time we observe adding lemma n-grams does not help, although lemma n-grams achieve very high accuracy by themselves. We believe the reason is that lemma n-grams are overlapping with word n-grams a lot, so they do not contribute more to the final prediction. We should keep in mind that good classifiers for ensemble learning need both accuracy and diversity. It remains unclear why function words (with accuracy of around 40%-50%) help more than POS n-grams or word embeddings, though.

We notice MLP improves the system performance over linear SVM as a combiner. For an individual feature type, MLP also performs better than linear SVM in most cases; however, we choose linear SVM as the base classifier, since it has better balance between speed and accuracy. MLP is roughly ten times slower than linear SVM when we run the experiments. This points us to the use of neural networks, since MLP is one of the simplest neural architecture. We would like to explore more about neural networks for NLI in future.

Another direction of future work may be towards a different architecture of combing various feature types. Ensemble methods have been studied quite a lot in text classification tasks; however, building an ensemble classifier is hardly an end-to-end task. We would like to explore how we can make the system smarter and learn by itself with less human input.

Finally, we hope the work in NLI would be of interest to the researchers from SLA/ESL. We hope the work we have done for NLI could be potentially useful for language teachers, and we would like to collaborate with them if they need anything from the view of computational linguistics.

Feature Type	Top Features Selected by Chi-square
Char3	h; vel; ink; n j; alo; pan; -t ; oup; oft; u w; owe; . .; kyo; fue; u ; nk ; 'm; 'm ; a ; he ; i '; u a; - ; & ; ..; , i; . ; gst; yme; i t; i ; wev; ho; gu; oym; yo; apa; you; gui; uid; tou; : ; rav; , ; ja; urk; ko; ou ; kor; jap
Char4	veli; ticu; germ; gste; ngst; ften; ofte; bbli; owev; weve; lopp; nk t; ymen; . ho; how; , i ; i th; oyme; ur g; you; r gu; pane; gui; joym; rkey; urke; guid; uide; tou; rave; deed; avel; trav; ita; ndee; in j; tour; ind; n ko; turk; pan ; alot; n ja; you ; orea; kor; jap; apan; japa
Char5	i thi; n ita; avel ; rean ; eed ,; oymen; howe; our g; k tha; orean; r gui; ur gu; rkey ; joyme; turke; urkey; uide ; njoym; guid; guide; in j; panes; pan ,; apane; ravel; anese; trave; deed ; trav; ital; indee; ndeed; tour; tour ; . ind; turk; in ko; n kor; inde; alot; alot ; orea ; in ja; you ; n jap; apan ; kore; korea; japa; japan
Char6	a tour; ravel ; eed , ; orean ; . howe; oyment; howev; orea ,; k that; nk tha; korean; r guid; ur gui; our gu; urkey ; turke; joymen; turkey; njoyme; enjoym; guide ; guide ; tour g; pan , ; apanes; japane; anese ; apan ,; panese; travel; trave; indeed; ndeed ; in ko; . ind; deed ,; tour ; in kor; n kore; . inde; indee; in ja; alot o; alot ; korea ; n japa; japan ; in jap; korea; japan
Char7	wever ,; a tour; a tour ; travel ; oyment ; . howev; . howe; korean ; howeve; k that ; korea ,; orea , ; nk that; ink tha; korean; enjoym; r guide; ur guid; our gui; turkey ; turkey; tour gu; joyment; njoymen; enjoyme; guide ; tour g; japane; japanes; apan , ; japan ,; panese ; travel; apanese; deed , ; in kor; ndeed ,; in kore; . inde; . indee; n korea; indeed; alot o; in jap; alot of; korea ; n japan; in japa; japan
Word1	u; jack; developped; infact; milan; pubblic; exemple; preparation; trip; 'm; youth; group; &; think; the; your; various; france; dont; ..; -; a; youngsters; he; germany; hence; his; italy; towards; traveling; particular; italian; often; however; thier; travel; i; korean; guide; enjoyment; turkey; :; japanese; indeed; tour; ,; alot; korea; you; japan
Word2	and hence; that you; jack of; the youth; it 's; led by; younger generation; the above; ; they; when compared; i 'm; a particular; group tour; you are; first ,; two reasons; a group; particular subject; korea .; in germany; second ,; now a; we; . second; japan .; as compared; , and; . ..; , that; in fact; i conclude; in italy; where as; in france; in turkey; a days; . however; i think; a tour; , i; however ,; think that; korea ,; tour guide; japan ,; indeed ,; in korea; . indeed; alot of; in japan
Word3	a lot of; have alot of; of all ,; conclude , i; , young people; master of none; , i think; tour guide .; enjoy a lot; , they can; , in japan; usage of; cars; of all trades; . i think; the younger generation; to conclude ,; on the one; each and every; the possibility to; i feel that; a group led; . therefore ,; i; reasons , i; the one hand; group led by; . to conclude; . in japan; for this reason; is , that; i conclude that; in korea .; jack of all; led by a; when compared to; . first ,; in a group; by a tour; are two reasons; . in fact; . second ,; in japan .; as compared to; a tour guide; now a days; in korea ,; . however ,; in japan ,; i think that; . indeed ,
Stem1	atleast; an; that; istanbul; intrest; taiwan; india; commun; fuel; tokyo; trip; group; infact; possibl; jack; milan; think; toward; advertiss; difer; the; exempl; youth; dont; variou; your; he; franc; hi; henc; germani; itali; particular; pubblic; youngster; often; thier; howev; italian; korean; guid; turkey; travel; japanes; tour; inde; alot; korea; you; japan
Stem2	all trade; when you; with out; have alot; feel that; you will; the italian; usag of; old age; each and; one hand; in india; peopl that; master of; group led; you have; mode of; to conclud; conclud that; and henc; everi thing; that you; when compar; possibl to; the youth; in group; jack of; younger gener; the abov; led by; enjoy lot; the subject; particular subject; you are; group tour; in germani; by tour; two reason; as compar; in fact; now day; in itali; where as; in franc; in turkey; think that; tour guid; in korea; alot of; in japan
Stem3	the new thing; alot of money; alot of thing; the statement that; and for thi; in olden day; youth of today; are my follow; in order to; the youth of; in today world; would say that; for these reason; for exampl consid; the older peopl; day by day; in thi way; for new thing; mode of transport; when you are; think that is; final conclud that; the usag of; accord to me; to my mind; all the subject; travel in group; the young peopl; more and more; you have to; think that in; tri for new; have alot of; master of none; usag of car; in group led; each and everi; the possibl to; on the one; of all trade; the younger gener; the one hand; group led by; for thi reason; jack of all; when compar to; led by tour; by tour guid; are two reason; as compar to
FW1	when; whether; to; about; by; some; amongst; it; can; into; every; than; there; atleast; must; three; across; or; why; upon; she; till; because; behind; will; could; of; though; my; would; whereas; might; they; their; this; him; that; olden; any; the; we; its; an; may; which; your; he; his; towards; you
FW2	that why; the he; all the; there three; you in; and he; some might; one should; to you; the may; the behind; any one; that that; that this; that in; you the; because you; his and; and that; you you; of the; which he; it to; you and; they can; what you; and towards; the which; he can; and you; he will; towards the; by myself; every one; in by; in olden; there two; he may; we can; in his; towards their; if you; you can; the you; you will; the of; when you; where as; that you; you to
FW3	some might that; there three as; you to and; as as with; the towards their; all but of; the of an; you to in; in the twenty; there in twenty; than there two; the you to; the in olden; some might with; to would that; you will to; you to the; they how to; for us to; you to to; if you to; in to this; but on the; that you can; we can the; the where as; above we can; their towards their; on of that; for these with; the these my; when you you; all as before; and for this; that in the; that you to; where as the; there two for; all in all; in all as; with the that; two for this; we can that; as would that; in the of; to in by; the of the; the that you; on the one; each and every
Dep0	compared_advmod_when; days_det_these; student_det_the; important_cop_; enjoyment_case_of; possibility_det_the; thing_det_every; subjects_det_the; taiwan_case_in; each_cc_and; usage_nmod_cars; self_nmod; enjoy_dobj_lot; hand_nummod_one; product_det_a; subject_det_the; knowledge_det_a; take_dobj_example; group_acl_led; conclude_mark_to; india_case_in; people_det_the; generation_det_the; feel_nsubj_i; generation_amod_younger; have_nsubj_you; group_det_a; preparation_det_a; youth_det_the; led_nmod_guide; reasons_nummod_two; tour_compound_group; group_case_in; subject_amod_particular; guide_case_by; days_det_a; germany_case_in; fact_case_in; italy_case_in; france_case_in; turkey_case_in; conclude_nsubj_i; poss_his; guide_det_a; think_nsubj_i; guide_compound_tour; korea_case_in; japan_case_in
Dep1	nn_acl_led; conclude_mark_to; nn_det_any; led_nmod_nn; youth_det_dt; generation_amod_jjr; vbn_nmod_guide; conclude_nsubj_fw; vbg_mark_in; subject_det_dt; group_det_dt; enjoyment_case_in; vbp_advmod_indeed; preparation_amod_jj; nn_case_towards; group_case_in; nn_det_a; tour_compound_nn; vbp_nsubj_that; preparation_det_dt; poss_your; nns_amod_various; vbp_nsubj_i; nn_amod_italian; nns_det_the; nn_nmod_korea; india_case_in; vb_dobj_alot; germany_case_in; vb_nsubj_you; reasons_nummod_cd; nn_amod_japanese; nn_nmod_japan; france_case_in; italy_case_in; vbd_nsubj_i; think_nsubj_prp; guide_case_in; nn_amod_particular; turkey_case_in; alot_nmod_nn; vbp_nsubj_you; guide_det_dt; guide_compound_nn; alot_nmod_nns; nn_compound_tour; korea_case_in; japan_case_in
Dep2	jjs_case_to; vbg_dobj_nn; vb_dobj_prp; vb_nsubj_prp; vbg_nsubj_nns; jj_mwe_in; vb_advcl_vbp; vbp_ccomp_jj; vbg_nmod_nns; jj_cop_vbz; nn_case_in; prp_case_vbg; jj_nsubj_prp; vbd_dobj_nn; nn_compound_nn; jj_xcomp_vb; jjr_conj_jjr; vb_aux_vbd; vb_nsubj_fw; vbp_nsubj_wdt; vbd_advmod_rb; vbp_advmod_rb; jj_advmod_rb; predet_pdt; nn_nmod_nn; vbd_nmod_nnp; jj_cop_vb; nnp_nmod_dt; vbp_expl_ex; nns_det; jj_cop_vbg; in_mwe_nn; vb_nsubj_nns; vb_aux_vbp; vb_advmod_ls; vbn_aux_vbz; vb_neg_rb; vbd_nsubj_fw; poss_nns; vbg_mark_in; jj_mark_to; nns_case_pos; vbp_nsubj_nns; vbp_nsubj_prp; vbp_advmod_ls; nns_det_dt; vbp_nsubj_fw; vbd_nsubj_prp; nn_det_dt

Table 4: Top features ranked by Chi-square on Train and Dev (separated by ";").

References

Steven Bird. 2006. Nltk: the natural language toolkit. In *Proceedings of the COLING/ACL on Interactive presentation sessions*. Association for Computational Linguistics, pages 69–72.

Serhiy Bykh and Detmar Meurers. 2014. Exploring Syntactic Features for Native Language Identification: A Variationist Perspective on Feature Encoding and Ensemble Optimization. In *Proceedings of COLING 2014, the 25th International Conference on Computational Linguistics: Technical Papers*. Dublin, Ireland, pages 1962–1973.

Radu Tudor Ionescu, Marius Popescu, and Aoife Cahill. 2014. Can characters reveal your native language? A language-independent approach to native language identification. In *Proceedings of the 2014 Conference on Empirical Methods in Natural Language Processing (EMNLP)*. Association for Computational Linguistics.

Scott Jarvis, Yves Bestgen, and Steve Pepper. 2013. Maximizing Classification Accuracy in Native Language Identification. In *Proceedings of the Eighth Workshop on Innovative Use of NLP for Building Educational Applications*. Association for Computational Linguistics, Atlanta, Georgia, pages 111–118.

Dan Klein and Christopher D Manning. 2003. Accurate unlexicalized parsing. In *Proceedings of the 41st Annual Meeting on Association for Computational Linguistics-Volume 1*. Association for Computational Linguistics, pages 423–430.

Can Liu, Chun Guo, Daniel Dakota, Sridhar Rajagopalan, Wen Li, Sandra Kübler, and Ning Yu. 2014. "My curiosity was satisfied, but not in a good way": Predicting user ratings for online recipes. In *Proceedings of the Second Workshop on Natural Language Processing for Social Media (SocialNLP)*. Dublin, Ireland, pages 12–21

Can Liu, Wen Li, Bradford Demarest, Yue Chen, Sara Couture, Daniel Dakota, Nikita Haduong, Noah Kaufman, Andrew Lamont, Manan Pancholi, Kenneth Steimel, and Sandra Kübler. 2016. IUCL at SemEval-2016 Task 6: An Ensemble Model for Stance Detection in Twitter. In *Proceedings of SemEval-2016*. San Diego, California, pages 394–400.

Shervin Malmasi. 2016. *Native Language Identification: Explorations and Applications*. Ph.D. thesis. http://hdl.handle.net/1959.14/1110919.

Shervin Malmasi and Mark Dras. 2014. Language Transfer Hypotheses with Linear SVM Weights. In *2014 Conference on Empirical Methods in Natural Language Processing (EMNLP)*. Doha, Qatar, pages 1385–1390.

Shervin Malmasi and Mark Dras. 2015. Multilingual Native Language Identification. In *Natural Language Engineering*.

Shervin Malmasi and Mark Dras. 2017. Native Language Identification using Stacked Generalization. *arXiv preprint arXiv:1703.06541* .

Shervin Malmasi, Keelan Evanini, Aoife Cahill, Joel Tetreault, Robert Pugh, Christopher Hamill, Diane Napolitano, and Yao Qian. 2017. A Report on the 2017 Native Language Identification Shared Task. In *Proceedings of the 12th Workshop on Building Educational Applications Using NLP*. Association for Computational Linguistics, Copenhagen, Denmark.

Shervin Malmasi, Marcos Zampieri, Nikola Ljubešić, Preslav Nakov, Ahmed Ali, and Jörg Tiedemann. 2016. Discriminating between Similar Languages and Arabic Dialect Identification: A Report on the Third DSL Shared Task. In *Proceedings of the VarDial Workshop*. Osaka, Japan.

F. Pedregosa, G. Varoquaux, A. Gramfort, V. Michel, B. Thirion, O. Grisel, M. Blondel, P. Prettenhofer, R. Weiss, V. Dubourg, J. Vanderplas, A. Passos, D. Cournapeau, M. Brucher, M. Perrot, and E. Duchesnay. 2011. Scikit-learn: Machine learning in Python. *Journal of Machine Learning Research* 12:2825–2830.

Jeffrey Pennington, Richard Socher, and Christopher D Manning. 2014. Glove: Global vectors for word representation. In *EMNLP*. volume 14, pages 1532–1543.

Radim Řehůřek and Petr Sojka. 2010. Software Framework for Topic Modelling with Large Corpora. In *Proceedings of the LREC 2010 Workshop on New Challenges for NLP Frameworks*. ELRA, Valletta, Malta, pages 45–50. http://is.muni.cz/publication/884893/en.

Bjrn Schuller, Stefan Steidl, Anton Batliner, Julia Hirschberg, Judee K. Burgoon, Alice Baird, Aaron Elkins, Yue Zhang, Eduardo Coutinho, and Keelan Evanini. 2016. The INTERSPEECH 2016 Computational Paralinguistics Challenge: Deception, Sincerity & Native Language. In *Interspeech 2016*. pages 2001–2005. https://doi.org/10.21437/Interspeech.2016-129.

Joel Tetreault, Daniel Blanchard, and Aoife Cahill. 2013. A Report on the First Native Language Identification Shared Task. In *Proceedings of the Eighth Workshop on Building Educational Applications Using NLP*. Association for Computational Linguistics, Atlanta, GA, USA.

Kristina Toutanova, Dan Klein, Christopher D Manning, and Yoram Singer. 2003. Feature-rich part-of-speech tagging with a cyclic dependency network. In *Proceedings of the 2003 Conference of the North American Chapter of the Association for Computational Linguistics on Human Language Technology-Volume 1*. Association for Computational Linguistics, pages 173–180.

Marcos Zampieri, Shervin Malmasi, Nikola Ljubešić,
Preslav Nakov, Ahmed Ali, Jörg Tiedemann, Yves
Scherrer, and Noëmi Aepli. 2017. Findings of the
VarDial Evaluation Campaign 2017. In *Proceedings
of the Fourth Workshop on NLP for Similar Lan-
guages, Varieties and Dialects (VarDial)*. Valencia,
Spain, pages 1–15.

Native Language Identification on Text and Speech

Marcos Zampieri[1], Alina Maria Ciobanu[2], Liviu P. Dinu[2]
[1]University of Wolverhampton, United Kingdom
[2]University of Bucharest, Romania
marcos.zampieri@uni-koeln.de

Abstract

This paper presents an ensemble system combining the output of multiple SVM classifiers to native language identification (NLI). The system was submitted to the NLI Shared Task 2017 fusion track which featured students essays and spoken responses in form of audio transcriptions and iVectors by non-native English speakers of eleven native languages. Our system competed in the challenge under the team name ZCD and was based on an ensemble of SVM classifiers trained on character n-grams achieving 83.58% accuracy and ranking 3rd in the shared task.

1 Introduction

Native language identification (NLI) is the task of automatically identifying non-native speakers' native language based on their foreign language production. As evidenced in Malmasi (2016) NLI is a vibrant research area in NLP and is usually modeled as single-label text classification.

NLI is based on the assumption that the mother tongue influences second language acquisition (SLA) and production. Corpora containing texts and utterances by non-native speakers are used to train systems that are able to recognize features that are prominent in the production of speakers of a particular native language. These features are subsequently used to identify texts (or utterances) that are likely to be written or spoken by speakers of the same language.

There are two important reasons to study NLI. Firstly, there is SLA. NLI methods can be applied to learner corpora to investigate the influence of native language in second language acquisition and production complementing corpus-based and corpus-driven studies. The second reason is a practical one. NLI methods can be an important part of several NLP systems including, for example, author profiling systems developed for forensic linguistics.

This paper presents the system submitted by the ZCD team to the NLI Shared Task 2017 (Malmasi et al., 2017). The organizers of the challenge provided participants with a dataset containing essays and spoken responses in form of transcriptions and acoustic features (iVectors) by non-native English speakers of eleven native languages taking a standardized assessment of English proficiency for academic purposes. Native languages included are: Arabic, Chinese, French, German, Hindi, Italian, Japanese, Korean, Spanish, Telugu, and Turkish. To discriminate between these eleven native languages we apply an ensemble of multiple linear SVM classifiers trained on character n-grams. The main motivation behind the choice of this approach is the success of linear SVMs and SVM ensembles in NLI and in similar text classification tasks such as dialect, language variety, and similar language identification as will be discussed in Section 2.

2 Related Work

There have been several NLI studies published in the past few years. Due to the availability of suitable language resources for English (e.g. learner corpora), the vast majority of these studies dealt with English (Brooke and Hirst, 2012; Bykh and Meurers, 2014), however, a few NLI studies have been published on other languages. Examples of NLI applied to languages other than English include Arabic (Ionescu, 2015), Chinese (Wang et al., 2016), and Finnish (Malmasi and Dras, 2014).

To the best of our knowledge, the NLI Shared Task 2013 (Tetreault et al., 2013) was the first

398

Proceedings of the 12th Workshop on Innovative Use of NLP for Building Educational Applications, pages 398–404
Copenhagen, Denmark, September 8, 2017. ©2017 Association for Computational Linguistics

Team	Approach	System Paper
Jarvis	SVM trained on character n-grams (1-9), word n-grams (1-4), and POS n-grams (1-4)	(Jarvis et al., 2013)
Oslo	SVM trained on character n-grams (1-7)	(Lynum, 2013)
Unibuc	String Kernels and Local Rank Distance (LRD)	(Popescu and Ionescu, 2013)
MITRE	Bayes ensemble of multiple classifiers	(Henderson et al., 2013)
Tuebingen	SVM trained on word n-grams (1-2), and POS n-grams (1-5), and syntactic features (dependencies)	(Bykh et al., 2013)
NRC	Ensemble of SVM classifiers trained on character trigrams, word n-grams (1-2), POS n-grams (2-4), and syntactic features (dependencies)	(Goutte et al., 2013)
CMU-Haifa	Maximum Entropy trained on word n-grams (1-4), POS n-grams (1-4), and spelling features	(Tsvetkov et al., 2013)
Cologne-Nijmegen	SVM classifier with TF-IDF weighting trained on character n-grams (1-6), word n-grams (1-2), and POS n-grams (1-4)	(Gebre et al., 2013)
NAIST	SVM trained on character n-grams (2-3), word n-grams (1-2), and POS n-grams (2-3), and syntactic features (dependencies and TSG)	(Mizumoto et al., 2013)
UTD	SVM trained on word n-grams (1-2)	(Wu et al., 2013)

Table 1: Top ten NLI Shared Task 2013 entries ordered by performance.

shared task to provide a benchmark for NLI focusing on written texts by non-native English speakers. A few years later, the 2016 Computational Paralinguistics Challenge (Schuller et al., 2016) included an NLI task on speech data. The NLI Shared Task 2017 combines these two modalities of non-native language production by including essays and spoken responses of test takers in form of transcriptions and iVectors.

The combination of text and speech has been previously used in similar shared tasks such as the dialect identification shared tasks organized at the VarDial workshop series (Zampieri et al., 2017) and described in more detail in Section 2.2.

In the next sections we present the most successful entries submitted for the NLI Shared Task 2013 and their overlap with methods applied to dialect, language variety, and similar language identification.

2.1 NLI Shared Task 2013

The aforementioned NLI Shared Task 2013 (Tetreault et al., 2013) established the first benchmark for NLI on written texts. Organizers of the first NLI task provided participants with the TOEFL 11 (Blanchard et al., 2013) dataset which contained essays written by students native speakers of the same eleven languages included in the NLI Shared Task 2017.

Twenty-nine teams participated in the competition, testing a wide range of computational methods for NLI. In Table 1 we list the top ten best

entries ranked by performance along with their respective system description papers.

The best system by Jarvis et al. (2013) applied a linear SVM classifier trained on character, word, and POS n-grams. Seven out of the ten best entries in the shared task used SVM classifiers. This indicates that SMVs are a very good fit for NLI and motivates us to test SVM classifiers in our ensemble-based system described in this paper.

2.2 Overlap with Dialect Identification

In the last few years, we observed a significant and important overlap between NLI approaches and computational methods applied to dialect, language variety, and similar language identification. So far the overlap between the two tasks has not been substantially explored in the literature.

Members of several teams that submitted systems to the NLI Shared Task 2013, some of them presented in Table 1, also participated in the dialect identification shared tasks organized within the scope of the VarDial workshop series held from 2014 to 2017. The three related shared tasks organized at the VarDial workshop thus far are the Discriminating between Similar Languages (DSL) task organized from 2014 to 2017, Arabic Dialect Identification (ADI) organized in 2016 and 2017, and German Dialect Identification (GDI) organized in 2017.

Next we list some of the teams that adapted systems from NLI to dialect identification in the past few years.

- Variations of the string kernels method by the Unibuc team (Popescu and Ionescu, 2013) competed in the ADI task in 2016 (Ionescu and Popescu, 2016) and in 2017 (Ionescu and Butnaru, 2017) achieving the best results.

- Cologne-Nijmegen's TF-IDF-based approach (Gebre et al., 2013) competed in the DSL shared task 2015 (Zampieri et al., 2015a) as team MMS ranking among the top 3 systems.

- A variation of NRC's SVM approach (Goutte et al., 2013) competed in the DSL 2014 (Goutte et al., 2014) achieving the best results.

- Bobicev applied Prediction for Partial Matching (PPM) in the NLI shared task (Bobicev, 2013) with results that did not reach top ten performance. A similar improved approached competed in the DSL 2015 (Bobicev, 2015) ranking in the top half of the table.

- A similar approach to the one by Jarvis (Jarvis et al., 2013) that ranked 1st place in the NLI task 2013 competed in the DSL 2017 (Bestgen, 2017), achieving the best performance in the competition.

- Variations of MQ's SVM ensemble approach (Malmasi et al., 2013) have competed in the DSL 2015 (Malmasi and Dras, 2015) and the ADI 2016 (Malmasi and Zampieri, 2016), achieving the best performance in both shared tasks.

This section evidenced an important overlap between NLI methods and dialect identification methods both in terms of participation overlap in the shared tasks and in terms of successful approaches. With the exception of Bobicev (2013), most teams that were ranked among the top ten entries in the NLI shared task were also successful at the VarDial workshop shared tasks.

Detailed information about all approaches and performance obtained in these competitions can be found in the VarDial shared task reports (Zampieri et al., 2014, 2015b; Malmasi et al., 2016b; Zampieri et al., 2017) and in the evaluation paper by Goutte et al. (2016).

3 Methods

In the next sections we describe the data provided by the shared task organizers and the ensemble SVM approach applied by the ZCD team.

3.1 Data

The organizers of the NLI Shared Task 2017 provided participants with data corresponding to eleven native languages: Arabic, Chinese, French, German, Hindi, Italian, Japanese, Korean, Spanish, Telugu and Turkish. The training dataset consists of 11,000 essays, orthographic transcriptions of 45-second English spoken responses, and iVectors (1,000 instances for each of the eleven native languages), while the development dataset was stratified similarly, containing 100 instances for each native language.

There were individual tracks in which only the essays or only the responses could be used and a fusion track in which both the essays and the speech transcriptions (including iVectors) could be used. The test dataset, containing 1,100 instances with essays, speech transcriptions and iVectors, was released at a later date.

The use of a dataset containing text and speech is the main new aspect of the 2017 NLI task so we decide to compete in the fusion track taking both modalities into account. The approach used in our submission is described next.

3.2 Approach

We built a classification system based on SVM ensembles, following the methodology proposed by Malmasi and Dras (2015).

The idea behind classification ensembles is to improve the overall performance by combining the results of multiple classifiers. Such systems have proved successful not only in NLI and dialect identification, as evidenced in the previous sections, but also in numerous text classification tasks, among which are complex word identification (Malmasi et al., 2016a) and grammatical error diagnosis (Xiang et al., 2015). The classifiers can differ in a wide range of aspects, such as algorithms, training data, features or parameters.

In our system, the classifiers used different features. We experimented with the following features: character n-grams (with n in $\{1, ..., 10\}$) from essays and speech transcripts, word n-grams (with n in $\{1, 2\}$) from essays and speech transcripts, and iVectors. For the n-gram features we

System	F1 (macro)	Accuracy
Essays + Transcriptions + iVectors	0.8358	0.8355
Essays + Transcriptions	0.8191	0.8191
Official Baseline (with iVectors)	0.7901	0.7909
Official Baseline (without iVectors)	0.7786	0.7791
Random Baseline	0.0909	0.0909

Table 2: ZCD results and baselines for the fusion track.

used TF-IDF weighting applied on the tokenized version of the essays and speech transcripts (provided by the organizers). As a pre-processing step, we lowercased all words.

We first trained a classifier for each type of feature using the essays as input data, and performed cross-validation to determine the optimal value for the SVM hyperparameter C, searching in $\{10^{-5}, ..., 10^5\}$. Further, for the n-gram features we kept only those classifiers whose individual cross-validation performance was higher than 0.8. Thus, our first ensemble consisted of individual classifiers using character n-grams (with n in $\{6, 7, 8\}$) from essays and speech transcripts.

For the second ensemble, we introduced an additional classifier using the iVectors as features. To combine the classifiers, we employed a majority-based fusion method: the class label predicted by the ensemble is the one that was predicted by the majority of the classifiers. We used the SVM implementation provided by Scikit-learn (Pedregosa et al., 2011), based on the Liblinear library (Fan et al., 2008).

On the development dataset, the first ensemble (essays + speech transcripts) obtained 0.83 accuracy, and the second ensemble (essays + speech transcripts + iVectors) obtained 0.84 accuracy.

4 Results

We submitted two runs of our system. The first run included the essays and the transcriptions of responses, whereas the second run included also the iVectors. We present the results obtained by the two runs along with a random baseline and the performance of the unigram-based official baseline system in terms of F1 score and accuracy in Table 2.

The best results were achieved by the second run, reaching 83.55% accuracy and 83.58% F1 score. As can be seen in Table 2, the iVectors bring a performance improvement of about 1.6 percentage points in terms of accuracy and F1 score.

Ten teams participated in the fusion track and our best run was ranked 3rd by the shared task organizers. Ranks were calculated using McNemars test for statistical significance, a common practice in many NLI shared tasks (e.g. DSL 2016 (Malmasi et al., 2016b), and the shared tasks at WMT (Bojar et al., 2016)).

The confusion matrix of our best submission is presented in Table 3. We observed that the best performance was obtained for Japanese and the worst performance was obtained for Arabic. Not surprisingly, most confusion occurred between Hindi and Telugu. Our initial analysis indicates that this confusion occurred because of geographic proximity and not by intrinsic linguistic properties shared by these two languages, as Hindi and Telugu do not belong to the same language family - Hindi is a Hindustani language and Telugu is a Dravidian language.

5 Most Informative Features

As briefly discussed in the introduction of this paper, NLI methods can provide interesting information about patterns in non-native language that can be used to study second language acquisition and L1 interference or language transfer. For this purpose, in Table 4 we present the top ten most informative character 8-grams for each of the eleven languages in the dataset according to our classifier.

It is not surprising that named entities are very informative for our system and highly discriminative for most native languages. For example, essays and responses from China often contain place names like *China, Taipei, Taiwan,* and *Beijing,* whereas those from Turkey contain *Istanbul* and, of course, *Turkey.* These features are very frequent in essays and responses by Chinese and Turkish speakers due to topical bias and not because of any intrinsic linguistic property of Chinese or Turkish. However, in other languages, interesting linguistic patterns can be identified by looking at these features.

	CHI	JPN	KOR	HIN	TEL	FRE	ITA	SPA	GER	ARA	TUR
CHI	91	3	2	0	0	0	2	0	0	1	1
JPN	2	93	2	0	1	1	0	0	1	0	0
KOR	4	14	77	0	0	1	1	1	0	1	1
HIN	1	0	1	80	18	0	0	0	0	0	0
TEL	0	0	1	18	78	0	0	1	0	2	0
FRE	2	0	0	2	1	87	5	0	2	1	0
ITA	0	0	0	1	0	6	85	3	3	2	0
SPA	1	1	2	2	1	4	7	77	2	2	1
GER	0	1	0	3	0	3	2	1	90	0	0
ARA	2	2	2	3	2	7	1	2	1	77	1
TUR	1	2	0	3	0	2	3	1	1	3	84

Table 3: Confusion matrix on the test set.

Language	Most Informative Features
Arabic	|alot of | alot of|y thing | statmen|statment|e alot o|tatment |ery thin|very thi|every th|
Chinese	| i think| taiwan |i think |beijing | beijing| taipei | in chin|in china|n china | chinese|
French	| indeed |. indeed| . indee|indeed ,|ndeed , | france |developp| french |to concl|o conclu|
German	| , that | and um | germany|germany | berlin |, that t|have to | have to| um yeah|um yeah |
Hindi	| towards|towards |as compa| as comp|various | various|s compar| enjoyme| mumbai | behind |
Italian	|hink tha|nk that |ink that| in ital|n italy |in fact |in italy| in fact|i think | italian|
Japanese	|in japan|n japan | in japa|apanese | japanes|japanese| japan ,|japan , |i disagr| japan .|
Korean	| korean |in korea| in kore|n korea | however|however |korea , | korea ,|. howev|. howeve|
Spanish	| mexico |oing to |going to| going t| diferen|le that | the cit|es that |diferent|ple that|
Telugu	|ing the |hyderaba| hyderab|yderabad|derabad | subject| we can | i concl|i conclu|where as|
Turkish	| turkey |istanbul|stanbul | istanbu| uh and |n turkey| in turk|in turke|s about | . becau|

Table 4: Top ten most informative character 8-grams for each language.

In the most informative features for French, for example, we find *developp* from the French *développé* which leads to a misspelling of the English word *developed*. In Arabic we observed a number of features that indicate misspellings. The Arabic alphabet is very different from the Latin one, making spelling English words particularly challenging for native speakers of Arabic. The top ten most informative features for Arabic include word boundary errors such as *every thing* for *everything*, and *alot* for *a lot*, as well as the omission of vowels such as *statment* for *statement*.

6 Conclusion

To the best of our knowledge, the NLI Shared Task 2017 fusion track was the first shared task to provide both written and spoken data for NLI. It was an interesting opportunity to evaluate the performance of NLI methods beyond written texts.

In this paper we highlighted the overlap between NLI and dialect, language variety, and similar language identification and used an approach that achieved high results in both tasks. We applied an SVM ensemble approach trained character n-grams achieving competitive results of 83.55% accuracy ranking 3rd in the fusion track.

Even though the results obtained by our approach were not low, we believe that there is still room for improvement. In previous shared tasks (e.g. NLI 2013, DSL 2015, and ADI 2016) we observed that SVM ensembles ranked higher in the results tables than our method did in the NLI 2017. We are investigating whether the combination of features or the implementation itself can be optimized for better performance.

Acknowledgements

We would like to thank the NLI Shared Task 2017 organizers for making the dataset available and for replying promptly to all our inquiries. We further thank the anonymous reviewers for their valuable feedback.

Liviu P. Dinu is supported by UEFISCDI, project number 53BG/2016.

References

Yves Bestgen. 2017. Improving the Character Ngram Model for the DSL Task with BM25 Weighting and Less Frequently Used Feature Sets. In *Proceedings of the Fourth Workshop on NLP for Similar Languages, Varieties and Dialects (VarDial)*. Valencia, Spain, pages 115–123.

Daniel Blanchard, Joel Tetreault, Derrick Higgins, Aoife Cahill, and Martin Chodorow. 2013. Toefl11: A corpus of non-native english. Technical report, Educational Testing Service.

Victoria Bobicev. 2013. Native language identification with ppm. In *Proceedings of the Eighth Workshop on Innovative Use of NLP for Building Educational Applications*. Atlanta, Georgia, pages 180–187.

Victoria Bobicev. 2015. Discriminating between similar languages using ppm. In *Proceedings of the Joint Workshop on Language Technology for Closely Related Languages, Varieties and Dialects (LT4VarDial)*. Hissar, Bulgaria, pages 59–65.

Ondrej Bojar, Rajen Chatterjee, Christian Federmann, Yvette Graham, Barry Haddow, Matthias Huck, Antonio Jimeno Yepes, Philipp Koehn, Varvara Logacheva, Christof Monz, et al. 2016. Findings of the 2016 Conference on Machine Translation. In *Proceedings of WMT*.

Julian Brooke and Graeme Hirst. 2012. Measuring Interlanguage: Native Language Identification with L1-influence Metrics. In *Proceedings of Language Resources and Evaluation (LREC)*. pages 779–784.

Serhiy Bykh and Detmar Meurers. 2014. Exploring Syntactic Features for Native Language Identification: A Variationist Perspective on Feature Encoding and Ensemble Optimization. In *Proceedings of COLING 2014, the 25th International Conference on Computational Linguistics: Technical Papers*. Dublin, Ireland, pages 1962–1973.

Serhiy Bykh, Sowmya Vajjala, Julia Krivanek, and Detmar Meurers. 2013. Combining shallow and linguistically motivated features in native language identification. In *Proceedings of the Eighth Workshop on Innovative Use of NLP for Building Educational Applications*. Atlanta, Georgia, pages 197–206.

Rong-En Fan, Kai-Wei Chang, Cho-Jui Hsieh, Xiang-Rui Wang, and Chih-Jen Lin. 2008. LIBLINEAR: A Library for Large Linear Classification. *Journal of Machine Learning Research* 9:1871–1874.

Binyam Gebrekidan Gebre, Marcos Zampieri, Peter Wittenburg, and Tom Heskes. 2013. Improving native language identification with tf-idf weighting. In *Proceedings of the Eighth Workshop on Innovative Use of NLP for Building Educational Applications*. Atlanta, Georgia, pages 216–223.

Cyril Goutte, Serge Léger, and Marine Carpuat. 2013. Feature space selection and combination for native language identification. In *Proceedings of the Eighth Workshop on Innovative Use of NLP for Building Educational Applications*. Atlanta, Georgia, pages 96–100.

Cyril Goutte, Serge Léger, and Marine Carpuat. 2014. The nrc system for discriminating similar languages. In *Proceedings of the First Workshop on Applying NLP Tools to Similar Languages, Varieties and Dialects (VarDial)*. Dublin, Ireland, pages 139–145.

Cyril Goutte, Serge Léger, Shervin Malmasi, and Marcos Zampieri. 2016. Discriminating Similar Languages: Evaluations and Explorations. In *Proceedings of Language Resources and Evaluation (LREC)*.

John Henderson, Guido Zarrella, Craig Pfeifer, and John D. Burger. 2013. Discriminating non-native english with 350 words. In *Proceedings of the Eighth Workshop on Innovative Use of NLP for Building Educational Applications*. Atlanta, Georgia, pages 101–110.

Radu Tudor Ionescu. 2015. A Fast Algorithm for Local Rank Distance: Application to Arabic Native Language Identification. In *Proceedings of the International Conference on Neural Information Processing*. Springer, pages 390–400.

Radu Tudor Ionescu and Andrei Butnaru. 2017. Learning to identify arabic and german dialects using multiple kernels. In *Proceedings of the Fourth Workshop on NLP for Similar Languages, Varieties and Dialects (VarDial)*. Valencia, Spain, pages 200–209.

Radu Tudor Ionescu and Marius Popescu. 2016. UnibucKernel: An Approach for Arabic Dialect Identification Based on Multiple String Kernels. In *Proceedings of the Third Workshop on NLP for Similar Languages, Varieties and Dialects (VarDial3)*. Osaka, Japan, pages 135–144.

Scott Jarvis, Yves Bestgen, and Steve Pepper. 2013. Maximizing classification accuracy in native language identification. In *Proceedings of the Eighth Workshop on Innovative Use of NLP for Building Educational Applications*. Atlanta, Georgia, pages 111–118.

André Lynum. 2013. Native language identification using large scale lexical features. In *Proceedings of the Eighth Workshop on Innovative Use of NLP for Building Educational Applications*. Atlanta, Georgia, pages 266–269.

Shervin Malmasi. 2016. *Native Language Identification: Explorations and Applications*. Ph.D. thesis.

Shervin Malmasi and Mark Dras. 2014. Finnish Native Language Identification. In *Proceedings of the Australasian Language Technology Association Workshop*.

Shervin Malmasi and Mark Dras. 2015. Language identification using classifier ensembles. In *Proceedings of the VarDial Workshop*.

Shervin Malmasi, Mark Dras, and Marcos Zampieri. 2016a. LTG at SemEval-2016 Task 11: Complex Word Identification with Classifier Ensembles. In *Proceedings of SemEval*.

Shervin Malmasi, Keelan Evanini, Aoife Cahill, Joel Tetreault, Robert Pugh, Christopher Hamill, Diane Napolitano, and Yao Qian. 2017. A Report on the 2017 Native Language Identification Shared Task. In *Proceedings of the 12th Workshop on Building Educational Applications Using NLP*. Copenhagen, Denmark.

Shervin Malmasi, Sze-Meng Jojo Wong, and Mark Dras. 2013. Nli shared task 2013: Mq submission. In *Proceedings of the Eighth Workshop on Innovative Use of NLP for Building Educational Applications*. Atlanta, Georgia, pages 124–133.

Shervin Malmasi and Marcos Zampieri. 2016. Arabic Dialect Identification in Speech Transcripts. In *Proceedings of the Third Workshop on NLP for Similar Languages, Varieties and Dialects (VarDial3)*. Osaka, Japan, pages 106–113.

Shervin Malmasi, Marcos Zampieri, Nikola Ljubešić, Preslav Nakov, Ahmed Ali, and Jörg Tiedemann. 2016b. Discriminating between similar languages and arabic dialect identification: A report on the third dsl shared task. In *Proceedings of the 3rd Workshop on Language Technology for Closely Related Languages, Varieties and Dialects (VarDial)*. Osaka, Japan.

Tomoya Mizumoto, Yuta Hayashibe, Keisuke Sakaguchi, Mamoru Komachi, and Yuji Matsumoto. 2013. Naist at the nli 2013 shared task. In *Proceedings of the Eighth Workshop on Innovative Use of NLP for Building Educational Applications*. Atlanta, Georgia, pages 134–139.

F. Pedregosa, G. Varoquaux, A. Gramfort, V. Michel, B. Thirion, O. Grisel, M. Blondel, P. Prettenhofer, R. Weiss, V. Dubourg, J. Vanderplas, A. Passos, D. Cournapeau, M. Brucher, M. Perrot, and E. Duchesnay. 2011. Scikit-learn: Machine Learning in Python. *Journal of Machine Learning Research* 12:2825–2830.

Marius Popescu and Radu Tudor Ionescu. 2013. The story of the characters, the dna and the native language. In *Proceedings of the Eighth Workshop on Innovative Use of NLP for Building Educational Applications*. Atlanta, Georgia, pages 270–278.

Björn Schuller, Stefan Steidl, Anton Batliner, Julia Hirschberg, Judee K. Burgoon, Alice Baird, Aaron Elkins, Yue Zhang, Eduardo Coutinho, and Keelan Evanini. 2016. The INTERSPEECH 2016 Computational Paralinguistics Challenge: Deception, Sincerity & Native Language. In *Proceedings of Interspeech*. pages 2001–2005.

Joel Tetreault, Daniel Blanchard, and Aoife Cahill. 2013. A Report on the First Native Language Identification Shared Task. In *Proceedings of the Eighth Workshop on Building Educational Applications Using NLP*. Atlanta, GA, USA.

Yulia Tsvetkov, Naama Twitto, Nathan Schneider, Noam Ordan, Manaal Faruqui, Victor Chahuneau, Shuly Wintner, and Chris Dyer. 2013. Identifying the l1 of non-native writers: the cmu-haifa system. In *Proceedings of the Eighth Workshop on Innovative Use of NLP for Building Educational Applications*. Atlanta, Georgia, pages 279–287.

Lan Wang, Masahiro Tanaka, and Hayato Yamana. 2016. What is your Mother Tongue?: Improving Chinese Native Language Identification by Cleaning Noisy Data and Adopting BM25. In *Proceedings of the International Conference on Big Data Analysis (ICBDA)*. IEEE, pages 1–6.

Ching-Yi Wu, Po-Hsiang Lai, Yang Liu, and Vincent Ng. 2013. Simple yet powerful native language identification on toefl11. In *Proceedings of the Eighth Workshop on Innovative Use of NLP for Building Educational Applications*. Atlanta, Georgia, pages 152–156.

Yang Xiang, Xiaolong Wang, Wenying Han, and Qinghua Hong. 2015. Chinese Grammatical Error Diagnosis Using Ensemble Learning. In *Proceedings of the 2nd Workshop on Natural Language Processing Techniques for Educational Applications*. pages 99–104.

Marcos Zampieri, Binyam Gebrekidan Gebre, Hernani Costa, and Josef van Genabith. 2015a. Comparing approaches to the identification of similar languages. In *Proceedings of the Joint Workshop on Language Technology for Closely Related Languages, Varieties and Dialects (LT4VarDial)*. Hissar, Bulgaria, pages 66–72.

Marcos Zampieri, Shervin Malmasi, Nikola Ljubešić, Preslav Nakov, Ahmed Ali, Jörg Tiedemann, Yves Scherrer, and Noëmi Aepli. 2017. Findings of the VarDial Evaluation Campaign 2017. In *Proceedings of the Fourth Workshop on NLP for Similar Languages, Varieties and Dialects (VarDial)*. Valencia, Spain, pages 1–15.

Marcos Zampieri, Liling Tan, Nikola Ljubešić, and Jörg Tiedemann. 2014. A Report on the DSL Shared Task 2014. In *Proceedings of the First Workshop on Applying NLP Tools to Similar Languages, Varieties and Dialects (VarDial)*. Dublin, Ireland, pages 58–67.

Marcos Zampieri, Liling Tan, Nikola Ljubešić, Jörg Tiedemann, and Preslav Nakov. 2015b. Overview of the dsl shared task 2015. In *Proceedings of the Joint Workshop on Language Technology for Closely Related Languages, Varieties and Dialects (LT4VarDial)*. Hissar, Bulgaria, pages 1–9.

Native Language Identification using Phonetic Algorithms

Charese Smiley
Indiana University
Bloomington, IN 47405
chsmiley@indiana.edu

Sandra Kübler
Indiana University
Bloomington, IN 47405
skuebler@indiana.edu

Abstract

In this paper, we discuss the results of the IUCL system in the NLI Shared Task 2017. For our system, we explore a variety of phonetic algorithms to generate features for Native Language Identification. These features are contrasted with one of the most successful type of features in NLI, character n-grams. We find that although phonetic features do not perform as well as character n-grams alone, they do increase overall F1 score when used together with character n-grams.

1 Introduction

Native Language Identification (NLI) is the task of automatically predicting the native language (L1) of a speaker given an unlabeled artifact such as a writing sample or speech transcript in a second language (L2). In a typical encounter with a non-native speaker, humans have a variety of contextual clues such as race, approximate age, style of dress, and accent to assist us in making a prediction about the person's native language. However, when predicting L1 relying on features that can be extracted from text alone, we must proceed without the assistance of these visual and acoustic signals. Acoustic cues can be an important source of information since speakers often transfer characteristics of their L1 onto L2. For example, a Japanese L1 speaker may transfer the rigid CV syllable structure onto English and epenthesize vowels into consonant clusters, which may also be reflected in writing. Thus, having phonetic information may prove useful in an NLI classification task. However, we need to make sure that the features we add can be acquired from text and do not contribute to data sparsity. For the IUCL system in the Native Language Identification Shared Task (Mal-

masi et al., 2017), we began with the premise that acoustic features lost in text are important for language identification and they can be reconstructed using pseudo-auditory features derived from phonetic algorithms that were developed for robust matching in text search. Additionally, we explore a dictionary lookup that provides a phonetic representation of the words in text.

English orthography is rich, complex, and at times idiosyncratic. Using phonetic algorithms, we can reduce some of this complexity by producing a phonetic representation of a word through a series of transformations that map characters and character sequences with similar pronunciation to a single representation such as mapping both <ph> and <f> → <f>. To our knowledge, phonetic algorithms have not been explored to generate features for NLI.

2 Related Work

The first NLI Shared Task was part of the 2013 Building Educational Applications (BEA) workshop (Tetreault et al., 2013). Participants received the training portion of the TOEFL11 corpus and were asked to identify the native language of the essay writer from among a closed set of 11 languages available in the corpus. Scoring was based on classification accuracy on an unseen test set in 3 tasks: 1 closed training task where only training data provided in the TOEFL11 corpus could be used, and 2 open training tasks. In the first open training task, researchers could use any training data except for the TOEFL11 corpus. In the second task, they could use any training data *including* the TOEFL11 corpus.

Both character-level and word-level n-grams have featured prominently in past work. Character n-grams ranging from lengths 1-9 have been used (Tetreault et al., 2013). Early work featuring

Proceedings of the 12th Workshop on Innovative Use of NLP for Building Educational Applications, pages 405–412
Copenhagen, Denmark, September 8, 2017. ©2017 Association for Computational Linguistics

character bigrams is that of Tsur and Rappoport (2007), which achieved 66% accuracy in 5-way classification. They suggested that character features can serve as a proxy for phonology and that learners' word choices in essays are influenced by their native language. That is, learners gravitate to words in the target language whose phonology matched that of their native language while avoiding words that do not. This tendency can be captured at the character level.

Word-level n-grams have been widely used in a variety of approaches (e.g. Bykh and Meurers, 2012; Jarvis et al., 2013). Traditionally, shorter n-grams with lengths of 1-3 characters are more useful for computational tasks due to the data sparsity that ensues as the length of the n-gram increases. Bykh and Meurers (2012), however, used longest recurring n-grams that appeared in 2 or more essays with good results, perhaps capturing longer collocations and set phrases used by learners from specific L1s. Wong and Dras (2009) and Jarvis et al. (2013) found that both character features and lexical features are effective but classification accuracy deteriorated when both feature types are used together.

Part-of-speech n-grams also feature widely in previous work (Koppel et al., 2005a,b; Wong and Dras, 2009). Lexical n-grams have been shown to outperform POS n-grams for classification accuracy (Bykh and Meurers, 2012). The traditional motivation for the use of POS n-grams is based on the assumption that they abstract away from the confounding effect of essay topic (Koppel et al., 2005a,b; Wong and Dras, 2009). However, POS tag sequences may still be topic dependent. For instance, an opinion piece may contain more personal pronouns than a scientific paper. Brooke and Hirst (2011) suggest that the essay prompts may lend themselves to responses in different registers and the register may manifest itself beyond the lexicon.

Additionally, a number of studies have used syntactic features: context-free grammar (CFG) production rules (Wong and Dras, 2011; Bykh and Meurers, 2014), Tree Substitution Grammar (TSG) fragments (Swanson and Charniak, 2012), and Stanford Dependencies (Malmasi and Cahill, 2015).

3 Data

For the 2017 shared task, similar to the 2013 shared task (Tetreault et al., 2013), the data consists of essays from the same 11 L1s, with the test data drawn from a similar distribution as the original TOEFL11 corpus. In addition to the written text, transcripts of speech and i-vector acoustic features were included in the data release as they have shown promising results for dialect identification (Malmasi et al., 2016; Zampieri et al., 2017). The NLI 2017 shared task contains tracks for essay, speech transcript, and i-vectors alone as well as a fusion task combining all features. The IUCL system focuses exclusively on the essay task.

This dataset consisted of 11 L1s: Arabic (ARA), Chinese (CHI), French (FRE), German (GER), Hindi (HIN), Italian (ITA), Japanese (JPN), Korean (KOR), Spanish (SPA), Telugu (TEL), and Turkish (TUR). There were a total of 11,000 training essays (1,000 for each L1) and 1,100 development essays (100 for each L1). Additionally, the data contained the test taker id, essay prompt, and speech prompt. The distribution of essays by essay prompt for the development set, shown in Figure 1, varies by L1 with Arabic and Korean having the most balanced distribution among prompts and Turkish and Italian having the least.

4 Acoustic Features

Our system utilizes phonetic features for NLI. We explore 3 algorithms that were developed for robust matching: Soundex (section 4.1), Double Metaphone (DMETA) (section 4.2), and the New York State Identification and Intelligence System (NYSIIS) (section 4.3).[1] Soundex relies on simple conversion rules that mostly ignore vowels and groups consonants together by place of articulation in the mouth. The approach abstracts over issues of 1-to-many sound-symbol correspondence in English. For example, the sound /ks/ can be written as both <ks> and <x> as in *tacks* and *tax*. Soundex converts the two spellings to two different representations. In contrast, the NYSIIS and the Metaphone family of algorithms (Philips, 1990, 2000) go a step further to incorporate more of the peculiarities of English spelling, which is necessary for better mappings of homophones.

---

[1]Features were generated using the Fuzzy library
`https://pypi.python.org/pypi/Fuzzy`

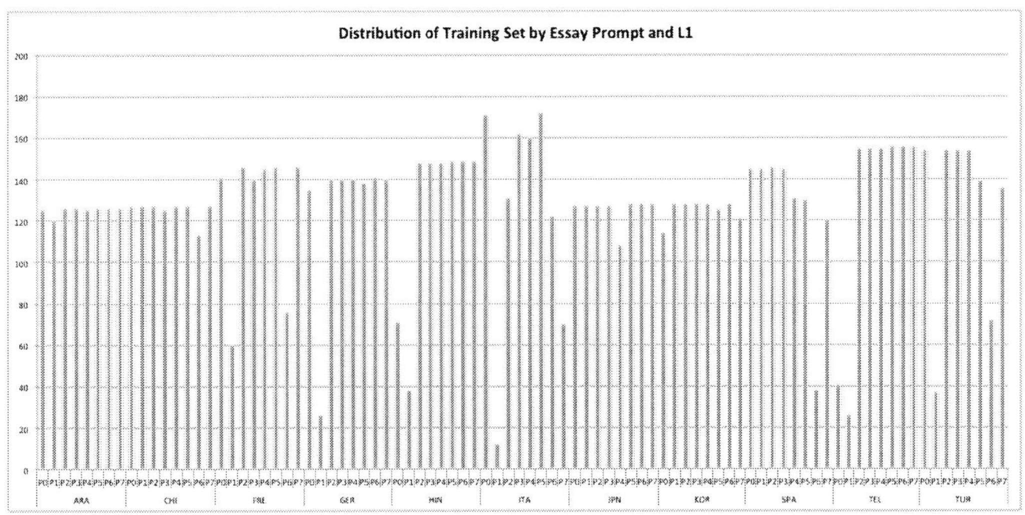

Figure 1: Distribution of data in the development set by number of essays per prompt for each L1.

Thus, all of these algorithms abstract away from specific types of acoustic distinctions, but they differ in which distinctions they ignore.

Finally, we also use the Carnegie Mellon University Pronouncing Dictionary (CMU) (section 4.4) which provides a lookup for the pronunciation of known words. This has the added benefit of providing more accurate mappings than a rule-based converter would and thus a better handling of known words. Moreover, the CMU dictionary can differentiate different vowel sounds where the other algorithms cannot.

4.1 Soundex

Soundex (Knuth, 1973) is an early algorithm first patented in 1918. Under Soundex, the first letter of a word is retained (including all vowels and consonants), all other consonants are mapped to the numbers 1-6, and all other vowels, along with consonants <h>, <w>, and <y>, are dropped. Consonants are converted to numbers within the algorithm as follows: 1: *b, f, p, v*, 2: *c, g, j, k, q, s, x, z*, 3: *d, t*, 4: *l*, 5: *m,n*, and 6: *r*.

This conversion ensures that the consonants are divided roughly along places of articulation with 1 for labials, 2 for coronals and dorsals (excluding <l> and <r>), 3 for dentals, 4 for laterals, 5 for nasals, and 6 for rhotics. Repeated numbers after conversion, such as <mn>, which becomes 55, are reduced to a single number (e.g., 5). All words are normalized to a starting letter plus 3 digits by either omitting any remaining characters for longer words or appending zeros until there are 3 digits for shorter words. Table 1 shows an example sentence from the training set written by a Turkish speaker converted to keys using Soundex and the other algorithms in this paper. One of the the advantages of the Soundex algorithm is that it is easy to implement the small number of rules mapping from letters to numbers. However, since it does not take into account English spelling rules, words that do not sound very similar can end up mapped to the same key. For example, *Cajun* and *Cigna* both map to C250 (Philips, 1990). For our purposes, this means that adaptations of vowels along with adaptations where the place of articulation does not change are not represented in the features.

4.2 Double Metaphone

The original Metaphone phonetic algorithm (Philips, 1990), uses an inventory of 16 consonants, 0BFHJKLMNPRSTWXZ, where 0 stands for /θ/ and X for /ʃ/ or /tʃ/. All 21 orthographic English consonants are mapped to these 16, by collapsing some letters like <d> and <t> to <t>. Metaphone contains a number of improvements over Soundex. For example, the letter <c> is sometimes pronounced as /s/ and sometimes as /k/ and the Metaphone algorithm covers many of such cases whereas Soundex does not due to its more simplistic mapping strategy.

Building on the Metaphone algorithm, the Double Metaphone (DMETA) algorithm (Philips,

Algorithm	Key
Original	Furthermore in the past since the mothers were frequently hausewifes, they were able to follow their chidren's education.
Soundex	F636 I500 T000 P230 S520 T000 M362 W600 F625 H212 T000 W600 A140 T000 F400 T600 C365 E323
DMETA	FR0R AN 0 PST SNK 0 M0RS AR FRKN HSFS 0 AR APL T FL 0R XTRN ATKX
NYSIIS	FARTARNAR IN T PAST SANC T MATAR WAR FRAGANTLY HASAF TAY WAR ABL T FAL TAR CADRAN EDACATAN
CMU	FER1DHER0MAO2R IH0N DHAH0 PAE1ST SIH1NS DHAH0 MAH1DHER0Z WER0 FRIY1KWAH0NTLIY0 HHAOSUWAYFS DHEY1 WER0 , EY1BAH0L TUW1 FAA1LOW0 DHEH1R CHIHDRAHNZ EH2JHAH0KEY1SHAH0N

Table 1: Sample sentence represented using various phonetic algorithms

2000) includes many changes and improvements over the original algorithm. Following Soundex, DMETA originally retains the first vowel in words and returns a key with a maximum of 4 letters. Additionally, it collapses all vowels to the letter *A*, and as such the words *Auto* and *Otto*, for example, are mapped to the same key. It also combines the letters <p> and <b>, treats <y> and <w> as vowels (thus eliminating them in post word-initial contexts) and includes a number of modifications to account for spelling influences from foreign words. Finally, the Double Metaphone algorithm returns multiple keys for words that could be pronounced in alternate ways. However, for the use in the IUCL system, we only choose the first key provided since the algorithm favors the most common American pronunciation over other alternatives. As an example, consider Spanish borrowings with <ll> that could be pronounced in an Americanized way as /l/ (e.g. *armadillo, flotilla*) or in the Spanish way as /j/ (e.g. *tortilla, paella*). This is an issue for a rather small number of words, roughly 10% based on Phillips' sample, but should not be of much consequence for our application.[2]

4.3 NYSIIS

Similar to the Double Metaphone algorithm, the NYSIIS algorithm extends Soundex by encoding each letter with consideration for English spelling nuances rather than strict reliance on place of articulation. Unlike the previous two algorithms, NYSIIS maintains the position of vowels within the word but collapses them by converting all vowels to <A>. Also, some versions of NYSIIS maintain the entire key rather than limiting it to the first *N* letters (e.g. exactly 4 letters for Soundex and 1-4 for DMETA). However, word final <s> and <a> are removed. For the IUCL system, we use the non-truncated version of the key. Thus, NYSIIS retains more information in comparison to the previous two conversion algorithms.

4.4 CMU Pronunciations

The Carnegie Mellon University Pronouncing Dictionary (CMU)[3] is an open source dictionary that contains pronunciations for more than 134,000 English words using a set of 39 phonemes and stress markers for vowels. The previous algorithms were designed to minimize the differences between homophones and near homophones. However, since this dictionary was developed for use in automatic speech recognition (ASR) applications rather than text search, the mappings are based on the common pronunciations of American English words. For unknown words, we the LOGIOS Lexicon Tool[4] which generates a CMU pronunciation using letter-to-sound rules. Using this tool, the misspelled word *hausewifes* in Table 1 is converted into the the pronunciation HHAOSUWAYFS.

Soundex, DMETA, and NYSIIS all fall under the category of fuzzy matching algorithms. The original intention for these algorithms were to improve recall when searching for names where the exact spelling is unknown or uncertain and they

---

[2]There is a newer version of the Metaphone algorithm, Metaphone 3 which is available for commercial use but the details remain unpublished.

[3]http://www.speech.cs.cmu.edu/cgi-bin/cmudict

[4]http://www.speech.cs.cmu.edu/tools/lextool.html

still enjoy widespread use in search applications. The main advantage for using algorithmic phonetic converters such as these is that they can produce a key as output no matter word is given as input. This has an advantage over dictionary-based methods like CMU which, under its pure implementation, fails when a word (such as a proper name or misspelling) falls outside of its internal list, however large. On the other hand, dictionary methods like CMU have the advantage of producing a more nuanced and accurate key for known words. This is especially true when it comes to representation of vowels. All of the other phonetic algorithms mentioned in this paper either collapse all vowels to a common representation or eliminate them in non-word-initial positions whereas in Table 1 we see that the CMU output most closely resembles the original words.

4.5 Experimental Setup

For all experiments, we use the C-Support Vector Classifier implementation in scikit-learn with a linear kernel.[5] For feature values, rather than using a frequency count matrix for features in the document, the TF-IDF score for the term is used instead. TF is the term frequency, i.e., the number of occurrences of a term in a document. IDF is the inverse document frequency, which is calculated by dividing the total number of documents in a corpus by the number of documents containing term t (if t is not equal 0). The application of TF-IDF weighting has been used to good effect in previous research (Gebre et al., 2013).

The benefit of using TF-IDF weighting in this task is that it dampens the effect of terms that are well dispersed throughout the corpus while emphasizing terms that occur less frequently and only within a smaller set of documents. For NLI, TF-IDF weighting is useful for capturing and amplifying the effects of vocabulary choices that are L1-specific. When using binary features, for example, only the presence or absence of a feature is recorded. This effectively weights rare features, such as low frequency words and spelling errors, the same as common features, such as function words. In contrast, TF-IDF gives a measure of the informativeness of a word since a word that appears in many documents will have a lower IDF than one that rarely occurs. Therefore, terms that

[5]http://scikit-learn.org/stable/
modules/generated/sklearn.svm.SVC.html

System	F1 (macro)	Accuracy
Random baseline	0.0909	0.0909
Essay baseline	0.7104	0.7109
Soundex	0.7455	0.7473
CMU	0.7629	0.7627
DMETA	0.7697	0.7727
NYSIIS	0.7830	0.7836
Char[†]	0.8206	0.8209
Char+CMU	0.8147	0.8145
Char+NYSIIS	0.8190	0.8191
Char+DMETA[†]	**0.8262**	**0.8264**
Char+Soundex	**0.8300**	**0.8300**

Table 2: Essay track results. Systems marked by † were submitted as part of the official NLI Shared Task. The remaining systems were submitted outside of the official testing phase.

receive a high TF-IDF score will occur with high frequency in a small number of documents.

All experiments were conducted using character n-grams of length 2-9. Additionally, we restricted the minimum document frequency to 5 documents and the maximum to 5% of documents in the training set.

5 Results

We show the results of the different feature sets in Table 2. All approaches perform well above the random baseline of 0.0909 (1/11) and above the shared task baseline of 0.7104 for the 11-way classification task. Results for the single feature runs show that none of the algorithms outperformed basic character n-grams (Char) features, which result in an F1 of 0.8206. Of the phonetic algorithms, NYSIIS shows the highest performance while Soundex and the CMU dictionary approach do not fare well, reaching an F1 of 0.7455 and 0.7697 respectively. This shows that the closest modeling of pronunciation is not helpful for the task. When we combine character-based features with the acoustic features, we observe that all combinations show improvements over the acoustic-only features. Additionally, combining with DMETA and Soundex results in higher performance than character n-grams alone, reaching an F1 of 0.8262 and 0.8300 respectively. The highest performing acoustic-only model, NYSIIS, shows the least improvement, which indicates that the features extracted from this particular conversion are harmful when combined with character n-grams. One

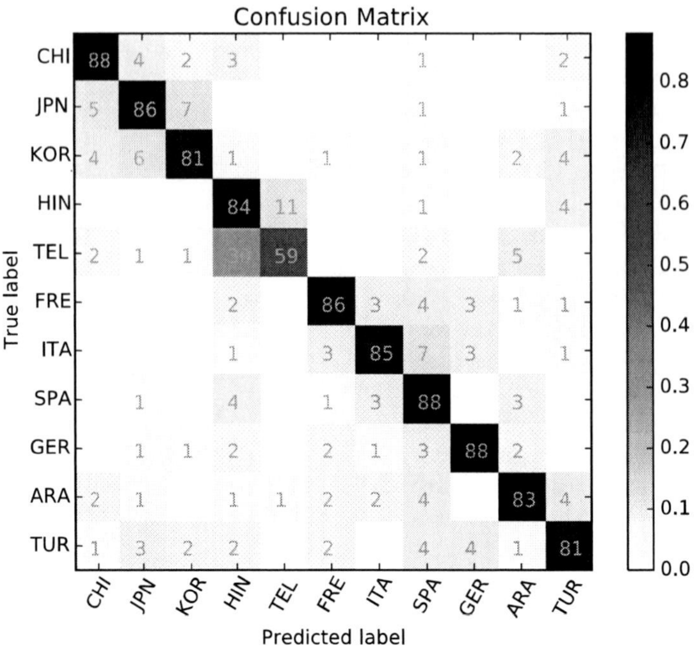

Figure 2: Confusion matrix for best official run, Char+DMETA

possible reason can be found in the higher number of features provided by NYSIIS as opposed to Soundex and DMETA since NYSIIS does not truncate the acoustic representation. However, this requires further investigation.

6 Discussion

Overall, we see that phonetic algorithms do not perform as well as character n-grams for NLI. One reason for this could be that by mapping characters to a simpler representation, important information is lost. For example, one of the most common misspellings for Arabic speakers is *becouse* but it would be rendered the same as *because* by all of the phonetic algorithms except for CMU. Information losses such as this could account for the reduced performance of phonetic algorithms as compared to character n-grams.

On the other hand, the advantage of phonetic algorithms is that commonly used phrases such as *for many reasons* (common among Arabic speakers) can be collapsed into one feature and captured even when minor spelling differences exist (especially if those errors have to do with vowels or consonant sounds that are close in place of articulation).

One of the most informative phrases in for Turk-

ish L1 writers was ATKX SSTM (DMETA) and E323 S235 (Soundex) which translates to 'education system'. Table 3 shows all of the variants of both words found in the training and development data with the variants for Turkish L1 writers shown in italics. Both DMETA and Soundex capture a wide range of variants including spelling errors and various parts-of-speech. As Table 3 demonstrates, Soundex is much more aggressive in combining words that do not sound as similar (e.g. *sixteen, scouting, skidding*) into a single key (S235). Overall, the power of DMETA and Soundex is that used in conjunction with other features, such as character n-grams, these types of features are able to take advantage of longer phrases even when they include spelling errors.

We reach the highest results in the official testing phase of the NLI Shared Task 2017 with the combination of character n-grams with DMETA features, which surpasses the character features by about 0.5% absolute and the DMETA features by about 5.6% absolute. Outside of the testing phase, our best run combined character n-grams with Soundex, surpassing character features by 0.9% absolute and Soundex alone by roughly 8.5% absolute. This shows that the phonetic conversion plus abstraction provides novel information that is

DMETA	education	educationaly, aducation, eeducational, educuation, *education*, aducational, edication, educationnal, *educations*, educationally, eduacation, edcation, ediocation, educationals, *educational*, edccationat
	system	systmatting, *systems*, *systematic*, *systematical*, sistm, systamatically, sistematically, systamatic, *systematically*, syustem, sistem, sistemsm, sistems, *system*, sysytem, systeme, systam, systme
Soundex	education	educationnal, educuation, educaction, *educating*, educaters, edicted, *educations*, edged, etcetera, educaded, edcation, educates, educationalisties, edcucation, eduactional, ethusiastic, *educated*, edecationat, *educaton*, euthusiastic, *educate*, educathion, educationally, eduaacation, educoated, educatoion, *education*, ettiquittes, etcetra, educatin, *educational*, edcated, educationaly, ediocation, educative, educaed, edcucate, edication, educat, edcuate, eductional, eductions, eduacte, ethusiastically, educationals, *eductaion*, *educatinal*, edxtra, eduction, eduaction, eeducational, etctec, educatipn, educateted, educatiuonal, educatied, *educators*, *educator*
	system	sixteens, sustaining, sestem, sistuations, seesighting, sstem, systemic, sostinable, *systems*, *systematic*, sixteen, *suggesting*, scitients, schedume, *sugestions*, *systematical*, *sustainable*, skidding, sustained, *sustainablity*, sketing, seggestion, sistematically, systamatic, sustan, sostitution, scation, sustanable, societyhence, sighting, sighteeing, *systematically*, skaiting, sustantiated, sustanining, *sections*, sistem, *succeeding*, sucseedments, sistemsm, sistems, section, *sugestion*, sightings, sustaine, *system*, sistm, sstems, sysytem, sustainment, *suggestions*, *succeding*, systamatically, skating, *sustainability*, *sustain*, sustances, ssudents, *section*, sexteen, systmatting, scating, sostantable, suggetions, sesation, systeme, scouting, systam, systme, suggesstion, syustem, *suggestion*, sistuation, skatting, sixtenn, systen, suceeding, sastained, successding, suggestiong

Table 3: Variants of "education system" in the corpus that are collapsed by DMETA and Soundex. Words in italics are taken from Turkish L1 essays.

not captured in spelling directly.

We had a closer look at the errors that our system makes. Figure 2 shows a confusion matrix for the best setting using character and DMETA features. The table shows that the main weak point of the learner lies in confusing Hindi and Telugu. This is not surprising given the fact that Indians are often multilingual and speak more than two languages. Additionally, English is often used as a lingua franca on the Indian subcontinent with frequent contact from speakers from a variety of L1s resulting in highly similar linguistic patterns.

7 Conclusion and and Future Work

This paper explored NLI using feature sets derived from 3 phonetic algorithms and one dictionary-based lookup. We have shown that our system IUCL can profit from having access to acoustic features in addition to character n-grams. In the future, we plan to further explore variants of phonetic conversions in which we do not abbreviate the words but rather segment them into acoustic n-grams. Will will also explore how features derived from phonetic algorithms can be combined with other lexical and syntactic features.

References

Julian Brooke and Graeme Hirst. 2011. Native language detection with 'cheap' learner corpora. In *Conference of Learner Corpus Research (LCR2011)*. Louvain-la-Neuve, Belgium.

Serhiy Bykh and Detmar Meurers. 2012. Native language identification using recurring n-grams – investigating abstraction and domain dependence. In *Proceedings of COLING 2012*. Mumbai, India, pages 425–440. http://www.aclweb.org/anthology/C12-1027.

Serhiy Bykh and Detmar Meurers. 2014. Exploring Syntactic Features for Native Language Identification: A Variationist Perspective on Feature Encoding and Ensemble Optimization. In *Proceedings* of COLING 2014, the 25th International Conference on Computational Linguistics: Technical Papers. Dublin, Ireland, pages 1962–1973.

Binyam Gebrekidan Gebre, Marcos Zampieri, Peter Wittenburg, and Tom Heskes. 2013. Improving native language identification with tf-idf weighting. In *the 8th NAACL Workshop on Innovative Use of NLP for Building Educational Applications (BEA8)*. pages 216–223.

Scott Jarvis, Yves Bestgen, and Steve Pepper. 2013. Maximizing Classification Accuracy in Native Language Identification. In *Proceedings of the Eighth Workshop on Innovative Use of NLP for Building Educational Applications*. Association for Computational Linguistics, Atlanta, Georgia, pages 111–118.

Donald E Knuth. 1973. *The Art of Computer Programming*, Addison-Wesley, Reading, MA, volume 3, chapter Sorting and Searching.

Moshe Koppel, Jonathan Schler, and Kfir Zigdon. 2005a. Automatically determining an anonymous author's native language. In *International Conference on Intelligence and Security Informatics*. Atlanta, GA, pages 41–76.

Moshe Koppel, Jonathan Schler, and Kfir Zigdon. 2005b. Determining an author's native language by mining a text for errors. In *Proceedings of the Eleventh ACM SIGKDD International Conference on Knowledge Discovery in Data Mining*. Chicago, IL, pages 624–628.

Shervin Malmasi and Aoife Cahill. 2015. Measuring feature diversity in native language identification. In *Proceedings of the Tenth Workshop on Innovative Use of NLP for Building Educational Applications (BEA)*. Denver, CO, pages 49–55.

Shervin Malmasi, Keelan Evanini, Aoife Cahill, Joel Tetreault, Robert Pugh, Christopher Hamill, Diane Napolitano, and Yao Qian. 2017. A Report on the 2017 Native Language Identification Shared Task. In *Proceedings of the 12th Workshop on Building Educational Applications Using NLP*. Copenhagen, Denmark.

Shervin Malmasi, Marcos Zampieri, Nikola Ljubešić, Preslav Nakov, Ahmed Ali, and Jörg Tiedemann. 2016. Discriminating between Similar Languages and Arabic Dialect Identification: A Report on the Third DSL Shared Task. In *Proceedings of the VarDial Workshop*. Osaka, Japan.

Lawrence Philips. 1990. Hanging on the metaphone. *Computer Language* 7(12).

Lawrence Philips. 2000. The double metaphone search algorithm. *C/C++ Users Journal* 18(6):38–43.

Benjamin Swanson and Eugene Charniak. 2012. Native Language Detection with Tree Substitution Grammars. In *Proceedings of the 50th Annual Meeting of the Association for Computational Linguistics (Volume 2: Short Papers)*. Association for Computational Linguistics, Jeju Island, Korea, pages 193–197. http://www.aclweb.org/anthology/P12-2038.

Joel Tetreault, Daniel Blanchard, and Aoife Cahill. 2013. A Report on the First Native Language Identification Shared Task. In *Proceedings of the Eighth Workshop on Building Educational Applications Using NLP*. Association for Computational Linguistics, Atlanta, GA, USA.

Oren Tsur and Ari Rappoport. 2007. Using Classifier Features for Studying the Effect of Native Language on the Choice of Written Second Language Words. In *Proceedings of the Workshop on Cognitive Aspects of Computational Language Acquisition*. Association for Computational Linguistics, Prague, Czech Republic, pages 9–16. http://www.aclweb.org/anthology/W/W07/W07-0602.

Sze-Meng Jojo Wong and Mark Dras. 2009. Contrastive Analysis and Native Language Identification. In *Proceedings of the Australasian Language Technology Association Workshop 2009*. Sydney, Australia, pages 53–61. http://www.aclweb.org/anthology/U09-1008.

Sze-Meng Jojo Wong and Mark Dras. 2011. Exploiting Parse Structures for Native Language Identification. In *Proceedings of the 2011 Conference on Empirical Methods in Natural Language Processing*. Association for Computational Linguistics, Edinburgh, Scotland, UK., pages 1600–1610. http://www.aclweb.org/anthology/D11-1148.

Marcos Zampieri, Shervin Malmasi, Nikola Ljubešić, Preslav Nakov, Ahmed Ali, Jörg Tiedemann, Yves Scherrer, and Noëmi Aepli. 2017. Findings of the VarDial Evaluation Campaign 2017. In *Proceedings of the Fourth Workshop on NLP for Similar Languages, Varieties and Dialects (VarDial)*. Valencia, Spain, pages 1–15.

A deep-learning based native-language classification
by using a latent semantic analysis
for the NLI Shared Task 2017

Yoo Rhee Oh, Hyung-Bae Jeon [*], **Hwa Jeon Song,**
Yun-Kyung Lee, **Jeon-Gue Park**, and **Yun-Keun Lee**
Speech Intelligence Research Group,
Electronics and Telecommunications Research Institute, South Korea
{yroh,hbjeon,songhj,yunklee,jgp,yklee}@etri.re.kr

Abstract

This paper proposes a deep-learning based native-language identification (NLI) using a latent semantic analysis (LSA) as a participant (ETRI-SLP) of the NLI Shared Task 2017 (Malmasi et al., 2017) where the NLI Shared Task 2017 aims to detect the native language of an essay or speech response of a standardized assessment of English proficiency for academic purposes. To this end, we use the six unit forms of a text data such as character 4/5/6-grams and word 1/2/3-grams. For each unit form of text data, we convert it into a count-based vector, extract a 2000-rank LSA feature, and perform a linear discriminant analysis (LDA) based dimension reduction. From the count-based vector or the LSA-LDA feature, we also obtain the output prediction values of a support vector machine (SVM) based classifier, the output prediction values of a deep neural network (DNN) based classifier, and the bottleneck values of a DNN based classifier. In order to incorporate the various kinds of text-based features and a speech-based i-vector feature, we design two DNN based ensemble classifiers for late fusion and early fusion, respectively. From the NLI experiments, the F1 (macro) scores are obtained as 0.8601, 0.8664, and 0.9220 for the essay track, the speech track, and the fusion track, respectively. The proposed method has comparable performance to the top-ranked teams for the speech and fusion tracks, although it has slightly lower performance for the essay track.

---

[*]Corresponding author

1 Introduction

Native-language identification (NLI) can be used to improve the performance of automatic speech recognition (ASR) for non-native speakers using native-language (L1) specific ASR systems. NLI can also be used in a computer-assisted language learning system using the L1-specific target-language errors. A considerable body of research on NLI has been reported (Malmasi, 2016; Malmasi and Dras, 2015) and the developed approaches can be classified into text-based NLI (Tetreault et al., 2013), speech-based NLI (Malmasi et al., 2016), and text and speech based NLI (Zampieri et al., 2017). Among them, this paper focuses on the NLI of text and speech data for the NLI Shared Task 2017 (Malmasi et al., 2017).

The first NLI Shared Task aims to identify the L1 of the text data of an essay response (Tetreault et al., 2013). Notably, a part of the 2016 Computational Paralinguistics Challenge focuses on speech-based NLI (Schuller et al., 2016). This year, the goal of the NLI Shared Task 2017 is to detect the L1 of the essay and speech responses of a standardized assessment of English proficiency for academic purposes among eleven L1s, Arabic, Chinese, French, German, Hindi, Italian, Japanese, Korean, Spanish, Telugu, and Turkish. To this end, there are 11,000 training data set, 1,100 development data set, and 1,100 test data set. In addition, each data set contains the text of an essay response, the transcription text and 800-dimensional i-vector feature of a speech response, and the L1 annotation of the participant of essay and speech responses.

In this paper, we propose a deep-learning based NLI method using a latent semantic analysis (LSA) as a participant (ETRI-SLP) of the NLI Shared Task 2017. First, the higher-rank of an LSA feature is used to detect L1 information; the

413

Proceedings of the 12th Workshop on Innovative Use of NLP for Building Educational Applications, pages 413–422
Copenhagen, Denmark, September 8, 2017. ©2017 Association for Computational Linguistics

lower-rank of an LSA feature is used to detect document topic information (Jeon and Lee, 2016b; Bellegarda, 2000). Second, we adopt a state-of-the-art machine learning methods, a deep-learning method (Jeon and Lee, 2016a; Chung and Park, in review), for L1 classification using various kinds of text-based features and a speech-based feature.

2 Feature extraction of the proposed method

2.1 Data preparation

For the text data of the NLI Shared Task 2017 such as the text of an essay response and the transcription text of a speech response, we use six unit forms for each text: (a) word 1-gram, (b) word 2-gram, (c) word 3-gram, (d) character 4-gram, (e) character 5-gram, and (f) character 6-gram. It is assumed that a word n-gram could reveal L1-specific words (e.g. 'kimchi' is a Korean food name) and L1-specific word sequences while a character n-gram could capture L1-specific typing errors, L1-specific character sequence patterns, etc.

First, each unit of a text is converted into a count-based vector and then entropy normalization (Jeon and Lee, 2016b; Bellegarda, 2000) is applied to the count-based vector. Next, the normalized count-based vector (Raw^{count}) is used to extract the 2000-rank features of a latent semantic analysis (LSA) (Jeon and Lee, 2016b; Bellegarda, 2000). The LSA feature is subsequently compressed into 10-dimensional features using a linear discriminant analysis (LDA), which is referred to as $Raw^{LSA2000/LDA10}$ hereafter. It is assumed that the high-rank LSA features could capture the L1 characteristics.

For a speech data set of the NLI Shared Task 2017, we only use the 800-dimensional i-vector feature of each speech response, which is supported by the organizers (Malmasi et al., 2017). In addition, we apply LDA normalization to the i-vector features.

2.2 Feature extraction

We extract five kinds of features from the Raw^{count} or $Raw^{LSA2000/LDA10}$ of each unit form of a text for an L1 classification: (a) the output prediction values (SVM_{output}^{count}) of a SVM classifier using the Raw^{count}, (b) the output prediction values ($SVM_{output}^{LSA2000/LDA10}$) of a SVM classifier using the $Raw^{LSA2000/LDA10}$, (c) the out-

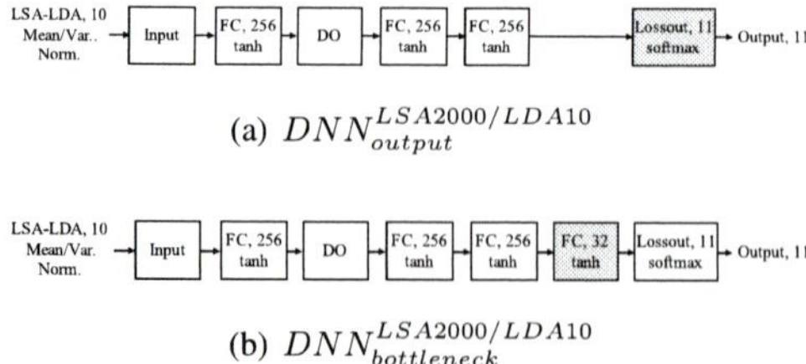

(a) $DNN_{output}^{LSA2000/LDA10}$

(b) $DNN_{bottleneck}^{LSA2000/LDA10}$

Figure 1: Configuration of the two DNNs for the $DNN_{output}^{LSA2000/LDA10}$ and the $DNN_{bottleneck}^{LSA2000/LDA10}$, respectively.

put prediction values ($DNN_{output}^{LSA2000/LDA10}$) of a DNN classifier using the $Raw^{LSA2000/LDA10}$, (d) the bottleneck (Grézl et al., 2007) values ($DNN_{bottleneck}^{LSA2000/LDA10}$) of the last hidden layer of a DNN classifier using the $Raw^{LSA2000/LDA10}$, and (e) the $Raw^{LSA2000/LDA10}$ itself.

For the SVM_{output}^{count} and $SVM_{output}^{LSA2000/LDA10}$, a linear kernel SVM is trained using SVM-Light tool (Joachims, 1999). In addition, two kinds of DNNs are trained for the $DNN_{output}^{LSA2000/LDA10}$ and $DNN_{bottleneck}^{LSA2000/LDA10}$, respectively, as shown in Fig. 1. In other words, the input features are normalized to a zero mean and unit variance and the output layer of each DNN is a softmax layer with eleven nodes that correspond to the eleven L1s. In order to prevent overfitting, dropout (DO) hidden layers are inserted. Moreover, each fully-connected (FC) hidden layer uses a hyperbolic tangent (tanh) activation function. As shown in Fig. 1(a), $DNN_{output}^{LSA2000/LDA10}$ consists of one input layer, four hidden layers, and one output layer. The first, third, and fourth hidden layers are FC layers where each layer contains 256 nodes, while the second hidden layer is a DO layer. On the other hand, the difference between $DNN_{bottleneck}^{LSA2000/LDA10}$ from $DNN_{output}^{LSA2000/LDA10}$ is that one additional hidden layer with 32 nodes is inserted before the output layer for bottleneck feature extraction, as shown in Fig. 1(b).

3 DNN based classifier for the NLI Shared Task 2017

For each text of the essay response and speech response transcription, thirty kinds of features are extracted by combining the six unit forms with the five feature types. Moreover, an 800-dimensional i-vector is extracted for each speech response signal. In order to combine the various features for

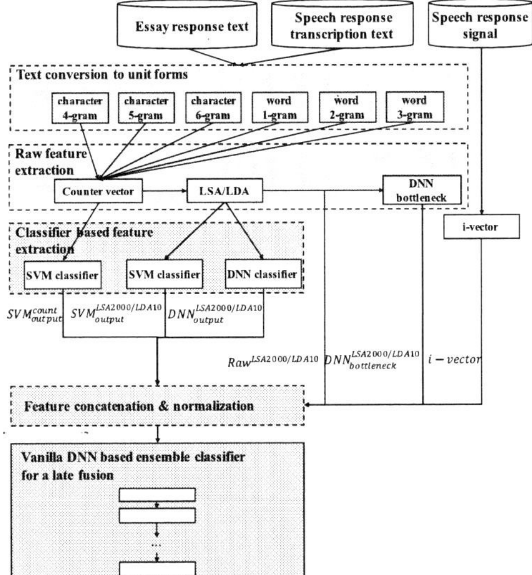

(a) A vanilla DNN based ensemble classifier for late fusion

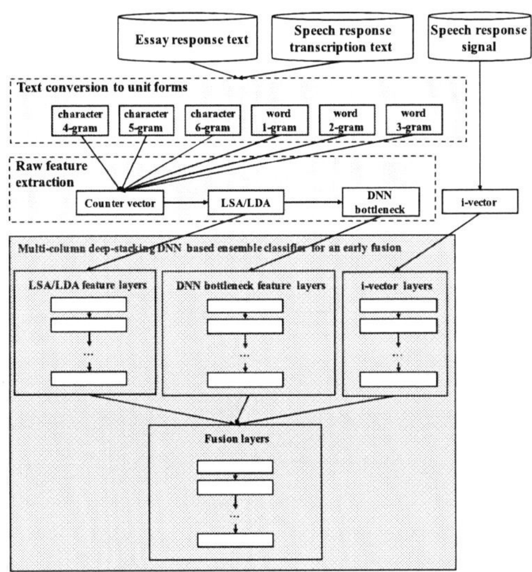

(b) A multi-column deep-stacking DNN based ensemble classifier for early fusion

Figure 2: The two kinds of DNN based ensemble classifiers for early fusion and late fusion, respectively.

the NLI Shared Task 2017, we design two DNN based classifiers: (a) a vanilla DNN based ensemble classifier for late fusion and (b) a multi-column deep-stacking DNN based ensemble classifier for early fusion, as shown in Fig. 2. Basically, each output layer of the proposed DNN based ensemble classifiers is a softmax layer with eleven nodes that correspond to the eleven native languages.

- **A vanilla DNN based ensemble classifier for late fusion**:

  A late fusion method (Snoek et al., 2005) is a feature combination method that generates a feature-based classifier corresponding to each feature and then performs classification using the output values of the feature-based classifiers. As shown in Fig. 2(a), the vanilla DNN based ensemble classifier is designed for late fusion using the output prediction values of the feature-based classifiers, SVM_{output}^{count}, $SVM_{output}^{LSA2000/LDA10}$, and $DNN_{output}^{LSA2000/LDA10}$. In other words, we concatenate the text-based and speech-based features including the output values of the feature-based classifiers and then apply the concatenated feature input data of the vanilla DNN based ensemble classifier for the fusion. Moreover, the vanilla DNN based ensemble classifier consists of one input layer, several hidden layers, and one output layer.

- **A multi-column deep-stacking DNN based ensemble classifier for early fusion**:

  An early fusion method (Snoek et al., 2005) is a feature combination method that fuses several kinds of features. As shown in Fig. 2(b), the multi-column (Ciresan et al., 2012) deep-stacking DNN based ensemble classifier is designed for early fusion. In other words, each feature is fed into the multi-column deep-stacking DNN and then linked to the corresponding feature layer. The node values of the last hidden layer of each feature-related layers are then connected to the input layer of the fusion-related layers. Moreover, the feature-related layers and fusion-related layers all have different configurations since the proposed multi-column deep-stacking DNN based ensemble classifier aims to efficiently combine heterogeneous features.

In particular, the overall network of the multi-column deep-stacking DNN based ensemble classifier is trained with a single objective function while the vanilla DNN based ensemble classifier is trained with multiple object functions such as (a) the objective functions for the feature-based classifiers and (b) the objective function for fusion. In this paper, SVM_{output}^{count}, $SVM_{output}^{LSA2000/LDA10}$, and $DNN_{output}^{LSA2000/LDA10}$ are used as feature-

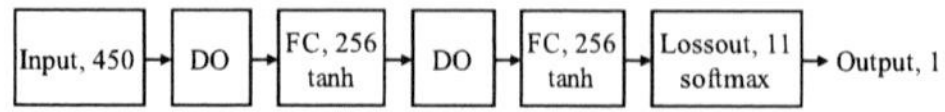

Figure 3: Configuration of the vanilla DNN based ensemble classifier for the essay track, where each block indicates a layer of the DNN and the number in a block indicates the number of nodes in the corresponding layer.

based classifiers for the vanilla DNN based ensemble classifier.

4 Results

This section presents the submitted experimental setups and the performances for the three tracks of the NLI Shared Task 2017: (a) the essay track using the texts of the essay responses, (b) the speech track using the transcription texts and i-vector features of the speech responses, and (c) the fusion track using both the texts of the essay responses and the transcription texts and i-vector features of the speech responses. In the experiments of the essay track, we also examine the performance of each unit form of a text while the feature combinations are examined in the experiments of the speech track. In addition, the performance is compared with the classification accuracy metric when evaluating the 1,100 development data set.

4.1 The experimental setup and its performances for the essay track

For the L1 detection of the essay track, we only used the vanilla DNN based ensemble classifier with the assumption that the text-related features were not extremely heterogeneous for each other. The submitted ETRI-SPL NLI system for the essay track was performed as follows.

We first transformed each text data into the six unit forms such as word 1/2/3-grams and character 4/5/6-grams. Then, we extracted the five features (SVM_{output}^{count}, $SVM_{output}^{LSA2000/LDA10}$, $DNN_{output}^{LSA2000/LDA10}$, $DNN_{bottleneck}^{LSA2000/LDA10}$, and $Raw^{LSA2000/LDA10}$) for each unit-transformed text. As a result, we obtained the thirty features for each text and then concatenated them into one 450-dimensional feature. The concatenated feature was then normalized to a zero mean and unit variance. After that, the normalized feature was fed into the input layer of a vanilla DNN based ensemble classifier. As shown in Fig. 3, the vanilla DNN based ensemble classifier for the essay track consisted of an input

Unit	Feature dimension	Norm. method	Accuracy
Official baseline			0.7236
word 1-gram $Raw^{LSA2000/LDA10}$	10	Mean/Var..	0.7764
word 2-gram $Raw^{LSA2000/LDA10}$	10	Mean/Var.	0.7909
word 3-gram $Raw^{LSA2000/LDA10}$	10	Mean/Var.	0.7045
character 4-gram $Raw^{LSA2000/LDA10}$	10	Mean/Var.	0.7736
character 5-gram $Raw^{LSA2000/LDA10}$	10	Mean/Var.	0.8064
character 6-gram $Raw^{LSA2000/LDA10}$	10	Mean/Var.	0.8164

Table 1: Performance comparison of each unit form of the $DNN_{output}^{LSA2000/LDA10}$ of the proposed method for the essay track when evaluating the development data, where 'Mean/Var.' indicates the normalization to the zero mean and unit variance.

layer, first and third DO hidden layers, second and fourth FC hidden layers, and an output layer. Each FC layer contained 256 nodes with a tanh activation function.

Prior to the performance comparison of the proposed ETRI-SPL NLI for the essay track, we evaluated the performance corresponding to each unit form. To this end, we extracted the six $Raw^{LSA2000/LDA10}$ features for the word 1/2/3-grams and character 4/5/6-grams, respectively. Then, we generated the vanilla DNN based ensemble classifier using each of the six features. After that, the six classifiers were evaluated for the development data. It was shown from the second, third, and fourth rows of Table 1 that the performances corresponding to the word n-grams were improved except for the word 3-gram when compared to the performance of the official baseline. It was noted that the performance degradation corresponding to the word 3-gram was occurred due to a data sparseness. Moreover, it was shown from the fifth, sixth, and seventh rows of the table that the performances corresponding to the character n-grams were improved according to the increase of the n-gram order. Especially, the performance corresponding to the character 6-gram outperformed among the others.

Next, we evaluated the performance corresponding to each feature type. In other words, we extracted each of the five feature types using the six unit forms of a text. After that, we generated the five vanilla DNN based ensemble classifiers corresponding to the feature types and then we measured the accuracy-based performance for the development data. As shown in the second, third, fourth, fifth, and sixth rows of Table 2, the accuracies were ranged from 0.8273 to 0.8364 for each classifier using the SVM_{output}^{count},

Feature	Feature dimension	Norm. method	Accuracy
Official baseline			0.7236
Late fusion: vanilla DNN based ensemble classifier			
(a) SVM_{output}^{count}	66	Mean/Var.	0.8345
(b) $SVM_{output}^{LSA2000/LDA10}$	66	Mean/Var.	0.8364
(c) $DNN_{output}^{LSA2000/LDA10}$	66	Mean/Var.	0.8345
(d) $DNN_{bottleneck}^{LSA2000/LDA10}$	192	Mean/Var.	0.8273
(e) $Raw^{LSA2000/LDA10}$	60	Mean/Var.	0.8318
(a)+(b)+(c)+(d)+(e) (**ETRI-SLP**)	450	Mean/Var.	0.8445

Table 2: Performance comparison of the proposed method for the essay track when evaluating the development set, where 'Mean/Var.' indicates the normalization to the zero mean and unit variance.

$SVM_{output}^{LSA2000/LDA10}$, $DNN_{output}^{LSA2000/LDA10}$, $DNN_{bottleneck}^{LSA2000/LDA10}$, and $Raw^{LSA2000/LDA10}$, respectively. Thus, it could be noted that each feature type successes to combine the six unit forms.

Finally, the accuracy of the proposed ETRI-SPL NLI for the essay track was 0.8445 using the thirty features by combining the six unit forms and the five feature types, as shown in the last row of the figure. When compared to the above rows of the figure, we concluded that the thirty features were well combined for the NLI.

4.2 The experimental setup and its performances for the speech track

For the L1 detection of the speech track using the transcription text and i-vector feature of a speech response, we used the multi-column deep-stacking DNN based ensemble classifier with the assumption that the text-related features were clearly heterogeneous to the speech-related i-vector feature. Moreover, we empirically selected the feature, $Raw^{LSA2000/LDA10}$, for the efficient combination with the text-related features and the i-vector feature. The submitted ETRI-SPL NLI for the speech track was performed as follows.

We first transformed each transcription text into the six unit forms and then extracted the $Raw^{LSA2000/LDA10}$ for each unit-transformed text. In addition, we used the 800-dimensional i-vector feature for each speech response signal. The text-related feature was then normalized to a zero mean and unit variance and the i-vector feature was normalized using a LDA normalization. As shown in Fig. 4(b), the $Raw^{LSA2000/LDA10}$ and i-vector features were fed into the LSA/LDA feature layers and the i-vector layers, respectively. The node values of the last hidden layer of each

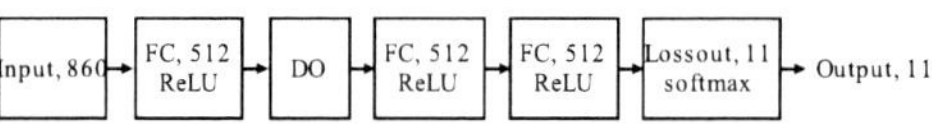

(a) Late fusion: vanilla DNN based ensemble classifier

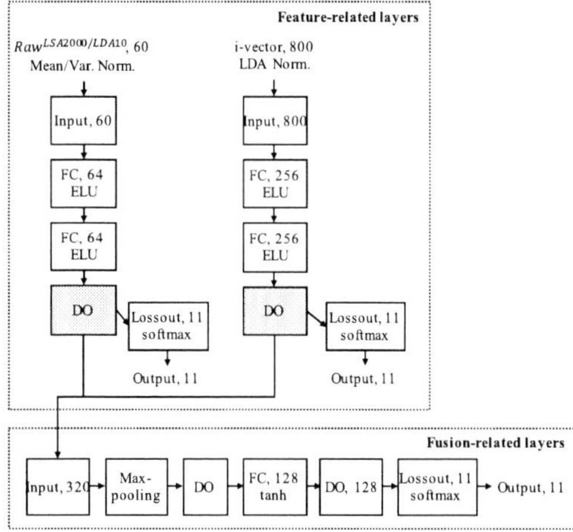

(b) Early fusion: multi-column deep-stacking DNN based ensemble classifier

Figure 4: Configuration of the two DNN based ensemble classifiers for the speech track, where each block indicates a layer of the DNN and the number in a block indicates the number of nodes in the corresponding layer.

feature layers were then connected to the input layer of the fusion layers. Each feature layers consisted of an input layer, the first and second FC hidden layers, the third DO hidden layer, and an output layer, where the FC layers contained 64 and 256 nodes for $Raw^{LSA2000/LDA10}$ and i-vector, respectively, with an exponential linear unit (ELU) activation function. And, the fusion layers consisted of an input layer, the first max-pooling hidden layer, the second and fourth DO hidden layers, the third FC hidden layer, and an output layer, where the FC layer contained 256 nodes with a tanh activation function.

Prior to the performance evaluation of the proposed ETRI-SPL NLI for the speech track, we evaluated the performance corresponding to each text-related feature, the i-vector feature, and the feature combinations using a vanilla DNN based ensemble classifier, as shown in Fig. 4(a). To this end, the extracted features were concatenated into one feature and then the concatenated feature was normalized using an LDA normalization since the i-vector feature was well matched with the LDA normalization rather than a normalization to a zero mean and unit variance. After that, the normalized feature was fed into the input layer of the vanilla

Feature	Feature dim.	Norm. method	Accuracy
Official baseline with transcription			0.5200
Official baseline with i-vector			0.7400
Official baseline with transcription & i-vector			0.7573
Early or Late fusion: vanilla DNN based ensemble classifier			
(a) SVM_{output}^{count}	66	LDA	0.4545
(b) $SVM_{output}^{LSA2000/LDA10}$	66	LDA	0.5827
(c) $DNN_{output}^{LSA2000/LDA10}$	66	LDA	0.5782
(d) $DNN_{bottleneck}^{LSA2000/LDA10}$	192	LDA	0.5764
(e) $Raw^{LSA2000/LDA10}$	60	LDA	0.5836
(f) i-vector	800	LDA	0.8082
(a)+(f) late fusion	866	LDA	0.5118
(b)+(f) late fusion	866	LDA	0.8245
(c)+(f) late fusion	866	LDA	0.6682
(d)+(f) early fusion	992	LDA	0.7345
(e)+(f) early fusion	860	LDA	0.8309
(b)+(c)+(f) late fusion	932	LDA	0.6627
(b)+(d)+(f) late fusion	1058	LDA	0.7127
(b)+(e)+(f) late fusion	926	LDA	0.8145
(c)+(d)+(f) late fusion	1058	LDA	0.6655
(c)+(e)+(f) late fusion	926	LDA	0.6609
(d)+(e)+(f) early fusion	1052	LDA	0.7155
(b)+(c)+(d)+(f) late fusion	1124	LDA	0.6673
(b)+(c)+(e)+(f) late fusion	992	LDA	0.6627
(b)+(d)+(e)+(f) late fusion	1118	LDA	0.7155
(c)+(d)+(e)+(f) late fusion	1118	LDA	0.6609
(b)+(c)+(d)+(e)+(f) late fusion	1184	LDA	0.6582
Early fusion: multi-column deep-stacking DNN based ensemble classifier			
(a)+(f)	866	Mean/Var./LDA	0.8109
(b)+(f)	866	Mean/Var./LDA	0.8527
(c)+(f)	866	Mean/Var./LDA	0.8473
(d)+(f)	992	Mean/Var./LDA	0.8491
(e)+(f)	860	Mean/Var./LDA	0.8591
(d)+(e)+(f)	1052	Mean/Var./LDA	0.8455
(d)'+(e)+(f) (ETRI-SLP)	1052	Mean/Var./LDA	0.8545

Table 3: Performance comparison of the proposed method for the speech track when evaluating the development data, where the underlined and the bolded represent the remarkable system and the submitted system, respectively. The 'early fusion' of the vanilla DNN based ensemble classifier indicates a classifier that uses no feature-based classifier. And, 'Mean/Var.' indicates a normalization to a zero mean and unit variance. The (d)' means the noisy data of the $DNN_{bottleneck}^{LSA2000/LDA10}$, which was an unexpected data.

DNN based ensemble classifier. The vanilla DNN based ensemble classifier consisted of an input layer, the first, third, and fourth FC hidden layers, the second DO hidden layer, and an output layer, where each FC hidden layer contained 512 nodes with a rectified linear unit (RELU) activation function. Also, it was noted that the number of nodes of the FC hidden layer was increased according to the increase of the dimension of the input feature data.

From the fourth row to the ninth row of Table 3, it was noted that the i-vector feature outperformed the text-related features. Among the text-related features, the LSA-LDA based features had better performances when compared to the count-based feature. From the tenth row to the fourteenth row of the table, the $SVM_{output}^{LSA2000/LDA10}$ and $Raw^{LSA2000/LDA10}$ improved the only i-vector feature when combining one text-related feature and the i-vector feature. However, it was shown from the fifteenth row to the twenty-fifth row of the table that the combination with two or more text-related features and the i-vector feature did not improve the combination with one text-related feature and the i-vector feature. It was summarized that there was no improvement on the combination with two or more text-related features since the text-related features had similar information using the same unit forms.

From the twenty-sixth row to the thirtieth row of the table, all the combinations of one text-related feature and the i-vector feature were improved using the multi-column deep-stacking DNN based ensemble classifier when compared to the use of one feature; only two features were improved using the vanilla DNN based ensemble classifier. Moreover, the thirty-first row of the table showed that the performance of the combination with the two text-related features and i-vector feature was slightly degraded; however, the degree of the performance degradation was marginal. Finally, the last row of the table presented the performance of the submitted system. In fact, the original intention was to combine the two text-related features and i-vector feature. Unfortunately, we found that the noisy data was inserted as the $DNN_{bottleneck}^{LSA2000/LDA10}$ after the submission. However, from the performance evaluation, we could examine that the multi-column deep-stacking DNN based ensemble classifier had the robust performance to a noisy data.

4.3 The experimental setup and its performances for the fusion track

For the L1 detection of the fusion track using the text of an essay response and the transcription text and i-vector feature of a speech response, we used the multi-column deep-stacking DNN based ensemble classifier. For the efficient combination with the text-related features and the speech i-vector feature, we empirically selected the $Raw^{LSA2000/LDA10}$ among non-classifier-based features. The submitted ETRI-SPL NLI for the fusion track was performed as

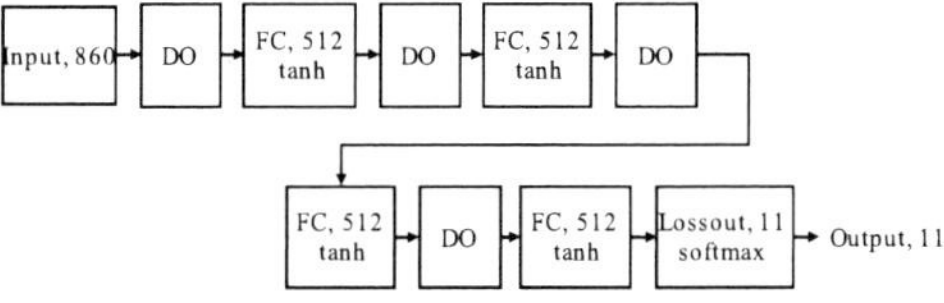

(a) Late fusion: vanilla DNN based ensemble classifier

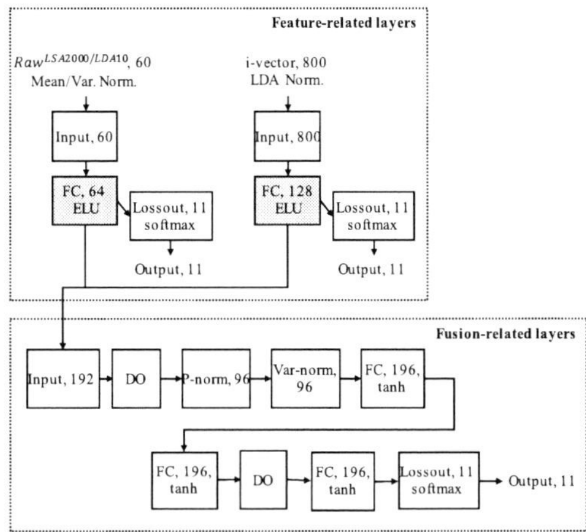

(b) Early fusion: multi-column deep-stacking DNN based ensemble classifier

Figure 5: Configuration of the two DNN based ensemble classifiers for the fusion track, where each block indicates a layer of a DNN and the number in a block indicates the number of nodes in the layer corresponding to a block.

Feature type	Feature dim.	Normalization method	Accuracy
Official baseline			0.7836
Late fusion: vanilla DNN based ensemble classifier			
(a) SVM_{output}^{count}	66	LDA	0.6309
(b) $SVM_{output}^{LSA2000/LDA10}$	66	LDA	0.8309
(c) $DNN_{output}^{LSA2000/LDA10}$	66	LDA	0.8518
(d) $DNN_{bottleneck}^{LSA2000/LDA10}$	192	LDA	0.8418
(e) $Raw^{LSA2000/LDA10}$	60	LDA	0.8291
(f) i-vectors	800	LDA	0.7900
(g) SVM_{output}^{count}	66	Mean/Var.	0.8582
(h) $SVM_{output}^{LSA2000/LDA10}$	66	Mean/Var.	0.8482
(i) $DNN_{output}^{LSA2000/LDA10}$	66	Mean/Var.	0.8400
(j) $DNN_{bottleneck}^{LSA2000/LDA10}$	192	Mean/Var.	0.8400
(k) $Raw^{LSA2000/LDA10}$	60	Mean/Var.	0.8473
(l) i-vectors	800	Mean/Var.	0.5864
(e)+(f) late fusion	860	LDA	0.9155
Early fusion: multi-column deep-stacking DNN based ensemble classifier			
(e)+(f) (ETRI-SLP)	860	Mean/Var./LDA	0.9164

Table 4: Performance comparison of the proposed method for the fusion track when evaluating the development data, where the bolded represent the submitted system. 'Mean/Var.' indicates a normalization to a zero mean and unit variance.

follows.

We first transformed each text of the essay and speech transcription into the six unit forms and then extracted the $Raw^{LSA2000/LDA10}$ for each unit-transformed text. To fuse an essay response and a speech response, the count-based vector of the speech transcription text was appended to the count-based vector of the essay text for each pair of an essay text and speech transcription text during the feature extraction of the $Raw^{LSA2000/LDA10}$. We also used the 800-dimensional i-vector feature of each speech response signal. The text-related features were then normalized to a zero mean and unit variance and the i-vector feature were normalized using a LDA normalization. As shown in Fig. 5(b), the $Raw^{LSA2000/LDA10}$ and i-vector features were fed into the LSA/LDA feature layers and the i-vector layers, respectively. The node values of the last hidden layer of each feature layers were then connected to the input layer of the fusion layers. Each feature layers consisted of an input layer, the FC hidden layer, and an output layer,

where the FC layers contained 64 and 128 nodes for $Raw^{LSA2000/LDA10}$ and i-vector, respectively, with an ELU activation function. And, the fusion layers consisted of an input layer, the first and sixth DO hidden layers, the fourth, fifth, and seventh FC hidden layers, the second p-norm pooling hidden layer, the third variance normalization hidden layer, and an output layer, where each FC layer contained 196 nodes with a tanh activation function and the p-norm and variance normalization layers contained 96 nodes.

Prior to the performance evaluation of the proposed ETRI-SPL NLI for the fusion track, we evaluated the performance corresponding to the $Raw^{LSA2000/LDA10}$, the i-vector feature, and the feature combination, respectively, using a vanilla DNN based ensemble classifier, as shown in Fig. 5(a). To this end, the extracted features were concatenated into one feature and then the concatenated feature was normalized using an LDA normalization. The normalized feature was then fed into the input layer of the vanilla DNN based ensemble classifier. The vanilla DNN based ensemble classifier consisted of an input layer, the first, third, fifth, and seventh DO hidden layers, the second, fourth, sixth, and eighth FC hidden layers, and an output layer, where each FC hidden layer contained 512 nodes with a tanh activation function.

It was shown from the second row to the seventh row of Table 4 that the LSA-LDA features had better performances than the count-based feature and i-vector feature when applying an LDA normalization. It was shown from the eighth row to the thirteenth row of the table that the count-based feature and i-vector feature were well matched with a normalization to a zero mean and unit variance and with an LDA normalization, respectively. From the fourteenth and fifteenth rows of the table, the two DNN based ensemble classifiers obtained the similar accuracies when using the same feature combination. It was noted from the experiments that the multi-column deep-stacking DNN based ensemble classifier worked better than the vanilla DNN based ensemble classifier when the features were heterogeneous and the performance differences were significant.

5 Performance of the test data set and discussions

This section first reports the official performance comparison based on the F1 (macro) score for the 1,100 test data set. Moreover, we present the official ranks that are grouped by a McNemar's test. Thus, we regard that the a same group has a comparable performance. After that, we conclude with our findings and discussions.

Table 5 and Fig. 6 present the performance comparisons and the confusion matrices of the submitted ETRI-SPL NLI systems for the essay track, the speech track, and the fusion track, respectively. For the essay track, the F1 (macro) scores are 0.7104, 0.8601, and 0.8818, for the baseline system, the ETRI-SPL system, and the ItaliaNLP (top-scored) system. In other words, the proposed system has the improved performance when compared to the baseline system; however, the proposed system has a slightly lower performance when compared to the top-scored system. For the speech track, the F1 (macro) scores are 0.7980, 0.8664, and 0.8755, for the baseline system, the ETRI-SPL system, and the UnibucKernel (top-scored) system. That is, the proposed system has the comparable performance to the top-scored system. For the fusion track, the F1 (macro) scores are 0.7901, 0.9220, and 0.9319, for the baseline system, the ETRI-SPL system, and the UnibucKernel (top-scored) system. That is, the proposed system also has the comparable performance to the top-scored system.

Track	Team	Rank group	F1 (macro)	Accuracy
Essay	Baseline	-	0.7104	0.7109
	ETRI-SLP	2	0.8601	0.8600
	ItaliaNLP (Top-scored)	1	0.8818	0.8818
Speech	Baseline	-	0.7980	0.7982
	ETRI-SLP	1	0.8664	0.8664
	UnibucKernel (Top-scored)	1	0.8755	0.8755
Fusion	Baseline	-	0.7901	0.7909
	ETRI-SLP	1	0.9220	0.9218
	UnibucKernel (Top-scored)	1	0.9319	0.9318

Table 5: Performance comparison based on the F1 and accuracy metrics of the proposed method for the essay, speech, and fusion tracks when evaluating the test data set. The first, second, third rows of each track indicate the official baseline system, the proposed system, and the top-scored system, respectively.

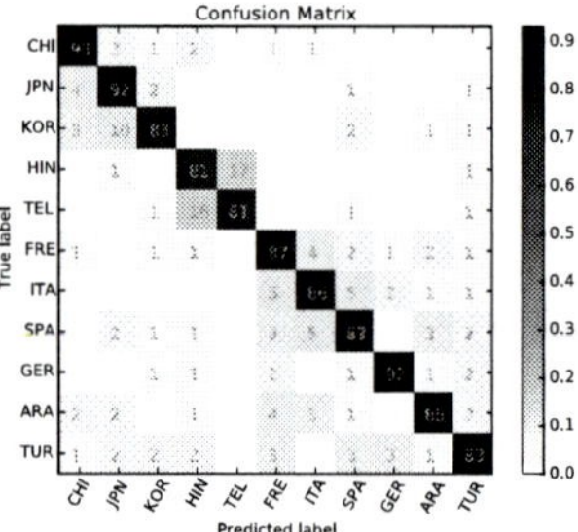

(a) Essay track

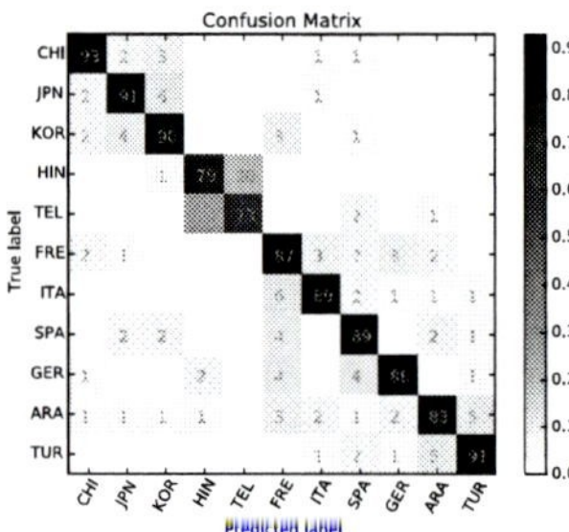

(b) Speech track

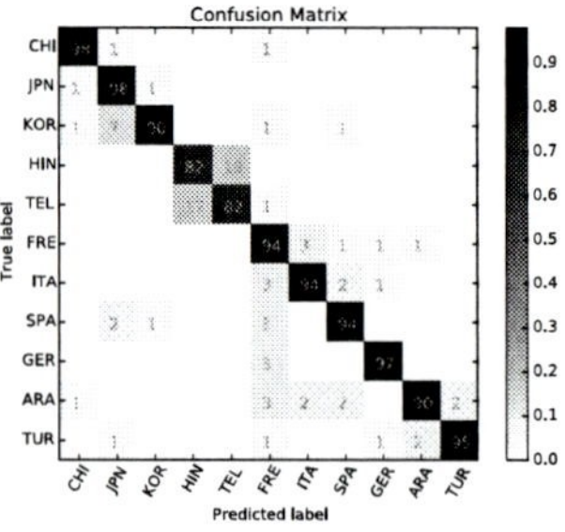

(c) Fusion track

Figure 6: Confusion matrixes of the ETRI-SLP NLI systems for the essay track, the speech track, and the fusion track, respectively, when evaluating the test data set.

In conclusion, we proposed the deep-learning based NLI using an LSA for the NLI Shared Task 2017. To this end, we extracted the LSA features using the six unit forms of character 4/5/6-grams and word 1/2/3-grams. Especially, we used 2,000-rank LSA features in order to capture the language information whereas the lower-rank LSA feature was used to the document topic-related applications. Next, the 2000-rank LSA feature was reduced into a 10-dimensional feature using LDA. It was noted from the NLI experiments that the LSA/LDA features performed well in the NLI Shared Task 2017 when compared to the count-based features, especially for the speech track.

For a fusion of the heterogeneous features such as the combination of a text-related feature and an i-vector feature, we designed two DNN based ensemble classifiers: (a) the vanilla DNN based ensemble classifier for late fusion and (b) the multi-column deep-stacking DNN based ensemble classifier for early fusion. The vanilla DNN based ensemble classifier was a late fusion classifier that combined the independently trained feature-related classifiers whereas the multi-column deep-stacking DNN based ensemble classifier was an early fusion classifier that combined the features in one fusion network. It was shown from the NLI experiments that the two DNN based ensemble classifiers had the comparable performances when the feature type and the performance were similar to each other. On the other hand, the multi-column deep-stacking DNN based ensemble classifier had a better performance when the the feature type and the performance were significantly different.

It was shown from the experiments on the NLI Shared Task 2017 that the F1 (macro) scores were obtained as 0.8601, 0.8664, and 0.9220, for the essay track, the speech track, and the fusion track, respectively. The performances for the speech and fusion tracks were comparable to the top-ranked systems whereas the performance for the essay track had a second-ranked performance.

Our findings from the NLI Shared Task 2017 were summarized as follows:

1. **Unit form for a text**
   We used the six unit forms of character 4/5/6-grams and word 1/2/3-grams. From the tenth row to the fourteenth row of Table 3, it was noted that the combination of the multiple text-related features had no improvement because the proposed text-related features were originated from the same unit forms. Therefore, we expected that the performance for the essay track would be improved if the additional unit forms were adopted.

2. **Feature type for a text: LSA-LDA feature**
   From the NLI experiments, it was noticed that the 2,000-rank LSA-LDA feature worked well for the NLI Shared Task 2017. Especially, LSA-LDA feature had a better performance than the count-based feature for the speech track. Moreover, the LSA-LDA feature worked well on both a normalization to a zero mean and unit variance and an LDA normalization whereas the count-based feature worked on the only normalization to a zero mean and unit variance.

3. **Normalization of an i-vector feature**
   It was observed from the experiments that the i-vector feature of a speech response signal worked well on an LDA normalization than a normalization to a zero mean and unit variance.

4. **DNN-based ensemble classifier**
   We attempted to use of a state-of-the-art deep learning method for the L1 classification by designing two DNN based ensemble classifiers: (a) the vanilla DNN based ensemble classifier for late fusion and (b) the multi-column deep-stacking DNN based ensemble classifier for early fusion. From the performance comparison of the other systems, it was seen that the proposed classifiers worked properly. Moreover, the multi-column deep-stacking DNN based ensemble classifier was better when the heterogeneous features had significant performance differences. In addition, we expected that the more detailed experiments of the DNN configurations and the feature combinations would improve the performance, especially using a more large amount data (Cheng et al., 2015).

Acknowledgements

This work was partially supported by the ICT R&D program of MSIP/IITP. [R0126-15-1117, Core technology development of the spontaneous speech dialogue processing for the language learning] and by Electronics and Telecommunications Research Institute (ETRI) grant funded by the Korean government. [17ZS1800, Development of self-improving and human-augmenting cognitive computing technology]

References

Jerome R Bellegarda. 2000. Exploiting latent semantic information in statistical language modeling. *Proc. IEEE* 88(8):1279–1296. https://doi.org/10.1109/5.880084.

Jian Cheng, Xin Chen, and Angeliki Metallinou. 2015. Deep neural network acoustic models for spoken assessment applications. *Speech Communication* 73:14 – 27. https://doi.org/10.1016/j.specom.2015.07.006.

Euisok Chung and Jeon Gue Park. in review. Sentence-chain based seq2seq model for corpus expansion. *ETRI Journal* .

Dan C. Ciresan, Ueli Meier, and Jürgen Schmidhuber. 2012. Multi-column deep neural networks for image classification. *CoRR* abs/1202.2745. http://arxiv.org/abs/1202.2745.

František Grézl, Martin Karafiát, Stanislav Kontár, and Jan Černocký. 2007. Probabilistic and bottle-neck features for lvcsr of meetings. In *Proc. IEEE International Conference on Acoustics, Speech and Signal Processing (ICASSP 2007)*. IEEE Signal Processing Society, pages 757–760. https://doi.org/10.1109/ICASSP.2007.367023.

HyungBae Jeon and Soo-Young Lee. 2016a. Initializing deep learning based on latent dirichlet allocation for document classification. *Neural Information Processing. ICONIP 2016. Lecture Notes in Computer Science* 9949. https://doi.org/10.1007/978-3-319-46675-0_70.

HyungBae Jeon and Soo-Young Lee. 2016b. Language model adaptation based on topic probability of latent dirichlet allocation. *ETRI Journal* 38(3):487–493. https://doi.org/10.4218/etrij.16.0115.0499.

T. Joachims. 1999. Making large scale SVM learning practical. In B. Schölkopf, C. Burges, and A. Smola, editors, *Advances in Kernel Methods - Support Vector Learning*, MIT Press, Cambridge, MA, chapter 11, pages 169–184.

Shervin Malmasi. 2016. *Native Language Identification: Explorations and Applications*. Ph.D. thesis. http://hdl.handle.net/1959.14/1110919.

Shervin Malmasi and Mark Dras. 2015. Multilingual Native Language Identification. In *Natural Language Engineering*. https://doi.org/10.1017/S1351324915000406.

Shervin Malmasi, Keelan Evanini, Aoife Cahill, Joel Tetreault, Robert Pugh, Christopher Hamill, Diane Napolitano, and Yao Qian. 2017. A Report on the 2017 Native Language Identification Shared Task. In *Proceedings of the 12th Workshop on Building Educational Applications Using NLP*. Association for Computational Linguistics, Copenhagen, Denmark.

Shervin Malmasi, Marcos Zampieri, Nikola Ljubešić, Preslav Nakov, Ahmed Ali, and Jörg Tiedemann. 2016. Discriminating between Similar Languages and Arabic Dialect Identification: A Report on the Third DSL Shared Task. In *Proceedings of the VarDial Workshop*. Osaka, Japan.

Björn Schuller, Stefan Steidl, Anton Batliner, Julia Hirschberg, Judee K. Burgoon, Alice Baird, Aaron Elkins, Yue Zhang, Eduardo Coutinho, and Keelan Evanini. 2016. The INTERSPEECH 2016 Computational Paralinguistics Challenge: Deception, Sincerity & Native Language. In *Interspeech 2016*. pages 2001–2005. https://doi.org/10.21437/Interspeech.2016-129.

C. G. M. Snoek, M. Worring, and A. W. M. Smeulders. 2005. Early versus late fusion in semantic video analysis. In *ACM International Conference on Multimedia*. pages 399?–402. https://doi.org/10.1145/1101149.1101236.

Joel Tetreault, Daniel Blanchard, and Aoife Cahill. 2013. A Report on the First Native Language Identification Shared Task. In *Proceedings of the Eighth Workshop on Building Educational Applications Using NLP*. Association for Computational Linguistics, Atlanta, GA, USA.

Marcos Zampieri, Shervin Malmasi, Nikola Ljubešić, Preslav Nakov, Ahmed Ali, Jörg Tiedemann, Yves Scherrer, and Noëmi Aepli. 2017. Findings of the VarDial Evaluation Campaign 2017. In *Proceedings of the Fourth Workshop on NLP for Similar Languages, Varieties and Dialects (VarDial)*. Valencia, Spain, pages 1–15.

Fusion of Simple Models for Native Language Identification

Fabio N. Kepler[*]
University of Pampa, Alegrete, Brazil
INESC-ID, Lisbon, Portugal
`fabio@kepler.pro.br`

Ramon F. Astudillo[*]
INESC-ID, Lisbon, Portugal
`ramon@astudillo.com`

Alberto Abad[*]
INESC-ID, Lisbon, Portugal
IST, University of Lisbon, Portugal
`alberto.abad@inesc-id.pt`

Abstract

In this paper we describe the approaches we explored for the 2017 Native Language Identification shared task. We focused on simple word and sub-word units avoiding heavy use of hand-crafted features. Following recent trends, we explored linear and neural networks models to attempt to compensate for the lack of rich feature use. Initial efforts yielded f1-scores of 82.39% and 83.77% in the development and test sets of the fusion track, and were officially submitted to the task as team L2F. After the task was closed, we carried on further experiments and relied on a late fusion strategy for combining our simple proposed approaches with modifications of the baselines provided by the task. As expected, the i-vectors based subsystem dominates the performance of the system combinations, and results in the major contributor to our achieved scores. Our best combined system achieves 90.1% and 90.2% f1-score in the development and test sets of the fusion track, respectively.

1 Introduction

Native Language Identification (NLI) is the task of identifying a person's native language (L1) based on that person's written or spoken content in a learned language (L2). The task has gained increased interest from various research communities, which led to the first shared task in 2013 (Tetreault et al., 2013). In 2016, a sub-challenge was held at Interspeech (Schuller et al., 2016) on identifying the native language based on spoken

responses in English, in contrast to the NLI shared task, which was based on written responses.

The NLI Shared Task 2017 is the next instance in this series of shared tasks (Malmasi et al., 2017), with the distinction of featuring both written and spoken based responses as available data. Spoken responses were available in the form of speech transcriptions and i-vectors, not actual audio files. Systems could compete in three tracks: ESSAYS, where only the provided written essays data could be used; SPEECH, where only the speech transcriptions and possibly i-vectors could be used; and FUSION, where all three datasets could be combined. The task provided a single development labeled dataset and two different unlabeled test sets: one for the ESSAYS and SPEECH tracks, and another for the FUSION track. Additionally, each system was allowed to participate in an open or closed sub-track depending on whether any external data was used or not, respectively.

In this paper we describe the approaches we took in the NLI Shared Task 2017, specifically in the FUSION closed track, where we participated as team L2F. After having officially submitted a system to the track, we performed further experiments and developed additional systems, including a late fusion one that performs 7 absolute points above the system we submitted.

The best performing systems on a variety of Natural Language Processing (NLP) and Information Retrieval problems, including NLI, are ensembles of complex models that employ a myriad of high-level features (Malmasi and Dras, 2017). There are, however, some systems with simple features that are able to surpass complex ensembles, like the previous state of the art in NLI by Ionescu et al. (2014).

One way of not relying on specially engineered features is to follow the current trend on using Neural Networks (NN) and Deep Learning (DL)

---
[*]All authors contributed equally.

423

techniques (and doing parameter tuning instead). Although DL approaches have achieved several state of the art results in NLP, this is not the case yet for NLI.

Our line of approach for this task was to benefit from the power of fusion systems while avoiding complex feature engineering and exploring the usefulness of DL techniques.

2 Related Work

There are several works on NLI based on essays, most of which are analyzed by Malmasi (2016). The current state of the art is the recent work of Malmasi and Dras (2017), which uses ensembles of several classifiers over a large set of features. The previous state of the art was the work of Ionescu et al. (2014), which used only character p-grams as features.

A recent trend has been the use of speech transcripts and audio features for tasks like dialect identification (Malmasi et al., 2016; Zampieri et al., 2017) or of only spoken responses for NLI, like in the 2016 Computational Paralinguistics Challenge (ComParE, Schuller et al. (2016)). The best performing system in ComParE 2016 was the work of Abad et al. (2016), which also employs a fusion of systems and highlights the importance of i-vectors acoustic features.

3 Methodology and Data

The NLI Shared Task 2017 combines the basic written essay approach with the spoken response approach by providing a written essay, a speech transcript, and an i-vector for each subject. For a thorough description of the datasets, including the number of samples for training, development and test, and the 11 L1 classes, see Malmasi et al. (2017).

Given that the task allowed for the fusion of all these data, we experimented with several approaches targeting a final fusion system, all of which we describe below.

3.1 Language Identification Techniques

Following the success in applying language identification techniques to L1 identification in speech (Abad et al., 2016), we explored language identification techniques in an initial stage. We trained the well known *langid* tool (Lui and Baldwin, 2011) using the data-sets provided in the shared task. The technique implemented in *langid* combines a Naive Bayes classifier with byte n-grams and no assumption over word boundaries. Unfortunately, no results outperforming the baseline could be attained with *langid*.

Character n-grams are a common feature in NLI systems and have been shown to provide strong results (Koppel et al., 2005; Ionescu et al., 2014). The low performance we attained with *langid* might therefore be related with particularities of the tool. It is also possible that specific tuning of algorithms for language identification might not be suitable for L1 identification.

3.2 Sub-word Features

Together with part-of-speech, character-level features are a commonly used feature for NLI (Malmasi, 2016). Upon manual inspection of the essays and speech transcriptions corpora of the shared task, it became clear that spelling or transcription errors were present with high frequency. This is a scenario in which sub-word units can play an important role for two main reasons. On the one hand, sub-word units help alleviate the effect of rare words that do not appear in the training corpus, also known as Out of Vocabulary Words (OOVs). On the other hand, they can capture systematic sub-word patterns, such as typographical or transcription errors, that can be specific to a particular L1 profile.

As an alternative to sub-word units based on character n-grams, we explored the use of the Byte Pair Encoding (BPE) approach (Sennrich et al., 2015). This simple approach, that has recently help to achieve state-of-the-art results in machine translation (Sennrich et al., 2015), provides a middle ground between character and word models. BPE is a well known compression technique that is here employed to iteratively merge the characters or sequences of characters that are most common into new tokens. The resulting vocabulary contains many or the original word tokens as well as fragments of frequent character sequences and individual characters.

Initial experiments explored the use of BPE tokens as a replacement for word tokens in the baseline system. This yielded however no notable improvements over the provided features. One possible limitation on the use of BPE features compared to Sennrich et al. (2015) is the lack of Recurrent Neural Networks to capture context. Without them, the use of sub-word units might destroy some useful information at the word token level. For this reason, further experiments included n-grams of BPE units as features with $n = 1, 2, 3$. It has to be taken into account that n-grams of BPE features might not only capture whole words but also sub-word patterns within and across word boundaries. The use of n-grams together produced however no improvements compared to the baseline system.

To provide some additional complementarity in the final ensemble, a Naive Bayes model was trained on the same features. Despite its simplicity, the model became competitive after introducing the n-gram features. Minor improvements over the baseline on the ESSAYS dataset were then attained by using BPE sub-word units (as we will see in Section 5, Table 1) and were kept for the final ensemble due to its complementarity. After determining the optimal features, the system parameters were tuned using the development set. A value of 10000 new BPE symbols was determined as optimal. The Naive Bayes classifier smoothing, equivalent to an uniform Dirichlet prior for the likelihood estimation, was set to $1e^{-4}$.

3.3 Neural Networks

Neural Networks are being successfully applied to a varying set of NLP problems. Following the current trend, we developed several architectures and tested them over the ESSAYS and FUSION tracks.

A common choice for treating sequence data like text are Recurrent Neural Networks (RNN), usually in their Long-Short Term Memory (LSTM) or Gated Recurrent Units (GRU) flavors, which are better able to capture long dependencies than plain RNNs. We decided to use GRUs (Chung et al., 2015) since they are faster to train and provide similar results to LSTMs.

We ended up building two networks: one for the ESSAYS tracks (NN-ESSAYS) and another for the FUSION track (NN-FUSION). The network for the FUSION track uses all available data as input: essays, transcripts, and i-vectors. The network for the ESSAYS track only uses the tokens in the essays.

Our final architecture for the NN-ESSAYS network is composed by the following layers:

- An embedding layer mapping input identifiers to a 300-dimensional space;

- A feed-forward layer with 300 units and ReLU (Nair and Hinton, 2010) activations;

- A bidirectional GRU layer with 300 units;

- A max-pooling layer applied across the time dimension;

- A feed-forward layer with 11 units (one for each language) and softmax activation.

The architecture for the NN-FUSION network is essentially similar but has to deal with the multiple inputs:

- The essay and transcript inputs each pass through the first four layers as in NN-ESSAYS before being concatenated;

- Each sample i-vector goes through a 400 units, ReLU activated feed-forward layer before being concatenated with the resulting concatenation above;

- A final softmax layer is then applied.

Several different architectures were tested, but none yielded results outperforming the baseline. As we will see in Section 5, the i-vectors dominate over the other features.

3.4 I-vector system

The success of the i-vector (Dehak et al., 2011a) framework in speaker recognition tasks has motivated the investigation of its application to other related fields, including language recognition (Martinez et al., 2011; Dehak et al., 2011b), where it has become the current *de facto* standard for acoustic Spoken Language Recognition (SLR), and more recently L1 recognition (Abad et al., 2016).

In the Total-variability modeling approach – so-called i-vector approach – the variability present in the high-dimensional GMM super-vector is jointly modeled as a single low-rank total-variability space. The low-dimensionality total variability factors extracted from a given speech segment form a vector, named i-vector, which represents the speech segment in a very compact and efficient way. Thus, the total-variability modeling is used as a factor analysis based front-end extractor.

In this work, the 800 dimensionality i-vectors provided in the task were used to build a new acoustic L1 classifier. First, we apply i-vector centering and whitening (Garcia-Romero and Espy-Wilson, 2011) that is known to contribute to a reduction of the channel variability. Moreover, the resulting centered and whitened i-vectors are normalized to be of unit length.

Second, we explored different classifiers on the top of the processed i-vectors. Like in Abad et al. (2016), in which log-linear and non-linear classifiers based on feed-forward networks were investigated, we could observe that the i-vector front-end already provides a very good separation of the classes which leads to similar results for the different modeling techniques.

In particular, we tried to model the distribution of i-vectors for each language with a single mixture Gaussian distribution with full covariance matrix shared across different target languages since it has proven very effective (Martınez et al., 2011; Abad et al., 2016). However, in this case, this approach showed very similar performance to the baseline classifier: a multi-class one-vs-rest logistic regression classifier. Consequently, we opted for the baseline logistic regression approach.

4   Calibration and Fusion Back-End

In this work, we carried out calibration and fusion of the systems at the output score level using the FoCal Multi-class Toolkit[1]. For that purpose, every single sub-system is forced to produce an 11-element score vector $\mathbf{s}_i$ corresponding to each of the target languages. Then, a Linear Logistic Regression (LLR) is trained to fuse the score outputs generated by the selected sub-systems in order to produce fused well-calibrated log-likelihoods $\mathbf{l}$ as follows:

$$\mathbf{l} = \sum_i \alpha_i \mathbf{s}_i + \mathbf{b}, \qquad (1)$$

where α_i is the weight for sub-system i and $\mathbf{b}$ is the language-dependent shift. For this challenge, the language with the highest fused log-likelihood is the hypothesized L1 language.

Notice that, in contrast to Abad et al. (2016), the use of a Gaussian Back-End to transform the score-vector of each individual sub-system before the LLR stage has not been applied, since it did not reveal to contribute for improved language identification in the validation experiments.

[1]https://sites.google.com/site/
nikobrummer/focalmulticlass

During the development of our systems, the LLR fusion parameters were trained and evaluated on the development set using a kind of 2-fold cross-validation: development data was randomly split in two halves, one for parameter estimation and the other for assessment. This process was repeated using 10 different random partitions so that the mean and variance of the systems' performance could be computed. This method allowed for a comparison and ranking of the different sub-systems under study. Then, for the trial submissions, no partition was made and all the development data was used to train the LLR fusion.

The final combined system for the FUSION track, which we call FINAL-FUSION, consists in the LLR fusion of the following 5 systems: i) ESSAY baseline; ii) speech transcriptions baseline; iii) the i-vector system described in Section 3.4; iv) the NN-ESSAYS system described in Section 3.3; and v) the BPE system described in Section 3.2. We also evaluated a LLR-FUSION system consisting in i), iv) and v) on the ESSAYS track.

5   Results

We first show the results over the development set in order to justify our approach choices, beginning with the ESSAYS track. The official evaluation metric is the macro averaged F1 score.

The organizers provided an already strong baseline at 72% F1 over essays. As we can see in Table 1, our BPE based systems and NN system were only able to be on par with the baseline, with the Naive Bayes using BPE n-grams only slightly surpassing it. However, as shown in Table 2, the Naive Bayes approach is indeed very complementary to the baseline. It performs well above the baseline for German, Italian, and Spanish, while performing much worse for Arabic and Telugu. The fusion system results confirms this hypothesis, showing the best result for all languages. The NN model also shows complementarity in a smaller scale that still provides a positive impact in the final ensemble.

Considering the FUSION track, both NN-FUSION and FINAL-FUSION systems significantly surpassed the baselines, as can be seen in Table 3. This is due mainly because of the use of the i-vectors in both systems. The NN-FUSION system without i-vectors, for example, performed 5 points worse than the baseline with no i-vector (not shown in the tables).

System	F1 (macro)	Accuracy
Baseline (1)	0.7230	0.7236
langid (2)	0.5469	
Naive Bayes 1-gram (3)	0.5912	0.5918
NN-ESSAYS (4)	0.7127	0.7145
Naive Bayes 1,2,3-grams (5)	0.7210	0.7227
Naive Bayes BPE 1,2,3-grams (6)	**0.7294**	**0.7309**
LLR-FUSION (1)+(4)+(6)	0.7949	0.7945

Table 1: Results for the ESSAYS track over the development dataset for the baseline, the *langid*, the Naive Bayes with and without BPE, the essay Neural Network (NN-ESSAYS), and the LLR-FUSION systems. The best result, excluding the LLR-FUSION, is highlighted in bold.

L1	Baseline	NB+BPE	NN-ESSAYS	FINAL-FUSION
ARA	**0.74**	0.67	0.65	0.76
CHI	**0.75**	0.74	0.74	0.84
FRE	0.74	**0.77**	0.72	0.81
GER	0.79	**0.85**	0.81	0.93
HIN	**0.69**	0.66	**0.69**	0.71
ITA	0.76	**0.83**	0.80	0.86
JPN	0.74	**0.76**	0.69	0.82
KOR	0.69	**0.70**	0.68	0.75
SPA	0.61	**0.68**	0.66	0.73
TEL	**0.73**	0.65	0.71	0.77
TUR	**0.72**	0.70	0.67	0.77
avg	0.72	**0.73**	0.71	0.79

Table 2: F1 (macro) scores on the ESSAYS track over the development dataset for the baseline, the Naive Bayes with BPE (NB+BPE), the essay Neural Network (NN-ESSAYS), and the FINAL-FUSION systems. The best result for each language, excluding the FINAL-FUSION, is highlighted in bold.

System	F1 (macro)	Accuracy
Baseline fusion	0.7500	0.7500
Baseline fusion+i-vectors	0.7809	0.7827
NN-FUSION	0.8238	0.8245
FINAL-FUSION	0.9011	0.9009

Table 3: Results for the FUSION track over the development dataset for the baselines, the fusion Neural Network (NN-FUSION), and the FINAL-FUSION systems.

5.1 Test set

As previously mentioned, the NLI Shared Task 2017 provided two test datasets, one for the ESSAYS and SPEECH tracks, and one for the FUSION track. We focused on the FUSION track test set for comparing the systems described above.

Table 4 shows the results of our two best single systems trained only on the ESSAYS dataset. The difference in performance is proportional to that on the development set shown in Table 1.

Table 5 shows the results on the FUSION track for our two fusion systems trained on all available data: essays, speech transcriptions, and i-vectors. The NN-FUSION was the only system we officially submitted to the task. After advancing with the other complementary systems and the FINAL-FUSION one, the results we achieved make it clear Neural Networks are not the best alternative for combining multiple sources of information, at least not in the simple way we approached it.

6 Discussion

Concerning the text component of the problem, we focused on simple word and sub-word features avoiding excessive use of hand engineered features. We also tested linear and recurrent neural networks based classifiers to attain complementary models. We then relied on fusion methods for combining our simple approaches and the task provided i-vectors.

Compared with the existing results, performance on the text component of the tasks was limited, with small improvements over the baseline. The obtained models were however complementary to each other and the baseline system, providing additional gains when ensembled. The use of BPE has shown as well to be a possible alternative to other sub-word units usually employed in NLI systems.

The outstanding performance of the i-vectors, consistent with findings of previous works, is the main driver in the final system's performance. The main improvements shown reside therefore in the alternative fusion strategy followed for the different systems.

Following the current trend, a possible line of work is to explore sub-word information combined with recurrent or convolutional neural architectures. In addition, more complex neural architectures can also be explored, like hierarchical classification models with attention, which are recently obtaining good results in other document classification problems.

Acknowledgements

Fabio Kepler gratefully acknowledge the support of NVIDIA Corporation with the donation of the Titan Xp GPU used for several experiments reported in this paper. This work was partially supported by Portuguese national funds through – Fundação para a Ciência e a Tecnologia (FCT) under Project UID/CEC/50021/2013.

References

Alberto Abad, Eugénio Ribeiro, Fábio Kepler, Ramón Fernández Astudillo, and Isabel Trancoso. 2016. Exploiting phone log-likelihood ratio features for the detection of the native language of non-native english speakers. In *Interspeech 2016*. pages 2413–2417.

Junyoung Chung, Caglar Gulcehre, Kyunghyun Cho, and Yoshua Bengio. 2015. Gated feedback recurrent neural networks. In Francis Bach and David Blei, editors, *Proceedings of the 32nd International Conference on Machine Learning*. PMLR, Lille, France, volume 37 of *Proceedings of Machine Learning Research*, pages 2067–2075. http://proceedings.mlr.press/v37/chung15.html.

Najim Dehak, Patrick Kenny, Réda Dehak, Pierre Dumouchel, and Pierre Ouellet. 2011a. Front-end factor analysis for speaker verification. *Audio, Speech, and Language Processing, IEEE Transactions on* 19(4):788–798.

Najim Dehak, Pedro A Torres-Carrasquillo, Douglas A Reynolds, and Reda Dehak. 2011b. Language recognition via i-vectors and dimensionality reduction. In *INTERSPEECH*. pages 857–860.

Daniel Garcia-Romero and Carol Y. Espy-Wilson. 2011. Analysis of i-vector length normalization in speaker recognition systems. In *Interspeech*.

Radu Tudor Ionescu, Marius Popescu, and Aoife Cahill. 2014. Can characters reveal your native language? A language-independent approach to native language identification. In *Proceedings of the 2014 Conference on Empirical Methods in Natural Language Processing (EMNLP)*. Association for Computational Linguistics.

Moshe Koppel, Jonathan Schler, and Kfir Zigdon. 2005. Automatically determining an anonymous author's native language. *Intelligence and Security Informatics* pages 41–76.

Marco Lui and Timothy Baldwin. 2011. Cross-domain feature selection for language identification. In *In Proceedings of 5th International Joint Conference on Natural Language Processing*. Citeseer.

Shervin Malmasi. 2016. *Native Language Identification: Explorations and Applications*. Ph.D. thesis. http://hdl.handle.net/1959.14/1110919.

Shervin Malmasi and Mark Dras. 2017. Native Language Identification using Stacked Generalization. *arXiv preprint arXiv:1703.06541* .

Shervin Malmasi, Keelan Evanini, Aoife Cahill, Joel Tetreault, Robert Pugh, Christopher Hamill, Diane Napolitano, and Yao Qian. 2017. A Report on the 2017 Native Language Identification Shared Task. In *Proceedings of the 12th Workshop on Building Educational Applications Using NLP*. Association for Computational Linguistics, Copenhagen, Denmark.

Shervin Malmasi, Marcos Zampieri, Nikola Ljubešić, Preslav Nakov, Ahmed Ali, and Jörg Tiedemann. 2016. Discriminating between Similar Languages and Arabic Dialect Identification: A Report on the

System	F1 (macro)	Accuracy
Baseline	0.7109	0.7112
NN-ESSAYS	0.7273	0.7269
Naive Bayes BPE 1,2,3-grams	0.7445	0.7404

Table 4: Results over the FUSION test dataset trained only on the ESSAYS for the baseline and our two best single systems.

System	F1 (macro)	Accuracy
Baseline fusion	0.7790	0.7790
Baseline fusion+i-vectors	0.7900	0.7900
NN-FUSION	*0.8377*	*0.8391*
FINAL-FUSION	0.9018	0.9018

Table 5: Results for the FUSION track over the test dataset for the baseline and our two fusion systems. The emphasized system, NN-FUSION, was the only officially submitted to the task.

Third DSL Shared Task. In *Proceedings of the VarDial Workshop*. Osaka, Japan.

David Martınez, Oldrich Plchot, Lukás Burget, Ondrej Glembek, and Pavel Matejka. 2011. Language recognition in ivectors space. In *Interspeech*. pages 861–864.

Vinod Nair and Geoffrey E Hinton. 2010. Rectified linear units improve restricted Boltzmann machines. In *Proceedings of the International Conference on Machine Learning*. pages 807–814.

Bjrn Schuller, Stefan Steidl, Anton Batliner, Julia Hirschberg, Judee K. Burgoon, Alice Baird, Aaron Elkins, Yue Zhang, Eduardo Coutinho, and Keelan Evanini. 2016. The INTERSPEECH 2016 Computational Paralinguistics Challenge: Deception, Sincerity & Native Language. In *Interspeech 2016*. pages 2001–2005. https://doi.org/10.21437/Interspeech.2016-129.

Rico Sennrich, Barry Haddow, and Alexandra Birch. 2015. Neural machine translation of rare words with subword units. *arXiv preprint arXiv:1508.07909* .

Joel Tetreault, Daniel Blanchard, and Aoife Cahill. 2013. A Report on the First Native Language Identification Shared Task. In *Proceedings of the Eighth Workshop on Building Educational Applications Using NLP*. Association for Computational Linguistics, Atlanta, GA, USA.

Marcos Zampieri, Shervin Malmasi, Nikola Ljubešić, Preslav Nakov, Ahmed Ali, Jörg Tiedemann, Yves Scherrer, and Noëmi Aepli. 2017. Findings of the VarDial Evaluation Campaign 2017. In *Proceedings of the Fourth Workshop on NLP for Similar Languages, Varieties and Dialects (VarDial)*. Valencia, Spain, pages 1–15.

Stacked Sentence-Document Classifier Approach for Improving Native Language Identification

Andrea Cimino, Felice Dell'Orletta
Istituto di Linguistica Computazionale "Antonio Zampolli" (ILC–CNR)
via G. Moruzzi, 1 – Pisa (Italy)
`{name.surname}@ilc.cnr.it`

Abstract

In this paper, we describe the approach of the *ItaliaNLP Lab* team to native language identification and discuss the results we submitted as participants to the essay track of NLI Shared Task 2017. We introduce for the first time a 2-stacked sentence-document architecture for native language identification that is able to exploit both local sentence information and a wide set of general–purpose features qualifying the lexical and grammatical structure of the whole document. When evaluated on the official test set, our sentence-document stacked architecture obtained the best result among all the participants of the essay track with an F1 score of 0.8818.

1 Introduction

Native Language Identification (NLI) is the task of identifying the native language (L1) of a writer based on their writing in another language. Since the seminal work by Koppel et al. (2005), within the Computational Linguistics community there has been a growing interest in the NLP–based Native Language Identification (henceforth, NLI) task. However, so far, due to the unavailability of balanced and wide–coverage benchmark corpora and the lack of evaluation standards it has been difficult to compare the results achieved for this task with different methods and techniques (Tetreault et al., 2012). The First Shared Task on Native Language Identification (Tetreault et al., 2013) was the answer to these mentioned problems.

In this paper, we describe our approach to the essay track of the 2017 Native Language Identification Shared Task (Malmasi et al., 2017). Participating teams of this task were asked to classify the native language of writers of 1,100 En-glish essays solely using the sample of their writings. 11,100 English essays from non-native English writing samples from a standardized, meaningful, and authentic assessment context of English proficiency for academic purposes (the Test Of English as a Foreign Language, TOEFL) (Blanchard et al., 2013) were provided as training data and the 11 native languages covered by the corpus are: Arabic, Chinese, French, German, Hindi, Italian, Japanese, Korean, Spanish, Telugu, and Turkish. Each essay in the TOEFL11 is labeled with an English language proficiency level.

Following the most common approaches and starting from the work of (Cimino et al., 2013), we tackled the Native Language Identification task as a text classification problem. The main novelty of our approach is the proposed classification architecture that combines a sentence and a document classifier in a 2-stacked sentence-document architecture. This system is able to exploit both local sentence information and a wide set of features extracted from the whole document. The features range across different levels of linguistic description, from lexical to morpho–syntactic and syntactic information.

The proposed method was prompted by our studies on sentence and document readability classification (Dell'Orletta et al., 2014), where we shown differences between document and sentence classification problems by focusing on the role of the features and their importance. For example, the classification of the readability of a sentence requires a higher number of features, mainly syntactic ones, and they have different weights with respect to the weights used in the document classification problem. In this work, we show how sentence local information can be exploited also in NLI task providing to the document classifier fruitful local information, thus making some features more effective.

Proceedings of the 12th Workshop on Innovative Use of NLP for Building Educational Applications, pages 430–437
Copenhagen, Denmark, September 8, 2017. ©2017 Association for Computational Linguistics

2 Related Work

Native Language Identification is most commonly tackled as a multi-class supervised classification task combining NLP–enabled feature extraction and machine learning: see e.g. (Tetreault et al., 2012), and (Malmasi and Dras, 2017). Among the different machine learning algorithms used, systems based on Support Vector Machines obtain the best accuracies. However, the most successful approaches made use of classifier ensemble methods to further improve performance. All recent state-of-the-art systems have relied on some form of multiple classifier system. Among the most recent works, (Ionescu et al., 2014) used multiple string kernels learning using only character n-gram features, reporting an accuracy of 85.3 on the TOEFL11 test set, 1.7 higher than the 2013 state of the art obtained by (Jarvis et al., 2013) in the first shared task on NLI (Tetreault et al., 2013). More recently, (Malmasi and Dras, 2017) made a systematic examination of ensemble methods. By exploiting a classifier stacking architecture, the authors obtained the current state-of-the-art results on three datasets from different languages. As in these previous works, the system presented in this paper uses a stcked architecture, but differently from the previous ones combines a sentence and a document classifier and it is able to exploit in a profitable way both local sentence information and global document information.

Typically, the range of features used is wide and includes characteristics of the linguistic structure underlying the L2 text, encoded in terms of sequences of characters, words, grammatical categories or of syntactic constructions, as well as of the document structure: note however that, in most part of the cases, the exploited features are task–specific. Differently, as in our first system (Cimino et al., 2013), we resort to a wide set of features ranging across different levels of linguistic description (i.e. lexical, morpho–syntactic and syntactic) without any a priori selection: the same set of features was successfully exploited in different tasks focusing on the linguistic form rather than the content of texts, such as readability assessment (Dell'Orletta et al., 2014) or the classification of textual genres (Dell'Orletta et al., 2012).

3 Description of the system

Our approach to the Native Language Identification Task was implemented in a software proto-type. The main novelty of our approach is the use of a stack of two SVM classifiers, each one operating on morpho–syntactically tagged and dependency parsed texts. The first classifier is a L1 *sentence classifier* that is aimed at classifying the native language of each sentence of a document. The predictions of the L1 sentence classifier are used as features by the L1 *document classifier*. In addition to the sentence classifier predictions, the second classifier exploits widely used features in native language identification that are used to build the final statistical model. This statistical model is finally used to predict the L1 language of unseen documents. The highest score of the document classifier represents the most probable L1 class. For this work we used LIBLINEAR (Fan et al., 2008) as machine learning library both for the sentence and the document classifiers. The documents were automatically POS tagged by the Part–Of–Speech tagger described in (Cimino and Dell'Orletta, 2016) and dependency–parsed by the DeSR parser (Attardi et al., 2009).

3.1 Training workflow

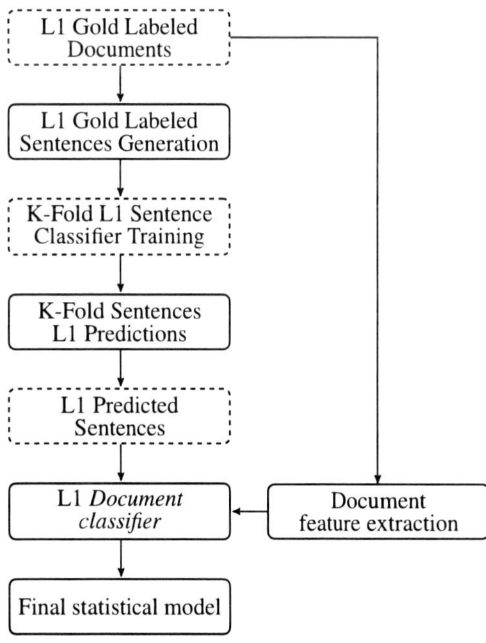

Figure 1: The training workflow of the 2-stacked sentence-document architecture.

Since the document classifier exploits the *predictions* of the sentence classifier in classification of unseen documents, we devised a specific training workflow that is shown in Figure 1. In the first step of the workflow, the L1 gold labels of the training documents are exploited to build an annotated corpus of L1 sentences where each sentence is labeled according to the label of its belonging document. Once the L1 gold labeled sentence corpus is generated, this is used to train the sentence classifier and used to create the training set of the document classifier. More precisely, the L1 sentence corpus is divided in k different folds [1] where each fold is used to provide the training examples for the sentence classifier. By exploiting widely used NLI features, the sentence classifier produces a specific statistical model for each of the k folds.

The statistical models are then used to predict the L1 language of the sentences that do not belong to the training examples of the generated folds. For this work we used the LIBLINEAR L2-regularized logistic regression as learning algorithm since the LIBLINEAR implementation provides the confidence of belonging to a specific class for unseen examples. In addition, features with frequency lower than 2 in the corpus where discarded. By merging the k folds of the L1 predicted sentences, a corpus of L1 predicted sentences is obtained and it is used by the document classifier during its training phase. The document classifier by exploiting widely used NLI features and the predictions of the sentence classifier produces its own statistical model that is finally used to predict the L1 language of unseen documents. The document classifier was trained using the LIBLINEAR L2-regularized L2-loss support vector classification that (Jarvis et al., 2013) have shown to have very good performances in NLI document classification. Features with frequency lower than 3 in the corpus where discarded.

Once the document classifier is trained, for the final settings the sentence classifier is trained using all the sentences of the L1 Gold sentence corpus, this in order to achieve the best possible accuracy in classification of unseen sentences.

The prediction workflow of unseen documents, shown in Figure 2, is similar to the training workflow with the exception that the k fold training procedure is not needed.

All the real valued features were scaled in the range $[0, 1]$ in order to reduce the training times and to maximize the classification performances.

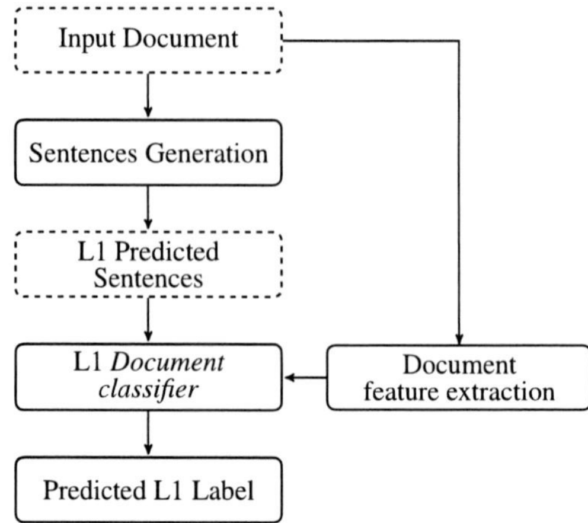

Figure 2: The test workflow of the 2-stacked sentence-document architecture.

3.2 Sentence and Document Features

Here are described the features used both by the sentence and the document classifiers. Hereafter we regard documents and sentences as *texts* in order to avoid ambiguities in the description of the features. In the description below some features are calculated as the normalized frequency and other as the normalized logarithm of the frequency. The choice was made according to empirical evaluation on the development set.

Raw and Lexical Text Features
Text Length, calculated as the number of tokens.
Word Length, calculated as the average number of characters per word.
Character n-grams, calculated as the logarithm of the frequency of each character n-gram in the text and normalized with respect to the text length. A smoothing term is added to the frequency of each n-gram in order to avoid 0 values for n-grams with 1 frequency.
Function word n-grams, calculated as the frequency of each function word n-gram in the text and normalized with respect to the number of tokens in the text. In this work we considered the words belonging to one of the following fine part-of-speech categories: determiners, coordinating conjunctions, preposition or subordinating conjunctions, interjections.
Word n-grams, calculated as presence or absence of a word n-gram in the text.
Lemma n-grams, calculated as the frequency of

---

each lemma n-gram in the text and normalized with respect to the number of tokens in the text.

Morpho–syntactic Features
Coarse grained Part-Of-Speech n-grams, calculated as the logarithm of the frequency of each coarse grained PoS n-gram in the text and normalized with respect to the number of tokens of the text.

Coarse grained Part-Of-Speech - Lemma n-grams: calculated as the frequency of the n-grams of the Coarse grained Part-of-Speech of the current token and its following token lemma. The frequencies are normalized with respect to the number of tokens of the text.

Syntactic Features
Linear dependency types n-grams, calculated as the frequency of each dependency n-gram in the text with respect to the surface linear ordering of words and normalized with respect to the number of tokens in the text.

Hierarchical dependency types n-grams calculated as the logarithm of the frequency of each hierarchy dependency n-gram in the text calculated with respect to the hierarchical parse tree structure and normalized with respect to the number of tokens in the text. In addition to the dependency relationship, the feature takes into account whether a node is a left or a right child with respect to its parent.

Head-dependents of the syntax tree: the distribution of head and its dependents in the syntax trees.

3.3 Document Classifier Specific Features

In addition to the features described in 3.2, the document classifier uses the following features.
Raw Features
Essay prompt, included in the TOEFL11 corpus.
Average sentence length and standard deviation, calculated in terms of number of tokens for each sentence in the document.
Type/Token Ratio. The Type/Token Ratio (TTR) is a measure of vocabulary variation which has shown to be a helpful measure of lexical variety within a text as well as style marker in an authorship attribution scenario: a text characterized by a low type/token ratio will contain a great deal of repetition whereas a high type/token ratio reflects vocabulary richness and variation. Due to its sensitivity to sample size, the TTR has been computed

for different chunk lengths. In this work we considered the first 100, 200, 300 and 400 tokens.

Sentence classifier predictions. Since the sentence classifier provides for each sentence the probability score of each L1 class, the following 55 features were calculated for each document: for each L1 language the *i*) average probability, *ii*) the standard deviation of the probabilities, *iii*) the probability product, *iiii*) the maximum probability and *iiiii*) the minimum probability of all the sentences.

3.4 Models

In order to test the performances of the proposed two-stacked sentence-document classifier, we conducted several experiments exploiting different configurations of our system. Table 1 reports the configurations selected for the official runs in terms of features and values of n-grams used. Stacked1 and Stacked2 use both the 2-stack classifier architecture, but the Stacked2 model does not include the *Functional word n-gram* features and the *head-dependents* features. Not-stacked1 and Not-stacked2 reflect the previous two configurations with the exception that the sentence classifier features were not introduced. The selection of these models was guided by the tuning performed on the official NLI Shared Task 2013 and 2017 test sets. Tables 2 and 3 report the results achieved by the selected models on the official 2013 test set and the 2017 development set.

Model	Prec.	Recall	F1-Score
Jarvis (2013)	-	-	0.836
Cimino (2013)	-	-	0.779
Stacked1	**0.853**	**0.851**	**0.851**
Not-stacked1	0.850	0.848	0.848
Stacked2	0.851	0.849	0.849
Not-stacked2	0.850	0.847	0.847

Table 2: Results obtained by our models on the NLI Shared Task 2013 official test set compared to the overall best run and our best run submitted in the NLI Shared Task 2013 edition.

Feature	Feature-Configuration	Stacked1	Stacked2	Not-stacked1	Not-stacked2
Sentence Classifier and Document Classifier features					
Character n-grams	up to 8	✓	✓	✓	✓
Word n-grams	up to 4	✓	✓	✓	✓
Lemma n-grams	up to 4	✓	✓	✓	✓
CPOS n-grams	up to 4	✓	✓	✓	✓
LEMMA-CPOS n-grams	up to 4	✓	✓	✓	✓
Functional word n-grams	up to 3	✓	✗	✓	✗
Linear dependency n-grams	up to 4	✓	✓	✓	✓
Hierarchical dependency n-grams	up to 4	✓	✓	✓	✓
Text Length	NA	✓	✓	✓	✓
Head-Dependents	NA	✓	✗	✓	✗
Document Classifier specific features					
Type Token Ratio	100,200,300,400	✓	✓	✓	✓
Essay Prompt	NA	✓	✓	✓	✓
Average Sentence Length	NA	✓	✓	✓	✓
Standard Deviation Sentence Length	NA	✓	✓	✓	✓
Average Sentence L1 Confidence	NA	✓	✓	✗	✗
Std. Dev. Sentence L1 Confidence	NA	✓	✓	✗	✗
Product of Sentence L1 Confidences	NA	✓	✓	✗	✗
Maximum Sentence L1 Confidence	NA	✓	✓	✗	✗
Minimum Sentence L1 Confidence	NA	✓	✓	✗	✗

Table 1: Configurations of our system used to train our classifier for the evaluation of the NLI Shared Task 2017 test set.

Model	Prec.	Recall	F1-Score
Stacked1	0.8551	0.8527	0.8525
Stacked2	**0.8567**	**0.8545**	**0.8544**
Not-stacked1	0.8552	0.8527	0.8526
Not-stacked2	0.8524	0.8500	0.8498

Table 3: Results obtained by our models on the NLI Shared Task 2017 official development set.

System	F1-Score	Accuracy
Random Baseline	0.0909	0.0909
Organizers baseline	0.7104	0.7109
Stacked1	0.8800	0.8800
Stacked2	**0.8818**	**0.8818**

Table 4: Results of our submitted models for the essay track on the NLI Shared Task 2017 official test set.

4 Results

Table 4 reports the F1-Score and the overall accuracy achieved by our stacked architecture with the feature configuration described in section 3.4 on the NLI Shared Task 2017 official test set. In addition the table reports the results achieved by two different baselines provided by the shared task organizers[2]: a random baseline and a classifier that uses only word unigrams as features. Figure 3 reports the confusion matrix of our best model (Stacked2) on the official NLI essay test set. In addition, Table 5 reports the results obtained by the non stacked version of our architecture. These runs were submitted to the organizers of the task after the official evaluation period.

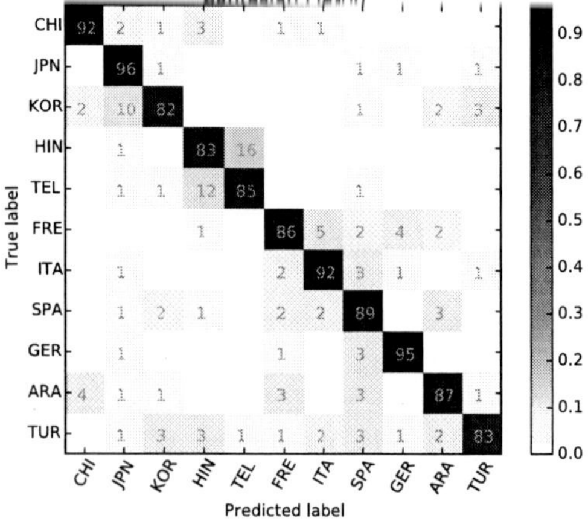

Figure 3: Confusion Matrix of the Stacked2 model on the NLI Shared Task 2017 official test set.

---

[2]A more detailed description of the baseline system is reported in (Malmasi et al., 2017).

System	F1-Score	Accuracy
Not-stacked1	0.8727	0.8729
Not-stacked2	0.8764	0.8765

Table 5: Results of our not-stacked systems for the essay track on the NLI Shared Task 2017 official test set.

4.1 Discussion

We tested different configurations of our architecture in order to evaluate the contribution on the accuracy of: *i)* the single components of the 2-stacked sentence-document architecture, *ii)* the lexical information and *iii)* the syntactic information. We carried out different experiments on the official NLI Shared Task 2017 development set and on the official NLI Shared Task 2013 test set that reflect the questions we wanted to answer, more specifically the questions are:

- (a) what are the performance obtained by using the 2-stacked sentence-document architecture and by using the sentence and document classifiers separately?

- (b) what is the contribution of the Lexical information on the stacked architecture and on the single components?

- (c) what is the contribution of the Syntactic information on the stacked architecture and on the single components?

In order to answer to these questions, we devised 3 different feature configurations: *All features*, that uses all the features described in section 3.2; *No Lexical*, that does not use the word n-grams features and the character n-grams features; *No Syntax*, that does not use the features extracted from the dependency syntax trees. For each configuration three different classifiers were trained: the Stacked classifier, the Document classifier (Not-Stacked) and the Sentence classifier (Sent). We tested the Sentence classifier in the document classification task by using two different approaches to assign the most probable L1 class of a document according to the predictions of the sentence classifier. The first is a vote approach (VOTE), where we decided to assign to a document the most frequent L1 predicted class among all the sentences of the document. The second is an average approach (AVG): since the sentence classifier assigns for each L1 class its confidence,

we took as L1 document class the one that had the highest average among all the probabilities of each sentence. In addition, we tested the accuracy of the Sentence classifier on sentence classification using as test sets the sentences belonging to the documents of the NLI 2017 development set and of the NLI 2013 test set.

2017 NLI development set			
Model	**Prec.**	**Recall**	**F1-Score**
All Features			
Stacked	0.8551	0.8527	0.8525
NotStacked	**0.8552**	**0.8527**	**0.8526**
Sent. (AVG)	0.7968	0.7900	0.7886
Sent. (VOTE)	0.7516	0.7436	0.7405
No Lexical			
Stacked	**0.8070**	**0.8036**	**0.8033**
Not-stacked	0.7947	0.7927	0.7923
Sent. (AVG)	0.7345	0.7182	0.7148
Sent. (VOTE)	0.6592	0.6409	0.6343
No Syntax			
Stacked	**0.8545**	**0.8527**	**0.8526**
Not-stacked	0.8519	0.8500	0.8498
Sent. (AVG)	0.8017	0.7936	0.7925
Sent. (VOTE)	0.7472	0.7409	0.7384

Table 6: Results of our experiments on the NLI Shared Task 2017 development set.

2013 NLI test set			
Model	**Prec.**	**Recall**	**F1-Score**
All features			
Stacked	**0.8537**	**0.8518**	**0.8516**
NotStacked	0.8502	0.8482	0.8480
Sent. (AVG)	0.7983	0.7909	0.7896
Sent. (VOTE)	0.7474	0.7418	0.7393
No Lexical			
Stacked	**0.8042**	**0.8018**	**0.8014**
Not-stacked	0.7840	0.7818	0.7814
Sent. (AVG)	0.7325	0.7200	0.7160
Sent. (VOTE)	0.6515	0.6373	0.6311
No Syntax			
Stacked	**0.8571**	**0.8555**	**0.8553**
Not-stacked	0.8513	0.8491	0.8489
Sent. (AVG)	0.7957	0.7891	0.7880
Sent. (VOTE)	0.7429	0.7373	0.7346

Table 7: Results of our experiments on the official NLI Shared Task 2013 test set.

Model	Prec.	Recall	F1-Score
2017 NLI development set			
Baseline	0.3533	0.3531	0.3515
All features	0.3937	0.3948	0.3936
2013 NLI test set			
Baseline	0.3541	0.3536	0.3519
All features	0.3946	0.3956	0.3946

Table 8: Performances of the sentence classifier on sentences belonging to the official NLI Shared Task 2017 development set and on the official NLI Shared Task 2013 test set.

Tables 6, 7 and 8 report the results of all the experiments. With the exception of the results obtained by the All features model on the 2017 development set, the stacked architecture always outperforms the not-stacked architecture in all the feature configurations used, showing that our devised stacked architecture is effectively able to exploit some information hidden in L2 sentences that are not fully captured at document level. For what concerns the sentence classifier when used as a document classifier, the average approach (AVG) always outperforms the results of VOTE version in all the configuration tested. We can see also that for each feature configuration there is a drop of only 5-6 points with respect to the 2-stacked classifier.

Table 8 reports the performances of the standalone sentence classifier on the L1 sentence classification task. For each dataset we report a baseline result calculated by using only word unigrams features. We have chosen this baseline following the approach used by NLI Shared Task organizers for calculating their baseline system. The baseline results are compared with the results achieved by the *All Features* configuration. As expected, the L1 sentence classification task is extremely more difficult than the L1 document classification task: the results achieved by the baseline system on the document classification task are extremely higher than the ones on the sentence classification task (+35% in terms of F1-Score). An interesting result to notice is the contribution in the sentence and document classification tasks of the features we used to develop our system. While we can observe an improvement of almost 14% (F1-Score) with respect to the baseline system on the L1 document classification task, only 4% (F1-Score) of improvement are achieved on the sentence classification task, confirming the complexity of the sentence classification task and the need of a specific process of feature selection for this task.

For what concerns question (b), we can observe that the lexical features (word n-grams and character n-grams) are extremely relevant for NLI. Both the *All Features Stacked* configuration and the *No Syntax Stacked* configuration report an accuracy of approximately 0.85% on the performed experiments, which is almost 5 points more than the results obtained by using the *No Lexical Stacked* configuration. The same drop in classification performance can be also observed when using the not-stacked architecture and the sentence classifier as document classifier with the AVG and the VOTE approaches.

Finally, for what concerns question (c) we can observe that surprisingly the syntax features bring almost or no contribution when joined with all the other features we used. When the results of the stacked, non-stacked and sentence rows achieved by the *All Features* configuration are compared with the respective ones achieved by the *No Syntax* configuration, no statistical difference in accuracy can be observed. In our opinion, this result is due to the correlation of lexical information and part-of-speech tag information, but a more in depth analysis would be required to analyze these results.

5 Conclusions

In this paper, we reported the results of our participation to the essay track of the Second Native Language Identification Shared Task. By resorting to a novel 2-stacked sentence-document architecture and to a set of general purpose features qualifying the lexical and grammatical structure of a text, we achieved very promising results and the first position in this shared task.

We have shown that our novel stacked architecture outperforms the results achieved by a single document classifier, showing that sentence local information is useful for NLI.

In future works, we would like to carry out a more in depth study of the sentence level classifier, focusing in particular on the features that most maximize its accuracy on L2 sentences. In addition, we want to investigate the combination of different sentence-document models in order to deepen the study of the interaction between the sentence and document levels in the task of native language identification.

References

Giuseppe Attardi, Felice Dell'Orletta, Maria Simi, and Joseph Turian. 2009. Accurate Dependency Parsing with a Stacked Multilayer Perceptron. In *Proceedings of the 2nd Workshop of Evalita 2009*.

Daniel Blanchard, Joel Tetreault, Derrick Higgins, Aoife Cahill, and Martin Chodorow. 2013. TOEFL11: A Corpus of Non-Native English. Technical report, Educational Testing Service.

Andrea Cimino and Felice Dell'Orletta. 2016. Building the state-of-the-art in POS tagging of Italian Tweets. In *Proceedings of Third Italian Conference on Computational Linguistics (CLiC-it 2016) & Fifth Evaluation Campaign of Natural Language Processing and Speech Tools for Italian. Final Workshop (EVALITA 2016), Napoli, Italy, December 5-7, 2016.*.

Andrea Cimino, Felice Dell'Orletta, Giulia Venturi, and Simonetta Montemagni. 2013. Linguistic Profiling based on General-purpose Features and Native Language Identification. In *Proceedings of the Eighth Workshop on Innovative Use of NLP for Building Educational Applications, BEA@NAACL-HLT 2013, June 13, 2013, Atlanta, Georgia, USA*. pages 207–215.

Felice Dell'Orletta, Simonetta Montemagni, and Giulia Venturi. 2012. Genre–oriented Readability Assessment: a Case Study. In *Proceedings of the Workshop on Speech and Language Processing Tools in Education (SLP-TED)*.

Felice Dell'Orletta, Martijn Wieling, Giulia Venturi, Andrea Cimino, and Simonetta Montemagni. 2014. Assessing the Readability of Sentences: Which Corpora and Features? In *Proceedings of the Ninth Workshop on Innovative Use of NLP for Building Educational Applications, BEA@ACL 2014, June 26, 2014, Baltimore, Maryland, USA*. pages 163–173.

Rong-En Fan, Kai-Wei Chang, Cho-Jui Hsieh, Xiang-Rui Wang, and Chih-Jen Lin. 2008. LIBLINEAR: A Library for Large Linear Classification. *Journal of Machine Learning Research* 9:1871–1874.

Radu-Tudor Ionescu, Marius Popescu, and Aoife Cahill. 2014. Can characters reveal your native language? A language-independent approach to native language identification. In *Proceedings of the 2014 Conference on Empirical Methods in Natural Language Processing, EMNLP 2014, October 25-29, 2014, Doha, Qatar, A meeting of SIGDAT, a Special Interest Group of the ACL*. pages 1363–1373.

Scott Jarvis, Yves Bestgen, and Steve Pepper. 2013. Maximizing Classification Accuracy in Native Language Identification. In *Proceedings of the Eighth Workshop on Innovative Use of NLP for Building Educational Applications*. Association for Computational Linguistics, Atlanta, Georgia, pages 111–118.

Moshe Koppel, Jonathan Schler, and Kfir Zigdon. 2005. Automatically Determining an Anonymous Author's Native Language. In *Intelligence and Security Informatics, IEEE International Conference on Intelligence and Security Informatics, ISI 2005, Atlanta, GA, USA, May 19-20, 2005, Proceedings*. pages 209–217.

Shervin Malmasi and Mark Dras. 2017. Native Language Identification using Stacked Generalization. *arXiv preprint arXiv:1703.06541* .

Shervin Malmasi, Keelan Evanini, Aoife Cahill, Joel Tetreault, Robert Pugh, Christopher Hamill, Diane Napolitano, and Yao Qian. 2017. A Report on the 2017 Native Language Identification Shared Task. In *Proceedings of the 12th Workshop on Building Educational Applications Using NLP*. Association for Computational Linguistics, Copenhagen, Denmark.

Joel Tetreault, Daniel Blanchard, and Aoife Cahill. 2013. A Report on the First Native Language Identification Shared Task. In *Proceedings of the Eighth Workshop on Building Educational Applications Using NLP*. Association for Computational Linguistics, Atlanta, GA, USA.

Joel R. Tetreault, Daniel Blanchard, Aoife Cahill, and Martin Chodorow. 2012. Native Tongues, Lost and Found: Resources and Empirical Evaluations in Native Language Identification. In *COLING 2012, 24th International Conference on Computational Linguistics, Proceedings of the Conference: Technical Papers, 8-15 December 2012, Mumbai, India*. pages 2585–2602.

Using gaze to predict text readability

Ana V. González-Garduño
University of Copenhagen
Department of Computer Science
fcm220@alumni.ku.dk

Anders Søgaard
University of Copenhagen
Department of Computer Science
soegaard@di.ku.dk

Abstract

We show that text readability prediction improves significantly from hard parameter sharing with models predicting first pass duration, total fixation duration and regression duration. Specifically, we induce multi-task Multilayer Perceptrons and Logistic Regression models over sentence representations that capture various aggregate statistics, from two different text readability corpora for English, as well as the Dundee eye-tracking corpus. Our approach leads to significant improvements over Single task learning and over previous systems. In addition, our improvements are consistent across train sample sizes, making our approach especially applicable to small datasets.

1 Introduction

When we read, our eyes move rapidly back and forth between fixations. These movements are called saccades. The distribution of fixations and saccades can provide us with important insight about the reader and the text being read. For example, long regressive eye movements, which typically involve regressing more than 10 letter spaces (Rayner, 1998), may indicate that the reader is facing some difficulty in understanding the text (Frazier and Rayner, 1982; Rayner, 2012). In addition, regressions have been shown to occur during the disambiguation of a sentence (Frazier and Rayner, 1982). This relationship between text and eye movements, has led to an influx of studies investigating the use of eye tracking data to improve and test computational models of language i.e. Barrett et al. (2016); Demberg and Keller (2008); Klerke et al. (2015). In this study we aim to incorporate eye movement data for the task of auto-

matic readability assessment. *Automatic readability assessment* is the task of automatically labeling a text with a certain difficulty level. An accurate and robust system has many potential applications, for example it can help educators obtain appropriate reading materials for students with normal learning capacities, as well as students with disabilities and language learners. It can also be used to assess the performance of machine translation, text simplification and language generation systems. Eye-tracking data has previously been used to evaluate readability models (Green, 2014; Klerke et al., 2015), however, our main contribution is to explore the way that eye tracking data can help improve models for readability assessment through multi-task learning (Caruana, 1997) and parser metrics based on the surprisal theory of syntactic complexity (Hale, 2001, 2016). Multi task learning allows the model to learn various tasks in parallel and improve performance by sharing parameters in the hidden layers.

The work most related to ours is by Singh et al (2016), who used eye tracking measures taken from the Dundee corpus in order to predict word by word reading times for each sentence. Subsequently, they used these word by word reading times as features for predicting readability. The two tasks were performed separately, and their feature representations were different from the ones presented here. In contrast, we present a model that predicts gaze *and* sentence-level readability simultaneously.

We use gaze data from the Dundee corpus (Kennedy et al., 2003) and two different datasets for the readability prediction task: aligned Wikipedia sentences used for the task of text simplification by Coster and Kauchak (2011) and the OneStopEnglish dataset used by Vajjala and Meurers (2014).

Proceedings of the 12th Workshop on Innovative Use of NLP for Building Educational Applications, pages 438–443
Copenhagen, Denmark, September 8, 2017. ©2017 Association for Computational Linguistics

Contributions This is, to the best of our knowledge, the first application of multi-task learning to readability prediction. Our model is also different from previous applications of multi-task learning to natural language processing in that we combine a classification task and a regression task. We experiment with two multi-task learning algorithms, namely hard parameter sharing for multi-layered perceptrons (Caruana, 1997) and a novel approach to hard parameter sharing between logistic and linear regression. We evaluate our models on Simple Wikipedia and the OneStopEnglish corpus. Finally, we present learning curves that show that the improvements are robust across different sample sizes.

2 Experiments

Data Our target task is sentence-level readability prediction, i.e. a binary classification problem of sentences into easy-to-read and hard-to-read.

Our main corpus is a sentence-aligned corpus of 137,000 simple versus normal English sentences from Wikipedia (Coster and Kauchak, 2011). Similar datasets have been used in the past, e.g., in Ambati et al. (2016) and Hwang et al. (2015). The easy-to-read sentences were taken from Simple Wikipedia and paired with sentences from the standard Wikipedia using cosine similarity.

In addition, we also evaluate our models on the OneStopEnglish corpus (Vajjala and Meurers, 2014), specifically the elementary-intermediate and elementary-advanced sentence pairs. This dataset has been used for readability assessment (Vajjala and Meurers, 2014) using the WeeBit model presented by (Vajjala and Meurers, 2012), so we compare our results with theirs.

Feature representation In this study, features known to affect the complexity of text, such as syntactic, lexical and total surprisal (Hale, 2001; Demberg and Keller, 2008), were used. Most of these features were extracted using a probabilistic top-down parser introduced by Roark (2001). After removing duplicate sentences and sentences with typos, the final corpus used was of about 80,000 sentence pairs. The features extracted are shown in table 1.

The *prefix probability* of word w_n is explained by Jelinek and Lafferty (1991) as the probability that w_n occurs as a prefix of some string generated by a grammar. It is the sum of the probabilities of

Features
1. Prefix probability -word1
2. Total surprisal - word1
3. Syntactic Surprisal -word1
4. Lexical Surprisal - word1
5. Ambiguity - word1
6. Prefix probability -word2
7. Total surprisal - word2
8. Syntactic Surprisal - word2
9. Lexical Surprisal - word2
10. Ambiguity - word2
11. Total surprisal – sent mean
12. Syntactic Surprisal – sent mean
13. Lexical Surprisal – sent mean
14. Ambiguity – sent mean
15. Total surprisal – sent sd
16. Syntactic Surprisal – sent sd
17. Lexical Surprisal – sent sd
18. Ambiguity – sent sd
19. Sentence length
20. Ave. Word length
21. Parse Tree height
22. Num of Subordinate clauses(SBARs)
23. Num of Noun phrases
24. Num of Verb phrases
25. Num of Prepositional phrases
26. Num of Adv phrases
27. Ratio nouns
28. Ratio verbs
29. Ratio adjectives
30. Ratio pronouns
31. Ratio adverbs
32. Ratio Det
33. Mean Age of Acquisition

Table 1: Features extracted for the readability data.

all trees from the first word to the current word. *Surprisal* is then the difference between the log of the prefix probability of w_n and w_{n-1}.

If we describe $\mathcal{D}(G, W[1, n])$ as the set of all possible leftmost derivations D with respect to probabilistic context free grammar G and whose last step used a production with terminal W_n. We can then express the prefix probability of $W[1, n]$ with respect to G as $PP_G(W[1, n]) = \sum_{D \in \mathcal{D}(G, W[1,n])} \rho(D)$, where $\rho(D)$ is the probability of the derivation of a certain tree.

The total surprisal of W_n is then defined as:

$$S_G(W_n) = -\log \frac{PP_G(W[1, n])}{PP_G(W[1, n - 1])}$$

Syntactic surprisal and *lexical surprisal* are calculated to account for high surprisal scores (Roark et al., 2009). As Roark et al. (2009) mentions, a word may surprise because it is unconventional, or because it occurs in an unusual context.

In order to separate the lexical and syntactic

components of surprisal, the incremental parser calculates partial derivations immediately before word W_n is integrated into the syntactic structure. Syntactic surprisal ($SynS_G(W_n)$) is defined as:

$$-\log \frac{\sum_{D\in\mathcal{D}(G,W[1,n])} \rho(D[1,|D|-1])}{PP_G(W[1,n-1])}$$

and lexical surprisal ($LexS_G(W_n)$) as:

$$-\log \frac{PP_G(W[1,n])}{\sum_{D\in\mathcal{D}(G,W[1,n])} \rho(D[1,|D|-1])}$$

Where $D[1,|D|-1]$ is the set of the partial derivations before each word is integrated into the structure $\mathcal{D}(G,W[1,n])$. Total surprisal turns out to be sum of syntactic surprisal and lexical surprisal.

We also obtain an entropy score using the parser. Entropy over a set of derivations $\mathcal{D}$, denoted as $H(\mathcal{D})$, quantifies the uncertainty over the partial derivations. We call this feature *Ambiguity*, defined as:

$$-\sum_{D\in\mathcal{D}} \frac{\rho(D)}{\sum_{D'\in\mathcal{D}} \rho(D')} \log \frac{\rho(D)}{\sum_{D'\in\mathcal{D}} \rho(D')}$$

Furthermore, features corresponding to the first and second words were included, as the initial words in a sentence allow the reader to make preliminary guesses of what the structure will be for the rest of the sentence, although these predictions can often turn out to be wrong. In addition, mean syntactic scores and standard deviations for all words in the sentence are included as features. We also include the mean age of acquisition for the words in a given sentence, using data from Kuperman et al. (2012). Finally, we include basic counts and ratios used previously in readability prediction such as sentence length, parse tree height, number of SBAR's, noun phrases, verb phrases, among others .

In order to predict gaze, we extract the features seen in Table 1 from the Dundee corpus. As mentioned earlier, these features offer a good representation of cognitive load, which is also reflected in reading times. A feature vector of size 33 was built for each sentence, and this information was used in order to predict an average first pass duration, regression path duration and total fixation duration.

First pass duration refers to the sum of all fixations on a region once the region is first entered until it is left. *Regression path duration* includes regressions made out of a region prior to moving forward in the text and *total fixation duration* is the sum of all fixations in the region including, regressions to that region. As mentioned in Rayner et al. (2006), these measures typically concern research questions focusing on sentence or discourse processing.

Logistic/linear regression and MLPs Logistic Regression (LR) models have been widely used in document level readability classification i.e. Feng et al. (2010) and (Xia et al., 2016). LR models are linear models and can be thought of as single-layer perceptrons with softmax or sigmoid activation functions. The objective is typically to minimize a cross-entropy loss function. The same architecture can be used for linear regression, however, when trained to minimize mean squared error. Here, we compare LR with a 3-layered Multi Layer Perceptron (MLP). For our MLP architecture, we use sigmoid activation at the input and output layers and use ReLu activation in the hidden layer. The hidden layer contains 100 neurons. All models presented here use the Adam optimizer, and a drop-out rate of 0.5. We also use Adam to learn logistic and linear regression models.

As already mentioned, we go beyond single-task LR and MLP models and present two multi-task learning architectures with heterogeneous loss functions (cross-entropy and minimum squared error). In multi-task learning (Caruana, 1997), the training signals of one task are used as an inductive bias in order to improve the generalization of another task. Specifically, we use the the task of gaze prediction in order to improve the generalization of readability prediction.

Multi-task MLP Our multi-task learning architecture is identical to that of Caruana (1997) and Collobert et al. (2011), i.e., two MLPs that share all parameters in their hidden layers. The only difference is that one of the MLPs in our case is trained to minimize a minimum squared error to predict gaze statistics.

Multi-task logistic and linear regression Our linear multi-task learning model is novel in that it combines a logistic and a linear regression model by tying their parameters. As mentioned earlier,

LR models can be thought of as single-layer perceptrons. We tie a single-layer perceptron with sigmoid activation to another single-layer perceptron with linear activation by sharing their single layer and giving a higher weight to our main task. While this is in fact a simpler model than the deep multi-task learning model above, this model has, to the best of our knowledge, not been suggested before, and in many ways, it is surprising that it works.

Baselines Ambati et al. (2016) obtained 78.87 percent accuracy on the Wikipedia dataset. They use features extracted from a Combinatory Categorical Grammar (CCG) parser. We also compare our results to Vajjala and Meurers (2014), who use their WeeBit model in order to predict readability at the sentence level. In addition, for the Wikipedia dataset, we include the best results from Singh et al. (2016) as it is the study most related to ours.

3 Results

Our results are shown in Table 2.

For the Wikipedia corpus, our best multi-task learning system shows an improvement in accuracy over previous work by about 8%. A big part of the improvement can be attributed to using a deep learning architecture. Single-task MLPs do about 8% better than logistic regression on this dataset, in absolute numbers. Multi-task learning buys us another .5%, absolute. For the advanced-elementary sentence pairs in the OneStopEnglish corpus, a slightly larger improvement is seen from multi-task learning to single-task. For all multi-task systems, there is an improvement over the corresponding single-task system with at least two of the gaze inputs. The best result was achieved using Multi-Task MLP. Inclusion of gaze data improved our results about 2.6 % over the best single-task result.

We performed various paired T tests in order to assess whether or not the improvements obtained using multi-task learning was significant. We compared the results of each MTL model to its corresponding STL model. We report p values using asterisks in Table 2. P values smaller than 0.001 are described using ***, ** indicate p values ranging from 0.001 to 0.01 and p values from 0.01 to 0.5 are shown with *. No asterisk indicates that there was no statistically significant changes.

SYSTEMS	WIKIPEDIA	OSE (A-E)	OSE (I-E)
PREVIOUS			
Singh	75.21	-	-
Ambati	78.87	-	-
Vajjala	66.00	61.0	51.0
SINGLE-TASK			
LR	78.17	67.23	58.72
MLP	85.95	67.53	59.30
MULTI-TASK LR			
1st pass	78.20	67.88	60.71***
Regression	78.15	68.10*	59.68
Total fix	78.60*	68.08**	60.80**
MULTI-TASK MLP			
1st pass	86.13	68.08 ***	61.70 ***
Regression	86.11	67.66	**61.91*****
Total fix	**86.45***	68.51 ***	61.27 ***

Table 2: Accuracy for all models. Most results obtained using MTL-MLP yield statistically significant improvements of STL-MLP ($p < 0.001$).

4 Discussion

Performance of features The features extracted using the probabilistic top down parser have previously been used in order to predict word by word reading times (Singh et al., 2016; Demberg and Keller, 2008), but have not been thoroughly explored in the task of readability prediction. Here, we used surprisal and entropy, along with other low-level features in order to predict the reading level of single sentences. Using the STL-MLP, we predicted readability using feature groups, separated by syntactic features and low level features. Our syntactic features include features 1-18, while our low level features are 19-33 in table 1. We found that low level features are more predictive for our datasets than syntactic features, however, it is a combination of both that yields the best results. These results can be seen in table 3.

Feature Set	Wikipedia	OSE I-E	OSE A-E
Syntactic Features	60.35	54.90	59.79
Low level Features	78.15	57.30	65.17
All Features	**85.95**	**59.30**	**67.53**

Table 3: Accuracy when predicting readability using features in groups. The results show, that a combination of both sets of features provide the best result.

In addition, we performed a single feature evaluation, where each feature was used to predict readability using the STL-MLP model. The 10 most predictive features for the Wikipedia dataset are presented in table 4. The results reaffirm the previous finding that although syntactic features are predictive of readability, low level features remain the most predictive.

Wikipedia	
Feature	Accuracy
Ratio Verbs	67.90
Ratio Adjectives	66.46
Sentence Length	61.96
Ratio Adverbs	57.53
Mean Age of Acquisition	57.34
Average Word Length	56.17
Ambiguity – sent SD	55.66
Lexical suprisal – sent SD	55.37
Num of verb phrases	55.13
Ambiguity Sent Mean	55.00

Table 4: Accuracy on Wikipedia dataset when predicting readability using single features.

Effects of using gaze data The main objective of this study was to explore how the use of eye tracking data improved our readability prediction model. Using the Dundee eye tracking corpus, we were able to learn models for predicting an average first pass duration, total regression to duration, and total fixation duration for a given sentence in our readability datasets. Using hard parameter sharing, we learned to predict a readability label and gaze simultaneously. This method allows us to exploit the information contained in one task to better generalize another. Our results demonstrate that gaze data does improve readability models significantly.

Learning curves In figure 1 we compare the learning curves for the best MTL and STL models for each dataset. We show the accuracy on both validation sets using varying amounts of train samples. The first train sample used consisted of 100 sentences. At this small sample size, the effect of the gaze data is more clear. For example, for the Wikipedia dataset the validation accuracy using 100 samples is about 74.5 % for the MTL MLP system, while for the STL MLP system, the accuracy is about 10 % lower. At about 20,000 samples the difference in performance between the two systems begins to level off, however, MTL remains slightly higher the entire time. This is in line with Caruana (1997), who mentions that the

improvements using MTL are typically stronger when using smaller sample sizes.

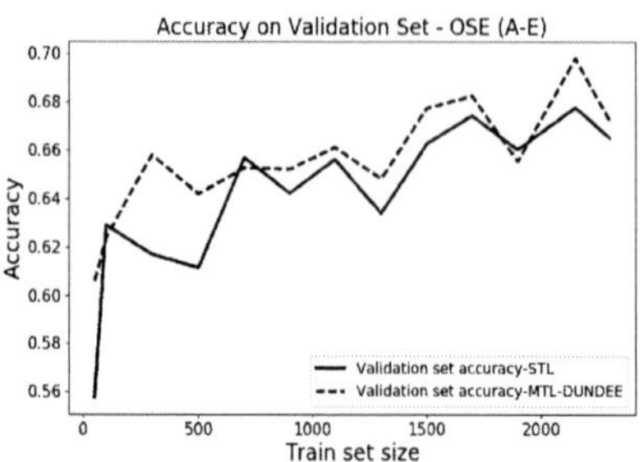
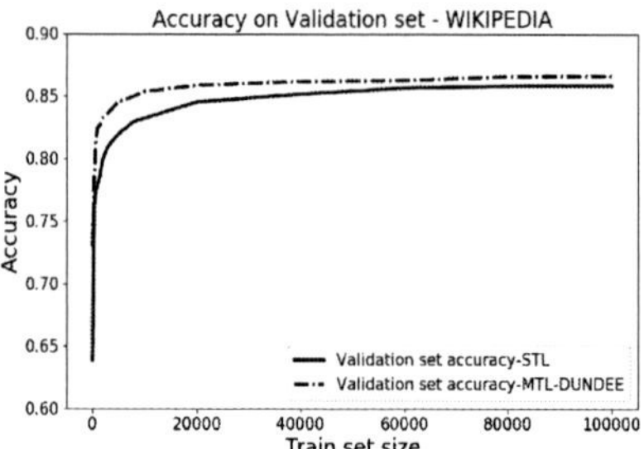

Figure 1: Learning curves for the OSE A-E and Wikipedia datasets varying the train sample size. The first sample size consisted of 100 sentences.

Similar results can be seen for the Advanced-Elementary sentence pairs. We begin training our model on about 100 samples and incrementally increased the train set size. Neither of the models achieve high accuracy, however, the MTL system improves the result about 5 %, and as the training set size increases, this trend persists. Similar results are observed for the Intermediate-Advanced pairs.

5 Conclusion

In this study, we have presented the first application of multi-task learning to predicting sentence-level readability. We presented two models: a deep learning model and a linear model. The linear multi-task learning model is novel and yields statistically significant results, however, the deep learning model performs better. We present a learning curve analysis showing that multi-task learning is more effective with small sample sizes, however, the improvements are robust across sample sizes.

References

Ram Bharat Ambati, Siva Reddy, and Mark Steedman. 2016. Assessing relative sentence complexity using an incremental ccg parser. In *Proceedings of the 2016 Conference of the North American Chapter of the Association for Computational Linguistics: Human Language Technologies*, pages 1051–1057.

Maria Barrett, Joachim Bingel, Frank Keller, and Anders Søgaard. 2016. Weakly supervised part-of-speech tagging using eye-tracking data.

Rich Caruana. 1997. Multitask learning. *Machine Learning*, 28(41).

Ronan Collobert, Jason Weston, Léon Bottou, Michael Karlen, Koray Kavukcuoglu, and Pavel Kuksa. 2011. Natural language processing (almost) from scratch. *Journal of Machine Learning Research*, 12(Aug):2493–2537.

William Coster and David Kauchak. 2011. Simple english wikipedia: A new text simplification task. In *Proceedings of the 49th Annual Meeting of the Association for Computational Linguistics:shortpapers*, pages 665–669.

Vera Demberg and Frank Keller. 2008. Data from eye-tracking corpora as evidence for theories of syntactic processing complexity. *Cognition*, 109(2):192–210.

Lijun Feng, Martin Jansche, Matt Huenerfauth, and Noémie Elhadad. 2010. A comparison of features for automatic readability assessment. In *Proceedings of the 23rd International Conference on Computational Linguistics: Posters*, pages 276–284. Association for Computational Linguistics.

Lyn Frazier and Keith Rayner. 1982. Making and correcting errors during sentence comprehension: Eye movements in the analysis of structurally ambiguous sentences. *Cognitive psychology*, 14(2):178–210.

Matthew J. Green. 2014. An eye-tracking evaluation of some parser complexity metrics. In *Proceedings of the 3rd Workshop on Predicting and Improving Text Readability for Target Reader Populations (PITR)*, page 38–46. Association for Computational Linguistics.

John Hale. 2001. A probabilistic earley parser as a psycholinguistic model. In *Proceedings of the second meeting of the North American Chapter of the Association for Computational Linguistics on Language technologies*, pages 1–8. Association for Computational Linguistics.

John Hale. 2016. Information-theoretical complexity metrics. *Language and Linguistics Compass*, 10(9).

William Hwang, Hannaneh Hajishirzi, Mari Ostendorf, and Wei Wu. 2015. Aligning sentences from standard wikipedia to simple wikipedia. In *Proceedings of the 2015 Conference of the North American Chapter of the Association for Computational Linguistics (NAACL)*.

Frederick Jelinek and John D. Lafferty. 1991. Computation of the probability of initial substring generation by stochastic context-free grammars. *Computational Linguistics*, 17(3):315–323.

Alan Kennedy, Robin Hill, and Joël Pynte. 2003. The dundee corpus. *Proceedings of the 12th European conference on eye movement*.

Sigrid Klerke, Sheila Castilho, Maria Barrett, and Anders Søgaard. 2015. Reading metrics for estimating task efficiency with mt output. In *Conference on Empirical Methods in Natural Language Processing*, page 6.

Victor Kuperman, Hans Stadthagen-Gonzalez, and Marc Brysbaert. 2012. Age-of-acquisition ratings for 30,000 english words. *Behavior Research Methods*, 44(4).

Keith Rayner. 1998. Eye movements in reading and information processing: 20 years of research. *Psychological Bulletin*, 124(3).

Keith Rayner. 2012. *Eye movements in reading: Perceptual and language processes*. Elsevier.

Keith Rayner, Kathryn H Chace, Timothy J Slattery, and Jane Ashby. 2006. Eye movements as reflections of comprehension processes in reading. *Scientific studies of reading*, 10(3):241–255.

Brian Roark. 2001. Probabilistic top-down parsing and language modeling. *Computational Linguistics*, 27(2).

Brian Roark, Asaf Bachrach, Carlos Cardenas, and Christophe Pallier. 2009. Deriving lexical and syntactic expectation-based measures for psycholinguistic modeling via incremental top-down parsing. In *Proceedings of the 2009 Conference on Empirical Methods in Natural Language Processing*, page 324–333. Association for Computational Linguistics.

Abhinav Deep Singh, Poojan Mehta, Samar Husain, and Rajakrishnan Rajkumar. 2016. Quantifying sentence complexity based on eye-tracking measures. In *Proceedings of the Workshop on Computational Linguistics for Linguistic Complexity*, page 202–212.

Sowmya Vajjala and Detmar Meurers. 2012. On improving the accuracy of readability classification using insights from second language acquisition. In *The 7th Workshop on the Innovative Use of NLP for Building Educational Applications*, page 163–173.

Sowmya Vajjala and Detmar Meurers. 2014. Readability assessment for text simplification. *International Journal of Applied Linguistics*, 165(2).

Menglin Xia, Ekaterina Kochmar, and E Briscoe. 2016. Text readability assessment for second language learners.

Annotating Orthographic Target Hypotheses in a German L1 Learner Corpus

Ronja Laarmann-Quante
Katrin Ortmann
Anna Ehlert
Maurice Vogel
Stefanie Dipper
{laarmann-quante, dipper}@linguistics.rub.de
{katrin.ortmann, anna.ehlert, maurice.vogel}@rub.de
Ruhr-University Bochum

Abstract

NLP applications for learners often rely on annotated learner corpora. Thereby, it is important that the annotations are both meaningful for the task, and consistent and reliable. We present a new longitudinal L1 learner corpus for German (handwritten texts collected in grade 2–4), which is transcribed and annotated with a target hypothesis that strictly only corrects orthographic errors, and is thereby tailored to research and tool development for orthographic issues in primary school. While for most corpora, transcription and target hypothesis are not evaluated, we conducted a detailed inter-annotator agreement study for both tasks. Although we achieved high agreement, our discussion of cases of disagreement shows that even with detailed guidelines, annotators differ here and there for different reasons, which should also be considered when working with transcriptions and target hypotheses of other corpora, especially if no explicit guidelines for their construction are known.

1 Introduction

Learner corpora cannot only be used to study the language of learners but they also have a strong connection to the development of educational applications. NLP tools can be trained on learner corpora to be later used in ICALL (intelligent computer-assisted language learning) systems, to provide immediate analyses of errors occurring in the input text (Meurers, 2015; for some examples, see Barbagli et al., 2016). To enable high-quality analyses in such a scenario, it is crucial that the underlying training data have been annotated mean-

ingfully and consistently. The identification and annotation of errors necessarily depends on a target hypothesis, i.e. the assumed correct form of the learner's utterance, be that stated implicitly or explicitly (Reznicek et al., 2013). The correct form itself can already serve as error annotation. This has the advantage that errors do not have to be cast into pre-defined categories, which might not capture all cases (Fitzpatrick and Seegmiller, 2004). However, as Reznicek et al. (2013) demonstrate, there is a possibly infinite number of target hypotheses for a single utterance, depending on the linguistic level that is corrected (orthography, grammar, lexis, etc.). They argue further that the usefulness of a target hypothesis depends on the research purpose, and that its construction must be comprehensible and transparent to other researchers.

In this paper, we present a new corpus resource which is tailored to research on orthography in texts produced by primary school children in Germany. It features a target hypothesis that strictly only corrects orthographic errors in order to keep them apart from other kinds of errors concerning grammar or semantics. Consider, for instance, the sentence in example (1):[1]

(1) Dodo *est das Eis
     Dodo eats the ice cream

The correct grammatical form of *<est>[2] in this context would be <isst> (3RD.PERS.SG.PRES. of '(to) eat'). However, there are two kinds of mistakes in the form *<est>: Firstly, the <s> has to be doubled, which is unambiguously an error on the level of orthography (see e.g. Eisenberg (2013) on

---

[1]The English translation in italics represents the intended meaning.

[2]Angle brackets mark graphemes, the asterisk indicates an erroneous form.

Proceedings of the 12th Workshop on Innovative Use of NLP for Building Educational Applications, pages 444–456
Copenhagen, Denmark, September 8, 2017. ©2017 Association for Computational Linguistics

German consonant doubling). Correcting this error results in the form <esst>, which is the 2ND.PERS.PL.PRES. form of '(to) eat', though. Now, the level of the second error, which is the use of <e> for <i>, is ambiguous. We see three possible analyses: (i) Given that <esst> does exist in the word's inflection paradigm, it is clear that only the grammatical context (agreement with *Dodo*, a proper name) reveals it as an error. One could hence say that a wrong inflectional form was chosen, which is not an issue of orthography but of grammar. (ii) Similarly, one could say that the form was inflected like a weak verb (in which case *esst* would indeed be 3RD.PERS.SG.PRES), which is also a matter of grammar rather than orthography. (iii) Finally, it is possible that the learner could not discriminate the phonemes /ɪ/ and /ɛ/. It is known that the discrimination and representation of lax vowels poses a challenge to primary school children, which is dealt with on the level of orthographic competence (May, 2013; Thelen, 2010). Thus, even for this word alone two different target hypotheses can be constructed: one which deals with orthography errors only (yielding <esst> as an acceptable word form of the intended lemma), and another one which deals with errors (possibly) attributable to grammar (yielding <isst>).

With our work currently focusing on orthography, we annotated our corpus with the first type of target hypothesis, i.e. the one that strictly only corrects orthographic errors. Keeping orthography errors apart from grammatical errors is important for two reasons: Firstly, the empirical questions we are pursuing concern the relationship of word properties and spelling errors. Mixing up grammatical and orthographic corrections would not allow to make statements about a child's orthographic competence only. Especially if we look at surface properties of the original and the target word like character n-gram frequencies, it is important to base the analysis on the word that the child in fact *targeted*, even if it is ungrammatical in this context. To analyze the interplay of grammatical and orthographic errors is then a possible second step.

Secondly, with regard to tool building, there are not many applications dealing with primary school children's orthography yet (but see Thelen, 2010; Berkling and Pflaumer, 2014; Berkling and Lavalley, 2015). Stüker et al. (2011) have shown, for instance, that for German, the generic state-of-the-art spellchecker Hunspell does not work well on spellings produced by primary school children. They proposed a phonetic-based approach combined with a language model. On their dataset of children's texts, this approach turned out more successful than Hunspell.

Robust spelling error detection and correction is a prerequisite for fully automatic applications dealing with spelling errors, such as the spelling error analysis tool we are currently developing (Laarmann-Quante, to appear). Such applications are needed to assist children individually in the acquisition of spelling competence. Our corpus shall provide a basis for further developments in this direction.

Both for the study of learner errors as well as for tool building, it is important that one can rely on the corpus annotations. Target hypotheses play a key role here. Rosen et al. (2014) (see also its discussion in Meurers, 2015) have shown that differing target hypotheses among annotators account for a considerable amount of disagreement in the choice of error tags. They conclude, in line with Reznicek et al. (2013), that an explicit target hypothesis is required for annotating learner errors. While target hypotheses in general are said to be hard to agree on (Lüdeling, 2008; Fitzpatrick and Seegmiller, 2004), minimal target hypotheses, i.e. minimal form changes that are required to make an utterance grammatical (Meurers, 2015), are generally presented as less problematic for inter-annotator agreement (see e.g. Reznicek et al. (2012) on the minimal target hypothesis in the Falko corpus). However, we are not aware of a study which systematically evaluates the agreement on such a minimal target hypothesis in a corpus. As example (1) above has shown, even form-driven distinctions include ambiguities which can lead to inconsistencies in the annotated data.

We therefore conducted a detailed inter-annotator agreement study on a subset of our corpus to evaluate the expected reliability of the target hypothesis annotations, and to raise awareness for potential inconsistencies, which even detailed annotation guidelines cannot fully cover. Moreover, even though many learner corpora are built from hand-written source texts, especially L1 corpora, errors or ambiguities that arise during the transcription are hardly ever addressed (but see Abel et al.,2014; Glaznieks et al., 2014). To deal with this issue, we also measured agreement on the transcription of our hand-written source data.

The remainder of the paper is structured as follows: Section 2 gives an overview of related work, Section 3 introduces our corpus, Section 4 explains our guidelines for the transcription and the target hypothesis, Section 5 presents our study on inter-annotator agreement and Section 6 concludes the paper with a summary and outlook. A full example of a transcribed and normalized text, including the scanned handwritten text, can be found in the Appendix.

2 Related Work

This paper deals with the orthographic annotation of a new corpus resource with two main novelties: Firstly, our target hypothesis (which we call "normalization") strictly only corrects orthographic errors, and secondly, we present a detailed analysis of the inter-annotator agreement for the target hypothesis. We review shortly how these two aspects have been handled by other corpora. While there is an abundant number of L2 learner corpora (see e.g. the 'Learner Corpora around the World' list maintained by the Centre for English Corpus Linguistics[3]), L1 written corpora are still relatively rare (see Abel et al. (2014) and Barbagli et al. (2016) for overviews). We restrict our discussion to an exemplary selection of corpora from both areas.

Not all L1 corpora present an explicit target hypothesis (e.g. Parr, 2010) but if they do, they typically only annotate one target hypothesis which corrects orthographic as well as grammatical and sometimes also lexical errors (Barbagli et al., 2016; Berkling et al., 2014; Berkling, 2016). In the corpora described in Berkling et al. (2014) and Berkling (2016), grammatical errors/corrections get an extra mark to be excluded from orthographic analyses but in the target hypothesis, only the grammatically correct form is given and spelling errors within the erroneous form are not considered. For instance, *<Dretet> is corrected to <tritt> '(he/she) kicks' while an orthographically correct (but grammatically incorrect form) would be <tretet>. Furthermore, one cannot see how ambiguous cases are handled, e.g. *<er schlaft> is treated as an orthography error and cor-

rected to <er schläft> 'he sleeps', although the same ambiguity applies as in example (1) above.[4]

Only in the *Osnabrücker Bildergeschichtenkorpus* (Thelen, 2000, 2010), words which contain both grammatical and orthographic errors are assigned two target hypotheses; e.g. *<ien> is assigned both <ihn> (orthographically correct) and <ihm> 'him' (grammatically correct). However, decisions about grammatical and orthographic errors are not consistent. For instance, at one point *(er/sie)* *<seht> (instead of <sieht> '(he/she) sees') is marked as a grammatical error, at another point as an orthographic one.

Two German L2 learner corpora are annotated with more than one target hypothesis: Falko (Reznicek et al., 2012) and EAGLE (Boyd, 2010). Falko treats orthographic and grammatical errors together at the first layer, though, and semantic/stylistic errors on the second. EAGLE provides a separate layer for spelling errors but only those resulting in non-words are considered.

All of the corpora have in common that there was no evaluation of the annotated target hypothesis and we are only aware of one corpus in which the transcription was evaluated (Abel et al., 2014; Glaznieks et al., 2014). The authors also report an evaluation of the orthographic error annotation but leave open if the evaluation only concerns the error categories themselves, or if the corrected forms have been evaluated as well. They achieved 80% accuracy, but state that they are not aware of numbers to compare with.

3 The Corpus

In her dissertation, Frieg (2014) evaluated the promotion of language skills with the help of "generative text production" in German primary school classes. To this end, she collected freely written texts from 15 classes of 7 different schools in North-Rhine Westphalia/Germany over a time period of over 2.5 years between 2010 and 2012. Children from grade 2–4, many of them with a migration background, produced texts at ten different points in time. Every two to four months, the children were asked to write down a picture story shown in a sequence of six pictures in their classrooms.[5] All the stories were taken from Schroff (2000) and deal with two children and their dog,

---

[3]https://uclouvain.be/en/
research-institutes/ilc/cecl/
learner-corpora-around-the-world.html,
last access on July 14, 2017

[4]The examples <Dretet> and <schlaft> are both taken from the corpus described in Berkling (2016).

[5]A sample text is shown in Appendix A.

who experience different adventures. Over the whole time course, eight different stories were used. For more information on the data collection, see Frieg (2014).

Our corpus is based on scans of the original handwritten texts collected in that research project. Basically, we used all the texts for which parental consent was given and which contained at least 15 readable words.[6] Moreover, we only included texts for which the entire scan was readable. This means that scans of bad quality or in which some lines were cropped were excluded altogether. Overall, our corpus comprises 1,845 texts[7] written by 251 children (47.0% female, 52.2% male, 0.8% unknown). On average, there are 7.4 texts (SD: 2.1) per child, with an average length 109.3 words (SD: 49.9). From the 1,741 texts that have been transcribed and normalized (i.e. assigned a target form) to date, 17.76% of the words contain one or more spelling errors (counted as mismatches of original and target word, see Section 4).

Each text is annotated with the following metadata: the child's ID, the grade in which the text was written, the ID of the class and school of the child, the topic of the picture story, the child's gender and age, language(s) spoken by the child, and whether they obtained additional tuition in German as a second language or in their mother tongue.

4 Transcription and Normalization Guidelines

In this section, we present the most important aspects of the guidelines we developed for transcribing the handwritten texts and for providing an orthographic target hypothesis, called "normalization". The full guidelines are published in Laarmann-Quante et al. (2017).

4.1 Transcription

The general rule for transcribing the texts to typewriting is to stick as closely as possible to the original input and not correct any spelling errors or word separations. In certain cases, the transcriber

is asked to decide in favor of the child, i.e. give the orthographically correct option a higher weight: if it is not possible to clearly decide which character(s) a stroke represents, whether a letter is uppercase or lowercase or if there is a space between words or not. Example (2) gives an example of such ambiguous cases. In the first word, the first letter could be a <d> or a capitalized <D>. Since the word refers to a proper name, the transcription with the uppercase letter <Dodo> is to be chosen. The second word could be read as <flpster> (a non-word) or as <fenster> 'window'. In this case, the transcriber should decide for the existing word.

(2) 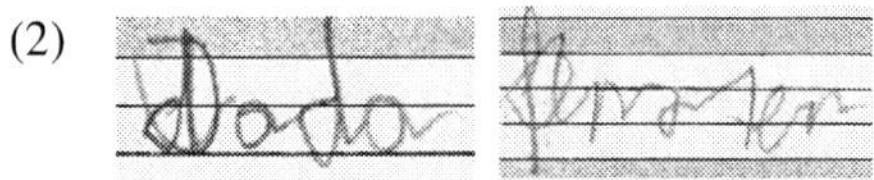

However, if a character is completely illegible or non-existent, it is represented by an asterisk (*), see example (3), which is transcribed as <ire Fre*ndin Lars> (with the target hypothesis of <Fre*ndin> being <Freundin> '(female) friend').

(3) 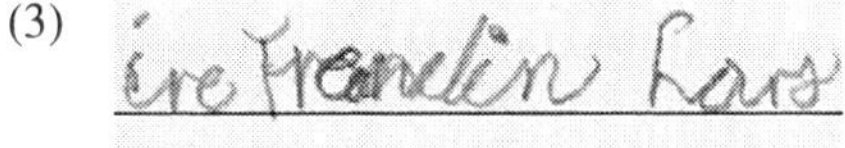

As we are only interested in the actual text the child wrote, graphical illustrations, comments of the teacher, blank lines and meta data like date information, etc. are ignored. Also, words crossed out by the child are not transcribed. If the child indicated a permutation of words or an insertion of one or more words, the words are inserted in the intended place. Besides the pure transcription of perceived characters, transcribers are asked to maintain information about the formatting of the text by marking the end of each line with a circumflex (^). At a later stage, this may help to explain certain word separations. The end of headlines is marked as well, to facilitate a subsequent grammatical analysis, because headlines often are incomplete sentences.

4.2 Normalization

The aim of the normalization is to provide an orthographic target hypothesis, i.e. the orthographically correct version, for each token. To decide whether a word form is orthographically correct,

---

[6]This means in particular that for at least 15 words, one had to be able to identify a target word. Some texts were shorter than 15 words altogether and some texts consisted (primarily) of non-identifiable letter strings.

[7]The final number of texts will probably be a little lower because we are still in the process of transcribing the texts and during this process some scans turn out to be unusable.

the *Duden*[8] is used as a reference. If the annotator cannot identify at all which word the child probably meant, the child's word is copied and a question mark ('?') is placed in front of it to mark it as a non-identifiable target.

It is important that only errors are corrected which can be clearly attributed to orthography and not to other phenomena such as sentence boundaries, inflection, agreement, syntax, semantics, etc. Example (4) shows an example sentence which contains both orthographic and grammatical errors.

(4)   Dodo bellt ein Vogel an Lea ist auf dem weg zu Schuhle auf einmal sid sie ire Fre*ndin Lars
Dodo barks at a bird Lea is on the way to school suddenly she sees her friend Lars

Following our guidelines, the target hypothesis is (5a) and not (5b):

(5) a.   Dodo bellt ein Vogel an Lea ist auf dem Weg zu Schule auf einmal sieht sie ihre Freundin Lars

      b.   Dodo bellt ein**en** Vogel an . Lea ist auf dem Weg zu**r** Schule . Auf einmal sieht sie ihr**en Freund** Lars

Any error which could be a purely grammatical one, like missing agreement (<bellt **ein** Vogel an>), false prepositions (<**zu** Schule>), is not corrected.[9] If a word contains both grammatical and orthographic errors, the orthographic errors are corrected but the grammatical errors are not. For instance, in *<Lea ging früh in die **Schuhlen**> 'Lea went to schools early' the superfluous <h> is corrected (<Schulen>) but not the inflection of *Schulen* (which should be *Schule*).[10]

Deciding in favor of the child is a principle that is also pursued in the normalization. For instance, letter case and word boundaries are only corrected

if there is absolutely no possibility that the child's version is correct. For instance, if the child wrote words separately that could in fact be written separately in a slightly modified context (as with verb particles for instance), it is regarded as a syntactical error and thus not corrected here. For example, <Ihr Hund wollte mit kommen> 'Her dog wanted to come with her' is not corrected to the more common form <mitkommen> because it would be correct if there were some words in between (e.g. <mit *in die Schule* kommen> 'come with her to school'. The same holds true for wrong letter case, e.g. if the first word after a sentence boundary mark was not capitalized: As many children only poorly mark sentence boundaries, one could argue that it was the wrong choice of punctuation mark instead (e.g. a period instead of a comma). Letter case is only corrected if the child wrote nouns and proper names in lowercase, or if it capitalized a word where one cannot at all argue for a (missing) sentence boundary.

Particular attention must be paid in cases of noun and verb inflection. Generally, a target word has to be an existing German word form. However, if a child e.g. mistakenly inflects a verb as a weak verb instead of a strong verb (like *treffen* → **trefften* instead of *trafen*, which is analogous to *meet* → **meeted* instead of *met*), this is considered a grammatical (morphological) error and, hence, is not corrected. Only the orthographic errors in such forms are corrected to an extent that a plausible word form is obtained which could be the result of an (incorrect) inflection of this word or derivation from a related word form. In some cases, the resulting word form does exist in the inflection paradigm (<esst>/<lauft> for <isst>/<läuft> is 2ND.PERS.PL.PRES. of 'eat'/'run') so the child may have picked the wrong form. In other cases, the word form does not exist at all (e.g. *<Wänder> for <Wände> 'walls', *<springte> for <sprang> 'jumped'). Here, the annotator is asked to mark the target hypothesis as non-existing by placing a tilde (∼) in front of the word (e.g.*schpringte* → ∼*springte*).

5   Inter-Annotator Agreement

To get a sense of the difficulty of the task, the effectiveness of the guidelines as well as the expected consistency of the transcription and normalization in the corpus, we conducted an inter-annotator agreement study.

---

[8]www.duden.de

[9]The only exception is the confusion of <das> (article/pronoun) and <dass> (conjunction) which is always corrected, because it is an error commonly counted in orthographic annotation schemes (Fay, 2010; Thomé and Thomé, 2004).

[10]Real-word errors can only be detected by considering the context. In such cases, the target word has to belong to the (probably) intended lemma. For instance, although <weg> is an existing word ('away'), the context could make clear that 'Weg' ('way') was meant, hence the real-word error is corrected.

| | Transcription | | | Normalization | |
Text ID	#char	perc	κ	#tok	perc
025-201112-I-Schule	971	98.04	.99	179	94.41
170-201112-IV-Weg	161	97.52	.99	31	83.87
207-200910-II-Weg	414	75.12	.86	82	71.95
324-201011-II-Jenga	314	95.54	.97	59	84.75
331-201011-III-Seilbahn	411	94.89	.97	69	91.30
416-201112-II-Fundbuero	891	98.54	.99	175	96.00
427-200910-I-Eis	248	96.37	.98	51	92.16
436-200910-I-Staubsauger	369	99.19	1.00	64	98.44
486-201011-I-Frosch	536	98.13	.99	99	86.87
604-201011-IV-Weg	712	98.03	.99	135	93.33
all texts taken together	5027	95.82	.98	944	90.78

Table 1: Number of characters (#char), percent agreement (perc) and Fleiss' κ for transcription, and numbers of tokens (#tok) and percent agreement for normalization among all four annotators for each text.

We pseudo-randomly picked ten texts from our corpus with the condition that the frequency distribution of the different topics was reflected in the selection. Four trained annotators then independently transcribed and normalized the ten texts. Transcription and normalization were carried out in a single step, i.e. a word was transcribed and then immediately normalized. The advantage is that firstly, as shown in example (2), normalization does to some extent influence the transcription, so carrying out the two steps together should lead to more consistent transcriptions and normalizations. Secondly, it turned out to be more time-efficient to carry out both steps at once. The transcription and normalization were written in a csv-file with one token per line. Clear technical mistakes were automatically corrected so that, for instance, whitespace that was accidentally added to a token would not be taken into account when computing agreement.

5.1 Agreement on Transcription

To evaluate agreement on the transcription, we chose a character-based procedure. We interpreted the transcription as an annotation task in which a region of pixels in the scan has to be assigned a tag. The tagset in this case consists of the letters of the alphabet, numbers and punctuation marks. In addition to raw percent agreement, we also computed chance-corrected agreement according to Cohen's κ (for pairwise comparisons) and Fleiss' κ (for comparisons of more than two annotators).

The transcription of each annotator was extracted from the csv-file and transformed into one long string with token boundaries indicated by spaces. The different transcriptions were then automatically aligned.[11] If one annotator transcribed a character (or a whitespace, i.e. a token boundary) where others did not, the missing characters were indicated by a '#' in the alignment. An example is given in (6), showing the scan and the transcriptions by the four annotators A1–A4.

(6)

```
A1:   mit#der Seil bahn und sie hate
A2:   mit#der seil bahn und sie hate
A3:   mit#der Seil#bahn und sie hate
A4:   mit der Seil bahn und sie hate
```

Table 1 shows the agreement results for each text.[12] Transcription agreement is generally very high (mostly > 94%, κ > .97). One can also observe a quite high variance with agreement rang-

---

[11] Only in the texts 207-200910-II-Weg and 331-201011-III-Seilbahn, parts of the alignments had to be corrected manually because in the former, one annotator accidentally left out two lines, and in the second, one word led to so different transcriptions (see example (7)) that the automatic alignment did not produce the optimal result.

[12] #char refers to the maximum number of characters that were transcribed, i.e. if one transcriber transcribed a character where the others did not (= empty string), this would still count in the maximum number of characters. Agreement was computed with the software tool R and the package "irr", https://cran.r-project.org/web/packages/irr/.

ing from 94.89–99.19%, indicating that there are simple, clearly-written texts as well as texts that are rather difficult to decipher. Text 207-200910-II-Weg sticks out with a much lower agreement result than the others. This is due to one annotator accidentally skipping two lines in the scan.

The agreement figures in Table 1 represent agreement between all four annotators, i.e. one annotator with a deviant transcription already results in considerably lower agreement scores. Table 2 shows the agreement between pairs, triples, and all four annotators. One can see that agreement is highest among annotators A1, A2 and A4: both as pairs and triples, they achieved $\kappa = .99$ (Cohen's κ in the case of pairs of annotators, Fleiss' κ with triples and all four annotators). These annotators had most experience with the texts and the guidelines: at the time of the agreement study, A1 and A2 had been working in the project for half a year, A3 for one month and A4 for more than 2 years. All in all, one can conclude that the transcriptions are very consistent.

| **Annotators** | **Transcription** | | **Norm.** |
	perc	κ	perc
A1+A2	99.26	.99	97.03
A1+A3	96.36	.96	93.43
A1+A4	99.30	.99	97.35
A2+A3	96.44	.96	93.01
A2+A4	99.28	.99	96.29
A3+A4	96.46	.96	92.80
A1+A2+A3	96.06	.97	92.06
A1+A2+A4	98.93	.99	95.34
A1+A3+A4	96.06	.97	91.84
A2+A3+A4	96.12	.97	91.31
A1+A2+A3+A4	95.82	.98	90.78

Table 2: Agreement results for pairs, triples, and all four annotators for transcription and normalization

5.2 Analysis of Disagreements in the Transcription

After the agreement study, the four annotators came up with a gold standard and categorized each disagreement. They identified seven categories, see Table 3.[13]

---

[13]Percent figures in Tables 3 and 4 do not add up to 100% due to rounding errors.

Category	Freq	Perc
careless mistake (CM)	112	53%
consequential error (CE)	28	13%
upper-/lowercase (UL)	27	13%
ambiguous case (A)	19	9%
word boundary (WB)	11	5%
guidelines not obeyed (G)	7	3%
influence of normalization (N)	4	2%
A or CM	2	1%
total	210	100%

Table 3: Sources of disagreements in the transcription

Careless mistakes (CM) have the largest share with 112 cases (53%) but 92 of them go back to the two missed lines by one of the annotators. Eight of the other 20 are due to forgotten linebreak marks, so only 12 actually refer to forgotten or confused characters. Whenever a disagreement automatically led to another disagreement, this is counted as a consequential error (CE), e.g. if a linebreak mark was forgotten, consequentially the whitespace following this linebreak mark was also missing. Upper-/lowercase (UL) and word boundaries (WB) were often ambiguous (see example (6)). While most of them could be resolved by majority vote or a second close look, three cases were particularly ambiguous and could only be decided after long discussion.

Eight of the other 19 ambiguous cases (A) refer to punctuation marks (period, comma or just a spot on the paper?), the others to characters (e.g. <v>/<w>, <u>/<a>). The hardest case is shown in example (7), presenting the scan and the four transcriptions (it was agreed that the gold transcription should be <Kn**lt>, and the target hypothesis, judging from the context, should be <knallt> 'bangs'):

(7)

Knalt, Kabolt, Ka*dt, Knalt

The seven cases of disagreement with regard to the guidelines (G) refer to highly specific cases where the numbers of the pictures or an ending formula like "The End" were not transcribed although it was asked for in the guidelines.

Finally, in four cases the transcription was influenced by the normalization (N): an erronous word was transcribed without the errors, according to the target hypothesis. It is often claimed that transcribing texts is difficult because one is tempted to correct errors when transcribing. Our figures do not support this claim, at least if one had some training (the overlooking of errors only happened to the annotator with the least training). In one case, the annotator had a different normalization in mind which influenced the transcription, see example (8):

(8) 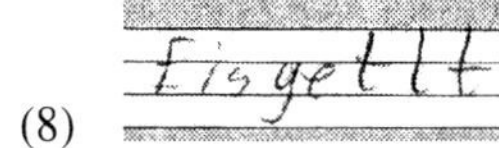

Three annotators transcribed <Eis getlt> and normalized it as <Eis geteilt> 'shared the ice cream', one annotator transcribed <Eis gellt> and normalized it as <Eisgeld> 'ice cream money'.

5.3 Agreement on Normalization

Agreement on normalization, i.e. the target hypothesis, was evaluated on a token basis. The normalized forms were automatically aligned token-wise, with a '#' indicating a split/merge or missing token. Choosing a correct target form for a transcribed word cannot be meaningfully interpreted as a categorization task, given that the theoretically possible number of targets is infinite. Therefore, chance-corrected agreement could not be computed, so we only report raw percent agreement. Table 1[14] shows the agreement between all four annotators for each text. One can see that overall, agreement is lower than for the transcriptions and that there is considerably more variation across the texts (83.87–98.44%, without the text with the two missed lines). The pairwise and three-way comparisons of annotators in Table 2 also show that agreement is highest among annotators A1, A2 and A4.

Since the annotators based the target hypothesis on their own transcriptions, missing tokens in the transcription automatically led to missing tokens in the normalization. Also, different transcriptions could lead to different normalizations. Therefore, we additionally computed normalization agreement of all four annotators for words with uniform transcriptions. Tokens that got the same transcription by all annotators (849 instances) showed a percent agreement of 96.70% (as compared to tokens that were transcribed by all annotators but possibly in different ways (912), with an agreement of 93.97%).

Normalization is clearly more demanding than transcription but the results seem satisfying.

5.4 Analysis of Disagreements in Normalization

Again, after the agreement study, a gold standard was constructed by the annotators, and seven categories were identified to classify the disagreements, see Table 4.

Category	Freq	Perc
token not transcribed (NT)	28	33%
token transcr. differently (DT)	16	19%
other word was meant (O)	12	14%
normalization wrong (W)	9	11%
mistake was overlooked (MO)	8	9%
unintuitive form req. (UF)	6	7%
word boundaries (WB)	3	4%
DT and UF	3	4%
total	85	100%

Table 4: Sources of disagreements in the target hypothesis

As discussed above, missing (NT) or different (DT) transcriptions have a big influence on the agreement on the target hypothesis (44 cases, i.e. 52% in total). Twelve tokens were normalized differently (DT) in that target words with different lemmas were chosen (e.g. <noch> 'still', vs. <nach> (preposition 'to')). Nine times a normalization was wrong (W): either a particular rule in our guidelines was not followed (e.g. *<hilt> was normalized to <hält> 'holds' instead of <hielt> 'held', which is phonetically more similar), or the target form was not standard German (e.g. <ist Zuhause> instead of <ist zuhause> 'is at home'). In eight cases, a spelling mistake was overlooked in the normalization (MO), and in six cases our guidelines were not followed in that they required to choose a form which was marked in some way or not the most intuitive one (UF): On the one hand, this concerns marked spellings that only recently have been adapted by the *Duden* (e.g. non-standard <kuckt> for

---

[14]As with characters (see footnote 12), #tok refers to the maximum number of tokens in the normalization. According to the gold standard, there were 939 target tokens in total, 198 (21.1%) of which contained orthographic errors, i.e. the transcribed and normalized token differed.

<guckt> 'he/she looks'). On the other hand, our requirement not to correct grammatical errors and certain capitalizations was not obeyed in five cases (e.g. <wegfahrt> was changed to <wegfährt> 'drive away', an agreement error); three of them were also mixed with a different transcription (DT and UF). Finally, three times word boundaries could be interpreted in different ways (WB), e.g. *Dann ist alles auf Mickel **drauf gefallen*** vs. ***draufgefallen*** 'Then everything fell down on Mickel'.

6 Conclusion and Future Work

In this paper, we propose a way of annotating orthographic target hypotheses in a new longitudinal L1 learner corpus of German with freely written texts from children of grades 2–4.

By annotating the corpus with a target hypothesis that strictly only corrects orthographic errors, it is tailored to research and tool development for orthographic issues in primary school. Having a target hypothesis for learner data is important in several ways: Firstly, it makes explicit what the annotator thought the child wanted to write. Secondly, it can be used to analyze in which way an observed spelling deviates from the correct spelling, and, hence, what kind of error the child made. Third, the standardized spelling can facilitate further (semi-)automatic processing of the texts.

Given the lack of evaluation of transcriptions and target hypotheses in existing corpora, we conducted a detailed inter-annotator agreement study on both tasks and discussed the sources of inconsistencies. Although agreement was very high and should allow for robust analyses and tool developments based on our corpus, we showed that some ambiguities always remain, even if the task only concerns 'minimal' changes and detailed guidelines are provided. Young children's handwriting has been shown to be difficult to decipher, and in some cases leading to different transcriptions. Similarly for normalization, different sources for disagreements or errors on the annotator's side were identified, which to some extent certainly generalize to other corpora and should be kept in mind.

When all texts are transcribed and normalized, our corpus will be made available[15]. It can be used for theoretical research on spelling acquisition but also in applied contexts, e.g. by teachers who want to look up frequently misspelled words. It is also intended for training, developing and evaluating automatic spelling correction and spelling assessment tools.

Our next step is to enrich the corpus with further annotations regarding word properties and orthographic errors (Laarmann-Quante et al., 2016). We also started to work on tools for automatic spelling error analysis (Laarmann-Quante, 2016, to appear). In the long term, we plan to consider grammatical errors as well.

Acknowledgments

This research is part of the project *Literacy as the key to social participation: Psycholinguistic perspectives on orthography instruction and literacy acquisition* funded by the Volkswagen Foundation as part of the research initiative "Key Issues for Research and Society". We would also like to thank the anonymous reviewers for their helpful comments.

References

Andrea Abel, Aivars Glaznieks, Lionel Nicolas, and Egon Stemle. 2014. KoKo: An L1 learner corpus for German. In *Proceedings of the Ninth International Conference on Language Resources and Evaluation (LREC 2014)*. Reykjavik, Iceland, pages 2414–2421.

Alessia Barbagli, Pietro Lucisano, Felice Dell'Orletta, Simonetta Montemagni, and Giulia Venturi. 2016. CItA: An L1 Italian learners corpus to study the development of writing competence. In *Proceedings of the Tenth International Conference on Language Resources and Evaluation (LREC 2016)*. Portorož, Slovenia, pages 88–95.

Kay Berkling. 2016. Corpus for children's writing with enhanced output for specific spelling patterns (2nd and 3rd grade). In *Proceedings of the Tenth International Conference on Language Resources and Evaluation (LREC 2016)*. Portorož, Slovenia, pages 3200–3206.

Kay Berkling, Johanna Fay, Masood Ghayoomi, Katrin Heinz, Rémi Lavalley, Ludwig Linhuber, and Sebastian Stücker. 2014. A database of freely written texts of German school students for the purpose of automatic spelling error classification. In *Proceedings of the Ninth International Conference on Language Resources and Evaluation (LREC 2014)*. Reykjavik, Iceland, pages 1212–1217.

---

[15]See `https://www.linguistics.rub.de/litkey/Scientific/Corpusanalysis/Resources.html`.

Kay Berkling and Rémi Lavalley. 2015. WISE: A web-interface for spelling error recognition for German: A description of the underlying algorithm. In *Proceedings of the Int. Conference of the German Society for Computational Linguistics and Language Technology (GSCL)*. Duisburg/Essen, Germany, pages 87–96.

Kay Berkling and Nadine Pflaumer. 2014. Phontasia — a phonics trainer for German spelling in primary education. In *Proceedings of the Fourth Workshop on Child Computer Interaction (WOCCI 2014)*. pages 33–38.

Adriane Boyd. 2010. EAGLE: An error-annotated corpus of beginning learner German. In *Proceedings of the Seventh Conference on International Language Resources and Evaluation (LREC'10)*. Valletta, Malta, pages 1897–1902.

Peter Eisenberg. 2013. *Das Wort*, volume 1 of *Grundriss der deutschen Grammatik*. Metzler, Stuttgart, 4th edition.

Johanna Fay. 2010. *Die Entwicklung der Rechtschreibkompetenz beim Textschreiben: Eine empirische Untersuchung in Klasse 1 bis 4*. Peter Lang, Frankfurt a. M.

Eileen Fitzpatrick and Milton Stephen Seegmiller. 2004. The Montclair electronic language database project. *Language and Computers* 52(1):223–237.

Hendrike Frieg. 2014. *Sprachförderung im Regelunterricht der Grundschule: Eine Evaluation der Generativen Textproduktion*. Dissertation, Ruhr-Universität Bochum. http://www-brs.ub.ruhr-uni-bochum.de/netahtml/HSS/Diss/FriegHendrike/diss.pdf.

Aivars Glaznieks, Lionel Nicolas, Egon Stemle, Andrea Abel, and Verena Lyding. 2014. Establishing a standardized procedure for building learner corpora. *Apples - Journal of Applied Language Studies* 8(3):5–20.

Ronja Laarmann-Quante. 2016. Automating multi-level annotations of orthographic properties of German words and children's spelling errors. In *Language Teaching, Learning and Technology*. ISCA, pages 14–22.

Ronja Laarmann-Quante. to appear. Towards a tool for automatic spelling error analysis and feedback generation for freely written German texts produced by primary school children. In *Proceedings of the Seventh ISCA workshop on Speech and Language Technology in Education (SLaTE)*.

Ronja Laarmann-Quante, Lukas Knichel, Stefanie Dipper, and Carina Betken. 2016. Annotating spelling errors in German texts produced by primary school children. In Annemarie Friedrich and Katrin Tomanek, editors, *Proceedings of the 10th Linguistic Annotation Workshop held in conjunction with ACL 2016 (LAW-X 2016)*. pages 32–42.

Ronja Laarmann-Quante, Katrin Ortmann, Anna Ehlert, Carina Betken, Stefanie Dipper, and Lukas Knichel. 2017. *Guidelines for the Manual Transcription and Orthographic Normalization of Handwritten German Texts Produced by Primary School Children*, volume 20 of *Bochumer Linguistische Arbeitsberichte (BLA)*.

Anke Lüdeling. 2008. Mehrdeutigkeiten und Kategorisierung: Probleme bei der Annotation von Lernerkorpora. In Grommes, P., Walter, M., editor, *Fortgeschrittene Lernervarietäten*, Niemeyer, Tübingen, pages 119–140.

Peter May. 2013. *Hamburger Schreib-Probe zur Erfassung der grundlegenden Rechtschreibstrategien: Manual/Handbuch Diagnose orthografischer Kompetenz*. vpm, Stuttgart.

Detmar Meurers. 2015. Learner corpora and natural language processing. In Sylviane Granger, Gaëtanelle Gilquin, and Fanny Meunier, editors, *The Cambridge Handbook of Learner Corpus Research*, Cambridge University Press, Cambridge, pages 537–566.

Judy M. Parr. 2010. A dual purpose data base for research and diagnostic assessment of student writing. *Journal of Writing Research* 2(2):129–150.

Marc Reznicek, Anke Lüdeling, and Hagen Hirschmann. 2013. Competing target hypotheses in the Falko corpus. In Ana Díaz-Negrillo, Nicolas Ballier, and Paul Thompson, editors, *Automatic Treatment and Analysis of Learner Corpus Data*, John Benjamins Publishing Company, Amsterdam, volume 59 of *Studies in Corpus Linguistics*, pages 101–124.

Marc Reznicek, Anke Lüdeling, Cedric Krummes, Franziska Schwantuschke, Maik Walter, Karin Schmidt, Hagen Hirschmann, and Torsten Andreas. 2012. Das Falko-Handbuch. Korpusaufbau und Annotationen, Version 2.01.

Alexandr Rosen, Jirka Hana, Barbora Štindlová, and Anna Feldman. 2014. Evaluating and automating the annotation of a learner corpus. *Language Resources and Evaluation* 48(1):65–92.

Corinne Schroff. 2000. *Lea, Lars und Dodo: Bilderbox*. SCHUBI Lernmedien.

Sebastian Stüker, Johanna Fay, and Kay Berkling. 2011. Towards context-dependent phonetic spelling error correction in children's freely composed text for diagnostic and pedagogical purposes. In *INTERSPEECH*. pages 1601–1604.

Tobias Thelen. 2000. Osnabrücker Bildergeschichtenkorpus: Version 1.0.0. http://tobiasthelen.de/uploads/Wissenschaft/ osnabruecker_bildergeschichtenkorpus_1_0_0.pdf.

Tobias Thelen. 2010. *Automatische Analyse orthographischer Leistungen von Schreibanfängern.* Dissertation, Universität Osnabrück. https://repositorium.uos.de/bitstream/urn:nbn:de:gbv:700-201006096307/1/thesis_thelen.pdf.

Günther Thomé and Dorothea Thomé. 2004. *Oldenburger Fehleranalyse OLFA: Instrument und Handbuch zur Ermittlung der orthographischen Kompetenz aus freien Texten ab Klasse 3 und zur Qualitätssicherung von Fördermaßnahmen.* isb Verlag, Oldenburg.

A   Full Example of Original Text, Transcription and Normalization

Original Text (Scan)

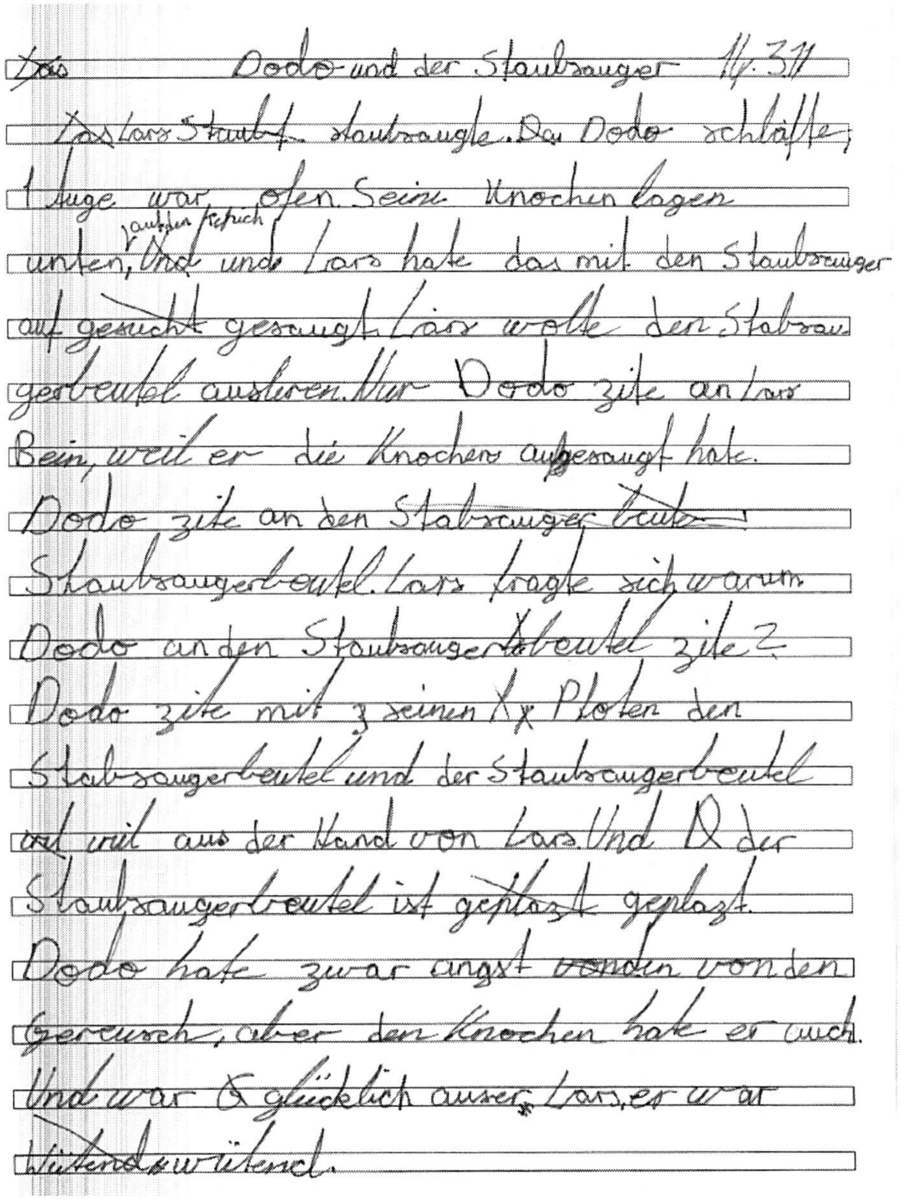

Figure 1: Example of an original text in the corpus

Transcription and Normalization

CHILD	TARGET	CHILD (cont.)	TARGET (cont.)
Dodo	Dodo	fragte	fragte
und	und	sich	sich
der	der	warum	warum
Staubsauger	Staubsauger	ˆ	
\h	\h	Dodo	Dodo
Lars	Lars	an	an
staubsaugte	staubsaugte	den	den
.	.	Staubsaugerbeutel	Staubsaugerbeutel
Dodo	Dodo	zite	˜ziehte
schläfte	˜schläfte	?	?
,	,	ˆ	
ˆ		Dodo	Dodo
1	1	zite	˜ziehte
Auge	Auge	mit	mit
war	war	seinen	seinen
ofen	offen	Pfoten	Pfoten
.	.	den	den
Seine	Seine	ˆ	
Knochen	Knochen	Stabsaugerbeutel	Staubsaugerbeutel
lagen	lagen	und	und
ˆ		der	der
unten	unten	Staubsaugerbeutel	Staubsaugerbeutel
auf	auf	ˆ	
den	den	viel	fiel
Tepich	Teppich	aus	aus
,	,	der	der
und	und	Hand	Hand
Lars	Lars	von	von
hate	hatte	Lars	Lars
das	das	.	.
mit	mit	Und	Und
den	den	der	der
Staubsauger	Staubsauger	ˆ	
ˆ		Staubsaugerbeutel	Staubsaugerbeutel
auf_gesaugt	aufgesaugt	ist	ist
.	.	geplazt	geplatzt
Lars	Lars	.	.
wolte	wollte	ˆ	
den	den	Dodo	Dodo
Stabsau-ˆgerbeutel	Staubsaugerbeutel	hate	hatte
ausleren	ausleeren	zwar	zwar
.	.	angst	Angst
Nur	Nur	von	von
Dodo	Dodo	den	den
zite	˜ziehte	ˆ	
an	an	Gereusch	Geräusch
Lars	Lars	,	,
ˆ		aber	aber
Bein	Bein	den	den
,	,	Knochen	Knochen
weil	weil	hate	hatte
er	er	er	er
die	die	auch	auch
Knochen	Knochen	.	.
aufgesaugt	aufgesaugt	ˆ	
hate	hatte	Und	Und
.	.	war	war
ˆ		glücklich	glücklich
Dodo	Dodo	auser	außer
zite	˜ziehte	Lars	Lars
an	an	,	,
den	den	er	er
ˆ		war	war
Staubsaugerbeutel	Staubsaugerbeutel	ˆ	
.	.	wütend	wütend
Lars	Lars	.	.

A Large Scale Quantitative Exploration of
Modeling Strategies for Content Scoring

Nitin Madnani　　**Anastassia Loukina**　　**Aoife Cahill**

Educational Testing Service
Princeton, NJ, 08541 USA
{nmadnani,aloukina,acahill}@ets.org

Abstract

We explore various supervised learning
strategies for automated scoring of content
knowledge for a large corpus of 130 different content-based questions spanning
four subject areas (Science, Math, English
Language Arts, and Social Studies) and
containing over 230,000 responses scored
by human raters. Based on our analyses, we provide specific recommendations
for content scoring. These are based on
patterns observed across multiple questions and assessments and are, therefore,
likely to generalize to other scenarios and
prove useful to the community as automated content scoring becomes more popular in schools and classrooms.

1 Introduction

Automatic scoring of free-text content-based
questions is a challenging task. Although it may
appear similar to the task of automatically scoring
student responses for writing quality (Page, 1966;
Landauer et al., 2003; Attali and Burstein, 2006),
it has important differences. Scoring for content
deals with responses to open-ended questions designed to test primarily what the student knows,
has learned, or can do in a *specific* subject area
such as Computer Science, Math, Biology, or Music with fluency being secondary. It is not important if the student makes some spelling mistakes
or grammatical errors as long as the desired specific information (e.g., scientific principles, trends
in a graph, or details from a reading passage) is
included in the response.

Assessing the content of student responses requires a different set of features that pay attention to whether students are using the right concepts, the right relationships between those con-

cepts, and whether they are providing the right
amount of detail. In addition, scoring for content
generally requires building separate scoring models for each question since each question usually
focuses on a specific set of concepts within a specific subject area. However, automated scoring for
writing quality can utilize "generic" scoring models that can be used to assess student responses independent of the question to which they were written since the aspects of writing being measured are
topic-independent (Attali and Burstein, 2006).

In this paper, we focus on a content scoring
approach that learns a scoring model by extracting a large number of sparse, binary features from
human-scored responses to a given question. The
model can then predict scores for previously unseen responses to the question. There are many
decisions that one needs to make for such an approach: what machine learning algorithm is likely
to give the best performance? Is it better to
use regression or classification? Is it worth al-
locating additional data and time for tuning the
hyper-parameters of the learning algorithm? For
many practical applications, the amount of human-
scored data available may not even be sufficient
for model training and evaluation let alone for
these types of meta-analyses.

We conduct analyses on a large corpus of *real*
student responses to identify patterns that are consistent across multiple questions and contexts and
are, therefore, likely to generalize to other scenarios. Our corpus contains 130 different questions spanning four different subject areas and
more than 230,000 human-scored responses. To
our knowledge, this is the largest collection of responses ever used in a study on automated content
scoring. The large number of questions allows us
to test many of our hypotheses in a rigorous manner and convert the answers into specific recommendations for the community that we hope will

457

Proceedings of the 12th Workshop on Innovative Use of NLP for Building Educational Applications, pages 457–467
Copenhagen, Denmark, September 8, 2017. ©2017 Association for Computational Linguistics

be useful in guiding further development of supervised content scoring models.

2   Related Work

Content scoring is sometimes also referred to in the literature as "short-answer" scoring. Although it is true that many content-based questions tend to be very specific and elicit responses that are relatively short, this is not always the case. Previously published studies have considered responses that span a range of lengths — from a few words (Basu et al., 2013) to a few dozen words (Madnani et al., 2013; Horbach et al., 2013) to a few hundred words (Madnani et al., 2016). Given that the primary facet of interest is the content of the response and not its length, we refer to the task as "content scoring" in the rest of the paper.

Content scoring approaches fall into two general categories: (a) **reference-based** where responses are scored on the basis of their similarity to reference answers provided by the authors of the question or selected from existing high-scoring responses (Alfonseca and Pérez, 2004; Nielsen et al., 2008; Meurers et al., 2011; Sukkarieh et al., 2011; Horbach et al., 2013; Pado and Kiefer, 2015). These studies generally use a small number of continuous-valued features, often with a single model trained for multiple questions. (b) **response-based** which use a large number of detailed features extracted from the student responses themselves (e.g., word n-grams, etc.) and human scores assigned to the responses to learn a supervised machine-learning model (Mohler et al., 2011; Dzikovska et al., 2013; Ramachandran et al., 2015; Zesch et al., 2015; Zhu et al., 2016). Response-based approaches generally require training a separate model for each question.

The choice of whether the reference-based approach is better than the response-based approach depends on the open-ended nature of the question and whether there is a sufficient number of human-scored responses available. Sakaguchi et al. (2015) — who explored the combination of the two approaches — observed that if sufficient human-scored data is available, response-based approaches often work better than reference-based approaches. Since several of the questions in our dataset are relatively open-ended and we have sufficient scored data available for all of them, we focus on the response-based approach in this paper.

Our study is different from the work we have discussed so far in that its goal is not simply to obtain the best performance for a given question or a set of questions. Instead, we focus on meta-analyses of scoring performance as a function of modeling strategies and data set characteristics. Some previous studies have considered the choice of learner in automated scoring for writing quality. Chen and He (2013) compared support vector classification, regression, and ranking for automatically scoring writing quality using a single dataset. Chen et al. (2016) reported that using support vector regression with a radial kernel produced better performance than a simple linear model. In addition, several studies (Feng et al., 2003; Haberman and Sinharay, 2010; Santos et al., 2012) have consistently reported that use of probabilistic classifiers such as cumulative logistic regression might be more appropriate for the task of automated scoring than linear regression since such models incorporate the assumption that the score is categorical in nature. All of these studies used a small number of continuous-valued features.

More generally in the machine learning literature, papers have analyzed and compared the performance of different learning algorithms on standard machine learning datasets from the UCI repository and/or synthetic datasets (Caruana and Niculescu-Mizil, 2006; Matykiewicz and Pestian, 2012; Doan and Kalita, 2015). These studies reported substantial variability in learner performance across problems which suggests that the learners that performed best for other applications may not necessarily do so for our task.

The work that might be closest to ours is that of Heilman and Madnani (2015) who explored the impact of the amount of training data available on content scoring performance across a range of questions. However, they used a much smaller set of 44 questions and did not investigate any questions about specific modeling strategies such as the choice of learning algorithm or the impact of hyper-parameter tuning.

2.1   Research Questions

We aim to answer the following specific questions about supervised learning specifically in the context of automated scoring of content:

1. What type of learner has the best performance for response-based automated content

Subject	N	Number of Responses	Score Range	Grade Level	Task Type	Response Lengths
Science	89	454–5824	0–4, 0–6, 1–5	6–10	Explanations and arguments embedded in inquiry science units that call for students to use evidence to link ideas.	47–320 chars
English Language Arts	23	737–2685	0–2, 0–3, 0–4	7–10	Summarization, argument development, and analysis of English reading passages.	105–506 chars
Math	15	669–3265	0–2, 0–3, 0–4	7–9	Explanation of how mathematical principles apply to given situations involving linear equations.	40–150 chars
Social Studies	3	3000–3100	0–3	9–12	Summarization of stories and passages focused on social issues.	150–180 chars

Table 1: A detailed breakdown of our corpus by subject. **N**: number of questions; **Number of Responses**: minimum and maximum number of human-scored responses available for questions on this subject; **Score Range**: ranges of possible scores that can be awarded to responses for questions on this subject according to the human-authored scoring rubrics; **Grade Level**: the grades of students whose responses were used for analysis; **Response Lengths**: minimum and maximum number of characters in responses to questions on a given subject.

scoring? Do non-linear learners offer a substantial advantage over linear models? Do margin-based methods such as support vector machines perform better than bagging ensembles like random forests?

2. How do probabilistic classifiers perform compared to regressors when predicting real-valued scores?

3. Do hyper-parameters matter? Is it worth spending extra time and effort to tune the hyper-parameters of any given learner over simply using the default values provided by the implementation being used?

3 Methodology

Before we provide more details of our corpus and the specific learning strategies, we would like to describe two factors that will be shared by all strategies in order to perform a controlled comparison: (a) the features and (b) the evaluation metric.

Features. Since the goal of this paper is to compare modeling strategies, we need to use the same fixed set of features for all strategies in order to obtain a meaningful comparison. We use a set of features that have been employed in many previously published response-based approaches to building content scoring models (Heilman and Madnani, 2015; Zesch et al., 2015; Sakaguchi et al., 2015;

Madnani et al., 2016). We extract the following features for all of the responses in our corpus:

(a) character n-grams including whitespace and punctuation (n=2–5)

(b) word n-grams (n=1,2)

(c) triples extracted over dependency parses obtained from ZPar (Zhang and Clark, 2011), and

(d) length bins (specifically, whether the log of 1 plus the number of characters in the response, rounded down to the nearest integer, equals x, for all possible x from the training set). For example, consider a question for which the responses in the training data are between 50 and 200 characters long. For this question, we will have 3 length bins numbered from 5 ($\lfloor \log_2 51 \rfloor$) to 7 ($\lfloor \log_2 201 \rfloor$). For a new response of length 150 characters, length bin 7 ($\lfloor \log_2 151 \rfloor$) would be the binary feature that gets a value of 1 with the other two bins getting the value of 0.

All of the features are binary (indicating presence or absence) and can be thought to indirectly approximate the requirements of content scoring we described earlier: good responses generally contain (a) the right concepts (approximately captured by words and bigrams), (b) the right syntactic relationships between those concepts (approximately captured by dependency triples), and (c) the right amount of detail (coarsely captured by length bins).

The character n-grams serve to capture spelling and morphological variations such that responses are not excessively penalized for misspellings or for using the incorrect morphological variants. For example, if the correct response to a question must contain the phrase "temperature increased", a candidate response containing the phrase "temprature increase" (with a misspelling and an incorrect verb form) can still get credit for that concept.

Metric. Human scores generally tend to be integers, while automated scores can be either integers or real values on a continuous scale. One advantage of the real-valued scores is that they allow for more fine-grained distinction than a small set of integers. In this paper, we predict real-valued scores on a continuous scale and evaluate the accuracy of the predicted scores by using mean squared error (MSE) as our default metric. Although some previous studies have used quadratically-weighted kappa (QWK) as another possible metric for evaluating content-scoring models, more recent work has shown that QWK may possess properties that render it less than suitable for automated scoring evaluation (Yannakoudakis and Cummins, 2015).

3.1 Data

Our corpus contains over 230,000 human-scored responses that were collected in response to 130 different questions. The questions spanned 4 subject areas: Science, English Language Arts, Math, and Social Studies and are administered as part of several different assessments. The 130 questions include the 10 content-based questions from the Automated Student Assessment Prize competition organized by the Hewlett Foundation that are publicly available.[1] The remaining questions are in active use in various classroom settings and are not publicly available. Table 1 shows a detailed breakdown of the corpus.

3.2 Learners

Table 2 summarizes the learners considered in this study. We choose learners that (a) have either

---

[1] https://www.kaggle.com/c/asap-sas/data

been shown to perform well with feature sets comparable to ours in previously published work — Mohler et al. (2011), Sakaguchi et al. (2015), and Zesch et al. (2015) all used support vector machines; Ramachandran et al. (2015) use a random forest regressor — or (b) are generally known to perform well with a large number of sparse features (Hastie et al., 2001; Fan et al., 2008; Chang and Lin, 2011). We use the scikit-learn (Pedregosa et al., 2011) implementations for all learners.

All the implementations incorporate some means of reducing learner variance either by design — random forests average over a large number of decision trees trained using bootstrapped samples — or by explicitly incorporating some form of regularization, e.g., an ℓ_2-penalty over the feature weights for logistic regression and a misclassification error penalty for SVMs.

The first four learners are classifiers. Since we are interested in predicting continuous values evaluated by using mean squared error, we would expect that classifiers that simply produce the most likely (integer) score would generally do worse than regressors, which produce continuous values. Therefore, for all four classifiers, we use the `predict_proba()` method of their scikit-learn implementations to obtain probability distributions[2] over the possible score points and then compute the expected value using the distribution as the final classifier prediction.[3] For the "Rescaled Support Vector Regressor", we simply rescale the predictions obtained from the regressor using the mean and standard deviation of the human scores for the training data. This form of post-processing has been shown to be particularly effective as evidenced by its use in many of the top submissions to the Kaggle automated scoring competitions.

3.3 Experiments

Although we have a fairly large number of responses for each question, we choose to use cross-validation instead of a single train-test split in or-

---

[2] scikit-learn has two implementations available for a support vector classifier with a linear kernel: one using LibSVM (Chang and Lin, 2011) and another using LibLinear (Fan et al., 2008). We use the former since the latter doesn't support probabilistic classification.

[3] The probabilities can vary in reliability depending on the calibration algorithm chosen to convert the predictions of the classifier into posterior probabilities (Platt, 1999; Zadrozny and Elkan, 2002). For this paper, we assume that scikit-learn provides reasonably well-calibrated implementations.

Learner	Type	Linear	Grid
Random Forest Classifier	Classifier	No	max_depth: $[1, 5, 10, \text{None}]$
Logistic Regression	Classifier	Yes	C: $[10^{-3}, 10^{-2}, \ldots, 10^3, 10^4]$
SVC (linear)	Classifier	Yes	C: $[10^{-3}, 10^{-2}, \ldots, 10^3, 10^4]$
SVC (RBF)	Classifier	No	C: $[10^{-3}, 10^{-2}, \ldots, 10^3, 10^4]$, γ: $[\frac{1}{\|F\|}, 10^{-7}, 10^6, \ldots, 10^{-3}]$
Random Forest Regressor	Regressor	No	max_depth: $[1, 5, 10, \text{None}]$
SVR (linear)	Regressor	Yes	C: $[10^{-3}, 10^{-2}, \ldots, 10^3, 10^4]$
SVR (RBF)	Regressor	No	C: $[10^{-3}, 10^{-2}, \ldots, 10^3, 10^4]$, γ: $[\frac{1}{\|F\|}, 10^{-7}, 10^6, \ldots, 10^{-3}]$
Rescaled SVR (RBF)	Regressor	No	C: $[10^{-3}, 10^{-2}, \ldots, 10^3, 10^4]$, γ: $[\frac{1}{\|F\|}, 10^{-7}, 10^6, \ldots, 10^{-3}]$

Table 2: Learners chosen for this study and their characteristics. "linear" and "RBF" refer to linear and radial basis function kernels. The **Grid** column shows the grid of possible values searched when tuning the hyper-parameters for each learner. C denotes the complexity parameter that controls the amount of regularization for the learner. γ denotes the kernel coefficient for the RBF kernel ($\frac{1}{\|F\|}$ — where $\|F\|$ refers to the number of features — is a commonly used value for γ and we include it in the grid). The max_depth parameter for random forests controls the maximum depth of the tree. Setting it to None tells scikit-learn to automatically compute that number based on internal calculations.

der to average over any possible biases that a single split might yield. We perform two sets of 5-fold cross-validation experiments for each of the eight learners. For both sets of experiments, the folds are stratified by the human scores, e.g., all train/test splits have similar distributions of human scores.

In the first set of cross-validation experiments, we train each learner using default hyper-parameters for each of the five folds. We compute the MSE for each of the five folds by comparing to the human scores and then use their average as the final MSE for the learner. For the second set of experiments, instead of using the default hyper-parameter values, we run scikit-learn's GridSearchCV over the (four-fold) "training" set *inside* each of the five top-level cross-validation runs in order to search a pre-specified parameter grid for values that yield the lowest estimated MSE. The learner with these tuned hyper-parameters is then used to make predictions on the fifth held-out fold as per usual. As before, we use the average MSE value across the five folds as the final MSE value for the learner.

Table 2 shows the hyper-parameter grids that we search for each of the eight learners in the second set of experiments. Although there are several hyper-parameters that can be tuned for each learner, we focus on parameters that are more likely to have a significant impact on performance, e.g., those that control regularization and, hence, over-fitting. Any parameters not included in the grids are assigned default values by scikit-learn.

Both sets of cross-validation experiments (with and without hyper-parameter tuning) were conducted using the SKLL toolkit which makes it easy to run scikit-learn experiments with multiple learners in batch mode.[4]

4　An Aside: Feature Characteristics

Before we delve into the analyses of modeling strategies, it might be instructive to explore some characteristics of our feature set. On average, we extract a total of $\sim$46,000 binary features for each question. As expected, the largest set of features are the character n-grams (about 3x as large as the word n-grams and the dependency triples). The length bin features constitute the smallest set with at most a dozen or so features.

We also wanted to explore how the number of features extracted for a given question varies by (a) the average length of a response for that question and by (b) the number of responses available for that question. Figure 1 shows correlations between the average number of features and the average response length and number of responses for

---

[4]`http://github.com/`
`EducationalTestingService/skll`

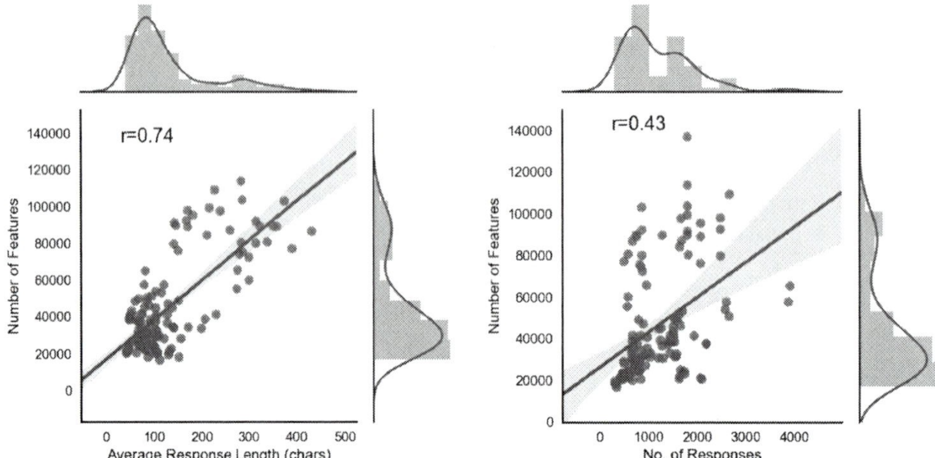

Figure 1: Joint distributions plots showing the impact of response length (in characters; left) and the number of available responses (right) on the number of features extracted for the questions in our corpus. Each plot is composed of a scatterplot with points denoting the 130 questions as well as histogram and density plots for each of the two variables being correlated. r = Pearson's correlation coefficient.

each question. As one might expect, the number of extracted features is larger for longer responses and for more numerous responses. We also observe that the average length of the response has a substantially larger impact on the number of extracted features than the number of responses available.[5] This intuitively makes sense since among the answers to the same question, there is a higher likelihood of newer words (and character sequences and dependency relations, etc.) being encountered *within* the same response as it grows longer, than across different responses.

5 Results

5.1 Effects of Modeling Strategies

Table 3 shows the mean squared error — averaged across all 130 questions in our corpus — for all eight learners both with and without tuned hyperparameters. We observe that the best performance is achieved by probabilistic support vector classifiers with linear and RBF kernels.

5.1.1 General Learner Properties

We first explored whether general properties of the learners such as being linear vs. non-linear or being a probabilistic classifier vs. a regressor had

Learner	Average MSE	
	not tuned	tuned
Logistic Regression	.401	.391
Random Forest Classifier	.385	.368
Random Forest Regressor	.356	.356
SVC (linear)	.336	.326
SVR (linear)	.514	.388
SVC (RBF)	.434	.321
SVR (RBF)	.723	.342
Rescaled SVR	.546	.343

Table 3: Average MSE across 130 questions for each of the eight learners using hyper-parameter values that are either **not tuned** (default) values or **tuned** via grid search. Lower values are better.

a statistically significant impact on model performance across different learners and questions.

We used a hierarchical mixed-effects linear model (Snijders and Bosker, 2011) implemented in R via the `lmerTest` package (Bates et al., 2015; Kuznetsova et al., 2016) to determine which modeling decisions have a statistically significant effect on model MSE over multiple questions. As our dependent variable, we used the standardized MSE value for each question and each learner. We also included the identity of each question and learner as a random factor to account for any random effects that might stem from characteristics

---

[5] We removed an extreme outlier from the left plot to minimize its impact on the correlation.

unique to any particular question or learner. We used the following learner properties as independent variables, specified as discrete factors with a fixed set of possible values (shown in quotes):

- **Type**. Is the learner a (probabilistic) "classifier" or a "regressor"?

- **Linearity**. Is the learner "linear" or "non-linear"?

- **Family**. Is the learner logistic regression ("LR"), a random forest ("RF"), or a support vector machine ("SVM")?

- **Tuning**. Are the learner hyper-parameters "tuned" or "not tuned"?

We generally focused on the main effects of each factor but also included interactions between the **Tuning** factor and the other factors.[6] The equation describing the mixed-effects model is shown below:

$$\begin{aligned} \mathrm{MSE} \sim\ & \mathrm{Type} * \mathrm{Tuning} \\ & + \mathrm{Family} * \mathrm{Tuning} \\ & + \mathrm{Linearity} * \mathrm{Tuning} \\ & + (1|\mathtt{question}) + (1|\mathtt{learner}) \quad (1) \end{aligned}$$

where MSE denotes the dependent variable; Type, Family, Linearity, and Tuning denote the learner factors we defined earlier, used here as fixed effects; the $*$ operator indicates an interaction between two factors; question and learner denote the question and learner identity respectively; and $(1|X)$ denotes the addition of a random intercept to the model for X. The reference values for the learner factors are: "classifier" (for Type), "SVM" (for Family), "non-linear" (for Linearity) and "tuned" (for Tuning).

The standardized coefficients for the model with all four fixed effects and the interactions are shown in Table 4. The coefficient in each row corresponds to the estimated difference in MSE (in number of standard deviations) relative to a learner

---

[6]Any other higher-level interactions cannot be consistently evaluated using our set of learners. For example, to consider the interaction between learner Type and Linearity, we would want several learners representing each of the four possible combinations of linear and non-linear regressors and classifiers. In our chosen set of learners, linear regressors are represented *only* by SVR (linear) which makes it impossible to tell whether any patterns observed for linear regressors are actually meaningful or just quirks of SVR (linear).

	Factor	**Coef.**	*p*-value
1	Intercept	$-.322$	.02
2	"linear"	.094	.47
3	"regressor"	.087	.43
4	"LR"	.205	.27
5	"RF"	.113	.38
6	"not tuned"	.596	<.00001
7	"LR": "not tuned"	$-.090$	.15
8	"RF": "not tuned"	$-.799$	<.00001
9	"linear": "not tuned"	$-.542$	<.00001
10	"regressor": "not tuned"	.395	<.00001

Table 4: Standardized coefficients and p-values for fixed factors and interactions included in the mixed-effects model (Equation 1). N=130 questions $\times$ 8 learners $\times$ 2 tuning conditions=2,080.

with the chosen reference values for the learner factors. Note that since lower values are better for MSE, positive coefficients actually indicate worse performance and vice versa.

These results clearly show that not tuning the hyper-parameters leads to significantly worse performance (higher MSE) irrespective of learner (row 6). They also show that tuning interacts significantly with learner family, with linearity, and with learner type. For example, row 8 shows that the difference between "tuned" and " not tuned" versions of "RF" is significantly lower than the corresponding difference for the reference learner family ("SVM"). Therefore, we can infer that not tuning has a significantly larger detrimental effect on SVMs than on random forests. Similarly, we can infer that not tuning is significantly worse for the (reference) non-linear learners than for linear ones (row 9), and for regressors than for the (reference) classifiers (row 10).

The results also show that overall there are no significant differences in performance due to linearity (row 2), learner type (row 3), and learner family (rows 4 and 5). We want to be particularly clear about the interpretation of these rows. For example, row 2 states that just because you pick a non-linear model does not *automatically* mean that you will obtain better performance than a linear model, and so on. The specifics matter. That is, these results do *not* say anything about the differences between the specific learner instantiations used in our study.

5.1.2 Comparing Specific Learners

In the previous section, we considered whether there are any general learner properties that would lead to consistently significant differences in performance. However, one may also reasonably ask which of the particular learners in our study turned out to be most accurate. To answer this question, we fit another mixed-effects model, which also used MSE as a dependent variable and question as a random factor, but uses the learner as a fixed factor instead of a random factor. Unlike the model described by Equation 1 — where we treated the chosen learners as a sample from the population of all possible learners — in this model we are specifically interested in the differences *within* this set of learners. This model is described by the equation:

$$\text{MSE} \sim \text{Learner} * \text{Tuning} + (1|\text{question}) \quad (2)$$

We set the reference learner to be the best performing one from Table 3 – the SVC with RBF kernel and tuned hyper-parameters. The model coefficients (not shown here due to lack of space) confirmed the consistently useful effect of tuning we observed in the previous section as well as the different effect sizes of tuning for different learners. They also showed that, among the tuned learners, the reference learner significantly outperformed all other learners except for SVC (linear) with tuned hyper-parameters. We discuss the implication of these results in §6 and conclude with practical recommendations in §7.

6 Discussion

In this paper, we considered the effect that different modeling strategies have on the accuracy of automated content scoring. We analyzed the performance of 8 different learners on a very large corpus of real student responses to evaluate both the impact of general learner characteristics as well as differences between specific learner instantiations.

We found that no individual learner characteristic had a consistent effect on model performance across all learners and questions. For example, SVM-based probabilistic classifiers with tuned hyper-parameters outperformed all other learners, but this was no longer the case for SVM-based regressors or even SVM-based learners with default hyper-parameters. Similarly, (linear) logistic regression performed worse than random forests, but an SVC with a linear kernel performed comparably to SVC with an RBF kernel. In other words,

our results indicate that no general family of learners is likely to be the most appropriate for this task out of the box: when choosing a learner, one should take into account *all* the factors considered in this study.

At the same time, we found that tuning hyperparameters significantly improves model performance for all learners even when a moderate number of responses is available to train the model for each question (the models in our study were trained on an average on 1,400 responses). Finally, we identified probabilistic support vector classifiers with linear or RBF kernel and tuned hyperparameters as the best performing learners across multiple questions in our corpus.

The sample of learners used in our paper is not exhaustive by any means. We focused on learners that have generally been shown to work well with similar features. There are other learners that we did not include in our study such as deep neural networks, nearest neighbor regressors etc. We leave the analysis of additional learner types for future work.

In addition to modeling choices, content scoring performance is also affected by data-related factors. In our analyses, we accounted for potential variation in baseline performance for each question by adding the question as a random factor to both mixed-effects models (Equations 1 and 2). We also conducted an additional exploratory study to evaluate whether the variation in performance of SVC (RBF), our best performing model, could be explained by specific question characteristics: the number of responses available, the number of different score levels, and the subject area. We found that the number of score levels had a moderate effect with model performance being higher for questions with a greater number of score levels, but there was no further effect of the number of responses available or of the subject area.

Of course, this does not mean that these parameters are not important for model performance. In fact, Heilman and Madnani (2015) reported a strong effect of the training size on the model performance for content scoring. A more likely explanation is that our data did not contain sufficient contrasts to establish such an effect: their study systematically considered training sets with N between 100 and 1,600, while in our study the N varied between 454 and 5,824 with the median at 1,350. It is also possible that the effects of the training size were confounded by other data-related factors. Furthermore, model performance may also be affected by the reliability of human scores, the context in which the assessment was delivered, and many other factors. We leave a more detailed exploration of such factors to future work.

7   Recommendations

Based on the observed results for general learner properties (§5.1.1) and for the specific learners (§5.1.2), we can provide the following recommendations to practitioners building automated content scoring models specifically when using features similar to ours:

1. It is generally beneficial to tune the hyper-parameters for every learner, if sufficient data and resources are available. [7]

2. If the goal is to pick a single learner that performs well for any question, the probabilistic SVC with an RBF kernel and with the C and γ parameters properly tuned via grid-search is likely to be a very good choice.

3. Not tuning the hyper-parameters has a substantial detrimental effect for non-linear SVMs, especially the regressors. If tuning is not possible due to lack of data or another reason, consider using random forests or probabilistic SVC with a linear kernel. If using scikit-learn/SKLL directly, these can be used "out of the box". However, if using another library, manually set the hyper-parameter values to be the same as the scikit-learn/SKLL defaults.

Acknowledgments

We would like to thank Beata Beigman Klebanov, Paul Deane, Guangming Ling, Brian Riordan, and the anonymous BEA reviewers for their useful comments and suggestions.

References

Enrique Alfonseca and Diana Pérez. 2004. Automatic Assessment of Open Ended Questions with a BLEU-inspired Algorithm and Shallow NLP. In *Advances in Natural Language Processing*, Springer, pages 25–35.

Yigal Attali and Jill Burstein. 2006. Automated essay scoring with e-rater V. 2. *The Journal of Technology, Learning and Assessment* 4(3):1–30.

Sumit Basu, Chuck Jacobs, and Lucy Vanderwende. 2013. Powergrading: a Clustering Aapproach to Amplify Human Effort for Short Answer Grading. *Transactions of the Association for Computational Linguistics* 1:391–402.

Douglas Bates, Martin Mächler, Ben Bolker, and Steve Walker. 2015. Fitting Linear Mixed-Effects Models Using lme4. *Journal of Statistical Software* 67(1):1–48.

Rich Caruana and Alexandru Niculescu-Mizil. 2006. An Empirical Comparison of Supervised Learning Algorithms. In *Proceedings of the International Conference on Machine Learning.* pages 161–168.

Chih-Chung Chang and Chih-Jen Lin. 2011. LIBSVM: A Library for Support Vector Machines. *ACM Transactions on Intelligent Systems and Technology* 2:1–27.

Hongbo Chen and Ben He. 2013. Automated essay scoring by maximizing human-machine agreement. In *Proceedings of the Conference on Empirical Methods in Natural Language Processing.* Seattle, Washington, USA, pages 1741–1752.

Jing Chen, James H. Fife, Isaac I. Bejar, and Andr A. Rupp. 2016. Building e-rater Scoring Models Using Machine Learning Methods. *ETS Research Report Series* 2016(1):1–12.

Tri Doan and Jugal Kalita. 2015. Selecting Machine Learning Algorithms Using Regression Models. In *Proceedings of the IEEE International Conference on Data Mining Workshops.* pages 1498–1505.

Myroslava Dzikovska, Rodney Nielsen, Chris Brew, Claudia Leacock, Danilo Giampiccolo, Luisa Bentivogli, Peter Clark, Ido Dagan, and Hoa Trang Dang. 2013. Task 7: The Joint Student Response Analysis and 8th Recognizing Textual Entailment Challenge. In *Proceedings of SemEval.* pages 263–274.

Rong-En Fan, Kai-Wei Chang, Cho-Jui Hsieh, Xiang-Rui Wang, and Chih-Jen Lin. 2008. LIBLINEAR: A Library for Large Linear Classification. *Journal of Machine Learning Research* 9:1871–1874.

Xin Feng, Neil Dorans, Liane N Patsula, and Bruce Kaplan. 2003. Improving the Statistical Aspects of E-rater ® : Exploring Alternative Feature Reduction and Combination Rules. *ETS Research Report Series* (June).

Shelby J. Haberman and Sandip Sinharay. 2010. The Application of the Cumulative Logistic Regression Model to Automated Essay Scoring. *Journal of Educational and Behavioral Statistics* 35(5):586–602.

---

[7] We would go so far as to recommend hyper-parameter tuning irrespective of task and the set of features used.

Trevor Hastie, Robert Tibshirani, and Jerome Friedman. 2001. *The Elements of Statistical Learning.* Springer New York Inc.

Michael Heilman and Nitin Madnani. 2015. The Impact of Training Data on Automated Short Answer Scoring Performance. In *Proceedings of the Workshop on Innovative Use of NLP for Building Educational Applications.* pages 81–85.

Andrea Horbach, Alexis Palmer, and Manfred Pinkal. 2013. Using the Text to Evaluate Short Answers for Reading Comprehension Exercises. In *Proceedings of the Second Joint Conference on Lexical and Computational Semantics (* SEM).* pages 286–295.

Alexandra Kuznetsova, Per Bruun Brockhoff, and Rune Haubo Bojesen Christensen. 2016. *lmerTest: Tests in Linear Mixed Effects Models.* R package version 2.0-33. https://CRAN.R-project.org/package=lmerTest.

Thomas K Landauer, Darrell Laham, and Peter W Foltz. 2003. Automated scoring and annotation of essays with the Intelligent Essay Assessor. *Automated Essay Scoring: A Cross-disciplinary Perspective* pages 87–112.

Nitin Madnani, Jill Burstein, John Sabatini, and Tenaha O'Reilly. 2013. Automated Scoring of a Summary-Writing Task Designed to Measure Reading Comprehension. In *Proceedings of the Workshop on Innovative Use of NLP for Building Educational Applications.* pages 163–168.

Nitin Madnani, Aoife Cahill, and Brian Riordan. 2016. Automatically scoring tests of proficiency in music instruction. In *Proceedings of the Workshop on Innovative Use of NLP for Building Educational Applications.* pages 217–222.

Pawel Matykiewicz and John Pestian. 2012. Effect of Small Sample Size on Text Categorization with Support Vector Machines. In *Proceedings of the Workshop on Biomedical Natural Language Processing.* pages 193–201.

Detmar Meurers, Ramon Ziai, Niels Ott, and Janina Kopp. 2011. Evaluating Answers to Reading Comprehension Questions in Context: Results for German and the Role of Information Structure. In *Proceedings of the TextInfer 2011 Workshop on Textual Entailment.* pages 1–9.

Michael Mohler, Razvan Bunescu, and Rada Mihalcea. 2011. Learning to Grade Short Answer Questions using Semantic Similarity Measures and Dependency Graph Alignments. In *Proceedings of ACL: HLT.* pages 752–762.

Rodney D Nielsen, Wayne H Ward, and James H Martin. 2008. Learning to Assess Low-Level Conceptual Understanding. In *Proceedings of the FLAIRS conference.* pages 427–432.

Ulrike Pado and Cornelia Kiefer. 2015. Short Answer Grading: When Sorting Helps and When It Doesnt. In *Proceedings of the Workshop on NLP for Computer Assisted Language Learning at NODALIDA.* 114, pages 42–50.

Ellis B Page. 1966. The imminence of... grading essays by computer. *The Phi Delta Kappan* 47(5):238–243.

F. Pedregosa, G. Varoquaux, A. Gramfort, V. Michel, B. Thirion, O. Grisel, M. Blondel, P. Prettenhofer, R. Weiss, V. Dubourg, J. Vanderplas, A. Passos, D. Cournapeau, M. Brucher, M. Perrot, and E. Duchesnay. 2011. Scikit-learn: Machine Learning in Python. *Journal of Machine Learning Research* 12:2825–2830.

John Platt. 1999. Probabilistic Outputs for Support Vector Machines and Comparisons to Regularized Likelihood Methods. *Advances in Large Margin Classifiers* 10(3):61–74.

Lakshmi Ramachandran, Jian Cheng, and Peter Foltz. 2015. Identifying Patterns For Short Answer Scoring Using Graph-based Lexico-Semantic Text Matching. In *Proceedings of the Workshop on Innovative Use of NLP for Building Educational Applications.* Denver, Colorado, pages 97–106.

Keisuke Sakaguchi, Michael Heilman, and Nitin Madnani. 2015. Effective Feature Integration for Automated Short Answer Scoring. In *Proceedings of NAACL: HLT.* pages 1049–1054.

Vdo Santos, M Verspoor, and J Nerbonne. 2012. Identifying important factors in essay grading using machine learning. In *Language Testing and Evaluation Series (International Experiences in Language Testing and Assessment),* volume 28, pages 295–309.

T.A.B. Snijders and R.J. Bosker. 2011. *Multilevel Analysis: An Introduction to Basic and Advanced Multilevel Modelling.* SAGE Publications.

Jana Z Sukkarieh, Ali Mohammad-Djafari, Jean-Francois Bercher, and Pierre Bessiére. 2011. Using a MaxEnt Classifier for the Automatic Content Scoring of Free-text Responses. In *Proceedings of the Conference on American Institute of Physics.* volume 1305, page 41.

Helen Yannakoudakis and Ronan Cummins. 2015. Evaluating the Performance of Automated Text Scoring systems. In *Proceedings of the Workshop on Innovative Use of NLP for Building Educational Applications.* pages 213–223.

Bianca Zadrozny and Charles Elkan. 2002. Transforming Classifier Scores into Accurate Multiclass Probability Estimates. In *Proceedings of the ACM SIGKDD International Conference on Knowledge Discovery and Data Mining.* pages 694–699.

Torsten Zesch, Michael Heilman, and Aoife Cahill. 2015. Reducing Annotation Efforts in Supervised

Short Answer Scoring. In *Proceedings of the Workshop on Innovative Use of NLP for Building Educational Applications*. pages 124–132.

Yue Zhang and Stephen Clark. 2011. Syntactic Processing Using the Generalized Perceptron and Beam Search. *Computational Linguistics* 37(1):105–151.

Mengxiao Zhu, Ou Lydia Liu, Liyang Mao, and Amy Pallant. 2016. Use of Automated Scoring and Feedback in Online Interactive Earth Science Tasks. In *Proceedings of the 2016 IEEE Integrated STEM Education Conference*.

Author Index